casa mundi

INSPIRATIONAL LIVING
AROUND THE WORLD

Florence, Italy

MASSIMO LISTRI RESIDENCE

Interiors by Marianna Gagliardi

The Florence home of Massimo Listri, who took all the photographs for this book, is outside time – or rather, suspended in time. Originally an annexe to an imposing 16th-century palazzo, it was redesigned by Listri and Marianna Gagliardi, who replaced its cramped spaces and post-war accretions with clean Cartesian lines, neoclassical styling, and baroque whimsy. After passing through an entrance hall with an archaeological flavour, and ascending a staircase in *pietra serena*, you pass two cabinets of curiosities and then reach the library-cum-gallery, which extends to the terrace over the garden. This pale blue, pearl grey and straw yellow room, with a shallow vaulted ceiling, is surrounded by Gothic Revival bookcases. The parchment-bound 'books' contain magazines.

Half-title page A mask from Oceania, in the library.

Preceding pages In the library, at the far left is a bust of Pietro Leopoldo, Grand Duke of Tuscany, carved by Luigi Pampaloni in 1841. The chairs are by Agostino Fantastici (1782–1845). On the table, next to a Russian gilt bronze lamp of 1870 (one of two in the room), are an Egyptian red porphyry vase and a Russian samovar of 1890. On the neoclassical mantelpiece are an African bronze head from Benin and two Ming dogs of Fo. The photograph, *Versailles*, is by Massimo Listri.

Right Also in the library is this purple and lilac velvet-covered sofa designed by Marianna Gagliardi. Massimo Listri's photograph, *Walhalla*, hangs above it, while a sculpture by Vitaliano De Angelis is just visible at the left.

Bronzes, seashells and coral flowers with elaborate gilt-bronze mounts are displayed in Listri's spectacular private cabinet of curiosities, below a vault decorated by Stefano Sieni and Maurizio Palma. For Listri, no sacrifice is too great when he covets an object to add to an interior that is worthy of Ariosto. The designer, Marianna Gagliardi, regards every house as a potentially exciting container to be filled with new life by a confluence of history, experience, skills and creativity.

Following pages
The library adjoins the drawing room and the sitting room.

At the end of the drawing room are two reliefs of Innocent XI and Urban VIII, and in the left foreground is a terracotta head of one of the Gonzagas. The stone corbel beyond dates from the 16th century.

MASSIMO LISTRI

casa mundi

INSPIRATIONAL LIVING AROUND THE WORLD

TEXT BY NICOLETTA DEL BUONO

With over 450 illustrations in colour

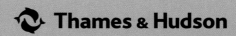
Thames & Hudson

A MAP OF THE DOMESTIC WORLD

Imago mundi – the image of the world – has always been at the centre of philosophical reflection and of mankind's search for the absolute. Always has been, and always will be, because the *imago mundi* cannot be reduced to a single, definitive, shared vision. Pierre d'Ailly, astronomer and cardinal under the antipope John XXIII, attempted to demonstrate the contrary in a celebrated work called *Imago mundi*, in which among other things he identified the location of the earthly paradise; but there is no one single vision, nor can there be a single immutable image even in the mind of God. Every land, every age, every culture, every community and every individual has a unique vision, which is the product of acquired knowledge, aspirations, symbols, and the collective imagination. As that great scholar of myths, Mircea Eliade, wrote, 'If the the land one lives in, the town, or the village, is the universe, the home becomes an *imago mundi*.' The home – *casa* – embodies the world as each person sees and experiences it; conversely, the world – *mundus* – finds in the home its symbolic, metaphorical equivalent.

Casa mundi – 'home of the world' – is the conceptual thread that links the pages of this book. Yet this volume is more than just another anthology of the world's most beautiful homes, however splendidly it may be produced. It is a sentimental and in its own way illuminating journey through some of the world's most beautiful old houses, romantic cottages, farmhouses, penthouses and lofts. All were visited and recorded by the enthusiastic, inquisitive, learned, implacable and responsive lens of Massimo Listri, one of the greatest of contemporary photographers of architecture and interiors.

Starting with the residence of Listri himself, the volume displays extreme differences in approaches to design, sources of aesthetic inspiration, moods and cultural expectations. Metropolitan or rural; Alpine or Mediterranean; classical or up-to-the-minute; exotic or vernacular; eclectic or rationalist; monothematic or open to influences ranging from monastic to lavish; reflecting a taste for minimalism or for excess and magical effects – these homes range from the Spartan to galleries brimming with art and exquisite antiques. Listri takes us through them as though a great fresco displaying the lifestyles of yesterday and today, explaining evolutions, modifications and superimpositions.

The following pages do not constitute a record, still less an encyclopaedia. Instead, they present an astonishing array of cultural choices in which each of us can find his or her dream home.

Opposite Dominating the corridor leading to the library in Massimo Listri's home are large photographs by him of works from Adolfo Wildt's physiognomical series. On the walls are framed discs of antique marble. The rhinoceroses on the console table are by a Thai artist. In the distance, on a Gothic Revival bracket, is a bronze sculpture of Helen by Canova.

DAVID FLINT WOOD HOUSE

C oconut Grove, the starfish-shaped
villa owned by David Flint Wood
and India Hicks, was built by Flint Wood
on the Hibiscus Hill estate on Harbour
Island, in the Bahamas.

Above and right The living room.
This white interior has the character
of old colonial residences on the islands.
The walls are pearly, the aviary is
snow-white, and the floorboards are
painted gloss white. Mahogany furniture
provides an eloquent note of colour
in this milky world.

Opposite The living room.

Above left and above Even the shutters are painted white. Standing out in all this colonial whiteness is a transparent acrylic Louis Ghost chair designed by Philippe Starck for Kartell.

Miami, Florida, United States

ELLA CISNEROS
PENTHOUSE

Interiors by Luis Bustamante

Overlooking Miami's Biscayne Bay is the penthouse of collector and businesswoman Ella Cisneros, where she keeps an impressive collection of contemporary art. The apartment, decorated by Spanish interior designer Luis Bustamante, extends over two floors.

Right The upper floor is a breathtaking open-air living room, with swimming pool and barbecue area and panoramic views. Raymond Jungles's architectural setting, in stone and mosaic, frames both the pool and a spectacular view of Biscayne Bay.

Left, above The living room. In the right foreground is *Concetto spaziale* by Lucio Fontana, an oil of 1960. The two lamps are by Romeo Sozzi for Promemoria.

Left, below In the corridor outside the living room is *Mouvement à trois vitesses* by Jesús-Rafael Soto, of 1965, in mixed media on wood. The Grand Repos armchair, designed by Jean Prouvé, is now made by Tecta.

Opposite Walls, ceiling and floor are in wood in the corridor, as they are throughout the interior. The leather chairs are by Sawaya & Moroni.

Left The drawing room is dominated by extensive shelves filled with remarkable objects. Much care has been taken over the lighting: table lamps are supplemented by the many ceiling-mounted spots that ensure optimal presentation of the numerous artworks.

Above The study, in a corner off the drawing room.

Above The dining room with its generous windows and large central table, over which hangs a Pierre ou Paul Dome pendant lamp by Ingo Maurer.

Right The kitchen. A Zettl'z ceiling lamp by Ingo Maurer illuminates the 1970 Nadine Charteret table.

Following pages At night, the view over Biscayne Bay through the living-room windows with their strong, rhythmical uprights sparkles like a scattering of Swarovski crystals, or an exclamation mark at the end of the dazzling sentence composed by this home.

These pages All the bedrooms open onto balconies through floor-to-ceiling windows. The made-to-measure furnishings are uncompromisingly rectilinear. The capacious, symmetrical cupboard units and chests of drawers have handles designed by architect Riccardo Bofill for Valli & Valli.

Bangkok, Thailand

RALF W. OHLEZ PENTHOUSE

Design by Yasuhiro Koichi
Interiors by Goh Swee Kiat

The great Japanese architect Yashuhiro Koichi, a master of evocative worlds in miniature, created this compact apartment perched on the top floor of a building in the Soi Lang Suan district of Bangkok. By mixing natural light with artificial, and emphasizing perspective, Koichi has created a jewel based on the principle of contrast. Inspired by Thailand's sumptuous gold and jewel-encrusted palaces, he invented elegant, original interiors that fuse two civilizations, the Orient and the West – for Koichi was in fact born in Germany.

Above A collection of Ming dynasty stone lions in a corner of the living room. The wall is panelled in bronze.

Opposite The entrance hall. A Han dynasty horse against a granite wall is reflected in mirrors. Below it, a pile of suitcases from the great days of travel support an 18th-century Cambodian vase. In the left foreground is a Ming dynasty Buddha of Compassion.

Above The living room, with its sofa
6 metres (18 feet) long. In the middle
of the room is a stone coffee table in
several sections. On the right are a
Flemish painting, Cambodian vases,
and stone sculptures. The rug is
18th-century Tibetan.

Opposite A traditional wooden headrest
sits on the sofa. The small iron Buddha
was made in Thailand in the 18th
century. Alternating slabs of granite
and teak cover the floor.

The walls of the master bedroom are panelled in bronze. An 18th-century Austrian painting hangs above the headboard. On the bed is a tray with a small collection of Ming dynasty brush-holders.

New York, New York, United States

IZHAR PATKIN RESIDENCE

A kaleidoscope of fantastical colour infuses panache into the New York home-cum-studio of versatile Israeli painter, sculptor and ceramist Izhar Patkin, who has redecorated it with found materials and objects of all kinds, mostly of Arab or Mediterranean origin. Patkin did all the work himself, redesigning his living and work spaces to create a vibrantly chromatic and perpetually changing narrative that unfolds around a central patio.

Right Glazed ceramic plates hand-painted by Patkin with the faces of great figures of the 20th century.

Opposite The dining room, with Patkin's oil painting, *Host Culture*, and lamps in recycled glass, again by Patkin. The cellophane sculpture near the window is by Thomas Lanigan Schmidt and dates from 1987. The hand-painted seats are by Kim MacConnel.

Opposite A painting by Kim MacConnel
fills one wall of the kitchen. The vases
on the shelf at the left are by Elsa Rady.
A large pendant lamp by Izhar Patkin
making use of old pieces of glassware
hangs from the ceiling.

Above left The house cat.

Above The bedroom. The floor lamp
in recycled coloured plastic is by Patkin,
and the rug is made to his design.
The armchair is by Kim MacConnel.

Above left The entrance. The collage of old photographs and lights on the back wall is by Patkin, as is the light unit on the right, assembled from fragments of coloured glass.

Above right A bathroom blue as an aquarium.

Opposite The master bedroom, with colourful ethnic furnishings.

Following pages Patkin's studio. In the right foreground is *Dulcinea* (1991), in wood and painted silver leaf; to the left of it *Don Quixote Part Two* (1987), in anodized aluminium, and in the background *Palagonia* (1989) in wax and gold leaf. The lamp is by Vivienne Westwood.

CASEY HOUSE

An 18th-century townhouse in Henrietta Street, this has a red brick façade with friezes and stuccowork and a typical Irish neoclassical doorway. The rooms are large, the staircases and balustrades are imposing, and the fireplaces are in marble or wood. When the property was acquired by performing artists Michael and Aileen Casey in 1975, it was completely abandoned. The couple at once set about restoring it with an eye to both style and history – a financially and physically daunting task that absorbed all their resources. The Caseys still live in a state of 'ambitious indigence', eschewing electricity – candles are the only source of light – as well as hot water and modern appliances. Original colours have been exposed on the plastered walls, which display portraits of the owners' Huguenot forebears. Throughout the house, there is a suggestion of aristocracy fallen on hard times that Henry Fielding or Laurence Sterne might have recognized.

Right In the library, a portrait of Bishop Hort hangs above the black marble fireplace. The table is piled with assorted books on architecture, military history, and religion.

Above The master bedroom reflects
a passion for military paraphernalia,
from the medals on the table to the
drum and uniform and the martial
prints on the walls.

Opposite The sitting room. On the walls,
where layers of old paint are exposed,
a large 19th-century portrait of the
Countess of Ormond hangs next to
an engraving of Queen Charlotte,
the consort of George III. The marble
bust dates from the 19th century.

Following pages A detail of the
sitting room.

Bangkok, Thailand

ZITZEWITZ PENTHOUSE

Imagine a majestic crystal crown atop one of Bangkok's tallest skyscrapers. By day it glitters against the milky sky of the Thai capital, and by night it glows with all the sensuous mystery of a Chinese lantern. Welcome to the home of a magnate in love with Thailand's heritage and customs. Inside this glass shell almost 8 metres (24 feet) high, walls and ceilings relate the history and culture of Thailand in an adventure that brims with erudite references and mythological connotations. Traces of the past mingle harmoniously with contemporary furniture covered with gold leaf, hinting at the owner's fondness for what today are often called 'modern antiques'. The dizzying height of the rooms gives everything a regal grandeur.

Right Detail of one of the panels depicting scenes from Thai history.

Opposite The living room looks out on Bangkok's skyscraper-studded skyline. Decorated columns support the ceiling and emphasize its height.

Opposite Looking down into the living room from the gallery. The floor is of Carrara marble; the lamps suggest the shapes of pagodas.

Right Another view of the living room. The sofa, with a glowing finish in gold leaf, was inspired by traditional Thai furniture. Panels referring to Thai history and legend decorate the walls.

The master bedroom. Dark tones and linear composition lend the room a masculine air, underlined by the massive, square-set volume of the cupboard, covered with gold leaf. The medallions on the ceiling depict animal gods of Thai mythology.

The spacious bathroom has walls
covered with local wood, a shower cabin,
and two bathtubs set head to foot.

Miami, Florida, United States

CLARK RESIDENCE

Design by René Gonzales

Interior and exterior conduct a dialogue in this apartment at Aqua on Allison Island, of which the wide terrace affords grand views over Biscayne Bay, Miami Beach and the downtown skyline. In a building by Alexander Gorlin, it was redesigned by René Gonzales. Clean lines and vaguely Zen-like volumes combine with deliberately neutral furnishings to focus attention on the panorama, framed by large windows, and the contemporary works of art that the owners collect.

Right A detail of the dining room.

Opposite The terrace looking out onto Miami Beach. Chairs and tables are by Paola Lenti.

Opposite From the living room there are
views of Biscayne Bay and Miami Beach.

Above The vast, all-white living room.
Grey 1 and *Grey 2* by Lynn Gelfman hang
on the wall. The sofa is by Living Divani
and the stools are African.

Opposite, above Like all the other interiors, the kitchen is characterized by rigor and functionalism.

Opposite, below A glimpse into the entrance hall, which is treated as a miniature art gallery. On the wall is *Rosa en la Tropical*, a photograph by Andrew Moore, and next to it are bottle-like sculptures in stainless steel.

Above The dining room. On the left-hand wall is *A Gleam of Knowledge* by José Alvarez. Peter Barrett's *Manifold* hangs on the back wall. The table is by Porro, the chairs are Lea, designed by Roberto Barbieri for Zanotta, and the lamp is by Robert Lewis.

Above The guest room.

Right The master bedroom. At the
foot of the bed, by Porro, is an African
wooden couch made by the Senufo
people. Alyson Shotz's series *Reflective
Mimicry* hangs above the headboard.

Bali, Indonesia

BEGAVAN GIRI

Design by Cheong Yew Kuan

The residential complex on the island of Bali known as Begavan Giri, or 'Wise Man's Mountain', stands near the village of the same name among flame-red plantations, waterfalls and freshwater springs venerated by local people. Its designer was Cheong Yew Kuan, who was commissioned by Bradley Gardner, the owner of an international chain of jewelry shops and residential developments. Bradley wanted a structure that would be part private home and part guest residence. Today, Begavan Giri with its five villas is one of the most elegant places in all Bali. Each villa has its own private pool, baths and gardens, laid out by landscape gardeners John Pettigrew and Thorston d'Heureuse in harmony with the natural environment, and each has a distinctive atmosphere.

Above A ground-level torch illuminates the wooden-floored terrace.

Right One of the swimming pools beside the villas, with a lush backdrop of foliage. The terrace has a slatted wooden floor.

Left A succession of water gardens
winds through the pavilions.

Above Stepping stones in the water
lead to the master suite in this exotic
gardenscape. The door was carved by
local craftsmen; there are oil lamps
in the niches.

Left In a villa bathroom. The tub is surmounted by an open carved wood canopy.

Opposite One of the bedrooms, with a fourposter bed shrouded in tulle mosquito netting.

One of the water gardens, fringed
by lush vegetation.

Right, above and below A tub and cushions on one of the terraces provide relaxation in close contact with nature.

Following pages Another terrace-level pool projects out into the luxuriant tropical vegetation.

Mustique, Caribbean

INDIGO HOUSE

Design by Jack Diamond

Canadian architect Jack Diamond built himself a house with a fairy-tale view over Pasture Bay on the Caribbean island of Mustique, the holiday paradise much beloved of celebrities and members of the international jet set. The concept hinges on the contrasting themes of water and sand, setting blue against white around a 'water courtyard' with an infinity pool.

Above The roof terrace.

Opposite The verandah and open-air dining area, seen from the courtyard.

Above The water courtyard and the
stone steps leading to it.

Opposite The area for daytime activities.
The unusual triangular structure of the
roof adds a sculptural note to a space
where the white of the plastered walls
and limestone floor contrasts with the
warm tones of the wooden furniture.

Above and opposite The infinity pool is surrounded by a luminous peristyle, through which the spacious area for daytime activities can be glimpsed.

Paris, France

FLORENCE PUCCI RESIDENCE

Interiors by Florence Pucci

A lovely Haussmannian building in the heart of Paris is where interior designer Florence Pucci has created her own apartment by transforming the original complex of small spaces into a series of intercommunicating rooms, which can be rearranged, thanks to screens and slideaway partitions, to suit the mood of the moment. Astutely positioned mirrors multiply space to infinity and add depth to the rooms, reflecting the many works of art, mainly by Chinese artists, and major pieces of modern design, displayed against white walls and ceilings.

Right A sitting room with a sofa 4 metres (12 feet) long covered in linen and lambskin. The white lacquer Berlingot pouffes were designed by Marie Leblon. In the left background is a Samurai lamp by Ingo Maurer. The coffee tables are by Florence Pucci, and the black chairs are a Verner Panton design produced by Vitra.

Left, above One end of the sitting room, with an LC2 sofa by Le Corbusier, Pierre Jeanneret and Charlotte Perriand, produced by Cassina. Beyond is the centre of the home, the drawing room, with Lui Wei's dominant *Celestial Mountain* photographs on the wall.

Left, below Another view of the sitting room and the long sofa.

Right A view of the drawing room showing the complex arrangement of spaces. The coloured Chinese dinosaur statues are by Sui Jiango. Antonio Citterio designed the Arne sofas and Harry pouffes for B&B. The Lazy chair and occasional tables by Patricia Urquiola were also created for B&B.

Left The slate-floored bathroom has a luminous tub with tap by Philippe Starck for Axor-Hansgrohe. The provocative photograph on the wall is by Qiu Zhijie.

Opposite The bedroom features a four-poster bed designed, like the bedside tables, by Florence Pucci. Also visible are Air Can lamps by Christophe Pillet for Mazzega and Louis Ghost chairs by Philippe Starck for Kartell.

Above and right Two views of a 'high-art' bathroom with washbasin and centrally placed tub in black marble. On the wall is *Chinese Landscape* by Huang Yan (1999). The RAR rocking chair, designed by Charles and Ray Eames in 1950, is made by Vitra. Beyond the door is the master bedroom.

Left In the drawing room. *Tattoo* by Qiu Zhijie (1994) is a digital print on canvas.

Opposite The kitchen and dining area. The grey lacquer and steel furniture was designed by Florence Pucci. The light fitting is a luminous sculpture by Daniel Baumann called *Vaisseau Céleste* (*Heavenly Vessel*) The chairs are by Verner Panton, produced by Vitra.

Malang, Java

ANHAR SETJADIBRATA HOUSE

Interiors by Anhar Setjadibrata

Located in the heart of colonial Malang, the loveliest town in eastern Java, the home of Indonesian designer Anhar Setjadibrata is a blend of inspiration, suggestion, tradition, travel, history, geography and anthropology. It was built in 1920 as the residence of a Javanese doctor and his German wife. The attractive exterior, in traditional Dutch colonial style, is largely untouched: the designer merely united the two parts of the original building into a single volume. Inside, however, the makeover is total. Walls have been moved or removed, ceilings and floors have been refitted, and the rooms flow into each other uninterruptedly to tell the story of a voyage in time and space. Room after room evokes the places and events of Asia.

Right Votive lamps before a wooden statue of Guan Yin, the Goddess of Compassion.

Opposite The room of the designer's daughter, Lucienne Setjadibrata. The enormous carved bed once belonged to a king of the island of Madura. Indian silks on the walls are complemented by a canvas by Raden Saleh, the father of modern Indonesian painting.

Above A detail of the 19th-century white marble altar in the entrance hall. The altar comes from Java, but shows considerable Chinese and European influence. Above it is a bronze Buddha from the ancient Chinese city of Li Jiang, resting on a rare carved wooden Chinese pedestal. A Dutch bronze vase holding incense sticks stands in the foreground.

Above right An antique carved wooden Chinese console table.

Opposite A 14th-century mythical animal in stone from the Hindu kingdom of Majapahit looks out over the pool and protects the home.

Opposite The door is flanked by scrolling 18th-century wooden carvings that were part of a Javanese palace gate. The child's table and chair in the foreground are from Madura. A Chinese carved wooden bed and 15th-century bronze Shiva are visible through the doorway.

Right A large stained-glass window opens onto the lush tropical garden.

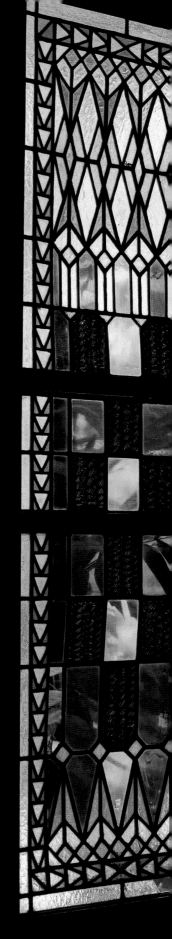

Above and opposite The dining room. The sixteen-seater dining table displays two marble lotus blossoms with flower arrangements. The sideboard, of the rare striped teak called *jati blirik*, was made in Java in colonial days by Chinese craftsmen. The backs of the chairs are carved with mythical Chinese dogs. Beyond the arch lie the pool and tropical garden.

Left A room leading to the bedrooms. The carved furniture is Indonesian and the vases are Chinese, as is the antique carved wooden console table on which they stand.

Right, above The entrance hall. On the altar is a small 19th-century bronze kilin lion from China and two containers in wood and bamboo for offerings of food. The massive 19th-century lead lions are from Portugal. The tiled floor dates from 1920, the year when the residence was built.

Right, below The Goddess of Compassion.

Following pages A view of the pool and of the entrance to the house. The sleeping Buddha, of wood, is from Burma. In the foreground beside the pool is a 14th-century carved stone slab on which votive offerings are placed for Shiva, Brahma and Vishnu.

Brussels, Belgium

D'AUWERE HOUSE

Design by Marc Corbiau
Interiors by Claire Bataille

Not far from Antwerp, in the heart of Flanders, Marc Corbiau designed the home of a collector of contemporary art in a modern idiom that pays due tribute to the heritage of local and classical architecture. Symmetries are Palladian yet constantly broken up, axes are slightly eccentric, and features such as the two flights of stairs are monumental but reduced to essentials. The materials used are of the highest quality, and meticulously detailed. The red bricks were fired to order in the United Kingdom, the stone for the floor was imported from Germany, and the rough stucco of the walls and stained teak flooring were carefully selected to enhance the sense of depth. Various works of contemporary art have been introduced into the rooms to define space without overwhelming it.

Right A corner of the house, which is set in a park laid out by landscape designer Jacques Wirth.

SOME OTHER OBJECTS

Left The red and black lacquer Chinese cupboard dates from the 18th century. A lacquer vase by Philippe Wolfers stands on the Printz table, and on the wall is a canvas by Lucio Fontana. Beyond the sliding door, with perfect Palladian proportions, one of the two dining rooms is set in a loggia-like structure that insulates it from the heat. One dining room is for use in winter, the other is for summer. The furniture is of teak, and the light fitting is by interior designer Claire Bataille.

Right The entrance hall and staircase. The table was designed by Christian Liaigre and the iron chair is by André Dubreuil. The large hanging light is by Emile-Jacques Ruhlmann.

Left, above The living room. Above the fireplace is *Ultramare* by Giovanni Anselmo (1990), a characterful example of Arte Povera. Chairs, armchairs and tables are by Josef Hoffmann.

Left, below The living room leads to the second dining room.

Opposite The swimming pool pavilion is at one end of the house. The windows are removable, and in summer the pavilion is completely open to the garden.

Normandy, France

CHATEAU OF
CHAMPS DE BATAILLE

Interiors by Jacques Garcia

The château of Champs de Bataille in Normandy was built by Alexandre de Créqui in the late 17th century, during the reign of Louis XIV. Today it belongs to Jacques Garcia, an interior designer with a particularly well developed sense of harmony, who has effected a scholarly restoration spiced by his own vivid aesthetic vision. In homage to its past glory, the château is open to the public; Garcia has a private corner pavilion where he likes to spend weekends.

Right A south-facing Moorish canopy erected outside the castle. The sunbeds enable guests to perfect their tans while enjoying a view of the large formal garden.

Above The spacious library, with
frescoed ceiling.

Opposite A terracotta bust of Bacchus,
attributed to Desjardins, stands on
a windowsill.

Above left and right Two bathrooms with period tubs and washbasins. In one the walls are papered, while in the other they are plastered.

Opposite Souvenirs from the Far East and North Africa in this guest room bear witness to Garcia's passion for exotic things – and characters.

Opposite Jacques Garcia's private swimming pool. Its air of Eastern mystery is reinforced by 18th-century columns purchased in Rajasthan. The fabrics are also from India.

Above A sinuous staircase winds up to Jacques Garcia's private pavilion. The 18th-century marble statue represents the Duchess of Alba, who was immortalized in a number of portraits by her lover, Goya.

Following pages The small library, where Garcia's guests gather to watch television or play cards and other games.

ERNESTO MENDOZA RESIDENCE

It should come as no surprise that fashion photographer Ernesto 'Nesti' Mendoza opted to leave New York and settle in Miami. The city's vibrant, tropical atmosphere is very reminiscent of Cuba, the Caribbean island where Mendoza was born and which still has a special place in his heart. The residence is in a building designed by Walter Chatham on Allison Island, in a sort of artists' colony designed by leading architects. In this apartment under the Florida sky, Mendoza, who studied architecture and graphic design, wanted interiors that would evoke the industrial spaces of Manhattan while preserving Miami's gentler modernist character. The area for daytime activities, created by incorporating an adjoining room, is the hub of the home. Suspended ceilings have gone, exposing pipes that suggest a loft, and one bathroom has been transformed into a bar. The effect is minimalist, reflecting Mendoza's passion for the purity of Le Corbusier and Mies van der Rohe.

Right The dining area. Arranged on the Jorge Pensi glass table are *Pupilles* II, IV, XI, XII and XIV, sculptures of 2000 by Markus Linnenbrink, who in the same year also painted *Multicolortrans*, which hangs on the wall. On the left are two Hudson chairs, designed by Philippe Starck for Emeco.

Following pages The spacious living area features a painting by Till Friewald of 2004. The daybed and Barcelona chairs are by Mies van der Rohe, made by Knoll, the table is by Le Corbusier, and the light fittings by Fontana Arte.

Left, above The studio.

Left, below The bedroom, an essay in neutral tones. The three paintings are by Jane Holsinger: *Windmill* (2001), *Encouragement* (2000), and *Two Girls* (2001).

Opposite In the bedroom the Sputnik hanging light is by Modulightor and the Glo-Ball table lamp is by Jasper Morrison for Flos.

An elegant bar, lit by Tom Dixon's Mirror Ball fittings, was created from a former bathroom. Outside the windows is the broad terrace.

A corner of the living area. Through the
windows you can see the terrace that
runs the entire length of the apartment.

Turin, Italy

VOENA RESIDENCE

Design by Paolo Genta Ternavasio

The Turin residence of a leading Italian art dealer, who runs important galleries in Milan and Rome, looks onto one of the Piemontese capital's broad late 19th-century avenues. Paolo Genta redefined volume and decoration in the huge apartment, creating sympathetic spaces for things both antique and ultra-modern, which are often stylistically and emotionally worlds apart. The result is a series of rooms with very varied iconography and moods.

Right A portrait of Baudelaire by Vik Munz thrones above the fireplace and Napoleon III carpet.

Following pages The eclectic living room, with its minimalist fireplace, displays a Louis XV sofa in shocking pink, a 1950s Italian reclining chair, a 17th-century double portrait by Pietro Paolini, and a portrait of Victor Amadeus I. The marble-topped metal coffee tables are by Angelo De Michelis.

Opposite A closet inspired by Japanese architecture leads to the master bathroom. The walls are in whitened black oak, with glass doors in which glimpses of the bathroom are reflected.

Above left and right Two views of the entrance hall, where yellow walls with relief plaster 'buttons' mimic the texture of upholstery. Playful imitation continues with Federico Zuccaro's plaster and rope chandelier, modelled on early 19th-century light fittings. The Carrara marble bust of Napoleon in the foreground is by Antoine-Denis Chaudet.

Above left The dining room. The
Louis XVI-style table and the crystal
chandelier above it both date from the
1940s. A work by Gilbert and George
hangs over the grey bardiglio marble
console table.

Above right Another view of the dining
room. The painting over the matching
bardiglio console table is by the New
York artist Peter Halley.

Opposite The dining room.

Left The master bathroom. The tub is set in marble and the lantern is of painted tin. An 18th-century lady keeps a watchful eye on events.

Opposite The fourposter bed in the master bedroom has hand-embroidered linen curtains. Two ox horns stand on the Boulle desk.

Venice, Italy

STEFANO CONTINI RESIDENCE

The Venice home of Stefano Contini, gallery owner and enlightened patron of the arts, is the perfect setting in which to share with friends and family one's love of creativity in all its forms. It occupies a noble palazzo (watched over by the heritage authorities) that looks onto the Grand Canal. This is no ordinary home. Space, light and movement from room to room are arranged so as to focus attention on the canvases and sculptures that Contini has assembled over the years. Restoration work, including the recovery of the terrazzo floors of a special Venetian type, was done with the utmost care. The walls have been treated so as to indicate the various functions of the rooms, and to provide a setting for Contini's important collection. The designer furniture was carefully chosen so as not to distract from the works of art.

Right In the living room overlooking the Grand Canal, Julian Schnabel's *Boni Lux* provides the centrepiece. Below it, on the cabinet, is *Leda and the Swan* by Fernando Botero. To the left, a plexiglass pedestal supports a bronze sculpture by Tony Cragg.

Opposite In the library is Graham Sutherland's *Interior*, depicting his studio on the Giudecca. The carpet was designed by Aldo Mondino.

Above *Star Hunter*, a work of the 1980s by Transavanguardia artist Mimmo Paladino, hangs next to one of the 19th-century frescoes that came to light during restoration work.

Left, above The entrance hall. Zoran Music's imposing triptych *Anchorite* hangs on the wall at the left. At the far end, on the divider that separates the entrance hall from the dining room, is Tamara de Lempicka's oil painting *Two Friends* (1928). A large work by Giambattista Crosato (1686–1758), *The Magnanimity of Scipio*, hangs on the right-hand wall. In the right foreground is a sculpture by Lorenzo Viani, *Female Torso*.

Left, below The Blue Room takes its name from the colour of floor and ceiling. The table is by Arman. The blue painting is *Il Solitario* (*The Loner*) by Mimmo Paladino.

The dining room is focused on the Doge table by Carlo Scarpa made by Gavina, and Vico Magistretti's Pollack chairs made by De Padova. At the head of the table is a Colber chair. Hanging on the back wall is Sandro Chia's 1987 painting *Orgasmo, Fantasmo, Sarcasmo*. Below it is Chia's Pesce sofa.

The Blue Room. In the left corner is a
blue velvet chair by Carla Tolomeo.

Christo and Jeanne Claude's sketch
for their Pont Neuf installation in Paris
hangs in the entrance hall.

Following pages The dining room. In the
unit that marks off the dining area from
the entrance *Steep Tease*, a bronze by
Giacomo Manzù, occcupies the centre;
on the right is *Toro* by Fernando Botero.
The abstract painting on the right-hand
wall is by Peter Halley.

ELLA CISNEROS HOUSE

Interiors by Luis Bustamante

For businesswoman and philanthropist Ella Cisneros, home and art go hand in hand. She collects homes, actively participating in the various stages of each project, with all the enthusiasm she devotes to collecting works of art, and has residences all over the world, including Madrid, Naples and Miami. This one, at Gstaad in the Bernese Oberland, is her retreat, where she can at last relax and think of herself. It is a classic chalet, conforming to local planning regulations – on the outside. Inside, the cosy mountain atmosphere is countered by a modern idiom suited to Cisneros's artistic temperament and the collections housed here, as in her other homes. Luis Bustamante created linear furniture, and chose rough local materials for surfaces, with occasional touches of colour.

Right The spa was excavated in the ground under the chalet. The three mattresses in the foreground conceal the whirlpool tub. The black table is by Romeo Sozzi for Promemoria. A photograph by Guido Albi Marini hangs on the wall on the left.

Left The contrast between modernity
and Alpine tradition is particularly
marked in the living room. The works
on the far wall are by Latin-American
photographers of the 1950s and 1960s.

Above Another corner of the living room.

The dining room. The table setting
features French porcelain decorated
with hunting scenes, Christofle silver,
and Lalique stemware. On the wall
is a painting by Richard Serra.

Above A conversation corner in the spa. On the back wall is a panoramic view of the Matterhorn and the western Swiss Alps. In front of the Minotti sofa is a table designed by Luis Bustamante. Guido Albi Marini's *Infinite Black Hole* hangs on the wall on the right.

Left A series of works by the young photographer Christian Geriath.

The guest room is given a very special
atmosphere by the old pine used
on its walls. The artworks are by
José Iraola.

The spa has an oak floor and walls of rough old pine. The tapware is by Dornbracht.

London, England

JUDITH GREER HOUSE

Design by Ettore Sottsass

Seattle-born patron of the arts and – with her husband, Richard – collector Judith Greer spent almost thirteen years in Tokyo, where she directed the Hara Museum of Contemporary Art; recently she published *Owning Art: The Contemporary Art Collector's Handbook*. When she moved to London, she purchased a Victorian townhouse and asked the *enfant terrible* of Italian design, the architect Ettore Sottsass, to rethink the interior. Sottsass, a founder member of the Memphis Group and one of the most creative and respected exponents of postmodernism, brought his trademark lightness of touch and irony to bear, imbuing this home-cum-museum with colour and purpose to make a perfect setting for the many works of art on the walls and in the gallery created on the top floor.

Right and opposite The spiral staircase, built to a design by Sottsass.

Left, above Simon Martin's *The Mysterious Suspicion* brings life to a wall in the kitchen.

Left, below The huge, light-filled living room has been enlarged by removing a dividing wall. The storage cupboards topped with coloured lights were designed by Sottsass, who took his cue from Coco Chanel's dress boxes. He also designed the large wooden playhouse.

Opposite The living room. The large painting on the wall at the right is *Doublonnage* by Yasumasa Morimura. Damien Hirst's round *Untitled* (1995) hangs next to the fireplace.

Following pages The study-library is separated from the dining room by a coloured sliding wall which is flat on one side and hollow on the other. Tables and armchairs are by Sottsass; the floor lamp is Tolomeo by Michele De Lucchi for Artemide. The painting is Yayoi Kusama's *Gentle are the Stairs to Heaven*; the sculpture, *Monkiness is the Whatness of all Monkey*, is by Simon Martin; in the right foreground on the red table is a ceramic television set – Ma Jun's *New China Series: Television*.

The top floor of the house has been converted into a gallery where Judith Greer exhibits pieces from her collection. She also makes it available for temporary exhibitions by non-profit organizations. The space is mainly dedicated to young emerging artists, who can meet important gallery owners at events held here.

Above *The Old In Out*, a sculpture by Sarah Lucas.

Right The large canvas is Lee Ufan's *Untitled*. The twelve photographs make up Gareth McConnell's series entitled *Meditation*. In the distance on the left-hand wall is *Centrepiece* by Gary Hume, near *Box* by Shimabuku. On the floor in the middle of the room is Gavin Turk's *Habitat*.

In the dining room Sottsass's large purple-toned laminate table goes well with the Pompeian red walls and with the sliding cupboards, also in laminate. The table itself is modular and can be extended to seat from sixteen to twenty-two diners. On the wall is *Fan Portrait*, by Yasumasa Morimura.

JAOUAD KADIRI PALACE

Design by Stuart Church
Interiors by Jaouad Kadiri

The most lavish palace built
in Marrakech in recent times
recreates in the heart of the Red City
a fairy-tale atmosphere drawn from
the western Indian kingdom of
Rajasthan. Here, all is grace and
harmony. As the sun sinks slowly in the
evening, India and Morocco fuse into a
single sumptuous decorative concept.

Right Ornate glass lamps.

Opposite A lotus pond is glimpsed
through latticework characteristic of
Moorish architecture. This is the Salon
du Crépuscule, or Sunset Room, which
symmetrically balances the Salon de
l'Aube (Sunrise Room). Burmese votive
vases are silhouetted against the water.

Above In the Salon de l'Aube.

Left An enfilade of arches. The Islamic shapes glow with the colours of medieval Indian art, which also governed the arrangement of the rooms, in a physical path that leads to spiritual awakening.

The entrance hall, also called the
Salon de la Siesta Collective (Room of
Communal Repose). It is an area where
guests can relax before Kadiri receives
them. The frames of the comfortable
Moroccan *sdairi* divans are of painted
cedarwood. The Murano glass lamps
were designed by Stuart Church. The
floor is of Moroccan *dess*, a mixture
of cement and natural pigments.

Opposite and above The master bedroom, with its carved wooden fourposter bed. Next to the bed is a splendid royal cradle from Rajasthan, with rattles in the form of tiny elephants, found in a Brussels antique shop. The giltwood hanging lamp was made by a craftsman in the Marrakech souk. On the floor is an antique Persian carpet.

Opposite The large divan in the reading
room nestles under a collection
of 18th-century portraits of Indian
royal personages.

Above Another view of the reading room.

Above The mirrors in the bathroom are of carved, gilt and inlaid wood. The setting of the tub, and the washbasin top, are of white Carrara marble.

Opposite A lavishly appointed dressing room with an upholstered divan made locally.

Athens, Greece

KIRIOS CRITON RESIDENCE

Interiors by Kirios Criton

A leading figure in Athens' cultural life, the Greek-born artist, critic, writer and interior designer Kirios Criton is always on the move. His Athens home is constantly changing, like its owner, and

it constitutes a web of influences and transformations in which objects appear as symbolic messengers. Hellenistic, pop and neobaroque coexist in a cheerful and ironic multisensual and multisensory eclecticism.

Above A detail of the sitting room.

Right In the drawing room, antique furniture coexists with pieces by Criton or his designer friends; surfaces are covered with leopardskin, damask and gold leaf; the classicizing figurines are by Stelios Triadis.

Left The walls of the living room are painted in shades of red and green. A neoclassical painting of a woman playing a musical instrument is held in the branches of a 'tree' coloured in the same green as the walls.

Above The chess table with an engraved glass top that stands beside the sofa.

Left A view into the dining room, through a frame of mouldings painted green and blue. The chair with a back in the form of an illustration of a Corinthian capital, by Fornasetti, evokes the classical world.

Opposite The rectangular shape of the dining room is subtly softened by the circular shapes of the table and the carpet by Criton. In the far right corner is an antique column. A figurine by Stelios Triadis stands on a bracket in the right foreground.

New York, New York, United States

CHARLES COWLES RESIDENCE

Design by Dana Nicholson

In the fashion-obsessed SoHo district of Manhattan, where galleries of contemporary art rub shoulders with the extravagant boutiques of emerging stylists, Charles Cowles, one of the New York art world's most brilliant figures, has set up his hideaway in a block built in the 1920s. A collector and former long-serving curator of the Seattle contemporary art museum, Cowles has established a gallery next to his residence. The loft, reached by a goods lift, was restored by Dana Nicholson, who created a sweeping open space for the living room, studio and dining room, separated by wooden columns supporting beams. The walls are white, to provide a neutral background for the artworks on display.

Right A substantial partition marks the living room off from the dining room. The sculpture on the left is by Manuel Neri, the painting on the partition by Matthew Weinstein. Below it is a rare Japanese vase.

Above The living room has Louis XVI
armchairs in which Cowles likes to
sit and read. The space is dominated
by a painting by Harry Kramer on the
right. A glass skull by William Morris
sits on the coffee table amid books on
photography, another of the owner's
passions. Beyond the columns in the
background is a wall sculpture by
Charles Arnoldi.

Opposite The exceptional collection
of photographs includes work by
Robert Mapplethorpe.

Following pages Charles Cowles'
venerable studio table marshals the
space in the large exhibition zone.

Opposite The functional white kitchen has a table of rough wood.

Above A shelf unit of pale wood shelters an impressive collection of valuable vases from different countries and cultures.

Florence, Italy

ROBERTO CAVALLI HOUSE

Design by Marianna Gagliardi

The Tuscan villa of flamboyant stylist Roberto Cavalli was built around a medieval tower-house, but its atmosphere of informal opulence fully reflects the bold, iconoclastic spirit of its owner. Inside, in spaces now like a volcano and now like a moonscape, Cavalli has filled the rooms with an astonishing collection worthy of a cabinet of curiosities. Paintings with gold backgrounds and wooden religious carvings of various dates mingle with ancient marbles, 18th-century grisailles, Orientalist paintings, Satsuma bronzes and vases, and horses – *cavalli* in Italian – of all kinds. Marianna Gagliardi has managed to give a specific theme to each room, and a sense of purpose to the house as a whole, without doing violence to its essential nature, which is based on free association. She has also created two new spaces for relaxation: a swimming pool with gymnasium where the lemon-house used to be, and a *calidarium*, or Turkish bath, with well concealed state-of-the-art technology.

Above right Rattan furniture from the 1920s in the winter garden. The 18th-century painting, *A Bird Seller*, is by Giacomo Francesco Todeschini.

Opposite The central tower, set in a luxuriant romantic garden, seen from the outdoor swimming pool.

Above left One corner of the living room in the tower shelters a 15th-century gold-ground painting, a 16th-century Tuscan painted wood Virgin and Child, and a 17th-century Tuscan walnut chair.

Above right and opposite The entrance to the tower.

Left The indoor swimming pool. The floor is of antique stone, while the urns are neoclassical.

Above A bowl with candles adds charm to the area of the swimming pool.

Above and right The *calidarium*. The marble bosses conceal computer controls for hydrotherapy. The niche on the right enshrines a large 17th-century marble medallion.

Opposite The master bedroom, with its lavish gilt decoration.

Above A 19th-century brass birdcage, set between 18th-century French stone garden sphinxes.

Following pages The portico, its openings glazed, has become the living room. A pair of unicorns flank the 16th-century fireplace in *pietra serena*. In the left foreground, a 1920s table with rounded ends supports two narwhal tusks and decorative glass by Gallé, Loetz and Daum. Above it, a painting by Giovanni Boldini hangs against the bronze-finished plaster wall. The carpets are mink.

Cortina, Italy

A CHALET IN CORTINA D'AMPEZZO

Interiors by Alberto Del Biondi and Tiberio Cerato

This chalet in Cortina d'Ampezzo is very different from traditional romantic Alpine architecture, and yet a feeling of crisp mountain air permeates these uncluttered interiors, not least because floor-to-ceiling windows remove all visual barriers between the living spaces within and the mountainscape of the Dolomites. The materials chosen for the interiors and furnishings by Alberto Del Biondi and Tiberio Cerato were all locally sourced, emphasizing the continuity between indoors and out. Stone and fragrant fir wood complement the valley's traditional fabric, boiled wool.

Right Fir wood cladding on ceiling and walls sets the tone in the living room. All the fabrics are boiled wool, except for the sheepskin pillows. The windows frame the dramatic majesty of the Cortina d'Ampezzo basin in a metaphor of the sublime.

Opposite The fireplace is set flush into the living room wall, which is made of hand-cut local stone. The television screen above can be concealed by a sliding screen of the same stone.

Right, above The dining area is entirely of wood. Above the rough fir table is a hanging light made from a deer's antlers.

Right, below Firewood in a niche next to the fireplace forms an eye-catching graphic pattern.

Opposite A characteristic feature of the interior design is the fluid movement between rooms, punctuated by differences in level and sliding doors.

Right, above The kitchen is closed off by a curtain of French brocaded velvet. The sink, with Cut taps by Boffi, was made from a single block of stone, which also supports an Alpes Inox hob.

Right, below On the dining table, a pewter tray holds three ox horns.

Following pages The fireplace end of the living room.

Opposite, above One of the guest rooms.

Opposite, below The master bedroom. The bed, with a fox fur coverlet and cushions in lamb and chamois, sits snugly under the sloping roof.

Above Another guest room. Plain fir wood forms the bed bases and seating. The blankets are of hand-stitched mohair, with horn buttons.

Careyes, Mexico

CASA TIGRE DEL MAR

Gianfranco Brignone's Mexican hideaway looks out on the Pacific Costa Careyes, or Turtle Coast, from towers that resemble a medieval fortress. And it is effectively a stronghold and retreat, where you can contemplate nature through one of the many windows, tend the fragrant garden of medicinal plants, escape from the madding crowd, and find solace among the local palms, some of which have been incorporated into the building itself.

Right The towers of Casa Tigre del Mar and the little garden with its medicinal plants.

Above One of the guest rooms.
It was built around two palm trees,
whose trunks pierce the ceiling from
which they emerge above the house.
Entwining them are their symbiotic
companions, lianas.

Opposite The entrance hall
and staircase.

Opposite The trunk of a palm tree rises to meet the straw-thatched roof of a *palapa*.

Above An open-air relaxation area. The contrasting reds and blues are a theme that runs throughout the house.

Left A guest room.

Above The floor of the pantry next to
the kitchen is bordered with a pattern
in black and white.

Above The terrace on the first floor.

Right A thatched *palapa*, supported on palm trunks, surrounded by a flower bed, looks onto the infinity pool, which is approached across a symbolic labyrinth.

Florence, Italy

GIANLUCA LELLI LOFT

Interiors by Gianluca Lelli

Gianluca Lelli, the youthful CEO of the Hilife property company, has set antique off against contemporary with an ironic touch within a former convent in the centre of Florence. His loft apartment is housed within its original brick walls and roofs; but in the way he fills this setting he is uncompromisingly modern. Thus the garage, which houses a sculpturesque Lamborghini, leads straight into the living room, sweeping away at a stroke all the hierarchical distinctions of traditional domestic spaces.

Above A corner of the living area, with a low Indian table and Arketipo armchairs. The ampersand-shaped wrought-iron bookcase was made by a Florentine blacksmith; the vase next to the audio speaker on the left is by Bruno Gamboni.

Opposite The main living space is 13 metres (some 40 feet) high. Originally the open courtyard of the convent, it was roofed over in the late 19th century. The sofas are by B&B, the audio-visual installation by Bang & Olufsen, and the photographs here and elsewhere by Massimo Listri.

Above The dining and kitchen areas.
The table and chairs are design classics:
the table is Eero Saarinen's Tulip, and
the chairs are by Harry Bertoia.

Right The island kitchen, of steel and
white Carrara marble, is by Arclinea.

Following pages A Lamborghini Gallardo
sits in the entrance hall-cum-garage,
which was originally the chancel of an
18th-century church. On the left are
Barcelona chairs by Mies van der Rohe
made by Knoll; the two resin floor lamps
in the corners are by Foscarini. The floor
is of Florentine *cotto*.

DOMENICO DOLCE HOUSE

Design by Rodolfo Dordoni

The villa built by Domenico Dolce for himself – with Stefano Gabbana – at Roquebrune-Cap Martin on the Côte d'Azur is in a perpetual state of transformation. Every year, Dolce adds something, modifying the interior or the outdoor areas. The geometrical plan has well defined, airy volumes and large windows opening to the world. The colours are Mediterranean, with white plaster, natural woods and steel. The overall design was conceived by Rodolfo Dordoni, in a style befitting a location like Roquebrune, which has such strong connections with architectural modernism (influential designers who were active here include Eileen Gray, Rob Mallet-Stevens and Le Corbusier). Dolce and Dordoni worked closely together to select the furniture, which pays tribute to the great names of 20th-century design: pieces by Alvar Aalto, Mies van der Rohe and Fornasetti find a congenial setting in these understated, clean-lined rooms.

Right The outdoor area linking the living room and dining room is an attractive space for breakfast or for aperitifs. The table and Fornasetti tea and coffee service form a rigorous study in black and white.

Above The living room is a place for
conversation or pre-dinner drinks. The
zebra-striped chairs by Alvar Aalto are
marketed in Italy by Mc Selvini. Helmut
Newton photographs look down from
the walls. On the far wall is an old
master painting of one of the Graces,
with a putto and pearls. Below it is a
bench covered in zebra skin.

Opposite On a wall in the guest suite
is a 17th-century painting symbolizing
the strength of man. The Aoy lamp is
by Achille Castiglioni for Flos. Further
photographs by Helmut Newton hang
in the corridor.

Left The dining room. Chairs designed by Mies van der Rohe in 1927, now made by Knoll, are grouped around the Ron Arad metal table. The *torchères* are 17th-century, from Sicily; the Murano glass chandelier was designed by Dolce & Gabbana.

Above Looking out to the garden from the verandah.

Following pages The pool, on the highest terrace of the estate, is set among lemon trees, palm trees and azaleas.

PALACE OF RODOLPHE D'ERLANGER

Musician, poet and painter, Baron Rodolphe d'Erlanger fell in love with Tunisia and Sidi Bou Said, so much so that in 1908 he built a home on a clifftop site overlooking the sea. The building is low and white and has the blue doors and windows that would soon become fashionable all over Tunisia. Baron d'Erlanger called in the finest Tunisian and Moroccan woodworkers and stuccodores to work on the interior, recreating the glories of Moorish art, with allusions to the Alhambra in Granada, the bays of the mosque in Cordoba, Moroccan stucco work, black and white Ottoman decorative motifs, and even ancient Rome. Today, the palace is owned by the state; the original decoration has been carefully conserved, in memory of a man who gave much to Sidi Bou Said.

Above left The courtyard with its blue woodwork on the upper floor is a tribute to the Medina in Tunis. While the columns on the first floor were made in Tunisia, the paving is Moroccan.

Opposite The first-floor gallery. The large windows with blue-painted frames look onto the main courtyard.

Opposite A view down into the corridor. In the *seghia*, or channel, perfumed water flowed from the fountain in the living room, where the baron loved to listen to *malouf* music, played by an orchestra that he had formed.

Right Two views of the living room, decorated with Tunisian stuccowork and Italian marble. From the fountain perfumed water flowed down the corridor, flanked by spaces with divans covered in antique silks.

Above The sitting room in one of the apartments, with Moroccan furniture.

Opposite Superb stuccowork by North African craftsmen, and four columns in Tunisian style, frame a divan draped with antique carpets and cushions.

Kyoto, Japan

YIEN EAST

This traditional Japanese home is a temple to the harmony of nature. Set in a romantic *shinden zukuri* garden, it is traversed by a bubbling stream. The intense pinks of camellias and azaleas and the paler tones of star magnolias stand out against the deep greens of the conifers and the softer shades of Japanese maples. The interior could be from a film by Yasujiro Ozu. Everything is in natural materials – wood, rice paper, parchment and stone – and strives almost philosophically to fuse what is inside us with what is around us.

Above A fountain carved out of a tree trunk at the entrance sets the note of anonymous artistic minimalism.

Right The entrance, looking towards the garden. The perimeter fence is made of bound branches. An uneven stone path leads up to the house.

Left The house is surrounded by a verandah. In front stands a *karikomi*, a hillock covered with moss and shrubs such as azaleas and rhododendrons, embodying Shintoist naturalism.

Above Lit candles in small protective boxes provide ritual illumination among the greenery.

Above The airy verandah that surrounds the house. On the floor are traditional modular *tatami* mats in woven and pressed rice paper.

Opposite, above The spacious rooms are separated by lightweight sliding panels, producing filigree-like images of the house's shifting volumes.

Opposite, below One of the rooms for daytime activities. Screens mark off spaces according to the moods and needs of the moment.

Left The dining area. A low red lacquer table is surrounded by large cushions used as seats on the *tatami*-covered floor. On the bench is a *raku* ceramic vase. A classic lamp with a rice paper shade hangs from the ceiling.

Following pages The stream that runs through the garden. The murmur of flowing water suggests harmony, providing a background note to the silence of the night in this tranquil residential district of Kyoto.

Tokyo, Japan

K HOUSE

Design by Nonframe/Ryota Ebisui

This U-shaped house was built for an addict to golf, a firm favourite with Japanese of all ages: a small putting green on the patio is visible through the windows, and other areas too are dedicated to the sport. Separate zones of the house are set aside for parents and children, the living room providing a space where the two generations can meet. The airy rooms, modern in style with just a hint of the Orient, are suffused by an intense light that is further emphasized by the white walls and dark accents of recesses, doors and projections. Tile floors conceal the heating and cooling systems.

Right The light-filled, double-height living room has Italian furnishings and light fittings. Visible above is the corridor that leads to the parents' and children's bedrooms.

Left, above A Chinese relief from an ancient temple, mounted on the right-hand wall, greets visitors in the entrance hall and protects the home from evil and bad luck.

Left, below Just beyond the entrance, zebrawood on the walls lends movement to the passages through the house.

Opposite The front door, seen from outside. The walls are faced with small, slightly uneven tiles that contrast attractively with the smoothness of the metal fittings.

The gangway-like corridor on the upper floor. One of the bedrooms can be seen in the background. Panes of glass take the place of a balustrade.

Opposite, above The study is packed with trophies, souvenirs, and the paraphernalia of golf.

Opposite, below An indoor driving range.

Above The putting green in the patio is surrounded by glass walls.

PETER HINWOOD RESIDENCE

P eter Hinwood is a voracious art
collector whose home occupies
the entire first floor of a grand house
in Mayfair. The rooms have the generous
dimensions characteristic of 18th-
century domestic architecture, making
them ideal for Hinwood's furniture,
some of which is massive. The strong
colours of the walls change from room
to room, setting off his eclectic Grand
Tour collection of rare objects from
all over the world.

Right In the bedroom, a small chest of
drawers in limed wood stands between
striped curtains.

Opposite Also in the bedroom, an
antique Moroccan mirror hangs
above a 19th-century French cupboard
with decoration in Moorish style.
The leather armchair in the left
foreground is English, from the reign
of George II; the imposing 18th-century
dresser on the left and the antique
armchair covered with striped fabric
in the right foreground are also English.
The occasional table is Moroccan.

The drawing room. Under the window in the background are a 19th-century kitchen table and an 18th-century English chair. Several of the Turkish tiles of which Hinwood is an avid collector are arranged on the mantelpiece. The lanterns and occasional tables are Moroccan.

Opposite Two views of the bedroom.
An African barber's sign hangs above
the 19th-century English brass bed.

Above Turkish tiles share the bathroom
shelves with other curiosities.

An amusing collection of engravings,
oil paintings and watercolours brightens
the kitchen walls.

Right, above and below Two views of
the entrance hall, which is painted
an intense shade of lavender and is
dominated by a console table with white
marble top and a large Indian painting.

Santo Domingo, Dominican Republic

HUGO TOLENTINO RANCHETA

Hugo Tolentino Dipp is one of the most distinguished residents of Los Samanes, in the Dominican Republic. He and his wife Sarah, an expert flower and landscape gardener, live in the Rancheta Caballona, which seems to sail like an ancient galleon through the verdant fruit and sugarcane plantations. It consists of three sections clad in pastel-painted palm wood and roofed with zinc, linked by corridors. The windows are unglazed, and the flooring is of roughly coloured concrete. The house was moved from its original site 80 kilometres (some 50 miles) away and re-erected in the garden created by Sarah Tolentino. The interior, with its colonial furnishings, naive paintings, hammocks, big terracotta jars and old European engravings, has all the vibrant fascination of the Caribbean.

Right The entrance door of one of the sections.

Opposite A corridor. The walls are covered in thin strips of painted palm wood and the floor is of coloured concrete.

Left The dining and sitting areas.
The dining chairs were made by
Dominican craftsmen; the armchairs
are of rattan.

Above Locally made antique jars
in the kitchen.

The guest room. In the hammock, visitors can take full advantage of the cool of the night.

Right, above The 19th-century bed in the master bedroom was made by Mexican craftsmen.

Right, below The master bathroom. Above 19th-century wood-edged tub are several *higueros*, half-coconuts polished and painted in bright colours.

London, England

WEINBERG HOUSE

Interiors by Anouska Hempel

The location is Chelsea, the elegant district of London on which many great architects, including Sir Christopher Wren, Sir John Soane and Norman Shaw, have left their mark. The house is that of insurance magnate and philanthropist Mark Weinberg. Inside, however, the decor is entirely the work of his wife, Anouska Hempel. A woman of many talents, she made her screen debut as an actress in 1969 in *On Her Majesty's Secret Service*, and she is regarded as one of the hundred most influential interior designers in the world. Her style-before-comfort philosophy strives above all for perfection in composition. Every majestic, historically resonant detail has its own precise location, governed by rigorous principles of symmetry, and by the recurrent contrast of flat surfaces filled with objets d'art, with expansive views towards the garden.

Previous pages, left A Victorian
oil painting.

Previous pages, right The living room.
Gold gleams from the large mirror,
the chest, and the neoclassical chairs
with their backs decorated with double-
lyre motifs. Note the concealed
ceiling lighting.

Above The library-study. The stepped
design of the sofa unit leads the viewer's
eye upwards to the portrait of a lady
painted in the 17th century in the style
of the great William Larkin (1580–1619),
whose work has only relatively recently
been rediscovered.

Opposite An arrangement of 18th-
century engravings of vases and ewers
frames the door of the bathroom.

Above left and right Engravings of
equestrian subjects from the 18th
century provide a leitmotiv in the
bathroom with its elegant burnished
decor.

Opposite The master bedroom. From
the head of the bed, with its elaborate
tasselled canopy and cover embroidered
in relief with floral motifs, a portrait of
a lady of the time of Charles I looks out.

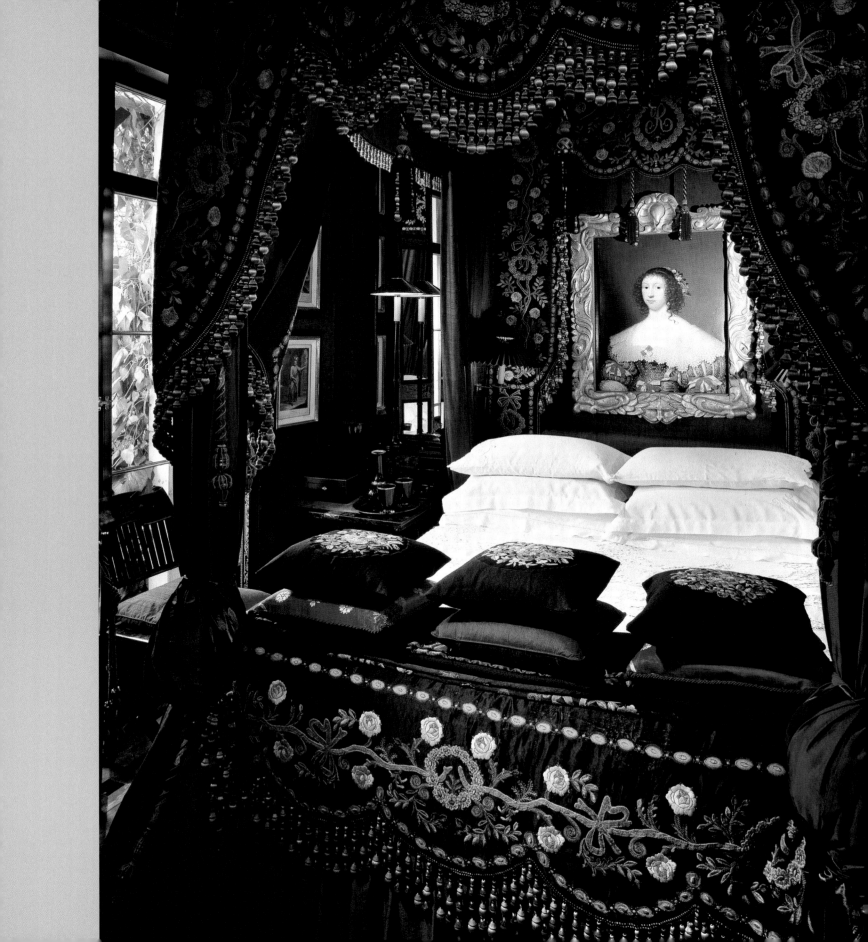

ORSOLA GAZZONI RESIDENCE

The bright colours of Mexico and the art of Henri Matisse set the tone in Orsola Gazzoni's apartment in a 19th-century palazzo located in Milan's bohemian Navigli district. The conventional bourgeois architecture is the setting for very unconventional colours, ethnic objects, contemporary artworks, and rich Tricia Guild fabrics that fill the rooms with life.

Right This still-life on the living room mantelpiece echoes the colours of a Matisse canvas. The small painting of a camel is by Fathi Hassan.

Opposite The enfilade through the rooms reveals an exciting sequence of colours. The magenta curtains are by Tad, the green ones by Tricia Guild.

Left The living room. Behind the sofa on the left, which is covered in a fabric by Tricia Guild, is *Senza titolo* (*Untitled*), a painting by Enzo Esposito of 2001. The cushions are by Tad, and the coffee table by Cappellini.

Above The entrance to the kitchen.

Left The Indian cupboard was painted by the Laboratorio Idarica Gazzoni. On top are a lamp and a vase by Tad.

Opposite The dining room. On the wall is a work by Sergio Barnils of 2001. The chairs are Indian and the table is Indonesian. The silver candlesticks are by Christofle.

Opposite The master bedroom. The
bedcover and cushions are by Romo,
and the bedside lamp by IKEA. Above
the wrought iron and rope head of the
bed is a work by Fathi Hassan.

Above The small mirror is Moroccan;
the red shelf is from IKEA.

LAURA SARTORI RIMINI RESIDENCE

Design by Laura Sartori Rimini

Architect-designer Laura Sartori Rimini's apartment occupies the attic floor of a 17th-century building at Celerina, near St Moritz, an Engadine village that has managed to retain much of its ancient character. The building was originally a farmhouse combined with a stable and barn (*talvo*). The attic used to be a grain loft, which was too low to be habitable. The floors of the three storeys were lowered to permit a rearrangement of the internal spaces without altering the external walls. All the old wood from the original house was saved and re-used in the attic apartment to clad the walls and ceilings, and to make new floors. The designer set up symmetries and contrasts to make the spaces seem larger and more unified, and then treated them as containers for the objects and furnishings she has carefully selected over the years in flea markets and antique shops around the world.

Right The living room. On the back wall, next to the 17th-century Lombard stone fireplace, is a portrait of an 18th-century gentleman. A 17th-century bench from Emilia stands in the middle of the room, affording a place for books and magazines. On the floor on either side are Turkish cushions. Chesterfield sofas and a 19th-century Ushak carpet complete the scene.

Left, above The entrance hall, with
its barrel-vaulted ceiling of Cimbrian
pine; the arch rests on two late 18th-
century fluted walnut columns. Kilims
cover the floor and table.

Left, below A corner of the living room.

Opposite The dining room. On the
floor on either side of the table are
two 17th-century still-lifes. Over
the table is a 19th-century wood
and iron chandelier.

Opposite The ceiling in the guest room is covered with linen to form a canopy. At the foot of the bed is a chest for candles, from a sacristy.

Above left The 19th-century rustic cupboard in the guest room comes from Central Europe.

Above right The bathroom. The iron and marble washbasin dates from the early 20th century, the mirror from the 19th century.

Paris, France

ALDA FENDI RESIDENCE

Interiors by Raffaelle Curi

In a not too distant past, Maurice Utrillo, Georges Braque, Picasso, Henry Miller, Man Ray and Cocteau walked the Boulevard Saint-Germain, and Alda Fendi has recreated that exciting early 20th-century atmosphere in a home conceived as an artist's studio. The interior designer she called in, Raffaele Curi, succeeded in capturing the spirit of the period with minimalist understatement. Central to it all is the great Dada artist Man Ray: a series of black-and-white photographs of him at work, by Dino Pedriali, are the keynote of the large, double-height living room, which is the heart of the interior.

This studio-like space is theatrically dominated by a tall double ladder, a reminder of the world of the stage from which Curi comes and with which he still has links.

Above The staircase, lit by Mayday lamps from Flos.

Right A tall black metal ladder designed by Raffaele Curi and made by Alimonti stands between the Raffles sofas by Vico Magistretti for De Padova in the living room.

Opposite and above The living room, alias studio. The wooden floor is marked with expressionist stains of paint. On either side of the fireplace are photographs by Dino Pedriali of Man Ray at work.

BJURÅKER FARM, HÄLSINGLAND

The Swedish painters Jonas Hertman, Anders Adel and Gustav Reuter achieved celebrity posthumously, but they would never have done so at all if a Hälsingland farmer had not reported to the heritage authorities that there were traces of religious paintings on the walls of his house and barn. It was soon discovered that most of the local farms were decorated with paintings dating from the 18th century, when the area produced linen that was much admired by King Gustav III: as their wealth grew, local farmers had had their homes painted by itinerant artists. The Bjuråker Farm, tucked away in the forest of Delsbo, is decorated throughout with rustic paintings by Gustaf Reuter (1699–1783) and his pupil Erik Ersson (1730–1800). The paintings were restored in the 1950s.

Above The main farmhouse at Bjuråker.

Right The walls of the dining room have a cycle of paintings depicting the life of Martin Luther, and a garland-bedecked ceiling in the Gustavian tradition. The paint, made with natural pigments extracted from leaves or roots, was applied to linen cloth attached to the wall.

A Gustavian vernacular sideboard and a painting representing Martin Luther, in one corner of the dining room.

The kitchen, warmed by a stove, was also used as a bedroom for the children, with a canopied bed for the older child and a cradle for the baby. The walls have paintings of stately cavalrymen. The artist Gustav Reuter had previously been in the infantry.

New York, New York, United States

THIERRY DESPONT HOUSE

Design by Thierry Despont

Thierry Despont is French by birth and cosmopolitan by inclination. A versatile, sophisticated architect and artist, he has a degree in fine art from Paris and a master's degree from Harvard. He has worked for Bill Gates, restored the Statue of Liberty, co-designed the galleries of the Getty Center in Los Angeles – and much more. In addition to all this, he paints, publishes illustrations, and holds one-man exhibitions. Despont's Manhattan home mirrors his passions and eclectic approach to history, architecture, art, and even science. He completely redesigned the interior of the building (moving the living room to the top floor), selected sober furniture, and coloured the walls in contrasting neutral and assertive tones.

Right The style of the living room alludes to *haut bourgeois* interiors in Paris of the 1930s and 1940s. The pieces upholstered in yellow and red mohair were designed by Despont, and the drawings on the walls are by him too. The black granite sculpture on the pedestal is by Benoit Luickx, and the glass composition at the back of the room is by Dale Chihuly.

Left, above and below The billiard room. The eye-catching wall covering is a tartan fabric designed by The Office of Thierry W. Despont. On the wall is a lithograph by John Register.

An Italian-made five-pin table
dominates the billiard room, below
a vintage French lamp. An engraved
glass armillary sphere, by the owner,
is perched on an antique tripod.

Above and right Surfaces in the bathroom are covered in Carrara and black Belgian marble. The charcoal drawing is by Despont.

The library-study showcases large pieces of natural history – some displayed with an ironic touch, like the rhinoceros skull into whose jaws Despont has inserted a wooden model hand. The photograph dates from the 19th century. An astrolabe brought back from a trip to Russia stands on the table.

Opposite The studio. The space is richly cluttered with models, drawings and paintings by Thierry Despont. An armillary sphere by Despont, of blown glass in an oxidized bronze frame, is engraved with fantastic representations of the heavens.

LARS SJÖBERG HOUSE

Art historian, curator of the National Museum in Stockholm, and consultant to IKEA, Lars Sjöberg acquired the Eckenberg house, built in Gustavian style in the 18th century by Carl August Ehrensvärd, and restored it with scholarly passion. The snow-white ceilings, panelled walls painted with trompe-l'oeil mouldings and pale floral garlands may look slightly dilapidated, but they still convey the glory and restraint of the elegant, minimalist style that King Gustav III preferred to the excesses of rococo.

Right The main entrance to the Eckenberg house.

Opposite The enfilade of rooms serves as a gallery for busts and neoclassical console tables.

Left The dining room. Floors painted
white or in pastel colours are typical
of the Gustavian style, and the chairs
are also characteristic of the period.
On the cupboard to the right of the tiled
stove is a bust of Lady Hamilton.

Above The corridor leading to the
kitchen. The medallion over the door
is by Johan Tobias Sergel. The rococo
longcase clock is Swedish, with an
English movement.

The master bedroom. The canopied
bed and gilt mirror coexist with
distinctively Gustavian elements such
as the white chair and the wallpaper
with floral motifs.

CHATEAU DU BREUIL

Interiors by Guy Thodorof

In the countryside not far from Paris stands the Château du Breuil. It is not a true castle but a fortified residence, originally a farm protected by an armed guard where from the 16th century onwards monks grew vegetables and raised livestock to feed the monasteries of the capital. The building itself is noble and solid, but time and commercial use had robbed the interiors of interest. When he was called in to rethink the decoration by the owner who purchased the property a decade ago, Guy Thodorof strove to create a residence that was real, although it had never actually existed: Flemish in style, aristocratic and eclectic, the house has a studied warmth, and the simple, welcoming atmosphere of a canvas by Jan van Kessel or Dirck Hals. Paintings, portraits, statues, antique furnishings,

Delft porcelain, old wood, marble, carpets, hangings, rich trimmings and decorated wallpaper blend with a refined historical sensitivity to shape and recount the story of a family with a glorious past.

Above The Château du Breuil is a country house guarded by a watchtower.

Right The living room still has the original beamed ceiling, now cleaned and made good. An 18th-century portrait of a Prussian noblewoman hangs above the Provençal walnut secretaire. On the right are Delft vases and a French portrait of a child in court dress (c. 1760). An imposing late Renaissance statue of a Roman emperor is set back behind curtains at the far right.

Left The decoration of the guest room is evocative of love, with portraits of young women and a series of engravings of amorous subjects. The wallpaper has a bold floral pattern. The neoclassical fall-front secretaire has drawers with ivory knobs; the bed too is neoclassical, from the early 19th century.

Above A miniature model of the living room of a Flemish house sums up the spirit behind the château's decoration.

Opposite A 17th-century Dutch portrait of a young man looks out above a cupboard made in Paris in the 18th century. The chairs are from Provence. The vases are Delft. The bust and wooden figurines date from the 16th century.

Above The drawing room. A family portrait by the 17th-century Dutch artist Jan Victoors hangs above the monumental fireplace. The orderly overcrowding of the furniture, the Delft tiles lining the fireplace, the brass chandelier and the richly draped purple curtains combine to evoke a flavour of Northern Europe.

Koh Samui, Thailand

KOH SAMUI RESIDENCE

Design by Bill Bensley

A world of its own, tucked away in a dream-like corner of a fairy-tale setting: such is the impression left by the Koh Samui Residence. Located on the Thai island of Samui, it was designed by Bill Bensley, the tall American architect who settled in Bangkok a few years ago. Scattered over a gentle hillside that runs down to golden beaches and a crystal-clear sea, Koh Samui comprises fifty-eight bungalows and two larger houses raised on stilts. Each building has its own style, excitingly marrying the local architecture with the standard of comfort required in the modern world. Every bungalow enjoys soul-satisfying views over the intense blue sea of the Gulf of Siam, each has its own infinity pool, and all are linked by a system of steps and gangways that lend a touch of adventure. Communal areas are large and symmetrically composed. The natural materials used, and the nearness to nature, engender an intensely relaxing sense of harmony.

Above right Some of the bungalows at Koh Samui, on a lush green slope above the sea.

Right Lit softly from below at night, the pitched roof of the 'hut' presents an impressive triangular silhouette.

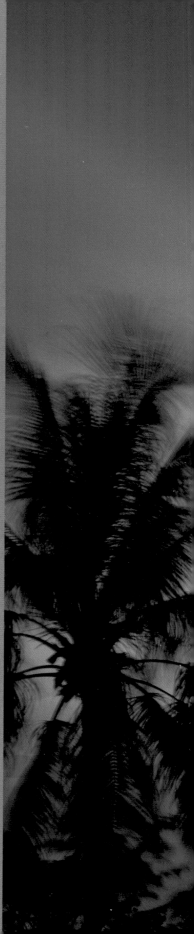

Left The 'hut' is the central element in the network of bungalows. This theatre-like space is open to the metaphysical marvel of a motionless sea and swept by delicious salty fragrances that mingle with the odours of the tropical forest. The unfussy, comfortably curvy sofas were designed by Bill Bensley.

Above The entrance to one of bungalows, with an understated abstract decorative motif.

Following pages The 'hut' seen from outside. Pillars, each made up of four tree trunks, support the roof, which is thatched with straw. A narrow 'fishpond' provides a boundary – in colour as well as medium – between the 'hut' and the surrounding forest.

Left, above and below The roof of a bungalow, and a detail of the interior. Bensley's decorative scheme focused on the natural materials to hand, especially wood, and involved local craft workers and businesses in the production of items in a style that elegantly blends the contemporary Western spirit with the heritage of the East.

A general view of the 'hut' shows how all the structural elements are joined without the use of any metal.

Left, above The swimming pool of a bungalow. Each pool is fed by a fountain of a different shape.

Left, below The spectacular wooden steps that lead to the spa through a forest of palm trees, mangoes and jackfruits.

Opposite One of the bungalows, with its private pool. Here as elsewhere in the complex, the dominant hue is turquoise, the colour of the sea of the Andaman Islands, west of Thailand.

Brussels, Belgium

VAN DE VELDE HOUSE

Interiors by Carlo Rampazzi

If ever there were any need to demonstrate that minimalism and maximalism can coexist in harmony, this house on the outskirts of Brussels would serve triumphantly as proof. The architecture is characterized by a restrained, unobtrusive modernism, austere and unemotional. Inside, on the other hand, exuberant colours and shapes, curvaceous lines and assertive baroque touches contrast with the cool, geometric spaces in a whirl of invention that shows the hand of a master of fantasy at work: Carlo Rampazzi, the inspired interior designer from the Ticino in Switzerland.

Right The house at dusk. Floor-to-roof windows on the two levels emphasize the linearity of the design.

Above In the dining area, the convex-fronted cupboard in red macassar was designed by Carlo Rampazzi and Sergio Villa and the cantilever chair with polished chrome base, upholstered in plaited silk, is by Most.

Above right The dining area looks out to the large garden. The table, from the Costantino Collection by Rampazzi and Villa, has sculptural bronze legs and a red faux crocodile-skin top. The leather-covered chairs are by Hurel.

Opposite The living area, centred on a large fireplace in modernist idiom, is filled with sunny colours. Between the sofa and the chairs, which include some from the La Nuova Tradizione line designed by Rampazzi for Colombostile, are two occasional tables on the axis of the fireplace. The coffee table – in silver sheet and macassar – displays a tray and candles designed and made by Rampazzi and Villa's furnishing workshop, Selvaggio.

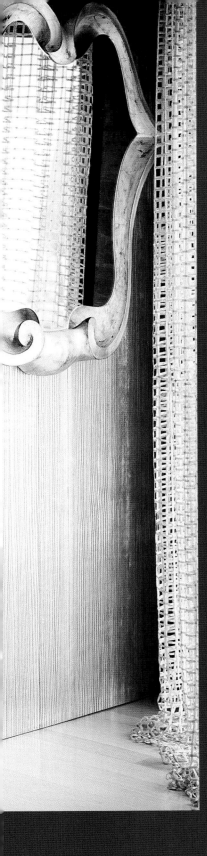

Left and below Two views of the exuberantly baroque bathroom. Sumptuous shapes and volumes, brilliantly coloured rare marbles, and works of art convey a sensation of sheer sensual pleasure.

Above and right The cool modernity of the swimming pool is tempered by the painting on the underside of the roof depicting a fluttering curtain open to a clear spring sky – a cheerful fiction to counteract the many grey days in the Northern European year. The load-bearing piers stand outside the walls, so that the space inside is completely unobstructed.

Malindi, Kenya

LION IN THE SUN

Design by Celeste dell'Anna and Stefano d'Alessandro

Flavio Briatore is a man courted by glossy magazines and women. To achieve success he chose a life of adventure, guided by the motto 'Think big'. Lion in the Sun, Briatore's home at Malindi in Kenya, fully reflects his penchant for grandeur but does so with simplicity, taking its cue from local African, colonial and occasionally Arab architecture. The original house was built in the 1990s to a design by Celeste dell'Anna, but it was steadily enlarged, to become a place where friendship and the holiday spirit flourish as if in a magical workshop. At the centre of the complex is a vast living room, open at one end, under a steep roof of *makuti* – a mixture of leaves and straw – designed by Stefano d'Alessandro, an architect familiar with all the secrets of African building techniques.

Right The living room. The double-flight staircase in the background leads to various conversation areas, and to the dining and breakfast area. The walls have decorations in Arab style and the floor is in dark local galena stone.

Left In one of the rooms Africa and Asia meet. The portrait of a Masai warrior is by a local Kenyan artist, the sideboard is Indian, the bowls on it are from Burma, and the kilim on the floor is from Iran.

Opposite This view of the living room shows the refined construction of the wooden staircase, decorated with rope motifs much favoured in East African Islamic crafts.

Opposite The living room opens onto a swimming pool; in the distance are canopied sitting areas and divans draped with brightly coloured fabrics and provided with mosquito nets.

Above A west-facing section of the mezzanine floor provides a romantic corner where diners can watch the African night fall among the mysterious whisperings of wild nature. Camphorwood flooring adds its own fascinating fragrance to the scene.

Miami, Florida, United States

MURANO PENTHOUSE

Design by René Gonzales

When two art-loving collectors were looking for a warm, functional home they could also use as a setting for their impressive collection of contemporary works, they turned to René Gonzales. Gonzales – whose designs include the Cisneros Fontanals Art Foundation – created a penthouse with an area of 600 square metres (6,500 square feet) and terraces giving panoramic views atop one of Miami Beach's most widely admired residential buildings. With his brief in mind, he chose a refined, understated style and tone of discreet, intellectual luxury. Instead of separate rooms, the spaces endlessly interpenetrate, linked by the materials used to create them. Teak, for example, is used for folding doors in the entrance hall, veneers a long buffet in the living room, forms the floor of the master bedroom, combines with stainless steel in the kitchen, and, finally, forms the dining room sideboard. The furniture includes pieces specially made for the apartment (bookcases, chests of drawers and bar), intriguing ethnic pieces, and pieces by major designers.

Right The living room is simple and understated. The Andy sofas were designed by Paolo Piva for B&B in 2002, the two coffee tables are by Monica Armani, and the Kangaroo chair was designed by George Nelson for Herman Miller in 1956. The three photographs on the walls are by Guido Albi Marini.

Above The teak and lacquer bathroom.

Right A bathroom with a couch on which to relax, and a view over the bay.

Following pages The dining room. The Doge dining table was designed in 1969 by Carlo Scarpa for Simon International; above it hang light fittings designed by Nasir Kassamali. On the back wall is *Giugno* (*June*), a photographic work by Guido Albi Marini.

The entrance hall is articulated by a
series of folding teak doors, designed
by Gonzales.

In the master bedroom, the focus
of attention is Guido Albi Marini's
photograph *Looking for the Self* (2005).

EMILIO MIGLIAVACCA HOUSE

Interiors by Emilio Migliavacca

The house that fashion designer Emilio – 'Milo' – Migliavacca built on Bali, with the help only of local workmen, is distinctly out of the ordinary. Foundations, ground floor and communal areas are in reinforced concrete, whereas the upper floors, which house the bedrooms, a cinema and the owner's studio, and the pillars that support the thatched roof are all of merbau, a robust local timber that resembles rosewood. The floors are covered with a special mixture of cement, glass, shards of mirror and mother-of-pearl invented by Migliavacca to give visitors the illusion of walking on a sort of magic carpet. Furnishings are in part colonial and in part decidedly vernacular, made locally.

Right An antique statue of Shiva stands at the entrance to greet visitors.

Opposite The octagonal house, on three levels, rises beyond the pool.

Left An early 20th-century Chinese opium bed in the living room.

Above An alabaster lamp covered with a Balinese dancer's headdress stands on a teak table.

Left, above A corner of a bedroom.

Left, below The bathroom.

Opposite A Hindu altar for votive offerings supports a painted wooden statue of Brahma and Chinese and local ceramics.

Cartagena, Colombia

LINA BOTERO HOUSE

Interiors by Lina Botero

Interior designer Lina Botero is the daughter of the artist Fernando Botero and Gloria Zea, curator of the Museum of Modern Art in Bogotá. When she was looking for a second home, she found it in the picturesque Spanish colonial district of Cartagena. The high-ceilinged two-storeyed house had been restored by Alvaro Barrera, who reinstated the original colours – hydrangea blue, salmon pink and ochre – which had long been hidden under white plaster. Lina Botero chose those shades when she laid out the ground floor, and selected plain furniture to fit in with the imposing colonial architecture.

Right The house is centred on a patio with a pool.

Left The living room, with salmon pink walls.

Above An antique terracotta pot on a colonial piece of furniture of painted wood.

Opposite The patio and pool.

Right, above Another view of the patio, showing the dining table.

Right, below A glimpse of the master bedroom. A painting by the Colombian artist Antonio Barrera hangs above the bed.

GERARD TREMOLET RESIDENCE

Interiors by Gérard Tremolet

Gérard Tremolet's Paris apartment on the fifth floor of a building in the ninth arrondissement is a riot of colour that brings to mind a souk in his native Algeria. Fuchsia, yellow and turquoise jostle in the living room, mauve pink tones the bedroom and pale green the bathroom. This kaleidoscopic ambience provides inspiration for the collections of women's accessories that the owner creates for Maison Lesage. Noted for his embroidery work, Tremolet stitches pearls, gold thread and butterflies onto dresses that grace the haute couture catwalks of Paris. At home, Tremolet applies the same eclectic spirit to mixing and matching his leather objects, fabrics, kilims, exotic furniture, antique furnishing accessories, and collections of unusual objects. Elephants, toiletries, hairpins, porcelain, glassware and jewelry both antique and modern proliferate. Souvenirs of distant lands mingle with toys and scale models, some peeking out from under the furniture.

Right A 19th-century candle-holder from a church is given small lampshades of brightly coloured satin, and the chair displays the vigorous pattern of leopard skin.

Opposite A mauve Louis XVI chair and a 19th-century Renaissance-style high-backed chair converse in the corridor.

The sitting room. On the left-hand wall,
a painting by Marie Kazan of 1930; on
the mantelpiece, candelabra, Chinese
vases of the 1920s, and a pair of
Austrian ceramic figurines.

Looking the other way in the sitting room. The portrait of a woman on the right-hand wall was painted by Stanislas Floch in 1937. It hangs between two enamelled snake wall lights. The cabinet is in Louis XV style. Two lamps in the form of lanterns stand on the floor in front of the early 20th-century Chinese sofa.

Left A Napoleon III-style secretaire and carved giltwood chair in the master bedroom, watched over by an 18th-century portrait of a country priest.

Above Beyond the curtain lies the bathroom.

BENJAMIN LIEBMANN HOUSE

Design by Louis Louw, Achilles Apostolellis and Johan Bergenthuin

The house of the eclectic South African lawyer and artist Benjamin Liebmann is in Houghton, an exclusive residential suburb of Johannesburg. Its themes are columns – large cylindrical ones – and the colour white, which highlights projections, recesses and architectural space, and draws attention to the African wood carvings of which Liebmann is an enthusiastic collector. Outdoor spaces are treated as rooms in the open air.

Above The swimming pool. Sliding doors between the interior of the house and the seating areas by the pool make it possible to keep the spaces separate or let them flow into one another.

Opposite The entrance. The bronze sculpture is *The Three Graces* by Paul Wunderlich.

Above The corridor. The carving from the Ivory Coast represents the Bird of Fertility.

Right The focal point of the living room is *Harmony of Opposites*, by Victor Passmore. In the background is Elizabeth Frink's *Goggle Head*.

Opposite A row of boots in front of an
mid-19th-century cupboard in the study.

Above A vase, saddle, and canopied bed
in the children's room.

HOUSE OF THE MONK THONDARA

Right: An old Burmese chaise longue.

Opposite: The teak facade of the monastery.

Opposite The altar before which offerings are placed. The statue depicts a dhyana Buddha.

Right, above Two bowls containing the monk's daily ration of rice sit on the rough wooden boards of the floor.

Right, below Old Burmese vases.

Above left The austere furnishings of a simple life, devoted to prayer.

Above right A traditional Burmese red lacquer table stands on a straw mat.

Opposite Thondara's mosquito-netted bed is on the ground, as required by the precepts of Buddhism.

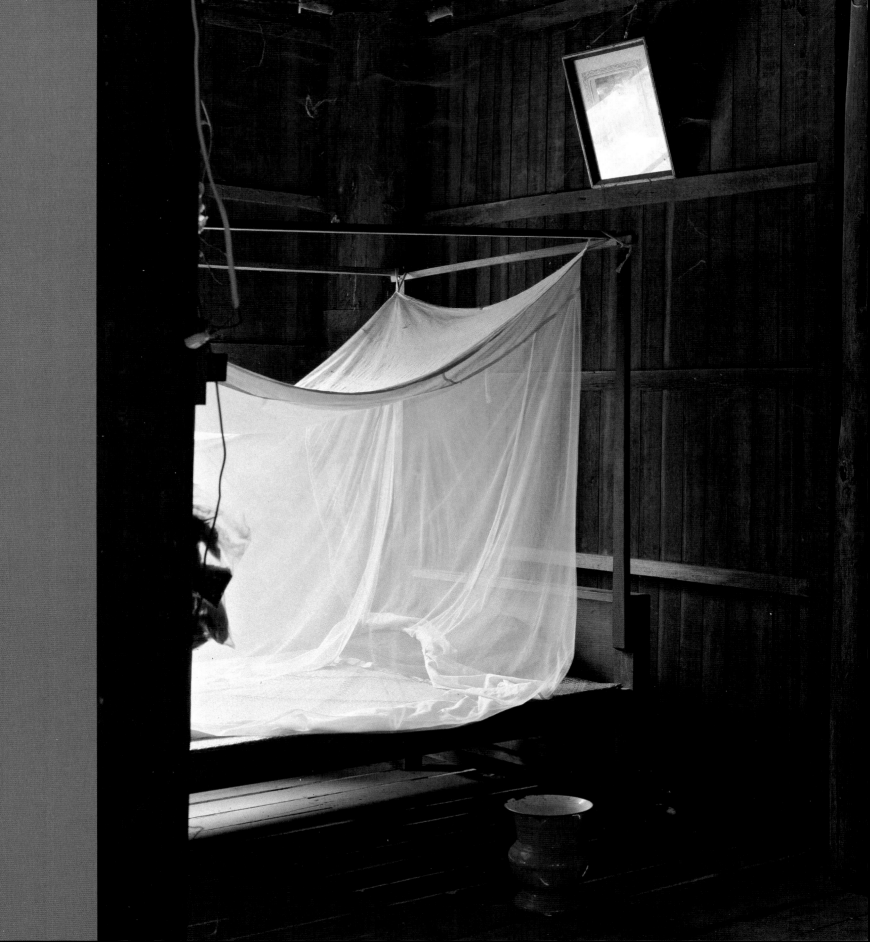

Los Angeles, California, United States

DAWNRIDGE, THE TONY DUQUETTE HOUSE

Interiors by Hutton Wilkinson

Dawnridge, the legendary home of artist and decorator Tony Duquette, tucked away in the lush green of Beverly Hills, has been restored to its former glory by the designer Hutton Wilkinson. The structure of the house remains the same. Almost all the pieces collected by Duquette in his lifetime had been sold at Christie's, but Wilkinson, Duquette's business partner and a proponent of the same theories of unusual beauty, managed to retain the stylistic unity, repopulating it with objects created by Duquette and paintings by his wife, Elizabeth Duquette. The dining room is the showplace of sumptuous jewels that Wilkinson designs for a limited clientele, and the setting for dinners he hosts to ensure that the spell cast by Duquette continues to bewitch.

Above A detail of the table set for guests.

Right The dining room's generous windows look out to the tropical garden, and the green hues and floral decor of the room (created on the site of a garage) suggest a garden. The table is set with antique Chinese lidded bowls in the shape of flowers, Venetian glass, imitation coral, and rock crystal. The Chinese display cabinet contains several pieces of jewelry by Duquette and Wilkinson.

Opposite The Camelot Room takes its
name from the models and sketches
Duquette made in the early 1960s for
the Broadway musical *Camelot*, which
earned him a prestigious Tony Award.
Duquette's console table and mirror
ornamented with horns evokes hunting;
the table supports votive rock crystals.
On the red lacquer cabinet against the
far wall is a three-dimensional model
of a design for *Camelot*.

Right, above On the screens designed by Duquette and Wilkinson in the living room, the 'suns' are made of hubcaps, with iron rays. On the far wall, a portrait of Tony Duquette painted by Martin Piks in 1965 hangs above Duquette's mixed media *Hem from a Priestess's Robe*. The figurine-filled green enamel display unit on the left was made by Duquette in 1941 for Elsie de Wolfe.

Right, below A shell-studded table lamp.

Opposite A bedroom, with fragments of antique Chinese architectural ornament on the walls. The bed was designed by Syrie Maugham for the actress Ina Claire; the paintings depict Birdcage, the Duquettes' Victorian home in San Francisco. On the floor is an antique Chinese rug.

Above left The bathroom. A birdcage transformed into a lamp hangs from the ceiling. The extravagant mirror reflects a window in a confusing way. Note the curious wall covering with a pattern of scales.

Above The master bedroom. The four-poster bed is draped with Thai silk and antique chintz. Art books on the shelves reflect the owner's interests.

Left A corner of the living room.
The gilt console and mirror with
their organic shapes were created
by Duquette in 1965. On the left is a
portrait of Elizabeth Duquette by Man
Ray, of 1947. The paintings are by her.

Opposite A door in the drawing room
sports a playful decoration inspired
by alchemy.

In a cool and sheltered bay north of Izmir, near the classical site of Pergamon, is the house of the theatre set designer Ezio Frigerio. Creator of spectacular sets for the world's most important opera houses, including the Metropolitan and Covent Garden, he is in love with the East and has a profound knowledge of Islamic art and thought. Here, well away from international tourist routes, Frigerio has created his own set. It is a house in which every window, arch and doorway is designed to frame the landscape, the seascape or the fragrant garden. Built of stone, it alludes to local tradition, but looks to a Turkey of the imagination, as conceived by Frigerio and Alexander Beliaev, the Russian designer who worked with him. Cappadocian stone was shaped by hand into columns, doors, windows, arches and lunettes; two terracotta domes were erected, without scaffolding; for the interiors, they chose hand-painted ceramic tiles of the type seen in mosques. For the furniture, Frigerio looked as far as Indonesia. He had teak screens made to filter the light, and selected fabrics from Turkey and Egypt and carpets from Persia, less common here than those from Anatolia. The result is brightly coloured, orderly, and welcoming. In this space poised between East and West Frigerio spends his summers with a few close friends and his partner, Franca Squarciapino, relaxing and reflecting on new projects.

Right The guest room has a domed ceiling. The oriental doors are antique; the bed is Hispano-Moresque.

Opposite An archway and openwork gate.

Turkey

EZIO FRIGERIO HOUSE

Design by Alexander Beliaev

Opposite The portico, paved with
Cappadocian stone.

Above left The master bedroom.
The carpet is Persian.

Above A pergola with a view of the sea.

Opposite A 17th-century Ottoman stone fountain in the living room. The antique ceramics and tiles come from Kutahya.

Left The fireplace in local stone decorated with Kutahya tiles is reminiscent of hearths in Cappadocia.

Following pages A guest room with curtained bed.

Paris, France

KUGEL RESIDENCE

Interiors by Louis-Charles de Rémusal

The apartment of a noted antique dealer in the heart of Paris has the compact volumes and layout typical of the aristocratic architecture of the Faubourg Saint-Germain. Living room and dining room have a view of the street, while the two bedrooms look onto the courtyard. The owner, assisted by the decorator Louis-Charles de Rémusal, retained the original layout with the exception of the door between living room and dining room, which was removed to create a more airy space. Colours characteristic of the 19th century were chosen – yellow, blue and green – and the light woodwork evokes Russia, where the owner's family came from. Other reminders of Russia are watercolours of St Petersburg and Fabergé-framed portraits of the imperial family.

Right The living room. A portrait of two brothers by the 19th-century Chilean artist Monvoisin hangs above the sofa. The lamps are mounted on Empire candlesticks.

A corner of the living room. The lion
head on the wall once decorated an
18th-century fountain; the portrait of
the 'leopard-girl' above it is by an early
18th-century Brazilian artist.

Right , above Another corner of the living room.

Right , below The point where living room and dining room meet.

Following pages The living room, looking towards the dining room. The double doors that once separated the two rooms have been removed.

Mustique, Caribbean

FELIX DENNIS RETREAT

Design by Arne Hasselqvist

Mustique can claim to be the original 'celebrity island'. Big names from the worlds of sports and entertainment and the international jet set continue to live on and visit the island. The home once owned by David Bowie was chosen by the British publisher, philanthropist and poet Felix Dennis as the place where he can live – and work in peace – for at least five months a year. Extrovert and controversial in this as in everything else, Dennis completely transformed the house, apart from the Las Vegas-style games room. To a flavour of China plus Indonesia with Scandinavian touches, he preferred eclecticism on a grand scale, embracing the Indies, Japan, and the colonial past.

Left Fossil nautilus shells decorate the paths in the garden and around the pool.

Right A belvedere with a telescope from which to explore the island and the surrounding Caribbean.

Above and opposite The retreat consists
of a series of pavilions designed by
Arne Hasselqvist that recall vernacular
Scandinavian architecture. Their
outlines are reflected in still pools filled
with colourful *koi* carp.

Opposite The entrance. A tribal mask
from Central Africa hangs above the
armchair from colonial times.

Above The verandah, with its
Indonesian-made furniture, is the
setting for a display of traditional art.

Right The master bedroom has a Japanese feel. A *tatami* mat covers the floor.

Following pages The extravagantly exuberant games room is the only interior to survive from the time when the house belonged to David Bowie.

Paris, France

GETRIDE HOUSE

Design by Pascal Mayer

S et in an elegant leafy area, this is the house of a couple devoted to collecting works of art. It has a strong Art Deco flavour, and its airy rooms are uncompromisingly masculine. Its understated luxury is expressed in stylish but austere materials – parchment, tropical woods, rough stone, black lacquer – and restrained colours such as beige, brown and mahogany. At the heart of the house is a dining room-cum-swimming pool. A sleek spiral staircase in the idiom of Le Corbusier curves up from the entrance hall. Every room displays works of modern and contemporary art, both paintings and sculptures, which the owners collect with passionate enthusiasm.

Above The entrance hall and staircase, designed by Pascal Mayer. The bronze sculpture is *The Watcher* by Igor Ustinov; the drawing on the wall is by Henri Matisse, of 1947.

Right The double-height living room with its floor-to-ceiling window. The walls are covered in parchment-effect leather; the white chairs are by Émile-Jacques Ruhlmann; and the lamps are by Igor Ustinov.

The dining room-cum-swimming pool.
By an ingenious hydraulic mechanism,
the bottom of the pool can be raised up
to increase the floor area. In this view
the pool has its full depth.

This view shows the effect when the bottom of the pool has just been raised to the level of the surrounding floor. Beyond the dining table is *Jarre Doré d'Automne* by Olivier Debré, of 1966.

Bali, Indonesia

LUCIO BRISSOLESE
HOUSE

Design by Ida Bagus Oka

For the sculptor and businessman Lucio Brissolese, Bali is a magic island. When he discovered it in 1982, it was love at first sight. Initially he lived on his yacht; then he moved on land, to a house in Balinese style that he built himself; then to another house, in Indonesian style; and finally to this exotic dwelling that has little to do with local architectural traditions. He designed the house with help from Ida Bagus Oka, creating a composition of rounded volumes with thatched roofs that blends perfectly with the vegetation and rocks in the garden, which is crisscrossed by flights of steps.

Right The ocean view can be savoured from the *balai*, a hut perched high above the waves. The two little tables are *balangs*, used by Balinese women to carry offerings of tropical fruits to the temple.

The *balai* pavilion with its *alang-alang* straw roof is set on an ocean terrace linked to the house by winding stone steps.

A chair and bench by Warisan
on the terrace.

Left A two-storeyed pavilion. The lower floor houses a bedroom, while the upper floor provides a room for yoga. The roofs are of *alang-alang* straw; the antique chaise longue is of teak.

Opposite The master bedroom with its curtained bed. The tall chest of drawers and the cupboard with decorated doors are Chinese, both antiques. A Buddha from Laos stands on the red lacquer Tibetan cabinet.

Paris, France

LASTIC RESIDENCE

Interiors by Rita Bormioli and Bernard Faguer

This home started life as an industrial workshop, and everything in it takes its cue from the massive metal structure, which could not be removed because it is load-bearing. Interior designers Rita Bormioli and Bernard Faguer therefore decided to treat it as a decorative and functional element, contrasting with the neutral tones of walls and furnishings. Another key feature of the project is the window, which now runs uninterruptedly throughout, giving views onto a small green courtyard. The informal atmosphere is like that of a New York loft, but here we are in the heart of Europe, and the casual mood that American designers strive for has acquired a dimension of Old World decorative refinement.

Right In the living room the burnished metal structure has been exploited both to articulate space and as a support for a television screen and spotlights. The low table is by Philippe Hurel and the halogen lamp by Ecart.

Above left A view that illustrates the spatial continuity of the 'loft' conceived by Bormioli and Faguer. Doors slide in and out of the walls as required, offering a range of possibilities.

Above right A Roman head and one of the original metal supports are juxtaposed in an elegant medley of classical and industrial archaeology, beautifully enhanced by pieces of contemporary design.

Opposite Another successful marriage. The Florentine Renaissance cabinet is offset by the geometrical lines of the metal structure and the rigorous plan of the space.

Opposite The bathroom, fitted with a
large whirlpool tub set in an oak frame.

Above This view of the living room shows
how exceptionally well it is lit by the
band of windows that runs along the
entire front of the building.

Paris, France

RÉMY LEFUR RESIDENCE

A sophisticated collector with a genuine passion both for the age of Louis XIV and for Post-Deco, Rémy Lefur chose a Gothic Revival shell for his Paris home. It was revealed when later accretions had been removed; and Lefur, although no great lover of the neo-gothic movement promoted by A. W. N. Pugin in the mid-19th century, immediately perceived the power of its personality and the flexible eclecticism that effortlessly embraces other aesthetic sensibilities. What better setting for Lefur's beloved Émile-Jacques Ruhlmann, Jean-Michel Franck and Adnet, the paintings of Christian Bérard and Suzanne Rogers, objects worthy of a cabinet of curiosities, and 17th-century armour than these white gothic mouldings, the gallery like the women's level in a church, the Gothic mullioned windows and the white ceiling beams decorated with ornate stalactites?

Right A detail of the living room ceiling, with plaster coffering.

Opposite The living room. Its height allows it to have a gallery, which is used for guests. The imposing 19th-century chandelier with three tiers of candles and the armchair upholstered in black and white maintain the Gothic Revival tone of the room. Other notes are struck by the Symbolist painting by Georges Roussel, *L'Homme et l'Ours* (*Man with a Bear*), the 1890 vases by Dunand, and the suit of armour used to clasp the curtains in a decorative drape.

Opposite The gallery overlooking the
living room is now a conversation area
for guests. The bookcases started life
as two Gothic Revival confessionals.

Above The intimate dining room opens
onto a small winter garden, reflecting
Rémy Lefur's love of nature. The paving
slabs came from an ancient chapel.

437

Above left and right Two bedrooms. The modern mood is announced by the 1940s Jensen chest of drawers with its trompe-l'oeil painted decoration and the table in the shape of a drum. The pattern used for the curtains appears elsewhere in the house.

Opposite Above the door to the living room is a theatrical internal balcony at one end of the guests' gallery. The walls are covered with a pale blue floral paper. Of the two mid-19th-century paintings, one depicts an edifying scene from a story, the other an Indian rajah.

Tuscany, Italy

JULIA SCARTOZZONI HOUSE

Interiors by Julia Scartozzoni

In the Chianti hills, where Bertolucci shot the most enchanting scenes of *Stealing Beauty* outside the castle of Brolio, interior designer Julia Scartozzoni bought and restored a farmhouse that had undergone much modification and extension over the years. The result is a delightful mosaic of chaotic spaces and a bizarre sequence of different levels, all under a single 15th-century roof. When she acquired it the property was in very poor condition, and the roof had to be dismantled and later reconstructed piece by piece, as did the first-floor loggia containing the main entrance, reached by stairs of *pietra serena*. Inside, the decor reflects the tastes of the owner, who began her career at a young age as a fashion designer and loves to paint fabrics and objects. Every item is unique, specially created for this house.

Above Detail of a hand-painted wooden panel over the fireplace. The vine motif appears in some form in every room.

Right The front of the farmhouse, with the entrance loggia and *pietra serena* staircase.

Left A small collection of chopping boards and kitchen tools.

Opposite The living room. Of the chairs, the one in the left foreground is 19th-century, while the leather-covered one beyond it dates from the early 20th century.

The wine-cellar is decorated with
traditional rural artefacts.

The kitchen. The 19th-century table is surrounded by chestnut benches from an old church and two old chairs, which don't match. Decorative baskets of every shape and size hang from the rafters.

PHILIP HEWAT-JABOOR HOUSE

Philip Hewat-Jaboor, art consultant to many museums, lives in London in a house that is very much like him. The atmosphere is almost theatrical, and the rooms are rich with pieces in curious marbles, for which he has a particular passion, as well as imperial porphyry from Egypt, alabaster and giltwood, and symbolic objects from ancient times. Furniture is sparse but valuable. Most items are antiques, but some were made to order by leading craft workshops. Philip Hewat-Jaboor's home is a fascinating, scholarly presentation of significant moments in art and history rather than a private residence.

Above Some of the smaller pieces in Hewat-Jaboor's impressive collection.

Opposite The library. The porphyry table with serpentine and Belgian black marble inlay round the edge is by Vitruvius. The chandelier is early 19th-century, and an English convex mirror of 1835 hangs above the 19th-century fireplace.

Left, above A 19th-century wall light, designed by the great British collector Thomas Hope for the Egyptian Room in his house.

Left, below Detail of a giltwood sofa by Thomas Hope.

The sitting room walls are painted
to simulate imperial porphyry from
Egypt. The sofa and pedestals are by
Thomas Hope. Porphyry vases stand
on the pedestals.

Opposite On the mantelpiece is a neoclassical mahogany cabinet. The Renaissance *pietra dura* and marble table was made in Rome; on it is an Egyptian alabaster canopic jar of the 6th century BC.

Above left *Meleager at the altar of Diana*, a bronze of 1720 by Giuseppe Piamontini, stands on the mantelpiece in the library.

Above On the wall beyond the sofa is an altar of *pietra dura* and ebony made in Rome in 1640.

Los Angeles, California, United States

CHOW HOUSE

Design by Humberto Artigas

The spacious, eclectic house that Michael and Eva Chow built in Los Angeles is in a sense an autobiography in stone and concrete. It took seven years, but the part-Chinese, part-Moorish residence succeeds in marrying diverse influences with grace. At the heart of the building is a covered central courtyard, clearly Chinese in inspiration, with a ceiling 10 metres (30 feet) high, onto which all the rooms open; an upper gallery leads to the bedrooms on the first floor. On one side, sliding doors give access to a portico beyond which lie the gardens and swimming pool. There is an air of austere luxury about this huge room with its limestone ceiling and floor and understated furniture. By comparison, the other rooms, where the Chows love to entertain, despite their size seem compact. Antique Chinese furniture stands alongside pieces by Pierre Chareau, Emile-Jacques Ruhlmann, Jean-Michel Franck and Dunand, and paintings – some of which Mr Chow obtained in payment for meals at his first restaurant in London – by Peter Blake, Ed Ruscha and Jean-Michel Basquiat. The Chows, who followed every stage of building closely, called in the Mexican architect Humberto Artigas to design the interior. Artigas created an extraordinary fully waterproof underground cinema and also managed the elegant juxtaposition of enormous antique Florentine doorways and ceilings, Mexican stone pilasters, and allusions to the Prado and Reina Sofía museums in Madrid and even to the Lanvin atelier in Paris.

Right The swimming pool and pool house, which has a guest room and gymnasium.

Following pages The vast hall has fireplaces at both ends. The painting by Julian Schnabel above the fireplace seen here is a portrait of Eva Chow. On the upper level is a gallery leading to the bedrooms. The piers and arches are of Mexican stone.

Left, above A 16th-century Flemish tapestry is the focus of attention in the library. The desks are by Ruhlmann and Jean-Michel Franck, the couch by Ruhlmann.

Left, below Above the matching fireplace in the hall, opposite the portrait of Eva Chow, is a portrait of Michael Chow by Jean-Michel Basquiat.

Opposite Over the library fireplace, which came from a Scottish castle, is *Mr. Chow L.A.*, painted by Ed Ruscha in exchange for meals at Chow's restaurant.

456

Left Two Le Corbusier armchairs and an Eileen Gray occasional table share the space of a sitting room with objects both antique and modern.

Above A gallery.

Opposite The gallery on the upper floor, with Keith Tyson's monumental *History Painting*. The floor is of antique French oak.

Above The fitness room. The table tennis table divides the space into zones for different types of activity.

461

JAMES GOLDSTEIN HOUSE

Design by John Lautner

S een from the lush vegetation of the steep, scenic slopes of Beverly Hills, the vast expanse of metropolitan Los Angeles shimmers in the night air. Up here is the house designed for James Goldstein by John Lautner, one of Frank Lloyd Wright's most talented pupils. (A new range was recently added by James Turell.) The structure has grown and developed over the years as its owner's needs have changed. Today, it is a glittering spiky diamond hidden in the forest that covers this area of Los Angeles. Shapes, materials, colours, and the use of space all hark back to Wright; but in what is almost a kind of deconstruction, volumes are sundered by dramatic expressionist slashes so that corners become a leitmotiv.

Sunlight floods in horizontally and vertically through vast automatically controlled windows, bringing the house to life as it highlights an endless series of surprising snapshots, bays, niches, angles and routes that unfold inside this beautiful, citadel-like residence.

Above and right The western side of the house, poised above Los Angeles, presents a spectacular trapezoidal roof that slopes down to the ground, partially covering the infinity pool. This bold sheet of reinforced concrete is stiffened by triangular divisions with great sculptural effect.

Above The living room. Nature and artifice, indoors and outdoors, come together in a harmonious blend of wood and concrete. The concrete coffering on the ceiling houses spotlights that illuminate the room. The concrete-base furniture was made to designs by John Lautner.

Opposite The structure reaches out into the void, creating striking corners with panoramic views.

Left Every feature, every centimetre of the house is sculptural in effect. The living room ceiling bends to meet the supporting pillars, creating a rugged space reminiscent of a sculpture by Donald Judd.

Above One of James Goldstein's many collections – this one of hats.

One of the fireplaces. The shuttered
concrete walls act like wood panelling,
against which the owner's many
works of art stand out with a fresh
decorative impact.

Above Beyond the glass and concrete table, designed by Lautner, is the area of the snack bar and kitchen, all looking out onto the rich vegetation of Beverly Hills. The roof, which in this part of the house is made of strips of wood, can be opened by remote control to give a view of the sunny California sky.

Following pages Corners are the major feature – virtually the symbol – of the house. They allow audacious leaps into the void and superb panoramic views over the lights of Los Angeles. Note the electrically controlled floor-to-ceiling windows and the spotlights inset in the floor that combine with the ones in the ceiling to highlight the building's profile when seen from outside.

First published in the United Kingdom in 2008 by
Thames & Hudson Ltd, 181A High Holborn,
London WC1V 7QX

www.thamesandhudson.com

Original edition © 2008 Magnus edizioni Srl
English translation © 2008 Magnus edizioni Srl
This edition © 2008 Thames & Hudson, London

British Library Cataloguing-in-Publication Data
A catalogue record for this book is available from the British Library

ISBN 978-0-500-51444-3

Printed and bound in Italy

Advanced Practice Palliative Nursing

Advanced Practice Palliative Nursing

Edited by

Constance Dahlin, MSN, ANP-BC, ACHPN, FPCN, FAAN
Patrick J. Coyne, MSN, ACHPN, ACNS-BC, FAAN, FPCN
Betty R. Ferrell, PHD, RN, MA, CHPN, FAAN, FPCN

UNIVERSITY PRESS

OXFORD
UNIVERSITY PRESS

Oxford University Press is a department of the University of Oxford. It furthers
the University's objective of excellence in research, scholarship, and education
by publishing worldwide. Oxford is a registered trade mark of Oxford University
Press in the UK and certain other countries.

Published in the United States of America by Oxford University Press
198 Madison Avenue, New York, NY 10016, United States of America.

© Oxford University Press 2016

Library of Congress Cataloging-in-Publication Data
Advanced practice palliative nursing/edited by Constance Dahlin, Patrick J. Coyne,
Betty Rolling Ferrell.
    p. ; cm.
Includes bibliographical references and index.
ISBN 978-0-19-020474-7 (alk. paper)
I. Dahlin, Constance, editor.   II. Coyne, Patrick, 1957–, editor.   III. Ferrell, Betty, editor.
[DNLM: 1. Hospice and Palliative Care Nursing—methods.   2. Advanced Practice
Nursing—methods. WY 152.3]
R726.8
616.02′9—dc23
2015008203

9 8 7 6 5 4 3 2

Printed by Sheridan, USA

Contents

Preface

Advancing Palliative Nursing

We dedicate this textbook to all advanced practice registered nurses (APRNs) who are forging new roles, developing new programs, and conducting innovative palliative research as well as nurses in educational programs. We know it takes courage, strength, skills, knowledge, and energy to do this with the ever-changing sands of healthcare.

As palliative nursing continues to mature, so too has advanced practice palliative nursing. In the late 1990s, there were only a few palliative APRNs. Most often, those of us who pioneered the advanced practice nursing role ventured into palliative care from oncology, critical care, or care of persons with HIV. We did not have a textbook devoted to our level of practice, which included advanced assessment skills, prescribing and ordering abilities, and clinical responsibilities. We learned by experience and trial (with some error) and gleaned knowledge from other colleagues and specialties.

Some 20 years later, there are more palliative advanced practice registered nurses providing care in all healthcare settings. As the shortage of physicians continues, APRNs will move into both primary and specialty care. The literature demonstrates that APRNs provide safe, cost-effective, and high-quality comprehensive care that many individuals appreciate.[1-7] Moreover, they will be part of promoting the "triple aim" of healthcare—improving the experience of healthcare, improving the health of populations, and reducing per capita costs.[8] It has been estimated that APRNs are providing some 140,000 home visits a year. There are over 1,000 APRNs certified in hospice and palliative nursing. There are some 2,000 APRN members of the Hospice and Palliative Nurses Association. And there are thousands of specialty APRNs providing palliative care within oncology, cardiology, and neurology, just to name a few.

The Institute of Medicine's report *Future of Nursing* recommends that nurses pursue their education and practice to the full extent of their practice.[9] The result is a growth of APRNs within professional organizations. We kept hearing the loud request for an advanced practice nursing text, in particular a text that reflected palliative nursing and not palliative medicine.

Given that palliative care has moved upstream, APRNs must be knowledgeable about the myriad of life-threatening conditions and illnesses from diagnosis to end stage. Some people felt there were enough palliative medicine books, but we wanted to ensure nurses had an advanced practice palliative nursing text to support their practice. We pursued a dream to produce a textbook that would meet this need.

This textbook of advanced practice palliative nursing builds on the *Oxford Textbook of Palliative Nursing*. It also builds on the tradition of collaboration and appreciation of our various expertise. But we realize the field of palliative care continues to establish itself as a specialty. The same is true for advanced practice nursing, although this is hampered by the variation in advanced practice nursing by state and location. Nonetheless, the text promotes consistency in practice by describing an integrated approach to care. As a result, we hope it strengthens understanding into the breadth and scope of advanced practice palliative nursing.

This reference textbook is the result of our colleagues' passion, commitment to the advancement of palliative nursing, and desire for improved care for patients and families. We appreciate our authors' contributions to this project. We understand that the time they devoted to this project took away from their own personal time, family time, or "down time."

The textbook's sections are organized by the range of settings where APRNs practice as well as on the most important physical and psychological symptoms for adults and children. These topics were determined based on our previous experience in educating our colleagues. The authors are practicing APRNs, who understand the practice of palliative care, and can speak to the issues of care delivery. We have encouraged authors to speak from nursing to represent the research by our nursing colleagues. The result is 62 chapters that cover comprehensive advanced practice nursing. The book is grounded in the domains of the National Consensus Project for Quality Palliative Care's *Clinical Practice Guidelines for Quality Palliative Care*, as well as the standards and competencies of the American Nurses Association and the Hospice and Palliative Nurses Association's *Palliative Nursing: Scope and Standards—An Essential Resource.*[10,11]

Audience

This text is intended for graduate nursing students, practicing palliative APRNs, and graduate-prepared advanced practice nurses interested in palliative care but who work in nonclinical settings such as research, academia, and administration. We think this text will provide a comprehensive resource to consider clinical issues and future directions for palliative APRN policy. We also hope it promotes role delineation and development within the spectrum of APRN practice. For practicing APRNs, the book promotes skills and competencies as a foundation for advanced practice palliative nursing practice. For educators, the book offers a curricular resource in preparing the next generation of palliative APRNs.

REFERENCES

1. American Academy of Nurse Practitioners. *Quality of Nurse Practitioner Practice*. Available at http://www.aanp.org/images/documents/publications/qualityofpractice.pdf. Accessed March 9, 2015.
2. American Academy of Nurse Practitioners. *Nurse Practitioner Cost Effectiveness*. Available at http://www.aanp.org/images/documents/publications/costeffectiveness.pdf. Accessed March 9, 2015.
3. National Governors Association. *The Role of Nurse Practitioners in Meeting Increasing the Demand for Primary Care*. Washington, DC; 2012:1–14.
4. Stanik J, N.R., White K, Johantgen M, et al. The quality and effectiveness of care provided by nurse practitioners. *J Nurse Pract.* 2013; 9(8): 492–500.
5. National Association of Clinical Nurse Specialists. *Impact of the Clinical Nurse Specialist Role on the Costs and Quality of Health Care.* Available at http://www.nacns.org/docs/CNSOutcomes131204.pdf.
6. Donald F, et al. A systematic review of the cost-effectiveness of nurse practitioners and clinical nurse specialists: what is the quality of the evidence? *Nurs Res Practice.* 2014; 2014: 28.
7. Kilpatrick K, et al. The effectiveness and cost-effectiveness of clinical nurse specialists in outpatient roles: a systematic review. *J Eval Clin Pract.* 2014; 20(6): 1106–23.
8. Berwick D, Nolan TW, W. J. The triple aim: care, health, and cost. *Health Affairs.* 2008; 27(3): 759–69.
9. Institute of Medicine. *The Future of Nursing: Leading Change, Advancing Health.* Washington, DC: The National Academies Press; 2011. Available at www.iom.edu/Reports/2010/The-Future-of-Nursing-Leading-Change-Advancing-Health.aspx.
10. American Nurses Association and Hospice and Palliative Nurses Association. In Dahlin C, Sutermaster DJ, eds. *Palliative Nursing: Scope and Standards of Practice—An Essential Resource for Hospice and Palliative Nurses.* 5th ed. Silver Spring, MD: American Nurses Association and Hospice and Palliative Nurses Association; 2014.
11. Hospice and Palliative Nurses Association. In Dahlin C, ed. *Competencies for Hospice and Palliative Advanced Practice Nurses.* 2nd ed. Pittsburgh, PA: Hospice and Palliative Nurses Association; 2014.

Acknowledgments

We appreciate our families: John, Madeline, Annika, Ellie, and Annie, who supported this project and understand our desire to create a foundation for palliative advanced nursing practice. We thank Andrea Hayward, our editorial assistant. We are indebted to Ellen Friedmann for her editorial assistance and are extremely grateful for her attention to detail.

Contributors

Tara A. Albrecht, PhD, ACNP-BC
Assistant Professor
Adult Health and Nursing Systems
Virginia Commonwealth University
School of Nursing
Richmond, Virginia

Elizabeth Archer-Nanda, DNP, APRN, PMHCNS-BC
Manager, Behavioral Oncology Program
Norton Cancer Institute
Louisville, Kentucky

Bernita D. Armstrong, DNP, MN, APRN-BC
Nurse Practitioner
Palliative Care Consultation Service
Pikeville Medical Center
Pikeville, Kentucky
Adjunct Faculty MN-FNP Program
East Tennessee State University
Johnson City, Tennessee

Vanessa Battista, MSN, RN, CPNP
Pediatric Advanced Care Team
The Children's Hospital of Philadelphia
Philadelphia, Pennsylvania

Ann Berger, MSN, MD
Chief of Pain and Palliative Care
National Institutes of Health Clinical Center
Bethesda, Maryland

Patricia Berry, PhD, RN, ACHPN, FPCN, FAAN
Professor and Director
Hartford Center of Gerontological Nursing Excellence
Oregon Health and Science University School of Nursing
Portland, Oregon

Leslie Blatt, MBA, MSN, APRN, PMHCNS-BC, ACHPN
Director Palliative Care Nursing
Yale New Haven Hospital
New Haven, Connecticut

Barton T. Bobb, MSN, FNP-BC, ACHPN
Virginia Commonwealth University Health System
Massey's Thomas Palliative Care Services
Richmond, Virginia

Marilyn Bookbinder, PhD, RN, FPCN
Director of Quality and Performance Improvement
MJHS, Institute for Innovation in Palliative Care
New York, New York

Tami Borneman, MSN, CNS, FPCN
Senior Research Specialist
City of Hope Comprehensive Cancer Center
Duarte, California

Christine Bosley, BSN, RN
Masters of Nursing Candidate 2015
UCLA School of Nursing
Los Angeles, California

Jeannine M. Brant, PhD, APRN, AOCN, FAAN
Oncology Clinical Nurse Specialist and Nurse Scientist
Billings Clinic
Billings, Montana
Affiliate Assistant Professor
Montana State University College of Nursing
Bozeman, Montana

Abraham A. Brody, PhD, RN, GNP-BC
Assistant Professor and Associate Director
Hartford Institute for Geriatric Nursing
New York University College of Nursing
New York, New York
James J. Peters Veteran's Administration Medical Center GRECC
Bronx, New York

Kathleen Broglio, DNP, ANP-BC, ACHPN
Senior Nurse Practitioner
Adult Ambulatory Palliative Care Services
Columbia University Medical Center
New York, New York

Marcia J. Buckley MSN, OCNS, ANP, ACHPN
Senior Nurse Practitioner
Palliative Care Consultation Service
University of Rochester Medical Center,
    Strong Hospital
Associate Professor of Clinical Nursing
University of Rochester School of Nursing
Adjunct Faculty
St. John Fisher College
Rochester, New York

Peggy S. Burhenn, MS, CNS, AOCNS
Professional Practice Leader
City of Hope Comprehensive Cancer Center
Duarte, California

Penelope R. Buschman MS, PMHCNS-BC, FAAN
Columbia University School of Nursing
New York, New York

Joan Carpenter, MN, CRNP, NP-C, GNP-BC, ACHPN
PhD Candidate
Hartford Center of Geriatric Nursing Excellence
University of Utah College of Nursing
Salt Lake City, Utah
Nurse Practitioner
Coastal Hospice and Palliative Care
Salisbury, Maryland

John D. Chovan, PhD, DNP, CNP, CNS, PMHNP-BC, ACHPN, AHN-BC
Assistant Professor and Director, DNP Program
Department of Nursing
Otterbein University
Westerville, Ohio
Nurse Practitioner
Mount Carmel Hospice and Palliative Care
Columbus, Ohio

Kimberly Chow, MSN, ANP-BC, ACHPN
Memorial Sloan-Kettering Cancer Center
New York, New York

Joan "Jody" Chrastek, DNP, RN, CHPN
Fairview Home Care and Hospice
University of Minnesota Masonic Childrens Hospital
Minneapolis, Minnesota

Nessa Coyle, PhD, RN, FAAN
Palliative Care and Ethics Consultant
New York, New York

Patrick J. Coyne, MSN, ACHPN, ACNS-BC, FAAN, FPCN
Director of Palliative Care
Medical University of South Carolina
Charleston, South Carolina

Amelia Cullinan, MD
Director, Outpatient Palliative Care Services
Section of Palliative Medicine
Dartmouth-Hitchcock Medical Center
Lebanon, New Hampshire

Sarah D'Ambruoso, MSN, RN, NP
Palliative Nurse Practitioner
University of California, Los Angeles
Los Angeles, California

Joan E. Dacher, PhD, RN, GNP
Professor of Nursing at The Sage Colleges
Advanced Practice Nurse Palliative Care Consultant
Troy, New York

Constance Dahlin, MSN, ANP-BC, ACHPN, FPCN, FAAN
Director of Professional Practice
Hospice and Palliative Nurses Association
Pittsburgh, Pennsylvania
Palliative Nurse Practitioner
North Shore Medical Center
Salem, Massachusetts

Mary E. Davidson MSN CNS
Palliative Care Program Manager
VA Healthcare System of Ohio
Cincinnati, Ohio

Janet Duncan, MSN, CPNP
Department of Psychosocial Oncology and Palliative Care
APN, Pediatric Palliative Care
Boston Children's Hospital and Dana-Farber Cancer Institute
Boston, Massachusetts

Charlene Earnhardt, MSN, RN, CNS
Cardiothroacic Services
University of California, Los Angeles
Los Angeles, California

Denice Economou PhD, RN, CHPN
Senior Research Specialist
City of Hope Comprehensive Cancer Center
Duarte, California

Justin Engleka MBA, CRNP, ACHPN
Associate Chief Nurse
VA Pittsburgh Healthcare System
Pittsburgh, Pennsylvania

Beth Fahlberg PhD, RN, AGPCNP-BC, CHPN
Clinical Professor
School of Nursing
University of Wisconsin-Madison
Madison, Wisconsin

Betty R. Ferrell, PhD, RN, MA, CHPN, FAAN, FPCN
Professor and Director of Nursing Research and Education
City of Hope Comprehensive Cancer Center
Duarte, California

Gretchen P. Fitzgerald, MSN, CRNP, NP-C, GNP-BC, ACHPN
OACIS Services/Palliative Medicine
Lehigh Valley Health Network
Allentown, Pennsylvania

Devon Fletcher, MD
Virginia Commonwealth University Health System
Massey's Thomas Palliative Care Services
Richmond, Virginia

Patricia Maani Fogelman, DNP
Director of Thoracic Medicine
GMC Nursing Grand Rounds
Associate Professor of Nursing
Columbia University
New York, New York

Maria Gatto, MA, APRN-BC, ACHPN, NP, HNP
Trinity Health System Director, Palliative Care
Trinity Health
Livonia, Michigan

Jennifer Gentry MSN, ANP-BC, GNP, ACHPN, FPCN
Duke University Hospital Palliative Care Consult Service
Department of Advanced Clinical Practice
Clinical Associate
Duke University School of Nursing
Durham, North Carolina

Janine A. Gerringer, MSN, CRNP
Ventricular Assist Device Coordinator
Geisinger Health System
Danville, Pennsylvania

Susan Gibson, MSN, FNP-BC, ACHPN
Nurse Practitioner
Visiting Nurse and Hospice Care Santa Barbara
Santa Barbara, California

Linda M. Gorman, MN, PMHCNS-BC, CHPN, FPCN
Palliative Care Clinical Nurse Specialist and Consultant
Los Angeles, California

Rosemary Gorman, MSN, ANP-BC, ACHPN
Salerno Medical Associates
East Orange, New Jersey

Marian Grant, DNP, RN, CRNP
Assistant Professor
University of Maryland School of Nursing
Baltimore, Maryland

Marlene Hardy-Gomez, MSN, CPNP-PC, ACHPN
Haslinger Family Pediatric Palliative Care Center
Akron Children's Hospital
Akron, Ohio

Amy Corey Haskamp, MSN, PCNS-BC, CPON
Pediatric Palliative Care
Riley Hospital for Children
Indiana University Health
Indianapolis, Indiana

Katherine A. Hinderer, PhD, RN, CCRN-K, CNE
Associate Professor
Department of Nursing
Salisbury University
Salisbury, Maryland

Rikki N. Hooper, MBA, MSN, FNP-BC, ACHPN
Four Seasons
Flat Rock, North Carolina

Anne Hughes, PhD, ACHPN, FAAN
Palliative Care, Pain Management and Ethics
Laguna Honda Hospital and Rehabilitation Center
San Francisco Department of Public Health
Clinical Professor of Nursing
University of California San Francisco
San Francisco, California

Susan Lysaght Hurley, PhD, GNP-BC, ACHPN
Director of Research/Hospice and Palliative Care Nurse
  Practitioner
Care Dimensions
Danvers, Massachusetts

Anne M. Ireland, MSN, RN, AOCN, CENP
Clinical Nursing Director, Solid Tumor Program
City of Hope Comprehensive Cancer Center
Duarte, California

Mimi Jenko, DNP, PMHCNS-BC, CHPN
Duke University
Doctorate of Nursing Practice
Durham, North Carolina

Anne Kinderman, MD
Director of Supportive and Palliative Care Service
San Francisco General Hospital
Assistant Clinical Professor of Medicine
University of California, San Francisco
San Francisco, California

Timothy W. Kirk, PhD
Assistant Professor
Department of History and Philosophy
City University of New York
York College
New York, New York

Kathie Kobler, MS, PCNS-BC, CHPPN
Pediatric Clincial Nurse Specialist
Pediatric Palliative Care
Advocate Children's Hospital, Park
  Ridge Campus
Park Ridge, Illinois

Lauren Koranteng, PharmD, CPE
Memorial Sloan-Kettering Cancer Center
New York, New York

Deborah A. Lafond, DNP, PPCNP-BC, CPON, CHPPN
PANDA Palliative Care Team
Division of Hospitalist Medicine
Children's National Health System
Washington, District of Columbia

Kerstin Lea Lappen, MS, CNS-BC, ACHPN, FPCN
Palliative CNS Lead
Abbott Northwestern Hospital
Allina Health
Minneapolis, Minnesota

MariJo Letizia PhD, ANP-BC, FAANP
School of Nursing
Loyola University Chicago
Chicago, Illinois

Maureen Lynch, MS, APN-BC, AOCN, ACHPN, FPCN
Nurse Practitioner
Division of Palliative Care
Dana Farber Cancer Institute
Boston, Massachusetts

Anne Mahler MS, GCNS-BC, ACHPN
Hebrew SeniorLife
Boston, Massachusetts

Polly Mazanec, PhD, ACNP-BC, AOCN, FPCN
Frances Payne Bolton School of Nursing
Case Western Reserve University
Cleveland, Ohio

Marlene E. McHugh DNP, FNP-BC, ACHPN, FPCN
Columbia University School of Nursing
New York, New York
Associate Director Palliative Care
Montefiore Medical Center
Bronx, New York

Sherrie Murray ANP-BC, FNP, MS
Nurse Practitioner
Internal Medicine
Capital Care Medical Group
Schenectady, New York
Assistant Professor of Nursing
The Sage Colleges
Troy, New York

Michele A. Naugle MS, CRNP, ACHPN
OACIS Services/Palliative Medicine
Lehigh Valley Health Network
Allentown, Pennsylvania

Peg Nelson, MSN, NP, ACHPN
Director of Palliative Care and Pain Services
St. Joseph Mercy Oakland
Pontiac, Michigan

Leiann Neubauer, RN
Carolinas Healthcare System
Mercy Hospital
Charlotte, North Carolina

Edith O'Neil-Page, MSN, RN, CNS, AOCNS
Clinical Nurse Specialist for Palliative Care
Ronald Reagan UCLA Medical Center
Los Angeles, California

James C. Pace PhD, MDiv, ANP-BC, FAANP, FAAN
Senior Associate for Academic Program
New York University College of Nursing
New York, New York

Judith A. Paice, PhD, RN, FAAN
Director of the Cancer Pain Program
Division of Hematology-Oncology
Northwestern University
Feinberg School of Medicine
Chicago, Illinois

Joan T. Panke, MA, NP ACHPN
Palliative Care Services
MedStar Washington Hospital
Washington, District of Columbia

Kathy Plakovic, MSN, FNP-BC, ACHPN
Palliative Care Nurse Practitioner
Edward Hospital
Naperville, Illinois

Barbara Reville, DNP, CRNP, ACHPN
Nursing Director
Division of Adult Palliative Care
Department of Psychosocial Oncology and Palliative Care
Dana-Farber Cancer Institute
Brigham and Women's Hospital
Boston, Massachusetts

Debbie Rochester-Gibbons, MPA
Administrator
Pain Medicine and Palliative Care
Mount Sinai Beth Israel
New York, New York

Gina Santucci, MSN, APRN-BC
Pediatric Advanced Care Team
The Children's Hospital of Philadelphia
Philadelphia, Pennsylvania

Robert Smeltz, MA, NP, ACHPN
Clinical Coordinator/Nurse Practitioner
Palliative Care Program
New York University School of Medicine
Bellevue Hospital
New York, New York

Angela Starkweather, PhD, ACNP-BC, CNRN, FAAN
Professor and Director, Center for Advancement in Managing Pain
University of Connecticut School of Nursing
Storrs, Connecticut

Lisa A. Stephens, MSN, APRN, ACHPN
Lead Nurse Practitioner
Section of Palliative Medicine
Dartmouth-Hitchcock Medical Center
Lebanon, New Hampshire

Virginia Sun, PhD, RN
Assistant Professor
City of Hope Comprehensive Cancer Center
Duarte, California

Ann Syrett MS, FNP-BC, ACHPN
Nurse Practitioner
Palliative Care Consultation Service
University of Rochester Medical Center, Strong Hospital
Rochester, New York

Andrea L. Tackett, MD
Chaplain
Palliative Care Team
Pikeville Medical Center
Pikeville, Kentucky

Cheryl Ann Thaxton, MN, CPNP, FNP-BC, CHPPN
Nurse Practitioner
Supportive & Palliative Care Team
Medical City Children's Hospital
Dallas, Texas

Patricia Thomas PhD, RN
Vice President Clinical Quality & Transformation/Chief Nursing Officer
Trinity Home Health Services
Livonia, Michigan

Charles Tilley, MSN, ANP-BC, ACHPN, CWOCN
Palliative Care Consultant
International Advanced Practice Palliative Care Partners, LLC
New York, New York

Sharon Verney, MSN, ANP, BC, GNP, BC
Nurse Practitioner
Hebrew Senior Life
Boston, Massachusetts

Beth Wagner MSN, CRNP, ACHPN
Nurse Practitioner
Palliative Care Team
Thomas Jefferson University Hospital
Philadelphia, Pennsylvania

Phyllis B. Whitehead, PhD, APRN, RN-BC, ACHPN
Clinical Nurse Specialist
Palliative Care Service at Carilion Roanoke Memorial Hospital
Assistant Professor
Virginia Tech Carilion School of Medicine
Roanoke, Virginia

Dorothy Wholihan, DNP, ANP-BC, GNP-BC ACHPN
Coordinator
Palliative Care Masters NP Specialty Program
New York University College of Nursing
New York, New York

Debra L. Wiegand, PhD, RN, CCRN, CHPN, FAHA, FPCN, FAAN
Associate Professor
School of Nursing
University of Maryland
Baltimore, Maryland

Clareen Wiencek, PhD, CNP, ACHPN
Associate Professor
University of Virginia School of Nursing
Charlottesville, Virginia

Elaine Wittenberg, PhD
Associate Professor
City of Hope Comprehensive Cancer Center
Duarte, California

Jacaline P. Wolf, CRNP, ACHPN
OACIS Services/Palliative Medicine
Lehigh Valley Health Network
Allentown, Pennsylvania

PART ONE

The Palliative Advanced Practice Registered Nurse

CHAPTER 1

History of the Advanced Practice Role in Palliative Nursing

Constance Dahlin and Patrick J. Coyne

Key Points

- Advanced practice nursing is synergistic with the principles of palliative nursing.

- Across all six population foci of advanced practice nursing, advanced practice registered nurses (APRNs) need current palliative care competencies in order to care for their patients across all settings.

- Palliative APRNs promote access to palliative care, facilitate evidence-based palliative practices, and deliver safe, quality palliative care.

Overview of the Advanced Practice Nurse in Palliative Care in the United States

Nursing and palliative care are intertwined. The foundation of modern nursing is grounded in care of the dying.[1] Florence Nightingale founded the practice of nursing while caring for soldiers in the Crimean War, many of whom were fatally injured.[2] Thus, the heart of nursing was the art of caring for seriously wounded individuals and serving as a midwife to dying patients.[2] As nursing moved to the United States, Clara Barton of the American Red Cross advanced nursing through the Civil War. Again, nursing practice was based in care of dying soldiers. Through the intervening centuries, nursing practice has evolved from caring for dying patients to caring for patients across the health and wellness continuum. Moreover, nursing has developed in its breadth and scope of practice for the registered nurse (RN), and in the evolution of graduate degree-prepared nurses. In the mid-20th century, the advanced practice roles of certified nurse midwife, nurse practitioner, clinical nurse specialist, and certified nurse anesthetist were developed. These roles play a significant part in hospice and palliative care.

The modern hospice movement was established in England by Dame Cicely Saunders. At St. Joseph's Hospice, Dr. Saunders followed her calling to promote compassionate care to the dying, calling on her background first as a nurse, then as a social worker. As a physician, she founded St. Christopher's Hospice to further develop hospice care.[2] These concepts traveled to the United States through the work of Dr. Florence Wald, then dean of the Yale School of Nursing.[3] Dr. Wald developed an expansive nursing curriculum that emphasized the nursing skills necessary for caring for dying patients, specifically pain and symptom management and communication.[3] Dr. Wald stated, "Hospice care is the epitome of good nursing care." She asserted, "It enables the patient to get through the end-of-life on their own terms. It is a holistic approach, looking at the patient as an individual, a human being. The spiritual role nurses play in the end-of-life process is essential to both patients and families."[3]

In 1982, the Medicare Hospice Benefit was enacted, offering benefits to patients with a terminal illness. Specific Medicare Hospice Conditions of Participation (CoPs) directed hospices to offer a certain set of services to patients and families.[4] Within the benefit, nursing has a prominent role as a core service. In programs across the United States, the majority of hospice care is provided by nurses visiting patients' homes. However, in its infancy, the Medicare Hospice Benefit did not recognize the different levels of nursing practice. It was not until recently that the Medicare Hospice Benefit even acknowledged that APRNs lead hospice teams and oversee the care of hospice patients. The most recent version of the CoPs (2011) clarifies the role of the APRN.

In addition, when the Medicare Hospice Benefit was started, care of dying patients was marked by a lack of consistency in care provision and little consensus on the defining characteristics of palliative care or quality indicators. Research from the nineties confirmed the worst fears about healthcare. The Study to Understand Prognoses and Preferences for Outcomes and Risks of Treatment (SUPPORT) demonstrated a failure to honor patients' preferences.[5] The study found a continued lack of communication between patients and their healthcare providers about end-of-life care. Seriously ill and dying patients reported high levels of pain, and despite patient preferences, aggressive care was continued.[5] Nurses were a major part of the intervention and conducted patient interviews for the study. However, there was inconsistency in the study: the use of APRNs and RNs varied. Because of the difference in education and training, the extent of nursing intervention would have been affected.[5] The lack of uniformity in scope of practice may have affected the nurses' communication skills, ultimately affecting the consistency of outcomes.

As the findings from SUPPORT were being disseminated in the mid-1990s, hospice concepts moved into the academic hospital setting in the form of palliative care.[6] Care focused on people with serious and life-threatening illnesses whose care was complicated, as well as terminally ill patients who were not ready for hospice.[6] Pioneer palliative care programs were developed across the country. Many of these palliative care services had a large presence of APRNs. With their enhanced graduate education and scope of

practice, APRNs offered a wide range of clinical services to patients and families, such as making diagnoses, taking histories, performing physical examinations, creating care plans, prescribing medications, and formulating treatment plans. APNs also had prominent roles in program development, research, and education of patients, families, colleagues, and health systems. The challenge was ensuring education and training for APNs to move into these roles. The development of the specialty of palliative APRN practice was just beginning. See Box 1.1 for a review of the specialty.

Most APRNs developed their own education plan as they moved into palliative care roles. Often education, practice expertise, and

Box 1.1	Timeline of Events Related to Advanced Practice Palliative Nursing, 1986–2014
1986	Establishment of the **Hospice Nurses Association**
1991	*Position Statement: Nursing and the Patient Self-Determination Act—Supporting Autonomy* released by the American Nurses Association
1993	Establishment of **National Board for Certification of Hospice Nurses**
1994	First examination for hospice nursing offered by National Board for Certification of Hospice Nurses
1995	Study to Understand Prognoses and Preferences for Outcomes and Risks of Treatments (SUPPORT) study released
1997	*Approaching Death: Improving Care at the End of Life* published by the Institute of Medicine
1998	Hospice Nurses Association becomes the **Hospice and Palliative Nurses Association** (HPNA)
	The National Board for Certification of Hospice Nurses becomes the **National Board for Certification of Hospice and Palliative Nurses** (NBCHPN)
	Peaceful Death: Recommended Competencies and Curricular Guidelines for End-of-Life Nursing Care published by the American Association of Colleges of Nursing
1999	Last Acts published *The Precepts of Palliative Care*
	Establishment of the Nursing Leadership Academy for End-of-Life Care to design an agenda for end-of-life care for the nursing profession
2000	*Statement on the Scope and Standards of Hospice and Palliative Nursing Practice* produced by HPNA
	When Children Die: Improving Palliative and End-of-Life Care for Children and Their Families and *Crossing the Quality Chasm: A New Health System for the 21st Century* released by the Institute of Medicine End-of-Life Committee
2001	*Professional Competencies for the Generalist Hospice and Palliative Nurse* created by HPNA
	Advanced Practice Nurses Role in Palliative Care—A Position Statement from American Nursing Leaders published
2002	*Scope and Standards of Hospice and Palliative Nursing Practice* published in collaboration with the American Nurses Association (ANA)
	Competencies for the Advanced Practice Hospice and Palliative Care Nurse created by HPNA
2003	First advanced practice nursing palliative and hospice examination administered within a partnership of NBCHPN and American Nurses Credentialing Center
2004	National Consensus Project for Quality Palliative Care *Clinical Practice Guidelines* (1st edition) released
2006	HPNA Position Statement—*Value of the Advanced Practice Nurse in Palliative Care* released (revised 2010, with name changed to *Value of the Advanced Practice Registered Nurse in Palliative Care*)
2007	HPNA and ANA released 4th edition of *Hospice and Palliative Nursing: Scope and Standards of Practice*
2009	National Consensus Project for Quality Palliative Care *Clinical Practice Guidelines* (2nd edition) released
	Core Curriculum for the Advanced Hospice and Palliative Registered Nurse (1st edition) published
2011	HPNA Position Statement—*The Nurse's Role in Advance Care Planning* released
2013	National Consensus Project for Quality Palliative Care *Clinical Practice Guidelines* (3rd edition) released
	Core Curriculum for the Advanced Practice Hospice and Palliative Registered Nurse (2nd edition) published
2014	*Palliative Nursing: Scope and Standards—An Essential Resource for Nurses* (5th edition) released by HPNA and ANA
	Competencies for the Hospice and Palliative Advanced Practice Nurse released by HPNA
	Dying in America—Improving Quality and Honoring Individual Preferences Near End of Life published by the Institute of Medicine

Adapted from *Palliative Nursing: Scope and Standards* (reference 31).

skills resulted from either oncology nursing or acquired immunodeficiency syndrome (AIDS) and human immunodeficiency virus (HIV) nursing. Other nurses moved from hospice care into palliative care. This was because these two specialties offered the most experience in pain and symptom management, counseling about progressive disease and death, and teamwork. Many APRNs learned aspects of a palliative approach through patient care over months to years without the benefit of an organized educational plan. It was often on-the-job skill building while developing individual models of care.

The release of essential reports about dying in America had an effect on advanced practice nursing. The 1997 Institute of Medicine (IOM) report *Approaching Death* described the state of end-of-life care in America.[4] This report recommended the subspecialty of palliative care, reviewed the use of medications for pain and symptom management, supported financial investment in palliative care, and appealed for healthcare professional education that included palliative care content in various curricula, textbooks, and training programs.[4]

The Precepts of Palliative Care were released by Last Acts, (formerly a Robert Wood Johnson-funded organization, now under the auspices of the National Hospice and Palliative Care Organization).[7] These precepts reaffirmed the comprehensive approach of palliative care as a specialized area of expertise. *The Precepts of Palliative Care* also stated that care should respect patient choices, affirmed that care utilizes the strengths of the interdisciplinary team, and encouraged the building of palliative care support through financing, outcomes, and research.[7]

In 2002, Last Acts published a state-by-state report card of end-of-life care in America, which captured a fairly bleak picture of palliative care in the United States.[8] It promoted much discussion about a unified response from the palliative care community. Other significant reports included two other IOM reports (*When Children Die* and *Crossing the Quality Chasm*) and a monograph by the National Hospice Work Group and the Hastings Center, in association with the National Hospice and Palliative Care Organization (NHPCO), entitled *Access to Hospice Care: Expanding Boundaries, Overcoming Barriers*.[9-11] These reports argued for significant changes in access to palliative care, promoting access for all ages, ensuring care in all health settings, and providing services for all progressive chronic, serious, or life-threatening illness and injuries.[9-11]

In 2014, the IOM released its report *Dying in America—Improving Quality and Honoring Individual Preferences Near End of Life*.[12] The report focuses on five areas for quality palliative care: (1) delivery of person-centered and family-focused palliative care; (2) clinician–patient communication and advance care planning; (3) professional education in palliative care; (4) policies and payment for palliative care; and (5) public education and engagement in palliative care.[12] These areas will provide a focus for healthcare improvement and moving care upstream to patients with serious illness rather than focusing just on the end-of-life. In addition, the report calls for more coordinated and collaborative care that is based in the community. APRNs will have a major role in the implementation of these areas and more broadly in moving palliative care into the community.

A significant development in the field was the 2004 release of the National Consensus Project for Quality Palliative Care's (NCP) *Clinical Practice Guidelines*, created by the five major hospice, palliative, and end-of-life professional organizations: American Academy of Hospice and Palliative Medicine (AAHPM), Center to Advance Palliative Care (CAPC), Hospice and Palliative Nurses Association (HPNA), Last Acts, and NHPCO. These guidelines established principles to improve and ensure the quality of palliative care in the United States.[13] They offer a framework for the future of palliative care, serving as a blueprint to create new programs, guide developing programs, and set high expectations for excellence for existing programs. The guidelines set ideal practices and goals that palliative care services should strive to attain rather than setting minimally acceptable practices. The guidelines have three specific aims: (1) to promote quality and reduce variation in new and existing programs, (2) to develop and encourage continuity of care across settings, and (3) to facilitate collaborative partnerships among palliative care programs, community hospices, and a wide range of other healthcare delivery settings.[14] Now in its third edition, the *NCP Clinical Practice Guidelines* are a collaboration of AAHPM, CAPC, HPNA, National Association of Social Work (NASW), National Palliative Care Research Center (NPCRC), and NHPCO and continue to move palliative care upstream. Moreover, the guidelines stress specialty education, training, and certification; specific to APRNs is the promotion of obtaining advanced certification within hospice and palliative nursing.[14,15]

Later in 2004, the first national meeting on palliative care research was convened in Bethesda, Maryland. The National Institutes of Health (NIH) held the first *State of the Science Conference on Improving End-of-Life Care*, which put forth statements to formulate future palliative research.[16] They concluded that (1) the definition of end-of-life care was vague and poorly understood and was experienced differently across subgroups of culture, healthcare settings, and disease populations; (2) the vague definition led to poor quality, fragmented care, and lack of continuity; and (3) research measures and interventions in use were inconsistent and lacked validation. In 2011, the National Institute for Nursing Research (NINR) convened a follow-up meeting that provided a summary of research initiatives and offered innovative methods to develop palliative metrics and measure quality.[17] It also emphasized the need for interdisciplinary research and training.[17]

Finally, there have been several significant events related to the quality of palliative care. APRNs are obligated to ensure the quality of palliative nursing practice, which requires an awareness of these developments and standards and an appreciation of how they affect care delivery, measurement of quality practice, and education. The National Quality Forum (NQF) is a nonprofit public–private partnership focused on quality care through the adoption of voluntary standards. Its goal is to develop meaningful information about care delivery, including timeliness, efficiency, safety, equality, and patient-centeredness.[18] In 2006, it published *A National Framework and Preferred Practices for Palliative and Hospice Care Quality: A Consensus Report*,[19] which built on the National Consensus Project for Quality Palliative Care's eight domains of care and put forth 38 preferred practices for hospice and palliative care.[19]

Related to the NQF was the formation of National Priorities Partnership (NPP). In 2008, NPP released the report *National Priorities & Goals—Aligning Our Efforts to Transform America's Healthcare*. It identified palliative care and end-of-life care as one of the six National Priorities that, if addressed, would significantly improve the quality of care delivered to Americans.[20] In 2010, the NPP convened a palliative and end-of-life meeting. It developed several areas on which to focus strategies to promote palliative care, including quality improvement stakeholders, insurers, consumer groups, certification groups, professional groups, and educational institutions.[21]

Within the federal structures of healthcare reporting, there has been work as well. The Measure Applications Partnership (MAP) is a public–private partnership convened by the NQF. MAP was created to provide input to the Department of Health and Human Services on the selection of performance measures for public reporting and performance-based payment programs. Each year the MAP clinician workgroup reviews measures for the government to use in its reporting programs.

There were other initiatives exclusive to nursing. The multifaceted project *Strengthening Nursing Education to Improve End-of-Life Care* was funded by the Robert Wood Johnson Foundation and focused on improving nursing knowledge about end-of-life.[22] The first component of the project reviewed nursing textbooks for end-of-life content, which was liberally defined as pain and symptom management, care of the dying patient, or spiritual care. This was completed in 1999 and demonstrated that written content in end-of-life nursing care was nearly nonexistent.[23] One result was *The Oxford Textbook of Palliative Nursing*, originally co-edited by Betty Ferrell and Nessa Coyle. Now in its fourth edition, with Judith Paice added as an editor, this nursing text serves as a reference for both the RN and the APRN.

The second component of the project examined end-of-life care content in nursing licensing examinations. This resulted in the creation of baccalaureate education competencies in end-of-life care that were disseminated within the American Association of Colleges of Nursing (AACN) document, *Peaceful Death: Recommended Competencies and Curricular Guidelines for End-of-Life Nursing Care*.[24] Previous research had clearly demonstrated that both RNs and APRNs felt they had inadequate preparation in end-of-life care.[25,26] These competencies have served as the basis for nursing education at both the graduate and undergraduate level. Palliative and end-of-life content questions now appear on the NCLEX examinations. It was hoped that more palliative care content would also appear on national advanced practice certification examinations.

The third component was to support key organizations to improve end-of-life education for nursing. The result was the Nursing Leadership Consortium on End-of-Life Care, funded by the Project on Death in America. The goal was to design an agenda for the nursing profession in end-of-life care.[22] The agenda emphasized (1) educating nurse leaders in strategies of planning and managing change and advocacy related to palliative care and end-of-life care; (2) creating a system of support, networking, and mentorship for nurses engaged in leadership and advocacy in palliative and end-of-life care; and (3) developing and implementing innovative strategies to advance the priorities of the Nursing Leadership Consortium on End-of-Life Care.[22]

An important collaboration between AACN and the City of Hope established the End-of-Life Nursing Education Consortium (ELNEC), which created a model of education for nurses.[27] The ELNEC curriculum, focusing on AACN's *Peaceful Death Competencies*, was created to educate nurses at all levels of practice and across all specialties. With a goal of developing a core

of expert educators and teaching resources to enhance end-of-life care competency, many versions have been developed over the past 15 years—core, graduate, oncology, critical care, geriatrics, pediatrics, and veterans.[27] Most recently, in 2013, the ELNEC Advanced Practice Registered Nurse Curriculum was developed, with the authors serving as consultants for its development. The goal is to offer education to new APRNs entering palliative care. In addition, there is a new curriculum for Doctor of Nursing Practice (DNP) faculty to teach them how to integrate palliative care into a DNP oncology curriculum. Current ELNEC versions include core, critical care, pediatrics, geriatrics, APRN, and DNP palliative oncology.[27]

In 2001, there was an important summit of national nursing leaders who represented clinical practice, academia, and research. The goal was to discuss advanced practice nursing in palliative care. The result was the document, *Advanced Practice Nurses Role in Palliative Care—A Position Statement from American Nursing Leaders*, which outlined the unique role of APNs in palliative care, and a companion monograph of pioneer APNs in the field. The position statement acknowledged the APN role in palliative care as a "valuable resource in national efforts to improve care and quality of life for Americans and their families living with advanced, life-limiting illness."[28] These concepts were later woven into the HPNA position statement *The Value of Advanced Practice Registered Nurses in Palliative Care*, first developed in 2006 and revised in 2010.[29]

Two graduate programs with a focus on specialist palliative nursing emerged.[7] In 1998, Ursuline College in Ohio offered preparation for the palliative clinical nurse specialist (CNS) and later New York University offered a program for nurse practitioners (NPs). Both of these were novel programs intended to promote specialist practice. The programs were successful for several years. However, in 2008, the National Council of State Boards of Nursing released the Licensure, Accreditation, Certification, and Education (LACE) model to increase the clarity and uniformity of APRN education and practice.[30] The LACE model stated that APRNs must be educated in one of six population foci: (1) family/individual across the focus of lifespan, (2) adult-gerontology, (3) pediatrics, (4) neonatal, (5) women's health/gender-related, or (6) psychiatric/mental health.[30] Thus, APRN education was focused on population-based and primary practice rather than disease-focused specialties. The result was that palliative care was no longer recognized as a primary practice, but as a subspecialty practice. Thus, both programs needed to revise their curricula, moving away from a primary focus on palliative care, to meet the population/primary care focus of the LACE model.

There are over 2,000 APNs within HPNA. To address the needs of palliative APRNs, there were several important events within the specialty. In 1998, the Hospice Nurses Association embraced palliative care and changed its name to the Hospice and Palliative Nurses Association. In 2002, the *Scope and Standards of Hospice and Palliative Nursing Practice* was published in collaboration with the American Nurses Association.[31] These delineated the actions of RNs and APNs. In 2014, these were updated as *Palliative Nursing: Scope and Standards*.[32] In this edition, primary palliative nursing and specialty palliative nursing were described. The different levels of advanced practice nursing within palliative care were delineated. One role is a clinical role, where the APRN practices in the role of clinical nurse specialist, nurse practitioner, certified nurse midwife, or certified nurse anesthetist. In a nonclinical role, the researcher, administrator, case manager, and educator are delineated as APNs.

Competencies for the Advanced Practice Hospice and Palliative Care Nurse were developed in 2002 by the HPNA.[33] The second edition of the *Competencies for the Hospice and Palliative Advanced Practice Nurse* was published in 2014.[33,34] The competencies are important because they are inclusive and address competencies for both the APN and the APRN.

In 2006, HPNA developed the *Standards for Clinical Practicum in Palliative Nursing for Practicing Professional Nurses*.[35] The goal of the standards is to ensure quality clinical palliative nursing for both RNs and APRNs by promoting improvement and standardization of palliative nursing education. Specific to advanced practice nursing is that a palliative program must have an Advanced Certified Hospice and Palliative Nurse (ACHPN) who leads the nursing education for graduate practicums and provides mentoring in the role development of an APRN. In addition, it sets the standard that palliative programs offering advanced nursing preceptorships or practicums have been established for at least 2 years. It emphasizes the importance of using the National Consensus Project's *Clinical Practice Guidelines* as a framework for education. Finally, it requires palliative care programs offering APRN practicums or preceptorships to use the *Palliative Nursing: Scope and Standards of Practice* and the *Competencies for the Hospice and Palliative Advanced Practice Nurse*.

Certification is a measure of specialty practice and serves as public recognition of an APN's expertise. In 2003, specialty certification at the APN level was first offered.[32] As a collaborative effort between the American Nurses Credentialing Center and the National Board for the Certification of Hospice and Palliative Nursing, the examination necessitated evaluation of the clinical nurse specialist role and the nurse practitioner role. The role delineation study found that the work of each role was similar and therefore only one examination was necessary. In the early 2000s, many nurses used the APN credential to establish palliative care as their primary practice. More importantly, a milestone was achieved when the Center for Medicare and Medicaid Services recognized the National Board of Certification of Hospice and Palliative Nurses as one of seven recognized national certifications for reimbursement eligibility. However, this was short-lived, because the implementation of the LACE model no longer allowed palliative care as a primary area of practice. Nevertheless, the role delineation to determine the difference between clinical nurse specialist and nurse practitioner practice was recently repeated and the results again found that the activities were similar, necessitating one examination. To date, approximately 1,000 APRNs have obtained the Advanced Certified Hospice and Palliative Nurse (ACHPN) credential.[36]

The APRN in Palliative Care

The palliative APRN role has evolved over the past 15 years. In particular, APRNs are practicing primary palliative care and specialty palliative care across the lifespan, across diseases, across settings, and across roles. The two roles of advanced practice nursing with palliative care are described in *Palliative Nursing: Scope and Standards of Practice*. One role is the "graduate-level prepared specialty nurse who is educated at the master's or doctoral level," but

Table 1.1 Types of APNs

APN Type	Educational Preparation	Roles
Graduate-level–prepared APN	Master's or Doctoral degree	Administrator Researcher Case Manager Academic Educator
Clinically educated APRN	Master's, Post-Master's, Doctoral degree	Clinical Nurse Specialist (CNS) Nurse Practitioner (NP) Certified Nurse Midwife (CNM) Certified Registered Nurse Anesthetist (CRNA)

does not practice in the clinical arena.[32(p 25)] The second role is the APRN clinically educated at a master's degree or above, working in a clinical setting.[32(p 27)] Table 1.1 explains the two roles, and Table 1.2 gives information about the settings where APNs practice.

The current state of education is lacking, but there are a number of resources; see Table 1.3, Table 1.4, and Table 1.5 for a review of sources of information for palliative APN practice. A number of national organizations, including the American Cancer Society, ELNEC, CAPC, and the HPNA, have recognized this gap in education and skill-building. HPNA offers palliative-focused continuing education for nurses at all levels. Since 2000, ELNEC has offered 2-day education programs focusing on eight modules. Recognizing the lack of APRN-specific education, in 2013, ELNEC launched a 2-day classroom APRN course focusing on six clinical modules (overview of palliative nursing, pain management, symptom management, communication, loss and grief, the final hours) and four program development models (business and finance, quality, education, and leadership).

Table 1.2 Roles and Settings for APNs

Clinical nurse specialist or Nurse practitioner	Hospice, home health agency, clinic, skilled care facility, hospital
Case manager	Insurance company, hospital (acute and rehabilitation), skilled care facility, hospice, home health agency, private practice
Educator	Academic setting, such as school of nursing and/or medicine, hospital, professional organization
Researcher	National research entity, such as National Institutes of Health or National Institute of Nursing Research, academic setting, such as school of nursing and/or medicine, academic medical setting, professional organization
Administrator	Hospice, home health agency, palliative care service
Policymaker	Professional organization, public organization, federal or state legislative body

Table 1.3 Professional Organizational Resources for APNs

American Nurses Association	*Nursing: Scope and Standards of Practice*
	Position Statement—Registered Nurses' Roles and Responsibilities in Providing Expert Care and Counseling at the End of Life (2010)
	Position Statement—The Nurse's Role in Ethics and Human Rights: Protecting and Promoting Individual Worth, Dignity, and Human Rights in Practice Settings (2010)
	Position Statement—Nursing Care and Do Not Resuscitate (DNR) and Allow Natural Death (AND) Decisions (2012)
Hospice and Palliative Nurses Association	*Palliative Nursing: Scope and Standards of Practice—An Essential Resource for Hospice and Palliative Nurses* (5th ed., 2014)
	Competencies for the Hospice and Palliative Advanced Practice Nurse (2nd ed., 2014)
	Position Statement—The Nurse's Role in Advance Care Planning (2011)
	Position Statement—The Value of the Advanced Practice Nurse (2015)
National Council of State Boards of Nursing	Consensus Model for APRN Regulations: Licensure, Accreditation, Certification & Education (2008)

There are few graduate programs that offer focused palliative care education, subspecialty, or certificate programs either at the master's or doctoral level.[37] Moreover, there are only a handful of APRN fellowships.[38] Most fellowships are offered at academic medical centers, with the majority for nurse practitioners and only one program for clinical nurse specialists. The result is that the majority of fellowships are using this training to increase their workforce. In other words, they educate future palliative

Table 1.4 References for the APN

National Consensus Project for Quality Palliative Care	*Clinical Practice Guidelines for Quality Palliative Care* (3rd ed. Pittsburgh, PA: National Consensus Project; 2013)
National Comprehensive Cancer Network	*NCCN Clinical Practice Guidelines in Oncology (NCCN Guidelines) Palliative Care Version 2* (2012)
National Institute of Nursing Research	*The Science of Compassion: Future Directions in End-of-Life & Palliative Care* (2011)
National Quality Forum	*Measure Applications Partnership—Performance Measurement Coordination Strategies for Hospice and Palliative Care Final Report* (2012)
Institute of Medicine	*The Future of Nursing: Leading Change, Advancing Health* (Washington, DC: National Academies Press; 2011)
	Delivering High-Quality Cancer Care: Charting a New Course for a System in Crisis (Washington, DC: National Academies Press; 2013)
Oxford University Press	*Oxford Textbook of Palliative Nursing* (4th ed.; New York, NY; 2015)
	Communication in Palliative Nursing (2012)

Table 1.5 APN Education Resources

End-of-Life Nursing Education Consortium (ELNEC)	*History, Statewide Effort and Recommendations for the Future Advancing Palliative Nursing Care* (Long Beach, CA: Archstone Foundation; 2012). Available at http://www.aacn.nche.edu/elnec/publications/ELNEC-Monograph.pdf

team members to then retain within their program. Most of these APRNs stay in hospital positions and do not move into rural or community settings. Outside of fellowships and observerships, there are few clinical experiences for APRNs. Of the few that exist, there are limitations in patient care exposure due to licensure, time, expense, and support for both clinical nurse specialists and nurse practitioners.

Graduate-level–prepared specialty nurses work in indirect roles, such as research, case management, administration, and education. Their settings of practice include academic research or education settings, schools of nursing, professional organizations, specialty clinics, and community settings. APNs in these roles promote all aspects of palliative care and palliative nursing by developing diverse programs for the public, insurers, and international communities, creating palliative care and nursing educational programs, and performing palliative care and palliative nursing research. There are many documents to frame such work, including the NQF's *A National Framework and Preferred Practices for Palliative and Hospice Care Quality: A Consensus Report*, the National Priorities Partnership's *Palliative and End-of-Life Convening Meeting Synthesis Report* strategies, and the National Consensus Project for Quality Palliative Care's *Clinical Practice Guidelines*. Although specialty palliative certification in these indirect roles does not exist, it is available in related areas, such as registered nurse, administrator, pediatric nurse, or perinatal loss expert.

APRNs making a midcareer change into palliative care may find it a difficult transition. Educational opportunities are limited. There are financial constraints, as education funds are shrinking and APRNs must use personal funds for travel and course registration fees. There are time constraints due to the need to continue clinical responsibilities while seeking further education. There are also limits imposed by the variations of APRN practice—specifically, licensure variability from state to state makes it difficult for APRNs to cross into other states to obtain direct clinical experience.

Within the role of research, the APN initiates, creates, participates in, or leads research projects. There are the formal research roles of identifying clinical problems, developing and conducting research studies, and overseeing recruitment and data collection. Informal research projects include quality improvement projects, translating research into practice, using research to create policies and procedures, educating others about the research process, and the use of evidence-based practice. Areas of research within palliative nursing have been established by the HPNA's *2015–2018 Research Agenda*, which focuses on the eight domains of care within the National Consensus Project for Quality Palliative Care's *Clinical Practice Guidelines*. These domains encompass palliative and end-of-life care for patients of all ages with any serious or advanced condition or disease, at any stage. For 2012–2015, the target domains include (1) structure and processes of care, (2) physical aspects of care, and (3) psychological and psychiatric aspects of care.[39] Moreover, the research agenda highlights the need for interdisciplinary research teams to obtain the multidimensional perspective needed to examine the complex issues within palliative care.[39] While all research in palliative care is important to patients, HPNA obtains input from members about current priority areas.

Within the role of educator, there are formal academic roles at schools of nursing. These may include tenured faculty positions, such as adjunct professor, assistant professor, associate professor, and professor. Nontenured positions include instructors, lecturers, and adjunct clinical positions. Educator roles may also include educational positions within professional organizations, such as director or coordinator of education for a professional nursing organization or another discipline. There may be education roles within palliative care and palliative care-related corporations, such as continuing education providers, pharmaceutical companies, or technical assistance companies, such as learning management systems. There may also be educational initiatives that offer regional, national, and international opportunities in palliative care and palliative nursing education. Some examples are the ELNEC and Education in Palliative and End-of-Life Care (EPEC) curricula.

Case managers can seek positions within healthcare organizations, insurers, or private companies. Case managers within hospitals are charged with increasingly difficult post-hospital care planning, with the emphasis on moving patients out of the hospital. In the community, there are more APN case managers who have the skills to accept or make plans for these complex patients. These may include geriatric specialists, hospice specialists, or case managers within home health, hospice, or specialty programs, such as cardiac disease or pulmonary disease.

Within the clinical roles of clinical nurse specialist, nurse practitioner, certified nurse midwife, and certified nurse anesthetist, many APRNs work in myriad health settings, including home, hospice, ambulatory and outpatient clinics, long-term care, skilled nursing facilities, community and rural hospitals, and academic medical centers (see Table 1.2). They have met or have been "grandmothered" into the requirements set by the National Council of State Boards of Nursing, or they may have completed a curriculum that combines population-specific issues with pain, palliative, or hospice concepts.

Within these clinical roles, the APRN has two functions—a consultant or a primary care provider. In the consultant role, the APRN offers expertise in the care and management of patients with chronic progressive, serious advanced illness, or life-limiting illness. In this role, the APRN offers advice but does not write orders, request diagnostic tests, or write prescriptions. Part of the consulting process involves educating colleagues about the appropriateness of moving palliative care upstream to diagnosis. The other part of consulting is performing expert care and offering expert opinion in the physical, psychological, spiritual, and emotional aspects of care. In a primary care role, the APRN takes on the responsibility for the patient. In this role, he or she is responsible for all aspects of care, from diagnostics to prescriptions, from admission to discharge, and everything in between.

There are opportunities and challenges within each role. As a consultant, the APRN has limited control over the patient's care; rather, it is hoped that through the collaborative process, recommendations, suggestions, and advice will be followed. However, in the consultant role, the APRN may be able to see more patients and carry a larger panel. As a primary provider, the APRN has more control but a larger burden of care. Patients may require more time and focus.

In addition, the APRN is part of an interdisciplinary team, as required by the definition of specialty palliative care stated in the NCP guidelines. The interdisciplinary team includes physicians, chaplains, registered nurses, nursing assistants, social workers, physical therapists, occupational therapists, speech and language pathologists, dieticians, and pharmacists. The team must work collaboratively and capitalize on each member's strengths and expertise. Effective team communication is essential, since this is a clear indicator of quality care and patient and family satisfaction.

The Future of Palliative APRNs

In the changing healthcare landscape, nurses, particularly APRNs, have been identified as an essential element of improving care and access, particularly as healthcare reform continues under the Affordable Care Act.[28,40,41] The Promoting Excellence *Advanced Practice Nurse Position Statement* acknowledged early on that APRNs offered promise for managing the changing needs of the aging population. Specifically, APRNs have the skills in clinical practice, education, and advocacy to develop palliative care in novel ways. Moreover, the 2011 IOM report *The Future of Nursing: Leading Change, Advancing Health* acknowledged the essential contributions of nursing at the bedside and in healthcare redesign with its four messages:[41]

1. Nurses should practice to the full extent of their education and training.

2. Nurses should achieve higher levels of education and training through an improved education system that promotes seamless academic progression.

3. Nurses should be full partners, with physicians and other healthcare professionals, in redesigning healthcare in the United States.

4. Effective workforce planning and policy making require better data collection and information restructure.

Each of these messages has important implications for hospice and palliative advanced practice nursing. APRNs should be practicing to the full extent of their education and training, but also to their scope of practice. There is much work to be done to promote the role within all types of programs. In addition, more nurses should be encouraged to pursue graduate education and training to promote palliative care within primary care practices, specialty clinics, and specialty programs. This promotes quality care and access to care. APRNs offer some innovative solutions in redesigning healthcare with population-focused initiatives. This allows them to create innovative models of care. APRNs may have a major role in workforce redesign and in restructuring care away from the hospital. Positions are being created in the community that allow APRNs to use their full range of skills.

The enactment of the Affordable Care Act places emphasis on the three Rs: right patient, right care, at the right time.[40] Indeed, all of the recommendations of the 2014 IOM report *Dying in America* involve areas where APRNs can have a direct impact.[12] By the nature of their care, they provide person-centered, family-focused care and engage in expert nurse–patient communication and advance care planning. APRNs are teaching the next generation of clinicians as well as their colleagues and the public about palliative care. They are integral to the role of payment and policies related to palliative care. With the goal of palliative care to keep patients at home and out of the hospital, APRNs are uniquely qualified and positioned to provide services, particularly in rural and community settings. They practice throughout the country in urban, suburban, community, and rural areas, with a focus on promoting wellness and alleviating suffering for patients and families living with illness. Within their scope of nursing practice, APRNs may diagnose, treat, prescribe for, and manage various health problems.

Within cancer care, there is a mandate for quality palliative care, and APRNs will be necessary to meet the growing demands of care. In 2012, the American Society of Clinical Oncology stated that palliative care should be offered to patients with advanced stages of lung cancer as well as for metastatic disease. In the same year, the American College of Surgeons, in collaboration with the Commission on Cancer, issued a statement that palliative services should be offered to all cancer patients across the cancer trajectory.[41] Finally, the 2013 IOM report *Delivering High-Quality Cancer Care: Charting a Course for a System in Crisis* suggests that scope of practice and reimbursement structures be created to promote comprehensive care.[42] This is because there is a shortage of oncology physicians and the interdisciplinary team will need to be maximally utilized based on their skills.

In cardiovascular care, there is a new emphasis on palliative care. In 2014, the American Heart Association and the American Stroke Association issued joint guidelines for palliative care in caring for patients with heart disease and stroke.[43] It recognized that palliative care should begin at the onset of such an event. In particular, this includes advance care planning, goal-setting, and family support, in particular for surrogate decision makers. Given the call for palliative care for all stroke patients, APRNs will have a large role in promoting the use of palliative care and providing it across settings. This will have an impact on the large numbers of nurses in cardiovascular nursing.

Despite this goal, clinical education and organized training in palliative care are seriously lacking. The National Consensus Project for Quality Palliative Care's *Clinical Practice Guidelines* offers a structure for future nursing education and research developed and initiated within the realm of advanced practice nursing in all aspects of palliative nursing. The provision of expert advanced palliative nursing requires clinical education and experience. The challenge for palliative APRNs will be developing skills and knowledge for their roles. For nurses entering a graduate program, there may be palliative care courses in pain and symptom management, advanced illness, and psychological coping. If an APRN is making a midcareer change into palliative care, there is a structure to allow development and mentorship in the palliative APRN role. While interprofessional education is appropriate for content and principles of palliative care, APRNs must receive coaching, mentoring, and education in specific palliative nursing principles and role-specific issues.

One consideration is determining learning practicums or preceptorships that offer population-based care delivery with supervised clinical training. One such program is a geropalliative care residency that offers 6 months of education for nurses to learn

about the palliative nursing necessary for care of older adults.[44] Another consideration is preparation for the diagnosis and management of advanced illness. It is hoped that more graduate nursing programs will offer palliative coursework, since all populations are affected by advanced illness, chronic progressive illness, and serious and life-threatening illness. Another challenge is financial concerns regarding salary support and the reimbursement structures that endorse the use of APRNs. However, many APRNs have created innovative financial structures and models of care to demonstrate that their salaries are offset by cost avoidance, lower readmission rates, or other measures.[45]

Furthermore, it is hoped that more innovative programs develop for midcareer transitions into palliative care. There are several examples of APRN-led palliative care programs: (a) a nurse practitioner-led primary care palliative care clinic,[46] (b) a nurse practitioner-led palliative care clinic imbedded in a health system,[47] and (c) a clinical nurse specialist-led initiative in an oncology clinic.[48] There is the potential for more community-based models to emerge in which palliative APRNs initiate or play a leading role in development and service delivery.

Conclusion

Undoubtedly, the field of palliative care will continue to mature to meet the needs of an aging and sicker population being cared for outside of the hospital. There are clearly more opportunities for APRNs in emerging models of healthcare. To meet this need, APRNs will need to be situated in primary care clinics, in homes providing care to frail elders, and in rural practices, as well as in accountable care organizations and medical homes/hospitals. Across these settings, APRNs will prevent unnecessary admissions and promote appropriate, safe, and timely discharges. In determining their roles and responsibilities, key areas for the APRN to determine will include knowledge, role clarification, palliative nursing competence, and a culture that embraces both advanced practice nursing and palliative nursing. Some of the issues APRNs will need to grapple with are (1) the clinical and didactic palliative care education required for clinical roles, (2) licensing, credentialing, and certification for both clinical and nonclinical roles, (3) qualifications to do either primary or specialty advanced palliative nursing, (4) creating supportive work environments, and (5) obtaining and ensuring appropriate financial support for their services.

References

1. Lynch M, Dahlin C, Hultman T, Coakley E. Palliative care nursing—defining the discipline? *J Hospice Palliat Nurs.* 2011; 13(2): 106–11.
2. Dahlin C, Lynch M. Evolution of the advanced practice nurse in palliative care. In: Dahlin CM, Lynch MT, eds. *Core Curriculum for the Advanced Practice Hospice and Palliative Registered Nurse.* 2nd ed. Pittsburgh, PA: Hospice and Palliative Nurses Association; 2013:3–12.
3. Yale Bulletin and Calendar. *American Academy Honors Three from YSN.* 2001. Available at http://www.yale.edu/opa/arc-ybc/v30.n11/story9.html. Accessed September 30, 2014.
4. Institute of Medicine. *Approaching Death: Improving Care at the End of Life.* Washington, DC: National Academies Press; 1997.
5. SUPPORT Principal Investigators. A controlled trial to improve care for the seriously ill hospitalized patients: The study to understand prognoses and preferences for outcomes and risks of treatment (SUPPORT). *JAMA.* 1995; 274(20): 1591–8.

6. The Robert Wood Johnson Foundation. *Pioneer Programs in Palliative Care: Nine Case Studies.* New York, NY: Milbank Memorial Fund; 2000.

7. Last Acts. *Precepts of Palliative Care.* Washington, DC: Last Acts; 1997.

8. Last Acts. *Means to a Better End: A Report on Dying in America Today.* Washington, DC: Last Acts; 2002.

9. Institute of Medicine. *When Children Die: Improving Palliative and End-of-Life Care for Children and Their Families.* Washington, DC: National Academies Press; 2002.

10. Institute of Medicine. *Crossing the Quality Chasm: A New Health System for the 21st Century.* Washington, DC: National Academies Press; 2001.

11. Jennings B, Ryndes T, D'Onofrio C, Baily MA. Access to Hospice Care: Expanding Boundaries, Overcoming Barriers. *Hastings Center Report.* 2003; Supplement 33(2): S1–59.

12. Institute of Medicine. *Dying in America—Improving Quality and Honoring Individual Preferences Near End of Life.* Washington, DC: National Academies Press; 2014.

13. National Consensus Project for Quality Palliative Care. *Clinical Practice Guidelines for Quality Palliative Care.* Pittsburgh, PA: National Consensus Project for Quality Palliative Care; 2004.

14. Dahlin C. National Consensus Project for Quality Palliative Care: Promoting Excellence in Palliative Nursing. In: Ferrell B, Coyle N, Paice J, eds. *The Oxford Textbook of Palliative Nursing.* 4th ed. New York, NY: Oxford University Press; 2014.

15. National Consensus Project for Quality Palliative Care. *Clinical Practice Guidelines for Quality Palliative Care.* 3rd ed. Pittsburgh, PA: National Consensus Project; 2013.

16. National Institutes of Health. NIH State-of-the-Science Conference Statement on Improving End-of-Life Care. *NIH Consens State Sci Statements.* 2004; 21(3): 1–26.

17. National Institute of Nursing Research. *The Science of Compassion: Future Directions in End-of-Life & Palliative Care.* 2011. Available at https://www.ninr.nih.gov/researchandfunding/scienceofcompassion#.U8FCJvldUUc. Accessed September 30, 2014.

18. Dahlin C. Providing quality palliative care. In: Dahlin C, Lynch M, eds. *Core Curriculum for the Advanced Practice Hospice and Palliative Registered Nurse.* 2nd ed. Pittsburgh, PA: Hospice and Palliative Nurses Association; 2013:13–23.

19. National Quality Forum. *A National Framework and Preferred Practices for Palliative and Hospice Care Quality: A Consensus Report.* Washington, DC: NQF; 2006.

20. National Priorities Partnership. *National Priorities & Goals—Aligning Our Efforts to Transform America's Healthcare.* 2008. Available at http://psnet.ahrq.gov/resource.aspx?resourceID=8745. Accessed September 30, 2014.

21. National Priorities Partnership. *Palliative Care and End-of-Life Convening Meeting Synthesis Report.* Washington, DC: National Quality Forum; 2010.

22. Dahlin C, Mazenec P. Building from our past: Celebrating 25 years of clinical practice in hospice and palliative nursing. *J Hospice Palliat Nurs.* 2011; 13(6S): S20–S8.

23. Ferrell BR, Virani R, Grant M. Analysis of end-of-life content in nursing textbooks. *Oncol Nurs Forum.* 1999; 26(5): 869–76.

24. American Association of Colleges of Nursing. Peaceful Death: Recommended Competencies and Curricular Guidelines for End-of-Life Nursing Care. 1997. Available at www.aacn.nche.edu/Publications/deathfin.htm. Accessed September 30, 2014.

25. White K, Coyne P, Lee J. Nurses' perceptions of educational gaps in delivering end-of-life care. *Oncol Nurs Forum.* 2011; 38(6): 711–7.

26. White K, Coyne PJ, White S. Are hospice and palliative care nurses adequately prepared for end-of-life care? *J Hospice Palliat Nurs.* 2012; 14(2): 133–40.

27. American Association of Colleges of Nursing. *About ELNEC.* 2013. Available at http://www.aacn.nche.edu/elnec/about/fact-sheet. Accessed September 30, 2014.

28. Promoting Excellence in End-of-Life. *Advanced Practice Nurses Role in Palliative Care: A Position Statement from American Nursing Leaders.* 2002. Available at http://www.promotingexcellence.org/downloads/apn_position.pdf. Accessed September 30, 2014.

29. Hospice and Palliative Nurses Association. HPNA Position Statement: Value of Advanced Practice Registered Nurses in Palliative Care. 2015. Available at http://www.hpna.org/DisplayPage.aspx?Title=Position%20Statements. Accessed September 30, 2015.

30. APRN Consensus Work Group & National Council of State Boards of Nursing APRN Advisory Group. *Consensus Model for APRN Regulations: Licensure, Accreditation, Certification & Education.* 2008. Available at https://www.ncsbn.org/Consensus_Model_for_APRN_Regulation_July_2008.pdf. Accessed September 30, 2014.

31. Hospice and Palliative Nurses Association, American Nurses Association. *Hospice and Palliative Nursing: Scope and Standards of Practice.* Silver Spring, MD: Hospice and Palliative Nurses Association/American Nurses Association; 2002.

32. American Nurses Association and Hospice and Palliative Nurses Association. *Palliative Nursing: Scope and Standards of Practice—An Essential Resource for Hospice and Palliative Nurses.* 5th ed. Silver Spring, MD: American Nurses Association and Hospice and Palliative Nurses Association; 2014.

33. Hospice and Palliative Nurses Association. *Competencies for the Hospice and Palliative APN.* Pittsburgh, PA: Hospice and Palliative Nurses Association; 2002.

34. Hospice and Palliative Nurses Association. *Competencies for the Hospice and Palliative Advanced Practice Nurse.* 2nd ed. Pittsburgh, PA: Hospice and Palliative Nurses Association; 2014.

35. Hospice and Palliative Nurses Association. *Standards for Clinical Practicum in Palliative Nursing for Practicing Professional Nurses.* 2006. Available at http://www.hpna.org/DisplayPage.aspx?Title=Standards%20for%20Clinical%20Practicum. Accessed September 30, 2014.

36. National Board for Certification of Hospice and Palliative Nursing. *ACHPN Map.* 2014. Available at https://www.nbchpn.org/Certificants_Map.aspx?Cert=APRN. Accessed September 30, 2014.

37. Hospice and Palliative Nurses Association. *Graduate Program Listing.* 2014. Available at http://www.hpna.org/DisplayPage.aspx?Title=Graduate%20Program%20Listing. Accessed September 30, 2014.

38. Hospice and Palliative Nurses Association. *Nursing Fellowships.* 2014. Available at http://www.hpna.org/DisplayPage.aspx?Title=Nursing%20Fellowships. Accessed September 30, 2014.

39. Hospice and Palliative Nurses Association. *Research Agenda 2012–2015.* Pittsburgh, PA; 2012. Available at http://www.hpna.org/DisplayPage.aspx?Title=Research. Accessed September 30, 2014.

40. Patient Protection and Affordable Care Act (PPACA), Public Law 111-148, §2702, Title III (B)(III) Section 3140,124, Stat. 119, 318-319, Consolidating amendments made by Title X of the Act and the Health Care and Education Reconciliation Act of 2010. 2010. Washington, DC.

41. American College of Surgeons, Commission on Cancer. *Cancer Programs Standards 2012: Ensuring Patient-Centered Care.* Chicago, IL: American College of Surgeons; 2012.

42. Institute of Medicine. *Delivering high-quality cancer care: Charting a new course for a system in crisis.* Washington, DC: The National Academies Press; 2013.

43. Holloway R, Arnold R, Cruetzfeldt C, et al. *Palliative Care and End of Life Care in Stroke: A Statement for Health Professionals from the American Heart Association/American Stroke Association. Stroke.* Dallas, TX: American Heart Association; 2014.

44. Lee SM, Coakley EE, Blakeney B, Brandt LK, Rideout ML, Dahlin C. The National AgeWISE Pilot. *J Nurs Admin*. 2012; 42(7/8): 356–60.

45. Coyne P. Evolution of the advanced practice nurse within palliative care. *J Palliat Med*. 2003; 6(5): 767–8.

46. Owens D, Eby K, Burson S, Green M, McGoodwin W, Isaac M. Primary palliative care clinic pilot project demonstrates benefits of a nurse practitioner-directed clinic providing primary and palliative care. *J Am Acad Nurse Practitioners*. 2012; 24(1): 52–8.

47. Deitrick LM, Rockwell EH, Gratz N, et al. Delivering specialized palliative care in the community: A new role for nurse practitioners. *Advances Nurs Sci*. 2011; 34(4): E23–E36.

48. Prince-Paul M, Burant CJ, Saltzman JN, Teston LJ, Matthews CR. The effects of integrating an advanced practice palliative care nurse in a community oncology center: a pilot study. *J Supportive Oncol*. 2010 Jan-Feb; 8(1): 21–7.

Fundamental Skills and Education for the Palliative Advanced Practice Registered Nurse

Dorothy Wholihan and Charles Tilley

Key Points

- The American Nurses Association and Hospice and Palliative Nurses Association document *Palliative Nursing: Scope and Standards of Practice* and the competencies defined by HPNA guide the education of advanced palliative nursing practice.

- The regulatory standards developed by the National Council of State Boards of Nursing and detailed in the Licensing, Accreditation, Certification, and Education (LACE) model define palliative care as an advanced practice registered nurse (APRN) specialty practice, which is achieved by professional board certification.

- Current educational programs for palliative APNs include master's, post-master's, doctoral, and continuing professional education programs.

Case Study

Melissa Johnson was a registered nurse who became working on the oncology floor of an urban academic medical center for six years. She attended an ELNEC training and several continuing education conferences in palliative nursing. Recognizing the many unmet needs of patients with advanced illness, she became increasingly interested in becoming a palliative advanced practice nurse. Knowing she wanted to work in the acute care setting, she planned to pursue a degree to become an acute care NP with a specialty in palliative care. The two major nursing schools in her area offered a master's NP program, as well as a new BSN-to-DNP program. She also heard about several online long-distance master's and DNP programs. Since she had so many options available, she consulted with academic advisors at the various schools to ascertain the best course of study for her professional goals and lifestyle needs.

Definition of Advanced Practice Nursing

Advanced practice registered nurses (APRNs) have played a pivotal role in palliative care over the past 15 years and will continue to shape the future of hospice and palliative care. Broadly defined and practice-focused, advanced practice nursing includes interventions that influence healthcare outcomes, including the direct care of individual patients, management of care for individuals and populations, administration of nursing and healthcare organizations, and the development and implementation of health policy.[1] The term "advanced practice" came to the forefront in the 1980s, with the expansion of graduate curricula and development of advanced practice specialty tracks within nursing programs.[2]

The American Association of Colleges of Nursing's *Peaceful Death Competencies*, The National Consensus Project, and the National Quality Forum: Roadmaps for Education

In the late 1990s, a national dialogue was ignited about the ability of the healthcare system to provide care to patients with life-threatening illness. In response to the dearth of end-of-life content in most nursing curricula at the time, combined with the realities of an aging population, the expense of unnecessarily prolonged dying driven by advanced technology, and public apprehension about suffering, the American Association of Colleges of Nursing, supported by the Robert Wood Johnson Foundation, assembled a panel of experts in 1997 to develop end-of-life competency statements.[3] This project, conducted in accordance with the mandate by the International Council of Nurses, detailed nurses' unique role in and responsibility for ensuring that individuals experience a peaceful death.[4] A roundtable of expert nurses and other healthcare professionals, on the premise that the precepts underlying hospice care are essential principles for all end-of-life care, developed an interdisciplinary approach to the educational preparation of nursing students for end-of-life practice. The panel developed 16 end-of-life competency statements to be included in multiple content areas, including health assessment, pharmacology, psychiatric–mental health nursing, nursing management courses, ethical/legal courses, cultural issues content, nursing research, and professional issues/healthcare settings.[3]

The *Clinical Practice Guidelines for Quality Palliative Care* were originally published in 2004 by the National Consensus Project for Quality Palliative Care (NCP).[5] The NCP started as a partnership of five national palliative care organizations: the American Academy of Hospice and Palliative Medicine, the Center to Advance Palliative Care, the Hospice and Palliative Nurses Association, the Last Acts Partnership, and the National Hospice and Palliative Care Organization, later joined by the National Palliative Care Research Center and the National Association of Social Workers. The *Clinical Practice Guidelines* aimed to reach professional consensus in making recommendations about the development of palliative care programs by creating clinical practice guidelines that improve the quality of palliative care in the United States. The third edition of the *Clinical Practice Guidelines*, published in 2013, further delineates the original eight domains identified.[5] Domain 1, Guideline 1.3 states that the interdisciplinary team includes palliative care professionals with the appropriate patient population-specific education, credentialing, and experience, and the skills to meet the physical, psychological, social, and spiritual needs of both patient and family. Of particular importance is assembling a team, which includes chaplains, nurses, pharmacists, physicians, and social workers, appropriately trained and, ideally, certified in hospice and palliative care, when such certification is available.[6]

Building on the work of the NCP, the National Quality Forum (NQF), a nonprofit public–private partnership focused on improving the quality of healthcare through setting voluntary consensus standards, developed *A National Framework and Preferred Practices for Palliative and Hospice Care Quality* (NQF Preferred Practices).[7] They incorporated the principles of the *Clinical Practice Guideline* domains into the framework, which were directly reflected in the preferred practices.

The NQF identified 38 preferred practices, including educational standards directly relatable to advanced practice education. NQF Preferred Practices 3, 4, and 5 directly addressed education.[7]

PREFERRED PRACTICE 3

♦ Provide *continuing education* to all healthcare professionals on the domains of palliative care and hospice care.

PREFERRED PRACTICE 4

♦ Provide *adequate training and clinical support* to assure that professional staff is confident in their ability to provide palliative care to patients.

PREFERRED PRACTICE 5

♦ Hospice care and specialized palliative care professionals should be *appropriately trained, credentialed, and/or certified* in their area of expertise.

The framework document recommends that "Palliative care programs ensure appropriate levels of education for all palliative care professionals. Advanced practice nurses, physicians, and rehabilitation therapists must have graduate degrees in their respective disciplines, with appropriate professional experience in hospice and palliative care."[7]

Institute of Medicine: *The Future of Nursing: Leading Change, Advancing Health*

In 2010, the Institute of Medicine published recommendations on how to transform the nursing profession.[8] This document was congruent with many palliative position statements already mentioned in this chapter, as it attempted to address the needs of an aging population, the growing number of people with chronic diseases, and the need for care coordination. Four key messages were pervasive throughout the eight recommendations, two directly related to the promotion and elevation of nursing education:[8]

1. Nurses should practice to the full extent of their education and training.

2. Nurses should achieve higher levels of education and training through an improved education system that promotes seamless academic progression.

3. Nurses should be full partners, with physicians and other health professionals, in redesigning healthcare in the United States.

4. Effective workforce planning and policy making require better data collection and an improved information infrastructure.

Specialty Palliative Care Versus Primary Palliative Care

The advent of specialty palliative care for advanced practice nursing has delineated primary palliative care and specialty palliative care. Primary palliative care may be provided by all healthcare professionals and includes the management of chronic illness, basic symptom management, communication, and the completion of advance directives. Specialty palliative care is provided by professionals with training and certification in palliative care and is focused on patients and families with more complex needs and advanced illness.[9]

All APRNs are educated to obtain the knowledge, skills, and competency to perform basic primary palliative nursing. However, additional graduate education and preparation promote practice at an advanced specialty level. More graduate programs are now including population-focused specialty palliative care education, as either elective courses or as more extensive and formal specialty course programs.[9]

Primary Nursing Practice

Since the essence of palliative care is embedded in all nursing practice, all nurses already practice primary palliative care. This is inherent in the definition of nursing as the alleviation of suffering through the diagnosis and treatment of human response, and advocacy in the care of individuals, families, communities, and populations. By the nature of their role, all nurses provide psychosocial support. They also have the skills to assess and assist advance care planning and to identify spiritual issues and cultural concerns.[9]

Many undergraduate baccalaureate programs offer specific courses in palliative care or incorporate elements of palliative nursing into required classes. After graduating from an accredited nursing program, registered nurses at the generalist level are required to pass the National Council Licensure Examination

(NCLEX-RN), which includes palliative care content. At places of employment, orientation and ongoing education programs can support further development of practice in these areas. [9]

Advanced Palliative Nursing Practice

As described in *Palliative Nursing: Scope and Standards of Practice*,[10] there are two roles in advanced practice palliative nursing practice. One advanced practice role is the graduate-level prepared specialty nurse educated at the master's or doctoral level in non-direct care roles (e.g., education, research, administration). These nurses practice in a variety of settings, such as academic medical centers, schools of nursing, specialty clinics, community settings, academic research or education settings, and various professional organizations. They promote educational programs in palliative care, palliative nursing research, and program development for diverse programs. Although advanced palliative nursing certification is not available in these areas, specialty hospice and palliative certification is encouraged. Currently offered are examinations for the registered nurse, administrator, pediatric nurse, and perinatal loss expert.[10]

The second, more common level of advanced palliative nursing practice is that of the APRN, a nurse educated at the master's level or above and practicing within one of the four roles defined by the 2008 *Consensus Model for APRN Regulation: Licensure, Accreditation, Certification, and Education (LACE)* document developed by the APRN Consensus Work Group & National Council of State Boards of Nursing APRN Advisory Committee.[11] According to this document, the APRN is a registered nurse educated at the master's, post-master's, or doctoral level in one of four roles: a clinical nurse specialist (CNS), nurse practitioner (NP), certified nurse midwife, or certified registered nurse anesthetist. Most hospice and palliative APRNs are CNSs and/or NPs. Nurse anesthetists and nurse midwives working in palliative care may practice in areas like pain management or perinatal palliative care.

Scope and Competencies of the Palliative APRN

The skills required for advanced practice in palliative care nursing have been defined by the professional organization that represents this discipline. The American Nurses Association and the HPNA have defined standards for practice in the document *Palliative Nursing; Scope and Standards of Practice—An Essential Resource for Hospice and Palliative Nurses*, which includes standards specific to advanced practice.[10] Last revised in 2014, the document is accompanied by a more specific delineation of competencies in the HPNA publication entitled *Competencies for the Hospice and Palliative APN*.[12] This document describes advanced core competencies that represent the knowledge, skills, and attitudes advanced practice hospice and palliative care nurses demonstrate when providing evidence-based care to patients and families experiencing life-limiting, progressive illness. This care encompasses the physical, psychosocial, emotional, and spiritual realms.[12] Thus, graduate education must include these competency domains.

Table 2.1 lists the basic areas of APRN competency as defined by the HPNA.[12]

Table 2.1 Areas of APN Expertise as Defined by the HPNA[10]

1. Clinical judgment
2. Advocacy and ethics
3. Professionalism
4. Collaboration
5. Systems thinking
6. Cultural competence
7. Facilitator of learning
8. Communication

Deficits in Nursing Education

Despite research documenting deficits in the care of patients with serious illness[13] and recommendations from many prestigious health organizations calling for improved palliative care,[14,15] the topics of palliative and end-of-life care have been historically neglected within both medical and nursing education. In a landmark study of nursing textbooks, Dr. Betty Ferrell and colleagues[16] first documented these deficits, finding that only 2% of nursing textbooks contained any reference to end-of-life care. White, Coyne, and White conducted a survey of 1,230 HPNA members and found that nurses believed formal education was important in palliative care.[17] In 2006, Paice and colleagues surveyed 131 of the existing 382 graduate nursing programs to evaluate the state of palliative care content in graduate nursing curricula.[18] The research revealed that faculty also reported that end-of-life care was an important facet of nursing education, but most perceived their own programs as only moderately effective in providing this content.[18]

Shea and colleagues[19] used the 106-item End-of-Life Nursing Education Consortium (ELNEC) examination to ascertain the knowledge level about end-of-life care of experienced nurses returning for graduate study. Results showed that, for the most part, these graduate students had no previous palliative care education (86.7%) and linked palliative care solely with end-of-life care. Although the researchers did not detail the areas of deficit, the mean score on the exam was reported at 68.73 (SD = 9.82), which the authors equated to a "D" grade. The graduate students who had been out of school longest had the lowest scores, possibly reflecting the dearth of palliative care content in earlier nursing curricula (this situation may have improved in more recent years). Since this study was conducted in 2010, it is hoped that scores will continue to improve as palliative care content increases.

Changes in APRN Education: The LACE Model

As described above, major changes in the education and licensing of advanced practice nurses came about with the proposal of the LACE model.[11] This document presents a uniform model of regulation of APRNs across the states. It establishes foundational requirements for educational tracks leading to APRN licensure. This model recategorizes APRNs, mandating that they have education and certification within a population focus. The consensus model specifies four advanced practice roles (registered nurse anesthetist, nurse midwife, clinical nurse specialist, and nurse practitioner); all these roles must fall within at least one of six population-based foci (family/individual across the lifespan, adult-gerontology, pediatric, neonatal, women's health/gender related, or psychiatric/mental health). After extensive national dialogue, the decision was made to define the adult population as "adult-gerontology" in order to increase the number of APRNs prepared to care for the growing older population.[20] This move has had a profound impact on the education of APRNs, in that all adult programs now have a melded adult-gerontology focus. Increasing geriatric curriculum in all adult programs will, it is hoped, result in increased palliative care content as well.

Current Educational Models: Master's Education in Palliative Care

As the specialty of palliative care has evolved over the past 20 years, so too have the educational models that form the basis of specialty advanced practice palliative nursing education. In 1998, the Breen School of Nursing at Ursuline College in Ohio offered the first MSN program for the preparation of palliative care clinical nurse specialists. The same year, a program specifically designed to prepare palliative care nurse practitioners was established at New York University. Both of these pioneering APRN programs included basic master's-level essential coursework, with additional specialized palliative care coursework and significant hours (500 or more) of palliative care clinical practice.[21]

Since these original programs were developed, several different models have been developed to integrate specialist palliative nurse education and clinical practice into master's programs. Framed as minors, certifications, and subspecialties, university programs have delivered content in a variety of formats, ranging from single-course didactic elective classes to extensive clinical and classroom-based specialty tracks. Quality can be standardized by using resources to assist with curriculum development. As the specialty palliative nursing organization, HPNA developed both scope and standards and competencies for advanced practice. In addition, HPNA established guidelines for clinical education entitled *Standards for Clinical Education of Hospice and Palliative Nurses.*[22] Many of the current palliative nursing education offerings and graduate-level programs are listed on the HPNA website.[23]

With the expanding need for palliative APRNs, several universities have developed post-master's certificate programs. Designed for practicing APRNs who wish to develop a new area of expertise, these programs are increasingly popular among working advanced practice nurses wanting to move into palliative care. A variety of formats exist, from purely didactic online programs to 12-credit academic programs with up to 500 clinical practicum hours. The reader is referred to the HPNA website for the most current listing of programs nationwide.[23]

Doctoral Education in Palliative Care—PhD and DNP

Doctoral education for the palliative care nurse provides the opportunity to contribute to the state of knowledge in the field. PhD programs in nursing provide the tools for nurses to design, conduct, analyze, and report theoretical and clinical research related to the care of those with advanced, progressive illness.[24] The DNP is a clinically based doctoral degree. Table 2.2 outlines the fundamental characteristics of both PhD and DNP programs of study.[1]

The PhD-Prepared Palliative Nurse

There is an urgent need for PhD-prepared nurses committed to increasing the body of knowledge within palliative nursing. *The Hospice and Palliative Nurses Associations (HPNA) 2012–2015 Research Agenda* highlights the need to integrate evidence into practice and guides nurse researchers in prioritizing research studies.[25] Within the framework of the eight NCP domains discussed earlier in this chapter, three priorities were identified from a survey of HPNA members who were asked to target the greatest gaps in palliative care knowledge. The three priority domains identified were (1) structure and process of care, (2) physical aspects of care, and (3) psychological and psychiatric aspects of care. In this document, HPNA also strongly recommended an interdisciplinary research team approach, which PhD-prepared nurses are uniquely positioned to lead, as they are among the frontrunners in developing interprofessional education models, embodying the teamwork competency.

HPNA is not alone in recognizing the dearth of research in end-of-life care and the need for evidence-based practice development. The American Academy of Hospice and Palliative Medicine partnered with the HPNA Research Advisory Group on an initiative called *Measuring What Matters.*[26] The purpose of the initiative is to provide measures for palliative care programs to use for program improvement, which would be a companion to the NCP guidelines previously discussed.

The science of palliative care has been targeted as a priority area for the National Institute of Nursing Research (NINR). In 2011, the NINR, the lead NIH funder of palliative care, conducted a State-of-the-Science Conference on Improving End-of-Life Care and affirmed its commitment to funding and supporting research in palliative care.[28] At time of publication, several major funding opportunities for palliative nursing were open. Table 2.3 provides a sample of the current funding opportunities for nurse researchers in palliative care.[26]

The DNP-Prepared Palliative Nurse

The DNP is a terminal degree for nurses interested in a clinical-focused, rather than research-based, doctorate. The development of this degree emerged from the need for highly educated, expert clinicians who could assume clinical leadership roles in shaping policy, developing clinical education and quality initiatives, and translating evidence at the point of patient contact.

There are currently two entry points for DNP education. The first is the post-bachelor's (BSN to DNP) that integrates the preparation of APRNs within the roles and population foci described above. The other option is the post-master's DNP, for the master's-prepared APRN who is already practicing. Palliative education can be integrated into either option. Students in the BSN-to-DNP program can add the specialty to their population focus, and post-master's students can gain the specialized knowledge while fulfilling the requirements for the doctoral degree.

Table 2.2 PhD and DNP Programs

	PhD	DNP
Focus	Nursing research	Nursing practice
Degree Objectives	To prepare nurse scientists to develop new knowledge for the science and practice of nursing. Graduates will lead interdisciplinary research teams, design and conduct research studies, and disseminate knowledge for nursing and related disciplines.	To create nursing leaders in interdisciplinary healthcare teams by providing students with the tools and skills necessary to translate evidence gained through nursing research into practice, improve systems of care, and measure outcomes of patient groups, populations and communities
Curriculum Focus	Emphasis on research methodology, theory and meta-theory. Cognates, courses in other disciplines that complement nursing science, are required. They provide knowledge of basic and social sciences that is relevant to the student's research focus.	Emphasis on translation of research to clinical practice. Specialized emphasis or tracks of practice: ♦ Direct care of individual patients ♦ Care of patient populations ♦ Practice that supports patient care
Point of Entry	BSN or MSN (or related master's degree)	BSN or master's in advanced practice nursing
Dissertation	Dissertation, including a dissertation defense, is required.	Dissertation requirements differ and must be grounded in clinical practice. They vary greatly and may include: ♦ No dissertation ♦ Thesis ♦ Capstone project
Clinical Requirements	Field research requirements vary.	Clinical practicum/residency requirements vary.
Employment Opportunities	Nurse scientist, nursing faculty	Healthcare administration, clinical nurse faculty

Adapted from American Association of Colleges of Nursing.[1]

The essential competencies of the DNP relate directly to the role of the palliative APRN, who often assumes systems-based responsibilities, such as patient and professional education, quality improvement, and team leadership. The DNP program requires a capstone project that demonstrates achievement of the DNP graduate's clinical competencies, emphasizes the translation of evidence into practice, and often provides the clinical scholarship leading to nursing policy change.[24] Several institutions have

Table 2.3 NINR Funding Opportunities for Palliative Care Research[28,61]

Funding Opportunity	Type of Grant*
Mechanisms, models, measurement, and management in pain research	R01, R03, R21
Building evidence: effective palliative/end-of-life care interventions	R01
Advancing the science of geriatric palliative care	R01, R03, R21

*Definition of grant types

R01: NIH's most commonly used grant program, used to support a discrete, specified, circumscribed research project. No specific dollar amount. Usually granted for 3–5 years.

R03: NIH Small Grant Program. Provides limited funding: Up to $50,000 for up to 2 years. Provides limited funding for a variety of types of projects, including pilot or feasibility studies, collection of preliminary data, secondary analysis of existing data, small self-contained research projects, development of new technology.

R21: Encourages new, exploratory and developmental research projects by providing support for the early stages of project development. Sometimes used for pilot and feasibility studies. Up to $275,000 for up to 2 years. No preliminary data are generally required.

successfully incorporated a formal palliative care specialty program into their DNP curriculum.[29,30]

Integrating palliative care content into master's and doctoral programs has been a challenge due to the high credit requirements of many programs. Lack of faculty expertise in palliative care has also been a barrier. The HPNA recently updated its *Core Curriculum for the Advanced Practice Hospice and Palliative Registered Nurse*,[27] which can serve as a guide for curriculum development. The core curriculum is designed around the major topics of Issues in Palliative Nursing, Dimensions of Care, Management of Common Serious or Life-Threatening Illnesses, and Considerations for Special Populations.

ELNEC developed several curricula in response to palliative care knowledge deficits among various levels of graduate faculty. Funding from the National Cancer Institute promoted the development of the ELNEC Graduate Curriculum, which provided end-of-life train-the-trainer education to graduate nursing faculty. Over the five years of the ELNEC Graduate Curriculum, 300 graduate nursing faculty members, representing 63% of the existing graduate schools of nursing, attended. Outcome data showed that thousands of graduate students have since been educated in this content. In addition, 65% of the faculty completing the course also used the materials to teach other audiences, such as undergraduates, nurses in clinical settings, and nurses in continuing education programs, and in faculty development programs.[31] The total hours of palliative care content added to graduate nursing curricula as a result of this initiative were reported as 18.4 (17.4 standard deviation) hours.[32]

More recently, in response to the changing trends in graduate education and the development of the DNP, the American Association of Colleges of Nursing and the City of Hope Medical Center collaborated on another grant from the National Cancer Institute. Together they developed *Integrating Palliative Oncology Care Into Doctor of Nursing Practice (DNP) Education and Clinical Practice* curriculum.[33] The aim of this grant is to offer national workshops to DNP nursing faculty and DNP clinical practitioners. The curriculum offers tools and resources to prepare the next generation of DNP graduates to provide excellent, compassionate, and evidence-based palliative care to those with cancer. Presentations cover information on integrating palliative care into core courses, clinical experiences, and DNP capstone projects.[33] This ongoing national faculty development initiative will assist educators to establish more formal palliative care specialty coursework, as well as integrate palliative care content into basic coursework at both the master's and DNP levels.

There are a limited number of postgraduate clinical nursing fellowships available. Barriers for APRN fellowship program development include the variation of state licensing requirements, low salaries, and inability to temporarily leave other positions. Most programs are sponsored by academic medical centers and may use the fellowships as workforce development within their institutions rather than an opportunity for APRNs to provide leadership in education and program development on a broader level. These programs are usually one-year postgraduate clinical fellowships for nurse practitioners, often offered alongside medical fellowships in major institutions where palliative care is well developed. However, few have been developed for midcareer APRNs. The HPNA website maintains a list of active NP fellowship programs.[34]

Continuing Education for the APRN

Along with formal academic programs, professional continuing education in palliative nursing has flourished over recent years. The most significant and far-reaching continuing education initiative has been the national ELNEC program, previously mentioned. ELNEC began in 2000 and continues today to educate nursing faculty, clinical nurses, researchers, and administrators in palliative care, including specialty content for those teaching pediatrics, oncology, critical care, geriatrics, and veterans' care. To date, over 20,000 nurses and other members of the interprofessional healthcare team have attended one of hundreds of national or international train-the-trainer courses held in every state across America and over 86 countries. The ELNEC curriculum also has been translated into eight languages to further its international reach.[35]

To target the education needs of the APRN, a two-day ELNEC APRN curriculum was developed. Recognizing both the clinical and the program development needs of APRNs, the curriculum includes the following clinical and program development modules: Overview, Pain Management, Symptom Management, Communication, Final Hours, Business & Finance, Quality Measurement, Education, and Leadership. The program offers breakout sessions for communication and palliative care program development important for both the generalist and the specialist palliative APRN. In addition, there are tracks for both adult and pediatric APRNs.[32] Participants are provided with diverse content that can be incorporated into various coursework within the specialist and graduate curriculum, so this course is attractive to nursing faculty as well.[35]

For graduate-prepared APNs who maintain a generalist practice outside of the clinical specialty realm, there is the ELNEC Core Curriculum. This content is divided into eight modules: Nursing Care at the End of Life; Pain Management; Symptom Management; Ethical/Legal Issues; Cultural Considerations in End-of-Life Care; Communication; Loss, Grief, Bereavement; and Preparation for and Care at the Time of Death. The ELNEC APRN content is expanded and includes advanced education in expert pain and symptom assessment/management and advanced communication techniques. Table 2.4 details the curricular topics of the ELNEC Core, ELNEC APRN, ELNEC Graduate, and ELNEC DNP courses.[36,37]

A plethora of other continuing education programs are available for APRNs interested in developing or expanding their palliative care skill set. There are various conferences, such as the annual assembly co-organized by American Academy of Hospice and Palliative Medicine and HPNA[38] and the annual Clinical Practice Forum organized by HPNA.[39] Nursing specialty organizations, such as the American Association of Critical Care Nurses and the Oncology Nursing Society, offer palliative care content at their annual conferences. Other clinical conferences include those organized by the Center to Advance Palliative Care, the National Hospice and Palliative Care Organization, and the American Society of Clinical Oncology. Several academic and clinical settings offer specialized immersion courses, such as the Harvard Medical School Center for Palliative Care and the Four Seasons Hospice. A unique program at the VCU Massey Cancer Center provides weeklong externships for experienced APRNs new to palliative care.[40] Extensive online education resources also exist and include Stanford University's eCampus Palliative Care curriculum[41] and the HPNA eLearning library.[42]

The Center to Advance Palliative Care[43] and the City of Hope Pain and Palliative Care Resource Center[44] are examples of extensive multifaceted repositories for practice and educational resources. Table 2.5 provides a sample of other available palliative care educational resources for APRNs interested in continuing educational opportunities.

Institutions throughout the country offer short-term, on-site clinical training programs.[45] Ranging from one day to several weeks, these programs offer a variety of experiences, including didactic classes, observership opportunities, bioethics training, individualized mentoring, and continuing education credits.

Future Directions in APRN Education

As palliative care continues to rapidly expand, graduate, postgraduate, and continuing education programs will also grow, affording APRN educators the opportunity for innovation and creativity. Several trends in APRN education are emerging.

Interprofessional education has become a mandate for the health sciences. Described as health professionals learning with and about each other in the educational and practice settings,

Table 2.4 ELNEC Curriculum Modules[31,33,36,37]

ELNEC Core	ELNEC APRN	ELNEC Graduate Faculty	Incorporating Palliative Care into DNP Curriculum
Introduction to Palliative Care	Overview of Palliative Care	Palliative Care in Advanced Practice Nursing	Overview: Palliative Care; Update on Cancer Care
Pain Management	Pain Management	Pain Management	Leading Teams in Pain and Symptom Management
Symptom Management	Symptom Management	Symptom Management	Interprofessional Teams
Communication	Communication	Communication	Enhancing Communication
Final Hours	Final Hours	Final Hours of Life	Changing Institutional Culture
Loss, Grief, and Bereavement	Business and Finance	Loss, Grief, and Bereavement	Principles of Business, Finance, and Economics to Improve Palliative Oncology Care
Ethical Considerations	Quality Management	Ethical Issues in Advanced Practice Nursing	Principles of Regulation, Outcomes Measurement, Guidelines, and Quality Improvement to Improve Palliative Oncology Care
Teaching Strategies	Education	Achieving Quality Care at the End-of-Life	Incorporating Palliative Care into Core and Clinical Coursework
Cultural Considerations in Palliative Care	Leadership		DNPs Leading Health Systems Change
Self-Care			

interprofessional education is interactive, cooperative, and experiential.[46] Four basic competencies, as developed by a collaborative expert panel, are Communication of Roles and Responsibilities, Demonstration of Values and Ethics in Collaborative Practice, Negotiation of Roles, and Interprofessional Teamwork.[47] Interprofessional courses in palliative care reflect some common themes: (1) interprofessional learners have stereotypes that can lead to tension and poor communication, and (2) interprofessional education can lead professionals to reevaluate the concepts of teamwork so they can work more creatively and constructively.[48,49] Given the holistic preparation and focus of advanced practice nursing, APRNs often play leading roles on interprofessional teams. APN educators must work to ensure that advanced practice nursing is well represented in interprofessional program planning, literature, and research.

Mentorship is an important aspect of palliative nursing education.[50] APRNs serve as mentors to nursing staff of all levels. APRNs frequently formally and informally mentor new practitioners in other fields, including medical students and residents, social workers, and other interdisciplinary team members. As palliative care programs continue to expand, experienced APNs must mentor both new graduates and experienced APNs moving into palliative care. A number of formal mentorship programs are available. HPNA is a co-sponsor of the annual Research Scholars Program, which mentors doctorally prepared nurses in their scientific endeavors.[51] In 2012, the HPNA launched its inaugural program of the Palliative Nursing Leadership Institute for the professional development of advanced nurses through a program of education and mentoring.[52]

Online and long-distance education have become the norm in many academic circles. Long-distance learning makes advanced education accessible to nurses in remote areas and provides a flexible platform for continuing education for nurses with varying responsibilities and work hours. However, this framework can create substantial challenges in teaching subjects that can be emotion-laden and necessitate interpersonal work. Advanced practice palliative nursing education requires significant direct role-playing for communication training. Use of online video streaming is one answer to this need for interactive work, and improving educational technology will undoubtedly influence the continuing development of online palliative care education.

Simulation, particularly in relation to teaching communication skills, has become increasing popular in palliative care education. Traditionally used as an evaluation tool in medical education, the Objective Structured Clinical Evaluation, in which an actor portrays a patient or family member, can be a powerful tool for teaching challenging communication skills.[53] Simulation is now a common component of many palliative care nursing educational programs.[54–56] Although these exercises are subjectively well received by students, who appreciate the opportunity for practice, the first randomized controlled trial of patient- and family-reported outcomes revealed disappointing results,[57] and further solid outcome research is needed to ascertain the efficacy of this teaching strategy.

A Call to Action for Palliative Care Nurse Educators

Since the mid-1990s, healthcare experts have called for improved palliative care for patients with serious illness, and major advances have been made in establishing palliative care as a recognized nursing and medical specialty. Yet much work remains

Table 2.5 Continuing Education Resources (Note: fees may apply)

Organization	Educational Opportunities	Website
HPNA	Conferences Books & products E-learning courses	www.gohpna.org
American Assoc. of Critical Care Nurses	Self-assessments E-learning Online resources & protocols	www.aacn.org
Hartford Institute for Geriatric Nursing	Webinars Podcasts CE courses	www.elearning.hartfordign.org/index.php?
Oncology Nursing Society	Conferences CE courses Online resources and guidelines Books & products	www.ons.org
American Society of Pain Management Nurses	Conferences Online education Books & products Webinars	www.aspmn.org
Center to Advance Palliative Care	Online resources Webinars Conferences	www.capc.org
Hospice Education Network	Interprofessional CE courses	www.hospiceonline.com/
California State Univ. Institute for Palliative Care	Online interprofessional courses Certification prep	www.csupalliativecare.org/programs/
National Center for Death Education	Online coursework Summer Institute	www.mountida.edu/academics/continuing-education/ncde/
American Academy of Hospice and Palliative Medicine	Conferences Webinars Online CE course Publications Online newsletter	www.aahpm.org
National Hospice and Palliative Care Organization	Webinars Conferences Online courses Pediatric resources Educational products	www.nhpco.org/education

to be done. There is evidence that palliative care in terminal illness not only improves quality of life but can prolong survival.[58] Healthcare reform has moved palliative care upstream and into the community. Progress has been made since the early descriptive studies about the deficits in care[13] and the initial Institute of Medicine report calling for sweeping changes in end-of-life care, *Approaching Death: Improving Care at the End of Life*.[14] Yet to many, progress has been slow, and much work is still to be done.

In September 2014, the Institute of Medicine released a new document, *Dying in America: Improving Quality and Honoring Individual Preferences Near the End of Life*, that revisits the state of palliative and end-of-life care.[59] The committee that compiled this new report writes, "Given the rapidly changing environment for

health care delivery, punctuated by the landmark passage of the Affordable Care Act in 2010, and the twin imperatives of improving the quality of health care while controlling costs, the time is ripe for a new examination of how individual values and preferences can be aligned while assuring compassionate care focused on the needs of individuals."[59]

This new Institute of Medicine report includes a chapter dedicated to education in palliative care.[59] While reporting that significant strides have been made in palliative care education since the initial report (mainly the establishment of the palliative care medical specialty), the committee concludes by identifying three remaining areas of need: insufficient attention to palliative care in medical and nursing school curricula, educational "silos" that impede the development of interprofessional teams, and deficits in equipping healthcare professionals with sufficient communication skills.

As previously described, work has been initiated in all these areas of APN education, and we can expect that these areas of education will garner further attention in light of the Institute's recommendations.

The recent changes in the structure of advanced nursing education (adaptation of the LACE model and rapid development of DNP programs) complicate educational efforts for specialized palliative care. There are currently not enough palliative care APRN programs to meet current workforce needs. However, these changes also present opportunities for innovative programs that can be integrated into generalist APRN as well as specialist educational efforts. Recent legislation introduced into Congress is evidence that policymakers are realizing the importance of palliative care education.[60, 61] The Palliative Care and Hospice Education Training Act of 2013 addresses the critical health workforce need by funding education centers to expand interdisciplinary training in palliative and hospice care. The act also funds advanced education nursing grants, academic career awards, and career incentive awards to support nurses and other healthcare providers who provide palliative and hospice care training.[63]

Conclusion

The discipline of palliative care is expanding, and its professional knowledge base is growing. The nursing profession has a mandate to educate its members, through formal academic programs and continuing professional education, in order to remain at the forefront of palliative care practice. The HPNA calls for nursing educators to take an active stance in promoting palliative care education for both specialist and generalist APRNs. Their position statement on the value of the APRN calls for nursing educators to become knowledgeable and expand the following:

◆ Continuing education to prepare and develop existing APRNs in palliative care competencies

◆ Integration of core palliative care competencies into programs for all APRN students, regardless of role or degree

◆ Provision of academic programs for specialized palliative care

◆ Provision of clinical mentoring in palliative care[62]

The current healthcare environment provides an exciting time to enter palliative care nursing, and many opportunities exist for nurses to take a leadership role in developing and leading palliative care programs in all settings. By providing advanced education for specialized clinical experts and expanding the primary palliative care knowledge base for generalist APRNs, palliative care educators can ensure that nursing remains at the forefront of this essential and rewarding work.

References

1. American Association of Colleges of Nursing. *AACN Position Statement on the Practice Doctorate in Nursing. 2004.* Available at http://www.aacn.nche.edu/publications/position/DNPpositionstatement.pdf. Accessed August 16, 2014.

2. Cockerham AZ, Keeling AW. A brief history of advanced practice nursing in the United States. In: Hamric AB, Hanson CM, Tracy MF, O'Grady E, eds. *Advanced Practice Nursing: An Integrative Approach.* 5th ed. St. Louis, MO: Elsevier Saunders; 2014.

3. American Association of Colleges of Nursing. *Peaceful Death: Recommended Competencies and Curricular Guidelines for End-of-Life Nursing Care.* 1997; www.aacn.nche.edu/Publications/deathfin.htm.

4. International Council of Nurses. *Basic Principles of Nursing Care.* Washington, DC: American Nurses Publishing; 1997.

5. National Consensus Project for Quality Palliative Care. *Clinical Practice Guidelines for Quality Palliative Care 2013.* Available at http://www.nationalconsensusproject.org/NCP_Clinical_Practice_Guidelines_3rd_Edition.pdf. Accessed August 16, 2014.

6. Horton J, Indelicato R. The advanced practice nurse. In: Ferrell B, Coyle N, eds. *Oxford Textbook of Palliative Nursing.* 3rd ed. New York, NY: Oxford University Press; 2010: 1121–9.

7. National Quality Forum. *A National Framework and Preferred Practices for Palliative and Hospice Care Quality.* Washington, DC: NQF; 2013.

8. Institute of Medicine of the National Academies. *The Future of Nursing: Leading Change, Advancing Health.* Available at http://www.iom.edu/Reports/2010/The-future-of-nursing-leading-change-advancing-health.aspx. Accessed September 10, 2014.

9. American Association of Colleges in Nursing. *Primary vs. Specialist Palliative Care.* Available at http://www.aacn.nche.edu/elnec/elnec-curricula/Primaryvs_Specialty-Palliative -Care.pptx. Accessed August 17, 2014.

10. American Nurses Association and Hospice and Palliative Nurses Association. *Palliative Nursing: Scope and Standards of Practice—An Essential Resource for Hospice and Palliative Nurses.* 5th ed. Silver Spring, MD: American Nurses Association and Hospice and Palliative Nurses Association; 2014.

11. APRN Consensus Workgroup, National Council of State Boards of Nursing APRN Advisory Committee. *Consensus Model for APRN Regulation: Licensing, Accreditation, Certification & Education (LACE).* 2008. Available at https://m.ncsbn.org/2276.htm. Accessed August 1, 2014.

12. Hospice and Palliative Nurses Association. *Competencies for the Hospice and Palliative APN.* Pittsburgh, PA: Hospice and Palliative Nurses Association; 2014.

13. SUPPORT Principal Investigators. A controlled trial to improve care for seriously ill hospitalized patients: the study to understand prognoses and preferences for outcomes and risks of treatment (SUPPORT). *JAMA.* 1995; 274: 1591–8.

14. Field MJ, Cassel CK. *Approaching Death: Improving Care at the End-of-Life.* Washington, DC: Institute of Medicine & National Academies Press; 1997.

15. Foley KM, Gelband H. *Improving Palliative Care for Cancer.* Washington, DC: Institute of Medicine & National Academies Press; 2001.

16. Ferrell BR, Virani R, Grant M. Analysis of end-of-life content in nursing textbooks. *Oncol Nurs Forum.* 1999; 26: 869–76.

17. White KR, Coyne PJ, White, SG. Are hospice and palliative nurses adequately prepared for end-of-life care? *J Hosp Pall Nurs.* 2012; 14: 133–40.

18. Paice JA, Ferrell BR, Virani R, Grant M, Malloy P, Rhome A. Graduate nursing education regarding end-of-life care. *Nurs Outlook.* 2006; 54: 46–52.

19. Shea J, Grossman S, Wallace M, Lange J. Assessment of advanced practice palliative care nursing competencies in nurse practitioner students: Implications for the integration of ELNEC curricular modules. *J Nurs Educ.* 2010; 49: 183–8.

20. Stanley J. Reaching consensus on a regulatory model: What does this mean for APRN's? *Journal for Nurse Practitioners.* 2009; 5: 99–104.

21. Sheehan DK, Malloy P. Nursing education. In: Ferrell BR, Coyle N, eds. *Oxford Textbook of Palliative Nursing.* 3rd ed. New York, NY: Oxford University Press; 2010:1193–209.

22. Hospice and Palliative Nurses Association. *Standards for Clinical Education of Hospice and Palliative Nurses.* 2006. Available at http://hpna.advancingexpertcare.org/wp-content/uploads/2015/08/HPNA-Clinical-Education-Standards.pdf. Accessed June 1, 2015.

23. Hospice and Palliative Nurses Association. *Graduate Program Listing.* Pittsburgh, PA: HPNA, 2013. Available at http://www.hpna.

org/DisplayPage.aspx?Title=Graduate%20Program%20Listing. Accessed August 1, 2014.

24. Pace JC, Lunsford B. The evolution of palliative care nursing education. *J Hosp Palliat Nurs*. 2011; 13: S8–S19.

25. Hospice and Palliative Nursing. *HPNA Research Agenda: 2-12-2015*. Available at http://www.hpna.org/DisplayPage.aspx?Title=Research. Accessed September 10, 2014.

26. American Academy of Hospice and Palliative Medicine. *AAHPM & HPNA: Measuring What Matters*. Available at http://aahpm.org/quality/measuring-what-matters. Accessed September 10, 2014.

27. Dahlin CM, Lynch MT. *Core Curriculum for the Advanced Practice Hospice and Palliative Registered Nurse*. 2nd ed. 2013. Pittsburgh, PA: Hospice and Palliative Nurses Association.

28. National Institute of Nursing Research. *End-of-Life and Palliative Care: The Science of Compassion*. Available at http://www.ninr.nih.gov/aboutninr/keythemes/themes-eolpc#.U_EUOIBdXok. Accessed August 10, 2014.

29. George Washington University School of Nursing. *Palliative Care Program Description*. 2014. Available at http://nursing.gwu.edu/sites/nursing.gwu.edu/files/downloads/DNP_PCNP.pdf. Accessed August 17, 2014.

30. University of Southern Alabama. *Doctor of Nursing Practice Program*. Available at http://www.southalabama.edu/nursing/dnp.html. Accessed August 17, 2014.

31. Malloy P, Paice J, Virani R, Ferrell BR, Bednash G. End-of-life nursing education consortium: 5 years of educating graduate nursing faculty in excellent palliative care. *J Profess Nurs*. 2008; 24: 352–7.

32. Paice J, Ferrell BR, Virani R, Grant M, Malloy P, Rhome A. Appraisal of the graduate end-of-life nursing education consortium training program. *J Palliat Med*. 2006; 9: 353–60.

33. City of Hope/American Association of Colleges of Nursing. *Integrating Palliative Oncology Care Into Doctor of Nursing Practice (DNP) Education and Clinical Practice* 2012. Available at http://www.aacn.nche.edu/elnec/DNP-Overview.pdf. Accessed August 2, 2014.

34. Hospice and Palliative Care Nurses Association. *Nursing Fellowships*. Available at http://www.hpna.org/DisplayPage.aspx?Title=Nursing%20Fellowships. Accessed August 12, 2014.

35. American Association of Colleges of Nursing. *ELNEC. End-of-Life Nursing Education Consortium: Fact Sheet*. 2014. http://www.aacn.nche.edu/elnec/about/fact-sheet. Accessed August 1, 2014.

36. American Association of Colleges of Nursing. *ELNEC Core*. Available at http://www.aacn.nche.edu/elnec/about/elnec-core. Accessed August 4, 2014.

37. American Association of Colleges of Nursing. *ELNEC APRN*. Available at http://www.aacn.nche.edu/elnec/elnec-curricula/aprn. Accessed August 4, 2014.

38. Hospice and Palliative Nurses Association. *Annual Assembly Program Description*. Available at https://www.hpna.org/DisplayPage.aspx?Title=Annual%20Assembly. Accessed August 1, 2014.

39. Hospice and Palliative Nurses Association. *Clinical Practice Forum*. Available at http://www.hpna.org/DisplayPage.aspx?Title=Clinical%20Practice%20Forum Accessed September 18, 2014.

40. Virginia Commonwealth University Massey Cancer Center. *Advanced Palliative Care Nursing Externship*. Available at http://www.massey.vcu.edu/patient-care/methods/palliative-care/training/advanced-nursing-externship/ Accessed September 18, 2014.

41. Stanford University School of Medicine. *Palliative Care*. Available at http://palliative.stanford.edu/. Accessed August 1, 2014.

42. Hospice and Palliative Nurses Association. *E-learning program description*. Available at https://www.hpna.org/DisplayPage.aspx?Title1=E-Learning. Accessed August 1, 2014.

43. Center to Advance Palliative Care. *Training and Education*. Available at http://www.capc.org/palliative-care-professional-development/Training/. Accessed August 10, 2014.

44. City of Hope. *Pain and Palliative Care Resource Center*. Available at http://prc.coh.org/. Accessed August 10, 2014.

45. Center to Advance Palliative Care. *Clinical Site Visit Directory*. Available at http://www.capc.org/palliative-care-professional-development/clinical-site-visit-directory Accessed August 10, 2014.

46. Barr H, Low H. *Introducing Interprofessional Education*. 2013. Fareham, England: Centre for the Advancement of Interprofessional Education.

47. Interprofessional Education Collaborative Expert Panel. *Core Competencies for Interprofessional Collaborative Practice: Report of an Expert Panel*. 2011. Washington, DC: Interprofessional Education Collaborative.

48. Mazanec P, Daly BJ, Bokar J, Wellman C. Integrating palliative care core into an interprofessional symptom management class for MSN students, oncology fellows, and palliative care fellows. *J Palliat Med*. 2014; 47: 443–4.

49. Koffman J, Higginson IJ. Assessing the effectiveness and acceptability of interprofessional palliative care education. *J Palliat Care*. 2005; 21: 262–9.

50. Ferrell B. Nurse mentors may improve palliative care. *Medscape* 2008. Available at http://www.medscape.com/viewarticle/572769. Accessed September 18, 2014.

51. HPNA. *Research Scholars Program* 2014. Available at http://www.hpna.org/DisplayPage.aspx?Title=Research%20Scholars%20Program Accessed September 18, 2014.

52. HPNA. *Palliative Nursing Leadership Institute* Available at http://www.hpna.org/DisplayPage.aspx?Title=Palliative%20Nursing%20Leadership%20Institute. Accessed September 18, 2014.

53. Hall P, Marshall D, Weaver L, Boyle A, Taniguchi A. A method to enhance student teams in palliative care: Piloting the McMaster-Ottawa team observed structured clinical encounter. *J Palliat Med*. 2011; 6: 744–50.

54. Rosenzweig M, Clifton M, Arnold R. Development of communication skills workshop for oncology advanced practice nursing students. *J Canc Educ*. 2007; 22: 149–53.

55. Curtis JR, Back AL, Ford DW, et al. Effect of communication skills training for residents and nurse practitioners on quality of communication with patients with serious illness: A randomized trial. *JAMA*. 2013; 310: 2271–81.

56. Bays AM, Engelberg RA, Back AL, et al. Interprofessional communication skills training for serious illness: Evaluation of a small-group, simulated patient intervention. *J Palliat Med*. 2014; 17: 159–66.

57. Temel JS, Grear JA, Muzikansky MA, et al. Early palliative care for patients with metastatic non-small cell lung cancer. *N Engl J Med*. 2010; 363: 733–42.

58. Institute of Medicine. *Committee on Approaching Death: Addressing Key End of Life Issues* 2014. Available at http://www.iom.edu/Activities/Aging/TransformingEndOfLife.aspx. Accessed August 17, 2014.

59. Committee on Approaching Death: Addressing Key End-of-Life Issues; Institute of Medicine. *Dying in America: Improving Quality and Honoring Individual Preferences Near the End-of-Life*, 2014. Available at http://www.nap.edu/download.php?record_id=18748# Accessed September 17, 2014.

60. American Cancer Society Cancer Action Network. *Legislative Initiatives 2013* Available at http://acscan.org/content/wp-content/uploads/2013/11/2013-ACSCAN-Quality-of-Life-Legislation.pdf. Accessed August 17, 2014.

61. HPNA. *Public Policy Recent Activity 2014*. Available at http://www.hpna.org/DisplayPage.aspx?Title=Recent%20Activity. Accessed August 17, 2014.

62. HPNA. *Position Statement: Value of the APRN in Palliative Care*. 2013. Available at https://www.hpna.org/pdf/PositionStatement_ValueOfAPNs.pdf. Accessed August 17, 2014.

63. S.641: Palliative Care and Hospice Education and Training Act 113th Congress (2013–2014). https://www.congress.gov/bill/113th-congress/senate-bill/641. Accessed December 5, 2015.

CHAPTER 3

Credentialing, Certification, and Scope of Practice Issues for the Palliative Advanced Practice Registered Nurse

Kerstin Lea Lappen

Key Points

- The *Consensus Model for APRN Regulation, Licensure, Accreditation, Certification, and Education* will have a significant impact on the practice of the advanced practice nurse, on the curriculum of advanced practice nursing educational programs, and on the U.S. healthcare system.

- Advanced practice registered nurses (APRNs) must understand credentialing requirements to practice safely, legally, and to the fullest extent of their scope.

- Specialty certification is a valuable endeavor to demonstrate the clinician's expertise and commitment to quality care and to the profession.

Case Study

Denise earned her graduate degree in nursing in 2002 with a specialty focus as a medical-surgical CNS. However, her credential title changed in 2008 to clinical nurse specialist in adult health. Denise's work experience had always been in hospice and pain management. In addition to achieving her CNS certification for entry to practice, she became board-certified as an advanced practice certified hospice and palliative nurse. She was hired to work as a consultant for a palliative care service in a large urban hospital. Denise was fortunate to live in a state that recognizes the CNS as an APRN who is able to bill for services and have prescriptive privileges. The state legislature recently voted to allow APRNs to practice independently, without a collaborative practice or prescriptive agreement with a physician. However, Denise was considering moving to another state to be closer to her children and grandchildren. She was worried about the negative impact and concerned about how her practice may change. She heard different stories from colleagues online about their trials and tribulations as they try to practice to the full extent of their scope in other states. She read some articles about the changing requirements for recertification and about something called the Consensus Model,

but she just felt confused by it all. "I'll worry about all that when I have to recertify in a year," she decided.

Introduction

In July 2001, Promoting Excellence in End-of-Life Care, a national program office of the Robert Wood Johnson Foundation, convened a group of advanced practice nurses (APNs) to discuss the state of palliative care advanced practice nursing in the United States. In this day-and-a-half-long meeting, pioneers in the field met to identify gaps in and barriers to practice and to develop strategies for the future. Participants represented the diversity of academic and practice settings: a graduate-level specialty palliative care nurse practitioner program, an urban trauma center, an acute care teaching hospital, an urban research cancer center, a geriatric practice, rural primary care and private practice, and long-term care facilities. *Advanced Practice Nurses Role in Palliative Care—A Position Statement from American Nurse Leaders*[1] was published in 2002 to spark conversation among nursing leaders about how to improve the state of palliative advanced practice nursing, to illustrate successful models of advanced practice palliative care nursing, and to promote the advanced practice nurse's role in providing palliative care. The final position statement called on leaders in the clinical professions, nursing educators, health service providers, healthcare payers, and public policy advocates to take the following actions:

- Continue to discuss the APN role, and opportunities and strategies to advance it in palliative care.

- Educate nursing educators about palliative care in order to develop curriculum and competencies for both APN students and existing APNs working in palliative care. Core palliative care competencies must be integrated into the education of all APN students, and clinical tracks must be developed for APN students who intend to specialize in palliative care.

◆ Work with payers of health services to recognize the specialty of palliative care and provide APNs with adequate and consistent compensation that is commensurate with the APN scope of practice, authority, and responsibility, regardless of practice setting or specialty.

◆ Call on the National Council of State Boards of Nursing (NCSBN) and individual state boards of nursing to work collaboratively to consistently recognize APN scopes of practice and privileges regardless of specialty and subspecialty.

◆ Ask health systems and health service providers to develop or expand practice opportunities for APNs in all settings that care for patients who may experience life-limiting illnesses.

◆ Hold APNs practicing in the specialty of palliative care accountable for the documentation and dissemination of outcomes of practice experience and roles, and for engaging in interdisciplinary research with an emphasis on translating findings into practice.

◆ Clarify the challenges that APNs face in training and licensure, along with regulatory and reimbursement barriers.

It was felt that with the development of registered nurse and advanced practice certification examinations and the creation of undergraduate and graduate advanced practice programs in palliative care, palliative care nursing would be on the road to being recognized as a specialty in all states.[1]

Advanced practice nursing and the specialty of hospice and palliative care have experienced significant changes in the years since that group met in 2002. The APRN is at an exciting crossroads in the American healthcare environment and the momentum has increased with three recent major developments.

First, in 2008, a collaborative effort between the NCSBN and the Advanced Practice Nursing Consensus Work Group developed uniform APRN regulations that culminated in the publication of the *Consensus Model for APRN Regulation: Licensure, Accreditation, Certification & Education* (the Consensus Model for short).[2] NCSBN launched the Campaign for Consensus, an ongoing initiative to promote adoption of the recommendations in the Consensus Model in all state jurisdictions, with the goal of full implementation by 2015 (as of 2014, only 10 states had fully adopted and implemented the NCSBN recommendations).

Second, in 2010, after a 2-year joint effort to assess the state of the nursing profession, the historical, cultural, regulatory, and policy barriers, and the future needs of the country, the Robert Wood Johnson Foundation and the Institute of Medicine (IOM) published the influential report *The Future of Nursing: Leading Change, Advancing Health*.[3] In addition to addressing challenges in the nursing education system, the blueprint outlines recommendations to remove legal barriers that affect APRN practice. To achieve this recommendation, the IOM specified directives for Congress, state legislatures, the Centers for Medicare and Medicaid Services (CMS), the Office of Personnel Management for Federal Employees, and the Federal Trade Commission and the Antitrust Division of the Department of Justice. It is a clear indication that those who influence public policy and cultural change, such as the IOM, now recognize the critical role APRNs will play in the healthcare landscape of the future. The document specifically instructs Congress to expand the Medicare program to include coverage of APRN services that are within the scope of practice under applicable state

law, just as physician services are now covered.[3] Other striking recommendations in the report include that Congress should limit federal funding for nursing education programs to only those programs in states that have adopted the Consensus Model, and that CMS require that hospitals that participate in the Medicare program remove barriers that limit clinical privileges and membership on medical staffs for APRNs.

Finally, coming on the heels of the Consensus Model and the IOM report, the implementation of the 2010 Affordable Care Act is bringing about an overhaul in healthcare that has not been seen since the creation of the Medicare and Medicaid programs in 1965. To meet the increased demand due to increased access to healthcare coverage, it is expected that APRNs will fill the gap of healthcare providers. APRNs who specialize in the field of hospice and palliative care will need to be used to the full extent of their scope to support the needs of a cultural shift and a changing U.S. demographic.

Understanding the Consensus Model: What Does it Mean and Why Care?

Currently, the profession of advanced practice nursing is a convoluted and complicated web of educational degrees, certifications, and regulations. Moreover, oversight occurs within multiple layers of hierarchies, including the CMS, state statutes and state boards of nursing, and individual institutional privileging and credentialing requirements. For the more than 200,000[2] APRNs who work in the United States and its territories, this lack of uniformity and cohesion creates confusion for employers and consumers, and barriers and inconsistencies in how and where APRNs may practice.

The Consensus Model has been endorsed by more than 40 nursing organizations and associations. It is the model for the future and was created to guide all states and jurisdictions in implementing and overseeing the uniform licensure, accreditation, certification, education, and practice of APRNs.[4] The Consensus Model is composed of seven major elements (Table 3.1). APRNs should understand their own state regulations regarding title, recognition, education, credentialing, licensing, and independence to practice. If the APRN were to change jobs or location of employment, would his or her scope of practice be more or less restricted? Indeed, could he or she practice at all? The following elements are addressed in the Consensus Model; the APRN should review these within his or her setting:

◆ **Title**: The purpose of a title is to differentiate professions, provide clarity to the consumer, and ensure consistent recognition regardless of location of practice.[4] The Consensus Model

Table 3.1 Seven Elements of the Consensus Model

I. Title
II. APRN Roles and Recognition
III. Licensure
IV. Graduate or Postgraduate Education
V. Certification
VI. Independent Practice
VII. Full Prescriptive Authority

has designated "advanced practice registered nurse" as the agreed-upon title. One would think something as basic as a title would be straightforward, but unfortunately this is not the case: there is wide variability across the country, with only about 60% of jurisdictions using the legal recognition of APRN. Other titles used include advanced practice nurse (APN), nurse specialist, and advanced registered nurse practitioner.

- **APRN Roles and Recognition:** There are four defined APRN roles with specific designated titles:

  - Certified nurse practitioner (CNP)

  - Clinical nurse specialist (CNS)

  - Certified registered nurse anesthetist (CRNA)

  - Certified nurse midwife (CNM)

  - CNPs and CNSs are the two that are most common in the field of hospice and palliative care.

- **Role Recognition Adoptions:** States vary in recognizing all four APRN roles, which certainly affects the ability of an APRN to move easily across state lines and continue to practice. Several states do not recognize the CNS role and have placed CNSs in a "nurse practitioner" designation.

- **Licensure:** State boards of nursing vary regarding required certifications, registrations, and licenses for permission to practice. Many states allow the APRN to practice with only an RN license and additional APRN certifications. The Consensus Model requires a separate APRN license in addition to the RN license. This additional licensure will ensure consistency in recognizing the APRN role from state to state and will give APRNs the flexibility to relocate for jobs and maintain their essential scope of practice.

- **Graduate or Postgraduate Education:** The Consensus Model requires that the APRN be educated by a nationally accredited program of nursing, with a minimum of a master's degree. The educational program must include the three core courses of advanced physiology/pathophysiology, health assessment, and pharmacology, with clinical and didactic experiences.[4] The educational path changed with the adoption of the Consensus Model in that all APRN students must be educated in one of six specific populations: family, adult/gerontology, neonatal, pediatrics, women's health, or psychiatric/mental health.[4] The selection of population focus will dictate what practice the APRN will be restricted to. For example, a CNP whose education was in women's health would not be able to practice in adult/gerontology without additional education and certification.

- **Certification:** The Consensus Model requires that all APRNs obtain certification to practice by passing a psychometrically sound and nationally accredited examination at the advanced practice nursing level that measures competency in the specific population of practice.[4] The organization providing the certification program must be nationally accredited by the American Board of Nursing Specialties or the National Commission for Certifying Agencies.[2] The APRN must also demonstrate ongoing competence to maintain certification. Specialty certification, such as advanced palliative and hospice care, is encouraged and recommended but is not a requirement of the Consensus Model.

- **Independent Practice:** The Consensus Model lobbies for the APRN to practice to the full stated scope without physician supervision. In many states, there has been legislation to promote this practice; however, it has been met with fierce resistance from the medical establishment. APRNs should be very familiar with the CMS requirement to work in collaboration with a physician with medical direction and appropriate supervision (though this supervision does not need to be direct) as required by the law of the state in which the services are furnished.[5] As part of the credentialing and privileging process, many state legislatures and/or individual institutions require the APRN to have a collaborative practice and/or prescribing agreement with a supervising physician. The Consensus Model makes the point that a hallmark of APRN practice is that of voluntary collaboration that emphasizes the interdependence and interreliance of healthcare professionals.[4] In the adoption of this element of practice without physician oversight, some states have specified a period of physician or APRN supervision of newly graduated APRNs to ensure a smooth transition with close mentoring and guidance.

- **Full Prescriptive Authority:** The ability for the APRN to prescribe pharmacologic and nonpharmacologic therapies without physician oversight and/or a written collaborative agreement is the element of the Consensus Model that has been met with the most opposition, primarily from organized medical groups. This is despite evidence that APRN outcome measures are equivalent to those of other medical providers.[4] Full prescriptive authority is key to being able to provide care to populations with limited access to healthcare.

The goal of the NCSBN is for all of the major elements of the Consensus Model to be adopted and fully implemented by 2015. To this end, the organization began the APRN Campaign for Consensus in 2009, making the necessary background information, resources, and model legislative language available online. Although approximately a fifth of the states have passed legislation in support of the Consensus Model, much work remains to be done. NCSBN is tracking each state's progress toward adoption of the seven elements. APRNs can access the most accurate and up-to-date status of adoption of the Consensus Model by checking the website: https//www.ncsbn.org/2567.htm.

Scope of Practice

"The advanced practice hospice and palliative registered nurse responds to the individual, professional, and societal needs related to the experience of serious or life-threatening illness through the nursing process."[6(p 21)] Through graduate-level education at the master's or doctorate level, APRNs differ from the generalists by being able to synthesize complex data, develop and implement advanced care plans, and provide leadership in hospice and palliative nursing. Besides the clinical focus of the CNS and CNP, advanced practice nurses in hospice and palliative care may also function as leaders/administrators, educators, researchers, consultants, case managers, program developers, and policymakers.

The Political Landscape of Advanced Practice Registered Nursing

APRNs have struggled with practice barriers imposed by restrictive legislation, often supported by the political influence of medical associations. These restrictions lack any evidence or data showing inadequacies or concerns about the safety and outcomes of practice by APRNs; in fact, there is much evidence to the contrary. Newhouse and colleagues completed a systematic review of published literature between 1990 and 2008 on the care provided by APRNs compared to physicians.[7] They concluded that patient outcomes of care provided by APRNs are similar in terms of safety, effectiveness, and quality—in some aspects, they are better than care provided by physicians alone. Patients' level of satisfaction with the care provided was also equivalent to that for physician care.[7] APRNs are also recognized for their inherent focus on collaborative practice.[8]

It is extremely significant that the Federal Trade Commission (FTC), which exists to monitor and prevent any unfair or deceptive acts or practices that would impair competition in the marketplace, including the healthcare industry, published a policy paper in March 2014 called *Policy Perspectives: Competition and the Regulation of Advanced Practice Nurses.*[8] The paper supports the ability of APRNs to practice to the full extent of their scope without unnecessary, unjustified, and restrictive supervisory requirements and collaborative practice agreements with physicians. The paper states, "APRN scope of practice limitations should be narrowly tailored to address well-founded health and safety concerns, and should not be more restrictive than patient protection requires."[8(p 4)]

The FTC recognizes that the scope of practice of any healthcare provider should be consistent with each professional's education and training, licensure and certification, and experience and capabilities. Current legislative or institutional requirements for physician supervision of the APRN to practice independently are identified by the FTC as a concern because they give one group of healthcare professionals control over another, resulting in restricted access to the market and potentially denying healthcare consumers the benefits of greater competition.[8]

In the policy paper, the FTC identified several concerns about the present state of APRN scope of practice where unwieldy and unwarranted restrictions, under the guise of "consumer protection," are actually contributing to less competition and, thus, less protection, including:

◆ Less access to safe and effective care, especially in underserved areas and populations that are experiencing, in particular, primary care provider shortages

◆ Impaired development of innovative models of healthcare delivery to meet the needs of the healthcare consumers

◆ Increased costs and less oversight of cost containment

◆ Less focus on the importance of measuring quality outcomes, with subsequent serious health and safety consequences

This report, along with the APRN Campaign for Consensus and the IOM recommendations discussed previously, have positioned APRN practice in its strongest standing to date. It remains to be seen how legislators, policymakers, and administrators will heed and implement these recommendations. APRNs can influence and support further changes and improvements in being able to practice to the fullest extent of their scope by getting involved with their professional organizations, as well as staying informed about and engaged in practice issues critical to APRN professional health.

The Professional Landscape of Advanced Practice Registered Nursing

The scope and standards of APRN practice are defined by the national professional nursing organizations specific to the population focus for which they were educated. The advanced practice registered nurse's clinical scope includes the tasks of performing advanced assessments; interpreting diagnostic studies; forming a differential diagnosis; prescribing pharmacologic and nonpharmacologic treatments and equipment; ordering additional diagnostic tests, consultants, and support services; and evaluating the response to treatment.[9]

APRNs are accountable to patients for the quality of the care they provide. They must be able to recognize the limits of their education, knowledge, and experience. They should know when to refer patients to other providers and practitioners for appropriate management when they are confronted by a situation that is outside their area of expertise. With this increased responsibility, no matter how long a nurse may have practiced as a registered nurse, when he or she becomes an APRN, there is usually a period of transition and uncertainty. Many questions may arise about what is now within the scope of practice for the APRN, such as:

◆ Does the advanced practice registered nurse role allow the APRN to prescribe, and if so, are there any restrictions on what classes of medications may be prescribed?

◆ If the APRN was trained in the population of family practice, given that his or her education and training was not in the population focus of adult/gerontology, can he or she provide care to an older adult entering the end stage of a chronic illness?

◆ Is the APRN's knowledge base adequate to diagnose and treat conditions for which he or she is seeing a patient?

◆ What are the limitations on the services that a CNS or CNP employed by a hospice program can provide, in light of CMS rules that dictate which medical providers may complete face-to-face assessments and recertification of terminal illness?

These and other questions may cause the hospice and palliative APRN some level of anxiety because the responsibilities and liabilities change with the increased scope of practice. The American Nurses Association (ANA) is the primary source for general guidelines about the scope and standards of advanced practice registered nursing.[9] Practice must, above all, be safe, quality-focused, and evidence-based. In a dilemma of what is considered appropriate practice within the accepted scope, the ANA advises the APRN to first consider the published scope and standards of practice. The ANA published a second edition of *Nursing: Scope and Standards of Practice* in 2010, and it includes specific information about the scope of the advanced practice registered nurse.[10]

Second, the APRN should determine the current state laws and regulations that dictate his or her practice limitations. In addition to the NCSBN website, each state's board of nursing is the source of up-to-date and pertinent legislation that governs the practice of APRNs in the jurisdiction where they work.

Third, APRNs should review the institutional policies and procedures that apply to their practice. Although CMS and state regulations provide the "outer limits" of APRN scope of practice, APRNs may find their practice further limited by the interpretation and application of those regulations in individual institutions/facilities or health systems. For instance, CMS may allow a CNS to prescribe, but the hospital where a CNS is employed may have very stringent collaborative agreement requirements or restrictions that limit the CNS's ability to prescribe medications. Although the professional credentialing process at a facility or institution may choose to be more restrictive, a motivated and informed cohort of APRNs can change practice at the ground level so that local rules and regulations mirror the rules and regulations of the larger governing body.

Finally, the APRN should do an objective review of his or her skills and expertise in a process of self-determination, taking into account the skills and expertise of other members of the healthcare team and available consultants. The prudent APRN should also consider risk management and potential liability issues in particular situations and consider consulting with the institution's risk management/legal department or the malpractice insurer for support and clarification regarding a scope of practice question. There are many good resources available that offer guidance to the APRN wanting to gain a deeper understanding of legal issues, including *Law and Ethics in Advanced Practice Nursing*.[11]

The APRN who practices in hospice and palliative care will find further information and guidance in the following resources specific to the specialty of palliative nursing:

◆ ANA and the Hospice and Palliative Nurses Association, *Palliative Nursing: Scope and Standards of Practice—An Essential Resource for Hospice and Palliative Nurses* (2014). A necessary resource for both APRNs and RNs, this revised second edition discusses in detail what is expected of all hospice and palliative registered nurse and advanced practice nurses. Practice accountabilities are divided into 16 standards with accompanying competencies, with additional competencies specified for APRNs. These standards provide the framework for guiding and evaluating the nurse's practice, along with behaviors and outcomes that would demonstrate whether he or she is meeting the minimal level of compliance with the standard.[6]

◆ Hospice and Palliative Nurses Association, *Competencies for the Hospice and Palliative Advanced Practice Nurse* (2014). Recently updated, this resource describes the explicit intellectual, interpersonal, technical, and moral competencies that are outcome-specific, measurable, and considered necessary for quality palliative nursing.[12] This second edition includes the following core characteristics applicable to the advanced practice nurse, which are further delineated by advanced core behaviors:

- Clinical judgment
- Advocacy and ethics
- Professionalism
- Collaboration
- Systems thinking

- Cultural and spiritual competence
- Facilitator of learning
- Communication
- Evidence-based practice and research

◆ Hospice and Palliative Nurses Association, *The Core Curriculum for the Advanced Practice Hospice and Palliative Registered Nurse* (2013). The second edition was published in 2013 to reflect the current evidence-based knowledge in advanced hospice and palliative nursing practice. The Core Curriculum provides a foundational work for the APRN and includes sections on role and practice concerns, management of common symptoms, psychosocial and spiritual aspects of care, and specific pathophysiology and disease-specific management. There is also information on vulnerable and special populations and an appendix with many references and tools for practice.[13]

◆ The National Consensus Project for Quality Palliative Care (NCP), *Clinical Practice Guidelines*, 3rd ed. (2013). This collaborative effort of six organizations, including the Hospice and Palliative Nurse Association, published a set of guidelines and recommendations for high-quality palliative care in eight domains of practice (Table 3.2). According to the National Consensus Project executive summary, "The purpose of the National Consensus Project for Quality Palliative Care is to promote the implementation of Clinical Practice Guidelines that ensure care of consistent and high quality, and that guide the development and structure of new and existing palliative care services."[14] Currently in its third edition, this updated edition builds on the work and developments that have occurred in hospice and palliative care since earlier guidelines were published in 2004 and 2009.

◆ American Association of Colleges of Nursing and City of Hope, *End-of-Life Nursing Education Consortium (ELNEC)*. This educational initiative was founded in 2000 by Dr. Betty Ferrell and colleagues to develop educational tools for undergraduate nursing faculty to ensure that topics in palliative care were taught as part of the nursing curriculum. Various versions of the curriculum have been developed for nurses in general practice and for special populations, such as veterans, pediatrics, geriatrics, and critical care units. ELNEC offers a course that addresses the unique needs of APRNs who are developing, leading, joining, or participating in a hospice and/or palliative care program or are incorporating palliative care into their current APRN role.[15]

Table 3.2 NCP 8 Domains of Care

I. Structure and Processes of Care
II. Physical Aspects of Care
III. Psychological and Psychiatric Aspects of Care
IV. Social Aspects of Care
V. Spiritual, Religious, and Existential Aspects of Care
VI. Cultural Aspects of Care
VII. Care of the Patient at End of Life
VIII. Ethical and Legal Aspects of Care

Credentialing

The terms "credentialing," "accreditation," "licensure," and "certification" are often misunderstood and thus are frequently used interchangeably and incorrectly. In a general sense, "credentialing" is an umbrella term that refers to several different processes overseen by a number of regulatory bodies (Table 3.3), such as licensure, certification, accreditation, recognition, and registration.[16]

Licensure involves a mandatory process by which a government agency grants time-limited legal status and permission for a person to engage in the practice of a profession in the public domain. Licensure signifies the provider has met minimal standards of competence, typically by passing a psychometrically sound examination. A license grants permission to use a particular title and provides protection of that title. It also defines a scope of practice for the profession. Licensure ultimately serves to protect the consumer and the public health, safety, and welfare.[17] To this end, the individual state boards of nursing must have processes in place for anyone to file a complaint against a nurse who they believe has acted in violation of nursing rules and the defined scope of practice. For instance, a consumer who has suffered harm from incompetent prescribing practices of an APRN could file a complaint with the board of nursing. The complaint would be investigated to determine if the APRN acted in an illegal or incompetent manner. If found to be at fault, discipline for the APRN would likely include restrictions, or even suspension of the professional license and thus the ability to practice.

A credential differs from licensure in that it is a designation issued by a nongovernmental agency or association that the public can look to for assurance that an individual provider has achieved specific standards of competence that have been defined and promoted by the profession. APRNs may be familiar with the credentials granted by the American Nurses Credentialing Center or the American Academy of Nurse Practitioners after passing an accredited certification exam. There are different kinds of credentialing applicable to the APRN, and these are important to understand and differentiate.

"Entry to practice" credentialing is the "end product" of an educational program, achieved after graduation and the successful completion of a psychometrically sound examination from an accredited certification organization in the area of practice the provider was educated in. Successful completion of the exam provides the APRN with the required certification to obtain licensure to practice according to state statute and grants the legal right to use a specific title.

"Professional" credentialing is the process by which safe, high-quality, and competent care by APRNs (and other providers) is determined and verified by the facility or institution in which the APRN will be working. The Joint Commission requires that

Table 3.3 Regulatory Bodies

- Federal and state law, including CMS laws
- Joint Commission standards
- State boards of nursing
- National certification associations and programs
- Professional organization statements
- Hospital and facility provider bylaws and policies

institutions have a systematic process to evaluate the provider who is applying for privileges[18] (see Chapter 4).

The credentialing application is extensive and typically includes the elements listed below. APRNs should begin keeping a portfolio immediately after graduation that contains these documents for quick reference for any questions and future recredentialing processes:

- Education, including proof of graduation and degree
- Previous work history
- Current licenses and certifications, DEA number
- Professional memberships
- Continuing education and competency assessments
- Collaborative practice and prescriptive agreements, if required
- Immunization status
- Any past or current disciplinary actions or suspensions from pertinent boards of practice
- Any past or current legal proceedings, both personal and professional
- Any physical, mental health, or chemical dependency issues that could affect one's ability to practice safely and competently
- References from peers

A credentialing committee at the institution reviews the application and, if approved, the APRN is granted privileges to practice. Clinical privileges are delineated to clarify specific sites where the APRN is able to practice and which practices and procedures the provider is allowed to provide, including prescriptive privileges. Clinical practice is often guided by, or in some cases is required to be based on, written guidelines and evidence-based protocols. There are many guidelines and evidence-based protocols in existence, so the APRN need not create something new; rather, he or she can adapt these to his or her setting. Depending on the specific practices and procedures the provider is requesting permission to perform, the committee may also require evidence of demonstrated competence.

Upon initial credentialing and privileging, APRNs can expect there to be a specified period of time in which their practice is closely monitored and evaluated, by direct peer feedback and/or medical record review. Reappointments typically occur every 2 years, and the APRN must provide evidence of continued competency.

Payer credentialing involves the application for authorization to bill for reimbursement through Medicare, Medicaid, and other for-profit and nonprofit insurance carriers. The paperwork for credentialing varies widely by payer, but all processes begin by obtaining a National Provider Identifier (NPI) number, which recognizes the APRN as a unique health care provider under the Health Insurance Portability and Accountability Act of 1996 guidelines and as one who maintains certifications and licensure. Applications for an NPI number are available to complete online at https://nppes.cms.hhs.gov/NPPES/Welcome.do (see Chapter 4 for more information).

The Value and Process of Specialty Certification

In most states, the CNP or CNS must obtain certification from a national, accredited certification organization after graduation from a master's or doctoral program in nursing in order to practice. Certification serves as a form of regulation by the state boards of nursing in recognizing a minimal level of competence. Certification is also now required for reimbursement for services through CMS and, as discussed previously, is required for practice, professional, and payer credentialing.

Specialty certification as an advanced certification hospice and palliative nurse (ACHPN) is available through the Hospice and Palliative Credentialing Center (HPCC), formerly known as the National Board for Certification of Hospice and Palliative Nurses (NBCHPN). It is voluntary for the individual APRN, but many employers require the additional specialty certification at the time of hire or require the nurse to obtain it within a specified timeframe. CMS added NBCHPN (now HPCC) to the list of recognized national certifying bodies for CNPs and CNSs. However, this was prior to the Consensus Model implementation, which now requires that the graduate student education program be focused on one of the six specific populations discussed earlier, with successful completion of the corresponding certification exam for entry to practice. In most states, hospice and palliative care is considered a "specialty" and the ACHPN examination is not accepted for entry to practice. The APRN should check with the individual state board of nursing and CMS to determine requirements for licensure and billing (see Chapter 4).

Some hospice and palliative APRNs wonder why they should work toward specialty certification in advanced hospice and palliative care when it might not be required. After all, it is an additional expense that may or may not be reimbursed by one's employer, and it is stressful and time-consuming to sit for an exam. But there are actually many benefits to obtaining certification in the specialty one practices in, and these perceived and actual values have been described in a study conducted by the American Board of Nursing Specialties.[19] They include:

◆ An expanded and deeper knowledge base. The exercise of studying for the exam actually contributes to learning new information about the specialty.

◆ A commitment to professional growth, enhanced feelings of personal accomplishment, professional satisfaction, and increased empowerment and confidence in the role

◆ Enhanced credibility and respect of coworkers; being seen as a staff resource

◆ The standard of practice is raised throughout the profession, which in the long run serves to improve patient care outcomes and safety.

◆ Employers have found that specialty certified nurses are desirable employees because certification reflects dedication to their profession and to providing the most relevant, evidence-based, and cutting-edge care to patients and their families.

◆ Financial benefits and professional growth. In addition to possible bonuses and salary increases, APRNs with specialty certification are often viewed as more competent and able to take on more responsibility, which can lead to career advancement and opportunities.

◆ Managers and employers have found that certified nurses help ensure a highly trained, progressive team, which elevates the perception of the medical facility or program. Hospitals applying for or renewing American Nurses Credentialing Center

Magnet status or programs seeking The Joint Commission for specialty certification in palliative care must have a greater percentage of certified providers.[19]

Specifics and Process of Attaining the ACHPN

Initial certification as an ACHPN is attained by passing a psychometrically sound, computer-based examination. The content of the examination has been developed from a national job analysis survey that identified the activities performed by hospice and palliative APRNs.[20] A taskforce of experienced hospice and palliative APRNs determined from the job analysis the activities and knowledge critical to the practice of the hospice and palliative APRN. These are specified in the Detailed Content Outline in the ACHPN Candidate Handbook,[20] which can be found online at http://www.nbchpn.org http://hpcc.advancingexpertcare.org. The content outline can be used to guide self-assessment and a study plan for the exam.

Although there is not a test question pertaining to each topic on the content outline, every question on the exam can be linked back to the outline. The questions are written by experienced APRNs in the field and are scrutinized by members of the HPCC APRN Exam Development Committee, with the guidance of a statistician from the professional testing agency that assists in the development, administration, scoring, and analysis of the certification examination. The examination includes 25 nonscored "pretest" or "trial" items that are not identified as such and are interspersed throughout the examination. Performance on the pretest questions does not affect the candidate's overall score. The results on the pretest questions are further evaluated with attention to statistical reliability and validity and are modified further before being approved for the exam or are retired if they do not meet the criteria.[20]

Recertification

HPCC certification must be renewed every 4 years through the Hospice and Palliative Accrual for Recertification process. It is the expectation that the APRN has continued to develop professionally with experience and exposure to new knowledge over that 4-year period. Continuing education and professional activities, along with a minimum number of practice hours, are the main requirements for certification renewal. Professional activities are converted to points, with a requirement to accrue 125 points in the 4-year period. Professional activities the APRN can complete for recertification include:[20]

◆ Continuing nursing education

◆ Continuing medical education

◆ Academic education

◆ Professional publications

◆ Professional presentations

◆ Item writer workshop participation

◆ Self-assessment examination completion

◆ Professional volunteer activities related to hospice and palliative care

◆ Clinical mentoring/preceptorship of graduate nursing students

In support of the goal to encourage continued competence in practice, a situational judgment exercise is also required for recertification. This is an open-book, online exercise that uses real-life, case-based scenarios to test the candidate's critical reasoning and clinical application beyond the level of the initial certification exam. As candidates are led through the scenario, they are asked to make decisions about what pertinent information to gather to guide decisions about the care and treatment of the patient and family. The cases involve more than just clinical decision making; they also address professional judgment, patient education, communication, ethics, and collaborative practice issues. Points are accrued toward recertification based on the score achieved.

To accomplish recertification efficiently, the APRN should organize dates and documentation during the 4-year accrual period. As most APRNs will also need to be gathering this information in order to recertify for their other primary practice certification, relicensure, and credentialing, it should not require significant extra work. Certification and credentialing agencies are moving to online documentation, which will make recordkeeping easier and more efficient, but it is still important for the APRN to keep copies of continuing education certificates of attendance and documentation to support other professional development activities. It is much better to acquaint oneself with the recertification requirements soon after initial certification rather than waiting for the deadline to be looming and discovering that meeting the recertification requirements will be difficult if not impossible.

Certification and recertification in advanced hospice and palliative care demonstrate professional commitment and mastery of the field. While they are not necessarily required to practice in the field, they speak to the APRN's professional commitment and dedication to the specialty.

Conclusion

It is an exciting and rapidly changing time for healthcare, and APRNs will need to rise to the challenge to provide efficient, cost-effective, and accessible care. The hospice and palliative care APRN will increasingly be called upon to meet the needs of an aging population. To practice safely, legally, and to the fullest extent of their scope, APRNs must have a working knowledge of the sometimes confusing world of credentialing, privileging, certification, and licensure. APRNs must understand potential changes to their own practice regarding the implementation of the NCSBN Consensus Model and the lifting of current restrictions to independent practice. APRNs practicing in the specialty of hospice and palliative care may best demonstrate their expertise and ongoing competence, in addition to professionalism, by achieving advanced certification in hospice and palliative care.

References

1. Promoting Excellence in End-of-Life-Care. *Advanced Practice Nurses Role in Palliative Care—A Position Statement from American Nurse Leaders.* Missoula, MT: Promoting Excellence in End-of-Life Care (a project of the Robert Wood Johnson Foundation); 2002. Avaialble at http://www.promoting excellence.org/downloads/apn_report.pdf. http://www.promotingexcellence.org/apn/pe3675.html. Accessed Oct 1, 2015.
2. National Council of State Boards of Nursing. *Consensus Model for APRN Regulation: Licensure, Accreditation, Certification &* *Education.* Available at https://www.ncsbn.org/Consensus_Model_for_APRN_Regulation_July_2008.pdf, July 7, 2008. Accessed July 30, 2014.
3. Institute of Medicine. *The Future of Nursing: Leading Change, Advancing Health.* Washington, DC: The National Academies Press; 2011.
4. Cahill M, Alexander M, Gross L. The 2014 NCSBN Consensus Report on APRN Regulation. *J Nurs Regul.* 2014; 4(4): 5–12.
5. Department of Health and Human Services Centers for Medicare and Medicaid Services. *Medicare Information for Advanced Practice Registered Nurses, Anesthesiologist Assistants, and Physician Assistants.* Available at http://www.cms.gov/Outreach-and-Education/Medicare-Learning-Network-MLN/MLNProducts/downloads/Medicare_Information_for_APNs_and_PAs_Booklet_ICN901623.pdf. Accessed September 29, 2014.
6. Dahlin CM, Sutermaster DJ, eds. *Palliative Nursing: Scope and Standards—An Essential Resource for Hospice and Palliative Nurses.* Silver Spring, MD: Co-published with HPNA and ANA/Nursebooks.org; 2014.
7. Newhouse RP, Stanik-Hutt J, White KM, et al. Advanced practice nurse outcomes 1990-2008: A systematic review. *Nurs Econ.* 2011; 29(5): 230–51.
8. Gilman DJ, Koslov TI. *Policy Perspectives: Competition and the Regulation of Advanced Practice Nurses.* 2014. Retrieved from the Federal Trade Commission website: http://www.ftc.gov/system/files/documents/reports/policy-perspectives-competition-regulation-advanced-practice-nurses/140307aprnpolicypaper.pdf. Accessed July 19, 2014.
9. American Nurses Association. Available at http://www.nursingworld.org/EspeciallyForYou/AdvancedPracticeNurses/Scope-of-Practice-2. Accessed July 30, 2014.
10. American Nurses Association. *Nursing: Scope and Standards of Practice.* 2nd ed. Silver Spring, MD: ANA/Nursebooks.org; 2010.
11. Kjervik D, Brous EA. *Law and Ethics in Advanced Practice Nursing.* New York, NY: Springer Publishing Company; 2010.
12. Dahlin C, ed. *Competencies For the Hospice and Palliative Advanced Practice Nurse.* 2nd ed. Pittsburgh, PA: HPNA; 2014.
13. Dahlin CM, Lynch MT, eds. *Core Curriculum for the Advanced Practice Hospice and Palliative Registered Nurse.* 2nd ed. Pittsburgh, PA: HPNA; 2013.
14. American Academy of Hospice and Palliative Medicine; Center to Advance Palliative Care; Hospice and Palliative Nurses Association; Last Acts Partnership; National Hospice and Palliative Care Organization. National Consensus Project for Quality Palliative Care: Clinical Practice Guidelines for quality palliative care, executive summary. *J Palliat Med.* 2004; 7(5): 611–627.
15. American Association of Colleges of Nursing. ELNEC website. Available at http://www.aacn.nche.edu/elnec. Accessed July 30, 2014.
16. Smolenski MC, Gagan MJ. Credentialing, certification, and competence: Issues for new and seasoned nurse practitioners. *J Am Acad Nurse Pract.* 2005; 17(6): 201–4.
17. Goudreau KA, Smolenski MC. Credentialing and certification: Issues for Clinical Nurse Specialists. *Clin Nur Spec.* 2008; 22(5): 240–4.
18. Kleinpell RM, Hravnak M, Hinch B, et al. Developing an advanced practice nursing credentialing model for acute care facilities. *Nurs Admin Q.* 2008; 32(4): 279–87.
19. American Board of Nursing Specialties. Specialty nursing certification: Nurses' perceptions, values and behaviors. 2006. Available at http://www.nursingcertification.org/pdf/white_paper_final_12_12_06.pdf. Accessed July 30, 2014.
20. Hospice and Palliative Credentialing Center. ACHPN® Candidate Handbook. Available at http://hpna.advancingexpertcare.org/wp-content/uploads/2014/12/HPCC-ACHPN-Handbook-January-2015_CM4.pdf. Accessed June 1, 2015.

CHAPTER 4

Reimbursement for the Palliative Advanced Practice Registered Nurse

Constance Dahlin

Key Points

- The advanced practice registered nurse (APRN) must identify potential opportunities for reimbursement as part of role and program development.
- The APRN must learn and stay current with federal guidelines pertaining to billing and documentation.
- To optimize reimbursement, the APRN must understand the complexity of billing and documentation.

Case Study

Cara Kelly was a new CNS who recently joined a developing palliative service in a community hospital. Because she has been acting in a resource role and her salary was under the department of nursing, she never needed to understand billing and reimbursement. Now she was expected to submit bills for her work on the consultative palliative care service. She has tried to understand the elements necessary to document her services for reimbursement. She learned the fundamentals of reimbursement language and coding. She attended a class that offered an overview of the basics of billing and reimbursement processes. She also scheduled time with the billing and coding department. Finally, she asked for ongoing meetings with the team. At the meetings, she and her fellow APRNs reviewed documentation notes to discuss best practices and accuracy of coding. She created a reference card with the inpatient hospital codes and the outpatient codes, elements of the particular visits, time estimates, and common diagnoses with their ICD codes. She requested quarterly review of her billing to ensure her competency and continued learning.

Introduction

Opportunities for indirect and direct reimbursement for palliative advanced practice nurses exist across all settings as well as in the creation of new models of care. Indirect reimbursement occurs through cost savings. APRNs who are unable to seek reimbursement (usually because they are located under departments

of nursing) provide services that can offset costs. Examples are reduction in length of hospital service days, appropriate utilization of resources, and preventing readmissions. While these are very important financial considerations, the focus of this chapter is on direct reimbursement.

Reimbursement for palliative services performed by advanced practice registered nurses is a valuable commodity in financial and business planning and hospital savings. It can immediately justify the palliative APRN's involvement and utilization within a team specifically since a portion of his or her salary can be recaptured through reimbursement. However, estimates reveal that fee-for-service reimbursement recaptures only about 60% of the palliative care practitioner's salary (physician and advanced practice nurse alike).[1] Reimbursement guidelines are established by the federal government and parameters for reimbursable services for Medicare and Medicaid patients, including settings of care, and billing and coding practices.

Unlike physician reimbursement, which is fairly straightforward, there are many aspects of and variations in reimbursement pertaining to the APRN. Specifically, there are regional variations of billing and coding practices within federal fiscal intermediaries, different bylaws within healthcare institutions, and state statutes governing APRN practice, scope of practice, and eligibility for reimbursement. Moreover, the guidelines established by the federal government often change as revisions or new healthcare acts alter the situations and circumstance in which APRNs can bill. To take advantage of billing and reimbursement, palliative APRNs must understand the fundamental aspects of reimbursement and stay informed regarding changing legislation and regulations.

History of APRN Reimbursement in the United States

Reimbursement for advanced practice nurses has been an evolving process, similar to gaining autonomous practice (Table 4.1). An overview of the history of APRN reimbursement fosters an understanding of the issues that influenced its development and the need for ongoing changes to capture a fiscal appreciation of

Table 4.1 History of APRN Billing

Prior to 1997	No APRN billing	◆ APRNs performed services under physician billing numbers
1997	Balanced Budget Act	◆ Removed restrictions of practice for reimbursement of services ◆ Recognized all APRNs—CNS, NP, CNM, and CRNA practice ◆ Allowed APRNs to apply for individual provider numbers to submit reimbursement for billing
2003	Medicare Modernization Act	◆ Broadened scope of reimbursable practice ◆ NPs to serve as attending of record for any patient
2007	Reinstatement of Medicare Modernization Act	◆ NPs can serve as attending for hospice patients ◆ NPs cannot certify terminal illness ◆ APRNs cannot order hospice or home health or DME for hospice and palliative patients (also in primary care) ◆ Certification in Advanced Hospice and Palliative Nursing recognized as one of the seven certifying organizations for reimbursement eligibility
2010	Affordable Care Act	◆ Delineated hospice benefit recertification and requirements for documentation ◆ Stated only NPs, not CNSs, could do the face-to-face visits

APRN practice. Until 1997, APRNs were not recognized within the Medicare reimbursement structure. Instead, their services were hidden because they were billed under a physician and his or her billing identification number.[2] This meant the APRN performed services for a patient but had to bring the physician into the room to oversee and supervise care. This was cumbersome and also diminished the autonomous role. In addition, it shrouded the amount of care that advanced practice nurses provided.

In 1997, the Balanced Budget Act (BBA) was passed. This was very significant because it removed the restrictions on APRN reimbursement. The BBA recognized all APRNs (clinical nurse specialists [CNSs], nurse practitioners [NPs], certified nurse-midwives [CNMs], and certified registered nurse anesthetists [CRNAs]).[3] It allowed APRNs to obtain their own identification numbers to use for submitting bills for reimbursement.[3] This important change impacted APRNs practicing in acute care settings and outpatient settings. By allowing APRNs to bill under their own identification numbers, it revealed the substantial volume of services provided by APRNs in these settings.

The Medicare Modernization Act of 2003 continued to move APRN practice forward. It recognized the specialty practice of APRNs and allowed them to provide a full range of services across all settings.[4] For the first time, it allowed an APRN, albeit only NPs, to serve in the role of attending physician for any hospice patient who chose to have the NP in the role. This meant patients who had relationships with NPs could have continuity of care across settings. It also meant NPs could serve as attending of record for palliative care patients throughout the disease trajectory. In 2007, there was further restatement of the Modernization Act. At this time, both NP practice and CNS practice were clarified and the ability to seek reimbursement was reinforced.[5,6] Moreover, hospice guidelines for APRN billing were established. Unfortunately, however, only NPs, not CNSs, were permitted to serve as the attending of record for hospice patients.[7] It is still not clear how this happened, but speculation is that the Center for Medicare and Medicaid Services (CMS) did not fully understand the difference between NPs and CNSs and perhaps thought they were the same. The result is that CNSs are unrecognized within

hospice care and cannot provide separate consultative services nor serve as the attending of record.

Most recently, the 2010 Patient Protection and Affordable Care Act reiterated NP and CNS reimbursement. Specifically, it delineated hospice care delivery in terms of benefit periods, recertification, and quality requirements.[8] There was no further discussion of the CNS's ability to serve as attending for hospice patients, so CNSs still may not serve in this role. APRNs are still unable to order hospice, home care, and durable medical equipment (DME). There was also no discussion of promoting universal practice to eliminate state-to-state variations. Clearly, there is more work to be done on a federal level surrounding APRN reimbursement, especially as healthcare reform occurs.

Reimbursement Structure Overview

Medicare is a federal health insurance program that covers persons aged 65 and older, as well as people who are younger than 65 with end-stage kidney disease and other disabilities. Medicare is divided into four benefits: Part A, Part B, Part C, and Part D (Table 4.2). Part A is the essential element of coverage and encompasses mostly hospital services as well as hospice and some home health services.[9] Part B is a voluntary benefit and encompasses provider services and some home health services and for which a person pays a premium for coverage.[10] Part C governs Medicare replacement programs that are contracted and enacted by commercial insurance plans.[11] Part D is also voluntary and relates to coverage for medications, with premium payments determined by level of coverage desired.[12]

Reimbursement for care of patients under all parts of Medicare is administered through the federal government, specifically CMS. The Department of Health and Human Services oversees CMS. CMS creates regulations that determine the necessary elements for documentation and billing practices for patients who have Medicare A and B. To assist in processing claims and working with local providers of healthcare services, CMS created 15 regional administration centers called Medicare Administration Centers (MACs)[13] (Fig 4.1). MACs perform a range of services ranging from providing education about billing and reimbursement,

Table 4.2 The Four Parts of Medicare[9–12]

Medicare Benefit	Part A	Part B	Part C	Part D
Type of Services	Hospital services	Professional services	Health programs that replace Medicare	Prescription drug programs
Universal or Voluntary	Universal coverage	Voluntary; premium	Voluntary; premium	Voluntary; premium
Coverage	Fully covered	Covered 80%	Varies by plan	Varies by plan

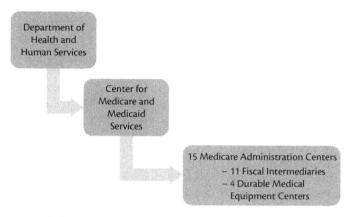

Figure 4.1 Organization of federal reimbursement oversight

issuing guidelines for reimbursement submission, and determining medical necessity, to processing Medicare claims.[13] Eleven MACs manage Medicare A and B claims and are known as fiscal intermediaries (FIs). Four of these are specifically responsible for the Medicare Hospice Benefit and the Medicare Home Health Benefit. Four MACs that manage durable medical equipment are known as DME regional centers or DMERCs.

Medicare Parts A and B oversee reimbursement in hospice and palliative care (Table 4.3). Medicare Part A is termed a hospital coverage. It covers institutional services such as hospital care, rehabilitation, and skilled nursing home services. It also includes hospice services and describes reimbursable services of NPs working with hospice patients. Medicare Part B is termed medical insurance. It covers medically necessary and preventive-type professional services provided by clinicians in all services and describes the reimbursable services of APRNs working with palliative, non-hospice patients.

Medicaid is a federal program for impoverished people. Such individuals, most often mothers and children as well as those in long-term care and with disabilities, must qualify under poverty definitions. Each state administers Medicaid, and some states have more robust programs than others. In particular, some states have a Medicaid Hospice Benefit and others do not. In the states that do, such benefits often mirror Medicare benefits.

Potential opportunities for reimbursable APRN services provided to patients with serious illness can be realized under both palliative care and hospice. The Medicare Hospice Benefit, which resides in Medicare Part A, is the best understood. It is an elected benefit for patients with advanced, serious, and life-limiting illnesses who want to focus on comfort and noncurative therapies.[7] In other words, "An individual is considered to be terminally ill if the medical prognosis is that the individual's life expectancy is 6 months or less if the illness runs its normal course."[8] Under the Medicare Hospice Benefit, NPs can bill for services for patients for whom they are serving as the attending of record; CNSs may not bill for their services provided to hospice patients.

Palliative care has no delineated benefit in Medicare guidelines, except that services must be medically necessary. Instead, it is defined as "patient- and family-centered care that optimizes quality of life by anticipating, preventing, and treating suffering. Palliative care throughout the continuum of illness involves addressing physical, intellectual, emotional, social, and spiritual needs and to facilitate patient autonomy, access to information,

Table 4.3 Medicare Part A and Part B[9,10]

Part A	Part B
Institutional services	**Professional services of clinicians**
Eligibility: Universal coverage for people ≥65 years old & people with certain disabilities. No copayments.	**Eligibility:** Voluntary. Copayment required. People ≥65 years old & people with certain disabilities.
Sites of care where services are covered:	**Types of services covered:**
◆ Hospital care	◆ Physicians, APRNs, PAs, psychologists, clinical social workers
◆ Skilled nursing facility	◆ DME
◆ Nursing home care (above custodial care)	◆ Outpatient dialysis
◆ Hospice	◆ Mental health services
◆ Home healthcare	◆ Outpatient hospital
◆ Inpatient rehabilitation	◆ Ambulance services
◆ Inpatient dialysis	◆ Rural health clinic and federally qualified health center services

and choice."[7] This definition allows palliative care to begin at diagnosis of a serious or life-threatening illness, life-limiting disease, and/or progressive chronic illness without limits on length of service.[14] Within palliative care, CNSs and NPs may bill for medically necessary services provided to patients across the illness trajectory in settings such as a hospital, skilled nursing facility, nursing home, comprehensive outpatient rehabilitation facility, ambulatory surgical center, community mental health center, rural health center, or federally qualified health center. Medicaid and commercial insurance plans often mirror the benefits outlined in Medicare.[15]

APRN Reimbursement Eligibility

There are five areas that determine the APRN's eligibility for reimbursement: education and certification, state authority, role delineation, source of salary, and institutional or organizational credentialing[16] (Fig 4.2 and Table 4.4). They are fairly straightforward.

Education pertains to the APRN's education at the master's level or higher in one of the four roles of advanced practice: CNS, NP, CNM, and CNA. APRN education should occur in one of the population foci as delineated by the National Council of State Boards of Nursing (NCSBN): (1) family/individual across the lifespan, (2) adult/gerontology, (3) neonatal, (4) pediatrics, (5) women's health/gender-related, and (6) psychiatric/mental health.[17,18] Coursework must include health assessment, pharmacology, and pathophysiology.

Within hospice and palliative care practice for both adults and children, the most common roles are CNSs and NPs. The APRN must also have national certification as an APRN in his or her population focus from a nationally recognized organization. Under

Figure 4.2 CMS eligibility criteria for APRN reimbursement

the APRN Licensing, Accreditation, Certification, and Education (LACE) model, palliative care nursing is no longer recognized as a primary area of focus, even though the National Board for Certification of Hospice and Palliative Nurses is one of the seven nationally eligible certifying organizations. However, subspecialty certification as an advanced practice hospice and palliative nurse is recommended and strongly endorsed by the National Consensus Project for Quality Palliative Care's *Clinical Practice Guidelines* and The Joint Commission's *Advanced Certification for Palliative Care*.[14,19]

Authority to practice beyond the registered nurse (RN) role as an APRN is the next area of eligibility. This means the APRN must have a state license to practice in an expanded role. For those in palliative care, this is usually the CNS or NP role. The licensing state must have statutes, rules, and regulations which delineate

Table 4.4 APRN Reimbursement Eligibility

Education and Certification	◆ *Education—Master's or doctoral degree* with coursework in health assessment, pharmacology, and pathophysiology in one of the four roles—clinical nurse specialist, nurse practitioner, certified midwife, or certified nurse anesthetist
	◆ *National certification* from a nationally recognized certification organization related to population focus of graduate education
Authority to Practice in Advanced Role	◆ *State license* to practice as APRN
	◆ *State APRN practice act, statutes, or regulations* within state APRN practices that grant authority to practice
Role Delineation	◆ A *job description* that delineates APRN practice
	◆ A *collaborative agreement* or practice agreement outlining tasks the APRN may perform in a particular setting, under what circumstances the APRN would refer to a physician, and the level of physician involvement or oversight. This can be part of the job description.
Basis of Salary	◆ All or *percentage of salary* (usually percentage of patient care hours) that is not part of Medicare Part A cost report
Organizational Credentialing	◆ Occurs at *institution where APRN will provide services.* For hospitals, this must now be through a medical staff office, not a human resources department.
	◆ *National Provider Identification (NPI) number*
	◆ Acceptance on Medicare, Medicaid, and commercial panels
APRN Prescriptive Authority	◆ *State* prescribing license and/or state-controlled substances registration
	◆ *Drug* Enforcement Administration (DEA) registration for controlled substances.

Adapted from Dahlin 2014 (Reference 16).

and allow the advanced practice role. These state regulations must describe specific services provided by the APRN that have been outlined by the NCSBN: the ability to take a patient history, complete a review of systems, perform a physical examination, determine diagnoses, and provide appropriate treatment for the patient. This establishes that these services would be provided by a physician in the absence of an APRN.[15] Prescriptive authority for the various classes of medications is included in state regulations. While such authority may promote more autonomous practice, it is not part of reimbursement eligibility. However, the complexity of decision making regarding medication use may influence reimbursement.

The reimbursement eligibility is also determined by scope of practice. One element of this is a clear job description that delineates the APRN's practice, with a description of skills, knowledge, and tasks performed. Federal guidelines dictate that there must be an accompanying collaborative practice agreement. Specifically, this outlines when the APRN would refer a patient to a physician as well as the physician's level of involvement or oversight.

There are many job descriptions for APRNs practicing in hospice and palliative care. It is best to have a job description that is consistent with other APRNs practicing in the employing healthcare organization but also includes the special aspects of palliative nursing. In addition, collaborative agreements ask for standards of practice, guidelines, and/or algorithms of practice. APRNs do not need to create new standards or competencies; they can refer to established references, such as *Palliative Nursing: Scope and Standards*, produced by the Hospice and Palliative Nurses Association (HPNA) and the American Nurses Association (ANA) as well as HPNA's *Competencies for the Hospice and Palliative APN*.[20,21] In addition, there are many well-known algorithms in the palliative nursing literature that can be adopted by a hospice or palliative care team.

Another critical aspect of APRN eligibility for reimbursement is salary. The source of the APRN's salary is critical to reimbursement issues. Specifically, an APRN must have all or a percentage of his or her salary that is not part of a Medicare A cost report. For palliative care APRNs in the hospital, this means their salary cannot come out of the department of nursing; otherwise, their care is part of bundled services. For hospice APRNs, their services are considered part of the Medicare Hospice Benefit under Part A with one exception: when the NP is serving as the attending of record, which would be separated out.

The last eligibility requirement is organizational credentialing. This is the professional credentialing done at the institution where the APRN provides services. This must be done through medical staff offices, not human resources or nursing. Specifically, this is a review of the APRN's compliance with necessary criteria for practice: proof of education, certification, licensing, malpractice insurance, and a National Provider Identification (NPI) number. Often, this also includes proof of state registration to prescribe medications as well as a Drug Enforcement Administration (DEA) registration for controlled substances. However, if an APRN is not writing prescriptions, a DEA registration may not be necessary. In addition, the credentialing will establish the APRN's acceptance on Medicare, Medicaid, and commercial insurance panels for purposes of reimbursement.

The Reimbursement Process

Reimbursement encompasses a several-step process: the provision of a healthcare service, documentation of that service, completion of a billing form, and submission of the bill. There are critical features to each step, and understanding the purpose of each step eases the process. First is the provision of a healthcare service. In performing a healthcare visit, the APRN must understand three points. Specifically, any service that the APRN will be submitting for reimbursement must (1) be necessary, (2) be of an advanced nature, (3) reflect standards of practice, and (4) include established visit components. In particular, the APRN must use advanced skills, such as those that in his or her absence would be performed by a physician and not an RN. This is clearly delineated by CMS. Services provided by an APRN are

> medical in nature, must be reasonable and necessary, be included in the plan of care and must be services that, in the absence of a nurse practitioner [and clinical nurse specialist] would be performed by a physician. If the services performed by a nurse practitioner [and clinical nurse specialist] are such that a registered nurse could perform them in the absence of a physician, they are not considered attending physician services and are not separately billable.[15,22]

Thus, APRN services that duplicate hospice or palliative RN services are not separately billable.

In performing services, it is extremely helpful to understand the elements necessary for visits. This is easiest to accomplish by having a template to follow. Critical elements of documentation include the who, what, where, when, how, and why of billing (Table 4.5).

Documentation

There is a convention to documentation. First, there is the nature of the presenting problem. Second is the history of the present illness. This includes a focus on the disease history or a symptom. If describing a symptom, the nurse should include its location, quality, severity, duration, timing, context, modifying factors, and/or associated signs and symptoms. Third is the review of systems, which encompasses 14 organ systems. So that it is more relevant to palliative care, there are some focused areas (Table 4.1). A review of systems can be long or short, depending on the type of visit. There are three types of review: (1) problem-focused, which includes one to five problems within an organ-specific system, (2) extended, which focuses on a specific problem and includes two to nine organ systems, and (3) comprehensive, which is based on the specific issue and a minimum of 10 other organ systems.[23] Then, there is the history section, which includes past medical history, social history, family history, and, for palliative care, spiritual history. Next is the physical examination, which includes a review of two to eight of the systems, again depending on the complexity of the visit. These systems are (1) constitutional, (2) eyes, ears, nose, mouth, and throat (known as EENMT), (3) cardiovascular, (4) respiratory, (5) gastrointestinal, (6) genitourinary, (7) musculoskeletal, (8) skin, and (9) neurological.[23]

Within consultations, the APRN must include the "four Rs": Request, Reason, Rendering of services, and Report. The request is the verbal or written wish for a consult. Contrary to public perception, any provider can make a request, though most often people only think of the attending physician. Other providers are

Table 4.5 Elements of Documentation for a Patient Visit

Element	Description	Identifying data
Who	Who was the patient seen by and which clinician saw the patient?	◆ Patient identification—name, medical record number ◆ APRN identification—name, credentials
What	What type of visit occurred and what was done during the visit?	◆ Consultation versus management ◆ Elements of visit—history, physical examination, medication review
Where	Where or in what setting did the visit occur?	◆ Hospital ◆ Home ◆ Skilled nursing facility ◆ Hospice
When	When did the visit occur and how long was it?	◆ Date ◆ Start and end times ◆ Total time
How	How was the time spent?	◆ History-taking ◆ Physical examination ◆ Procedures, test review ◆ Family meeting, counseling, etc.
Why	Why was the consult requested (specifically explaining the medical reason for a consult request or a follow-up visit)?	◆ Medical reason, such as symptom, issue, or problem ◆ Referring clinician ◆ Palliative trigger

Adapted from Dahlin 2014 (Reference 16).

defined by CMS and include osteopaths, APRNs, physician assistants, rehabilitation therapists, psychologists, and/or social workers. The reason is the specific purpose of the consult, which may include (but is not limited to) symptom management, pain management, psychosocial support, goals of care determination, code status, and/or disposition. The rendering of services is the actual consultative visit. The report is the record of the consultation. This can be a consultative note or letter sent back to the referring provider.

For subsequent follow-up visits, documentation depends on the complexity of the visit. It should include a SOAP note (subjective, objective, assessment, and plan). The "S" includes the chief complaint, history of present illness, family history, and spiritual assessment. The "O" includes vital signs, physical examination, medications, and diagnostic studies. The "A" includes the APRN's impression, with a summary description of the status of the patient's presenting problem(s) and differential diagnosis(es). The "P" includes the plan, which is a summary of the management actions to be taken, incorporating education and counseling, diagnostic testing, and therapeutic interventions.

Time is also an important aspect of documentation. This includes the length of a visit. For hospital visits, the time begins when the APRN arrives at the floor and ends when he or she leaves the floor. This includes review of the chart, talking with other providers involved with the care, reviewing laboratory and radiology studies, patient interview and examination, and documentation time. When in the clinic or outpatient setting, time includes only the APRN's face-to-face time with the patient in an examination/consult room.

Billing

A bill for palliative care has various elements that offer details of the encounter. First is a procedure description, which includes an evaluation and management (E/M) code and/or a procedure code.[23,24] The E/M code is determined by the setting of the visit, type of visit, and patient type. According to CMS, evaluation and management should include the nature of the presenting problem and the history of the present illness, with a focus on a symptom and its description, with details on its location, quality, severity, duration, timing, context, modifying factors, and/or associated signs and symptoms. Then, there is the description of the diagnosis, which takes into consideration the reason for the encounter, symptoms and physical findings, and the diagnoses. Finally, within palliative care, there is a professional code that specifies that the care is related to palliative care. For palliative care, these are the GV and the GW codes. A GV code is a professional code that signifies that care for the palliative care patient is related to a terminal illness, but services are not related to hospice. A GW code is a professional code that signifies that care is unrelated to the patient's terminal condition.

The services an APRN can provide include a range of visit types. They can include a transfer of care, whereby the APRN assumes responsibility for the patient and serves as the attending of record. The APRN can also perform initial consultations, whereby he or she is asked to advise on the patient's symptoms, conditions, diseases, or illness. The APRN can also perform follow-up or subsequent visits. Finally, the APRN can perform discharge services or death pronouncement visits.

The Two Categories of Billing

There are two types of billing: independent billing and "incident to" billing. Independent billing occurs when the APRN provides care and services under his or her own license and NPI number. This is also known as direct billing and has the

Box 4.1 Palliative Care Review of Systems Documentation

Constitutional: Fever; fatigue; drowsiness; weight loss

Eyes: Vision changes

Ears, Nose, Mouth, Throat: Excess or absence of secretions; oral symptoms; swallowing

Cardiovascular: Chest pain; swelling of extremities/face/neck; paroxysmal nocturnal dyspnea; orthopnea

Respiratory: Dyspnea; cough; hiccups

Gastrointestinal: Changes in appetite; presence of nausea/vomiting/dyspepsia; abdominal pain; constipation; diarrhea

Genitourinary: Urinary frequency; urinary pain; urinary retention; urinary incontinence

Musculoskeletal: Weakness; stiffness; joint pain; muscle pain; no pain

Integumentary/Skin: Dry skin; pruritus; rash; decubitus ulcers; bruising

Neurological: Delirium; agitation; sedation; balance or gait issues

Psychiatric: Anxious; depressed mood; hallucinations; insomnia

Endocrine: Steroid side effects; cold/heat intolerance

Allergic/Immunological: Immunosuppression; neutropenia

Hematological/Lymphatic: Bruising; bleeding; lymphedema; lymphadenopathy

Adapted from Dahlin 2014 (Reference 16).

consultations, or subsequent visits under independent billing. Most important is that the APRN does not need a supervisory note from a physician. However, some healthcare organization bylaws require this.

"Incident to" billing occurs when the APRN provides an integral aspect of care, such as a commonly rendered service, but services are billed under the physician's NPI number.[15] There are various guidelines for "incident to" billing. Specifically, the physician initiates the course of treatment and care plan for each new problem and the APRN follows that treatment plan for the specific problem. If there is a new problem, the physician must initiate a new course of treatment and care plan. The physician must be physically present in the office suite and immediately available; the physician cannot be only telephonically available. There are also restrictions to "incident to" billing. It is not allowed when the APRN sees patients in the hospital, and it is not allowed for hospice patients in any setting.

It is important to understand the difference between independent billing and "incident to" billing and when they can be used (Table 4.6). Sometimes, APRNs and physicians may perform shared visits where they both may see a patient. How the visit is billed is determined by the setting, the range of services performed, and documentation. When these situations occur, the physician and APRN must talk before they bill to determine whose documentation will best support the bill.

Coding

Coding is complex and a learned skill. While it is beyond the scope of this chapter to provide all the details of coding, there are many resources provided by CMS. First is the determination of whether the patient is new or established. In the inpatient setting, the definition of a new patient refers to the new patient for whom the APRN provides a consultation, known as the initial evaluation. Each admission for a new problem constitutes a new patient even if the patient has been seen before. However, if a patient is readmitted for the same problem, he or she is considered an established patient. In the outpatient setting, a new patient is one who is new to the APRN; is new to the practice; or is a patient who

fewest restrictions.[15] The rate is specified for Medicare patients as being 80% of the lesser of either the actual charge or 85% of the physician's fee schedule amount. The APRN can see a patient in any setting and can perform initial evaluations,

Table 4.6 Independent Billing Versus "Incident to" Billing

Circumstance	Independent Billing	"Incident to" Billing
NPI number used	Individual NPI used on bill	Physician's NPI number on bill
Settings	All settings	Restricted to outpatient settings only, including office, home, or skilled nursing facility Not allowed in hospital or hospice
Consultation	Able to do	Unable to do
Assumption of care	Yes	No
Subsequent visits	Able to do	Able to do for established problems. For a new problem, a physician must perform.
Physician co-signature or supervision note	Not necessary	Necessary or that referring to plan of care set by physician
Reimbursement	85%	100%
Shared visits	Yes, except consultation	Yes

has not been seen in 3 years. If the APRN sees a patient who has been seen before in the practice, this is not a new patient.

An established patient is a patient known to the palliative APRN, whom the patient sees for a subsequent or follow-up visit. In the hospital, this is the patient who is seen as a new patient at the first visit and then as an established patient after that. In the outpatient setting, an established is defined as the patient who is known to the palliative APRN and the practice and has received services within the past 3 years.

There are some features to consider in determining billing codes, including the setting, the complexity and severity of the patient's condition, and the average time of a visit. The setting determines a set of codes specific to a site known as Current Procedural Terminology (CPT) codes.[23,24] They include codes for the hospital, the outpatient setting, a skilled facility, and the home. Their numbering signifies the setting almost in the same way as a ZIP code designates a location. In addition, within each set of codes, there are levels from problem-based or least intensive to very complex to most complex. Included in the decision to use a specific code is consideration of how complex the decision making was in treating the patient, the patient's stability, and a time range for care delivered in the visit. The least complex visits are problem-based and shorter in duration. From there, visits become more expanded with an increase in complexity and the amount of time they necessitate. Finally, the APRN needs to consider medical decision making. This relates to the number of diagnoses and the complexity of data needed to manage and create a care plan.

As part of the billing process, after a CPT code is used, further description of a visit is delineated by the International Classification of Diseases (ICD) code. ICD codes are specific codes for symptoms and diagnoses.[25] Internationally, ICD-10 codes have been used since 1990. The United States has been slow to adopt them and is still using ICD-9 codes. CMS has mandated that by October 1, 2015, all organizations use ICD-10 codes for inpatient codes. ICD-10 codes are a major change from ICD-9 codes. Instead of being three to five numbers long, ICD-10 codes are four to seven characters long and are all alphanumeric. ICD-10 codes are much more specific, with more capacity for new diagnoses, procedures, and technology. They require more precise categorization in terms of stage of care, more specificity in diagnosis, and more detail in anatomy (e.g., lateral or medial; left or right), associated or related conditions, and cause of injuries or problems. Because there are over 160,000 codes, APRNs must become familiar with the common symptoms and diagnoses used in hospice and palliative care. Billing departments can assist in compiling a list of commonly used codes and diagnoses pertaining to palliative care that can aid in learning the codes. Moreover, billing departments can review actual paper or electronic bills for accuracy and can coach APRNs in this area.

Distinct Palliative Care Reimbursement Situations

Several types of visits in palliative care deserve attention. Common in palliative care are family meetings, time-based visits, death pronouncements, and transitional care management. Family meetings are an essential tool in palliative care. They are frequently requested and often are conducted by palliative care APRNs. The components of family meetings are covered in Part Four of this text, Communication. In terms of reimbursement, specific details need attention when documenting the meeting. The APRN should state the following:

1. Who requested the family meeting and the topic to be covered

2. Who attended the family meeting. It is ideal if the patient attends the meeting. CMS Guidelines require it; often, however, the patient chooses not to attend, or cannot attend if he or she is cognitively impaired with delirium or dementia, or is unconscious.

3. Whether the visit was only a family meeting or if it included some aspects of a physical examination

4. The topics discussed and the plan for follow-up

5. The start and stop time of the meeting

6. The percentage of time spent in counseling. This is usually written as "greater than 50% of time spent in the family meeting discussing [a specific topic]."

Another common type of visit in palliative care is time-based billing. Time-based billing results from situations in which the APRN offers counseling. The topics for counseling include diagnosis, the need for diagnostic studies, test results, potential treatment options as well as risks and benefits, plan for initiation of treatment, prognosis, code status, and patient and family education, as well as referrals, such as to a particular specialist, home care, or hospice. Similar to family meetings, there are documentation requirements delineating the topic of counseling, start and stop time, percentage of time spent in counseling, and the focus of the counseling (e.g., pain management, advance care planning).

Death pronouncements are an important task that APRNs perform. Federal law requires that an individual be officially pronounced dead. All licensed independent practitioners, defined as physicians, APRNs, and physician assistants, may perform these visits. Correspondingly, Medicare will reimburse APRNs for pronouncement visits. The APRN first performs the "death pronouncement," which is the confirmation that death has occurred. The APRN verifies the absence of respirations and cessation of the heartbeat. The APRN then completes the death certificate. These visits are billed under the discharge code. Care includes reasonable and necessary care up to the time of death. The challenge is that many state statutes or organizational bylaws may not allow APRNs to perform a death pronouncement. Therefore, the APRN may provide services through the time of death, but a physician may have to do the death pronouncement. In this situation, the APRN may not bill for the visit.

The last type of visit is transitional care management visits. These codes were added by CMS in 2013 and are known as Transitional Management Codes. These codes are different from face-to-face encounters and are billed as regular visits or consults to establish a palliative or hospice care plan. When the patient leaves an acute care hospital, psychiatric hospital, inpatient rehabilitation facility, long-term care facility, or skilled nursing facility, the discharging clinician, which may be an APRN, informs the patient of the need for follow-up. The APRN and the patient together determine who will render follow-up care. This is very important as there have often been many providers, and only one can serve and bill for the follow-up care. The patient returns to his or her home, domiciliary, rest home, or assisted living facility.[26]

Table 4.7 Potential Reimbursement Opportunities for APRNs by Site and Visit Type

Type of Visit	Acute Inpatient	Rehabilitation	Hospice	Home
Consultation	Yes	Yes	Yes	Yes
Initial visit	Only if serving as attending of record	Only if serving as attending of record	Only if serving as attending or record	N/A
Subsequent or follow-up visits	Yes	Yes	Yes	Yes
Discharge	Yes	Yes	Yes	Yes
Death	Yes	Yes	Yes	Yes

Adapted from Dahlin 2014 (Reference 16).

The APRN may provide the post-discharge care. These services are offered by a provider in 30-day periods. An APRN can deliver care under independent "incident to" billing. A requirement is that some meaningful contact must be made by the second business day following discharge. Such communication may include e-mail and interactive technology. Depending on the patient's complexity, a face-to-face visit at home must occur within 7 to 14 days. Activities also include reviewing discharge information, reviewing diagnostic test results or determining the need for further diagnostic tests, providing family and caregiver education, and determining the need for other referrals. There are other rules that concern readmissions to the hospital within a certain time period and clarity of the transitional management codes.

Summary of Potential Opportunities for Reimbursement

Across all settings, there are many opportunities for APRN reimbursement (Table 4.7). APRNs can bill for services they provide in the hospital if they are credentialed as part of a physician practice. They can be employed under various departments, such as internal medicine, primary care, palliative care, and geriatrics. They can perform consultations and subsequent visits for these patients. In the clinic, APRNs can perform visits as a consultant as part of a clinic-based palliative care team or as a palliative care specialist within a specialty medical group.[24] APRNs can also provide consultative services in a skilled nursing facility as part of a consultative practice within the facility or from outside it. At home, a palliative APRN may provide palliative care services as part of a home-based or clinic-based palliative care service or as an independent consultant. Finally, an APRN may provide palliative care services to non-hospice patients as part of hospice, or an NP may provide services to hospice patients if he or she is serving as the attending of record.

Conclusion

The changing healthcare terrain over the past 20 years has offered new opportunities for APRNs. The acknowledgment and legitimization of APRN practice has had a tremendous effect on reimbursement. This has promoted the use of APRNs in practice and simultaneously provided important information about the number of APRNs who practice across the country. It has also opened

possibilities for APRNs to practice in new ways, as reimbursement promotes autonomy. Clearly, there is still work to be done in reimbursement as healthcare reform continues. However, APRNs can now make the business case for playing a prominent role on palliative care teams. Whether through direct or indirect reimbursement, APRNs can provide quality care, reduce costs, and increase patient satisfaction, all of which are important measures and translate into financial rewards.

References

1. Center to Advance Palliative Care. A guide to building a hospital-based palliative care program. New York: Center to Advance Palliative Care; 2004.
2. U.S. House. 101st Congress. H.R. 3299, Omnibus Budget Reconciliation Act of 1989. Available from www.govtrack.us/congress/bills/101/hr3299. Accessed September 28, 2014.
3. U.S. House. 105th Congress. H.R. 2015, Balanced Budget Act of 1997, Public Law 105-33.Available from www.govtrack.us/congress/bills/105/hr2015. Accessed September 28, 2014.
4. U.S. House. 108th Congress. H.R. 1, Medicare Prescription Drug, Improvement, and Modernization Act of 2003, P. L. 108-173. Available from www.gpo.gov/fdsys/pkg/PLAW-108publ173/html/PLAW-108publ173.htm. Accessed September 28, 2014.
5. Centers for Medicare and Medicaid Services, Department of Health and Human Services. Transmittal 15. NPs serving as hospice patient attending physicians. Washington, DC: CMS Manual System; 2007. Available from http://www.cms.gov/Regulations-and-Guidance/Guidance/Transmittals/downloads/R75BP.pdf. Accessed September 28, 2014.
6. Centers for Medicare and Medicaid Services, Department of Health and Human Services. Transmittal 75. Nurse practitioner (NP) services and clinical nurse specialist (CNS) services. Washington, DC: CMS Manual System; 2007. Available from www.cms.gov/Regulations-and-Guidance/Guidance/Transmittals/downloads/R75BP.pdf, Accessed September 28, 2014.
7. Federal Register. Medicare and Medicaid programs: Hospice conditions of participation, Final Rule, 73(109), 2008, pp. 32088–32220. Available from www.gpo.gov/fdsys/pkg/FR-2008-06-05/pdf/08-1305.pdf. Accessed September 28, 2014.
8. Centers for Medicare and Medicaid Services, Department of Health and Human Services. Transmittal 141. New hospice certification requirements and revised conditions of participation (CoPs). Washington, DC: CMS Manual System; 2011.
9. Centers for Medicare and Medicaid Services. What does Medicare Part A cover? 2014. Available from www.medicare.gov/what-medicare-covers/part-a/what-part-a-covers.html. Accessed September 28, 2014.
10. Centers for Medicare and Medicaid Services. What does Medicare Part B cover? 2014. Available from www.medicare.gov/

what-medicare-covers/part-b/what-medicare-part-b-covers.html. Accessed September 28, 2014.

11. Centers for Medicare and Medicaid Services. About Medicare plans. 2014. Available from http://www.medicare.gov/ sign-up-change-plans/medicare-health-plans/medicare-health-plans. html. Accessed September 28, 2014.

12. Centers for Medicare and Medicaid Services. How to get drug coverage. 2014. Available from http://www.medicare.gov/ sign-up-change-plans/get-drug-coverage/get-drug-coverage. html#1360. Accessed September 28, 2014.

13. Centers for Medicare and Medicaid Services. Medicare administrative contractors. 2013. Available from http://www.cms.gov/Medicare/ Medicare-Contracting/Medicare-Administrative-Contractors/ MedicareAdministrativeContractors.htmls. Accessed September 28, 2014.

14. National Consensus Project for Quality Palliative Care. *Clinical Practice Guidelines for Quality Palliative Care*. 3rd ed. Pittsburgh, PA: National Consensus Project; 2013.

15. Centers for Medicare and Medicaid Services, NHIC. Part B. Physician assistant, nurse practitioner, clinical nurse specialist, certified nurse-midwife billing guide. Washington, DC: CMS; 2010.

16. Dahlin C. *A Primer in APRN Reimbursement*. Pittsburgh, PA: Hospice and Palliative Nurses Association; 2015.

17. APRN Consensus Work Group, National Council of State Boards of Nursing APRN Advisory Committee. *Consensus Model for ARPN Regulation: Licensure, Accreditation, Certification, and Education*. 2008. Available from www.nursingworld.org/ ConsensusModelforAPRN. Accessed September 28, 2014.

18. National Council of State Boards of Nursing APRN Advisory Committee. *ARPN Regulation: Licensure, Accreditation, Certification, and Education*. 2008. Available from www.ncsbn.org/Consensus_Model_for_APRN_ Regulation_July_2008.pdf. Accessed September 28, 2014.

19. The Joint Commission. Advanced certification in palliative care. 2011. Available from http://www.jointcommission.org/certification/ palliative_care.aspx. Accessed September 28, 2014.

20. American Nurses Association and Hospice and Palliative Nurses Association. *Palliative Nursing: Scope and Standards – An Essential Resource for Nurses*. 5th ed. Silver Spring, MD: American Nurses Association and Hospice and Palliative Nurses Association; 2014.

21. Hospice and Palliative Nurses Association. *Competencies for the Hospice and Palliative APN*. Pittsburgh, PA: Hospice and Palliative Nurses Association; 2014.

22. Centers for Medicare and Medicaid Services. Medicare claims processing manual, Chapter 12—Physicians/nonphysician practitioners. 2012. Available from http://www.cms.gov/ Regulations-and-Guidance/Guidance/Manuals/downloads/ clm104c12.pdf. Accessed September 28, 2014.

23. Department of Health and Human Services. Evaluation and management services guide. 2010. Available from http://www.cms. gov/Outreach-and-Education/Medicare-Learning-Network-MLN/ MLNProducts/downloads/eval_mgmt_serv_guide-ICN006764.pdf. Accessed September 28, 2014.

24. Centers for Medicare and Medicaid Services, NHIC. J14—A/B MAC. Part B. Physician assistant, nurse practitioner, clinical nurse specialist, and certified nurse-midwife billing guide. Washington, DC: NHIC; 2013.

25. Centers for Medicare and Medicaid Services. Introduction to ICD-10. A guide for clinicians. Washington, DC: eHealth; 2013. Available from http://cms.gov/Medicare/Coding/ICD10/Downloads/ICD-10-Intro-Guide.pdf. Accessed September 28, 2014.

26. Department of Health and Human Services, Centers for Medicare and Medicaid Services. Transitional care management services.Washington, DC: Medicare Learning Network; 2013. Available from http://www.cms.gov/Outreach-and-Education/ Medicare-Learning-Network-MLN/MLNProducts/Downloads/ Transitional-Care-Management-Services-Fact-Sheet-ICN908628.pdf. Accessed September 28, 2014

CHAPTER 5

Data Utilization for the Palliative Advanced Practice Registered Nurse

Marilyn Bookbinder and Debbie Rochester-Gibbons

Key Points

- Various types of data and related terms are used frequently in palliative care. Advanced practice registered nurses (APRNs) should be familiar with the opportunities for, and barriers to, their use.

- APRNs must develop competencies in data to use in U.S. healthcare reform.

- There are many examples of APRNs using data to add more value to their patient care and practices.

Hiding within those mounds of data is knowledge that could change the life of a patient, or change the world.

—Atul Butte, Stanford

Defining Data

Data are plain facts. When data are processed, organized, structured, or presented in a given context to be useful, they are called information. Pieces of information can be used in an analysis of a problem, such as the diagnosis of a health problem. Data are also facts stored and processed by a computer.[1] Data can also be described by type:

- Quantitative data are measurable and can be expressed in statistical form with numbers.

- Qualitative data are narrative or subjective and often describe attitudes, beliefs, and feelings. They are not arrived at by statistical or other quantitative techniques. Rather, the goal is to understand behavior in a natural setting and the perspective of research participants within the context of their everyday life. Methods used for conducting inquiry include interviewing, observation, ethnography, participant observation, and focus groups.

- Research data can be quantitative or qualitative information that is collected, observed, or created for purposes of analysis to produce original research results. Research data are generated for different purposes and through different processes and may be grouped into different categories. Each category of research may require a different type of data management plan.

Defining the types of data and their uses is a huge task. To organize the concepts, we borrowed from others in the field of implementation science, informatics, and biomedical engineering and organized information as "small" and "big" data.[2]

Small data are individual-level pieces of information specific to an individual or circumstance. They are specific and take a microscopic view of an individual or event. One familiar example of small data is the information entered into the electronic health record (EHR) for a new patient admission. This can include the individual's demographics, medical, social, and psychosocial history, findings from physical exams, allergies, and medications.

Big data are patterns of data and information at the population level. The goal of big data is to obtain a macroscopic view of health. Large datasets can help us recognize patterns that are not readily apparent and allow us to go from pieces of data to collective wisdom and knowledge shared by individuals and groups. One example of big data that is high on the radar screen of most APRNs today is the Centers for Medicare and Medicaid Services (CMS)-driven Meaningful Use initiative, described more in the next section. Table 5.1 lists some frequently used terms and phrases associated with data and their definitions.

APRNs Are Poised to Lead Healthcare Reform

Since 2010, two landmark federal initiatives, the Affordable Care Act (ACA) and the CMS-driven Meaningful Use initiative, as well as professional nursing organization imperatives, have poised APRNs in the next decade to maximize their education, scope of practice, and influence to use information wisely for their patients, their profession, and the healthcare industry.

The ACA

The signing of the ACA created enormous pressures on federal, professional, and healthcare organizations to reform and give Americans more access to affordable, quality health insurance and to reduce the growth in healthcare spending in the United States.[3]

Table 5.1 Data Definitions and Related Phrases

Categorical data	Categorical data are qualitative and suited to classification into categories. Further divisible into nominal (names), ordinal (levels of quality, development), and dichotomized (mutually exclusive).
Continuous data	Data that have an infinite number of possible values
Data	Plural of datum. A collection of information or facts processed and interpreted to yield information.
Database	An organized collection of data. A medical database is all the information that exists in the practice at any time.
Data adjustment	For useful results, data often need to be modified before analysis—for example, for age, for sex, or for difficulty or for number of attempts.
Data aggregation	A collection of protected health information used to conduct data analysis relating to the healthcare operations of the entity
Data analysis	Submission of data to statistical analysis; includes sorting into categories and determining relationships between variables
Data capture	A mechanism for collecting specified segments or categories of data from a stream of automatically recorded data, some of which may be irrelevant for the specific purpose
Data processing	The collection of data, processing of the data to obtain usable information, and communication of this usable information
Derived or compiled data	Examples include text and data mining and 3D models.
Diagnostic data	Lists of diagnoses and data of clinical signs, clinical pathology results, and pathology lesions used in making diagnoses
Dimensional data	Numerical or quantitative data. May be explicit and therefore continuous, or grouped into approximate groups (e.g., nearest whole number)—that is, discrete data.
Discrete data	Data that have finite (usually whole integer) values and therefore fall naturally into groups of similar values; opposite of continuous data
e-measurement	The secondary use of electronic data to populate standardized performance measures. The prerequisites include standardized performance measures in an electronic format; clinical information systems that capture structured, coded data; and administrative and clinical workflows that facilitate consistent documentation or capture of the data needed to populate the electronic measures.
Experimental data	Data obtained from lab equipment; often reproducible, but can be expensive (e.g., gene sequences, chromatograms, magnetic field data)
Incidence data	Data related to the occurrence of specific disease incidents
Non-normal data	Data whose frequency distribution is markedly different from that of normal data
Normal data	Data that manifest graphically as a bell-shaped curve distributed symmetrically about the peak value
Observational data	Data captured in real time, usually irreplaceable (e.g., sensor data, survey data, sample data, neurological images)
Ordinal data	A type of data containing limited categories with a ranking from the lowest to the highest (e.g., none, mild, moderate, severe). Subjects placed in order from high to low. For instance, an employer might rank applicants for a job on their professional experience, giving a rank of 1 to the subject who has the least experience, 2 to the next highest, and so on. This rank does not tell us by how much subjects differ.
Paired data	Values that fall normally into pairs and can therefore be expected to vary more between pairs than within pairs
Preexisting data	Data that were in existence before the commencement of a study. Of limited value unless they are exactly the data required, they have been collected adequately, and a group of pre-existing controls with their corresponding data can be identified.
Prevalence data	Disease occurrences are recorded against the size of the population at risk at the time.
Ratio-level data	A higher level of data than the interval level because the ratio has an absolute zero point that we know how to measure. Thus, weight is an example of the ratio scale because it has an absolute zero that we can measure.
Raw data	Data as they are collected, before any calculation, ordering, etc., has been done

Adapted from The Free Dictionary website (http://medical-dictionary.thefreedictionary.com/data)

The Institute of Medicine's landmark *Future of Nursing* report (2010) suggests that the ACA puts consumers back in charge of their healthcare, giving Americans a new "Patient's Bill of Rights" and the stability and flexibility they need to make informed choices about their health and insurance plans. The report describes the positive outcomes from studies of APRNs in delivering safe, high-quality primary care and why healthcare organizations have increased their roles and responsibilities in patient care.[4]

Meaningful Use Guidelines

Another powerful driver for APRNs in the use of data was the American Recovery and Reinvestment Act of 2009 (Recovery Act), including the Health Information Technology for Economic and Clinical Health Act (HITECH Act), which established programs under Medicare and Medicaid to provide incentive payments to eligible professionals, eligible hospitals, and critical access hospitals for the adoption and meaningful use of Certified Electronic

Health Record Technology. As of November 2013, more than 93% of all eligible hospitals had registered to participate in the incentive programs. APRNs are at the heart of this initiative, along with physicians and other providers. Meaningful use guidelines are meant to support those eligible by using the EHR information in a meaningful way to help improve the quality and safety of the nation's healthcare system and its consumers. It can be viewed as a national effort to collect big data to control the cost of healthcare while delivering quality care. Implementation is planned over 5 years. Stage 1 of the EHR incentive program began in 2011, with Stages 2 and 3 to be established by future CMS rules. For more information about meaningful stages and expectations, go to http://www.hrsa.gov/healthit/meaningfuluse/MU%20Stage1%20 CQM/mu.html.

After 2015, Medicare will require that all eligible professionals and hospitals meet meaningful use or they may be subject to a financial penalty. HITECH's incentives and assistance programs seek to improve the health of Americans and the performance of their healthcare system with a focus on five goals:

◆ Improve the quality, safety, and efficiency of care while reducing disparities

◆ Engage patients and families in their care

◆ Promote public and population health

◆ Improve care coordination

◆ Promote the privacy and security of patient information

The new meaningful use standards are changing the way professionals document medical information. To meet the detailed criteria developed by CMS, thorough charting and documentation are essential for everyone involved in patient care. Meaningful use will also affect how providers engage patients and families in care. To do this, APRNs and others will need to approach and treat patients with certain goals in mind, including the following:

◆ **Providers will have a broader view of patient data.** The EHR's interface can offer providers better information about tests, screening tools, or treatments that may have been missed. EHRs can reveal lapses in testing or preventive screenings and alert the provider so that necessary treatments are not overlooked.

◆ **More hands-on patients.** Through patient portals and other online tools, patients will have digital access to their own records, lab results, and medication lists. This means patients will take a more informed and leading role in their own plan of care.

◆ **More collaboration and coordination between providers.** The ultimate goal of EHR use is to provide one, real-time, current picture of a patient's health that can be viewed by providers, hospitals, and clinics across the United States. Having this current information on hand makes it easier for providers to compare treatments and decide what will work best for a particular patient.[5]

Professional Nursing Imperatives Improving Quality

The 2011 report by the American Nurses Association, *Advanced Practice Nursing: The New Age in Health Care*, reminds us of the powerful position of advanced practice nurses to produce revenue and have influence over patient outcomes. Nurse practitioners

(NPs) and clinical nurse specialists (CNSs) are being reimbursed by Medicare, Medicaid, and private insurers and have prescriptive authority in all 50 states. In 22 states and the District of Columbia, NPs can practice independently without physician involvement, and 39% of NPs nationwide have hospital privileges. In 19 recent studies, results confirmed that NPs delivered care equivalent to physician-provided care "and, in some studies, more effective care among selected measures than that provided by physicians." NPs also consistently demonstrated better results for patient follow-up, satisfaction, consultation time, and providing screening, assessment, and counseling.[6-8]

In June 2014, Press Ganey, a recognized leader in performance improvement for nearly 30 years, announced the acquisition of the American Nurses Association's National Database of Nursing Quality Indicators (NDNQI), the leading quality improvement and nurse engagement tool in the United States, managed by the University of Kansas School of Nursing since 2001. Press Ganey, also a vendor for patient satisfaction reporting of the patient experience, is partnering with more than 11,000 healthcare organizations worldwide and 98% of U.S. Magnet-designated hospitals to ultimately improve the overall healthcare experience. Use of NDNQI data strengthens the ability of nurses and leaders in their mission to reduce patient suffering, improve the patient experience, and make improvements on 18 nursing-sensitive measures, including hospital-acquired conditions and adverse events subject to the CMS non-payment rule—such as pressure ulcers, falls, and bloodstream infections. With a robust comparative database, organizations can compare themselves to peer institutions, both nationally and regionally, in key quality areas. NDNQI also measures characteristics of the nursing workforce that have been related to the quality of patient care, such as staffing levels, turnover, and registered nurse education and certification. Organizations contributing to NDNQI have demonstrated improved nursing quality: infection rates decreased by 87% in 2 years; injury fall rates decreased by 17% in 4 years; and hospital-acquired pressure ulcer rates decreased by 24% to 59% in 2 years.[9] Coupled with Press Ganey's broad benchmarking data, and advanced analytics, "the addition of NDNQI in approximately 2,000 hospitals nationwide is the largest provider of unit-level performance data to hospitals, offering those accountable for making changes in structure and process more targeted insights into nursing performance to improve the overall patient experience and outcomes." Nurse leaders claim that this strategic alignment will enhance the power of nursing data, generate even better normative comparisons, and allow for expanded linkages to outcomes.[10]

APRNs in every role, including management, administration, education, informatics, and direct patient care, will move their thinking from volume-based care to value-based care. They will need the ability to understand results from nursing quality indicators and "retain nursing staff to maintain their vital role in new coordinated models of care." For more information, visit www.ndnqi.org.

APRNs are also leading healthcare reform by assuming new executive roles, such as deputy chief information officers, senior nurse informaticists, and nursing informatics executives. These nurse leaders are joining forces to educate, train, coach, and mentor APRNs on how to integrate technologies to manage information and improve healthcare. APRNs can assess their levels of competency in data management and translation to lead and support new models for delivering patient care in all settings. Specific competencies in informatics address the following:

◆ **Education/coaching**: Can APRNs translate technical and scientific health information to meet patients' information and learning needs? Can they assess patient and caregiver educational needs? Can they coach patients and caregivers in positive behavioral change?

◆ **Decision making**: Can APRNs demonstrate information literacy and analytic skills in situations that require complex decision making?

◆ **System design**: To what extent can APRNs contribute to the design of clinical information systems?

◆ **Evaluation**: Can APRNs use technology to evaluate the quality, safety, and efficiency of nursing care?

APRNs who demonstrate the ability to generate revenue and who have the knowledge and skills to use data in leadership, care delivery, informatics, finance, and education will soar in the next decade and lead others to create better (faster and less expensive) workflows and improved patient outcomes. For more about the decades of contributions by advanced practice nurses to informatics, analytics, and the role of translating big data into knowledge and patient outcomes, we refer readers to the Healthcare Research Information website at http://www.ncbi.nlm.nih.gov/pmc/articles/PMC3717442/.

Barriers to Using Data

Several studies have highlighted the barriers facing APRNs when trying to use data as care providers in their daily practice. We will discuss the obstacles they face using research results, information on the Internet, and data needed for decision making in daily clinical practice.

In a systematic review of 63 studies spanning nearly two decades (1991–2009) that was reported in *Implementation Science*, nurse researchers examined the state of knowledge of the validated BARRIERS scale and nurses' use of research and its usefulness to improve practice. They found that barriers were consistent over time and across geographic locations despite varying sample size, response rate, study setting, and the assessment of quality research.

Approximately one-third of the sample included APRN-level positions. The most frequently reported barriers to using research were related to knowledge and skills in research, their setting, and the presentation of the research. Further, nurses reported not having the skills to read research, particularly evaluating the merit and statistical sections, not having the protected time needed at work to read research, and not having the authority to use the findings or support from other colleagues, including physicians, to implement a research-based change.[11]

The researchers concluded that the BARRIERS scale, although reliable as reflected in assessments of internal consistency and identifying general barriers to research utilization, was less useful for planning implementation interventions. They recommend that barriers be identified in real time and be specific to the particular context of implementation and the intended evidence to be translated. Similar results were found in a Magnet-designated community hospital study and its 1,100 nurses. Barriers to using research data included the characteristics of the organization, including lack of protected time and practice authority as the greatest barriers.[12]

In another study, researchers explored the barriers experienced by NPs and other nurses when trying to use the Internet to find best practices. In this smaller purposive sample of 29 practicing nurses and 4 APRNs from general practices in northern England, investigators examined which information sources the nurses used in their daily clinical decision making. Decisions were categorized into seven clinical areas: assessment, diagnosis, intervention, referral, communication, service delivery and organization, and information seeking. The majority of the nurses reported their uncertainty in making decisions about what they read and instead relied on personal experience or simply obtained advice and information from physicians or other colleagues nearby.[13]

Human sources of information were overwhelmingly preferred to text or online resources. Despite encounters with evidence-based resources through continuing professional development, the nurses rarely used them to seek answers to routine clinical questions. In most decisions, nurses were trying to get answers about how to best communicate to patients the risks and benefits associated with various interventions. This study supports the need for expert clinical resources, such as CNSs or specialty-level NPs who can provide information, in "real time" in clinical areas for adult learners.

Reasons cited for not using the Internet included lack of knowledge and skills to use the Internet and computer, lack of time to conduct searches and download the key information from an overwhelming amount of data, and uncertainty about the quality of the information. Findings from these studies support previous nursing research on barriers to using data over the past three decades and concluded that most nurses still lack the knowledge, skill, and time to use evidence in daily practice.

Roles of APRNs and Data Utilization

The Department of Veterans Affairs,[14] the Geisinger Health System,[15] and Kaiser Permanente[16] are recognized healthcare delivery organizations that maximize advanced practice nurses' scope of practice. APRNs in these organizations work in a range of practice settings with exposure to small individual data, specialty databases, and big datasets from national samples. Some exemplary roles are described below.

NPs can provide primary and subspecialty-level care to patients. They might practice independently and collaborate closely with doctors and other healthcare professionals. Together or alone, they are responsible for accurate documentation to ensure patient safety, improved goals, and reimbursement. They perform comprehensive physical examinations, diagnose and manage common health conditions, order diagnostic tests, and prescribe therapeutic medications and treatments. NPs may provide family healthcare as well, or they may limit their practice to a specific population, such as adults, children, or the elderly. NPs, depending on their role, technology environment, and resources, may have access to data at the individual and population levels.

CNSs are experts in a specific area of nursing, such as oncology or cardiology. They can focus on specific patient populations or individual patients. CNSs often provide consultation, leadership, education and management skills in healthcare settings, such as emergency room care. They might be experts in a specific type of problem, such as pain or end-of-life care. Whatever the role, the CNS performs basic nursing practices but with a greater depth of knowledge and skill. Inherent in their role is the translation of research for the education and training of other nurses and patient and family populations. They typically have skills in evaluation and using research to improve quality care and develop evidence-based practices that raise the standard of care for organizations and their processes, interventions, policy, protocols, and research.

As direct care providers, APRNs might focus their use of data in a defined scope of practice, such as geriatrics or palliative care. With support from peers, professional resources, a national computerized patient record system, and collaboration within the framework of interdisciplinary care teams, APRNs in this health model, especially those who are ready to generate revenue and be self-supporting, have exciting potential to lead healthcare reform in the decades ahead.

As healthcare researchers, APRNs conduct research that involves nursing issues and outcomes of care, including patient and family satisfaction with care. Master's prepared nurses have the opportunity to be principal investigators and co-investigators of research projects, as well as translate their findings into practice. As one of the largest research organizations in the United States, the Department of Veterans Affairs, for example, offers funded research opportunities and encourages nurse researchers and clinicians to disseminate their findings in literature and through presentations and publication.

As educators, APRNs have the opportunity to guide the future generation of NPs and CNSs by participating in and leading research through affiliations with nursing schools. APRNs in exemplary organizations can hold university faculty positions and offer leadership as preceptors, and in developing curriculums for observerships, internships, residency and fellowship programs.

As health information technology leaders, APRNs can establish the linkages needed among nurses, informatics, analytics, and patient outcomes. They can improve workflows and help reduce the barriers nurses face in documenting routine care. These linkages are critical to capturing the data needed to populate nursing-sensitive indicators and use health information technology to promote positive outcomes.[17]

As healthcare leaders, APRNs shape policy, facilitate access to healthcare, and influence resource management. Exemplary organizations encourage their leaders to be involved in professional nursing organizations and to share and benchmark data at conferences and other local, regional, and national committees and taskforces. We end this section by offering readers a self-assessment tool that may help to determine areas of proficiency and deficiency and specific learning needs using data (Table 5.2).

Increasing Competencies of APRNs in Data Utilization

The American Association of Colleges of Nursing sets standards for U.S. accredited graduate school curriculums. The association's 2011 report incorporates data utilization exercises into the quality standards that prepare APRNs in nine knowledge and skill areas.[18] Skill areas address how to lead change to improve quality outcomes, advance a culture of excellence through lifelong learning, build and lead collaborative interprofessional care teams,

navigate and integrate care services across the healthcare system, design innovative nursing practices, and translate evidence into practice.

APRNs represent less than 8% of our workforce in hospitals and outpatient and community settings. Given that the average age of U.S. practicing nurses is approximately 50 years, we can assume that most may not have had exposure or training in the process of accessing, reading, translating, and using data to create best practices and improve delivery systems.

The Institute of Medicine's report on the quality areas needed to improve the American healthcare system is over a decade old, yet only minimal improvements in quality and safety have been reported, according to nurse leaders. To boost improvement efforts, the Quality and Safety Education for Nurses initiative was developed to integrate quality and safety competencies into nursing education. Leaders argue that the current challenge is for nurses to move beyond the application of Quality and Safety Education for Nurses competencies to individual patients and families and incorporate systems thinking in quality and safety education and healthcare delivery.[19]

APRNs with administrative support can use financial and administrative data to justify aspects of their APRN role. Figure 5.1 is the outline of a financial proposal for a new program. In Figure 5.2, a new NP created a dashboard of indicators to monitor volume, quality, and safety of a new service. In Figure 5.3, an NP and nurse manager piloted a fast-track program to reduce walk-ins for a rapidly growing chronic pain service. In Figure 5.4, a CNS demonstrated the positive patient outcomes of her Reiki program. Each of these APRNs partnered with a mentor to develop these projects. Mentors for these APRNs were administrators, directors of nursing, peers, and physician collaborators.

The next examples are related to quality concerns voiced by APRNs in both educator and NP inpatient practitioner roles. In the Case Study and Figure 5.5, APRNs piloted two peer review exercises. The case study of individual patient data was reviewed with peers for the purpose of improving the plan of care. An APRN director recognized the need for better comprehensive documentation by NPs caring for palliative patients in the community. Case reviews were done at interdisciplinary team meetings over a 4-month period. Documentation improved, and fewer cases were rejected for reimbursement because of inadequate documentation.

Case Study

Mr. Li was a 65-year-old Chinese-American man, diagnosed a year earlier with lung cancer. The patient has been told he has "lung disease." Despite the fact that his disease was clearly advancing, the family insisted that he not be told of his diagnosis or prognosis. Mr. Li lost 20 lbs. in the previous two months and was having difficulty swallowing. He was in pain and expressed shortness of breath. He had a recent long hospital stay resulting in progressive deconditioning, weakness, and functional decline. He lived with his wife in a second-floor apartment. His two sons were both married and lived in the area. He denied any religious affiliation. The home healthcare team was increasingly frustrated with the fact that Mr. Li was not able to fully participate in decisions about his care. As Mr. Li's disease progressed, he became weaker and unable to move from the bed. When asked how he was feeling, he always

Table 5.2 Self-Assessment of Data Utilization

Data Sources	Assess your level of confidence/competence to:				
Administrative and financial data	Lacking	Improving	Competent	Good	Excellent
1. Review budgets and variance reports	1	2	3	4	5
2. Translate billing reports	1	2	3	4	5
3. Develop a justification for additional staff or new program	1	2	3	4	5
4. Use the computer and software: Excel, Word, PowerPoint, timelines, table of organization	1	2	3	4	5
5. Participate in an informatics group to redesign your EHR	1	2	3	4	5
6. Perform a needs assessment (gap analysis)	1	2	3	4	5
7. Conduct a brainstorming session	1	2	3	4	5
8. Design a workflow	1	2	3	4	5
9. Access policies, procedures, and standards of care	1	2	3	4	5
10. Develop a dashboard for your patient caseload of volume statistics and quality indicators	1	2	3	4	5
11. Develop an evidence-based protocol	1	2	3	4	5
12. Understand CPT coding guidelines/rules (how to bill)	1	2	3	4	5
13. Understand profit-and-loss statements; review a business plan	1	2	3	4	5
14. Manipulate data to look at patterns (by using software or spreadsheets)	1	2	3	4	5
15. Redesign staffing model based on needs, resources, and revenue	1	2	3	4	5
16. Develop a database to capture complaints	1	2	3	4	5
Quality data					
17. Develop a quality improvement study	1	2	3	4	5
18. Read quality reports and develop action plans	1	2	3	4	5
19. Develop a graph or table with data	1	2	3	4	5
20. Participate in a shared governance or magnet committee	1	2	3	4	5
21. Understand best-practice benchmarks and metrics	1	2	3	4	5
22. Interpret patient satisfaction scores and develop an action plan for improvement	1	2	3	4	5
23. Use Survey Monkey™ to gather information and summarize results	1	2	3	4	5
24. Write up a case study for morbidity/mortality meeting	1	2	3	4	5
25. Develop a competency measuring knowledge and skills	1	2	3	4	5
26. Display data in a control or Pareto chart	1	2	3	4	5
Research data					
27. Conduct a literature search	1	2	3	4	5
28. Compile data into graphs or tables	1	2	3	4	5
29. Join a research committee	1	2	3	4	5
30. Participate in a journal club and determine the level of evidence of a research study	1	2	3	4	5
31. Write an abstract on a project with data	1	2	3	4	5
32. Give a presentation displaying data	1	2	3	4	5
33. Evaluate a student's progress using a standardized tool	1	2	3	4	5
34. Participate in peer review	1	2	3	4	5
35. Co-author a manuscript about clinical practice	1	2	3	4	5
36. Critique a research study for an evidence-based practice project	1	2	3	4	5

Financial Summary

Total Program

	Approved Budget	Actual
Revenues (by source)		
I. Salaries and Benefits		
II. OTPS		
III. Overhead		
IV. Equipment		
V. Consultants		
Total		
Explanation of major variances:		

Problem/Issue: A Nurse Manager and Director were asked to explain the financial cost/benefit of a new infusion program.

Methods: A simple summary of key aspects of the program was compiled against dollars budgeted. Variances were discussed in preparation.

Outcome: The financial summary and quality outcomes of the program helped the team explain costs and participate objectively in presenting their business case for the program.

Figure 5.1 Sample program expense sheet

whispered "fine" and denied any symptoms. His wife was tearful about her husband's diminished appetite. She believed he would be cured if only he would "eat" and that he needed to "try harder." The nurse observed the patient experienced difficulty swallowing and potentially aspirated when given soft food. When (through an interpreter) the nurse attempted to explain the distress and risks involved, Mrs. Li appeared unable to understand.

The team identified three options: they could talk to family hospice services, consider inpatient management, or continue with acute care home care services. During a subsequent home visit by the home care nurse and social worker, the home care team

discussed the services that a hospice program could offer the patient and family. The family, patient, and primary medical doctor were agreeable. The home health nurse contacted the nurse at hospice, who was the patient's primary nurse, and shared the care plan with her. The patient transitioned to a hospice program without difficulty. Over the next week, the team worked with the family regarding symptom management and intake of food and fluids. The goals of care were discussed and the family wished to move forward with a palliative care plan. The patient was successfully managed at home with twice-weekly RN visits and weekly social work visits. The patient experienced more shortness of breath and

DASHBOARD														
CORE INDICATORS	JAN	FEB	MAR	APR	MAY	JUN	JUL	AUG	SEPT	OCT	NOV	DEC	TOTAL	Variance YTD 2014 to 2015
Total Visits														
New Pt. Visits														
Follow-up visits														
Occurrences/Incidents														
Discharges														
Complaints														
Patient Satisfaction														
Other														

Problem/Issue: A novice NP starting a new service wanted to prepare a dashboard including volume and quality outcomes for a monthly meeting with Administration.

Methods: Monthly report data are summarized onto the dashboard.

Outcome: The NP expressed feeling more confident when reporting on service statistics and issues needing attention with a supervisor. Trends and changes are reviewed and recognized early. The NP's monthly billing report is also discussed with the administrator. The NP was applauded by the team for her vigilance to quality care and an organized billing approach that generated revenue beyond her salary line. As a result, she was given approval to hire a per diem NP to cover the consistently high-volume days.

Figure 5.2 New consultation service dashboard

told his wife he knew he was dying and wished to die outside of the home. The interdisciplinary team worked with the patient and family to arrange for inpatient hospice. The patient was transferred to inpatient hospice, symptoms were managed, and he died peacefully 48 hours after admission, with the family at his bedside.

The second (Fig 5.5) was a peer review tool piloted by NPs in an Advanced Practice Committee following a review of the literature. The two processes were instrumental in raising the knowledge levels of individuals and a group of practitioners in a specific specialty, working toward advanced certification in palliative care.

Date: _____ Patient: _____

Provider: _____Last Visit: _____

Reason for walk-in:

    1. Out of medications:

    2. Renewal request not ready:

    3. Lost/stolen medications:

    4. Needs prior authorization:

    5. Prescription written incorrectly; medication error:

    6. Early refill:

    7. Appointment canceled by practice:

    8. Patient missed appointment:

    9. Change in medical condition:

    10. Discharged from hospital:

    11. OTHER: _____

Patient pain grade: /10 B/P_____ P_____ RR_____ Sat: (prn) _____

New pain or change in pain: _____

_____

Review of medications: _____

_____

Aberrant behavior: _____

_____

Pertinent physical findings: _____

_____

Assessment: _____

_____

Plan: _____

_____

Problem/Issue: A chronic pain clinic had >10 patients walking in each day for prescription refills, after several days of closing the clinic following a hurricane.

Methods: An NP recommended starting a fast-track clinic to accommodate the patient overflow and avert negative patient outcomes, such as withdrawal symptoms from running out of opioid medication.

Outcome: The NP assessed patients using a brief documentation tool that was scanned into the electronic record. The program was successful and a full-time position was created over time.

Figure 5.3 Fast-track walk-in documentation form: pain management outpatient clinic

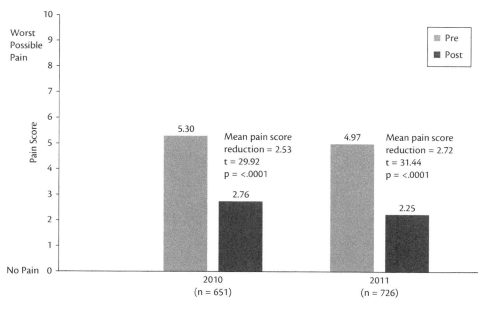

Figure 5.4 Documenting orthopedic patient response to Reiki therapy following surgery

In the next two examples, inpatient pain management NPs learned the value of using two quality tools to increase efficiency and target improvements in patient satisfaction: the Pareto chart and control chart. Using a Pareto chart (Fig 5.6), an NP identified specific patient diagnoses that were consistently associated with high sustained pain (i.e., 3 consecutive days of moderate to severe pain). Sickle cell patients and chronic pain patients were more frequently admitted through the emergency department and referred to the hospitalist team, who then called a pain consultation. The NP developed a standard protocol for patients with these diagnoses entering the emergency department, reducing delays in pain management and increasing patient reports of comfort. In

Practice Setting: _____				
Legend: Y=yes N=no NA=not applicable				
	Patient 1	Patient 2	Patient 3	Patient 4
Date of review				
Subjective: History of present illness, review of systems				
Characteristic and course of complaints				
Significant history (medical/surgical, social, pysch)				
Treatment/alleviating factors				
Objective: Physical exam				
Pertinent physical findings				
Assessment:				
Rationales for differential diagnosis are documented				
Plan of care:				
1. Diagnostic/laboratory tests				
2. Treatment plan				
Purpose: The chart review is a mechanism by which the nurse practitioner, his/her peer nurse practitioner, and the collaborating physician/provider systematically review assessment, diagnosis, and treatment decisions for the purpose of education, patient care quality improvement, and compliance with NYS practice standards. A quarterly review of **4 NP** encounters is completed and kept as a permanent record in the practice area. **Nurse Practitioner:** _____				

Figure 5.5 Sample pilot peer review sheet

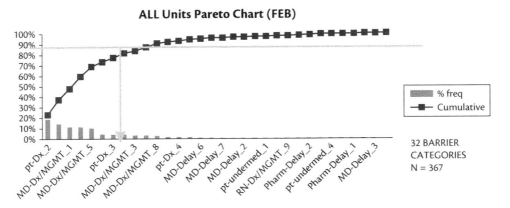

Figure 5.6 Pareto chart

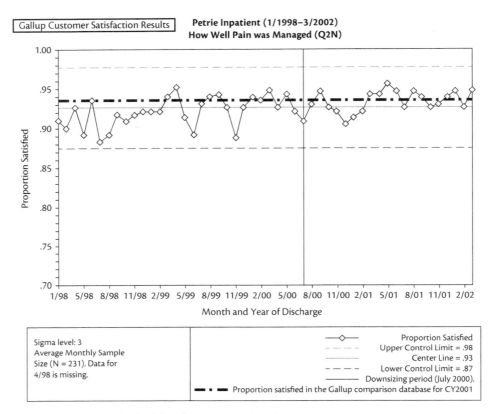

Figure 5.7 Control chart showing statistical control and stability of process: Managing pain

Figure 5.7, a CNS in pain management used control charts from standardized satisfaction surveys to demonstrate a stable process and how well pain was managed, and helped others see the value of using data to support pain protocols and build staff morale.

One way APRNs can increase their knowledge and skills in the translation of research into evidence-based practice (EBP) is to enroll in a class, such as the Johns Hopkins Nursing EBP Course, a self-learning online course. The course is offered in five modules.[20] Module 1 defines what EBP is and why it is important for nurses to learn. Module 2 is the development of questions about a problem in practice and plans for how to get started, how to form your team, and how to get the work done. This is the methods module and helps the learner create the rules and a timeline for each step. Module 3 relates to the evidence. Once the problem question is written, this step helps the learner look for evidence. This module explains what evidence is appropriate and how to find it. In Module 4, the learner summarizes the evidence. Tools are provided to the learner to help evaluate the studies, the strength of the evidence, and what kind of practice change, if any, is appropriate. Module 5, the translation step, is thought to be the hardest part of the EBP process. Learners are guided through how to implement a change in practice and learn the difference between leading change and managing transitions and developing a systematic action planning process.

Healthcare leaders in economics predict that 130% more family nurse practitioners will be needed by 2020. Many will enroll

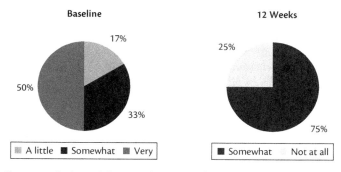

Figure 5.8 Patient satisfaction with treatment for neuropathic pain

in DNP programs to meet professional goals to become independent practitioners. APRNs entering DNP programs will have opportunities to be mentored by faculty in the research and data utilization process as DNP students typically develop EBP projects first hand, using a recognized EBP model. Figures 5.8 and 5.9 illustrate the efforts of two oncology NPs to perform a quality improvement study that would improve the screening, assessment, and treatment of patients with neuropathic pain receiving chemotherapy. The NPs increased their competency in using and conducting research. They developed an algorithm that began with screening by nursing assistants, followed by referral to the NP for a full neuropathic assessment, treatment using evidence-based pharmacology, and follow-up evaluations.

Figure 5.9 describes a nurse manager's efforts to improve patient satisfaction ratings in pain management on her unit. The Pain Service NP, hospitalists, and nurse manager reviewed all patients and their pain data daily, identifying those with high-sustained pain (i.e., patients with pain levels of 5 or greater). Patients having three consecutive days without a significant decrease were primarily chronic pain patients referred to the pain service. Although decreases occurred, the unit continued to have about one-third of patients with moderate to severe pain. This finding increased awareness of all unit staff about making earlier referrals to the pain service, and other approaches to managing the patient's pain flares and attention to the patient's hospital experience.

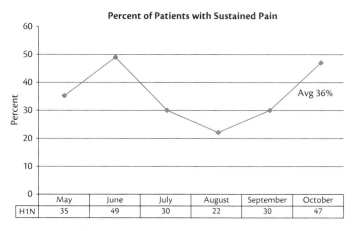

Figure 5.9 Identifying patients with moderate to severe pain for earlier referral to pain management

Future of APRNs and Data Utilization

The Affordable Care Act domino effect is here, with an additional 30 million people with health insurance who will need to access care. The number of primary care providers is inadequate, and APRNs (NPs) will be in demand to help with this problem. Nurse-managed health centers are a well-established community-based model providing primary healthcare services, under the leadership of an advanced practice nurse. They emphasize health education, health promotion, and disease prevention, and their target population is usually the underserved. Unlike "Minute Clinics," which are also led by NPs, these centers are not-for-profit and usually have sliding scales for payment. There are at least 200 of these nurse-managed health centers currently operating in 37 states, with an estimated 2 million patient encounters per year. APRNs of the future will need to have skills in using administrative, financial, quality, and research data to build viable care centers with best practices and economic models that can be sustained.[21]

APRNs of the future will be collaborating with researchers using telemedicine to improve a patient's clinical health status. Telemedicine researchers evaluate information exchanged from one site to another via electronic communications, including applications and services that use two-way video, email, smartphones, wireless tools, and other forms of telecommunications technology. Timothy Landers, RN, CNP, PhD, assistant professor at the Ohio State University and a Robert Wood Johnson Foundation Nurse Faculty Scholar, is a nurse researcher leading the field in testing the Fitbit One and its ability to collect personal health outcomes. This clip-on device is an activity monitor that measures activity level, including steps taken, stairs climbed, distance walked, calories burned, and sleep. The Fitbit smartphone app syncs with a small activity monitor and displays personal activity data. This use of small data will enable patients and clinicians to be more aware of changes in activity and lifestyles.[22] APRNs in direct patient care roles are positioned to use individual patient information to make smart clinical assessments and diagnoses and search for best practices for specific diagnoses. Using the same technology, APRNs in management positions can support data collection at the group level, providing the big data that could be useful in evaluating workplace designs in relationship to the activity levels of workers.

Conclusion

Data are all around you and represent a huge task: they can be your enemy or your friend. Make them your friend. Understand what type of data you need to know about. Learn how to read and translate reports and use the data you are responsible for wisely. Ask your supervisor what your key role is in improving outcomes. Gain competency in those areas and keep improving yourself and those around you.

Pressures to be smarter and more efficient with data will increase. Meaningful use is here to offer hospitals incentives to capture data geared toward promoting quality.

APRNs are expected to be knowledgeable about each component at the various stages. Be the one who knows what is ahead, and be prepared to lead others. Report cards measuring patient satisfaction and other indicators of quality are shaping behavior by forcing providers to "look in the mirror." Drill down the data to the practice level where you can make a difference in scores and create partnerships to move those scores up. Find out what the benchmarks are in your practice area and start a team so that you can compare and improve. The barriers facing APRNs in data utilization have not changed in 20-plus years. APRNs will need new forums for mentorship and education in data utilization in the decades ahead.

References

1. Definition of data by medical dictionary. The Free Dictionary website. Available at http://medical-dictionary.thefreedictionary.com/data Published 2009. Accessed November 3, 2014.

2. NINR's first symptoms research methodologies boot camp focused exclusively on Big Data. National Institute for Nursing Research website. Available at https://www.ninr.nih.gov/newsandinformation/newsandnotes/predoctoral-bigdata-2014. Published September 19, 2014. Accessed November 4, 2014.

3. ObamaCare Facts: Facts on the Affordable Care Act website. Available at http://obamacarefacts.com/obamacare-facts.php Published 2014. Accessed November 3, 2014.

4. The Future of Nursing: Leading Change, Advancing Health. Institute of Medicine website. Available at http://www.iom.edu/Reports/2010/The-Future-of-Nursing-Leading-Change-Advancing-Health.aspx#sthash.mjjduTPj.dpuf. Published October 5, 2010. Accessed November 10, 2014.

5. Meaningful Use initiative. Centers for Medicare & Medicaid Services (CMS) website. Available at http://www.cms.gov/Regulations-and-Guidance/Legislation/EHRIncentivePrograms/Downloads/DataBrief_November2013-.pdf. Published November 2013. Accessed November 3, 2014.

6. Chenoweth D, Martin, N, Pankowski J, et al. A benefit-cost analysis of a worksite nurse practitioner program: First impressions. *J Occup Environmental Med.* 2005; 47(11): 1110–6.

7. Eibner CE, Hussey PS, Ridgely MS, et al. *Controlling Health Care Spending in Massachusetts: An Analysis of Options.* RAND Corporation, August 2009. Available at www.rand.org/pubs/technical_reports/TR733.html. Accessed November 4, 2014.

8. Naylor MD, Kurtzman ET. The role of nurse practitioners in reinventing primary care. *Health Affairs.* 2010; 29(5): 893–9.

9. Turn nursing quality insights into improved patient experiences. The Press Ganey website. Available at http://www.pressganey.com/ourSolutions/performance-and-advanced-analytics/clinical-business-performance/ndnqihttp://journals.lww.com/jncqjournal/toc/2004/01000. Published 2014. Accessed November 14, 2014.

10. Dykes P, Collins S. Building linkages between nursing care and improved patient outcomes: The role of health information technology. *OJIN: The Online Journal of Issues in Nursing.* September 30, 2013; 18(3).

11. Kajermo KN, Boström AM, Thompson D. The BARRIERS scale—the barriers to research utilization scale: A systematic review. *Implementation Science.* 2010; 5: 32. doi: 10.1186/1748-5908-5-32.

12. Atkinson M, Turkel M, Cashy J. Overcoming barriers to research in a magnet community hospital. *J Nurs Care Qual.* 2008; 23(4): 362–8.

13. McCaughan D, Thompson CA, Cullum NA, Sheldon TA, Raynor P. Nurse practitioner and practice nurses' use of research information in clinical decision making: qualitative findings from a national study. *Family Practice.* 2005; 22: 490–7.

14. Stony Brook Helps Veterans Become Nurses. The Robert Wood Johnson Foundation website. Available at http://www.rwjf.org/en/culture-of-health/2014/11/stony_brook_helpsve.html. Published November 11, 2014. Accessed November 16, 2014.

15. Northwest Patients to Gain Easy Access to Clinicians Notes. The Robert Wood Johnson Foundation website. Available at http://www.rwjf.org/en/library/articles-and-news/2014/04/northwest-patients-gain-access-to-clinicians-notes.html. Published April 8, 2014. Accessed November 4, 2014.

16. Kaiser Permanente and UCSF Add Substantial Genetic, Health Information to NIH Online Database. The Robert Wood Johnson Foundation website. Available at https://www.ucsf.edu/news/2014/02/112161/kaiser-permanente-and-ucsf-add-substantial-genetic-health-information-nih-online. Published February 16, 2014. Accessed November 4, 2014.

17. Cipriano PF. The future of nursing and health IT: The quality elixir. *Nurs Econ.* 2011; 29(5): 286–289.

18. The Essentials of Master's Education in Nursing. The American Association of Colleges of Nursing website. Available at http://www.aacn.nche.edu/education-resources/MastersEssentials11.pdf. Published March 21, 2011. Accessed November 16, 2014.

19. Dolansky MA, Moore SM. Quality and safety education for nurses (QSEN): The key is systems thinking. *OJIN: The Online Journal of Issues in Nursing.* September 30, 2013; 18(3).

20. JHN Evidence-Based Practice Course. The Institute for Johns Hopkins Nursing website. Available at http://www.hopkinsmedicine.org/institute_nursing/continuing_education/ebp/ebp_course_description.html Published 2014. Accessed November 16, 2014.

21. Kovner C. Walani S. Initiative on the future of nursing: Nurse managed health centers. Available at http://www.thefutureofnursing.org/resource/detail/nurse-managed-health-centers-nmhcs

22. Landers T. Big Data and the Great Challenges of Health and Medicine. The Robert Wood Johnson Foundation website. http://www.rwjf.org/en/blogs/human-capital-blog/2013/05/big_data_and_thegre.html. Published May 20, 2013. Accessed November 16, 2014.

PART TWO

The Palliative Advanced Practice Registered Nurse Across Healthcare Settings

The Palliative Advanced Practice Registered Nurse in the Acute Care Setting

CHAPTER 6

Palliative Care in the Emergency Department

Angela Starkweather

Key Points

- The role of the palliative advanced practice registered nurse (APRN) in the Emergency Department (ED) incorporates expert provision of care that addresses the physical, psychological, emotional, and spiritual needs of patients with life-limiting illness and their family members.

- The ED often serves as a port of entry to palliative care services for patients with chronic life-limiting disease and individuals with complex symptoms and/or care coordination, as well as people at the end-of-life.

- Models of palliative care in the ED may incorporate hospital-based palliative care team consultations, ED-based palliative APRN champions, and partnerships with external agencies that provide palliative care/hospice services.

- The palliative APRN can use systematic methods to identify patients with the greatest need for palliative care services or to initiate consultation/referral to palliative care in the ED setting.

- The palliative APRN has an important role in ED and telephonic communication because of the critical nature and timing of conversations that influence patient and family interactions with the healthcare team and ED palliative care outcomes.

Introduction

This chapter outlines the role of the palliative APRN in the emergency department (ED) and highlights the integration of palliative care in the ED setting as well as common barriers to implementation. Various models that may be used are described, along with strategies to operationalize the provision of palliative care to patients in the ED. Methods to identify patients at the greatest need for palliative care and the evaluation of palliative care services are discussed, along with guidelines for delivering notification of death by telephone. Finally, this chapter offers a case study that demonstrates the important role of the palliative APRN in the ED as well as approaches that positively influence patient and family interactions with the healthcare team and directly contribute to quality ED palliative care outcomes.

The goal of emergency medicine has traditionally focused on preserving life by providing rapid resuscitation and stabilization of acutely presenting health conditions or injuries. However, many patients present to the ED with life-limiting disease and/or injuries that necessitate an alignment of the clinician's prognostic evaluation, the patient's values, and realistic goals of care. When management strategies need to shift the focus from cure to comfort and symptom management and/or life-prolonging approaches are deemed to be medically futile, palliative care can be initiated in order to relieve suffering and provide the means for the most dignified and comfortable dying experience as possible. Palliative care recognizes death as an inevitable process and transforms the focus of care to providing comfort and addressing the needs of patients and families.[1]

Palliative care encompasses the physical, psychological, emotional, and spiritual needs of patients and their family members from diagnosis to cure or death from a life-threatening disease. Core services of palliative care have been described as (1) including a holistic assessment and management strategies provided by a team of individuals to address patient and family needs, (2) promoting proactive patient–family communication that fosters patient-centered decisions, (3) providing assessment of patient and family variables that affect disposition, and (4) offering support for families after a patient's death.

The palliative APRN has an important role in promoting care that is aligned with patient wishes and preferences in the ED setting. Major challenges to healthcare professionals in the ED include balancing the goal to cure against the context of life-limiting disease/injuries and incorporating physical, psychological, emotional, and spiritual needs in the provision of ED care. The palliative APRN can fill these gaps in care and address the multiple challenges to palliative care implementation that are frequently encountered in the ED setting as well as other areas of healthcare. Given the demands of making healthcare decisions in the ED, palliative APRNs can play an instrumental role in ensuring that patients and families are fully informed and understand the prognosis and its implications for management options; they can also foster a plan of care that is guided by the patient's values.

The Role of the Palliative APRN in the ED

As defined by the Hospice and Palliative Credentialing Center, hospice and palliative nursing practice is the "provision of nursing care for the patient and family, with emphasis on their physical, psychological, emotional and spiritual needs when experiencing a life-limiting illness and through bereavement."[2] Palliative APRNs hold a unique body of knowledge regarding the provision of palliative care as delineated by the specialty competencies.[3] The role of the palliative APRN in the ED can be operationalized using the competency domains and areas of expertise.

Specific to the ED setting, the palliative APRN plays a major role in identifying patients with palliative care needs. Unlike other settings in which the diagnosis is known and the plan of care is clear, patients arriving to the ED are often confronted with options of undergoing a range of diagnostic tests and procedures before the net benefit can be considered regarding the patient/family goals of care, life expectancy, or improvement in quality of life. The palliative APRN can play an instrumental role in eliciting information from the patient and family that can inform decisions regarding the workup and plan of care in the ED. Palliative APRNs facilitate decisions that are aligned with the patient's values in the context of life-limiting disease/injury as well as patient and family wishes and preferences when cure is no longer possible.

The unique perspective of the palliative APRN also provides a foundation for advancing palliative care in the ED setting. The traditional goals of ED care focused on the provision of curative treatments. When confronted with a life-limiting disease or injury, the palliative APRN guides the delivery of patient-centered care. The palliative APRN's assessment of the physical, psychological, emotional, and spiritual needs of the patient and family can have dramatic implications for the course of care provided. The role of the palliative APRN in the ED setting incorporates a process of negotiation among healthcare professionals, the patient, and family members to define realistic goals of care in the context of the patient's wishes and preferences.

A critically important role and prerequisite skill for aligning the goals of care with patient and family wishes and preferences is initiating difficult conversations. Palliative APRNs have exquisite skill in eliciting information from patients and family members as well as guiding crucial conversations that can inform the provision of care in the ED. The ED setting may be the first place in which the patient's prognosis is fully understood by the patient and family. Assisting the patient and family as they encounter limitations in life-preserving measures and the possibility or reality of death is a major role of the palliative APRN in the ED setting.

Coordination of care is another major role of the palliative APRN in the ED. This role incorporates navigating the healthcare system and accessing resources for the patient and family that support palliative care. Care transitions represent one of the most significant challenges to continuity of care and increase the risk of readmission. Ensuring that all providers involved in the care of the patient are informed of the palliative care plan and making certain that adequate resources are provided to address the trajectory of declining health status, distressing symptoms, and caregiver needs are important aspects in the palliative APRN's coordination of care.

The ED as a Gateway to Palliative Care

As many patients with life-limiting illness spend months or years in a chronic disease state, the ED frequently manages urgent issues for patients and families that arise during the disease trajectory or as they are receiving palliative or end-of-life care.[4] When patients decline or approach end-of-life, symptoms can change rapidly, requiring immediate evaluation and intervention.[5] Without adequate preparation and supplies, symptoms such as pain, dyspnea, and/or nausea and vomiting may become difficult to manage at home, in an assisted living facility, or in an outpatient setting. Even for patients who have clear goals of care, symptoms can become unmanageable and families often need support for their loved one's physical and psychological distress. The ED is often the only place that can provide immediate access to medical evaluation and treatment, particularly during non-business hours.

In addition to managing the urgent needs of patients who are already receiving palliative care, EDs serve as a critical gateway for identifying patients who would benefit from palliative care services.[6] This is especially true for patients who are at the end-of-life, when the need for care coordination is the greatest, the patient's symptom burden is escalating, and there is a high level of family and/or caregiver distress. There has been an increasing recognition of the need to integrate palliative care strategies in the ED because care decisions initiated in this setting determine the subsequent course of treatment.[7] Although aggressive stabilization strategies may be initiated when the patient arrives in the ED, once the prognosis becomes clear and it is evident that stabilization efforts will not increase the potential of recovery, a discussion needs to take place concerning the patient's values in light of impending and unpreventable death. These discussions will inform decisions on whether to continue with life-prolonging measures so that family members can gather or to immediately implement strategies for comfort at the end-of-life.[8] The ability to have these discussions in the ED environment is quite challenging, however, due to the rapid pace of care and the limited information available about the patient's pre-emergency condition, prognosis, and care coordination, as well as contextual issues, such as whether the decline was expected or unexpected, and/or agreement on the course of care by family members.

The palliative APRN can facilitate communication among healthcare providers, patients, and family members regarding realistic goals of care in the context of life-limiting disease/injury. Palliative APRNs promote patient-centered care by presenting management options that are informed by patients' wishes and preferences regarding their care at the end-of-life. Palliative care consultation in the ED has been shown to reduce distressing symptoms, increase patient and family satisfaction, and decrease costs of care.[9] Since hospital-based palliative care consultation typically occurs more than a week into a patient's hospital stay, there has been a great interest in advancing the role of the palliative APRN in the ED through direct care and consultation services. Palliative APRNs in the ED can play an instrumental role in designing systems to identify patients who need palliative care as well as integrating palliative services in the ED, where major decisions regarding the goals of care are made.

Barriers to Providing Palliative Care in the ED

Inadequate palliative care staffing and coverage have been found to be major barriers for providing palliative care in the ED.[8] Efforts to establish sustainable models of palliative care delivery in the ED have been emerging to address this issue. Employing full-time palliative APRNs to provide direct care in the ED or using hospital-based palliative APRNs to provide consultation are two ways to increase access to palliative care services in the ED setting.

Although there are many good reasons to integrate palliative care in the provision of ED services, several barriers to implementation have been noted, including provider education, communication, environment, and personal beliefs.[8] While the integration of palliative care services in the ED can be challenging, there are resources available to assist in developing and strengthening clinicians' skills and reducing system issues.

Lack of education and training of physicians, APRNs, and nursing staff has been a fundamental barrier for implementing palliative care in ED settings. However, various nursing organizations have stepped up to improve the situation for APRNs, including the Education on Palliative and End-of-Life Care Project,[10] the End-of-Life Nursing Education Consortium, and the Initiative for Pediatric Palliative Care.[11] Curricula are also available through webinars, online modules, videos, and conferences, as well as through continuing education and self-study materials.[12] The palliative APRN can play a key role in disseminating palliative care education in the ED setting and can help design institutional standards of care and outcomes for palliative care as well as policies, procedures, and protocols for successful implementation of palliative care services.

Communication in the ED can be challenging due to lack of privacy, the patient's impaired decision-making capacity, incomplete medical records or lack of access to records, and inability to contact the patient's primary care provider or family/surrogate decision maker. Communicating a grave prognosis or change in the patient's condition can be difficult due to time constraints, lack of patient and/or family understanding of the diagnosis, prognosis, or treatment options, and lack of space or time for family meetings. Palliative APRNs may lead these conversations using their unique skills for eliciting key information about patient wishes and preferences, initiating difficult conversations regarding the patient's prognosis, and negotiating realistic goals of care among healthcare providers, patients, and family members.

Environmental constraints can also impede communication and the provision of palliative care services. The ED environment is often fast-paced, with loud noises and a steady stream of personnel, patients, and families. Providing a quieter and more controlled environment may promote dialogue and create a stronger sense of shared decision making. Palliative APRNs can play an instrumental role in assisting the patient and family to understand the implications of the prognostic information, realistic goals of care, and options in the provision of care. The presence of the palliative APRN through this process and in coordinating care can help to meet the psychological, emotional, and spiritual needs of the family in the ED environment.

The personal beliefs of the provider may be a barrier to providing palliative care. Emergency providers may see palliative care as incongruent with their overall mission and scope of practice. Medicolegal concerns may also be a barrier: defensive medicine and decision making based on doing the most possible in order to avoid litigation have been a longstanding trend in emergency medicine. Providers may be unprepared to provide palliative care or may lack access to palliative care services or consultation.[8] To directly address these issues, there are more palliative APRNs certified in advanced hospice and palliative nursing moving into the ED who can serve as champions of palliative care services in the ED setting. Palliative APRNs in the ED can play a major role in providing direct patient care, designing education and training for other healthcare providers, and implementing strategies to advance palliative care in the ED. In addition, palliative medicine is now an official subspecialty of the American Board of Emergency Medicine, so there will likely be less resistance by providers in viewing palliative care as an essential aspect of emergency services.

Models of Palliative Care Delivery in the ED

In response to the growing number of patients with advanced illness cared for in the ED, several health systems have initiated programs to deliver ED-based palliative care, consultation, and/or coordination. There are typically three types: ED-based consultation programs initiated by the inpatient (hospital-based) palliative care team, services initiated by palliative care champions in the ED, such as the palliative APRN, and ED partnerships with hospice providers.[1]

Hospital-based palliative care teams routinely cover ED consultations, and the ED may provide a significant source of outpatient referrals or inpatient admissions to the palliative care team and/or unit. However, with increasing palliative care consultations throughout the hospital and time constraints in providing care on the inpatient side, ensuring timely consultation in the ED can be challenging. Regardless, patient management through palliative care services has been shown to decrease the number of ED visits.[13] Billing and administrative data support the fact that ED-based palliative care consultation decreases hospital length of stay and costs for those who are admitted to and die in the hospital.[14]

A greater number of hospice and palliative nurse champions in the ED are becoming available in response to the recognized need, in part because an increasing number of palliative APRNs are moving to the ED setting. An added benefit of having ED-based palliative APRNs is the ability to identify patients who may need palliative care as they arrive in the ED, so that crucial conversations about the goals of care can take place early on. Education in palliative care practice is necessary so that uniform access to palliative care services can be provided in the ED. As more clinicians and healthcare systems are taking the opportunity to become adept at meeting the needs of palliative care patients in the ED, it is anticipated that there will be greater coordination of care. Palliative APRNs in the ED setting can play an instrumental role in advancing palliative care education and strengthening systems for the provision of palliative care in the ED, as well as in coordination of care and tracking palliative care outcomes.

ED partnerships with hospice providers can also provide a system for increasing access to palliative care services. When patients are identified in the ED as requiring end-of-life care, the palliative APRN can initiate referral and transfer to a hospice facility or hospice services.[15] Coordination of care can be easier to implement when a partnership is established between providers and institutions. An important competency of palliative APRNs is building systems and resources to ensure quality care during transitions and to support the patient and family while making these difficult decisions and through the process of bereavement.

Identifying Patients Who Need Palliative Care in the ED

One of the major challenges to efficient implementation of palliative care services in the ED is identifying patients early in the patient encounter. Patients at high risk for needing palliative care can be identified through triggers or high-risk characteristics. Palliative APRNs may be responsible for devising such triggers in the electronic health record as well as educating triage nurses and emergency medical service personnel on appropriate assignment to palliative care champions in the ED. Triggers for palliative care consultation are listed in Table 6.1 and may include elderly patients with life-limiting conditions, such as advanced dementia, severe congestive heart failure, chronic obstructive pulmonary disease, advanced malignancy, and/or AIDS with at least moderate functional status limitations.[16] Additional criteria have been found to be applicable in identifying patients in need of palliative care, such as having recent losses in activities of daily living, high symptom distress, poor functional status, and high levels of caregiver burden.[17] Questions on these topics may be incorporated as part of the triage process to assist in identifying patients who need palliative care services and to inform assignment to the ED-based palliative APRN.

When these factors are present on ED admission, a palliative care consultation may be beneficial. In addition, triggers may be embedded in the electronic health record to automatically ask the provider if a palliative care consultation is necessary. Other triggers or prognostic indicators may include the Karnofsky Performance Scale, Palliative Performance Scale (PPS), Palliative Prognostic Score (PaP), or Palliative Prognostic Index (PPI).[18] These indicators can be used to consult palliative care services as well as initiate case management to assist in coordination of care.[19]

In addition, the Center to Advance Palliative Care developed a primary and secondary list of indicators that can be used to screen for the need for palliative consultation services both on admission to the ED and for patients already admitted to the hospital.[20] The primary list entails the life-limiting conditions described above and loss of function, as well as multiple, frequent admissions, high physical and/or psychological symptom severity for 24 to 48 hours, and complex care requirements. This checklist provides a framework for supporting the need for palliative care or consultation and may promote more timely involvement so that the care received is congruent with the patient's values. Coordinating the ED system with triggers or indicators of the need for palliative care can be a major role of the palliative APRN and can help drive the delivery of palliative care in the ED setting.

Delivery of Palliative Care in the ED

Palliative APRNs play a vital role in the early recognition of critically ill patients requiring palliative care in the ED because the trajectory of resuscitation and stabilization using invasive diagnostic or treatment procedures as well as inpatient hospitalization is often set in the ED. Immediately upon the patient's presenting to the ED with a life-threatening emergency, full resuscitative efforts occur unless the patient rejects treatment or an advance directive is in place. When resuscitative efforts cannot stabilize the patient's condition and offer virtually no chance of clinical benefit, prolonged survival, or quality-of-life improvement, the palliative APRN and family/surrogate decision maker should decide whether to make the transition from curative to palliative treatment. In a patient with advanced illness who is unlikely to benefit, the palliative APRN should address the goals of care before initiating aggressive interventions.

APRNs play a vital role in facilitating communication regarding the patient's prognosis, patient and family wishes and preferences, and realistic goals of care in the ED. By following the steps in Box 6. 1, he or she can promote communication and decision making for patients with acute devastating events who are near the end-of-life. This process starts with determination of the patient's decision-making capacity, identification of surrogates, and interpretation of advance directives.[21] In addition, communication to empower the patient, family, or surrogate decision maker at the end-of-life should include the following:[22]

1. Assess the family/surrogate decision maker's understanding of what is happening to the family member.

2. Provide an honest view of the patient's prognosis.

3. Elicit the family/surrogate decision maker's best judgment of the patient's values regarding end-of-life decisions.

Table 6.1 Triggers for Identifying Patients Who Need Palliative/End-of-Life Care

Indicator	Characteristics
Potentially life-limiting or life-threatening condition	Advanced dementia, severe congestive heart failure, chronic obstructive pulmonary disease, advanced malignancy, AIDS with at least moderate functional status limitations
Frequent admissions	More than one admission for same condition within several months or increasing frequency
Presentation due to difficult-to-manage physical or psychological symptoms	Moderate to severe symptom intensity/distress for more than 24–48 hours
Complex care requirements	Functional dependence, complex home support, high level of caregiver burden
Failure to thrive	Decline in function, feeding intolerance, or unintended decline in weight
Karnofsky Performance Scale	Performance status as predictor of survival
Palliative Performance Scale (PPS)	Predicts approximate 6-month survival
Palliative Prognostic Score (PaP)	Predicts 30-day mortality
Palliative Prognostic Index (PPI)	Predicts <3-week mortality

Box 6.1 Steps of Communication in Palliative Care/End-of-Life

Decision-making capacity, surrogates, and advance directives

1. Determine decision-making capacity of the patient.

2. Identify the legal surrogate decision maker.

3. Elicit patient values as expressed in completed advance directives.

Transition from curative treatment to palliative/end-of-life care

1. Determine patient's/surrogate's understanding of prognosis, limitations of curative treatment, and expected goals of care.

2. Convey provider's understanding of patient's condition, prognosis, and treatment options with recommendation.

3. Share decisions regarding withdrawing/withholding resuscitative efforts, using available resources to address patient/family physiological, psychological, social, and spiritual needs.

4. Consider options for organ donation.

5. Revise goals of treatment as necessary.

Adapted from Limehouse WE, Feeser R, Bookman KJ, Derse A. A model for emergency department end-of-life communications after acute devastating events-Part II: Moving from resuscitative to end-of-life or palliative treatment. *Acad Emerg Med*. 2012; 19: 1300–8.

4. Communicate medical information in small increments using understandable language.

5. Build trust and make decisions with the family that incorporate the patient's values, beliefs, and preferences in determining the goals of care.

When the goals of care shift from curative treatment to comfort measures, addressing symptom management becomes paramount. APRNs play a vital role in this process. First, they can make sure the patient and family are prepared. They can ensure that symptom management strategies are used and anticipatory guidance is provided regarding expected symptoms and stages of dying. These educational topics are critical for reducing unnecessary ED visits. Education and planning should include the patient, family members, and other caregivers as well as the primary care and specialty providers involved in the patient's care. Clear instructions should be provided about accessing care when necessary. Communication should also take place between the palliative care team and the primary care provider and on-call provider regarding palliative care/end-of-life management and goals of care in case a subsequent ED visit is inevitable.

Evaluation of Palliative Care in the ED

The evaluation of palliative care services may involve operational, clinical, and patient/family satisfaction indicators (Table 6.2). Operational indicators are those that affect the operational aspects of providing palliative care in the ED. These include the number of palliative care consultations and referrals, the response time of the palliative care team, and the number of clinicians who are certified in the specialty of palliative care.

Clinical indicators represent actions carried out in the clinical setting that incorporate palliative measures. These include the number of patients screened for palliative care needs, documentation of advance directives, end-of-life decisions, and communication with patients and family concerning palliative/end-of-life care.

Patient and family satisfaction indicators are subjective assessments of how well the palliative care team addressed palliative care needs and the overall delivery of palliative care. These indicators may include the level of care provided to address communication and decision making, symptom management, and end-of-life support. Acquiring information from each of these realms is important to inform the quality of palliative care delivery from an organizational, clinician, and individual patient/family level. The APRN may play a role in creating such assessments, initiating their use, following up with patients and families, or evaluating and reporting the data.

Telephonic Communication—Notification of Death

Communicating the death of a family member is a difficult skill, particularly for providers with limited interactions with the patient or family. Although it is usually preferable to notify the family in person, APRNs must weigh the benefits of truthfulness against the risk of potential harm resulting from abrupt disclosure of the bad news. Factors to consider in making this decision include whether the death was expected or not, how well the provider knows the patient and the family, the relationship of the contact person to the patient, the anticipated emotional reaction of the contact person based on prior information, whether the contact person will be alone when receiving the information, the contact person's level of understanding, and the distance, availability of transport, and time of day.[23] When the decision is made to make a notification of death by telephone, the call should be made as soon as possible following the death.

There are several key steps for the APRN to follow. First, after positively identifying the patient and confirming death, obtain relevant information about the patient (name, age, gender, patient identity numbers, and circumstances of death). Second, establish the relationship of the contact person to the deceased patient; obtain the full name, address, and telephone numbers of the person(s) who need to be informed from the chart and/or nursing staff. Third, find a quiet or private area with a phone and thoroughly review the information to be conveyed. When making the phone call, follow the steps listed in Table 6.3 to ensure best practice.[23,24]

Case Study

Mrs. Casey was a 52-year-old woman found unconscious at home by her husband. She was transported to the ED via ambulance and remains unresponsive. En route, the paramedics intubated her and provided basic life support, noting that both pupils were sluggish and her heart monitor was showing multiple paroxysmal ventricular contractions (PVCs). When she arrived at the ED, she immediately received a brain computed tomography (CT) scan and labs.

The CT revealed a massive intracerebral hemorrhage—a devastating neurological injury in which no hope of recovery is possible. Her husband was at the bedside and, upon questioning, he stated that his wife had high blood pressure and frequent migraines but was otherwise healthy. The neurosurgeon on call provided a grim prognosis and signed off on the case. The palliative APRN, Andrea, was called to provide support to the husband.

Without decision-making capacity, Mrs. Casey's surrogate decision maker was her husband. Andrea's initial priority was to ensure that Mr. Casey understood his wife's condition, her prognosis, and the treatment options available. Andrea appropriately explained that while emergency medical treatments were keeping her alive at this time, his wife would not survive this injury and any further interventions will only prolong her dying. Specifically, Andrea explained that there were two directions: (1) sustaining life through artificial means is a short-term measure until brain death or cardiovascular arrest occurs or (2) discontinuing life-prolonging therapies so that comfort measures can be instituted during the progression to a natural death. Mr. Casey said that his wife's greatest fear was being in a coma and that she would not want to live in a way in which she could not care for herself.

The husband recalled watching a television program with his wife recently that showed cardiopulmonary resuscitation. After watching the program, he and his wife had a discussion about what they would want if there was clearly no chance of recovery from illness or injury. At the time, his wife had stated that she hoped he would be able to let her go since she was certain she would be going to a better place rather than having to live out a life that was dependent on everyone else.

There was no advance directive present in the chart and the husband did not recall his wife completing an advance directive document. However, Mr. Casey's remarks regarding his wife's wishes and preferences provided adequate information to suggest that she would have made the decision to withdraw life-sustaining measures.

At this point, the husband asked if he should call his two sons to come to the hospital as they were college students living in different areas of the state. Recognizing that Mrs. Casey would face imminent death upon withdrawal of life-sustaining medical treatment, the APRN directed the focus of care to support the family. While immediate withdrawal of mechanical ventilation would have avoided any further suffering and use of resources that would not contribute to the recovery of the patient, this approach did not

Table 6.2 Metrics for Informing Quality Outcomes in ED Palliative Care

Metric Type	Parameters
Operational	Number of palliative care/hospice consultations/referrals
	Time from call for consultation to documented consultation
	Discharge status/disposition
	% palliative care patients returning to ED within 30 days
	% palliative care patients readmitted to hospital within 30 days
	Mean/median length of stay in ED
	% of patients admitted to palliative care services/unit
	Number of board-certified palliative care providers
	Hospital direct costs
Clinical	% of patients screened for need of palliative care services
	% of patients with advance directives in the EMR
	% of patients for whom the healthcare decision maker is documented in the EMR
	% of patients with documented pain assessment on presentation
	% of patients prescribed opioids with bowel regimen on discharge
	% of patient families with documented offer of spiritual support after ED death
	% of patient caregivers screened for caregiver strain
	% of patients with documented family meeting
	% of patients with documented family contact
Patient/family satisfaction	% of patients reporting excellent level of satisfaction with palliative care services/coordination
	% of patients reporting excellent pain/symptom management
	% of patients discharged from ED who reported they were informed about their condition/prognosis/treatment options
	% of surrogates/families who reported excellent end-of-life care after ED death
	% of patient families who perceived that the management decisions were congruent with the patient's values

Adapted from Quest T, Herr S, Lamba S, Weissman D, the IPAL-EM Advisory Board. Demonstrations of clinical initiatives to improve palliative care in the emergency department: A report from the IPAL-EM initiative. *Ann Emerg Med.* 2013; 61: 661–7.

Table 6.3 Steps for Telephonic Communication

Determine next of kin as listed in the electronic health record or other source and ask an identifying question.	Identify yourself and ask to speak to the contact person indicated in the chart. If that person is not available, ask the identity of the person you are talking to and his or her relationship to the patient.
	Avoid responding to any direct questions until you have verified the identity of the person to whom you are speaking.
	Do not give death notification to minor children.
	If you reach an answering machine or voice mail, only leave specific contact information for the family to call back. If you are unable to make contact within 1 to 2 hours, contact a hospital representative (e.g., social worker) to assist you in locating family or others.
Determine what the contact person knows about the patient's illness/injury.	Speak clearly and slowly, allowing time for questions.
	If you do not have a prior relationship with the person you are speaking with, ask what he or she knows about the patient's condition.
	"What has the team (in some places APRNs are the clinicians) told you about _____'s condition?"
Provide a warning shot.	"I'm afraid I have some bad news."
	Find out where the person is and if there is anyone with him or her.
Use clear and direct language, avoiding medical jargon.	"I'm sorry, _____has just died." Use the word "died" or "dead." Other terms, such as "expired," "passed away," or "didn't make it," can be misinterpreted.
Assess the person's emotional response.	Provide time for the person to respond.
Ask the family if they would like to come to the hospital to view the body.	If the family chooses to come to see the body, arrange to meet with them personally when they arrive. If you are unable, make arrangements for a colleague such as a social worker or chaplain to meet them.
	Provide contact information for the clinical team member who can meet with them and answer questions about the patient's death and other administrative issues.
Ask if you can contact anyone else for them.	"Is there anyone else that you'd like me to contact about _____'s death?"

Adapted from End of Life/Palliative Care Educational Resource Center; Fast Facts #76 & #77: Telephone Notification of Death—Part 1 & 2. 2nd ed.

provide time for the family to say their last good-byes and deal with the psychological and emotional aspects of the unexpected death of their family member, nor time to discuss potential organ procurement and donation with the husband, which required following appropriate protocols.

In this scenario of an imminent fatal outcome, the ethical values of beneficence and nonmaleficence extend to the patient as well as the patient's family. Confronted with an unexpected fatal event, it is often unreasonable to expect a grieving family to make immediate decisions. However, Andrea promoted a treatment plan that would allow the patient's family time to be present with her during the dying process.

Andrea discussed the pros and cons of having the patient's sons see their mother in this condition and, together, Mr. Casey and Andrea decided that allowing her sons to see that all possible measures have been taken would provide emotional comfort and closure for them. Andrea offered to call Mr. Casey's sons, but he insisted that he wanted to communicate with them directly and make sure that they have the means to travel to the hospital. Andrea then offered information on the next steps. This includes the dying process, either in the ED or perhaps transfer to a medical unit. After the discussion, the plan was created with the husband to continue mechanical ventilation until after the sons arrived and had time with their mother; however, if cardiac arrest occurred before they arrive, decompressions will not be initiated.

In addition, the husband was informed that since the patient had a catastrophic brain injury and required ventilation, the local organ procurement organization was contacted as part of the hospital procedures. ED staff left discussion of organ donation to a trained designated requestor or the organ procurement organization representative, which depends on the state.

The husband was very decisive about his wife wanting to donate her organs, and her wishes were further indicated on her driver's license. The patient's sons arrived and they both agreed that their mother would want to proceed with organ donation, as she had mentioned this on several occasions. She told the story of her childhood friend who had died at an early age because she required a heart transplant and a donor was not available in time. The family members expressed their comfort in knowing that their mother's last act was one of giving, something she would have wanted. The family members said their last good-byes to their wife and mother before she was transferred to the intensive care unit for organ procurement.

This case demonstrates the vital role of the APRN in the ED. It also illustrates the decision-making process regarding palliative care/end-of-life care in a patient with an acute event. Advance directives were not available to help inform decisions, but the husband had previously discussed situations such as living in a coma and being incapacitated as well as whether his wife would want cardiopulmonary resuscitation when facing a terminal prognosis.

Although not all scenarios are as clear-cut as this one, the APRN has a vital role in initiating such conversations in the ED and determining advance care planning. Often the patient's prognosis may not be clear until more invasive measures have taken place, which makes it challenging for the APRN to make the transition from the goals of cure to relieving suffering and providing comfort in death. In other situations, families may not agree with the goals of care, thus requiring lengthy discussions between the APRN and the family. The scenario also demonstrates the process of shared decision making between the provider and family. Once the prognosis is clear and the family understands the prognosis, this process can become much easier. However, establishing trust is imperative. Demonstrating that decisions will be made based on what the patient and family need, rather than the provider's goals, can take time. The APRN can serve as a consistent clinician in these discussions. See Chapter 38, Introducing Palliative Care; Chapter 39, Advance Care Planning; and Chapter 41, Communication at Time of Death for further information.

Conclusion

The ED is an important setting for the initiation of palliative care. The quickly changing status of patients makes access to palliative services an important element of care. Moreover, communication is different from other departments, as often patients present without family members. The palliative APRN has a significant role in identifying patients who need palliative care, assessing the patient's physical, psychological, emotional and spiritual needs, initiating difficult conversations, and coordinating care.

Palliative APRNs are experts in designing and implementing system-based standardized methods for advancing palliative care services in settings such as the ED. Working with the interprofessional team, the palliative APRN may be the leader in developing triggers for recognizing palliative care needs in ED patients. This process can make the system of triage and referral more efficient so that crucial conversations can take place early in the ED visit. The palliative APRN can initiate difficult conversations and negotiate realistic goals of care among the patient, family, and other providers involved in the patient's care, a process that often takes time to build trust and constant presence as the patient and family work through difficult decisions.

Using a holistic assessment of the patient and family, the palliative APRN offers a unique perspective in the ED that is focused on patient-centered care and congruence between the goals of care and the patient's wishes and preferences. Coordination of palliative care is also a major role of the palliative APRN in the ED, which is critical for ensuring quality and safety throughout care transitions. The palliative APRN also has expertise in designing outcomes for system improvement using quality indicators to evaluate how palliative care is being used and implemented in the ED. This is a critically important process to achieve the best use of palliative care services and to improve the ways it is implemented in the ED setting.

References

1. Quest T, Herr S, Lamba S, Weissman D, the IPAL-EM Advisory Board. Demonstrations of clinical initiatives to improve palliative care in the emergency department: A report from the IPAL-EM initiative. *Ann Emerg Med.* 2013; 61: 661–7.
2. Hospice and Palliative Credentialing Center. *ACHPN Candidate Handbook.* Available at http://hpna.advancingexpertcare.org/wp-content/uploads/2014/12/HPCC-ACHPN-Handbook-January-2015_CM4.pdf. Accessed January 1, 2015.
3. Hospice and Palliative Nurses Association. C Dahlin, ed. *Competencies for the Hospice and Palliative Advanced Practice Nurse.* 2nd ed. Pittsburgh, PA: Hospice and Palliative Nurses Association; 2014.
4. Wu FM, Newman JM, Lasher A, Brody AA. Effects of initiating palliative care consultation in the emergency department on inpatient length of stay. *J Palliative Care.* 2013; 16(11): 1362–7.
5. Wallace EM, Cooney MC, Conroy M, Twomey F. Why do palliative care patients present to the emergency department? Avoidable or unavoidable? *Am J Hospice Palliative Care.* 2012; 30(3): 253–6.
6. Beynon T, Gomes B, Murtagh FEM, et al. How common are palliative care needs among older people who die in the emergency department? *Emerg Med.* 2011; 28: 491–5.
7. Grudzen CR, Stone SC, Morrison RS. The palliative care model for emergency department patients with advanced illness. *J Palliative Care.* 2011; 14(8): 945–50.
8. DeVader TE, Albrecht R, Reiter M. Initiating palliative care in the emergency department. *J Emerg Med.* 2012; 43(5): 803–10.
9. Lamba S, Nagurka R, Zielinski A, Scott SR. Palliative care provision in the emergency department: Barriers reported by emergency physicians. *J Palliative Med.* 2013; 16(2): 143–7.
10. Emanuel LL, Quest T, eds. *The EPEC Project. The Education in Palliative and End-of-life Care for Emergency Medicine (EPEC-EM) curriculum.* Chicago, IL: Northwestern University; 2008.
11. Chan G, Bryant NE, Lamba S, Weissman DE, Quest TE, Todd KH, IPAL-EM Project. *Clinical Practice Guidelines: A Technical Assistance Resource from the IPAL-EM Project.* Available at http://ipal-live.capc.stackop.com/downloads/ipal-em-clinical-practiceguidelines.pdf. Accessed August 1, 2014.
12. Shearer FM, Rogers IR, Monterosso L, Ross-Adjie G, Rogers JR. Understanding emergency department staff need and perceptions in the provision of palliative care. *Emerg Med Austral.* 2014; 26: 249–55.
13. Lawson BJ, Burge FI, McIntyre P, Field S, Maxwell D. Can the introduction of an integrated service model to an existing comprehensive palliative care service impact emergency department visits among enrolled patients? *J Palliative Med.* 2009; 12(3): 245–52.
14. Grudzen CR, Richardson LD, Major-Monfried H, Kanarian B, Ortiz JM, Morrison S. Hospital administrators' views on barriers and opportunities to delivering palliative care in the emergency department. *Ann Emerg Med.* 2013; 61: 654–60.
15. Lamba S, Quest TE. Hospice care and the emergency department: Rules, regulations and referrals. *Ann Emerg Med.* 2011; 57: 282–90.
16. Glajchen M, Lawson R, Homel P, DeSandre P, Todd KH. A rapid two-stage screening protocol for palliative care in the emergency department: A quality improvement initiative. *J Pain Symptom Manag.* 2011; 42(5): 657–60.
17. Richards CT, Gisondi MA, Chang C, et al. Palliative care symptom assessment for patients with cancer in the emergency department: Validation of the screen for palliative and end-of-life care needs in the emergency department instrument. *J Palliative Care.* 2011; 14(6): 757–64.
18. Ouchi K, Wu M, Medairos R, et al. Initiating palliative care consults for advanced dementia patients in the emergency department. *J Palliative Care Med.* 2014; 17(3): 346–50.
19. O'Mahoney S, Blank A, Simpson J, et al. Preliminary report of palliative care and case management project in an emergency department for chronically ill elderly patients. *J Urban Health.* 2008; 85: 443–51.
20. Weissman DE, Meier DE. Identifying patients in need of a palliative care assessment in the hospital setting: A consensus report from the Center to Advance Palliative Care. *J Palliat Med.* 2011; 14(1): 17–23.
21. Limehouse WE, Feeser R, Bookman KJ, Derse AA. A model for emergency department end-of-life communications after acute devastating events—Part I: Decision-making capacity, surrogates and advance directives. *Acad Emerg Med.* 2012; 19(9): 1061–5.
22. Limehouse WE, Feeser R, Bookman KJ, Derse A. A model for emergency department end-of-life communications after acute devastating events—Part II: Moving from resuscitative to end-of-life or palliative treatment. *Acad Emerg Med.* 2012; 19: 1300–8.
23. Osias RR, Pomerantz DH, Bresnilver JH. Telephone notification of death—Part 1. 2nd ed. *Fast Facts and Concepts* 2006;76.
24. Osias RR, Pomerantz DH, Bresnilver JM. Telephone notification of death—Part 2. 2nd ed. *Fast Facts and Concepts* 2006;77.

CHAPTER 7

Palliative Care in the Intensive Care Unit Setting

Clareen Wiencek

Key Points

- Palliative care is now an expected component of high-quality care in the intensive care unit (ICU).

- The palliative advanced practice registered nurse (APRN) has the ideal skill set to influence clinical outcomes in the intensive care unit (ICU).

- The palliative APRN needs to acquire knowledge about pain and symptom management, resuscitation outcomes, withdrawal and withholding of life-sustaining treatments, and quality improvement activities in the ICU.

Case Study

The palliative APRN responded to a consult for an 87-year-old female patient, Mrs. S., who had suffered a massive intracerebral hemorrhage. The patient had multiple comorbidities but had been living at home with her grandson, John, prior to the acute event. Mrs. S. was minimally responsive, intubated and mechanically ventilated, and on vasopressor support. She was a full code as a default due to the absence of an advance directive. The APRN was consulted to help with goals of care and was informed that the patient's grandson was unreasonable and abrasive. After an examination of the patient, the palliative APRN met with the intensivist and John. She started the meeting by asking John what he understood about his grandmother's condition and what the doctors had told him, and affirming John's obvious love and devotion for his grandmother. In addition, the APRN asked what a typical "good day" looked like for his grandmother and what activities gave her joy. During that meeting, she began to establish trust with John and began to deescalate some of the aggressive behavior. The APRN assured him that the ICU team was doing everything they could to support his grandmother and did not press for a change in code status during the first encounter. Over several days, trust continued to increase but the patient's condition did not improve. The team and John agreed that more aggressive intervention would be more harmful than helpful to his grandmother and agreed to a DNR order. The APRN helped John to consider his grandmother's quality of life and dignity and to begin to think about possible withdrawal of the ventilator rather than performing a tracheostomy and continued support in light of grave neurological outcomes.

The palliative APRN made recommendations on how to manage the patient's agitation and sedation while on the ventilator. Over one weekend, John contacted the APRN and told her that he was ready to withdraw the ventilator. He shared that his grandmother had come to him in a dream and asked that he let her go. The palliative APRN worked with the intensivist and bedside nurse to allow John time with his grandmother and then premedicated the patient prior to extubation and removal of the ventilator. Spiritual care was offered and taken prior to the withdrawal. Mrs. S. died peacefully 4 hours later with her grandson at her side in the ICU. John expressed gratitude to the palliative APRN and ICU team for the compassionate care of his beloved grandmother. His memory of a good death was preserved through the skilled delivery of palliative care.

Introduction

The early ICUs of the 1950s were opened to care for the sickest patients and to concentrate the knowledge and skills of the nurses and physicians who worked there. The aim was rescue and survival of the most critical patients in a more efficient and effective physical space.[1] This mission has not changed over the past 60 years, but technological and medical advances have transformed those early units into modern, high-tech centers within acute care hospitals. At first glance, palliative care may seem an incongruous fit for the ICU due to the fundamental difference between the ICU goals of cure and rescue and the palliative goals of quality of life and symptom management. However, after a decade of explosive growth in acute care-based palliative care programs and considerable expansion of the evidence base, palliative care in the ICU setting is no longer a novelty but an essential component of high-quality care.[2,3] Most critical care professional societies have issued position statements, protocols, or clinical practice guidelines that delineate the how and why of integrating palliative care in the care of the critically ill.[4–7] The Center to Advance Palliative Care (CAPC) launched the Improve Palliative Care in the ICU (IPAL-ICU) initiative in 2010, and it is an excellent resource for quality improvement.[8] Given the ongoing shift in acceptance and viewpoints, the palliative APRN is ideally suited to deliver high-quality outcomes for critically ill patients and their families through the full integration of palliative care in the ICU setting, whether in the integrative or consultative role.[8]

All critically ill patients and their families have palliative care needs based on the National Consensus Project definition:

> Palliative care means patient- and family-centered care that optimizes quality of life by anticipating, preventing and treating suffering. Palliative care throughout the continuum of illness involves addressing physical, intellectual, emotional, social, and spiritual needs and to facilitate patient autonomy, access to information, and choice.[9]

This more expansive definition, broadening beyond just end-of-life care, has yet to be widely accepted in the ICU setting. However, all critically ill patients and their families have needs consistent with this definition: for goal-oriented care that is aligned with their goals, preferences, and values; for the management and relief of distressing symptoms related to the underlying critical illness and to the procedures and interventions inherent in that treatment; for regular and effective communication between the critical care team and the patient and surrogate decision makers, so common in the ICU setting; and for deliberate planning for care transitions.[2]

The commonality of palliative needs in the critically ill and the palliative interventions to meet those needs can be driven by APRNs when they are allowed to practice to the full scope of their education, licensure, and certification. Full scope of practice was just one of the changes called for by the Institute of Medicine's 2010 report, *The Future of Nursing: Leading Change, Advancing Health.*[10] The palliative APRN, when practicing to full scope, can improve care for those patients who will survive the life-threatening episode and for those who will die in the ICU. Although palliative care is broader than just terminal care, death is common in the ICU: one in five Americans die in the ICU or during an ICU-related admission.[11]

The findings of the landmark SUPPORT[12] study (Study to Understand Prognoses and Preferences for Outcomes and Risks of Treatments) and the 1997 IOM[13] report *Approaching Death: Improving Care at the End of Life* revealed that Americans do not die well. The SUPPORT investigators found that 50% of the more than 9,000 seriously ill patients enrolled in the study died with unrelieved pain and experienced an undesirable ICU admission in the last week prior to death.[12] Multiple studies since have reported limitations in the care of the critically ill. These discrepancies include unrelieved pain and other symptoms, inadequate communication and goal setting, divergence in goals of treatment, clinician burnout and moral distress, and inefficient resource utilization.[5,14] Since death is common in the ICU and usually occurs after a course of aggressive, life-sustaining interventions, experts assert that an ICU admission is actually a therapeutic trial, and only when it fails do providers, patients, and families entertain a change in goals from survival at all costs to palliation.[5] It is time to change that paradigm and fully integrate palliative care from time of admission. The palliative APRN can lead this transformation.

Although death remains common in the ICU setting, especially in medical units, the site of death is shifting. Teno and colleagues analyzed the care of Medicare beneficiaries in 2000, 2005, and 2009.[15] Between 1989 and 2007, home deaths increased from 15% to 24%. However, the rate of ICU use in the last month of life increased from 24.3% to 29.2% in 2009. It is commonly agreed that hospitals are not the preferred place of death, as patients strongly prefer to return home, but only after the full trial of advanced, aggressive medical technologies, such as those found in the ICU. As noted by Rothman, "in the mid-20th century death and dying was removed and rendered invisible once through hospitalization and again through the intimidating locked doors of the ICU."[1(p 2459)] The locked doors have opened for most ICUs, partially thanks to the American Association of Critical-Care Nurses (AACN)'s efforts to promote open visitation,[16] and it is now time for palliative care to be fully present.

Palliative care APRNs must take up the challenge presented by the mix of technology widely accepted in today's ICUs and the expanding evidence base that the critically ill and their families not only could benefit from palliative care but should expect it. Also, it is the greater awareness that palliative care does have a place in the ICU that has led prominent stakeholders to call for more systematic integration. These stakeholders include the Joint Commission, the Institute for Healthcare Improvement, the Critical Care Societies Collaborative, and the Institute of Medicine.[14] Toward the goal of optimizing the palliative APRN's impact in the ICU, this chapter focuses on four dimensions: pain and symptom management, communication, withdrawal of life-sustaining treatments and resuscitation outcomes, and quality improvement activities. The case study at the beginning of the chapter shows how the APRN can affect outcomes for ICU patients.

Pain and Symptom Management

Pain: Prevalence and Clinical Practice Guidelines

Pain is a common symptom in the critically ill. Despite over 20 years of research and quantification of the pain experience, the incidence of significant pain is still 50% or higher in both medical and surgical ICU patients, and preemptive analgesia for painful procedures is only used 20% of the time in ICU patients.[17–20] The seminal work by Puntillo[17] in 1990 was one of the first studies to describe the pain experience of critically ill patients, and the multicenter Thunder Project II provided strong evidence of the high incidence, up to 80%, of procedural pain in this population and the inadequate management and relief.[21] Such common procedures as turning, tracheal suctioning, line insertion, and dressing changes were found to be associated with significant levels of pain.[21] The stress response evoked by unrelieved pain in the critically ill can lead to impaired tissue perfusion, hyperglycemia, lipolysis, and impaired wound healing, thereby increasing not only patient discomfort but risk of prolonged morbidity.[19]

The evidence that most critically ill patients experience pain and that pain continues to be undermanaged led to the development of the "Clinical Practice Guidelines for the Management of Pain, Agitation and Delirium (PAD) in Adult Patients in the Intensive Care Unit" by the American College of Critical Care Medicine, the consultative body of the Society of Critical Care Medicine.[19] These 2013 guidelines were issued to define best practices for optimizing management of pain, agitation, and delirium in the critically ill; however, the authors report that only 60% of ICUs in the United States have implemented PAD guidelines, and compliance to such protocols remains low.

There are several reasons behind the continued prevalence of suboptimal pain management in the critically ill. One of the main reasons is the conflict in goals between rescue and comfort.[19] Many ICU nurses and providers, especially those in training, may be concerned about and therefore reluctant to use medications, such as opioids, that could impact hemodynamic stability, threaten end-organ perfusion and function, or induce oversedation and respiratory depression.[19,22,23] Second, critical care practitioners may not have the experience or knowledge about the use of opioids and adjuvant medications, including routes other than the parenteral route widely used in the ICU setting.[14,19,23] Third, there is a growing number of evidence-based management bundles and checklists used in the ICU setting that may complicate the delicate balance between treatment goals and quality of life for the patient.[19] Finally, the preponderance of nonverbal patients in the ICU limits the gold standard of patient self-report, resulting in the use of surrogate reports or interpretations and therefore potentially leading to a reluctance to administer pain medications in doses adequate for relief.[24] The palliative APRN practicing in the ICU must be aware of and accommodate to these realities of pain management, especially when in the consultative role. Table 7.1 lists the major recommendations from the PAD guidelines for pain management, and Chapter 23 provides a full discussion of pain management principles.

Pain and Special Patient Populations: Nonverbal Patients

The prevalence of critically ill patients unable to self-report pain is high due to a multitude of factors that include severity of illness, neurological dysfunction or injury, intentional sedation, metabolic disturbances, and vital organ dysfunction. This prevalence poses a challenge to optimal pain management for the palliative APRN. Since these patients cannot self-report, the APRN must use standardized scales and multiple measures on which to base assessment and management.[19,23,24] The palliative APRN should assess for behavioral signs of pain, such as grimacing, furrowed brow, restlessness, and delirium. Generally, vital signs as physiologic indicators are not sensitive for discriminating pain from other distressing triggers.[24] No single strategy will be sufficient unto itself, and the APRN must be aware that vital signs that are within normal ranges do not indicate an absence of pain.[24] In fact, the APRN should assume that pain is present for those on neuromuscular blockade and recommend appropriate analgesic therapy.[24]

Clinical practice guidelines call for a hierarchy of pain assessment techniques in the adult, nonverbal patient: self-report, ruling out potential causes of pain, observing patient behaviors, using surrogate reporting, and attempting an analgesic trial.[24] A therapeutic trial is indicated if a pathologic or procedural reason exists for pain. For mild to moderate pain, a non-opioid analgesic should be given initially; if the patient's behaviors improve, continue the regimen. If the pain-related behaviors do not improve, the APRN should order a trial dose of a short-acting opioid and observe the effect. If there is no change in behavioral indicators of pain, the dose should be increased by 25% to 50% and the nurse should observe the effect.[24]

The palliative APRN may use proxy reports of pain as a basis for management in the nonverbal patient. Proxy reports remain controversial; families often overestimate pain.[23] Even so, family members can provide valuable information, such as a history of chronic back pain, that can influence pain management outcomes.

Multiple scales are used to assess pain in the nonverbal adult population, but two scales are more commonly used and have sound psychometrics: the Behavioral Pain Scale (BPS) and the

Table 7.1 The PAD Guidelines for Adult ICU Patients: Pain Management

Recommendation	Level of Evidence
Pain should be routinely monitored in all ICU patients.	+1B
The Behavioral Pain Scale (BPS) and the Critical-Care Pain Observation Tool (CPOT) are the most valid and reliable scales for patients unable to self-report.	B
Vital signs should not be used alone for pain assessment.	-2C
Preemptive analgesia or nonpharmacologic interventions should be administered prior to chest tube removal.	+1C
Preemptive analgesia and/or nonpharmacologic interventions may be administered to alleviate pain associated with invasive and potentially painful procedures in the ICU.	+2C
Intravenous (IV) opioids should be considered as first-line medications to treat non-neuropathic pain in critically ill patients.	+1C
All available IV opioids, at equianalgesic doses, are equally effective.	C
Non-opioid analgesics should be considered to decrease the amount of opioids.	+2C
Consider enterally administered gabapentin or carbamazepine in addition to IV opioids for neuropathic pain.	+1A
Consider thoracic epidural anesthesia/analgesia for patients undergoing abdominal aortic aneurysm surgery.	+1B
Suggest thoracic epidural analgesia for patients with traumatic rib fractures.	+2B
No recommendation due to lack of evidence for regional analgesia over systemic analgesia in medical ICU patients.	0

[19] Adapted from Barr, Fraser, Puntillo et al (2013).

Key:

Quality of evidence: High (level A), Moderate (level B), Low/very low (C)

Strength of recommendation: Strong (1) or weak (2)

For or against an intervention: For (+) or against (-)

Critical-Care Pain Observation Tool (CPOT). These two scales are the most reliable and valid behavioral pain scales for assessing and monitoring pain in nonverbal medical, surgical, or trauma ICU patients and should be used at standardized intervals.[19,23,24]

Pain and Special Patient Populations: Renal and Hepatic Failure

It is estimated that up to 25% of all ICU patients present with or develop acute renal failure, depending on the setting and the definition.[25] Although evidence is limited by the lack of common definition, the RIFLE criteria have improved classification and standardization: **R** (risk of injury), **I** (injury), **F** (failure), **L** (sustained loss), and **E** (end-stage features). In addition to patients with acute renal failure, chronic kidney disease is prevalent in the ICU setting. It has been reported that chronic pain affects 50% of hemodialysis patients.[26,27]

If opioids are used by the palliative APRN to manage pain in this population, certain medications must be avoided or used with caution. However, there is a lack of hard pharmacokinetic data that support specific treatment guidelines.[26] Meperidine, codeine, dextropropoxyphene (propoxyphene), and morphine should be avoided due to toxicity and/or the accumulation of active, nondialyzable metabolites.[26,27] Oxycodone and hydromorphone should be used with caution. Oxycodone undergoes hepatic metabolism, but 19% is excreted unchanged in the urine. Hydromorphone should be used prudently in patients who are not on dialysis due to the rapid accumulation of its active metabolite.[26] Fentanyl and methadone are considered to be the safest opioids for patients in renal failure.[26,27] Broadbent and colleagues recommended the following guide for dosing of opioids in patients with renal failure: normal dosing if creatinine clearance is more than 50 mL/min, 75% of normal dosing if creatinine clearance is 10 to 50 mL/min, and 50% of baseline dose if creatinine clearance is less than 10 mL/min.[27]

The critically ill patient with hepatic failure also presents challenges in terms of optimal pain and symptom management. The greater the hepatic dysfunction, the greater the impairment in drug metabolism and removal.[28,29] The efficiency of drug removal by the liver depends on blood flow, plasma protein binding, and hepatic enzymes. Advanced liver dysfunction alters the effects of many medications as a result of changes in pharmacokinetics, abnormal accumulation of the free drug in plasma, and end-organ response. The palliative APRN should be aware that the majority of pain medications are largely metabolized by the liver and that opioid clearance is reduced and drug bioavailability increased in hepatic failure. Fentanyl is the preferred opioid in this population.[30] Given the variability in response, the right dose and interval of any opioid are those tolerated by the patient. Dosing should be based on close and frequent assessment of the patient's response.[30] Box 7.1 provides guidelines on how to optimize pain management in patients with hepatic failure.[28,30]

Symptom Management: Agitation and Delirium

Agitation is common in critically ill patients.[19] The palliative APRN should assess for possible causes of agitation when developing the treatment plan, such as pain, delirium, hypoxemia, or withdrawal from alcohol or opioids. Strong evidence now exists that prolonged deep sedation is associated with adverse outcomes and that light sedation from which the patient can be aroused and

can follow simple commands is preferred.[31,32] Indeed, most ICUs have established treatment protocols with this goal. Due to the growing evidence that benzodiazepine use is strongly correlated with delirium in the acutely ill patient, patterns of use are changing. Currently, the dominant medications used for sedation of the critically ill patient are midazolam and propofol (Diprivan), with decreasing use of lorazepam, rare use of diazepam and barbiturates, and growing use of dexmedetomidine (Precedex).[19]

The palliative APRN caring for patients in the ICU should be familiar with the pharmacokinetics and side effects of propofol and dexmedetomidine due to their common use in this setting. Propofol is an intravenous sedative that binds to multiple central nervous system receptors to block neural impulses. It has sedative, hypnotic, anxiolytic, antiemetic, and anticonvulsant properties. Propofol does not possess any analgesic properties, so analgesics must be co-administered. This drug causes dose-dependent respiratory depression and hypotension but has rapid redistribution and a short duration, making it an ideal adjuvant for mechanical ventilator-related sedation that allows for daily sedation interruption protocols.[19,33] Dexmedetomidine is a selective alpha-receptor agonist with sedative, analgesic or opioid-sparing, and sympatholytic properties that was approved in the United States over 10 years ago for short-term sedation (<24 hours) at a maximum dose of 0.7 micrograms/kg/hour. Its pattern of sedation differs significantly from other sedatives as patients are more easily arousable, but its onset is also quick (in about 15 minutes). Dexmedetomidine produces minimal respiratory depression and therefore is the only sedative approved in the United States for administration in non-intubated patients. However, patients' ventilator and oxygenation status must still be closely monitored as the drug can cause loss of oropharyngeal muscle tone, putting the patient at risk of airway obstruction. The most common side effects of dexmedetomidine are hypotension and bradycardia. The opioid-sparing effects of this sedative may reduce opioid requirements in the critically ill patient.[19]

Agitation can be distressing for the critically ill patient, family members, and the team. Preferred agents in the ICU have changed over the past decade based on research, and strong evidence now supports the use of subjective sedation scales at regular intervals.

Box 7.1 Guidelines to Optimize Pain Management in Patients with Hepatic Failure

1. Reduce long-term acetaminophen dosing to 2 to 3 g/day.

2. A one-time acetaminophen dose of 3 to 4 g/day may be safe.

3. Use reduced doses of NSAIDs and opioids in patients with cirrhosis.

4. Avoid using NSAIDs in patients with compensated or decompensated cirrhosis due to the risk of inducing acute renal failure from prostaglandin inhibition.

5. Avoid using opioids in patients with a history of encephalopathy.

6. Avoid using codeine and meperidine at all times.

7. Decrease hydromorphone dose by 50% of normal dose and administer it at prolonged dosing intervals.

The most valid and reliable sedation assessment tools for adult ICU patients are the Richmond Agitation-Sedation Scale (RASS) and the Sedation-Agitation Scale (SAS).[19] These two scales demonstrated a high degree of interrater reliability and had robust methodology and sampling method. Table 7.2 gives the complete recommendations from the American College of Critical Care Medicine's PAD guidelines on how to manage agitation and delirium.

Delirium is also highly prevalent in critically ill patients, affecting up to 80% of mechanically ventilated patients.[19] Strong evidence now exists that even one episode of delirium is an independent predictor of adverse clinical outcomes, such as increased mortality, increased hospital length of stay, higher costs of care, and long-term cognitive impairment.[34–36] Delirium is a syndrome associated with a change or fluctuation in mental status, inattention, and either disorganized thinking or an altered level of consciousness.[19] Hypoactive delirium and hyperactive delirium exist, with hypoactive being more common, and ICU clinicians often underestimate its clinical presence.[19] Formerly referred to as ICU psychosis, it is no longer considered a benign condition in the ICU or acute care setting.

The ideal treatment for delirium is prevention and the use of standardized screening. The palliative APRN should be familiar with the Confusion Assessment Method for the ICU (CAM-ICU) and the Intensive Care Delirium Screening Checklist (ICDSC), which are the most valid and reliable instruments for the screening and monitoring of delirium in ICU patients.[19] Moderate-quality evidence exists that routine monitoring for delirium is feasible and that monitoring compliance rates exceed 90%.[19] There is

mixed or a lack of evidence that haloperidol is effective as a preventive measure. Full recommendations can be found in Table 7.2.

Symptom Management: Dyspnea

Dyspnea is a prevalent symptom in the critically ill population.[37] Puntillo and other members of the IPAL-ICU Advisory Board conducted a comprehensive literature review related to palliation of pain, dyspnea, and thirst.[37] Optimal treatment for dyspnea was found to be identification and amelioration of the underlying condition, patient positioning, and, sometimes, supplemental oxygen. As for other symptoms, the use of a standardized symptom assessment scale is correlated with better outcomes. The Respiratory Distress Observation Scale is the only reported behavioral scale for assessment of dyspnea. A systematic review by Lorenz and colleagues focused on the management of dyspnea at end-of-life.[38] Strong evidence supported the use of beta agonists and opioids in patients with chronic obstructive pulmonary disease and weak evidence supported the use of opioids to relieve dyspnea in patients with cancer.

Several options are available for the treatment of dyspnea in end-of-life patients. Systemic opioids, either oral or parenteral, are considered first-line medications. Opioid receptors are found in the respiratory centers of the brain and peripherally in the respiratory tract and lung tissue. Clinicians have suggested that nebulized opioids would result in less systemic absorption, leading to a safer clinical profile. However, robust trials and systematic reviews have found these to be no more effective than placebo.[39] Guidelines from the American College of Chest Physicians recommend the use of systemic opioids for relief of dyspnea.[40] A robust

Table 7.2 PAD Guidelines for Adult ICU Patients: Agitation and Delirium

Recommendation	Level of Evidence
Light level of sedation is associated with improved clinical outcomes.	B
Use a light level of sedation unless clinically contraindicated.	+1B
The RASS and SAS are the most reliable and valid sedation assessment tools.	B
Sedation strategies using non-benzodiazepines (propofol or dexmedetomidine) may be preferred over benzodiazepines to improve clinical outcomes in mechanically ventilated adult ICU patients.	+2B
Delirium is associated with increased mortality and prolonged length of stay.	A
Use routine monitoring of delirium in the ICU patient.	+1B
The CAM-ICU and the ICDSC are the most reliable and valid delirium monitoring tools.	B
Preexisting dementia, history of hypertension or alcoholism, and high severity of illness are significantly associated with delirium in the ICU patient.	B
Perform early mobilization of adult ICU patients to reduce the incidence and duration of delirium.	+1B
Do not suggest that either haloperidol or atypical antipsychotics be administered to prevent delirium.	-2C
No recommendation for using a combined pharmacologic and nonpharmacologic prevention protocol	0,C
There is no published evidence that treatment with haloperidol reduces the duration of delirium in adult ICU patients.	No evidence
Atypical antipsychotics may reduce the duration of delirium.	C

[19] Adapted from Barr, Fraser, Puntillo et al (2013).

Key:

Quality of evidence: High (level A), Moderate (level B), Low/very low (C)

Strength of recommendation: Strong (1) or weak (2)

For or against an intervention: For (+) or against (-)

Cochrane Review concluded that evidence does not support the routine use of benzodiazepines in patients with dyspnea without coexisting anxiety.[41] However, the treatment of underlying conditions that exacerbate dyspnea, such as edema or inflammation, can provide benefit if treated with glucocorticoids, bronchodilators, and diuretics.[39]

Symptom Management: Other Considerations

Although pain, dyspnea, and thirst are three of the most distressing and prevalent symptoms reported by critically ill patients,[37] other distressing symptoms can occur. These include anxiety, depression, nausea and vomiting, and sleep disturbances. The appropriate chapters in this text provide full discussions, as these are not unique to the ICU. What *is* unique is the impact that the delicate balance between the ICU goals of rescue and hemodynamic stability and the palliative goals of comfort and quality of life has on treatment plans. The palliative APRN needs to be aware of the medications and alternate routes that can be used in the ICU for patients across the continuum of survival to end-of-life, because barriers exist to medication administration and choice of agents.[39] The choice of pharmacologic agents to treat symptoms must be considered after clear goals of care are established between the patient/family, ICU team, and palliative team.

Although symptom management requires a multimodal approach, pharmacologic agents are often used by the palliative APRN to relieve general symptoms. The route of administration is predominantly intravenous, but if this route no longer exists, medications can be given by the buccal, sublingual, rectal, nebulized, or transdermal route. Liquid concentrates, sometimes referred to as Intensol (i.e., lorazepam Intensol), are up to 10 times more potent and can be given orally in very small volumes. These are considered high-alert medications by the Institute for Safe Medication Practices. Topical agents may be used with the intent of systemic absorption to control symptoms at end-of-life, but the APRN should be cautious about using compounded formulations because evidence is lacking to support efficacy. Frail or cachetic patients may have lower absorption and therefore inadequate symptom management due to low body fat stores. Transdermal fentanyl patches must be used with caution in this scenario or not at all. Rectal medications should be avoided in patients with thrombocytopenia, neutropenia, diarrhea, abdominal-perineal resection, and anorectal disease. Although many agents can be given by this route, patient comfort and choice must be considered. The subcutaneous route may be used as an alternate to the intravenous route but does result in slower drug absorption rates. These are limited to volumes of 1 mL or less, but continuous infusions can be administered if more than 1 mL is needed and have been shown to provide more stable symptom control. Limited evidence supports the use of nebulized morphine, fentanyl, and hydromorphone, and these should not be used as a regular alternative to parenteral or oral formulations. Nebulized lidocaine has been shown to be effective for intractable cough at end-of-life.[39]

The Palliative APRN's Role in Communication

Skilled communication is at the core of effective palliative care integration across all settings and is especially critical in the ICU. The transition from goals of rescue and cure to goals of comfort—or mixed goals combining elements of intensive care and palliative care—can be a turbulent time for patients, families, and the ICU team. The palliative APRN is ideally equipped with communication skills to help all stakeholders navigate this transition. As mentioned earlier in this chapter, the ICU setting is unique due to the delicate balance, and the potential divide, between ICU goals of rescue and the palliative goals of comfort and optimal quality of life. The ICU is the epitome of the technological imperative, so for a patient or family to request, or a consultant to suggest, the withdrawal or withholding of such technology can be a source of conflict unless grounded with expert listening and communication skills. Communication between ICU clinicians and families has been described as a delicate dance with many complex issues embedded in the relationship.[42] Skill is needed to deal with that complexity.

Regular communication between critically ill patients and their families and the ICU team is now considered an essential component of high-quality care.[2,5,43] Many studies have shown the value of proactive, structured clinician–family communication in the ICU on the establishment of goals of care. These same studies have demonstrated a positive impact on family members' psychological well-being, consensus among surrogate decision makers and the ICU team, and utilization of ICU resources.[2,43-47] Yet, regular meetings between families and ICU clinicians, as the standard of care, remain the exception and not the rule in many ICUs.[2]

The fact that practice is lagging behind evidence in this case may be due to the high incidence of surrogate decision makers in the ICU. It is estimated that as many as 95% of critically ill patients lack decision-making capacity, requiring families to step forward to make often-difficult treatment decisions.[5] Prognostic uncertainty also exists, although at least one study reported that 87% of surrogate decision makers preferred that physicians discuss an uncertain prognosis, as they consider this uncertainty to be an unavoidable feature of critical illness.[48]

The palliative APRN can use specific, evidence-based approaches to facilitate communication and goal setting in the ICU and to remove the obstacles to family conferences. Competing time demands, lack of space, cultural differences, language barriers, and clinicians who are inadequately trained in communication skills are barriers to family conferences in the ICU setting.[49] Families are more satisfied with ICU communication when relational comments outweigh informational content (i.e., physiological data), when clinicians spend more time listening to, and less time talking at, the family members, when the family members feel their perspective is valued, and when their emotions are acknowledged and supported.[5] The APRN can use the "Care and Communication Bundle"[2] developed by the IPAL-ICU project. This bundle is a systematized set of activities that culminate in a structured family meeting. It entails several crucial steps, including timeframes that are evidence-based. Strategies for improving communication in the ICU are shown in Box 7.2.

Finally, authentic teamwork that involves communication among all team members, regardless of rank or position, is essential to improve palliative care integration in the ICU. Experts assert that interdisciplinary collaboration, based on open communication and mutual respect, is the single most important element for success.[2] The palliative APRN should drive such team collaboration based on an understanding of the ICU culture and the

Box 7.2 Evidence-Based Communication Strategies

1. Train clinicians in communication skills.

2. Conduct family meetings early in the ICU course.

3. Increase proportion of time spent listening to family members.

4. Use VALUE mnemonic during family meetings:

    a. Value statements by family members.

    b. Acknowledge emotions.

    c. Listen to family members.

    d. Understand who the patient is as a person.

    e. Elicit questions from the family members.

Adapted from Troug, Campbell, Curtis et al.[5]

evidence behind proactive, structured communication between patients, families, and the ICU team.

Resuscitation Outcomes and the Withholding and Withdrawal of Life-Sustaining Treatments

A strong working knowledge of resuscitation outcomes and guidelines for withdrawal of life-sustaining treatments is a required element of the palliative APRN's practice in the ICU. This knowledge is essential for optimal outcomes in patient/family meetings, for prognostication, and to achieve congruence between the patient's preferences for treatment and the ICU treatment goals.

Since cardiopulmonary resuscitation (CPR) was first reported in a 1960 study,[50] overall survival to hospital discharge has remained essentially unchanged for decades.[51] The American Heart Association issued 2013 consensus recommendations to improve survival after in-hospital cardiac arrest.[51] The current prevalence of in-hospital cardiac arrests outside the ICU setting is 3.66 in 1,000 adult admissions and 1.14 in pediatric. It is estimated that 45% of adult and 65% of pediatric arrests occur in ICUs. Adult survival to discharge after an in-hospital cardiac arrest is 18%, with a 1-year survival of 6.6%. These findings are essentially the same since the results that Weil and Freis reported in 2005 in their analysis of over 14,000 in-hospital cardiac arrests.[52] The overall survival in their study was 17%, and though neurological recovery was good in survivors (60% had good cerebral performance), in-hospital cardiac arrest in end-stage disease was associated with a low probability of survival.[52] The findings reported in a large study by Peberdy and colleagues of 14,720 cardiac arrests were similar.[53] Variables associated with failure to survive to discharge after an in-hospital cardiac arrest were sepsis, serum creatinine level of more than 1.5 mg/dL, metastatic cancer, dementia, and dependent functional status on admission.[54]

Thus, even after decades of refining CPR techniques and the presence of highly trained teams in hospitals, resuscitation outcomes as reported remain poor. However, the setting for advance care planning and palliative care teams is shifting. The American Heart Association has raised concerns that the current culture of hopelessness in outcomes after in-hospital cardiac arrests may lead to the early withdrawal of life-sustaining treatment and has noted that CPR outcomes should be interpreted with caution due to the lack of consistency in reporting these events.[51] Also, the rising use of therapeutic hypothermia is changing resuscitation outcomes. Three studies, conducted between 2002 and 2011 with a total of 1,391 subjects, show better outcomes in the setting of the shockable rhythms of ventricular tachycardia and ventricular fibrillation; survival in this population ranged from 55% to 66%. For patients presenting with asystole or pulseless electrical activity, 8% had a favorable outcome from therapeutic hypothermia.[55–57] Worse outcomes were associated with advanced age, low ejection fraction, seizures, and hemodynamic instability.[55]

The palliative APRN should keep abreast of resuscitation outcomes in the ICU as a basis for discussions about whether to withhold or withdraw life-sustaining treatment. Such decisions are commonly made in the ICU setting, and the palliative APRN may be consulted to drive such decisions. There is no ethical distinction between withholding or withdrawing life-sustaining treatment, and experts consider that it is morally and legally permissible for a patient or his or her surrogate to make such life-limiting choices.[5,58,59] Withdrawal of life-sustaining treatment has broad support in the United States and is based on three principles: withdrawing and withholding are equivalent, allowing death and killing are clearly distinct, and the doctrine of double effect.[5]

Even though there is no ethical distinction between withholding and withdrawing treatment, clinicians are generally more comfortable with the former. The decision to offer or discontinue an intervention should be based solely on a honest risk/benefit analysis in light of the patient's goals and preferences. High courts have upheld a person's right to refuse any unwanted medical treatment, even if life-sustaining.[5] Thus, withdrawing such treatment, even if death follows, is considered to be allowing the person to die from the underlying condition and not to be killing. Finally, the principle of double effect applies to withdrawing or withholding life-sustaining treatment. The philosophical doctrine of double effect draws a moral distinction between giving medications with the intent to allow a natural death free from suffering and giving medications with the direct intent to kill the patient.[5,58]

If the palliative APRN is coordinating withdrawal of life-sustaining treatment, several principles guide care. First, words matter. The APRN should be careful to use the words "withdrawal of technology," avoiding the phrase "withdrawal of care." Language is important, especially to family members who will live with the memory of their loved one's death.[5] Second, there is no single, universally accepted protocol for withdrawal of treatment, so the APRN should be aware of unit or system policies and procedures.[3] Acceptable strategies include non-escalation of current therapies and withdrawal of some or all current support. The process of withdrawal may be gradual or immediate. Communication with the family and among the team should occur prior to removal of life-sustaining treatment. Third, the palliative APRN should anticipate symptom management needs, especially respiratory distress, if the patient is removed from mechanical ventilation and extubated. The possibility of stridor and airway compromise should be anticipated, and interventions, such as racemic epinephrine, should be readily available. Cook and Rocker[3] found that no or only a low risk of physical distress is associated with discontinuation of renal replacement therapy and inotropes or vasopressors, but a risk of dyspnea is associated with removal of the endotracheal tube and mechanical ventilation. Again, the APRN should be prepared for distressing symptoms in order to act quickly.

Finally, the multidisciplinary team members, such as the chaplain or social worker, should be recruited to offer additional support for the family and the ICU team.[3] Cook and Rocker outline activities of dignity-conserving care in the setting of withdrawal of life-sustaining technology: awareness of one's attitudes and assumptions, dignity-enhancing behaviors such as sitting down and not rushing, using compassion to be sensitive to the suffering of others, and engaging in dialogue that acknowledges the personhood of the patient.[3] The palliative APRN can serve as a role model for these dignity-enhancing behaviors to the ICU team when such treatments are withdrawn.

The Palliative APRN's Role in Quality Improvement in the ICU

Due to several national initiatives, the palliative APRN has multiple resources for quality improvement in the ICU. In 2002, the Robert Wood Johnson Foundation established the Promoting Palliative Care Excellence in Intensive Care project. The aim was to balance medically aggressive or even futile care with goal-directed palliative care. Seven domains were identified for quality improvement: patient- and family-centered decision making, communication, continuity of care, emotional and practical support, symptom management, spiritual support, and emotional and organizational support for ICU clinicians. APRNs can access this initiative's bundled indicators to evaluate the quality of palliative care in their ICU.[60] Also, the palliative APRN could use the PAD guidelines to monitor the quality of outcomes related to the management of pain, agitation, or delirium in the ICU population. AACN has identified palliative and end-of-life care as one of its major voice initiatives. AACN became the repository for the ICU Palliative Care tools developed under the Robert Wood Johnson Foundation initiative, and these materials are available on the website, www.aacn.org.[42]

National educational programs are also available that could form the basis for quality improvement. The End-of-Life Nursing Education Consortium (ELNEC) was established over 10 years ago with the goal to educate nurses, thereby improving the care of patients at end-of-life. An ELNEC curriculum specific to critical care was developed in 2006. In a statewide effort to educate critical care nurses, ELNEC was shown to be an effective strategy to improve end-of-life care in the ICU.[61]

The IPAL-ICU project at the Center to Advance Palliative Care[62] provides a wealth of resources for the palliative APRN to use in quality improvement initiatives. In the Improvement Tools section, there are templates for family meetings, pocket cards to use for family conferences, professional education materials, and other resources. The palliative APRN who seeks to improve the integration of palliative care in the ICU should become familiar with this valuable resource.

Summary

Palliative care is now considered an essential component of high-quality critical care. ICU patients experience serious or life-threatening illnesses and the associated symptom burden. Distressing symptoms are common in the critically ill and are amenable to the intervention of palliative APRNs. Palliative APRNs, whether in a consultative or integrative role, can improve outcomes for the critically ill in the areas of pain and symptom management, communication enhancement and family meeting structures, withholding and withdrawing of life-sustaining treatments, and the planning and implementation of quality improvement activities. The palliative APRN has the skills to help patients and families and the ICU team navigate the often-tumultuous transition from the ICU goals of rescue to the more palliative goals of comfort and quality of life. The time is now for the full integration of these two disciplines.

References

1. Rothman DJ. Where we die. *N Engl J Med*. 2014; 379(26): 2457–60.
2. Nelson JE, Cortez TB, Curtis JR, et al. Integrating palliative care in the ICU: The nurse in a leading role. *J Hospice Palliat Nurs*. 2011; 13(2): 89–96.
3. Cook D, Rocker G. Dying with dignity in the Intensive Care Unit. *N Engl J Med*. 2014; 370(26): 2506–14.
4. American Association of Critical Care Nurses (AACN); Medina J, Puntillo K, eds. *Protocols for Practice: Palliative Care and End-of-Life Issues in Critical Care*. Sudbury, MA: Jones and Bartlett Publishers; 2006.
5. Troug RD, Campbell ML, Curtis JR, et al. Recommendations for end-of-life care in the intensive care unit: a consensus statement by the American College of Critical Care Medicine. *Crit Care Med*. 2008; 36(3): 953–63.
6. Lanken PN, Terry PB, Delisser HM, et al. An official American Thoracic Society clinical policy statement: palliative care for patients with respiratory distress and critical illnesses. *Am J Respir Crit Care Med*. 2008; 177(8): 912–27.
7. Selecky PA, Eliasson CA, Hall RI, et al. Palliative and end-of-life care for patients with cardiopulmonary diseases: American College of Chest Physicians position statement. *Chest*. 2005; 128(5): 3599–610.
8. Nelson JE, Bassett R, Boss RD, et al. Models for structuring a clinical initiative to enhance palliative care in the intensive care unit: a report from the Improve Palliative Care in the ICU (IPAL-ICU) Project and the Center to Advance Palliative Care. *Crit Care Med*. 2010; 38(9): 1765–72.
9. National Consensus Project for Quality Palliative Care. *Clinical Practice Guidelines for Quality Palliative Care*. 3rd ed. Pittsburgh, PA: National Consensus Project for Quality Palliative Care, 2013.
10. Institute of Medicine. The Future of Nursing: Leading Change, Advancing Health. Available at http://www.iom.edu/~/media/Files/ReportFiles/2010/The-Future-of-Nursing/FutureofNursing 2010 Report Brief. Accessed July 19, 2014.
11. Angus DC, Barnato AE, Linde-Zwirble WT, et al. Use of intensive care at the end of life in the United States. *Crit Care Med*. 2004; 32(3): 638–43.
12. SUPPORT Principal Investigators. A controlled trial to improve care for seriously ill hospitalized patients. The study to understand prognoses and preferences for outcomes and risks of treatments (SUPPORT). *JAMA*. 1995; 274: 1591–8.
13. Field MJ, Cassell CK, eds. *Approaching Death: Improving Care at the End of Life*. Washington, DC: National Academy Press; 1997.
14. White KR, Roczen ML, Coyne PJ, Wiencek C. Acute and critical care nurses' perceptions of palliative care competencies: A pilot study. *J Contin Educ Nursing*. 2014; 45(6): 265–77.
15. Teno JM, Gozalo PL, Bynum JPW, et al. Change in end-of-life care for Medicare beneficiaries: site of death, place of care, and health care transitions in 2000, 2005, and 2009. *JAMA*. 2013; 309: 470–7.
16. Family visitation in adult intensive care units. Available at http://www.aacn.org/WD/practice/docs/practicealerts/family-visitation-adult-icu-practicealert.pdf. Accessed July 19, 2014.

17. Puntillo KA. Pain experiences of intensive care unit patients. *Heart Lung.* 1990; 19(5): 526–33.
18. Chanques G, Sebbane M, Barbotte E, et al. A prospective study of pain at rest: Incidence and characteristics of an unrecognized symptom in surgical and trauma versus medical intensive care unit patients. *Anesthesiology.* 2007; 107: 858–60.
19. Barr J, Fraser GL, Puntillo K, et al. Clinical practice guidelines for the management of pain, agitation, and delirium in adult patients in the Intensive Care Unit. *Crit Care Med.* 2013; 41(1): 263–306.
20. Erstad BL, Puntillo K, Gilbert HC, et al. Pain management principles in the critically ill. *Chest.* 2009; 135: 1075–86.
21. Puntillo KA, White C, Morris AB, et al. Patients' perceptions and responses to procedural pain: Results from the Thunder Project II. *Am J Crit Care.* 2001; 13: 292–301.
22. Griffiths RD, Jones C. Seven lessons from 20 years of follow-up of intensive care unit survivors. *Curr Opin Crit Care.* 2007; 13: 508–13.
23. Chow K. Ethical dilemmas in the Intensive Care Unit. *J Hosp Palliat Nurs.* 2014; 16(5): 256–60.
24. Pain assessment in the patient unable to self-report. Available at http://www.aspmn.org/Organization/documents/PainAssessmentinthePatientUnabletoSelfReport.pdf. Published 2006. Revised 2011. Accessed November 1, 2014.
25. Bellomo R, Kellum JA, Ronco C. Defining and classifying acute renal failure: from advocacy to consensus and validation of the RIFLE criteria. *Intens Care Med.* 2007; 33(3): 409–13.
26. Opioid use in renal failure. Available at http://www.eperc.mcw.edu/EPERC/FastFactsIndex/ff_161.htm. Accessed July 19, 2014.
27. Broadbent A, Khor K, Heaney A. Palliation and chronic renal failure: opioid and other palliative medications—dosage guidelines. *Progress in Palliative Care.* 2003; 11(4): 183–90.
28. Chandok N, Watt KDS. Pain management in the cirrhotic patient: the clinical challenge. *Mayo Clin Proc.* 2010; 85(5): 451–8.
29. Bernal W, Wendon J. Acute liver failure. *N Engl J Med.* 2013; 369: 2525–34.
30. Opioid use in liver failure. Available at http://www.eperc.mcw.edu/EPERC/FastFactsIndex/ff_260.htm. Accessed July 19, 2014.
31. Girard TD, Kress JP, Fuchs BD, et al. Efficacy and safety of a paired sedation and ventilator weaning protocol for mechanically ventilated patients in intensive care (Awakening and Breathing Controlled trial): A randomized controlled trial. *Lancet.* 2008; 371: 126–34.
32. Treggiari MM, Romand JA, Yanez ND, et al. Randomized trial of light versus deep sedation on mental health after critical illness. *Crit Care Med.* 2009; 37: 2527–34.
33. Carson SS, Kress JP, Rodgers JE, et al. A randomized trial of intermittent lorazepam versus propofol with daily interruption in mechanically ventilated patients. *Crit Care Med.* 2006; 34: 1326–32.
34. Pun BT, Ely EW. The importance of diagnosing and managing ICU delirium. *Chest.* 2007; 132: 624–36.
35. Shehabi Y, Riker RR, Bokesch PM, et al. SEDCOM (Safety and Efficacy of Dexmedetomidine Compared with Midazolam) Study Group: Delirium duration and mortality in lightly sedated, mechanically ventilated intensive care patients. *Crit Care Med.* 2010; 38: 2311–8.
36. Girard TD, Jackson JC, Pandharipande PP, et al. Delirium as a predictor of long-term cognitive impairment in survivors of critical illness. *Crit Care Med.* 2010; 38: 1513–20.
37. Puntillo K, Nelson JE, Weissman D, et al. Palliative care in the ICU: relief of pain, dyspnea and thirst: a report from the IPAL-ICU Advisory Board. *Intensive Care Med.* 2014; 40(2): 235–48.
38. Lorenz KA, Lynn J, Dy SM, et al. Evidence for improving palliative care at the end-of-life: A systematic review. *Ann Intern Med.* 2008; 148(2): 147–59.
39. Leung JG, Nelson S, Leloux M. Pharmacotherapy during the end of life: Caring for the actively dying patient. *AACN Adv Crit Care.* 2014; 25(2): 79–88.
40. Mahler DA, Selecky PA, Harrod CG, et al. American College of Chest Physicians consensus statement on the management of dyspnea in patients with advanced lung or heart disease. *Chest.* 2010; 137(3): 674–91.
41. Simon ST, Higginson IJ, Booth S, Harding R, Bausewein C. Benzodiazepines for the relief of breathlessness in advanced malignant and non-malignant diseases in adults. *Cochrane Database Syst Rev.* 2010; 1: CD007354.
42. Munro CL, Savel RH. Communicating and connecting with patients and their families. *Am J Crit Care.* 2013; 22(1): 4–6.
43. Fox MY. Improving communication with patients and families in the Intensive Care Unit. *J Hosp Palliat Nurs.* 2014; 16(2): 93–8.
44. Daly BJ, Douglas SL, O'Toole E, et al. Effectiveness trial of an intensive communication structure for families of long-stay ICU patients. *Chest.* 2010; 138(6): 1340–8.
45. Lilly Cm, De Meo DL, Sonna LA, et al. An intensive communication intervention for the critically ill. *Am J Med.* 2000; 109(6): 469–75.
46. Bradley CT, Brasel KJ. Developing guidelines that identify patients who would benefit from palliative services in the surgical intensive care unit. *Crit Care Med.* 2009; 37(3): 946–50.
47. Delgado EM, Callahan A, Paganelli G, et al. Multidisciplinary family meetings in the ICU facilitate end-of-life decision making. *Am J Hosp Palliat Care.* 2009; 26(4): 295–302.
48. Evans LR, Boyd EA, Malvar G, et al. Surrogate decision-makers' perceptions on discussing prognosis in the face of uncertainty. *Am J Respir Crit Care Med.* 2009; 179: 48–53.
49. Gay EB, Pronovost PJ, Bassett RD, Nelson JE. The intensive care unit family meeting: making it happen. *J Crit Care.* 2009; 24(4): 629. e1–12.
50. Kouwenhoven WB, Jude JR, Knickerbocker GG. Closed-chest cardiac massage. *JAMA.* 1960; 173: 1064–7.
51. Morrison L, Neumar R, Zimmerman J, et al. Strategies for improving survival after in-hospital cardiac arrest in the United States: 2013 consensus recommendations. A consensus statement from the American Heart Association. *Circulation.* 2013;127:epub.
52. Weil MH, Fries M. In-hospital cardiac arrest. *Crit Care Med.* 2005; 33(12): 2825–30.
53. Peberdy MA, Kaye W, Ornato JP, et al. Cardiopulmonary resuscitation of adults in the hospital: a report of 14720 cardiac arrests from the National Registry of Cardiopulmonary Resuscitation. *Resuscitation.* 2003; 58(3): 297–308.
54. CPR survival in the hospital setting. Available at http://www.eperc.mcw.edu/EPERC/FastFactsIndex/ff_179.htm. Accessed July 19, 2014.
55. Laish-Farkash A, Matetzky S, Oieru D, et al. Usefulness of mild therapeutic hypothermia for hospitalized comatose patients having out-of-hospital cardiac arrest. *Am J Cardiol.* 2011; 108: 173–8.
56. The Hypothermia After Cardiac Arrest Study Group. Mild therapeutic hypothermia to improve the neurologic outcome after cardiac arrest. *N Engl J Med.* 2002; 346(8): 549–56.
57. Dumas F, Grimaldi D, Zuber B, et al. Is hypothermia after cardiac arrest effective in both shockable and nonshockable patients? Insights from a large registry. *Circulation.* 2011; 123: 877–86.
58. Berlinger N, Jennings B, Wolf S. *The Hastings Center Guidelines for Decisions on Life-Sustaining Treatment and Care Near the End-of-Life: Revised and Expanded second edition.* New York, NY: Oxford University Press; 2013.
59. Wiegand DL, Grant MS. Bioethical issues related to limiting life-sustaining therapies in the Intensive Care Unit. *J Hospice Palliat Nurs.* 2014; 16(2): 60–4.
60. Curtis JR, Nielsen EL, Treece PD, et al. Effect of a quality improvement intervention on end-of-life in the intensive care unit: a randomized trial. *Am J Respir Crit Care Med.* 2011; 183: 348–55.
61. Grant M, Wiencek C, Virani R, et al. End-of-life care education in acute and critical care: the California ELNEC project. *AACN Adv Crit Care.* 2013; 24(2): 121–9.
62. IPAL-ICU Project. Available at http://www.capc.org/ipal-icu. Accessed July 19, 2014.

CHAPTER 8

Palliative Care in the Medical, Surgical, and Geriatric Patient Care Unit

Phyllis B. Whitehead

Key Points

- More than 50% of all deaths occur in the acute care setting, where the focus is on active, curative treatment, not on managing symptoms and establishing realistic goals of care.

- Palliative advanced practice registered nurses (APRNs) are uniquely qualified to care for seriously ill patients by providing comprehensive, effective, compassionate, and cost-effective care that improves end-of-life care in acute care settings.

- Palliative APRNs orchestrate interdisciplinary care plans focused on alleviating suffering and promoting healing to enhance the quality of life for seriously ill patients and their loved ones.

Introduction

Seriously ill hospitalized patients represent a specialized patient population that greatly benefit from the expanded skills and knowledge of palliative APRNs. These patients and their loved ones have unique needs that are often unaddressed in a busy healthcare system. By the year 2030, almost one in five adults will be over the age of 65 years and have at least one chronic illness.[1-3] Often, chronically ill patients have uncertain prognoses and poorly predictable disease trajectories, resulting in numerous emergency department visits and hospital admissions.

Hospitals have become places where patients go for "state-of-the-art" diagnostic and therapeutic interventions, procedures, complex surgeries, and powerful medications to support life at all costs. The modern acute care setting is overwhelmingly complicated and difficult to navigate for patients and their families, with countless specialists; it is often compared to a "conveyer belt" approach to care.[4] Specialization of care may result in a sole focus on incremental improvement of a specific organ. This emphasis does not take into account "the big picture" of the patient's overall clinical condition or the way that organ interactions affect the disease process.

Additional barriers that interfere with providing effective end-of-life care in acute care settings include (1) a lack of communication among clinicians, patients, and caregivers; (2) a focus on life prolongation and technology; and (3) unrealistic expectations on the part of patients and their loved ones.[1,5] To address these challenges, inpatient specialty palliative care programs have grown dramatically over the past decade. APRNs have become an integral part of these growing programs and are well-prepared to care for complex acutely ill patients. APRNs may serve as the patient's attending provider or as a pain or palliative consultant. Their numerous acute care roles include (1) direct clinical care, (2) expert coaching and guidance to colleagues, (3) ethical decision-making skills, (4) collaboration, (5) clinical and professional leadership, (6) research skills, (7) consultation, and (8) education.[6,7]

Today, medical-surgical patients are sicker, with many comorbid conditions. One of the most challenging barriers in acute care settings is the lack of communication and coordination of patient care.[8] APRNs are well positioned to address this barrier. For example, while making rounds on their patients, APRNs can model effective communication with the patient and family, nursing staff, and medical teams. APRNs can address pain and symptom management of patients while coaching and mentoring their colleagues on the most current evidence-based standards of care. Furthermore, APRNs can identify seriously ill patients, earlier in their disease trajectory, who will benefit from aggressive pain and symptom management as well as goals-of-care discussions that otherwise may go unaddressed.

An illustration of this holistic approach to patient care is the unitary-caring praxis conceptual model for the palliative care APRN embedded within the eight domains of the National Consensus Project for Quality Palliative Care (Fig 8.1).[3,9] The use of a model guided by nursing theory can enhance the care of seriously ill patients while promoting spiritual and emotional healing when physical healing may not be possible. A theoretical framework resembling the unitary-caring praxis provides guidance for the APRN in caring for seriously ill patients by translating

Figure 8.1 APRN unitary-caring praxis framework

national guidelines into a comprehensive but practical approach to palliative care.

Chronic Kidney Disease

Case Study 1: Paul

Paul was a 97-year-old Caucasian male who had been on hospice care at home for the preceding 3 weeks. His past medical history included dementia (diagnosed in 2010), hypertension, chronic kidney disease stage 3 (glomerular filtration rate 30–59 mL/min), coronary artery disease, chronic diastolic heart failure, and squamous cell skin cancer of the right ear, right face, and right hand, untreated per his family's request. Paul's past medical history also included benign prostatic hypertrophy with urinary obstruction, chronic solar dermatitis, osteoarthritis, acute-on-chronic renal failure, and colon cancer (diagnosed in 2005). Paul's past surgical history included colectomy (2005) and exploratory abdominal laparotomy (2010). His medications included amlodipine, metoprolol, lisinopril, topical Flagyl as needed for wound odor control, and oxycodone as needed for pain.

Paul presented to the emergency department with increased confusion and falls. His daughter, Nancy, reported Paul had been more confused and eating and drinking less for the past week. She also stated that his falls had increased. His review of systems revealed no fever, chest pain, or shortness of breath. According to Nancy, Paul had been having more difficulty swallowing his medications over the past few weeks.

Nancy also reported several episodes of bleeding from Paul's skin cancer lesions, which was a great concern to her. She also described how the hospice registered nurse came out to help with the wound care and medication management. She and the hospice nurses

performed local wound care several times a week, mainly to contain the drainage and bleeding. However, Nancy wished no further diagnostic studies regarding the skin cancer and stated, "I don't want to put him through any additional distress of unnecessary treatments and interventions." She wanted the admitting physician to investigate for any easily treatable causes of Paul's confusion.

Nancy had been caring for her father for the past 12 years, first at his home and then at her home. He had been living with her for the past 5 years. His wife and siblings were deceased. Nancy was married with two adult children and four adult grandchildren. She was solely responsible for Paul's care and shared that her husband had expressed frustration that she was spending all of her time with Paul. She was considering nursing home placement as she was not sure she could care for him any longer. Overall, Paul was declining, with a very poor appetite, weight loss (20 pounds over the past 8 weeks), weakness and fatigue, and increased confusion and falls.

Based upon the conversation with Nancy and the review of the diagnostics and laboratory values (creatinine 1.83 mg/dL and estimated glomerular filtration rate 29 mL/min/1.73 m^2) (Table 8.1), a palliative care consult was ordered for Paul to discuss goals of care, as well as his pain and symptoms. A family meeting was scheduled and the palliative APRN, Stacey, reviewed the role of palliative care in Paul's care. Stacey asked Nancy to share her understanding of Paul's condition. After listening to Nancy's understanding of Paul's condition, she explained that a stroke, cerebral bleed, and infection had all been ruled out as sources of his encephalopathy. Stacey clarified that the confusion and decline were related to Paul's dementia, and his other underlying heart and kidney diseases were not reversible.

Nancy said she knew Paul's prognosis was limited since he had been enrolled in hospice for the past 6 weeks. She wanted to focus on comfort/quality of life and did not want to pursue life-sustaining interventions or procedures, including resuscitation, dialysis, and mechanical ventilation. However, when Paul fell, Nancy did not notify Paul's hospice before calling 911 for assistance and instead revoked Paul's hospice benefit and came to the hospital for evaluation.

Stacey recommended transferring Paul to the hospital's palliative care unit for symptom management while a disposition plan was established. Since the focus was on comfort and no surgical intervention, a wound care consult was placed. The purpose was to

Table 8.1 Stages of Chronic Kidney Disease

Stage	Glomerular Filtration Rate (GFR)	Status
1	>90	Normal kidney function
2	60–89	Declining GFR with comorbidities
3	30–59	Decline, incidence of anemia, malnutrition, poor quality of life, consider palliative care consult
4	15–29	Pre-dialysis, preparation for dialysis
5	<15	Renal replacement therapy, kidney transplant, or hospice care

Adapted from references 16 and 18

create a plan to manage odor and drainage of the large fungating and necrotic lesions on Paul's face and hand.

Nancy said she could not continue to care for Paul at her home. Stacey reviewed disposition options with her, including long-term care with hospice versus skilled nursing care. Unfortunately, there were no local residential hospice facilities in Nancy's community. Stacey consulted the palliative care social worker to assist Nancy in disposition planning. In the meantime, Paul was transferred to the palliative care unit.

The APRN observed Paul cry out in pain upon positioning, and per the nursing staff, wound dressing changes were reported to be very painful for Paul. Stacey changed Paul's medications since he had dysphagia. She scheduled oxycodone orally (20:1 concentrate) 10 mg for pain every 4 hours and 30 minutes prior to dressing changes to address his pain.

Over the next 72 hours, Paul continued to decline. He was unable to eat or drink. Stacey discussed artificial hydration and nutrition with Nancy, who shared that Paul never wanted a feeding tube. Nancy stated that she knew Paul was dying and that even though he was 97 years old, it was hard to lose her father. Stacey encouraged Nancy to speak with the hospital chaplain or the palliative care bereavement counselor. Nancy expressed appreciation for the additional support and met with each of them.

The nursing staff and the APRN closely assessed Paul for any signs of pain and agitation as well as the effectiveness of his medications. They documented that Paul's pain was better controlled with the scheduled oxycodone but required dose titration over the next day. Stacey and the palliative care team (physician, nurses, social worker, counselor, chaplain, and pharmacist) made rounds daily and collaborated to provide intensive psychosocial and spiritual care to Paul and Nancy. Paul died peacefully 4 days after he came to the palliative care unit. Nancy expressed deep appreciation of the care Paul received.

End-Stage Renal Disease

With the growing elderly population, the number of patients with acute kidney injury, stage 4 and 5 chronic kidney disease, or end-stage renal disease (ESRD) and comorbidities is increasing.[10-12] Mortality among ESRD patients is 10 to 100 times greater than in the general population when matched for age and gender.[11] The number of patients receiving dialysis is increasing by up to 10% annually, and the number of those older than 75 years undergoing dialysis has doubled over the past 20 years.[11] In 2000, the American Society of Nephrology and Renal Physicians Association published the first clinical practice guideline encouraging palliative care for ESRD patients. It was revised in 2010 to include information on an integrated prognostic model predicting the mortality of hemodialysis patients (available at http://touch-calc.com/calculators/sq).[12,13]

It is clear that patients, loved ones, and hospitals need to be prepared to have end-of-life conversations, ideally before dialysis is initiated but most certainly when patients are functionally and physically declining despite dialysis. APRNs need to feel comfortable having the discussion with patients and their families regarding whether dialysis may offer a better quality and quantity of life compared to conservative management of symptoms.[11] For example, patients older than 80 years who start dialysis experience a significant loss of functionality within the first 6 months of treatment, requiring caregiver support or placement in a nursing home.[10] Unfortunately, randomized clinical trials evaluating the benefits of dialysis for older adults are lacking.[11,14]

Paramount is the collaboration with the hospital's nephrologists and the dialysis nurses to implement the American Society of Nephrology and Renal Physicians Association's published clinical practice guidelines for palliative care counseling and symptom management. Early palliative care involvement and integration into routine ESRD management are preferred for creating trusting relationships with patients and their loved ones. Several instruments have been developed by Cohen and colleagues—the Dialysis Discontinuation Quality of Dying (DDQOD) and the Dialysis Quality of Dying Apgar (QODA)—which help distinguish between good and bad deaths for dialysis patients and may assist with end-of-life discussions.[14,15]

Palliative care renal literature and guidelines suggest that the elements of good end-of-life care for ESRD patients include (1) advance care planning for agreed level of care and preferred place of care, (2) appropriate transition from life-sustaining to comfort care, including potential withdrawal of dialysis, (3) ongoing dialogues with patients and caregivers regarding prognosis and treatment options, and (4) aggressive symptom management throughout disease progression.[12]

Physical assessment includes (1) skin turgor and color changes (i.e., gray-bronze color), (2) oliguria or anuria, (3) edema and/or ascites, (4) jugular vein distention, (5) fluid accumulation in the lungs, (6) blood pressure and orthostatic changes, (7) fluid retention resulting in weight gain, (8) hypocalcemia, (9) dry, flaky skin, (10) ammonia-smelling breath, (11) tremors/seizures, (12) easy bruising, and (13) signs of anemia.[16] Routine laboratory tests should be ordered, including blood urea nitrogen (BUN), creatinine, hemoglobin, hematocrit, calcium, phosphorus, sodium, and potassium. Other diagnostic testing may involve imaging (computed tomography [CT] or magnetic resonance imaging [MRI]), renal arteriograms, and kidney, ureters, and bladder (KUB) radiographs.[16] The APRN should assess for common symptoms, such as nausea and vomiting, anxiety, depression, constipation, diarrhea, pruritus, pain, fatigue, and anorexia. Morphine should be avoided; fentanyl, methadone, and oxycodone are preferred in the treatment of pain.[16,17]

All reversible causes should be eliminated, especially in the treatment of acute renal failure. For ESRD, dialysis discussions should cover lifestyle changes, dietary restrictions, symptom management, potential complications, transplant option, and whether dialysis will continue until the patient dies or under what circumstances dialysis will be discontinued.[16,18] Once a decision is made to stop dialysis, all nonessential medications must be stopped to avoid toxicities and to stop or at least minimize fluid volume. Patient and family education must be provided on what to expect, especially alleviating the fear of "drowning in fluids" that accompanies stopping dialysis. The patient's diet should be liberalized so he or she can enjoy foods and beverages that have been restricted. The patient who has stopped dialysis has a prognosis usually measured in days to a few weeks. The APRN should review disposition planning options with the patient and family, including home with hospice, long-term care facility with hospice, or a residential hospice facility, and provide guidance in this decision.

Dementia

Dementia is a common diagnosis on medical, surgical, and geriatric units. Frequently, families do not understand that dementia is a life-limiting condition. APRNs are uniquely positioned to initiate conversations to help families understand the disease trajectory for dementia patients. The incidence of dementia is growing; it occurs in approximately 1% of all people 65 years of age and 50% of people aged 90 years.[19] Worldwide, 24 million individuals are living with dementia, and this number is predicted to double over the next 20 years.[19] Dementia, specifically Alzheimer's disease, is the fifth leading cause of death.[20] Dementia is a progressive, incurable condition that causes limitations in life and should be recognized as a life-limiting condition.[19,21-23]

Dementia can have many causes, such as Alzheimer's disease, vascular dementia, advanced Parkinson's or Huntington's disease, Lewy body disease, and excessive and chronic alcohol use.[23] Impairments in mental and physical functioning, such as memory loss, language impairment, personality changes, dysphagia, and inability to perform activities of daily living, characterize the condition.[19,23] There are seven stages of dementia (Table 8.2). The APRN should be familiar with these stages to help clinicians and families understand the role of palliative and hospice care for patients and their loved ones.

One challenge for the acute care APRN is the difficulty of identifying dementia as a life-limiting illness and the importance of getting a palliative care consult for the patient. Evidence shows patients with end-stage dementia are less likely to be referred to palliative care than other non-oncological end-stage disease patients (9% vs. 25%), and dementia patients are likely to be prescribed fewer palliative medications (28% vs. 51%).[24] Caregivers' burden can be worsened when periods of stability are interrupted by acute exacerbations—in contrast to the more predictable decline in patients with advanced cancer.[24] Advance care planning and goal setting should be initiated early in the disease progression, while the patient can provide guidance to loved ones. Due to the progression of dementia, it can be challenging for family and clinicians to know when to initiate palliation as a goal.

Table 8.2 Stages of Dementia

Stage	Impairment Level
1	No impairment
2	Very mild decline—unnoticeable memory lapses
3	Mild decline—noticeable memory and concentration problems; losing items
4	Moderate decline—forgetfulness of events; difficulty performing tasks
5	Moderate to severe decline—gaps in memory, thinking; needs help with activities of daily living
6	Severe decline—loss of awareness of recent experiences; remembers own name but has difficulty with others
7	Very severe decline—total care; swallowing impaired; hospice eligible

Adapted from references 23 and 26.

The use of functionality and cognition scales, such as the Minimum Data Set 2 (MDS-2) or the Functional Assessment Staging (FAST) instruments, can be helpful in quantifying the stage and identifying appropriate palliative and/or hospice patients.[22,25] Both pain (39%) and dyspnea (46%) are common symptoms at end-of-life for many dementia patients.[26] They should be aggressively treated on a first-line basis with an opioid, such as morphine. Patients with dementia receive less analgesia than patients who are cognitively intact. They often cannot express themselves verbally and hence receive suboptimal palliative care.[19] The APRN should integrate the use of behavioral pain assessment tools, such as the Pain Assessment in Advanced Dementia Scale (PAINAD). The American Society of Pain Management Nursing's "Position Statement on Pain Assessment in Patients Unable to Self-Report" recommends using patient self-report of pain if possible, review of known pain etiologies from the medical history, observation of pain-related behaviors, and family or proxy reports to assess for pain in the dementia patient.[26] Agitation may affect up to half of end-stage dementia patients, necessitating a calm environment and the treatment of reversible causes, such as pain, dyspnea, and constipation.[26,27] The APRN should assess for cognitive changes, including delirium. Tools such as the Mini-Mental State Examination (MMSE), the Short Portable Mental Status Questionnaire (SPMSQ), the Delirium Observation Screening Scale, and the Confusion Assessment Method (CAM) can be used to screen for cognitive changes and delirium to enhance symptom management.[26]

Infections, such as pneumonia from aspiration, urinary tract infections, or pressure ulcers from lack of mobility are a natural part of the disease progression.[26] The nurse must discuss with caregivers the role of antibiotics in the context of a life-prolonging intervention, especially in the late stages of the disease. Antibiotics are not benign and can cause complications, such as *Clostridium difficile* infection, so an early dialogue is warranted about the use of oral and/or intravenous antibiotics as contingent on the patient's goals of care.[25,26]

Due to the prevalence of dysphagia (93%),[23] malnutrition and dehydration are common. Conversations on the use of artificial hydration and nutrition should start early and continue as the disease progresses. There are many resources, such as the video from the University of North Carolina School of Medicine Palliative Care Resources on feeding options (http://www.med.unc.edu/pcare/resources/feedingoptions), to provide patients and their loved ones with accurate information on the benefits and risks of artificial nutrition versus careful hand feeding so the patient and/or caregivers can make informed decisions. A speech-language pathologist referral should be considered to determine the safest oral intake/diet recommendations for the patient.

Frequently, loved ones ask how we can allow the patient to "starve to death." A candid discussion on the natural dying process for a dementia patient is imperative. Using a careful selection of words, such as "fasting," and explaining that this process is not uncomfortable, can be helpful for caregivers. Comparing the fasting state to a time when the loved one has been ill and did not have a desire to eat may also be helpful. It is important to emphasize the patient will be offered comfort foods and/or sips of beverages, despite the risk of aspiration, along with frequent oral care. Providing the information and allowing loved ones time to process it while providing empathy are essential APRN skills.

Hip Fractures

Elderly patients hospitalized for hip fractures are common on medical-surgical units. In 2010, 258,000 hospital admissions were for hip fractures among patients aged 65 and older.[28] By 2030, hip fractures are projected to increase by 12.6% to 289,000 admissions.[28] APRNs need to be familiar with the care of these patients, including pain and symptom management as well as the importance of initiating an early goals-of-care discussion with the patient (if possible) and family. Although one may not consider consulting palliative care for a hip fracture alone, it may be appropriate if the patient has multiple comorbidities (e.g., heart failure, dementia, chronic pulmonary and kidney disease) and is frail even at baseline. Hip fractures in a patient greater than 65 years old should trigger a palliative care consult.

Having a goals-of-care conversation with the patient and family can align the patient's priorities of care (cure vs. quality of life) while ensuring that both surgical and conservative intervention options are fully discussed, including the benefits and risks (mortality) of each. Many times the patient's main priority is to ambulate again, so surgery may be the better option if, realistically, rehabilitation is possible. It is important for patients and their loved ones to understand that pain and symptom management can be achieved via medical management.

In Case Study 1, although Paul did not sustain a fracture, he was at high risk because of his frequent falls. Hip fractures increase especially after the age of 60, and then exponentially after the age of 80.[28–30] Approximately 30% of community-dwelling senior citizens age 65 and up fall annually, with higher numbers in institutions.[30] Hip fractures are disabling and a major cause of morbidity and mortality in elderly individuals.[28] Common risk factors for falls include (1) cognitive dysfunction; (2) bowel/bladder incontinence; (3) medications, such as opioids, sedatives, and diuretics; (3) impaired balance; (4) environmental hazards, such as throw rugs and slippery floors; (5) pets; and (6) weakness.[26]

Chronic Obstructive Pulmonary Disease

Case Study 2: Lucy

Lucy was a 56-year-old African-American female admitted to the hospital for acute-on-chronic hypoxic respiratory failure secondary to COPD and acute-on-chronic heart failure. Her past medical history was notable for breast cancer status post left mastectomy, lung cancer status post right upper lobe lobectomy, lymphoma, hypertension, atrial fibrillation on warfarin (chronic heart failure; ejection fraction 50%), tricuspid and mitral valve regurgitation, COPD (on 4 liters home oxygen), pulmonary hypertension, and hypothyroidism. Upon arrival at the hospital from the assisted living facility, Lucy stated that she felt "sick as a dog" and short of breath. This was Lucy's fifth admission over the past 4 months for dyspnea, pneumonia, weakness, and fatigue.

Lucy's chest x-ray on admission revealed a right basilar aeration (partially improved) and otherwise stable cardiomegaly, prominent central pleural vasculature, and chronic interstitial changes. Her significant laboratory values were carbon dioxide 38 mEq/L and white blood cells $12.8 \times 10^3/\mu L$. Lucy was admitted to a regular/non-monitored bed for treatment of her shortness of breath and was treated with ipratropium bromide and albuterol sulfate inhalations (Duoneb) overnight. Her trazodone and mirtazapine were held to minimize her sedation.

Lucy had four adult children, three daughters and one son. She was married but had been estranged from her husband for the past 5 years. Lucy had been disabled for the past 15 years and was covered by both Medicare and Medicaid. Lucy's parents were alive and had been caring for her between hospitalizations and admissions to skilled nursing facilities. She had not completed an advance directive.

The following morning, Lucy was noted to have increased difficulty breathing, audible crackles, and productive sputum. A second chest x-ray showed mild vascular congestion, patchy infiltrates bilaterally, and small bilateral pleural effusions. A few days later, Lucy showed more signs of pneumonia, with resolution of her crackles and rales and the development of more rhonchi on exam. She was started on levofloxacin and the dosage of her intravenous diuretics was increased. Lucy experienced increasing somnolence and became disoriented toward the evening. Arterial blood gas analysis showed that she had significant respiratory acidosis with metabolic alkalosis compensating. Noninvasive ventilation (BiPap) was started.

Overnight, Lucy pulled at the BiPap equipment, requiring continual nursing and respiratory therapy support. Despite aggressive interventions, Lucy continued to decline, with her oxygen levels desaturating into the 70s. Lucy became unresponsive. Her medical team decided that her COPD was end-stage and her prognosis was grim. A palliative care consult order was placed. The palliative APRN, Johnny, scheduled a family meeting with Lucy's husband, children, and parents.

After reviewing palliative care services and listening to the family members' understanding of Lucy's medical condition, Johnny explained the role of a medical surrogate decision maker and clarified who legally had the authority, under current state laws, to act as Lucy's surrogate. The estranged husband deferred to Lucy's adult children, who all agreed that she would not want life-prolonging measures (e.g., mechanical ventilation, including BiPap, or chest compressions) and the focus should be on her comfort. Her code status was changed to a "Do Not Resuscitate." Her family decided to continue the antibiotics but agreed to stop if Lucy began to have any adverse symptoms, such as diarrhea. The decision was made to transfer her to the palliative care unit for pain and symptom management and not to return her to the intensive care unit if her condition declined.

Johnny prescribed Lucy a low dose of scheduled morphine (1 mg intravenously every 4 hours) to treat her dyspnea, scheduled dexamethasone (4 mg intravenously every morning), and as-needed lorazepam (1 mg intravenously every 4 hours as needed) for her anxiety. Johnny reinforced the importance of using the morphine as first-line treatment for Lucy's dyspnea. After morphine and dexamethasone were started, Lucy's oxygen was able to be lowered to her baseline 4 liters via nasal cannula. Lucy's family remained at her bedside, requesting the support of the palliative care chaplain and bereavement counselor.

Overnight, unexpectedly, Lucy began to interact with her family and staff. She answered simple questions and was able to drink and eat. By day 3, Lucy was able to direct her own care. She agreed with the care plan of focusing on her comfort and confirmed that she never wanted to use mechanical ventilation devices again or to return to the hospital. She decided to return to her nursing facility as a long-term-care resident with hospice. Lucy was discharged after she completed an advance directive naming her son as her medical power of attorney and the appropriate state form designating that she did not want life-sustaining interventions (i.e., Medical Order for Life Sustaining Treatment [MOLST] form). Johnny helped complete the discharge and ensured that Lucy had the appropriate oral medication prescriptions to manage her medical conditions, dyspnea, and other symptoms at the long-term care facility with hospice.

Chronic obstructive pulmonary disease (COPD) is the third leading cause of death in the United States and is predicted to become the third leading cause of death worldwide by 2020.[18,31,32] The death rate due to COPD continues to rise.[33,34] COPD is commonly seen later in life after exposure to risk factors such as cigarette smoking, tuberculosis, and noxious gaseous/particulate matter, and a history of respiratory infections. COPD is progressive and incurable; it is punctuated by acute exacerbations characterized by airflow obstruction caused by chronic inflammation.[32]

The last years of life for COPD patients are tainted by progressive functional decline, poor quality of life, and oxygen dependency.[33,34] Death usually occurs from acute exacerbations of COPD, such as lung infections, respiratory failure, and secondary complications from comorbidities.[33] Hospital admissions increase with age, with patients older than 80 years at the highest risk of hospitalization (14 times greater than 40- to 49-year-old patients).[34]

Common symptoms are anxiety, cough, sputum production, dyspnea, and fever. The prevalence of dyspnea is 90% to 95% in COPD patients like Lucy.[31] Physical assessment findings include (1) audible wheezing, (2) abnormal breath sounds (rhonchi, crackles), (3) decreased breath sounds, (4) paradoxical respirations, (5) tachypnea and tachycardia, (6) dyspnea, (7) "blue bloater" (classic sign of bronchitis), (8) "pink puffer" (sign of emphysema), (9) accessory muscle use, (10) fever, (11) cough, (12) cyanosis, (13) dependent edema, (14) weight loss, (15) fatigue, (16) sleep deprivation, (17) changes in mental status, (18) depression, and (19) anxiety.[31]

Laboratory tests routinely ordered include chemistries to monitor elevated serum carbon dioxide levels and arterial blood gas analysis for acidosis, hypercapnia, and hypoxemia. Pulse oximetry may be helpful in detecting hypoxemia. Chest radiographs and chest CT are useful in revealing fibrosis, effusions, hyperinflated lungs, and hyperlucent areas reflecting bullae.[31] The APRN should review and use these lab results to facilitate an advance care planning discussion, including whether they align with the patient's stated goals of care.

Low-dose opioids are the first line for the treatment of dyspnea, whereas benzodiazepines the first line for treating anxiety, and best practice suggests a low-dose opioid (which may be contrary to how clinicians have been trained).[31,35] Optimizing medication management of the underlying pulmonary disease is key to good palliative treatment of the COPD patient. Table 8.3 discusses pharmacologic management of COPD.

COPD is a common primary diagnosis for an acute care admission, and APRNs need to be familiar with staging and treatment management, so they can care for these complex patients and their loved ones. The common disease progression includes frequent admissions and escalation of care, such as intensive care. (Multiple admissions to the hospital for the same reason should trigger a palliative care consult.) The disease trajectory is challenging, as is prognostication, because death frequently occurs before the patient is perceived as terminal.[32] COPD grading per the Global Initiative for COPD (GOLD)[18,31] is a helpful tool in prognostication (Table 8.4).

The National Institute for Health and Clinical Excellence and the American Thoracic Society both endorse early involvement of

Table 8.3 Pharmacologic Management of COPD

Medication	Onset of Action	Mechanism of Action	Dosing Schedule
Albuterol	5–15 mins	Smooth muscle relaxant (SMR)	Varies
Levalbuterol	5–10 mins	SMR	Varies
Ipratropium	<15 mins	SMR	Varies
Formoterol	<10 mins	SMR	BID
Arformoterol	7–20 mins	SMR	BID
Tiotropium	<30 mins	SMR	Daily
Budesonide	Varies	Anti-inflammatory	BID/TID
Fluticasone/salmeterol inhaler	2 hours	SMR/anti-inflammatory	BID
Budesonide/formoterol inhalation	2 hours	SMR/anti-inflammatory	BID
Aminophylline	Varies	SMR	Daily
Theophylline	Varies	SMR	Daily
Roflumilast	Up to 8 hours	Anti-inflammatory	Daily
Prednisone	1-2 hours	Anti-inflammatory	Daily
Methylprednisolone	1-2 hours	Anti-inflammatory	Daily
Fluticasone	Up to 2 weeks	Anti-inflammatory	BID

Adapted from references 31 and 35.

Table 8.4 COPD Grading per GOLD

Airflow Limitation	Post-bronchodilator Spirometry	Descriptors
GOLD 1 Mild	$FEV_1 \geq 80\%$ of predicted normal values $FEV_1/FVC < 70\%$ confirms COPD diagnosis.	♦ Mild airflow limitation ♦ May be unaware that lung function has started to decline ♦ May not have COPD symptoms ♦ May have symptoms of chronic cough and excessive mucus ♦ Rarely seek treatment
GOLD 2 Moderate	$50 \leq FEV_1 < 80\%$ predicted values	♦ Airflow limitation worsens. ♦ May notice symptoms, particularly shortness of breath upon exertion ♦ Cough and sputum production ♦ Many people typically seek treatment at this stage.
GOLD 3 Severe	$30 \leq FEV_1 < 50\%$ predicted values	♦ Airflow significantly worsens. ♦ Shortness of breath becomes more evident and COPD exacerbation is common. ♦ Decrease in activity tolerance and increase in fatigability
GOLD 4 Very Severe	$FEV_1 < 30\%$ of predicted normal values **or** $FEV_1 < 50\%$ of predicted normal values plus chronic respiratory failure	♦ Quality of life is greatly impaired. ♦ COPD exacerbations are life-threatening. ♦ Airflow limitation is severe. ♦ Chronic respiratory failure is often present at this stage and may lead to complications, such as cor pulmonale and/or, eventually, death. ♦ Hospice eligible

FEV_1 = forced expiratory volume in 1 second; FVC = forced vital capacity

Adapted from references 18 and 31.

palliative care services in caring for COPD patients, but, unfortunately, palliative care conversations are not occurring.[32] The APRN is in a unique position to facilitate dialogues with patients so they understand they have a life-limiting illness.[32,36] COPD patients must understand their disease progression, future care, and end-of-life treatment options.[32] The APRN should provide honest but balanced information, striving to maintain optimism and realism. To maintain hope, the APRN should allow the patient time to process the poor prognosis while redirecting him or her from hope of recovery toward hope of quality time and optimal symptom management.[32]

Surrogate or Proxy Decision Making

Because seriously ill patients like Lucy, with end-stage COPD, lose their decision-making capacity, the APRN may have to rely on loved ones to advocate for the patient's wishes.[36,37] State laws vary in the extent to which they authorize proxy decision making; they also differ as to which family members have priority in the decision making. Thus, the APRN should be familiar with the state's surrogate decision-making laws and regulations. The acute care APRN should initiate family meetings early during the hospital stay, so that priorities of care can be established.

During the family meeting, the APRN needs to provide an accurate summary of the medical care to date, all of the medical treatment options being considered, and the potential outcomes, including prognosis. The APRN should summarize what the medical teams are recommending as the best care option(s), while focusing on the patient's preferences and values. For example, "In light of what we have talked about so far, what do you think Lucy would want to do?"[38] The goals of the meeting are to minimize the surrogate decision maker's burden of responsibility and to remain focused on the patient's wishes, not the decision maker's wishes.[36-38]

Whether the APRN is serving as the patient's attending or as a consultant, there is an expanding palliative care role in the acute care setting.[39,40] APRNs are defining hospitals' end-of-life policies and procedures as well as creating triggers for appropriate palliative care consults. APRNs provide optimal symptom management, maximize patient and family function throughout treatment, and ensure seamless transitions to end-of-life care when cure is no longer possible or desirable.[6]

With the majority of deaths occurring in acute care settings, where the focus of care is on active, curative treatment and not on managing symptoms or establishing realistic goals of care, palliative APRNs must be able to advocate for seriously ill patients and their loved ones.[1,2] Patients need APRNs who are skilled in the science of palliative medicine as well as the art of holistic healing. With the ever-changing healthcare environment, palliative APRNs are essential in providing specialized interventions to meet the diverse needs of acute care patients.

References

1. Garner KK, Goodwin JA, McSweeney JC, Kirchner JE. Nurse executives' perceptions of end-of-life care provided in hospitals. *J Pain Symptom Management.* 2013; 45(2): 235–43.

2. Gott M, Ingleton C, Gardiner C, et al. How to improve end of life care in acute hospitals. *Nursing Older People.* 2009; 21(7): 26–9.

3. Reed SM. A unitary-caring conceptual model for advanced practice nursing in practice care. *Holistic Nursing Practice.* 2010; 24(1): 23–34.

4. Hillman KM. End-of-life care in acute hospitals. *Australian Health Rev.* 2011; 35: 176–7.

5. Aslakson RA, Wyskiel R, Thornton I, et al. Nurse-perceived barriers to effective communication regarding prognosis and optimal end-of-life care for surgical ICU patients: A qualitative exploration. *J Palliative Med.* 2012; 15(8): 910–5.

6. Mauricio RV, Okbuysen-Cawley R. The caring continuum: Role of the pediatric critical care advanced practice nurse in palliative care program development. *Critical Care Nursing Quarterly.* 2010; 33(3): 292–7.

7. Skalla KA. Blended role advanced practice nursing in palliative care of the oncology patient. *J Hospice Palliative Nurs.* 2006; 8(3): 155–63.

8. Fernandez R, Tran D, Johnston M, Jones S. Interdisciplinary communication in general medical and surgical wards using two different models of nursing care delivery. *J Nurs Management.* 2010; 18: 265–74.

9. National Consensus Project for Quality Palliative Care. *Clinical Practice Guidelines for Quality Palliative Care.* 3rd ed. Pittsburgh, PA; 2013.

10. Arulkumaran N, Szawarski P, Philips BJ. End-of-life care in patients with end-stage renal disease. *Nephrology Dialysis Transplantation.* 2012; 27: 879–81.

11. Koshy AN, Mace R, Youl L, Challenor S, Bull R, Fassett RG. Contrasting approaches to end of life and palliative care in end kidney disease. *Indian J Nephrol.* 2012; 22(4): 307–9.

12. McAdoo SP, Brown EA, Chesser AM, Farrington K, Salisbury EM. Measuring the quality of end of life management in patients with advanced kidney disease: Results from the Pan-Thames Renal Audit Group. *Nephrology Dialysis Transplantation.* 2011; 27: 1548–54.

13. Moss AH. Revised dialysis clinical practice guideline promotes more informed decision-making. *Clin J Am Soc Nephrol.* 2010; 5: 2380–3.

14. Mid-Atlantic Renal Coalition and the Kidney End-of-Life Coalition. Clinical algorithm & preferred medications to treat pain in dialysis patients. MidAtlantic Renal Coalition and the Kidney End-of-Life Coalition. Available at http: //www.kidneysupportivecare.org/Files/PainBrochure9-09.aspx2009. Published March 13, 2009. Accessed July 7, 2014.

15. Renal Physicians Association. *Shared Decision-Making in the Appropriate Initiation and Withdrawal from Dialysis. Clinical Practice Guideline.* 2nd ed. Available at http: //www.renalmd.org/catalogue-item.aspx?id=682. Published September 25, 2010. Accessed July 11, 2014.

16. Gorman L. Renal conditions. In: Dahlin CM, Lynch MT, eds. *Core Curriculum for the Advanced Practice Hospice and Palliative Registered Nurse.* 2nd ed. Pittsburgh, PA: Hospice and Palliative Nurses Association; 2013: 353–68.

17. Quill TE, Bower KA, Holloway RG, et al. Pain management. In: *Primer of Palliative Care.* 6th ed. Chicago, IL: American Academy of Hospice and Palliative Medicine; 2014:17.

18. Maxwell TL. Caring for those with chronic illness. In: Ferrell B, Coyle N, eds. *Oxford Textbook of Palliative Nursing.* 3rd ed. New York, NY: Oxford University Press; 2010:690–7.

19. Brorson H, Plymoth R, Ormon K, Bolmsjo I. Pain relief at the end of life: Nurses' experiences regarding end-of-life pain relief in patients with dementia. *Pain Management Nursing.* 2014; 15(1): 315–23.

20. Smith LW, Amell E, Edlund B, Mueller M. A dimensional analysis of the concept of suffering in people with dementia at end of life. *J Hospice Palliative Nurs.* 2014; 16(5): 263–70.

21. Boogaard JA, van Soest-Poortvliet MC, Anema JR, et al. Feedback on end-of-life care in dementia: The study protocol of the follow-up project. *BMC Palliative Care.* 2013; 12(29): 1–8.

22. Coleman AME. End-of-life issues in caring for patients with dementia: The case for palliative care in management of terminal dementia. *Am J Hospice Palliative Med.* 2012; 29(1): 9–12.

23. Dahlin CM, Cohen AK, Goldsmith T. Dysphagia, xerostomia, and hiccups. In: Ferrell B, Coyle N, eds. *Oxford Textbook of Palliative Nursing.* 4th ed., New York, NY: Oxford University Press; 2015:191–216.

24. Costa-Requena G, Espinosa Val M, Cristofol R. Caregiver burden in end-of-life care: Advanced cancer and final stage of dementia. *Palliative and Supportive Care.* 2014: 1–7.

25. Parsons C, McCorry N, Murphy K, et al. Assessment of factors that influence physician decision making regarding medication use in patients with dementia at the end of life. *Int J Geriatric Psychiatry.* 2014; 29: 281–90.

26. Smeltz R. Neurological conditions. In: Dahlin CM, Lynch MT, eds. *Core Curriculum for the Advanced Practice Hospice and Palliative Registered Nurse.* 2nd ed. Pittsburgh, PA: Hospice and Palliative Nurses Association; 2013:389–418.

27. Quill TE, Bower KA, Holloway RG, Shah MS, Caprio TV, Storey CP. Delirium, depression and anxiety, and fatigue. In: *Primer of Palliative Care.* 6th ed. Chicago, IL: American Academy of Hospice and Palliative Medicine; 2014:91–111.

28. Yoon B, Baek J, Kim MK, Lee Y, Ha Y, Koo K. Poor prognosis in elderly patients who refused surgery because of economic burden and medical problem after hip fracture. *J Korean Med Sci.* 2013; 28: 1378–81.

29. Alarcon T, Gonzalez-Montalvo JI, Gotor P, Madero R, Otero A. A new hierarchical classification for prognosis of hip fracture after 2 years' follow up. *J Nutrition Health Aging.* 2010; 15(10): 919–23.

30. Kristensen MT. Factors affecting functional prognosis of patients with hip fracture. *Eur J Physical Rehab Med.* 2011; 47(2): 257–64.

31. Bouxman SR. Pulmonary conditions. In: Dahlin CM, Lynch MT, eds. *Core Curriculum for the Advanced Practice Hospice and Palliative Registered Nurse.* 2nd ed. Pittsburgh, PA: Hospice and Palliative Nurses Association; 2013:331–51.

32. Momen N, Hadfield P, Kuhn I, Smith E, Barclay S. Discussing an uncertain future: End-of-life care conversations, in chronic obstructive pulmonary disease. A systematic literature review and narrative synthesis. *Thorax.* 2012; 67: 777–80.

33. Chou W, Lai Y, Huang Y, Chang C, Wu W, Hung Y. Comparing end-of-life care for hospitalized patients with chronic obstructive pulmonary disease and lung cancer in Taiwan. *J Palliative Care.* 2013; 29(1): 29–35.

34. Chou W, Lai Y, Hung Y. Comparing end-of-life care in hospitalized patients with chronic obstructive pulmonary disease with and without palliative care in Taiwan. *J Research Med Sci.* 2013; 18(7): 594–600.

35. Quill TE, Bower KA, Holloway RG, et al. Dyspnea. In: *Primer of Palliative Care.* 6th ed. Chicago, IL: American Academy of Hospice and Palliative Medicine; 2014:50–51.

36. Wittenberg-Lyles E, Goldsmith J, Ferrell B, Ragan SL. *Communication in Palliative Nursing.* New York, NY: Oxford University Press; 2013.

37. Gamino LA, Ritter RH. *Ethical Practice in Grief Counseling.* New York, NY: Springer Publishing Company; 2009.

38. Quill TE, Bower KA, Holloway RG, et al. Goal setting, prognosticating, and surrogate decision making. In: *Primer of Palliative Care.* 6th ed. Chicago, IL: American Academy of Hospice and Palliative Medicine; 2014:139–64.

39. Vasilevskis EE, Knebel RJ, Dudley RA, Wachter RM, Auerbach AD. Cross-sectional analysis of hospitalist prevalence and quality of care in California. *J Hospital Med.* 2010; 5(4): 200–7.

40. Goodrich K, Krumholz H, Conway P, Lindenauer P, Auerbach AD. Hospitalist utilization and hospital performance on six publicly reported patient outcomes. *J Hospital Med.* 2012; 7(6): 482–8.

CHAPTER 9

Palliative Care in the Oncology Unit

Anne M. Ireland

Key Points

◆ Early introduction of palliative care for patients with metastatic disease and/or high symptom burden is recommended.

◆ Advanced practice registered nurses (APRNs) are appropriately prepared to assess for, plan, implement, and evaluate palliative care interventions.

◆ Palliative care clinical competencies need to be integrated into curriculums so we are prepared to provide standardized and evidence-based primary palliative care services, reserving our palliative care specialists for truly difficult problems.

Case Study

Mary was a 26-year-old unmarried woman who had been diagnosed with stage IV melanoma 3 months earlier. She was admitted over the weekend with intractable pain and dyspnea. The palliative APRN met her on Monday morning rounds.

On reviewing her medical records, the palliative APRN observed that Mary presented with stage IV disease with metastases to the lungs and bones. She had undergone three cycles of CVD (cisplatin, vinblastine, and DTIC), but recent scans revealed widespread progressive disease. She rated her pain at 7/10 on patient-controlled analgesia with morphine at a basal rate of 2 mg/hr, with a 2-mg bolus once an hour as needed. Oxygen saturation was 94% on 2 liters of oxygen.

The palliative APRN visit focused on establishing a bond with Mary and her parents, Ben and Jill, and working to improve her symptoms. With her permission, her parents stayed in the room during the initial assessment. She was "desperate" to be more comfortable but also wanted to be able to think and function coherently. The palliative APRN made it clear to her that she could be more comfortable, but it was going to take some adjustment in her current medications. The benefits of morphine were discussed—both for her pain and her breathing. She reported that she was tolerating the morphine fine, except for its constipating side effects. Mary was assured that the constipation could be countered with a good bowel regimen. Work began on improving her pain control. The palliative APRN reviewed the number of breakthrough doses she had attempted since her admission and

adjusted her morphine dosage up to 3 mg/hr and gave her a 3-mg bolus every 20 minutes. Simultaneously, her bowel regimen was increased to include stool softeners and laxatives. An as-needed antiemetic was prescribed, given the likelihood that the increased opioid dosage would cause nausea and vomiting. The palliative APRN informed Mary that the first few days of titration might make her more sedated than she wanted, but she would adjust to the sedative effects to some degree over time. The palliative APRN reinforced the principle of patient-controlled analgesia—that she was in control of how much she needed or wanted, and efforts to balance her pain control with the level of sedation would be undertaken moving forward.

The next focus was her dyspnea. While the morphine might have helped with this, her chest x-ray from the preceding day revealed a large left pleural effusion and moderate right pleural effusion. The palliative APRN consulted with the oncologist to ask if he would consider tapping the effusions to improve her respiratory status. When he said yes, the palliative APRN made arrangements with the interventional radiology department to perform bilateral pleural taps later in the day or on Tuesday morning at the latest.

As the APRN left the room with them, Ben and Jill shared that Mary was the second of three daughters in their family. She was the first person in their family to go to college and then on to graduate school; she recently moved out of state to begin her career. Shortly after her move, she was diagnosed with melanoma and elected to return to her parent's home to begin treatment. In her parent's words, she was the "golden child." Their home was a one-hour drive away from the hospital. Their older daughter (28) lived out of state; their younger daughter (23) lived nearby but was finding being with her sister at this time very difficult. They shared that they were very aware of the gravity of their daughter's illness but were not prepared for what was ahead. The palliative APRN reassured them there were resources to help them feel better prepared. They agreed to meet with the social worker and confirmed that a chaplain would also be helpful for them.

The palliative APRN discussed the plan and conversations with the nurse caring for Mary. The RN had already had a brief conversation with Mary's parents and agreed to reinforce the plan of care for the day and ensure that both the social worker and the chaplain visited.

On Tuesday, Mary's pain control was markedly improved, with a self-reported level of 2/10. Oxygen saturation was 99% after the pleural taps and she did not feel she needed the oxygen all the time. A plan was made to meet to discuss next steps. With Mary's permission, Ben and Jill were included in the conversation. It was a difficult conversation. Mary and her parents were advised that the cancer had progressed in her bones and lungs, which meant that the treatment she had received was not working. The oncologist reviewed other treatment options, anticipated side effects, and the likelihood of the treatment extending her life. While there were investigational protocols that Mary could consider, she was clear she did not want to spend her remaining time in a hospital. She wanted to go home to be with her family and dog. In collaboration with the case manager, a plan was begun to discharge her home with hospice.

By Thursday, planning was compete. All the home hospice equipment had been delivered to Mary's house. Her hospital bed was in the family room that looked out over the ocean; there was an adjacent bathroom. Although Mary was not wearing the oxygen all the time, it had been delivered and set up, anticipating that she would need it in the future. The hospice agency had visited with Mary's parents and her sister. The hospice nurse and social worker on their team would meet with them frequently, initially, to help them better understand what to expect as Mary's disease progressed. Ben and Jill contacted their pastor and advised him they were coming home with Mary, and he told them he would visit them as often as they needed him. Mary was discharged to home hospice on Thursday afternoon. She benefited from palliative radiation to a lytic lesion in her right femur and also had an additional pleural tap for her recurrent left pleural effusion. Two months later, Mary passed away comfortably in her home, surrounded by her family and with her dog on her bed. She had returned for outpatient services several times.

Bereavement follow-up revealed that Mary's family felt supported during the transitional care process. As difficult as it was for them to have her decide to stop treatment, they saw her make a decision that she felt was best for her. Although she stopped treatment, she was actively engaged in managing her symptoms so she could continue to enjoy her life until the very end. She had taken a few trips with her college friends, visited the family cottage on the east coast, where she spent a lot of time as a child, and even had spent a day at the beach watching her sisters surf.

Introduction

Oncology nursing started in the mid-1960s when chemotherapy and radiation therapy clinical trials for patients with cancer started to develop.[1] Oncology nurses began to organize as a specialty, and with the chartering of the Oncology Nursing Society (ONS) in 1975, they began to create a professional organization with a focus on nurses who cared for patients with cancer.[2] Over time, hospitals established specialized inpatient oncology units and employed nurses with expertise in chemotherapy administration and the symptoms that ensued. In the early years, there was a strong focus on managing nausea and vomiting, preventing and treating oral mucositis, managing diarrhea, and preventing the life-threatening consequences of neutropenia. Patients with advanced cancer diagnoses were also admitted to these newly created oncology units, so the care of patients requiring pain and symptom management at the end-of-life quickly fell within the realm of oncology nursing as well.

By the early 1980s, the specialty of oncology nursing had evolved to the point that the ONS pursued the development of an oncology nursing certification examination. In 1984, the Oncology Nursing Certification Corporation administered its first oncology certification exam, which appropriately included content on end-of-life care. The most recent blueprint has content on symptom management (22%), palliative and end-of-life care (11%) and psychosocial dimensions of care.[3]

Despite the long-term association between patients with advanced cancer and the oncology specialty, patients are dying on our oncology units in pain and with nausea, anxiety, depression, shortness of breath, and many other symptoms.[4] In light of this, several national and international organizations have advocated for the inclusion of palliative care practices into oncology practice.[5-8] The premise of this advocacy is a fundamental belief that patients and their families should have ready access to—and deserve the components of—palliative care throughout their disease trajectory and not just at the end-of-life. In 2010, Hui and colleagues reported survey findings from both National Cancer Institute (NCI)-designated cancer centers and non-NCI cancer centers. Most of the responding organizations reported they had a palliative care program, although the scope of services and degree of integration varied.[9] They found that NCI cancer centers were significantly more likely to have a palliative care program (92% vs. 78%; $p = .002$), at least one palliative care physician (92% vs. 74%; $p = .04$), an inpatient palliative care consultation service (92% vs. 56%; $p < .001$), and an outpatient palliative care clinic (59% vs. 22%: $p < .001$). Only 23% of the centers had dedicated palliative care beds, and 37% had hospice beds. The median duration from referral to death was 7 days for both inpatient consultation teams and units and 90 days for outpatient clinics.

While there has been significant growth in the development of palliative care programs in hospitals, additional efforts are needed to realize the vision of the American Society of Clinical Oncology (ASCO), which is "the integration of palliative care in the model and vision of comprehensive cancer care by 2020."[8]

Does Palliative Care Make a Difference?

Based on a review of randomized controlled trials of palliative care, ASCO published a Provisional Clinical Opinion stating that palliative care should be integrated into standard oncology care early in the course of illness for patients with metastatic cancer and/or high symptom burden.[10] These studies reported that patients referred to palliative care demonstrated improved overall quality of life, symptom management, patient satisfaction, and caregiver burden. Temel and colleagues (2010) reported that early referral to palliative care services for patients with metastatic non-small-cell lung cancer reduced overall healthcare utilization, with more timely referrals to hospice, fewer hospital readmissions for symptom control, and reduced use of futile intensive care.[11] They also reported that the patients who received this early integrated palliative care had a survival advantage of 2 months. Bakitas and colleagues (2009), in their randomized controlled trial of the effects of a palliative nurse practitioner intervention on several clinical outcomes in patients with advanced cancer, found that patients had improved quality of life and mood but did not have significant improvements in symptom intensity or reduced days in the intensive care unit or emergency department.[12] While there remain some differences in findings related to financial and survival advantages, there is consensus that palliative care within the context of oncology care is important. Palliative care has been shown to reduce symptom burden, improve quality of life, and increase the odds of dying at home.[11, 12] These outcomes alone are compelling reasons to move toward an integrated model of care where patients with cancer also receive palliative care.

The National Comprehensive Cancer Network (NCCN) provides guidelines on palliative care to "help assure that each patient with cancer experiences the best quality of life possible throughout the illness trajectory by providing guidance for the primary oncology team."[5] These guidelines are an essential resource for both the primary oncology team and the palliative care team. They provide detailed guidance on initial palliative care assessment, pain and symptom management, advance care planning, special palliative care interventions for patients with intractable symptoms, care of the imminently dying, a peaceful death, and after-death care interventions. The NCCN guidelines reinforce the standards of palliative care, as outlined by ASCO in the publication by Ferris and colleagues (2009):

- Institutions should develop processes for integrating palliative care into cancer care, both as part of usual oncology care and for patients with specialty palliative care needs.

- All cancer patients should be screened for palliative care at their initial visit, at appropriate intervals, and as clinically indicated.

- Patients and families should be informed that palliative care is an integral part of their comprehensive cancer care.

- Educational programs should be provided to all healthcare professionals and trainees, so that they can develop effective palliative care knowledge, skills, and attitudes.

- Palliative care specialists and interdisciplinary palliative care teams, including board-certified palliative care physicians, advanced practice registered nurses, physician assistants, social workers, chaplains, and pharmacists, should be readily available to provide consultative or direct care to patients/families who request or require their expertise.

- Palliative care quality should be monitored by institutional quality improvement programs.

The Delicate Dance Between Oncology Care and Palliative Care

In the past, the oncology community has been reluctant to adopt the concept of palliative care. Practitioners have long confused palliative care with hospice care and do not want their patients to perceive they are giving up on them or on treating their disease. The patient's desire to continue to "fight the good fight" is a reality in the oncology field, and physicians are, in fact, obligated to continue to offer therapeutic options that hold some chance of therapeutic response. Despite this, ASCO published a statement on individualized care for patients with advanced cancer and issued "a clarion call for oncologists as individual practitioners, and for our profession in general, to take the lead in curtailing the use of ineffective therapy and ensuring a focus on palliative care and relief of symptoms throughout the course of illness."[13(p 759)] Oncologists are also concerned about their patients' feeling abandoned if/when they transfer their care to palliative care practitioners. Oncologists commonly have long-standing relationships with their patients, do not like transferring a patient's care during the end-of-life timeframe, and frequently see it as their responsibility to continue to provide care throughout the entire disease. A confounding issue in all of this occurs when oncologists lack the skills required to engage in the difficult conversations about moving to end-of-life care. While medical schools are striving to include communication skills in their curricula, there remains great variability in the amount of time allotted to this subject.

Palliative Care Competency with Oncology

In 1999, Weissman and colleagues published an eloquent document that highlighted recommendations for incorporating palliative care education into the acute care hospital setting.[14] The report included critical aspects of provider education concerning palliative care in inpatient settings and identified specific barriers to improving the delivery of care. Weissman's Acute Care Hospital Working Group recommended the following: (1) that end-of-life care be integrated into all aspects of medical education; (2) that medical faculty who teach in acute care settings appreciate that dying is a normal part of the life cycle and demonstrate a sense of "privilege" when attending to patients and families at this vulnerable time; (3) that students be taught how to attend to distressing physical, psychological, and spiritual symptoms; and (4) that providers understand the value of the interdisciplinary team. The list of barriers is bold and lengthy, including inappropriate attitudes, lack of knowledge, poor practice behavior, and the impact of the rapidly changing system of healthcare economics. Sadly, many of these recommendations have not yet been fully embraced, and barriers still exist in our academic medical settings.

Both medical and nursing schools in the United States have placed a limited emphasis on end-of-life care. In 2007, Dickinson collected data from medical schools and baccalaureate nursing programs in the United States. Essentially, all the schools reported offering content on death and dying, with over 90% student participation, but both professional programs offered, on average, less than 15 hours. Over 87% of the schools offered palliative care content.[15] The author concluded that the programs were exposing students to the issues, though not in an in-depth way. More recently, White and Coyne reported that more than half of the 714 ONS members they surveyed reported they had had less than 2 hours of continuing education regarding end-of-life care in the past 2 years.[16] Determining the exact content, quantity, and frequency of continuing education should be a focus of oncology nursing organizations, as we strive to ensure that the nursing staff is skilled and knowledgeable about general palliative care and are confident about accessing palliative care experts when patients' needs exceed their skills or their scope of practice.

While the opportunity to expand palliative care skills and knowledge through certification is relatively accessible, it seems more appropriate that the skills and education should be fully integrated into the basic curriculum, rather than being an option for oncology providers and oncology nurses. Given that many oncology patients experience significant symptom burden and half of them die of their disease, oncology practitioners should all be equipped and competent to deliver the care the majority of oncology care. However, palliative APRNs can offer support for difficult symptoms and situations.

Teamwork and Communication

In addition to individual palliative care knowledge, oncology practitioners must understand what other team members and disciplines bring to the care of the patient. An organization with a palliative care consult team or a palliative care unit might include any or all of the following: physicians, advanced practice registered nurses, social workers, psychologists, chaplains, pharmacists, psychiatrists, and anesthesiologists. Having a clear understanding of each team member's role is critical to ensure appropriate consultation based on the patient's and family's need; that understanding should also provide clarity on who may best manage specific issues or concerns. In many cases, a patient and family may need more intensive guidance from one discipline and less from another. In a highly functioning team, each member knows the boundaries of his or her own scope of practice and when to seek input from another team member.

The ability to communicate effectively with the patient and family is critical to a smooth transition to palliative care. It is not uncommon for healthcare professionals to soften the information given to patients in an attempt to protect them from hurtful, sad, or bad news. But as Fallowfield (2002) stated, "the truth may hurt but deceit hurts more."[17] Having skills in how to have difficult conversations is of paramount importance, and it should not be assumed that any team member comes equipped with them. Quill's (2000) article on how to initiate an end-of-life discussion with seriously ill patients provides excellent insight into the provider's perspective, as well as that of the patient. He points out that, as difficult as it is for clinicians to begin these conversations, healthcare professionals must be mindful that the patient may want to avoid the topic as well.[18]

Several models for promoting and improving oncology nurses' communication skills have been published, with a focus on providing a framework for difficult conversations and facilitating goals of care discussions.[19–23] Many organizations now teach "how to" have difficult conversations, and several of these involve simulated clinical scenarios where clinicians practice skills and get and give feedback. Box 9.1 includes an outline of several frameworks designed to teach and support communication skill development within the team, as well as with patients and families.

Challenges with Integrating Palliative Care into Oncology Care

While leaders in both palliative and oncology care are advocating for improved integration of palliative care into oncology care, the reality is that barriers exist regardless of the model in place. Bruera and Hui (2012) describe the MD Anderson Supportive and Palliative Care Program in Houston, Texas, which offers a range of services, including a mobile team, an acute palliative care unit, and a supportive care center for outpatients. Despite the scope of services, they report that their referrals remained "heterogeneous and delayed."[24] Patients admitted to the palliative care unit had a median stay of 7 days and a median survival of 21 days, with more than 70% of the patients discharged alive. Notably, patients with advanced solid tumor diagnoses were referred a median of 48 days before death, and those with hematologic malignancies were

---

Box 9.1 Resources for Communication Skill Training and Development

COMFORT: Communication Training Curriculum (www.clinicalcc.com)

- Module 1: Communication
- Module 2: Orientation and Opportunity
- Module 3: Mindful Presence
- Module 4: Family
- Module 5: Openings
- Module 6: Relating
- Module 7: Team

ONCOTALK: Improving Oncologists' Communication Skills (http://depts.washington.edu/oncotalk/learn/)

- Module 1: Fundamental Communication Skills
- Module 2: Giving Bad News
- Module 3: Managing Transitions to Palliative Care when Chemotherapy is Failing
- Module 4: Talking about Advance Care Plans and Do Not Resuscitate Orders
- Module 5: Discussing Treatment Options and Informed Consent
- Module 6: Conducting a Family Conference
- Module 7: Handling Requests for Therapies that You Feel Are Futile
- Module 8: Cultivating your Communication Skills

---

referred a median of 14 days before death.[24] They indicated that the term "palliative care" itself appeared to be a barrier. Simply changing the program name from "palliative care" to "supportive care" resulted in a significant referral increase.[24]

Role of the Palliative APRN

Bakitas and colleagues (2004) described the role of advanced practice registered nurses in one of the first palliative care demonstration projects for patients with advanced cancer. APRNs in hospital, community, and hospice settings collaborated to improve cancer patient care in a project called ENABLE (*E*ducate, *N*urture, *A*dvise *B*efore *L*ife *E*nds), aimed at symptom management, enhancing communication between patient/family and clinicians; offering support for family, friends, and caregivers; addressing the emotional and spiritual needs of the dying; and understanding the administrative structures required to deliver quality care.[25] This sentinel study affirmed the role of the APRN in the delivery of palliative care for patients with advanced cancer.

In 2014, Fox described the role of the acute care nurse practitioner as it relates to the implementation of the American College of Surgeons Commission on Cancer's standard on palliative care services.[26] The new standard stipulates that palliative care services be available to patients either onsite or by referral. The palliative care services should include team-based planning and pain and non-pain symptom management; facilitate communication among patients, families, and team members; and provide continuity of care, spiritual care, psychosocial support, bereavement support, and hospice care.[26] Fox posits that the educational preparation, scope, and standards of nurse practitioner practice place the acute care nurse practitioner in "the perfect position" to deliver quality palliative care to patients in the acute care setting.[26] Since APRNs may be employed in a variety of healthcare settings (private practice, long-term care facilities, home health, and hospice agencies), they can greatly influence the provision of palliative care. With the ability and licensure to assess, plan, implement, and evaluate palliative care interventions, APRNs should be an integral component in delivering quality palliative care.

APRN Practice on the Oncology Unit

As we strive to ensure integration of palliative care at the beginning of oncology care, specific approaches and assessments should be incorporated into clinical care. The NCCN guidelines detail three distinct aspects of care: palliative care screening, palliative care assessment, and palliative care interventions.[5] Box 9.2 provides questions to consider when performing an initial screening. The "surprise question," despite its simplicity, helps identify cancer patients who have a greatly increased risk of 1-year mortality.[27] These questions should be considered at every visit; if/when the patient has a positive screen, an interdisciplinary care plan to address the patient's and family's needs should be developed.

For patients meeting the screening criteria, the oncology team should perform a comprehensive palliative care assessment, evaluating the benefits and risks of anticancer therapy; the presence and severity of physical symptoms and psychosocial or spiritual distress; personal goals and expectations; educational and informational needs; and cultural factors affecting care.[5] NCCN provides specific interventions within each assessment area (see Box 9.3 for the list of symptoms included in the guidelines). The algorithms divide patients into three groups based on life expectancy: years to months, months to weeks, and weeks to days. Acknowledging the lack of precision around life expectancy, the panel recommended this approach to guide appropriate palliative care interventions.[5]

The ONS designed "Putting Evidence into Practice" (PEP) to provide nurses with evidence-based interventions for patient care and teaching on symptomatic concerns common in cancer patients.[28] Teams consisting of nurse scientists, advanced practice registered nurses, and staff nurses summarized and synthesized the available

---

Box 9.2 Palliative Care Screening Questions

1. Ask yourself the "surprise question": *Would I be surprised if this patient dies in the next 12 months?*

2. Does the patient have poorly controlled symptoms?

3. Does the patient have serious comorbid physical, psychiatric, and/or psychosocial concerns?

4. Does the patient have moderate to severe distress related to cancer diagnosis and therapy?

5. Does the patient have metastatic solid tumor?

6. Is the patient/family requesting palliative care?

Box 9.3 NCCN Guidelines for Palliative Care

Symptoms
- Pain
- Dyspnea
- Anorexia/cachexia
- Nausea and vomiting
- Constipation
- Malignant bowel obstruction
- Sleep/wake disturbances, including insomnia and sedation
- Delirium

Social support/resource management

Goals and expectations, educational and informational needs, and cultural factors affecting care for patient and family

Advance care planning

Response to requests for hastened death

Care of the imminently dying patient

Palliative sedation

After-death interventions

Source: http://www.nccn.org/professionals/physician_gls/pdf/palliative.pdf

---

evidence in numerous PEP topic areas (Box 9.4). The published resources detail the interventions that have demonstrated effectiveness in preventing or treating the outcome of interest. The classification system indicates the effectiveness and recommendation level of each intervention: red indicates the intervention is not effective, yellow indicates the effectiveness of the intervention is not established, and green indicates the intervention is effective and recommended. While some of the PEP topics included may be more prevalent in patients receiving chemotherapy/biotherapy and/or radiation therapy, many of them are common in the palliative care and hospice settings as well. In some topic areas, PEP resources include a review and summary of instruments to measure the specific symptom as well.

Freeman (2013) developed a pocket-sized tool, "CARES," to provide guidance on the management of common symptoms patients experience during the last days or hours of life. The tool includes prompts and recommendations for both nursing and medical interventions to assist in **C**omfort, **A**irway Management, **R**estlessness and delirium, **E**motional and spiritual support, and **S**elf-care.[29] The content of the tool complements the education provided by the Hospice and Palliative Care Nurses Association, certification examinations, and the End-of-Life Nursing Education Consortium programs. The use of the acronym CARES was intentional, with the intent of elevating the importance and respect for the unique skills required to care effectively for the dying and the family. The use of this tool by registered nurses and advanced practice registered nurses can improve the fundamental care provided to patients in their last few days of life.[29]

Pain Management

Despite decades of clinical research and many publications, clinical practice guidelines, and pain management algorithms, more

Box 9.4 Oncology Nursing Society "Putting Evidence into Practice" (PEP) Topics

Anorexia

Anxiety

Caregiver strain and burden

Cognitive impairment

Constipation

Depression

Diarrhea

Dyspnea

Fatigue

Hot flashes

Lymphedema

Mucositis

Nausea and vomiting

Pain

Peripheral neuropathy

Prevention of bleeding

Prevention of infection

Radiodermatitis

Skin reactions

Sleep/wake disturbances

Source: http://www2.ons.org/Research/PEP

than half of patients with advanced cancer have pain.[30] This is not because of knowledge, but because it is not applied. APRNs must be knowledgeable about the principles of pain management and be confident enough to escalate opioid doses as needed to achieve adequate pain control. NCCN guidelines provide detailed content on pain assessment and management as well as recommendations for managing the adverse effects of opioids in the adult with cancer, in the palliative care patient, and in the imminently dying.[5,31] The ONS PEP topics include content on acute pain, breakthrough pain, chronic pain, and refractory/intractable pain. Beyond the use of analgesics, treatment includes the use of gabapentin, tramadol, hypnosis/hypnotherapy, and music/music therapy as "likely to be effective." Effectiveness is not yet established for interventions such as acupressure, acupuncture, ketamine, massage/aromatherapy, morphine mouthwash, paravertebral block, perioperative drug combinations, pregabalin, preoperative dexamethasone, progressive muscle relaxation and guided imagery, reflexology, remifentanil patient-controlled analgesia, therapeutic touch, and topical anesthetics.

Freeman's model provides practical guidance on ways to promote comfort, such as eliminating unnecessary procedures and tests and modifying the environment to reduce unwanted stimuli.[29] While these issues may seem obvious, they are often not attended to and can contribute to poor pain control.

NCCN guidelines include palliative sedation as an available option and an effective symptom-control treatment for imminently dying patients with refractory symptoms and a life expectancy of hours to days. Informed consent, ethical consultation, and referral to a palliative care expert are recommended before initiating palliative sedation.

Dyspnea

Dyspnea has several definitions, many of which are similar and describe an uncomfortable awareness of breathing. Causes of dyspnea in cancer patients may be directly related to the disease itself (pulmonary parenchymal involvement with primary or metastatic tumor, lymphangitic carcinomatosis, airway obstruction, pleural tumor, pleural effusion, ascites, hepatomegaly, phrenic nerve paralysis, pulmonary leukostasis, or superior vena cava syndrome) or secondary to another problem (cachexia, electrolyte abnormalities, anemia, pneumonia, pulmonary aspiration, pulmonary emboli, neurologic paraneoplastic syndromes).[32] In the general cancer population, dyspnea is estimated to occur in 15% to 55% of patients at diagnosis and as many as 80% during the last week of life.[33] Despite its prevalence in this patient population, there is a paucity of research on effective interventions.

Based on extensive review of the literature and guided by the PEP rating system, ONS limits its "recommended for practice" intervention for dyspnea in patients with terminal or advanced cancer to the use of immediate-release oral parenteral opioids. While morphine has been most extensively studied, other opioids have been studied and demonstrate effect. Generally speaking, patients who are opioid-naïve should be given smaller doses initially. In patients who are already taking other opioids, the supplemental dose required to achieve relief of dyspnea is not clear, but many studies reported either 25% or 50% of the equivalent 4-hour opioid dose to be effective.

Interventions for which there are currently insufficient, poor-quality, or conflicting data include the use of extended-release morphine, nebulized medications (opioids, furosemide, and lidocaine), supplemental oxygen, acupuncture, and cognitive-behavioral approaches. Patients receiving these interventions may report a significant improvement in breathlessness and quality of life. Further trials are needed to strengthen these interventions before they can be recommended for practice.

In patients whose life expectancy is years to months, the NCCN guidelines include the use of temporary ventilator support for a severe reversible condition, oxygen therapy, benzodiazepines for anxiety, and psychosocial and emotional support for patients and family. In patients who are imminently dying, they recommend the following: reduce excessive secretions with scopolamine, hyoscyamine, or atropine; implement oxygen therapy if subjective report of relief; institute sedation as needed; discontinue fluid support; and consider low-dose diuretics if fluid overload is a concern.

Bone Marrow Transplantation
Palliative Care

Bone marrow transplantation (BMT) has made significant advances in the past several years as new therapies have emerged and advances in supportive care have been developed. However, mortality from BMT remains high and the symptom burden significant. While transplant teams have been leaders in the management of infections, mucositis, nutrition, and pain, many BMT programs have been reluctant to engage or collaborate with palliative experts.[34] Several publications confirm that palliative care services are used earlier and more frequently for patients with solid tumors than for those with hematologic malignancies.[35]

Symptom Management in BMT

Oral mucositis is a significant problem in patients undergoing transplantation, affecting both quality of life and survival. Along with the associated pain, there is an increased risk of infection, alteration in nutritional status, and increased risk of graft-versus-host disease.

The NCCN Task Force recommendations for the prevention and management of oral mucositis in cancer patients provides a detailed review of assessment tools, prevention approaches, and treatment strategies for cancer patients receiving chemotherapy, radiation therapy, and stem cell transplantation.[36]

While oral hygiene and dental health are important components of prophylaxis, most transplant patients report significant oral mucositis at some time during their treatment. Palifermin has been shown to significantly reduce the severity and duration of mucositis in transplant patients. It has also been shown to decrease the need for intravenous opioids for pain control and the need for parenteral nutrition. The NCCN guidelines currently only recommend its use as preventive therapy in patients receiving regimens containing total body irradiation before autologous stem cell transplantation. The cytoprotectant amifostine may also help in both the prevention and treatment of mucositis in transplant patients.

Transfusion Dependence

If patients relapse after transplant, many maintain a good quality of life with occasional transfusions. The decision to continue with transfusions becomes a conversation for the transplant team, patient, and family regarding the merits of ongoing transfusion support. Several studies have demonstrated the cost effectiveness of outpatient transfusions and the impact on quality of life they provide.

Conclusion

Caring for patients with advanced cancer or significant symptom burden, in any phase of treatment, requires that healthcare team members have expert assessment skills and knowledge of interventions and measures most likely to improve the patient's symptoms. Knowledge of common symptoms and effective interventions is a significant component of the healthcare team's role. Balancing disease-focused care with efforts to improve quality of life can be one of the most challenging tasks in caring for cancer patients and their families. A team member's ability to engage in conversations where patients can share their goals and plans for the future will be essential in determining the best course of action.

Palliative care as a component of oncology care is a logical progression for both specialties, and healthcare professionals have made significant progress in the past decade. Advanced practice registered nurses are well positioned to influence the care of patients in this new paradigm by initiating the conversation, as necessary, and then supporting the transition to palliative care, when appropriate. Collaboration between oncology APRNs and palliative APRNs is essential.

References

1. Henke-Yarbro C. The history of cancer nursing. In: McCorkle R, Grant M, Frank-Stromborg M, Baird SB, eds. *Cancer Nursing: A Comprehensive Textbook*. 2nd ed. Philadelphia, PA: Saunders; 1996:12–24.
2. Oncology Nursing Society. History. Available at http://www2.ons.org/about/History. Accessed July 1, 2015.
3. Oncology Nursing Certification Corporation. OCN® Test Blueprint. Available at http://www.oncc.org/TakeTest/Certifications/media/oncc/docs/certification/ocn_blueprint.pdf. Accessed July 1, 2015.
4. Seow H, Barbera L, Sutradhar R, et al. Trajectory of performance status and symptom scores for patients with cancer during the last six months of life. *J Clin Oncol*. 2011; 29(9): 1151–8.
5. NCCN Clinical Practice Guidelines in Oncology: Palliative Care. V1. 2014. Available at http://www.nccn.org/professionals/physician_gls/pdf/palliative.pdf
6. IOM National Cancer Policy Board. *Improving Palliative Care for Cancer*. Washington, DC: Institute of Medicine; 2001.
7. World Health Organization. Pain Relief and palliative care. In: *National Cancer Control Program: Policies and Managerial Guidelines*. 2nd ed. Geneva, Switzerland: World Health Organization; 2002:83–91.
8. Ferris FD, Bruera E, Cherny N, et al. Palliative cancer care a decade later: accomplishments, the need, next steps—from the American Society of Clinical Oncology. *J Clin Oncol*. 2009; 27(18): 3052–8.
9. Hui D, Elsayem A, De La Cruz M, et al. Availability and integration of palliative care at US cancer centers. *JAMA*. 2010; 303(11): 1055.
10. Smith TJ, Temin S, Alesi ER, et al. American Society of Clinical Oncology Provisional Clinical Opinion: The integration of palliative care into standard oncology care. *J Clin Oncol*. 2012; 30(8): 883.
11. Temel JS, Greer JA, Muzikansky MA, et al. Early palliative care for patients with metastatic non-small-cell lung cancer. *N Engl J Med*. 2010; 363(8): 733–42.
12. Bakitas M, Lyons KD, Hegel MT, et al. Effects of a palliative care intervention on clinical outcomes in patients with advanced cancer—the Project ENABLE II randomized controlled trial. *JAMA*. 2009; 302(7): 741–9.
13. Peppercorn JM, Smith TJ, Helft PR, et al. American Society of Clinical Oncology Statement: toward individualized care for patients with advanced cancer. *J Clin Oncol*. 2011; 29(6): 755–60.
14. Dickinson G. End-of-life and palliative care issues in medical and nursing schools in the United States. *Death Studies*. 2007; 31(8): 713–26.
15. White K, Coyne P, Lee J. Nurses' perceptions of educational gaps in delivering end-of-life care. *Oncol Nurs Forum*. 2011; 38(6): 711–7.
16. Weissman DE, Block SD, Blank L, et al. Recommendations for incorporating palliative care education into the acute care hospital setting. *Acad Med*. 1999; 74(8): 871–7.
17. Fallowfield LJ, Jenkins VA, Beveridge HA. Truth may hurt but deceit hurts more: communication in palliative care. *Palliat Med*. 2002; 16(4): 297–303.
18. Quill TE. Initiating end-of-life discussions with seriously ill patients—addressing the "elephant in the room." *JAMA*. 2000; 284(19): 2502–7.
19. McGuigan D. Communicating bad news to patients: a reflective approach. *Nurs Stand*. 2009; 23(31): 51–7.
20. Grant M. Communication. In: Dahlin C, Lynch A, eds. *Core Curriculum for the Advanced Hospice and Palliative Registered Nurse*. 2nd ed. Pittsburgh, PA: Hospice and Palliative Nurses Association; 2012:61–76.
21. Baer L, Weinstein E. Improving oncology nurses' communication skills for difficult conversations. *Clin J Oncol Nurs*. 2013; 17(3): E45–E51.

22. Peereboom K, Coyle N. Facilitating goals-of-care discussions for patients with life-limiting disease—Communication strategies for nurses. *J Hospice Palliat Nurs.* 2012; 14(4): 251–8.

23. Goldsmith J, Ferrell B, Wittenberg-Lyles E, Ragan S. Palliative care communication in oncology nursing. *Clin J Oncol Nurs.* 2012; 17(2): 163–7.

24. Bruera E, Hui D. Conceptual models for integrating palliative care at cancer centers. *J Palliat Med.* 2012; 15(11): 1263–7.

25. Bakitas M, Stevens M, Ahles T, et al. Project ENABLE: a palliative care demonstration project for advanced cancer patients in three settings. *J Palliat Med.* 2004; 7(2): 363–72.

26. Fox K. The role of the acute care nurse practitioner in the implementation of the Commission of Cancer's standards on palliative care. *Clin J Oncol Nurs.* 2014; 18(Suppl): 39–44.

27. Moss AH, Lunney JR, Culp S, et al. Prognostic significance of the "surprise" question in cancer patients. *J Palliat Med.* 2010; 13(7): 837–40.

28. Oncology Nursing Society. Putting Evidence into Practice. Available at http://www2.ons.org/Research/PEP

29. Freeman B. CARES—an acronym organized tool for the care of the dying. *J Hospice Palliat Nurs.* 2013; 15(3): 147–53.

30. Van den Beuken-van Everdingen MH, de Rijke JM, Kessels AG, Schouten HC, van Kleef M, Patijn J. Prevalence of pain in patients with cancer: A systematic review of the past 40 years. *Ann Oncol.* 2007; 18(9): 1437–49.

31. NCCN Clinical Practice Guidelines in Oncology: Adult Cancer Pain Version 2. Available at http://www.nccn.org/professionals/physician_gls/pdf/pain.pdf

32. DiSalvo WM, Joyce MM, Tyson LB, Culkin AE, Mackay K. Putting evidence into practice: evidence-based interventions for cancer-related dyspnea. *Clin J Oncol Nurs.* 2008; 12(2): 341–52.

33. Ripamonti C, Fusco F. Respiratory problems in advanced cancer. *Supportive Care in Cancer.* 2002; 10(3): 204–16.

34. Chung HM, Lyckholm LJ, Smith TJ. Palliative care in BMT. *Bone Marrow Transplant.* 2009; 43, 265–73.

35. Epstein AS, Goldberg GR, Meir DE. Palliative care and hematologic oncology: The promise of collaboration. *Blood Rev.* 2012; 26: 233–9.

36. Bensinger W, Schubert M, Ang KK, et al. NCCN Task Force Report: Prevention and management of mucositis in cancer care. *J National Comprehensive Cancer Network*, 2008; 6 (Suppl 1): S1–S21.

CHAPTER 10

Palliative Care in the Cardiac Specialty Unit

Beth Fahlberg

Key Points

◆ Cardiac patients have unique needs, experiences, pathophysiologies, and devices that necessitate a specialized approach to palliative care.

◆ Appropriate individualized decisions may be facilitated by including the palliative advanced practice registered nurse (APRN) in discussions among cardiac team members, patients, and families.

◆ An understanding of common cardiac diagnoses, tests, treatments, and medications, as well as the cardiac patient's and provider's mindset, will facilitate effective teamwork between the palliative APRN and the cardiac team.

Case Study 1

RB was a 72-year-old retired bank executive whose history included MI with cardiogenic shock and coronary artery bypass graft 15 years earlier. He had been admitted 9 months previously with a new MI after being fatigued for several months. At that point, his ejection fraction was 20% and he was not a good candidate for surgery or stent, so his medications were adjusted to make him more comfortable, and an ICD was placed 2 months later to prevent sudden death.

After the ICD was placed, RB was hospitalized for heart failure (HF) three times and his ICD shocked him on five separate occasions for ventricular fibrillation. To prevent additional shocks, his cardiologist prescribed the antiarrhythmic drug amiodarone. However, 1 month after starting this medication, RB developed worsening shortness of breath caused by amiodarone pulmonary toxicity, necessitating its discontinuation and the use of oral prednisone and continuous home oxygen to treat his symptoms.

The prednisone exacerbated RB's HF, and with little amiodarone left in his body, he started having more arrhythmias. This time, his ICD shocked him five times in a row, every 2 minutes. He was alert the whole time, crying out in distress. When the paramedics arrived, they deactivated the ICD by placing a magnet on it and transported him to the hospital with continuous cardiac monitoring and ACLS drugs ready for immediate use. An electrophysiologist and device nurse interrogated his ICD as soon as he arrived and found that he had received two shocks for slow ventricular tachycardia and three more that were unexplained, likely due to a

faulty lead. His daughter, who was with him during the episode at home, told them she would never forget that horrible experience.

RB's cardiologist placed a palliative care consult to clarify goals of care and to facilitate a meeting between the team and the patient and family to discuss treatment options: replacement of his malfunctioning ICD with a biventricular pacemaker and ICD that might also improve his functional status, or hospice with his ICD turned off.

The cardiologist explained that cardiac resynchronization from biventricular pacing had a 60% chance of improving his quality of life and functional status. However, the procedure also came with several important risks, including kidney injury, pacer pocket infection, and HF exacerbation. It was also likely that RB would continue to receive shocks from the new ICD periodically, since he continued to have ventricular arrhythmias and could not take any additional antiarrhythmic medications.

When the palliative APRN met RB, she was most concerned that he showed signs of severe anxiety any time the ICD was mentioned. She knew that patients could develop post-traumatic stress disorder after repeated ICD shocks, and when she explored his feelings about the ICD, RB cried, "I just want this thing out of my body!" When asked about his goals of care, he exclaimed "I'm so tired of this! I just want to go home and be left in peace! My dad died in his sleep. That's the way to go. This life I've got now is hell on earth!"

Based on RB's goals, and with the agreement of the cardiac team, the palliative APRN facilitated hospice referral, his ICD remained off, and he was discharged 2 days later with home hospice. He died suddenly 5 weeks later while watching a football game with his family.

Introduction

Heart disease is the leading cause of mortality in the United States, accounting for approximately 600,000 deaths per year.[1] Even so, palliative specialists infrequently participate in the care of patients who have heart disease,[2] and patients with heart problems represent only 11.5% to 15% of Medicare patients who die with the support of hospice.[3]

The purpose of this chapter is to describe the role of the palliative APRN in an acute cardiac unit. The palliative APRN working in this setting must understand the cardiac care culture and mindset and barriers to the use of palliative care in the cardiac setting, as well as the trajectory of cardiac disease, common symptoms, and other considerations that are covered in this chapter.

While the role of specialty palliative care in cardiac patient care is still being defined, the palliative APRN has a unique set of skills and perspectives that are needed in cardiology. Thus far, most palliative care efforts have focused on heart failure, yet palliative care is also needed in acute care cardiac specialty units where many patients and families are faced with decisions about tests and treatments that may pose significant risk with questionable benefit. Many of the patients are in their 80s and 90s and have multiple comorbidities (illness, dementia, or frailty). The palliative APRN working in a cardiac setting needs to have a basic understanding of common cardiac medications, tests, and treatments as well as the risks and benefits of each, or tools for risk stratification. Table 10.1 and Table 10.2 will serve as valuable clinical resources for the palliative APRN working with cardiac patients.

Palliative Care for Cardiac Patients

Over the past decade, the idea of palliative care for heart failure patients has been widely promoted and has gained increasing acceptance within HF specialty care.[3–5] A recent publication described a vision for palliative care in HF as a seamless collaborative process that includes both specialists in HF and palliative care:

> Ideally, the HF clinician would offer primary palliative care, with the support of palliative specialists as needed, until the patient reaches stage C and possibly D. At that time, the patient could be referred to specialist-level PC to assist when symptoms and decision making become more complex.[6]

However, despite increasing conceptual acceptance of this ideal model of care, translating palliative care specialty models into the care of HF patients has been more problematic.

Many different barriers to palliative care implementation in cardiac care have been described. These include cardiac providers' lack of understanding of the difference between hospice and palliative care as well as how and when to refer patients.[2,7] At the same time, smaller palliative care teams who begin to receive consults from cardiology may quickly become overwhelmed by the number of patients they are asked to see and the complexity of the situations they may encounter. As a result of these and other barriers, most palliative care for cardiac patients is currently being implemented using a primary or integrated palliative care model by cardiac nurses and primary care providers. However, evidence is beginning to accumulate showing that HF outcomes can be improved through the use of both primary and specialty palliative care. A model of joint patient and family visits that includes both cardiac and palliative specialists looks promising.[2] This joint model has been used to guide descriptions of the palliative APRN role on the cardiac specialty unit in this chapter. According to the 2013 American College of Cardiology/American Heart Association (ACC/AHA) heart failure management guidelines, "The core elements of comprehensive palliative care for heart failure delivered by clinicians include expert symptom assessment and management. Ongoing care should address symptom control, psychosocial distress, health-related quality of life, preferences about end-of-life care, caregiver support, and assurance of access

to evidence-based disease-modifying interventions. The heart failure team can help patients and their families explore treatment options and prognosis. The heart failure and palliative care teams are best suited to help patients and families decide when end-of-life care (including hospice) is appropriate. Assessment for frailty and dementia is part of this decision care process offered to the patient and family."[8] Specifically, "Evaluation for cardiac transplantation or MCS (mechanical circulatory support) in experienced centers should include formal palliative care consultation, which can improve advance care planning and enhance the overall quality of decision making and integrated care for these patients, regardless of the advanced HF therapy selected."[8(p 108)]

While these guidelines describe an ideal, their practical implementation is still in its infancy. Therefore, many of the suggestions in this chapter are based on limited evidence and the anecdotal reports of HF nurses and palliative care clinicians who are on the front lines, doing their best to implement new guidelines and the best evidence they have in complex and at times heart-wrenching situations.

Role of the Palliative APRN in Cardiac Care

Palliative APRNs can play a key role in promoting quality of life and facilitating "a good death" for cardiac patients. They can encourage the development of positive memories and prevent traumatic end-of-life experiences and complicated grief for their family members by promoting:

◆ Open, honest communication about what to expect using a "hope for the best, prepare for the worst" approach and shared decision making[9]

◆ Current, specific documentation of patient preferences for emergency care and resuscitation that can be easily retrieved by any provider in any setting, including the community

◆ Early conversations about end-of-life choices, such as specialist palliative care referral, hospice, and resuscitation options, including specific preferences about devices

◆ Patient and family decision-making meetings when patients are faced with high-risk options or advanced treatments, such as ventricular assist devices, transplant, and risky treatment choices[8]

◆ Support for family members and patients with complicated or advanced heart problems, such as ventricular assist device (VAD), and while waiting for transplant

◆ Early hospice referral when the patient with advanced HF has chosen to forgo further procedural and device "fixes"

◆ Cardiac-specific, guideline-based policies, orders, and training for specialty palliative care and hospice providers

◆ Access to outpatient palliative care and hospice for patients who choose that their cardiac devices, such as implantable cardioverter defibrillator (ICD) and VAD, remain active until they die

Barriers to Palliative Care Referrals for Cardiac Patients

While palliative care has become recognized as a guideline-based intervention in advanced HF, the number of patients being

Table 10.1 Medications Used in HF, with Palliative Care Considerations

Drug	Dosing	Benefit	Decisions	Risk	Monitoring	Self-Care
Diuretics, Loop *Furosemide* 20–40 mg 1 or 2 times/day Up to 600 mg/day *Torsemide* 10–20 mg 1 or 2 times/day Up to 200 mg/day[1] *Bumetanide* 0.5–1 mg 1 or 2 times/day Up to 10 mg/day[1]	Titrate dose to maintain dry wt. Second daily dose should be taken early to avoid nocturia. Diuretics work best when the patient is lying down. Try dosing in early a.m. before getting up & early afternoon before nap.	Maintenance dose controls fluid status. Higher doses or addition of metolazone provide diuresis. Alternatives to furosemide used in diuretic resistance.	Symptom improvement vs. worsening renal function & diuretic resistance. Diuretic resistance: ↑ oral dose Add metolazone IV bolus IV infusion	Worsening renal function. Risk of dehydration with poor intake, anorexia, nausea, vomiting. Diuretics may need to be paused or taken only when wt ↑ until intake improves.	↑ or ↓ K+ & Mg++ Adjust replacement as diuretic dose is titrated. ↑ Creatinine Obtain wt daily or several times weekly & with symptom exacerbation & ↓ oral intake.	Wt monitoring ↓ sodium diet Dose adjusted often; current dose may not be on the bottle. Need for both maintenance and PRN orders for diuretics and K supplements.
Diuretics, Thiazide-like *Metolazone*	Dosed PRN when above dry wt, taken with furosemide	Potent diuretic to treat fluid overload	Requires daily communication with pt, especially when initiating treatment	Can cause marked diuresis and K+ loss. Carefully follow labs & fluid status.	Relief of dyspnea & orthopnea Wt, K+, signs of dehydration	Wt monitoring ↓ sodium diet
ACE Inhibitors *Enalapril* *Lisinopril*	Titrated up to highest tolerable dose used in randomized controlled trials. Cough in 5–20% of pts. Angiotensin receptor blocker can be substituted.[8]	Prevent HF sx & ↑ survival in all pts with ↓EF	In advanced HF may need to stop ACE for symptomatic hypotension, yet it is a key drug in sx management.[8]	↓ renal function Risk of ↑ K+ with ↓ renal function/K-sparing diuretics.[23]	K+, Cr. ↑ dose may ↑ creatinine if > 30% ↑ consult cardiac specialist about discontinuing/reducing dose[23]	Discontinuation can cause rapid deterioration of heart function and symptoms.
Beta-blockers *Metoprolol* *Carvedilol* *Atenolol*	HF: Titrated up to highest tolerated dose guided by randomized controlled trial doses. Should not be stopped suddenly: reflex tachycardia.	↓ EF: ↓ risk of HF sx, ↑survival CAD: controls ischemic sx by ↓cardiac work. Arrhythmia treatment & HR control in AF. HTN.	Consider ↓ dose or stopping with symptomatic ↓ HR (<55) ↓ BP (SBP <80).	Bradycardia Hypotension Fatigue Worsening respiratory function in asthma/chronic obstructive pulmonary disease Blunting of hypoglycemia in diabetes	Monitor HR, BP at each visit and symptoms of light-headedness, fatigue	Pt should know how to check pulse, and do this periodically or if symptomatic.

Drug	Dosing	Benefit	Decisions	Risk	Monitoring	Self-Care
Digoxin	HF: No loading doses needed. Low dose less frequently if high risk for toxicity (i.e., elderly, renal failure). May need to ↓ dose with progressive wt loss & cachexia in advanced HF. Goal digoxin level: 0.5–0.9 ng/mL.[8]	HR control in AF, as adjunct to beta-blocker or calcium channel blocker. May ↑ functional status, ↑ quality of life & ↓ hospitalization in pt with HF & low EF if pt symptomatic after GDMT in place.	Risk vs. benefit: May help HF sx but toxicity risk, particularly with ↓ K^+, ↓ Mg^{++}, ↓ body mass, ↓ renal function, ↑ age[8]	Toxicity: Bradyarrhythmias, heart block, GI & neuro sx. Contraindicated in heart block without pacemaker. Numerous drug interactions.	HR should be ≥ 60 (lower may indicate toxicity) Digoxin levels K^+, Mg^{++}, renal function	Accurate dosing essential to avoid toxicity.
Anticoagulant **Anti thrombotic agents** *Warfarin/Coumadin* "should be individualized based on shared decision making after discussion of absolute and relative risks of stroke and bleeding and the pts values and preferences."[24(p 12)]	Complex dosing guided by algorithms & INR results, often by anticoagulation service or cardiology. Typical INR goals: 2–3 AF, other thrombosis treatment & prevention 2.5–3.5 mechanical valve	Reduces risk of embolic stroke in AF, prosthetic valve, thrombus	High risk: previous CVA, TIA. Risk calculators: CHA_2DS_2-VASc- Use for nonvalvular AF, 2 or greater anticoagulation recommended.[24] Anticoagulation bleeding risk: HAS-BLED ATRIA	↓ INR: stroke ↑ INR: bleeding Heparin bridge needed for invasive tests & treatments. Risk of bleeding/hemorrhagic stroke in pt at risk for falls. Aspirin or other antiplatelets may be used when risk outweighs benefit.	INR fluctuates with changing health status, diet, medication changes. Many drug interactions.	Warfarin: Complex dosing, many interactions. INR blood test ≥1x/week when starting, monthly when stable.[24] Vitamin K balanced diet.
Lipid-Lowering Agents *Statins*	Dosed to achieve lipid level goals	↓ cardiovascular events[8]	Consider discontinuing in pts with limited life expectancy.	Myositis: muscle aches. Stop drug, check for ↑ creatinine kinase.	Lipid levels	Lifestyle: diet, exercise, wt loss

ACE = angiotensin-converting enzyme; BP = blood pressure; EF = ejection fraction; GDMT = guideline-directed medical therapy; HF = heart failure; HR = heart rate; ICD: Implantable cardioverter-defibrillator; INR = International Normalized Ratio.

Table 10.2 Treatments for HF, with Palliative Care Considerations

Name	Purpose	Description	Decisions	Benefits	Risks	Psychosocial	Comments
Cardiac resynchronization therapy (CRT)	Biventricular pacemaker or ICD paces both ventricles at the same time to improve cardiac output when ventricles are out of sync.	This is not an emergent treatment, so ensure adequate time for decision making.	Indications: EF ≤ 35% on GDMT + EKG QRS ≥ .15 sec + moderate to severe functional symptoms[8,25]	60% chance of improved quality of life & symptoms	Quality of life may not improve. Pt & family need to weigh cost/risk/benefit ratio carefully.	Not appropriate with noncardiac conditions significantly limiting life expectancy/functional status	Most pts fitting criteria are also candidates for ICD. Combined device should be considered in anticipation of symptom progression.[25]
Implantable cardioverter-defibrillator (ICD): Device information & settings should be easily available to all emergent care providers. Device nurse & company representative are contacts for issues, detailed risk/benefit information, & deactivation of shocking functions.	Prevent recurrence of SCA in survivor.[26] Primary prevention in pt with sustained or symptomatic VT/VF > 2 days after MI if no ongoing ischemia.[27] Primary prevention of SCA in systolic HF & EF <30% following revascularization (if appropriate) & clinically stable on GDMT.[26]	ICD has both pacing and shocking capabilities as well as recording cardiac arrhythmias. Its programs pace slow & fast HRs & shock fast HRs. Device function is tested and settings are adjusted during procedure. With ICD, heart is stimulated to go into arrhythmia with treatment by device while pt under anesthesia & continuously monitored with external defibrillation & ACLS if needed.	Appropriate if: Consistent with goals, preferences, & advance directives. Discussion of shock deactivation while nearing end-of-life. Replacement or repair of ICD with battery depletion, device failure or recall.	May prolong life in pts at high risk for SCA. Life-saving nature of device may alleviate anxiety for pt & family; "safety net." Pacing functions may alleviate fatigue throughout end-of-life. Deactivation of pacing function may result in rapid death if pt is pacer-dependent. Device interrogation is needed to determine risks.	Implantation risks: Device or lead malfunction/recall. Inappropriate, recurrent shocks.[25] Infection < 1% risk initial, 2.6–7% with replacement[28] often requires surgical removal/replacement.[25] Dye used in lead placement may injure kidneys, especially if prior renal impairment. Lead displacement (1%), usually treated by surgically repositioning device.[25] Lead replacement complications in 15%.[28] Extreme pain with shocks "kicked in the chest by a horse." Shocks while actively dying.	ICD-related psychological distress more common if: Age <50 Female Preexisting psychiatric condition ≥ 5 shocks Poor social support can cause anxiety or post-traumatic stress disorder.[29] Anxiety symptoms usually improve over time after implantation.[30] 73% worry about battery life[28] or device failure.	Using optimal HF GDMT & follow-up self-care. No other issues greatly increasing procedural risk. Arm movement restrictions after placement to prevent lead dislodgement. Follow-up device checks by phone and in clinic, approx. every 3 months & with problems/shocks.
Mechanical circulatory support: Ventricular assist device (VAD) Mean cost $201K (±106K) for index hospital stay; additional inpt costs in first yr $26K (± 52K)[20]	Pumps blood to support cardiac output in severe ventricular failure. May be used with left ventricle (most common), right ventricle, or both.	Requires constant energy supply outside the body. Risk of infection at entry site. Pt cannot lie on the exit-site side. Pt cannot swim or take a bath. Ongoing need for anticoagulants. Withdrawal of VAD may not be widely discussed; practices vary between VAD centers & providers. Withdrawal of ICD shock function is appropriate in same discussions.[31]	Palliative care consult recommended for pts being considered for VAD.[8] Palliative medicine consult before destination therapy "preparedness planning"; discussion of possible situations unique to destination therapy. Device failure Poor quality of life after VAD implant Catastrophic VAD-related events Debilitating comorbidities[32]	May improve survival, functional status & symptoms in advanced HF. Initially developed as "bridge to transplant" but is now commonly used long term as "destination therapy." Recent studies have shown improved heart function in some pts during VAD therapy, which may allow them VAD withdrawal at some point.	Mortality: In-hospital: 10% 1 year: 26% Readmission all cause: 81% Cardiac 43% Number of readmissions: 2 (±2)[20] Pump thrombus, with death, pump exchange or transplant 5–12%[21] Infection Bleeding Embolism Pump failure	Adjustment disorders[31] Self-care involvement is high: equipment care & response to alarms. Constant connection to power supply: worry and anxiety. Exit-site care Infection control Exercise Nutrition Fluid balance Medications Self-monitoring[31] pt/caregiver response to alarms	Self-care priorities may need to be redefined at end-of-life. Exercise & nutrition may become less important. Some meds may be less important. Drive line & exit wound care still needed.[31] Close communication with VAD coordinator is important when working with these pts.

Heart transplant					
Replacement of weak damaged heart with a new heart from a brain-dead donor Medicare pays for 40% of heart transplants. Average payment: $375K yr;[33] $45K later yrs.[34] Transplant is initially more expensive than VAD, but in the long term may be more cost-effective with better outcomes.[34]	Extensive workup required to ensure patient is healthy and will be able to engage in the extensive self-care required. Surgery is sudden, based on organ availability. If a donor organ is not healthy, the surgery may be cancelled. Postop patients require lifetime rigorous immunosuppressant therapy and many medications to prevent complications.	Palliative care consult recommended for pts being considered for transplant.[8] Risk of worsening health or death while on waiting list. Pretransplant mortality 12.4%[34] 55% wait ≤ 1 yr; 66% wait ≤ 3 yrs for HTx.[34] 13.9% taken off list.[34] Median survival 11.6 years after transplant. Survival rates: 88% at 1 yr, 81% at 3 yrs, 75% at 5 yrs, 56% at 10 yrs[34]	Mortality: 12% in first year 25% in 5 years. 44% in 10 years Mortality causes at ≤ 3 mo/1 year: Infection 1.4%/2.3% CV/Cerebrovascular events 1.3%/3% 2 yr Graft failure 1.1%[34] 62.7% on life support to survive until HTx: 36.2% IV inotropes 35.6% LVAD 5.9% IABP Rejection: 23% 1st yr 45% in 5 yrs[34] Hospitalization: 36.3% 1st yr 61.1% in 4 yrs[34] Immunosuppressant risks: diabetes mellitus, hypertension, ↑lipids, renal failure, malignancy Post-HTx: lymphoproliferative disorder (often fatal): 5.4% at 5 years[35] Lowest survival rates: age 18–34, black, no VAD	Patient engagement is critical: medications, follow-ups. Ongoing uncertainty. Dashed hopes from "false alarms": pt called & prepped, transplant cancelled. Post-transplant: Positive: pride, hope, gratitude, altruism, faith, optimism, control over new challenges, normalcy.[36] Negative: fear, grief, depression, frustration, mood swings, discrimination Social support is very important. It may negatively influence pt by preventing person from regaining independence.[36]	Post-transplant period: uncertainty about quality of life, health, future, whether personality will change.[37] <30% of HTx recipients return to work.[38] 2,400 HTx per year; 130 HTx with other organs (lung, kidney, liver). Recipient must be near transplant center while on waiting list.

EF = ejection fraction; GDMT = guideline-directed medical therapy; HF = heart failure; HTx = heart transplant; HR = heart rate; ICD = implantable cardioverter-defibrillator; SCA = sudden cardiac arrest; VAD = ventricular assist device.

referred to specialist palliative care and hospice remains low.[6,10] Cardiologists' use of specialty palliative care teams and hospice has been limited by a number of important issues, such as:

1. Cardiologists' perception that cardiac symptom control is often most effectively accomplished using guideline-based cardiac therapies to treat the underlying problem, and that appropriate use of complex medications for symptom control requires specialty cardiac training and experience[6]

2. The many options to treat advanced HF symptoms, including medications, interventional procedures, surgeries, and devices.[6] Acute cardiac events often precipitate a need for these treatments, necessitating rapid decision-making processes. The urgency of the situation and guideline-based algorithms often dictate a rapid course of action. Importantly, low mortality rates are often the primary measure of quality cardiac care and interventional effectiveness.

3. The misperception that specialty palliative providers mainly guide patients into hospice. At present, palliative specialists are often brought into the cardiac patient's care when all treatment options have been exhausted and the end is near, sometimes only hours or days away. The cardiac team can benefit from a broader understanding of the role of specialty palliative care upstream in the cardiac disease trajectory, facilitating decisional support, holistic care, symptom management, and support.[5,6]

4. Lack of consistent access to hospices prepared to provide guideline-based care for HF patients, or those who require current guideline-based treatments for symptom management and patient-centered care. Cardiac patients who may have difficulty accessing hospice include those wishing to keep their ICD active, those approaching the end-of-life who are VAD-dependent, and patients on inotrope infusions.[3]

The palliative APRN working in a cardiac specialty unit should understand these issues, as well as what dying looks like in cardiology. Shared understanding between cardiac and palliative care providers in terms of viewpoints, knowledge, and experiences will promote effective implementation of team-based palliative care in cardiac settings. The role of the palliative APRN within the cardiac care team is still in its infancy, yet there is great promise for this role as APRNs bridge the divide between cardiology and specialty palliative care on cardiac specialty units.

Unpredictability of the Cardiac Trajectory as a Barrier to Palliative Care

An ongoing barrier to the use of palliative care and hospice for HF patients is the unpredictability of the cardiac trajectory. The cardiac patient often has fluctuating symptoms and functional status with a subtle decline over time and often an unexpected end. Heart disease may affect someone for 30 days or 30 years, and during an acute care hospitalization it can be very difficult to predict which is more likely. This can have a marked impact on patients, who may not know what their future holds or when they should ensure that their legacy and end-of-life "business" are complete. Indeed, we rarely talk with patients about ensuring that their business is complete and that they have a chance to leave a legacy and say goodbye. These anticipatory rituals are consistent with a certain death, not the unexpected death so common in cardiac patients.

The uncertainty of the cardiac trajectory can have serious consequences for patients, as well as for the loved ones who survive them. Families may live for years feeling ambiguous about their loved one's future and their own prospects and plans, not knowing how long their situation will last, or how to anticipate or prepare for what's to come. Even if the patient and family can see what is coming, their distress may be compounded when healthcare providers are not honest with them about the prognosis. This is particularly troublesome when the provider has communicated only messages of hope for a transplant, VAD, or other "fix," failing to provide anticipatory guidance about the very real risk of sudden death.

Case Study 2

JD was a 34-year-old survivor of Hodgkin's lymphoma. Ten years after his remission, he was diagnosed with Adriamycin-induced cardiomyopathy, with an ejection fraction of 15%. He was on guideline-directed medical therapy and was on the transplant list for the preceding month. He was clinically stable and was scheduled for a biventricular ICD placement in 2 weeks. However, he was unable to work, so his wife was working overtime in addition to caring for their two young children and trying to do all of the household chores that JD did in the past.

One night when cooking dinner with his family, JD suddenly collapsed on the kitchen floor. His wife called 911 and started CPR, yelling at him and crying the whole time, while his kids watched, not knowing what was going on. When the emergency technicians arrived, JD was in a fine ventricular fibrillation. Despite multiple shocks and ACLS drugs, he could not be resuscitated.

After his death, JD's wife tried to keep the family going, but she struggled with what she thought should be simple tasks, such as paying the bills and accessing their online bank accounts. JD had never compiled their account information in one place, and the passwords were all in his head, so she is still trying to piece together their financial records and she is frequently surprised by late payment bills and calls from collection agencies. She is angry with JD for not planning ahead more. She's also worried about the kids. The younger one wakes at night terrified, reliving her memory of seeing her father die. The older child has become detached and acts indifferent, but his mother can tell there are some deep wounds.

Ambiguous Dying

The last several years of life for a person with HF have been described as "ambiguous dying." Providers are often uncertain about whether the patient is dying, and when death is likely to occur.[11] As seen in Case Study 2, patients can be very sick, yet their providers are unlikely to describe them as "dying" or to talk with them about planning for the possibility of a sudden death.[11] This ambiguity about when or whether someone is dying also makes it difficult for providers to know what to say when about the prognosis, or to apply hospice admission criteria, which assume a predictable dying trajectory, as was characteristic of cancer in past decades. This ambiguity is also seen in patients, who typically overestimate their life expectancy.[12]

The cardiac disease trajectory is a "stuttering" one, with symptom exacerbations and remissions punctuated by significant "events," such as a new myocardial infarction (MI), arrhythmia, or infection, any of which could lead to death.[4,11,13] The cardiac patient usually has several other serious chronic conditions, such as diabetes, chronic obstructive pulmonary disease, dementia, and renal failure, some of which have contributed to or been a consequence of their heart problems.[14]

When the patient is stable, the body's physiologic systems and compensatory mechanisms are finely balanced in homeostasis. However, it takes only a slight insult to the person's health, such as getting the flu, for a rapid downward spiral to begin. In many cases, cardiac patients die within a few days of being stable. The palliative APRN who understands the uncertainties of heart disease can use events that prompt hospitalization as a signal for discussions about goals of care, preparing for the "what ifs," and for reviewing whether hospice referral is appropriate at that time.

The Cardiology Mindset

Cardiac events are often sudden, prompting cardiac providers to spring into action. Since day 1 of our healthcare careers, we have been trained to do cardiopulmonary resuscitation (CPR) in response to a patient dying. And we don't call it "dying"; we call it a "code," "cardiac arrest," "ventricular fibrillation," or "asystole." Those working in cardiac specialty units are trained in cardiac monitoring, are certified in Advanced Cardiac Life Support (ACLS), and have to demonstrate competency in providing appropriate care in a cardiac emergency. Therefore, we are constantly on the alert and prepared to jump into action at any moment to intervene when the patient is "crashing" so that he or she won't die. We have difficulty trying to conceive of the cardiac patient who is "actively dying" because the processes that cause this, usually arrhythmias and cardiogenic shock, happen quickly and prompt us to action. Not intervening in some way is difficult for us, as it goes against our training and mindset of "doing something." As a result, it can be very difficult for cardiac providers to accept, understand, or implement the idea of letting "nature take its course." When confronted with a patient who has an acute cardiac event, but who is on Do-Not-Resuscitate (DNR) status with comfort care only, it can be difficult to switch from a life-saving to a palliative care mindset.

Advance Care Planning in a Cardiac Population

One of the challenges of providing palliative care to a cardiac population is that advance care planning is often not straightforward. Resuscitation options in cardiac patients can (and should) be complex. In addition, many life-saving treatments and devices, such as cardiac interventions, surgery, VAD, and transplant, can alleviate symptoms and prolong life in even the sickest cardiac patients, and these should be acknowledged as an important part of cardiac decision making.

DNR Decisions: The Cardiac Patient's Perspective

The DNR decision may be more complicated for cardiac patients and family than it is in other patient populations. A cardiac patient may have survived cardiac arrest because someone did CPR and shocked him with an automated external defibrillator (AED). After the initial hospitalization and recovery, the patient often reports a happy, healthy life for years afterward, with an ICD providing a safety net in case cardiac arrest happens again. The patients often express their gratitude to the person who did CPR and state that the additional years were a gift they did not take for granted.

With this experience in mind, the cardiac survivor with advanced HF may not be interested in a DNR order. He or she is likely to remember the positive outcome and assume that the next time CPR is needed, the outcome will be the same. But this does not take into account the patient's changes in health.

Cardiac technologies and treatment developments have outpaced communication, documentation, and policies for cardiac patients, particularly those with devices like ICDs and VADs. Therefore, the one-size-fits-most approach to advance care planning that is reflected in most legal documents may not fit the cardiac patient very well. He or she may want more options, considering what he or she has previously experienced, as well as the risks and benefits of each.

Unfortunately, most advance care planning documents and DNR orders do not easily accommodate "special requests." In light of this, it may be time to consider moving toward a menu-type approach to advance care planning for cardiac patients, which may also be appropriate in other populations. Options on the emergency cardiac care menu may include:

- Chest compressions
- Emergency drugs
- ICD shock and pacing
- External shock
- External pacing
- Rescue breathing
- Mechanical ventilation
- Mechanical circulatory support
- Coronary angioplasty and stent
- Dialysis

The palliative APRN working with cardiac patients should be prepared to address the risks, burdens, and benefits of each option for the individual and to legally document and effectively communicate the patient's specific goals of care and preferences.

Advanced HF

One of the greatest challenges in working with cardiac patients can be determining when they are at the end of the testing and treatment process and ready to consider hospice. While a 6-month prognosis can be challenging to accurately determine, a pattern of worsening functional status with little improvement, despite guideline-directed medical therapy (GDMT) titration, is a key indicator of limited life expectancy that has consistently emerged in the research.[13,15,16] Other signs of a poor prognosis include:

- Recurrent and/or recent HF hospital admissions
- Unintentional weight loss (pattern of decreasing dry weight) and cachexia

- ICD shocks or ventricular arrhythmias
- Presence of third heart sound (S3) in patient with reduced ejection fraction
- Recent withdrawal of angiotensin-converting enzyme (ACE) inhibitors and/or beta-blockers due to medication intolerance[8]

The use of hospice in patients with advanced HF, as well as in patients who are not interested in pursuing advanced treatment options, may prevent unwanted hospital admissions and futile tests and treatments, while reducing healthcare costs.[6]

Preventing the readmission of HF patients is now one of the top organizational priorities at hospitals across the United States. In 2012, the Affordable Care Act began implementing Medicare reimbursement penalties for all hospitals with HF 30-day readmission rates above the national benchmark.[6] As stated before, the trajectory of advanced HF is characterized by recurrent hospital admission.[8] Palliative specialty care and early hospice referral are consistently identified as keys to reducing readmission rates. An understanding of the financial implications of HF readmission and the use of evidence-based palliative care strategies to reduce these readmissions can provide leverage for palliative APRNs looking for palliative care program funding.

Palliative Management of Cardiac Symptoms

As illustrated in the first case study, pain is not the most common cause of physical distress among cardiac patients in the later stages of heart disease. Fatigue, functional limitations, and difficulty breathing are common and bothersome physical symptoms of heart disease. These symptoms may have an insidious onset, slowly worsening over time. Patients may report "a lack of energy," "slowing down," "having to pace myself," or difficulty sleeping, and it can be difficult for both patients and providers to distinguish whether these symptoms are due to heart problems or another cause. Therefore, palliative APRNs must understand the common symptoms specific to HF and/or cardiology patients, and interventions that will be most appropriate to the underlying cause of these symptoms.

Dyspnea and Difficulty Sleeping

Dyspnea is a common and distressing symptom in cardiac patients. It can be exacerbated by exertion or lying supine, or it may occur when sleeping. People with dyspnea on exertion often reduce their activity to avoid this symptom; therefore, an accurate assessment of the patient's actual recent physical activity is a key element of the history that can help identify problems and treat symptoms. Orthopnea (shortness of breath that is exacerbated when lying flat) is a hallmark sign of fluid overload in the cardiac patient, indicating a need for diuresis. This feeling of suffocation or drowning prompts patients to sit up so they can breathe, then to prop themselves up in bed with pillows or sleep in a recliner. In paroxysmal nocturnal dyspnea, another sign of fluid overload that occurs while sleeping, the patient wakes up at night unable to breathe or feeling claustrophobic. This is also alleviated by sitting upright or getting up.

The patient who reports difficulty sleeping should be carefully assessed for signs of fluid overload. The typical constellation of signs and symptoms includes a recent increase above the patient's dry weight, jugular vein distention, hepatic congestion, ascites, hepatojugular reflux, edema, and crackles in the lungs. The absence of edema and crackles should not be used as sole indicators of fluid status, as they may be absent in the patient with chronic HF who has fluid overload. A rise in the brain natriuretic peptide blood level can useful in identifying fluid overload as the source of dyspnea.

Fluid overload-related dyspnea requires diuresis for symptom management.[17] This is usually accomplished with loop diuretics (see Table 10.1). Morphine and lorazepam can be used to alleviate feelings of air hunger and anxiety while diuresis is being accomplished, but these drugs should not be used as the sole treatments for fluid-related dyspnea, as they will only mask the cause of the symptoms rather than treating it, with ongoing symptom distress.

Another source of dyspnea that should not be ignored is the occurrence of a new cardiac event, such as a new MI and/or acute pulmonary edema. The sudden onset of new symptoms should prompt rapid assessment and treatment as well as communication with the family consistent with the patient's goals and plan of care.

An exception to the use of diuretics in treating fluid-related dyspnea may be the person who is actively dying as the result of a new cardiac event and whose expected prognosis is hours to a day. Diuretics are unlikely to provide symptomatic benefit if this person is in cardiogenic shock, as the weakened heart will not adequately perfuse the body, severely limiting the absorption, distribution, and metabolism of drugs like diuretics and preventing excretion of excess fluid. In this situation, small doses of opioids and benzodiazepines in the opioid-naïve cardiac patient may provide comfort while the patient and family say goodbye.[17]

Cardiac Pain

In the cardiac patient who reports pain, it is important to distinguish between "cardiac" and "noncardiac" pain, as the causes, treatments, and short-term implications are very different. In addition, assessment should not be limited to using the word "pain," as this may not prompt the patient to report his or her cardiac symptoms. Patients may perceive their cardiac ischemic symptoms in different ways and may describe their symptoms with terms like "discomfort," "pressure," or "heaviness."

Cardiac "pain" or "discomfort" is usually a sign of poor perfusion to the heart muscle (ischemia or infarction). It is most commonly aggravated by exertion and alleviated with rest (or stopping the activity), nitroglycerin, oxygen, and morphine. Cardiac symptoms may indicate serious problems, such as a new MI; therefore, in the absence of a treatment plan for symptomatic relief, the patient should be promptly evaluated for the cause and treated until the symptoms are completely relieved. Prompt treatment of cardiac symptoms with a goal of complete relief and ongoing prevention with medications that promote coronary perfusion will promote positive patient outcomes, including better quality of life and functional status.

Stable cardiac symptoms often present the same way from one time to the next, but the symptoms may differ markedly between patients. Women, people with diabetes, and older adults are at higher risk for atypical cardiac symptoms or silent ischemia. In the absence of chest discomfort, patients with silent ischemia may have other symptoms, such as shortness of breath, lightheadedness, gastrointestinal upset, or falls. Dramatic presentations with these types of symptoms should raise a high index of suspicion for a new cardiac event, prompting rapid evaluation and treatment or implementation of the agreed-upon plan.

Noncardiac Pain

Noncardiac pain is common in people with heart disease, usually associated with coexisting conditions such as arthritis, diabetic neuropathy, and back problems. However, non-steroidal anti-inflammatory drugs (NSAIDs) should be avoided in heart disease patients if possible, because they carry a higher risk of serious cardiovascular events, such as MI, stroke, and death.[18] NSAIDs block renal prostaglandin synthesis, which can compromise renal function and contribute to fluid retention in patients with HF and older adults. Many cardiac patients take anticoagulants and antiplatelet medications, which are also contraindications to NSAIDs because of the additive risk of bleeding. When patients with heart disease require NSAIDs, naproxen may be the safest alternative. It should be used at the lowest dose possible for the shortest time possible.[18,19]

New Cardiac Event

If a new event occurs, a cardiac patient's proxy, goals of care, and advance care plan should be immediately available to direct treatment decisions. The majority of cardiac patients die suddenly, so a rapid change in the patient's condition should prompt quick intervention from the cardiac team and palliative APRN, consistent with the patient's wishes. If the patient has chosen a comfort approach, the team's interventions should be directed toward promoting open, honest, empathetic communication and comfort for the patient and support for the family, realizing that the period when the patient is "actively dying" may be short and the end may come suddenly.

If an advance care plan has not been identified or if the patient has elected to have some or all resuscitative or life support measures employed, the palliative care team should facilitate communication about the patient/family decisions and the need for monitoring and intensive care. The palliative APRN can assist in clarifying the code status with the physician and begin preparing for resuscitation or activating a rapid response. The palliative APRN can ensure that the family members have adequate support and resources to promote their psychological, spiritual, and physical well-being throughout this challenging period.

Emerging Roles for Palliative APRNs in Cardiology

Family Support During and After Resuscitation

The palliative APRN with an understanding of ACLS may play an important role in supporting and providing information to the family of a cardiac patient during a code or rapid response. Offering the family the option of being present during resuscitation is widely accepted. However, the family should be accompanied by a clinician who can explain what is happening, assist with contacting support systems, and facilitate decision making.[20,21]

Anticipatory guidance may be used early in the code to begin preparing the family for the possibility that the patient may die, and about their ability to stop resuscitation efforts at some point. As the code progresses, the palliative APRN can provide explanations about what is happening, explain some of what the family members are seeing and hearing, according to their needs, and

answer questions. It can be comforting for the family to know that the team did all they could to save their loved one. This type of support during a family-witnessed resuscitation can prevent complicated grief and post-traumatic stress disorder in bereaved family members.[22] The palliative APRN is an ideal person for the important yet underimplemented role of family liaison for the code and rapid response teams.

The Palliative APRN as an Integral Member of the Cardiac Interdisciplinary Team

In this chapter we envision the role of palliative APRNs on the cardiac specialty unit, yet this vision has been limited to patients with advanced HF. As this role becomes established, there is ample opportunity for expansion of the role to include decisional support and holistic symptom management care for many more types of cardiac patients. The role of the palliative APRN in the care of patients being worked up for VAD is currently being identified. Another avenue that may emerge soon in cardiac palliative care is decisional support for any high-risk cardiac patients who are considering their testing and treatment options. These roles will require more advanced understanding of cardiology as well as the risks, benefits, and nuances of different options. The palliative APRN role on the cardiac specialty unit is in its infancy.

Conclusion

As seen in this chapter, there are many ways that the patient with cardiac disease in the acute care setting can benefit from specialist palliative care. The palliative APRN can play an important role in the care of patients on the acute cardiac specialty unit by promoting a focus on comfort, quality of life, communication, shared decision making, advance care planning, and family support. Cardiac patients and their families are challenged by needs, experiences, and pathophysiologic changes that are unique to this population, affecting their quality of life, decisions, and the advance care plans that are appropriate for them. An understanding of the cardiac provider's mindset and common cardiac diagnoses, tests, treatments, and decisions will enable the palliative APRN to become a trusted, effective member of the interdisciplinary cardiac team so that one day specialty palliative care will be available to all cardiac patients from diagnosis to death.

References

1. Murphy SL, Xu J, Kochanek KD. Deaths: final data for 2010. *National Vital Statistics Reports.* 2013; 61(4): 1–117.
2. Lindvall C, Hultman TD, Jackson V. Overcoming the barriers to palliative care referral for patients with advanced heart failure. *J Am Heart Assoc.* 2014; 3(1): e000742. doi:10.1161/JAHA.113.000742.
3. Goodlin SJ. Hospice care following heart failure admission: what next? *J Card Fail.* 2012; 18(6): 478–9. doi:10.1016/j.cardfail.2012.03.004.
4. Goodlin SJ, Hauptman PJ, Arnold R, et al. Consensus statement: palliative and supportive care in advanced heart failure. *J Card.Fail.* 2004; 10(3): 200–9. doi:10.1016/j.cardfail.2003.09.006.
5. Buck HG, Zambroski CH. Upstreaming palliative care for patients with heart failure. *J Cardiovasc Nurs.* 2012; 27(2): 147–53. doi:10.1097/JCN.0b013e318239f629.
6. Gelfman LP, Kalman J, Goldstein NE. Engaging heart failure clinicians to increase palliative care referrals: overcoming barriers,

improving techniques. *J Palliat Med.* 2014; 17(7): 753–60. doi:10.1089/jpm.2013.0675.

7. Kavalieratos D, Mitchell EM, Carey TS, et al. "Not the 'grim reaper service'": an assessment of provider knowledge, attitudes, and perceptions regarding palliative care referral barriers in heart failure. *J Am Heart Assoc.* 2014; 3(1): e000544. doi:10.1161/JAHA.113.000544.

8. Yancy CW, Jessup M, Bozkurt B, et al. 2013 ACCF/AHA Guideline for the Management of Heart Failure. *Circulation.* Available at http://circ.ahajournals.org/. Accessed June 8, 2013.

9. Allen L, Stevenson LW, Grady KL, et al. Decision making in advanced heart failure: a scientific statement from the American Heart Association. *Circulation.* 2012; 125(15): 1928–52. doi:10.1161/CIR.0b013e31824f2173.

10. Unroe KT, Greiner M, Hernandez F, et al. Resource use in the last 6 months of life among Medicare beneficiaries with heart failure, 2000–2007. *Arch Intern Med.* 2011; 171(3): 196–203. doi:10.1001/archinternmed.2010.371.

11. Bern-Klug M. The ambiguous dying syndrome. *Health Soc Work.* 2004; 29(1): 55–65. Available at http://www.ncbi.nlm.nih.gov/pubmed/15024919.

12. Allen LA, Yager JE, Funk MJ, et al. Discordance between patient-predicted and model-predicted life expectancy among ambulatory patients with heart failure. *JAMA.* 2008; 299(21): 2533–42.

13. Lunney JR, Lynn J, Foley DJ, Lipson S, Guralnik JM. Patterns of functional decline at the end-of-life. *JAMA.* 2003; 289(18): 2387–92. doi:10.1001/jama.289.18.2387.

14. Havranek EP, Masoudi F, Westfall K, Wolfe P, Ordin DL, Krumholz HM. Spectrum of heart failure in older patients: Results from the National Heart Failure Project. *Am Heart J.* 2002; 143(3): 412–7. doi:10.1067/mhj.2002.120773.

15. Chiarantini D, Volpato S, Sioulis F, et al. Lower extremity performance measures predict long-term prognosis in older patients hospitalized for heart failure. *J Card Fail.* 2010; 16(5): 390–5. doi:10.1016/j.cardfail.2010.01.004.

16. Buck HG, Riegel B. The impact of frailty on health related quality of life in heart failure. *Eur J Cardiovasc Nurs.* 2011; 10(3): 159–66. doi:10.1016/j.ejcnurse.2010.06.001.

17. Fahlberg B, Panke J. *Compendium of Treatment of End Stage Non-Cancer Diagnoses: Heart Failure.* 2nd ed. Pittsburgh, PA: Hospice and Palliative Nurses Association; 2011:16–24.

18. Solomon DH. Nonselective NSAIDs: Adverse cardiovascular effects. *UpToDate* 2014. Accessed July 28, 2014. Available at http://www.uptodate.com/contents/nonselective-nsaids-adverse-cardiovascular-effects.

19. Trelle S, Reichenbach S, Wandel S, et al. Cardiovascular safety of non-steroidal anti-inflammatory drugs: network meta-analysis. *BMJ.* 2011; 342(jan11_1): c7086. doi:10.1136/bmj.c7086.

20. Carr JJ, Hendel RC, White RD, et al. 2013 appropriate utilization of cardiovascular imaging: a methodology for the development of joint criteria for the appropriate utilization of cardiovascular imaging by the American College of Cardiology Foundation and American College of Radiology. *J Am Coll Cardiol.* 2013; 61(21): 2199–206. doi:10.1016/j.jacc.2013.02.010.

21. Porter J, Cooper SJ, Sellick K. Attitudes, implementation and practice of family presence during resuscitation (FPDR): a quantitative literature review. *Int Emerg Nurs.* 2013; 21(1): 26–34. doi:10.1016/j.ienj.2012.04.002.

22. Kentish-Barnes N, Davidson JE, Cox CE. Family presence during cardiopulmonary resuscitation: an opportunity for meaning-making in bereavement. *Intensive Care Med.* 2014. doi:10.1007/s00134-014-3396-3.

23. Paul S, ed. *AAHFN Heart Failure Nursing Certification: Core Curriculum Review.* 1st ed. Mt. Laurel, NJ: American Association of Heart Failure Nurses; 2012.

24. January CT, Wann LS, Alpert JS, et al. *2014 AHA/ACC/HRS Guideline for the Management of Patients With Atrial Fibrillation: Executive Summary. A Report of the American College of Cardiology/American Heart Association Task Force on Practice Guidelines and the Heart Rhythm Society.* 2014. doi:10.1161/CIR.0000000000000040/-/DC1. Accessed August 7, 2014.

25. UpToDate. Implantable Cardioverter Defibrillator. 2013. Available at http://www.uptodate.com/contents/implantable-cardioverter-defibrillators-beyond-the-basics. Accessed August 7, 2014.

26. Russo AM, Stainback RF, Bailey SR, et al. ACCF/HRS/AHA/ASE/HFSA/SCAI/SCCT/SCMR 2013 appropriate use criteria for implantable cardioverter-defibrillators and cardiac resynchronization therapy: a report of the American College of Cardiology Foundation appropriate use criteria task force. *J Am Coll Cardiol.* 2013; 61(12): 1318–68. doi:10.1016/j.jacc.2012.12.017.

27. Kusumoto FM, Calkins H, Boehmer J, et al. HRS/ACC/AHA Expert Consensus Statement on the use of implantable cardioverter-defibrillator therapy in patients who are not included or not well represented in clinical trials. *Circulation.* 2014:94–125. doi:10.1161/CIR.0000000000000056.

28. Boston Scientific: ICD Longevity Facts & Stats. 2012. Available at www.bostonscientific.com/templatedata/imports/HTML/intl/Longevity/facts.html. Accessed July 20, 2014.

29. Sears SF, Hauf JD, Kirian K, Hazelton G, Conti JB. Posttraumatic stress and the implantable cardioverter-defibrillator patient: what the electrophysiologist needs to know. *Circ Arrhythm Electrophysiol.* 2011; 4(2): 242–50. doi:10.1161/CIRCEP.110.957670.

30. Kapa S, Rotondi-Trevisan D, Mariano Z, et al. Psychopathology in patients with ICDs over time: results of a prospective study. *Pacing Clin Electrophysiol.* 2010; 33(2): 198–208. doi:10.1111/j.1540-8159.2009.02599.x.

31. Ben Gal T, Jaarsma T. Self-care and communication issues at the end-of-life of recipients of a left-ventricular assist device as destination therapy. *Curr Opin Support Palliat Care.* 2013; 7(1): 29–35. doi:10.1097/SPC.0b013e32835d2d50.

32. Swetz KM, Freeman MR, AbouEzzeddine OF, et al. Palliative medicine consultation for preparedness planning in patients receiving left ventricular assist devices as destination therapy. *Mayo Clin Proc.* 2011; 86(6): 493–500. doi:10.4065/mcp.2010.0747.

33. Specialty Society Lists of Five Things Physicians and Patients Should Question (for physicians). *Choosing Wisely* 2014. Available at http://www.choosingwisely.org/doctor-patient-lists/.

34. HRSA. *Organ Procurement and Transplantation Network/Scientific Registry of Transplant Recipients 2012 Annual Data Report: Heart.* 2012. Available at srtr.transplant.hrsa.gov/annual_reports/2012/flash/05_heart_13/v2files/assets/downloads/publication.pdf.

35. Wasson S, Zafar MN, Best J, Reddy HK. Post-transplantation lymphoproliferative disorder in heart and kidney transplant patients: a single-center experience. *J Cardiovasc Pharmacol Ther.* 2006; 11(1): 77–83. Available at http://www.ncbi.nlm.nih.gov/pubmed/16703222. Accessed August 3, 2014.

36. Conway A, Schadewaldt V, Clark R, Ski C, Thompson DR, Doering L. The psychological experiences of adult heart transplant recipients: a systematic review and meta-summary of qualitative findings. *Heart Lung.* 2013; 42(6): 449–55. doi:10.1016/j.hrtlng.2013.08.003.

37. Sadala MLA, Stolf NG, Bocchi E, Bicudo MAV. Caring for heart transplant recipients: The lived experience of primary caregivers. *Heart Lung.* 2013; 42(2): 120–5. doi:10.1016/j.hrtlng.2012.09.006.

38. What is a heart transplant? National Heart Lung & Blood Institute 2012. Available at www.nhlbi.nih.gov/health/health-topics/topics/ht/. Accessed July 28, 2014.

CHAPTER 11

Palliative Care in the Solid Organ Transplant Unit

Edith O'Neil-Page, Charlene Earnhardt, Sarah D'Ambruoso, and Christine Bosley

Key Points

- Palliative advanced practice registered nurses (APRNs) have a high potential to care for individuals undergoing solid organ transplant, since 28,000 transplants occur annually across the United States.

- While the need for palliative care is well documented, many barriers prevent access to palliative care for patients, families, and care providers.

- Because suffering is a common occurrence for individuals undergoing solid organ transplantation, palliative APRNs have a role in ameliorating patients' physical and psychological symptoms.

Introduction

Many diseases or congenital abnormalities of the heart, liver, lung, and kidney may be incompatible with life or medically irreversible, necessitating organ support by mechanical means or replacement through transplantation. Although transplant surgery has not historically been associated with palliative care, organ replacements and/or transplantations are palliative in that they offer extension of life and increased quality of life through achievement of identified life goals.

Retrieval of organs and tissue for transplantation may occur in several ways: through donation from related living donors, from a cadaver, or from a donor declared as "brain dead" through appropriate procedures of circulatory and ventilator support. Donation after cardiac death entails retrieval of organs following the discontinuation of mechanical ventilation, allowing cardiac death.[1,2]

As the demand for organs increases and the number harvested through donation after cardiac death increases, ethical issues may arise for physician providers, APRNs, and critical care nurses to ensure that families are aware of and understand the process. Involvement of the palliative care team with a palliative APRN has been found to be instrumental in ensuring quality of care through withdrawal of life support and end-of-life.[1-3]

The first successful organ transplant was performed over six decades ago with the transplantation of a kidney to the identical twin of the recipient.[4] More than 601,928 cases have been performed since 1998 in the United States, and today, organ transplant is the standard of care for end-stage failure of the kidneys, lungs, liver, and heart.[3] In 2012, a total of 28,954 patients received organ transplants (Table 11.1).[5,6] According to the World Health Organization, transplantation saves lives when other medical treatments are either unavailable or nonexistent. For instance, kidney transplantation may yield substantial survival rates in combination with acceptable quality of life when evaluated against other end-stage renal disease treatments. Challenges occur as a result of multiple pressures on the system for transplantation. The need for organs exceeds availability and access to delivery systems and/or the supportive needs required to sustain survival. In addition, quality of selection, delivery systems, and processes are integrated with safety concerns for both donors and recipients.[7]

When a decision is made to pursue organ transplant, patients must be referred by a physician to an appropriate delivery system and demonstrate they no longer respond to medical therapy for the specific disease. A thorough medical examination follows, including in-depth psychological and social support system assessments. If the individual meets the requirements and is accepted for organ transplantation, the case is added to the Organ Procurement and Transplant Network (OPTN) wait list. The OPTN is a unique public–private partnership that links all of the professionals involved in the donation and transplantation system with the goal of increasing the effectiveness and efficiency of organ sharing and equity in the national system of organ allocation and to increase the supply of donated organs available for transplantation.

Palliative care is defined "as a multidisciplinary or an interdisciplinary intervention focusing on optimizing quality of life and maximizing life function independent of prognosis,"[8] which is what successful transplantation offers. However, palliative care is more often confused with hospice services and is correlated with a maximum expected prognosis of 6 months or less.[8,9] Thus, many transplant providers and patients may decline palliative services.

Table 11.1 Number of Transplants Performed in the United States

	To Date Total since 1999	2014	2013	2012	2011	2010	2009
All donor types	601,929	9,339	28,954	28,054	28,539	28,662	28,458
Deceased donor	472,225	7,523	22,967	22,187	22,518	22,101	21,849
Living donor	129,704	1,816	5,987	5,867	6,021	6,561	6,609

Moreover, families and patients may hold unrealistic expectations of survival, despite the severity of disease, paired with fear, resulting in unwillingness to plan for end-of-life.

Since these patients receive care in an intensive care unit (ICU), screening tools and triggers can help identify patients appropriate for palliative care, such as those undergoing transplant. One study suggests that development of palliative care screening criteria resulted in improved utilization of ICU resources, without changing mortality.[10] As a result of this and other studies, the advent of "advance care planning" and the development of "preparedness planning" have become more evident.[3,11–14]

Heart Failure and Transplantation

Case Study 1

Mr. K, an active 50-year-old man, was seen in his primary care physician's office for intermittent shortness of breath over the preceding 2 weeks. He stated he had been sleeping on two pillows at night and believed his symptoms were caused by anxiety; he denied chest pain, productive cough, wheezing, or syncope. He was started on oral alprazolam 0.25 mg twice per day by his primary physician, which initially improved his shortness of breath. Over the next week, he became increasingly dyspneic and was unable to independently perform activities of daily living (ADLs). A cardiology consult was ordered as well as an echocardiogram. To rule out amyloidosis, a cardiac angiogram with biopsy was performed and showed a significantly worse ejection fraction. The following day, Mr. K suffered a cardiac arrest followed by the initiation of extracorporeal membrane oxygenation. Overnight, Mr. K's neurological status improved and hemodynamics stabilized. His family and physician decided to initiate a percutaneous ventricular assist device (PVAD) as a bridge to an orthotopic heart transplant (OHT). Due to the patient's unstable cardiovascular condition and need for rapid medical intervention, palliative care was not consulted.

Three days after Mr. K's cardiac arrest, the PVAD was inserted; he was weaned off the ventilator and was extubated without incident during the day shift. Overnight, he became increasingly short of breath and required endotracheal reinsertion. Over the next week, Mr. K did not tolerate ventilator weaning. An interdisciplinary family meeting was held regarding nutrition and pulmonary status. It was agreed that a tracheostomy was needed, as well as a small-bore feeding tube.

The following day, Mr. K became hypotensive, requiring vasoactive medications and continuous renal replacement therapy. A renal biopsy was performed to rule out amyloidosis. The medical team met again with the patient and family to discuss the positive results of the kidney biopsy. The decision was made to continue vasoactive medications and ventilator support, as well as starting chemotherapy to treat his renal amyloidosis, with the goal of renal transplantation in the future.

Throughout these interventions, Mr. K continued to maintain a positive attitude with his family by his side. His wife returned to work and started spending more time with their two young children, one of whom was developmentally disabled. His mother and father consistently remained at the bedside for emotional support, yet Mr. K's spirit declined. He communicated to his family his exhaustion and inability to continue to live in his current state. His parents became very upset with this and decided to move into an apartment closer to the hospital to be more available. After discussion of this episode with the medical team, antidepressants were initiated.

After Mr. K spent 5 weeks as an inpatient without improvement, the interdisciplinary team consulted palliative care due to Mr. K's wishes to "stop all of this and die naturally." During the interdisciplinary meeting, the oncologist stated it was too early to evaluate improvement from chemotherapy, and the cardiologist verbalized that, without improvement, Mr. K would not be an OHT candidate. His mother and father stated their son wanted to keep fighting, and when asked directly, Mr. K agreed he wanted to continue treatment. After the meeting, Mr. K communicated to the bedside nurse he could not disappoint his parents by refusing treatment.

At the interdisciplinary transplant meeting the next week, it was agreed Mr. K was not a candidate for OHT. A family conference was planned with Mr. K and his wife only, per his request. Mr. K communicated to his wife that he loved her and their children but felt he could no longer continue to fight and did not want to continue to live "hooked up to machines." The difficult decision was made with the medical team to discontinue the PVAD and to provide comfort measures per Mr. K's request. Mr. K died peacefully, accompanied by his family.

Advanced chronic heart failure (HF) or end-stage heart failure (ESHF) refers to disease characterized by objective signs of structural heart disease (left ventricular ejection fraction less than 30%, evidence of low cardiac output and high filling pressures) as well as subjective symptom burden (moderate to severe dyspnea at rest or with minimal exertion and severe fatigue and reduced functional capacity).[15] Patients with these symptoms are typically refractory to optimal medical management and are at high-risk for hospital admission. Guidelines developed by the American Heart Association/American College of Cardiology on the evaluation and management of patients with ESHF require patient referral to a cardiac transplantation center and evaluation for candidacy for advanced therapies, OHT, or replacement of a patient's native heart with a cadaver organ, and/or mechanical circulatory support (MCS).[16] Evaluation variables include hemodynamic and functional status as well as social support networks and psychiatric history.[17] A multidisciplinary team determines the patient's eligibility for transplant. In addition, a palliative care consult is required.

Long-term MCS refers to durable devices that augment or replace the native heart's pump function, such as ventricular assist devices (VADs) or total artificial hearts.[16] Patients may receive MCS as a bridge to transplant (BTT), a bridge to recovery (BTR), or destination therapy (DT). There are three generations of left ventricular assist devices (LVADs), two of which are approved by the U.S. Food and Drug Administration for DT as well as BTT therapy. The HeartMate II LVAD, the most widely used durable device, provides continuous, nonpulsatile flow. A recent cost-effectiveness study demonstrated that LVAD as BTT therapy is comparable to heart transplant in terms of ratio of survival benefit to overall cost.[18]

More than 3,800 OHTs take place annually, with the majority taking place in the United States.[17] Of the more than 2,800 Americans who are annually placed on the list for cardiac transplantation, nearly 15% die every year awaiting transplant. The average survival of OHT recipients is a median of 10.9 years. Those who survive the first year after transplantation have a median survival of 13.4 years.[17] This is in comparison to OHT-eligible patients receiving optimal medical management, whose life expectancy is estimated at 1.1 years, with less than 40% surviving a year. Patients waiting for an LVAD as BTT for more than 6 months on average survive about 3.8 additional years.[19] The latest data from INTERMACS, the national registry of patients with MCS, suggest that survival rates have remained stable over the past 5 years, with 80% of patients living at least 1 year after the implant and 70% living at least 2 years after the implant.[20]

A retrospective review of transplant recipient data from 2006 to 2011 found that 82% of patients awaiting OHT at Status 1A or 1B (the highest United Network for Organ Sharing [UNOS] acuities) required circulatory support while awaiting transplant, either inotropic or mechanical.[17] Thus, the likelihood of receiving MCS while awaiting OHT is high. When patients with LVADs eventually receive OHT, they can expect to live a total of 12.3 years.[19] These LVAD patients are at high risk for death in the immediate postimplantation period, which accounts for about 65% of LVAD mortality within the first year after implantation.[21,22] Furthermore, as the advanced HF population ages, many no longer qualify for OHT and are instead considered for MCS as DT, accounting at this time for more than 40% of all devices placed. See Table 11.2 for survival rates.[20]

Among OHT recipients, risk for reduced survival is higher in patients whose cardiomyopathy was caused by valvular disorders or congenital heart defects, and in those who require a second transplant or who required MCS prior to transplant (Table 11.3).[17] Those at risk for mortality within the first 5 years after transplantation include older patients, those for whom this is a second transplant, those whose cardiomyopathy was ischemic in origin, mismatch of HLA, hepatitis B positivity in the recipient, and female donor/male recipient combinations.[17] Post-transplantation complications include graft rejection and infection due to a profoundly immunosuppressed state.[17]

In terms of MCS survival, the REMATCH trial demonstrated a 48% reduction in mortality among non-OHT eligible patients

Table 11.2 Survival of Heart Transplant Recipients Based on Their Status at the Time of Transplant

Recipient UNOS Status at Trans	Years After Transplant	Number Functioning/ Alive	Survival Rate (%)
1A	1	2,101	85.7
1B	1	1,839	87.3
2	1	1,425	90.6
1A	3	2,373	75.2
1B	3	2,407	80.3
1	3	50	78.5
2	3	1,764	81.9
1A	5	1,006	68.8
1B	5	1,048	72.7
1	5	2,284	72.1
2	5	1,686	74.0

Data show 1-year survival based on 2002–2004 transplants, 3-year survival based on 1999–2002 transplants, and 5-year survival based on 1997–2000 transplants. Retrieved from http://optn.transplant.hrsa.gov on July 25, 2014.

who were randomly selected to receive LVAD implantation compared to those managed medically.[17] More than half of the LVAD recipients survived for longer than 1 year, as opposed to only 25% of the patients receiving optimal medical management.[17] Other large trials investigating the second- and third-generation LVAD devices have found similar survival benefits, and other large trials are under way without reportable data as of this writing.[17] Patients requiring long-term biventricular support do not have a durable VAD device option at this time. In-hospital support can be maintained with a Thoratec paracorporeal VAD or a Centrimag VAD, or patients may be eligible to receive a total artificial heart.[17]

For patients living with MCS devices, the most frequent adverse events are hospitalization, bleeding, infection, cardiac arrhythmia, respiratory failure, right heart failure, neurologic dysfunction, renal dysfunction, and psychiatric episode.[20] Catastrophic neurologic events constitute the greatest risk for mortality in MCS patients after the first 3 months after the implant.[21,23] Patients who received continuous-flow LVADs versus those who received pulsatile devices were found to have better outcomes in terms of fewer strokes and fewer device failures, an effect that was sustained 24 months after implantation. In general, patients who are referred for OHT/MCS in a "healthier" state typically have better survival than those who receive transplants or other high-technological therapies in a more advanced, less compensated state.[17]

Studies have generally reported significant improvements in functional status, exercise capacity, and self-reported quality of life among patients living with MCS devices, either as DT or BTT/BTR.[23] Rogers and colleagues reported significant improvements in exercise tolerance over baseline among MCS recipients, with more than 60% reporting improvements from a baseline of "low" or "very low" to "moderate" or "very high," an effect that was sustained for 24 months following implantation (for DT patients). More than 80% of MCS-DT patients experienced an improvement in New York Heart Association functional class IV symptoms

Table 11.3 Heart Transplant Recipient Survival with Regard to Initial Presenting Diagnosis in the United States

Recipient Diagnosis Category	Years After Transplant	Number Functioning/ Alive	Survival Rate (%)
Cardiomyopathy	1	2,452	89.4
Congenital heart disease	1	301	82.1
Coronary artery disease	1	2,148	87.1
Other cardiac disease	1	1	*
Retransplant/ graft failure	1	170	82.8
Valvular heart disease	1	111	85.5
Other	1	95	88.2
Cardiomyopathy	3	2,978	81.1
Congenital heart disease	3	417	73.7
Coronary artery disease	3	2,804	78.4
Other cardiac disease	3	2	*
Retransplant/ graft failure	3	182	66.5
Valvular heart disease	3	136	74.6
Other	3	79	77.2
Cardiomyopathy	5	2,647	74.3
Congenital heart disease	5	368	68.1
Coronary artery disease	5	2,674	71.8
Retransplant/ graft failure	5	158	57.9
Valvular heart disease	5	130	71.7
Other	5	50	65.6

Heart Kaplan-Meier patient survival rates for transplants performed 1997–2004.

*Patient survival was not computed due to N < 10. 1-year survival based on 2002–2004 transplants, 3-year survival based on 1999–2002 transplants, 5-year survival based on 1997–2000 transplants.

Based on OPTN data as of July 25, 2014. Retrieved from http://optn.transplant.hrsa.gov on July 25, 2014.

to functional class I or II, which was also sustained through the 24-month mark.[24] However, other studies have shown that more than 40% of MCS patients still reported "some problems" with performing usual activities 24 months after implantation, with a small percentage (4.2%) reporting "severe problems."[20] More than 20% of MCS patients reported having "some problems" with self-care 24 months after implant, with a small percentage (1%) reporting "severe problems."[20]

Self-reported quality of life using the EQ5D Visual Analog Scale, with 0 being the worst and 100 being the best, remained relatively high for patients at 24 months after implant, with a mean score of 70, as compared to a mean score of 40 before the implant.[20] Similarly, Sandau and colleagues[25] found in a qualitative study of 11 patients living with continuous-flow LVAD devices (as BTT/ BTR or DT) that quality of life was conceptualized by patients in five domains (physical, cognitive, spiritual, social, and emotional realms) and that patients generally experienced improvements in all domains after implantation. The study also identified a more crystalized definition of quality of life among patients living with MCS as "Being well enough to do and enjoy day-to-day activities that are important to me," and the researchers pointed out that most existing quality-of-life questionnaires do not assess patients on their cognitive (memory function) and spiritual (existential) domains.[25]

Despite the clear need for symptom management and advance care planning in this population, palliative care remains underused among ESHF patients.[26] Kavallieratos and colleagues (2014) found, in in-depth interviews with 18 cardiologists, primary care providers, and palliative care providers, that most cardiology and primary care providers interviewed had limited understanding of palliative care and understood palliative care to be appropriate only for those patients nearing death. Other barriers to timely palliative care referrals included the innate uncertainty in HF prognostication, a lack of clear criteria for generating palliative care referrals across the HF disease spectrum, and difficulty distinguishing "usual care" for HF symptoms from palliative care.[8] Bakitas and colleagues[26] found, in a retrospective chart review of palliative care consultations in ESHF patients, that consultations took place an average of 21 days prior to death, with consultations most frequently being requested for goals of care, decision making, and hospice referral/discussion. Hupcey[27] and others have called for palliative care providers to increase awareness and continue peer education efforts to assist providers in determining when and how best to use palliative care in this population.[8]

A major barrier to referring ESHF patients for palliative care consultation is due to the innate unpredictability in HF severity at the level of the individual.[28,29] The trajectory of HF is not linear or predictable; rather, it is characterized by periods of stability and acute exacerbation, where decline occurs, with some recovery, but not the same functional status.[15] This trajectory is further complicated by end-of-life scenarios that run the gamut of possibility—from sudden cardiac death due to lethal arrhythmia occurring in seconds to minutes to slow death by gradual, progressive pump failure occurring over weeks to months.[15]

Several predictive models for determining risk for mortality from HF have been developed, many of which consider multiple variables, such as demographic data as well as functional status and disease stage.[28,29] Models validated in ambulatory populations include the Heart Failure Survival Score and the Seattle Heart Failure Model, and those validated for use with hospitalized patients include the EVEREST Risk Model, the EFFECT score, the ADHERE score, and the ESCAPE Discharge Score.[15,29] However, these models' accuracy in predicting risk for death and their applicability across the HF population spectrum are considered modest at best.[28,29] Clinicians are advised to acknowledge the uncertainty of prognosis and the imperfection of available mortality prediction algorithms for most HF patients when discussing goals of care with these patients.[15,29]

Advanced practice registered nurses can play an essential role in review and management of patients with advanced HF. Strachen and colleagues[30] clearly identify a "requirement for a palliative approach" in symptom management and have developed a tool to assist toward that end. The reduction of suffering and improvement of quality of life by integrating interdisciplinary communication across the trajectory of disease, treatment, and outcomes is paramount in assessment and implementation of appropriate care for the HF patient[30] and is clearly consistent with the advanced practice nursing role.[30]

Disease-Specific Advance Care Planning with ESHF Patients: Preparedness Planning

Preparedness planning is a mode of advance care planning that is tailored to the needs of the patient undergoing heart transplant evaluation with possible implantation of a mechanical assist device as a BTT.[13] The preparedness planning approach is a method of open dialogue about specific potential health states in an effort to promote informed consent as well as to guide future healthcare shared decision making.[13] These hypothetical health states are related to the known complications of MCS devices, such as repeat admissions, thromboembolic events, gastrointestinal hemorrhage, infection, and right ventricular failure.[23,31] Preparedness planning also addresses hypothetical health situations in which the patient's quality of life is not improved by the VAD, such as the need for hemodialysis, right heart failure, and decision making about deactivation. Preparedness planning attempts to document the values and preferences of patients whose future disease trajectory is uncertain and is vastly compromised by living with an invasive machine.[13] Patients' expectations about improved quality of life must be documented and revisited on a regular basis to ensure that the MCS device is improving quality of life in measurable, tangible ways.[13,32,33]

Ongoing Palliative Care for Patients Living with MCS as DT

Qualitative research conducted with ESHF patients who receive MCS as DT point to significant gains in self-reported functional status and exercise tolerance, but also to the ongoing difficulties of adjusting to life with an invasive device, such as new dependence on caregiver support in performing activities of daily living.[34] Other qualitative research among caregivers of MCS-DT patients has revealed high levels of emotional distress due to the perceived caregiving needs of the MCS patient and the durability and lifespan of the device, including anxiety about device failure and, among some spousal caregivers, guilt or regret at consenting to device placement.[35] The importance of respite services for caregivers who are at high risk for caregiver burnout and ongoing palliative and supportive care of the patient and family is paramount. Patients continue to live with an end-stage disease with an uncertain trajectory and thus continue to be at risk for psychosocial and existential symptom burden, as well as for catastrophic complications of the device itself and sudden death due to device failure.[13,34,36] Goals of care and advance care planning discussions should continue after implantation to reflect

patients' current clinical status and help patients and families understand their prognosis and set realistic goals.[13,29,33] Advance care planning after implantation should continue the conversations begun before implantation with the preparedness plan and should include explicit instructions for managing catastrophes/emergencies and complications.[13,29,37] Palliative APRNs may also assist patients and families in understanding device withdrawal or deactivation and can provide reassurance about symptom management and comfort care at the end-of-life.[29,33,36,37]

End-Stage Lung Failure and Transplantation

The first successful lung transplant (LTx) procedure was performed over 50 years ago. The patient survived 18 days, eventually dying of renal failure and malnutrition. Until the 1980s, lung transplantations were fraught with poor outcomes, including graft failures and patient deaths.[38] With the introduction of improved surgical techniques and the arrival of cyclosporine, patient outcomes improved dramatically. To date LTx, whether single, bilateral, or heart and lung, is considered the only established treatment with the potential to prolong survival and improve quality of life in this patient population. See Table 11.4 for contraindications for LTx.

LTx is a respected strategy for advanced chronic obstructive pulmonary disease (COPD), idiopathic pulmonary fibrosis, cystic fibrosis, emphysema due to alpha-1 antitrypsin deficiency, and idiopathic pulmonary arterial hypertension. These diseases prompt the majority of LTx operations worldwide. Data from OPTN (Table 11.5) demonstrate that survival varies according to preexisting diagnosis, with the 5-year survival rate only half that of all other serious diagnoses.

LTx should be a consideration for patients with advanced lung disease whose clinical status continues to decline despite maximal medical treatment. These patients are symptomatic, with poor functional status and a poor life expectancy. Once a patient is found eligible as a transplant candidate, he or she is placed on a waiting list managed by UNOS. The patient is given a Lung Allocation Score, which is a score ranging from 0 to 100 if older than 12 years of age. It is a weighted combination of the predicted risk of death during the following year on the waiting list and the predicted likelihood of survival during the first year after the transplant (Table 11.6).[40]

In 2012, 1,942 LTx procedures were performed in North America, with 1,837 patients surviving to discharge (6% mortality). Of the patients who survived to discharge, the mean survival rate of single lung transplants and double lung transplants was 81% at year 1 and 63% at year 3, depending on the diagnosis that led to the operation (see Table 11.5). Patients who undergo a second lung transplant have a significantly higher 1-year mortality rate. Evidence shows that, on average, one in six patients will die awaiting a lung for transplantation.[41–43]

Lung transplant patients and their families face many challenges while encountering a chronic downward trajectory of their disease process. Patients often require hospitalization, mechanical ventilation, and temporary support on extracorporeal membrane oxygenation (ECMO). Many centers are using ECMO successfully as a BT in carefully selected patients. Support with venovenous ECMO can be done while awake and free of mechanical ventilation. As an intervention, venovenous ECMO is a recognized treatment that can allow the patient to be weaned from the ventilator,

Table 11.4 Contraindications to Lung Transplantation

Absolute Contraindications
Malignancy in the past 2 years, with the exception of cutaneous squamous and basal cell tumors
Untreatable advanced dysfunction of another major organ system (e.g., heart, liver, or kidney)
Non-curable chronic extrapulmonary infection, including chronic active viral hepatitis B, hepatitis C, and human immunodeficiency virus
Significant chest wall/spinal deformity
Documented nonadherence or inability to follow through with medical therapy or office follow-up, or both
Drug or alcohol dependency
Untreatable psychiatric or psychological condition associated with the inability to cooperate or comply with medical therapy
Absence of a consistent or reliable social support system
Relative Contraindications
Older than 65 years
Critical or unstable clinical condition
Severely limited functional status with poor rehabilitation potential
Severe obesity (BMI > 30)
Mechanical ventilation (carefully selected candidates on mechanical ventilation without other acute or chronic organ dysfunction, who are able to actively participate in a meaningful rehabilitation program, may be successfully transplanted)

Data from reference 39.

undergo physical therapy, and improve or maintain nutritional status.[43,44] ECMO is no longer considered a heroic death stay, but rather an innovative approach that bridges transplant and promotes improved outcomes by allowing the patient to regain strength and muscle mass prior to surgery.[45]

End-Stage Liver Disease and Transplantation

Case Study 2

TR was a 59-year-old female with a history of substance abuse, diabetes mellitus, hypertension, thyroid disease, liver cirrhosis, and hepatitis C. She received interferon and ribavirin for 6 months, which she tolerated. She underwent esophageal banding. A subsequent ultrasound in 2012 revealed a 2.4-cm liver lesion. A follow-up MRI indicated it had grown to 4.3 cm; 3 months later it was 6.5 cm. TR was treated with transarterial chemoembolization. Upon admission, the patient was febrile and tachycardic. She was given ciprofloxacin 400 mg IV q12h and metronidazole 500 mg IV q8h. She had patient-controlled analgesia with hydromorphone and ondansetron for nausea. Her condition worsened, with increasing fever and hemoptysis. Further evaluation revealed a hepatopulmonary fistula and associated pneumonia.

She underwent an evaluation for liver transplant and had a MELD score of 18. TR was admitted to the ICU and continued to experience multiple acute exacerbations with compromised liver and kidney function. She experienced confusion and lethargy and could

not eat or communicate clearly with her family. Immobility and declining nutritional status produced a deterioration of skin integrity and several lesions developed and became infected. Due to her continued decline, the patient was removed from the waiting list.

Following this deterioration, palliative care was consulted for pain and symptom management as well as discussion about goals of care. Several family meetings were held to explain her situation to the family. The family expressed significant concern regarding her delisting and continued deterioration. They wanted her to continue to fight and "get better." Her pain and symptoms were consistently evaluated. TR became increasingly debilitated and, with the support of palliative care, the family agreed to withdraw procedures that were causing more burden than benefit. Over a period of 3 days, TR evidenced an increase in comfort and died peacefully with her family at the bedside.

Liver transplantation is described in the literature as a "life-saving procedure for patients with chronic end stage liver disease."[5] For patients with end-stage liver disease or acute liver failure, transplantation has become a feasible option, and patients and families may have high expectations of survival following liver transplantation.[46] According to the OPTN/Scientific Registry of Transplant Recipients annual report of 2012, over 6,256 patients received liver transplants; in the same timeframe more than 65,000 persons were living with transplanted livers.[47] The liver is the most frequently transplanted organ in the United States and is identified by patients and families as a "successful life-saving procedure for patients with irreversible liver disease." Liver disease is the 12th most common cause of mortality in the United States, and access to liver transplantation has had a strong impact on the treatment of advanced liver disease.[48]

Although liver transplantation is considered a "valid treatment" for end-stage liver disease, the process for liver transplant is complicated. Many potential recipients are confronted with long waiting times for transplantation, and other candidates cannot stay healthy enough to remain eligible for a transplant. Up to 17% of candidates die while waiting for a liver.[48]

Evaluation focuses on physiological, medical, psychosocial, and emotional strengths and weaknesses in regard to a healthy lifestyle and adherence to lifelong immunosuppressive medications. In addition, maintaining disease stability throughout the waiting process can take its toll on families and patients alike.[49]

In 2013 the American Association for the Study of Liver Diseases and the American Society of Transplantation developed Practice Guidelines to reflect the major advances in liver transplantation management. Those guidelines delineate indications and contraindications (Table 11.7 and Table 11.8). Imperative for a successful transplant is the presence of a committed caregiver throughout the process to assist with personal, financial, and social support. Challenges may be physically as well as emotionally demanding and require that the caregiver maintain adequate self-care.[49,50]

Candidates who are denied transplantation and have not been referred to palliative care may demonstrate higher hospital readmission rates. These patients may not understand their health status completely, what will happen next, or their options for care. It is generally believed that fewer than 10% of patients are referred to palliative care for pain and symptom management when removed from the waiting list.[51] Some data suggest that referrals to palliative care are "rare" despite a median survival of 2 months and many medical needs. Yet the professional literature continues to

Table 11.5 1- to 5-Year Survival for Lung Transplant Based on Primary Diagnosis in the United States

Recipient Diagnosis Category	Years After Transplant	Number Functioning/ Alive	Survival Rate (%)
Alpha-1-antitrypsin deficiency	1	169	84.1
Congenital heart disease	1	16	76.2
Cystic fibrosis	1	461	85.2
Emphysema/COPD	1	1,049	86.2
Idiopathic pulmonary fibrosis	1	544	79.0
Other lung disease	1	246	82.0
Primary pulmonary hypertension	1	91	75.4
Retransplant/graft failure	1	57	65.6
Other	1	55	73.3
Alpha-1-antitrypsin deficiency	3	176	60.6
Cardiomyopathy	3	1	*
Congenital heart disease	3	22	53.7
Cystic fibrosis	3	419	64.1
Emphysema/COPD	3	1,051	65.1
Idiopathic pulmonary fibrosis	3	351	55.6
Other lung disease	3	204	59.5
Primary pulmonary hypertension	3	92	59.0
Retransplant/graft failure	3	37	39.5
Other	3	43	68.3
Alpha-1-antitrypsin deficiency	5	138	47.7
Cardiomyopathy	5	1	*
Congenital heart disease	5	21	40.9
Coronary artery disease	5	1	*
Cystic fibrosis	5	305	46.8
Emphysema/COPD	5	658	47.4
Idiopathic pulmonary fibrosis	5	207	40.0
Other lung disease	5	160	51.4
Primary pulmonary hypertension	5	70	44.8
Retransplant/graft failure	5	27	26.9
Other	5 Year	28	44.5

* Graft survival was not computed due to N < 10. 1-year survival based on 2002–2004 transplants, 3-year survival based on 1999–2002 transplants, 5-year survival based on 1997–2000 transplants. Organ Procurement and Transplantation Network, lung Kaplan-Meier graft survival rates for transplants performed 1997–2004. Based on OPTN data as of July 18, 2014. Retrieved July 25, 2014.

identify utilization or referral to palliative care as important[12] and widely recommended and states that it "helps ensure patients receive care aligned with their wishes."[52]

End-Stage Renal Failure and Transplantation

Case Study 3

JA was a 39-year-old female with an 8-year history of acute renal failure. She was treated with dialysis and a subsequent kidney transplant. The wound from the transplant did not heal. Multiple infections developed and the wound became necrotic. JA was admitted to the hospital with purpuric and necrotic lesions that had developed around the edges of the surgical wound. Because her history included systemic lupus erythematosus, biopsy samples were taken from some of these lesions and they were confirmed to be calciphylaxis. The lesions spread rapidly to all open wounds, her tongue, mouth, face, and neck. They were treated intralesionally with thiosulfate and hypobaric oxygen therapy, with no results. She could not take liquids and oral care was excruciatingly painful. JA's mental clarity became an issue and her decision-making ability waxed and waned. Her mother was identified as the temporary surrogate decision maker.

Table 11.6 Clinical Characteristics Used for Lung Allocation Score

Predictors of Waiting List Survival	Predictors of Post-transplant Survival
Diagnosis	Diagnosis
Age	Age
BMI	Creatinine at transplant (mg/dL)
Diabetes	New York Heart Association Functional Class
Forced vital capacity	
Pulmonary arterial systolic pressure	Forced vital capacity
Oxygen requirements at rest	Pulmonary capillary wedge pressure ≥ 20 mmHG
Six-minute walk distance (feet)	
Continuous mechanical ventilation	Mechanical ventilation
PCO_2	

Adapted from http://optn.transplant.hrsa.gov/converge/resources/allocationcalculators.asp?index=87 with permission. Retrieved October 30, 2014.

During this time, the palliative APRN continued with conversations exploring the meaning of "full code" and described potential outcomes. Throughout the admission period of 7 weeks, when JA was coherent, she frequently stated she was "a fighter" and did not wish to "let go." She expressed commitment to a "full code status" that included cardiopulmonary resuscitation, intubation, and full life support. When JA was close to the end of her life, her mother asked that her medication be lightened. A discussion occurred in which JA was able to express that she was "being strong because that's what my family wants." The mother had never heard this

Table 11.7 Indications for Liver Transplant

Acute Liver Failure
Complications of cirrhosis
Ascites
Chronic gastrointestinal blood loss due to portal hypertensive gastropathy
Encephalopathy
Liver cancer
Refractory variceal hemorrhage
Synthetic dysfunction
Liver-based metabolic conditions with systemic manifestations
Alpha$_1$-antitrypsin deficiency
Familial amyloidosis
Glycogen storage disease
Hemochromatosis
Primary oxaluria
Wilson disease
Systemic complications of chronic liver disease
Hepatopulmonary syndrome
Portopulmonary hypertension

From reference 51.

Table 11.8 Contraindications to Liver Transplant

Model for End-Stage Liver Disease (MELD) score <15
Severe cardiac or pulmonary disease
AIDS
Ongoing alcohol or illicit substance abuse
Hepatocellular carcinoma with metastatic spread
Uncontrolled sepsis
Anatomic abnormality that precludes liver transplantation
Intrahepatic cholangiocarcinoma
Extrahepatic malignancy
Fulminant hepatic failure with sustained ICP > 50 mm Hg or CPP < 40 mm Hg
Hemangiosarcoma
Persistent noncompliance
Lack of adequate social support

From reference 51.

message from JA. After further conversation, JA's code status was changed to DNR/DNI, sedation for comfort, and withdrawal of all life-prolonging medical support. JA died peacefully 2 days later.

End-stage renal disease (ESRD) is a very debilitating chronic condition that requires continual intervention for the patient to survive. It involves significant "lifestyle, dietary and fluid restrictions" in the management of the patient's illness. Maintenance of fluid and electrolyte balance with adequate nutrition as well as active function can be challenging for those of any age. It can be particularly challenging for young to middle-aged adults who receive kidney transplants.[4,53]

According to the National Kidney Foundation, 122,737 people are currently waiting for organ transplants in the United States, and the number continues to increase annually.[47] Of these, 100,602 are waiting for kidney transplants and 71% are between the ages of 18 and 49. The additions to the waiting list greatly exceed the number of available organs, and it is estimated that "14 people die each day while waiting for an organ"[4] (Table 11.9).

For patients with ESRD, organ transplantation can provide "improved quality of life" and "longer survival rates" than hemodialysis can.[47] Patients who are unable or unwilling to adhere to lifelong regimens of immunosuppressant medications face risks of graft rejection, resulting in hospital admission. Some recipients are not always aware of the need for precise administration of these medications: even occasional missed doses can be detrimental to the organ and result in graft failure. Research indicates that there are five main risk factors: socioeconomic issues, complicated dosing and administration regimens, lack of knowledge and understanding, side effects of the medications, and personal considerations, such as work or school. Involving the participant in medication management improved adherence.[54] Interventions that were most beneficial included behavioral, educational, and emotional components and encouraging individual participation.[46]

Table 11.9 Kidney Transplants in the United States

	To Date since 1988	2014	2013	2012	2011	2010	2009
All donor types	356,691	5,408	16,895	16,488	16,815	16,900	16,829
Deceased donor	232,505	3,673	11,163	10,868	11,043	10,622	10,442
Living donor	124,186	1,735	5,732	5,620	5,772	6,278	6,387

Data over the past 5 years have remained constant, with well over 16,000 transplants (all donor types). Based on OPTN data as of July 25, 2014.

Table 11.10 Unadjusted Graft and Patient Survival at 3 Months, 1 Year, 3 Years, 5 Years, and 10 Years

Organ and Survival Type		Follow-up Period				
		3 Months	1 Year	3 Years	5 Years	10 Years
		Tx 2006–2007	Tx 2006–2007	Tx 2004–2007	Tx 2002–2007	Tx 1997–2007
Kidney: Deceased Donor	Graft survival	95.3%	91.0%	80.1%	69.3%	43.3%
	Patient survival	98.1%	95.6%	89.1%	81.9%	61.2%
Kidney: Living Donor	Graft survival	98.1%	96.3%	89.6%	81.4%	59.3%
	Patient survival	99.5%	98.5%	95.3%	91.0%	77.1%
Pancreas Alone	Graft survival	85.3%	75.5%	59.5%	51.5%	34.7%
	Patient survival	98.9%	97.8%	92.3%	88.7%	76.1%
Pancreas After Kidney	Graft survival	87.1%	80.0%	65.2%	53.4%	36.9%
	Patient survival	98.8%	97.0%	91.6%	84.5%	67.5%
Kidney–Pancreas	Kidney graft survival	96.0%	92.5%	86.1%	78.6%	58.3%
	Pancreas graft survival	88.7%	84.8%	79.4%	73.4%	55.0%
	Patient survival	97.9%	95.7%	91.7%	87.2%	71.4%
Liver: Deceased Donor	Graft survival	91.2%	84.3%	74.2%	68.4%	54.1%
	Patient survival	94.3%	88.4%	79.3%	73.8%	60.0%
Liver: Living Donor	Graft survival	90.9%	86.0%	79.0%	72.9%	62.6%
	Patient survival	94.9%	91.0%	84.9%	79.0%	69.9%
Heart	Graft survival	92.8%	87.9%	80.6%	73.7%	54.2%
	Patient survival	93.1%	88.3%	81.5%	74.9%	56.0%
Lung	Graft survival	91.6%	81.6%	63.5%	51.5%	26.2%
	Patient survival	92.3%	83.3%	66.2%	54.4%	28.6%
Heart–Lung	Graft survival	85.5%	80.5%	61.5%	43.1%	26.2%
	Patient survival	85.5%	80.6%	61.7%	44.9%	29.0%
Kidney–Liver	Kidney graft survival	89.8%	83.0%	71.9%	64.4%	48.1%
	Liver graft survival	90.2%	83.7%	72.4%	66.0%	52.7%
	Patient survival	93.3%	87.4%	76.5%	71.4%	58.9%
Kidney–Heart	Heart graft survival	94.7%	92.6%	82.6%	76.0%	57.5%
	Kidney graft Survival	90.5%	88.2%	78.5%	72.0%	48.7%
	Patient survival	97.2%	95.8%	84.7%	77.6%	58.8%
Liver–Intestine	Intestine graft survival	71.4%	58.7%	55.3%	53.0%	36.7%
	Liver graft survival	71.4%	58.7%	55.3%	53.4%	36.7%
	Patient survival	73.3%	63.3%	58.2%	58.0%	39.0%

This table demonstrates that patient survival decreases over time, with a gradual decline. Graft survival also decreases, and those patients may be eligible for retransplant.

Source: OPTN/SRTR data as of May 4, 2009. Multiple organ transplants are excluded except where specified. Living donor transplants are excluded unless explicitly listed. Heterotopic heart and liver transplants are excluded. Graft survival follows individual transplants until graft failure. Patient survival follows patients from first transplant of this type until death. http://www.ustransplant.org/annual_reports/current/113_surv-new_dh.htm Retrieved July 25, 2014.

Conclusion

End-stage diseases of heart, liver, lung, and kidney commonly result in transplant and have similar post transplant survival rates (Table 11.10). Interventions using devices or transplantation are often the last step in the process and are indicated for the purpose of prolonging life, controlling symptoms, and improving quality of life. Maximization of organ function is imperative in this first stage of qualification for the transplant process, which may take days or weeks. If the organ should completely fail or compromise other organs, the patient may not qualify for the waiting list.[53] A palliative care team, ideally an interdisciplinary team, can identify the needs and concerns of the patients and the family.[55] The exploration of life's meaning and spiritual and faith concerns is important in that the team needs to be aware of the patient's commitment to the transplantation process and also to identify how the patient wishes to live if the organ is rejected. Early palliative care intervention for patients undergoing organ transplant maximizes quality of life and reduces suffering.[56] It can improve quality of life and may extend survivorship as well.

Collaboration between intensive care specialists and primary palliative care providers is shown to be beneficial through integration of the patient's personal goals, psychosocial support for the family and patient, and medical treatment.[57] Improved quality of life and positive patient and family outcomes are often associated with early discussion of goals and clear communication of prognosis through palliative care consultation.[59] Furthermore, palliative care reduces the number of late hospital admissions and subsequent painful procedures or treatments and is critical to improved patient care.[46,59–62] It is important for the APRN to build relationships with the transplant team and patients, thereby reducing physical, psychological, and spiritual suffering.

References

1. Prommer E. Organ donation and palliative care: can palliative care make a difference? *J Palliat Med.* 2014; 17(3): 368–71. doi: 10.1089/jpm.2013.0375.
2. Everidge CS. Donation after cardiac death: ethical dilemmas and implications for advanced practice nurses. *Dimens Crit Care Nurs.* 2012; 31(4): 228–34. doi: 10.1097/DCC.0b013e318256d7dc.
3. HPNA Position Statement: The Role of Palliative Care in Organ and Tissue Donation. 2013.
4. National Kidney Foundation: News. Available at http: //www.kidney.org/news/newsroom/factsheets/Organ-Donation-and-Transplantation-Stats.cfm. Accessed July 9, 2014.
5. Varma V, Mehta N, Kumaran V, Nundy S. Indications and contraindications for liver transplantation. *Int J Hepatol.* 2011. doi: 10.4061/2011/121862.
6. National Data, Organ Procurement Transplant Network. Available at optn.transplant.hrsa.gov/converge/data/citing.asp
7. WHO. Human organ and tissue transplantation. Available at http: //www.who.int/ethics/topics/human_transplant_report/en/. Accessed July 9, 2014.
8. Kavalieratos D, Mitchell EM, Carey TS, et al. "Not the 'Grim Reaper Service'": an assessment of provider knowledge, attitudes, and perceptions regarding palliative care referral barriers in heart failure. *J Am Heart Assoc Cardiovasc Cerebrovasc Dis.* 2014; 3(1): 1–2. doi: 10.1161/JAHA.113.000544.
9. Autor S, Storey S, Ziemba-Davis M. Knowledge of palliative care. *J Hosp Palliat Nurs.* 2013; 15(5): 307–15.
10. Nelson JE, Curtis JR, Mulkerin C, et al. Choosing and using screening criteria for palliative care consultation in the ICU: a report from the Improving Palliative Care in the ICU (IPAL-ICU) Advisory Board. *Crit Care Med.* 2013; 41(10): 2318–27. doi: 10.1097/CCM.0b013e31828cf12c.
11. Luckett T, Sellars M, Tieman J, et al. Advance care planning for adults with CKD: A systematic integrative review. *Am J Kidney Dis.* 2014; 63(5): 761–70. doi: 10.1053/j.ajkd.2013.12.007.
12. Park IK, Jun HJ, Park SJ, et al. Differences in end-of-life care decision making between patients with and without cancer. *Am J Hosp Palliat Med.* 2014. doi: 10.1177/1049909114542646.
13. Swetz KM, Kamal AH, Matlock DD, et al. Preparedness planning before mechanical circulatory support: a "how-to" guide for palliative medicine clinicians. *J Pain Symptom Manage.* 2014; 47(5): 926–35.e6. doi: 10.1016/j.jpainsymman.2013.06.006.
14. HPNA position statement: The Nurse's Role in Advance Care Planning. 2013. Hospice and Palliative Nurses Association, Pittsburgh, PA. Available at hpna.advancingexpertcare.orgeducation/position-statements.
15. Allen LA, Stevenson LW, Grady KL, et al. Decision making in advanced heart failure: A Scientific Statement from the American Heart Association. *Circulation.* 2012; 125(15): 1928–52. doi: 10.1161/CIR.0b013e31824f2173.
16. Hunt SA, Abraham WT, Chin MH, et al. 2009 Focused update incorporated into the ACC/AHA 2005 Guidelines for the Diagnosis and Management of Heart Failure in Adults: A Report of the American College of Cardiology Foundation/American Heart Association Task Force on Practice Guidelines developed in collaboration with the International Society for Heart and Lung Transplantation. *J Am Coll Cardiol.* 2009; 53(15): e1–e90. doi: 10.1016/j.jacc.2008.11.013.
17. Katz JN, Waters S, Hollis IB, Chang PP. Advanced therapies for end-stage heart failure. *Curr Cardiol Rev.* 2014; 10: 63–72.
18. Alba AC, Alba LF, Delgado DH, Rao V, Ross HJ, Goeree R. Cost-effectiveness of ventricular assist device therapy as a bridge to transplantation compared with nonbridged cardiac recipients. *Circulation.* 2013; 127(24): 2424–35. doi: 10.1161/CIRCULATIONAHA.112.000194.
19. Long EF, Swain GW, Mangi AA. Comparative survival and cost-effectiveness of advanced therapies for end-stage heart failure. *Circ Heart Fail.* 2014; 7(3): 470–8. doi: 10.1161/CIRCHEARTFAILURE.113.000807.
20. Kirklin JK, Naftel DC, Pagani FD, et al. Sixth INTERMACS annual report: a 10,000-patient database. *J Heart Lung Transplant.* 2014; 33(6): 555–64. doi: 10.1016/j.healun.2014.04.010.
21. Lietz K. Destination therapy: patient selection and current outcomes. *J Card Surg.* 2010; 25(4): 462–71. doi: 10.1111/j.1540-8191.2010.01050.x.
22. Miller LW, Lietz K. Candidate selection for long-term left ventricular assist device therapy for refractory heart failure. *J Heart Lung Transplant.* 2006; 25(7): 756–64. doi: 10.1016/j.healun.2006.03.007.
23. Slaughter MS, Rogers JG, Milano CA, et al. Advanced heart failure treated with continuous-flow left ventricular assist device. *N Engl J Med.* 2009; 361(23): 2241–51. doi: 10.1056/NEJMoa0909938.
24. Rogers JG, Aaronson KD, Boyle AJ, et al. Continuous flow left ventricular assist device improves functional capacity and quality of life of advanced heart failure patients. *J Am Coll Cardiol.* 2010; 55(17): 1826–34. doi: 10.1016/j.jacc.2009.12.052.
25. Sandau KE, Hoglund BA, Weaver CE, Boisjolie C, Feldman D. A conceptual definition of quality of life with a left ventricular assist device: results from a qualitative study. *Heart Lung J Crit Care* 2014; 43(1): 32–40. doi: 10.1016/j.hrtlng.2013.09.004.
26. Bakitas M, MacMartin M, Trzepkowski K, et al. Palliative care consultations for heart failure patients: How many, when, and why? *J Card Fail.* 2013; 19(3): 193–201. doi: 10.1016/j.cardfail.2013.01.011.
27. Hupcey JE. The state of palliative care and heart failure. *Heart Lung J Crit Care* 2012; 41(6): 529–30. doi: 10.1016/j.hrtlng.2012.09.003.

28. Allen LA, Gheorghiade M, Reid KJ, et al. Identifying patients hospitalized with heart failure at risk for unfavorable future quality of life. *Circ Cardiovasc Qual Outcomes.* 2011; 4(4): 389–98. doi: 10.1161/CIRCOUTCOMES.110.958009.

29. Whellan DJ, Goodlin SJ, Dickinson MG, et al. End-of-life care in patients with heart failure. *J Card Fail.* 2014; 20(2): 121–34. doi: 10.1016/j.cardfail.2013.12.003.

30. Strachan PH, Joy C, Costigan J, Carter N. Development of a practice tool for community-based nurses: The Heart Failure Palliative Approach to Care (HeFPAC). *Eur J Cardiovasc Nurs.* 2014; 13(2): 134–41. doi: 10.1177/1474515113519522.

31. Caccamo M, Eckman P, John R. Current state of ventricular assist devices. *Curr Heart Fail Rep.* 2011; 8(2): 91–8. doi: 10.1007/s11897-011-0050-z.

32. Bruce CR. A review of ethical considerations for ventricular assist device placement in older adults. *Aging Dis.* 2013; 4(2): 100–12.

33. Rizzieri AG, Verheijde JL, Rady MY, McGregor JL. Ethical challenges with the left ventricular assist device as a destination therapy. *Philos Ethics Humanit Med.* 2008; 3: 20. doi: 10.1186/1747-5341-3-20.

34. Ottenberg AL, Cook KE, Topazian RJ, Mueller LA, Mueller PS, Swetz KM. Choices for patients "without a choice": Interviews with patients who received a left ventricular assist device as destination therapy. *Circ Cardiovasc Qual Outcomes.* 2014; 7(3): 368–73. doi: 10.1161/CIRCOUTCOMES.113.000660.

35. Kitko LA, Hupcey JE, Gilchrist JH, Boehmer JP. Caring for a spouse with end-stage heart failure through implantation of a left ventricular assist device as destination therapy. *Heart Lung J Crit Care.* 2013; 42(3): 195–201. doi: 10.1016/j.hrtlng.2012.10.004.

36. Byram EK. Upstream palliative care for the patient with a left ventricular assist device as destination therapy. *Dimens Crit Care Nurs.* 2012; 31(1): 18–24. doi: 10.1097/DCC.0b013e31823a537c.

37. Brush S, Budge D, Alharethi R, et al. End-of-life decision making and implementation in recipients of a destination left ventricular assist device. *J Heart Lung Transplant.* 2010; 29(12): 1337–41. doi: 10.1016/j.healun.2010.07.001.

38. Hardy JD, Webb WR, Dalton M, Walker GR. Lung transplantations in man. *JAMA.* 1963; 186(12): 99–108.

39. Orens JB, Estenne M, Arcasoy S, et al. International Guidelines for the Selection of Lung Transplant Candidates: 2006 Update—A Consensus Report From the Pulmonary Scientific Council of the International Society for Heart and Lung Transplantation. *J Heart Lung Transplant.* 2006; 25: 745–55. doi: 10.1016/j.healun.2006.03.011.

40. Yusen RD, Christie JD, Edwards LB, et al. The Registry of the International Society for Heart and Lung Transplantation: Thirtieth Adult Lung and Heart-Lung Transplant Report—2013; Focus Theme: Age. *J Int Soc Heart Lung Transplant.* 2013; 32(10): 965–78. doi: 10.1016/j.healun.2013.08.007.

41. Yelle MT, Stevens PE, Lanuza DM. Waiting narratives of lung transplant candidates. *Nurs Res Pract.* 2013; 2013: 1–4. doi: 10.1155/2013/794698.

42. International Society of Heart and Lung Transplant. Quarterly Report, 2014. Available at ishlt.org.

43. Gottlieb J. Lung transplantation for interstitial lung diseases and pulmonary hypertension. *Semin Respir Crit Care Med.* 2013; 34(3): 281–7. doi: 10.1055/s-0033-1348462.

44. Javidfar J, Iribarne A, Jurado J, et al. Extracorporeal membrane oxygenation as a bridge to lung transplantation and recovery. *J Thorac Cardiovasc Surg.* 2012; 144(3): 716–21. doi: 10.1016/j.jtcvs.2012.05.040.

45. Lang G, Taghavi S, Aigner C, et al. Primary lung transplantation after bridge with extracorporeal membrane oxygenation: a plea for a shift in our paradigms for indications. *Transplantation* 2012; 93(7): 729–736. doi: 10.1097/TP.0b013e318246f8e1.

46. Lamba S, Murphy P, McVicker S, Harris Smith J, Mosenthal AC. Changing end-of-life care practice for liver transplant service patients: Structured palliative care intervention in the surgical intensive care unit. *J Pain Symptom Manage.* 2012; 44(4): 508–19. doi: 10.1016/j.jpainsymman.2011.10.018.

47. Organ Procurement and Transplantation Network. Available at: http: //optn.transplant.hrsa.gov. Accessed July 23, 2014.

48. Cox-North P, Doorenbos A, Shannon SE, Scott J, Curtis JR. The transition to end-of-life care in end-stage liver disease. *J Hosp Palliat Nurs.* 2013; 15(4): 209–15. doi: 10.1097/NJH.0b013e318289f4b0.

49. Goetzinger AM, Blumenthal JA, O'Hayer CV, et al. Stress and coping in caregivers of patients awaiting solid organ transplantation. *Clin Transplant.* 2012; 26(1): 97–104. doi: 10.1111/j.1399-0012.2011.01431.x.

50. Martin P, DiMartini A, Feng S, Brown R, Fallon M. Evaluation for liver transplantation in adults: 2013 practice guideline by the American Association for the Study of Liver Diseases and the American Society of Transplantation. *Hepatology.* 2014; 59(3): 1144–65.

51. Poonja Z, Brisebois A, van Zanten SV, Tandon P, Meeberg G, Karvellas CJ. Patients with cirrhosis and denied liver transplants rarely receive adequate palliative care or appropriate management. *Clin Gastroenterol Hepatol.* 2014; 12(4): 692–8. doi: 10.1016/j.cgh.2013.08.027.

52. Ahluwalia SC, Bekelman DB, Huynh AK, Prendergast TJ, Shreve S, Lorenz KA. Barriers and strategies to an iterative model of advance care planning communication. *Am J Hosp Palliat Med.* 2014. doi: 10.1177/1049909114541513.

53. Finnegan-John J, Thomas VJ. The psychosocial experience of patients with end-stage renal disease and its impact on quality of life: Findings from a needs assessment to shape a service. *ISRN Nephrol.* 2012; 2013: 1. doi: 10.5402/2013/308986.

54. Low JK, Williams A, Manias E, Crawford K. Interventions to improve medication adherence in adult kidney transplant recipients: a systematic review. *Nephrol Dial Transplant.* 2014; 30(5): 752. doi: 10.1093/ndt/gfu204.

55. Rosenberger EM, Dew MA, DiMartini AF, DeVito Dabbs AJ, Yusen RD. Psychosocial issues facing lung transplant candidates, recipients and family caregivers. *Thorac Surg Clin.* 2012; 22(4): 517–29. doi: 10.1016/j.thorsurg.2012.08.001.

56. Strand JJ, Mansel JK, Swetz KM. The growth of palliative care. *Minn Med.* 2014; 97(6): 39–43.

57. Aslakson RA, Curtis JR, Nelson JE. The changing role of palliative care in the ICU. *Crit Care Med.* 2014; 42(11): 2418. doi:10.1097/CCM.0000000000000573.

58. Bernacki RE, Block SD, for the American College of Physicians High Value Care Task Force. Communication about serious illness care goals: A review and synthesis of best practices. *JAMA Intern Med.* 2014; 174(12): 1994–2003. doi: 10.1001/jamainternmed.2014.5271.

59. Fauci J, Schneider K, Walters C, et al. The utilization of palliative care in gynecologic oncology patients near the end-of-life. *Gynecol Oncol.* 2012; 127(1): 175–9. doi: 10.1016/j.ygyno.2012.06.025.

60. O'Connor TL, Ngamphaiboon N, Groman A, et al. Hospice utilization and end-of-life care in metastatic breast cancer patients at a comprehensive cancer center. *J Palliat Med.* 2014; 18(1): 50–55. doi: 10.1089/jpm.2014.0238.

61. Mulvey CL, Smith TJ, Gourin CG. The use of inpatient palliative care services in patients with metastatic incurable head and neck cancer. *Head Neck.* Oct. 21, 2014. doi: 10.1002/hed.23895.

62. Fawole OA, Dy SM, Wilson RF, et al. A systematic review of communication quality improvement interventions for patients with advanced and serious illness. *J Gen Intern Med.* 2013; 28(4): 570–7. doi: 10.1007/s11606-012-2204-4.

The Palliative Advanced Practice Registered Nurse in the Ambulatory Care Setting

CHAPTER 12

The Advanced Practice Registered Nurse in Outpatient Palliative Cancer Care

Barbara Reville

Key Points

♦ Leaders in the fields of palliative care and oncology advocate full integration of palliative care into usual oncology care.

♦ Models of palliative care outside the acute care setting have demonstrated benefits in the domains of symptom management, psychosocial and spiritual distress, and support for patients at illness transition points.

♦ Advanced practice registered nurses (APRNs) have a stake in strategic planning for outpatient services alongside administrators and oncology clinicians.

♦ The therapeutic relationship between the palliative care APRN and patients and families is the focal point of patient-centered palliative nursing.

Introduction

Advanced practice nursing at the intersection of outpatient oncology and palliative care is the focus of this chapter. The chapter opens with a review of relevant evidence and national directives to integrate outpatient oncology and palliative care early in the illness course. Next, the different conceptual models for palliative care in oncology settings are explained. Finally, key categories of nursing intervention to relieve patient suffering, maintain collaborative relationships with the oncology team, and measure outcomes of practice are presented.

Palliative care is universally recognized as a pillar of comprehensive cancer care throughout the illness trajectory, not just at the end-of-life. This view has evolved in recent years in response to emerging evidence. Currently, leaders in the fields of palliative care and oncology advocate full integration of palliative care into usual oncology care.[1-7] Ferris and colleagues defined "palliative cancer care" as:

[T]he integration into cancer care of therapies to address the multiple issues that cause suffering for patients and their families and have an impact on the quality of their lives. Palliative cancer care aims to give patients and their families the capacity to realize their full potential, when their cancer is curable as well as when the end of life is near.[6(p 3055)]

As the nature of cancer becomes increasingly chronic, most oncology care occurs in the outpatient or community setting, not the acute care setting.[5] While palliative care for cancer patients and families in the hospital or hospice setting is widely available at U.S. cancer centers, specialty palliative care services for outpatients are less common.[7,8] Specialty outpatient practice represents a "new frontier" for palliative care professionals to operationalize longitudinal care over the illness course rather than primarily managing acute issues during an inpatient encounter.[2,4,5,7(p 823)] Models of nonhospice palliative cancer care outside the acute care setting have demonstrated benefits in the domains of symptom management, psychosocial and spiritual distress, and support for patients and families at transition points of the illness.[1,3,9-17]

While there is strong support among oncology and palliative care organizations for collaboration, there is no standard model of care delivery for outpatient palliative cancer care.[3,6,8,18] However, innovative endeavors by palliative care physicians and APRNs have demonstrated the feasibility of outpatient practice models, patient and provider satisfaction, and positive patient outcomes.[10,11,14-21]

The APRN is well suited to provide care that is complementary to physician management in nonhospital settings.[22-26] Nursing's practice of whole-person care aligns with palliative care's patient- and family-centered focus.[27-29] The Hospice and Palliative Nurses Association's position statement declares that the APRN is "uniquely qualified and positioned to address the myriad needs of individuals facing life-threatening, progressive illness" in any primary care setting.[30(p 1)]

According to the Oncology Nursing Society, the scope of practice defined for oncology APRNs encompasses attention to the palliative care needs of patients and families.[31] Therefore, the APRN with education as a clinical nurse specialist, a nurse practitioner, or a blended role and clinical skills in oncology can provide primary palliative care of the oncology patient.[23,26-30] However, specialty training and certification as a hospice and palliative advanced practice registered nurse is required for expert-level palliative care practice.[23,26,28-31]

Integration of Oncology and Palliative Care—A National Priority

The professional oncology community aspires to full palliative care integration into comprehensive cancer care by the year 2020.[6,8] National opinion leaders and professional groups in oncology joined the groundswell of support for integrative care models and new standards for quality cancer care. While palliative care awareness is growing, timely referral for and access to services remain inadequate.[2,32]

According to the Institute of Medicine's report *Dying in America*, our increasingly aging and culturally diverse populations who are living with advanced serious illness deserve access to palliative care.[32] The Institute of Medicine charged the healthcare professions to train clinicians to adopt palliative care's person and family focus, to encourage more frequent clinician-initiated communication about end-of-life decisions with patients, and to build more basic palliative care training programs for doctors and nurses. The report recommended that healthcare systems develop better access to integrated palliative care models and expert-level palliative care providers, offer incentives for reducing hospital admissions and costs, and ensure quality, efficiency, and information transfer.

The National Comprehensive Cancer Network's (NCCN) clinical guidelines reflect the profession's commitment to full integration of care.[33] The guidelines direct institutions to develop programs whereby patients can access credentialed palliative care professionals, including APRNs, concurrent with oncologic care. Further, these programs should be monitored for quality outcomes.

The Evidence for Outpatient Palliative Cancer Care

Several major findings galvanized the oncology field's perception that palliative care can improve the cancer patient's illness experience in a variety of ways from the time of diagnosis.[1,5,9,10,14,15,17,18] While the following reviews are not exhaustive, they provide an historical overview of this body of work. The cumulative results build a strong case for earlier involvement of palliative care in the outpatient setting.

In 2009, Bakitas and colleagues reported on a nursing-led intervention involving multiple patient education, psychosocial support, and problem-solving sessions followed by telephone case management for a rural population of outpatients from time of diagnosis with stage III or IV cancer diagnoses until death.[14] The study intervention ran concurrently with usual oncologic care. Quality of life, symptom intensity, and mood were measured at baseline, at 1 month, and every 3 months while on the study. The electronic medical record supplied data on use of the hospital, intensive care unit, and emergency department as proxy measures for use of aggressive care at the end-of-life. The patients in the study group reported higher quality of life and better mood than the controls, without a difference in mortality or use of acute care services.

Another nurse investigator, Prince-Paul, led a pilot study to explore the effects of concurrent care by a palliative APRN in a community oncology setting.[15] Similar measures as in the aforementioned Bakitas study for physical and psychosocial symptoms, including spiritual well-being and use of healthcare services, were measured in a sample of advanced cancer patients. There were no significant differences between the group who received palliative APRN care and those who did not on symptoms, quality of life, depression, or spiritual well-being. However, patients in the APRN group had lower mortality at 4 months and were significantly less likely to be hospitalized. This work affirmed the value of the APRN and suggested a feasible, cost-effective model for centers without resources to hire an entire team.

A rising number of cancer survivors are alive today.[5] The survival of nearly 12 million Americans with a cancer history lends credence to progress in anticancer modalities and care. While most of these individuals encounter healthcare providers outside the acute care setting, many are coping with symptoms of a physical, psychological, or spiritual nature stemming from their cancer illness. These community-dwelling cancer patients are not eligible for hospice care but may need palliative care.

Data analyses on 4,980 cancer patients seen by palliative care providers offered an overview of nonhospice palliative care needs in the ambulatory setting.[5] Patients' diagnoses were mostly solid tumors, including lung and gastrointestinal, and some hematologic cancers. Forty percent of the sample required hospital care in the previous 6 months, 49% had performance status indicative of limitations in daily function, and 40% had substantial functional decline. Most had a provider estimate of survival of less than 6 months, and 88% reported fair or poor quality of life. One-third of the sample did not have a healthcare surrogate identified and 97% had not completed a physician order about end-of-life preferences. As to symptoms, 95% had at least one symptom and 67% had three or more symptoms. In summary, these outpatients were encountering palliative care when in decline without earlier attention to symptoms or decision making. These findings suggest that earlier intervention during the disease course is warranted.

Muir and colleagues reported on the effect of adding one half-day palliative care clinic alongside a busy community oncology center on quality outcomes, referral volume, provider satisfaction, and time saved for oncologists.[18] Over the first 2 years of clinic operation, the investigators noted a decrease in patients' symptom severity scores on the Edmonton Symptom Assessment System, high provider satisfaction, and an 87% increase in referrals. The issue of saving specialty cancer resources is germane because the existing oncologist workforce is insufficient to meet the growing need as the American population ages.[34]

In 2010, Temel and colleagues added impressive evidence to the emerging case for early outpatient intervention in advanced cancer.[10] In this trial, newly diagnosed lung cancer patients with metastatic disease were randomized to receive usual cancer care with or without early palliative care provided by board-certified palliative care physicians and APRNs. The researchers measured quality of life using a lung-cancer-specific tool (Functional Assessment of Cancer Therapy-Lung) and mood at baseline and 3 months. They searched electronic medical records to assess use of aggressive end-of-life care (use of chemotherapy within 14 days of death, no hospice care or hospice enrollment within 3 days of death), documentation of end-of-life preferences, and survival. Significant findings among the intervention group were higher quality-of-life scores, less depression, less aggressive care at the end-of-life, and a remarkable 2.7-month survival advantage.[10] The accumulated evidence in favor of palliative care had reached the tipping point.[1]

Policy Shift Favoring Early Palliative Care for Cancer Patients

In 2012, the American Society of Clinical Oncology responded to the mounting evidence in favor of palliative care by directing its members to eschew the perception that palliative care is merely end-of-life care.[1] Further, they advised oncology professionals to consider involving palliative care early in the illness for patients with metastatic cancer and/or multiple symptoms. The National Cancer Institute (NCI) articulated the full continuum of palliative care as follows: "palliative care is given throughout a patient's experience with cancer."[35,36]

The Commission on Cancer (CoC) of the American College of Surgeons added a new palliative care standard as a requirement for hospital cancer program accreditation in 2012.[3,37] This standard requires that "palliative care services are available to patients either on-site or by referral."[37(p 70)] Table 12.1 lists the palliative care services that fulfill the CoC standard. An interdisciplinary team, including a specialty-trained and/or certified hospice and palliative medicine physician and nurse, along with other professionals, is recommended.[28,29]

The broadening of the oncology profession's perception of palliative care beyond an end-of-life care paradigm helped set the stage for expansion of outpatient models of care in cancer centers and the community.[4,5,7,18,34,38] In 2010, a survey of NCI-designated cancer centers revealed that most (98%) had some palliative care service (e.g., a palliative care physician, a consultation team, or a palliative care clinic) as compared to only 78% of non-NCI-designated centers.[8] Nurses were represented on palliative care teams in 47% of all programs in the sample, although level of training or certification was not reported.

Outpatient palliative care clinics specifically for oncology patients were twice as common among NCI-designated centers but were still available for only about 66% of centers.[8] The oncology clinic was the site of palliative care delivery in 23% of the centers with outpatient care. Growth of outpatient palliative cancer programs that need APRN providers can be anticipated in coming years.[4]

Another survey of outpatient palliative care targeted 12 academic medical centers where palliative care was well established.[38] Most were not full-time operations and reported nearly 500 patient visits annually, usually referred by oncologists. Team members most often included physicians. More than half of the programs reported APRN staff, followed by social workers (45%) and registered nurses (36%). Funding came from a mixture of billing revenues and institutional support.

Models of Outpatient Palliative Cancer Care: Opportunity and Challenge

The use of language to communicate what "palliative care" means to oncology providers and patients has evolved along with the field.[2,4,11,38] The APRN practicing in an oncology setting should be mindful of both the attitudes and adoption of palliative care conveyed by word choices. In some settings the term "palliative care" is avoided altogether. For example, "simultaneous care model" implies that palliative care is not an alternative to oncologic care.[2,7] The term "supportive care" is frequently used synonymously with palliative care and is favored by oncologists wary of the stigma of the latter term.[2,11,39] The term "supportive care" can also connote early intervention closer to the time of diagnosis of metastatic or highly symptomatic cancer.

There are three principal models of outpatient palliative care associated with a health system or hospital: a stand-alone clinic, a co-located clinic, and an embedded clinic.[4] Definitions for each are listed in Table 12.2. These models are advantageous for cancer centers committed to support onsite palliative care services and earn CoC accreditation.[40] More than one model may operate successfully within a single institution.[11]

APRNs have a stake in strategic planning for outpatient services alongside administrators and oncology clinicians.[29] Items to negotiate include responsibility for clinic costs, space and time allotments for palliative care providers, billing revenue flow, and referral processes.[4,11,40] The CoC palliative care services standard requires that a palliative care team member join the institution's cancer committee.[37]

Table 12.1 Commission on Cancer: Palliative Care Program Requirements

Interdisciplinary, team-based care of patient and family
Pain and symptom management
Communication among providers, patients, family
Continuity of care across all services and settings
Provision of spiritual comfort
Provision of psychosocial support for patient and family
Provision of bereavement support to families and professional care providers
Conversation about hospice care if patients have poor prognosis or at the end-of-life

Sources: Commission on Cancer (2012), reference 37; American College of Surgeons (2011), reference 3; Fox (2014), reference 29.

Table 12.2 Definitions of Outpatient Palliative Care Clinic Models

Clinic Model	Referral Sources	Operations
Stand-alone clinic	From anywhere in health system, depending on scope of services	Separate palliative care administrative structure and cost center, space, staff, scheduling, and billing
Co-located clinic	Predominantly from host specialty but can accept from other specialties	Shared space and services with host from a specialty that frequently consults palliative care. Responsibility for operational costs is negotiable.
Embedded clinic	Collaboration with host clinic for exclusive, onsite palliative care services. Referral process and scope of practice well defined.	Host clinic assumes all operational costs.

Sources: Barbour et al. (2012), reference 40; Bruera & Hui (2012), reference 11.

Clear communication about the nature and scope of the palliative care involvement between palliative care and oncology teams is essential for fruitful collaboration.[18] In a consultant role, the palliative care provider renders clinical opinions, providing only recommendations.[40] In a co-management role, palliative care personnel see patients on a "limited" basis to manage specific issues (e.g., symptoms) at the request of the oncology team.[11,18] A primary care role involves ongoing or longitudinal care involvement for higher-demand patients (e.g., early intervention palliative care).[41-43] In any scenario, patients can be seen individually by the palliative care provider or jointly with the oncology team.[40] A uniform policy is advisable to clarify provider accountability for patient follow-up and medication prescribing, especially for opioid use.

Challenges to realizing integrated palliative cancer care can hamper a program's success either at its outset or during growth.[5,11,24] First, there is limited evidence on how to best integrate primary and secondary palliative care and when to involve specialty-level palliative care.[5,44] Second, APRN practice may be subject to limitations due to regulations or institutional policy.

Primary palliative care skills are essential to all oncology clinicians, including oncology APRNs.[44] Oncology teams consult specialty-level palliative care providers for more complicated or refractory symptoms, complex psychosocial-spiritual issues, conflict situations, or ethical dilemmas. Without a clear triage or referral schema, palliative care providers can be overwhelmed by too many consults or, conversely, can be underused due to confusion about when to initiate consults.[16]

Palliative care programs use referral criteria or "triggers" as a process of care that educates providers about when to consult palliative care.[33,45] Table 12.3 lists oncology referral criteria for palliative care. These can also be applied to screen incoming consults

to ensure that requests are appropriately directed to palliative care.[40,44]

Palliative APRNs may encounter practice barriers due to variations in states' scope of nursing regulations, such as limits to independent practice without physician supervision, or prescriptive authority.[24] Lower reimbursement for services compared to physicians may drive institutional decisions about practice model, or referral protocols may limit APRNs from initiating new consults.[18] To overcome such barriers, it is important for APRNs to contribute to planning structures and processes of outpatient care.

Case Study Part 1

Mack, a 45-year-old married landscaper with cancer at the base of the tongue, developed severe neuropathic facial pain during chemoradiation. The pain became refractory to his home pain regimen of extended-release oxycodone. During an oncology clinic visit, the team consulted the palliative APRN associated with their clinic to co-manage Mack's pain and see the patient during future oncology visits. The palliative APRN recommended an opioid rotation from oxycodone to methadone and prescribed a daily bowel regimen.

Unique Role of the Palliative APRN

APRNs provide palliative care as expert clinicians, educators, leaders, administrators, and researchers.[23,24,26-30] Their unique role combines a holistic perspective on human responses to serious illness with the art of creating a healing presence and the use of evidence-based interventions to prevent, diagnose, and ameliorate the suffering of patients and families.[27] Guidelines for APRN intervention can be found in *The Clinical Practice Guidelines for Quality Palliative Care* and the Hospice and Palliative Nurses Association's APRN competencies.[46,47]

Nurses often work alongside non-nursing providers. Whether the palliative APRN is the only nurse on a palliative care team or the sole palliative care clinician in an oncology clinic, it is important to maintain "a nursing orientation."[27(p 108)] When nurses "unconsciously use a medical or institutional model as their perspective for organizing care," they limit their potential contribution.[48(p 27)] The key principles of advanced nursing practice are reviewed in the following sections.

Establishing and Maintaining Relationships

The palliative APRN in the outpatient oncology setting must establish "linkages" or collaborative relationships and observe proper consultation etiquette to be successful.[7(p 828)] Oncologists and the oncology team ultimately decide the timing and extent of palliative care consultation.[2,11,18] Should other issues outside the consult's scope arise, the APRN must communicate these to the oncology team before proceeding to an extensive consultation. For example, a request for help treating a symptom is a typical limited consultation. A more extensive consultation request might include broaching goals of care and support for a hospice transition. Clear communication establishes and maintains trust and respects the oncology care plan and role boundaries.

The therapeutic relationship between the palliative APRN and patients and families reflects the patient-centered approach of

Table 12.3 Triggers for Palliative Care Consultation

Disease Factors	Patient Factors	Hospitalization Factors
Disease progression during treatment	Substance abuse history	≥2 admissions in 3 mos.
Limited treatment options	Cognitive impairment	≥5 days in ICU without evidence of progress
Decline in functional status in last 60 days	Limited social support	Frequent emergency department visits
Life expectancy ≤ 6 months	Need to clarify treatment decisions or goals of care	
Advanced comorbidities	Request for palliative care	
Uncontrolled symptoms	Language barriers	
Complex or refractory pain - Escalating opioid use - Neuropathic pain	Uncontrolled psychosocial or spiritual distress	

Sources: National Comprehensive Cancer Network (2014), reference 33; Walling et al. (2008), reference 54; Reville et al. (2013), reference 45.

nursing and palliative care.[15,27,48] Prince-Paul described how a palliative APRN embedded in oncology practice accomplished this: "The [palliative APRN] established a trusting relationship with the patients through clinical expertise, repeated contact and communication, an active presence, and emotional support; this connection may have ultimately improved outcomes."[15(p 26)] Over time, "an emotional climate" for sharing of psychological and spiritual concerns and regrets offers patients comfort without altering their situation.[49(p 164)]

Jacobsen and colleagues advocate "continuity outpatient palliative care," a concept for long-term palliative care presence that builds a trusting provider–patient relationship.[43(p 1)] This is consistent with the aforementioned primary care role and is ideal for early palliative care involvement. In this scenario, initial patient encounters focus on building rapport and assessing symptom or coping issues.[41,42] Over subsequent patient encounters, the palliative APRN should ask about life prior to the illness and the cancer's impact on emotions and should intervene as necessary with advice on adaptive coping strategies (e.g., meditation, problem solving, or gratitude).[49,50]

The APRN should elicit the patient's illness understanding, his or her expectations for cancer treatment, and preferences for receiving frank prognostic information.[49–51] Assessing the role of family caregivers in medical decision making is preliminary to talks about advance care planning and, eventually, code status and end-of-life wishes. As the illness evolves or with clinical setbacks, the trust and the caring foundation the palliative APRN has created with the patient allows access to more sensitive topics. Ongoing communication about key patient disclosures with the referring oncology team is advised. A successful joint care plan requires alignment of information the patient hears from both oncology and palliative care providers.

Case Study Part 2

Over the course of subsequent visits with Mack, the palliative APRN ascertained that his goals were to remain home with his wife and 3-year-old son, Mack, Jr., to continue working, and to pursue any and all treatment options. A recent hospital stay was very stressful for Mack's wife, who felt torn between remaining at the hospital with Mack or home to care for Mack, Jr. The palliative APRN communicated these concerns to the oncology team and suggested a visit with the oncology social worker to discuss coping strategies with Mack and his wife, and to consider a home care referral.

Practicing Essential Communication Skills

The palliative APRN in the oncology clinic uses his or her communication expertise to establish and maintain relationships as described above and during serious conversations at illness turning points.[43,49,51–53] While the primacy of this practice must be stated, full discussion of APRN communication skills is outside the scope of this section.

Oncology referrals to palliative care to address goals of care are recommended at transition points in the illness and when treatment options are dwindling.[1,33,54] These "sentinel events" include (1) admission to an intensive care unit; (2) use of mechanical ventilation; (3) metastasis to the central nervous system; (4) start of a new chemotherapy regimen; (5) need for hemodialysis; (6) placement of a cardioverter-defibrillator; (7) placement of gastric tube; and (8) impending major surgery.[54(p 3900)] Psychosocial or spiritual shifts in awareness of the patient's inevitable death generate equally traumatic transitions.[25] At these turning points, a goals-of-care discussion or family meeting is warranted.

Goals-of-care discussions ideally involve the patient and family and the oncology team.[15,18] Social work or pastoral care colleagues bring another perspective and considerable communication skills, especially for psychosocial distress, existential questions, or conflict. The palliative APRN may facilitate the meeting or provide specific information, such as hospice eligibility.

Case Study Part 3

Four months after initiation of chemoradiation, Mack was hospitalized with delirium, dehydration, weight loss, worsening functional status, and acute renal dysfunction. Imaging studies indicated disease progression. The delirium improved with intravenous hydration and opioid dose adjustment. However, the oncology team had no further treatment options and felt hospice was Mack's best option.

The oncologist scheduled a family meeting soon after discharge with Mack, his wife, the oncology social worker, and the palliative APRN. Mack was emphatic in his desire for more chemotherapy in hopes of life prolongation. The oncologist warned of organ dysfunction and side effects, as well as low likelihood of longer life.

The palliative APRN recalled Mack's initial goal to remain at home with his family and asked if this was still his foremost goal. The APRN expressed concern that more treatment might cause complications and need for hospitalization. Mack replied that he preferred never to return to the hospital. The conversation turned toward an elaboration of Mack's wish for death at home with support for his family and attention to his comfort. He did not want life-prolonging measures like cardiopulmonary resuscitation. The social worker outlined how hospice care aligned with Mack's wishes and would reduce his wife's stress. A hospice referral was made. Mack died peacefully at home 4 weeks later.

In this chapter's case study, a limited symptom management consult evolved following sentinel events in the illness course to an extensive goals-of-care conversation. The APRN's co-management role with oncology complemented disease management and supported the patient's and family's quality of life. The APRN's caring relationship over the illness course facilitated a transition in goals of care.

Screening for Pain and Non-pain Symptoms

The NCCN guidelines instruct oncology teams to screen all patients for uncontrolled symptoms, advanced comorbidities, poor performance status, and specific oncologic problems (e.g., hypercalcemia, spinal cord compression, or cachexia).[33] Common symptoms to assess include pain, dyspnea, anorexia, nausea and vomiting, constipation, fatigue, sleep disorders, and delirium. A management plan is needed for any issue identified during initial assessment.

Symptom screening tools aid clinicians performing comprehensive evaluations, reduce variations in care, and supply baseline data for quality measures. The palliative APRN should elicit symptom intensity, quality, associated symptoms, and level of distress using tools validated in the oncology population or in common use by the oncology team.[55] Examples include the Memorial Symptom Assessment Scale, Edmonton Symptom Assessment System, the 0–10 visual analogue scale, and the McCorkle Symptom Distress Scale.[5] Management strategies for common symptoms can be found elsewhere in this text.

Coping Support and Distress Management

The CoC cancer program accreditation standards require universal screening for psychosocial distress during an initial oncology clinic visit by clinician interview or questionnaire.[3,37,56] Should patients indicate moderate or high distress, evidence in writing of an in-depth assessment, plan of care, or referral is required. Any member of the oncology team, including psychosocial-spiritual care providers, can complete this assessment. Each program must develop its own process of care to comply with this standard. Smith and colleagues used an electronic patient report system that triggered referrals in outpatient oncology.[21]

The NCCN guidelines recommend palliative care referrals for distress scores above 4 on a 0-to-10 scale.[33] Other criteria for referral include evidence of caregiver deficits, poor social support, family conflict, spiritual concerns, and risk factors for complicated grief. The palliative APRN can help the oncology team by performing in-depth psychosocial assessments that comply with the clinic standard. Assisting patients with coping is consistent with the APRN role, as are medication management and referral to psychosocial and spiritual professionals.

Staff distress can occur in high-volume oncology settings, especially among staff exposed to cumulative patient losses.[57] The palliative APRN can help to identify compassion fatigue and moral distress and collaborate with the oncology team on resources to support staff.

Promoting Care Continuity and Coordination

A team approach shares the work of caring for the myriad physical and psychological concerns of patients with serious illness. The palliative APRN can benefit from networking about services within the institution and in the community that provide cancer care—for example, home care and hospice agencies, physical rehabilitation services, specialists in interventional pain modalities, nutrition professionals, mental health resources, and others.[40]

The palliative APRN serves as a bridge between the disciplines in the interest of full integration between oncology and palliative care. Ideally, the APRN communicates regularly with his or her inpatient palliative care colleagues to learn about incoming referrals from the hospital, to track progress of hospitalized patients, and to provide collegial support and education. At the same time, the APRN can participate in oncology clinic forums for education, quality improvement, and patient care coordination.

Measuring Outcomes for Quality and Sustainability

The Joint Commission awards advanced certification to palliative care programs that establish data-driven performance improvement processes to improve and validate operations. Measures must be evidence-based and must include patient satisfaction feedback and a plan to address sentinel events.[58]

It is best if outcome measures align with oncology priorities and use data already collected in routine practice or processes. For example, data on physical symptoms using standardized scoring systems are useful to measure improvement from before to after consultation.[6] Psychosocial measures include quality-of-life and depression scores, caregiver burden and perceptions of care, and distress scores.[18] Indicators of acute care utilization (e.g., readmission rates, emergency department visits, and timing of hospice enrollment prior to death) show the impact of palliative care integration.[10,11,19] Operational measures (e.g., consult volume, wait time to see new referrals, professional fee revenues, or time saved for oncologists) will interest stakeholders and help anticipate staffing needs.[40] Palliative care providers can also survey their oncology colleagues for feedback on the collaboration.

Summary

Palliative APRNs practicing in oncology outpatient settings are leading the way for full integration of these disciplines into comprehensive, high-quality cancer care. Reports from many innovative endeavors have demonstrated beneficial patient outcomes and institutional goals.

There are various models for care delivery. For patients who need specialized palliative care input, the palliative APRN may consult, co-manage, or play a primary care role in collaboration with the oncology team. Ongoing communication is essential to establish and cultivate linkages to referring oncology providers.

The APRN is advised to contribute to strategic assessment, planning, and evaluation of new programs to ensure that they address gaps in care and adhere to national practice standards. Finally, APRNs should advocate for structures and processes of care that prioritize patient- and family-centered care and support an expanded scope of advanced nursing practice.

References

1. Smith TJ, Temin S, Alesi ER, et al. American Society of Clinical Oncology provisional clinical opinion: The integration of palliative care into standard oncology care. *J Clin Oncol.* 2012; 30(8): 880–7.

2. Bruera E, Hui D. Integrating supportive and palliative care in the trajectory of cancer: Establishing goals and models of care. *J Clin Oncol.* 2010; 28(25): 4013–7.

3. American College of Surgeons. New commission on cancer accreditation standards gains strong support from four national cancer advocacy organizations. http://www.facs.org/news2011/coc-standards0811.html. Updated 2011. Accessed August 1, 2014.

4. Barbour LT, Cohen SE, Jackson VA, et al., eds. *Models for Palliative Care Outside the Hospital Setting.* 1st ed. New York, NY: Center to Advance Palliative Care; 2012, A Technical Assistance Module from the IPAL-OP Project.

5. Kamal AH, Bull J, Kavalieratos D, Taylor DH, Downey W, Abernethy AP. Palliative care needs of patients with cancer living in the community. *J Oncol Pract.* 2011; 7(6): 382–88.

6. Ferris FD, Bruera E, Cherny N, et al. Palliative cancer care a decade later: Accomplishments, the need, next steps: from the American Society of Clinical Oncology. *J Clin Oncol.* 2009; 27(18): 3052–8.

7. Meier DE, Beresford L. Outpatient clinics are a new frontier for palliative care. *J Palliat Med.* 2008; 11(6): 823–8.

8. Hui, D, Elsayem, A, De La Cruz, M, et al. Availability and integration of palliative care at US cancer centers. *JAMA.* 2010; 303(11): 1054–61.

9. Wright AA, Zhang B, Ray A, et al. Associations between end-of-life discussions, patient mental health, medical care near death, and caregiver bereavement adjustment. *JAMA.* 2008; 300(14): 1665–73.

10. Temel JS, Greer JA, Muzikansky A, et al. Early palliative care for patients with metastatic non-small-cell lung cancer. *N Engl J Med.* 2010; 363: 733–42.

11. Bruera E, Hui D. Conceptual models for integrating palliative care at cancer centers. *J Palliat Med.* 2012; 15(11): 1261–9.

12. Douglas SL, Daly BJ. Effect of an integrated cancer support team on caregiver satisfaction with end-of-life care. *Oncol Nurs Forum.* 2014; 41(4): E248–55.

13. Robison J, Du Pen AR. The outpatient setting. In: Ferrell BR, Coyle N, eds. *Oxford Textbook of Palliative Nursing.* 3rd ed. New York, NY: Oxford University Press; 2010:923–33.

14. Bakitas M, Lyons KD, Hegel MT, et al. Effects of a palliative care interventions on clinical outcomes in patients with advanced cancer. *JAMA.* 2009; 302(7): 741–9.

15. Prince-Paul M, Burant CJ, Saltzman JN, Teston LJ, Matthews CR. The effects of integrating an advanced practice palliative care nurse in a community oncology center: A pilot study. *J Support Oncol.* 2010; 8(1): 21–7.

16. Gibson S, Bordofsky M, Hirsch J, Kearney M, Solis M, Wong C. Community palliative care: One community's experience providing outpatient palliative care. *J Hosp Palliat Nurs.* 2012; 14(7): 491–9.

17. Follwell M, Burman D, Le LW, et al. Phase II study of an outpatient palliative care intervention in patients with metastatic cancer. *J Clin Oncol.* 2009; 27(2): 206–13.

18. Muir JC, Daly F, Davis MS, et al. Integrating palliative care into the outpatient, private practice oncology setting. *J Pain Symptom Manage.* 2010; 40(1): 126–35.

19. DiMartino LD, Weiner BJ, Mayer DK, Jackson GL, Biddle AK. Do palliative care interventions reduce emergency department visits among patients with cancer at the end-of-life? A systematic review. *J Palliat Med.* 2014; 17: 1–16.

20. Owens D, Eby K, Burson S, Green M, McGoodwin W, Isaac M. Primary palliative care clinic pilot project demonstrates benefits of a nurse practitioner-directed clinic providing primary and palliative care. *J Am Acad Nurse Pract.* 2012; 24(1): 52–8.

21. Smith SK, Rowe K, Abernethy AP. Use of an electronic patient-reported outcome measurement system to improve distress management in oncology. *Palliat Support Care.* 2014; 12(1): 69–73.

22. Coyne PJ. The evolution of the advanced practice nurse within palliative care. *J Palliat Med.* 2003; 6(5): 769–70.

23. Meier DE, Beresford L. Advanced practice nurses in palliative care: A pivotal role and perspective. *J Palliat Med.* 2006; 9(3): 624–7.

24. Heinle R, McNulty J, Hebert RS. Nurse practitioners and the growth of palliative medicine. *Am J Hosp Palliat Med.* 2014; 31(3): 287–91.

25. Duggleby W, Berry P. Transitions and shifting goals of care for palliative patients and their families. *Clin J Oncol Nurs.* 2005; 9(4): 425.

26. Skalla KA. Blended role advanced practice nursing in palliative care of the oncology patient. *J Hosp Palliat Nurs.* 2006; 8(3): 155–63.

27. Lynch M, Dahlin C, Hultman T, Coakley EE. Palliative care nursing: defining the discipline? *J Hosp Palliat Nurs.* 2011; 13(2): 106–11.

28. Kazanowski M, Sheldon LK. Working together: Including palliative care with oncology care. *Clin J Oncol Nurs.* 2014; 18S(1): 45–8.

29. Fox K. The role of the acute care nurse practitioner in the implementation of the Commission on Cancer's standards on palliative care. *Clin J Oncol Nurs.* 2014; 18S(1): 39–44.

30. Hospice and Palliative Nurses Association. HPNA position statement: Value of the advanced practice registered nurse in palliative care. Available at http: //hpna.org/DisplayPage. aspx?Title=Position%20Statements. Published June 2013. Accessed September 2, 2014.

31. Oncology Nursing Society. The role of the advanced practice nurse in oncology care. Oncology Nursing Society. Available at https: // www.ons.org/about-ons/ons-position-statement/education/APRN. Published January /2014. Accessed September 4, 2014.

32. Pizzo PA, Walker DM, Bomba P, et al. *Dying in America: Improving Quality and Honoring Individual Preferences near the End of Life.* Washington, DC: Institute of Medicine; 2014:1–6.

33. National Comprehensive Cancer Network. Clinical practice guidelines in oncology. palliative care. NCCN Guidelines Version 1.2014. Available at http: //www.nccn.org/professionals/physician_ gls/f_guidelines.asp. Published April 18, 2014. Accessed June 2, 2014.

34. Levit L, Balogh E, Nass S, Ganz PA. *Delivering High-Quality Cancer Care: Charting a New Course for a System in Crisis.* Washington, DC: Institute of Medicine; 2013:1–412.

35. National Cancer Institute. Palliative care in cancer. Available at http: //www.cancer.gov/cancertopics/factsheet/Support/ palliative-care. Published March 16, 2010. Accessed September 2, 2014.

36. Mahon MM. US survey finds higher availability of palliative care programs, palliative physicians and consultation teams and palliative outpatient services in national cancer institute centres compared to non-NCI centres. *Evid Based Nurs.* 2010; 14(4): 105–6.

37. Commission on Cancer, ed. *Standard 2.4 palliative care services.* Chicago, IL: American College of Surgeons; 2012.

38. Rabow MW, Smith AK, Braun JL, Weissman DE. Outpatient palliative care practices. *Arch Intern Med.* 2010; 170(7): 654–5.

39. Dalal S, Palla S, Hui D, et al. Association between a name change from palliative to supportive care and the timing of patient referrals at a comprehensive cancer center. *Oncologist.* 2011; 16: 105–11.

40. Barbour LT, Cohen SE, Jackson VA, et al, eds. *Getting Started: The Outpatient Palliative Care Clinic.* 1st ed. New York, NY: Center to Advance Palliative Care; 2012A, Technical Assistance Module from the IPAL-OP Project.

41. Jacobsen J, Jackson VA, Dahlin C, et al. Components of early outpatient palliative care consultation in patients with metastatic nonsmall cell lung cancer. *J Palliat Med.* 2011; 14(4): 459–64.

42. Yoong JY, Park ER, Greer JA, et al. Early palliative care in advanced lung cancer: A qualitative study. *JAMA Intern Med.* 2013; 173(4): 283–90.

43. Jacobsen J, Kvale E, Rabow M, et al. Helping patients with serious illness live well through the promotion of adaptive coping: A report from the Improving Outpatient Palliative Care (IPAL-OP) initiative. *J Palliat Med.* 2014; 17(4): 1–6.

44. Quill TE, Abernethy AP. Generalist plus specialist palliative care-creating a more sustainable model. *N Engl J Med.* 2013; 368(13): 1173–5.

45. Reville B, Reifsnyder J, McGuire DB, Kaiser K, Santana AJ. Education and referral criteria: Impact on oncology referrals to palliative care. *J Palliat Med.* 2013; 16(7): 786–9.

46. National Consensus Project for Quality Palliative Care. *Clinical Practice Guidelines for Quality Palliative Care.* Pittsburgh, PA: National Consensus Project for Palliative Care; 2009.

47. Hospice and Palliative Nurses Association. In C Dahlin, ed. *Competencies for the Hospice and Palliative Advanced Practice Nurse.* 2nd ed. Pittsburgh, PA: Hospice and Palliative Nurses Association; 2014.

48. Reed SM. A unitary-caring conceptual model for advanced practice nursing in palliative care. *Holist Nurs Pract.* 2010(January/ February): 23–34.

49. Goldsmith J, Ferrell B, Wittenberg-Lyles E, Ragan SL. Palliative care communication in oncology nursing. *Clin J Oncol Nurs.* 2013; 17(2): 163–7.

50. Edmonds KP, Ajayi TA, Cain J, Yeung KN, Thornberry K. Establishing goals of care at any stage of illness: The PERSON mnemonic. *J Palliat Med.* 2014; 17(10): 1.

51. Peereboom K, Coyle N. Facilitating goals-of-care discussions for patients with life-limiting disease-communication strategies for nurses. *J Hosp Palliat Nurs.* 2012; 14(4): 251–8.

52. Svarovsky T. Having difficult conversations: The advanced practitioner's role. *J Adv Pract Oncol.* 2013; 4(1): 47–52.

53. Campbell TC, Carey EC, Jackson VA, et al. Discussing prognosis: Balancing hope and realism. *Cancer J.* 2010; 16: 461–6.

54. Walling A, Lorenz KA, Dy SM, et al. Evidence-based recommendations for information and care planning in cancer care. *J Clin Oncol*. 2008; 26(23): 3896–902.

55. Ferrell B, Levy MH, Paice J. Managing pain from advanced cancer in the palliative care setting. *Clin J Oncol Nurs*. 2008; 12(4): 575–81.

56. Commission on Cancer, ed. *Standard 3.2 psychosocial distress screening*. Chicago, IL: American College of Surgeons; 2012.

57. Carton ER, Hupcey JE. The forgotten mourners: Addressing health care provider grief—a systematic review. *J Hosp Palliat Nurs*. 2014; 16(5): 291–303.

58. The Joint Commission. Advanced Certification for Palliative Care Programs. Available at www.jointcommission.org/certification/palliative_care.aspx. Updated 2015. Accessed June 30, 2015.

CHAPTER 13

The Advanced Practice Registered Nurse in the Palliative Care Clinic

Lisa A. Stephens and Amelia Cullinan

Key Points

◆ The palliative advanced practice registered nurse (APRN) in a palliative care clinic provides continuity of care and symptom management concurrent with disease-modifying treatment that enhances patient satisfaction and reduces healthcare utilization.

◆ The palliative APRN offers collaborative decision support at key points along the disease trajectory to offer patient-centered, preference-sensitive treatment options.

◆ The palliative APRN's longitudinal relationship with the patient and family, as well as with the other members of the patient's healthcare team, enhances their coping and fosters resilience.

Case Study

Eileen O'Henry was a 35-year-old woman with a history of asthma and obesity, status post gastric bypass surgery. She was admitted to the hospital with progressive, severe shortness of breath. She was diagnosed with pulmonary hypertension due to dermatomyositis-associated interstitial lung disease. Six years prior to her diagnosis, Eileen left her position as a bank manager and moved closer to her aged, ailing parents, with her fiancé and his two sons. She was estranged from her two sisters, who both struggled with alcoholism. Over the next 2 years, her mother and then her father died. One year prior to her admission, her fiancé died suddenly after a viral illness, leaving behind his 14- and 11-year-old sons. In the aftermath of that loss, their mother continued the previous custody arrangement, allowing the boys to stay with Eileen every other weekend.

In the first year after her diagnosis, despite treatment for her dermatomyositis, Eileen's pulmonary hypertension progressed significantly, resulting in cor pulmonale and NYHA functional class III-IV disease. In the setting of chronic steroid use, she gained over 100 pounds, reaching a BMI of 38. She was admitted for initiation of vasodilator therapy (epoprostenol), which resulted in significant headache and muscle/joint pain. During this admission, she learned that she had been denied transplant listing by two different regional heart/lung transplant centers due to her weight. Faced with the progression of her disease and lack of apparent options to treat it, she presented as hopeless and distressed. Her pulmonologist requested a consultation from the inpatient palliative care team to establish a longitudinal relationship for ongoing goals-of-care discussions, pain management, and psychosocial support. For continuity, she was seen by the outpatient APRN during that admission. The consulting palliative APRN then followed her closely in the outpatient clinic along her disease trajectory.

Over the course of the second year of her illness, Eileen was seen monthly by the palliative APRN. Eileen's severe dyspnea made it difficult to navigate the medical complex, so the APRN traveled to the medical infusion suite to see her during her monthly infusion therapy for dermatomyositis, which it was hoped would stabilize enough to again pursue heart/lung transplantation. A co-management model allowed the palliative APRN to assess and manage Eileen's pain and symptoms and provide appropriate prescriptions and nonpharmacologic interventions. Eileen suffered from musculoskeletal pain (headache, jaw pain, shoulder aches) due to epoprostenol but was fearful about addiction to opioids given her family history. The palliative APRN provided education regarding opioid misconceptions and counseling regarding coping strategies during her monthly visits. The patient was also followed closely by the palliative care outpatient social worker. Knowledge of community resources on the part of the APRN and the social worker enhanced Eileen's access to community services and allowed her to stay home longer. Emotionally, Eileen struggled to maintain hope without a certain plan for heart/lung transplant. She told the social worker, "I feel as if I have no past (referencing the death of her fiancé and parents), no future (referencing survival without a transplant) and the present sucks." Both the palliative APRN and social worker helped to enhance Eileen's resilience in the face of physical debility and medical uncertainty and supported her in coming to terms with her changing physical abilities as a stepmother.

As she began the third year of her illness, now 37 years old, Eileen suffered increasingly with dyspnea and pain and worsening functional ability. Eileen's pulmonary, cardiology, and rheumatology teams shared with her that her disease was not responding as they had hoped. A transplant was no longer a possibility. She began to ask theoretical questions about stopping treatment of her pulmonary hypertension, stating, "I don't think I can do this anymore," but she was not ready to stop life-prolonging treatments out of concern that her stepsons would think she was a "quitter."

In response to Eileen's distress, the palliative APRN organized and led a multidisciplinary outpatient team meeting to discuss Eileen's goals of care. Eileen and her close friend, along with her primary pulmonologist, cardiologist, and rheumatologist, were in attendance. Eileen described the misery of her home situation and made the request that someone "give me an achievable goal or let me go." Her subspecialists responded that ongoing therapy of her pulmonary hypertension would only slow the rate of her inevitable decline and death. She then asked what would happen if her epoprostenol was discontinued. She was told that she might die quickly and might suffer significantly worsened dyspnea or chest pain after withdrawal. She was offered the option of admission to the medical center's cardiology floor for withdrawal of the drug in a monitored setting, with the expectation that she would die, which she accepted. She requested the admission be arranged after one last Christmas with her stepsons, at a time when all of her medical subspecialists, including the palliative APRN, could be present.

When Eileen was ultimately admitted, as requested, the palliative APRN was on call that weekend and her primary cardiologist, pulmonologist, and rheumatologist were also available. Before the epoprostenol was withdrawn, she spent a wonderful day and a half with her close family and dear friend at her side. Each family had an opportunity to say goodbye to her. The palliative social worker assessed how each of the family members was coping and ensured they had adequate supports going forward. The palliative APRN was the primary clinician responsible for Eileen's comfort medications during the withdrawal process and provided intensive emotional support to the nursing staff through the process. Eileen died peacefully several hours after her epoprostenol was discontinued, with her stepsons, aunt and uncle, and best friend at her side.

Concurrent Care from Diagnosis Onward

The prevalence of inpatient palliative care programs is rapidly rising in the United States. From 2000 to 2011, among hospitals with over 50 beds, the number of palliative care teams increased by more than 150%.[1] While hospital-based palliative care has grown substantially over the years, continuity across all settings has been lacking. Outpatient palliative care often extends the impact of an inpatient program "upstream" by providing concurrent care from the time of diagnosis across the illness to end-of-life. The most common model of outpatient clinics has been the academic medical center model of outpatient palliative care clinics as a growth of inpatient palliative care services. However, there are new models emerging from a more community-based perspective. In these settings, palliative care clinics are developing from a breadth of community partnerships, such as hospice, home health agencies, independent practices, and community service agencies.

All along a patient's disease trajectory, a palliative care clinic can enhance continuity of care, improve symptom management, increase patient satisfaction, and reduce healthcare utilization, particularly at the end-of-life.[2] As the above case demonstrates, the initial palliative care consultation was requested during an inpatient admission, but the referring team recognized that this patient needed longitudinal care. The patient, Eileen, had a high symptom burden, poor social support. Her goals were to continue pursuing disease-modifying treatment with the hope of prolonging her life. Her prognosis was poor and she was overwhelmed. Outpatient palliative care clinics are often started as an extension of the inpatient palliative care team to enhance the quality and continuity of care throughout the disease trajectory.[3]

Palliative APRNs play a pivotal role in the delivery of high-quality palliative care concurrent with disease-modifying treatments. A key component of quality is continuity of care, which is enhanced by a continuous patient–APRN relationship. This promotes the APRN's ability to provide ongoing assessment and management of pain and symptoms, counseling regarding adjustment to illness, advance care planning, and education regarding the side effects of treatments and medications. Moreover, the palliative APRN is poised, through education and experience, to assess the patient's emotional history and coping and to provide supportive counseling and screening for spiritual concerns.[4-6] A recent pilot study, looking at the effects of integrating a palliative APRN into a community oncology center, found that, when compared to usual care, patients were six times less likely to be hospitalized and possibly even lived longer.[4] In this study, the palliative APRN was integrated into the care of patients with advanced cancer at the time of diagnosis and followed the patient and family throughout the disease trajectory. This study demonstrates the value of a continuous relationship with a palliative APRN who has specialized knowledge and experience.

The trust that is built by the palliative APRN over time also acts as a foundation for the difficult conversations that will come later in the disease trajectory. A preexisting relationship brings comfort to the patient and family when these conversations are revisited in times of crisis. Since most patients are ambulatory at the time of diagnosis and continue treatments on an outpatient basis, an outpatient palliative care clinic is the ideal place for the APRN to develop such relationships. In addition to improving patient satisfaction and quality of life and decreasing hospital admissions, concurrent palliative care has been proven, in a population of lung cancer patients, to increase survival.[7-9] Box 13.1 lists the benefits of outpatient palliative care services.[10]

Core Services and Practice Considerations

The first step in building a palliative care clinic is to determine the primary population of patients to be served and the core services to be provided. This focus may be determined by a perceived need within a targeted population or by the expertise of the palliative care APRN. Most palliative care clinics serve patients with serious or life-threatening illness who have one or more of the following needs: complex pain and symptom management, complex medical decision support, assistance with goals of care clarification, assistance with advance care planning, and/or complex social and family dynamics, including substance abuse issues and mental health issues. It is important to determine whether outpatient palliative care services will be provided to a certain disease-specific

Box 13.1 Benefits of Palliative Outpatient Services

- Allows early involvement of palliative care at the time of diagnosis
- Improves symptoms and quality of life
- Improves patient satisfaction with care
- May reduce unwanted healthcare utilization/hospital admissions
- Builds relationship before a crisis
- May increase skills of other caregivers and providers
- Early intervention for advance care planning
- Decision support at key points along the disease trajectory
- Improves transitions of care
- Earlier hospice involvement

Adapted from Spragens L, Jones A. Community-based opportunities for extending the palliative care continuum. [Presentation handout]. 2011.

population, based on a needs assessment that reveals challenges with patient populations, or will be based on pain and symptoms.[11]

Smith and colleagues,[3] in a survey of outpatient palliative care clinics, found that the most common reasons for referral were management of pain and non-pain symptoms, determining goals of care, and support for psychological issues. However, when the survey respondents were asked to rank the services actually provided, they listed determining goals of care first, followed by pain and non-pain symptom management, then social support. The authors suggest that the likely reason for the difference in services requested and those provided is that palliative care team members "uncover" unmet needs. Defining the delivery model and core services is imperative to help guide referral sources and define the mission of the clinic. However, addressing unmet needs is often welcomed by the referring providers and patients and families. Prior to initiating an outpatient clinic, there must be well-defined descriptions of appropriate palliative patients, triggers that may warrant referral, and clear expectations of the services to be provided.

APRNs' scope of practice may determine their role in a palliative care clinic. Specifically, individual state nurse practice acts and statutes, as well as institutional bylaws, will need to be considered when designing the palliative care clinic. Furthermore, there may be differences between the role of a clinical nurse specialist and a nurse practitioner in state nurse practice acts. Some states may allow autonomy through full independent practice without physician oversight; other states may have more restrictive practice acts requiring physician supervision. Of course, to participate in federal billing and reimbursement, all APRNs will need a collaborating physician. Another important aspect of a palliative care clinic is prescription medications. There is state variation on prescriptive authority, with some states more progressive than others.[12] The APRN in a more restrictive state will need to develop a plan for prescription writing.

Despite these differences by state, the palliative APRN can function at the highest scope of practice and provide advanced knowledge of the physical, emotional, social, and spiritual needs of seriously ill patients. Moreover, APRNs institute comprehensive care and provide communication to healthcare providers. In states where APRNs have full independent practice, collaborative practice with physician colleagues is still an important consideration for palliative care. Indeed, for optimizing the management of patients who need highly complex symptom management, a physician colleague can co-manage patients to assist with problem solving and decision making.

The shortage of board-certified hospice and palliative medicine physicians should not be a barrier to finding the right fit with a collaborating physician. If the palliative APRN is providing palliative care services to primarily heart failure or oncology patients, he or she may choose to collaborate with a cardiologist or an oncologist. A non-hospice and palliative medicine collaborating physician provides expertise in complex diagnostic and specific disease management issues that may arise, while the palliative APRN provides expertise on the assessment and treatment of symptoms and offers psychosocial and spiritual counseling as well as coordination of care.

Models of Outpatient Palliative Care Clinics

Across the United States, a wide variety of models are used to deliver outpatient palliative care services, ranging from outpatient clinics to home and nursing home visits. Once the scope of services is determined, the setting for the care can easily be identified. New models are emerging in the growth of community-based outpatient palliative care clinics. Three current models have been identified for a palliative care clinic: embedded, standalone, and co-located[13] (Table 13.1).

The embedded model is often used to start a palliative care clinic. Several successful and innovative embedded models have been described that use a palliative APRN as the core team member.[4,5,14,15] Embedding a palliative APRN in an outpatient clinic has been associated with measurable benefits, such as improved symptom management, decreased emergency department visits and hospital admissions, and possibly a decrease in mortality rate.[4,5]

In the embedded model, palliative care is available as standard treatment for any patient with a life-limiting illness in the clinic. This patient-centered approach allows the palliative APRN to get a "foot in the door" with reluctant referrers and patients, decreasing the perception that palliative care is only for the imminently dying. Fairly quickly, referrers note the benefits of being supported in the arenas of complex symptom management, coordination of care, and complex goals-of-care discussions. Often, in the embedded clinic model, the palliative APRN becomes an informal teacher for other healthcare providers by modeling complex conversations or coaching other providers through these conversations, thus enhancing the care delivered. The embedded clinic model not only enhances the satisfaction of the referrers but can also provide support to the palliative APRN, who, by practicing in collaboration with others, develops specialty-level knowledge of the disease state.

There are several disadvantages of an embedded clinic model centered on lack of control for patient flow issues. The palliative APRN's schedule is dependent on another clinician's timeliness, and there is a higher likelihood of unscheduled add-on

Table 13.1 Models of Palliative Care Clinics

	Standalone Clinic	**Co-located**	**Embedded Clinic**
Overview	Unique clinic operation. Overhead and support likely to be in a distinct cost center.	Sublet or subsidized tenant, with possible shared services, but independent patient populations	Service extension of an existing clinic, with shared or designated space
Source of Patients	Independent	Independent, but may reflect higher mix from "host" clinic	Dependent; a subset of the "host" specialty; may also allow other patients to be served
Cost Structure	Full cost center with provider staff + support + rent & operating expenses	Mixed options; often some overhead & support may be "in kind" or subsidized by "host" or system	Most support provided by "host" clinic.

Used with permission: Barbour LT, Cohen SE, Jackson V, et al. Getting started: The outpatient palliative care clinic. A technical assistance monograph from the IPAL-OP project. 2012. Available at http://ipal.capc.org/downloads/the-outpatient-palliative-care-clinic.pdf. Accessed September 12, 2014.

appointments and a higher number of cancellations. Despite these inefficiencies, embedding an APRN in a clinic is often a cost-effective way to establish credibility and build relationships while slowly increasing referrals, possibly with a goal of developing a sustainable standalone clinic.

The standalone clinic allows for a broader patient population. A palliative care service may only have the funding to provide a full-time APRN in the clinic. Additional team members, such as a chaplain or social worker, may be available for only a percentage of a full-time equivalent position or may be supported fully by the institution at large. Palliative care physicians may also see patients in tandem with the palliative APRN or may just consult on occasion. In a standalone clinic, the palliative APRN becomes an important consultant. Patients and families will see the added value of the palliative APRN separate from their oncologist or pulmonologist.

Some palliative care clinics are co-located in a cancer clinic or an HIV or congestive heart failure clinic. The advantage to the host clinic is quick and easy access to the palliative APRN and other palliative care team members. This model may save costs for the palliative care service in terms of overhead and allow more incremental growth.[13]

Outpatient palliative care services can also be provided as a combination of embedded and standalone clinics. In institutions with close proximity among specialty outpatient clinics, palliative APRNs can float to multiple different clinics in the same day. An example might include seeing his or her own panel of patients in a standalone clinic, traveling to see others in the oncology infusion suite, and then joining a heart failure clinician for a joint visit. Advantages include in-time coordination and collaboration of care, allowing those patients who have long days with infusions or have a harder time getting from place to place to have palliative care services come to them. This approach has the value of being extremely patient-centered by going to where the patient is, but it can be inefficient, as the palliative APRN loses valuable documentation time while in transit between clinics. The palliative APRN is again at the discretion of another clinic's schedule changes or appointment delays. For certain populations, however, having the palliative APRN travel to the patient is indispensable. Some instances include the reluctant or fearful patient who might not be willing to come to a standalone clinic visit, or a patient with complex chronic illness who does not yet understand the role that palliative care can play in his or her care.

No matter what the type of palliative care clinic, there may come a time when it is difficult for a patient to travel to a clinic. In these situations, the APRN must have knowledge about community resources to ease the transition of care to the home. Home palliative care services may include hospice when appropriate or desired; home health when the homebound criteria are met and/or the patient declines hospice; and home palliative care from either hospice or independent providers. See Chapter 19, The Palliative Advanced Practice Registered Nurse in the Home Setting, and Chapter 17, The Palliative Advanced Practice Registered Nurse within a Hospice Organization.

Role of Other Team Members

Other team members may be embedded in the palliative care clinic or may require referral, notably social work and chaplaincy. In addition to providing in-depth counseling and support, social workers can help patients to complete advance directive forms and assist with finding resources for those with financial, insurance, or transportation needs. If a social worker and chaplain are not fully dedicated to a palliative care clinic, a plan must be in place for timely referrals. Early joint visits with the chaplain or social worker can facilitate rapport, allowing for subsequent visits to be completed separately from the palliative APRN. Ideally, the palliative APRN will have institutional or local access to nutrition services, rehabilitative therapies, such as physical therapy, occupational therapy, and speech and language pathology, chronic pain management (if not covered by the palliative APRN), child life specialists, and grief counseling for their patients.

Funding

A variety of funding sources are generally necessary to run a palliative care clinic. APRN billing and reimbursement will vary depending on whether a clinic is an independent practice, a hospital-owned clinic, or part of another entity. See Chapter 4, Reimbursement for the Palliative Advanced Practice Registered Nurse, for details on billing and coding issues. Typically, given low rates of reimbursement and relatively low clinic appointment volumes, billing revenues do not cover the full cost of an outpatient clinic practice and at least one other source of funding will be needed. In a survey of 20 outpatient palliative care practices, funding sources varied among the programs, but the most common was a combination of institutional support and billing revenues.[3] Commonly, justification for a palliative APRN may include cost avoidance through decreased hospital admissions, decreased emergency department visits, decreased lengths of stay, and early admission to hospice. This cost avoidance may translate into financial support from the institution at large. Embedding an APRN in an oncology or primary care clinic has shown such cost avoidance through decreased healthcare utilization.[4,5] Philanthropy, research, and private foundation support are also common funding sources. Funding will be required for staff (medical and nonmedical), overhead (space and supplies), billing, budgeting and information systems, and tracking of outcomes.[11]

Launching the Palliative Care Clinic

Establishing Visit Times

Once a model is chosen for the palliative care clinic, funding has been located, and a staffing plan has been identified, decisions should be made about clinic flow and practice, in particular establishing visit times. Visit times may need to be longer to accommodate travel time, lack of support staff, and documentation time. A recent survey of 20 outpatient palliative care programs showed that new consultation times were 40 to 120 minutes, with an average of 65 minutes, and follow-up visit times were 20 to 90 minutes, with an average of 37 minutes.[3] In one oncology-embedded APRN-run palliative care clinic, the initial visits are scheduled for 90 minutes.[14] In general, a good rule is to begin with 90 minutes for a new patient or new consultation and 45 minutes for a follow-up visit, unless more time is needed to travel from clinic to clinic. These appointment times provide a cushion for those days when a follow-up patient may have complex issues and extensive care coordination is needed. Clinic times may be adjusted on a case-by-case basis or shortened if needed to accommodate same-day appointments.

Referrals and Scheduling

Referrals can come from many sources, such as registered nurses, physician's assistants, physicians, social workers, rehabilitation therapists (physical therapy or occupational therapy), chaplains, other APRNs, or patient and family self-referral. Scheduling guidelines, developed by the palliative care team members, should be established prior to the startup of the palliative care clinic. Screening for inappropriate referrals should be outlined within these guidelines. In some practices, screening questions can be used by the scheduling secretary: the reason for the consult and the urgency.[11] These questions, as well as self-referrals, may trigger the palliative APRN to interview the patient or referring provider about the appropriateness of the consultation. Some self-referred patients may not have a serious, life-limiting illness but are looking for a new opioid prescriber or may be asking for patient care coordination that would be better provided by their primary care provider's team.

As a way of building clinic volumes or to reach a specific high-needs population, outpatient palliative care clinics can be part of disease-specific or algorithm-driven triggered consultations. Scheduling pathways can then be developed for automatic referrals in these groups. As an example, an automatic palliative care consultation could be scheduled for patients with newly diagnosed stage IIIB or stage IV lung cancers, pancreatic cancer, New York Heart Association (NYHA) stage III or IV heart failure, advanced chronic obstructive pulmonary disease, or amyotrophic lateral sclerosis. Automatic referrals require close collaboration with the specialty group. These automatic referrals not only make palliative care consultation part of the routine care provided by the specialty group but also decrease the perception that palliative care is only for patients at the very end-of-life.

Patient Care Responsibilities

The palliative APRN should explicitly communicate with referring clinicians about role expectations. The role may vary on a case-by-case basis, ranging from consultation only to co-management and even sometimes assuming primary responsibility for the patient.[11]

Co-management is an ideal model for providing specialty palliative care for patients with serious illness. These patients have intense needs, and a co-management approach allows team members to lean on each other along the disease trajectory to off-load work and support each other emotionally, decreasing the risk of burnout. This collaboration also avoids a "handoff" when the patient's care needs tip toward a more palliative focus, away from disease-modifying therapies. This integrated, co-management model prevents the patient from feeling abandoned and enhances the concept that palliative care is an "extra layer of support" that is offered to many patients at the time of diagnosis.[16]

Other providers may request consultation for a specific issue only (such as pain management) or for the palliative APRN to take over full care of the patient. Consultation-only requests that require the referring provider to implement recommendations may not improve symptom control outcomes.[8] The embedded model is the ideal setting for a consultation-only role as the APRN can work closely with the referring provider to guide the implementation of the recommendations. Assuming sole care for a patient can be time-intensive for the palliative APRN. However, it may be appropriate for a patient who has no primary care provider and is no longer receiving disease-modifying treatment or is referred to hospice care without a primary care provider.[13] Defining these roles up front, at the time of consultation, not only helps the patient clarify whom to call with specific issues but also improves collaboration between team members, ultimately benefiting the patient and increasing satisfaction among all team members.

The Initial Outpatient Consultation

Prior to the visit, the APRN should gain a comprehensive understanding of the patient's medical history, likely prognosis, and disease trajectory through chart review and discussion with primary specialists and/or the primary care provider. See Chapter 38 for a guide to introducing palliative care to the patient and family in the initial visit. The underlying goal of the initial visit is to introduce the patient and family to the role of palliative care to establish rapport and to screen for and address the most pressing needs, whether those are physical symptoms, emotional distress, or decision-making support.

During the initial visit, the palliative APRN performs a comprehensive assessment of symptoms using tools like the Edmonton Symptom Assessment System or the Memorial Symptom Assessment Scale, with a focus on pain and physical symptoms and psychological symptoms, such as depression and anxiety. The APRN may also need to institute pain interventions and initiate opioid prescribing agreements and guidelines. The APRN should also assess, to the extent possible, the patient's and family's understanding of the illness and prognostic awareness, mentally bookmarking areas of significant disconnect between what the patient believes and what chart review has revealed. In addition, it is useful to know about any particular information or decision-making preferences.[17] Chapter 39, Advance Care Planning, can assist the APRN in counseling regarding end-of-life preferences and the timing of such conversations. The palliative APRN should perform a social assessment to determine the patient's and family's coping strengths and deficiencies.

After the initial consultation, the palliative APRN can identify longitudinal goals for addressing the identified areas of need and can suggest a frequency of follow-up visits. For example, if a patient is emotionally resilient, fully understands his or her disease trajectory and prognosis, and has no symptom issues, the palliative APRN might offer to see the patient every 1 to 2 months, in conjunction with surveillance, restaging diagnostics, or visits with the primary specialist. If, however, the palliative APRN identifies a number of areas of need, or there is a high likelihood that symptom burden may change rapidly due to beginning new disease-directed therapies (chemotherapy or radiation), the patient might need to be seen as soon as a few days or a week following the consult.

Above all, the palliative APRN should set realistic expectations for herself or himself in an initial consultation to avoid forcing an agenda upon the patient and family members, potentially alienating them. The philosophy of promoting quality of life, maximizing functional status, optimizing psychosocial coping, and assisting with care management can guide care and help the patient and family understand the support of palliative care. If the patient/family is willing to return, the palliative APRN has succeeded and the work can continue. Box 13.2 lists unique components of the initial consultation note.

Subsequent Outpatient Visits

Depending on the disease type and trajectory, the middle phase of outpatient palliative care work may last weeks, months, or even years. During this time, in addition to ongoing symptom

---

Box 13.2 Unique Components of the Outpatient Palliative Medicine Consult Note
◆ **Understanding of illness**
◆ **Goals of care:** Hopes, worries, and priorities
◆ **Preferences:** Communication, decision making, and advance directives
◆ **Social context:** Place of residence, important family members, occupation, and hobbies
◆ **Emotional history:** Existing coping strategies and their effectiveness; sources of strength, pride, meaning, and connection; areas of significant personal distress (e.g., financial concerns, worries about family members' coping)
◆ **Spiritual history:** Consider including a screening tool for this area.

management as indicated, the palliative APRN should work on fostering resilience and developing prognostic awareness in the patient and caregivers.[18,19] This work increases the patient's tolerance for difficult discussions and lays a foundation of trust in the relationship for the later, challenging work of end-of-life decision making. The APRN should partner with the patient in celebrating the happy moments and solving problems through the tough times, effectively banking a store of goodwill in the relationship that increases the patient's willingness to engage in less comfortable conversations when they are needed.

Once patients and families can rely upon adequate coping skills and have appropriate prognostic awareness, they have the emotional energy to participate in legacy work: preparing for leave-taking. For those patients with adequate coping and strong familial and financial supports at diagnosis, this work may be engaged in much earlier, but for some particularly challenged patients or family members, the capacity may never evolve.[20]

Fostering Resilience

In the initial consultation, or early in the course of the relationship, the APRN should inquire about, explicitly name, and validate the patient's existing and past coping strategies and assess how well they worked in the past and are working now. If past strategies are no longer effective, offer alternatives and offer to brainstorm how new behaviors might work for the patient.[18] Table 13.2 lists different coping strategies patients might employ. The palliative APRN relies on his or her ability to synthesize the coping history, prognosis, and emotional response to the illness in order to reflect core strengths back to the patient. This approach will not only foster resiliency in the patient but strengthen the patient–APRN relationship.

In addition to identifying existing coping styles and developing new ones, the palliative APRN should foster the experience of positive emotion. Experiencing positive emotions minimizes the autonomic sympathetic fear response, increasing a patient's sense of safety and willingness to try new behaviors.[21] When patients report happy events, the APRN should celebrate those moments with them, and at other times, help them to recognize and enjoy those things they are grateful for.

Finally, the palliative APRN should strategically interpose challenging conversations or difficult encounters with more light-hearted interludes or matter-of-fact visits. This careful titration of discomfort is critical to avoid overwhelming the patient's and family's ability to cope and fosters the resilience needed to engage in the next difficult conversation to come.

Identification of High Emotional Distress

One challenge is handling patients who struggle to adapt to these circumstances and require more in-depth services. The palliative APRN should identify the patient with high emotional distress when they are first screened in palliative care and enlist the help of a skilled social worker or other counselor to engage more intensively in counseling around coping strategies. Box 13.3 lists a number of "red flag" characteristics that should prompt referral to a social worker or other clinician skilled in problem-solving therapies or cognitive-behavioral therapy.[22]

Table 13.2 Sample Coping Behaviors and Examples

Distraction	Do activities to take one's mind off worries.	Watch TV, read, talk with friends, listen to music.
Optimism	Stay positive about the future. Try to have times when one almost forgets about the cancer.	Think about future possibilities. Make plans for the future. Hope for good things.
Gratitude	Acknowledge benefits that one has received.	Express thankfulness to family, friends, or physicians. Appreciate small things.
Joy	Enjoy moments of beauty and excellence.	Watch the sunset. Appreciate a well-played game of basketball.
Meditation	Engage in meditation, relaxation, or spirituality.	Listen to meditation tapes. Do progressive muscle relaxation. Go to church. Take a walk in nature.
Humor	Laugh about the situation.	Make jokes, appreciate the funny or ironic side of life. Help others to laugh.
Flow	Engage in tasks that take one's mind off worries and increase gratification.	Engage in hobbies, play games, do puzzles, engage in work.
Problem solving	Identify problems and generate solutions.	Research treatment options. Make plans for family financial security. Do advance care planning. Engage in legacy work.
Intellectualization	Think about abstract ideas and avoid focusing on emotions.	Contemplate the meaning of life or death. Read about the illness and discuss details with family or physicians.

Used with permission from Jacobsen J, Kvale E, Rabow M, et al. Helping patients with serious illness live well through the promotion of adaptive coping: A Report from the Improving Outpatient Palliative Care (IPAL-OP) initiative.

Coping and Denial

A common reason for referral is concern that the patient is in "denial." In the face of life-threatening illness, patients cope by avoiding their painful new reality as a way of preserving psychological equanimity. Denial is adaptive until proven otherwise, and the palliative APRN should not seek to correct the denial by forcing the patient to discuss topics that are clearly causing discomfort. The palliative APRN in the clinic is afforded multiple visits over time to support a patient's transition from denial to adaptive acceptance.

Deepening Prognostic Awareness

Most patients experience an acute stress response driven by a nervous system sympathetic discharge when they are first told they have a life-limiting illness. For many patients, this sympathetic

Box 13.3 Correlates of High Emotional Distress in the Face of Terminal Illness

◆ Pessimism

◆ Regrets about past behaviors

◆ Marital strain

◆ History of severe psychiatric illness or suicidal ideation/attempts

◆ Passive coping style

◆ Expectation of few familial or community supports

◆ Feelings of isolation or hopelessness

◆ High level of disruption from normal life activities

◆ Tendency to blame others for personal misfortunes

◆ History of ineffective coping in response to past stressors

◆ Lack of trust in healthcare providers

Adapted from Weisman AD, Worden JW. The existential plight in cancer: Significance of the first 100 days. *International Journal of Psychiatry in Medicine*. 1977.

response overloads their cognitive capacities and much of what they are subsequently told may be heard but not comprehended. Over time, the majority of patients pass through this sympathetically charged, fear-driven stage and into a cognitively intact phase in which they have achieved an accurate understanding of their prognosis. Having this awareness facilitates goal-directed medical decision making, as when discontinuing chemotherapy prior to enrolling in hospice, or when electing not to pursue an implanted defibrillator in NYHA class IV heart failure.[23]

The minority of patients who struggle with this comprehension phase should be referred to a palliative care clinic to assist with improving prognostic awareness and establishing a relationship for future decision support. With the combination of education and experience in compassionate nursing care and expertise in symptom management, the APRN is well prepared to address "a patient's capacity to understand his or her prognosis and the likely illness trajectory" (prognostic awareness).[14] When palliative care has been involved early in the course of the disease, or when the patient has a slowly progressive disease, the palliative APRN has time to work on fostering resilience, as described above. The APRN can intermittently test the patient's tolerance for discussions of prognosis by asking him or her to imagine worse health states, making use of a "hope for the best, prepare for the worst" framework: "I'm really hopeful that this new chemotherapy regimen will do the trick, and I also wonder, though, if we should plan for what you might do if it doesn't."

When the patient's disease progresses rapidly, or when he or she is referred late to palliative care, the patient may be faced with decisions that depend upon adequate prognostic understanding, even if he or she is not there yet. The palliative APRN should consider "naming the dilemma" as a way of aligning with the patient, but ensuring the conversation is opened. "I can tell that talking about a time when your cancer is worse is really hard to do and I wish we didn't have to, but I worry that if we don't we won't be able to make good decisions together. Can you help me think about a way to discuss this that would feel OK to you?"[19]

Supporting the Resilience of Referring Clinicians

Palliative APRNs are well positioned to support their referring colleagues and reduce the risk of compassion fatigue and burnout. The palliative APRN can lighten the referring APRN's or physician's workload and time pressures by handling intensive symptom management or by exploring goals and preferences.[24] As a co-manager of complex cases, the palliative APRN serves as a mentor for difficult communication and the palliative care team-at-large acts as a supportive community for other APRNs and physicians. The palliative APRN can also support the resiliency of other referring APRNs through relationship building that fosters informal discussions of complex cases, which may lead to requests for formal case reviews. Providing shadowing experiences for new APRNs during orientation can also bolster APRN colleagues' confidence in discussing palliative care services with patients and their families.

Comprehensive, Coordinated, Continuous Care

An important aspect of quality palliative care is to provide a coordinated assessment and continuity of care along the disease trajectory. The National Consensus Project *Clinical Practice Guidelines for Quality Palliative Care* discuss domains of quality that form the basis of practice. Under Domain 1, Structure and Processes of Care, there is an emphasis on coordinated assessment and continuity of care across all healthcare settings.[25] Patients may have complex pain or symptoms requiring frequent medication adjustments and education; they may have multiple specialists involved in their care and experience increased vulnerability during transitions of care. The palliative APRN is well-suited to address this challenge and provide continuity of care.

A skilled coordinating registered nurse is a critical support to the APRN. This registered nurse is primarily responsible for phone triage, ensuring that patients' symptoms are managed and psychosocial needs are met in a timely manner in between visits. The nurse also communicates with patients' other providers and helps to coordinate hospital admissions. The registered nurse acts to "extend" the reach of the APRN, handling basic symptom assessment and management (such as bowel medication titration), using appropriate guidelines to allow him or her to practice within his or her professional nursing scope of practice. When patients are undergoing dose titration of pain medications or require close monitoring for other reasons, the coordinating nurse can make routine phone calls to check in with the patient, ensuring that the correct protocol is followed and optimal results are achieved. Because this registered nurse acts as the "right hand" of the APRN, he or she should be located in the clinic to ensure optimal communication and collaboration with the APRN or physician he or she is working with that day. Depending on workload, he or she may also assist with checking patients in before visits, reconciling medications, assessing and evaluating the effectiveness of interventions, monitoring for adverse effects of medications, and screening for new symptoms or problems.

Another important aspect of providing coordinated care and continuity of care is through the interdisciplinary meeting. The expectation for an inpatient palliative care staff is similar to that for outpatient palliative care staff: the need to meet at least weekly to discuss patients and to review new consults and particularly challenging situations. This ensures that the palliative care roles are defined, that handoffs through transition of care are thorough, and that care goals are in alignment. This meeting also provides support to clinicians in the ongoing clinical care.

When providing quality palliative care in the outpatient setting, access to a specialty palliative care provider should be available 24 hours a day, 7 days a week. This service is helpful not only for patients who have active symptoms but also for referring providers who may need phone consultation about a complex symptom management situation. This is especially important when the palliative APRN dispenses prescriptions to enable follow-up care.

Approaching End-of-Life: Late Work

As a patient's life approaches its close, the palliative APRN partners with other clinicians and discusses the perceived benefits and burdens of further disease-directed therapy. This discussion may trigger awareness that the patient's goals need further clarification. Chapter 40, Family Meetings, offers a thorough review of conducting these discussions. In general, a goals-of-care discussion must be informed by the patient's values and goals and the medically available and/or appropriate treatment options that will meet those goals.

Most patients choose to continue disease-directed therapy as long as they perceive the treatment as beneficial (i.e., it is helping them to meet their goals) and not significantly limiting their quality of life. When a patient's scales tip such that the benefit is outweighed by the burdens, it is often the palliative APRN who learns, through the longitudinal relationship developed in the clinic, that a transition to purely palliative therapies is needed. Some patients may be perceived by their primary specialists as desiring inappropriately aggressive care. Palliative APRNs can elucidate the reasons for these choices: in one typical scenario, a patient is willing to temporarily accept an otherwise unacceptably low quality of life in order to meet certain goals, such as living long enough to be present for a major life event, like the birth of a grandchild. By sharing these motivations with the treatment team(s), the palliative APRN can ease some of the moral distress experienced by clinicians who worry the patient "just doesn't get it."

Increasingly, palliative APRNs are incorporated into the care team of patients with multiple chronic illnesses and multiple specialty providers. The palliative APRN is well-positioned to arrange and facilitate multidisciplinary meetings in the outpatient setting. The palliative APRN serves to translate medical information to the patient and family and helps to elicit the patient's goals, which are reflected back to the medical team. The benefits to patients are clear, given the often fragmented care and communication they experience because they have multiple specialists.

In addition to supporting patients through the transition to end-of-life care, the palliative APRN is in an optimal position to support the patient's primary provider, who may be struggling with anticipatory grief at the thought of losing a patient or guilt that he or she could not cure or forestall the disease's progression. The palliative APRN helps team members to cope through debriefing conversations that allow for expression of emotions and for thorough discussion of the patient's goals and preferences. Knowledge and acceptance of the patient's goals facilitate adaptive coping in the provider.

Referrals to Hospice

The rapport and trust developed over time in the longitudinal relationship described in this chapter becomes the foundation for emotionally charged discussions closer to the end-of-life. Helping a patient and family make the transition to hospice is one of those complex conversations. In addition to skill in communicating empathically, the palliative APRN should have a thorough understanding of hospice eligibility criteria for the patient's diagnosis and the services provided in the patient's community. Assuming hospice eligibility criteria are met, a patient should be referred to hospice once he or she is no longer receiving disease-modifying therapy or when coming back and forth to the clinic has become burdensome. At the time of the hospice referral, the palliative APRN should review the patient's medication list to identify medications that might not be covered on hospice and suggest alternatives, and should prepare for crisis events in the home by prescribing medications for crescendo pain, dyspnea, seizures, or agitation.

Prior to making a hospice referral, the palliative APRN should identify which provider will oversee the patient's care once on hospice. To promote quality care within the transition, the palliative APRN should be explicit that he or she remains available as a consultant to the hospice medical director and should state whether he or she will serve as the attending physician of record for hospice care. This ongoing consultative relationship helps patients and families feel that they are not being abandoned once a referral to hospice is made and provides expert-level guidance to the clinician managing the patient's care going forward. It is important that the attending physician of record feel comfortable with the current plan of care and feel prepared to manage any foreseeable complex pain or symptom issues. Carefully communicated handoffs, at the time of hospice referral, are imperative to ensure a smooth transition.

Conclusion

Embedded in the culture of nursing and APRN education are the skills of communication, assessment and management of symptoms, psychosocial and spiritual support, and coordination of care. The palliative APRN in the clinic draws on these skills, improving patient satisfaction and decreasing healthcare utilization. The longitudinal APRN–patient relationship enhances communication with patients and families, thereby improving the ability to offer patient-centered, preference-sensitive treatment options. Palliative APRNs deliver coordinated, comprehensive care that can lessen the burden of illness on patients and families and may improve the resilience of the clinicians who co-manage these patients with the palliative APRN.

References

1. Center to Advance Palliative Care. Growth of palliative care in U.S. hospitals: 2013 snapshot. 2013. Available at http://www.capc.org/capc-growth-analysis-snapshot-2013.pdf. Accessed September 11, 2014.
2. Rabow M, Kvale E, Barbour L, et al. Moving upstream: A review of the evidence of the impact of outpatient palliative care. *J Palliat Med.* 2013; 16(12): 1540–9.
3. Smith AK, Thai JN, Bakitas MA, et al. The diverse landscape of palliative care clinics. *J Palliat Med.* 2013; 16(6): 661–8.
4. Prince-Paul M, Burant CJ, Saltzman JN, Teston LJ, Matthews CR. The effects of integrating an advanced practice palliative care nurse in a community oncology center: A pilot study. *J Support Oncol.* 2010; 8(1): 21–7.
5. Owens D, Eby K, Burson S, Green M, McGoodwin W, Isaac M. Primary palliative care clinic pilot project demonstrates benefits of a nurse practitioner-directed clinic providing primary and palliative care. *J Am Acad Nurse Pract.* 2012; 24: 52–8.
6. Heinle R, McNulty J, Hebert RS. Nurse practitioners and the growth of palliative medicine. *Am J Hosp Palliat Care.* 2013; 31(3): 287–91.
7. Bakitas MA, Doyle Lyons K, Hegel MT, et al. The project ENABLE II randomized controlled trial to improve palliative care for patients with advanced cancer. *JAMA.* 2009; 302(7): 741–9.
8. Rabow M, Dibble SL, Pantilat SZ, McPhee SJ. The comprehensive care team: A controlled trial for outpatient palliative medicine consultation. *Arch Intern Med.* 2004; 164: 83–91.
9. Temel JS, Greer JA, Muzikansky A, et al. Early palliative care for patients with metastatic non-small-cell lung cancer. *N Engl J Med.* 2010; 363(8): 733–42.
10. Spragens L, Jones A. Community-based opportunities for extending the palliative care continuum. [Presentation handout]. 2011. Available at http: //www.capc.org/palliative-care-across-the-continuum/community-based/. Accessed September 11, 2014.
11. Barbour LT, Cohen SE, Jackson V, et al. Getting started: The outpatient palliative care clinic. A technical assistance monograph from the IPAL-OP project. 2012. Available at http: //ipal.capc.org/downloads/the-outpatient-palliative-care-clinic.pdf. Accessed September 12, 2014.
12. American Academy of Nurse Practitioners. Nurse practitioner state practice requirements. 2014. Available at http: //www.aanp.org/component/content/article/66-legislation-regulation/state-practice-environment/1380-state-practice-by-type. Accessed November 8, 2014.
13. Barbour LT, Cohen SE, Jackson V, et al. Models for palliative care outside the hospital setting: A technical assistance monograph from the IPAL-OP project. 2012. Available at http: //ipal.capc.org/downloads/overview-of-outpatient-palliative-care-models.pdf. Accessed September 12, 2014.
14. Meier DE, Beresford L. Outpatient clinics are a new frontier for palliative care. *J Palliat Med.* 2008; 11(6): 823–8.
15. Bakitas MA, Bishop MF, Caron P, Stephens L. Developing successful models of cancer palliative care services. *Semin Oncol Nurs.* 2010; 26(4): 266–84.
16. Vergo MT, Cullinan AM. Joining together to improve outcomes: Integrating specialty palliative care into the care of cancer patients. *J Natl Compr Canc Netw.* 2013; 11(Supplement 4): S1–S9.
17. Parker SM, Clayton JM, Hancock K, et al. A systematic review of prognostic/end-of-life communication with adults in the advanced stages of a life-limiting illness: patient/caregiver preferences for the content, style, and timing of information. *J Pain Symptom Manage.* 2007; 34(1): 81–93.
18. Jacobsen J, Kvale E, Rabow M, et al. Helping patients with serious illness live well through the promotion of adaptive coping: A report from the Improving Outpatient Palliative Care (IPAL-OP) initiative. *J Palliat Med.* 2014; 17(4): 463–8.
19. Jackson VA, Jacobsen J, Greer JA, Pirl WF, Temel JS, Black AL. The cultivation of prognostic awareness through the provision of early palliative care in the ambulatory setting: A communication guide. *J Palliat Med.* 2013; 16(8): 894–900.
20. Block SD. Psychological considerations, growth, and transcendence at the end-of-life—The art of the possible. *JAMA.* 2001; 285(22): 2898–905.

21. Tugade MM, Fredrickson BL, Feldman Barrett L. Psychological resilience and positive emotional granularity: Examining the benefits of positive emotions on coping and health. *J Pers.* 2004; 72(6): 1161–90.

22. Weisman AD, Worden JW. The existential plight in cancer: Significance of the first 100 days. *Int J Psychiatry Med.* 1977; 7(1): 1–15.

23. Knight SJ, Emanuel L. Processes of adjustment to end-of-life losses: A reintegration model. *J Palliat Med.* 2007; 10(5): 1190–8.

24. Muir J, Daly F, Davis M, et al. Integrating palliative care into the outpatient, private practice oncology setting. *J Pain Symptom Manage.* 2010; 40(1): 126–35.

25. National Consensus Project for Quality Palliative Care. The Clinical Practice Guidelines for Quality Palliative Care. 3rd ed. 2013. Available at http: //www.nationalconsensusproject.org/ NCP_Clinical_Practice_Guidelines_3rd_Edition.pdf. Accessed November 5, 2014.

CHAPTER 14

The Advanced Practice Registered Nurse in Primary Care

Rosemary Gorman and Dorothy Wholihan

Key Points

- Advanced practice registered nurses (APRNs) providing primary care require a generalist palliative care skill set.

- An aging population with multiple comorbidities may require complex symptom management.

- A primary care practice with long-term patient–provider relationships is the optimal setting for advance care planning.

Introduction

Primary care is defined by the Institute of Medicine (IOM) as "the provision of integrated, accessible healthcare services by clinicians who are accountable for addressing a large majority of personal healthcare needs, developing a sustained partnership with patients, and practicing in the context of family and community."[1] A patient will see his or her primary care provider (PCP) for routine physicals, preventive care, care of stable chronic illness, as well as common health-related issues. APRNs most commonly nurse practitioners, frequently act in the role of primary care providers. The APRN who assumes the role of the PCP acts as the initial contact point for patients experiencing a health-related problem. The APRN PCP directs and coordinates specialist care as needed. PCPs aim for continuity of care that leads to the development of longstanding relationships. Since primary care takes a long-term, lifespan approach, the implementation of palliative care may be appropriate intermittently in a patient's health trajectory.

The recent implementation of the Affordable Care Act has resulted in the need for increased training of PCPs to provide care to the newly insured, and many anticipate that nurse practitioners will fill this need, especially for vulnerable populations.[2,3] Many new patients will have been previously underserved, and many will be older adults. Current demographics reflect a growing older adult population within our country, as baby boomers become seniors. By 2050, the older adult population is expected to exceed 88.5 million people, more than twice the number in 2010.[4] Due to advances in medical therapies and technology, our population is living longer and living with chronic illness. The combination of these factors results in an urgent need for APRN

PCPs with primary palliative care skills. However, this chapter will discuss the palliative care issues facing both generalist and specialist APRNs.

The current trend in primary care is to transform the delivery of primary care through the development of patient-centered medical homes (PCMHs). This concept focuses on a model of care, not simply a place of care. The Agency for Health Care Research and Quality describes the five functions and attributes of a PCMH as:

1. Comprehensive care: This includes the provision of care for prevention and wellness, acute care and care for chronic disease. The medical home, or practice, may contain multiple specialty providers within the practice or can simply have established relationships with individual specialists within the community. Comprehensive care includes care for mental health as well as physical health and may also include pharmacists, nutritionists, and social workers. By the holistic nature of their practice, APRNs are well-suited to coordinate comprehensive care in the medical home setting.

2. Patient-centered care: This concept focuses on patients learning to manage and participate in their own care. It focuses on holistic care based on a partnership. The medical home emphasizes teaching and patient involvement in the care plan so that care is always patient-centered.

3. Coordinated care: The PCMH coordinates care across the healthcare continuum. It is the responsibility of the PCMH to establish close communication between all care providers, including hospital and subacute care and community providers, inclusive of home care, dialysis, or daycare. The PCMH coordinator assists in arranging the plan of care that is most consistent with the patient's needs and involves discussion with the patient.

4. Accessible services: The PCMH must have accessible hours and contact information to meet the needs of the patient. This may include daily time for walk-in appointments, extended evening hours, as well as telephone or e-mail access to the care provider.

5. Quality and safety: The PCMH has a commitment to provision of high-quality care by providing evidence-based medicine,

undergoing ongoing quality assessment as well as monitoring, and responding to patient satisfaction measurements.[5]

The PCMH model is in direct alignment with the core concepts of palliative care, providing holistic, high-quality care that is consistent with patient needs and includes patient input. To provide holistic, consistent care, a PCP must provide generalist palliative care services. According to *Palliative Nursing: Scope and Standards*,[6] as nurses, all APRNs practice primary palliative care. Basic palliative care is inherent in the definition of nursing: alleviation of suffering through the diagnosis and treatment of human response. Furthermore, all nurses provide psychosocial and spiritual support and assist with advance care planning within the context of a patient's cultural background. Quill and Abernethy recommend that the palliative care skill set for primary care should include basic management of pain and physical symptoms, basic management of anxiety and depression, together with basic discussions regarding prognosis, goals of treatment, suffering, and code status. They suggest that referrals to palliative care specialists be used for refractory or complex symptoms, assistance with conflict resolution, and assistance with cases of near futility.[7] Specialty palliative APRNs are distinguished by their ability to synthesize complex data, develop and implement advanced plans, and provide leadership in hospice and palliative nursing.[6] The Health Resources and Services Administration (HRSA) anticipates that the full implementation of the Affordable Care Act will result in increased access to, and demand for, primary care and an estimated shortage of PCPs. The need for primary care-trained nurse practitioners will increase. Hence, primary care nurse practitioners will also need to develop a basic skill set for palliative care.[8]

Who Needs Palliative Care?

The National Consensus Project for Quality Palliative Care defines palliative care as "patient and family centered care that optimizes quality of life by anticipating, preventing, and treating suffering. Palliative care involves addressing physical, intellectual, emotional, social, and spiritual needs throughout the continuum of illness, as well as facilitating patient autonomy and access to information and choice."[9] APRN PCPs must be cognizant that palliative care is not the same as hospice care. Moreover, in primary care, both are important and will support the care offered by the PCP.

Palliative care is applicable early in the course of illness and is also appropriate in conjunction with treatment intended to prolong life. Palliative care focuses on the management of both physical and emotional symptoms experienced by those with serious illness. Palliative care helps to match treatment with a patient's self-identified goals. Since primary care is comprehensive care, basic palliative care must be incorporated as an integral part of primary care. When it is time for hospice, the APRN PCP will need to work with the hospice nurses to develop a plan of care and will often continue to order medications and supervise the plan of care.

Today's APRN PCPs must understand primary palliative care principles. Vigilant symptom management for patients with multiple comorbid diseases can optimize quality of life and minimize unnecessary admissions. Communication skills essential to the determination of individual and family goals can ensure

person-centered care. The awareness of, and ability to connect with, community resources assists patients to access appropriate services, which can help them remain at home, and the APRN can provide expert guidance in the ongoing management of complex cases.

The specialist palliative APRN has an important role in collaborating with PCPs in the community. Inpatient palliative care specialist consultants can assist with appropriate discharge and follow-up planning, providing essential but often-neglected care coordination by maintaining clear, open communication with community providers. As outpatient palliative care specialty clinics and office practices develop and expand, palliative APRNs in these settings need to increase awareness among PCPs about their contributions and how they can develop partnerships for patient care. Team care can then be translated to the community outpatient settings. Research has shown that integrating APRN palliative care into community oncology clinics can improve outcomes in terms of hospital admissions and mortality in patients receiving aggressive treatment.[10] Outpatient palliative care clinics can also improve access to early outpatient palliative care, as evidenced by a pilot project that evaluated a primary palliative care clinic.[11] In this study, Owens and colleagues found that care for patients with life-limiting illnesses and the continuity and primary care provided by a palliative APRN resulted in a significant decrease in the use of the emergency department.[11]

Palliative APRNs also need to develop their teaching skills. Providing interprofessional educational opportunities for care partners can facilitate development of working relationships, increase professional awareness of the benefits of palliative care, and improve the general levels of palliative care knowledge among PCPs. In addition, both primary care nurse practitioners and palliative APRN specialists are well-suited to provide public education in order to increase public awareness of the benefits and availability of palliative care in the community.

The aging of America's baby boomers will have a significant impact on healthcare. The prediction is that there will be 72 million older adults by 2030: this is more than twice the number in 2000. It is estimated that the population aged 85 and over may grow to 19 million by 2050.[12] Technological advances in both the pharmaceutical and medical device industry have improved medical care and have resulted in the increased survival of individuals with chronic conditions. Nearly three in four individuals aged 65 and over have multiple chronic conditions.[13] Diseases previously considered terminal, such as HIV, end-stage renal disease, liver failure, heart failure, chronic obstructive pulmonary disease (COPD), and cancer, are now chronic long-term health problems, with basic healthcare managed by APRN PCPs, with specialty consultation as needed.

Progressive chronic disease can have an uncertain illness trajectory, characterized by intermittent disease exacerbations and progressive decline in functional status, together with an associated high symptom burden.[14] This care requires palliative interventions to maintain quality of life. There is a dearth of evidence for the management of patients with multiple coexisting chronic conditions, which adds to the complexity of the treatment and difficulty with prognostication. Research is lacking, and currently there are no appropriate clinical practice guidelines.[14] The principles of palliative care can guide the APRN PCP in basic symptom management and the establishment of treatment plans based on realistic goals.

Integrating Palliative Care into the Primary Care of Common Chronic Illness

Heart Disease in Primary Care

The Centers for Disease Control and Prevention (CDC) identifies heart disease as the number one cause of death in the United States, with 5.1 million people identified as having heart failure, and half of these patients diagnosed with heart failure dying within 5 years.[15] The symptom burden identified by those with heart failure has been reported to include general discomfort and fatigue, anorexia, dyspnea, depression, and anxiety. In addition, patients with advanced congestive heart failure routinely have multiple comorbidities and multiple symptoms. See Chapters 16, The Advanced Practice Registered Nurse Practice in a Specialty Outpatient Setting, and 48, Withdrawal of Cardiology Technology, for more detail.

COPD in Primary Care

Identified as the third leading cause of death in the United States, COPD is identified by the CDC as affecting more than 15 million Americans.[16] According to the American Lung Association, research indicates that COPD is underdiagnosed, and as many as 24 million Americans have impaired lung function.[17] COPD is a crippling disease and significantly affects quality of life. Breathlessness is the primary symptom of advanced COPD and can be accompanied by pain, fatigue, and insomnia. Anxiety, depression, and social isolation contribute to psychological suffering and the high symptom burden.[18] The palliative care needs of this population are often complex and are discussed in Chapter 49 with regard to specific symptoms and treatment withdrawal issues.

Cancer and Survivorship in Primary Care

As of January 2012, the American Cancer Society estimated that there are 13.7 million cancer survivors living in the United States, and this number may likely rise to 18 million by January 2022.[19] Although their disease may have been eradicated, many survivors suffer from emotional sequelae or treatment side effects attributed to medications, radiation, or surgery. These side effects may not occur until years after treatment was completed. Cardiac problems, neuropathy, osteoporosis, and liver or lung problems can arise, as well as an increased risk of other cancers. Anxiety and depression can also have a significant impact on quality of life. PCPs are frequently not familiar with chemotherapeutic agents and the possible long-term effects, making long-term management complicated. In 2006, the IOM introduced the Cancer Survivorship Care Planning Fact Sheet based on its 2005 report *From Cancer Patient to Cancer Survivor: Lost in Transition*.[20] The IOM began recommending that cancer patients receive a Survivorship Care Plan from their oncology team. This recommended treatment plan contains valuable information for PCPs, including specific information about the cancer diagnosis and treatment; a schedule for follow-up, including necessary screening tests; and information about possible late side effects and signs of recurrence or of a new cancer. The American Society of Clinical Oncology (ASCO) promotes the use of treatment summaries and care plans and has initiated a practice-based quality improvement program to improve care coordination and survivorship, specifically completion of a treatment summary.[21]

In support of the improved survivorship plan, ASCO has issued evidence-based clinical practice guidelines for common symptom issues facing cancer survivors, including fatigue,[22] anxiety and depression,[23] and chemotherapy-induced peripheral neuropathy,[24] the first set of guidelines in a planned series on survivorship care. The APRN PCP should maintain awareness of ongoing survivorship issues in coordinating care with oncology.

See Chapters 12, The Advanced Practice Registered Nurse in Outpatient Palliative Cancer Care, 36, Symptom Clusters in Various Solid Tumors and Hematologic Malignancies, and 52, Recurrent Disease and Long-Term Survivorship for more detail on specific care issues.

Frailty

The significant expected increase in the number of the oldest creates a focus on frailty. Frailty is defined as "a clinically recognizable state of increased vulnerability resulting from aging-associated decline in reserve and function across multiple physiologic systems such that the ability to cope with every day or acute stressors is compromised."[25] Operationally, Fried and colleagues defined frailty as meeting three out of five phenotypic criteria indicating compromised energy, in an attempt to make the concept of frailty distinct from and independent of medical comorbidities (Box 14.1).[26]

APRN PCPs should recognize and address frailty as a syndrome and understand its effect on functionality and prognosis, as it may have clear implications in terms of treatment decisions and goals of care. Unfortunately, frailty is no longer a diagnosis that can be used for referral to hospice care, but its impact on functional status can significantly exacerbate a concomitant diagnosis that could serve as the primary hospice diagnosis.

Frailty is associated with an increased vulnerability to adverse clinical outcomes and is a risk indicator for falls, admission to an institution or hospital, and mortality,[26] Hence, this condition warrants proactive palliative care interventions. The recognition of this syndrome can promote appropriate care planning and potentially reduce medical interventions that would exacerbate the patient's decline. Knowledge about frail elders can also lead to successful palliative management of the symptom burden contributing to decline. Optimization of community resources and early advance care planning are essential. Palliative care's interdisciplinary team approach provides physical as well as psychological symptom management, together with spiritual support, all resulting in an improved quality of life.[27]

Box 14.1 Criteria of Frailty

- Low grip strength
- Low energy
- Slowed walking speed
- Low physical activity
- Unintentional weight loss

1 or 2/5—prefrail; 3–5/5—frail

From reference 25.

Dementia

According to the Alzheimer's Association,[28] Alzheimer's disease accounts for 60% to 80% of the cases of dementia and is now the sixth leading cause of death in the United States. There are more than 5 million people living with Alzheimer's disease, which significantly affects the provision of primary care. Early recognition is key, and dementia should be addressed as a terminal disease. Patients with Alzheimer's disease and other dementias and their caregivers require complex symptom management and support.

Dementia is an incurable and life-limiting illness; it is characterized by a slow progressive decline of cognitive abilities and functional decline that ultimately limits participation in activities of daily living. This neurodegenerative disorder leads to severe cognitive deficits, gradual functional decline, and death. Currently, there is no cure or therapy to halt or reverse this devastating disease. Challenging behaviors attributed to the disease itself or sundowning behavior likely may be related to unmet symptom treatment needs. These behaviors are distressing to patients and caregivers alike.[29] The inability to manage the behaviors may contribute to the fact that 70% of persons with advanced dementia die in nursing homes.[30]

Burdensome interventions, distressing symptoms, high caregiver burden, and poor end-of-life care have been suggested in multiple studies,[31] making dementia patients optimal candidates for palliative care. Challenging prognostication issues and strict requirements for hospice admission leave dementia patients and their caregivers with few resources. The slowly debilitating nature of this disease means that APRN PCPs provide care for long periods. The APRN PCP should guide care in line with palliative care principles that focus on proactive management of symptoms, caregiver support, and advance care planning. Emphasis is placed on early recognition and management of behaviors and assistance with often painful medical decision making. Coordination of care among providers can also ensure that benefit versus burden is fully understood when treatment goals are determined.

Case Study

Dave was a 75-year-old man with a 6-year history of Alzheimer's disease. He was recently moved from his home, where he had been cared for by a live-in caregiver for the last 3 years, to an assisted living facility near his daughter's home. His past medical history was positive only for hypertension. His daughter was called to take him to the hospital for evaluation of acute behavioral disturbance; he was subsequently admitted to the inpatient psychiatric unit for medication adjustment. When the daughter arrived the following day, the nurse practitioner told her that the medical workup was positive for a urinary tract infection (UTI), antibiotics had been started, and her father would be released the following day. There was no need for further medication adjustment, as his sudden behavioral changes could be attributed to the infection.

The APRN caring for Dave at the assisted living facility provided education to the staff concerning unmet needs/infection, and all understood that often-sudden behavioral changes were likely not attributable to progressive dementia but could have other causes, with UTI as a primary suspect. This education might have prevented an unnecessary hospital admission.

Renal Disease

The incidence of chronic kidney diseases is rising. Dialysis is now being offered to older and more medically complex patients.[32] Statistics from the 2013 U.S. Renal Data System Annual Report note that over 615,000 Americans are being treated for kidney failure; of these, 430,000 are dialysis dependent.[33] Moderate to severe cognitive impairment is present in two-thirds of patients receiving dialysis.[34] Individuals with end-stage renal disease experience a high symptom burden, and many of their symptoms are left untreated.[32] The myriad of symptoms may include uncontrolled pain, lack of energy, pruritus, dyspnea, edema, dry mouth, muscle cramps, restless leg syndrome, sleep disturbance, and constipation. If these symptoms go untreated, quality of life is decreased.[35] The estimated 5-year survival for dialysis patients over the age of 65 years is a mere 18%, but few patients in this population have completed advance directives.[32] PCPs who may have long-term relationships with these patients need to be cognizant of the overall risks versus benefits of aggressive treatment and counsel their patients, focusing on the individual's values and goals of care. Patients with end-stage renal disease underuse palliative care, but the large symptom burden, poor quality of life, and lack of advance directives make these patients appropriate candidates for referral to palliative care. The trusted PCP may be most suitable to suggest referral to palliative care specialists. See Chapter 8, Palliative Care on the Medical, Surgical, and Geriatric Patient Care Unit, and Chapter 16, The Advanced Practice Registered Nurse in a Specialty Outpatient Setting to learn more about renal care.

Advance Care Planning in Primary Care

A patient's relationship with a PCP develops over time; patients with chronic illness can experience a long trajectory, with multiple exacerbations of each chronic disease. Given their longstanding relationships with patients, PCPs are well-suited to facilitate values-based communication concerning goals of care. Advance care planning is a process that is ideally developed over multiple interactions, not during a period of crisis. Changes in a patient's condition warrant evolving discussions of treatment, including the specific impact of the treatment on the patient's quality of life and ongoing reassessment of advance care planning. An informed PCP can take into account the synergistic symptom burden, along with the patient's specific goals and values, and counsel the patient accordingly.

Patient-centered care requires that patients are well-informed about their condition. The success rate of proposed treatment, the overall prognosis with and without treatment, and the expected impact on quality of life are all important aspects for an individual to consider in making a decision regarding treatment and goals of care. Such information may help patients establish their priorities, make informed decisions regarding treatment, and ultimately formulate an advance directive. This advance care planning is best done in the primary care setting because the established ongoing patient–practitioner relationship in the primary care setting gives the practitioner insight into the patient's support system and values. This familiarity opens the door for an honest, non-intimidating discussion about values, ultimately leading to an advance care plan.

In the quest to avoid repeat hospital admissions, Medicare now reimburses PCPs for transitional care management (TCM). This involves follow-up on patients discharged from an inpatient facility and their transition to home, as well as a face-to-face visit within a required timeframe. This face-to-face visit allows the practitioner to discuss the condition or exacerbation of the condition precipitating the admission, the treatment that was rendered, and its impact on the patient's quality of life and/or functional status. The potential for repeat exacerbations and the implications for further care can also be discussed. For example, an end-stage COPD patient who was recently hospitalized with an exacerbation requiring intubation may verbalize a request to never endure intubation again, leading to a pertinent goals discussion and the implementation of an advance directive document.

The purpose of an advance directive is to deliver care consistent with a patient's wishes; it focuses on autonomy and empowers patients when they are no longer able to make decisions for themselves.[36] Chronically ill and dying patients can be spared multiple, unwanted care transitions and physical and emotional suffering when advance directives are completed and appropriate care is in place. Making critical decisions during a crisis adds to the emotional stress that a family experiences during a difficult time. Advance care planning can lighten this burden for the family.[37] See Chapter 39, Advance Care Planning, for information on the process.

Legislative efforts are beginning to mandate that palliative care be offered to those with chronic disease or life-limiting illnesses. Effective January 1, 2009, California enacted the Terminal Patients' Right to Know End-of-Life Options Act, California Law AB 2747, making this state the first in the nation to require full disclosure and counseling about available end-of-life options in law and medicine. In 2011, New York State amended the Public Health Law by adding Section 299c, the Palliative Care Information Act, requiring physicians and nurse practitioners to offer information and counseling to patients with advanced life-limiting conditions or illnesses. In 2013, Massachusetts, Rhode Island, Maryland, Connecticut, and New Hampshire discussed legislation directed at increasing access to palliative care.[38] Although not all these legislative initiatives passed, a definite policy trend is emerging.

Professional Barriers to Completion of Advance Directives in Primary Care

Research conducted by the Agency for Research and Quality reflects that even though patients value advance care planning discussions and expect professionals to initiate these discussions, fewer than 50% of severely and terminally ill adults have a documented advance directive in their medical record.[39] Studies reveal that elderly patients with chronic illness were substantially more satisfied with their PCP when advance directives were discussed.[40] Professional barriers to completion of advance directives are found in Box 14.2.[41,42]

APRN Discomfort with Advance Care Planning/End-of-Life Discussions

Historically, nursing school education has not included palliative or end-of-life education, and exposure was "informal" at best.[43] The Liaison Committee on Medical Education (LCME) now requires end-of-life medical education,[44] but this has not occurred in graduate nursing programs. Medical schools' interpretation of this mandate varies widely and can include as little as 2 hours to as many as 80 hours over a 4-year curriculum. This required education can range from occasional lectures and short courses to palliative care rotations.[45] While there is an attempt to improve didactic palliative education, education about communication, advance directive discussions, and direct exposure to dying patients continue to be lacking.[44]

More than any other health professional, nurses are likely to spend the greatest amount of time with patients at the end-of-life. However, this exposure does not give an APRN the knowledge and skill to care for patients with a life-limiting illness. APRN programs, with the exception of specialty palliative APRN tracks, offer limited if any exposure to palliative care competencies. Healthcare professionals who have established long-term relationships with their patients may face the difficulty of "letting go." Furthermore, end-of-life preferences can be complicated and influenced by religion, race, and culture, requiring providers to be culturally sensitive to the population they serve. When discussions about advance directives become a routine part of a primary care visit, the interactions can be calm and nonthreatening. APRNs can improve their comfort and competence in addressing goals of care through formal academic or continuing education programs that emphasize communication skills. The use of simulation has become increasingly popular in teaching communication strategies. See Chapter 2 for discussion of strategies to improve palliative APRN education.

Strategies to improve completion rates of advance directives in primary care include improved reimbursement, increased patient awareness, and educational efforts geared to improving communication skills among providers. Chapter 39 discusses advance directives. Box 14.3 lists educational resources available to facilitate advance care planning discussions in primary care settings.

Billing and Coding

Legislation was introduced during the 2009 healthcare reform process to reimburse practitioners for time spent counseling Medicare patients on end-of-life options, including how to prepare an advance directive. Some opponents of the larger healthcare reform process took this opportunity to exploit public fears of the dying process and misconstrued this counseling legislation as government rationing of healthcare, promoting this issue in the press as a "death panel." As a result, this counseling proposition was dropped from the legislation. A similar rule was introduced in 2010; after being initially approved, it was quickly reversed by a new Congress.[48] As a result, PCPs are challenged to include these discussions without specific reimbursement.

Inadequate time and lack of reimbursement are barriers to the completion of advance directives in primary care. Yet, advance

---

Box 14.2 Barriers to Completion of Advance Directives

♦ Lack of time and lack of reimbursement for extensive discussions with patients and family

♦ Challenges of prognostication in chronic disease

♦ Practitioner discomfort with the topic, which leads to patient-initiated discussions rather than practitioner-initiated discussions

♦ Lack of education on end-of-life discussions

♦ Reluctance of the provider to "let go"

Data from references 41 and 42.

Box 14.3 Educational Resources for Advance Care Planning Discussions in Primary Care

1. Leading discussion points[48]

2. Center to Advance Palliative Care Fast Facts[46]

   Fast Fact #06 and #011: Delivering Bad News, parts 1 and 2

   Fast Fact #017: Patient-Centered Interviewing

   Fast Fact #021: Hope and Truth Telling

   Fast Fact #023 and #024: Discussing DNR Orders, parts 1 and 2

   Fast Fact #065: Establishing End-of-Life Goals: The Living Will Interview

   Fast Fact #162: Advance Care Planning in Chronic Illness

3. End-of-Life Nursing Education Consortium (ELNEC): ELNEC is a national education initiative to improve palliative care. ELNEC offers a 2-day course to prepare APRNs to deliver appropriate end-of-life care. Participants receive advanced education in pain and symptom assessment/management and communication.[47]

Box 14.4 Advance Directive Patient-Friendly Tools

The *Five Wishes* tool is available in 26 languages and Braille; it is written in simple language and is legal in 42 states. Available through Aging with Dignity (http://agingwithdignity.org).

PREPARE is a patient-friendly online resource to assist individuals in making complex medical decisions. Videos are used to help identify values and how to communicate them with family and physician. The content is written at a fifth-grade reading level and is easy to use (http://prepareforyourcare.org).

Mydirectives.com is a free online advance care planning service. My Directives is the first advance care platform to receive "meaningful use" certification from Health and Human Services (HHS), making it eligible for incentive payments from Medicare and Medicaid (https://www.mydirectives.com/en/about/company/).

---

care planning discussions and the completion of Provider Orders for Life-Sustaining Treatment (POLST) are appropriate for any patient with a chronic, serious, or life-threatening illness. These conversations can be time-consuming, and there is no specific CPT code to bill for these conversations. Furthermore, such discussions can be overwhelming, and the patient may want to consult with family members, necessitating multiple visits over time. PCPs with heavily booked schedules will need to make time for these discussions. In particularly challenging cases, referral to palliative care specialists may be appropriate, and PCPs should be knowledgeable about specialist resources in their community.

To bill for these discussions, documentation must meet specific criteria under Medicare regulations. Private insurers may have specific codes making these discussions reimbursable with specific criteria. Evaluation/management and diagnosis codes are based on location, complexity, and effort. When counseling/information-giving represents more than 50% of the patient visit, it may be most appropriate to bill by time, and the provider should select an evaluation and management code that corresponds to the total time of the face-to-face visit. In the outpatient/office setting, billing by time is limited to the face-to-face time spent with the patient. The *Medicare Claims Processing Manual* specifies that only physicians, physician assistants, or APRNs will be reimbursed for counseling. Documentation must reflect the amount of time spent with the patient and the nature of the counseling/information-giving. Explicit description of the complicating factors or prognosis is advisable. Acceptable diagnostic codes may be either pathophysiological or symptom-related.[49] Further details of reimbursement for APRN palliative care are detailed in Chapter 4, Reimbursement for the Palliative Advanced Practice Registered Nurse.

Appropriate tools for advance directive formulation can help to improve completion rates. Tools must be appropriate for the patient's literacy level and language. The APRN PCP should consider using tools that are available in multiple languages and are written at a fifth-grade reading level or accompanied by interactive resources.[50] Box 14.4 provides both online and print suggestions. Advance care planning is covered in Chapter 39.

Prognostication

"How long do I have?" This is the question most frequently asked by patients facing a terminal illness or debilitating condition. Prognosis is a prediction of the outcome of a disease based on medical knowledge and experience.[51] Prognosis can affect treatment decisions as well as eligibility for hospice care. Diseases that result in chronic organ failure can have multiple exacerbations, any of which could result in death, making prognostication extremely difficult even for skilled palliative care specialists. The rate of decline in functional status can be a key indicator in determining prognosis. These tools can help palliative care specialists with prognostication:

a. The Palliative Performance Scale (PPS) is a reliable and valid tool for the measurement of performance status in palliative care. It uses the patient's functional status to predict survival. The PPS evaluates ambulatory status, activity level, evidence of disease, ability to perform self-care, and level of consciousness.[52] Periodic measurements document the evolving physical deterioration of an individual. The rapidity of the functional decline likely corresponds with rapid deterioration and ultimately a shorter survival.[53]

b. The surprise question: "Would I be surprised if this patient died in the next year?" This simple question has been recognized

---

Box 14.5 Mobile Application for Prognostication

I. MPI (Multidimensional Prognostic Index), a prognostic tool based on a standard geriatric assessment, predicts short- and long-term mortality in the elderly.

II. Qx Calculate, an app focused on highlighting tools used in clinical practice that affect diagnosis, treatment, and prognosis. It includes prognostic indicators for heart failure, lymphoma, myeloma, hemodialysis, COPD, transient ischemic attacks, pancreatitis, and many others.

Box 14.6 Center to Advance Palliative Care Fast Facts Related to Prognostication

Fast Fact #213: Prognosis in HIV and AIDS

Fast Fact #191: Prognostication in Patients Receiving Dialysis

Fast Fact #189: Prognosis in Decompensated Chronic Liver Failure

Fast Fact #150: Prognostication in Dementia

Fast Fact #143: Prognostication in Heart Failure

Fast Fact #141: Prognosis in End-Stage COPD

Fast Fact #099: Chemotherapy: Response and Survival

Fast Fact #013: Determining Prognosis in Advanced Cancer

---

as a tool to improve end-of-life care in both primary care and dialysis populations. A "no" answer to this question can serve to identify patients with a poor prognosis who would be appropriate for palliative care.[54]

c. Mobile applications containing prognostic indicators exist for a multitude of individual medical conditions.

Boxes 14.5 and 14.6 list other resources available to assist with prognostication in advanced illness.

Conclusion

Growing evidence demonstrates the benefits of early palliative care for patients with serious illness, and palliative care shares many common goals with primary care. Each addresses the patient with serious illness within the context of community, with a focus on care over time, and emphasizing symptom support and communication.[55]

APRN PCPs are well-suited to incorporate palliative care into their practices. The unique blend of medical knowledge with an educational background based on a holistic nursing model makes the APRN a prime candidate to assume the role of PCP, able to deliver high-quality, low-cost, patient-centered healthcare. Practicing within a primary care framework allows the APRN to establish an ongoing relationship with the patient and family, which facilitates an honest, trusting bond and positions the APRN to monitor the patient's progress over time. This ongoing relationship can allow the primary care APRN to discuss goals of care with an educated patient/family in a nonemergent environment, revising the advance care plan as needed. APRNs who integrate palliative care into their primary care practices should understand the range of disease trajectories and multidimensional symptoms, as well as the communication skills needed for advance care planning and end-of-life decision making. Once adept at these skills of symptom management and care planning, primary care APRNs can perform an integral role in incorporating palliative care and serving as a role model to others within their practice.

References

1. AHRQ. Primary care workforce: Facts and figures 2012. Available at http://www.ahrq.gov/research/findings/factsheets/primary/pcworkforce/index.html. Accessed August 1, 2014.
2. Kaiser Family Foundation. Improving access to adult primary care in Medicaid: Exploring the potential role of nurse practitioners and physician assistants. 2011. Available at http://kff-medicaid-issue-brief/improving-access-to-adult primary-care-in/. Accessed August 14, 2014.
3. Pohl JM, Hanson C, Newland JA, et al. Unleashing nurse practitioners' potential to deliver primary care and lead teams. *Health Affairs.* 2010; 29: 900–5.
4. Vincent GK, Velkoff VA. The next four decades. The older population in the United States: 2010 to 2015. Population estimates. 2010. Available at http://www.census.gov/prod/2010pubs/p25-1138.pdf. Accessed August 13, 2014.
5. AHRQ. *Patient-centered medical home.* 2014. Available at http://pcmh.ahrq.gov/page/defining-pcmh. Accessed August 2, 2014.
6. Dahlin C. *Palliative Nursing: Scope and Standards of Practice.* Silver Spring, MD: American Nurses Association and Hospice and Palliative Nurses Association; 2013.
7. Quill T, Abernethy AP. Generalist plus specialist palliative care: creating a more sustainable model. *N Engl J Med.* 2013; 368: 1173–5.
8. Health Resources and Services Administration (HRSA). *Projecting the supply and demand for primary care practitioners through 2020.* 2013. Available at http://bhpr.hrsa.gov/healthworkforce/supplydemand/usworkforce/primarycare. Accessed August 4, 2014.
9. National Consensus Project for Quality Palliative Care. *Clinical practice guidelines for quality palliative care.* 3rd ed. 2013. Available at http://www.nationalconsensusproject.org. Accessed August 1, 2014.
10. Prince-Paul M, Burant CJ, Saltzman JN, Teston LJ, Matthews CR. The effects of integrating an advanced practice palliative care nurse in a community oncology center: a pilot study. *J Support Oncol.* 2010; 8(1): 21–7.
11. Owens EK, Burson S, Green M, McGoodwin W, Isaac M. Primary palliative care clinic pilot project demonstrates benefits of a nurse practitioner-directed clinic providing primary and palliative care. *J Am Acad Nurse Practitioners.* 2012; 24(1): 52–8.
12. Administration on Aging. *Projected future growth of the older population.* Available at http://agingstatistics.gov. Accessed July 20, 2014.
13. Tinetti ME, Fried TR, Boyd, CM. Designing health care for the most common chronic condition: multimorbidity. *JAMA.* 2012; 307: 2493–4.
14. Maxwell TL. Caring for those with chronic illness. In Ferrell BR, Coyle N, eds., *Oxford Textbook of Palliative Nursing.* 3rd ed. New York, NY: Oxford University Press; 2010:687–99.
15. Centers for Disease Control and Prevention. *Heart Failure Fact Sheet.* 2014. Available at http://www.cdc.gov/DHDSP/data_statistics/fact_sheets/fs_heart_failure.htm. Accessed August 4, 2014.
16. American Lung Association. *COPD Fact Sheet.* 2011. Available at http://www.lung.org/lung-disease/copd/resources/facts-figures/COPD-Fact-Sheet.html. Accessed August 4, 2014.
17. Janssen DJ, Spruit MA, Uszko-Lencer NH, et al. Symptoms, comorbidities, and health care in advanced chronic obstructive pulmonary disease or chronic heart failure. *J Palliat Med.* 2011; 14: 735–43.
18. Spathis A, Booth S. End of life care in chronic obstructive pulmonary disease: in search of a good death. *Intl J COPD.* 2008; 3: 11–29.
19. Siegel R, Desantis C, Virgo K, et al. Cancer treatment and survivorship statistics. *CA Cancer J Clin.* 2012; 62: 220–41.
20. Hewitt M, Greenfield S, Stovall E, eds. *From cancer patient to cancer survivor: Lost in transition.* 2005. Available at http://www.nap.edu/catalog.php?record_id=11468. Accessed August 4, 2014.
21. McCabe MS, Bhatia S, Oeffinger KC, et al. American Society of Clinical Oncology statement: Achieving high-quality cancer survivorship care. *J Clin Oncol.* 2013; 31: 631–9.
22. Bower J, Bak K, Berger A, et al. Screening, assessment, and management of fatigue in adult survivors of cancer: An American

Society of Clinical Oncology clinical practice guideline adaptation. *J Clin Oncol.* 2014; 32: 1840–50.

23. Anderson BL, DeRubeis RJ, Berman BS, et al. Screening, assessment, and care of anxiety and depressive symptoms in adults with cancer: An American Society of Clinical Oncology guideline adaptation. *J Clin Oncol.* 2014; 32: 1605–19.

24. Hershman D, Lacchetti C, Dworkin R, et al. Prevention and management of chemotherapy-induced peripheral neuropathy in survivors of adult cancers: American Society of Clinical Oncology clinical practice guideline. *J Clin Oncol.* 2014; 32: 1941–67.

25. Xue Q. The frailty syndrome: Definition and natural history. *Clin Geriatr Med.* 2014; 27: 1–15.

26. Fried LP, Tangen CM, Watson J. Frailty in older adults: Evidence for a phenotype. *J Gerontol.* 2001; 56(3): M146–56.

27. Koller K, Rockwood K. Frailty in older adults: Implications for end-of-life care. *Cleveland Clin J Med.* 2013; 80: 168–74.

28. Alzheimer's Association. *Alzheimer's facts and figures.* 2014. Available at http://www.alz.org/alzheimers_disease_facts_and_figures.asp. Accessed August 4, 2014.

29. Gallagher M, Long CO. Advanced dementia care: Demystifying behaviors, addressing pain, and maximizing comfort. *J Hospice Palliatr Nurs.* 2011; 13: 70–8.

30. Ersek M, Carpenter JG. Geriatric palliative care in long term care settings with a focus on nursing homes. *J Palliat Med.* 2013; 16: 1180–7.

31. Van der Steen JT. Dying with dementia: What we know after more than a decade of research. *J Alzheimers Dis.* 2010; 22: 37–52.

32. O'Connor NR, Corcoran AM. End-stage renal disease: Symptom management and advance care planning. *Am Family Physician.* 2012; 85: 705–10.

33. National Kidney Foundation. *End-Stage Renal Disease in the United States.* 2014. Available at http://www.kidney.org. Accessed August 4, 2014.

34. Murray AM. Cognitive impairment in the aging dialysis and chronic disease populations: an occult burden. *Adv Chron Kidney Dis.* 2008; 15:123–32.

35. Claxton RN, Blackhall L, Weisbond S, et al. Undertreatment of symptoms in patients on maintenance hemodialysis. *J Pain Sympt Manag.* 2010; 39: 211–8.

36. Tung EE, Vickers KS, Lackore K, et al. Clinical decision support technology to introduce advance care planning in the primary care setting. *Am J Hosp Palliat Med.* 2011; 28: 230–5.

37. Hinders D. Advance directives: Limitations to completion. *Am J Hosp Palliat Med.* 2011; 24: 286–9.

38. Warner E. *Palliative in Practice.* 2013. Available at http:// palliativeinpractice.org/2013/07/. Accessed August 1, 2014.

39. Detering KM, Hancock AD, Reade MC, et al. The impact of advance care planning on end of life care in elderly patients: randomized control trial. *BMJ* 2010; 340. http://dx.doi.org/10.1136/bmj.c1345

40. Tierney WM, Dexter PR, Gramelspacher GP. The effect of discussions about advance directives on patients' satisfaction with primary care. *J Gen Intern Med.* 2001; 16: 32–40.

41. Slort W, Schweitzer BP, Blankenstein AH, et al. Perceived barriers and facilitators for general practitioner–patient communication in palliative care: A systematic review. *Palliat Med.* 2011; 25: 613–29.

42. Spoelhof GD, Elliott B. Implementing advance directives in office practice. *Am Family Physician.* 2012; 85: 461–6.

43. Block SD. Medical education in end-of-life care: The status of reform. *J Palliat Med.* 2002; 5: 243–8.

44. Billings ME, Engelberg R, Curtis JR, et al. Determinants of medical students' perceived preparation to perform end-of-life care, quality of end-of-life care education, and attitudes toward end-of-life care. *J Palliat Med.* 2010; 13: 319–26.

45. Horowitz R, Gramling R, Quill T. Palliative care education in US medical schools. *Med Educ.* 2014; 48: 59–66.

46. Center to Advance Palliative Care. *Fast Facts.* Available at https:// www.capc.org/fast-facts/ Accessed August 10, 2015.

47. End-of-Life Nursing Education Consortium (ELNEC). Available at http://www.aacn.nche.edu/elnec. Accessed August 10, 2014.

48. Zeytinoglu M. Talking it out: Helping our patients live better while dying. *Ann Internal Med.* 2011; 154: 830–2.

49. Von Gunten C. *Coding and billing for physician services in palliative care.* 2001. Available at https://www.capc.org/fast-facts/ (formerly http://www.eperc.mcw.edu/EPERC/FastFactsIndex/ff_048.htm. Accessed August 10, 2014).

50. Fischer SM, Sauala A, Min S, et al. Advance directive discussions: Lost in translation or lost opportunities. *J Palliat Med.* 2001; 15: 86–92.

51. Sudore RL, Knight SJ, McMahan RD, et al. A novel website to prepare diverse older adults for decision making and advance care planning: A pilot study. *J Pain Symp Manag.* 2014; 47: 674–86.

52. Glare PA, Sinclair CT. Palliative medicine review: Prognostication. *J Palliat Med.* 2008; 11: 84–94.

53. Chan E, Wu H, Chan Y. Revisiting the palliative performance scale: Change in scores during disease trajectory predicts survival. *Palliat Med.* 2012; 27: 367–74.

54. Moss AH, Lunney JR, Culp S, et al. Prognostic significance of the "surprise" question in cancer patients. *J Palliat Med.* 2010; 13: 837–40.

55. McCormick E, Chia E, Meier D. Integrating palliative care into primary care. *Mt Sinai J Med.* 2012; 79: 579–85.

CHAPTER 15

The Advanced Practice Registered Nurse in the Geriatric Outpatient Setting

Joan E. Dacher and Sherrie Murray

Key Points

- A growing number of older adults in the United States are living longer, but with multiple chronic illnesses and disabilities. These result in frailty, high illness burden, and high healthcare utilization at the end-of-life. Palliative advanced practice registered nurses (APRNs) can play a role in the care of these older adults.[1]

- The principles of geriatric care, in tandem with *The Clinical Practice Guidelines for Quality Palliative Care* developed by the National Consensus Project for Quality Palliative Care,[2] provide guidance to the APRN caring for medically complex older adults in the outpatient setting, with an emphasis on patient- and family-centered care delivered by a coordinated care team.

- APRN practice in the geriatric outpatient setting will include the delivery of primary care, care coordination, interdisciplinary team communication, assisting patients to navigate the healthcare system, advocacy, and patient education, while providing evidence-based practice.[3]

- Among the common problems encountered by the APRN working with geriatric patients in the community setting are fatigue, sleep disturbances, depression, anxiety, grief, cognitive impairment, disability or change in functional status, polypharmacy, and post-hospitalization medication adherence.[4–7]

Introduction

The appropriateness of palliative care for older adults is evidenced by the demographic profile of older Americans as well as the data that speak to the efficacy and cost of the care provided. A model for providing palliative care is well-established and can be found in the nexus between the principles of palliative care and gerontology.

There is a strong, evidence-based case for ensuring that older adults have access to palliative care. With the appropriate education, knowledge, and skills, APRNs are well situated to play a pivotal role in providing palliative care to older adults in outpatient settings.

The growth of the total numbers of older adults in the United States, their state of health with regard to chronic illness and disability, and the stated desire of this population to live out their lives in the community make a case for ensuring that older adults have access to palliative care. Since 1900, the population aged 65 and older has grown faster than other segments of the population, in part due to increased longevity, the result of medical advances. Projecting into the future, the growth in this segment of the population will continue to expand.[8] With longevity come issues of disability, chronic illness, and access to appropriate care. Increased longevity is a mixed blessing. It is the result of health improvements but in turn results in frailty, a high illness burden, and heavy use of healthcare at the end-of-life.

The prevalence of acute and chronic health conditions increases with age. According to the U.S. Census Bureau, overall, individuals 65 and older represent 50% of all cancer diagnoses in the United States.[1] Dementia, specifically Alzheimer's disease, disproportionately affects older adults, and the rate increases with age.[1] Functional limitations and disability are associated with advanced age. The APRN working in this area should be knowledgeable about the physiological changes of aging and how they contribute to limitations and disabilities. Among the common issues confronting the APRN working with older adults with complex serious illness in the community setting are fatigue, sleep disturbances, depression, anxiety, grief, cognitive impairment, and disability or change in functional status.[4] Polypharmacy and post-hospitalization medication adherence are risk factors for worsening of disease, repeat admission, and death.[5–7] Injury prevention is a critical preventive health need. A fall can be a catalyst for a sequence of events that contribute to an increased demand for healthcare, a loss of independence, and a need for pain and symptom management. Falls can be the outcome of numerous clinical factors, including age-related changes in postural control, gait, and vision, diseases that affect sensory input, musculoskeletal changes, and medication use.[9] The clinical picture is further complicated by the patient's living environment. Each of these is a focal area for assessment by the APRN.

Ethics of Care for Older Adults in the Community Setting

Decision making in regard to the appropriate course of care for older adults living with acute and chronic illness is complex. At the macro or systems level of consideration, attention must be given to the efficacy of care, resource utilization and deployment, and the prominence of cure over care.[10] Heavy use of healthcare does not result in better care, greater patient satisfaction, or increased ability to remain independent.[4,5] The increased prevalence of chronic illness is significant; management of chronic illness has emerged as the expected healthcare need among older adults. When working with the older adult in the community, questions emerge about the appropriate use of services.[11,12] Management requires an approach that takes into account pharmacologic intervention, physical response and symptoms, safety, mobility, social and emotional well-being, and the ability to maintain the highest possible level of functional capacity. These concerns prompt ethical questions about what constitutes appropriate care for older adults, as well as the circumstances in which care is delivered. Care for community-dwelling older adults is shifting toward becoming more responsive and coordinated, with a focus on offering opportunities for participation in advance care planning. The APRN working with this population must bear in mind the larger ethical questions and the ways they drive patient's and family's decisions. This establishes a context for care that is especially important for geriatric patients, who are at higher risk for morbidity and mortality.

Health Policy and Support for Palliative Care for Older Adults

While the 2010 Patient Protection and Affordable Care Act (PPACA) is an opportunity to address issues of chronic illness, quality of care, the rising cost of care, and all issues that disproportionately affect older adults, it falls short in addressing access to palliative care. In its initial inceptions, the bill included support for provider reimbursement for an advance care planning conversation with Medicare patients. Amid criticism and concerns about healthcare rationing and Medicare "death panels," portions of the act were omitted in the final version; policy changes related to end-of-life care are absent from the final document, and thus the opportunity to address a critical need of healthcare in the United States was lost.[13] Other provisions of the PPACA offer the opportunity to address quality issues for which palliative care could be of benefit.[14]

Money allocated to reduce the cost of care and the move toward bundled care costs have resulted in affordable care organizations (ACOs)[15] and primary care medical homes (PCMHs), two models designed to coordinate care for patients with complex care needs and to provide support for the transition of care from one setting to another.[16] The APRN in the outpatient geriatric setting who is working within the larger ACO or the PCMH can play a critical role in delivering care to the older adult with comorbidity and advanced chronic illness, especially in the transition to the community, and in avoiding readmission and extraordinary interventions for the management of complex comorbidities. Some states have recognized certified Medicaid provider nurse practitioners as appropriate to take on the leadership of PCMHs.[17] The goal of the ACO is to reduce fragmented and uncoordinated care[18] through the use of an integrated team for care delivery. Care is best delivered to older adults in the context of a team and a coordinated approach to quality and safety. The APRN is an ideal partner for this, and the geriatric clinic provides a setting in which to support these goals and meet the needs of older adults with complex medical conditions.

ACOs and PCMHs are conceptually aligned with palliative care as well, offering additional opportunity for the APRN working in the geriatric clinic to integrate concepts of palliative care into practice. The literature suggests that an integrated model of palliative care can result in cost savings and is well-positioned to assist in these models of healthcare delivery. Palliative care teams have shown they can align services to meet patient and family needs while employing existing resources and reducing cost burden,[19] presenting an opportunity to incorporate palliative care as a viable model for the development of ACOs and PCMHs.

The APRN's Role in Providing Palliative Care for the Older Adult

This is a critical juncture for continuing to expand the role of the APRN in palliative care for older adults in the outpatient or community setting. Funding exists for educating APRNs in palliative care through the educational arm of the PPACA. Nurse practitioners are needed across the continuum of care from inpatient, nursing home, and community/outpatient settings.[13] The use of APRNs in these settings is cost-effective, as suggested in Bauer's study of nurse practitioners in nursing homes,[20] and can be effectively delivered using a collaborative practice model with other health professionals.[21] Nurse practitioner co-management of geriatric clients is similarly shown to have better outcomes.[22] Evidence supports the value and role of geriatric clinical nurse specialists in improving patient outcome and providing cost-effective care.[23] The geriatric clinical nurse specialist is educated to work in a large scope of practice in direct and indirect roles, including patient education, diagnosis and treatment of symptoms, staff education, program and policy development, and quality and safety improvement.[24] A strong case has been made for the importance of the generalist, primary care, or acute care APRN to have the knowledge base in palliative care to best serve older adult clients wherever they are encountered.[25]

The Nexus Between Gerontology and Palliative Care

There is ample guidance for the APRN engaged in delivering palliative care to older adults. Gerontology offers a comprehensive approach to the study of aging, and geriatric medicine as a subset of gerontology provides practitioners with recommendations and principles for comprehensive assessment and treatment. Such assessment and treatment address all aspects of the older adult's life: physical, cognitive, psychosocial, financial, and environmental conditions that converge and drive the need for care. Often comprehensive assessment is conducted by an interdisciplinary team and treatment is offered within the context of the team. Findings may include multiple medical comorbidities, including recognized geriatric conditions (dementia, falls, functional impairment, failure to thrive) that are associated with high healthcare utilization.[26] A comprehensive approach to the care of older adults with multiple comorbidities is key because these patients are at risk for receiving a great deal of healthcare interventions with questionable outcomes in terms of efficacy, satisfaction with care, and quality of life. This is the very population for which palliative care is most appropriate. The principles of geriatric care as described in the literature are listed in Box 15.1.[27,28]

These principles of geriatric care are synergistic with *The Clinical Practice Guidelines for Quality Palliative Care* developed by the National Consensus Project for Quality Palliative Care.[2] These guidelines are the foundation for evidence-based practice in palliative care and, like the principles of geriatric care, are based on the belief that the most appropriate care is holistic and comprehensive and ensures that the patient and family are integral to care planning and decision making. The synergy extends to the prominence of the interdisciplinary team in addressing the complexities of care. Eight domains for palliative care are delineated within the guidelines and provide structure for the delivery of palliative care.

Optimal outcomes for the older adult in need of community-based palliative care can be achieved when the principles of geriatric care and the guidelines for quality palliative care are applied simultaneously to clinical practice. The resultant practice model addresses all the needs of the patient and family and takes into account the dynamic nature of acute and chronic illness as experienced by an older adult. The experiences of family and caregivers are also attended to within this framework; families figure prominently in the assessment of the patient and are understood to be full participants in the palliative care experience.

The intersection between the principles of geriatric care and the guidelines are multifaceted, with significant conceptual overlap. When considered as a conceptual whole, this integrated practice model for geriatric palliative care provides an alternative paradigm for the care of older adults in the community setting from the point of diagnosis of chronic illness to the end-of-life. Figures 15.1 and 15.2 illustrate the diverse ways two selected domains and the guidelines converge. A unique domain for palliative care is at the center of each figure. Branching out from these are the various geriatric principles, followed by examples of the application of each for practice.

Case Studies and Application of Principles and Domains

Case Study 1

Mr. W was a 90-year-old white male living at home with his wife. His diagnoses included coronary artery disease, hypertension, and early dementia. His medications included ASA 81 mg QD, lisinopril 10 mg QD, and Aricept 10 mg QD. His wife, a frail 88-year-old, had mild cognitive impairment but was able to manage their basic needs within the home. The couple needed assistance for some

---

Box 15.1 Principles of Geriatric Care

- Aging is not a disease.
- Geriatric care is multidisciplinary.
- Medical conditions are chronic, with multiple comorbidities, and multifactorial.
- Care is patient- and family-focused. Ask the patient and family what the primary concerns and goals of care are. Consider these within the context of the developmental tasks of aging.
- Understand who the primary decision maker will be.
- Before offering options for care, consider the available evidence regarding the patient's prognosis and important outcomes. Weigh the risks and benefits of options against the goals of care.
- Consider the prognosis and evaluate the patient's and family's understanding of the prognosis.
- Consider possible drug–drug interactions and treatment-related risks (safety, long-term benefit vs. short-term harm).
- Discuss the risks, burden, and benefits of options with the patient and family. Assess their understanding.
- Discuss the patient's prognosis and offer clinical evidence within the context of the patient's ethnic, cultural, spiritual, and family values.
- Offer reassessment of the benefits of treatment, feasibility, adherence, and alignment with preferences.
- Provide a comprehensive general health assessment with emphasis on areas of importance to the geriatric patient:

  a. Medications and the potential for interactions in face of the patient's comorbidities
  b. Recent and impending life changes
  c. Objective measure of overall sense of social and personal well-being, and quality of life
  d. The patient's ethnic, cultural, spiritual, and family values
  e. Available physical and instrumental support: family, friends, others. Is there a caregiver network in place?
  f. Availability of a social network and social connections
  g. The patient's level of physical function and independence, mobility, and balance
  h. The patient's physical living environment: is there a match between the patient's physical ability and the demands of the environment? Assess the risks of the patient's environment and the use and availability of services. Can care be offered in the least restrictive environment?
  i. The patient's cognitive status and ability to participate in decision making
  j. The patient's nutritional status and needs
  k. Ethical issues and end-of-life planning

From references 27 and 28.

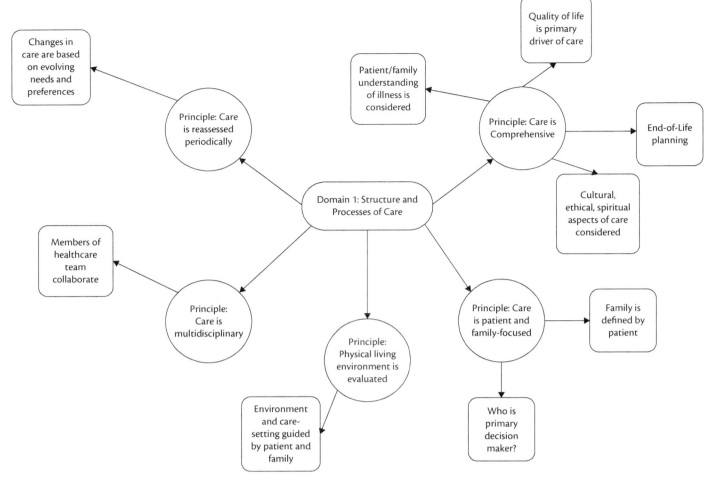

Figure 15.1 Domain 2: Physical Aspects of Care

activities of daily living and relied on the support of 24-hour nurses' aides. A home care nurse visited monthly to monitor medications and their overall condition. Mr. W had advance directives as well as a community DNR and a completed MOLST form that specifies comfort care only. Recently Mr. W was noted to have new-onset slurred speech and weakness on his left side. This prompted a call to the nurse by the aide. The nurse case manager visited and evaluated the patient using the FAST scale from the American Stroke Association, evaluating for facial droop, arm weakness, speech difficulties, and time of onset of symptoms.[29] She verified a blood pressure of 150/94 and a regular pulse of 76.

The geriatric APRN was notified and the patient was given an extra dose of ASA 81 mg, as he was beyond the window of opportunity for treatment with tPA.[30] The APRN reviewed the advance directives and consulted the physician and social worker at the geriatric clinic. After reviewing the options, she phoned the son, who was the healthcare proxy. The decision was made to bring the patient to the outpatient geriatric center the next day for care, as the son wanted him to have an evaluation that included a full workup for stroke. The son believed this action was most consistent with his father's advance directives.

At the clinic, the APRN evaluated the patient's status. The EKG showed no evidence of atrial fibrillation or acute changes from his previous EKG. His bloodwork included a PTT, PT, INR, CBC with platelet count, cardiac markers, electrolytes and renal function, lipid panel, and vital signs with oxygen saturation.[30] His physical exam included complete neurological and functional evaluations and a geriatric mental health exam. The NIH screening tool was used to evaluate his stroke, and a bedside swallow evaluation tool was used as well.[31] Mr. W was found to have an adequate swallow and was believed to be over 12 hours from the onset of symptoms. During this visit, the plan of care was discussed with the patient and son, including the option of radiologic testing. The decision was made to send him for a CAT scan of the head so an ischemic stroke could be confirmed.[30]

The following day the son returned to the clinic for a care planning meeting with the team. The plan included monitoring and management of blood pressure to maintain a BP of less than 140/90; an increased dose of ASA to 160 mg per day; and evaluation by PT, OT, and ST for safety at home and nutritional needs.[32] They discussed adding a statin pending the results of the lab work and a discussion of the risk/benefits in light of the patient's age. Since the patient's advance directives expressed his wish to remain at home and avoid hospitalization, the son made clear that Mr. W would not be hospitalized even if his condition worsened. The son discussed concerns regarding the increased

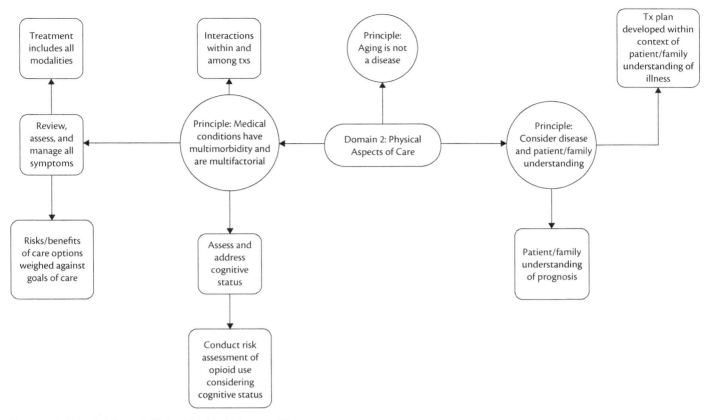

Figure 15.2 Domain 3: Psychological and Psychiatric Aspects of Care

burden on his mother and shared that he would temporarily move in with them. The team agreed that a regular diet with thin liquids was appropriate as the patient showed no evidence of aspiration on evaluation. The APRN planned to educate the caregivers in the home on aspiration prevention using the Hartford Institute for Geriatric Nursing Preventing Aspiration Guideline.[33] During the team meeting, the APRN offered the son a referral to a local Alzheimer's disease caregiver support group.

To further ensure high-quality care with respect to the goals of care, the APRN visited the home, spoke with the aides, and provided education about the new plan of care. She emphasized the need to call the APRN or covering team in the event of a change in status and not 911. The plan was placed in writing in the home, next to the MOLST and DNR.

In general, response to this case can be guided by the following principles of geriatric care:

◆ Care is interdisciplinary/multidisciplinary.

◆ Medical conditions are chronic, with multiple comorbidities, and multifactorial.

◆ Care is patient- and family-focused.

◆ Understand who the primary decision maker will be.

◆ Provide comprehensive assessment that considers physical state, emotional state, quality of life, well-being, sources of primary support, and optimal level of physical function.

Domain 1: Structure and Process of Care

Palliative care is based on comprehensive assessment of the patient; change in status drives reevaluation of care. The assessment and plan of care reflect the understanding and desires of the patient and family and are focused on promoting quality of life as they define it. The plan of care includes consideration of the physical environment to ensure safety and functional needs are met. Care is interdisciplinary and involves all members of the team, the patient, and the family. The APRN is responsible for reviewing these regularly with the patient and family, taking into account the patient's cognitive ability to continue to participate in decision making.

Domain 2: Physical Aspects of Care

Pain and symptom management is a primary focus of palliative care. Assessment is evidence-based, documented, and performed by trained professionals. While Mr. W did not need active pain and symptom management, this was part of the ongoing assessment, as was evaluation of his neurological symptoms. Should Mr. W require pain management, appropriate administration and safe use in the home will be critical considerations in light of both his and his wife's cognitive status. In the outpatient setting, pain is assessed at each visit with the primary provider. As Mr. W's primary symptoms were neurological, it was appropriate to use the FAST and the NIH Stroke Scale in the clinic or at home (recommended by the American Stroke Association) for screening and response at recommended intervals.[29]

Domain 3: Psychological and Psychiatric Aspects of Care

In the presence of a change in cognitive and mental status, they are evaluated using developmentally appropriate tools. Care includes identification and recognition of loss, grief, and depression in patients and family. Differentiating between grief and depression is important because their definitions, clinical features, and interventions are different.[34] Education and support are provided for patient, family, and staff. The use of a Geriatric Mental Status Exam with Mr. W on an ongoing basis provided for evidence-based practice and ensured that care was developmentally and cognitively appropriate.[35]

Domain 4: Social Aspects of Care

Continued change in status will require ongoing assessment and evaluation of needs. Additional assistance may be needed in the home to allow aging in place; this will prompt an evaluation of financial resources and a meeting with the patient and his wife and son to discuss the goals of care and options for achieving those goals. Advance care planning is reevaluated to ensure that remaining at home and avoiding hospitalization remain a priority. Services like home-based meal programs, social or medical model senior day care programs, and transportation services, as well as coordination of services through local government programs for the elderly, support the desire to remain in the community and avoid social isolation.

Case Study 2

Mrs. T was an 84-year-old woman who presented to her primary care provider with radicular pain radiating from her lower back down her right leg. She was independent in all activities and had an active social life in her community. Her primary support was her son and family, who lived up north. Her medical history was significant for hypercholesterolemia, for which she received Zocor 10 mg QD, osteoporosis treated with calcium supplements, and mild cognitive impairment treated with Aricept 10 mg QD. She declined treatment for depression.

Her radicular pain had developed 2 months earlier, resulting in limitations of physical activity. She was referred to a rheumatologist and L/S spine x-rays were negative, showing only degenerative changes consistent with age. Conservative management included PT and a series of cortisone injections. These proved to be ineffective. Reevaluation revealed L/S spine bony destructive changes consistent with metastatic disease. A bone scan revealed metastatic spread to the pelvis and right femur. Pathology results of the bone biopsy showed small cell carcinoma of the lung. A CT of the chest showed a right upper lobe mass. Palliative radiological treatment effectively reduced most of the radicular pain. Mrs. T was referred to a palliative APRN for symptom management. For relief of her nausea she was prescribed Zofran ODT 4 mg tablets q8h PRN. The patient had been placed on NSAIDs previously and was intolerant of these drugs due to gastrointestinal side effects. She had been taking acetaminophen PRN but with little relief. She was started on oxycodone 5 mg q6h as needed for pain.[36] A safety plan was implemented by physical therapy that included home support and services with a move closer to her son. A new assessment offered a prognosis of 12 to 18 months with appropriate

advance care planning. She agreed to a trial of palliative chemotherapy. With chemotherapy she experienced nausea, vomiting, loss of weight, change in cognition, and new onset of a DVT, with minimal response. She decided to discontinue therapy.

A new pain regimen was initiated and included OxyContin 10 mg q12h to promote comfort and function. A dose of 5 mg of oxycodone q4h was continued for breakthrough pain.[36] The ondansetron ODT was continued for nausea as needed. A new plan included pain control, nutritional issues, mild exacerbation of her mild cognitive impairment, unresolved family issues, grief related to the recent cancer deaths of her husband and another son, safety issues, and coping. The APRN assessed Mrs. T's nutritional risk using the Mini-Nutritional Assessment Short-Form (MNA®-SF).[37] She was offered a referral to social work to address her depression and grief and spiritual support, both of which she declined. An evaluation of the home was conducted using the CDC Check for Safety Home Fall Prevention Checklist for Older Adults,[38] and recommendations were made regarding assistive and adaptive devices.

Over the next 6 months, Mrs. T's disease progressed with an increase in pain and continued weight loss. The patient and her family were instructed in the safe use of opioids. She developed SOB and a deep nonproductive cough along with lower limb swelling. She raised the question of a return to treatment as an option to cure her disease. While her family supported her decision to forgo treatment, she herself was unsure. The risks and benefits of treatment were addressed by the palliative APRN. Mrs. T declined further treatment and reaffirmed her desire to remain at home even in the face of increased severity of symptoms. To enhance her safety at home, Mrs. T agreed to an increase in the hours of an aide.

About 6 weeks prior to her death and a year after diagnosis, Mrs. T began to experience significant decline, including severe SOB, lower-extremity edema, increased pain in her back and hip, increased periods of fatigue and sleeping, loss of appetite, and weight loss. A review of medications was conducted by the APRN to eliminate unnecessary medications in light of her prognosis. The palliative APRN discussed goals of care with the primary care team, the patient, her son, and other family members. The patient found oxygen helpful but declined hospice. She died 6 weeks later with home health support.

Domain 1: Structure and Process of Care

The care for Mrs. T was interdisciplinary and coordinated and subsequent reevaluations were provided as needed. All aspects of her status were considered, including presenting symptoms, prior history, and response to past treatment. Prognosis and quality-of-life considerations weigh heavily in consideration of care planning. Goals are set by the patient and family, and Mrs. T was the primary decision maker until the end of her life.

Domain 2: Physical Aspects of Care

Symptoms may involve multiple systems, and specialist-level expertise is needed to achieve relief. Validated assessment tools are used to guide evidence-based practice. When opioids are prescribed, a risk/benefit assessment is conducted regularly, with appropriate patient and family education. Mrs. T's pain and symptoms were managed conservatively with OxyContin 10 mg q12h based on her request that she remain cognizant.[36] By "starting low and going slow" with increases in doses, Mrs. T had excellent pain management, without changes in cognition, including delirium. Medications that were not essential to managing her cancer and symptoms were discontinued (including Aricept) to reduce the possibility of toxicity.

Domain 3: Psychological and Psychiatric Aspects of Care

The palliative care team assesses and responds to the patient's psychological distress. Mrs. T had a premorbid diagnosis of depression and was assessed as experiencing unresolved grief related to the death of her husband and son, her own diagnosis, and other complex family issues. She was offered support and treatment and declined them. There are several tools to assess depression that would have been appropriate for use, including the Geriatric Depression Scale.[39] Despite her distress, Mrs. T was able to enjoy time spent with her family and friends and found great joy in her grandchildren. This love was reciprocated and she had the opportunity to meet the developmental task of aging, generativity, through these intergenerational relationships.

Domain 4: Social Aspects of Care

The goal of this domain is to support the patient and family in addressing broadly defined social needs. These include goals for care, grief, response to illness, communication, caregiving needs, and access to medication, equipment, and community resources. Mrs. T's social concerns reflected her desire to stay connected with neighbors and family and remain active in the community. The palliative APRN ensured that Mrs. T had access to the services and assistance she required.

Domain 7: Care of the Patient at the End-of-Life

This domain recognizes the complex needs of the patient and family at the end-of-life. Education and support is provided to the family and other caregivers about the dying process. In anticipation of the dying process, the palliative APRN worked with the family and hospice to ensure that all appropriate medications were in the home and that family members who would be in attendance at the end-of-life knew how to administer them. The palliative APRN continued communication and care coordination to Mrs. T's last days.

Case Study 3

Mrs. P was an 82-year-old female with a two-day history of SOB and swelling of the lower extremities. One week prior, she was seen by her primary care nurse practitioner for worsening SOB and was diagnosed with heart failure. Because of a history of renal failure, her diuretic dose was increased, with only short-term relief. She returned to the geriatric clinic for worsening symptoms.

Her past medical history was significant for type 2 DM, stage IV chronic kidney disease, and kidney cancer. Her chronic kidney disease was nearing stage 5, with a GFR of 15 mL/min. She was status post left nephrectomy and adrenalectomy. Prior conversations had included the possibility of hemodialysis in the future. A recent CT of the chest and abdomen showed no evidence of metastatic disease or cancer. Mrs. P lived independently in the community and relied on her daughter for support for healthcare provider visits. Though she described herself as "slowing down," she stated her quality of life was satisfactory and described herself as healthy. She had decision-making capacity, though she included her daughter in all discussions.

Mrs. P had a history of CAD, for which she had undergone stenting twice, and a history of CHF and an EF of 40. She was involved in an outpatient CHF program and was well educated about her disease. Due to weight gain and increased swelling in her lower extremities and abdomen, she sought further care. The APRN's assessment determined probable recurrence of CHF. Mrs. P's medications were reviewed; she was on Lopressor 12.5 mg BID, irbesartan 150 mg QD, as well as bumetanide 0.5 mg QD[40] (Table 15.1).

The APRN reviewed the patient's advance care planning documents. Though her out-of-hospital medical orders for life-sustaining treatment (POLST/MOLST) stated she did not want hemodialysis, the patient and her daughter said they would like to discuss whether this was an option to stabilize her condition and increase her comfort. Though dialysis would not reverse her kidney disease, and despite the burdens, both Mrs. P and her daughter decided to proceed with hemodialysis.

The APRN was able to do bloodwork while the patient was in the office and obtain a chest x-ray, which revealed CHF. The APRN called the cardiologist and renal physician to coordinate a plan of care and discussed with Mrs. P what would happen next. She was prescribed oral bumetanide 1 mg BID as she was still making urine and there could be some response to the new diuretic dosing.[41,42] Side effects of the medication were discussed with the patient and her daughter, as well as a plan to monitor electrolytes, renal function, and urine output. Mrs. P. needed a fistula; the primary care nurse practitioner discussed this with the renal physician, who thought it would be prudent to have access for possible dialysis earlier than a fistula would be available. The renal physician would work toward having a dialysis slot for Mrs. P. The APRN coordinated a visit with the renal physician in his office, as well as with the cardiologist.

The daughter was concerned about her mother's increased weakness and believed she could not safely return home. The palliative APRN called visiting nurses to set up services to monitor

Table 15.1 Adverse Effects of Using Diuretics for Chronic Kidney Disease

Condition	
Hypotension	Most common when initiating therapy or increasing diuretic use
Decrease in the glomerular filtration rate (GFR)	Most common with concurrent use of angiotensin receptor blockers and angiotensin-converting enzyme inhibitors
Electrolyte abnormalities	
Hypokalemia Hypomagnesemia Hyponatremia	Occurs with loop diuretics, sodium intake dependent
Hyperkalemia	Occurs with loop and thiazide diuretics
Hypocalcemia	Occurs with thiazide diuretics
Hypercalcemia	Occurs with loop diuretics

Mrs. P at her daughter's home. Mrs. P was reluctant at first to leave her own home but believed this would be temporary until she improved. The out-of-hospital medical orders for life-sustaining treatment (POLST/MOLST) were changed to reflect the new plan of care. The patient had a home visit from the palliative APRN as well as the visiting nurse, who was able to see that Mrs. P was responding to the increase in her diuretics. The APRN repeated her bloodwork due to the change in medication. She reviewed whether Mrs. P had any symptoms of postural hypotension. The diuretic medication was adjusted based on her response to the dose and in discussion with the cardiologist and renal physician. Once Mrs. P's condition had stabilized, the APRN provided some anticipatory guidance with the patient and the daughter regarding the next steps in her care and the management of her chronic disease. The patient was seen by a vascular surgeon in order to have a central line and a fistula placed after her acute phase had resolved. If the patient had developed increased SOB, confusion, or nausea and vomiting due to uremia[41,43] (Table 15.2), the plan would have changed based on her medical status, up to and including hospitalization. Referral was made to the nurse educator at the local dialysis center to prepare and educate the patient and her daughter regarding dialysis. Both patient and daughter stated that the goals of care remained symptom management and optimal quality of life in light of the new treatment. The plan of care was reviewed; additional education and anticipatory planning were provided for support and care in light of this change in status and the potential increase in care needs.

Domain 1: Structure and Processes of Care

A primary criterion for this domain is that care is interdisciplinary and coordinated and reflects comprehensive assessment. Patient and family understanding of the illness, expectations of treatment, and goals of care are assessed. Quality of life is a prime consideration throughout. When developed, the plan of care is based on comprehensive assessment and in collaboration with the patient and family. With any change in condition, the priorities for care are reevaluated. In light of Mrs. P's prior cancer diagnosis and the presence of complex chronic conditions, comprehensive assessment was integral to developing an appropriate

Table 15.2 Symptoms of Uremia in the Patient with Chronic Kidney Disease: When Dialysis Should Be Initiated and GFR Is <15 mL/min

Nutritional deterioration, including fatigue, anorexia, and weight loss
Excessive thirst
Visual disturbance
Muscle cramps
Pruritus
Mental status changes
Metabolic abnormalities, such as anemia or acidemia and electrolyte abnormalities, may be present
Poorly controlled cardiovascular problems can precipitate symptoms of uremia

Adapted from Medscape (2013) and reference 43.

patient-centered plan of care. Though 82 years old and with a significant medical history, this patient enjoyed an active life and perceived herself to be healthy. Her decision to address her shifting renal function with dialysis was made within the context of understanding that this was a palliative measure and would not "cure" her renal disease. The primary care nurse practitioner took a palliative care approach and coordinated communication and care across all healthcare providers. Communication was intentional and regular, resulting in a plan of care that reflected patient decision making with input from the family.

Domain 2: Physical Aspects of Care

The goal of this domain is safe and timely management of physical symptoms over time. Patient and family understanding of the illness and possible interventions is assessed and education is provided. In this care, the primary care nurse practitioner provided timely and appropriate physical care in response to the patient's change in status. This was done from the perspective of managing her comorbidities and the goal of palliative intervention. Through a process of enhanced communication with all providers and coordination of care, the nurse enhanced the likelihood that care would support the patient's goal for care. The recognition that Mrs. P had the capacity to remain independent was key to providing appropriate palliative interventions; the disease was addressed, but within the context of her larger life. Providing education about the course of treatment is a way to support the patient's quality of life and need for ongoing management of her illness and symptoms for a disease that cannot be cured, the hallmark of good geriatric nursing and palliative nursing in the outpatient setting.

Domain 8: Ethical and Legal Aspects of Care

Ethical and legal aspects of care are addressed though an assessment of the patient's and family's choices for care. There is a defined process for eliciting values, care preferences, religious beliefs, and cultural considerations that is sensitive to the needs of the patient and family, and this should be revisited over time. Appropriate documents are completed to meet legal standards for implementation. As Mrs. P's disease progressed, her decisions regarding palliative treatment with hemodialysis changed. In this case the APRN recognized that care decisions are dynamic and provided the patient and her daughter the opportunity to reevaluate prior decisions and update legal documents. The APRN is ethically obligated to do this and to ensure patient autonomy as well as meet the ethical principles of beneficence and nonmaleficence.

Conclusion

The increase in the total number of older Americans has resulted in an aging population that is living longer and will experience multiple chronic illnesses along with physical and functional impairment prior to the end-of-life.[11] The implication of this is the need for increased access to a model of palliative care that is designed to meet the unique needs of an older population. APRNs will be essential to meeting the palliative healthcare needs of this population across the continuum of care and are poised to provide cost-effective and high-quality care for the frail elderly. While more research is needed to fully understand the parameters and specifics of what is needed in geriatric palliative care,[44,45] the evidence currently available suggests that the APRN has a crucial role. Resources are available to the APRN to enhance knowledge and skills and support practice in this area. *The Clinical Practice Guidelines for Quality Palliative Care*[2] is an essential document for APRNs working in this realm, as are the "Guiding Principles for the Care of Older Adults with Multimorbidity."[27,28] Other resources include clinical tools from the Center to Advance Palliative Care,[46] the *Try This* series from the Hartford Institute for Geriatric Nursing,[47] and the Fast Facts series from the Center to Advance Palliative Care.[48]

References

1. West L, Cole S, Goodkind D, He W. 65+ in the United Sates: 2010. Current population reports. U.S. Census Bureau. Washington, DC: U.S. Government Printing Office; 2014:23–212. Available at http://www.census.gov/content/dam/Census/library/publications/2014/demo/p23-212.pdf. Accessed July 1, 2014.

2. Clinical Practice Guidelines for Quality Palliative Care. 3rd ed. Pittsburgh, PA: National Consensus Project for Quality Palliative Care; 2013. Available at http://www.nationalconsensusproject.org/NCP_Clinical_Practice_Guidelines_3rd_Edition.pdf. Accessed September 1, 2014.

3. Horton J, Indelicato RA. The advanced practice nurse. In: Ferrell B, Coyle N, eds. *Oxford Textbook of Palliative Nursing*. 3rd ed. New York, NY: Oxford University Press; 2010:1121–1129.

4. Combs S, Kluger B, Kutner JS. Research priorities in geriatric palliative care: nonpain symptoms. *J Palliat Med*. 2013; 16(9): 1001–7.

5. Mansur N, Weiss A, Hoffman A, Gruenewald T, Beloosesky Y. Continuity and adherence to long-term drug treatment by geriatric patients after hospital discharge. *Drugs & Aging*. 2008; 25(10): 861–70.

6. Fulton MM, Allen ER. Polypharmacy in the elderly: A literature review. *J Am Acad Nurse Practitioners*. 2005; 17(4): 123–32.

7. Mallet L, Spinewine A, Huang A. Prescribing in elderly people, 2: The challenge of managing drug interactions in elderly people. *The Lancet*. 2007; 370(July 14): 185–91.

8. A profile of older Americans: 2013. Administration on Aging website. http://www.aoa.gov/Aging_Statistics/Profile/2013/docs/2013_Profile.pdf Published 2013. Accessed July 23, 2014.

9. Miller KE, Zylstra RG, Standbridge JB. The geriatric patient: a systematic approach of maintaining health. *Am Fam Physician*. 2000; 61(4): 1089–104.

10. Kelley A. Epidemiology of care for patients with serious illness. *J Palliat Med*. 2013; 16(7): 730–3.

11. Wennberg J, Fisher E, Goodman D, Skinner J. Tracking the care of patients with severe chronic illness. Lebanon, NH: The Dartmouth Atlas of Health Care; 2008. Available at http://www.dartmouthatlas.org/downloads/atlases/2008_Chronic_Care_Atlas.pdf Published 2008. Accessed July 23, 2014.

12. Meir DE, Morrison RS. Improving value in health care: the case for palliative care. Available at http://www.cms.gov/Medicare/Quality-Initiatives-Patient-Assessment-Instruments/QualityMeasures/Downloads/Improving-Value-in-Health-Care-The-Case-for-Palliative-Care.pdf. Published April 8, 2014. Accessed July 23, 2014.

13. Giovanni LA. End-of-life care in the United States. *Nurs Econ*. 2012; 30(3): 125–6.

14. Sherman DW, Cheon J. Palliative care: A paradigm of care responsive to the demands for health care reform in America. *Nursing Econ*. 2012; 30(3): 153–66.

15. Fletcher D, Panke J. Opportunities and challenges for palliative care professionals in the age of health reform. *J Hosp Palliat Nurs*. 2012; 14(7): 452–9.

16. AHRQ. Ensuring that patient-centered medical homes effectively serve patients with complex health needs. Available at http://pcmh.ahrq.gov/page/ensuring-patient-centered-medical-ho mes-effectively-serve-patients-complex-health-needs Published October 2011. Accessed October 25, 2014.

17. ANA Issue Brief. Solving the crisis in primary care. Available at http://www.nursingworld.org/MainMenuCategories/Policy-Advocacy/Positions-and-Resolutions/Issue-Briefs/APRNs-as-PCPs.pdf. Published 2010. Accessed October 28, 2014.

18. Graham MC. Advocacy in practice: accountable care organizations the future of health care? *Nurse Practitioner*. 2011; 36(8): 11.

19. Byock I, Twohig JS, Merriman M. Promoting excellence in end-of-life care: a report on innovative models of palliative care. *J Palliat Med*. 2006; 9(1): 137–52.

20. Bauer JC. Nurse practitioner as an underutilized resource for health reform: evidence based demonstration of cost-effectiveness. *J Am Acad Nurse Pract*. 2010; 22(4): 228–31. doi: 10.1111/j.1745-7599.2010.00498.x

21. Ettner SL, Kotlerman J, Afifi A, et al. An alternative approach for reducing the costs of patient care: a controlled trial of the multi-disciplinary doctor-nurse practitioner (MDNP) model. *Med Decis Making*. 2006; 26(1): 9–17.

22. Reuben DB, Ganz DA, Roth CP, McCreath HE, Ramirez BA, Wenger NS. Effect of nurse practitioner comanagement on the care of geriatric conditions. *J Am Geriatr Soc*. 2013; 61(6): 857–67.

23. Conley DM, Burket TL, Schumacher S, Lyons D, DeRosa SE, Schirm V. Implementing geriatric models of care: a role of the gerontological clinical nurse specialist-part I. *Geriatric Nurs*. 2012; 33(3): 229–34.

24. American Association of Colleges of Nursing. Adult-gerontology clinical nurse specialist competencies. Available at http://www.aacn.nche.edu/geriatric-nursing/adultgeroCNScomp.pdf. Published 2010. Accessed October 26, 2014.

25. McHugh ME, Arnold J, Buschman PR. Nurses leading the response to the crisis of palliative care for vulnerable populations. *Nurs Econ*. 2012; 30(3): 140–7.

26. Comprehensive geriatric assessment. Wolters Kluwer Health, Up To Date. Available at http://www.uptodate.com/contents/comprehensive-geriatric-assessment?source=search_result&search=comprehensive+geriatric+assessment&selectedTitle=1%7E52. Updated December 30, 2013. Accessed September 1, 2014.

27. Weston C, Addleman K, Douglas J, et al. Guiding principles for the care of older adults with multimorbidity: an approach for clinicians: American Geriatrics Society Expert Panel on the Care of Older Adults with Multimorbidity. *J Am Geriatr Soc*. 2012; 60(10): E1–E25.

28. Villar F. Successful ageing and development: the contribution of generativity in older age. *Ageing & Society*. 2012; 32: 1087–105.

29. Get With The Guidelines Clinical Tools. The American Stroke Association. Available at http://www.heart.org/HEARTORG/HealthcareResearch/GetWithTheGuidelines/GetWithTheGuidelines-Stroke/Get-With-The-Guidelines-Stroke-Clinical-Tools_UCM_303743_Article.jsp. Updated March 2, 2013. Accessed October 28, 2014.

30. Stroke Treatments for Professionals. American Stroke Association. Available at http://www.strokeassociation.org/STROKEORG/AboutStroke/Treatment/Stroke-Treatments_UCM_310892_Article.jsp. Updated October 1, 2014. Accessed November 3, 2014.

31. AHA/ASA Presidential Advisory. The American Stroke Association. Available at http://www.heart.org/HEARTORG/HealthcareResearch/FocusonQuality/e-Communications/AHAASA-Presidential-Advisory_UCM_460822_Article.jsp. Updated February 13, 2014. Accessed October 30, 2014.

32. Dalen JE. Aspirin to prevent heart attack and stroke: what's the right dose? *Am J Med*. 2006; 119: 198–202. doi:10.1016/j.amjmed.2005.11.013 http://iranep.org/Articles/ASA%20right%20dose%20AJM%202006.pdf Accessed November 3, 2014.

33. Preventing Aspiration in Older Adults with Dysphagia Assessment Tools. Try This: Best Practices in Nursing Care to Older Adults. Hartford Institute for Geriatric Nursing. Available at http://

consultgerirn.org/uploads/File/trythis/try_this_20.pdf. Revised 2012. Accessed October 28, 2014.

34. #043 Is It Grief or Depression?, 2nd ed. Fast Facts and Concepts. Available at http://www.eperc.mcw.edu/EPERC/FastFactsIndex/ ff_043.htm. Updated April 2009. Accessed October 30, 2014.

35. Mental Status Assessment of Older Adults: The Mini-Cog. Try This: Best Practices in Nursing Care to Older Adults. Hartford Institute for Geriatric Nursing. Available at http://consultgerirn.org/ uploads/File/trythis/try_this_3.pdf Revised 2013. Accessed October 30, 2014.

36. Pharmacological Management of Persistent Pain in Older Persons. American Geriatrics Society Panel on the Pharmacological Management of Persistent Pain in Older Persons. The American Geriatric Society. Available at http://www.americangeriatrics.org/ files/documents/2009_Guideline.pdf. Updated 2014. Accessed October 28, 2014.

37. Assessing Nutrition in Older Adults. Try This: Best Practices in Nursing Care to Older Adults. Hartford Institute for Geriatric Nursing. Available at http://consultgerirn.org/uploads/File/trythis/ try_this_9.pdf. Revised 2012. Accessed October 28, 2014.

38. Check for Safety: A Home Fall Prevention Checklist of Older Adults. CDC Foundation, MetLife Foundation, Department of Health and Human Services Centers for Disease Control and Prevention. Available at http://www.cdc.gov/homeandrecreationalsafety/pubs/ English/booklet_Eng_desktop-a.pdf. Published 2005. Accessed October 30, 2014.

39. Brown EL, Raue R, Halpert KD, Adams S, Titler MG. Evidence-based guideline detection of depression in older adults with dementia. *J Geront Nurs*. 2009; 35(2): 11–5.

40. National Kidney foundation K/DOQI Guidelines. Guideline 1, Goals on Antihypertensive Therapy in Chronic Kidney Disease. Available at http://www2.kidney.org/professionals/KDOQI/ guidelines_bp/guide_1.htm. Updated 2012. Accessed October 30, 2014.

41. Medscape. Uremic Clinical Presentation. Available at http:// emedicine.medscape.com/article/245296-clinical. Updated November 6, 2013. Accessed November 1, 2014.

42. National Kidney Foundation K/DOQI Guidelines. Guideline 12, Use of Diuretics in Chronic Kidney Disease. Available at http://www2. kidney.org/professionals/KDOQI/guidelines_bp/guide_12.htm. Updated 2012. Accessed October 30, 2014.

43. Tattersall J, Dekker F, Heimburger O, et al. When to start dialysis: updated guidance following publication of the Initiating dialysis early and Late (IDEAL) study. *Nephrol Dial Transplant*. 2011; 26(7): 2082–6. doi: 10.1093/ndt/gfr168

44. Hanson LC, Winzelberg G. Research priorities for geriatric palliative care: Goals, values and preferences. *J Palliat Med*. 2013; 16(10): 1175–9.

45. Morrison RS. Research priorities in geriatric palliative care: An introduction to a new series. *J Palliat Med*. 2013; 16(7): 726–8.

46. Center to Advance Palliative Care: Clinical Tools. Available at http://www.capc.org/signup?tool=/clinical-tools/. Accessed July 20, 2014.

47. Hartford Institute for Geriatric Nursing: Try This series. Available at http://consultgerirn.org/. Accessed July 10, 2014.

48. End-of-Life/Palliative Resource Center (EPERC) at the Medical College of Wisconsin: Fast Facts series. Available at http://www. eperc.mcw.edu/EPERC.htm. Accessed July 10, 2014.

The Palliative Advanced Practice Registered Nurse in the Specialty Outpatient Setting

Linda M. Gorman

Key Points

- The palliative advanced practice registered nurse (APRN) in a specialty practice cares for patients with chronic illnesses to manage their symptoms and address goals of care throughout the disease trajectory. This is especially important in the outpatient setting.

- Those with end-stage renal disease (ESRD) have a variety of uncomfortable symptoms that are often underrecognized and undertreated.

- As HIV/AIDS has moved from a terminal to a chronic illness, the APRN in the HIV clinic can address the uncomfortable symptoms that can reduce adherence to treatment.

- Loss of mobility, speech, and potentially cognitive functioning in amyotrophic lateral sclerosis (ALS) demonstrates the need for palliative care involvement for advance care planning earlier in the disease course.

- Breathlessness is one of the most distressing symptoms in chronic nonmalignant lung disease, and the patient needs to be prepared for treatment options earlier in the disease course to ensure that treatment meets the patient's goals.

Introduction

The APRN has a key role in the management of many chronic, progressive illnesses. Palliative care for these patients involves addressing high symptom burdens, functional limitations, and increasing caregiver stress.[1] The palliative APRN in a specialty practice setting is aware of the disease progression and how to prepare the patient for each phase of the illness. This support is needed in the outpatient setting, where long-term management influences quality of life, treatment compliance, and prevention of complications.

This chapter examines four outpatient populations where the palliative APRN can make significant contributions: renal disease, HIV, neurologic disease, and lung disease. Routine early involvement of the palliative APRN can ensure the patient receives this expertise throughout the trajectory, not just at the end-of-life. Palliative APRNs may consult on a range of complex progressive chronic illnesses that have no cure to provide expertise in goals of care and advance care planning and to treat complex symptoms, including ongoing pain.

Palliative care in specialty clinics is expanding, but there are barriers that can contribute to underuse of the services. These include:

- Delayed referrals due to unpredictable disease trajectories in comparison to cancer, resulting in periods of stability with sudden exacerbations

- Specialists' as well as patients' and families' failure to understand the difference between hospice and palliative care, the benefits of early palliative care, and the appropriate time to involve palliative care

- Patients' and families' unrealistic expectations of treatment outcomes, particularly if there are many options that may prolong life, especially with advancing technology

- Lack of knowledge about end-stage disease

- Hesitancy by some clinicians to add other professionals to the patient's ongoing care

Palliative APRNs in a specialty clinic can be introduced at two distinct times: at the point of diagnosis or at the development of specific symptoms or disease progression. The APRN may consult separately or as part of joint visits. Joint visits with palliative care and the specialty team promote better collaboration and improve communication between the professionals and the patient.[2] In addition, joint visits demonstrate support of palliative care as part of the treatment plan. Some chronic disease models are now including palliative care in the rehabilitation outpatient program as well.[3]

The Patient with End-Stage Renal Disease

Case Study

Mr. R was a 79-year-old patient with ESRD along with, as well as diabetes, peripheral vascular disease, and heart failure. Mr. R had been on hemodialysis for 3 years. He adapted to life on dialysis, fitting in social activities around his 3-days-a-week dialysis schedule. He noticed increasing fatigue, irritability, and arthritis pain, but he attributed them to old age. The previous week, one of his longtime dialysis buddies suffered a cardiac arrest during dialysis and died. This unexpected death caused Mr. R to be increasingly withdrawn and quiet during treatment. The palliative APRN who was new to the nephrology practice noticed his change in behavior and asked to speak with him. Mr. R shared that he never before thought about dying prior to witnessing his friend die. Mr. R admitted that he had considered dialysis life-saving and anticipated living many years; dying wasn't something he thought about. The palliative APRN encouraged Mr. R to share his concerns and then asked him to consider his wishes and goals. Over subsequent visits, the patient was able to confirm his wish not to be resuscitated during dialysis. He was also able to describe what symptoms would lead him to consider stopping dialysis.

The U.S. Renal Data System[4] reports that the public health impact of kidney disease has been underappreciated. High mortality rates, a substantial burden of physical, psychosocial, and spiritual symptoms, and the increasing prevalence of decisions to withhold or discontinue dialysis all highlight the care needs of this population. People over 75 years old make up the fastest-growing segment of the end-stage renal disease (ESRD) population, and these patients have a high mortality rate.[5–8]

Disorders of the kidney have an impact on many body systems, and a number of chronic illnesses influence the development of kidney failure. Heart disease and diabetes are the major contributors. Kidney failure leads to uremia, a syndrome characterized by a glomerular filtration rate (GFR) of less than 15 mL/min, and adversely affects every body system. Uremia literally means "urine in the blood." ESRD is a terminal illness when a transplant is not an option.

Management of the high symptom burden in these patients, whether or not they are receiving dialysis, is an important reason for palliative care involvement.[9,10] Another focus is decision making about treatment choices in the face of this very serious diagnosis. Clinicians can use the Renal Physician Association guidelines for shared decision making (Box 16.1) for guidance in planning patient care.[11] These guidelines give detailed information about the burdens and benefits of treatment throughout the disease trajectory.

A unique characteristic of the ESRD population is that much of the treatment occurs in dialysis centers, many of which are not connected to local hospitals and palliative care specialists.[1,12] Moreover, ESRD patients commonly die in the hospital, during a crisis, without any advance care planning.[13] A common scenario is discontinuing dialysis in the intensive care unit after the onset of overwhelming complications.[14]

Palliative care involvement is important for patients discontinuing dialysis as well as those receiving dialysis. Another population in need of palliative care are patients with uremia who may

Box 16.1 Renal Physicians Association Guidelines on Appropriate Initiation and Withdrawal of Dialysis: Recommendation Summary for Adults

1. Develop a physician–patient relationship for shared decision making.

2. Fully inform patients with acute kidney injury (AKI), stage 4 and 5 chronic kidney disease (CKD), and ESRD about their dialysis, prognosis, and all treatment options.

3. Give all patients with AKI, stage 5 CKD, or ESRD an estimate of prognosis specific to their overall condition.

4. Institute advance care planning.

5. If appropriate, forgo (withhold initiating or withdraw ongoing) dialysis for patients with AKI, CKD, or ESRD in certain well-defined situations.

6. Consider forgoing dialysis for AKI, CKD, or ESRD patients who have a very poor prognosis or for whom dialysis cannot be provided safely, as in advanced dementia or unstable hypotension.

7. Consider a time-limited trial of dialysis for patients who require dialysis but who have an uncertain prognosis, or for whom a consensus cannot be reached about providing dialysis.

8. Establish a systematic, due process approach for conflict resolution if there is disagreement about what decision should be made with regard to dialysis.

9. To improve patient-centered outcomes, offer palliative care services and interventions to all AKI, CKD, and ESRD patients who suffer from burdens of their disease.

10. Use a systematic approach to communicate about diagnosis, prognosis, treatment options, and goals of care.

From reference 11 (with permission).

not be dialysis candidates. These patients are generally older, have many comorbidities, are not transplant candidates, and are managed conservatively without dialysis. This is sometimes called non-dialysis medical therapy. Care includes attention to fluid balance, treatment of anemia, and correction of acidosis and hyperkalemia without dialysis.[15] Unlike withdrawal of dialysis in which imminent death is expected, some patients receiving non-dialysis medical therapy can live for months to years with appropriate supportive care.[15] Although dialysis is a life-sustaining therapy, there is evidence that it does not increase life expectancy in elderly patients with severe illness.[16,17] Such patients may have a slower progression of renal disease, so this should also be taken into consideration before rushing to start dialysis.[7]

Symptoms in Patients with Renal Disease

There is a significant symptom burden in ESRD that can have a negative impact on all aspects of life. The symptom burden can be complicated by multiple medication side effects, potential vitamin deficiencies, and intermittent electrolyte imbalances, which are common in uremia and/or its treatment.

Jablonski found an average of 5.67 uncomfortable symptoms reported by patients undergoing dialysis.[18] The most common were fatigue, sleep disorders, cramps, muscle weakness, and joint pain. Patients undergoing conservative management reported significant symptom burden from uremia, with the average number of symptoms varying from 6.8 to 17.[15] Box 16.2 lists common symptoms in uremia.

Uremia itself is painless, but there are many other sources of pain in patients treated with or without dialysis. Pain is often underappreciated and undertreated in this population.[19] Sources of pain include joint pain, cramps, headaches, abdominal pain, and chest pain. Pain may be related to comorbidities, such as peripheral vascular disease, neuropathies, and coronary artery disease, or to treatment side effects or complications, such as osteomyelitis, cramping during dialysis, access device problems, and calciphylaxis (also known as calcific uremic arteriopathy, an extremely painful complication caused by calcium deposits on the skin). Pharmacologic treatment of pain needs to incorporate understanding of how the drugs are metabolized in the presence of impaired renal clearance.[19,20] See Chapter 23, Pain, for further details.

When dialysis is being discontinued at the end-of-life, the most frequent symptoms include pain, delirium, dyspnea, nausea, and itching. The most frequent reasons for discontinuing are failure to thrive, medical complications, and access failures.[21] These factors can have an impact on symptoms as well. Table 16.1 reviews basic principles for symptom management during withdrawal of dialysis. For further discussion, see Chapter 50, Discontinuation of Life-Sustaining Therapies. Discontinuing dialysis requires intensive end-of-life care, as the time to death averages 8 days.[5]

For ESRD patients who are not on dialysis, symptoms of uremia may be similar to those in patients discontinuing dialysis, but they may be less intense. The symptom burden and severity increase in the months prior to death.[15]

Communication

Starting dialysis is a form of life support and needs to be addressed as such. These discussions should be part of the informed consent process for dialysis. They include the burdens, benefits, potential alternatives, and discontinuation options, especially in the very elderly, frail population.[24] See Chapter 39, Advance Care Planning, for further discussion. Hospice care is underused in this population but may be very helpful. The palliative APRN can introduce hospice when patients are considering discontinuing dialysis, receiving conservative treatment, or develop a second terminal illness while receiving dialysis. Barriers to hospice referrals may be due to the short timeframe to death after discontinuation of dialysis and inaccurate knowledge about hospice appropriateness.[25,26] See Chapter 38, Introducing Palliative Care.

Box 16.2 Common Symptoms in Uremia

- Pain
- Shortness of breath
- Nausea/vomiting
- Fatigue
- Itching
- Irritability

Table 16.1 Basic Principles for Discontinuation of Dialysis

- Formulate a treatment plan addressing the reduction of the risk of toxic symptoms in the presence of escalating renal failure.

- Discontinue all nonessential medications to reduce risk for side effects and toxicities (e.g., statins, antibiotics). The rationale is that the more medications the patient takes, the greater likelihood of toxicities.

- Anticipate that administration of fluids in the face of no urine output will promote volume overload. Therefore, discontinue hydration and tube feelings early in the process. There may be cultural and religious situations in which they cannot be discontinued, but amounts may be greatly reduced to 10 mL/hr.

- Wait for renal failure symptoms, such as pain, agitation, and itching, to occur before starting treatment in order to reduce the risk of toxicities from multiple nonessential medications.

- Consult a pharmacist to ensure that medications given are not metabolized via the kidneys.

- Educate patient and family on what to expect from discontinuing dialysis. Address fears, especially fear of "drowning in fluid" without dialysis.

From references 10, 22, 23.

The Patient with Advanced HIV/AIDS

Case Study

Ms. S was a 30-year-old woman with a long history of heroin addiction. Two years ago, she was told she was HIV positive. She adhered to her ART medication regimen. She had not used heroin in over 1 year and was compliant in her methadone program. She recently obtained custody of her 5-year-old child. She struggled with chronic joint pain as well as headache. Ms. S was referred to the palliative APRN in the HIV clinic for symptom management. The patient was guarded and suspicious because she felt her regular doctor "dumped" her to another practitioner. The patient expressed feeling that her regular doctor had given up on her. The palliative APRN took the time to establish a relationship with Ms. S by identifying the current stressors in her life and confirming her goals as well as reinforcing her accomplishments in the prior year. Ms. S agreed to try non-opioid analgesics and make some adjustments in her drug regimen to address her discomforts. In addition, the palliative APRN taught her some alternative treatments for pain, including guided imagery and acupressure.

The impact of HIV on healthcare and palliative care has been substantial. Recent developments in treatments have changed HIV from an eventually terminal illness to a chronic condition. The presence of HIV in the body follows stages from initial exposure to the virus to advanced disease. The presence of HIV in the body initially causes a glandular fever-like illness and the person seroconverts to being HIV positive in 6 to 12 weeks. The clinical latency period can last for many years, especially if the person is taking antiretroviral therapy (ART). When the CD4 count drops below 200/mm,[3] the patient has progressed to AIDS. A badly damaged and weakened immune system is now vulnerable to infections and infection-related cancers called opportunistic illnesses (OIs).[27]

Once a person is HIV positive, the goal is to prevent new infections and progression to AIDS. The patient needs frequent lab monitoring, promotion of prophylaxis strategies, and prevention and treatment of infections. Management of side effects from treatment, reduction of risk factors, and early treatment of infections will promote long-term survival with HIV. Compliance with ART treatment is the most significant predictor of the patient's long-term prognosis by promoting CD4 T-cell recovery.[27] Problems with adherence include treatment complexity, treatment side effects, younger age, presence of mental illness, and lack of support. Comorbidities and complications often seen in this population include anemia, altered body fat distribution, bone disorders like osteoporosis, and hepatitis A, B, and C.

HIV and AIDS continue to be stigmatized in some areas of society, which adds to stress as well as social isolation. The population of HIV-positive patients may include a higher percentage of people with histories of intravenous drug abuse as well as psychiatric disorders, which can create more challenges in promoting safe practices and compliance with treatment.[28,29]

In the early days of HIV/AIDS care, the illness was a terminal condition. Palliative care and hospice provided symptom management and offered compassionate care for the dying.[30] While ART has extended life for people living with HIV/AIDS, it has also increased prognostic uncertainty, posed socioeconomic challenges to patients, and complicated decision making about advance care planning in a younger population faced with many challenges.[31] Incorporating palliative principles into HIV/AIDS overall management can provide support for these challenges. Patients are likely to receive lifelong treatment, so the patient must incorporate this into his or her lifestyle. Active treatment and palliative care need to work together to achieve the patient's goals.[30]

The World Health Organization (WHO)[32] recognizes that palliative care is essential for people living with HIV/AIDS because of the symptom burden and potential suffering. WHO recommends including palliative care in every stage of HIV disease, with or without ART. Simms and colleagues recommend instituting palliative care within 6 months of diagnosis to prevent suffering and reduce the risk of noncompliance.[33]

Symptoms in HIV/AIDS Population

Patients with HIV/AIDS present a spectrum of distressing physical and psychological symptoms that involve every body system. An important goal is to promote adherence with ART, as treatment may contribute to some of the symptoms. Pain in HIV is underreported and undertreated, especially in those with a substance abuse history and/or psychiatric illness.[29] Pain can be complex due to the many comorbidities, treatment side effects, and viral characteristics. There may be multiple types of pain with different etiologies and treatment requirements, with a high incidence of chronic pain. Pain can result from a variety of etiologies, including from the virus itself, causing arthritis, arthralgias, skin conditions, and stomatitis. Neuropathies are a common source of pain due to viral invasion of nervous tissue. Mouth and throat pain can be caused by infections. See Chapter 23, Pain, for further information. In addition to pain, Merlin and associates found a median of eight symptoms in HIV patients.[29] Some of the symptoms may be experienced by patients in any stage of HIV/AIDS. Common symptoms are summarized in Table 16.2.

Psychiatric symptoms of depression, bipolar disorder, substance use disorders, withdrawal symptoms, and co-occurring disorders (substance abuse and another psychiatric disorder) may be preexisting or occur as a response to the stress of the illness.[34]

Communication

Many patients with HIV/AIDS are younger and less prepared for facing serious or potentially terminal illness. Yet, discussion about goals and values needs to be a continuing part of treatment, especially if the disease progresses. Burdens of ongoing

Table 16.2 Common Symptoms Other than Pain in HIV/AIDS

Symptom	Etiology	Characteristics
Fatigue	◆ Anemia, vitamin deficiencies, side effects from medications, diarrhea, cachexia	◆ Contributes to social isolation, poor adherence to treatment
Anemia and weight loss	◆ Viral load ◆ ART side effect ◆ Mouth discomfort from infections ◆ Depression	◆ These symptoms also contribute to fatigue and decreased muscle mass and muscle strength.
Cough	◆ Variety of respiratory infections	◆ Can be acute or chronic as well as productive or nonproductive
Fever	◆ Common as CD4 count declines as well as with any infection	◆ Common initial presenting symptoms ◆ Maintenance of hydration is important. ◆ Contributes to fatigue, malaise
Dyspnea	◆ Respiratory infections ◆ Generalized weakness	◆ Contributes to chronic cough, fatigue
Diarrhea	◆ Side effect of ART ◆ Many OIs	◆ Can lead to incontinence, social isolation, dehydration, fatigue
Skin lesions	◆ Generally caused by a variety of OIs	◆ Many varieties of skin lesions, including fungal infections, herpes zoster

From references 27 and 29.

treatment will need to be weighed against benefits, as well as what fits the patient's lifestyle. Long periods of stable disease can make advance care planning more difficult to suggest, but eventually many patients will have to prepare for advancing disease. See Chapter 39, Advance Care Planning.

The Patient with Amyotrophic Lateral Sclerosis (ALS)

Case Study

Deana Larson was a 50-year-old woman who was diagnosed with ALS 2 years earlier. Since she was having more difficulty ambulating, she maintained her job by working from home. She had recently experienced more difficulty speaking, so she relied more and more on texts and emails to communicate with her office to avoid embarrassment. Over the previous few months, she had increasing difficulty managing her secretions. She regularly communicated electronically with the palliative APRN in the ALS clinic to monitor her symptoms and address her concerns. Through this communication Ms. Larson was able to share her fears of the progressive disease and wanted to consider the burdens and benefits of pursing a PEG. The patient consented to a home visit by the palliative APRN to have an in-depth discussion about the future treatment options.

ALS is the most common degenerative disorder of the motor neuron system in adults.[35] ALS is a progressive neurological disorder characterized by loss of independence and declining ability to communicate.[36] Both the upper and lower motor neurons are involved, leading to eventual wasting and atrophy of all voluntary muscles, including the muscles used for respiration. With loss of voluntary muscle action, there is progressive muscle weakness and paralysis, with a high symptom burden. Initial symptoms are loss of fine motor skills and weakness. As the motor neurons die, the ability of the brain to control muscle movement is lost. Eventually the disease affects the swallowing and respiratory muscles as well as speech. The cause is unknown, there is no cure, and the main treatment is symptomatic. The average life expectancy is 3 to 4 years, though some patients have been known to live much longer—often on mechanical ventilation. The usual cause of death is related to respiratory failure. Life expectancy is influenced by the patient's goals for the degree of aggressive treatment in advanced disease.

Once dysphagia begins, it usually necessitates nutritional support (e.g., percutaneous gastrostomy tube [PEG]), which may actually improve the patient's quality of life as eating may have become exhausting. Noninvasive ventilator support may be needed and progresses to invasive intubation if the patient wishes to pursue this aggressive treatment. Incorporating tools to promote communication and socialization will enhance the patient's quality of life and will allow an ongoing discussion of goals, since loss of ability to speak is common.[37]

Palliative care has been part of the treatment for the ALS patient but has generally been reserved for advanced stages of the disease, specifically when respiratory insufficiency is apparent and end-of-life issues around ventilator support and hospice are being considered.[36,38] The American Academy of Neurology Report of the Quality Measurement and Reporting Subcommittee does not specifically mention palliative care but supports the team approach, with emphasis on good symptom management and advance care planning.[37]

Symptoms in the ALS Population

Assessing the symptom burden in these patients can be challenging due to the patient's impaired communication ability. Pain, a common symptom that is generally due to muscle atrophy and weakness, is often poorly understood and undertreated.[39] Loss of muscle mass, muscle spasms, and spasticity result in postural imbalance and cause pain in muscles and joints as they compensate for more affected areas.[36] Complaints of pulling sensations and "charley horse"-type leg cramps are common.[40] Treatment often begins with antispasmodics rather than analgesics. As the disease progresses, immobility causes pain from skin breakdown and inactivity. Table 16.3 lists other common symptoms in ALS.

Communication

Discussion about the degree of invasive and noninvasive ventilatory support and artificial nutrition is best incorporated early in the care of these patients, particularly because of the risks of altered communication ability. The potential for cognitive decline later in the disease course is another reason to have these discussions early. In the ALS population, treatment decision making is even more complex than in many other life-limiting diseases because aggressive interventions can prolong life significantly.[35] In addition, once the patient is on a ventilator, it is unlikely he or she will be able to be weaned off.[36] Discussion of options for end-of-life care without invasive respiratory support needs to be included in the advance care planning so the patient and family can make informed choices once the disease advances. Ventilator discontinuation can be discussed prior to placement. See Chapter 49, Withdrawal of Respiratory Technology.

The Patient with Nonmalignant Lung Disease

Case Study

Mr. Hawkins was 75 years old when he spent 3 months in the hospital for respiratory failure related to his 30-year history of COPD. He required a ventilator for several weeks. After being weaned off the ventilator and spending several months in a rehabilitation facility, he was discharged home with follow-up by his pulmonary team. The pulmonologist included the palliative APRN in the patient's first visit after hospitalization. The palliative APRN introduced the topic of advance care planning. This patient had never completed an advance directive. He said he was satisfied with the treatment approach he received in the hospital and would want the same approach if this happened again. This information provided the pulmonologist with the opportunity to discuss how future events may have different outcomes, and the patient needs to consider his goals if he cannot be removed from a ventilator in the future. The patient was unable to confirm his wishes at that point but agreed to follow-up visits with the APRN to continue the discussion.

Chronic nonmalignant lung disease encompasses a variety of pathologies, all of which have a high mortality rate and symptom

Table 16.3 Common Symptoms of ALS

Symptom	Etiology	Characteristics
Fatigue/muscle weakness/muscle spasms	◆ Progressive muscle weakness and debility ◆ Depression	◆ Inability to complete ADLs ◆ Social isolation
Dyspnea	◆ Weakened respiratory muscles	◆ Coughing, orthopnea, morning headache, poor sleep
Sialorrhea (excessive salivation/drooling)	◆ Difficult-to-manage secretions due to impaired swallowing mechanisms	◆ Increased risk for aspiration ◆ Coughing, choking sensation ◆ Causes embarrassment and social isolation
Dysphagia	◆ Loss of voluntary muscle control	◆ May have trouble with chewing and swallowing ◆ High risk for aspiration
Emotional lability (also referred to as pseudobulbar affect or involuntary emotion expression disorder)	◆ Upper motor neuron dysfunction ◆ Depression	◆ Excessive/inappropriate crying, laughing ◆ Difficulty being understood due to dysarthria can exaggerate these.
Anxiety/depression	◆ Facing this progressive disease contributes to fears of choking and complete dependence.	◆ Emotions can be challenging to assess due to altered communication and facial expressions.

From references 36 and 40.

burden.[41] These conditions include chronic obstructive pulmonary disease (COPD), interstitial lung disease, such as pulmonary fibrosis, and cystic fibrosis. COPD is by far the most common. These conditions all affect lung function by obstructing or fibrosing lung tissue. Most of these patients will die of their disease. These respiratory diseases are characterized by sudden deterioration from acute infections or other complications. These may require acute hospitalization, often in the intensive care unit, and short-term ventilator care. Appropriate escalation of treatment may be successful earlier in the patient's illness but will become less effective and increasingly burdensome as the disease progresses.[41]

Generally, there is slow decline with each hospitalization. This cycle tends to continue throughout the disease trajectory. The patient may struggle from one crisis to another for many years before sudden deterioration and death over a few days.[42] Many patients with lung disease have to cope with complex and intrusive treatments, which may include multiple drug treatments, nebulized medications, side effects from long-term steroid use, physiotherapy, oxygen therapy, and in some cases noninvasive ventilation and nutritional support.

Despite the high symptom burden and progressive disease, palliative care is available inconsistently for this population, despite studies demonstrating the benefit in patients with advanced chronic respiratory disease.[43-45] The physical and psychosocial needs of patients with chronic nonmalignant lung disease have been compared to those with lung cancer. Actually, compared with patients dying from unresectable, non-small-cell lung cancer, end-stage COPD patients have a significantly worse quality of life.[41,46]

In 2008, the American Thoracic Society established guidelines for the use of palliative care in chronic respiratory disease.[47] Included was the availability of palliative care at any point during the course of a progressive or chronic respiratory disease or critical illness when the patient becomes symptomatic. One study revealed that the introduction of palliative care for COPD patients led to the identification of symptoms that had been unidentified and as well as undertreated prior to the consultation.[45]

Some triggers for palliative care consultation to consider include oxygen dependence, cachexia/weight loss, frequent hospital admissions, and FEV_1 (forced expiratory volume in 1 second) of less than 30% predicted.[48] With chronic respiratory illness, it has been found that a perceived poor quality of life does not necessarily correlate with a clear willingness to refuse invasive or noninvasive mechanical ventilation.[49]

Symptoms in Nonmalignant Lung Disease Populations

Palliative care for respiratory disease is often complex because of the high level of symptoms experienced and the variable and sometimes unpredictable trajectories. In many patients, loss of dignity and self-respect, social isolation, and psychological problems will progress slowly over time, well before advanced disease occurs. Keen assessment skills are necessary because this population has a tendency not to complain about symptoms. Over time, there is an adaptation as well as a belief that the symptoms are normal or that no treatment is available.[50]

Despite medical therapy, most patients with moderate to severe COPD, interstitial lung disease, and cystic fibrosis experience pain, fatigue, and dyspnea, with the majority not getting relief from dyspnea toward the end-of-life.[41] These patients have substantial disability, which often leads to a vicious cycle of breathlessness, reduced physical activities, and deconditioning of muscles, with secondary problems of social isolation, loss of autonomy, depression, and anxiety.

Breathlessness, acute or chronic, is the most frequent symptom and is one of the most frightening. Blinderman and colleagues found that one-third of COPD patients reported significant pain that reduced their quality of life.[51] Treatment often includes opioids with close monitoring. However, some clinicians are reluctant to prescribe opioids to treat pain out of fear that the drugs will worsen ventilation. Table 16.4 lists common symptoms.

Communication

The distressing future probability of respiratory failure may be difficult to address with patients. COPD patients, in particular, may view the illness as a way of life because of the slow decline

Table 16.4 Common Symptoms of Chronic Respiratory Disease

Symptoms	Characteristics
Breathlessness	◆ Most common symptom ◆ May be unrelated to hypoxia ◆ Can be triggered by other symptoms like coughing, inadequate secretion clearance, anxiety ◆ Pulmonary rehabilitation can teach breathing techniques to regain a sense of control over this symptom.
Pain	◆ Often includes chest pain, pain from comorbidities, osteoporosis due to chronic steroid use ◆ Pain can inhibit secretion clearance and increase breathlessness.
Fatigue	◆ Chronic breathlessness is a major contributor. ◆ Fear of breathlessness may inhibit physical activity, which exacerbates fatigue.
Cough	◆ Interferes with sleep, communication
Anxiety/ depression	◆ Chronic breathlessness contributes to many psychosocial symptoms.
Sleep disturbances	◆ Frequent awakening due to coughing, secretion, hypoxia ◆ Causes irritability, increased fatigue, daytime sleepiness

From references 3 and 52.

rather than a progressive, life-limiting illness. Ongoing discussions about this information is critical with each exacerbation. Communication about goals can be challenging when the patient is feeling better and not experiencing distressing symptoms. Yet when symptoms like breathlessness are acute, decisions are often made out of fear rather than based on the patient's goals. Most patients with nonmalignant respiratory disease will eventually be faced with decisions about ventilatory support. If the patient chooses invasive ventilatory support, time limitations and discontinuation should be part of the conversation. See Chapter 49, Withdrawal of Technology—Respiratory.

Conclusion

Palliative care in non-cancer diagnoses is expanding but is challenging due to the unpredictability of disease trajectories. Professionals in these specialties may be less knowledgeable about incorporating palliative care into treatment. Palliative care is in its infancy, with many specialty organizations just developing guidelines. Research is showing that, in patients with the chronic illnesses discussed in this chapter, uncomfortable symptoms are often underrecognized and undertreated. Expertise in addressing chronic pain and other undertreated symptoms and incorporating advance care planning throughout the disease will lead to more recognition of the benefits of involving palliative care. Each of the conditions discussed in this chapter can benefit from the incorporation of palliative care throughout the disease trajectory. The APRN with palliative care expertise is in a position to support and lead specialty practices to include palliative care throughout the disease trajectory, including the outpatient setting. As palliative care becomes more accepted in these specialties, the palliative APRN will continue to find opportunities to bring his or her specialized skills to these diseases.

References

1. Kurella Tamura M, Meier DE. Five policies to promote palliative care for patients with ESRD. *Clin J Am Soc Nephrol.* 2013; 8(10): 1783–90.
2. Linvall C, Hultman TD, Jackson VA. Overcoming the barriers to palliative care referral for patients with advanced heart failure. *J Am Heart Assoc.* 2014; 3: e000742.
3. Janssen DJ, McCormick JR. Palliative care and pulmonary rehabilitation. *Clin Chest Med.* 2014; 35(2): 411–21.
4. U.S. Renal Data System. *2013 Annual Data Report: Atlas of Chronic Kidney Disease and End-Stage Renal Disease in the United States.* Bethesda, MD: National Institutes of Health, National Institute of Diabetes and Digestive and Kidney Diseases; 2013. Available at http://www.usrds.org/adr.aspx.
5. Germain MJ, Cohen LM, Davison SN. Withholding and withdrawal from dialysis: What we know about how our patients die. *Semin Dial.* 2007; 20(3): 195–9.
6. Kurella Tamura M, Covinsky KE, Collins AJ, Chertow GM. Octogenarians and nonagenarians starting dialysis in the United States. *Ann Intern Med.* 2007;146: 177–83.
7. Schmidt RJ. Informing our elders about dialysis: Is an age-attuned approach warranted? *Clin J Am Soc Nephrol.* 2012; 7(1): 185–91.
8. Murtagh FE, Addington-Hall J, Edmonds P, et al. Symptoms in the month before death for stage 5 chronic kidney disease patients managed without dialysis. *J Pain Symptom Manage.* 2010; 40: 342–52.
9. Koncicki HM, Swidler MA. Decision making in elderly patients with advanced kidney disease. *Clin Geriatr Med.* 2013; 29(3): 641–55.
10. Swidler M. Considerations in starting a patient with advanced frailty on dialysis: complex biology meets challenging ethics. *Clin J Am Soc Nephrol.* 2013; 8(8): 1421–8.
11. Renal Physicians Association. Shared decision-making in the appropriate initiation of and withdrawal from dialysis: Clinical practice guidelines. 2nd ed. Rockville, MD; 2010. Available at http://www.renalmd.org/catalogue-item.aspx?id=682.
12. Tong A, Cheung KL, Nair SS, Kurella Tamura M, Craig JC, Winkelmeyer WC. Thematic synthesis of qualitative studies on patient and caregiver perspectives on end-of-life care in CKD. *Am J Kidney Dis.* 2014; 63(6): 913–27.
13. Davison SN. Advance care planning in patients with chronic kidney disease. *Semin Dial.* 2012; 25(6): 657–63.
14. Davison SN. The ethics of end-of-life care for patients with ESRD. *Clin J Am Soc Nephrol.* 2012; 7(12): 2049–57.
15. O'Connor NR, Kumar P. Conservative management of end-stage renal disease without dialysis: A systematic review. *J Palliat Med.* 2012; 15: 228–35.
16. Misra M. Oreopoulos D, Vonesh E. Dialysis or not? A comparative survival study of patients over 75 years of age with chronic kidney disease stage 5. *Nephrol Dial Transplant.* 2008; 23(5): 1768–9.
17. Ishikawa H. Ogihara N, Tsukushi S, Sakamoto J. Withdrawal from dialysis and palliative care for severely ill dialysis patients in terms of patient-centered medicine. *Case Rep Nephrol.* 2013. http://www.hindawi.com/journals/crin/2013/761691/.
18. Jablonski A. Level of symptom relief and the need for palliative care in the hemodialysis population. *J Hosp Palliat Nurs.* 2007; 9: 50–60.
19. Davison SN, Koncicki H, Brennan F. Pain in chronic kidney disease: a scoping review. *Semin Dial,* 2014; 27(2): 188–204.
20. Mid-Atlantic Renal Coalition and the Kidney End-of-Life Coalition. Clinical algorithm and preferred medications to treat pain in dialysis patients. Richmond, VA; 2009. Available at http://www.kidneysupportivecare.org/Files/PainBrochure9-09.aspx.
21. Mailloux L. Initiation, withdrawal and withholding dialysis. In: Chambers E, Brown E, Germain MJ, eds. *Supportive Care of the Renal Patient.* Oxford, England: Oxford University Press; 2010:231–40.
22. Davison SN, Rosielle DA. Clinical care following withdrawal of dialysis. *J Palliat Med.* 2012; 15:1271–2.

23. Gorman LM. *Compendium of Treatment of End-Stage Non-cancer Diagnoses: Renal.* 2nd ed. Pittsburgh, PA: Hospice and Palliative Nurses Association; 2011.

24. Akbar S, Moss AH. The ethics of offering dialysis for AKI to the older patient: Time to re-evaluate? *Clin J Am Soc Nephrol.* 2014. http://cjasn.asnjournals.org/content/early/2014/05/07/CJN.01630214. abstract.

25. Cohen LM, Ruthazer R, Germain MJ. Increasing hospice services for elderly patients maintained with hemodialysis. *J Palliat Med.* 2010; 13: 847–54.

26. Germain MJ, Davison SN, Moss AH. When enough is enough: the nephrologist's responsibility in ordering dialysis treatments. *Am J Kidney Dis,* 2011; 58: 135–43.

27. Woodruff R, Cameron D. HIV/AIDS in adults. In: Hanks G, Cherny NI, Christakis NA, Fallon M, Kassa S, Portenoy RK, eds. *Oxford Textbook of Palliative Medicine.* 4th ed. Oxford, England: Oxford University Press, 2010: Section 12.2.

28. Tsao JC, Soto T. Pain in persons living with HIV and comorbid psychologic and substance use disorders. *Clin J Pain,* 2009; 25(12): 307–12.

29. Merlin JS, Cen L, Praestgaard A, et al. Pain and physical and psychological symptoms in ambulatory HIV patients in the current treatment era. *J Pain Symptom Manage.* 2012; 43(3): 638–45.

30. Sherman DW, Kirton CA. Patients with acquired immunodeficiency syndrome. In: Ferrel BR, Coyle N, eds. *Oxford Textbook of Palliative Nursing.* 3rd ed. New York, NY: Oxford University Press; 2010:767–815.

31. Selwyn PA, Rivard M, Kappel D, et al. Palliative care for AIDS at a large urban teaching hospital: program description and preliminary outcomes. *J Palliat Med.* 2003; 6(3): 461–74.

32. World Health Organization. Palliative care. Available at. www.who. int/hiv/topics/palliative/PalliativeCare/en.

33. Simms V, Higginson IJ, Harding R. What palliative care-related problems do patients experience at HIV diagnosis? A systematic review of the evidence. *J Pain Symptom Manage.* 2011; 42(5): 734–53.

34. Perry BA, Westfall AO, Molony E, et al. Characteristics of an ambulatory palliative care clinic for HIV-infected patients. *J Palliat Med.* 2013; 16(8): 934–7.

35. Borasio GD, Lorenzi S, Rogers A, Voltz R. Palliative care in non-malignant neurological disorders. In: Hanks G, Cherny NI, Christakis NA, Fallon M, Kassa S, Portenoy RK, eds. *Oxford Textbook of Palliative Medicine.* 4th ed. Oxford, England: Oxford University Press; 2010: Section 12.5.

36. Blackhall LJ. Amyotrophic lateral sclerosis and palliative care: where we are, and the road ahead. *Muscle Nerve.* 2012; 45(3): 311–8.

37. Miller RG, Brooks BR, Swain-Eng RC, et al. Quality improvement in neurology: amyotrophic lateral sclerosis quality measures. Report of the Quality Measurement and Reporting Subcommittee of the American Academy of Neurology. *Amyotroph Lateral Scler Frontotemporal Degener.* 2014; 15(3-4): 165–8.

38. Corr B, Frost E, Markey F. Access to palliative care services by Irish ALS patients. *Amyotroph Lateral Scler.* 2003; 4: 219–20.

39. Bebe P, Oliver D, Stodart J, et al. Palliative care in amyotrophic lateral sclerosis: a review of current international guidelines and initiatives. *J Neurol Neurosurg Psychiatry.* 2011; 82(4): 413–8.

40. Houseman G. Symptom management of the patient with amyotrophic lateral sclerosis—A guide for hospice nurses. *J Hosp Palliat Nurs.* 2008: 10(4): 207–13.

41. Boland J, Martin J, Wells AU, Ross JR. Palliative care for people with non-malignant lung disease: Summary of current evidence and future direction. *Palliat Med.* 2013; 27(9): 811–6.

42. Leach RM. Palliative care in non-malignant, end stage respiratory disease. In: Hanks G, Cherny NI, Christakis NA, Fallon M, Kassa S, Portenoy RK, eds. *Oxford Textbook of Palliative Medicine.* 4th ed. Oxford, England: Oxford University Press; 2010: Section 12.3.

43. Batzlaff CM, Karpman C, Afessa B, Benzo RP. Predicting 1-year mortality rate for patients admitted with an acute exacerbation of chronic obstructive pulmonary disease to an intensive care unit: an opportunity for palliative care. *Mayo Clin Proc.* 2014; 89(5): 638–43.

44. Moens K, Higginson IJ, Harding R. Are there differences in the prevalence of palliative care-related problems in people living with advanced cancer and eight non-cancer conditions? A systematic review. *J Pain Symptom Manage.* 2014: May. http://www. sciencedirect.com/science/article/pii/S0885392414000773.

45. Schroedl C, Yount S, Szmuilowicz E, Rosenberg SR, Kalhan R. Outpatient palliative care for chronic obstructive pulmonary disease: A case series. *J Palliat Med.* 2014:June. http://www.ncbi.nlm. nih.gov/pubmed/24933590.

46. Gore JM, Brophy J, Greenstone MA. How well do we care for patients with end-stage chronic obstructive pulmonary disease (COPD)? A comparison of palliative care and quality of life in COPD and lung cancer. *Thorax.* 2000; 55: 1000–6.

47. Lanken PN, Terry PB, Delisser HM, et al. An official American Thoracic Society clinical policy statement: palliative care for patients with respiratory diseases and critical illnesses. *Am J Respir Crit Care Med.* 2008; 177(8): 912–27.

48. Patel K, Janssen DJ, Curtis JR. Advance care planning in COPD. *Respirology.* 2012; 17(1): 72–8.

49. Carlucci A, Guerrieri A, Nava S. Palliative care in COPD patients: Is it only an end-of-life issue? *Eur Respir Rev.* 2012; 21(126): 347–54.

50. Habraken JM, Pols J, Bindels PJ, Willems DL. The silence of patients with end-stage COPD: a qualitative study. *Br J Gen Pract.* 2008; 58(557): 488–9.

51. Blinderman CD, Homel P, Billings JA, Tennstedt S, Portenoy RK. Symptom distress and quality of life in patients with advanced chronic obstructive pulmonary disease. *J Pain Symptom Manage,* 2009; 38(1): 115–23.

52. Bourke SJ, Peel ET. Palliative care of respiratory diseases. In: Bourke SJ, Peel ET, eds. *Integrated Palliative Care of Respiratory Disease.* New York, NY: Springer, 2013:3–15.

The Palliative Advanced Practice Registered Nurse in the Community

CHAPTER 17

The Palliative Advanced Practice Registered Nurse Within a Hospice Organization

Rikki N. Hooper

Key Points

◆ Advanced practice registered nurses (APRNs) in hospice organizations are in an ideal position to extend palliative care in the community, achieving improved symptom management, communication, collaboration, decreased use of hospital services at the end-of-life, and earlier hospice transitions.

◆ Palliative APRNs within a hospice organization have multiple roles in following patients through their disease course to the end of their life.

◆ APRN encounters are reimbursable services across settings and services through Medicare, private insurance, and Medicaid programs.

Case Study 1

Larry, a 53-year-old man, had rarely used the medical system until shortly after his 50th birthday, when he collapsed at work one day, having complained to his co-workers that he thought he had a stomach virus. His workup, however, revealed a myocardial infarction (MI). Over the subsequent week Larry was also diagnosed with diabetes mellitus (DM). He had two further MIs, culminating in cardiac arrest from ventricular fibrillation and subsequent in-hospital resuscitation. He underwent emergent cardiac surgery to bypass seven vessels. These events left him with ischemic cardiomyopathy and a left ventricular ejection fraction (LVEF) of 35%. He returned to work after discharge but his fatigue became progressively worse. He began to complain of pain in his feet and edema of his lower legs, impeding his ability to work. Within 6 months, he could not work because of frequent hospital admissions and profound fatigue. He was found to be anemic. Four months later, the etiology of his anemia was revealed: bleeding from arteriovenous malformations in his small bowel. This required surgical repair, during which he was transferred between three different hospitals. He received a total of 56 units of packed red blood cells and developed acute renal failure, for which hemodialysis was initiated. Upon discharge, he received home health services and received hemodialysis three times weekly.

One month later, he was readmitted for repair of a fractured right hip after falling at home. After surgery, he developed decubitus ulcers on both his heels, which became progressively worse after he was discharged to a skilled nursing facility (SNF). On his second readmission to the hospital for sepsis, he was referred to the palliative care team for help with pain management and establishing goals of care. He was discharged home to the care of his family, having decided that he did not want to return to the SNF. The community palliative CNS was asked to see Larry at home for ongoing symptom management and discussions regarding his goals of treatment. Her initial visit with the patient, his wife, and his sister-in-law, a disabled medical assistant, revealed the following additional information.

Social History: Married to Jeannie, 26 years his junior, from the Philippines (a "mail-order bride," per the patient). No children. He is the fourth child of six siblings, all of whom live locally, but not all are amicable with each other. Previously worked as a diesel truck mechanic for a local construction company for 28 years. Previously enjoyed gardening and woodworking.

Advance Care Planning: Healthcare power of attorney designating wife as primary surrogate decision maker, his sister Gail and sister-in-law Jane as secondary proxies. Living will indicating a desire for no prolongation of life with artificial feeding and hydration, nor resuscitation should he have a terminal or incurable condition. Currently Full Code.

Spiritual History: Raised within the Southern Baptist faith, but over the years has professed atheism to his family, who are strong believers, causing them some distress. He is noncommittal when asked about its importance to him currently.

Symptoms:

Pain: (a) Bilateral pain in lower legs, burning into the feet, constant, worse with walking, 8/10 currently, 6/10 at best with current medications. (b) Right upper leg aching, with occasional sharp pain along incision site, 5/10 most of the time. (c) Pain across sacrum/buttocks, numbness and burning at times, 6/10 currently, 2/10 at best when off his back for more than an hour. (d) Left wrist/hand related to an IV catheter left in for an extended period of time causing nerve damage.

Constipation: irregular BMs, described as "hard, difficult to push."

Nausea: associated with dialysis (currently six times weekly), feels unable to eat at these times, and gets a bad taste in his mouth.

Fatigue: feels tired all the time, no energy to do anything, doesn't feel any better even if he gets a decent night's sleep.

Insomnia: sleeps only a couple of hours at a time, then has to change position, awoken by pain.

Functional Status: PPS (Palliative Performance Scale) 40%, spends 80% of his time in bed, has a hospital bed in living room. Requires assistance with personal care, putting on clothes, changing position in bed, standing, walking or using his wheelchair. Able to feed himself; wife prepares meals for him.

Community Services: Home health agency providing RN weekly for wound care, nursing assistant providing personal care services three times weekly, and physical therapy twice weekly.

Equipment: Hospital bed with air mattress, Hoyer® lift, bedside commode, walker, motorized chair, wheelchair, oxygen concentrator and portable tanks, and home dialysis machine.

Medications: Fentanyl topical patch 25 mcg/hr q72h; oxycodone/acetaminophen 5/325 mg q4h PRN pain (using 6 doses daily); carvedilol 3.125 mg daily; ferrous sulfate 325 mg daily; furosemide 160 mg BID; metolazone 2.5 mg daily 30 min prior to furosemide; spironolactone 25 mg BID; pantoprazole 40 mg daily; aspirin 81 mg daily; ascorbic acid 1 g daily; potassium chloride 10 mEq three times daily; guaifenesin 600 mg BID, isosorbide mononitrate ER 60 mg daily; nitroglycerin 0.4-mg tabs PRN for chest pain; Humulin U500® 44 units three times daily and per sliding scale before meals and at bedtime; Levimir® 90 units BID.

Allergies: Meperidine (causes renal failure), metoprolol (causes swelling), statin medications (cause myalgias).

Physical Exam: Vital signs: BP 115/54, HR 102 bpm, RR 19/min, O_2 sat 97% on 2 L/min of oxygen. GEN: No distress. PULM: B clear, diminish at bases, no crackles, wheezes or rubs were present. CARD: S_1S_2 heard with no murmurs or rubs noted. GI: Obese, soft and non-tender to palpation with hypoactive bowel sounds. EXT: Without cyanosis or clubbing, edema noted in both lower extremities, +1 on L, +2 on R, both feet were wrapped in gauze bandages. Stage 3 decubitus ulcers on both heels, R worse than L. NEURO: A & O×3. Accurate historian with family assistance. Decision-making capacity intact.

This examination was consistent with the hospital discharge summary. This comprehensive assessment allowed the NP to develop an initial relationship with the patient and family, demonstrating a genuine desire to help with his symptoms and improve his quality of life by assessing the whole person. Moreover, it promoted a patient-centered process for collaborative decision making and the mutual establishment of a treatment plan.

Pain: Increase fentanyl dose to 50 mcg/hr to provide longer-acting analgesia effect. Switch breakthrough medication from oxycodone/acetaminophen to hydromorphone, as this had been more effective in the hospital. Start dose at 2 mg q2h as needed to evaluate the effect. Initiate a trial of baclofen at 5 mg three times daily for muscle spasms in both his legs and left arm, with careful monitoring due to renal impairment.

Constipation: Trial of prunes or prune juice while monitoring blood glucose levels. Added sennosides 1 tab daily. Patient and family education about opioid medications often causing constipation, coupled with his decreased mobility and the need for monitoring.

Nausea: Acknowledged this as side effect of constipation, but since it was generally associated with hemodialysis, trial of prochlorperazine 10 mg q6h as needed to be taken prior to starting hemodialysis prophylactically.

Fatigue: Review potential medications as well as risks and benefits. Decision made to hold on medication until evaluation of the management of other symptoms.

Insomnia: Probable etiology is pain. However, trial of trazodone 25 mg at bedtime, to help sleep and mood.

They further discussed collaboration with the home health nurse regarding his plan of care, including wound treatments and glucose control. In her role as a consultant, the CNS explained that she would not replace his cardiology, nephrology, endocrinology, and internal medicine specialty providers but instead would be collaborating with them. She suggested that she visit again in a week or two to review the effects of their interventions, gave instructions regarding how to contact her should other issues arise in the meantime, and explained that they would be working together as a team to improve Larry's quality of life. The CNS encouraged Larry to think about what would improve this most before her next visit. In this encounter, the CNS acted in the role of both educator and consultant, becoming a case manager in many ways.

Over the subsequent 8 weeks, the CNS worked diligently to address Larry's symptoms, achieving control of his nausea with prochlorperazine every morning before dialysis and once during dialysis. His overall pain control improved dramatically (reduced from 8/10 to 4/10) using a combination of fentanyl 100 mcg/hr patch, baclofen 10 mg three times daily, and hydromorphone 4 mg q2h as needed. He used between two and four doses daily depending on whether he had physical therapy or underwent hemodialysis. He reported improved consecutive hours of sleep using his analgesia medications and trazodone 50 mg at bedtime. His bowels were regular with sennosides 3 tablets every night. His quality of life was improved through the use of a wheelchair so he could "supervise" and watch family members work in his vegetable garden.

After 2.5 months, the CNS received a phone call from Larry's family stating that Larry had experienced an episode where he became quite unresponsive, pale, and diaphoretic. It lasted about 3 minutes and Larry was refusing to let them call an ambulance. He stated that he wanted to stay in his home despite their overt requests to get him to the hospital. They asked for a visit that day and the CNS was able to rearrange her schedule to do so. Family members met her in the driveway, expressing their concern that he might be dying and that his spiritual salvation was heavy on their minds. She suggested meeting with Larry alone, which they agreed was a good plan. The CNS asked Larry about the symptoms he had experienced. He stated he felt nauseated without chest pain but that the feelings were "just like the first heart attack." He expressed feeling a sense of "slipping away" but that he wasn't ready to go yet. The CNS explored these statements further from a spiritual perspective and asked Larry about his reluctance to go back to the hospital. He expressed his desire to stay at home and avoid dying in the hospital, particularly since he had spent many months of the past 3 years there. He preferred the quality of his life at home to that in the hospital, even if more interventions might prolong his life. When the CNS asked Larry about the option of hospice care at home, he said he didn't want to have more people coming into his house. He felt comfortable with the current team, as he trusted them and was not ready to stop dialysis. They agreed to see how things went over the next few days.

The CNS shared Larry's wishes with the family. To allay their fears regarding his spiritual faith, she had offered to have a chaplain visit, but he declined. She further explained his tenuous situation and his clear desire to stay at home and forgo resuscitation. The CNS signed and left an out-of-facility Do Not Resuscitate order. A plan was instituted to keep Larry at home. She educated the family on the use of nitroglycerin for chest pain and increased the frequency of his hydromorphone to every hour as needed. She encouraged the family to call if Larry experienced further symptoms or distress. Following the visit, the CNS communicated with staff at the nephrology and cardiology offices and with the home health nurse. Over the next few days, Larry's condition waxed and waned. He was able to meet with all his brothers and sisters, nieces and nephews, passing on personal messages. He was able to get outside to the garden with help from family members. He did experience some hypotension and associated diaphoresis during hemodialysis. The dialysis nurse suggested a hospital admission and he refused. The CNS frequently communicated with family members until Larry died 1 week later at home, as was his wish.

Case Study 2

John's diagnosis of stage IV non-small-cell lung cancer came as a surprise to him at the age of 73. Despite having smoked a pack a day for 20 years, he hadn't smoked in 30 years when his diagnosis was made. He had developed an unrelenting cough for several weeks, although he was otherwise healthy. A biopsy of the left lower lobe mass revealed that the non-small-cell type was sarcomatoid, a relatively rare form of malignancy, accounting for only 1.3% of non-small-cell cancers. Pleural studding was noted, as were several small pericardial masses; pleural fluid from a small pleural effusion was positive; and lymphadenopathy was noted in the hilar nodes. His daughter and son, Jamie and Tony, supported his decision to pursue chemotherapy and radiation therapy with the goal of shrinking the tumors in the pleural space. However, they were concerned about the toll it could take on him. Their mother, his first wife, had died from a malignant brain tumor when they were teenagers. Jamie and Tony had observed how their mother become progressively weaker through treatments and suffered from many symptoms, including pain and nausea.

John embarked on his palliative treatment course, requiring hospitalization for profound dehydration secondary to chemotherapy-induced vomiting and diarrhea after only two treatments. During that admission, he was referred to a member of the palliative care team. However, he was transferred to an SNF the same day, so care was transferred to the facility APRN. She met with the patient and his wife, Maria, to discuss his care. They reviewed his nutritional state, his function, and his goals for medical treatment. She determined that John had an advance directive, completed prior to his current marriage, designating his daughter Jamie as his surrogate decision maker for healthcare and his son Tony as the alternate. He confirmed that this was unchanged. John reiterated that he did not want his life prolonged by artificial means if/when his condition was determined to be terminal. He also acknowledged knowing that his cancer treatment was palliative in nature. He did not want to change his code status, however, citing the fact that his wife wanted him to remain a full code. Maria told the CNS that she believed a miracle would occur and that John's cancer would be cured. She explained that she and her family in Latin America were praying for this miracle, and forgoing resuscitation would not allow this to occur.

John was in pain; he complained of discomfort around his thorax and his low back in addition to generalized joint discomfort in his knees and hips with ambulating. He described the pain as aching mostly, with occasional sharper moments. The CNS prescribed oxycodone 5 mg q4h as needed to begin with and planned to evaluate its effectiveness within the week. Adequate analgesia was necessary so that John's physical therapy could be maximized to achieve his goal of being strong enough to go home. His functional status had declined during his extended episodes of dehydration and compromised nutritional intake. He was weak and unable to walk unassisted even a few steps. He required help with bathing and dressing. He and his wife were hopeful that therapy would help him gain strength, enabling him to go home and eventually be able to receive more chemotherapy.

John's symptoms subsided and he regained enough strength to return home after 3 weeks. His chemotherapy regimen was adjusted to minimize side effects, and he was able to complete his radiation treatment course. The CNS had offered to have the palliative care team follow him at the outpatient clinic but he and his wife declined, stating they felt able to deal with things.

Two months passed until a referral for hospice care was received for John. His oncologist had suspended further chemotherapy due to John's weakness and inability to tolerate further treatments. The hospice admissions nurse met with John, Maria, and Jamie to discuss services. Since they wanted to return to the hospital for aggressive interventions and continue IV fluids at home, it was agreed that their goals of medical care were not consistent with the hospice philosophy. They agreed to have the palliative NP see them at home because John was too weak to travel to the outpatient clinic.

At her first visit, the NP met with Maria and Jamie first, per their request, prior to seeing John. She reviewed their understanding of his medical condition and their goals of medical care. Maria appeared defensive, immediately saying they were not "giving up," despite being told by the oncologist that John had just a few weeks to live. The NP acknowledged Maria's hopes for a miracle to occur and encouraged her to continue her prayers for John's suffering to be relieved. Maria agreed that her husband was suffering: his pain was not well managed and he was weak and tired, sleeping a good portion of the day. Moreover, he was not eating or drinking much, taking in only minimal amounts despite Maria's attempts to give him small pieces of fruit and soft foods, such as scrambled egg, with Ensure® a couple of times daily. Jamie shared that John was having a lot of pain in his lower chest. She explained that her father had not reacted well to opioid analgesics, experiencing many side effects, though she wasn't sure what they were.

While Maria left to attend to John, Jamie told the NP that there was tension in the family situation. She and her brother Tony felt that her father needed to focus on comfort at this point and have hospice care. However, their stepmother didn't agree and wanted him to continue aggressive treatments. Maria's goals were to get him stronger so that he could have more chemotherapy to live longer. John acquiesced to his wife's wishes, Jamie said, adding that her brother was really quite angry at the situation. The NP confirmed that Jamie was indeed the healthcare power of attorney. Jamie stated that while she was trying hard to "keep the peace" in the family, she was prepared to override her stepmother's wishes if necessary. She also relayed that John's living will did indeed state that he would not want life-prolonging measures taken if it became apparent that his condition were irreversible. They discussed talking about this further with John at a later visit.

During her visit with John, the NP noted tenderness to touch at the costal margin on the left side of his chest. He denied shortness of breath but admitted that his pain was "pretty bad," although he was unable to rate it. He confirmed his profound fatigue and lack of appetite, citing the fact that "nothing tastes good" as his main reason for not eating. He stated his bowels were irregular, with movements occurring only every 3 or 4 days.

Understanding that symptom management would build trust in her relationship with John and his wife, the NP explained her desire to first address his distressing physical symptoms. They discussed Maria's desire to avoid opioid analgesics and agreed on a plan of giving routine acetaminophen as a first step. The NP prescribed acetaminophen 500 mg four times daily. They also agreed that Maria could use a heating pad for short periods of time and adjust his position to make him more comfortable. The NP explained her concern that acetaminophen may not be strong enough to treat John's pain, but since John was willing to try it, she agreed. They discussed a schedule of offering John small amounts of food every few hours and of his drinking small amounts of more fluids. Maria agreed that the NP could return the following week for reevaluation. Again, however, the couple stated they were not interested in hospice. Prior to leaving, the NP reiterated her consultant role in John's care. Unlike the hospice program, palliative care did not have the ability to respond personally in an emergency as a general rule, but there would be provider availability by phone.

The NP was able to comprehensively assess the situation holistically as the palliative care consultant. Her assessment determined that there were cultural differences because Maria was from a Latin American country. In addition, spiritual discord was present: John's family had a Christian faith and Maria had a Catholic belief system. Further, there were social issues: Tony especially resented Maria, who was much younger even than him and his sister, and the way he felt that she provided care for his father. The NP initiated treatment for symptoms following her clinical evaluation. She acted as an educator, explaining the rationale behind effective treatment of symptoms, while acknowledging the cultural backgrounds of both the patient and family members. She practiced collaboration with the referring provider by calling the oncologist to talk with him and gain a clear understanding of the medical picture and potential treatment options. She further communicated with the home health nurse, who stated that home health services would cease that week.

Over the subsequent 3 weeks, the NP worked with Maria and John on symptom management interventions. John also spent 2 days in the hospital receiving a blood transfusion and was discharged on total parenteral nutrition (TPN) at the suggestion of a home health nurse with a different agency. His pain worsened and the NP was asked to return to meet with the whole family. Friction was clearly present between Tony and Maria. The NP addressed questions specifically to John as much as possible. He agreed that his pain was bad and that he needed stronger pain medicines. Maria again shared her concern that stronger pain medicine would make him sleep more and decrease the amount of food and drink he could take in. The NP stressed the importance of managing pain to improve his breathing, energy levels,

and rest. She taught them that higher levels of pain often cause increased fatigue and more sleep. She advocated for John's desire to treat the pain, even if it meant he slept more, while respecting the cultural aspect of Maria's need to feed John. Maria agreed to try hydrocodone/acetaminophen 5/325 mg, which John had taken previously, at a half tab three times a day routinely and q4h as needed.

With all family members present, the NP asked John specifically about his goals of care in light of his advanced disease, and whether he would want attempts at resuscitation to be made. He looked to Maria for answers, but the NP stressed needing to know what his feelings and desires were. John was able to say that he did not feel that he would be able to take more chemotherapy treatments. He further declared that while he knew his life expectancy was short, he wanted to live as long as he could with as much quality as possible. They agreed to continue this conversation over the coming weeks. After the meeting, Tony shared his concern that Maria would not give his father the analgesia as prescribed if it made him sleepier. The NP assured him that she would maintain ongoing discussions with Maria in order to advocate for his father's wishes.

The following week John was a little more comfortable but he experienced more nausea, particularly when he took the liquid hydrocodone/acetaminophen. Maria remembered that John's primary care provider, a physician assistant, had at one time said that he was allergic to codeine. Maria asked if there was something that wasn't a narcotic medication, so they agreed to try naproxen 200 mg q8h routinely, though the NP again stressed her concern that this would not be strong enough to treat John's pain. She answered Maria's questions about natural interventions for nausea and pain and agreed that trying ginger tea might help with nausea. Maria expressed her gratitude that the NP was respecting her wishes and desires for her husband. She acknowledged that she was still hoping for a miracle but admitted that she had not seen any improvement in John's condition with the current interventions. She also shared that he had said that he did not want to take any more chemotherapy, and she agreed that it would not contribute to his quality of life now. The NP acknowledged the meticulous care she was providing to her husband. She suggested that they were getting close to the point where they could use more help at home. Maria said she would think about this before their next visit.

The following week, John complained of increased pain, now in both sides of his chest, and his back. He stated that he was "done playing around with medicine." He wanted to be comfortable and didn't care what that took. The NP explained to Maria that it seemed like it was time to involve the hospice team, and she agreed. Maria asked if the NP could continue to see him, as she felt comfortable with her care. John was admitted to the hospice program that afternoon, with the NP serving as his attending of record.

The NP collaborated with the RN case manager, social worker, and chaplain, explaining the family situation from all aspects—physical, psychosocial, and spiritual. She demonstrated leadership of the team, collaborating with her physician colleague regarding the certification for hospice care. Over the following 3 weeks, the NP directed John's care at home, discontinuing the TPN and reinstating IV fluids every other day, since Maria was very concerned about him being thirsty. As the team continued educating Maria, she was able to see that the fluids were not contributing to John's quality of life and agreed to stop them in the second week of service. John became less responsive during that week. He was able to talk with his children and his wife, requesting that they all try to get along for his sake. They agreed to do this and were able to come together with the help of the hospice team social worker. The chaplain worked closely with Maria and her spiritual distress over the lack of the miracle she prayed for. He encouraged her to continue to pray for healing, and to consider the possibility that the miracle of healing would appear in a different way, through a peaceful death. A few days later John died peacefully at home, with his wife by his side and the hospice RN present.

Palliation of distressing symptoms at the end-of-life through hospice care has been available to people with terminal illnesses in the United States since the early 1970s, after interest was sparked during a 1963 visit by Dame Cicely Saunders from England. However, it did not become reimbursable until 1982, so it was initially organized and provided by volunteers, mostly nurses. The number of people accessing these services has increased over the past 30 years, with more than 1.2 million people being served in 2005,[1] 1.46 million in 2011, and 1.56 million by 2012. Between 2001 and 2007, the number of Medicare decedents receiving hospice care increased from 18.8% to 30.1%, and by 2011 it had grown to 44.6%.[2] While it is encouraging to see this growth in the number of people accessing hospice services at the end-of-life, it is still being provided for only a short period of time.[3,4]

The traditional benefit structure supported by Medicare is limiting for patients desiring treatments or interventions deemed to be aggressive or "curative" in nature, even when they clearly are referred to as palliative (e.g., palliative chemotherapy). With the median length of stay decreasing from 19.7 to 18.7 days between 2010 and 2012,[3] it is clear that there is still work to do in determining how to provide the best care at the end-of-life. In March 2014 it was announced that the Centers for Medicare and Medicaid Services (CMS) would begin testing the concurrent provision of curative therapies and hospice service,[4] giving some indication that this is being recognized. With increased focus on acute healthcare utilization, particularly in the last year of life, it has been shown that hospice admission has a significant impact on hospital admission and readmission rates for patients with serious illness, generally a population with higher rates.[5]

Unfortunately, the majority of palliative care teams began, and still exist, in the hospital setting; 63% of hospitals with more than 50 beds have a palliative care program, the availability having more than doubled over the last decade.[6] However, smaller hospitals often do not have the resources to be able to provide their own palliative care team. Thus, local hospice organizations have an opportunity to provide specialty consultation services within the hospital. When combining this with a community-based palliative care program, they can achieve increased and improved continuity of care,[7] enhancing communication across the continuum of care. Ongoing symptom management is possible, and earlier involvement in the disease trajectory allows relationships to be built before a crisis occurs.[8]

As healthcare has advanced, it has become abundantly clear that Americans are living longer, and as the average lifespan has increased so has the number of people suffering from chronic progressive diseases. They often have multiple conditions and are requiring longer and more sustained care.[3] This slow, progressive disease trajectory places burdens on families and presents challenges for the healthcare system. It is predicted that, on average, the debilitating progression will last between 2 and 3 years, depending on gender, before death occurs.[9] The Center to Advance Palliative Care report, *Improving Palliative Care in Nursing Homes*, states that 70% of Americans said that they would prefer to die in their own home—yet only 25% actually do, with 50% of all deaths occurring in the hospital.[1] The remaining 25% of deaths happen in nursing homes or skilled nursing facilities (SNFs), though this is projected to increase to over 40% by the year 2030.[9] By comparison, of patients enrolled in hospice programs, 70% died at their place of residence: 42% in their own home, 22.8% in SNFs, and 5.5% in other residential facilities. Other patients died in a hospice inpatient unit or at an acute care facility.[1] Clearly, hospice providers are making patients' goals to die in their place of residence a reality more of the time. It makes sense that hospice organizations take on a more active role in improving care for the dying in other settings[10] and for providing care earlier in the disease trajectory.

Palliative care is not restricted to purely end-of-life care, as are hospice programs. It is appropriate and relevant for these patients regardless of their prognosis, when the disease is not curable or may involve years of suffering before death occurs.[3,9] This patient population tends to use hospital systems more during their last years of life, bouncing back and forth with exacerbations of their chronic conditions, often with no specific follow-up plan upon discharge. It is not surprising, then, that one in five patients receiving Medicare is readmitted within 30 days of hospital discharge, half of them before they have seen any outpatient provider.[11]

However, other factors can have a significant impact on care, such as the proximity of relatives.[12] Informal caregivers may not be able to take time away from work to care for family members as frequently as necessary. In fact, the number of informal caregivers overall is decreasing,[13] with changing demographics and all available adults needing to be employed. As family caregivers feel pulled in many different directions, and their stress levels rise, the caregiving reduces their quality of life and emotional well-being, increasing the risk that the patient will be admitted to the hospital.[14] Caring for families can be combined with caring for patients, and just as nurses can lead the interdisciplinary team within the hospice program, they can do so within palliative care.[14] Providing community-based palliative care services offers many benefits, not only to the patient and family but also to the hospice organization, referring providers, and the community as a whole.

Pain, dyspnea, anxiety, and depression are all common symptoms experienced by patients with life-limiting illness.[10] Often these symptoms take people to the hospital, but patients can potentially have symptoms managed well, avoiding hospital admissions and remaining safe and cared for in their place of residence (home, SNF, or other residential care setting).[8] This leads to improved patient and family satisfaction and decreased costs overall, with fewer unnecessary tests being performed,[10] fewer days in the hospital, and less time away from work for patients or family members.

Use of Advanced Practice Registered Nurses in Hospice-Based Palliative Care

A well-organized, consistent approach that is comprehensive and proactive in providing intensive symptom management is necessary.[15] Advanced practice registered nurses, usually clinical nurse specialists (CNSs) or nurse practitioners (NPs), are in a unique position to care for this patient population, although there may be a role for certified nurse midwives in perinatal palliative care programs. Using the nursing process, they can address the complex issues of the seriously ill patient by synthesizing complex data to develop and implement patient-centered care plans.[16] APRNs combine palliative nursing's focus on the whole person[17] and their advanced education to perform comprehensive physical evaluations and order and interpret diagnostic tests, in addition to prescribing medications, depending on the specific state's advanced practice nurse certifying regulations.[9,16,18,19] The APRN acts as a case manager, involves other members of the interdisciplinary team when appropriate, educates the patient and family, empowering them to participate fully in the plan of care, and encourages them to self-manage where possible.[7,20] As part of the assessment process, the APRN explores the patient's value system and actively participates in discussions regarding goals of medical treatment, explaining treatment options in the setting of the patient's advanced illness and values. This discussion includes choices regarding end-of-life care, including resuscitation, and the APRN has a duty to advocate for the patient's preferences.[21] The ability of the APRN to receive reimbursement for services rendered enhances his or her value as an important member of the interdisciplinary team. Table 17.1 compares the NP and CNS roles and how they might be applicable in a palliative care service based in a community hospice organization.

The model of using advanced practice nurses in palliative care is not new; the British Macmillan Nurse Model has existed for many years. In this model, advanced practice and specialty training offers registered general nurses (RGNs) an in-depth knowledge of advanced disease pathophysiology, as well as the psychological, social, and spiritual needs of patients with a life-threatening disease.[9] Originally developed for nurses caring for cancer patients, the Macmillan model has nurses follow patients throughout their disease, from diagnosis onward, whether it is thought to be curable or not. The model provides continuity for patients and families; it involves home visits and the nurse's presence at attending physician specialist appointments when an advocate might be beneficial. Macmillan nurses identified the following components as part of their role[9]: expert practitioner, consultant, educator, researcher, and leader. These components are also found in the 2014 second edition of *Competencies for Advanced Practice Hospice and Palliative Registered Nurse* published by the Hospice and Palliative Nurses Association (HPNA), with the addition of case manager, advocate, program developer, and policymaker.[16,22]

APRNs have consistently demonstrated commitment to providing excellent care to vulnerable populations in the United States: the frail, poor, rural, and culturally diverse populations.[9] They have performed this care with a high degree of autonomy, collaborating with physician colleagues when appropriate but exercising their excellent skills in critical thinking and implementing strategies to provide improved care.[18] APRNs apply an evidence-based approach to care delivery incorporating physical, emotional, psychosocial, and spiritual or existential aspects.[23] Using this multifaceted assessment, the APRN can use the holistic approach to advance care planning with patients and families. Spiritual assessments can be particularly useful in this area.[24] These components of practice are highlighted in the first case study in this chapter, which outlines the care of a homebound patient with multiple chronic diseases by an APRN working in a community-based palliative care program as part of a hospice organization.

Home Palliative Care Visits Within a Hospice Organization

When patients are cared for at home with palliative care, some studies have reported that they are more likely to die at home and families are less likely to experience complicated or prolonged grief, or even post-traumatic stress disorder.[10] With education, the skills of caregivers, formal and informal, are increased when palliative care is involved over a longer period of time.[11] Awareness of this type of care becomes more widespread when care is delivered at home—within the medical community through collaboration with other providers, and through informal channels in the wider community.[11]

Table 17.1 Comparison of Hospice Roles for NP and CNS

Nurse Practitioner	Clinical Nurse Specialist
Focuses on providing direct clinical care along the wellness–illness continuum across settings. May lead a nursing team or a program.	Focuses on integrating care across the continuum, through patient, nurse, and system spheres. Often more in nursing management or leadership positions, may consult on clinical cases. May lead a nursing team or a program.
Primarily focused on clinical collaboration with the nursing team	Able to educate nursing staff and lead patient care improvement projects. May be more focused on quality improvement.
Often has prescriptive authority	May or may not have prescriptive authority
Always required to have a collaborative practice agreement with a physician per the Centers for Medicare and Medicaid Services	Generally does not need to have a collaborative or supervisory agreement with a physician
Able to see hospice patients for the face-to-face visit Medicare requirement, or act as attending of record, facilitating continuity of care	May only make clinical hospice visits, to provide consultation for nursing staff

Adapted from references 16, 22, and 26.

Home visits are billable and reimbursable, when medically necessary, under the Medicare Part B program for outpatient services, and other private insurance companies. See Chapter 4, Reimbursement for the Palliative Advanced Practice Registered Nurse, for more detail. Home visits offer opportunities to perform more in-depth needs assessment for homebound patients. They can be made as part of a purely consultative service for symptom management or a more comprehensive ongoing service providing disease management and/or case management. This could be included as part of a "bridge" or "transitions"[11] program prior to hospice when patients have a shorter life expectancy, or as part of a palliative care program offering services to those with a longer life expectancy. The term "transitions" has recently been more frequently associated with reduction of readmission rates to hospitals, so care should be taken to be clear about the definition of "transitions" being used. Palliative care team members can also provide this type of service in advanced illness management, acting as "transitions coaches," educating patients on managing their own symptoms, and empowering them to take control of their own health and wellness. These clinicians increase control and therefore improve quality of life and satisfaction when palliative care assessments and principles are incorporated into delivery models.[8]

Providing home visits through community-based palliative care does, of course, present challenges, not least of which may be geography. In some areas, having to travel long distances can decrease the number of patients that the APRN can see daily and may consequently increase costs. These expenditures may be offset by earlier transition into hospice. Geography may limit the ability of the APRN to have expedient access to diagnostic testing or data when making clinical decisions. However, this limitation allows APRNs to truly focus on and treat the whole person, rather than the data. Palliative APRNs in hospice organizations must become experts in all facets or components of palliative care—the physical, psychosocial, emotional, and spiritual aspects of suffering.

Case Study 1 highlights the APRN's many dimensions. Larry's care involved both a CNS and an NP as APRNs. Hospice organizations are less likely to employ CNSs because face-to-face visits for hospice patients can only be provided by NPs. A larger agency may have enough patients to support a CNS in a palliative care program alone, but smaller agencies appreciate the flexibility of being able to use an NP across both programs. The case demonstrates how APRNs can use their unique skills to care for a patient throughout the disease trajectory. The CNS provided both the patient and family with education and advocacy throughout the course of care. Although it would have been beneficial to have been involved earlier in Larry's care, the CNS demonstrated the impact that palliative care could have with a patient with chronic life-limiting illness. The case shows how APRNs can combine the medical and nursing components of practice effectively.

SNF Visits for Palliative Care Provided by a Hospice Organization

Community-based palliative care is certainly not limited to home care for patients. More than 25% of deaths occur in SNFs,[13] and SNFs offer opportunities to improve the quality of life for the residents and to build more formal relationships between SNFs and hospice organizations through the provision of palliative care.[13]

SNFs face many challenges in providing high-quality care to the residents. Medicare reimbursement focuses more on rehabilitation services than palliation of symptoms,[13] and residents often have more than one chronic disease process, making their cases more complex to manage. The use of palliative care or hospice services varies widely across states, with usage rates of between 10% and 30%.[1] These rates are all lower than desirable, considering the progressive serious illnesses experienced by the patients. In addition, residents often experience many transfers between care settings during their last years of life; these are often disrupting and disorienting, with suboptimal communication between settings.[13] This is frustrating for staff and places the resident at risk, particularly when medication reconciliation is incomplete or inaccurate. Increased focus on these transitions is occurring, along with improved advance care planning and establishing goals of medical care, the basic tenets of palliative care, in order to improve the overall care for residents. A survey by the American Medical Directors Association revealed that 81% of residents in SNFs had no documentation of code status or the existence/absence of an advance directive.[13] Since the principles of palliative care align closely with recent initiatives to change the culture in SNFs, incorporating palliative care principles in those settings can be done effectively through palliative care services associated with hospice organizations providing service to the SNF.

Staff education regarding the recognition of terminal decline and symptom management can improve beliefs about hospice services and significantly increase the hospice referral rates in a facility.[1] Staff turnover in SNFs is, however, high for many reasons: the work is difficult and demanding, the pay is low, there is increasing regulatory scrutiny,[13] and nurses are frustrated with the quality of care they feel forced to provide. This rapid turnover can reduce hospice referral rates, so lowering turnover rates is part of the challenge for hospice and palliative care organizations. It is estimated that 90% of SNFs are understaffed, with almost 80% of direct care being provided by nursing assistants.[13] Staff retention rates could be increased by educating staff regarding ways they can improve care for residents, educating them on the principles of pain and symptom management, improving communication skills, and providing educational materials for staff and families about advance care planning. Improved continuity of care with facility staff and palliative care/hospice services leads to improved quality of care and potentially decreased hospital admissions for symptom-related issues.[4] Again, APRNs are in an ideal position to provide these interventions because they can relate to nursing staff at their level using a common language and shared philosophy.[25] Connecting nursing interventions to medical conditions through ongoing education and communication is important to improve the assessment and critical thinking skills of facility staff. Education provided by physicians is not as readily accepted by nursing staff, as they often feel intimidated. Incorporating palliative care education into nursing education through curriculum change is important, but the principles taught in End-of-Life Nursing Education Consortium (ELNEC) curricula give APRNs tools to use in SNFs.[13]

Many of these principles also apply to providing care to patients in assisted living facilities. Although the facilities can vary widely in their structure, there are many opportunities for APRNs to meet the needs of residents within palliative care. Assisted living facilities are often the first step in a patient's journey into a

Table 17.2 The APRN Across Care Settings

Setting	Palliative Care	Hospice
Home	Provide direct care assessments, manage symptoms, prescribe medications, order medical equipment and home health (under physician). Bill Medicare Part B and private insurance.	Provide direct care assessments. NPs only may serve as attending of record and perform face-to-face visits for patients under the Medicare Hospice Benefit.
Assisted living facility	Provide direct care assessments, manage symptoms, write orders, order medical equipment and home health (under physician). Bill Medicare Part B and private insurance.	Provide direct care assessments. NPs only may serve as attending of record and perform face-to-face visits for patients under the Medicare Hospice Benefit.
Skilled nursing facility	Provide direct care assessments, manage symptoms, write orders, order medical equipment and home health (under physician). Bill Medicare Part B and private insurance.	Provide direct care assessments. NPs only may serve as attending of record and perform face-to-face visits for patients under the Medicare Hospice Benefit. However, a physician must be the facility's attending provider.
Hospice inpatient unit	May provide information to assist in transition to hospice or provide continuity of care. Palliative care patients would not be in an inpatient unit.	Provide direct care assessments. NPs only may serve as attending of record and perform face-to-face visits for patients under the Medicare Hospice Benefit.

Adapted from reference 26.

conjugate living situation and recognition of his or her decline in functional status.

By educating staff in the basic principles of palliative care, APRNs will be able to focus on their roles as leader, educator, and case manager, providing oversight of nursing interventions while being a consultant in more complex situations and assisting in the management of hospice patients within the facility. APRNs promote increased continuity of care during transitions while following patients through their disease trajectory, particularly if chosen by the patient or family to serve as the attending of record delineated under the Medicare Hospice Benefit.[26] (See Chapter 1, History of the Advanced Practice Role in Palliative Nursing, and Chapter 4, Reimbursement for the Palliative Advanced Practice Registered Nurse, for more details.)

Continuity of Care: Serving in the Role of Attending of Record

Serving as the attending physician of record can enhance the continuity of care not only in SNFs, but in the community at large. APRNs provide continuity of care to patients under palliative care as they make the transition to hospice care at home. Maintaining a relationship with a clinical provider who is familiar with their care, and whom they trust, decreases the vulnerability and anxiety felt by the patient and family.

Case Study 2 highlights this continuity of care and the changing role of the APRN in the patient's care. It 2 highlights the important role that the APRN plays in the interdisciplinary team, collaboratively integrating the principles of palliative care throughout this patient's disease trajectory and promoting quality of life as being central to all decisions regarding treatment.[9] It further demonstrates the APRN's ability to direct the patient's care within a team, and the flexibility necessary to act as both consultant and primary care provider at different parts of the disease trajectory. The importance of continuity of care is highlighted, particularly when complex medical and social situations exist, with communication between team members being imperative.

Table 17.2 compares the APRN role across settings in palliative care and hospice programs. Reimbursement is different when the APRN is a consultant or a hospice provider. There are also restrictions on the hospice CNS in terms of reimbursement and serving as the attending of record. For more details, see Chapter 4, Reimbursement for the Palliative Advanced Practice Registered Nurse.

Conclusion

Palliative care patients can be seen in many different settings in the community: home, SNFs, and assisted living facilities or other residential facilities, as well as outpatient palliative clinics or specialty clinics. APRNs in the community can provide a more holistic approach. Community APRNs in hospice programs must have astute clinical assessment skills as well as a wide knowledge of medications appropriate for the home. This promotes the patient's ability to stay at home. In addition, the palliative APRN working in a community hospice must be nonjudgmental; patients present in all sorts of conditions in many different living conditions, and with variable family dynamics. The APRN often is presented with many psychosocial challenges. Visiting patients at home or outside the acute care setting necessitates flexibility but maximizes reimbursement. Losses are common in this type of program, unless there is some other subsidy to support it—from a local hospital or SNF, through increased hospice enrollment, or through grant funding. Opportunities for grant funding can and should be sought for research projects, innovative programs, and so forth through endowment funds or state or federal institutions. Research continues to find alternative funding models for community-based palliative care. The goal for palliative care is to provide the best quality of life for patients and families,[15] and this is most effectively achieved through the combination of medical and nursing interventions provided by APRNs. The ability of the APRN to follow patients in the community provides a continuity of care that is unique, and transitions can be relatively seamless for patients and their families, thus decreasing stress in a very stressful time.

References

1. Workgroup Report on Hospice Care, Palliative Care and End-of-Life Counseling. Maryland Health Commision Workgroup. July 6, 2010. Available at www.oag.state.md.us/Healthpol/Hospice_and_Palliative_Care_Workgroup_Report.pdf. Accessed April 21, 2014.

2. NHPCO Facts and Figures: Hospice Care in America. NHPCO. Alexandria, Virginia. 2012. Available at www.nhpco.org/sites/default/files/public/Statistics_Research/2013_facts_Figures.pdf. Accessed September 16, 2013.

3. NHPCO. Hospice Care in America: Facts and Figures. NHPCO, Alexandria, Virginia. 2013. Available at www.nhpco.org/sites/default/files/public/Statistics_Research/2013_Facts_Figures.pdf. Accessed September 29, 2014.

4. Brooks M. CMS testing curative along with palliative care in hospice. Medscape. March 24, 2014. Available at http:www.medscape.com/viewarticle/822473. Accessed April 21, 2014.

5. Tangeman J, Rudra CB, Kerr C, Grant PC. A hospice-hospital partnership: Reducing hospitalization costs and 30-day readmission rates among seriously ill adults. *J Palliat Med.* 2014; 17(9): 1005–10.

6. Center to Advance Palliative Care. A state-by-state report card on access to palliative care in our nation's hospitals. 2011. Available at www.capc.org/reportcard/summary. Accessed September 29, 2014.

7. Hanson LC. Where will palliative care go next? *J Palliat Med.* 2014; 14(9): 980.

8. Deitrick LM. Delivering specialized palliative care in the community; A new role for nurse practitioners. *Advances in Nursing Science.* 2011; 34(4): E23–E36.

9. Kuebler K. The palliative care advanced practice nurse. *J Palliat Med.* 2003; 6(5): 707–12.

10. Meier DE, McCormick E. Palliative care. UpToDate.com. Wolters Kluwer Health, March 2014. Available at www.uptodate.com/contents/palliative-care-benefits-services-and-models-of-care. Accessed April 21, 2014.

11. Spragens L, Jones A. Community-based Opportunities for Extending the Palliative Care Continuum. Presented at AAHPM Annual Meeting, 2011, Vancouver, Canada. Available at www.capc.org/palliative-care-cross-the-continuum/community-based-opportunities-for-extending-the-palliative-care-continuum.ppt. Accessed April 21, 2014.

12. Kelley A. Factors that Influence Treatment Choices: Implications for Services Across the Palliative Care Spectrum. Shown May 29, 2014. www.CAPC.org. Accessed April 21, 2014.

13. Center to Advance Palliative Care. Improving Palliative Care in Nursing Homes. New York, NY: CAPC, June 2007. Available at www.capc.org/capc-resources/capc_publications/nursing_home_report.pdf. Accessed April 21, 2014.

14. Cloyes K, Carpenter J, Berry P, Reblin M, Clayton M, Ellington L. "A true human interaction." Comparison of family caregiver and hospice nurse perspectives on needs of family hospice caregivers. *J Hospice Palliat Nurse.* 2014; 16(5): 282–90.

15. Byock I. Hospice and palliative care: a parting of the ways or a path to the future? *J Palliat Med.* 1998; 1(2): 165–76.

16. American Nurses Association and Hospice and Palliative Nurses Association. Dahlin C, Sutermaster DJ, eds. *Palliative Nursing Scope and Standards of Practice: An Essential Resource for Hospice and Palliative Nurses.* Silver Spring, MD: ANA & HPNA; 2014.

17. Meier D, Beresford L. Advanced practice nurses in palliative care: a pivotal role and perspective. *J Palliat Med.* 2003; 9(3): 624–7.

18. Coyne P. The evolution of the advanced practice nurse within palliative care. *J Palliat Med.* 2003; 6(5): 769–71.

19. APRN Consensus Work Group & National Council of State Boards of Nursing APRN Advisory Committee. Consensus Model for APRN Regulation: Licensure, Accreditation, Certification & Education. Chicago, IL: National Council of State Boards of Nursing. July 7, 2008. Available at http://www.nursingworld.org/consensusmodel. Accessed September 30, 2014.

20. Bakitas M, Lyons K, Hegel M, et al. Effects of a palliative care intervention on clinical outcomes in patients with advanced cancer: The project ENABLE II randomized controlled trial. *JAMA.* 2009; 302(7): 741–9.

21. American Nurses Association. Position Statement: Nursing Care and Do Not Resuscitate (DNR) and Allow Natural Death (AND) Decisions. March 12, 2012. Available at http://www.nursingworld.org/MainMenuCategories/EthicsStandards/Ethics-Position-Statements.aspx. Accessed September 29, 2014.

22. Hospice and Palliative Nurses Association. Dahlin C, ed. *Competencies for Advanced Practice Hospice and Palliative Care Nurses.* Pittsburgh, PA: HPNA; 2014.

23. Dahlin C, Lynch M. Evolution of the advanced practice nurse in palliative care. In Dahlin CM, Lynch MT, eds. *Core Curriculum for the Advanced Practice Hospice and Palliative Registered Nurse.* 2nd ed. Pittsburgh, PA: HPNA; 2013:3–12.

24. Chrash M, Mulich B, Patton C. The APN role in holistic assessment and integration of spiritual assessment for advance care planning. *J Am Acad Nurse Practitioner.* 2011; 23(10): 530–6.

25. Villars P. A nurse practitioner is valuable in hospice and palliative care. KevinMD.com. February 20, 2010. Available at www.kevinmd.com/blog/2012/02/nurse-practitioner-valuable-hospice-palliative-care.html. Accessed May 3, 2013.

26. Centers for Medicare and Medicaid Services. October 1, 2011. Available at www.cms.gov/Regulations-and-Guidance/Guidance/Manuals/downloads/bp102c09.pdf. Accessed June 30, 2014.

CHAPTER 18

The Advanced Practice Registered Nurse in Hospice

Susan Gibson

Key Points

- An advanced practice registered nurse (APRN) in hospice is a leader and advocate for hospice care of the terminally ill.

- An APRN in hospice works within an interdisciplinary, holistic, and compassionate model of care focused on promoting quality of life.

- The delivery of expert end-of-life care within the hospice model demands that APRNs function at the highest level of their training and expertise.

Case Study 1: Hospice NP

Jerry Davis was a 47-year-old man with metastatic colorectal cancer admitted to home hospice at the residential care facility where he had recently moved. He agreed to have the hospice NP, Lilly Moore, serve as his attending physician. His past medical history was remarkable for unresectable colorectal cancer with a diverting colostomy, a colovesicular fistula, and metastases to his liver; an unrepaired umbilical hernia; and a dual diagnosis of paranoid schizophrenia and substance abuse disorder. His code status was DNR. His medication list included two 10/325-mg hydrocodone/APAP q4h PRN and Risperdal Consta 50 mg IM every 2 weeks. His family and social history included current alcohol and tobacco use and distant cocaine and amphetamine use; intermittently homeless; unemployed; mother and stepfather in touch but living out of state. Consultation with Jerry's psychiatrist from the County Mental Health Department revealed that prior to his cancer diagnosis he was stable on his current psychiatric medications. Staff liked him for his kind and gentle nature. Lilly incorporated the impact of his dual diagnosis when creating a treatment plan. His major issues were as follows.

Pain management complicated by auditory hallucinations, altered perception and thought processes: Jerry insisted on only taking two hydrocodone/APAP pills q4h despite a poor response and increasingly higher doses of long-acting morphine. Lilly added immediate-release morphine q2h PRN. Jerry was happy with the plan, and his pain control improved. Doses were periodically increased until his death, based on his report and the care team's and Lilly's assessment. His desire for alcohol also increased, so Jerry was connected with the local Alcoholics Anonymous group, who were able to visit him at the residential care facility; a volunteer was arranged to take him to meetings. He was also allowed to smoke tobacco on the patio.

Symptom management and personal care needs complicated by paranoia with auditory hallucinations, personal space concerns, and difficulty with acceptance and trust: Clinical staff were frequently misled by Jerry's affable manner, which masked his underlying paranoia; as a result, symptoms of constipation, nausea, and vomiting often went undetected. Poor hygiene was also an issue, as Jerry insisted on being independent with his colostomy. Lilly implemented interdisciplinary meetings to help the nursing and facility staff assess symptoms more accurately and respond appropriately to Jerry's needs. In consultation with his psychiatrist, olanzapine ODT was initiated as an antiemetic and antipsychotic for its low side-effect profile in spite of its cost.

Emotional and spiritual support complicated by severe mental illness: Jerry avoided talking about his death. Lilly recognized that as Jerry's disease progressed, his psychological state deteriorated. Disorganized and distorted thinking, delusions, and auditory hallucinations all increased. In addition to working closely with the hospice social worker and chaplain, integrative therapies such as massage, Reiki, and music therapy were intensified. His tobacco and alcohol use increased, and he frequently left the facility, returning disheveled and disoriented. Lilly recognized that Jerry was entering the final phase of the dying process, exhibiting a hyperactive terminal delirium. An alarm was placed on his door so that when he left his room the staff were alerted and available to respond to his needs. Skilled communication was necessary to ensure the team understood that he was not restricted to his room, but this was to be used as a signal that he had left it and needed something. By this time he was permitted to drink alcohol on site and smoke on the patio with supervision.

Very soon after this occurred Jerry became bed-bound, unable to swallow, and more confused and agitated. Lilly discontinued all oral medications, initiating morphine and midazolam subcutaneous infusions and IM chlorpromazine injections. Reiki, massage, and music therapy were continued. Jerry died peacefully, with staff and family surrounding him. Despite the challenges, Lilly remembers his gentle spirit and the lessons he taught her.

Lilly Moore, in her role as the hospice NP attending of record, demonstrated clinical judgment, advocacy and ethical reasoning, professionalism, collaboration, systems thinking, cultural competence, and facilitation of learning, communication, and evidence-based practice.

Case Study 2: Hospice CNS

John Brown was a CNS working for a home hospice provider. He was called one day by one of the nurse case managers for consultation on a particular case. The nurse reported that her patient, Mrs. G, was a 75-year-old woman originally from Japan admitted to hospice the week before for end-stage COPD. Her past medical history included a recent left hip fracture and repair, and chronic low back pain related to a motor vehicle accident several years ago. The patient had been started on routine extended-release morphine with immediate-release morphine for breakthrough pain prior to her hospice admission. Over the previous week her hip and back pain had worsened, resulting in several increases in her long-acting morphine dose. The patient had been alert and oriented, eating, and up to the bedside commode with assistance, but was now confused, sleepy, shaking, and constipated.

John made a home visit. He found a woman who was lethargic and confused, with brief involuntary jerks of both upper and lower extremities, and reporting 9/10 pain. John recognized signs of opioid toxicity, including myoclonus and dysphoria. In addition, he noted that Mrs. G's primary language was Japanese, so communication with her and her family caregivers was difficult. Using his knowledge of advanced pharmacology and pain management, John identified opioid rotation as the appropriate intervention. In collaboration with the hospice medical director, the long-acting morphine was discontinued. Methadone 5 mg q12h was initiated with immediate-release morphine for breakthrough pain. John also added bisacodyl daily suppositories for 3 days for constipation. This new plan of care was communicated to the hospice nurse and to the patient and family using the telephone language translation services.

Three days later John received another urgent call from the nurse because the family was unable to wake Mrs. G up. John immediately thought of over sedation due to the long half-life of methadone and that a medical error had occurred. John made another home visit, confirming his theory. In collaboration with the hospice medical director, new orders were communicated to the nurse, including holding the methadone, using the immediate-release morphine for signs or symptoms of pain, and making daily visits until the patient was awake and more stable. By day 3 the methadone was restarted at 2.5 mg q12h as the patient was awake and able to swallow.

Mrs. G continued on hospice services for another month, requiring only two more increases of her methadone dosage. She died peacefully with her family at her side.

The events that occurred were discussed by the team at the next weekly interdisciplinary team meeting. It was agreed that a root cause analysis should be conducted. John conducted a critical analysis, identifying multiple issues, including a complex pain management scenario; no bowel program initiated with a patient on routine opioids; a lack of knowledge of methadone pharmacology by the nurse; and a lack of process around the initiation and titration of methadone in the home setting with family caregivers

of hospice patients. While noting that there were no policies or procedures in place system-wide to prevent a recurrence, John created a clinical practice change. John conducted a needs assessment testing nursing's knowledge of opioid pharmacology, including methadone. He researched the current evidence related to identifying complex pain syndromes. He then developed a nursing education plan addressing triggers identifying a complex pain patient, assessment and management of pain using opioid therapy, and the unique characteristics of methadone. Subsequently he developed new policies, protocols, and procedures to be initiated in two areas, identification of complex pain patients and methadone initiation in the home setting. These new policies included an automatic trigger for a CNS consultation. A standard bowel program for use with all patients taking opioids was initiated.

John also conducted an in-service on the use of the telephone language translation line. Finally, he developed an evaluation process using chart audits to measure the outcomes of the new policies. He incorporated the new policies into an education plan for the nursing staff.

In his role as a hospice CNS, John demonstrated clinical judgment, advocacy and ethical reasoning, professionalism, collaboration, systems thinking, cultural competence, communication, evidence-based practice, and facilitation of learning.

Introduction

APRNs have a unique skill set ideally suited to working with the terminally ill receiving hospice services. Hospice APRNs have the opportunity to work to the full extent of their potential while providing compassionate care to dying individuals and their families. The work is challenging, but APRNs who master the necessary skills will ultimately reap the benefit of deep personal and professional growth.

Death is inevitable and can occur at any time, but in the United States it is predominantly associated with aging, and the aging population is growing. It is estimated that by 2030, 20% of the population will be over the age of 65.[1] In the United States, prior to death, most terminally ill individuals find themselves caught in a fragmented healthcare system, relying on complex medical interventions and burdened by rising costs. In contrast, when given a choice about end-of-life care, many Americans would prefer medical care that is coordinated and comprehensive; they want their care to reflect their wishes for comfort and quality of life; and they want information about what lies ahead for them and their family.[2] Hospice is the healthcare delivery model that provides this type of care. The demand for hospice services will likely increase, resulting in an increased demand for a skilled workforce.

Overview of the APRN in Hospice

The clinical APRN is an evolving role in hospice care. With a shortage of hospice and palliative medicine physicians,[3] the demand for advanced practice registered nurses (APRNs) will continue to grow. Most APRNs providing clinical care in hospices are either nurse practitioners (NPs) or clinical nurse specialists (CNSs). APRNs work in influential positions in hospice programs throughout the United States. In addition to clinical care, there are other roles for advanced practice nurses (APNs) in hospice, such as chief executive officer, chief operating officer, director, administrator, quality and performance improvement officer, and manager, to name a few. APNs in these roles combine a tradition of advocacy and teaching, a broad clinical knowledge base, and their critical thinking skills to make complex decisions related to the structure and processes of patient care in the hospice setting.[4] This includes issues related to "organizational and workforce excellence, compliance with laws and regulations, stewardship and accountability, and quality and performance improvement."[5]

As leaders at all organizational levels in hospice, APRNs understand the importance of patient-centered, whole-person, interdisciplinary care delivered within a framework of high-quality, evidence-based practice.[6] A basic requirement of palliative nursing, and indeed any leadership role, is expert communication skills[7] and collaboration. Specific tasks that rely on these skills are gathering and relaying information, negotiating, teaching, and resolving conflicts. Due to the multidimensional nature of hospice care, APRNs often lead interdisciplinary teams, requiring a high level of expertise and a strong understanding of clinical and professional issues across all disciplines involved. APRNs should understand the need to work collaboratively, with an appreciation for the expertise of others within nursing and other disciplines,[6] to ensure that individuals and their families receive high-quality end-of-life care under hospice services. APRNs in leadership roles must bring the unique care needs of hospice patients to the attention of the larger healthcare community through advocacy and education. Discussing end-of-life care even at an institutional level can be fraught with pitfalls, so the APRN must have expert guidance and coaching skills and a solid knowledge of the ethical issues associated with end-of-life care in the hospice setting.

The Hospice APRN

APRNs practicing in clinical roles as CNSs and NPs in hospice are educated and certified in their primary role or population focus in one of six population foci according to the *Licensure, Accreditation, Certification, and Education (LACE)* model.[8] A broad scope of practice of the primary role is preferred to accommodate the diverse population accessing hospice services. To demonstrate their specialty practice, hospice APRNs should obtain certification as an advanced certified hospice and palliative nurse (ACHPN). A hospice APN who is not a CNS or NP should obtain certification as a certified hospice and palliative nurse (CHPN).[9]

Hospice Model of Care

Hospice is a model of healthcare delivery that provides palliative care, defined by the National Consensus Project (NCP) for Quality Palliative Care as "patient and family-centered care that optimizes quality of life by anticipating, preventing, and treating suffering. Palliative care throughout the continuum of illness involves addressing the physical, intellectual, emotional, social and spiritual needs and to facilitate patient autonomy, access to information, and choice."[10] Since its inception, hospice care has not only matured into an advanced model of care for terminally ill patients but has also become a philosophy of care. As "the model for quality, compassionate care at the end of life,"[2] hospice is a type of care that focuses on all dimensions of quality of life for both the patient and family. The modern hospice movement started in England in

the 1960s and migrated to the United States in the 1970s. The first American hospice was opened in 1974, in part due to the vision of an APN, Dr. Florence Wald, Dean of the Yale School of Nursing. As a distinguished APN, she, along with two pediatricians and a chaplain, started the first home hospice program in New Haven, Connecticut.[11]

Today in the United States, hospice services are a guaranteed Medicare Part A benefit for individuals over the age of 65 with a prognosis of 6 months or less to live if their terminal disease takes its natural course and they choose to focus on comfort only rather than curative interventions.[2] The Centers for Medicare and Medicaid Services (CMS) oversees the provision of hospice services. Medicaid and many commercial and private insurance companies mirror the Medicare Hospice Benefit (MHB) for individuals below the age of 65. The delivery of hospice care in the United States has grown and developed in the past 40 years. (Table 18.1 is an overview of hospice providers.)

These agencies vary considerably in their organizational structure (not-for-profit vs. for profit), the communities they serve (rural vs. urban), size (from large to small), and setting (standalone and independent vs. beds within a nursing home).[12-14] Hospice services are provided in any setting, anywhere along the age continuum, to individuals with a variety of diseases. However, as illustrated in Table 18.2, in 2012 66% of individuals received care at their place of residence, 84.5% were over the age of 65,

Table 18.1 Overview of Hospice Providers in the United States

	1982	2012
Annual number of patients accessing hospice services[12]	25,000	1,600,000
Number of hospice providers	100s	5560[14]
Type of hospice agency[14]		
Freestanding/independent		57.4%
Part of a hospital system		20.5%
Part of a home health agency		16.9%
Part of a nursing home		5.2%
Operate inpatient facility or residence		25.0%
Agency size: average daily census[14]		
1–25 patients per day		20.0%
26–100 patients per day		33.3%
>100 patients per day		46.7%
Tax status[14]		
Not for profit		31.9%
For profit		63.1%
Government		4.9%
Geographic population served[14]		
Rural		31.5%
Urban		22.7%
Rural/urban		45.8%

Adapted from NHPCO FY2012 National Summary of Hospice Care, reference 14.

Table 18.2 Hospice Patient Demographics

Site of Care at Time of Death	2011	2012	Primary Diagnosis	2011	2012
Patient's place of residence	66.4%	66.0%	Cancer	37.0%	36.9%
Private residence	41.6%	41.5%	Non-cancer diagnosis	62.3%	63.1%
Nursing home	18.3%	17.2%	Debility unspecified	13.9%	14.2%
Residential facility	6.6%	7.3%	Dementia	12.5%	12.8%
Hospice inpatient facility	26.1%	27.4%	Heart disease	11.4%	11.2%
Acute care hospital	7.4%	6.6%	Lung disease	8.5%	8.2%
Patient age			Other	4.8%	5.2%
<24 years	0.4%	0.4%	Stroke or coma	4.1%	4.3%
25–34 years	0.4%	0.4%	Kidney disease (End Stage Renal Disease)	2.7%	2.7%
35–64 years	16.0%	15.7%	Liver disease	2.1%	2.1%
65–74 years	16.3%	16.3%	Non-amyotrophic lateral sclerosis motor neuron	1.6%	1.6%
75–84 years	27.6%	27.7%	Amyotrophic lateral sclerosis	0.4%	0.4%
>85 years	39.3%	40.5%	HIV/AIDS	0.2%	0.2%

Table adapted from NHPCO FY2012 National Summary of Hospice Care, reference 14.

and approximately 63% had a non-cancer diagnosis spanning all organ systems.[13,14]

APRNs and Hospice Care

APRNs, with their roots firmly established in nursing theory, are well prepared to provide expert end-of-life care to dying individuals receiving hospice services. Theoretical concepts that are shared by nursing practice and hospice care include whole-person care, health and its impact on quality of life, and being present and bearing witness, all delivered within a collaborative practice framework.[2,15] In hospice, APRNs combine these common theoretical concepts with the skills needed to provide expert care at the end-of-life. The Hospice and Palliative Nurses Association (HPNA) developed the *Palliative Nursing: Scope and Standards* which establish the competencies necessary to meet these standards. These standards are divided into Standards of Practice for Palliative Nursing, which incorporates the nursing process, and Standards of Professional Performance.[16] The competencies are advanced clinical judgment, use of evidence and research, expert communication skills, collaboration, knowledge of ethical principles and professional standards, respect for cultural and spiritual diversity, advocacy, systems thinking, and an understanding of the importance of ongoing education for creating a professional practice that delivers expert end-of-life care.[9]

These standards and associated competencies are closely aligned with both the eight domains of quality palliative care as outlined in the NCP *Clinical Practice Guidelines for Quality Palliative Care*[10] and the National Hospice and Palliative Care Organization's (NHPCO) *Standards of Practice for Hospice Programs*.[5] The NHPCOs standards stipulate that for hospice providers to provide high-quality patient- and family-centered palliative care, they must incorporate either the NCP *Clinical Practice Guidelines* or the NHPCO *Standards of Practice*

for Hospice Programs into the delivery of hospice services.[5] Shared concepts across all of these guidelines, standards, and competencies are easily identified when they are placed side by side (Table 18.3).

In addition, familiarity with the hospice local coverage determinations (LCDs), which are published by the local geographic area's Medicare administration contractor, and the hospice conditions of participation (COPs) criteria set forth by the CMS is essential. The LCDs are guidelines for determining eligibility and prognosis.[2] The COPs delineate the services that a certified hospice provider must provide to a patient as it relates to his or her terminal diagnosis and related conditions, and also set the standards for the delivery of hospice services, such as clinical record-keeping and staff credentials. To receive reimbursement from the CMS, a hospice provider must comply with these standards and requirements.[17] Private insurers usually follow the CMS hospice guidelines for eligibility, the type of services provided, and reimbursement. The NHPCO works closely with these agencies to create these guidelines and requirements.

All of these essential components of professional practice combine to create a complex and comprehensive knowledge base for APRNs practicing in hospice care. These guidelines, standards, and competencies guide the hospice APRN. With the patient and family as the unit of care, Figure 18.1 demonstrates these components, clearly showing the multifaceted dimensions of professional practice that contribute to the provision of expert end-of-life care by APRNs within the hospice model of care.

An extensive clinical knowledge base is also essential for practice in a hospice setting. APRNs will be expected to provide care for diverse patients of all ages in a variety of settings, with any and all terminal illnesses, and within a finite reimbursement system. Such a broad sphere of practice demands creativity, flexibility, and a high level of critical thinking skills to produce good outcomes in such a multitude of situations.

Table 18.3 Hospice APRN Scope, Standards, and Competencies and Hospice Care Standards and Guidelines

Palliative Nursing: Scope and Standards[16]			HPNA Competencies for the Advanced Practice Nurse[9]	NHPCO Standards of Practice for Hospice Programs[5]	NCP Clinical Practice Guidelines for Quality Palliative Care[10]
Communication	*Education	Standards of practice	Clinical judgment	Clinical excellence and safety	Physical care
		Evidence-based practice and research	Evidence-based practice and research		Care of the patient at the end-of-life
		Collaboration			
		Leadership			
		Environmental health			
		Ethics	Advocacy and ethics	Ethical behavior and consumer rights	Ethical and legal
		Quality of practice	Professionalism	Organizational excellence	Structure and processes of care
		Evidence-based practice and research	Systems thinking	Workforce excellence	
		Resource utilization	Collaboration	Standards	
		Professional practice evaluation	evidence-based practice and research	Compliance with laws & regulations	
		Collaboration	Systems	Stewardship & accountability	
		Leadership		Performance measurement	
		Collaboration	Cultural and spiritual	Patient- and Family-centered care	Cultural
		Standards of practice	Evidence-based practice and research	Standards	Psychological & psychiatric
				Inclusion and access	Social
					Spiritual, religious, & existential

* Facilitator of learning.

Hospice services are predominantly provided to individuals over the age of 65.[14] However, hospice services are also provided to newborns, young children, adolescents, young adults, and middle-aged individuals.[14] Understanding each age group's developmental stages and challenges is critical. Caring for individuals across the age continuum ensures that APRNs will encounter a multitude of disease states. This demands a comprehensive knowledge of many illnesses and conditions; their pathophysiology, manifestations, and progression; and associated pharmacology.

The APRN will encounter a wide diversity of patients, such as military veterans; individuals with developmental disabilities; individuals with mental illness and personality disorders; prison inmates; the lesbian, gay, bisexual, transgender, and intersex community; individuals with substance use disorders; individuals who are homeless; and individuals of a low socioeconomic status. Cultural competence and knowledge of issues specific to these populations are essential.

The setting in which hospice services are provided plays an important role in the delivery of hospice care. Sixty-six percent of individuals receiving hospice care are in their place of residence, such as a private home, a nursing home, an assisted living facility, a residential care facility,[14] a prison, or even a homeless shelter.[18] In addition, there are hospice houses, which vary in population demographics. Some provide strictly residential routine hospice care, others provide only general inpatient hospice care, and others provide a mixture of both.

Caring for an individual in his or her home presents different challenges than in an acute care setting. Stepping into a person's home is a privilege, as the APRN is a guest. In the private home, family members are usually the primary caregivers. They are often stressed and overwhelmed, with little ability to assess symptoms and then apply interventions. In other home settings, paid caregivers, often with limited scope of practice and frequently minimal training, are providing the care. Hospice houses, depending on the population they serve, may have only paid unlicensed caregivers or highly skilled licensed and unlicensed personnel, or a mixture of both. All of these scenarios present advantages and disadvantages in terms of symptom assessment and management, medication administration, and delivery of personal care, which the APRN will have to incorporate into the plan of care.

The hospice APRN must determine the knowledge and expertise of the caregivers in different settings. Moreover, each physical location in which hospice services are provided, other than a private home, will have regulatory oversight by state and federal licensing agencies based on their designation. The hospice APRN must understand how these regulations affect his or her practice. For example, nursing homes often have strict regulations regarding the use of certain antipsychotics, thus influencing the APRN's choice of medications in these facilities. In another example, many residential care facilities do not have the licensed staff to dispense medications like opiates or cannot give them on an as-needed basis. In both of these cases, the hospice APRN must

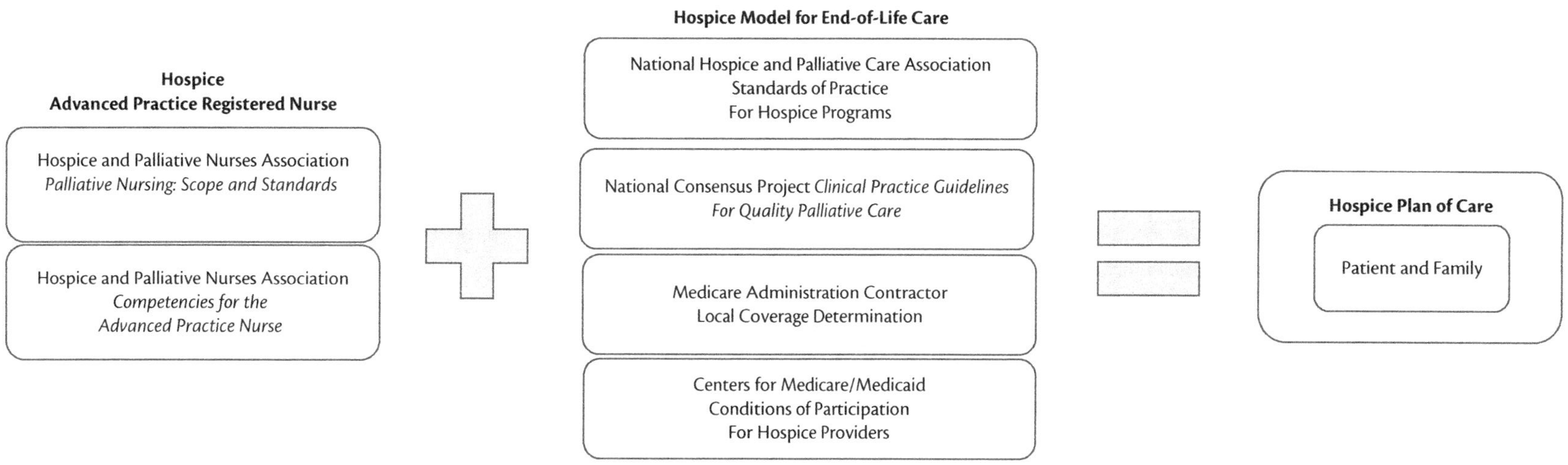

**Hospice
Advanced Practice Registered Nurse**

Hospice and Palliative Nurses Association
Palliative Nursing: Scope and Standards

Hospice and Palliative Nurses Association
*Competencies for the
Advanced Practice Nurse*

Hospice Model for End-of-Life Care

National Hospice and Palliative Care Association
Standards of Practice
For Hospice Programs

National Consensus Project *Clinical Practice Guidelines
For Quality Palliative Care*

Medicare Administration Contractor
Local Coverage Determination

Centers for Medicare/Medicaid
Conditions of Participation
For Hospice Providers

Hospice Plan of Care

Patient and Family

Figure 18.1 Overview of the requirements for expert professional practice for the hospice APRN

Table 18.4 Levels of Care with the Medicare Hospice Benefit

Levels of Hospice Care[19]	Description[19]	Daily Reimbursement Rates for FY2014 Hospice Care by CMS[20]
Routine home care	Routine hospice care at home	$156.06
Continuous home care	Hospice provider provides crisis intervention in the home. The patient receives hospice care consisting of continuous nursing care for a minimum of 8 hours a day. The patient may also receive continuous hospice aide or homemaker care. Used for only brief periods with a goal of keeping the terminally ill individual in the home.	$910.78
Inpatient respite care	Individual receiving hospice care is transferred to a contracted facility for a short period to give family/caregivers a respite. The individual continues to receive routine hospice care while in the facility.	$161.42
General inpatient care	An individual receiving hospice care is transferred to an inpatient hospice facility (or bed) for acute pain control or acute or chronic symptom management that cannot be managed in other settings.	$694.19

balance regulatory restrictions with recommended standards of care to develop an appropriate care plan.

In addition to physical location, the four CMS-mandated hospice levels of care that a hospice provider must offer strongly influence the delivery of hospice care. These four levels of care are routine home care; continuous home care for patients in crisis; inpatient respite care, usually provided in a contracted facility, for patients whose families need respite from caregiving; and general inpatient care for patients in crisis who cannot be managed at home.[19] Table 18.4 shows the differences and the associated variance in reimbursement from the CMS.[20] In July 2015, the first significant changes to hospice reimbursement since the Medicare Hospice benefit went into effect in 1983 were initiated with new legislation approved by Congress. The changes to be implemented on January 1, 2016 include a two-tiered routine home care rate and a service intensity add-on payment. The two-tiered payment model for routine home care means that hospices will receive a higher rate for the first 60 days of hospice care and a lower rate for any additional days of hospice care. The service intensity add-on payment will reflect the higher acuity and needs of dying patients and their families in the last seven days of life. It will be calculated retrospectively based on nursing and social work visits and will be equal to the continuous home care hourly rate up to four hours per day. These reimbursement changes reflect the reality of short lengths of stay and a higher intensity of care in the last week of life that many hospices encounter. [21] Clearly, the hospice APRN must be able to assess the patient's and family's needs and the skill of the caregivers, then incorporate this information into a care plan that meets regulatory oversight, all within a finite monetary compensation to the hospice provider.

This leads us to the additional limitation of a capitated reimbursement for hospice services, which also affects the treatment plan. Appropriate resource utilization while achieving good outcomes is a standard of professional practice. The hospice organization is responsible for the cost of all the care of an individual as it relates to his or her terminal diagnosis. Therefore, an extensive knowledge of pain and symptom management options is necessary to enable the creation of a care plan that provides comfort in any setting to any individual in a fiscally responsible manner. For example, the hospice APRN must know the cost and relative efficacy of different medications. In the medical management of a

bowel obstruction, it is acceptable to use inexpensive drugs, such as scopolamine or glycopyrrolate, rather than the more expensive drug octreotide.[22]

Barriers to Care

APRNs must be aware of some of the barriers to accessing hospice services, including lack of healthcare provider and community knowledge, the predominant culture's death-denying beliefs, the influence of an individual's culture, and insurance issues, among others.[2] The delivery of end-of-life care in a hospice setting is governed by financial restraints and regulatory issues, as discussed previously. APRNs must integrate these factors into their clinical decision making when creating, maintaining, or changing hospice programs. Providing compassionate, evidence-based, patient- and family-centered care within these confines can be challenging. The NHPCO has an extensive compilation of resources designed to help hospice providers and clinicians achieve good clinical outcomes within these regulatory and financial constraints.[23]

Opportunities

APRNs working in hospice have a remarkable opportunity to directly influence the provision of expert end-of-life care at all levels of delivery. APRNs have the education to work with public policy to promote high-quality hospice care, to develop and manage healthcare agencies providing hospice services, to work as educators and researchers to ensure high-quality, evidence-based practice, and to provide expert direct patient care. With the expected growth in the demand for hospice services, there is enormous potential for APRNs to continue and expand their presence.

The Role of the Hospice NP

APRNs working in hospice have functioned as primary care providers, expert clinicians, leaders, educators, researchers, advocates, consultants, collaborators, and coordinators of care. However, most hospices use NPs rather than CNSs due to reimbursement issues. Since the 1970s NPs have been considered a resource that is effective, cost-conscious, and essential to the delivery of healthcare in the United States.[24] By the 1980s, it was acknowledged that geriatric NPs in hospice and home care had the potential to improve outcomes, such as better case management and increased use of advanced interventions, and in general to raise nursing's awareness of the unique characteristics of aging.[25] The real impetus to use NPs in hospice occurred in 2003 with the Medicare Prescription Drug Improvement and Modernization Act. CMS revised the definition of the hospice attending of record to include NPs, defining this position as "the Doctor of Medicine or Osteopathy, or Nurse Practitioner selected by the individual as the person who has the most significant role in the creation and provision of the individual's plan of care."[26] With this legislation, NPs could serve as the primary medical provider for hospice patients; assess and diagnose; implement plans of care, including writing and signing orders; and prescribe medications as defined within the statutes of the specific nurse practice act of the state in which the NP practices. The COPs stipulate that patients may be given a choice between a physician and NP as the attending of record if the patient does not already have a designated primary care clinician. The primary role of NPs in this role is the healthcare provider who is recognized by the hospice patient to have the most influence over his or her care. NPs acting in this capacity work alongside physician colleagues to provide expert patient care to patients at the end-of-life. However, NPs still cannot certify or recertify a terminal illness or 6-month prognosis.[26]

Another push to increase the use of NPs occurred with the implementation of the Patient Protection and Affordable Care Act (PPACA) of 2010. Embedded within the PPACA is the requirement for a face-to-face visit to be made by a physician or an NP to all hospice patients prior to the 180th-day recertification and prior to each subsequent recertification.[27] This has created an additional role for the hospice NP as the primary clinician performing these visits; in fact, many hospice providers have hired NPs solely to perform these visits. This act mandates that the NP be employed by the hospice provider in order to perform these visits but does not have to be the attending of record.[27] Sound physical assessment abilities, comprehensive information gathering, knowledge of prognostic indicators and eligibility requirements, and expert communication skills are necessary to perform this function well.

As a hospice attending of record, NPs practice in the role of leader of the interdisciplinary team, although their presence does not replace the hospice medical director.[28] In collaboration with the hospice interdisciplinary team and the patient and family, hospice NPs develop the plan of care, provide oversight in its implementation, and lead the evaluation of outcomes (see Case Study 1). The primary focus is on the clinical management of patients, which requires expert clinical judgment, an in-depth knowledge of a host of diseases, and extensive knowledge of pain and symptom assessment and management. Superb physical assessment and diagnostic reasoning are critical skills in a hospice setting. Lack of access to sophisticated diagnostic tools, such as x-rays, computed tomography (CT) scans, magnetic resonance imaging (MRI), and ultrasound, due to cost and the burden of travel at the end-of-life, means that the hospice NP must be able to elicit the pertinent history and know the physical assessment findings indicating serious conditions like effusions, ascites, bowel obstructions, and so forth. The APRN must be able to recognize the risks, benefits, and burdens of treatment and where the individual is on the illness trajectory; know the cost of interventions; be able to apply current clinical research to clinical practice; and be able to

synthesize complex data into a comprehensive care plan specific to the individual's needs and goals. The use of standard tools to assist with prognostication, to assess physical symptoms, and to identify psychosocial and spiritual issues is indispensable.

Prognostication is also an important skill. However, NPs are legally prohibited from certifying or recertifying a terminal illness or determining a 6-months-or-less prognosis.[26,28] Nonetheless, it will be their clinical judgment on which the hospice medical director will base the determination of eligibility and prognosis in order to ensure that the hospice provider remains within the LCD hospice eligibility guidelines. Understanding the implications of related conditions and comorbidities in determining the patient's prognosis is part of this skill. Estimation of prognosis is also essential to keep the patient and family informed of where he or she is on the illness trajectory. In addition, as medical care in general becomes more complex, relying on advanced therapies to extend life, hospice NPs serving as the attending of record must be prepared to manage patients on hospice with interventions already in place, such as ventricular assist devices, intravenous vasopressor therapy, pulmonary hypertension infusions, and ventilators, among other treatments.

Expert practice is built on strong communication skills.[7] Hospice NPs must recognize the communication needs of their patients, families, team members, and other caregivers. Communication skills to be mastered include listening, collecting and conveying information, being present, and bearing witness.[7] They must be adept at conducting meetings with patients and families, other healthcare providers, and team members. Issues addressed in these meetings include pain and symptom assessment and management, advance care planning, giving bad news, code status, goals of care (including the use and discontinuation of life-sustaining therapies and artificial hydration and nutrition), and transition to death. Requests for euthanasia, assisted suicide, and palliative sedation will be encountered, and hospice NPs should know the legal, ethical, and moral issues surrounding these topics. They should be able to respond openly and compassionately to the suffering of individuals and families. With recognition of the influence of culture on the experience of dying, advocacy and the application of ethical analysis are essential steps in working through these issues. Hospice NPs serve as mentors to their interdisciplinary colleagues, modeling expert clinical, ethical, and professional behaviors.

Serving in the role of the attending of record, NPs shoulder the responsibility for the patient's care. This carries significant weight at a highly emotional and often difficult time for patients and families. In addition, providing expert clinical care is challenging given the confines of limited reimbursement and often inexperienced caregivers. NPs providing care to hospice patients have the moral and ethical obligation to provide the best symptom management while conserving resources; thus, they must examine not only the benefit, burden, and risk of each intervention but also the cost and ease of administration. Hospice NPs need to use all of their critical thinking skills to create a plan of care that is effective, compassionate, evidence-based, and cost-conscious.

An additional legal limitation that hospice NPs may encounter is whether they have the scope of practice within their state to sign the forms generally known as Medical Orders for Life Sustaining Treatments. Known in many states as the Physician/Provider/Medical Orders for Life Sustaining Treatments (POLST/MOLST) forms, these allow patients to have more control over their death. NPs may also sign death certificates, depending on organizational bylaws and state statutes. This varies from state to state, potentially impeding the delivery of care if the NP cannot sign these documents.

The Role of the Hospice CNS

Hospice providers since the 1980s have recognized the important contribution of CNSs to end-of-life care in the areas of nursing education, research, and the care of increasingly complex patients.[29] CNSs working in hospice have functioned as educators, expert clinicians, researchers, consultants, administrators, advocates, coordinators, case managers, leaders, program developers, and policymakers (see Case Study 2). CNSs have three core areas of practice: managing the care of complex and vulnerable populations, educating and supporting interdisciplinary staff, and facilitating change and innovation in healthcare systems.[30] There is more variability for CNS practice, and similarly to NP practice, state statutes and regulations vary, including prescriptive authority.[24]

CNSs are the ideal clinicians to serve in the role of RN case manager, caring for complex patients receiving hospice services, such as patients with ventricular assist devices, those receiving intravenous vasopressor or pulmonary hypertension therapy, those on ventilators, or those receiving other life-prolonging therapies that require a high level of critical thinking. Other direct patient care scenarios that would use CNSs' advanced clinical skills are complex pain and symptom management patients, individuals with difficult wounds, patients with a comorbid serious mental illness, and developmentally disabled individuals, to name a few. CNSs caring for complex patients combine their comprehensive knowledge of multiple disease states and expert assessment skills with their ability to synthesize data to create individual comprehensive care plans. Standards of practice include the incorporation of validated assessment tools for pain, other symptoms, and psychosocial and spiritual needs. CNSs have the skills necessary to assist the attending of record in prognostication and the recertification process. Hospice CNSs are also familiar with the current research as it relates to end-of-life care and can incorporate this information into the patient's plan of care.

CNSs working in this role manage the multiple interventions related to direct patient care as well as the social, emotional, and spiritual issues that accompany the use of advanced technological therapies at the end-of-life. CNSs must be skilled in communication,[7] as they will be expected, in collaboration with the attending of record and other members of the interdisciplinary team, to conduct patient and family meetings, to give bad news, to participate in team meetings, to discuss the discontinuation of therapies, to negotiate conflicts, and to prepare the patient and family for the actively dying phase. Deep listening and bearing witness are nonverbal communication tools that CNSs will be expected to master to ensure patient autonomy.[7] CNSs, with their understanding of the ethical dilemmas related to end-of-life care and their ability to sort through these complex issues, along with a knowledge of the importance of culture in end-of-life care, play a crucial role in the care of complex patients.

CNSs are also especially suited to the role of consultant and educator to the patient, family, caregivers, nurses, and other members of the interdisciplinary team. Patients, their families, and other caregivers have a multitude of educational needs. Patients are usually dependent on others for the majority of their care at the end-of-life as changes in cognition, fatigue, pain, and other symptoms impair their ability to care for themselves. Thus, the majority of care falls to others, and with the bulk of hospice care being performed in the place of residence, the caregivers are often not adept at performing the often complex functions of end-of-life caregiving. Learning needs include symptom and medication management, taking care of personal care necessities, and the emotional and spiritual concerns individuals face at the end of life. CNSs combine their communication skills with their knowledge of adult learning styles to teach these caregivers the skills they need to perform these tasks.

Nursing education and research related to providing end-of-life care in a hospice setting are two significant areas of focus for CNSs. The goal is to improve patient outcomes, and CNSs who assume the role of educator in hospice must be familiar with the HPNA *Palliative Nursing: Scope and Standards* and *Competencies for the Hospice and Palliative APN*, licensed vocational nurse, and certified nursing assistant.

Regardless of the setting in which hospice care occurs, CNSs must be able to identify knowledge gaps and the educational needs of nursing staff. To identify areas of concern in patient care in the hospice setting, CNSs must have a broad understanding of a multitude of disease states and the specialty nursing knowledge necessary to care for all individuals regardless of their terminal diagnosis, combined with an understanding of the nursing process and its relationship to the unique needs of dying patients relative to all the domains of quality of life. In addition, the heavily regulated CMS oversight of hospice care mandates that CNSs be well versed in all the regulatory and licensing requirements that pertain to hospice nursing care.

Identifying needs and concerns is only the first step. CNSs must also be adept at implementing change in nursing practice. Using their expertise in conducting research and integrating current evidence into clinical practice, CNSs take on the roles of change agent and mentor, recognizing the unique challenges encountered by nurses providing end-of-life care in a hospice setting.

With an increasingly complex patient population entering hospice, the role of the CNS has huge growth potential. CNSs have been widely used for their positive influence on patient outcomes in the acute care setting, but there is limited evidence indicating their use in hospice care. It is unclear why this is the case: the increased use of CNSs would seem to be both prudent and appropriate to ensure high-quality end-of-life care. Hospice providers who use them will find themselves leaders in end-of-life care.

Conclusion

The demand for hospice services will grow, and the roles available to APRNs in hospice are rich and varied, as hospice care is not limited by age, setting, disease, or population. Even though the work is challenging, demanding that APRNs work to their fullest professional capacity, caring for dying individuals and their families is a great privilege that offers many rewards.

References

1. Centers for Disease Control and Prevention. The State of Aging and Health in America, 2013. Atlanta, GA: Centers for Disease Control and Prevention, US Department of Health and Human Services; 2013. Available at www.cdc.gov/aging.

2. Egan City KA, Labyak MJ. Hospice palliative care for the 21st century: A model for quality end-of-life care. In: Ferrell BR, Coyle N, eds. *Oxford Textbook of Palliative Nursing*. 3rd ed. Oxford, New York: Oxford University Press; 2010:13–52.

3. Lupu D. Estimate of current hospice and palliative medicine physician workforce shortage. *J Pain Symptom Management*. 2010; 40(6): 899–911.

4. Horton JR, Indelicato RA. The advanced practice nurse. In: Ferrell BR, Coyle N, eds. *Oxford Textbook of Palliative Nursing*. 3rd ed. Oxford, New York: Oxford University Press; 2010:1121–9.

5. National Hospice and Palliative Care Organization. Quality and Standard Committee. *Standards of Practice for Hospice Programs NHPCO 2010*. Alexandria: VA. 2010. Available at www.nhpco.org. Accessed July 17, 2014.

6. Tracy MF, Hanson CM. Leadership. In: Hamric AB, Hanson CM, Tracy MF, O'Grady ET, eds. *Advanced Practice Nursing. An Integrated Approach*. 5th ed. St. Louis, MO: Elsevier Saunders, 2014:266–98.

7. Wittenberg-Lyles E, Goldsmith J, Ferrell B, Ragan SL. Preface. In: *Communication in Palliative Nursing*. Oxford, New York: Oxford University Press; 2013:ix–xv.

8. National Council of State Boards of Nursing and APRN Advisory Committee. APRN Regulation: Licensure, Accreditation, Certification, and Education. 2008. Available at www.ncsbn.org/Consensus_Model_for_APRN_Regulation_July_2008.pdf. Accessed April 27, 2014.

9. Hospice and Palliative Nurses Association (HPNA). *Competencies for the Hospice and Palliative Advanced Practice Nurse*. 2nd ed. Pittsburgh, PA: HPNA; 2014.

10. National Consensus Project for Quality Palliative Care. *Clinical Practice Guidelines for Quality Palliative Care*. 3rd ed. Pittsburgh, PA: National Consensus Project; 2013.

11. National Hospice and Palliative Care Organization. *History of Hospice*. Alexandria, VA. Available at http://www.nhpco.org/history-hospice-care. Accessed September 29, 2014.

12. National Hospice and Palliative Care Organization. Patients served by hospice in the US: 1982–2012. Available at http://www.nhpco.org/sites/default/files/public/Statistics_Research/Graph_of_hospice_1982_2012.pdf. Retrieved September 2014.

13. Neuman K. Assessing payment adequacy: hospice services. The Medicare Payment Advisory Commission. 2011. http://www.medpac.gov/documents/december-2011-meeting-presentation-assessing-payment-adequacy-hospice-services.pdf. Retrieved September 2014.

14. National Hospice and Palliative Care Organization. *FY2012 National Summary of Hospice Care*. Alexandria, VA: NHPCO; Available at http://www.nhpco.org/sites/default/files/public/NDS_2012_National_Summary_20131106.pdf Accessed June 1 2015.

15. Nursing theories: an overview. *Current Nursing*. Available at http://currentnursing.com. Updated 2012. Accessed July 13, 2014.

16. American Nurses Association and Hospice and Palliative Nurses Association. *Palliative Nursing: Scope and Standards—An essential resource for nurses. 2014*. Silver Spring, MD: Nursesbooks, 2014.

17. Centers for Medicare and Medicaid Services (CMS). *Medicare Hospice Benefits*. Baltimore, MD: US Department of Health and Human Services; 2013. Available at http://www.medicare.gov/pubs/pdf/02154.pdf. Retrieved July 18, 2014.

18. Tribe C. Hospice for the homeless. Street Sights. Available at http://www.streetsights.org/2011/hospice-for-the-homeless/. Published 2011. Accessed July 18, 2014.

19. US Government Publication. 42 CFR-418 Hospice Care. Available at http://www.nhpco.org/cms-medicare-hospice-regulations. Retrieved August 31, 2014.

20. Medicare Learning Network (MLN). Update to Hospice Payment Rates. 2013. Available at http://www.cms.gov/Outreach-and-Education/Medicare-Learning-Network-MLN/MLNMattersArticles/Downloads/MM8416.pdf. Retrieved September 21, 2014.

21. National Hospice and Palliative Care Organization. *CMS Final Rule Implements New Payment Structure for Hospice*. Available at http://www.nhpco.org/press-room/press-releases/cms-releases-fy2016-hospice-wage-index-final-rule. Retrieved August 23, 2015.

22. Von Gunten CF, Muir JC. *Medical Management of Bowel Obstructions*. 2nd ed. Fast Facts and Concepts. August 2005; 45. Available at http://www.eperc.mcw.edu/fastfact/ff_045.htm.

23. National Hospice and Palliative Care Organization. Regulatory and Advocacy. Available at http://www.nhpco.org. Accessed September 21, 2014.

24. Cockerham AZ, Keeling AW. A brief history of advanced practice nursing in the United States. In: Hamric AB, Hanson CM, Tracy MF, O'Grady ET, eds. *Advanced Practice Nursing. An Integrated Approach*. 5th ed. St. Louis, MO: Elsevier Saunders; 2014:1–26.

25. Ebersole P, Enloe CH. Geriatric nurse practitioner: vital to hospice and home health. *Caring*. 1983; 2(6): 48–50.

26. Medicare Learning Network. Nurse Practitioners as Attending Physicians in the Medicare Hospice Benefit. 2004. Provider Inquiry Assistance. Available at http://www.cms.gov. Published 2004. Updated 2013. Accessed July 18, 2014.

27. Centers for Medicare and Medicaid Services. The Patient Protection and Affordable Care Act 2010. Available at https://www.cms.gov. Published 2010. Accessed July 18, 2014.

28. Centers for Medicare and Medicaid Services. Coverage of Hospice Services under Hospital Insurance. Medicare Benefit Policy. Available at www.cms.gov. Updated 2012. Accessed July 18, 2014

29. Snap J. Hospice responds to increasingly complex patient needs. Medscape. Available at http://www.medscape.org/viewarticle/505167. Published 2005. Accessed July 18, 2014.

30. Lewandowski W, Adamle K. Substantive areas of clinical nurse specialist practice: a comprehensive review of the literature. *Clin Nurse Specialist. 2009*;23:73–90.

The Palliative Advanced Practice Registered Nurse in the Home Setting

Gretchen P. Fitzgerald, Michele A. Naugle, and Jacaline P. Wolf

Key Points

◆ There are many models using palliative advanced practice registered nurses (APRNs) in the home setting.

◆ The palliative APRN in the home setting offers quality palliative care and cost-effective management.

◆ The APRN must understand the components of a successful and sustainable program in the home setting.

Introduction

APRNs are educated in both clinical and psychosocial aspects of care, making them well qualified to provide palliative care. By bringing their expertise to the home environment, APRNs improve access to palliative care for complex chronically ill patients and their families. As a result, patients receive individualized care and experience an improved quality of life. Palliative care practices that use APRNs have proved to be both successful and sustainable, demonstrating that this is an effective model for palliative care in the home.

Development of Palliative Care in the Home

As the number of people living with chronic illness continues to escalate, there may be an increased demand for palliative care services. Over the years, the indications for palliative care have expanded to include not only patients with cancer, but also patients with organ failure and dementia. Often patients struggle with multiple comorbidities, including geriatric syndromes, which involve atypical disease presentation, unpredictable exacerbations, and loss of functional independence.[1,2] The multiple psychosocial issues of the chronically ill create additional hardships, making it more challenging for the patient to cope as the disease progresses. Poor functional status results in restricted access to medical care, leading to increased symptom burden.[3] Even if patients are not homebound by the definition of Medicare,

traveling to the office of their providers may be a hardship. A service that provides home visits for palliative care improves both access to care and symptom management.[4]

Models of Palliative Care in the Home

In the past, most patients received palliative care only during hospital stays. Palliative care in the home offers a continuum of care for patients in the community. Alternatively, palliative care at home can establish goals of care before an acute crisis, as well as offer continued support when the patient makes the transition home from the hospital. Over the past several years, a variety of models of home-based palliative care have developed. Many of these models resulted in improved symptom management and patient and family satisfaction, but not all of them were cost-effective or sustainable.[5–7]

The sustainability of a palliative care program often relies on indirect savings, such as reduced hospital admissions, reduced emergency department visits, and earlier admissions to hospice. Considering that palliative care in the home addresses symptom exacerbations, self-management skills, psychosocial burdens, and goals of care earlier in the disease progression, it is not surprising that some programs have seen a cost savings by decreasing emergency department visits, hospital admissions, and caregiver burden.[8–11] The overall success of a program depends not only on its sustainability but also on its ability to meet the needs of the local community. Because there are unique needs of communities, one model is not applicable to all settings. Thus, there are a variety of models throughout the United States.

Some palliative care programs are focused on interventions by registered nurses in a care coordinator, case manager, and/or educator role. Outcomes include increased satisfaction, improved preparation for end-of-life decisions, and decreased symptom burden, but only some of these programs showed financial sustainability through decreased hospital admissions and shorter length of hospital stay.[12–15] Compared to standard home care, palliative care embedded in home care agencies did show improved results.[16] Unfortunately, these models require the patient to meet the Medicare criteria for home care services. Many patients who would benefit from palliative care do not have acute care issues that require skilled nursing visits, nor do they technically meet the criteria of being homebound. Although additional home visits made by a registered nurse, in addition to standard care through a medical clinic, resulted in higher patient satisfaction, it was more costly to the practice.[15] This may be attributed to the fact that registered nurses are unable to bill for their services. One study described an interdisciplinary program in which the registered nurse was responsible for patient education only, and the physician's recommendations were based on surveys and on a social worker's assessment.[17,18] This model resulted in decreased physician visits but not in a reduction of emergency department visits or hospital admissions. Although there was improvement in some symptoms and patients appreciated having access to a palliative care professional, quality of life and satisfaction were not improved.[17,18]

Other palliative care programs caring for the chronically ill population involve a disease management approach. These network-based programs are led by physicians and often include registered nurses and social workers. The clinical expertise of the team is enhanced by the direct involvement of a physician trained in palliative medicine. Studies of this model of care found that symptoms significantly decreased in severity.[4,19] The goal of involving a variety of disciplines is to address the medical and psychosocial issues in patients with end-stage illnesses, which decreases psychosocial distress.[20] Program sustainability has been established through decreased hospital admissions[21,22] and increased hospice length of stay.[19]

Models of Palliative Care in the Home Using APRNs

As the advances of medical technology increase longevity, older adults are experiencing more chronic illnesses for a longer period of time. Forty-one percent of people over the age of 65 have three or more chronic conditions.[23] Despite the best efforts by programs like those discussed previously, gaps remain that leave patients without access to palliative care. For example, many areas lack palliative care services, and even where programs exist, there is a shortage of palliative care specialists, making it difficult to staff the programs.[24] APRNs can be essential members of the palliative care team as they are "uniquely trained to offer expertise in palliative care in clinical, research, educational, and consulting roles."[25] APRN education includes communications skills, symptom management, psychosocial and spiritual assessment, and coordination of care.[24] Certification in advanced hospice and palliative nursing further distinguishes the expertise of the APRN in palliative care.

Specialized initiatives embedded in home care or hospice programs using APRNs have shown success. For example, in the Transitional Care Model, APRNs coordinated care for patients with heart failure.[26] Their role was to smooth the transition of care from the hospital, help manage other comorbidities that affect heart failure, teach self-management skills by focusing on the patient's goals, and address psychosocial issues to improve quality of life.[27] By approaching the patient holistically, the APRNs identified each patient's unique needs and provided an individualized

management approach. This approach resulted in improved quality of life and patient satisfaction, as well as fewer readmissions and lower costs for up to a year after the patient's initial episode of heart failure.[26] Although it was focused on patients with heart failure, this model can be applied to the development of a palliative care program.

Different Settings of the Home-Based Palliative Care Program

Some home-based palliative care programs are embedded in a home care or hospice agency. The Transitional Care Model program mentioned previously had APRNs in a home care agency, allowing them access to the interdisciplinary team.[26,27] Although both standard home care and palliative home care diminish symptom distress and functional dependence, only palliative home care with APRNs decreases hospital admissions.[28] However, a limitation regarding palliative care programs within home care agencies is the requirement for the patient to have a skilled nursing need and to be homebound. Since the APRN cannot bill as an employee of the agency, there is an increased expense in employing an APRN as opposed to a registered nurse. Due to the concern regarding sustainability, one study suggested that instead of home care employing an APRN specialized in oncology or palliative care, the home care nurses should strengthen the collaboration with the oncology APRN in the oncology practice.[28]

The benefits of the interdisciplinary team also apply to programs designated as extensions of hospice agencies, offering some of the benefits of the hospice approach earlier in the terminal illness. However, since an APRN cannot bill when employed by a hospice, the palliative care program would have to focus on indirect benefits, such as increasing the hospice census and the hospice length of stay, in order to maintain sustainability. Not only can an APRN provide a pre-hospice consult for the patients and families, but an APRN can also educate the physicians, resulting in more appropriate referrals to hospice services. This model has been shown to be sustainable through the indirect financial benefits to the hospice agency.[5]

More commonly, a palliative care program is a clinical practice supported by a hospital or health network often embedded in a palliative care, oncology, or other specialty department. The team usually consists of physicians, APRNs, and social workers. As recommended in the National Consensus Project (NCP) Clinical Practice Guidelines 1.1, teams may also include interdisciplinary members or have access to different disciplines through partnerships in the health network.[29] Some of these models reported positive results, including improved symptom management, decreased costs, decreased hospital admissions, and decreased caregiver burden.[4,9,11,30,31] Table 19.1 provides a comparison of APRN models for home-based palliative care. The APRN's role in these practices may include coordinating the practice, conducting telephone interventions with patients or caregivers, or providing direct clinical care in the home.

Different Roles of the APRN

The scope of practice of both clinical nurse specialists (CNSs) and nurse practitioners (NPs) differs by state in the United States. CNSs traditionally were trained for roles in education, research,

Table 19.1 APRN Models of Home-Based Palliative Care

	Home Care/Hospice Agency	Office-Based Practice
Benefits	Access to interdisciplinary team[27]	Decreased cost to hospital system[4,9,11]
	Decreased hospital admissions[28]	Decreased hospital admissions[11]
	Increased hospice census[5]	Improved symptom management[9]
	Increased hospice length of stay[5]	Decreased caregiver burden[4,9]
	Sustainability through indirect financial benefit to hospice[5]	Partially sustainable through billing[2,11,38]
Burdens	Higher expense of APRN vs. RN if APRN is employee of agency[28]	Lack of resources for nonbillable interdisciplinary team members
	Must meet Medicare criteria for home care services	Often requires supplemental funding for sustainability[2,38]

and policy development, while NPs were traditionally trained for a role in providing primary care to the underserved population.[32] Over the years, the roles and education of both have expanded, and both play an important role in palliative care.

APRNs can act in a coordinator role in a palliative care program without using their full scope of practice. Through coordinating referrals, triaging phone calls from patients, and maintaining the collaborative relationship with the providers, the APRN can be an important member of the team.[2] In other palliative care programs, the APRN's role focuses only on education and telephone interventions. This may be due to lack of resources or due to the practice location, as it is less efficient to make home visits in rural communities. Through telephone interventions, the focus is to educate and empower patients to improve their self-management skills.[33] Although these programs resulted in improved patient satisfaction, they did not show significant results in improvement of symptom severity or cost-effectiveness.[33-35] The lack of improvement is not surprising, considering these programs were not maximizing the palliative APRN's full scope of practice. The lack of success also suggests that palliative care is best performed face to face, due to the complexity of each patient, including multiple comorbidities, emotional stress, and psychosocial needs.

Other palliative care programs take advantage of the APRN's full scope of practice and expertise. These skills include clinical assessment and symptom management while considering all aspects of the patient's illness, including psychosocial distress and functional capabilities. Compared to the standard practice of registered nurse visits and phone calls, even just two visits from APRNs decreased readmissions among coronary artery bypass graft patients.[36] One program found that adding a psychosocial counselor who focused on providing caregiver support did not result in significant changes in caregiver stress, suggesting that APRNs already incorporate adequate caregiver support into their comprehensive visits.[37] Even a short intervention of 12 weeks, including one to three contacts with an APRN, resulted in decreased caregiver burden as well as decreased costs to the hospital system.[9] Total and variable costs were lowered through decreases in inappropriate hospital admissions, hospital lengths of stay, and probability of a 30-day readmission.[11,31] Considering that patients with chronic complex illness will continue to experience a decline in their health status as their disease progresses, a decrease in the use of hospital resources is a substantial finding and demonstrates the significance of an APRN intervention. Most home-based programs are not sustainable on billing profits alone due to the small number of patients who are seen daily because of

time spent traveling, as well as assessing and managing patients with complex issues. Some programs cannot survive without the support of a hospital network or grants to supplement the income from visits.[2,38] Therefore, demonstrating cost-effectiveness to the hospital network through indirect benefits supports the argument for developing and maintaining a palliative care home-based program.

By focusing on each patient's goals and viewing the patient and family as a unit, the APRN can develop a patient-centered plan of care. Even one visit is useful in providing insight into the home environment and subsequently recognizing any barriers to self-management.[30] The patient-centered plan of care is shared with the primary care provider and specialists to create a "shared care" model of collaboration to improve palliative care for complex patients.[11,39] Complex chronically ill patients require a team of providers to adequately care for their multiple needs. The APRN is skilled not only at coordinating the care between providers but also modeling "best practice" by providing expert palliative care in the home.[39] However, the future of this model of care will depend on policies that support the intense collaboration required to care for this patient population.[39]

OACIS: A Model Using Palliative NPs in the Home

OACIS (Optimizing Advanced Complex Illness Support) is an example of a successful and sustainable model using NPs in the home.[11] Box 19.1 lists characteristics of a home-based palliative care program. OACIS is a medical practice of the Lehigh Valley Health Network in Allentown, Pennsylvania, that specializes in palliative care and encompasses the continuum of care, including the hospital, the clinic, and the home. The home division of OACIS is based on an NP practice model with a medical director. This is distinct from home care, as the patient does not need to be homebound, nor does the patient require skilled nursing care as defined by Medicare.

Before this program was developed, palliative care leaders in the network noted that many patients with complex illness and palliative care needs were no longer eligible for home care services because they remained at their baseline functional status. Furthermore, these patients were not yet eligible for hospice care, due to either their prognosis or their goals of care. Although these patients required additional supportive care, none was available to them through the home care model. Therefore, an NP-based model using house calls was initiated based on the fact that NPs

---

Box 19.1 Characteristics of a Home-Based Palliative Care Practice

- Use of APRNs, as well as other clinical providers
- Patient-centered/family-focused palliative care plan
- Home clinical assessment
- Symptom management
- Patient and caregiver support
- Advance care planning and goals-of-care discussions
- Psychosocial support and connection with community resources
- Patient and family education
- Care management and coordination
- Collaboration with primary care physician and specialist providers
- Collaboration with other palliative care members: social worker, nurse coordinator
- Access to other members of the interdisciplinary team
- Continuity of care between inpatient palliative care service and home

---

Table 19.2 Elements of the Home-Based Palliative APRN Role[40]

Care management and coordination of patient-centered/family-focused palliative care plan	Education about illness and treatments
Psychosocial support of patient and family	Discussion and completion of advance care planning documents
Clinical management of advanced illness and comorbidities	Collaboration with other community agencies and services

clinical coordinator who is responsible for prioritizing referrals, triaging calls from patients, and coordinating care with providers. To maintain a continuum of care, the clinical coordinator monitors patient admissions to hospitals and other facilities. OACIS also includes an inpatient palliative care service, allowing continuity of care between the community and the hospital.[11]

Elements of the APRN Role in the Home

One model of the APRN role for palliative care in the home involves four interconnected components: care management and coordination, clinical management, psychosocial support of patient and family, and education.[40] Each influences the others, creating a model for complex patients, such as those involved with the OACIS program and other palliative care programs. Table 19.2 lists the elements of the palliative APRN's role in the home.[40]

Care Management and Coordination

An essential aspect of the palliative APRN's role is the consideration of the patient's multiple comorbidities, psychosocial issues, and goals of care to help create a unique patient-centered treatment plan to maintain the patient's quality of life (NCP Guidelines Domain 1.2).[29] The objective of the treatment plan is to accurately describe the patient's story and values and how these influence the patient's care. As the patient's clear understanding of the situation is crucial, the APRN spends time explaining the "big picture." Having these conversations in the home allows patients to feel more in control of the situation, often leading to increased candor and clarity in defining their goals of care.

This patient-centered treatment plan is subsequently communicated to the multiple providers and agencies involved, creating a collaborative relationship and team approach. The APRN has the clinical and psychosocial skills to perform this collaboration effectively, developing a respectful and reciprocal relationship with other providers.[40] The patient-centered treatment plan changes with any significant alteration in the patient's situation, whether it is clinical, psychosocial, or related to the patient's goals of care. With strong knowledge in disease pathophysiology and trajectory, psychosocial assessment skills, and coordinating capabilities, APRNs excel at this role.

have the skill set to clinically care for this population, assess psychosocial issues, and provide guidance for end-of-life decisions. In addition, NPs in Pennsylvania are licensed independent providers who are eligible to bill insurance for their services, thereby contributing to the sustainability of the program. (See Chapter 4, Reimbursement for the Palliative Advanced Practice Registered Nurse.) NPs also have the appropriate skills to develop strong alliances with primary care providers and other specialists involved, to ensure a collaborative approach.[11]

Although an NP's scope of practice depends on state statutes and regulations, in Pennsylvania the role includes the diagnosis and management of symptoms, which is especially important in the home. Although a collaborating physician is always available by phone, the NP must possess the expertise and confidence to work independently in the home. The OACIS NP completes an in-home comprehensive palliative care consultation, including clinical, psychosocial, and spiritual assessment. In addition, the patient's values and goals of care are discussed, involving family and caregivers as appropriate. Subsequently, a comprehensive plan of care is developed in collaboration with the patient's primary care and specialist providers, as well as any involved community services, such as home care. By supervising and adjusting this individualized plan of care, the NP guides the patient's symptom management and helps the patient and family determine goals of care to prevent crises and unnecessary hospital admissions. Patients receiving services from the OACIS team have fewer hospital admissions, shorter hospital stays, lower medical costs, and a decreased probability of hospital readmission within 30 days of discharge.[11]

Although palliative care programs will differ, the core team of OACIS includes the APRNs, physicians, and social workers. The social worker assists patients with the more complex psychosocial needs by connecting them to resources and providing counseling (NCP Guidelines 4.2).[29] The OACIS team is supported by a nurse

Case Study 1

Bert was an 82-year-old male with multiple comorbidities, including CHF, chronic kidney disease, diabetes, and COPD. His finances were limited, and he moved in with his son and disabled daughter-in-law in their home. The son experienced caregiver stress since he was the primary caregiver for both his father and his wife and worked part time. Prior to being involved with palliative care services, the patient was hospitalized four times in nine months. With the support from the palliative APRN, his hospital admissions decreased to one per year for four years. This was due to the strong collaboration among all of his providers, who worked to keep his symptoms under control and to avoid exacerbations. As his disease progressed, he made a clear decision not to return to the hospital, but refused hospice care for personal reasons. By coordinating care with his providers, home care, and his family, the APRN was able to keep him comfortable at home throughout the progression of his renal disease. When his disease process significantly impaired his functional status, he accepted hospice care and died peacefully with his family surrounding him.

One of the biggest challenges for palliative APRNs is to consider the patient's unique situation and the "big picture" while describing and presenting it in a way that is understandable to the patient, family, and other providers. In Bert's case, it was critical to ensure that everyone understood Bert's goals to remain at home and his personal definition of quality of life. His situation was constantly changing due to a multitude of factors, so the frequent communication by the APRN with the patient's son and providers made it possible for him to maintain his quality of life at home.

Clinical Management

Although the palliative APRN encourages collaboration among all team members, he or she also enhances the patient's care with expertise in palliative care. This leads to a more robust plan of care. This plan has to be constantly monitored and altered as the disease progresses or the symptoms worsen. The APRN helps to manage these symptoms and disease processes through follow-up visits and phone calls, allowing timely interventions to prevent hospital admissions.[40] This is in contrast to a one-time consult or phone interventions without direct clinical assessments.

Furthermore, although working as a team is the ideal situation, often the urgency of a crisis requires a provider to make clinical decisions independent of the other team members. Due to their educational background and scope of practice, APRNs can independently alter the palliative treatment plan as appropriate. Often, the APRN is visiting the patient more frequently than other health providers and may notice changes in the patient's clinical situation that, untreated, would result in a clinical exacerbation. Being alert to the patient's usual state of health and signs of potential exacerbations is beneficial in helping to prevent hospital admissions.

One aspect of symptom management is obtaining the patient's perspective on the exacerbation. By involving the patient as part of the team, the APRN can better understand the significance of a particular symptom and the subsequent effect on the patient's quality of life. By determining obstacles to self-management, future exacerbations and hospital admissions can be prevented. In addition, determining the patient's priorities and main concerns helps to lend perspective to the overall situation.

Case Study 2

Regina is a 62-year-old female with CHF and COPD. Although home care nurses and her primary care provider educated her and

her partner about her medications and her disease processes, she often did not take her medications correctly, nor did she understand how her diet affected her symptoms. Additional time during a palliative care home visit was spent reinforcing self-management skills and exploring obstacles to achieving these goals. Through creative educational methods presented by the APRN, Regina's understanding of her disease process and medications improved, and so did her self-management skills. However, her COPD was progressing and steroids were required to improve her dyspnea. Her situation was fragile, for although the steroids improved her functional status, this treatment resulted in increased fluid retention. Through close monitoring and constant medication adjustments by the palliative APRN, her symptoms have been managed at home without hospital admissions for the past year.

As a patient's disease continues to progress over time, one of the roles of the APRN is to determine the patient's appropriateness for hospice. Although this is a multiple-step process that includes the patient's goals as well as emotional readiness to accept mortality, the progression of disease has to meet the hospice guidelines. The APRN has the clinical and palliative expertise to determine appropriateness and helps to refer patients to hospice earlier in their disease process so that they can benefit from services for more than the national median hospice length of stay of 18.7 days.[41]

Psychosocial Support

Home visits by the palliative APRN offer patients and families a time of undivided attention to build a trusting relationship. The APRN can be physically and emotionally present in the patient's home, allowing the patient and family members to freely discuss their concerns and needs. Home visits give the APRN a unique perspective, providing insight for the patient's overall care. This insight into the patient's daily routine, burdens, and challenges allows the APRN to support, guide, and empower the patient and family members to determine and achieve their goals of care. By focusing on the patient's needs and definition of quality of life, the APRN can reduce stress and anxiety around end-of-life care.[40]

Case Study 3

Henrietta was a 75-year-old woman with pancreatic cancer. Her symptoms included anemia, fatigue, pain, and weight loss. She had been married to her elementary-school sweetheart for 50 years and had been a second-grade teacher. At the end of the initial visit she said, "I was not the one who wanted your services, my husband did." His concerns included her weight loss, inactivity, and general decline. However, she was more concerned about upsetting her grandchildren when her physical appearance began to change. As her symptoms progressed, Henrietta required paracentesis for ascites and more frequent visits from the palliative APRN. These visits provided an opportunity for a trusting relationship to develop. One day, when the APRN phoned the patient, she responded, "I have been waiting for your call," illustrating the growth of this relationship. With continued phone calls and visits by the APRN, as well as support from her church and family, she was able to feel more confident and comfortable with the physical changes she experienced as her disease progressed. This allowed her to continue to be a "teacher" to her grandchildren. Support was offered for both the patient and her husband throughout the journey. Although her husband was not ready to "allow the cancer to win," the APRN provided support through active listening, which allowed him to express his fears and grief.

During the home visit, the APRN provided active listening and was emotionally present with the patient and the family in a safe environment. This provided Henrietta and her family an opportunity to develop a trusting relationship with the APRN and accept the support offered to them. The unique and supportive care provided by the palliative APRN allowed the patient to die with dignity.

Patient and Family Education

The palliative APRN in the home setting is in an excellent position to provide information to patients and families about disease progression and life-prolonging care. He or she has the expertise to offer individualized guidance related to specific aspects of a patient's disease and comorbidities, symptom management, and available resources to support both the patient and family through the transition to end-of-life care.

The APRN assists in advance care planning by engaging patients and families to reflect on their values, understand their disease process and progression, and develop a palliative care plan. This is accomplished during home visits, in family meetings, and in coordination and collaboration with other services and providers. The APRN shares this information with the patient's providers to maintain continuity of care.[40]

If the patient and the family are interested, an out-of-hospital order for life-sustaining treatment (commonly known as POLST [Physician/Provider Orders for Life Sustaining Treatment], MOLST [Medical Orders for Life Sustaining Treatment], or other state-specific acronyms) is discussed. These out-of-hospital orders serve as a guide for family and caregivers, emergency personnel, and hospital staff, reflecting the patient's wishes regarding aggressive life-prolonging care, including resuscitation, mechanical intubation, use of antibiotics, and artificial nutrition and hydration. Depending on the state, an out-of-hospital order for life-sustaining treatment such as POLST or MOLST documents may be honored by emergency medical services. The APRN should ensure that copies are distributed and placed in a prominent and easily accessible location in the home.

Case Study 4

Maggie was an 85-year-old woman with end-stage dementia. She was well cared for by her husband at home, with the assistance of the county aide services, who provided caregiver relief for a few hours each day. The palliative APRN determined Maggie was FAST Stage 7e.[42] Maggie had lost the ability to speak intelligibly, to ambulate, to sit without assistance, to control her bowel and bladder function, and to smile. She tolerated a daily routine and feedings. She had a history of aspiration and seizures and had been on a puréed diet for many years. Her husband, Randell, was clear that he would not want any aggressive life-prolonging care for Maggie, but he was not aware that a gastric feeding tube could be an option should she experience increased episodes of aspiration. The APRN talked to him about the process of placement of a gastric feeding tube, the implications for prolonging life

without improvement in quality of living, and the continued risk of aspiration in end-stage dementia. In addition, the symptoms associated with aspiration and management of the symptoms to provide comfort was explained. Randell decided to decline gastric feeding, and this led to a conversation about how to best support both Maggie and her family in the event that she had a sudden life-threatening aspiration. A plan was made in collaboration with the primary care provider so that an immediate referral to hospice would be placed in the case of sudden aspiration.

Several months later, Maggie developed symptoms of aspiration, including shortness of breath, fever, and lung congestion. Randell called the primary care provider, who made a referral to hospice. Maggie died a few days later at home with her family at her side.

Timely education about disease process and the possibility of complications helps prepare the patient and family. This information helped Maggie's family to develop a plan of care honoring her wishes. To effectively communicate the patient's goals of avoiding heroic measures to all providers, a document was dictated into the hospital electronic medical record. A well-developed plan allowed the patient to remain at home, avoiding an unwanted hospital admission, and created a smooth transition to hospice.

Programmatic Characteristics of Palliative Care in the Home

Referral Process

Referrals to palliative care programs can be received from a variety of sources, including community primary care providers, specialty providers, hospital discharge planning staff, and home care services, as well as patients and caregivers themselves. Referrals should be managed by a clinically trained professional to assess eligibility and triage symptom management concerns and psychosocial needs. Proper consultation etiquette suggests that the primary care provider be alerted if he or she has not initiated the referral. This establishes collaboration, which is an important aspect of any home palliative care program.

The criteria for patient eligibility for palliative care differ between programs and are influenced by the needs of the local community. Criteria often include adults with advanced complex illness, including metastatic and progressing cancer, organ failure, and dementia. Eligibility for palliative care should take into consideration the patient's clinical presentation, health care utilization, and psychosocial needs, to best determine his or her level of acuteness and complexity.

Patient Encounters

The patient's length of stay in a palliative care program is dependent on symptom burden, disease progression, and the psychosocial needs of the patient and family. Some initial consults may only require one visit due to an immediate transition to hospice. Visit frequency for each patient varies and should be determined at each appointment, depending on the patient's current clinical and psychosocial needs as well as the staff and resources of each practice. Visits can be scheduled in between appointments with the patient's primary care provider or specialist to maintain continuity of care.

The amount of time spent completing initial palliative care consults and subsequent visits depends on the complexity and acuteness of the patient's needs. Upon meeting the patient and family for the first time, the APRN explains the palliative care home-based service and clarifies the APRN's role. A working relationship with the patient and family is subsequently established, with the focus of care being patient-centered and patient-driven. With this approach, patients often prioritize their greatest health concerns early in the visit. Time is allowed for patients to describe their experience of living with chronic illness, their coping mechanisms, and their life's journey.

Effects of Catchment Area

Geography is an important consideration for both size of caseload and number of visits per day. In addition to the length of time spent with each patient, the travel time between patients restricts the number of patient visits each day. Travel time is affected by whether the catchment area is urban, suburban, or rural. Practices with multiple providers should consider regionalization of providers to improve efficiency.

Preparation and Communication

In preparation for a patient encounter, the APRN should review the patient's medical record and consult providers to clearly understand the patient's overall situation and prognosis. Important aspects of palliative care documentation may include emphasis on an extensive history of present illness, a thorough social history, a functional assessment, and documentation of discussions about the patient's values and goals of care and the emotional struggles with these decisions. These are the specific sections of the clinical note that make palliative care documentation distinct from a typical office visit note and illustrate the contribution of palliative care toward the overall plan of care. After the encounter, the APRN should communicate these findings with all providers and involved community agencies to ensure continuity of care.

A palliative care team should meet regularly to discuss and collaborate on difficult cases. This allows input from the entire interdisciplinary team to help formulate the basis of the palliative care plan (NCP Guidelines 1.1).[29] Team meetings can also provide an opportunity for team members to help recognize and alleviate caregiver stress (Box 19.2).

Summary

Palliative APRNs are instrumental in providing comprehensive care for patients with advanced complex illness. Their advanced education and nursing experience allow them to offer a unique patient-centered approach to care in the home. The palliative APRN provides individualized care through undivided attention and understanding of the patient's comorbidities, support system, and home environment. The palliative APRN maintains continuity of care with the patient, supporting the development of a trusting relationship, which encourages conversations regarding values and goals. Through their ability to manage symptoms, to address psychosocial issues, to provide guidance through education, and to discuss goals of care, palliative APRNs improve the quality of care for patients with advanced complex illness.

Box 19.2 Development Considerations of a Home-Based Palliative Care Program

Patient Population
- Needs assessment of the community
- Consideration of appropriate patient population
- Geographic catchment area

Palliative Care Services
- Role of palliative care service—consultative, co-management, primary provider, or mix of all three
- Access of palliative care team after hours and on weekends
- Scheduling—frequency and duration of patient encounters
- Team members, including clinical staff, support staff, and interdisciplinary team
- Design of a comprehensive palliative care clinical note

Community Collaboration
- Establishment of relationships with primary care physicians and specialists
- Establishment of relationships with community services—county services, home health agencies, hospices

Administrative
- Reimbursement process
- Development of data and metrics upon which to measure success
- Staff continuing education and certification

References

1. Goldstein NE, Morrison RS. The intersection between geriatrics and palliative care: a call for a new research agenda. *J Am Geriatrics Soc.* 2005; 53(9): 1593–8.
2. Holley APH, Gorawara-Bhat R, Dale W, Hemmerich J, Cox-Hayley D. Palliative access through care at home: experiences with an urban, geriatric home palliative care program. *J Am Geriatrics Soc.* 2009; 57(10): 1925–31.
3. Wajnberg A, Ornstein K, Zhang M, Smith KL, Soriano T. Symptom burden in chronically ill homebound individuals. *J Am Geriatrics Soc.* 2013; 61(1): 126–31.
4. Ornstein K, Wajnberg A, Kaye-Kauderer H, et al. Reduction in symptoms for homebound patients receiving home-based primary and palliative care. *J Palliat Med.* 2013; 16(9): 1048–54.
5. Bookbinder M, Glajchen M, McHugh M, et al. Nurse practitioner-based models of specialist palliative care at home: sustainability and evaluation of feasibility. *J Pain Symptom Management.* 2011; 41(1): 25–34.
6. Gomes B, Calanzani N, Curiale V, McCrone P, Higginson IJ. Effectiveness and cost-effectiveness of home palliative care services for adults with advanced illness and their caregivers. *Cochrane Database of Systematic Reviews.* 2013(6). doi: 10/1002/14651858.CD007760.pub2.
7. Gomes B, Calanzani N, Higginson IJ. Benefits and costs of home palliative care compared with usual care for patients with advanced illness and their family caregivers. *JAMA.* 2014; 311(10): 1060–1.

8. Brumley R, Enquidanos S, Jamison P, et al. Increased satisfaction with care and lower costs: results of a randomized trial of in-home palliative care. *J Am Geriatr Soc.* 2007; 55(7): 993–1000.

9. Higginson IJ, McCrone P, Hart SR, Burman R, Silber E, Edmonds PM. Is short-term palliative care cost effective in multiple sclerosis? A randomized phase II trial. *J Pain Symptom Management.* 2009; 38(6): 816–26.

10. Hughes SL, Cummings J, Weaver F, Manheim L, Braun B, Conrad K. A randomized trial of the cost effectiveness of VA hospital based home care for the terminally ill. *Health Services Res.* 1992; 26(6): 801–17.

11. Lukas L, Foltz C, Paxton H. Hospital outcomes for a home-based palliative medicine consulting service. *J Palliat Med.* 2013; 16(2): 179–84.

12. Aiken LS, Butner J, Lockhart CA, Volk-Craft BE, Hamilton G, Williams FG. Outcome evaluation of a randomized trial of the Phoenix Care Intervention: program of case management and coordinated care for the seriously chronically ill. *J Palliat Med.* 2006; 9(1): 111–26.

13. Chan CW, Chui YY, Chair SY, et al. The evaluation of a palliative care programme for people suffering from life-limiting diseases. *J Clin Nurs.* 2014; 23(1-2): 113–23.

14. Hopp FP, Trzcinski E, Roth R, et al. Cost analysis of a novel interdisciplinary model for advanced illness management. *Am J Hospice Palliat Care.* 2014; Feb 21 [Epub ahead of print].

15. Uitdehaag MJ, Van Putten PG, Van Eijck CHJ, et al. Nurse-led follow-up at home vs. conventional medical outpatient clinic follow-up in patients with incurable upper gastrointestinal cancer: a randomized study. *J Pain Symptom Management.* 2014; 47(3): 518–30.

16. Ranganathan A, Dougherty M, Waite D, Casarett D. Can palliative home care reduce 30-day readmissions? Results of a propensity score matched cohort study. *J Palliat Med.* 2013; 16(10): 1290–3.

17. Rabow MW, Schanche K, Petersen J, Dibble SL, Mcphee SJ. Patient perceptions of an outpatient palliative care intervention. *J Pain Symptom Management.* 2003; 26(5): 1010–5.

18. Rabow MW, Dibble SL, Pantilat SZ, McPhee SJ. The comprehensive care team: a controlled trial of outpatient palliative medicine consultation. *Arch Intern Med.* 2004; 164(1): 83–91.

19. Kerr CW, Tangeman JC, Rudra CB, et al. Clinical impact of a home-based palliative care program: a hospice-private payer partnership. *J Pain Symptom Management.* 2014; April 18 [Epub ahead of print].

20. Groh G, Vyhnalek B, Feddersen B, Führer M, Borasio GD. Effectiveness of a specialized outpatient palliative care service as experienced by patients and caregivers. *J Palliat Med.* 2013; 16(8): 848–56.

21. Labson MC, Sacco MM, Weissman DE, Gornet B, Stuart B. Innovative models of home-based palliative care. *Cleveland Clinic J Med.* 2013; 80(E-Suppl. 1): E-S30–S35.

22. Wong RC, Tan PT, Seow YH, et al. Home-based advance care programme is effective in reducing hospitalisations of advanced heart failure patients: a clinical and health care cost study. *Ann Acad Med Singapore.* 2013; 42(9): 466–71.

23. U.S. Census Bureau, P23-212, *65+ in the United States: 2010.* Washington, DC: U.S. Government Printing Office; 2014.

24. Heinle R, McNulty J, Hebert RS. Nurse practitioners and the growth of palliative medicine. *Am J Hospice Palliat Med.* 2014; 31(3): 287–91.

25. Quagilietti S, Blum L, Ellis V. The role of the adult nurse practitioner in palliative care. *J Hospice Palliat Nurs.* 2004; 6(4): 209–14.

26. Naylor MD, Brooten DA, Campbell RL, Maislin G, McCauley KM, Schwartz JS. Transitional care of older adults hospitalized with heart failure. *J Am Geriatr Soc.* 2004; 52(7): 1228.

27. Mccauley KM., Bixby MB, Naylor MD. Advanced practice nurse strategies to improve outcomes and reduce cost in elders with heart failure. *Disease Management.* 2006; 9(5): 302–10.

28. McCorkle R, Benoleil JQ, Donaldson G, Georgiadou F, Moinpour C, Goodell B. A randomized clinical trial of home nursing care for lung cancer patients. *Cancer.* 1989; 64:1375–82.

29. National Consensus Project for Quality Palliative Care. *Clinical Practice Guidelines for Quality Palliative Care.* 3rd ed. Pittsburgh, PA: NCP. 2013. Available at http://www.nationalconsensusproject.org/Guidelines_Download2.aspx

30. Boling PA, Chandekar RV, Hungate B, Purvis M, Selby-Penczak R, Abbey LJ. Improving outcomes and lowering costs by applying advanced models of in-home care. *Cleveland Clinic J Med.* 2013; 80(E-Suppl. 1): E-S7–S14.

31. Smith KL, Ornstein K, Soriano T, Muller D, Boal J. A multidisciplinary program for delivering primary care to the underserved urban homebound: looking back, moving forward. *J Am Geriatrics Soc.* 2006; 54(8): 1283–9.

32. Rose S, All A, Gresham D. Role preservation of the clinical nurse specialist and the nurse practitioner. *Internet J Adv Nursing Practice* 2002; 5(2). Available at https://ispub.com/IJANP/5/2/7413

33. Bakitas M, Lyons KD, Hegel MT, et al. Effects of a palliative care intervention on clinical outcomes in patients with advanced cancer: the project ENABLE II randomized controlled trial. *JAMA.* 2009; 302(7): 741–9.

34. Bakitas M, Bishop MF, Caron P, Stephens L. Developing successful models of cancer palliative care services. *Semin Oncol Nurs.* 2010; 4: 266–84.

35. Bruera E, Yennurajalingam S, Palmer JL, et al. Methylphenidate and/or a nursing telephone intervention for fatigue in patients with advanced cancer: a randomized, placebo-controlled, phase II trial. *J Clin Oncol.* 2013; 31(19): 2421–7.

36. Hall MH, Esposito RA, Pekmezaris R, et al. Cardiac surgery nurse practitioners prevent coronary artery bypass graft readmissions. *Ann Thorac Surg.* 2014; 97(5): 1488–95.

37. Walsh K, Jones L, Tookman A, et al. Reducing emotional distress in people caring for patients receiving specialist palliative care: randomised trial. *Br J Psychiatry.* 2007; 190: 142–7.

38. Stuart B, D'Onofrio N, Boatman S, Feigelman G. CHOICES: promoting early access to end-of-life care through home-based transition management. *J Palliat Med.* 2003; 6(4): 671–83.

39. Marshall D, Howell D, Brazil K, Howard M, Taniguchi A. Enhancing family physician capacity to deliver quality palliative home care: an end-of-life, shared care model. *Canadian Family Physician.* 2008; 54: 1703e1–1703e6.

40. Dietrick L, Rockwell E, Gratz N, et al. Delivering specialized palliative care in the community: a new role for nurse practitioners. *Advances Nurs Sci.* 2011; 34(4): E23–E36.

41. National Hospice and Palliative Care Organization. Facts and Figures: Hospice Care, 2013 edition. Alexandria, VA: NHPCO. Available at http://www.nhpco.org/sites/default/files/public/Statistics_Research/2013_Facts_Figures.pdf. Published October 2013. Accessed July 20, 2014.

42. Riesberg B. Functional Assessment Staging (FAST). *Psychopharmacol Bull.* 1988; 24: 653–659.

CHAPTER 20

The Palliative Advanced Practice Registered Nurse in the Nursing Home

MariJo Letizia

Key Points

- The nursing home is a major setting for death and dying in the United States, and this trend is likely to increase in upcoming years.

- Palliative advanced practice registered nurse (APRNs) are ideally suited to direct and deliver palliative care to patients and their families in nursing homes, but they need education and skills to do so.

- Palliative APRNs must ensure that high-quality palliative care is provided to patients in nursing homes, in accordance with recommended practices, in order to promote their quality of life.

Introduction

In the United States today, people are living longer despite the occurrence and progression of chronic diseases. By the year 2030, one in five people in the United States will be 65 years of age or older, totaling over 70 million,[1] in part due to the aging baby boom generation. However, while people are living longer, many cannot maintain independent living in a home setting, especially when they are near or at the end-of-life. In these cases, long-term care is often provided in a nursing home.

A nursing home is a long-term care facility serving as a place of residence for patients who cannot care for themselves. Room and board are provided with 24-hour custodial and nursing care. Nursing homes were first built in the United States in the 1930s, and an expansion of these facilities occurred in the 1960s when Medicare was established. Currently, over 17,000 nursing homes are in operation across the United States. Each state regulates the licensing of these facilities. The cost of daily room and board and nursing home care is paid out of pocket by the patient and/or family, with long-term care insurance, or with state Medicaid funding. The number of patients living in U.S. nursing homes is quite high, with an estimated 1.5 million people residing in these facilities before their death.[2] The vast majority of patients are 65 years old or older. The need for nursing home beds is expected to increase dramatically in the near future: by the year 2030 more

than 3 million people are expected to reside in a long-term-care setting.[3]

The nursing home is a major setting for death and dying in the United States and this trend is likely to continue. While approximately 28% of patients die in nursing homes currently, the number is expected to increase in coming years. The median length of stay for a nursing home patient is 463 days.[2] The median and mean length of stay before death is reported as 5 months and 13.7 ± 18.4 months, respectively; 53% of patients die within 6 months of nursing home placement.[4] In most cases, patients die of chronic, progressive, and debilitating diseases, such as dementia and heart disease.[2] Prior to death, these patients often experience a decline in functional status that includes cognitive decline and physical frailty.

Because the nursing home is the final place of residence for many elderly patients who have life-limiting illnesses, high-quality palliative care must be carefully planned and delivered in these facilities. Of particular importance is the incorporation of approaches that improve the quality of living and the quality of dying of these patients, particularly as they reach the end of their lives. One proposed solution to meet the needs of this expanding population is to increase the number of APRNs who can provide direct patient evaluation and management at the advanced practice level, and who can also improve care at the system level.

Challenges in Providing Palliative Care in Nursing Homes

An estimated 80% of nursing home patients are deemed appropriate for palliative care, but palliative approaches are underused in long-term-care settings.[5] All essential components of palliative care as delineated in consensus documents by experts and professional organizations can be included in the care provided to appropriately identified patients in nursing homes. Fundamentally, these components include ongoing evaluation and management of pain and other symptoms; careful communication about goals of care, including advance care planning, so that care can be aligned with patient/family-stated preferences; and incorporating culturally appropriate approaches to care, including psychosocial and spiritual support. However, a number of challenges may influence the delivery of palliative care in nursing homes.

Staff Variables

Nursing staff may experience challenges in providing palliative care in nursing homes, including the need to adapt to a higher level of patient acuity than in years past. Patients in these facilities are living longer with more complex comorbid conditions and more highly aggressive interventions, including the use of intravenous fluids and medications; peritoneal dialysis and hemodialysis; ventilator support, such as positive-pressure devices and tracheostomies; advanced wound care approaches; and extensive polypharmacy. Staff members who have had a long tenure in these facilities may be familiar and comfortable with a more stable patient population but need to adjust to a higher level of patient care needs.

The care provided by nursing home staff can be affected when turnover occurs, potentially leading to a higher nurse-to-patient ratio. Nursing homes may be understaffed, with a pattern of high turnover among all team members, including direct care providers as well as administrators.[3] A higher rate of turnover in these settings may be related to lower pay, more difficult work, less professional respect, and greater understaffing than in other types of healthcare facilities.[2]

Education of nursing staff is another important variable to consider in the delivery of care in nursing homes. Many staff members are either licensed professional nurses (LPNs or LVNs) or registered nurses (RNs) who have completed an associate or diploma program for their basic nursing training. The curricula in these programs may focus more specifically on task-oriented care rather than the person-centered care currently needed in long-term-care settings.[6] Likewise, these nurses may not have been formally educated with a strong foundation in providing care for highly complex patients in nursing homes, particularly during acute changes in condition and when they are near the end-of-life.

All too often, palliative care is not universally included as a content area in prelicensure nursing education programs at the diploma, associate, or baccalaureate levels. Yet all nursing staff in nursing homes must have the knowledge, skill, and comfort to care for patients who are living with, and dying from, life-limiting illnesses. Strategies to achieve this learning include continuing education programs, orientation programs for new employees, on-the-job apprenticeship training, and support for staff to enroll in formal university coursework in palliative care. In addition to those providing direct care, facility administrators, including the director of nursing, medical director, and director of therapies, influence system issues that affect the provision of palliative care; these individuals can also benefit from education about palliative care.

Underidentification of Patients

Challenges abound in identifying patients in long-term care settings who might benefit from palliative care approaches. For patients with advanced chronic diseases, a specific focus on prognostication is thought to be neither helpful nor required for the initiation of palliative care. Instead, attention to a new or rapid decline in functional status, including changes in the ability to perform activities of daily living, may be a more helpful trigger in this patient population.[3] Other clinical findings that may indicate an appropriate shift to palliative care include declining cognition, decreased oral intake, and/or weight loss in light of progressive illness. Repeated emergency department evaluations and/or repeated hospital admissions are other important triggers. Long-term-care patients with advanced-stage disease or multiple comorbidities and those who do not respond favorably to evidence-based pharmacologic or nonpharmacologic treatments to correct or cure the underlying condition are also likely to benefit from palliative approaches.

National experts suggest that providers consider one simple question in order to better identify patients who are appropriate for palliative care: "Would you be surprised if this patient were to die in the next 12 to 24 months?" If the answer is "no" and death is anticipated during this timeframe, a shift in focus to full supportive care may be appropriate. In the nursing home, the APRN then considers discontinuing diagnostic tests that will not change the plan of care, discontinuing medications no longer deemed essential or helpful, and instituting a Do Not Hospitalize (DNH) order.

Influence of State and Federal Regulation

Regulatory issues may also contribute to the underuse of palliative care in nursing homes. The Omnibus Budget Reconciliation Act 1987, also known as the Federal Nursing Home Reform Act, continues to influence the delivery of care in these settings. This legislation introduced minimal standards for patient care; specifically, facilities with Medicaid and Medicare funding are required to demonstrate that each patient receives, and the facility provides, the necessary care and services to attain or maintain the highest practicable physical, mental, and psychosocial well-being, in accordance with the comprehensive assessment and plan of care. This language might be incorrectly interpreted as requiring a plan for restorative care for all nursing home patients, in order to ensure that those patients' conditions improve and/or that they avoid a decline and achieve a high state of functioning. However, patients with advanced, incurable diseases do reach a point in which a decline in function is both expected and unavoidable. For example, patients diagnosed with dementia often proceed along a normal course of disease progression, ultimately leading to a decrease in oral intake and hydration, weight loss, and weakness. These findings, indicative of a predicted decline in condition and function, are not inherently indicators of substandard care in this patient population.

The current Centers for Medicare and Medicaid Services (CMS) agency manual defines palliative care as "patient and family-centered care that optimizes quality of life by anticipating, preventing, and treating suffering. Palliative care throughout the continuum of illness involves addressing physical, intellectual, emotional, social, and spiritual needs and to facilitate patient autonomy, access to information, and choice."

To avoid regulatory scrutiny and to promote appropriate palliation, physicians and APRNs must be diligent in their documentation as they evaluate and treat patients who are near or at the end-of-life in the long-term care setting. In particular, for those patients in whom lack of improvement or decline in status is evident, the provider's progress notes must describe the evidence of decline in the patient's status, including expected assessment findings on the history and physical exam, as well as results of appropriate diagnostic testing. The defined and expected findings of disease progression are taken into account as palliative management strategies are incorporated in the plan of care. In particular, the medical providers' communication with staff members in the facility is of utmost importance, so that the patient's care plan is consistently updated to reflect changes in the patient's condition. Such changes lead to decisions about interventions that are implemented by staff and then revised in accordance with the patient's response. In the case of progressive disease, supporting documentation also includes communication that has taken place with the patient and family that the underlying disease is not curable and a decline in the patient's condition is anticipated. In these cases, it is essential to document discussions with the patient, family, and members of the interdisciplinary team regarding goals of care and treatment approaches.

The care provided to patients in nursing homes that participate in Medicare and Medicaid funding must comply with all uniform state and federal regulations. The CMS is responsible for monitoring the quality of care and enforcing the standards that have been set. Monitoring includes an on-site evaluation by state surveyors at least annually, as well as the investigation of complaints should they occur. These surveys are unannounced and involve a team of healthcare professionals. The focus of the team's survey includes assessment of patients' conditions, rights, and needs; assessment of the facility's policies and procedures; assessment of medication management and skin care; and assessment of the facility environment, including food service. Information is gathered from the medical record, interviews with the patient (or the patient's legal representative), and communication with facility staff and medical providers caring for the patient. If an inspection reveals a failure to meet a standard(s), the facility may be issued a deficiency citation that requires action, called a plan of correction (POC). The POC must include the following: (1) corrective actions for those patients affected by the deficiency; (2) the plan for identification of other patients who are also potentially affected by the deficiency; and (3) the plan to ensure that the deficiency will not recur. The POC must also include use of the facility's quality assurance program to monitor the systems, policies, and procedures for ongoing compliance.

Deficiencies are classified as ranging in scope from being isolated and less serious, to being widespread and very serious. Deficiencies are also judged according to severity, ranging from "no actual harm with potential for minimal harm" to the patient, to "immediate jeopardy to resident health or safety." Remedies imposed are based on the scope and severity of detected deficiencies and include the following: requiring in-service training for the staff; fines to the facility, or denial of payments for services provided; replacement of the facility administrator with temporary management; or installation of a state monitor in the facility. Ultimately, the failure of the facility to comply with standards can result in the CMS revoking the facility's certification.

In 2012, the CMS made changes in the surveyor guidance regarding end-of-life care provided to patients in long-term-care facilities. Specifically, for patients approaching the end of life, the following must be accomplished and documented: (1) identifying the patient's prognosis on the basis of a comprehensive assessment; (2) advising and educating the patient and family about palliative care approaches, including hospice care; (3) advance care planning that includes the patient, family, and interdisciplinary team; and (4) delineating patient preferences regarding care. Advance care planning must include a discussion with the patient and family regarding treatment approaches, including hospitalization, if acute changes in condition occur. The plan of care must be reviewed and revised on a consistent basis, demonstrating that the services provided to the patient align with the wishes of the patient and family.

Medical Record Documentation in the Long-Term-Care Setting

Components of documentation in patients' nursing home medical records are quite different than in other healthcare settings, and the APRN must understand these unique requirements. The Resident Assessment Instrument (RAI) provides a uniform mechanism for gathering, documenting, and analyzing comprehensive assessments of each patient's functional status, health needs, and preferences for care. Assessments include interviews with the patient as well as staff observations of the patient and data from the patient's chart. Using RAI, members of the interdisciplinary team can develop a plan of care, review and evaluate achievement of the goals of care, and revise the plan as needed. The RAI consists of three components: the Minimum Data Set (MDS), the Care Assessment Areas (CAAs) (formerly named Resident Assessment Protocols), and Utilization Guidelines that provide instructions on the use of the RAI, including the synthesis of information from the MDS.

Minimum Data Set

The MDS is a lengthy standardized instrument regarding the comprehensive assessment of patients' conditions and care. The MDS is completed for each patient within 14 days of admission to the facility, quarterly in the first year, annually in years after the first, with any significant change in the patient's condition, and upon the patient's discharge from the facility or death. MDS items are divided into three general categories: (1) physical (e.g., medical condition, mood, vision), (2) functional (e.g., activities of daily living, behavior), and (3) psychosocial (e.g., preferences, goals of care, interests). Data documented on the MDS form the basis for further assessment of the patient and for developing his or her plan of care.

Information on the MDS directly affects payments to the facility. The level of reimbursement for care provided to the patient is based on the patient's acuity and use of resources considering the patient's needs. Each patient is evaluated according to a reimbursement utilization group category. The eight major groups are (1) rehabilitation plus extensive services, (2) rehabilitation, (3) extensive services, (4) special care high, (5) special care low, (6) clinically complex (including components such as dialysis and oxygen therapy), (7) behavioral symptoms and cognitive performance problems, and (8) physical function reduced. This structure of compensation is based on a model of restorative care, with facilities receiving a far higher level of reimbursement for providing skilled care services. A financial disincentive exists when the facility focuses on palliative care, because approaches such as advance care planning and the provision of psychosocial support are not well reimbursed.[3]

MDS findings are also used to evaluate the quality of care provided to the patient. This is achieved via the MDS-based quality indicators (QIs) and quality measures (QMs). QIs are the conditions and aspects of care related to the patient's health status and level of function, as delineated in the MDS, that demonstrate the presence or absence of quality care practices. QIs comprise 18 physical and clinical categories, such as the prevalence of pressure ulcers, restraint use, pain, and falls in the facility. QMs are numeric values assigned to the QIs, in accordance with published nursing home quality indicators. For example, one MDS-based QM is the percentage of patients in the facility who have an indwelling catheter when compared to the prior assessment. The QMs are intended to provide an objective measure for patients and their families as they compare the quality of care provided in nursing homes. The "Five-Star Quality Rating System" is available to the public on the Medicare.gov "Nursing Home Compare" website. The ratings are developed based on specific quality measures as noted above, the average hours of nursing staff providing care in the facility, the results of state surveys, and an overall composite rating. However, because the prime focus of surveys relates to restorative measures, the information reported on this website does not include measures indicating the provision of high-quality palliative care to those with advanced illness.

Care Assessment Areas

Information on the MDS delineates potential or actual problems that then serve as a "trigger" to the staff, leading to further evaluation of the patient. CAAs provide a mechanism to systematically review 20 common triggered areas of concern, conditions, and symptoms experienced by nursing home patients, including delirium, urinary incontinence, falls, pressure ulcer, and pain. Using the CAAs, additional assessment is undertaken by the staff, including an examination of a host of underlying factors that cause or contribute to the problem. This holistic assessment of potential and actual problems, along with an analysis of findings, then leads to the development of the patient's written and active plan of care. To enact the plan of care, goals of care are communicated among interdisciplinary team members, who work together with the patient and family to achieve those goals.

Ideally, the CAAs provide an important mechanism to identify patients appropriate for palliation and to implement a plan of palliative care. For example, in a patient diagnosed with progressive dementia, a change in the patient's cognitive patterns is noted on the MDS and triggers the related area on the CAA. This trigger leads the team to evaluate components of mental status changes, including a description of the current problem, underlying and/or reversible cause(s) and/or contributing factors, and risk factors related to the problem. From this analysis, the team delineates appropriate interventions, including diagnostic testing, and considers the need for consultation with additional disciplines or referral to additional medical providers. Evaluation of a trigger also includes reviewing the goals of care, which may include improving the patient's status, preventing further deterioration, maintaining the current status, or focusing on reduction of symptoms in light of an expected further decline in condition when the disease(s) is irreversible.

The APRN in the Nursing Home

The APRN is a central member of the team providing care to patients in long-term care settings. Considering the many challenges faced in providing palliative care to these patients, one important proposed solution is a stronger inclusion of APRNs in nursing homes. Nurse practitioners and clinical nurse specialists have been directing and delivering care in nursing homes since the 1970s. Throughout the 1990s, the proportion of nursing homes with nurse practitioners and physician assistants doubled, from less than 10% to greater than 20%,[7] with approximately 1,400 nurse practitioners employed in these facilities during that timeframe.[8] This number is expected to continue to grow in light of the increased need and demand for providers as well as the historical and ongoing limitation of physician availability in long-term care settings.[9]

APRNs are ideally suited for both direct and indirect care roles in nursing homes. Having been prepared with the graduate-level education, they possess a high level of knowledge and skill, demonstrated in part by obtaining national certification in advanced nursing practice. As direct care providers, nurse practitioners have particular expertise in assessing, diagnosing, and managing patients with complex health conditions, with a focus on interdisciplinary coordination of care. Clinical nurse specialists have particular expertise in affecting systems of care, including planning for, implementing, and evaluating improvements in quality and safety. All APRNs are expected to have honed their communication skills so they can serve as advocates for patients and their families. The APRN's role also includes educating patients, families, and staff; evaluating and using evidence-based practices; and providing support and consultation for patients, staff, and the facility.

Considering the strong preparation of APRNs and their roles in positively affecting the care provided to patients and families in nursing homes, a panel of clinical experts has recommended the following strategies for increasing the impact of these providers: (1) increase the presence of APRNs in nursing homes, (2) require geriatric content in APRN educational preparation, (3) delineate resident, facility, and practitioner factors that influence the number and type of reimbursable APRN visits per day, (4) restructure APRN reimbursement to account for nonbillable activities related to resident care, and (5) provide the technical assistance necessary to facilitate APRN practice in nursing homes.[10]

APRN Practice Models in the Nursing Home

A variety of practice models exist for APRNs practicing in nursing homes. Some APRNs are employed by the nursing home itself; in these cases, the APRN can develop a close familiarity and working relationship with the administration, staff, patients, and families. Other APRNs who evaluate and manage patients in nursing homes are employed as independent providers, having been hired by their own practice group, a physician group, or a larger healthcare system. These individuals may provide care at more than one facility. Some APRNs are employed by a hospice and/or palliative care program; these individuals also generally provide care to patients in more than one facility.

The way in which APRNs bill and receive reimbursement for services provided in a nursing home depends, in part, on their practice model. Providers who serve as the patient's primary care attending and those who serve as a palliative care consultant use fee-for-service billing under Medicare Part B, Medicaid, or private insurance. Regardless of the practice model, APRNs provide high-quality care to long-term care patients along with their physician colleagues, following regulatory and facility policies. This includes reviewing the patient's plan of care, including the results of diagnostic testing, current medications and nonpharmacologic treatments, including approaches to nutrition, and progress in any skilled therapies and/or therapeutic or restorative activities.

The physician at the nursing home completes a comprehensive history and physical examination of the patient within 72 hours of admission and then reevaluates the patient within 30 days. APRNs providing direct care complete an initial comprehensive assessment of the patient's medical stability and subsequently can alternate visits with the physician every 30 days for a period of 1 year. After the first year of residency, the patient is evaluated every 60 to 90 days for chronic disease management. During these visits, providers monitor the patient for changes in condition and can carefully focus on the alignment of the patient's goals of care with the specific plan of care. The APRN also evaluates patients for periodic assessments and when they experience changes in condition and/or episodic illnesses. During these visits, the APRN is attentive to the patient's functional status, especially in light of the expected trajectory of the patient's medical diagnosis or diagnoses.

APRN Outcomes

Multiple investigations over the past several years have established the effectiveness of APRNs in providing cost-effective, high-quality care to patients residing in nursing homes; specific outcomes noted in published literature demonstrate the value of the APRN in long-term-care settings[11-13] (Box 20.1). One compelling systematic review of four research investigations posed the following research questions: (1) Do APRNs improve the quality of care, quality of life, functional and health status, health services use, and satisfaction of older adults living in long-term-care residential settings? (2) Do APRNs improve the quality of life and satisfaction of family members of older adults in long-term-care residential settings? (3) Do APRNs improve the skills, quality of care, and job satisfaction of healthcare staff in long-term-care residential settings? Data analysis revealed several positive outcomes attributed to the APRNs, including a reduction in depression, incontinence, pressure ulcers, restraint use, and aggressive behaviors. Patients reported a high level of meeting their stated personal goals, and family members were highly satisfied with the care provided by the APRN. Nursing home staff was satisfied with the education and consultation provided by the APRN, and with the APRN's assistance they reported improved skills, a higher quality of care delivery, and enhanced job satisfaction.[14]

Reducing Emergency Department Visits and Repeat Admissions

When palliative care is provided to nursing home patients, a specific goal often includes avoiding unnecessary emergency department visits and hospital admissions. This is especially true if those visits lead to interventions that that are inconsistent with the patient's goals of care and/or likely to increase

---

Box 20.1 Effectiveness of APRNs Providing Palliative Care in Long-Term-Care Settings

1. More thorough pain and symptom assessment, with improved pain and symptom control

2. Enhanced communication among patients, families, and providers in the facility

3. Heightened levels of respect for patient and family preference of care

4. Improved access to care because of availability to evaluate and treat patients on a timely basis

5. Increased levels of satisfaction among patients, family, and physicians

6. Fewer unnecessary laboratory and diagnostic tests

7. Greater appropriate reductions in medication use when polypharmacy is evident

8. Reduction of problems like falls and fall-related injuries, incontinence, pressure ulcers, and aggressive behavior

9. Enhanced clinical skill level, confidence, and morale of nursing home staff, including an increased sense of being appreciated[28]

10. Reduced total cost of caring for these patients[28]

---

the patient's discomfort. In particular, while no convincing evidence exists that hospital admission improves outcomes of patients who are near or at the end-of-life,[15] upwards of 40% of patients residing in nursing homes are hospitalized within 30 days of their death.[2] Working in concert with other members of the interprofessional team, the APRN can provide reasonable interventions in the nursing home when patients experience acute changes in their condition, such as treatment of infection, which may be preferred over hospital admission in this patient population.

A number of negative consequences result from repeated hospital admissions of nursing home patients, including fragmentation in the continuity of care, duplication of diagnostic workups, more frequent medical errors, and higher costs. In one investigation of nearly 500,000 patients, 19.0% met at least one of the following criteria defined as "particularly problematic": (1) hospitalization occurring in the last 3 days of life, (2) hospitalization associated with a lack of continuity in care, and (3) repeated hospitalizations.[16] Challenges of avoiding hospital admission among nursing home patients with advanced disease, particularly when they experience an acute change from their baseline status, include fear of legal ramifications if a patient is not sent to the hospital; decisions made to hospitalize patients by on-call providers who are not familiar with the patients; the need for nursing staff to more closely monitor the patient if he or she is not hospitalized; and additional requirements of staff to provide treatments such as intravenous fluid when the patient remains in the facility rather than being transferred to the hospital. Another challenge relates to financial incentives; for example, following a 3-day hospital stay, patients can return to the nursing home under the Medicare Skilled Care Benefit, in which the level of reimbursement provided to the patient and the facility is higher. Conversely, the nursing home does not receive an increase in reimbursement for providing a higher level of care for patients with higher acuity and care needs.

Understanding these challenges may help the APRN to identify mechanisms to reduce rates of repeated emergency department visits and repeat hospital admissions. For example, one initiative demonstrating positive outcomes in preventing repeat admissions is the Interventions to Reduce Acute Care Transfers (INTERACT) II program. This program focuses on staff recognition of changes in the patient's status so that unnecessary hospital admissions can be avoided.[17] The INTERACT program, facilitated by APRNs, has led to a 17% reduction in hospital admissions.

Delineating Goals of Care in the Nursing Home

While true across all care settings, close attention to advance care planning is especially important in nursing homes. Patient preferences must be ascertained, documented, and followed. However, patients in nursing homes who cannot communicate about their needs, wishes, and goals must have a surrogate decision maker to speak on their behalf. If a power of attorney for healthcare is not available, the facility must implement a mechanism for a substitute decision maker in accordance with state law.

The APRN can be instrumental in creating policies in the nursing home that make advance care planning part of the standard practice with every patient admitted to and residing in the facility. Upon the patient's admission to the facility, the APRN is in an ideal position to initiate a discussion regarding goals of care with each patient and his or her family. Likewise, throughout the patient's stay these goals can be reassessed on an ongoing basis. For instance, meetings can be routinely scheduled with patients and their families along with key members of the nursing home interdisciplinary team, including the APRN, nursing home administrator, director of nursing, director of rehabilitation services, and social worker. During these meetings, information can be reviewed and clarified as necessary regarding the patient's current condition in light of his or her advance directives. Expressed goals of care related to the patient's preference to elect or decline life-sustaining treatments are then translated into particular treatment approaches. For example, the plan of care may focus solely on comfort, focus on rehabilitation to enhance function, or focus on particular life-prolonging interventions.

Designating a surrogate decision maker in the form of a power of attorney for healthcare is especially important before the nursing home patient becomes acutely ill or loses his or her decision-making capacity. In particular, it's important that providers initiate and continue discussions with patients who, because of advanced frailty and multiple life-limiting illnesses, are expected to have a decreased life expectancy.[18] In the long-term care setting, preferences regarding a Do Not Resuscitate (DNR) or Do Not Hospitalize (DNH) order are especially important to discuss and then document according to the patient's stated preference. However, a DNR or DNH order does not preclude the need for discussions with the patient and family regarding other medical treatments.

Clinical Issues of Patients in the Nursing Home

The APRN in the nursing home participates in the evaluation and management of clinical problems commonly experienced by this patient population. Because many of these patients have conditions that are not curable, the APRN focuses on ongoing assessment of symptoms, management of symptoms according to evidence-based practices, and evaluation of selected interventions. Attention to the psychosocial needs of the patient and family is an essential component of the plan of care. Religious, cultural, and/or ethnic traditions are honored, and social service team members assist with providing information to patients and families about resources like pastoral care and bereavement support.

The APRN recognizes that patients with progressive disease reach a point in which they cannot respond to interventions intended to allay or improve an expected decline in cognition, function, and nutrition. While palliative approaches are appropriate and recommended early in the course of life-threatening illness, such approaches are particularly important when the patient is at or near the end-of-life. Regardless of the underlying condition, the presence of certain factors has been linked to the likelihood of a 6-month prognosis (Box 20.2).[19]

Regardless of the prognosis, the assessment and management of pain is of utmost importance. In nursing homes, the presence of pain is a quality indicator that is included in the MDS; for example, facilities are required to report the percentage of patients with moderate or severe pain. Despite the more recent emphasis on the management of pain, as many as 40% to 80% of patients in nursing homes experience pain, and this symptom is consistently undertreated.[20] The consequences of pain are well known, including disturbance in appetite, sleep, mobility, mental status, and activities of daily living. Pharmacologic and nonpharmacologic strategies must be included in the patient's plan of care, with close attention to alleviation of this symptom.

Long-term-care patients are frequently diagnosed with the following three conditions that can affect cognition and functional status: dementia, delirium, and depression. An estimated 66% of patients in nursing homes are diagnosed with dementia.[3] Especially in the advanced and end stages, palliative care interventions are particularly appropriate for patients with dementia. Functional decline becomes more apparent and problematic, including the risk of agitation, falls, decreased intake of food and fluids, and wandering. Although the majority of surrogate decision makers request comfort as a goal of care for their family members

---

Box 20.2 Factors Linked to Likely 6-Month Prognosis

1. Weight loss not due to reversible causes
2. Recurrent or intractable infections
3. Recurrent aspiration and/or inadequate oral intake due to intractable dysphagia
4. Progressive decline in Karnofsky Performance Status
5. Progressing dementia by objective measures
6. Progressive pressure ulcers (stage 3 or 4) despite optimal care

with dementia, burdensome approaches, such as hospital admission and artificial hydration and nutrition, are often employed.[21] The APRN is well positioned to implement system-wide and patient-specific strategies so that preferences regarding goals of care are closely aligned with management strategies for patients with advanced dementia who have lost their decision-making capacity.

Delirium, manifested by agitation and aggressive behavior, is another troublesome problem experienced by patients in nursing homes. This common diagnosis is not part of the typical process of aging and can result in morbidity and mortality. Delirium affects cognition, behavior, and functional status and often contributes to hospital admission. The APRN evaluates patients for underlying factors that may be the cause of a new onset of delirium, especially pain and/or other untreated symptoms, depression, dehydration, infection, and polypharmacy. Diagnostic testing may be appropriate if the results are expected to reveal a treatable cause. Treatment approaches include correcting the underlying contributing factors and tailoring drug therapy to the presenting symptoms. For example, antipsychotic medications may be required for patients with more acute or severe signs and symptoms. As with all patients, keeping delirious patients safe and free from harm is a central component of care.

Depression is an underdiagnosed and undertreated condition in nursing homes. Because of this, some experts have recommended universal screening of long-term-care patients. Depression negatively affects patients' quality of life, including resultant problems of fatigue, insomnia, and poor appetite with diminished oral intake that can lead to dehydration, malnutrition, and weight loss. In the nursing home, depression can be manifested as, as well as lead to social isolation and disinterest in activities in the facility. In developing the plan of care, the APRN considers antidepressant medication along with nonpharmacologic approaches to care, including psychotherapy.

Infection Prevention and Control

The risk of infection is a major consideration for APRNs providing care in a nursing home. The patients may be at increased risk because of a higher level of exposure to certain pathogens, a diminished immune response, general debility, and antibiotic resistance. The APRN considers infection as a differential diagnosis in patients with a new onset or increased level of confusion or agitation, and/or an acute change in functional status. While fever may be blunted in an elderly patient, updated guidelines from the Infectious Disease Society of America propose the following parameters of fever among patients in nursing homes: (1) a single oral temperature above 100°F (37.8°C); (2) repeated oral temperatures above 99°F (37.2°C) or rectal temperatures above 99.5°F (37.5°C); and (3) an increase in temperature of more than 2°F (1.1°C) over baseline.[22]

Particular types of infection can occur more frequently and be more problematic in nursing homes, including urinary tract infections, influenza, Clostridium difficile (C. diff), and pneumonia. If diagnosed, a determination is made regarding treatment of the patient in the facility versus in the hospital. The most frequent cause of urinary tract infection is urinary incontinence and indwelling catheters; therefore, removal of urinary catheters is important. Because patients are at risk of contracting influenza from staff and facility visitors, they are vaccinated in the fall season. During influenza outbreaks in a facility, patients may be confined to their rooms, and units with affected patients may be closed. C. diff can be especially problematic in nursing homes, because of (1) a higher incidence of fecal incontinence, leading to a higher transmission rate, and (2) the diminished ability of this patient population to tolerate the effects of diarrhea and resultant dehydration. Staff must follow evidence-based practice guidelines to treat patients diagnosed with C. diff, including enteric precautions. Healthcare-associated pneumonia acquired in a long-term-care facility is a leading cause of death in this patient population. The pneumococcal vaccine is an important mechanism for preventing streptococcal pneumonia in this population.

Nutrition and Hydration

CMS standards require nursing homes to provide patients with appropriate hydration and nutrition. A new onset of anorexia and/or weight loss triggers the need for reassessment of the patient; the plan of care must be reviewed if the patient experiences a weight change of 5% in 30 days or 10% in 6 months. Because normal aging often includes a pattern of slow weight loss, a patient is deemed to have "clinically significant" weight loss when a decrease of body weight by 5% over 6 to 12 months is detected. The APRN determines and documents those cases in which weight loss is unavoidable; for these patients, changes in nutrition are an expected consequence but not a cause of the dying process. In patients who are near or at the end-of-life, diagnostic testing is generally not helpful or recommended, as more laboratory findings regarding nutrition are nonspecific and can often be influenced by underlying diseases. Likewise, data derived from calorie counts and daily weights are not necessary when that information will not change the plan of care. Reasonable treatment approaches include involving other members of the interdisciplinary team, including the speech therapist, who can evaluate the patient's ability to swallow, and the dietitian, who can consider and recommend oral nutritional supplements. The APRN evaluates the patient for thirst; if it is present, the APRN reviews medications to determine if any may be contributing to this symptom. Artificial nutrition and hydration, including intravenous fluids and a gastrostomy feeding tube, have not been shown to improve clinical outcomes in this patient population.[23] Instead, consideration is given to lifting dietary restrictions and transitioning to pleasure feeding with aspiration precautions.

Hospice Care in the Nursing Home

Although hospice programs may provide nonhospice palliative care services and consultation in nursing homes, patients with a prognosis of 6 months or less qualify for hospice service in these facilities. Hospice care provided to eligible patients in nursing homes is reimbursed by Medicare and Medicaid. Over 17% of all hospice patients across the United States reside in a nursing home; likewise, more than 33% of all nursing home patients currently receive this care.[24] However, the hospice benefit is underused in the nursing home, particularly among those patients whose prognosis is difficult to predict.

The Conditions of Participation[25,26] define the requirements of hospices in providing care in nursing homes. The current Conditions, effective as of 2008, require the following of hospices who deliver care to nursing home patients: confirm patient's eligibility, election, and duration of benefits; complete written and signed contract with the facility; include hospice plan of care for each patient; coordinate services; and orient and train nursing staff. In 2013, the CMS emphasized the need for a partnership between the hospice program and the nursing homes, ensuring that the quality of care provided in a nursing home is equivalent to that provided to that same patient were he or she in a personal home setting.[27] For nursing home patients who elect the hospice benefit, the facility and the hospice agency are jointly responsible for developing, implementing, and evaluating a coordinated plan of care. This responsibility includes delineating which is responsible for particular aspects of the plan of care as well as the plan for communication between them regarding care services provided to the patient and family. The facility maintains the responsibility for the overall care of the patient and must notify hospice if the patient experiences an acute change in condition.

Value-added services demonstrated by hospice, beyond standard palliative care approaches in the plan of care, include volunteer, pastoral care, and bereavement services, and patient and family access to hospice staff who have specific training and skills in providing end-of-life care. Research investigations have demonstrated fewer hospital admissions, fewer unmet needs, and improved pain and non-pain assessment and management when patients are admitted to hospice in the nursing home.[28]

Case Study

Lois was a 91-year-old female admitted to the nursing home in the summer. She had been hospitalized several weeks prior to this admission following a fall at an assisted living facility that was associated with progressive weakness. A workup revealed elevated calcium and parathyroid hormone levels, leading to diagnoses of hypercalcemia and hyperparathyroidism. The APRN performed a comprehensive medical stability visit on the day Lois was admitted to the nursing home.

The patient reported a pattern of increasing weakness and fatigue over the past weeks despite attempting to alternate rest/sleep. She is frustrated but says she is "accepting" of these symptoms, stating, "After all, I'm 91 years old." She sleeps fairly well during the night but doesn't wake up feeling rested. Weakness and fatigue prevent her from being independent in ADLs, and she is afraid of falling even while using a rolling walker. She denies pain, but her appetite and oral intake have diminished greatly over the past weeks; she denies nausea but reports constipation. Her past medical history includes hypertension, coronary artery disease, GERD, and breast cancer; medications include aspirin, Pepcid, and HCTZ. The patient is a widow of many years, with one son and daughter-in-law who live nearby; another son lives out of town. Code status is DNR; her elder son is the surrogate decision maker. Living will document delineates no CPR, artificial ventilation, feeding tube, or dialysis.

Physical exam findings revealed the following: *General:* Vital signs stable; no acute distress. *Eyes:* conjunctiva clear, PERRLA. *ENT:* hearing impaired; lips/gums pink, nasal and oral mucosa pink; mouth is dry. Neck supple and symmetrical without masses or lymph enlargement; trachea midline; no thyromegaly. *Cardiac:* PMI present and non-displaced, RRR without murmur; pedal pulses palpable without peripheral edema. *Respiratory:* lungs clear. *Neurological:* recent and remote memory intact. Affect appropriate. Diagnostic testing included a calcium level of 11.9.

The diagnosis and plan included the following: *Primary hyperparathyroidism* with hypercalcemia, labile status. Start cinacalcet 30 mg po BID, low-calcium diet; dietitian consult. Renal consult. BMP in one week. *Coronary artery disease, stable.* Continue aspirin 81 mg po QD. *Hypertension, stable.* Discontinue HCTZ (can contribute to hypercalcemia); start lisinopril 10 mg po QD. GERD, stable. Continue famotidine 20 mg po BID. *Constipation, labile.* Start Miralax 17 g po QD.

For the next several weeks, Lois participated in restorative therapies, with continued weakness and fatigue. The dietitian recommended oral nutritional supplements that Lois tolerated, but her appetite and intake of food and fluids were poor, ranging from 25% to 50% for most meals. The APRN ordered megestrol as a trial approach for appetite stimulation. From the time of admission to the nursing home, the APRN and nephrologist collaborated in titrating the cinacalcet dose in accordance with weekly calcium levels. In the middle of the summer, because of increasing levels of calcium despite cinacalcet dose adjustment, the nephrologist recommended an ultrasound and nuclear medicine scan of the parathyroid that revealed a parathyroid adenoma. A surgeon recommended against surgical removal of the adenoma, citing concerns about the expected extended length of the procedure and Lois's high risk of perioperative complications. In a subsequent goals-of-care conference with the APRN, Lois expressed her agreement with continued medical management in an attempt to keep her as free of symptoms as possible; she reiterated her wish to avoid aggressive interventions, and her family supported her preference. Lois continued to have pastoral care provided by her friend, a Catholic priest. At this point, she asked for the sacrament of the Anointing of the Sick.

Near the end of the summer, despite cinacalcet dosing adjustments to a maximum of 90 mg BID, Lois's calcium level reached a critical level. To avoid unnecessary symptoms and as a time-limited approach, 0.9% saline was provided IV at 60 cc/hr for 7 days. Lois responded well to this therapy; within 10 days her calcium level had stabilized and the IV fluids were discontinued.

At the beginning of the fall, Lois experienced a new onset of cough, congestion, and low-grade fever, prompting the NP to order a chest x-ray, revealing bibasilar infiltrates. Lois was started on oral antibiotics and IV fluids. She responded to these therapies but then experienced a fall without injury. A cognitive evaluation focusing on fall safety awareness revealed an MMSE score of 27/30. An evaluation by physical therapy led to initiation of muscle strengthening and gait training, but Lois did not have the energy to participate in therapy. Despite nutritional supplementation, an increase in the dose of megestrol, and encouragement of foods and fluids, the dietitian noted a new 5% weight loss over 1 month and an albumin level of 2.9. The APRN then discontinued the megestrol and documented that Lois's current findings were expected considering the progressive and incurable nature of her disease.

By the end of the fall, Lois experienced progressive lower extremity edema that was uncomfortable, making it difficult for her to transfer from the bed. This finding abated partly with the APRN's orders for Furosemide and potassium supplementation. At this time, the APRN convened a family meeting, where Lois expressed interest in a Do Not Hospitalize (DNH) order. She stated, "I just don't feel like eating and my body just can't take it anymore." Lois and her family were informed of the availability of hospice care in the facility, which would include bereavement support in addition to other additional care providers, but they declined this service. Over the next several weeks, the APRN noted clinical changes indicating that Lois was actively dying. Medications for symptom control, including lorazepam, morphine, and scopolamine, were ordered on an as-needed basis, as Lois was quite comfortable. She died peacefully in the nursing home, surrounded by her family and members of the staff who had come to consider her as family, over Thanksgiving weekend.

Conclusion

APRNs are very well positioned to advance the delivery of evidence-based palliative care to patients in nursing homes. Their education about advanced chronic disease management and their communication skills promote collaboration with patients, families, and other members of the healthcare team. In their care of patients in nursing homes, APRNs lead and participate in advance care planning, including identifying appropriate patients for palliative care; they also evaluate and manage symptoms in accordance with patients' goals and preferences of care.

While challenges exist, including unique staffing and regulatory considerations, ample evidence confirms numerous positive outcomes when APRNs are involved in the care of patients in nursing homes. With the expectation that even greater numbers of individuals will be residing in nursing homes in the future, a tremendous opportunity exists for APRNs to affect the quality of living and dying of patients in these facilities.

References

1. Letizia M, Jones T. An educational intervention for nurse practitioners providing palliative care in nursing homes. *J Hospice Palliat Nurs.* 2012; 14(5): 351–8.
2. Carlson L, Meier D. Strategies and innovative models for delivering palliative care in nursing homes. *J Am Med Directors Assoc.* 2011; 12(2): 91–8.
3. Meier D, Lim B, Carlson M. Raising the standard: palliative care in nursing homes. *Health Affairs.* 2010; 29(1): 136–40.
4. Kelly A, Conell-Price J, Covinsky K, et al. Length of stay for older adults residing in nursing homes at the end of life: lengths of stay for nursing home decedents. *J Am Geriatr Soc.* 2010; 58(9): 1701–6.
5. DuBois J, Reed P. The nurse practitioner and policy in end-of-life care. *Nurs Sci Q.* 2014; 27: 70–6.
6. Wetle T, Shield R, Teno J, et al. Family perspectives on end-of-life care experiences in nursing homes. *Gerontologist.* 2005; 45(5): 642–50.
7. Intrator O, Feng Z, Mor V, et al. Employment of nurse practitioners and physician assistants in U.S. nursing homes. *Gerontologist.* 2005; 45(4): 486–94.
8. Rosenfeld P, Kobayashi M, Barber P, et al. Utilization of nurse practitioners in long-term care: findings and implications of a national survey. *J Am Med Directors Assoc.* 2004; 5(1): 9–15.
9. DuBois J, Reed P. The nurse practitioner and policy in end-of-life care. *Nurs Sci Q.* 2014; 27: 70–6.
10. Bourbonniere M. Expanding the knowledge base of resident and facility outcomes of care delivered by advanced practice nurses in long-term care: expert panel recommendation. *Policy Politics & Nursing Practice.* 2009; 10(1): 40–63.
11. Ploeg J, Kaasalainen S, McAiney C. Resident and family perceptions of the nurse practitioner role in long term care settings: a qualitative descriptive study. *BMC Nursing.* 2013; 12: 24b.
12. Sangster-Gormley E, Carter N, Donald F. A value-added benefit of nurse practitioners in long-term care settings: increased nursing staff's ability to care for residents. *Nurs Leadership.* 2013; 26(3): 24–37.
13. Bauer J. Nurse practitioners as an underutilized resource for health reform: evidence-based demonstrations of cost-effectiveness. *J Am Acad Nurse Pract.* 2010; 22(4): 228–31.
14. Donald F, Martin-Misener R, Carter N, et al. A systematic review of the effectiveness of advanced practice nurses in long-term care. *J Adv Nurs.* 2013: 69(10):2148–61.
15. Goldfeld K, Grabowski D, Caudry D, et al. Health insurance status and the care of nursing home residents with advanced dementia. *JAMA Intern Med.* 2013; 173(22): 2047–53.
16. Gonzalo P, Teno J, Mitchell S, et al. End-of-life transitions among nursing home residents with cognitive issues. *N Engl J Med.* 2011; 365: 1212–21.
17. Ouslander J, Lamb G, Tappen R. Interventions to reduce hospitalizations from nursing homes: evaluation of the INTERACT II collaborative quality improvement project. *J Am Geriatr Soc.* 2011; 59: 745–53.
18. Davis J. The use of innovative advance directives programs in nursing homes. *The Health Care Manager.* 2013; 32(4): 370–9.
19. Agarwal K. Failure to thrive in elderly adults: Management. In: Schmader K, Billings J, eds. Available at www.UpToDate.com. Accessed July 11, 2014.
20. Kaasalainen S, Martin-Misener R, Carter N, et al. The nurse practitioner role in pain management in long-term care. *J Adv Nurs.* 2009; 66(3): 542–51.
21. Rabins P, Hicks K, Black B. Medical decisions made by surrogates for persons with advanced dementia within weeks or months of death. *AJOB Prim Res.* 2011; 2(4): 61–5.
22. High KP, Bradley SF, Gravenstein S, et al. Clinical practice guidelines for the evaluation of fever and infection in older adult residents of long-term care facilities: 2008 update by the Infectious Diseases Society of America. *Clin Infect Dis.* 2009; 48: 149–71.
23. Lopez R, Amella E, Strumpf N, et al. The influence of nursing home culture on the use of feeding tubes. *Arch Intern Med.* 2010; 170(1): 83–8.
24. Miller C, Lima J, Gozalo P, Mor V. The growth of hospice care in U.S. nursing homes. *J Am Geriatr Soc.* 2010; 58(8): 1481–8.
25. Centers for Medicare and Medicaid Services. Medicare Benefit Policy Manual Chapter 9—Coverage of Hospice Services Under Hospital Insurance. Vol CMS Publication 100-02, Chap. 9, 10, 20.1, 40.1.3, 2012.
26. Federal Register. Medicare and Medicaid Programs: Hospice Conditions of Participation, Final Rule, 73(109). 2008:32088–32220.
27. Hwang D, Teno J, Clark M. Family perceptions of quality of hospice care in the nursing home. *J Pain Symptom Management.* 2014; doi: 0.1016/j.jpainsymman.2014.04.003.
28. Kiely DK, Givens JL, Shaffer ML, et al. Hospice use and outcomes in nursing home residents with advanced dementia. *J Am Geriatr Soc.* 2010; 58: 2284–91.

CHAPTER 21

The Palliative Advanced Practice Registered Nurse in the Rehabilitation Setting

Anne Mahler and Sharon Verney

Key Points

◆ Rehabilitation settings provide care for patients with a broad range of complex palliative care needs.

◆ There are multiple similarities in palliative care and rehabilitation philosophies, including the need to provide patient-centered care with the focus on improving quality of life.

◆ The role of the advanced practice registered nurse (APRN) in rehabilitation encompasses relationships with other team members, advanced assessment skills, expert knowledge of symptom management, and involvement in systems improvement.

Introduction

Each year, more than 10 million Americans are admitted to a post-acute facility, including some of the frailest and most vulnerable elders. The patient entering rehabilitation usually comes from another facility. Care transitions represent a time of heightened vulnerability for the patient and confusion for the family. The Association of Rehabilitation Nurses' White Paper[1] on Care Transitions recognizes transitions from the hospital to post-acute care, and again from post-acute care to home, as times of potential crisis. APRNs possess the optimal skills to provide comprehensive, compassionate care coordination for patients requiring rehabilitation and who are moving through the medical system.

The APRN attends to the patient's transition, coordinates interdisciplinary team involvement, and ensures appropriate medical care and follow-up, including coordination of chemotherapy, radiation, and orthopedic appointments. The APRN performs medication reconciliation, educates the patient and family, and creates a comprehensive care plan. Examples of evolving educational needs include caring for new diabetic complications, deep vein thrombosis (DVT) treatment, and wound care and surgical

site care. If the palliative care patient needs to move to an acute care setting from rehabilitation, the APRN ensures that the patient's goals of care are communicated to the acute facility.

Most often, patients are discharged from the rehabilitation setting. From 2013 to early 2014,[2] 77% of all skilled nursing facility (SNF) discharges were to a home setting, 12% to the acute hospital, and 9% to long-term care. Two percent of the SNF patients died during the SNF stay. Wherever the palliative patient is discharged, the APRN should coordinate care for the patient before discharge. When the APRN facilitates patient- and family-centered discharge planning, their needs are more easily identified and discharge goals can be devised that will increase their feelings of preparedness.[3,4] The APRN may be involved with prescription writing and ensures that the patient is discharged with an accurate medication list, advance care planning documents, and follow-up appointments. The APRN ensures continuity through communication with the healthcare provider who is overseeing the care in the next location. The Association of Rehabilitation Nurses[5] states that nurses in the rehab setting are concerned about the patient's quality of life and recognize that technological advances might be compromising it. It acknowledges that advanced medical technology may prolong life but not improve the quality of life. APRNs support the Association of Rehabilitation Nurses' commitment to patient autonomy and the position that all patients have the right to full resuscitation, to request Do Not Resuscitate orders, to request discontinuation of life-support measures, or to refuse recommended treatment, as long as the patient is considered capable.

A palliative patient with endstage illness may die in the rehabilitation facility. When this occurs, the APRN works with the patient, family, and rehabilitation staff to provide comprehensive and comfort-focused end-of-life care. The APRN's knowledge of symptom management is vital to optimize quality of life for the patient and family. Supporting the team during this time of transition from improving the patient's functional abilities to providing comfort-focused end-of-life care can be challenging for the APRN.

While attending to the patient and family, the APRN may need to simultaneously support a team that is grieving. The APRN, social worker, and chaplain will be helpful in supporting all staff during and after the death of their patient.

Rehabilitation and Rehabilitative Nursing

Rehabilitation involves a process that includes comprehensive assessment, goal setting, development of a plan of care, and frequent reevaluation.[6] Rehabilitation, in its purest sense, is defined as the process of helping a person reach his or her fullest physical, psychological, social, vocational, and educational potential consistent with his or her physiological or anatomical impairment, environmental limitations, desires, and life plans.[7] It has been described as a philosophy of practice and attitude toward caring for persons with disabilities and chronic health problems[1] and is designed to help the patient and family make the most of each day within the course of an illness.

Rehabilitation nursing[5] is a specialty practice that involves the diagnosis and treatment of individuals' responses to actual or potential health problems resulting in altered functional ability and altered lifestyle. The goal of rehabilitation nursing is to assist individuals with disabilities and chronic illnesses requiring restoration, maintenance, and promotion of optimal health. It requires the focus, ability, and dedication to caring for a person holistically, is patient-centered, and is an active process that involves supporting adaptation to changes in life circumstances.[6] The patient and family are considered active partners in identifying and setting collaborative goals.[8] Nursing supports the patient's existing abilities and facilitates the use of adaptive strategies. Rehabilitation nurses provide comprehensive and compassionate end-of-life care, including the provision of comfort and the relief of pain.[5] The advanced practice rehabilitation nurse merges the roles of direct care provider, educator, consultant, researcher, and manager when providing care.[9] The APRN may be an[10] adult, geriatric, or family practice nurse practitioner or clinical nurse specialist, or a palliative and hospice NP or CNS. As a primary care provider, the APRN has a key role on the primary care team, providing clinical leadership and encouraging a collaborative practice with the entire rehabilitation team.[11] The APRN may provide palliative care consultation with pain and symptom management.

Locations for Rehabilitation

Patients can receive rehabilitative care and services in a variety of settings. The aim of this chapter is to identify the processes and practice of rehabilitation in the acute rehabilitation setting, known as an inpatient rehabilitation facility (IRF), and in an SNF, also referred to as subacute rehabilitation. When patients are approaching discharge from a hospital, a screening process occurs that helps direct the patient to the level and location of rehabilitation that would be most helpful to him or her. Table 21.1 identifies the differences in rehabilitation models.

Patients and their family members often enter the rehabilitation setting with the expectation of a full return to a previous baseline of mobility, prevention of secondary disabilities, or some minimal improvement to allow return home. In IRFs, the focus of care is patients who have complex medical and functional problems and high premorbid baseline abilities, such as the person who has experienced multiple traumatic injuries. For a patient to qualify for IRF, the Centers for Medicare and Medicaid guidelines require the patient to need hospital-level care and intensive rehab.[12] Medicare identified 13 medical conditions that must be present in at least 60% of patients admitted to the IRF, including stroke, spinal cord injury, amputation, major multiple trauma, fracture of the femur, Parkinson's disease, and brain injury.

Approximately 30% to 35% of patients admitted to an SNF rehab unit have a diagnosis of "medical complexity," which includes patients with oncological diagnoses, infections, and medical and surgical complications. The second most common group of patients to seek subacute rehabilitation are people with an orthopedic condition or surgery, followed by significantly fewer patients with primary cardiac, pulmonary, and neurological needs.[2]

Often the SNF resident is older and frailer and has a greater number of chronic conditions. For this population, the restoration of functional abilities or enhancing residual capacity can be critical to the person with functional challenges secondary to chronic conditions. Javier identified the SNF as serving as a transitional program of care before the person is discharged from medical services.[7] While many people who use SNF services do move back home, the stay is usually longer than in the IRF. Discharge may

Table 21.1 Patient Criteria: Inpatient Rehabilitation Facility and Skilled Nursing Facility

	Inpatient Rehabilitation Facility	Skilled Nursing Facility
Functional status	◆ Patient has some degree of ADL and mobility impairment. ◆ Patient is cognitively able to participate in therapies. ◆ Significant functional improvement is expected.	◆ Patient has some degree of ADL and mobility impairment or other skilled need. ◆ Some functional improvement is expected.
Nursing and medical services	◆ Requires acute medical management ◆ Requires 24-hour rehabilitation nursing care	◆ Requires involvement of skilled nursing staff to meet medical needs
Therapies	◆ Requires two or more therapies, one of which must be physical or occupational therapy	◆ Requires one or more therapies OR has daily skilled nursing need
Number of therapy hours required and tolerated	◆ Tolerates at least 3 hours per day of therapy, 5 days a week	◆ No minimum number of tolerated hours required; skilled nursing need is sufficient
Discharge	◆ Probable discharge to community	◆ Possible discharge to community

From references 12 and 14.

be to home, family homes, or long-term care facilities. Aragon reported that almost one-third of elders receive care in an SNF in their last 6 months of life, and 1 in 11 will die while in the SNF setting.[13]

Case Study 1

Aaron Vargus is an 84-year-old male who was admitted to an SNF after a hospitalization for pneumonia. He has had three hospital admissions in the past 6 months, and all of the hospitalizations had required intubation. Recently, he was intubated in the ICU and it was difficult to wean him from the ventilator. He has a past medical history that includes chronic respiratory failure, hypertension, and COPD. On admission he stated to the CNS, "I want to live for my wife, but I might be dying of lung disease." The hospital physician felt he would have very little chance of weaning from future intubation because of severe lung disease.

Mr. Vargus lives with his wife, who helps with ADLs. He has stairs to get into his home and additional stairs to get to his bedroom. He was unable to get out of bed without being short of breath. He was evaluated by physical therapy and occupational therapy. He was unable to perform the Timed Up and Go test, which is a test that times the patient from sitting to walking 3 meters and then walking back and sitting back down. The CNS started Mr. Vargus on lorazepam 0.5 mg PO and albuterol inhaler 90 mcg 2 puffs before he participated in therapies.

Mr. Vargus coughed frequently and became more short of breath with oral intake. The CNS suspected he was aspirating and ordered a modified barium swallow (MBS). He was evaluated by the SLP and the MBS confirmed he was aspirating. The SLP recommended a change to a purée texture and added thickener to his fluids. Immediately Mr. Vargus experienced an easier time with meals, resulting in increased intake and conservation of energy.

Team meetings were held weekly to update goals. One issue was Mr. Vargus's inability to negotiate stairs given his severe lung disease. Mr. Vargus's family organized his house so that he could live on the first floor. At the end of Mr. Vargus's rehabilitation stay, he was able to take a few steps to get out of bed, transfer to a commode, and eat moderate meals. He could wash his face and brush his teeth but required assistance with the rest of his bathing and dressing tasks. His wife was trained to assist with his ADLs and mobility to maximize his independence while preserving his safety and comfort. Social services provided resources for more services at home as Mr. Vargus's needs became greater. The CNS ordered a visiting nurse with a potential bridge to hospice for his return home.

Characteristics of the Rehabilitation Setting

One of the core tenets of rehabilitation is the vital role that the interdisciplinary team plays. While the patient and family caregivers are at the center of the team, they require the expertise of all members (Table 21.2). Effective team collaboration and communication occur through weekly meetings, which include updates on the patient's progress as well as identification of support systems and barriers that the patient may rely on or encounter.

Table 21.2 Interdisciplinary Team Members and Roles

Discipline	Role/Tasks
Physician	Manages the medical care of the patient
Physiatrist	Medical provider who specializes in rehabilitation
Nurse (RN or APRN)	Provides holistic care, including assessment, medication administration, and patient-specific treatments based on effective communication
Pharmacist	Assists in managing medications
Physical therapist	Uses exercise, therapeutic modalities, and mobility devices to maximize functional independence and positioning
Occupational therapist	Uses adaptive equipment and exercise to improve ADLs
Speech and language pathologist (SLP)	Helps restore and maintain cognition, communication, and swallowing
Registered dietitian	Works with the patient to ensure adequate nutrition
Social worker	Offers support to patients and families and options for external resources; coordinates transition plan
Case manager	Coordinates discharge planning; helps with coordinating team and family meeting
Recreational therapist	Provides entertainment activities for the patient that promote adaptation and engagement and limit social isolation
Psychologist/ Psychiatrist	Specializes in diagnosis and treatment of mental illness; provides/recommends counseling for mental health
Chaplain	Provides spiritual guidance and counseling for patient and family
Prosthetist and orthotist	Provide and fit the patient with artificial limbs and orthotics

From references 7, 15, 16, and 17.

Nursing and rehabilitation therapies both play a critical role in the patient's care. Patient care often begins at the bedside with nursing, with medication administration, dressing changes, and wound care, as well as ongoing assessment of the patient's status, response to treatment, and adaptation to the consequences of illness or disease. The APRN uses the nursing assessments to initiate and modify treatment plans, while identifying and communicating expected outcomes and potential complications with the nursing staff.

Adaptive equipment is essential to assist in compensating for physical deficits, such as decreased coordination, balance, flexibility, range of motion, and strength. Equipment enables the patient to maintain functional independence with less reliance on caregivers and family. The rehabilitation setting is the optimal setting to ensure proper fitting and training with adaptive equipment. The ability to communicate is also supported through adaptive equipment, as is environmental modification aimed at maximizing mobility and safety (Table 21.3).

Table 21.3 Adaptive Equipment

Equipment	Intended Goal
Wheelchairs and scooter	Increase mobilization and improve energy conservation
Walkers	Accommodate balance deficits
Canes	Assist with stability when walking
Hospital bed	Increase ease in positioning, edema management, improved bed mobility
Built-up/weighted plates and utensils	Stabilize upper extremity tremors and fine motor deficits
Communication devices (e.g., sound amplifiers and communication boards)	Enhance interaction with caregivers and family, improve expression of patient's needs and wishes
Splints/orthotics	Maximize range of motion and increase joint stability
Hand reacher	Retrieval of items
Long-handled shoe horn	Decrease effort and minimize flexion when donning shoes
Dressing stick	Improve independence in ADLs (e.g., pulling up pants, item retrieval)
Transfer boards	Enable surface-to-surface transfers with minimal lower extremity weight-bearing
Mechanical lift	Transfer ease for severely dependent patient
Environmental modifications: grab bars, shower bed, raised toilet seat	Safe transfer and energy conservation

The Patient in the Rehabilitation Setting

The patient with life-limiting illness in the rehabilitation setting may experience a variety of symptoms and stressors, including pain, anxiety, depression, decreased mobility, increased dependence, fear, and a loss of hope. Many patients who enter rehab experience a threat to their physical and spiritual well-being from the functional impact of their illness or disease. Worsening mobility and function result in uncertainty about the future. Whether the loss is acute, such as a stroke, or more chronic and progressive, as with heart failure or lung disease, most people must learn to adapt to a different functional baseline.[18]

Palliative Care in the Rehabilitation Setting

Historically, the goals of palliative care and of rehabilitation appeared to have few similarities. In rehabilitation, the concept of maintaining or improving physical function and independence for as long as possible is recognized for its role in improving the patient and caregiver's quality of life. There is little published that addresses the role of palliative care, and its effect, in the general rehabilitation setting. One study[19] demonstrated that palliative care consultation, along with root cause conferences for patients readmitted to the hospital from an SNF, demonstrated a decreased hospital readmission rate. As the understanding of palliative care has evolved, however, there is a growing recognition that rehabilitation's core goal of promoting a patient's quality of life is synonymous with a palliative philosophy of care.

The National Consensus Project[20] defined the philosophy of palliative care as one that expands the traditional disease model of medical treatments to include the goals of optimizing function, and helping with decision making. Both palliative care and rehabilitation mandate an interdisciplinary team approach to patient care, driven by collaborative goal setting by the patient, family, and team to improve patient comfort and function. Quality of life for the patient can be significantly improved through improved function and physical activity, decreased dependence on others, and decreased symptoms.[21,22] One study found that a patient-centered model, with the focus of therapy on addressing deficits, resulted in improvement in patients' health-related quality of life.[23] Improvement in quality of life requires that the patient be engaged and that goals reflecting the patient's values and views are incorporated into care.[24]

Rehabilitation for the Palliative Patient

Rehabilitation may be able to provide a reasonable level of independence and comfort, with goals and approaches focused on comfort and function.[25] The challenge exists in determining when a functional decline is a sign that the person is at the end-of-life and entering the dying process. Significant deterioration in all aspects of functioning, especially within the areas of physical, cognitive, and social function, occurs within the last 2 months of life. The majority of patients experience increased weakness and fatigue, pain, dyspnea, and anorexia.[26] When the patient's remaining time is limited and function is unlikely to improve, the goals of rehabilitation shift to maximizing home safety and helping the patient and caregiver with activities of daily living (ADLs) and mobility. Maintaining a balance between function and comfort is key and dependent on the person's goals.

The Oncology Population

Functional losses in the cancer patient may be due to the disease itself or complications of the treatments. In traditional cancer rehabilitation, the early goal is to help a person return to his or her premorbid level of function after cancer therapies, or to maintain function during months of cancer treatment. Many hospitalized patients with advanced cancer who are experiencing a functional decline are often referred to subacute rehab.[27] Dietz[7] identified four types of cancer rehabilitation, dependent on the person's stage of disease: preventive, restorative, supportive, and palliative. Preventive rehabilitation attempts to preclude functional decline. Restorative rehabilitation refers to the effort to return the patient to his or her premorbid functional status. Supportive rehabilitation strives to maximize function after permanent impairments caused by disease or treatment. Palliative rehabilitation's primary goal is to reduce dependence in mobility and self-care with the provision of comfort and support.

The Pulmonary Population

Pulmonary rehabilitation is indicated for patients who may be experiencing distressing symptoms or are living with decreased functional abilities and increased dependence due to pulmonary disease. Pulmonary rehabilitation is a comprehensive intervention based on a thorough assessment followed by individualized therapies, including exercise training and education.[28] The person with advanced chronic obstructive pulmonary disease has many palliative care needs. These include an increased symptom burden, with dyspnea, anxiety, pain, depression, and cough being common. Gilbert[29] identified the value of early discussion of advance directives for the person with advanced chronic obstructive pulmonary disease; this offers the opportunity for the patient to consider his or her own end-of-life wishes and serves as an intervention that may ease tension, fear, and stress.

The Neurology Population

The palliative care issues of the person who has suffered a stroke are numerous and may include pain from central post-stroke pain or hemiplegic shoulder pain, fatigue, and the potential for seizures. There are many psychosocial issues, with a 40% incidence of depression, as well as the common occurrence of anxiety, apathy, sexual dysfunction, altered body image, and social dysfunction.[30] The caregiver burden is often profound and long-lasting. Concerns arise regarding fears of dying, as well as issues about meaning, connection, and purpose. A palliative approach can begin to help the patient in reframing hope and beginning the processes of acceptance and adjustment. According to Blacquire,[31] when palliative care was incorporated into the rehabilitation of stroke patients, control of pain and dyspnea was rated most successful, with a slightly less but still positive change in levels of anxiety and depression. The highest satisfaction levels were evident in communication, provision of respectful care, and support of the patient's dignity.[31]

The Geriatric Population

Geriatric rehabilitation is a specialty within the rehabilitation field. Unique problems and challenges are associated with aging, including multiple comorbidities, polypharmacy, and frailty. Geriatric rehabilitation has been described as operating at the intersection of geriatric medicine, rehabilitation medicine, and palliative care.[32] Disabilities in the elderly commonly have multiple causes. The rehabilitation approach to care has subtle but significant differences with elders. Special attention needs to be paid to the elderly person's ability to communicate, including hearing, vision, and cognitive abilities. Attention to the prevention of delirium, malnutrition, and falls is important. Assessment tools designed specifically for the elderly, such as the Geriatric Depression Scale,[33] can provide more individualized screening for the elderly person in rehab.

Rehabilitation for the person who has had a hip fracture begins with a commitment to managing pain. Musculoskeletal pain affects participation in ADLs, with undertreated hip pain during rehab influencing long-term outcomes, including a negative impact on health-related quality of life 1 year after surgery.[34] Pain, depression, and anxiety have been identified as outcome indicators, with 50% of patients with good functional ability prior to fracture unable to gain full independence. In elderly persons, falls are considered one of several geriatric syndromes, and hip fractures have been labeled a geriatric illness. Hung[35] found that 13% of elderly persons with hip fractures died within 6 months of fracture and 24% died within a year. For the person with severe functional dependence, such as the person with advanced dementia who may be bedbound at baseline, treatment options should be explored. The patient's baseline function and goals of care should inform the discussion about the options of operative versus non-operative care for the patient.

Patient and Family Assessment

The APRN in the rehabilitation setting conducts comprehensive, problem-focused, multidimensional assessments of patients and families experiencing health problems stemming from altered functional ability resulting from physical disability or chronic illness.[36,37] Patients, in the context of suffering, disability, and terminal illness, may struggle with the meaning of illness. Rehabilitation patients and families often have significant psychosocial and spiritual needs. Moving from independence to dependence often results in many feelings of loss: loss of control, loss of authority, loss of identity, and loss of role and place in the world.[38] Depression, anxiety, hopelessness, or frustration is not uncommon. This is especially true for the rehabilitation patient who is challenged to integrate the old self into the new self.[39] A necessary component of rehabilitation is the identification of these losses and the development of a different set of coping skills. Spiritual assessment helps identify the person's supports and coping skills and may be formal or informal. For further discussion, see Chapter 44, The Role of the Advanced Practice Registered Nurse in Spiritual Care, and Chapter 47, Interdisciplinary Team Collaboration and the Provision of Spiritual Care.

Culture influences a person's response, behavior, and participation in the rehabilitation process. A cultural assessment contributes to the development of a patient-specific care plan that provides insight into how the person views illness and disability. The meaning that the disability has to the patient and his or her view and value of independence and the need for control contribute to effective patient–staff partnering. Other aspects of culture that inform rehabilitation and adaptation include the patient's role in the family, who the decision maker is, and the attitude toward the use and value of Western and Eastern medicine, as well as home remedies.

In the rehabilitation arena, there is the need for a broad social assessment because the patient will need a support circle. The patient and/or caregiver's learning abilities and educational needs should be determined to create the best plan of care, particularly when arranging for discharge. An assessment of caregiver stress and burden is essential in organizing comprehensive post-discharge care. The presence of risk factors for increased caregiver burden, including increased anxiety of both caregiver and patient, high dependency of the patient, depression of the caregiver, and poor family support, should be assessed. The results of these assessments will assist in the identification and provision of additional physical and emotional support as needed for the patient and caregiver.[41,42]

Multiple tests and tools are available to assess function in the rehabilitation setting (Table 21.4). These assessments can provide objective measurements that assist the patient and therapy staff determine appropriate levels of intervention that will help the patient attain realistic goals. They are used to measure frailty as well as fall risk, and to measure the person's ability to complete functional tasks. Valid tools focus on the patient's ability to maintain a safe level of independence in daily life.

Common Symptoms in the Rehabilitation Setting

Pain management is the highest priority for attaining or maintaining the best quality of life for the palliative rehabilitation patient. Unrelieved pain prevents the patient from fully

Table 21.4 Sampling of Assessment Tools for the Palliative Care Patient in Rehabilitation

Assessment Tool	Description	Purpose
Edmonton Functional Assessment Scale[42]	Assesses the status of communication, pain, mental status, dyspnea, balance, mobility, locomotion, ADLs, fatigue, and motivation; each item evaluated on a 4-point rating scale	Documents the degrees of functional performance for the patient with advanced cancer
Katz Index of Independence in Activities of Daily Living[43]	Rates patient's ability in six areas: bathing, dressing, toileting, transfer, continence, and feeding; cumulative score of 0 (very dependent) to 6 (independent)	Assesses the ability of patients to perform ADLs
Timed Up and Go test[44]	Measures the time for the patient to arise from sitting, walk 10 feet, and return to sitting; <10 seconds indicates a person freely mobile, with >20 seconds indicating impaired mobility	Assesses mobility and fall risk
Tinnetti Balance Assessment[45]	Measures eight tasks involved in balance, including sitting and standing balance, measured on a 3-point scale for each task	Measures an older adult's gait and balance abilities

benefitting from the rehabilitation process. Neuropathic pain, such as with diabetic neuropathies or spinal stenosis, and chronic pain, such as with osteoarthritis, must be recognized and its treatment incorporated into the plan of care. Both short-term and long-term functional outcomes are reduced when pain is undertreated in rehabilitation.[14,35,36] Inadequately controlled pain in the rehab setting impedes the recovery process: patients in pain will avoid ambulating and participating in therapy sessions, and will have sleep disturbances and daytime fatigue.[46] Loss of appetite, anxiety and depression, and an increased potential for delirium are consequences of pain that interfere with a person's ability to participate in rehabilitation. While the concern exists that opioids can contribute to the risk of delirium, the risk of delirium alone should not be a deterrent for adequate pain control, as severe pain can also contribute to the incidence of delirium. In rehab, there is the challenge of managing a patient's pain without causing excessive sedation. The interdisciplinary team plays a vital role in pain management. Table 21.5 describes modalities physical and occupational therapists can offer for pain management.

Table 21.5 Modalities for Managing Acute and Chronic Pain

Modalities	Effects	Types of Conditions
Electrical stim/TENS	Decreases pain Increases circulation	Joint pain, wound healing
Short-wave diathermy	Decreases pain Decreases inflammation Increases circulation	Joint contracture, wound healing, joint pain
Hot packs	Increase circulation	Muscle spasm
Cold packs	Decrease edema Decrease pain	Joint pain, swelling in joint
Ultrasound	Increases circulation Decreases inflammation	Tendinitis, wound healing

The APRN's Role in Managing Rehabilitation Complications

Postural changes in blood pressure are a common problem for patients in rehabilitation. The reasons for the blood pressure changes vary from patient to patient, but they may be caused by prolonged bedrest and deconditioning, dehydration, and polypharmacy. The role of the APRN includes reviewing the medication list and possibly discontinuing medications that contribute to hypotension. Ensuring that the patient has adequate hydration and offering compression stockings to promote venous return if appropriate are interventions the APRN might order for palliation. Midodrine, an alpha receptor agonist that acts on blood vessels to raise blood pressure, should be used with caution as it may cause a significant, potentially harmful, elevation in blood pressure in some patients. The steroid fludrocortisone should also be used with caution. As with all medications, every patient should have an individualized plan of care that incorporates patient history, drug tolerance, existing comorbidities, and the patient's goals and preferences.[47]

DVT is another distinctive complication that patients in rehabilitation are at risk for. Whether due to the decreased motion and function associated with generalized immobility, a recent joint replacement, or stroke, there is a significant incidence of DVT in this population. The APRN should review the potential risks, harm, and benefit that anticoagulation might offer or cause. Assessing the individual's risk factors for DVT development, such as a previous history of DVT, dehydration, or the presence of certain malignancies, is important when discussing the options for care.[48] While prevention of a DVT is extremely important, recognizing that the process of having blood drawn can be traumatic for the patient with a significant cognitive impairment underscores the importance of activity and ambulation. Physical and occupational therapists can work to increase mobility through ambulation or other activity that will increase muscle action and circulation, which in turn decreases the risk of clot formation.

Bowel and bladder dysfunction is a common complication that patients experience during rehabilitation. Patients may have recently had surgery that resulted in a temporary or permanent ostomy. The patient and caregiver will need support and education in beginning the process of mastering self-care with the ostomy. Equally challenging is the process of beginning the emotional and psychological adjustment to a period of life with an ostomy, with its accompanying altered body image.

Frequently, patients experience urine retention and require a Foley catheter. Depending on the cause of the urinary retention, voiding trials may be initiated. The APRN should educate the patient and staff on the need for the patient to be well hydrated. The APRN should review the patient's medications to ensure that the patient isn't taking any medications that could be contributing to urinary retention. Medications like tamsulosin hydrochloride and bethanechol are often used to help with urinary retention not caused by obstruction. If the urinary retention is due to a neurogenic bladder, the patient and/or caregiver will need education and support in learning to care for an indwelling catheter, or in the art of intermittent self-catheterization. The APRN also is vigilant for signs and symptoms of a urinary tract infection in the person prone to urinary retention.

Maintaining skin integrity is an integral part of rehabilitation. Often the rehabilitation patient has had significant changes from his or her prior activity level, resulting in more time in bed or seated in a wheelchair. The therapy staff will maximize the activity level and ensure proper fitting of the wheelchair with a pressure-relieving cushion. The APRN also must ensure that skin integrity is monitored when the patient is prescribed new splinting devices and orthotics, and that thorough staff education is completed on proper donning and doffing of equipment. The APRN must attend closely to surgical wounds and pressure ulcers to maximize patient comfort and prevent infections.

Lymphedema is swelling that occurs in limbs when lymph node drainage is compromised. It is progressive, and patients are typically treated by physical therapists and occupational therapists who are certified in lymphedema management. When the lymphedema is mild, elevating the limb and initiating an exercise program may be the appropriate treatment intervention. As the effects of lymphedema increase, compression and manual massage drainage may be indicated. For long-term management of lymphedema, patients and caregivers are instructed on how to provide their own manual lymph drainage or apply compression.[49]

Case Study 2

Conner Graham was an 85-year-old male living at home with hospice. His admitting hospice diagnosis was advanced scleroderma. His daughter Christine, who lives close by, often assists with grocery shopping. One day, Mr. Graham's hospice nursing assistant arrived at his home to find him on the floor, complaining of left hip pain. Mr. Graham was evaluated at the ED and a pelvic CT scan revealed fractures of the left acetabulum and inferior pubic rami. He was admitted to the hospital for pain management. The consulting orthopedic surgeon recommended no surgical intervention but rather 6 weeks of non-weight-bearing to his left lower extremity.

Mr. Graham and his daughter decided to discontinue the hospice benefit for a stay in rehabilitation. Upon admission, goals of care were discussed with the NP. Mr. Graham stated he did not want resuscitation, nor did he want to return to the hospital. The NP discussed the potential to develop a DVT secondary to his immobility. After reviewing the side effects, risks, and benefits of anticoagulation, Mr. Graham chose to forgo anticoagulation due to painful injections and multiple blood draws. Mr. Graham complained of significant nausea and left hip pain. The NP ordered hydromorphone 2 mg po q6h PRN and ondansetron 4 mg po q8h PRN. Physical and occupational therapy evaluations revealed decreased strength in both upper extremities and the right lower extremity, resulting in his inability to maintain non-weight-bearing status when using a walker.

Mr. Graham continued to have nausea and his oncologist was consulted. She recommended the use of an off-label medication, granisetron, which improved his nausea. After 3 weeks, however, Mr. Graham had not made any functional gains. The team met to discuss his wishes for discharge: the ability to transfer to a wheelchair, to a toilet, and into a car. The NP called the orthopedic surgeon to convey Mr. Graham's goals and how his non-weight-bearing status was now the primary barrier to achieving these goals. The surgeon changed his orders to weight-bearing as tolerated. Mr. Graham progressed with physical and occupational therapy and soon was able to safely transfer without assistance. The NP wrote a prescription for a wheelchair and made a referral back to hospice, and Mr. Graham returned home.

Setting Goals in the Rehabilitation Setting

Goal setting is a central component of rehabilitation. Determining goals in the rehabilitation setting can be a challenge due to conflicting viewpoints of patients, family members, and staff and the emotional intensity of potential and actual loss. However, patient-centered and patient-driven rehabilitation goals have demonstrated greater patient satisfaction, shorter stays, and improved motivation.[25,50] The shift to a holistic team approach, with increased focus on the patient's attainment of goals rather than resolution of a problem, represents a paradigm shift. The International Classification of Functional Disability, a 2001 framework for measuring health and disability, moved beyond a purely medical or biological conceptualization of dysfunction and emphasized the concept that simply knowing the health condition does not predict function.[25] Functional goals should be realistic and specific to each person's unique state. Joint goal setting helps the therapists target interventions to priority areas where meaningful gains can be achieved. When the rehabilitation plan reflects the patient's expressed needs, values, and expectations, there will be better outcomes, including an improved sense of hope. Personal goals in rehabilitation are tied to dignity and self-worth; a person who is debilitated and deconditioned frequently has concerns about being a burden. By setting realistic goals, patients have a better sense of control and a chance to achieve optimal functional capacity within the limits of the disease.[29]

The focus for many patients with worsening chronic illness, especially in the SNF setting, is on preserving independence for as long as possible. The APRN's role in goal setting includes collaborating with the patient and family in identifying, clarifying, and advocating for their wishes and preferences. The APRN has the knowledge and responsibility for identifying prognostic indicators that help the patient, family, and rehab team recognize goals that are realistic. (See Chapter 40, Family Meetings.)

Case Study 3

Mary Lancaster was an 80-year-old female, recently admitted to an SNF rehab unit. This was her 15th admission since she suffered a left thalamic CVA with residual right hemiparesis 10 years earlier. Mrs. Lancaster had complicated and prolonged rehabilitation stays. Her multiple comorbidities included chronic osteoarthritis, peripheral neuropathy, atrial fibrillation, and heart failure. She had a PEG tube placed 1 year earlier due to worsening dysphagia. She lived with her frail 82-year-old spouse. Over the past 10 years, Mrs. Lancaster displayed the fiercest determination to return home independently, and she always made just enough gains each time to make this possible. When it appeared that Mr. Lancaster would be unable to manage the tube feeding in the home due to a mild but worsening cognitive impairment, Mrs. Lancaster worked aggressively with SLP until she decided that she had met her goal of having sufficient oral intake, with minimal risk of aspiration.

Mrs. Lancaster's wish has always been to live as long as possible, but she also chose to have her code status reflect her wishes not to be resuscitated. A recent rehab admission with worsening heart failure resulted in profound weakness and fatigue. Mrs. Lancaster chose to have her goal of care shift completely to comfort: to stop the intermittent tube feedings and not be hospitalized. Even as her ability to swallow and speak became significantly diminished, she continued to direct her care. The therapists and nursing staff grieved along with Mr. Lancaster. The NP who had worked with her for years commented that caring for Mrs. Lancaster had made her a better NP. It was this NP who had the quiet, supportive conversation with Mr. Lancaster when it was clear that his wife's time was getting shorter. As they both silently cried together, Mr. Lancaster expressed appreciation that his wife could live her last days at this rehabilitation unit and die among staff members who had cared for her for the past 10 years.

The NP managed Mrs. Lancaster's pain and dyspnea with morphine elixir 10 mg (20 mg/1 cc) every hour PRN. The patient remained comfortable, with her husband and staff respecting her wishes for peace, comfort, and care from those she loved. She died in the rehab setting that she considered a second home. The family rallied around the frail surviving spouse, and staff supported each other during a time of bereavement.

Conclusion

Many patients arrive at the rehabilitation unit in pain, unsure of what another hospital stay with its associated worsening physical dependence will mean, and hoping that a short stay in rehab will return them to a previous baseline of improved health and function. Many of these patients have multiple palliative care needs. The functional losses that accompany chronic, progressive disease have a life-altering impact on patients and their families. These losses may lead to the inability to return to a familiar home setting, a worsening sense of self-worth, altered roles and relationships, and a sense of despair and loss of hope. Patients in pain need expert symptom management along with psychosocial and spiritual support. In particular, they may need assistance in finding meaning in their illness and need a partner to help navigate their rehabilitation journey and provide knowledgeable, compassionate support.

The APRN in rehab has the responsibility and the opportunity to work with the patient and family during this time of transition and uncertainty. Recognizing that the patient can participate more fully in all aspects of rehabilitation when troublesome symptoms are controlled, the APRN applies his or her expertise in symptom management. The APRN supports the patient by conducting goals of care and discharge planning conversations, providing education and support as the patient attempts to adjust to a new, potentially more limited functional role. The APRN functions as a critical member of the interdisciplinary, patient-centered rehab team. By learning what the patient and family wish for and value, and by subsequently managing the complex responses to illness that stem from the patient's altered functional abilities, the APRN can offer comprehensive care that will enhance the patient's ongoing health.

References

1. Camicia M, Black T, Farrell J, Waites K, Wirt S, Lutz B, with the Association of Rehabilitation Nurses Task Force. The essential role of the rehabilitation nurse in facilitating care transitions: A white paper by the Association of Rehabilitation Nurses. *Rehabil Nurs.* 2014; 39: 3–15.
2. Uniform Data System for Medical Rehabilitation. Standard Facility Report, volume 28, Quarter 1, April 2013–March 2014.
3. Loupis Y, Foxx S. Family conferences in stroke rehabilitation: A literature review. *J Stroke Cerebrovasc Dis.* 2013; 22(6): 883–93.
4. McGilton K, Davis A, Naglie G, et al. Evaluation of patient-centered rehabilitation model targeting older persons with a hip fracture, including those with cognitive impairment. *BMC Geriat.* 2013; 13(136). Available at http://www.biomedcentral.com/1471-2318/13/136, Accessed July 1, 2014.
5. Association of Rehabilitation Nurses. Scope of rehabilitation nursing practice. Available at http://www.rehabnurse.org/about/content/Scope-of-Practice.html Updated 2014. Accessed August 1, 2014.
6. Booth S, Jester R. The rehabilitation process. In: Jester R, ed. *Advancing Practice in Rehabilitation Nursing.* Oxford, England: Blackwell Publishing; 2007:1–13.
7. Javier N, Montagnini ML. Rehabilitation of the hospice and palliative care patient. *J Palliat Med.* 2011; 14(5): 638–48.
8. Koc A. Rehabilitation nursing: Applications for rehabilitation nursing. *Int J Caring Sci.* 2012; 5(2): 80–6.
9. Association of Rehabilitation Nurses. Role of the APRN. The APRN: Role description. Available at http://www.rehabnurse.org/pubs/role/Role-Advanced-Practice-Rehab-Nurse.html. Updated 2014. Accessed August 1, 2014.
10. Association of Rehabilitation Nurses. Position statement on advanced practice nursing. Available at http://www.rehabnurse.org/advocacy/content/Postition-Statement-AdvPractice.html. Revised 2014. Accessed August 1, 2014.
11. Meier D, Beresford L. Advanced practice nurses in palliative care: A pivotal role and perspective. *J Palliat Med.* 2006; 9(3): 624–7.
12. Center for Medicare and Medicaid. Inpatient rehabilitation facility prospective payment system: Payment system fact series. November 2013. Available at http://www.cms.gov/Outreach-and-Education/Medicare-Learning-Network. MLN/MLNProducts/downloads/InpatRehabPaymtfctsht09-508.pdf. Accessed August 1, 2014.
13. Aragon K, Covinsky K, Miao Y, et al. Use of Medicare post hospitalization skilled nursing benefit in the last 6 months of life. *Arch Intern Med.* 2012: 172(20): 1573–9.
14. Medicare's post-acute payment system: A review of the issues and policy proposals. National Health Policy Forum. Available at http://www.nhpf.org/library/issue-briefs/IB847_PostAcutePayment_12-07-12.pdf. Published December 7, 2012. Accessed July 20, 2014.

15. American Occupational Therapy Association. The role of occupational therapy in end of life care. *Am J Occup Ther*. 2011; 65(suppl): 66–75.

16. American Board of Physical Medicine and Rehabilitation. Definition of physical medicine and rehabilitation. Available at www.abpmr.org/consumers/pmr_definition.html. Accessed August 1, 2014.

17. Cheville A. Rehabilitation of patients with advanced cancer. *Cancer*. 2001; 92(4): 1039–48.

18. Cruetzfeldt C, Holloway R, Walker M. Symptomatic and palliative care for stroke survivors. *J Gen Intern Med*. 2011; 27(7): 853–60.

19. Berkowitz R, Jones RN, Rieder R, et al. Improving disposition outcomes for patients in a geriatric skilled nursing facility. *J Am Geriat Soc*. 2011; 59(6): 1130–6.

20. National Consensus Project for Quality care. *The Clinical Practice Guidelines for Quality Palliative Care*, 3rd ed. 2013. Available at http://www.nationalconsensusproject.org/NCP_Clinical_Practice_Guidelines_3rd_Edition.pdf. Accessed September 20, 2014.

21. Quaglietti S, Blum L, Ellis V. The role of the adult nurse practitioner in palliative care. *J Hosp Palliat Nurs*. 2004: 6(4): 209–14.

22. Kasven-Gonzales N, Souverain R, Miale S. Improving quality of life through rehabilitation in palliative care: Case report. *Palliat Support Care*. 2010; 8: 359–69.

23. McPhail S, Nalder E, Hill AM, Haines T. Physiotherapists have accurate expectations of patients' future health-related quality of life after first assessment in a subacute rehabilitation setting. *Biomed Res Int*. 2013; doi.10.1155/2013/340371.

24. National Alliance for Quality Care. Fostering successful patient and family engagement: Nursing's critical role. 2013. Available at http://www.naqc.org/WhitePaper-PatientEngagement. Accessed August 1, 2014.

25. Santiago-Palma J, Payne R. Palliative care and rehabilitation. *Cancer*. 2001; 92(4): 1049–53.

26. Elmquist M, Jordhoy M, Bjordal K, Kassa S, Jannert M. Health-related quality of life during the last 3 months of life in patients with advanced cancer. *Support Care Cancer*. 2009; 17: 191–8.

27. Dy S, Liste D, Barbe C, Knight L. A quality improvement initiative for improving of referrals from a cancer center to subacute rehabilitation. *J Pain Symptom Manage*. 2014; 48: 127–31.

28. Janssen D, McCormick J. Palliative care and pulmonary rehabilitation. *Clin Chest Med*. 2014; 35(2): 411–21.

29. Gilbert C, Smith C. Advanced parenchymal lung disease: Quality of life and palliative care. *Mt Sinai J Med*. 2009; 76(1): 63–70.

30. Kitzmuller G, Haggstrom T, Asplund K. Living in an unfamiliar body: the significance of the long-term influence of body changes on the perception of self after stroke. *Med Health Care Philos*. 2013; 16(1): 19–29.

31. Blacquiere D, Bhimji K, Meggisen H, Sinclair J, Sharma M. Satisfaction with palliative care after stroke: A prospective cohort study. *Stroke*. 2013; 44(9): 2617–9.

32. Van Dam E, Groenewegan-Sipkema K, Spruit-van Eijk M, Chavannes N, Achterberg W. Geriatric rehabilitation for patients with advanced COPD: Programme characteristics and case studies. *Int J Palliat Nurs*. 2013; 19(3): 141–6.

33. Geriatric Depression Scale. Available at http://consultgerirn.org/uploads/File/trythis/try_this_4.pdf. Revised 2012. Accessed August 1, 2014.

34. Kristensen M. Hip fracture-related pain strongly influences functional performance of patients with an intertrochanteric fracture upon discharge from the hospital. *Phys Med Rehab*. 2013; 5(2): 135–41.

35. Hung W, Egol K, Zuckerman J. Hip fracture management: Tailoring care for the older patient. *JAMA*. 2012; 307(20): 2185–94.

36. Hospice and Palliative Nurses Association. *Competencies for the Hospice and Palliative Advanced Practice Nurse*. 2nd ed. Pittsburgh, PA: HPNA; 2014.

37. Association of Rehabilitation Nurses. Position statement on advanced practice nursing. Available at http://www.rehabnurse.org/advocacy/content/Postition-Statement-AdvPractice.html. Revised 2014. Accessed August 20, 2014.

38. Coyle N. The hard work of living in the face of death. *J Pain Symptom Manage*. 2006; 32(3): 266–74.

39. Rieg L, Mason C, Preston K. Spiritual care: Practical guidelines for rehabilitation nurses. *Rehabil Nurs*. 2006; 31(6): 249–54.

40. McCullagh E, Brigstocke G, Donaldson N, Kalra L. Determinants of caregiver burden and quality of life in caregivers of stroke patients. *Stroke*. 2005; 36(10): 2181–6.

41. Kamel A, Bond A, Froelicher E. Depression and caregiver burden experienced by caregivers of Jordanian patients with stroke. *Int J Nurs Pract*. 2012: 18(2): 147–54.

42. Edmonton Functional Assessment Scale. Available at http://consultgerirn.org/uploads/File/trythis/try_this_2.pdf. Revised 2012. Accessed September 20, 2014.

43. Katz Index of Independence in Activities of Daily Living. Available at http://www.npcrc.org/files/news/edmonton_functional_assessment_tool_EFAT.pdf. Accessed July 20, 2014.

44. Timed Up and Go test. Available at http://www.cdc.gov/homeandrecreationalsafety/pdf/steadi/timed_up_and_go_test.pdf. Accessed August 30, 2014.

45. Tinnetti Balance Assessment. Available at http://consultgerirn.org/uploads/File/Tinetti_Assessment_Balance.pdf. Accessed September 20, 2014.

46. Shyu Y, Chen MU, Chen MC, Wu C, Su J. Post-operative pain and its impact on quality of life for hip-fractured older people over 12 months after hospital discharge. *J Clin Nurs*. 2009: 18(5): 755–64.

47. Figueroa J, Basford J, Low P. Preventing and treating orthostatic hypotension: As easy as A, B, C. *Cleve Clin J Med*. 2010; 77(5): 298–305.

48. Kappelle J. Preventing deep vein thrombosis after stroke: strategies and recommendations. *Curr Treat Options Neur*. 2011; 13(6): 629–35.

49. National Lymphedema Network. Position statement of the national lymphedema network: the diagnosis and treatment of lymphedema. Available at http://www.lymphnet.org/pdfDocs/nlntreatment.pdf. Updated February 2011. Accessed September 20, 2014.

50. Schleinich M, Warren A, Nekolaichuk C, Kassa T, Watanabe S. Palliative care rehabilitation survey: a pilot study of patients' priorities for rehabilitation goals. *Palliat Med*. 2008; 22(7): 822–30.

CHAPTER 22

Palliative and Hospice Care in Rural Areas: Access and Delivery

Bernita D. Armstrong and Andrea L. Tackett

Key Points

♦ Individuals with serious illness who live in rural areas face unique challenges.

♦ The palliative advanced practice registered nurse (APRN) has the potential to affect the care of these individuals.

♦ The palliative care team should become a vital resource for the patient and family and the medical community.

Introduction

Rural communities are unique unto themselves and thus pose special challenges to effecting change. Some of the obstacles to rural palliative care include an absence of family caregivers, because younger family members have migrated to larger communities; financial hardships for patients and healthcare facilities; lack of qualified or specially trained palliative care professionals; inadequate funding for palliative-trained specialists, especially nurses; increased travel expenses for the patient and family; and lack of grief and bereavement specialists and resources. Reimbursement agencies (such as Medicare, Medicaid, and commercial insurers) do not consider the higher costs required to provide services in rural communities.[1]

Palliative care is a basic human right for all individuals regardless of geographic location, socioeconomic status, or racial or cultural background.[2] Access to healthcare and specifically palliative and hospice care in the rural community is challenged by geography, provider availability, and rural culture. Rural dwellers (those who live in open country and settlements with fewer than 2,500 residents) may perceive themselves as vulnerable and easily harmed either by their illness or mistrust their interactions with the medical community.

In a healthcare context, vulnerable groups, such as those in rural areas, have an increased risk of, or susceptibility to, adverse health outcomes, as evidenced by higher morbidity, premature mortality, and diminished quality of life. Low socioeconomic level and lack of external and environmental resources may contribute to disease susceptibility and are therefore indicators of

vulnerability.[3] The purpose of this chapter is to describe barriers to access and delivery of palliative and hospice care in rural and remote areas, discuss the unique characteristics of rural culture, and offer suggestions for developing a rural community palliative care program.

The Center to Advance Palliative Care (CAPC) defines palliative care as "specialized medical care focused on providing relief from the pain, symptoms and stress of a serious illness whatever the diagnosis. It is appropriate at any age and at any stage of a serious illness, and can be provided together with curative treatment." However, the association of palliative care with the end-of-life and hospice has created an "identity problem." The fundamental difference between palliative and hospice care needs to be clearly defined, as approximately seven out of ten Americans are "not at all knowledgeable" about palliative care, and most healthcare professionals believe it is "synonymous with end-of-life care."[4] As a result, many people who could benefit from the treatment of physical and psychological symptoms and spiritual issues relating to a chronic life-limiting illness are not being referred to, or accepting, palliative care.

Significant barriers exist in the United States, as well as in other countries, that limit access to healthcare and palliative care for rural dwellers. In the past, health officials believed that the main challenge in providing healthcare to rural residents was a lack of physicians and palliative care providers.[5] In response, health centers were built and rural healthcare became a specialty for physicians and APRNs. With the declining number of family practice physicians, changes in reimbursement, and a limited number of professionals who desire to work in rural areas, APRNs have assumed the role of primary care provider for many of these patients.[6,7] According to the American Nurses Association, the Affordable Care Act will foster the growth of independent practices for the APRN, as their skills will be in demand to meet the healthcare needs of those in rural regions and other health disparity areas.[8]

However, rural care delivery is different from urban care delivery. The *Report Card: America's Care of Serious Illness* produced by the CAPC states that "geography is destiny."[9] While the prevalence of palliative care teams in hospitals has experienced steady growth from 2000 to 2010, the Dartmouth Atlas indicates that hospitals with fewer than 50 beds who offer palliative care are extremely limited.[10] According to the CAPC, in the most recent data analysis, 1,635, or 66%, of U.S. hospitals with more than 50 beds have a palliative care team—an increase of 148.5% since 2000. The prevalence of palliative care teams in U.S. hospitals is lowest in the South, with only 52.7% of hospitals reporting a palliative care team, and highest in the Northwest, with 75.4% of hospitals reporting a palliative care team.[11] Research from small rural hospitals has shown clinical and financial findings to support the need for and benefit of rural palliative care programs.[12,13] Even though hospital-based palliative care programs are increasing, rural dwellers experience significant barriers to accessing palliative care such as pain control and hospice services.[14]

The National Institute of Health's 2002 report characterizes rural older adults as an "underserved population with limited access to care."[15] Many of the studies evaluating rural palliative care and identification of the needs of the rural dwellers have occurred outside the United States, in Canada, Australia, New Zealand, and the United Kingdom.[16–20] Identified barriers include the geographical dispersion of residents, inadequate financial resources, limited support systems, and lack of qualified medical, psychosocial, and spiritual support to meet the needs of the patient, caregiver, and family. These research findings are consistent with the studies conducted in the United States and share the same barriers to access and delivery of palliative care.

The Rural Community

There is no standard definition of "rural"; in fact, the U.S. government uses three definitions. The U.S. Census Bureau uses "rural" to encompass all population, housing, and territory not included within an urbanized area (UA) of 50,000 or more people or an urban cluster (UC) of 2,500 to 50,000 people.[21] The Office of Management and Budget uses metropolitan statistical areas (MSAs) to define urban and rural areas. An MSA is a city with 50,000 or more residents and a surrounding metropolitan area of at least 100,000 people. All non-MSA areas are considered rural. The U.S. Department of Agriculture Economic Research Service defines rural as an area that "comprises open country and settlements with fewer than 2,500 residents."[22] According to the U.S. Census Bureau, in the 2010 Census, 19.3% of the population was classified as rural (59,492,276), while greater than 95% of the land area was classified as rural; 80.7% of the population was classified as urban (249,253,271), while 5% of the land was classified as urban.[23] In addition to rural designation, areas may be known as "frontier." According to the National Rural Health Association, "frontier" is defined as an area with fewer than six people per square mile.[24]

No matter the definition one chooses, a rural area involves a small population spread over a large distance. The distance and the terrain present unique barriers to healthcare service delivery, including palliative care.

Many rural people have deep spiritual roots that are not typical of mainstream religious practices; some are specific to the rural region itself.[25] Such beliefs may present a challenge to those not familiar with them. It is important to approach the rural patient and family with a willingness to listen, rather than judge, to keep the path to trust open. Purposeful listening and being fully present are vital to the spiritual and emotional care of the rural palliative care patient.

Many rural individuals—religious or otherwise—believe that disease or illness is "sent on them" because of something they have done in the past.[26] One patient stated repeatedly: "I don't know what I did to make God send this on me!" The healthcare provider took the time to listen to the patient's fears and attempted to explain that God did not send cancer to punish her for unknown sins or fears. In a controlling sect in a rural community, two patients were reported to have extreme reactions to oncology treatment. One patient chose to have chemotherapy as part of her aggressive oncology care regime. She bewailed the fact that when she lost her hair, she was shunned by her religious community. Another young woman of the same sect refused chemotherapy based on the threat of being shunned, and died in her mid-thirties.

The "old ways," grounded in spiritual faith and natural medicine, differ greatly from the aggressive medical treatments found in hospitals serving rural areas today. Ironically, urban hospitals are far more likely to include holistic healthcare, such as prayer, meditation, essential oils, herbs, pet therapy, music therapy, and art. Rural hospitals have shown a tendency to focus on aggressive medical care only, viewing palliative care as failure. Rural clinicians and patients need to be educated about the benefits of palliative care; such care is not "giving up" or "quitting," but providing the best care possible so that every patient can have his or her best quality of life.[27,28]

In rural communities, the healthcare provider may encounter clients with simplistic views, especially patients who have rarely, or never, come to see providers for their healthcare needs. For example, in a family meeting to create a care plan, the patient or family members may have trouble understanding details the provider is sharing but may be too proud to ask for clarification. A palliative care team can bridge the gap between the patient/caregiver and healthcare providers, eliminating confusion and frustration. They can work with patients who have never received healthcare but who have been diagnosed with a life-threatening illness and do not know what to do or how to cope with the diagnosis. In these situations, it often takes time to develop trust among the clinician, patient, and medical community, and the palliative care team may serve as a vital intermediary.[29]

Access and Coordination of Care

Chronic disease is identified as the primary cause of death for 87% of people older than 65.[30] It is estimated that adults over the age of 70 have, on average, at least three chronic illnesses.[31] As of 2007, the elderly make up 7.5 million of the 50 million people living in rural America.[32] As the population ages, the number of adults who experience multiple chronic illnesses, cognitive impairment, and related disability and increasing dependency will increase. Many of these older adults in the rural community will be cared for in their home by family members with the support of both formal and informal care systems. There are both benefits and challenges to providing home palliative care.

According to Hanson and colleagues, the benefits of palliative care in the rural setting include "primary family caregivers sometimes personally know the formal care provider; flexibility in organizational support; other family members provide a range of support; church members provide many types of support; and neighbors and friends often help out with chores." Challenges to end-of-life care relate to limited resources and caregiver stressors, specifically the following: "service boundaries lead to limited hours or availability of formal services; lack of qualified caregivers; lack of continuity of care; and primary family caregiver stress."[33]

Accessing and coordinating palliative care services can be difficult in rural areas. The goal is for palliative care to be centered in the home, but the needs of the patient and caregivers must be acknowledged and addressed. Ventura and colleagues found that patients' and caregivers' concerns included better communication, spiritual, psychosocial, practical, and information support; lack of respite care; isolation; and loss of autonomy.[34] In the rural community, these needs are met through both formal and informal care providers.

Formal care refers to healthcare services commonly provided in the rural areas by a generalist practitioner, a nurse practitioner, or a physician assistant. Studies by Weinhold and Gurtner showed that older rural dwellers had fewer care choices, with a narrow range and scope of available services, compared to urban dwellers.[35] Wilson and colleagues demonstrated a lack of specialized palliative care and home care in rural areas, and Madigan and colleagues noted fewer hospice providers.[36,37]

Informal care refers to services that are provided by unpaid family members, friends, volunteers, or organizations. Informal care and networks may be a necessity rather than a choice. They reflect some of the strengths of rural relationships, such as social solidarity, close-knit relationships, and community commitments, and may result in high-quality, integrated palliative and end-of-life services despite scarce resources[38] (Table 22.1).

Rural Palliative Care Program

A rural palliative care program must be based on a thorough understanding of the rural community, its beliefs and customs, prevalent medical diagnoses, and available community resources, including financial and human capital. Rural dwellers tend to be poorer, with a per capita income that is $7,417 less than the income of those in urban areas. Rural and frontier Americans are more likely to live below the poverty level and to rely heavily on the federal food stamp program. Disparity in incomes is even greater for minorities living in rural areas. Compared to the urban population, rural dwellers are less likely to have employer-provided healthcare coverage or prescription drug coverage or to be covered by Medicare benefits, which in turn will limit medical service availability.[39]

There are 2,157 health professional shortage areas in rural and frontier areas and U.S. territories, compared to 910 in urban areas. Although nearly one-fourth of the population lives in these areas, only about 10% of physicians practice in rural America. In urban areas, there are nearly 60 dentists per 100,000 persons versus 40 per 100,000 in rural areas. Mental health services are limited in terms of both mental health infrastructure and the supply of professionals.[3] Twenty percent of nonmetropolitan counties lack mental health services versus 5% of metropolitan counties. Nonmetropolitan counties have, on average, fewer than two mental health organizations, while metropolitan counties report an average of more than 13.[39]

Table 22.1 Risk Assessment for Barriers to Palliative Care

Patient Risk Factors	Yes	No
Uninsured?		
Underinsured?		
No prescription plan or only partial plan?		
On disability?		
Prisoner?		
Homeless?		
Over 65 years old?		
Under 18 years old?		
Unable to communicate verbally?		
Unable to speak English?		
Unable to read or write?		
Undocumented immigrant?		
Mental illness, including depression?		
Caregiver for someone else?		
Have a primary care physician?		
Does he/she spend time in bed during the waking hours?		
Caregiver		
Does the patient have a caregiver?		
Is the patient's caregiver elderly?		
Does the patient's caregiver work?		
Living conditions		
Does the patient live in an unsafe neighborhood (i.e., Is hospice/home health unable to visit during night/day due to safety concerns?)?		
Does the patient live in a nursing facility?		
Stairs to bathroom?		
Running water?		
Electricity?		
Telephone?		
Food stamps?		
Rural location?		
Transportation		
Does the patient have reliable transportation?		
Knowledge, planning		
Does the patient have a living will/advance directive?		
Does the patient know about hospice care?		

Source: From reference 14, with permission.

Designing a Rural Palliative Care Program

An important first step in designing a successful palliative care program in a rural community is performing a community assessment, focusing on local assets, resources, and stakeholders who recognize the need for palliative and hospice services. Offering stakeholders and champions a role in designing and implementing the program goals and objectives will ensure the momentum and success of the program.[40]

Understanding the nature of family and community support is crucial to the success of the program. Studies have found that rural dwellers are accepting of barriers to healthcare due to their rurality and therefore are reticent about seeking care. Rural residents tend to *make do* with available resources, *solve their problems* independently, and be *self-reliant*. The sense of *community belonging* in rural culture means that "neighbors know and look out for each other," and individuals in *close-knit communities* fear sharing their health-related issues and seek care due to privacy issues. These attributes are a source of strength and personal control for rural dwellers and thus may be a challenge to integrating palliative care into the community.[41] However, acceptance and knowledge of the unique beliefs, customs, and rituals of each culture will promote acceptance of the APRN and the palliative care program.

For a palliative care program to succeed in a rural community, the healthcare providers must possess cultural competency and communication skills and be able to deliver effective care for patients with diverse values, beliefs, and behaviors. Mass media can be used as a health promotion tool to build community trust. The goal of public education and social marketing is to help people change their health behaviors by acquiring information and education they lack or through verbal and visual messaging that can shift the individual's thinking, attitudes, and values. Effective use of the media requires positioning oneself as an expert in palliative care and being available *formally* and *informally* to explain, promote, and be a resource for information, referrals, and services[42] (Table 22.1).

The ethnographic work by Averill has demonstrated that dedicated professionals can provide excellent palliative care despite scarce resources.[43] However, not all healthcare can be provided in the rural community itself, and travel may present unique barriers and challenges for the patient and family. As the expert in palliative care, the APRN must understand whom to contact for services; how and where to obtain medications, equipment, and supplies; and ways to offer appropriate care that is within the financial means of the rural population. The APRN must also appreciate the benefits and burden of care, recognize when care needs exceed the rural area's capacity, and when referral to a larger town or city is appropriate and necessary.

Commuting for Care

Distance, roadways, and weather conditions are significant factors when deciding to commute for specialized healthcare services not available in the rural community. Often, it is not the mileage alone but the road conditions (e.g., curves, elevation) and weather conditions (e.g., flooding, mud, snow and ice) that make it daunting for a provider to make a house call or for the patient to make a clinic visit. In a mountainous area, a 50-mile commute may take 3 hours. Early in the disease process, this may be acceptable to the patient, but as the disease progresses and treatments continue, the patient may decide the time burden is too much, may choose not to leave the community for care, or may relocate to the urban area to be closer to specialized services. The costs for transportation, food, and lodging, as well as time commitments, are important considerations.[44]

Transportation is a common barrier for the rural dweller, as public transportation may not exist or may exist for local areas only. Moreover, such transportation may be costly and time-consuming. The patient may already be experiencing financial hardships due to treatment and must then rely on family and friends for support and transportation. Family and friends must take time from work to drive the patient to the city and stay with the patient for either the day or several days, depending on the treatments required. Financial support is generally shared by family and friends. Many treating facilities have agreements with agencies where patients can stay or eat at a reduced rate.

Commuting may be anxiety-provoking for the patient who feels he or she is a burden to the family and community. Travel can also create significant anxiety for the caregiver. Strategies for coping with commuting include careful preparation for the trip, maximizing a routine, managing time, and maintaining significant relationships. Anticipation of weather and traffic delays, planning

Table 22.2 Media Technologies and How Information Can Be Shared

Mass Media	Media Technologies	Examples
Broadcast media	Radio, television	Guest speaker on radio and television community programs; public information spots
Print media	Newspaper, magazine, pamphlets, books	Opinion editorial, article, fact sheet, flyers (placed in pharmacy, medical offices, food store, church bulletin, club newsletter), booklet *"What is palliative and hospice care?"* with contact information
Outdoor media	Billboards, signs	Advertisement with program & contact information; ground signs for outdoor events and near office
Public speaking	Events—speaker and/or organizer	PowerPoint presentations, lectures (formal and informal) for healthcare practitioners and community
Digital media	Internet forums Social network Blogging and microblogging Podcasts Video sharing	Establish an e-mail account and web page specific to your palliative care program on Facebook, Twitter, LinkedIn, YouTube.

for food and rest stops, scheduling pain medications and other pharmacologic agents to maintain analgesic coverage during the commute, and sharing quality time together may decrease the patient's anxiety.[45] The issue of continuing the care plan once the patient returns home may also cause anxiety.

"Lost to Care" and "Abandonment"

Being "lost to care" in their own community is another concern for patients who choose to travel out of the area for care. Such patients may lose contact with their local provider. The APRN can bridge this gap by assuming "ownership" of the patient's case (case manager) when the patient is referred, while the patient is under the care of providers in distant cities, and when the patient returns to the community. Frequently, the APRN serves as the communication link by providing continuity of care for the patient and family. Communication, either in person or by telephone, is paramount with this patient population to prevent the patient from being "lost to care."[46]

First, individuals may not be aware of the palliative care services that are available in their own community. If there are no defined palliative care services, their primary healthcare professional is expected to provide these services and coordinate their care. If their healthcare professional lacks primary palliative care education and training, the treatment plan that was established when the patient was discharged may not be continued. The patient may experience untreated, undertreated, or overtreated pain and symptoms, both physical and psychological.

The patient who does not have a primary care provider and was not referred to a primary care provider by the discharging facility is at a great disadvantage. If this is not recognized by the family and friends, the patient will truly be "lost to care." To avoid these situations, a *rural–urban referral system* needs to be established. The APRN formulates and maintains a list of contacts in other facilities, contacts the facility when a patient is referred, maintains verbal and written contact during the admission, and anticipates the time of discharge and needs when the patient returns to the rural community.

Second, the unfamiliar language of palliative care may be a barrier to rural patients, family members, and healthcare professionals who equate palliative care to hospice care. Softer terms, such as *supportive care* rather than *palliative care, forgo treatments* rather than *stop treatments, comfort measures only* rather than *stopping all treatments,* and *allow natural death* rather than *do not resuscitate,* have been shown to be more comfortable terminology for the patient and family.[47]

Third, navigating the bureaucratic system may be a challenge in rural areas. It can be difficult to know what agency to contact for help with securing medical services, financial resources to pay for medications and living expenses, home health services, and equipment. This lack of information can cause emotional stress for the patient and family who have been self-sufficient and have always been able to "do whatever it takes" to make things work. A community resource information flyer and/or magnet can be developed, including the name of the facility or organization, contact, address, and telephone numbers. If there are no hospice services available, the APRN should coordinate alternate providers for services, such as grief services, to be provided by the funeral home or local clergy; pain and symptom management, to be provided by emergency medical personnel or community members with medical skills; and support services, such as meals, respite care, transportation,

and performing errands, to be coordinated through local churches and service organizations. The development of coordinated palliative services and focused education for the healthcare professionals and community will help to alleviate this stress and ultimately change the cultural attitude toward palliative care.

Sites of Care and Workforce

The limited number of healthcare professionals trained in primary or specialty palliative care, homecare and volunteer services, nursing home beds, and/or alternate sites of care may create barriers to rural palliative care. If the family cannot care for the patient, it may be difficult to locate a skilled nursing facility close to the patient's home. This scenario is common in rural areas like Alaskan villages and Appalachia and other mountainous regions. Many rural dwellers prefer to die at home, in their community or village, with family and friends present at the time of death. The work of DeCourtney and colleagues with Alaskan native villagers has shown that a culturally sensitive palliative care program can be developed to provide end-of-life care and meet the goals of the Alaskan villagers to live their final days in their village.[48] While home has been thought to be the preferred site of death, other studies have found that this might not be true; dying in a local hospital or nursing home may be preferred if the care providers are known to the patient and family.[49]

The shortage of healthcare professionals and facilities in rural communities continues to be an issue for the APRN to coordinate and provide continuity of care. MacDowell and colleagues conducted a nationwide survey of 1,031 rural hospital CEOs to determine if they perceived a shortage of healthcare professionals in their area. Seventy-five percent of the responders reported shortages of all healthcare professionals; the survey did not address palliative care specialists.[50] To address the shortage of rural physicians in the United States, the "Conrad State 30" program was developed to recruit foreign-trained physicians to work in rural areas in exchange for permanent residence. A similar program exists for advanced practice registered nurses and nursing faculty to serve in critical shortage facilities and accredited schools of nursing. The program pays 60% of their unpaid nursing student loans for 2 years of service and an additional 25% of the original balance for an optional third year.[51]

Cassel and colleagues reported on the benefits of rural palliative care for hospitals and dedicated palliative care practitioners. Palliative care programs save hospitals money through cost avoidance (decreased daily costs, decreased length of stay, increased hospice referrals), are associated with a decreased in-hospital death rate, and generate income for the palliative care practitioner.[52]

Family and Community Support

The challenge for the APRN and the palliative care team in the rural community is to coordinate formal and informal services to meet the needs of patients and caregivers. As noted earlier, rural dwellers tend to be reticent to seek care, possibly due to their inability to access and understand healthcare information (low health literacy), which impedes their acceptance of healthcare interventions.

Patients and caregivers reported poor communication with healthcare providers, feeling that the providers did not have the time to listen or were not familiar with their condition or current situation.[53] Communication is paramount to the peace of mind of the patient and caregiver. Communication begins with the team members. The team determines who is responsible for various services, provides contact information (address, telephone number, and contact person), and lets the patient and family know when they can expect these services. This information helps the patient and family to gain a sense of control.

Frequently, the APRN is the leader of the palliative care team (officially or unofficially) and is responsible for the coordination and access to care from the patient's and family's perspective. By holding a family meeting to explore goals of care, the APRN can ensure that the patient's and family's perceived needs are met, including medical, financial, equipment, spiritual, and other information specific to the patient's/family's culture and belief systems. As part of the family meeting, the palliative care team should discuss each member's perception of the shared information, should determine what services are needed, should make referrals, and within 24 hours should provide the patient and family with a written plan of care.

Providing information about the patient's illness, how the condition will progress, the patient's life expectancy, and specific treatment decisions is an important aspect of care. Some patients expressed concern about what would happen to their spouse when they died.[54] Other caregivers wanted information in writing about their caregiving role and complementary and alternative treatments.[55] Health literacy levels are reported to be low in the rural population; many individuals have never had an ill loved one or been in a caregiving role. They can be confused about the disease and the process, and their understanding and perceptions are often overshadowed by cultural beliefs and rituals.

Loneliness, isolation, and loss of autonomy in older ill adults who live in rural areas have been related to higher depression scores, lower quality of life, lower social support, and particularly lower emotional support.[56] Some patients felt their isolation and lack of communication were a result of the stigma of their disease; other patients felt their loss of autonomy was due to their inability to interact and participate with their family in usual activities and holidays.[57,58]

Teamwork is essential to the delivery of rural palliative care. The independence, cooperation, and collaboration evident in rural communities are the strengths that allow the APRN and healthcare professionals, family, and community to meet the needs of the patient, even though resources may be lacking.

Competencies for the Rural APRN

The importance of competencies for palliative providers has been reported by Schrader, Nelson, and Eidsness from their work with palliative care teams on the South Dakota prairie.[59] Whether palliative services are delivered using a specialist or generalist model, educational needs are essentially the same. Pain and symptom management, spiritual issues, advance directives, psychosocial issues, and family support were identified as critically important. Barriers to professional development for rural practitioners include geographic and professional isolation, time constraints, workload, and no one to fill in during their absence. Various modalities exist to acquire training and maintain skills; one-on-one and classroom presentations appear to be both the most rewarding for rural healthcare practitioners and the least accessible.

One study demonstrated an 8-year ongoing collaborative effort by urban and rural palliative care practitioners to develop a rural palliative care program. Urban practitioners traveled to the rural community to educate and train rural healthcare professionals to deliver palliative care services. The goals of the program were to develop a rural palliative care program and enhance the knowledge base of rural providers. Program evaluation determined that the goals were met: a palliative care program for rural and remote communities was developed, and healthcare providers felt they had a greater capacity to deliver palliative care in the rural setting.[60]

Reymond and colleagues conducted workshops with 3-month follow-up of rural and remote community providers. Program evaluation revealed significant improvement in the participants' confidence regarding their palliative care knowledge and skills. Costs were relatively inexpensive, as the workshops were conducted in their locale.[61]

Telemedicine, also known as telehealth or health information technology, is a rapidly developing application of clinical medicine using telephone, computers, the Internet, and other networks to advance the delivery of rural and remote healthcare. Telehealth has facilitated the exchange of information and knowledge regardless of geographic or environmental barriers while reducing access time and costs. The study by Holland and colleagues demonstrated positive results for rural palliative care and hospice patients and families, such as improved quality of life, satisfaction with care, reduced hospital readmissions, and reduced healthcare costs, using health information technology.[62] As APRNs become more comfortable with the use of computer technology and sharing of education and information, new models of palliative care for rural and older adults will be developed.

The Reality of Rural Life

Imagine a patient in a rural area with no access to healthcare. The patient receives a terminal diagnosis after going to a city following a bad fall. The patient views the healthcare providers as haughty and only wanting money. A specialist offers aggressive treatment that may cure the patient's disease. After several meetings and treatments, the patient gradually lets down his defenses and finds he not only trusts this clinician, but has also developed a sense of dependency on her because she offers a possible cure. However, the treatments no longer work and actually make the patient sicker. At some point, the patient is told there is nothing more to be done and he should go home and die. Imagine the sense of abandonment and betrayal a patient experiences when a specialist who has finally gained his trust discharges him when aggressive care ceases to be of benefit! As one patient asked this author's team leader at an initial meeting, "Are you going to kick me to the curb, too?"

The remedy is to begin palliative care early, soon after the diagnosis, and to collaborate with rural care providers. A shift toward seeing palliative care as part and parcel of care, rather than a last resort, is very welcome. This way, palliative care becomes a flexible companion instead of giving up, a bridge to support the patient and family throughout the journey, whatever its length. Palliative care should be woven seamlessly into treatment to reduce families' stress levels and improve patients' quality of life in their final days.[63]

This chapter's case study represents a perfect example of the beauty and challenges to practice in rural Appalachia. Although she was geographically isolated, the patient had strong family ties and a devoted 21-year old daughter, willing to uphold her mother's final wishes.

Case Study

Anna was a 47-year-old female who presented to the ED with a 2-month history of shortness of breath, weakness, and increasing fatigue. Palliative Performance Status was 50%. In the ED she was found to be in respiratory distress; she required ventilator support and ICU admission. Diagnostic workup revealed non-small-cell lung cancer, stage IV. Anna was unemployed, had no medical coverage, and had limited financial resources and limited family and social support systems. Subsequent to her diagnosis, she received numerous treatments (chemotherapy and radiation, antibiotics, and blood products) with a total of six hospital admissions, four of the six requiring ICU admission and ventilator support. During the fifth admission to ICU, she was unable to protect her airway. Anna agreed to a tracheostomy and a PEG tube was placed. The palliative care team once again met with Anna and her family to discuss transfer to a long-term acute care hospital or a nursing home that provided ventilator support, with the hope of weaning her off the ventilator. However, she lived in a rural area and the closest facility that provided services to ventilator-dependent patients was at least 2 hours away. The family had very limited financial resources and difficulty obtaining transportation. Because the patient felt she was at the end of her life, she did not want to spend her remaining time in a hospital or nursing home several hours away from her family, and she declined the transfer.

The palliative APRN searched for in-home patient and family support services. Calls were made to the two hospice agencies that served the area. Both agencies stated that because the patient was on a home ventilator, which was considered aggressive treatment, she did not qualify for hospice admission. Contact with the three home health agencies that served the patient's area revealed they did not offer home ventilator support services. The third agency had a home ventilator program; however, at the time of referral, they did not have a nurse qualified to fill this position. To provide services to the patient, they would need to hire a nurse, but until then they would not be able to see her.

A long discussion was held with the patient and her daughter concerning options for discharge. The daughter stated she would care for her mother, if she could be taught how to care for the tracheostomy and ventilator. The palliative APRN worked with the durable medical equipment company that provided the home ventilator and their respiratory technicians. The nursing staff taught the patient's daughter how to care for the patient and the ventilator. Anna was discharged home, and the palliative APRN and the medical equipment company continued formal and informal support. Several months later, one of the home health agencies received approval to provide nurse aides and RN support, however, they were unable to assist with managing the ventilator.

Seven months after discharge home, Anna was admitted to the hospital for end-of-life care. She had accomplished her goal to be at home with her family during the last days of her life.

Conclusion

Palliative care is both a specialty and a philosophy of care that has evolved over many decades. Central to its practice is the development of an informed and compassionate approach to care for the chronically ill patient and family. Palliative care views the patient and family as a unit. Its goal is to improve the quality of life for both by treating pain and other symptoms; providing time-intensive communication; supporting complex medical decision making; ensuring practical, spiritual, and psychological support; and coordinating care across all settings. In larger communities where resources are "just around the corner," this is easily accomplished. However, for rural communities, where 80% of palliative care is provided by non-physician providers, the challenge for the APRN and members of the healthcare team is to design a community-based palliative care program to create a seamless transition from a curative care model to a comfort care model while meeting the needs, wishes, and expectations of the patient and family.

References

1. Rural Assistance Center. Why is hospice and palliative care an issue in rural areas? *Heal Hum Serv Inf Rural Am.* 2014. Available at http://www.raconline.org/topics/hospice-and-palliative-care/faqs#rural. Accessed June 18, 2014.
2. Brennan F. Palliative care as an international human right. *J Pain Symptom Manage.* 2007; 33(5): 494–9.
3. Brundisini F, Giacomini M, DeJean D, Vanstone M, Winsor SSA. Chronic disease patients' experiences with accessing health care in rural and remote areas: a systematic review and qualitative meta-synthesis. *Ont Health Technol Assess Ser.* 2013; 13(15):1–33.
4. Center to Advance Palliative Care. *2011 Public Opinion Research on Palliative Care.* CAPC; 2011:1–14.
5. Klugman CM, Dalinis M. *Ethical Issues in Rural Health Care.* Baltimore, MD: The Johns Hopkins University Press; 2008.
6. Kuebler KK. The palliative care advanced practice nurse. *J Palliat Med.* 2003; 6(5): 707–14.
7. Emnett J, Byock I, Twohig JS. Advanced Practice Nursing: Pioneering Practices in Palliative Care. Promoting Excellence in End-Of-Life Care, a National Program Office of The Robert Wood Johnson Foundation. 2002:1–13. Available at http://www.rwjf.org/en/grants/programs-and-initiatives/P/promoting-excellence-in-end-of-life-care.html. Accessed June 21, 2014.
8. Lathrop B. The Affordable Care Act: primary care and the doctor of nursing practice nurse. *OJIN.* 2014;19(2). Available at http://www.nursingworld.org/MainMenuCategories/ANAMarketplace/ANAPeriodicals/OJIN/TableofContents/Vol-19-2014/No2-May-2014/Articles-Previous-Topics/Affordable-Care-Act-Doctor-of-Nursing-Practice.html. Accessed June 16, 2014.
9. Morrison RS. Report Card: America's care of serious illness. A State-by-State Report Card on Access to Palliative Care in Our Nation's Hospitals. 2011. Available at http://www.capc.org/reportcard/pdf/state-by-state-report-card-pdf. Accessed June 12, 2014.
10. The Dartmouth Institute for Health Policy and Clinical Practice. The Dartmouth Atlas of Health Care. 2011. Available at www.dartmouthatlas.org. Accessed June 21, 2014.
11. CAPC.org. Growth of palliative care in U.S. hospitals 2012 Snapshot. 2012. Available at http://www.getpalliativecare.org.
12. Armstrong B, Jenigiri B, Hutson SP, Wachs PM, Lambe CE. The impact of a palliative care program in a rural Appalachian community hospital: a quality improvement process. *Am J Hosp Palliat Med.* 2013; 30(4): 380–7.
13. Mcgrath LS, Gar D, Frith KH, Hall WM. Cost effectiveness of a palliative care program in a rural community hospital. *Nurs Econ.* 2013; 31(4): 176–83.

14. Lyckholm LJ, Coyne PJ, Kreutzer KO, Ramakrishnan V, Smith TJ. Barriers to effective palliative care for low-income patients in late stages of cancer: report of a study and strategies for defining and conquering the barriers. *Nurs Clin North Am.* 2010; 45(3): 399–409.

15. National Institute of Health. Strategic research plan and budget to reduce and ultimately eliminate health disparities, Vol 1: Fiscal years 2002-2006. 2002:1–33. Available at http://www.nimhd.nih.gov/documents/VolumeI_031003EDrev.pdf. Accessed August 16, 2014.

16. Kaasalainen S, Brazil K, Wilson DM, et al. Palliative care nursing in rural and urban community settings: A comparative analysis. *Int J Palliat Nurs.* 2011; 17(7): 344–52.

17. Robinson CA, Pesut B, Bottorff JL. Supporting rural family palliative caregivers. *J Fam Nurs.* 2012; 18(4): 467–90.

18. Sach J. Issues for palliative care in rural Australia. *Collegian.* 1997; 4(41): 22–7.

19. Smyth D, Farnell A, Dutu G, Lillis S, Lawrenson R. Palliative care provision by rural general practitioners in New Zealand. *J Palliat Med.* 2010; 13(3): 247–50.

20. Evans R, Stone D, Elwyn G. Organizing palliative care for rural populations: A systematic review of the evidence. *Fam Pract.* 2003; 20: 304–10.

21. U.S. Bureau of the Census. Geographic Terms and Concepts—Urban and Rural. 2013. Available at http://www.census.gov/geo/reference/gtc/gtc_urbanrural.html. Accessed June 24, 2014.

22. U.S. Department of Agriculture. What is Rural? 2013. Available at http://www.ers.usda.gov/topics/rural-economy-population/rural-classifications/what-is-rural.aspx#.VBjpbBZ0a3M. Accessed June 24, 2014.

23. U.S. Bureau of the Census. How many people reside in urban or rural areas for the 2010 Census? What percentage of the U.S. population is urban or rural? *United States Census 2010.* 2012. Available at http://2010.census.gov/2010census/contact/. Accessed June 20, 2014.

24. Natural Rural Health Association. *Providing Hospice and Palliative Care in Rural and Frontier Areas.* Kansas City, MO: National Rural Health Association; 2005. Available at http://www.nhpco.org/sites/default/files/public/InfoCenter/RuralToolkit_Chp_2.pdf.

25. Behringer B, Krishnan K. Understanding the role of religion in cancer care in Appalachia. *South Med J.* 2011; 104(4): 295–6.

26. Hutson SP, Dorgan KA, Phillips AN, Behringer B. The mountains hold things in: The use of community research review workgroups to explore cancer disparities in Southern Appalachia. *Oncol Nurs Forum.* 2007; 34(6): 1133–9.

27. West H. Is palliative care "giving up"? No, it can actually improve both quality of life and survival. 2010. Available at http://cancergrace.org/cancer-treatments/2010/07/30/is-palliative-care-giving-up/.

28. Solomon N. Palliative care: Letting go, not giving up. St. Louis University, 2004. Available at http://www.slu.edu/readstory/more/3949. Accessed July 28, 2014.

29. Dorgan KA, Hutson SP, Gerding G, Duvall KL. Culturally tailored cancer communication, education, and research: the highways and back roads of Appalachia. *Prev Chronic Dis.* 2009; 6(2): A68.

30. Centers for Disease Control and Prevention. Health, United States, 2010. 2010. Available at http://www.cdc.gov/nchs/data/hus/hus10.pdf. Accessed July 20, 2014.

31. Alliance for Aging Research. Medical never-never land: Ten reasons why America is not ready for the coming age boom. 2002. Available at http://agingresearch.org/content/article/detail/698/. Accessed June 24, 2014.

32. Older Americans 2012: Key Indicators of Well-Being. *Fed Interag Forum Aging-Related Stat.* 2012. Available at http://www.raconline.org/topics/aginghttp://agingstats.gov/Agingstatsdotnet/Main_Site/Data/2012_Documents/Docs/EntireChartbook.pdf.

33. Hansen L, Cartwright JC, Craig CE. End-of-life care for rural-dwelling older adults and their primary family caregivers. *Res Gerontol Nurs.* 2012; 5(1): 6–15.

34. Ventura AD, Burney S, Brooker J, Fletcher J, Ricciardelli L. Home-based palliative care: a systematic literature review of the self-reported unmet needs of patients and carers. *Palliat Med.*

35. 2014; 28(5): 391–402. Available at http://www.ncbi.nlm.nih.gov/pubmed/24292156. Accessed September 18, 2014.

35. Weinhold I, Gurtner S. Understanding shortages of sufficient health care in rural areas. *Health Policy (New York).* 2014. Available at http://linkinghub.elsevier.com/retrieve/pii/S0168851014001997. Accessed August 18, 2014.

36. Wilson DM, Justice C, Sheps S, et al. Planning and providing end-of-life care in rural areas. *J Rural Health.* 2006; 22(2): 174–81.

37. Madigan EA, Wiencek CA, Vander Schrier AL. Patterns of community-based end-of-life care in rural areas of the United States. *Policy Polit Nurs Pract.* 2009; 10(1): 71–81.

38. Hughes PM, Ingleton CM, Noble B, Clark D. Providing cancer and palliative care in rural areas. *J Palliat Care.* 2004; 20: 44–9.

39. Office of Rural Health Policy. *Rural Healthy People 2010—"Healthy People 2010: A Companion Document for Rural Areas."* 2010. Available at http://sph.tamhsc.edu/srhrc/docs/rhp-2010-volume2.pdf. Accessed August 26, 2014.

40. Greenhalgh T, Robert G, Bate P, Macfarlane F, Kyriakidou O. *Diffusion of Innovations in Health Service Organizations: A Systematic Literature Review.* Malden, MA: Blackwell; 2005.

41. Tessaro I, Smith SL, Rye S. Knowledge and Perceptions of Diabetes in an Appalachian Population. *Prev Chronic Dis.* 2005; 2(2): A13.

42. Mason DJ, Leavitt JK, Chaffee MW. *Policy & Politics in Nursing and Health Care.* St. Louis, MO: Elsevier; 2012. Available at http://evolve.elsevier.com.

43. Averill J. Keys to the puzzle: recognizing strengths in a rural community. *Public Health Nurs.* 2003; 20(6): 449–55.

44. Pesut B, Robinson CA, Bottorff JL, Fyles G, Broughton S. On the road again: patient perspectives on commuting for palliative care. *Palliat Support Care.* 2010; 8(2): 187–95.

45. Reif S, Golin CE, Smith SR. Barriers to accessing HIV/AIDS care in North Carolina: rural and urban differences. *AIDS Care.* 2005; 17(5): 558–65.

46. Hauser JM. Lost in transition: the ethics of the palliative care handoff. *J Pain Symptom Manage.* 2009; 37(5): 930–3.

47. Venneman SS, Narnor-Harris P, Perish M, Hamilton M. "Allow natural death" versus "do not resuscitate": three words that can change a life. *J Med Ethics.* 2008; 34(1): 2–6.

48. DeCourtney CA, Jones K, Merriman MP, Heavener N, Branch PK. Establishing a culturally sensitive palliative care program in rural Alaska Native American communities. *J Palliat Med.* 2003; 6(3): 501–10.

49. Robinson CA, Pesut B, Bottorff JL. Issues in rural palliative care: views from the countryside. *J Rural Health.* 2010; 26(1): 78–84.

50. MacDowell M. Glasser M, Fitts M, Neilsen K, Hunsaker M. A national view of rural health workforce issues in the USA. *Rural Remote Heal.* 2013; 10(3): 1–16.

51. U.S. Department of Health and Human Services. Nurse Corps Loan Repayment Program. Available at http://www.hrsa.gov/loanscholarships/repayment/nursing/. Accessed November 11, 2014.

52. Cassel JB, Webb-Wright J, Holmes J, Lyckholm L, Smith TJ. Clinical and financial impact of a palliative care program at a small rural hospital. *J Palliat Med.* 2010; 13(11): 1339–43.

53. Sharpe L, Butow P, Smith C, McConnell D, Clarke S. The relationship between available support, unmet needs and caregiver burden in patients with advanced cancer and their carers. *Psychooncology.* 2005; 14(2): 102–14.

54. Jo S, Brazil K, Lohfeld L, et al. Caregiving at the end of life: perspectives from spousal caregivers and care recipients. *Palliat Support Care.* 2007; 5: 11–7.

55. Jones I, Kirby A, Ormiston P, et al. The needs of patients dying of chronic obstructive pulmonary disease in the community. *Fam Pract.* 2004; 21(3): 310–3.

56. Theeke LA, Goins RT, Moore J, Campbell H. Loneliness, depression, social support, and quality of life in older chronically ill Appalachians. *J Psychol.* 2012; 146(1-2): 155–71.

57. Osse BHP, Vernooij-Dassen MFJ, Schadé E, Grol R. Problems experienced by the informal caregivers of cancer patients and their needs for support. *Cancer Nurs.* 2006; 29(5): 378–88.

58. Osse BHP, Vernooij-Dassen MJFJ, Schadé E, Grol RPTM. The problems experienced by patients with cancer and their needs for palliative care. *Support Care Cancer.* 2005; 13(9): 722–32.

59. Schrader SL, Nelson ML, Eidsness L. Palliative care teams on the prairie: composition, perceived challenges & opportunities. *S D Med.* 2007; 60(4): 151–53.

60. Kelley ML, Habjan S, Aegard J. Building capacity to provide palliative care in rural and remote communities: does education make a difference? *J Palliat Care.* 2004; 20(4): 308–15.

61. Reymond L, Charles M, Israel F, Read T, Treston P. A strategy to increase the palliative care capacity of rural primary health care providers. *Aust J Rural Heal.* 2005; 13: 156–61.

62. Holland DE, Vanderboom CE, Ingram CJ, et al. The feasibility of using technology to enhance the transition of palliative care for rural patients. *Comput Inform Nurs.* 2014; 32(6): 257–66. Available at http://www.ncbi.nlm.nih.gov/pubmed/24814998. Accessed September 24, 2014.

63. Ledwick M. Palliative care isn't "giving up"—it improves quality of life and dignity, and maybe even survival. *Cancer Res.* 2010. Available at http://scienceblog.cancerresearchuk.org/2010/08/23/palliative-care-isnt-giving-up-it-improves-quality-of-life-and dignity-and-maybe-even-survival/. Accessed August 12, 2014.

PART THREE

PAIN AND SYMPTOM MANAGEMENT FOR THE PALLIATIVE ADVANCED PRACTICE REGISTERED NURSE

SECTION A

Physical Symptoms

CHAPTER 23

Pain

Judith A. Paice

Introduction

Pain is greatly feared by those experiencing a life-threatening illness. In most cases, patients and their loved ones can be reassured that this symptom can be relieved, but in some cases pain can be extremely challenging to control. This is in part because the subjectivity of the pain experience, along with the absence of specific laboratory or imaging markers, complicates assessment and management. The biopsychosocial model of pain provides a framework that can guide APRNs in understanding the many variables that contribute to the experience of pain (Fig. 23.1).[1,2] Biological, psychological, social, and spiritual factors should be considered part of a complete assessment and serve as a guide for development of a comprehensive plan of care.

The palliative APRN is in a unique position to provide this "whole person" care. Blending knowledge of the common pain syndromes seen in life-threatening illness, sophisticated assessment skills, and awareness of interventions used to relieve pain, while employing stellar education and communication strategies, the APRN can provide safe and effective pain relief for the majority of palliative care patients with pain.

Goals of Pain Management

The goals of comprehensive and effective pain management include prevention of pain, relief of pain, improved function and quality of life, safety, and the prevention of adverse societal effects (such as diversion). In a perfect world, all pain would be prevented. Yet, acute pain serves as an important warning sign. Therefore, although preventing acute pain is neither reasonable nor desired in

all circumstances, there are situations in palliative care where the APRN can work to develop strategies to prevent pain. Procedural pain, such as that experienced with bone marrow aspiration or other interventions, can be reduced or prevented with adequate local and/or systemic analgesics, education, and preparation. There is ample evidence that unrelieved postoperative pain correlates with chronic pain syndromes, such as post-mastectomy pain.[3] Thus, prevention of acute pain may preclude or limit persistent pain syndromes.

When pain cannot be prevented, relief is imperative. This requires a balance among analgesia, increased function, and safety, and these goals are based on the state of the patient's illness. For the actively dying, the scale may tip towards analgesia, with less emphasis on function. For the patient who is a long-term survivor, the goal of enhanced function supersedes complete pain control.[4,5] Regardless of the patient's overall stage of disease, safety needs are paramount. Adverse effects must be prevented, minimized, or controlled. Medications must be used by the patient, and only the patient, in a manner that will limit untoward events. This includes preventing access to controlled substances by family, friends, caregivers, or others for inappropriate use (sharing with others, or selling the medications).[6–8]

Pain Syndromes in Palliative Care

An awareness of common pain syndromes seen in life-threatening illness assists the APRN in identifying the etiology and guides treatment.[9] Differentiating acute from chronic syndromes will help determine the course and treatment options.[10] Specific pain syndromes common in those with cancer have been identified, but unfortunately the types of pain associated with other life-threatening illnesses have not been fully categorized (Box 23.1).[10–13] Understanding the etiology may lead to treatment options beyond analgesic therapies, such as radiotherapy for new bone metastases or surgery to repair joints affected by avascular necrosis (discussed later in this chapter).

Another strategy for grouping pain syndromes is by their quality: somatic, neuropathic, visceral, or mixed.[14] Understanding the quality of the patient's pain informs the analgesic regimen. One paradigm is as follows:

◆ Somatic pain—usually managed by non-opioids and opioids

◆ Neuropathic pain—treated with adjuvant analgesics and opioids (little or no response to non-opioids)

◆ Visceral pain—controlled by opioids and corticosteroids

Biopsychosocial Model of Pain

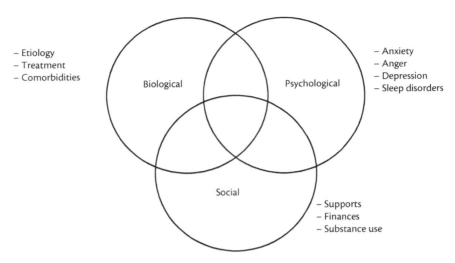

Figure 23.1 The biopsychosocial model of pain (from references 1 and 2)

Box 23.1 Selected Cancer Pain Syndromes

Tumor-Related Pain Syndromes

- Bone metastases
- Hepatic capsule distention due to metastases
- Plexus involvement by tumor

Treatment-Related Pain Syndromes

Surgical Pain Syndromes

- Post-amputation phantom pain
- Post-thoracotomy pain
- Post-mastectomy pain

Radiation-Related Pain Syndromes

- Chest pain/tightness
- Cystitis
- Enteritis
- Fistula formation
- Myelopathy
- Osteoporosis
- Osteoradionecrosis
- Pelvic fractures
- Peripheral nerve entrapment
- Plexopathies
- Proctitis
- Secondary malignancies

Chemotherapy-Related Pain Syndromes

- Chemotherapy-induced peripheral neuropathy
- Osteonecrosis from corticosteroids

Stem Cell Transplant-Mediated Chronic Graft-versus-Host Disease

- Scleroderma-like skin changes
- Eye pain and dryness
- Oral pain and reduced jaw motion
- Dysuria
- Dyspareunia, vaginal pain
- Paresthesias
- Arthralgias, myalgias

Hormonal Therapy-Related Pain Syndromes

- Osteoporotic compression fractures
- Arthralgias

Pain Unrelated to Tumor or Treatment

- Comorbid conditions, such as diabetic neuropathy, arthritis

From references 10–13.

Pain Assessment

The APRN is uniquely trained to obtain a comprehensive pain assessment in palliative care. This includes a thorough history, a careful physical examination, and in some cases interpretation of laboratory values or imaging results.[15] The history can be guided by the biopsychosocial model, considering all components of the pain experience. Box 23.2 provides a sample template for a comprehensive pain assessment.

While conducting a thorough history, it is useful to consider those patients at risk for inadequate assessment and management of pain (Box 23.3).[11,16,17] The use of tools designed for special populations can improve the accuracy of assessment findings. Table 23.1 provides a list of instruments designed to assess pain in adult populations at risk for inadequate assessment.[18,19]

The physical examination begins when first meeting the patient. Observing the patient's gait while he or she approaches the examination room or evaluating his or her posture while sitting or lying in bed provides essential information. Pay special attention to nonverbal cues of pain. This is followed by close inspection of painful sites, evaluating areas of trauma, skin breakdown, changes in bony or joint structures, and trophic changes, such as reduced hair growth or thickened nails. Palpate areas for tenderness or masses (including signs of obstipation). Perform range of motion in affected extremities to determine if there are contractures or disorders of the joint that elicit pain. Auscultation can reveal crackles, rhonchi, or decreased breath sounds that may signal painful respiratory complications (such as pneumonia) or hyperactive bowel sounds, suggesting bowel obstruction. Percussion can assist in revealing fluid accumulation in ascites. A careful neurological evaluation can identify allodynia, dermatomal distribution of pain and other sensorimotor changes.

Coupled with a thorough physical examination, radiographic studies and laboratory evaluation may be useful in identifying the etiology of pain. However, these tools may not be readily accessible in all settings, they may place the patient at-risk for discomfort

Box 23.2 Template for Comprehensive Pain History Documentation

Chief Report

Mr. Johnson is a 56-year-old African-American male diagnosed with metastatic non-small-cell lung cancer (NSCLC) after experiencing a chronic cough that did not resolve with antibiotic therapy; we were asked to see him by Dr. Washington for concerns related to back pain. Briefly, he was diagnosed with NSCLC 8 months ago and underwent 4 courses of chemotherapy (carboplatin and pemetrexed). He recently developed right hip pain and was found to have a pathologic fracture of the right femur that was treated with open reduction and internal fixation and XRT 3 months ago. He now presents with low back pain and right rib pain—which are consistent with sites of metastatic disease on recent PET scan.

Pain History

Location(s), referral, radiating pattern

Duration

Intensity (last 24 hours, at rest, with movement)

Quality

Timing

Aggravating/alleviating factors

Other symptoms associated with pain

Functional changes/interference with daily activities

Current therapies

◆ Medications—duration, response

◆ Radiation therapy

◆ Other—nerve blocks, vertebroplasty, PT/OT, acupuncture, etc.

Prior treatment, response, adverse effects, reason for discontinuing

◆ Medications—dose, duration, adverse effects

◆ Radiation therapy (sites)

◆ Other—nerve blocks, vertebroplasty, PT/OT, acupuncture, etc.

Past Medical History

The PMH includes *relevant* serious illness, chronic diseases, surgical procedures, and injuries the patient has experienced.

Social History

Marital status/partnered

Children/grandchildren

Type of home (stairs), who lives in home, who provides support

Work history, education

Substance Use History

Smoking

ETOH

Recreational drug use

Family history of addictive disease

Physical or sexual abuse, especially as preteen or teenager

Medication History

Current medications, including prescription and nonprescription medications, name and dosage for each.

Review of Systems

Perform a Review of Symptoms (ROS) that may occur along with pain. May use Edmonton Symptom Assessment Scale (ESAS) or other symptom assessment tool in place of ROS. The following is the ROS for Mr. Johnson.

GENERAL: endorses fatigue, sleep

HEENT: xerostomia, denies dysphagia

CV: denies chest pain

RESP: denies SOB, cough

GI: last BM *x* days ago, consistency *x*, appetite [poor/good], nausea and vomiting

GU: denies urgency, frequency, incontinence, or dysuria

MS: denies tripping or falls

NEURO: denies neuropathy

SKIN: denies rash or open wounds

PSYCH: endorses feeling sad/depressed, finds strength through [name the focus, strategy, or intervention]

Performance Status

May use ECOG, Karnofsky, or other tool. This helps determine function and prognosis and track change over time.

Physical Exam

List the physical assessment findings that are "remarkable" or contribute to understanding the pain experience and/or etiology.

Patient Goals

What the patient hopes to achieve if pain is relieved (e.g., return to work, play with grandchildren, go to church).

Impression/Problem List

1.

2.

3.

Recommendations/Plan

1.

2.

3.

Box 23.3 Groups at Risk for Inadequate Assessment and Undertreatment of Pain

- Infants and children
- Elderly
- Cognitively-impaired
- Nonverbal individuals
- People with mental health disorders
- Minorities
- Non-English-speaking individuals
- Long-term survivors
- Socioeconomically disadvantaged
- Uninsured
- Those with current or past substance use disorders

From references 11, 16, 17.

(e.g., lying on a hard table during a lengthy scan), and they may increase the financial burden to patients and families. These diagnostic tools should not be employed if they are not going to alter the course of therapy.

Pharmacologic Management of Pain

There are three broad categories of medications used to relieve pain: non-opioids, opioids, and adjuvant analgesics. In most cases, a strong analgesic regimen employs multimodal therapies, including more than one pharmacologic agent along with nonpharmacologic strategies. The palliative APRN with prescribing privileges must adhere to safe prescribing principles as well as bearing in mind financial and regulatory concerns.

Table 23.1 Assessment Tools for Special Adult Populations

Tool	Intended Population
Assessment of Discomfort in Dementia (ADD)	Dementia
Behavioral Pain Scale (BPS)	Intensive care, unresponsive adults
Checklist of Nonverbal Pain Indicators (CNPI)	Dementia
Critical Care Pain Observation Tool (CPOT)	Intensive care, unresponsive adults
Doloplus 2	Dementia, palliative care
Nursing Assistant-Administered Instrument to Assess Pain in Demented Individuals (NOPPAIN)	Dementia
Pain Assessment Scale for Seniors with Limited Ability to Communicate (PACSLAC)	Dementia
Pain Assessment in Advanced Dementia (PAINAD)	Dementia

From references 18 and 19.

Non-opioids

Acetaminophen (also called paracetamol) is analgesic and antipyretic and is found in a variety of combination prescription and over-the-counter compounds. These may include admixtures with opioids (e.g., acetaminophen with codeine, hydrocodone, or oxycodone), or over-the-counter cold, sinus, or sleep remedies (e.g., acetaminophen with diphenhydramine). Hepatic toxicity can result from excessive use, and a firm limit on daily consumption has not been established.[20,21] Some sources recommend no more than 2,000 mg per day, while others suggest up to 3,000 mg may be safe. This needs to be tailored to the patient. Altered hepatic function, excessive alcohol intake, and other comorbid factors may place some patients at elevated risk, and these individuals should be advised to avoid acetaminophen. Renal toxicity is another potential adverse effect of this agent. Acetaminophen is available in oral formulations, including liquids and suppositories, and more recently an injectable formulation has been used to treat pain and fever.[22] The adult dosage (adults weighing >50 kg) is 1 g given intravenously q6h with a maximum of 4 g per day; patients with renal or hepatic disease should be given a decreased dose or should avoid this drug. The price may preclude use in many palliative care settings.

Nonsteroidal anti-inflammatory drugs (NSAIDs) are analgesic, antipyretic, and anti-inflammatory. They are generally useful for nociceptive or musculoskeletal pain syndromes.[21,23] Adverse effects include gastrointestinal bleeding (which can be prevented with the addition of a prostaglandin analog or a proton pump inhibitor), renal dysfunction, platelet aggregation abnormalities (generally reversible when stopping the drug, except for aspirin, which has an irreversible effect on platelets), and cardiovascular events, such as myocardial infarction and stroke in those at risk.[24-26] Most NSAIDs are available in oral formulations, some in liquids or suppositories. Ketorolac is available for parenteral use and is highly potent; however, prolonged use is contraindicated due to an elevated risk of adverse effects.

Opioids

Opioids are useful in treating nociceptive and neuropathic pain, although higher doses are generally required to relieve nerve pain.[27] A wide array of opioids is available, allowing rotation when one opioid is ineffective or produces uncontrolled adverse effects. Immediate-release agents provide faster onset to provide rescue when breakthrough pain occurs, and controlled-release products allow more constant control of pain. Various routes of administration allow personalized care when oral delivery is not feasible. Table 23.2 lists opioids available in the United States.[11,27-29] Prevention and management of adverse events is crucial, as is education of patients, family members, and caregivers regarding safe use of these agents.

There are significant differences between opioids. Codeine is a prodrug and must be metabolized to morphine by the action of the CYP2D6 enzyme.[30,31] Inadequate analgesia can result in patients who are poor metabolizers, while increased toxicity and overdose have been reported in individuals (or a breastfeeding baby) who are ultra-rapid metabolizers of this enzyme.[32,33] Tramadol is a weak opioid agonist and a serotonin-norepinephrine reuptake

Table 23.2 Opioid Analgesics: Available Formulations and Equianalgesic Guidelines

OPIOID EQUIANALGESIC TABLE

DRUG	DOSAGE FORM/STRENGTHS	APPROXIMATE EQUIVALENCE	
		IV/SQ	ORAL
Codeine (a prodrug dependent on CYP2D6—significant percentage of people are poor metabolizers and cannot obtain relief)	**Tablets:** Codeine—15, 30, 60 mg **Codeine/Acetaminophen Tablets** ◆ Generic—15/300 mg ◆ Tylenol #3 and generics—30/300 mg ◆ Tylenol #4 and generics—60/300 mg **Codeine/Acetaminophen Liquid** ◆ Solution—12/120 mg per 5 mL (Also available with guaifenesin, butalbital, caffeine and other agents)		200 mg
Fentanyl Parenteral		100 mcg	
Fentanyl **Transdermal** Long-acting; Not for opioid-naïve patients	**Fentanyl Transdermal** Duragesic® andw generic—12, 25, 50, 75, 100 mcg/hr ◆ Not for postop/acute pain ◆ 12–24 hours for full onset ◆ 12–24 hours to leave system		100 mcg patch q 2–3 days ≈ 200 mg oral morphine q 24 hrs
Fentanyl **Transmucosal Immediate-Release Fentanyl (TIRF)** Not for opioid-naïve patients Requires TIRF-REMS compliance https://www.tirfremsaccess.com/TirfUI/rems/home.action	**Transmucosal-Buccal Oral Lozenge** ◆ Actiq® and generic—200, 400, 600, 800, 1200, 1600 mcg ◆ Fentora®—100, 200, 400, 600, 800 mcg **Fentanyl Buccal Strip** Onsolis®—200, 400, 600, 800, 1200 mcg **Sublingual Tablet** ◆ Abstral® Fentanyl SL –100, 200, 300, 400, 600, 800 mcg **Sublingual Spray** Subsys®—100, 200, 400, 600, 800 mcg spray **Fentanyl Nasal Spray** Lazanda˚ –100, 200, 400 mcg	– – –	See package inserts
Hydrocodone	**Hydrocodone/Acetaminophen Tablets** ◆ Examples: Vicodin®—5/300 mg; Vicodin® ES—7.5/300 mg, Lorcet® or Vicodin® HP—10 mg/300 mg ◆ Lortab®—2.5/500 mg, 5/500 mg 7.5/500 mg, 10/500 mg ◆ Norco®—5/325 mg, 7.5/325 mg, 10/325 mg **Liquid:** Hycet®—7.5/325/15 mL **Hydrocodone/Ibuprofen Tablets** ◆ Vicoprofen® and generic—7.5/200 mg	– – –	20–30 mg
Hydromorphone	**Tablets** ◆ Hydromorphone (Dilaudid® and generic)—2, 4, 8 mg **Liquid:** Hydromorphone (Dilaudid®)—1 mg/mL **Injection**—1, 2, 4 mg/mL ◆ Dilaudid® HP—10 mg/mL **Suppository:** Hydromorphone—3 mg **Extended Release** (Exalgo)—8, 12, 16, 32 mg q 24 hrs	1.5 mg – – –	7.5 mg – – –
Methadone	Equivalency ratios for methadone are complex because of its long half-life, potency, and individual variations in pharmacokinetics.	– – –	Consult with Pain/Palliative Care Specialist

(continued)

Table 23.2 (Continued)

OPIOID EQUIANALGESIC TABLE

DRUG	DOSAGE FORM/STRENGTHS	APPROXIMATE EQUIVALENCE	
		IV/SQ	ORAL
Morphine	**Immediate-Release Tablets**	10 mg	30 mg
	◆ Morphine Sulfate Immediate Release—15, 30 mg		
	Sustained-Release Tablet:		
	◆ Generic—15, 20, 30, 50, 60, 80, 100, 200 mg q 12 hrs		
	◆ MS Contin®—15, 30, 60, 100, 200 mg q 8 or 12 hrs		
	◆ Avinza®—30, 45, 60, 75, 90, 120 mg q 24 hrs		
	◆ Kadian® –10, 20, 30, 40, 50, 60, 70, 80, 100, 130, 150, 200 mg q 12–24 hrs		
	Generics Oral Liquid		
	◆ Morphine Sulfate Immediate-Release Solution—2 mg/mL, 4 mg/mL, 20 mg/mL		
	Suppository: Rectal Morphine Sulfate (RMS)—5, 10, 20, 30 mg		
Oxycodone	**Immediate-Release Tablets**	– – –	20 mg
	◆ Oxycodone IR—5, 10, 15, 20, 30 mg		
	◆ Roxicodone®—5, 15, 30 mg		
	Oxycodone/Acetaminophen Tablets		
	◆ Percocet®—2.5/325, 5/325, 7.5/325, 7.5/500, 10/325 mg		
	◆ Roxicet®—5/325, 5/500 mg, 10/650		
	Sustained-Release Tablets		
	◆ OxyContin®—10, 15, 20, 30, 40, 60, 80 mg		
	Liquid: Oxycodone—20 mg/mL		
Oxymorphone	**Tablets**	1 mg	10 mg
	◆ Opana®—5, 10 mg		
	◆ Generic IR—5, 10 mg		
	◆ Opana® ER—5, 7.5, 10, 15, 20, 30, 40 mg q 12 hrs		
	◆ Generic ER—7.5, 15 mg		
Tramadol Dual-Action Analgesics (opioid and SNRI reuptake inhibitor)	**Tramadol Hydrochloride Tablets**	– – –	300 mg
	◆ Ultram® and generic—50 mg		
	◆ Ultracet® and generic—37.5/325 mg acetaminophen		
	Tramadol® ODT: Rybix® ODT—50 mg		
	Extended Release		
	◆ Ultram® ER and generic—100, 200, 300 mg q 24 hrs		
	◆ Ryzolt® –100, 200, 300 mg q 24 hrs		
Tapentadol (dual-action opioid and norepinephrine reuptake inhibior)	**Tapentadol Tablets**		150 mg
	◆ Nucynta®—50, 75, 100 mg		
	◆ Nucynta®ER—50, 100, 150, 200, 250 mg q 12		

From references 11, 27–29. Reprinted with permission from ELNEC.

inhibitor. Due to this dual action, it has a ceiling of 300 mg per day, and naloxone will not completely reverse overdose.[34] Tramadol should be avoided in patients with seizure risk or suicidal ideation. Dizziness is the most common adverse effect. Tapentadol is also an opioid agonist and norepinephrine reuptake inhibitor, with little action on serotonin reuptake. Caution is warranted when adding antidepressants that act on the serotonin system to either tramadol or tapentadol to prevent serotonin syndrome. As

with tramadol, naloxone will not completely reverse the effects of overdose with tapentadol.

Methadone can be a highly effective analgesic: it may prevent or limit hyperalgesia, it appears to be useful for neuropathic pain, and it is inexpensive. Several challenges complicate the use of methadone, and several guidelines recommend a palliative care consultation when considering its use. As a result, palliative APRNs must be highly skilled in the use of this opioid. Specific

Box 23.4 Methadone Prescribing Recommendations

◆ Start low:

   ◆ 10 mg or less per day in divided doses (q8h or q12h)

   ◆ Regardless of whether patient is opioid naïve or tolerant

◆ Provide breakthrough medications—not methadone.

◆ Increase no more than 25–50% weekly, generally no more often than every 3–7 days.

◆ Use caution when combining with benzodiazepines or other sedating drugs, especially at night.

◆ Use caution in patients with sleep apnea, respiratory infection.

From references 38, 39.

Box 23.5 Selected Chemotherapeutic Agents that Can Prolong QTc in Combination with Methadone (and degree of risk)

Abarelix (severe)

Dasatinib (severe)

Degarelix (major)

Doxorubicin (major)

Epirubicin (major)

Lapatinib (severe)

Pazopanib (major)

Sunitinib (severe)

Toremifend (severe)

From reference 35.

issues in methadone use include the long and variable half-life, which complicates dose escalation and conversions; the prolonged QTc that can result; lack of clarity on equianalgesic ratios; and many drug–drug interactions.[35–40] Box 23.4 provides guidelines for use of this drug.[38,39] Table 23.3 lists potential drug–drug interactions with methadone involving medications commonly employed in palliative care.[35,39] Box 23.5 lists chemotherapeutic agents that can result in prolonged QTc when given in combination with methadone.[35]

When analgesia is incomplete despite appropriate titration of the opioid, or when adverse effects persist despite aggressive management, opioid rotation is warranted.[41,42] Box 23.6 provides general guidelines for opioid rotation. An excellent handbook is available to guide the APRN who is new to equianalgesic dosing: *Demystifying Opioid Conversion Calculations*.[28] And although online calculators are available, the palliative APRN

must thoroughly understand the calculations to provide safe dosing and to teach others appropriately.

Adjuvant Analgesics

Adjuvant analgesics include agents that have other purposes but have been found to be analgesic, primarily in the management of neuropathic pain. Table 23.4 includes common agents, starting doses, and potential adverse effects.[11,21,43–47] Because these agents act via different mechanisms, patients with complex pain may require multimodal therapy that includes one agent from each drug class. There are few studies exploring the efficacy of these drugs in the palliative care setting, and results often conflict with observations from clinical practice.

Corticosteroids are important adjuvant analgesics for the relief of neuropathic pain as well as some visceral pain syndromes that involve inflammation around masses (e.g., ovarian or gastrointestinal malignancies).[46] These agents can be highly effective in reducing the tumor burden of lymphoma, which can open airway or gastrointestinal obstructions from this malignancy. Added benefits

Table 23.3 Selected Methadone Drug–Drug Interactions

Inducers (decrease methadone levels)	Inhibitors (increase methadone levels)
◆ Abacavir	◆ Cimetidine
◆ Amprenavir	◆ Ciprofloxacin
◆ Barbiturates	◆ Diazepam
◆ Carbamazepine	◆ Diltiazem
◆ Cocaine	◆ Disulfiram
◆ Dexamethasone	◆ Fluconazole
◆ Efavirenz	◆ Grapefruit
◆ Heroin	◆ Haloperidol
◆ Lopinavir + Ritonavir	◆ Ketoconazole
◆ Nelfinavir	◆ Macrolides (erythromycin, clarithromycin)
◆ Nevirapine	◆ Metronidazole
◆ Phenytoin	◆ Omeprazole
◆ Rifampin	◆ Sorafanib
◆ Spironolactone	◆ SSRIs (fluoxetine, paroxetine, nefazodone, sertraline)
◆ St. John's wort	

From references 35, 39.

Box 23.6 Opioid Rotation/Switching Opioids

Step 1

   ◆ Calculate the equianalgesic dose using a standard table or online calculator.

   ◆ Reduce dose by 25–50% to account for incomplete cross-tolerance between opioids.

Step 2

   ◆ Consider an additional increase or decrease of 15–30% based upon medical and psychosocial characteristics.

   ◆ Consider adverse effects, risk of withdrawal.

   ◆ Frequently reassess and titrate.

   ◆ Provide an oral rescue dose of 10–20% of 24-hour dose.

From references 41, 42.

Table 23.4 Adjuvant Analgesics

Drug Class	Daily Adult Starting Dose (Range)	Routes of Administration	Adverse Effects
Antidepressants	Nortriptyline 10–25 mg q hs	PO	Anticholinergic effects
	Venlafaxine 37.5 mg bid	PO	Nausea, dizziness
	Duloxetine 30 mg q d		Nausea
Antiepilepsy drugs	Gabapentin 100 mg tid	PO	Dizziness
	Pregabalin 50 mg tid	PO	Dizziness
	Clonazepam 0.5–1 mg q hs, bid or tid	PO	Sedation
Corticosteroids	Dexamethasone 2–20 mg q d	PO/IV/SQ	"Steroid psychosis" Dyspepsia
Lidocaine	Lidocaine patch 5% q day	Topical	Rare skin erythema
	Lidocaine infusion	IV/SQ	Perioral numbness, cardiac changes
N-Methyl-D-aspartic acid antagonists	Ketamine (see text for dosing)	PO/IV	Hallucinations

From references 11, 21, 43–47.

of corticosteroids include improved appetite for approximately 2 weeks and activation, which can relieve fatigue and possibly depression.[48] A recent study explored the use of methylprednisolone for pain in advanced cancer and found the treatment to be ineffective.[49] Study design issues, including inclusion criteria, limit the extrapolation of these findings to most people with cancer pain. Important drug–drug interactions with dexamethasone are listed in Box 23.7.

Lidocaine and other local anesthetics have been limited by the lack of an oral formulation. Topical solutions and patches may relieve more superficial pain syndromes. Spinal delivery, either alone or in combination with opioids and other agents, can be useful, but administration requires specialists to insert catheters and potentially complicated and/or expensive delivery systems (e.g., catheter care, external or implanted pumps). Infusions of parenteral lidocaine, particularly in the face of intractable neuropathic pain, may be effective. Box 23.8 provides a protocol for using parenteral lidocaine.[50]

Ketamine is an N-methyl-D-aspartic acid antagonist that is thought to be useful in relieving neuropathic pain, in reducing opioid doses when high doses appear ineffective, or in the management of opioid-induced hyperalgesia.[51–53] Although often

Box 23.7 Drug–Drug Interactions Involving Dexamethasone: Potential to Decrease Chemotherapy Levels

Erlotinib

Gefitinib

Ibrutinib

Lapatinib

Pazopanib

Ruxolitinib

Sorafenib

Sunitinib

Temsirolimus

Box 23.8 Lidocaine Infusion Guidelines: Virginia Commonwealth University

Thomas Palliative Care Guidelines

Lidocaine Infusion for Severe Pain

Purpose

Lidocaine infusion has been reported as an effective intervention in individuals having refractory pain, in which opioids are not effective.

Protocol

1. Challenge and infusion: Prior to a lidocaine infusion, a lidocaine challenge is routinely done. Lidocaine 100 mg IV over a half-hour period is used. If effective (improvement in pain score), an infusion of 0.5–2 mg/kg per hour will be initiated. This infusion may be titrated by 20%/hour, not to exceed 2 mg/kg/hour. Doses above 2 mg/hour are rarely needed. Lidocaine 2,000 mg in 500 mL/D5W can be ordered to have available if the test dose is successful.

2. Monitoring: During infusion, observe and document vital signs and pain intensity every 15 minutes.

3. Goals of therapy
   a. Pain relief
   b. Decrease opioids rapidly and to the lowest dose possible; safe administration with minimal side effects

4. Side effects are rare when given in low doses. The most serious side effect is an allergic reaction.
   a. An allergic reaction may include difficulty breathing and irregular heartbeat or other signs of anaphylaxis.
   b. The common side effects are numbness around the mouth, dryness, or a sense of being intoxicated.

c. Other potential side effects may include hives, hallucination, muscle twitches, and in rare cases seizures.

5. Long-term therapy may be initiated with lidocaine or mexiletine.

6. **Contraindication**: Hypersensitivity to lidocaine or other amide anesthetics (mepivacaine, prilocaine, dibucaine, and procainamide). Add precautions: bradycardia, congestive heart failure, heart block, hypovolemia, liver disease, renal impairment, shock, Wolff-Parkinson-White syndrome.

Original 2008; Reviewed April 2010, October 2012, September 2013.

Source: Ferrini R, Paice, J. How to initiate and monitor infusional lidocaine for severe and/or neuropathic pain. *J Support Oncol.* 2004; 2(1), 90–94. Available at http://www.oncologypractice.com/jso/journal/articles/0201090.pdf.

used in intraoperative and postoperative settings, ketamine's use in palliative care has been hampered by the lack of a commercially available preparation. Box 23.9 provides a sample protocol for use in palliative care. Palliative APRNs with prescribing privileges should check state and institutional rules regarding their ability to prescribe this medication. Studies are under way to investigate the efficacy of ketamine in relieving depression at the end-of-life.

The role of cannabinoids in relieving pain is often questioned, and palliative APRNs will be asked by professionals, patients, and the public about the use of these compounds. Research is limited, in part because of inadequate funding and lack of availability of an approved study drug. Most professional organizations have not endorsed cannabis for medical use but agree that more research is needed.[54–56] As the APRN reviews current literature, it is helpful to understand the different formulations of cannabinoids. This is particularly important as more states approve either medical or recreational use of cannabinoids. Box 23.10 clarifies the variety of formulations of cannabinoids.[54,55,57]

Box 23.9 Ketamine Protocol for Oral or Parenteral Administration in Palliative Care

Purpose

This is an adjunct medication often considered for pain refractory to opioids or intractable side effects from opioids, particularly if the pain is neuropathic in nature or if a high degree of morphine tolerance is suspected.

Definition

Ketamine is an *N*-methyl-D-aspartate receptor (NMDA) agent that may be opioid-sparing.

Protocol

Oral dosing

◆ The typical starting dose is 10–15 mg po q6h. Reversal of morphine tolerance may occur at low doses such as this, while management of neuropathic pain is likely to require higher doses.

◆ There is no commercially available oral product. The injectable product may be diluted from its standard concentration of 50 mg/mL or 100 mg/mL with cherry syrup or cola to mask the bitter taste when given orally.

◆ Consider decreasing long-acting opioid by 25–50%.

◆ Dosing may be increased *daily* by 10 mg q6h until pain is relieved or side effects occur. Do not increase doses more frequently than every 24 hours.

◆ Major side effects include dizziness, a dreamlike feeling, and auditory or visual hallucinations. If intolerable side effects occur, ketamine should be decreased to the previous dose or discontinued. Resolution may not occur for 24 hours.

◆ Oral doses as high as 1,000 mg per day have been reported in the neuropathic pain literature, with average oral doses of 200 mg per day in divided doses required for pain relief.

IV dosing

◆ Ketamine may be given intravenously or subcutaneously if the oral route is not available.

◆ Some facilities allow a ketamine challenge. A trial of 10 mg IV can be considered, which may be repeated in 15–30 minutes.

◆ The starting infusion dose of 0.2 mg/kg/hr can be increased by 0.1 mg/kg/hr q6h, with upward titrations to 0.5 mg/kg/hr or 800 mg in 24 hrs.

◆ Consider decreasing long-acting opioid dose by 25–50%.

◆ The injectable solution is irritating and the subcutaneous needle may need to be changed daily.

◆ For side effects of hallucinations or a dreamlike state, benzodiazepines can be given prophylactically or Haldol can be given when the effects occur.

Box 23.10 Formulations of Cannabinoids

Endocannabinoids

- Endogenous neurotransmitters—arachidonic acid derivatives (e.g., anandamide)

Phytocannabinoids (also called botanical cannabis)

- Compounds found in *Cannabis sativa* plant (e.g., THC, CBD)
- Primarily smoked, vaporized, ingested

Synthetic cannabinoids

- Laboratory-produced congeners of THC, CBD
- Dronabinol (Marinol)—tablet, approved in U.S. for chemotherapy-induced nausea and vomiting and AIDS-associated anorexia
- Nabilone (Cesamet)—approved in U.S. for chemotherapy-induced nausea and vomiting
- Nabiximols—oral spray indicated for neuropathic pain, spasticity (not yet approved in U.S.)

From references 54, 55, 57.

Nonpharmacologic Interventions for Pain

The biopsychosocial model clarifies the need for both pharmacologic and nonpharmacologic techniques to relieve pain. The findings from the complete pain history and physical examination help the palliative APRN in designing a treatment plan that incorporates appropriate interventions. Many of these interventions require the expertise of specialists and other team members, including radiologists, surgeons, psychologists, physical therapists, chaplains, social workers, and many others. Close communication with these consultants and team members will ensure continuity of care and will increase the chances of meeting the patient's goals for pain relief. Education is an essential component of all successful pain relief regimens.[2,58,59] Table 23.5 lists selected nonpharmacologic interventions.[58,60–67] Challenges to the incorporation of these interventions into the treatment plan include lack of reimbursement, limited access to practitioners with expertise in these interventions, and reluctance on the part of some patients and family members to accept these techniques.

Safe Practices

Pain management in palliative care will include the use of drugs with a high potential for abuse. To provide safe and effective pain control, palliative APRNs must work to prevent misuse and diversion.[6]

Safe Storage

Education of patients and their family members regarding safe storage and disposal is essential. Studies suggest that patients, including oncology patients, are not employing these practices.[68,69] Medications should be kept locked, not stored in the medicine cabinet or out on the kitchen counter. Medications should never be shared and should be used only for pain relief.

Table 23.5 Biopsychosocial Model: Nonpharmacologic Interventions

Biological	Psychological/Social/Spiritual
Disease-modifying therapies ◆ Chemotherapy ◆ Radiation therapy	Cognitive-behavioral therapies
Kyphoplasty/vertebroplasty	Mindfulness/Meditation
Nerve blocks	Guided imagery
Ablative procedures	Hypnosis
Physical/occupational and other rehabilitation therapies	Biofeedback
Exercise	Prayer
Heat/cold/bracing/orthotics	Music
Massage	Art therapy
Acupuncture and other integrative procedures	Support groups

From references 2, 58, 60–67.

Many find that these medications enhance sleep, improve mood, and relieve anxiety, particularly during initial exposure, in part due to the sedating effect. But tolerance quickly develops to the soporific effect and patients will find the need to escalate doses to obtain the original response. This can lead to serious complications, including oversedation or other toxicities as the dose is increased. Compounding this is the stigma held by many about taking psychotropic medications, which are more appropriate in managing anxiety, depression, sleep issues, or other mood disorders.[7]

Safe Disposal

Safe disposal of medications prevents access by others (e.g., children, pets, individuals with intent to use the drugs recreationally or to sell these agents) and limits impact on the environment.[70] Municipalities are detecting medications in the water supply, in part as a result of drugs being flushed into the sanitary system. The Environmental Protection Agency advises against flushing medications (http://water.epa.gov/scitech/swguidance/ppcp/upload/ppcpflyer.pdf).

The Drug Enforcement Agency (DEA) offers a twice-yearly National Prescription Drug Take-Back Program, and a new law will allow collection receptacles in places such as law enforcement stations, hospitals, and pharmacies (http://www.deadiversion.usdoj.gov/fed_regs/rules/2014/2014-20926.pdf).

The Food and Drug Administration (FDA) recommends that if a take-back program is not available, medications (except for controlled substances) should be mixed with moistened kitty litter or used coffee grounds, placed in a sealed plastic bag, and thrown away in the trash. Empty pill bottles or other packaging should be blacked out so that the drug or individual cannot be identified. However, the FDA still requires that if a take-back program is not available, opioids must be flushed down the sink or toilet due to safety concerns (http://www.fda.gov/Drugs/Resources ForYou/Consumers/BuyingUsingMedicineSafely/Ensuring SafeUse ofMedicine/SafeDisposalofMedicines/ucm186187.htm#Flushing_list).

Safe Prescribing

Because there is no absolute predictor for who might misuse medications, chronic pain management experts recommend the use of "universal precautions." Although studies are lacking regarding their efficacy, particularly in palliative care, many prescribers are adopting all or some of these recommendations.[8,71,72] Box 23.11 outlines key aspects of universal precautions.[73] Numerous tools are available to screen for misuse or high-risk behaviors (e.g., CAGE, Current Opioid Misuse Measure [COMM], Opioid Risk Tool [ORT]). Few have been validated in a palliative care population.

Random urine drug testing through toxicology screening can help determine if patients are taking illicit drugs or not taking the drugs prescribed. However, caution is advised in the interpretation of these results; false negatives and positives abound. For example, a patient receiving transdermal fentanyl will have a test result that is negative for opioids. The palliative APRN obtaining random urine toxicology must seek expert advice regarding interpretation of the results before making decisions regarding whether a patient should no longer be prescribed an opioid.

Prescription drug monitoring programs are now available in 49 states. Although the information provided by each state varies, most allow prescribers to view the controlled substances that have been prescribed for a particular patient, the date and number of tablets/patches dispensed, the method of payment (insurance vs. self-pay), the pharmacy where the drug was dispensed, and the name of the prescriber. Although sometimes viewed as a method to "catch" offenders, more often these programs help identify the medications taken by patients who do not bring in their medications or do not know the name of the drug (e.g., the "blue pill") (http://www.deadiversion.usdoj.gov/faq/rx_monitor.htm).

Palliative APRNs must be aware of the DEA schedule system so they can comply with prescribing regulations in their own state and institution. Table 23.6 lists substances that may be used in palliative care for pain and symptom control. Ongoing review of this schedule system is vital; for example, hydrocodone was recently rescheduled from III to II. Prescribers can no longer call in this medication by telephone or fax, and refills cannot be ordered. Lack of awareness of these changes can result in delays in patients obtaining needed medications. For more information see http://www.deadiversion.usdoj.gov/fed_regs/rules/2014/fr0822.htm.

Box 23.11 Universal Precautions

Assess:

◆ Pain

◆ Risk for addiction/diversion

Opioid management agreements or "contracts"—limited evidence in palliative care

Adherence monitoring

◆ Urine drug testing

◆ Pill counts

◆ Prescription monitoring programs

From reference 73.

Table 23.6 Controlled Substances—Schedules

Schedule	Examples
Schedule I	Heroin
	Lysergic acid diethylamide (LSD)
	Marijuana
Schedule II/IIN (2/2N)	**Schedule II**
	Codeine
	Fentanyl (Sublimaze®, Duragesic®)
	Hydrocodone
	Hydromorphone (Dilaudid®)
	Methadone (Dolophine®)
	Meperidine (Demerol®)
	Morphine
	Opium
	Oxycodone (OxyContin®, Percocet®)
	Pentobarbital
	Schedule IIN
	Amphetamine (Dexedrine®, Adderall®), Methamphetamine (Desoxyn®)
	Methylphenidate (Ritalin®)
Schedule III/IIIN (3/3N)	Codeine/acetaminophen (Tylenol with Codeine®) Buprenorphine (Butrans®, Suboxone®)
	Ketamine
	Depo®-Testosterone
Schedule IV	Tramadol (Ultram®)
	Alprazolam (Xanax®)
	Clonazepam (Klonopin®)
	Diazepam (Valium®)
	Lorazepam (Ativan®)
	Midazolam (Versed®)
Schedule V	Cough preparations containing not more than 200 milligrams of codeine per 100 milliliters or per 100 grams (Robitussin AC®, Phenergan with Codeine®)

Adapted from http://www.deadiversion.usdoj.gov/schedules/#define

Risk evaluation and mitigation strategies (REMS) have been instituted to advance safe prescribing of a variety of substances. Two of these strategies involve opioids and have implications for APRNs who might prescribe these agents. Use of the strategy for transmucosal immediate-release fentanyl products (TIRF REMS) (https://www.tirfremsaccess.com/TirfUI/rems/home.action) is required for prescribers of these products. An online educational module and exam can be completed for provider enrollment in this program. When these medications are prescribed for an individual patient, he or she signs an online agreement affirming that he or she understands appropriate use of these products. The strategy for extended-release and long-acting opioid analgesics is highly recommended to improve the knowledge of both providers and patients (http://www.er-la-opioidrems.com/IwgUI/rems/home.action).

Despite all of these measures and safeguards, there may be times when patients exhibit what seems to be aberrant drug-taking behavior. The palliative APRN must assess further requests for early or frequent refills. Box 23.12 describes the differential diagnosis for these requests so that the underlying problem can be appropriately addressed.[74–76]

Case Study

Mr. Johnson was a 66-year-old African-American man with metastatic non-small-cell lung cancer for whom a full pain assessment was conducted. He recently developed right hip pain and was found to have a pathologic fracture of the right femur, which was treated with open reduction and internal fixation and XRT 3 months prior. This pain had resolved, but he then presented with low back pain and right rib pain—these were consistent with sites of metastatic disease on his PET scan. The back pain was distributed over the low lumbar area, described as aching without radiculopathy. The intensity was 2 at rest but 8 when standing for more than a few minutes. The rib pain was also aching and throbbing and was worse when lying on that side or taking a deep inspiration. He had been given hydrocodone/acetaminophen with little relief, although he took less than the prescribed dose. He denied adverse effects. Further investigation revealed no personal history of substance misuse, but his son had died from a heroin overdose. He was extremely worried about becoming addicted and anxious regarding constipation. Review of the prescription drug monitoring program revealed only a few refills of small amounts of hydrocodone, all prescribed by his oncologist. Urine toxicology was negative except for opioids.

Extensive education provided by the palliative APRN reassured Mr. Johnson about safe medication use and storage. Constipation prevention and management were discussed and a bowel program was initiated. The hydrocodone/acetaminophen was changed to oxycodone to reduce potential toxicities associated with excess acetaminophen. After consistent use of oxycodone, a fentanyl patch was added to provide a baseline level of relief. Radiotherapy was consulted for palliation of bone metastases. A home palliative nurse was consulted to ensure his environment was safe, to provide ongoing assessment of pain, and to reinforce teaching. Transition to hospice occurred when disease progressed, and he died peacefully.

Conclusion

Effective pain management in palliative care requires knowledge of common pain etiologies, as well as skill in conducting a thorough assessment. The palliative APRN who is devising a treatment plan must consider the available pharmacologic and nonpharmacologic therapies, using the biopsychosocial model as a guide. Consulting with other team members is imperative to provide optimal control. Safety is crucial: the palliative APRN must use tools such as prescription drug monitoring programs and urine toxicology. Education of patients and families regarding appropriate use, storage, and disposal of pain medications is essential.

References

1. Sutton LM, Porter LS, Keefe FJ. Cancer pain at the end of life: a biopsychosocial perspective. *Pain*. 2002; 99(1-2): 5–10.
2. Syrjala KL, Jensen MP, Mendoza ME, Yi JC, Fisher HM, Keefe FJ. Psychological and behavioral approaches to cancer pain management. *J Clin Oncol*. 2014; 32(16): 1703–11.
3. Schreiber KL, Martel MO, Shnol H, et al. Persistent pain in postmastectomy patients: comparison of psychophysical, medical, surgical, and psychosocial characteristics between patients with and without pain. *Pain*. 2013; 154(5): 660–8.
4. Merlin JS, Childers J, Arnold RM. Chronic pain in the outpatient palliative care clinic. *Am J Hosp Palliat Care*. 2013; 30(2): 197–203.
5. Paice JA, Von Roenn JH. Under- or overtreatment of pain in the patient with cancer: how to achieve proper balance. *J Clin Oncol*. 2014; 32(16): 1721–6.
6. Francoeur RB. Ensuring safe access to medication for palliative care while preventing prescription drug abuse: innovations for American inner cities, rural areas, and communities overwhelmed by addiction. *Risk Manag Healthc Policy*. 2011; 4: 97–105.
7. Volkow ND, McLellan TA. Curtailing diversion and abuse of opioid analgesics without jeopardizing pain treatment. *JAMA*. 2011; 305(13): 1346–7.
8. Blackhall LJ, Alfson ED, Barclay JS. Screening for substance abuse and diversion in Virginia hospices. *J Palliat Med*. 2013; 16(3): 237–42.
9. Breivik H, Cherny N, Collett B, et al. Cancer-related pain: a pan-European survey of prevalence, treatment, and patient attitudes. *Ann Oncol*. 2009; 20(8): 1420–33.
10. Glare PA, Davies PS, Finlay E, et al. Pain in cancer survivors. *J Clin Oncol*. 2014; 32(16): 1739–47.
11. Paice JA, Ferrell B. The management of cancer pain. *CA Cancer J Clin*. 2011; 61(3): 157–82.
12. Paice JA. Chronic treatment-related pain in cancer survivors. *Pain*. 2011; 152: S84–S89.
13. Bennett MI, Rayment C, Hjermstad M, Aass N, Caraceni A, Kaasa S. Prevalence and aetiology of neuropathic pain in cancer patients: a systematic review. *Pain*. 2012; 153(2): 359–65.

14. Rayment C, Hjermstad MJ, Aass N, et al. Neuropathic cancer pain: Prevalence, severity, analgesics and impact from the European Palliative Care Research Collaborative-Computerised Symptom Assessment study. *Palliat Med.* 2013; 27(8): 714–21.

15. Hui D, Bruera E. A personalized approach to assessing and managing pain in patients with cancer. *J Clin Oncol.* 2014; 32(16): 1640–6.

16. Fisch MJ, Lee JW, Weiss M, et al. Prospective, observational study of pain and analgesic prescribing in medical oncology outpatients with breast, colorectal, lung, or prostate cancer. *J Clin Oncol.* 2012; 30(16): 1980–8.

17. Kwon JH. Overcoming barriers in cancer pain management. *J Clin Oncol.* 2014; 32(16): 1727–33.

18. Bjoro K, Herr K. Assessment of pain in the nonverbal or cognitively impaired older adult. *Clin Geriatr Med.* 2008; 24(2): 237–62.

19. Herr K, Bjoro K, Decker S. Tools for assessment of pain in nonverbal older adults with dementia: a state-of-the-science review. *J Pain Symptom Manage.* 2006; 31(2): 170–92.

20. Chun LJ, Tong MJ, Busuttil RW, Hiatt JR. Acetaminophen hepatotoxicity and acute liver failure. *J Clin Gastroenterol.* 2009; 43(4): 342–9.

21. Vardy J, Agar M. Nonopioid drugs in the treatment of cancer pain. *J Clin Oncol.* 2014; 32(16): 1677–90.

22. Yeh YC, Reddy P. Clinical and economic evidence for intravenous acetaminophen. *Pharmacotherapy.* 2012; 32(6): 559–79.

23. Nabal M, Librada S, Redondo MJ, Pigni A, Brunelli C, Caraceni A. The role of paracetamol and nonsteroidal anti-inflammatory drugs in addition to WHO Step III opioids in the control of pain in advanced cancer. A systematic review of the literature. *Palliat Med.* 2012; 26(4): 305–12.

24. Masso Gonzalez EL, Patrignani P, Tacconelli S, Garcia Rodriguez LA. Variability among nonsteroidal anti-inflammatory drugs in risk of upper gastrointestinal bleeding. *Arthritis Rheum.* 2010; 62(6): 1592–601.

25. Takeuchi K. Pathogenesis of NSAID-induced gastric damage: importance of cyclooxygenase inhibition and gastric hypermotility. *World J Gastroenterol.* 2012; 18(18): 2147–60.

26. McGettigan P, Henry D. Cardiovascular risk with non-steroidal anti-inflammatory drugs: systematic review of population-based controlled observational studies. *PLoS Med.* 2011; 8(9): e1001098.

27. Caraceni A, Hanks G, Kaasa S, et al. Use of opioid analgesics in the treatment of cancer pain: evidence-based recommendations from the EAPC. *Lancet Oncol.* 2012; 13(2): e58–68.

28. McPherson ML. *Demystifying Opioid Conversion Calculations: A Guide for Effective Dosing.* Bethesda, MD: American Society of Health-System Pharmacists; 2010.

29. Portenoy RK, Ahmed E. Principles of opioid use in cancer pain. *J Clin Oncol.* 2014; 32(16): 1662–70.

30. Prommer E. Role of codeine in palliative care. *J Opioid Manag.* 2011; 7(5): 401–6.

31. Racoosin JA, Roberson DW, Pacanowski MA, Nielsen DR. New evidence about an old drug—risk with codeine after adenotonsillectomy. *N Engl J Med.* 2013; 368(23): 2155–7.

32. Bateman DN, Eddleston M, Sandilands E. Codeine and breastfeeding. *Lancet.* 2008; 372(9639): 625.

33. Madadi P, Koren G, Cairns J, et al. Safety of codeine during breastfeeding: fatal morphine poisoning in the breastfed neonate of a mother prescribed codeine. *Can Fam Physician.* 2007; 53(1): 33–5.

34. Tassinari D, Drudi F, Rosati M, Tombesi P, Sartori S, Maltoni M. The second step of the analgesic ladder and oral tramadol in the treatment of mild to moderate cancer pain: a systematic review. *Palliat Med.* 2011; 25(5): 410–23.

35. Kapur BM, Hutson JR, Chibber T, Luk A, Selby P. Methadone: a review of drug–drug and pathophysiological interactions. *Crit Rev Clin Lab Sci.* 2011; 48(4): 171–95.

36. Chatham MS, Dodds Ashley ES, Svengsouk JS, Juba KM. Dose ratios between high dose oral morphine or equivalents and oral methadone. *J Palliat Med.* 2013; 16(8): 947–50.

37. Krantz MJ, Martin J, Stimmel B, Mehta D, Haigney MC. QTc interval screening in methadone treatment. *Ann Intern Med.* 2009; 150(6): 387–95.

38. Parsons HA, de la Cruz M, El Osta B, et al. Methadone initiation and rotation in the outpatient setting for patients with cancer pain. *Cancer.* 2010; 116(2): 520–8.

39. Chou R, Cruciani RA, Fiellin DA, et al. Methadone safety: a clinical practice guideline from the American Pain Society and College on Problems of Drug Dependence, in collaboration with the Heart Rhythm Society. *J Pain.* 2014; 15(4): 321–37.

40. Chou R, Weimer MB, Dana T. Methadone overdose and cardiac arrhythmia potential: findings from a review of the evidence for an American Pain Society and College on Problems of Drug Dependence clinical practice guideline. *J Pain.* 2014; 15(4): 338–65.

41. Mercadante S, Caraceni A. Conversion ratios for opioid switching in the treatment of cancer pain: a systematic review. *Palliat Med.* 2011; 25(5): 504–15.

42. Swarm RA, Abernethy AP, Anghelescu DL, et al. Adult cancer pain. *J Natl Compr Canc Netw.* 2013; 11(8): 992–1022.

43. Mishra S, Bhatnagar S, Goyal GN, Rana SP, Upadhya SP. A comparative efficacy of amitriptyline, gabapentin, and pregabalin in neuropathic cancer pain: a prospective randomized double-blind placebo-controlled study. *Am J Hosp Palliat Care.* 2012; 29(3): 177–82.

44. Baron R, Brunnmuller U, Brasser M, May M, Binder A. Efficacy and safety of pregabalin in patients with diabetic peripheral neuropathy or postherpetic neuralgia: Open-label, non-comparative, flexible-dose study. *Eur J Pain.* 2008; 12(7): 850–8.

45. Smith EM, Pang H, Cirrincione C, et al. Effect of duloxetine on pain, function, and quality of life among patients with chemotherapy-induced painful peripheral neuropathy: a randomized clinical trial. *JAMA.* 2013; 309(13): 1359–67.

46. Paulsen O, Aass N, Kaasa S, Dale O. Do corticosteroids provide analgesic effects in cancer patients? A systematic literature review. *J Pain Symptom Manage.* 2013; 46(1): 96–105.

47. Saarto T, Wiffen PJ. Antidepressants for neuropathic pain: a Cochrane review. *J Neurol Neurosurg Psychiatry.* 2010; 81(12): 1372–3.

48. Yennurajalingam S, Frisbee-Hume S, Palmer JL, et al. Reduction of cancer-related fatigue with dexamethasone: a double-blind, randomized, placebo-controlled trial in patients with advanced cancer. *J Clin Oncol.* 2013; 31(25): 3076–82.

49. Paulsen O, Klepstad P, Rosland JH, et al. Efficacy of methylprednisolone on pain, fatigue, and appetite loss in patients with advanced cancer using opioids: a randomized, placebo-controlled, double-blind trial. *J Clin Oncol.* 2014; 32(29): 3221–8.

50. Ferrini R, Paice JA. How to initiate and monitor infusional lidocaine for severe and/or neuropathic pain. *J Support Oncol.* 2004; 2(1): 90–4.

51. Okamoto Y, Tsuneto S, Tanimukai H, et al. Can gradual dose titration of ketamine for management of neuropathic pain prevent psychotomimetic effects in patients with advanced cancer? *Am J Hosp Palliat Care.* 2013; 30(5): 450–4.

52. Bell RF, Eccleston C, Kalso EA. Ketamine as an adjuvant to opioids for cancer pain. *Cochrane Database Syst Rev.* 2012; 11: CD003351.

53. Bredlau AL, Thakur R, Korones DN, Dworkin RH. Ketamine for pain in adults and children: a systematic review and synthesis of the literature. *Pain Med.* 2013; 14(10): 1505–17.

54. Bostwick JM. Blurred boundaries: the therapeutics and politics of medical marijuana. *Mayo Clinic Proc.* 2012; 87(2): 172–86.

55. Bostwick JM, Reisfield GM, DuPont RL. Clinical decisions. Medicinal use of marijuana. *N Engl J Med.* 2013; 368(9): 866–8.

56. Volkow ND, Compton WM, Weiss SR. Adverse health effects of marijuana use. *N Engl J Med.* 2014; 371(9): 879.

57. Portenoy RK, Ganae-Motan ED, Allende S, et al. Nabiximols for opioid-treated cancer patients with poorly-controlled chronic pain: a randomized, placebo-controlled, graded-dose trial. *J Pain.* 2012; 13(5): 438–49.

58. Thomas ML, Elliott JE, Rao SM, Fahey KF, Paul SM, Miaskowski C. A randomized, clinical trial of education or motivational-interviewing-based coaching compared to usual care to improve cancer pain management. *Oncol Nurs Forum.* 2012; 39(1): 39–49.

59. Kim HS, Shin SJ, Kim SC, et al. Randomized controlled trial of standardized education and telemonitoring for pain in outpatients with advanced solid tumors. *Support Care Cancer.* 2013; 21(6): 1751–9.

60. Kwekkeboom KL, Cherwin CH, Lee JW, Wanta B. Mind-body treatments for the pain-fatigue-sleep disturbance symptom cluster in persons with cancer. *J Pain Symptom Manage.* 2010; 39(1): 126–38.

61. Collinge W, MacDonald G, Walton T. Massage in supportive cancer care. *Semin Oncol Nurs.* 2012; 28(1): 45–54.

62. Toth M, Marcantonio ER, Davis RB, Walton T, Kahn JR, Phillips RS. Massage therapy for patients with metastatic cancer: a pilot randomized controlled trial. *J Altern Complement Med.* 2013; 19(7): 650–6.

63. Greer JA, Traeger L, Bemis H, et al. A pilot randomized controlled trial of brief cognitive-behavioral therapy for anxiety in patients with terminal cancer. *Oncologist.* 2012; 17(10): 1337–45.

64. Balboni MJ, Babar A, Dillinger J, et al. "It depends": viewpoints of patients, physicians, and nurses on patient-practitioner prayer in the setting of advanced cancer. *J Pain Symptom Manage.* 2011; 41(5): 836–47.

65. Sharp DM, Walker MB, Chaturvedi A, et al. A randomised, controlled trial of the psychological effects of reflexology in early breast cancer. *Eur J Cancer.* 2010; 46(2): 312–22.

66. Cheville AL, Basford JR. Role of rehabilitation medicine and physical agents in the treatment of cancer-associated pain. *J Clin Oncol.* 2014; 32(16): 1691–702.

67. Alemann G, Kastler A, Barbe DA, Aubry S, Kastler B. Treatment of painful extraspinal bone metastases with percutaneous bipolar radiofrequency under local anesthesia: feasibility and efficacy in twenty-eight cases. *J Palliat Med.* 2014; 17(8): 947–52.

68. Reddy A, de la Cruz M, Rodriguez EM, et al. Patterns of storage, use, and disposal of opioids among cancer outpatients. *Oncologist.* 2014; 19(7): 780–5.

69. Tanabe P, Paice JA, Stancati J, Fleming M. How do emergency department patients store and dispose of opioids after discharge? A pilot study. *J Emerg Nurs.* 2012; 38(3): 273–9.

70. Okie S. A flood of opioids, a rising tide of deaths. *N Engl J Med.* 2010; 363(21): 1981–5.

71. Nuckols TK, Anderson L, Popescu I, et al. Opioid prescribing: a systematic review and critical appraisal of guidelines for chronic pain. *Ann Intern Med.* 2014; 160(1): 38–47.

72. Dev R, Parsons HA, Palla S, Palmer JL, Del Fabbro E, Bruera E. Undocumented alcoholism and its correlation with tobacco and illegal drug use in advanced cancer patients. *Cancer.* 2011; 117(19): 4551–6.

73. Starrels JL, Becker WC, Alford DP, Kapoor A, Williams AR, Turner BJ. Systematic review: treatment agreements and urine drug testing to reduce opioid misuse in patients with chronic pain. *Ann Intern Med.* 2010; 152(11): 712–20.

74. Chou R, Fanciullo GJ, Fine PG, et al. Clinical guidelines for the use of chronic opioid therapy in chronic noncancer pain. *J Pain.* 2009; 10(2): 113–30.

75. Kircher S, Zacny J, Apfelbaum SM, et al. Understanding and treating opioid addiction in a patient with cancer pain. *J Pain.* 2011; 12(10): 1025–31.

76. Cheatle MD, O'Brien CP, Mathai K, Hansen M, Grasso M, Yi P. Aberrant behaviors in a primary care-based cohort of patients with chronic pain identified as misusing prescription opioids. *J Opioid Manag.* 2013; 9(5): 315–24.

CHAPTER 24

Dyspnea

Kathleen Broglio

Key Points

- Dyspnea is a prevalent sensory/affective symptom that affects individuals with advanced diseases and often worsens toward the end-of-life.

- The palliative advanced practice registered nurse (APRN) should assess dyspnea using a biopsychosocial approach, with the understanding that dyspnea affects the entire person.

- The palliative APRN should use multimodal (pharmacologic, nonpharmacologic, and psychoeducational) approaches to dyspnea management.

Case Study Part 1

Maria was a 76-year-old Hispanic woman with COPD and CHF. She had been oxygen-dependent on 3 liters via nasal cannula for the preceding 6 months. Two months earlier she began to experience disabling dyspnea and could not walk more than 30 feet without having to sit and rest. Although her oxygen saturation and pressure of carbon dioxide (pCO_2) did not change, her sense of breathlessness had an impact on all parts of her life. Her appetite was affected because it took too much energy to eat. Maria worried about dying. Her only outings were her multiple medical appointments.

Introduction

Dyspnea is a prevalent symptom for individuals with advanced disease that is undertreated and has a negative impact on the patient's quality of life. The phrase "total dyspnea,"[1] modeled after the concept of "total pain,"[2] aptly describes the domains affected by dyspnea—physical, psychological, social, and spiritual.[1] Acute dyspnea in advanced disease can be considered a palliative care emergency.[3] APRNs must accurately assess the situation, treat the underlying cause when possible, and manage dyspnea to enhance the patient's quality of life and alleviate suffering.

Definition

Dyspnea, also called "breathlessness," has been defined by the American Thoracic Society as "a subjective experience of breathing discomfort that consists of qualitatively distinct sensations that vary in intensity."[4] The group adds that the "experience of

dyspnea derives from interactions of physiological, psychological, social, and environmental factors and may induce secondary physiological and behavioral responses."[4] Dyspnea is a symptom that often arises from physiologic impairment from the disease process or therapies[5] and may be independent of physiologic signs of respiratory compromise, such as tachypnea.[4]

McCaffery's original description of the subjectivity of "pain as being what the person says it is when experienced"[6] is similarly articulated in the American Thoracic Society's definition of dyspnea. That is, dyspnea is perceived only by the person experiencing it and involves the person's perception and interpretation of the meaning.[4] Similar to pain, dyspnea has a sensory component and an affective component, subdivided into the degree of unpleasantness and its emotional impact on the individual.[7]

Descriptive qualities of dyspnea have been separated into three categories (air hunger, work, and tightness); each may arise from different pathophysiologic processes.[7] Descriptions of dyspnea in those with chronic obstructive pulmonary disease (COPD) and heart disease have been clustered into categories describing the rate and depth of breathing, obstructive or restrictive qualities, effort or work of breathing, or feelings of distress.[8,9] These descriptors highlight the sensory effects of dyspnea as well as the affective components of dyspnea. In individuals with COPD, descriptors have included "frightening," "worried," "depressed," and "awful," thus highlighting the affective component of dyspnea.[10] Dyspnea descriptions in individuals with advanced cancer have included "air hunger," "breathlessness," "gasping," "exhaustion,"[11] "not enough air," "short of breath," "suffocation," "choking," and "drowning."[12]

Prevalence

In studies conducted in the northeastern United States, dyspnea was the most prevalent symptom in those with COPD ($n = 100$)[13] and the third most prevalent symptom in those with congestive heart failure (CHF) ($n = 103$).[14] In a study of those with advanced AIDS, COPD, CHF, advanced cancer, and renal disease, 50% of the individuals experienced dyspnea.[15]

Dyspnea is a common reason for emergency department (ED) visits for individuals with advanced disease. In a systematic review of 18 studies, dyspnea was one of the most common reasons for visits to the ED by oncology patients.[16] In a retrospective study of ED visits of individuals with cancer, dyspnea was the fourth most common reason for the visit during the last 6 months of life and the second most common reason in the final 2 weeks of life.[17] In a study of deaths in the ED in North Carolina, dyspnea was the second most common chief complaint.[18]

Dyspnea is a prevalent symptom and often part of symptom clusters in advanced disease.[11,13–15,19,20] Dyspnea was associated with fatigue, sleep, anxiety, and depression that interfered with activities of daily living and enjoyment in a study of individuals with advanced cancer.[11] In a qualitative study of individuals with lung cancer and their caregivers, dyspnea, coughing, and fatigue were part of a symptom cluster that negatively affected the quality of life.[20] Solano and colleagues have postulated that dyspnea may be one of the symptoms that are part of a common pathway at the end-of-life.[15]

Classifications of Dyspnea

The palliative APRN must understand the multifactorial etiologies of dyspnea. Dyspnea may arise from underlying cardiac or pulmonary diseases, mismatch in perfusion and oxygenation, fatigue, weakness/deconditioning, and psychological distress.[5] Increased respiratory effort in obstructive processes, increases in ventilatory requirements, restrictive processes, ventilatory mismatch, fatigue, or musculoskeletal weakness may cause dyspnea.[5] Pulmonary cases of dyspnea can be from malignant or nonmalignant sources, whereas cardiac causes of dyspnea are generally related to nonmalignant pathology. Side effects of surgery and treatments can cause dyspnea. Systemic causes of dyspnea may be secondary to advancing disease. Psychological states can also provoke dyspnea[5,21] (Table 24.1).

The qualities and intensity of dyspnea may vary across disease states.[19,22–26] In a cross-sectional and longitudinal study[19,23] and a cohort study,[24] individuals with COPD or lung cancer experienced breathlessness. Those with COPD had higher levels of breathlessness over time, whereas those with lung cancer experienced worsening dyspnea toward the end-of-life.[19,23,24] Dyspnea was reported in 25% of individuals in their first year after diagnosis with cancer.[25] In a consecutive cohort hospice study, dyspnea was worse in those with non-cancer diagnoses but increased significantly for individuals with cancer in the last 10 days of life.[26] In a qualitative study of individuals with cancer, COPD, heart failure, and motor neuron disease, there were individual variations in

the experience of dyspnea,[22] pointing to the need for the palliative APRN to personalize treatment.

Pathophysiology and Mechanisms of Dyspnea

Mechanisms and pathways associated with the sensation of dyspnea are not well understood. It is generally accepted that dyspnea emanates from changes in activity in central chemoreceptors.[21] Both hypercapnia and hypoxia can induce a sense of "air hunger" independent of changes in respiratory activity.[27] Changes in mechanoreceptor activity in the lung, chest wall, upper airway, and facial receptors can also contribute to dyspnea.[21] It has been hypothesized that changes within the airway itself and the associated activity of pulmonary receptors generate a sense of tightness and constant respiratory discomfort.[28] Dyspnea can arise from increased sense of work of breathing in those with fatigue, weakened respiratory muscles, or obstructive diseases.[21,29] Neuromechanical dissociation, a mismatch between incoming information from the respiratory system and outgoing commands from the brain center, can also cause dyspnea[21,29] (Box 24.1).

Neural imaging, although in its infancy, may lead to a better understanding of the central processes involved in perception of and response to breathlessness,[30,31] which are not fully explained by currently accepted mechanisms. Similar neural networks may mediate both pain and dyspnea[30] and may play a role in the emotion-related human brain network.[32]

Case Study Part 2

During a visit with the pulmonary APRN, Maria reported increased dyspnea when she was worried or fatigued. Oxygen was not sufficient during these times. She never tried any medications for dyspnea and had never been on any medications for pain other than over-the-counter analgesics. The pulmonary APRN referred her to palliative care. The palliative APRN's clinical assessment revealed that anxiety and fatigue significantly increased Maria's sense of dyspnea. Maria also screened positive for depression related to her physical condition.

Table 24.1 Potential Causes of Dyspnea in Advanced Disease*

Pulmonary	Cardiac	Systemic	Treatment-related	Psychological
Airway obstructions	CHF	Cachexia	Surgical	Anxiety
Carcinomatosis	Ischemia	Steroid myopathy	◆ Lobectomy	Panic
Chest wall infiltrations	Pericardial effusion	Hepatomegaly	◆ Pneumonectomy	
COPD	Pulmonary hypertension	Ascites	Chemotherapy	
Interstitial lung disease		Anemia	◆ Pulmonary or cardiac toxicity	
Effusions		Metabolic abnormalities	Radiation side effects	
Embolism		Obesity	◆ Pneumonitis	
Pneumonia		Hyperventilation	◆ Fibrosis	
Pneumothorax		Neuromuscular abnormalities	◆ Pericarditis	
Superior vena cava obstruction				
Tumor				

* Only partial list of more common causes. Adapted from Chan et al., 2010. Ref 10.

Central chemoreceptor changes

◆ Hypoxia

◆ Hypercapnia

Mechanoreceptor stimulation

◆ Lung, chest wall, upper airway, facial area

Respiratory muscle effort

◆ Increased sense of breathing due to fatigue/obstructive processes

Neuromechanical disassociation

◆ Mismatch between respiratory and brain command center

* Does not fully explain causes

Clinical Assessment

The palliative APRN's clinical assessment of dyspnea initially focuses on eliciting the underlying pathology, either from previous consultations or by appropriate assessment and diagnostic workup. A biopsychosocial assessment is imperative because the individual's experience and interpretation of dyspnea and preferences for treatment may vary and change with disease progression.[22]

Experts recommend dyspnea assessment and tracking over time.[4,33,34] The palliative APRN can adapt the PQRST mnemonic for pain assessment to guide dyspnea assessment:[35]

P: provoking/palliating factors

Q: quality/characteristics

R: relationship to other symptoms, such as anxiety and fatigue

S: severity, using a unidimensional scale

T: timing (constant or intermittent)

In patients with cancer, the palliative APRN should assess for not only the effects of tumor burden, but also the posttreatment effects of radiation and chemotherapy that may contribute to dyspnea. For patients with cardiac, pulmonary, or motor neuron diseases, the palliative APRN should inquire about the appropriate use of disease-modifying therapies that affect the respiratory system. Lifestyle factors should be explored, as exposure to environmental toxins like tobacco smoke may contribute to dyspnea.

Multiple dyspnea assessment tools have been developed, but they have been unidimensional or disease-specific or have not addressed dyspnea's affective component or dyspnea in advanced disease. The American Thoracic Society and the American College of Chest Physicians have not endorsed the use of any specific scale.[4,33] The modified Borg Scale,[36] visual analogue scale (VAS),[37] and numeric rating scale (NRS)[38] are unidimensional scales that measure dyspnea severity but do not elicit affective components of dyspnea. Patient self-assessment tools in those with advanced disease, the Memorial Symptom Assessment Scale (MSAS)[39] and the Edmonton Symptom Assessment System (ESAS),[40] measure the severity of multiple symptoms.

Psychometrically valid tools, such as the Dynspnoea-12, tested in those with heart failure, COPD, and interstitial lung disease,[41] and the Cancer Dyspnea Scale (CDS), tested in those with cancer,[42] address both the physical and affective components of dyspnea. For patients who cannot report, the Respiratory Distress Observation Scale (RDOS) is a validated, simple-to-use tool that may help the clinician to evaluate the trend and response to treatment.[43] Caregivers' reports may be useful if the patient cannot report the severity of dyspnea.[44]

The clinical interview and the use of psychometrically validated tools for dyspnea assessment should be coupled with physical examination and diagnostic testing as appropriate. In considering the choice of diagnostic testing for evaluating the respiratory system, the palliative APRN should understand potential causes for dyspnea related to the disease state. Further diagnostic testing should be coupled with consideration of the goals of care and the effects of additional information on the individual outcomes (Box 24.2).

Management

The palliative APRN must optimally manage both the disease and the dyspnea. Discussion of disease management is beyond the scope of this chapter, but treatments for dyspnea secondary to COPD[45,46] and CHF secondary to fluid overload[47,48] should be optimized to decrease dyspnea. Treatment of underlying conditions is warranted for those with cancer when the benefit outweighs the risk and if consistent with goals of care. Nonpharmacologic and pharmacologic measures should be used to decrease symptom distress.[4,33] Toward the end-of-life, dyspnea management may preclude the treatment of the underlying pathology. Although there has been progress in understanding the mechanisms of dyspnea, the treatment of dyspnea has not progressed significantly.[4] The palliative APRN can manage dyspnea and improve quality of life despite the lack of high-quality studies and gaps in evidence for recommended therapies[49-52] (Table 24.2).

Pharmacologic Management
Opioids

Dyspnea has been compared to pain in terms of the need to address it as a basic human right for treatment—the evidence is there for opioid therapy, and to deny it is to deny a human right.[53] Opioids are the first-line treatment for dyspnea.[4,33] Opioids may reduce dyspnea by decreasing the respiratory drive, by altering responses to hypoxia and hypercapnia, and through changes in bronchoconstriction.[54] Morphine, the most widely studied opioid, has been shown to be effective for dyspnea.[55-57] In a systematic review and meta-analysis, where three out of eight randomized controlled trials could be evaluated through meta-analysis, opioids were efficacious for dyspnea.[55] Other studies have confirmed the efficacy of compounded subcutaneous oxycodone[58] and hydromorphone[59] for dyspnea in advanced cancer. Small studies have confirmed the efficacy of fentanyl for refractory breathlessness.[60] Results from a randomized controlled trial comparing morphine, oxycodone, and a placebo for dyspnea in heart failure failed to demonstrate efficacy nor did it demonstrate any adverse effects from opioid use.[61] In a multisite randomized controlled trial of patients with chronic dyspnea, 54% of participants had COPD and were treated

---

Box 24.2 Assessment of Dyspnea

Clinical Interview

- PQRST (provoking/palliating, quality, relation to other symptoms, severity, timing)
- Use of disease-modifying therapies that affect respiratory system when indicated
- Lifestyle factors—smoke exposure

Selected Assessment Tools*

Unidimensional tools—measure severity

- Modified BORG
- Visual analogue scale
- Numeric rating

Patient self-assessment tools in advanced disease—measure severity of multiple symptoms

- Memorial Symptom Assessment Scale
- Edmonton Symptom Assessment System

Disease-specific tools—address physical/affective components

- Dyspneoea-12 (COPD, heart failure, interstitial lung disease)
- Cancer Dyspnea Scale

Observation scale—for patients unable to report

- Respiratory Distress Observation Scale

Physical Examination

- General—pallor, cachexia, ascites, edema
- Respiratory—respiratory rate, oxygen saturation, breathing pattern, breath sounds
- Cardiac—pulse rate, heart sounds, jugular venous pressure

Laboratory—Diagnostic Testing**

- Hemoglobin, oxygen saturation, pCO_2, basic metabolic panel
- Chest x-ray
- CT or perfusion scans, echocardiograms

---

* There are many more than listed; no specific one endorsed for use by American Thoracic Society or American College of Chest Physicians.

** Dependent on goals of care.

Table 24.2 Selected Treatment Options for Dyspnea in Advanced Disease

Intervention	Comment
Pharmacologic Opioids (IV, SC, PO)	First-line treatment for dyspnea related to cancer, COPD; efficacy in CHF not determined. Optimal dosing has not been determined. Starting morphine doses range from 0.5 mg to 10 mg orally q4h; other opioids may also be effective if morphine is contraindicated.
Benzodiazepines	Not first-line recommendation, but potentially useful for dyspnea refractory to other measures or in dyspnea-associated anxiety
Furosemide	Nebulized furosemide may be useful in COPD.
Oxygen	Beneficial for hypoxemia; may be beneficial for those not hypoxemic; trial is warranted
Noninvasive ventilation	May be useful for exacerbations of COPD, and in those with hypercapnia
Interventional Pleurodesis	May decrease dyspnea due to pleural effusions
Tunneled catheter	May decrease dyspnea due to pleural effusions
Bronchial stenting	May decrease dyspnea secondary to obstructions
Nonpharmacologic Rehabilitation	Breathing training—COPD Pulmonary rehabilitation—efficacy in COPD, some evidence in cancer
Psychoeducational	Counseling, education, relaxation, Internet-based self-management—may increase self-efficacy
Fans	Low-risk treatment, may be beneficial
Acupuncture	Equivocal evidence

Results from studies of patients with COPD,[56,64] cancer,[56,65] or heart failure[61] evaluating the use of opioids for dyspnea failed to demonstrate a relationship between opioids and respiratory compromise. In a qualitative interview study, men with chronic heart failure were willing to use opioids for dyspnea from a trusted provider but had concerns about providers' willingness to use them.[66]

There have been limited studies to confirm the dose needed to manage dyspnea. This is partially due to the inherent difficulty of conducting randomized controlled trials in vulnerable populations and the heterogeneity of the patient population with dyspnea. The proposed doses of morphine for opioid-naïve patients with dyspnea range from 0.5 to 1 mg orally q4h[52] to 5 to 10 mg orally q3-4h[67] to 10 mg of extended-release oral morphine daily, with titration to 30 mg daily for chronic dyspnea.[56] Based on the variation of proposed doses, palliative APRNs should use the same approach as when treating pain—"start low and go slow." There is an exception, however, when managing dyspnea toward the end-of-life in an acute care setting, where opioids may be given intravenously and the dose titrated rapidly. The dose should be adjusted for those who are older and frail with multiple comorbidities. Although it has not been specifically studied for dyspnea, the palliative APRN should use opioids other than morphine for those with renal dysfunction due to accumulation of morphine metabolites M-3-gluconoride and M-6-gluconoride, which may add to the adverse effects of opioids.[68]

with extended-release once-daily morphine (10 mg to 30 mg),[56] which remained effective over time.[57]

Opioids are still underused due to fears about respiratory depression.[4,33] In semistructured interview studies, practitioners were reluctant to use opioids in patients with COPD due to fears of decreasing respiratory drive,[62,63] but patients and caregivers derived benefit and believed opioids should be continued.[63]

Nebulized opioids may be attractive to individuals who may not want to take oral medications.[69] Results from studies of nebulized morphine were equivocal, whereas those from studies of hydromorphone and fentanyl showed possible benefit in those with cancer.[70] Due to a lack of robust studies, results from a systematic review of nebulized or intranasal fentanyl do not support its use for breathlessness.[60,69] Therefore, the use of nebulized opioids should be evaluated on a case-by-case basis;[70] it may be considered if oral or parenteral opioids fail to provide benefit.

Benzodiazepines

Benzodiazepines have been used for dyspnea and may treat the affective response to dyspnea. However, in a systematic review of benzodiazepines for dyspnea, the analysis from seven studies in advanced cancer and COPD did not show a significant benefit regardless of type, dose, or route.[71] Anxiolytics (including benzodiazepines) have not been recommended by the American and Canadian thoracic societies for dyspnea in patients with COPD.[4,46] However, benzodiazepines have been shown to be effective in some recent small studies.[12,72,73] In a prospective nonrandomized study of hospitalized patients with cancer, combined use of lorazepam and opioids (morphine and hydromorphone) demonstrated a significant reduction in dyspnea without any increased respiratory depression.[72] In a retrospective review of hospitalized patients receiving palliative care, those who received benzodiazepines and opioids had better relief from dyspnea than those receiving only opioids.[73] Results from a randomized controlled trial demonstrated that oral midazolam was superior to oral morphine for dyspnea in a 5-day period for ambulatory patients with advanced cancer and dyspnea.[12]

Benzodiazepines may be used for dyspnea refractory to opioids or other nonpharmacologic measures, although quality studies are needed to further evaluate their potential efficacy.[71] Lorazepam is recommended due to its relatively short half-life and availability in liquid form.[74] Dosing can start as low as 0.25 mg orally or sublingually q4h. Individuals with significant anxiety, who may not be approaching the end-of-life, may benefit from treatment of anxiety with agents such as selective serotonin reuptake inhibitors.

Furosemide

In a recent review of nebulized medications for dyspnea, furosemide showed potential benefit in those with dyspnea related to COPD.[70] In a double-blind randomized controlled trial, nebulized furosemide as an adjunct was beneficial for dyspnea for those with an exacerbation of COPD seen in the ED.[75] However, in a systematic review of the use of furosemide for dyspnea in cancer, only two small randomized controlled trials were identified, and furosemide was not beneficial for dyspnea.[76] Given the paucity of studies, the use of nebulized furosemide should be reserved for those who do not respond to first-line therapies.

Oxygen

Oxygen is generally the first treatment clinicians consider when someone is dyspneic. The use of oxygen is warranted if dyspnea is related to a physiologic event limiting the delivery of necessary oxygen to the body, such as for those with COPD. However, in advanced disease, the oxygen saturation and carbon dioxide status may not correlate with the perception of dyspnea. In systematic reviews,[77,78] dyspnea was improved with the use of oxygen therapy in those with COPD who were mildly hypoxemic or not hypoxemic and would not have qualified for home oxygen therapy. Ameer and colleagues concluded that due to the quality of the studies, the evidence is inconclusive to recommend oxygen for long-term use in those with COPD who are not hypoxemic at rest.[78] Abernethy and colleagues compared the effects of oxygen versus room air delivered by nasal cannula in those with advanced disease in a multisite randomized controlled trial and found that the subjective feeling of dyspnea was relieved in those who were treated with air by nasal cannula at the same rates as those treated with oxygen therapy, thus questioning the need for oxygen therapy.[79] There have not been any high-quality studies assessing the efficacy of oxygen use in those with CHF, but nocturnal oxygen for those with comorbid obstructive sleep apnea may provide benefit.[80] The palliative APRN's best approach may be a time-limited trial of oxygen therapy to evaluate the response in dyspneic individuals with advanced disease who are not hypoxemic or only mildly hypoxemic.

Noninvasive ventilation has been studied in those with acute exacerbations of COPD. In a systematic review, dyspnea was improved in three of four randomized controlled trials, but due to limitations in the studies the use of noninvasive ventilation needs to be further studied before it can be recommended.[81] Nava and colleagues compared the effects of noninvasive ventilation with oxygen therapy in individuals with advanced cancer. Noninvasive ventilation provided benefit, especially to hypercapnic patients, and decreased the use of morphine. The number of deaths from enrollment until 6 months after discharge was less in the hypercapnic group using noninvasive ventilation versus those on oxygen.[82] Noninvasive ventilation may provide benefit for those with advanced disease and dyspnea, but further research is needed to evaluate its efficacy in different disease states.[83] The treatment of dyspnea related to motor neuron diseases poses additional challenges, as individuals must make decisions related to the use of both noninvasive and invasive ventilation not only to manage dyspnea, but also to prolong life.

Interventional Therapy

The palliative APRN may consider referrals for interventional therapies to reduce dyspnea if consistent with goals of care. Mechanical or chemical pleurodesis may reduce dyspnea secondary to pleural effusions. For those with more advanced disease, the placement of a tunneled catheter for management of pleural effusions may be the most effective option.[84,85] Disease-modifying therapies, such as chemotherapy and radiation therapy, should be explored as first-line treatments for obstructions secondary to tumor burden.[86] Those with malignant airway obstructions may benefit from interventional bronchoscopy and/or stenting.[87] However, the increased risk of infection secondary to stenting should be balanced against the possible benefit.

Nonpharmacologic Management

Treatment for dyspnea is best managed using a multimodal approach. When considering the inclusion of nonpharmacologic treatment, it is important to consider individual beliefs, the perceived relevance, insurance coverage, short-term benefits, convenience in administration, and caregiver involvement.[88]

Therapies

Breathing training techniques,[46,89] the use of walking aids,[46] and the use of neuromuscular electrical muscle stimulation[46,89] have been beneficial for dyspnea in those with COPD, but access may be limited by insurance issues. In a meta-analysis of 11 studies, pulmonary (respiratory) rehabilitation therapy was beneficial for dyspnea in those with COPD.[90] Results from an integrative review of systematic studies showed that inspiratory muscle training was beneficial for dyspnea when used alone and in combination with pulmonary rehabilitation in individuals with COPD.[91] The evidence for the use of pulmonary rehabilitation in those with cancer is sparse, but results from studies of individuals with non-small-cell lung cancer demonstrated significant reduction in dyspnea.[92-94] In one of the studies, 81% also had COPD,[92] so this may account for the positive response. Exercise therapy may be an effective adjunct strategy in those with cancer, but further studies are needed to confirm efficacy.[95]

Psychoeducational Interventions

The authors of a systematic review on noninvasive interventions for lung cancer concluded that nursing intervention programs may improve dyspnea.[96] Counseling, education, and relaxation techniques to manage breathlessness have been beneficial in individuals with lung cancer.[97] In a randomized controlled trial of an Internet-based self-management support program compared to face-to-face care and general health education for individuals with COPD, dyspnea was not reduced, but there was satisfaction with participation in the program and increased self-efficacy.[98] A cognitive-behavioral program was effective in improving quality of life and ability to cope with breathlessness in a group of individuals with advanced COPD.[99] A common theme in these programs is the inclusion of education and support, which may increase self-efficacy and improve self-management of dyspnea.

Breathlessness Intervention Services

A comprehensive approach to treating dyspnea includes palliative care specialists and respiratory physiotherapists who work together to manage dyspnea.[100,101] These clinics may operate independently and may treat individuals irrespective of diagnosis.[101] Although these services may not be available to the palliative APRN working in rural settings, including respiratory physiotherapists in the assessment and management of dyspnea may improve outcomes.

Fans

The use of fans has been advocated for the relief of dyspnea. It has been hypothesized that cool air on the nasoreceptors decreases the subjective feeling of dyspnea. In a randomized controlled crossover trial evaluating the use of a handheld fan on the leg and face, results showed a positive effect on dyspnea with the use of the fan on the face.[102] Due to its low risk and cost, a trial of a fan is warranted, except for those with facial pain secondary to trigeminal neuralgia or a neuropathic process that may be aggravated with the air on the face.

Acupuncture

Acupuncture may be beneficial for dyspnea, but most studies have been small and heterogeneous and lacked a control group.[103] Results from a recent randomized controlled trial in individuals with COPD showed a reduction in dyspnea on exertion.[104] However, results from two systematic reviews did not find enough evidence to recommend acupuncture.[55,89] If available without undue burden to the individual, acupuncture may be a consideration as part of a multimodal therapeutic approach.

Dyspnea Management at the End-of-Life

Dyspnea may worsen in both pulmonary and nonpulmonary disease states toward the end-of-life. The palliative APRN should optimize pharmacologic management at this time to relieve suffering. In the acute care setting, the use of an opioid infusion may treat both dyspnea and pain and may be rapidly titrated. Benzodiazepines in combination with opioids may improve moderate to severe dyspnea.[65,73] Although there may be concern that opioids and benzodiazepines may hasten death, the principle of the double effect justifies their use to relieve dyspnea at the end-of-life.[33,67] In home care settings, use of sublingual or rectal routes of opioids and benzodiazepines may alleviate dyspnea at the end-of-life. For a select few who experience intractable dyspnea, the use of palliative sedation may be a consideration if dyspnea cannot be controlled with opioids and benzodiazepines (see Chapter 51, Palliative Sedation).

Case Study Part 3

The palliative APRN started Maria on morphine 5 mg PO q4h PRN dyspnea. She was transitioned to extended-release oral morphine 15 mg daily, which significantly reduced the dyspnea. A selective serotonin reuptake inhibitor was started to manage her anxiety and depression. A short course of pulmonary rehabilitation therapy improved her overall condition. RN case management reinforced principles of medication adherence and self-management. After 3 months, her dyspnea worsened due to disease progression and her functional status declined. She was hospitalized with pneumonia. Despite optimal antibiotic therapy and a trial of noninvasive ventilation, her conditioned worsened. Maria did not want an ICU level of care or mechanical ventilation. Antibiotics were discontinued and she was placed on oxygen at 3 liters per nasal cannula, a continuous intravenous infusion of morphine, and IV lorazepam for dyspnea PRN. Atropine 1% was administered sublingually for increased oropharyngeal secretions. She died peacefully with her family at the bedside.

Patient and Family Education

Palliative APRNs are in an optimal position to provide consistent ongoing information and education, which are essential components of care. Patients and families should understand the potential causes of dyspnea and the treatments that may address the underlying pathology and those that provide symptomatic relief. Discussions should include information about multimodal treatment, including pharmacologic and nonpharmacologic modalities.[105] Myths may need to be dispelled regarding the use of opioids and anxiolytics.[54,106] Patient and caregiver involvement is key to provide personalized treatment.[88] Caregivers may experience psychological distress secondary to increased caregiving.[107]

They may feel isolated, especially when there are longer trajectories of illness, and may benefit from social work involvement and referral to community support agencies.[107] Given the multidimensional nature of dyspnea, a multimodal plan that is patient- and family-centered is essential to ensure appropriate effective management.

Conclusion

The effective treatment of dyspnea combines the optimal treatment of the underlying pathology (when appropriate) and the associated distress. During the clinical assessment, the palliative APRN should address the severity and characteristics of dyspnea and the impact of dyspnea on the patient's life. Queries about symptom clusters that may affect the distress of dyspnea should be incorporated into each clinical encounter. Pharmacologic and nonpharmacologic approaches can decrease dyspnea and its associated distress. Further research is necessary to optimize understanding and treatment of dyspnea. Palliative APRNs are in key roles to contribute to the further development of this evidence base.

References

1. Abernethy AP, Wheeler JL. Total dyspnea. *Curr Opin Support Palliat Care*. 2008; 2(2): 110–3. doi: 10.1097/SPC.0b013e328300cad0
2. Saunders C. A personal therapeutic journey. *BMJ*. 1996; 313: 1599–601.
3. Schrijvers D, van Fraeyenhove F. Emergencies in palliative care. *Cancer J*. 2010; 16(5): 14–520. doi: 10.1097/PPO.0b013e3181f28a8d
4. Parshall MB, Schwartzstein RM, Adams L, et al. An official American Thoracic Society statement: update on the mechanisms, assessment, and management of dyspnea. *Am J Respir Critic Care Med*. 2012; 185(4): 435–52.
5. Kamal AH, Maguire JM, Wheeler JL, Currow DC, Abernethy AP. Dyspnea review for the palliative care professional: assessment, burdens, and etiologies. *J Palliat Med*. 2011; 14(10): 1167–72. doi: 10.1089/jpm.2011.01019
6. McCaffery M. Nursing practice theories related to cognition, bodily pain, and man-environment interactions. Los Angeles: University of California at Los Angeles Students' Store; 1968:95.
7. Lansing RW, Gracely RH, Banzett RB. The multiple dimensions of dyspnea: review and hypotheses. *Respir Physiol Neurobiol*. 2009; 167(1): 53–60. doi: 10.1016/j.resp.2008.07.012
8. Caroci, AS, Lareau SC. Descriptors of dyspnea by patients with chronic obstructive pulmonary disease versus congestive heart failure. *Heart Lung*. 2004; 33(2): 102–10.
9. von Leupoldt A, Balewski S, Petersen S, et al. Verbal descriptors of dyspnea in patients with COPD at different intensity levels of dyspnea. *Chest*. 2007; 132(1): 141–7.
10. Williams M, Cafarella P, Olds T, Petkov J, Frith P. The language of breathlessness differentiates between patients with COPD and age-matched adults. *Chest*. 2008; 134(3): 489–96. doi: 10.1378/chest.07-2916
11. Reddy SK, Parsons HA, Elsayem A, Palmer JL, Bruera E. Characteristics and correlates of dyspnea in patients with advanced cancer. *J Palliat Med*. 2009; 12(1): 29–36. doi: 10.1089/jpm.2008.0158
12. Navigante AH, Castro MA, Cerchietti LC. Morphine versus midazolam as upfront therapy to control dyspnea perception in cancer patients while its underlying cause is sought or treated. *J Pain Symptom Manage*. 2010; 39: 820–30.
13. Blinderman CD, Homel P, Billings JA, Tennstedt S, Portenoy RK. Symptom distress and quality of life in patients with advanced chronic obstructive pulmonary disease. *J Pain Symptom Manage*. 2009; 38(1): 115–23. doi: 10.1016/j.jpainsymman.2008.07.0006
14. Blinderman CD, Homel P, Billings JA, Portenoy RK, Tennstedt S. Symptom distress and quality of life in patients with advanced congestive heart failure. *J Pain Symptom Manage*. 2008; 35(6): 594–603.
15. Solano JP, Gomes B, Higginson IJ. A comparison of symptom prevalence in far advanced cancer, AIDS, heart disease, chronic obstructive pulmonary disease and renal disease. *J Pain Symptom Manage*. 2006; 31(1): 58–69.
16. Vandyk AD, Harrison MB, Macartney G, Ross-White A, Stacey D. Emergency department visits for symptoms experienced by oncology patients: a systematic review. *Support Care Cancer*. 2012; 20(8):1589–99. doi: 10.1007/s00520-012-1459-y
17. Barbera L, Taylor C, Dudgeon D. Why do patients with cancer visit the emergency department near the end of life? *CMAJ*. 2010; 182(6): 563–8. doi: 10.1503/cmaj.091187
18. Leak A, Mayer DK, Wyss A, Travers D, Waller A. Why do cancer patients die in the emergency department? An analysis of 283 deaths in NC EDs. *Am J Hosp Palliat Care*. 2013; 30(2): 178–82. doi:10.1177/1049909112445306
19. Bausewein C, Booth S, Gysels M, Kuhnbach R, Haberland B, Higginson IJ. Understanding breathlessness: cross-sectional comparison of symptom burden and palliative care needs in chronic obstructive pulmonary disease and cancer. *J Palliat Med*. 2010; 13(9): 1109–18.
20. Molassiotis A, Lowe M, Blackhall F, Lorigan P. A qualitative exploration of a respiratory distress symptom cluster in lung cancer: cough, breathlessness and fatigue. *Lung Cancer*. 2011; 71: 94–102.
21. Chan K, Tse DMW, Sham MMK, Thorsen AB. Palliative medicine in malignant respiratory diseases. In: Hanks G, Fallon M, Cherny NI, Christakis NA, Portenoy RK, Kaasa S, eds. *Oxford Textbook of Palliative Medicine*. 4th ed. New York: Oxford University Press; 2010. Available at http://online.statref.com/Document.aspx?fxId=109&docId=595.
22. Gysels M, Higginson IJ. The lived experience of breathlessness and its implications for care: a qualitative comparison in cancer, COPD, heart failure and MND. *BMC Palliat Care*. 2011; 10: 15.
23. Bausewein C, Booth S, Gysels M, Kühnbach R, Haberland B, Higginson IJ. Individual breathlessness trajectories do not match summary trajectories in advanced cancer and chronic obstructive pulmonary disease: results from a longitudinal study. *Palliat Med*. 2010; 24(8): 777–86. doi: 10.1177/0269216310378785
24. Weingaertner V, Scheve C, Gerdes V, et al. Breathlessness, functional status, distress, and palliative care needs over time in patients with advanced chronic obstructive pulmonary disease or lung cancer: a cohort study. *J Pain Symptom Manage*. 2014; 48(4): 569–81. doi: 10.1016/j.jpainsymman.2013.11.011
25. Molassiotis A, Wengström Y, Kearney N. Symptom cluster patterns during the first year after diagnosis with cancer. *J Pain Symptom Manage*. 2010; 39: 847–58.
26. Currow DC, Smith J, Davidson PM, Newton PJ, Agar MR, Abernethy AP. Do the trajectories of dyspnea differ in prevalence and intensity by diagnosis at the end of life? A consecutive cohort study. *J Pain Symptom Manage*. 2010; 39(4): 680–90. doi: 10.1016/j.jpainsymman.2009.09.017
27. Moosavi SH, Golestanian E, Binks AP, Lansing RW, Brown R, Banzett RB. Hypoxic and hypercapnic drives to breathe generate equivalent levels of air hunger in humans. *J Appl Physiol*. 2003; 94(1): 141–54.
28. Binks AP, Moosavi SH, Banzett RB, Schwartzstein RM. "Tightness" sensation of asthma does not arise from the work of breathing. *Am J Respir Crit Care Med*. 2002; 165(1): 78–82.
29. Nishino T. Dyspnoea: underlying mechanisms and treatment. *Br J Anaesth*. 2011; 106(4): 463–74. doi: 10.1093/bja/aer040
30. Pattinson KTS, Johnson MJ. Neuroimaging of central breathlessness mechanisms. *Curr Opin Support Palliat Care*. 2014; 8(3): 225–33. doi: 10.1097/SPC.0000000000000069

31. Herigstad, M, Hayen A, Wiech K, Pattinson, KTS. Dyspnoea and the brain. *Respir Med*. 2011; 105: 809–17.

32. von Leupoldt A, Sommer T, Kegat S, et al. Dyspnea and pain share emotion-related brain network. *Neuroimage*. 2009; 48(1): 200–6. doi: 10.1016/j.neuroimage.2009.06.015

33. Mahler DA, Selecky PA, Harrod CG, et al. American College of Chest Physicians consensus statement on the management of dyspnea in patients with advanced lung or heart disease. *Chest*. 2010; 137: 674–91.

34. Mularski RA, Campbell ML, Asch BB, et al. A review of quality of care evaluation for the palliation of dyspnea. *Am J Respir Crit Care Med*. 2010; 181(6): 534–8. doi: 10.1164/rccm.200903-0462PP

35. Twycross RG. The assessment of pain in advanced cancer, *J Med Ethics*. 1978; 4: 112–6.

36. Borg G. Perceived exertion as an indicator of somatic stress. *Scand J Rehabil Med*. 1970; 2(2): 92–8.

37. Gift AG. Validation of a vertical visual analogue scale as a measure of clinical dyspnea. *Rehabil Nurs*. 1989; 14(6): 323–5.

38. Gift AG, Narsavage G. Validity of the numeric rating scale as a measure of dyspnea. *Am J Crit Care*. 1998; 7(3): 200–4.

39. Portenoy RK, Thaler HT, Kornblith AB, et al. The Memorial Symptom Assessment Scale: an instrument for the evaluation of symptom prevalence, characteristics and distress. *Eur J Cancer*. 1994; 30A(9): 1326–36.

40. Bruera E, Kuehn N, Miller MJ, Selmser P, Macmillan K. The Edmonton Symptom Assessment System (ESAS): a simple method for the assessment of palliative care patients. *J Palliat Care*. 1991; 7(2): 6–9.

41. Yorke J, Moosavi SH, Shuldham C, Jones PW. Quantification of dyspnea using descriptors: development and initial testing of the Dyspnoea-12. *Thorax*. 2010; 65(1): 21–6. doi: 10.1136/thx.2009.118521

42. Tanaka K, Akechi T, Okuyama T, Nishiwaki Y, Uchitomi Y. Development and validation of the Cancer Dyspnoea Scale: a multidimensional, brief, self-rating scale. *Br J Cancer*. 2000; 82(4): 800–5.

43. Campbell ML, Templin T, Walch J. A Respiratory Distress Observation Scale for patients unable to self-report dyspnea. *J Palliat Med*. 2010; 13(3): 285–90. doi: 10.1089/jpm.2009.0229

44. Hui D. Morgado M., Vidal M, et al. Dyspnea in hospitalized advanced cancer patients: subjective and physiologic correlates. *J Palliat Med*. 2013; 16(3): 274–80. doi: 10.1089/jpm.2012.0364

45. Bouxman SR. Pulmonary conditions. In: Dahlin CM, Lynch MT, eds. *Hospice and Palliative Nurses Association Core Curriculum for the Advanced Practice Hospice and Palliative Registered Nurse*. 2nd ed. Pittsburgh, PA: Hospice and Palliative Nurses Association; 2013:331–51.

46. Marciniuk DD, Goodridge D, Hernandez P, et al. Managing dyspnea in patients with advanced chronic obstructive pulmonary disease: a Canadian Thoracic Society clinical practice guideline. *Can Respir J*. 2011; 18(2): 69–78.

47. Yancy CW, Jessup M, Bozkurt B, et al. 2013 ACCF/AHA guideline for the management of heart failure: a report of the American College of Cardiology Foundation/American Heart Association Task Force on Practice Guidelines. *J Am Coll Cardiol*. 2013; 62(16): e147–239. doi: 10.1016/j.jacc.2013.05.019

48. Wilson MA. Heart failure. In: Dahlin CM, Lynch MT, eds. *Hospice and Palliative Nurses Association Core Curriculum for the Advanced Practice Hospice and Palliative Registered Nurse*. 2nd ed. Pittsburgh, PA: Hospice and Palliative Nurses Association; 2013:311–29.

49. Dorman S, Jolley C, Abernethy A, et al. Researching breathlessness in palliative care: consensus statement of the National Cancer Research Institute Palliative Care Breathlessness Subgroup. *Palliat Med*. 2009; 23(3): 213–27. doi: 10.1177/0269216309102520

50. Johnson, MJ, Abernethy AP, Currow DC. Gaps in the evidence base of opioids for refractory breathlessness. a future work plan? *J Pain Symptom Manage*. 2012; 43(3): 614–24. doi: 10.1016/j.jpainsymman.2011.04.024

51. Currow DC, Higginson IJ, Johnson MJ. Breathlessness—current and emerging mechanisms, measurement and management: A discussion from an European Association of Palliative Care workshop. *Palliat Med*. 2013; 27(10): 932–8. doi: 10.1177/0269216313493819

52. Rocker G, Horton R, Currow D, Goodridge D, Young J, Booth S. Palliation of dyspnoea in advanced COPD: revisiting a role for opioids. *Thorax*. 2009; 64(10): 910–5. doi: 10.1136/thx.2009.116699.

53. Currow DC, Abernethy AP, Ko DN. The active identification and management of chronic refractory breathlessness is a human right. *Thorax*. 2014; 69(4): 393–4. doi: 10.1136/thoraxjnl-2013-204701

54. Horton R,G. What is the role of opioids in treatment of refractory dyspnea in advanced chronic pulmonary disease? In: Goldstein NE, Morrison RS, eds. *Evidence-Based Practice of Palliative Medicine*. Philadelphia, PA: Elsevier; 2013:111–9.

55. Ben-Aharon I, Gafter-Gvili A, Leibovici L, Stemmer SM. Interventions for alleviating cancer-related dyspnea: a systematic review and meta-analysis. *Acta Oncol*. 2012; 51(8): 996–1008. doi: 10.3109/0284186X.2012.709638

56. Currow DC, McDonald C, Oaten S. et al. Once-daily opioids for chronic dyspnea: a dose increment and pharmacolvigilance study. *J Pain Symptom Manage*. 2011; 42(3): 388–99.

57. Currow DC, Quinn S, Greene A, Bull J, Johnson MJ, Abernethy AP. The longitudinal pattern of response when morphine is used to treat chronic refractory dyspnea. *J Palliat Med*. 2013; 16(8): 881–6. doi: 10.1089/jpm.2012.0591

58. Kawabata M, Keisuke K. Continuous subcutaneous infusion of compound oxycodone for the relief of dyspnea in patients with terminally ill cancer: a retrospective study. *Am J Hosp Palliat Care*. 2013; 30(3): 305–11. doi: 10.1177/1049909112448924

59. Charles M, Reymond L, Israel F. Relief of incident dyspnea in palliative cancer patients: a pilot randomized, controlled trial comparing nebulized hydromorphone, systemic hydromorphone, and nebulized saline. *J Pain Symptom Manage*. 2008; 36: 29–38.

60. Simon ST, Koskeroglu P, Gaertner J, Voltz R. Fentanyl for the relief of refractory breathlessness: a systematic review. *J Pain Symptom Manage*. 2013; 46: 874–86.

61. Oxberry SG, Torgerson DJ, Bland JM, Clark AL, Cleland JG, Johnson MJ. Short-term opioids for breathlessness in stable chronic heart failure: a randomized controlled trial. *Eur J Heart Fail*. 2011; 13(9): 1006–12. doi: 10.1093/eurjhf/hfr068

62. Young J, Donahue M, Farquhar M, Simpson C, Rocker G. Using opioids to treat dyspnea in advanced COPD: attitudes and experiences of family physicians and respiratory therapists. *Can Fam Physician*. 2012; 58(7): e401–7.

63. Rocker G, Young J, Donahue M, Farquhar M, Simpson C. Perspectives of patients, family caregivers and physicians about the use of opioids for refractory dyspnea in advanced chronic obstructive pulmonary disease. *CMAJ*. 2012; 184(9): e497–504. doi: 10.1503/cmaj.111758

64. Ekström MP, Bornefalk-Hermansson A, Abernethy AP, Currow DC. Safety of benzodiazepines and opioids in very severe respiratory disease: national prospective study. *BMJ*. 2014; 348: g445. doi: 10.1136/bmj.g445

65. Clemens KE, Quednau I, Klaschik E. Is there a higher risk of respiratory depression in opioid-naïve palliative care patients during symptomatic therapy of dyspnea with strong opioids? *J Palliat Med*. 2008; 11(2): 204–16. doi: 10.1089/jpm.2007.0131

66. Oxberry SG, Jones L, Clark AL, Johnson MJ. Attitudes to morphine in chronic heart failure patients. *Postgrad Med J*. 2012; 88(1043): 515–21. doi: 10.1136/postgradmedj-2011-000074rep

67. Lanken PN, Terry PB, Delisser HM, et al. An official American Thoracic Society clinical policy statement: palliative care for patients with respiratory diseases and critical illnesses. *Am J Respir Crit Care Med*. 2008; 177(8): 912–27. doi: 10.1164/rccm.200605-587ST

68. Niscola P, Scaramucci L, Vischini G, et al. The use of major analgesics in patients with renal dysfunction. *Cur Drug Targets*. 2010: 11: 752–8.

69. Bausewein C, Simon S. Inhaled nebulized and intranasal opioids for the relief of breathlessness. *Curr Opin Support Palliat Care.* 2014;8(3): 208–12. doi: 10.1097/SPC.0000000000000071

70. Boyden JY, Connor SR, Otolorin L, Nathan SD, Fine PG, Davis MS, Muir JC. Nebulized medications for the treatment of dyspnea: a literature review. *J Aerosol Med Pulm Drug Deliv.* 2014 June 10. [Epub ahead of print]

71. Simon ST, Higginson IJ, Booth S, Harding R, Bausewein C. Benzodiazepines for the relief of breathlessness in advanced malignant and non-malignant diseases in adults. *Cochrane Database Syst Rev.* 2010; (1):CD007354.

72. Clemens KE, Klaschik E. Dyspnoea associated with anxiety-symptomatic therapy with opioids in combination with lorazepam and its effect on ventilation in palliative care patients. *Support Care Cancer.* 2011; 19: 2027–33. doi: 10.1007/s00520-010-1058-8

73. Gomutbutra P, O'Riordan DL, Pantilat SZ. Management of moderate-to-severe dyspnea in hospitalized patients receiving palliative care. *J Pain Symptom Manage.* 2013; 45(4): 885–91. doi: 10.1016/j.jpainsymman.2012.05.004

74. Quill TE, Bower KA, Holloway RG, et al. Dyspnea. In: *Primer of Palliative Care.* 6th ed. Chicago, IL: American Academy of Hospice and Palliative Medicine; 2014:52.

75. Sheikh Motahar Vahedi H, Mahshidfar B, et al. The adjunctive effect of nebulized furosemide in COPD exacerbation: a randomized controlled clinical trial. *Respir Care.* 2013; 58(11): 1873–7. doi: 10.4187/respcare.02160

76. Jeba J, George R, Pease N. Nebulised furosemide in the palliation of dyspnoea in cancer: a systematic review. *BMJ Support Palliat Care.* 2013; doi: 10.1136/bmjspcare-2013-000492

77. Uronis H, McCrory DC, Samsa G, Currow D, Abernethy A. Symptomatic oxygen for non-hypoxaemic chronic obstructive pulmonary disease. *Cochrane Database Syst Rev.* 2011; 6: 78.

78. Ameer F, Carson KV, Usmani ZA, Smith BJ. Ambulatory oxygen for people with chronic obstructive pulmonary disease who are not hypoxaemic at rest. *Cochrane Database of Syst Rev.* 2014; 6: CD000238. doi:10.1002/14651858.CD000238.pub2

79. Abernethy AP, McDonald CF, Frith PA, et al. Effect of palliative oxygen versus room air in relief of breathlessness in patients with refractory dyspnea: a double-blind randomised controlled trial. *Lancet.* 2010; 376(9743): 784–93. doi: 10.1016/S0140-6736(10)61115-4

80. Clark AL, Johnson MJ, Squire I. Does home oxygen benefit people with chronic heart failure? *BMJ.* 2011; 342:d234. doi: 10.1136/bmj.d234.

81. Smith TA, Davidson PM, Lam LT, Jenkins CR, Ingham JM. The use of non-invasive ventilation for the relief of dyspnoea in exacerbations of chronic obstructive pulmonary disease; a systematic review. *Respirology.* 2012; 17(2): 300–7. doi: 10.1111/j.1440-1843.2011.02085.x

82. Nava S, Ferrer M, Esquinas A, et al. Palliative use of non-invasive ventilation in end-of-life patients with solid tumours: a randomised feasibility trial. *Lancet Oncol.* 2013;14(3): 219–27. doi: 10.1016/S1470-2045(13)70009-3

83. Gifford AH. Noninvasive ventilation as a palliative measure. *Curr Opin Support Palliat Care.* 2014; 8(3): 218–24. doi: 10.1097/SPC.0000000000000068

84. Monsky WL, Yoneda KY, MacMillan J, et al. Peritoneal and pleural ports for management of refractory ascites and pleural effusions: assessment of impact on patient quality of life and hospice/home nursing care. *J Palliat Med.* 2009;12(9): 811–7. doi: 10.1089/jpm.2009.0061

85. Olden AM, Holloway R. Treatment of malignant pleural effusion: PleurX catheter or talc pleurodesis? A cost-effectiveness analysis. *J Palliat Med.* 2010; 13(1): 59–65. doi: 10.1089/jpm.2009.0220

86. Grosu HB, Eapen GA, Morice RC, et al. Stents are associated with increased risk of respiratory infections in patients undergoing airway interventions for malignant airways disease. *Chest.* 2013; 144(2): 441–9. doi: 10.1378/chest.12-1721

87. Casal RF. Update in airway stents. *Curr Opin Pulm Med.* 2010; 16(4): 321–8. doi: 10.1097/MCP.0b013e32833a260

88. Ellis J, Wagland R, Tishelman C. et al. Considerations in developing and delivering a nonpharmacological intervention for symptom management in lung cancer: the views of patients and informal caregivers. *J Pain Symptom Manage.* 2012; 44(6): 831–42. doi: 10.1016/j.jpainsymman.2011.12.274

89. Bausewein C, Booth S, Gysels M, Higginson IJ. Non-pharmacological interventions for breathlessness in advanced stages of malignant and non-malignant diseases. *Cochrane Database Syst Rev.* 2008; 2: CD005623. doi:10.1002/14651858.CD005623.pub3

90. Lacasse Y, Martin S, Lasserson TJ, Goldstein RS. Meta-analysis of respiratory rehabilitation in chronic obstructive pulmonary disease. A Cochrane systematic review. *Eura Medicophys.* 2007; 43(4): 475–85.

91. Bailey CD, Wagland R, Dabbour R, et al. An integrative review of systematic reviews related to the management of breathlessness in respiratory illnesses. *BMC Pulm Med.* 2010; 10: 63. doi: 10.1186/1471-2466-10-63

92. Cesario A, Dall'Armi V, Cusumano G, et al. Postoperative pulmonary rehabilitation after lung resection for NSCLC: a follow-up study. *Lung Cancer.* 2009; 66: 268–9.

93. Glattki GP, Manika K, Sichletidis L, Alexe G, Brenke R, Spyratos D. Pulmonary rehabilitation in non-small cell lung cancer patients after completion of treatment. *Am J Clin Oncol.* 2012; 35(2): 120–5. doi: 10.1097/COC.0b013e318209ced7

94. Li XH, Zhu JL, Hong C, Zeng L, Deng LM, Jin LY. Effects of systematic rehabilitation programs on quality of life in patients undergoing lung resection. *Mol Clin Oncol.* 2013; 1(1): 200–8.

95. Koelwyn GJ, Jones LW, Hornsby W, Eves ND. Exercise therapy in the management of dyspnea in patients with cancer. *Curr Opin Support Palliat Care.* 2012; 6(2): 129–37. doi: 10.1097/SPC.0b013e32835391dc

96. Rueda JR, Solà I, Pascual A, Subirana Casacuberta M. Non-invasive interventions for improving well-being and quality of life in patients with lung cancer. *Cochrane Database Syst Rev.* 2011; 9: CD004282. doi: 10.1002/14651858.CD004282.pub3

97. Chan CW, Richardson A, Richardson J. Managing symptoms in patients with advanced lung cancer during radiotherapy: results of a psychoeducational randomized controlled trial. *J Pain Symptom Manage.* 2011; 41(2): 347–57. doi: 10.1016/j.jpainsymman.2010.04.024

98. Nguyen HQ, Donesky D, Reinke LF, et al. Internet-based dyspnea self-management support for patients with chronic obstructive pulmonary disease. *J Pain Symptom Manage.* 2013; 46(1): 43–55.

99. Howard C, Dupont S, Haselden B, Lynch J, Wills P. The effectiveness of a group cognitive-behavioural breathlessness intervention on health status, mood and hospital admissions in elderly patients with chronic obstructive pulmonary disease. *Psychol Health Med.* 2010; 15(4): 371–85. doi: 10.1080/13548506.2010.482142

100. Farquhar M, Higginson IJ, Fagan P, Booth S. Results of a pilot investigation into a complex intervention for breathlessness in advanced chronic obstructive pulmonary disease (COPD): brief report. *Palliat Support Care.* 2010; 8:143–9. doi: 10.1017/S1478951509990897

101. Booth S, Moffat C, Farquhar M, Higginson IJ, Burkin J. Developing a breathlessness intervention service for patients with palliative and supportive care needs irrespective of diagnosis. *J Palliat Care.* 2011; 27(1): 28–36.

102. Galbraith S, Fagan P, Perkins P, Lynch A, Booth S. Does the use of a handheld fan improve chronic dyspnea? A randomized, controlled crossover trial. *J Pain Symptom Manage.* 2010; 39(5): 831–8. doi: 10.1016/j.jpainsymman.2009.09.024

103. Towler P, Molassiotis A, Brearley SG. What is the evidence for the use of acupuncture as an intervention for symptom management in cancer supportive and palliative care: an integrative overview of reviews. *Support Care Cancer.* 2013; 21: 2913–23. doi:10.1007/s00520-013-1882-8

104. Suzuki M, Muro S, Ando Y, et al. A randomized, placebo-controlled trial of acupuncture in patients with chronic obstructive pulmonary disease (COPD): the COPD-acupuncture trial (CAT). *Arch Intern Med.* 2012; 172(11): 878–86.

105. Hernandez P. What nonopioid treatments should be used to manage dyspnea associated with chronic obstructive pulmonary disease? In: Goldstein NE, Morrison RS, eds. *Evidence-Based Practice of Palliative Medicine.* Philadelphia, PA: Elsevier; 2013:120–5.

106. Abernethy AP, Kamal A, Maguire JM, Currow D. What interventions are effective for managing dyspnea in cancer? In: Goldstein NE, Morrison RS, eds. *Evidence-Based Practice of Palliative Medicine.* Philadelphia, PA: Elsevier; 2013:103–10.

107. Malik FA, Gysels M, Higginson IJ. Living with breathlessness: a survey of caregivers of breathless patients with lung cancer or heart failure. *Palliat Med.* 2013; 27(7): 647–56.

CHAPTER 25

Bowel Symptoms
Constipation, Diarrhea, and Obstruction

Kimberly Chow and Lauren Koranteng

Key Points

- Constipation, diarrhea, and malignant bowel obstruction are highly prevalent and distressful symptoms in advanced illness.

- The palliative advanced practice registered nurse (APRN) plays a vital role in assessing, treating, educating, and supporting patients and families with a high symptom burden from bowel dysfunction throughout the disease trajectory.

- Bowel symptoms do not occur in isolation from other symptoms, and proper management requires a global understanding of the patient's experience.

Case Study

MA was a 41-year-old female diagnosed with metastatic ovarian carcinoma status post multiple lines of chemotherapy with periods of disease stability mixed with progression. Throughout treatment, her complaints of abdominal pain gradually worsened, requiring initiation and titration of opioid therapy. Although her pain improved, her appetite and activity level began decreasing. Rather than her usual bowel movement every other day, MA began waiting 5 or 6 days; she attributed this to her decreased oral intake. One evening, she woke up with severe abdominal pain and distention. She was admitted for symptom management and further workup. MA's oncologist recommended a palliative care consult to assist with symptom management and psychosocial support.

The palliative APRN met with MA for an initial assessment and discussed her treatment course up until this admission, her "normal" bowel patterns prior to diagnosis, her activity level at home, her daily oral intake of food and fluids, and her medications. MA was married with two sons, age 7 and 10, and spent her days caring for her family; this is what brought her the most joy.

On medication review, the APRN learned that MA's opioid regimen had nearly tripled over the past month, without any corresponding changes in her bowel regimen of a stool softener and stimulant laxative. On physical examination, her abdomen was soft, mildly tender, and distended, with hypoactive bowel sounds.

Abdominal x-ray revealed stool throughout the colon without evidence of obstruction. Her bowel regimen was titrated to achieve bowel movements and she was discharged home.

MA required two additional admissions for pain, this time with nausea and vomiting. On her third admission, her abdominal exam revealed increased distention, pain on light palpation, significant ascites, and hyperactive bowel sounds with borborygmi, and she was found to have a complete small bowel obstruction. The palliative APRN recommended nasogastric tube placement for symptom relief, intravenous opioid therapy, and haloperidol for nausea. The oncology team, the APRN, and a social worker met with MA and her husband to discuss potential interventions. After hearing the risks of surgery with little promise of benefit, MA and her husband requested gastrostomy tube placement for symptom relief and return home with hospice as soon as possible to spend her remaining time with her family.

Introduction

This chapter discusses three common bowel symptoms that are highly prevalent and distressful for palliative care patients: constipation, diarrhea, and obstruction. These symptoms rarely occur in isolation from other clinical manifestations of disease and can affect a person's quality of life and eligibility for treatment; they may even be life-threatening. The APRN must approach care with a global understanding of the patient's individual needs, primary illness, disease-related complications, and past and current treatments.[1] Assessment and management are always provided with respect for the patient's culture, privacy, and goals of care.

Constipation

Constipation remains a largely subjective symptom that is often quantified by individuals based on what they perceive to be their normal bowel function.[2,3] Four suggested domains for diagnosis are (1) life-long history of constipation using the Rome Criteria; (2) clinical changes causing or exacerbating constipation;

(3) subjective symptoms, including bloating or incomplete defecation; and (4) objective changes, such as frequency and consistency of stools.[4] Constipation is a highly distressing symptom for patients, families, and providers and can lead to a multitude of physical signs and symptoms, including anorexia, nausea, vomiting, abdominal pain, distention, and obstruction.[5-7]

The American Gastroenterology Association defines constipation as, "difficult or infrequent passage of stool, at times associated with straining or a feeling of incomplete defecation."[8,9] The identification and the management of constipation in palliative care have historically been complicated by the lack of a universal definition as well as disparities between patient and provider opinions.[2-4]

Incidence

Constipation affects approximately 14% of the general population worldwide and 27% to 30% of people in North America.[8,10] Incidence increases in the palliative care population and has been reported in 30% to 100% of patients.[5,11,12] An estimated 72% to 87% of patients on opioid therapy will report constipation at some point during treatment.[2] Despite its high prevalence in acute and chronic illness, constipation often remains underrecognized, underreported, and undertreated by providers at every level, with the consequence of unnecessary hospital admissions, distress, and anxiety.[2,11]

Pathophysiology

Potential causes of constipation may be related to structure, disease, or personal factors and are grouped into primary or secondary causes.[12-15] Primary (e.g., idiopathic or functional) constipation occurs without an identifiable underlying cause.[8,9,14] Gastrointestinal motility is often intact, with reports of difficulty evacuating, hard stools, or dysfunction of the pelvic floor muscles or anal sphincter.[8]

Secondary causes of constipation (Box 25.1) are the result of medications, personal factors, or disorders that may be structural, metabolic, or neurologic in nature. In advanced illness, constipation is often multifactorial from decreased activity, anorexia, polypharmacy, older age, side effects of disease and treatment, and psychological effects of disease. Current recommendations support treating the multiple contributing factors rather than

single risk factors, and the APRN should be aware of the common etiologies.[7,10]

Assessment

A subjective assessment requires a thorough history of current and past bowel patterns.[16] The APRN should document stool volume, frequency, and appearance, along with the presence of accompanying symptoms, such as flatus, nausea, vomiting, and anorexia.

The APRN may want to consider the elements of the Constipation Assessment Scale (CAS), a quick, reliable, and validated tool commonly used in palliative care. It assesses for eight symptoms that measure the severity of constipation: (1) abdominal distention or bloating; (2) change in amount of gas passed rectally; (3) less frequent bowel movements; (4) oozing liquid stool; (5) rectal fullness or pressure; (6) rectal pain with bowel movements; (7) smaller stool size; and (8) urge, but inability to pass stool.[1,12,18,19] Medication reconciliation can help the APRN to identify common medications (Table 25.1) that may contribute to constipation.

When conducting a physical exam, the APRN should always be mindful of privacy and cultural sensitivity.[1,16] Assessment includes looking for oral lesions and thrush, which can affect diet and nutrition. The abdomen should be assessed for bowel sounds, distention, tenderness, and organomegaly. Fecal masses may be palpable on rectal exam.[15] Unless the patient is immunocompromised, rectal exams help rule out fecal impaction, impaired sphincter tone, anal fissures, tumor, and/or hemorrhoids.[1]

Further workup of constipation should be dictated by life expectancy (Box 25.2).[22] For palliative care patients, extensive imaging and bloodwork may be costly and provide little benefit. Results

---

Box 25.1 Secondary Causes of Constipation

- Medications (e.g., opioids, anticholinergics)
- Personal factors (e.g., time, privacy, diet, activity, fluid intake)
- Endocrine/metabolic disorders (e.g., diabetes, hypercalcemia, hypothyroidism)
- Cancer-related (e.g., tumor obstruction, spinal cord compression, electrolyte imbalances, cerebral tumors)
- Neurologic disease (e.g., cerebrovascular disease, Parkinson's disease)
- Psychological disorders (e.g., anxiety, depression, somatization)

From references 7, 8, 10, 12, 16, 17.

Table 25.1 Drugs/Drug Classes Associated with Constipation

Drugs/Drug Class	Examples
Antacids	Calcium carbonate
Anticonvulsants	Carbamazepine, Oxcarbazepine, Phenobarbital
Antidepressants	Amitriptyline, doxepin
Antihistamines	Diphenhydramine
Antiparkinsonian agents	Benztropine, bromocriptine
Barium sulfate	
Calcium channel antagonists	Verapamil
Cholestyramine	
Clonidine	
Diuretics	Furosemide, hydrochlorothiazide
Nonsteroidal anti-inflammatory agents	Ibuprofen, naproxen
Opioids	Morphine, hydromorphone
Serotonin receptor antagonists	Ondansetron, granisetron
Phenothiazines	Promethazine
Polystyrene sodium sulfonate	
Vinca alkaloids	Vincristine

From references 12, 15, 20, 21.

Box 25.2 Differential Diagnosis of Constipation

- Psychological disorders (e.g., anxiety, depression)
- Irritable bowel syndrome
- Colonic obstruction (e.g., malignant, nonmalignant)
- Surgical adhesions
- Electrolyte imbalance
- Ileus
- Spinal cord compression

From references 15, 20.

Table 25.3 Options for Prophylactic Management of Constipation

Start with a basic regimen based on the patient's status and preference and titrate to effect.

Patients on opioid therapy should be on constipation prophylaxis unless contraindicated:

Option 1	Senna 17.2 mg at bedtime or 17.2 mg oral (PO) twice daily if taking opioids.
	Consider stool softener: docusate 100 mg PO twice daily if indicated.
Option 2	Polyethylene glycol 17 g PO once daily
Option 3	Lactulose 30 mL PO once or twice daily
Option 4	Bisacodyl 1 tablet PO once daily

From references 21, 25, 26.

may lead to unintentional findings that can complicate the clinical picture and prolong the hospital stay. Thus, workup should match the patient's goals of care. Table 25.2 lists laboratory studies and radiologic imaging to consider.[16,18]

Management

Pharmacologic Management

Optimal pharmacologic management of constipation involves a combination of effective and appropriate prophylactic and treatment doses.[6,23] Table 25.3 offers prophylactic options to consider. The choice of agents is influenced by factors like cost, patient preference, availability, and side effects.

New studies on constipation in advanced disease have emerged. A recent prospective randomized controlled trial demonstrated that docusate plus sennosides was no more efficacious than sennosides alone in managing constipation in hospice patients. The trial was performed over 10 days and showed no difference in terms of number of bowel movements per day, difficulty evacuating bowels, and completeness of evacuating bowels; however, the docusate group did note softer stools.[24] While findings are promising and may potentially lead to a decreased pill burden for palliative care patients, results should be used in combination with clinical judgment.

Table 25.4 lists the various classes of laxatives and bowel preparations, initial and maximum daily doses, and special considerations for the APRN. The APRN must also be aware of safe prescribing techniques and complexities in medication use (Table 25.5).

Nonpharmacologic Interventions

A nonpharmacologic approach is a key part of the care plan and takes into account personal factors that promote optimal bowel

Table 25.2 Additional Constipation Assessment Measures

Laboratory Workup	Radiologic Exam
• Complete blood count (CBC)	Abdominal radiograph (x-ray)
• Thyroid-stimulating hormone (TSH)	• Rule out obstruction
• Calcium (Ca)	• Differentiate between stool and tumor
• Serum creatinine (Cr)	• Provides very little definitive information

From references 11, 15, 20.

function. Examples include routine upright positioning, increasing activity, and an effective combination of fiber and fluid intake when appropriate.[1,12] Toileting should allow privacy and ample time.[16] Unless completion of assessment is urgent, the APRN should not interrupt the patient's toileting to complete assessment.

Management Interventional Techniques

Disimpaction can cause severe pain, so proper premedication should be provided.[16] Aside from manual disimpaction, the next intervention to relieve severe constipation would be surgery.

Patient and Family Education

Participating in his or her own plan of care can be extremely helpful to ensure compliance and empowers the patient to detect changes and communicate them to the care team. Education on the nonpharmacologic interventions mentioned here should be reviewed, and caregivers should also be educated about the physical, psychological, and social impact that constipation can have on the patient. Patients and caregivers should be educated on proper bowel prophylaxis and signs of constipation to report. They can benefit from being aware of, and participating in, self-care activities, increasing physical activity, and keeping food diaries.

Diarrhea

Diarrhea has commonly been classified as an increase in stool frequency and liquidity; for the majority of the general population, it is self-limited and does not require medical attention.[20] The objective definition is the passage of three or more unformed stools within a 24-hour period.[34] Acute diarrhea occurs within 24 to 48 hours of exposure to the offending agent or event and usually subsides within 1 to 2 weeks.[12,20,35] Most cases have a short duration and are infectious in nature. Onset of chronic diarrhea may not occur immediately and can persist for over 30 days.[35] While significantly less prevalent than constipation in the palliative care population, diarrhea is a highly distressing symptom, with both physical and psychosocial effects. The goal of management is to determine and treat the underlying etiology while simultaneously providing supportive care.

Subjectively, patients may describe any change in stool frequency, volume, or consistency as diarrhea; this should be clarified. When bowel movements are intense and variable, patients

Table 25.4 Medications for Constipation

Generic Name (*Brand Name*)	Initial Dose (Init)	Comments
Bulk-Forming Agents—Absorb liquid in the GI tract and increase the bulk consistency of stool. *Not recommended if unable to tolerate large volume of liquids.*		
Psyllium (*Metamucil*)	*Init*: 2.5 g PO 1–3 times daily	◆ Drink with 8 ounces of liquid. ◆ Separate dose by at least 2 hrs from other medications. ◆ Onset of action: 12–72 hrs
Methylcellulose (*Citrucel*)	*Init*: 2 g 1–3 times daily as needed *MDD*: 6 g	◆ Use caution in dehydrated patients. ◆ Onset of action: 24–48 hrs
Stimulant Laxatives— Stimulate myenteric plexus and initiate peristaltic activity and inhibit water absorption		
Senna (*Senokot*)	*Init*: 17.2 mg PO at bedtime *MDD*: 68.8 mg	◆ Previously used in combination with docusate ◆ May cause cramping ◆ Onset of action: 6–12 hrs
Bisacodyl (*Dulcolax*)	*Init*: 5 mg PO *or* 1 suppository *or* enema (10 mg) PR once daily *MDD*: 15 mg PO	◆ May cause cramping ◆ Onset of action: 6–8 hrs (oral); 0.25–1 hr after rectal administration
Castor oil (*Emulsoil*)	*Init*: 15–60 mL PO once daily as needed *MDD*: 60 mL	◆ May cause cramping ◆ Onset of action: 2–6 hrs
Surfactant/Detergent Laxatives—Lower surface tension of stool to allow mixing of aqueous and fatty substances; alter intestinal mucosal permeability		
Docusate salts (*Colace*)	*Init*: 50–300 mg PO in single or divided doses *MDD*: 240 mg PO for docusate calcium; 360 mg PO for docusate sodium	◆ Onset of action: 24–72 hrs ◆ New study suggests no significant benefit of docusate with sennosides and to consider use on an individual basis.
Osmotic Laxatives—Cause fluid retention, distending the colon to increase peristalsis		
Lactulose (*Kristalose, Chronulac, Constulose, Enulose*)	*Init*: 15–30 mL once daily *MDD*: variable	◆ Mix with beverage to improve flavor ◆ Costly ◆ May cause flatulence and cramping ◆ Onset of action: 24–48 hrs
Sorbitol	*Init*: 30–45 mL (27–40 g) PO once daily *MDD*: 45 mL PO; 120 mL PR	◆ Less expensive than lactulose ◆ May cause abdominal pain, cramping, and diarrhea ◆ Onset of action: 0.25–1 hr
Magnesium citrate (*Citroma*)	*Init*: 150–300 mL PO as a single or divided dose *MDD*: 300 mL PO as a laxative	◆ Chill to improve taste ◆ May cause cramping ◆ Onset of action: 3–6 hrs
Magnesium hydroxide (*Milk of Magnesia*)	*Init*: 15–60 mL PO daily, preferably at bedtime *MDD*: 60 mL	◆ May dilute with water prior to administration ◆ Onset of action: 0.5–8 hrs
Magnesium sulfate (*Epsom Salt*)	*Init*: 10–30 g PO as single or divided doses *MDD*: NA	◆ Dissolve in a full glass of water prior to intake; may use lemon juice for taste ◆ Onset of action: 3–6 hrs
Polyethylene glycol (*Miralax*)	*Init*: 17 g daily *MDD*: 34 g PO daily	◆ Mix with 8 ounces of water, juice, coffee, or tea, ◆ Onset of action: 24–96 hrs
Lubricant Laxatives—Penetrate and soften stool and interfere with reabsorption of water in the colon		
Mineral oil (*Fleet Mineral Oil*)	*Init*: 45 mL PR as single dose *MDD*: 45 mL	◆ Avoid oral formulation due to risk of lipid pneumonitis. ◆ Adverse effects: mild abdominal pain, fecal urgency, cramps ◆ Onset of action: within 0.25 hr
Other Agents		
Linaclotide (*Linzess*)	*Init*: 145 mcg PO once daily *MDD*: 290 mcg	◆ Take on empty stomach at least 0.5 hr before the first meal of the day. ◆ May cause diarrhea

(continued)

Table 25.4 (Continued)

Generic Name (*Brand Name*)	Initial Dose (Init)	Comments
Lubiprostone (*Amitiza*)	*Init:* 24 mcg PO twice daily *MDD:* 48 mcg	◆ May experience nausea, diarrhea, headache, abdominal pain, distention, flatulence ◆ Take with food and water.
Methylnaltrexone (*Relistor*)	*Init:* Administered SC based on weight: <38 kg: 0.15 mg/kg/day 38 to <62 kg: 8 mg/day 62–114 kg: 12 mg/day	◆ For opioid-induced constipation ◆ High cost of administration ◆ Onset of action: 0.5–1 hr

MDD = maximum daily dose

From references 2, 12, 21, 25–32.

may have discomfort and anxiety and experience social isolation. Uncontrolled, persistent diarrhea can cause increased weakness, malnutrition, dehydration, and electrolyte imbalances that may be debilitating and even life-threatening. In patients continuing to receive active treatment, severity of symptoms may result in dose reduction or even discontinuation of disease-targeted therapies. The APRN should be mindful of treatments that commonly cause diarrhea in order to provide prompt evaluation and intervention.

Incidence

The incidence of diarrhea varies in developed versus developing countries based on access to evaluation and treatment.[8] In the palliative care population, the incidence also varies by disease and treatment modalities. In HIV-positive patients, diarrhea has been reported in 6% to 54% of the population as early as diagnosis.[36] In older, frail adults, approximately 10% to 60% of patients receiving enteral feedings will suffer from diarrhea.[34]

Diarrhea occurs frequently throughout the cancer treatment trajectory. The incidence and the severity of chemotherapy-induced diarrhea vary based on the agent and dose, with rates as high as 50% to 80% with certain regimens.[37] Radiation to the abdominal or pelvic fields has been associated with diarrhea of any level in up to 70% of patients, with more severe cases seen in 20% of this population.[12,15,35] Diarrhea also affects approximately 7% to 10% of cancer patients admitted to hospice.[9,12,37]

Pathophysiology

The pathophysiology of diarrhea is described by the specific cause or causes of increased stool water content and output. Potential

Table 25.5 Special Considerations for Constipation

Safe Prescribing	Complex Medication Use
◆ Individual bowel regimens are based on careful assessment and monitoring.	◆ Cost of medication versus pill burden should be considered and discussed.
◆ Assess for obstruction prior to initiating bowel stimulants.	◆ Estimated $800 million per year is spent on nonprescription laxatives.
◆ Use caution with over-the-counter medications as they may be contraindicated or duplicates of an already prescribed regimen.	◆ Improper use of enemas and suppositories may lead to bleeding, infection, electrolyte imbalance, and other adverse effects.

From references 8, 16, 33.

causes are listed in Table 25.6 and include increased fluid secretion, decreased fluid absorption, or bowel hypermotility.[12,20]

Assessment

A careful history and assessment are crucial. The APRN should assess the frequency, appearance, and number of stools and temporal correlation with medications, treatment, or meals. Secondary effects of diarrhea, such as fatigue, weakness, abdominal pain or cramping, dehydration, dizziness, weight loss, and skin breakdown, should also be identified. Constipation with a sudden onset of diarrhea is suspicious for fecal impaction or obstruction with overflow diarrhea.[12,15] Medications should be reviewed for offending agents, such as laxatives, antibiotics, and chemotherapeutic agents.[9,20]

The APRN should assess for signs of dehydration, including dry oral mucosa, skin appearance, and changes in mental status, secondary to severe diarrhea. The physical assessment includes looking for oral candidiasis, hyperactive or hypoactive bowel sounds, abdominal distention, and tenderness. A rectal examination is performed if there is concern for fecal impaction.[15]

Additional testing may include stool specimen examination for pus, blood, fat, ova, or parasites as appropriate. Cultures and

Table 25.6 Pathophysiology of Diarrhea

Type	Causes
Increased fluid secretion (most difficult to control and often not preventable)	◆ Inflammation ◆ Hormones ◆ Enterotoxins ◆ Chemotherapy, radiotherapy
Decreased fluid absorption	◆ Medications (e.g., antibiotics) ◆ Hyperosmolar preparations/enteral feedings ◆ Laxative overuse ◆ Dietary: high-sorbitol diet, lactose intolerance ◆ Fistulas
Bowel hypermotility	◆ Gastrointestinal malignancies ◆ Adhesions, fistulas ◆ Biliary/pancreatic or bowel obstructions ◆ Chemotherapy

From references 12, 20.

sensitivity testing can rule out opportunistic infections, such as *Clostridium difficile* or other gastrointestinal infections.[12] An evaluation for electrolyte imbalance should be considered. If obstruction is suspected, an abdominal x-ray may be indicated[15] (Box 25.3).

Management

Management first considers treatment of the underlying cause. If this does not lead to resolution of diarrhea, symptom management to thicken stool and slow peristalsis may be necessary. Adequate hydration should be ensured and modification of medications or dietary factors should be considered.[35]

Pharmacologic Management

Identifying the cause of diarrhea guides pharmacotherapy. Treatment for specific causes of diarrhea includes pancreatic enzymes for steatorrhea or pancreatic insufficiency; cholestyramine for excess fecal bile acids or radiation-associated diarrhea; histamine antagonists for carcinoid syndrome; antibiotics; and mesalazine for ulcerative colitis.[15] Various nonspecific medications (Table 25.7) can be used for the general treatment of diarrhea and unless contraindicated, may help control the extent of symptoms (Table 25.8).

Nonpharmacologic Interventions

Nonpharmacologic interventions begin with dietary modifications, including a focus on oral rehydration, as tolerated. Bowel rest or consuming clear liquids and simple carbohydrates can often give the gastrointestinal tract a much-needed rest. Proactive management should be provided for patients undergoing treatments highly associated with diarrhea. Keeping a food log to help determine any food sensitivities is encouraged. Common products that are irritating to normal bowel function are dairy products, caffeine, and high-fiber, spicy, and high-fat foods.[15]

Management Interventional Techniques

For patients with limited mobility, fecal incontinence and persistent diarrhea in the acute care setting may warrant consideration

---

Box 25.3 Differential Diagnosis of Diarrhea

- Viral (e.g., noroviruses, rotaviruses)
- Bacterial (e.g., *Salmonella, Shigella, Escherichia coli, Listeria, Clostridium*)
- Protozoal (e.g., *Giardia lamblia, Cryptosporidium*)
- Medication (e.g., antibiotics, magnesium-containing agents, laxatives, chemotherapy)
- Inflammation (e.g., ulcerative colitis, Crohn's disease)
- Functional (e.g., irritable bowel syndrome, diverticulosis, anxiety)
- Malabsorption syndromes (e.g., sprue, pancreatic insufficiency, lactase deficiency)
- Treatment-related (e.g., post-gastrectomy dumping syndrome, fistulas)

From references 12, 15, 38.

---

of rectal catheter placement to divert stool away from both impaired and healthy skin. Patients on anticoagulation and antiplatelet therapy have an increased risk of gastrointestinal hemorrhage with rectal tubes and should be monitored closely.[45] The APRN should advocate for appropriate treatments that are in line with the patient's goals of care and improve quality of life as defined by the patient.

Patient and Family Education

Persistent diarrhea can be quite debilitating and distressing for patients and their families. Implementing changes in the home environment may help the patient feel more secure and comfortable. The goal is to minimize or prevent accidents by attempting to plan and time activities based on predictable bowel patterns. Access to the bathroom be unobstructed, and the availability of a commode may be helpful and reduce the risk of injury. Beds can be protected with padding, which may be more dignified for the patient compared to wearing diapers. Meticulous skin and perineal care is essential and should be emphasized to patients and caregivers. Application of skin ointment may help with irritation, and odor management with aromatherapy may be soothing for the patient.

Bowel Obstruction

Incidence/Definition

A malignant bowel obstruction is defined as an obstruction beyond the ligament of Treitz that is related to an intra-abdominal primary cancer with incurable disease or from a non–intra-abdominal primary cancer with clear intraperitoneal disease.[12,46,47] Malignant bowel obstruction occurs in approximately 5% to 51% of women with ovarian cancer and 10% to 20% of patients with advanced gastrointestinal cancers. Depending on the type of malignancy, median survival after onset varies between 30 and 90 days; being aware of the median survival can aid in prognosticating and decision making.[47–49]

Pathophysiology

Malignant bowel obstruction can occur at single or multiple levels and can be classified as mechanical or functional, partial or complete.[48] It can affect bowel function significantly and is considered an oncologic emergency due to the risk of perforation, sepsis, or necrosis.

Intra-abdominal tumors may be intraluminal or intramural. They can impair bowel function by occluding the lumen, causing intussusception, or impairing peristalsis. Malignant adhesions can create multiple points of obstruction, as they kink the bowel from an extramural site.[46,48] Duodenal obstruction is most related to cholangiocarcinoma and pancreatic malignancies, while distal obstruction is largely associated with primary colon and ovarian carcinomas.[48] In rare cases, obstruction is treatment-related from nonmalignant adhesions following surgery or radiation.

Assessment

A combination of subjective and objective findings often aids in diagnosing the presence and level of obstruction. The APRN should understand the different characteristics of the location of the bowel obstruction. Duodenal obstruction presents with severe

Table 25.7 Pharmacologic Management of Diarrhea

Generic name (*Brand name*)	Initial Dose (Init)	Comments
Bulk-forming agents—Absorb liquid in the gastrointestinal tract and increase the bulk consistency of stool		
Methylcellulose (*Citrucel*)	*Init:* 2 g 1–3 times daily as needed *MDD:* 6 g	◆ Take with water to reduce risk of choking. ◆ Use caution in dehydrated patients. ◆ Onset of action: 24–48 hr
Cholestyramine (*Questran*)	*Init:* 2–4 g 2–4 times daily *MDD:* 24 g	◆ Bile acid-binding resin ◆ For chologenic diarrhea
Opioid agents—If cause of diarrhea is unknown and low suspicion for infection		
Codeine	*Init:* 10–60 mg PO 2–4 times daily *MDD:* Variable	◆ Avoid use in diarrhea caused by poison or bacteria.
Diphenoxylate/Atropine (*Lomotil*)	*Init:* 5 mg/0.05 mg (2 tablets) PO, then 1 tablet (2.5 mg/0.025 mg) after each loose stool *MDD:* 20 mg	◆ Avoid use in diarrhea caused by poison or bacteria. ◆ Onset of action: 0.75–1 hr
Loperamide (*Imodium*)	*Init:* 4 mg PO initially, followed by 2 mg after each unformed stool *MDD:* 16 mg	◆ Avoid use in diarrhea caused by poison or bacteria.
Opium tincture	*Init:* 50 mg/5 mL 0.6 mL (range: 0.3–1 mL per dose) PO 4 times a day *MDD:* 6 mL	◆ 25 times stronger than paregoric or camphorated tincture of opium ◆ Monitor stools. ◆ Do not abruptly discontinue after prolonged use.
Camphorated tincture of opium (paregoric)	*Init:* 2 mg/5 mL 5–10 mL PO 1–4 times daily *MDD:* N/A	◆ 1/25 the strength of opium tincture ◆ Monitor stools. ◆ Do not abruptly discontinue after prolonged use.
Adsorbents—Naturally occurring minerals that have adsorptive capacities		
Kaolin-pectin mixture (Kaopectate)	*Init:* 15–30 mL PO after each loose bowel movement *MDD:* 120 mL per 12 hrs	◆ May decrease the absorption of drugs that chelate with aluminum ◆ Onset of action: 24–48 hr
Polycarbophil (*Fiber-lax*)	*Init:* 1,000 mg PO 1–4 times daily *MDD:* 6.000 mg PO	◆ Some products may contain calcium. ◆ Onset of action: 12–72 hr
Salicylates—May have antisecretory, antimicrobial, and anti-inflammatory effects		
Bismuth subsalicylate (*Pepto-Bismol*)	*Init:* 524 mg PO every 30–60 minutes, as needed *MDD:* 4.2 g	◆ For nonspecific acute diarrhea ◆ Avoid in salicylate hypersensitivity. ◆ FDA approved for proctitis and ulcerative colitis ◆ May discolor stool
Somatostatin analogues—Inhibit diarrhea caused by hormone-secreting tumors of the pancreas and gastrointestinal tract		
Octreotide (*Sandostatin*)	*Init:* 300–600 mcg/day SC in 2–4 divided doses	◆ May cause diarrhea, abdominal pain, nausea, and drowsiness ◆ High cost of administration
Other agents		
Ranitidine (*Zantac*)	*Init:* 150 mg twice daily *MDD:* 300 mg	◆ May be given with pancrelipase ◆ Reduces gastric acidity
Pancrelipase (*Creon*)	*Init:* Dose varies by brand	◆ Individualize dose ◆ May be given with ranitidine or other H2 blocker
Vancomycin (*Vancocin*)	*Init:* 125 mg daily for 10 days	◆ Diarrhea due to *Clostridium difficile*
Metronidazole (*Flagyl*)	*Init:* 400 mg 3 times daily for 10–14 days	◆ Diarrhea due to *Clostridium difficile*
Cyproheptadine (*Periactin*)	*Init:* 4 mg 3 times daily	◆ Carcinoid syndrome diarrhea

MDD = maximum daily dose
From references 27, 39–44.

Table 25.8 Special Considerations for Diarrhea

Safe Prescribing	Complex Medication Use
◆ High-volume stool should not be masked with prescription or over-the-counter antidiarrheal agents.	◆ Cost of administration of treatment
◆ Severe diarrhea with rapid dehydration can lead to acute renal injury and, in extreme cases, shock. Further evaluation is imperative.	◆ Outpatient parenteral support may be necessary.
	◆ Cases of diarrhea accompanied by fever, nausea, vomiting, neutropenia, bleeding, or evidence of sepsis may require hospital admission.
◆ Send stool specimen prior to suppressing output with medications.	

From references 34, 35, 43.

vomiting and emesis often containing undigested food. Pain or distention will often not be noted on examination. Obstructions of the small and large intestine both present with hyperactive bowel sounds with borborygmi. Nausea and vomiting will be more severe with obstruction higher along the gastrointestinal tract, whereas obstructions of the large intestine will produce delayed emesis with abdominal distention and colicky pain.[12,47,48,50,51]

Radiologic imaging should be employed only if suspected findings can be treated. There tends to be an overreliance on abdominal x-rays, which are more cost-effective but less accurate than contrast radiographs.[48] Computed tomography (CT) scans remain the gold standard for diagnosis, with an accuracy of 94% in identifying the etiology of obstruction[12,47] (Box 25.4).

Management

Symptoms associated with malignant bowel obstruction have historically been difficult to manage, as nausea, vomiting, colic, and abdominal pains are quite persistent and bothersome. A number of medical and surgical interventions exist, but the best treatment remains undetermined and should always be based on the patient's goals of care, symptom burden, and prognosis.[12,46,48,52]

Pharmacologic Management

The goal of pharmacologic management in obstruction is to provide symptomatic relief while minimizing the adverse effects of medications. Treatment includes analgesics, antisecretory drugs, glucocorticoids, and antiemetics; individualized treatment is encouraged.[53,54] Pharmacologic management options are listed in Table 25.9 and may be the sole treatment or used for symptom relief while anticipating surgical interventions.

Box 25.4 Differential Diagnosis of Malignant Bowel Obstruction

◆ Ileus

◆ Pseudo-obstruction

◆ Ogilvie syndrome

◆ Intra-abdominal sepsis

From references 12, 15.

For persistent pain, opioid analgesics are recommended. APRNs should remember that opioids tend to exacerbate colicky pain and anticholinergic agents should be considered for pain relief.[53,55] Given the challenges with oral medications, parenteral, sublingual, and transdermal routes should be considered (Table 25.10).

Nonpharmacologic Interventions

During the workup and evaluation of potential treatment options, patients should avoid oral intake of food and fluids that may worsen symptoms and increase the risk of perforation with complete obstruction. The APRN may prefer a period of bowel rest to avoid unnecessary surgical interventions. Thirst and the desire for oral intake may be highly distressing, and support as well as meticulous mouth care should be provided.

Management Interventional Techniques

Multiple factors are associated with the selection of intervention, and several options exist. Surgical intervention in advanced cancer is controversial and is determined by performance status, extent of disease, level of obstruction(s), presence of ascites, and goals of care.[47,50,62] Patients with progressive cancer despite tumor-directed therapy pose the greatest risk for surgeons.[48,50] In advanced cancer, often the risk of surgery outweighs any potential benefit, which may be difficult for patients and families to understand and accept.

Endoscopic procedures, such as gastric or colonic stenting, present a less invasive option and have been associated with quicker recovery in patients with a single focus of obstruction or locally advanced disease.[48] Stenting is contraindicated in patients with already established perforation or for rectal tumors, as symptoms of tenesmus and incontinence may worsen.[48,63] Risks include stent migration and perforation.[47,62,63]

Management in patients with a poor prognosis, overt ascites, and carcinomatosis with multiple levels of obstruction is primarily supportive; placement of a venting gastrostomy tube can help to relieve symptoms. This may or may not allow the patient to tolerate some oral intake for pleasure and decreases pressure in the abdomen.[64] Nasogastric tubes are often used as a temporary bridge to surgery and can be quite uncomfortable. These tubes provide short-term symptomatic relief in patients who do not qualify for a gastrostomy tube due to severe ascites or tumor infiltration of the stomach.[48,52]

Patient and Family Education

Patients and caregivers should be taught about the signs and symptoms of obstruction early in the disease course, especially in gastrointestinal and gynecologic malignancies, where obstruction is highly prevalent.[49] Patients may feel that lack of bowel movements is expected in the setting of decreased food and fluid intake and may go weeks without reporting early or late signs of obstruction. Malignant bowel obstruction is often indicative of the late stages of disease, and access to psychoeducation and support for both patients and caregivers cannot be emphasized enough.

Conclusion

Bowel symptoms do not occur in isolation and are often accompanied by decreased appetite, fatigue, and general

Table 25.9 Pharmacologic Management of Obstruction

Generic name (*Brand Name*)	Initial Dose (Init)	Comments
Chlorpromazine (*Thorazine*)	*Init*: 10–25 mg q4–6h as needed *MDD*: 1,000 mg	◆ To control nausea and vomiting ◆ Sedating ◆ Monitor for extrapyramidal symptoms (EPS). ◆ Onset of action: 0.5–1 hr
Haloperidol (*Haldol*)	*Init*: 0.5–1 mg q12h or q4–6h as needed *MDD*: 100 mg PO	◆ To control nausea and vomiting ◆ Monitor for EPS. ◆ Onset of action: 0.5–1 hr
Metoclopramide (*Reglan*)	*Init*: 10 mg q6–8h *MDD*: 60 mg PO; single dose not to exceed 20 mg	◆ Prokinetic; avoid in definitive or complete obstruction ◆ May cause sedation, fatigue, and restlessness ◆ Onset of action: 0.5–1 hr
Prochlorperazine (*Compazine*)	*Init*: 10 mg PO q4–6h as needed *or* 25 mg PR q6–12h as needed *MDD*: 50 mg/day PR; 40 mg/day PO or IM	◆ EPS, especially at high doses ◆ Onset of action: 0.5–1 hr
Hyoscyamine (*Levsin*)	*Init*: 0.25–0.5 mg IV *or* SQ q6h as needed *or* 0.125–0.25 mg PO or SL q4h as needed *MDD*: 1.5 mg	◆ May cause blurred vision, confusion, constipation, dizziness, drowsiness, ileus, mydriasis, nausea/vomiting, nervousness, palpitations, sinus tachycardia, urinary retention/hesitancy, weakness ◆ Onset of action: IV: 2–3 minutes; PO: 20–30 minutes
Octreotide (*Sandostatin*)	*Init*: 50–100 mcg IV/SQ q8h *MDD*: Variable	◆ High cost of administration ◆ May cause diarrhea, abdominal pain, flatulence, nausea, constipation ◆ Onset of action: 0.5 hr
Scopolamine transdermal patch (*Transderm Scop*)	*Init*: 1.5 mg transdermal q72h; 0.3–0.6 mg IV *or* SQ q4h as needed *MDD*: 2.4 mg IV 1 transdermal patch q72h	◆ May cause drowsiness or somnolence ◆ Onset of action: transdermal, 4 hr; IV, 15–20 min
Dexamethasone (*Decadron*)	*Init*: 4 mg 1 or 2 times daily *MDD*: Variable	◆ Long-term use not recommended

From references 44, 53, 55, 57–60.

malaise. Patients may experience loss of dignity that can lead to social isolation if not addressed. Adequate support and education can empower patients to play an active role in their disease process and can help build trust between the patient, family, and APRN. The APRN must understand conditions, medications, and situations that induce bowel symptoms in order to provide appropriate care throughout the disease trajectory. Crafting an individualized plan of care tailored to specific patient needs is an essential piece of quality care and promotes quality of life.

Table 25.10 Special Considerations for Malignant Bowel Obstruction

Safe Prescribing	Complex Medication Use
◆ Agents that promote gastrointestinal motility should be avoided with complete obstruction and used cautiously with partial obstruction. ◆ Monitor patients on opioids and anticholinergics for side effects.	◆ Combination regimens can improve quality of life but often require inpatient admissions due to cost and lack of availability in the community. ◆ Patient's goals of care should be reviewed.

From references 35, 43, 55, 56, 61.

References

1. Librach SL, Bouvette M, De Angelis C, et al. Consensus recommendations for the management of constipation in patients with advanced, progressive illness. *J Pain Symptom Manage*. 2010; 40(5): 761–73.

2. Candy B, Jones L, Goodman ML, Drake R, Tookman A. Laxatives or methylnaltrexone for the management of constipation in palliative care patients. *Cochrane Database of Systematic Reviews*. 2011, Issue 1. Art. No.: CD003448. DOI: 10.1002/14651858.CD003448.pub3.

3. Clark K, Urban K, Currow DC. Current approaches to diagnosing and managing constipation in advanced cancer and palliative care. *J Palliat Med*. 2010; 13(4): 473–6.

4. Clark K, Currow DC. Constipation in palliative care: what do we use as definitions and outcome measures? *J Pain Symptom Manage*. 2013; 45(4): 753–62.

5. Strassels SA, Maxwell TL, Iyer S. Constipation in persons receiving hospice care. *J Pain Symptom Manage* .2010; 40(6): 810–20.

6. Ishihara M, Iihara H, Okayasu S, et al. Pharmaceutical interventions facilitate premedication and prevent opioid-induced constipation and emesis in cancer patients. *Support Care Cancer*. 2010; 18: 1531–8.

7. Davis MP. Cancer constipation: are opioids really the culprit? *Support Care Cancer*. 2008; 16: 427–9.

8. Fabel PH, Shealy KIM. Diarrhea, constipation and irritable bowel syndrome. In: DiPiro JT, Talbert RL, et al., eds. *Pharmacotherapy: A Pathophysiologic Approach*. 9th ed. USA: McGraw-Hill Education; 2014:531–47.

9. American Gastroenterological Association. Medical Position Statement on Constipation. Available at http://www.gastrojournal. org/article/S0016-5085(12)01545-4/fulltext#sec1. Updated March 4, 2014. Accessed August 12, 2014.

10. Clark K, Lam LT, Agar M, Chye R, Currow DC. The impact of opioids, anticholinergic medications and disease progression on the prescription of laxatives in hospitalized patients: a retrospective analysis. *Palliat Med.* 2010; 24(4): 410–8.

11. Clark K, Currow, DC. Assessing constipation in palliative care within a gastroenterology framework. *Palliat Med.* 2011; 26(6): 834–41.

12. Economou DC. Bowel management: constipation, diarrhea, obstruction, and ascites. In: Ferrell B, Coyle N, J Paice eds. *Oxford Textbook of Palliative Nursing.* 4th ed. New York: Oxford University Press; 2015:217–36.

13. Clark K, Smith JM, Currow DC. The prevalence of bowel problems reported in a palliative care population. *J Pain Symptom Manage.* 2012; 43(6): 993–1000.

14. Clemens KE, Faust M, Jaspers B, Mikus G. Pharmacological treatment of constipation in palliative care. *Supportive and Palliative Care.* 2013; 7(2): 183–91.

15. Sykes NP. Constipation and diarrhea. In: Walsh D, ed. *Palliative Medicine.* USA: Saunders Elsevier; 2009:846–54.

16. McHugh ME, Miller-Saultz D. Assessment and management of gastrointestinal symptoms in advanced illness. *Prim Care Clin Office Pract.* 2011; 38: 225–46.

17. Agar M, Currow D, Plummer J, et al. Changes in anticholinergic load from regular prescribed medications in palliative care as death approaches. *Palliat Med.* 2009; 23: 257–65.

18. Nagaviroj K, Chai Yong W, Fassbender K, Zhu G, Oneschuk D. Comparison of the constipation assessment scale and plain abdominal radiography in the assessment of constipation in advanced cancer patients. *J Pain Symptom Manage.* 2011; 42(2): 222–8.

19. McMillan SC, Williams FA. Validity and reliability of the constipation assessment scale. *Cancer Nurs.* 1989; 12(3): 183–8.

20. Richter JM. Approach to the patient with constipation. In: Goroll AH, Mulley AG, ed. *Primary Care Medicine.* 7th ed. Philadelphia, PA: Lippincott Williams & Wilkins; 2014:529–34.

21. Bharucha AE, Pemberton JH, Locke GR. 3rd American Gastroenterological Association technical review on constipation. *Gastroenterology.* 2013; 144: 218–38.

22. National Comprehensive Cancer Network. NCCN Clinical Practice Guidelines in Oncology: Palliative Care. Version 1.2015. Available at http://www.nccn.org/professionals/physician_gls/PDF/palliative.pdf. Accessed August 12, 2015.

23. Droney J, Ross J, Gretton S, et al. Constipation in cancer patients on morphine. *Support Care Cancer.* 2008; 16: 453–9.

24. Tarumi Y, Wilson M, Szafran O, Spooner G. Randomized, double-blind, placebo-controlled trial of oral docusate in the management of constipation in hospice patients. *J Pain Symptom Manage.* 2013; 45: 2–13.

25. Twycross R, Sykes N, Mihalyo M, Wilcock A. Stimulant laxatives and opioid-induced constipation. *J Pain Symptom Manage.* 2012; 43(2): 306–13.

26. Hurdon V, Viola R, Schroder C. How useful is docusate in patients at risk of constipation? A systematic review of the evidence in the chronically ill. *J Pain Symptom Manage.* 2000; 19: 130–6.

27. Gattuso JM, Kamm MA. Adverse effects of drugs used in the management of constipation and diarrhoea. *Drug Saf.* 1994; 10(1): 47–65.

28. Costilla VC, Foxx-Orenstein AE. Constipation: understanding mechanisms and management. *Clin Geriatr Med.* 2014; 30(1): 107–15.

29. Clausen MR, Mortensen PB. Lactulose, disaccharides and colonic flora. Clinical consequences. *Drugs.* 1997; 53: 930–42.

30. Agra Y, Sacristan A, Gonzalez M: Efficacy of senna versus lactulose in terminal cancer patients treated with opioids. *J Pain Symptom Manage.* 1998; 15: 1–7.

31. Wong BS, Camilleri M. Lubiprostone for the treatment of opioid-induced bowel dysfunction. *Expert Opin Pharmacother.* 2011; 12(6): 983–90.

32. Brick N. Laxatives or methylnaltrexone for the management of constipation in palliative care patients. *Clin J Oncol Nurs.* 2013; 17(1): 91–2.

33. Hjalte F, Berggren AC, Bergendahl H, Hjortsberg C. The direct and indirect costs of opioid-induced constipation. *J Pain Symptom Manage.* 2010; 40(5): 696–703.

34. Cherny NI. Evaluation and management of treatment-related diarrhea in patients with advanced cancer: a review. *J Pain Symptom Manage.* 2008; 36(4): 413–23.

35. von Gunten CF, Gafford E. Treatment of non-pain related symptoms. *Cancer J.* 2013; 19(5): 397–404.

36. Simms VM, Higginson IJ, Harding R. What palliative care-related problems do patients experience at HIV diagnosis? A systematic review of the evidence. *J Pain Symptom Manage.* 2011; 42(5): 734–53.

37. Shaw C, Taylor L. Treatment-related diarrhea in patients with cancer. *Clin J Oncol Nurs.* 2012; 16(4): 413–7.

38. Richter JM. Evaluation and management of diarrhea. In: Goroll AH, Mulley AG, ed. *Primary Care Medicine.* 7th ed. Philadelphia, PA: Lippincott Williams & Wilkins; 2014:517–28.

39. Phillips J. Kaopectate reformulation and upcoming labeling changes. *Drug Topics.* 2004; 148: 58.

40. Kent AJ, Banks MR. Pharmacological management of diarrhea. *Gastroenterol Clin North Am.* 2010; 39: 495–507.

41. Brunton LL, Chabner BA, Knollmann BC. *Goodman & Gilman's The Pharmacological Basis of Therapeutics*, 12th ed. China: The McGraw-Hill Companies; 2011. Available at http://accessmedicine. mhmedical.com/content.aspx?bookid=374&sectionid=41266200. Accessed July 4, 2014.

42. Prommer E. Role of codeine in palliative care. *J Opioid Manage.* 2011; 7(5): 401–6.

43. Craig DS. Constipation and diarrhea. In: Strickland JM, ed. *Palliative Pharmacy Care.* USA: American Society of Health-System Pharmacists, Inc.; 2009:115–25.

44. Mercadente S. The role of octreotide in palliative care. *J Pain Symptom Manage.* 1994; 9(6): 406–11.

45. Mulhall AM, Jindal SK. Massive gastrointestinal hemorrhage as a complication of the Flexi-Seal fecal management system. *Am J Crit Care.* 2013; 22(6): 537–43.

46. Wright FC, Chakraborty A, Helyer L, Moravan V, Selby D. Predictors of survival in patients with non-curative stage IV cancer and malignant bowel obstruction. *J Surg Oncol.* 2010; 101: 425–9.

47. Laval G, Marcelin-Benazech B, Guirimand F, et al. Recommendations for bowel obstructions with peritoneal carcinomatosis. *J Pain Symptom Manage.* 2014; 48(1): 75–91.

48. Soriano A, Davis MP. Malignant bowel obstruction: individualized treatment near the end of life. *Cleveland Clinic J Med.* 2011; 78(3): 197–206.

49. Lefkowits C, Binstrock AB, Courtney-Brooks, M, et al. Predictors of palliative care consultation on an inpatient gynecologic oncology service: are we following ASCO recommendations? *Gynecol Oncol.* 2014; 133: 319–25.

50. Olson TJP, Pinkerton C, Brasel KJ, Scwarze ML. Palliative surgery for malignant bowel obstruction from carcinomatosis. *JAMA Surg.* 2014; 149(4): 383–92.

51. Yeo HL, Lee SW. Colorectal emergencies: review and controversies in the management of large bowel obstruction. *J Gastrointest Surg.* 2013; 17: 2007–12.

52. Lynch M, Dahlin C, Bakitas M. Bowel obstruction and delirium: managing difficult symptoms at the end of life. *Clin J Oncol Nurs,* 2011; 16(4): 391–8.

53. Ripamonti, C. Twycross R, Baines M, et al. Clinical-practice recommendations for the management of bowel obstruction in patients with end-stage cancer. *Supportive Care in Cancer,* 2001; 9: 223–33.

54. Sykes N. Constipation and diarrhea. In: Hanks G, Cherny NI, Christakis NA, et al., eds. *Oxford Textbook of Palliative Medicine*. 4th ed. Oxford: Oxford University Press; 2010:833–50.

55. Ripamonti C, Mercadente S, Groff L, et al. Role of octreotide, scopolamine butylbromide, and hydration in symptom control of patients with inoperable bowel obstruction and nasogastric tubes: a prospective randomized trial. *J Pain Symptom Manage*. 2000; 19: 23–34.

56. Ripamonti C, Easson AM, Gerdes H. Management of malignant bowel obstruction. *Eur J Cancer*. 2008; 44(8): 1105–15.

57. Ripamonti C, Mercadente S. Pathophysiology and management of malignant bowel obstruction. In: Hanks G, Cherny NI, Christakis NA, et al., eds. *Oxford Textbook of Palliative Medicine*. 4th ed. Oxford, UK: Oxford University Press; 2010:850–63.

58. Laval, G. Girardier J, Lassauniere JM, et al. The use of steroids in the management of inoperable intestinal obstruction in terminal cancer patients: do they remove the obstruction? *Palliat Med*. 2000; 14: 3–10.

59. Tuca A, Guell E, Martinez-Losada E, Codorniu N. Malignant bowel obstruction in advanced cancer patients: epidemiology, management, and factors influencing spontaneous resolution. *Cancer Management and Research*. 2012; 4: 159–69.

60. Laval G, Rousselot H, Toussaint-Martel S, et al. SALTO: a randomized, multicenter study assessing octreotide LAR in inoperable bowel obstruction. *Bull Cancer*. 2012; 99: E1–E9.

61. Marukami H, Matsumoto H, Nakamura M, Hirai T, Yamaguchi Y. Octreotide acetate-steroid combination therapy for malignant gastrointestinal obstruction. *Anticancer Res*. 2013; 33: 5557–60.

62. Abbott S, Eglinton TW, Ma Y, et al. Predictors of outcome in palliative colonic stent placement for malignant obstruction. *Br J Surg*. 2014; 101: 121–6.

63. Alford T, Ghosh S, Wong C, Schiller D. Clinical outcomes of stenting for colorectal obstruction at a tertiary centre. *J Gastrointest Canc*. 2014; 45: 61–5.

64. Mori M, Bruera E, Dev R. Complications of a gastrostomy tube used for decompression of an inoperable bowel obstruction in a patient with advanced cancer. *J Pain Symptom Manage*. 2009; 38(3): 466–72.

CHAPTER 26

Anorexia and Cachexia

Robert Smeltz

Key Points

♦ Because cachexia and anorexia syndrome is present in most advanced chronic and life-limiting illnesses, the palliative advanced practice registered nurse (APRN) should be vigilant in assessing for its presence.

♦ Assessment of cachexia and anorexia syndrome requires subjective and objective measures and must take into account the multiple dimensions of the individual.

♦ Treatment of cachexia and anorexia syndrome requires a multimodal approach using pharmacologic and nonpharmacologic interventions, treating both physical and psychosocial symptoms.

Introduction

This chapter defines anorexia and cachexia and their interplay as a syndrome, as seen in most advanced stages of disease. The assessment of anorexia and cachexia is fundamental in establishing an effective treatment plan. A first step in treatment of cachexia and anorexia is setting goals and educating patients and families on the limits of reversing anorexia and cachexia in advanced disease. The use of a multimodal approach with pharmacologic and nonpharmacologic measures delivered by an interdisciplinary care team geared at treating the whole person is the key strategy to addressing cachexia and anorexia syndrome.

Cachexia is defined as a

multifactorial syndrome characterized by an ongoing loss of skeletal muscle mass (with or without loss of fat mass) that cannot be fully reversed by conventional nutritional support and leads to progressive functional impairment. The pathophysiology is characterized by a negative protein and energy balance driven by a variable combination of reduced food intake and abnormal metabolism.[1]

Anorexia in cancer and advanced chronic illness is a decrease in nutritional intake, often accompanied by a loss of appetite. Cachexia and anorexia are often seen together, and this is referred to as cachexia and anorexia syndrome (CAS). CAS is seen in cancer, heart disease, kidney failure, chronic lung diseases, and HIV/AIDS. Weakness, weight loss, and anorexia are seen in 60%, 53%, and 46% of patients with advanced cancer, respectively. The prevalence increases to 86%, 74%, and 56%, respectively, in the last 1 to 2 weeks of life in advanced cancer.[2] Cachexia is seen in 10.5% of patients with congestive heart failure.[3] Anorexia is seen in 15% to 30% of elderly persons in the community.[4]

CAS is a difficult symptom to treat and often becomes refractory toward the end-of-life. Most pharmaceuticals have limits in terms of efficacy and/or side effects. Dietary counseling seems like a logical choice with no adverse effects, but it is not clear that outcomes are improved. This chapter discusses the role of the palliative APRN in treating CAS. The pathophysiology of CAS, identifying underlying causes, and the importance of using a multimodal approach to treatment are outlined. A review of the psychosocial assessment and how CAS affects the patient and family is offered. Finally, strategies the palliative APRN can offer as part of education and support are described.

Palliative APRN Considerations

The palliative APRN plays an important role in assessment, diagnosis, and treatment of anorexia and cachexia. This includes coordinating the patient's interdisciplinary care, advocating for the patient, and educating the patient and family.[5] The palliative APRN can identify the goals of care in terms of how they relate to addressing CAS and can help the family understand what is realistic within the limits of the disease at its current point in the disease trajectory. The palliative APRN can help the family explore pharmacologic and nonpharmacologic treatment measures and identify a regimen that takes into account the patient's goals as well as caregiver burden.

Pathophysiology

CAS is produced by multiple factors, including decreased appetite, alterations in metabolism, and increased catabolism. The decrease in appetite is likely multifactorial as well, resulting from decreased drive to feed, early satiety, decreased intestinal motility, and nausea. Decreased food intake results in some of the weight loss but does not explain all of the wasting seen in CAS. There are also disturbances in metabolism resulting in loss of lean body mass and body fat.[6] This is evidenced by visceral organs not showing the signs of wasting in CAS that are seen in starvation.[7] Also, in CAS there is greater loss of lean body mass, unlike initial stages of starvation, where fat is lost.

CAS is believed to be caused, in part, by pro-inflammatory cytokines (interleukin [IL]-1, IL-2 and IL-6, interferon-gamma, and tumor necrosis factor-alpha [TNF-α]) in patients with cancer.[8] There are other peptides and pathways that influence appetite and catabolism, which could also be affected by cancer.

TNF appears to increase lipolysis in rat models, but its impact on patients with cancer in terms of weight loss and decreased appetite is not clear.[8] IL-6 is a pro-inflammatory cytokine, but like TNF and the other cytokines, it is difficult to understand the specific roles in CAS since there is overlap and redundancy. It is likely that the effects of several cytokines cause CAS, and inhibiting one cytokine has little to no effect on CAS.

Glucagon and other hormonal peptides and neuropeptides play a role in CAS. Specifically, glucagon administration has been shown to reduce food intake, and glucagonemia is associated with some cancers. Corticotropin-releasing factor (CRF) is seen in some cancers, and its presence decreases gastric emptying as well as food intake and appetite. There are several other neuropeptides that appear to affect feeding and weight, but their role in CAS and implications in the treatment of CAS are not known.[8]

Cancer cell metabolism may play a role in CAS. The uncontrolled metabolism and growth of cancer cells inhibit delivery of sufficient oxygen, which prevents creation of energy from the Krebs cycle; instead, the Cori cycle is used to create energy. This creates lactic acid, which needs to be processed in the liver, requiring further energy expenditure. This essentially helps to increase the resting energy expenditure.[7]

CAS is seen in several serious illnesses in addition to cancer. The process of aging likely contributes to CAS in the elderly population.[4] Gastric emptying is decreased in older patients.[9] Senses, including smell, taste, and sight, may be altered, which may have an impact on appetite. CAS in amyotrophic lateral sclerosis and dementia is not well understood. It is at least partially related to decreased mobility and decreased nutritional intake secondary to the progression of the neurologic disease.

CAS is also seen in advanced heart disease. Pro-inflammatory cytokines appear to be involved.[10] Decreased circulation to the intestines can decrease motility and absorption, which can further contribute to anorexia and cachexia, respectively. There is an increase in muscle protein breakdown.[11] Decreased insulin sensitivity could also play a role in CAS in patients with heart disease.[12]

Inflammatory responses appear to play a role in CAS in chronic obstructive pulmonary disease (COPD).[13] The increased work of breathing likely increases energy expenditure, contributing to CAS. Impaired oxidative capacity in COPD appears to alter protein turnover, worsening CAS further.[14]

Assessment

The goal of assessment is to identify the presence of cachexia, weight loss, and/or anorexia. The presence of cachexia is identified with weight loss disproportionate to, or without, anorexia. Reversible causes of anorexia and cachexia should be sought.

The assessment of anorexia and cachexia includes the patient's report of appetite, disturbances in taste and smell, early satiety, and nausea. Appetite can be assessed on a Likert scale.[15] There are screening tools, but most of them are not practical for daily clinical practice, like the Mini-Nutritional Assessment tool. The Simplified Nutritional Appetite Questionnaire is more practical clinically, but it lacks the sensitivity and specificity of the lengthier assessment tools.[16]

The patient's food intake should be assessed either through patient report or direct quantification of food eaten over a period of time.[1] The number of meals the patient eats per day and the size or the percentage of the meals eaten should be recorded. A variety of tools can be used. The patient can keep a food diary or use applications on computers or handheld devices for tracking food consumption, or healthcare providers can do a calorie count.

Secondary causes of reduced food intake should be assessed. These include pain, stomatitis, constipation, dyspnea, depression and anxiety, and poor dietary habits. More information on the assessment and treatment of these symptoms can be found throughout this textbook.

The patient's weight should be monitored. Fluid retention should be considered when evaluating weight changes. Muscle mass can be assessed through the mid-arm muscle area. Muscle strength can be assessed using handgrip, upper extremity, and lower extremity strength testing. More precise muscle strength can be achieved with upper-limb handgrip dynamometry.[17]

Laboratory tests and imaging can be used to measure nutritional status, inflammation, and body composition. Prealbumin is one of the better measures for assessing malnutrition. A low prealbumin level indicates low protein stores indicative of chronic anorexia. C-reactive protein (CRP) measures systemic inflammation, but cachexia can be present without an increase in CRP. Cross-sectional imaging (computed tomography [CT] or magnetic resonance imaging [MRI]), dual energy x-ray imaging (DEXA), anthropometry (mid-arm muscle area), and bioimpedance analysis are tests that can measure muscle mass. However, it is not clear how useful these tests are in treating CAS.[1]

The palliative APRN must assess the patient's functional status. This can be accomplished through patient report on activities or provider assessment using the Karnofsky scale, the Palliative Performance Scale, or similar measures. In addition, the psychosocial effects of anorexia and cachexia should be assessed.

Cachexia and Anorexia Management

Identifying the goals of care and how they relate to management of CAS is important. The palliative APRN can initiate a goals of care discussion, so that he or she can inform the patient and family what is realistic, within the limits of the disease. The patient and family may want to treat CAS to increase body mass, weight, and functional status or to improve appetite for the sake of the pleasure of eating, or they may be simply looking for a way to help the patient. An understanding of the natural progression of disease and the pharmacologic and nonpharmacologic measures (Table 26.1) to treat CAS will help when counseling the patient and family to clarify and meet their goals.

Pharmacologic Management

Megestrol acetate (MA) is a synthetic progestin used as an antineoplastic agent and to stimulate appetite.[18] The Cochrane Collaboration has done reviews of MA, the most recent in 2013.[19] The meta-analysis considered outcomes like weight gain, improved quality of life, increased appetite, increased body mass, adverse effects, and death in patients with cancer, AIDS, or COPD and the elderly. The analysis found an increase in appetite and modest weight gain compared to placebo, but there was also an increase in thromboembolic events and mortality. There was no improvement in quality of life. Currently, MA is the most effective

Table 26.1 CAS Management

	Intervention	Implementation	Comments
Pharmacologic	Megestrol	800 mg PO qd	Shown to improve appetite and weight. Increased risk of blood clots and increased mortality. Patients should be aware of this potential adverse effect before implementing.
	Dronabinol	Starting dose is 2.5 mg PO bid (qd in elderly).	Treats anorexia in HIV/AIDS, treats therapy-related nausea in cancer patients
	Glucocorticoids	Starting dose: 4 mg PO qd	Use of this regimen is limited due to side effects. Used often to treat anorexia and cachexia near the end-of-life.
Nonpharmacologic	Dietary counseling	Refer to dietitian in complex cases. Provide instruction to reduce size of meals but increase frequency.	No evidence that this will result in sustained weight gain or improved quality of life in advanced cancer patients. Patients with COPD did benefit from nutritional counseling in terms of increased oral intake, weight gain, and increased strength.
	Oral care	Oral hygiene can prevent oral infection. Keeping the mouth moist can improve mastication and prevent infection.	Low-risk and low-cost interventions

pharmaceutical for CAS, but patients should be aware of the side effects and limits of the drug before they start taking it.

The American Geriatric Society recommends avoiding MA in the elderly.[20] One study found improved appetite and weight gain (mostly adipose tissue) with the use of MA over placebo in the elderly.[21] This was a small, randomized, double-blind trial with 3 months of treatment and 3 months of follow-up without treatment and a 4-year survival analysis. Currently, MA is not recommended for patients with cardiac cachexia.[12]

The typical dosage of MA is 800 mg once a day, or 625 mg for the concentrated formulation.[18] Other doses have been studied and showed some benefit; there is increased weight gain with higher doses.[19] MA reaches peak plasma concentrations in 1 to 5 hours. It is metabolized by the liver and excreted by the kidneys and in the feces.

Dronabinol and other cannabinoids have been used to improve appetite in CAS resulting from multiple etiologies. Dronabinol, a synthetic cannabinoid, has been approved to treat anorexia related to HIV/AIDS.[22,23] There is no evidence to support the use of dronabinol and cannabinoids in CAS related to cancer,[24] but dronabinol is approved to treat cancer treatment-related nausea that is refractory to first-line antiemetics.[23]

The starting dose is 2.5 mg before lunch and supper; however, 2.5 mg once daily should be considered for geriatric patients and in patients who experience side effects with more frequent daily dosing. The maximum dosage is 20 mg per day in divided doses.[23] The most common side effects involve the central nervous system and include feeling high, somnolence, and confusion. The initial half-life is 4 hours, but the terminal elimination half-life is 25 to 36 hours. Steady-state plasma levels are reached in 2 weeks.[23]

Glucocorticoids have shown some efficacy in improving appetite and weight gain, but no better than MA and with a worse toxicity profile.[25] The toxicity may be limited if the drug is given for short periods of time; however, the beneficial effects wear off after the steroids are stopped.[25] Glucocorticoids may be a better intervention for patients near the end-of-life. Doses as low as 4 mg per day of dexamethasone were used.[26]

Mirtazapine is known to produce increased appetite and weight gain as a side effect.[27] Although it is being studied, there is currently insufficient evidence to support the clinical use of mirtazapine in treating CAS related to cancer or other chronic illnesses.[28] Nonsteroidal anti-inflammatory drugs (NSAIDs) have been studied for their effectiveness in managing CAS. The drugs studied include celecoxib, ibuprofen, and indomethacin. Currently there is insufficient evidence to recommend their use in clinical practice.[29]

Thalidomide is thought to work by anti-inflammatory mechanisms, blocking cytokines or cytokine production and thereby treating the underlying causes of cachexia. Insufficient evidence exists to support the use of thalidomide, and its use is not recommended due to toxicities in the absence of efficacy.[30]

There currently is insufficient evidence to support the efficacy of eicosapentaenoic acid (EPA), an omega-3 fatty acid, but early studies show promise.[31] Further research will need to be done to determine if EPA is effective. It is thought that EPA could inhibit tumor-induced lipolysis and muscle protein degradation by suppressing cytokines.

Ghrelin, a peripheral hormone that is secreted from the stomach, is being studied as a treatment for CAS. The release of ghrelin stimulates the release of growth hormone and stimulates orexigenic neurons in the hypothalamus, which is known to increase appetite. Ghrelin has been shown to increase appetite in healthy subjects.[32] It has shown benefit in patients with renal failure, heart failure, and COPD.[12,32,33] However, ghrelin is currently not approved by the U.S. Food and Drug Administration for any indication.

L-Carnitine given with celecoxib was compared with L-carnitine with celecoxib and MA. Both treatments were effective in increasing lean body mass and increasing physical daily activity. However, it was not compared to placebo, and the number of people finishing the study was less than 60.[34] Another study looked at five types of treatment, with over 300 patients enrolled. The only group that showed a statistically significant increase in lean body mass was the one taking a combined medication regimen, including L-carnitine, MA, EPA, and thalidomide.[35] Despite the problems of these studies, they suggest that multiple-drug regimens should be looked at more closely, but cannot yet be recommended for clinical practice.

Nonpharmacologic Management

Dietary counseling can play an important role in patients with anorexia and cachexia. Counseling has been shown to increase calorie intake in cancer patients in one study; however, the increase in weight did not reach statistical significance and appeared to be fat tissue.[36] Dietary counseling includes education on modifying familiar or favorite foods to match patients' changing tastes and needs, adding nutritional supplements, and decreasing the size and increasing the frequency of meals.

There is no conclusive evidence to support increased survival, significant weight gain, or improved quality of life with dietary counseling in cancer patients, but the risks are low and patients and families may value this kind of support. There is some evidence to support dietary counseling in patients with COPD. With therapy mainly in the form of nutritional supplements, patients with COPD experienced increased caloric intake, increased weight, and increased grip strength.[13]

Providing good oral care to reduce the risk of mucositis and oral mucosal infections can prevent these causes of decreased oral intake. This includes good oral hygiene. Patients at risk (those with reduced immunity, receiving radiation therapy, or receiving chemotherapy) or with mucositis should use a mouth rinse, like bicarbonate solution or chlorhexidine (alcohol-free) regularly. Using sucralfate-based saliva substitutes can provide needed moisture to the mouth to aid with mastication and prevent dryness. Using an antifungal or antibiotic agent in the presence of oral infection should be considered.

Exercise has shown some benefit in improving symptoms related to CAS.[37] More evidence is needed to make recommendations on the types and quantity that work best, but it is likely this could be tailored to the patient. It is important for patients to avoid exercise that causes pain or is too strenuous; safety is always the first consideration.

Artificial Enteral and Parenteral Feeding

Parenteral feeding should be used only if the patient's gastrointestinal tract is not functioning and the patient has a good prognosis.[5] Parenteral feeding is often used temporarily prior to treating the gut dysfunction. Patients with advanced cancer likely will not see benefit from parenteral feeding and are apt to have more complications.[38]

Patients with advanced cancer receiving enteral feeding did not show significant benefit either.[38] Tube feedings don't improve survival in patients with advanced dementia.[39] Artificial enteral feeding is often used in certain disease processes, such as severe dysphagia associated with stroke, when the patient's quality of life is acceptable and it meets his or her goals of care. Also, patients with head and neck cancers who have lost the ability to swallow as a result of the disease or treatment can benefit from enteral feeding through a percutaneous endoscopic gastrostomy (PEG) tube.

Multimodal Approach

CAS is a syndrome with multiple components contributing to the symptoms, so it is reasonable to suspect that multiple modes of treatment, including pharmacologic, nonpharmacologic, and psychosocial measures, will be needed to address the CAS.[40] There

are no good studies that would allow recommendations to be made for specific treatment regimens; however, available evidence suggests a trend that a multimodal approach could help.[40]

Identifying the patient's goals of care related to treating CAS is an initial step in using a multimodal approach. This will help tailor the interventions and will determine if using a pharmaceutical like MA is prudent. The goals will also inform the instructions provided during nutritional counseling. If patients want to maintain weight during disease-directed therapies, they should eat small meals several times a day, paying attention to the nutritional content of the food. However, if goals are geared toward comfort, instructing patients and families to focus on comfort feeding is important.

Existence of other symptoms and comorbidities will help to inform choices for a multimodal approach. For example, if patients are nauseated in addition to having CAS, antinausea agents with appetite-stimulating properties may be a wise choice. Patients who experience early satiety with nausea may benefit from metoclopramide. Patients with increased risk for thrombi should avoid MA. For patients who are depressed, mirtazapine may be considered.

Use of nutritional supplements like L-carnitine, EPA, protein, and vitamins should be explored with patients. There are few if any adverse reactions to these supplements, but caution should be used since there may be unknown drug interactions. There is not sufficient evidence to direct dosing recommendations. Patients should be aware of the limited efficacy these supplements could have on advanced diseases.

Nonpharmacologic measures should be part of a multimodal approach. The combination of pharmaceuticals, supplements, oral care, exercise, and dietary counseling should be directed by the patient's goals.

Psychosocial Support

CAS not only affects the body but also has psychosocial implications for patients and families. Patients, who are already having to make psychosocial adjustments as a result of their underlying diseases, are also suffering from the social isolation caused by their anorexia and cachexia. They may avoid social situations to avert pressure to eat.[41] The patient may have a desire to please, and eat when pressured, but this can strain relationships. Family members can also experience a sense of rejection, guilt, or helplessness when the patient refuses offers of food.

Food not only sustains life, but also plays a central role in most cultures, traditions, and celebrations. It is often a symbol of nurturing. Preparing food is one way we take care of the ones we love. Seeing patients eat less over time can be a reminder of the imminence of death.

Patients with CAS and their family members may express concern about the patient's decreased appetite, changing appearance, prognosis, and changes in social interactions.[42] Addressing these concerns is important to patients and families,[43] but healthcare professionals may not have the knowledge or training to do so.[44] APRNs specializing in palliative care need to develop expertise in addressing the physical and psychosocial sequelae of CAS.

The palliative APRN can arrange a family meeting to discuss the role of food in the patient's care. This will create an opportunity for the patient and the family to discuss their views about eating food in light of the patient's condition and disease. The APRN can establish goals of care as they relate to nutritional intake. This becomes a good time to educate both the patient and family on the impact that progressive illnesses have on appetite and weight loss.

End-of-Life Considerations

During the final hours to days of life, it is not uncommon for patients to eat and drink little to nothing. The patient or family may make requests at this time to address the patient's poor nutritional intake or weight loss. This often includes requests for parenteral hydration. Simply discussing the options available to treat anorexia and cachexia misses an opportunity to explore what the patient and family really want. It is likely the family is seeking a way to provide care to their loved one. Finding meaningful ways for family members to do just that introduces hope that may not have been realized.

The goals of care discussion can be a great starting point to help the family identify more effective and meaningful ways of helping their loved one. When goals of care are directed toward treating symptoms and promoting comfort, educating the family about the difference between little or no intake of nutrients at the end-of-life and starvation is important. Starvation is what happens when someone who has the desire to eat is deprived of food; his or her body is otherwise capable of processing food and nutrients if they were available. When a patient does not eat at the end-of-life, it is due to the patient's lack of desire to eat. The body also increasingly becomes unable to properly process food due to decreased motility and absorption in the intestines.

It is important for families to see the hope they provide to their loved one by their presence and commitment to care. Having some useful routines of care that family members can provide at the end-of-life goes a long way in comforting both the patient and the family. This includes an oral regimen of providing moisture through mouth swabs every couple of hours. Providing food to the patient should happen only if the patient desires it, taking into consideration the patient's safety. Any food provided should be the right consistency, texture, and amount. Sometimes a taste is all that is needed; this is referred as to pleasure feeding or eating. If the sensation of taste is all that is desired, flavored ices can be effective. Safety always needs to be considered along with goals and comfort.

Case Study

MM was a 62-year-old male with recently diagnosed pancreatic cancer who opted to pursue chemotherapy. Before starting treatment for his cancer, he was hospitalized for failure to thrive. His appetite became very poor, and he was diagnosed with a partial post-outlet obstruction due to disease progression. He was made NPO for safety. This caused him discomfort, because, as he stated, he derived a lot of pleasure from eating. The palliative APRN was asked to evaluate him.

Physical assessment revealed bowel sounds. His abdomen was flat and there was no abdominal tenderness. At 5-foot-11 and 155 pounds, he had lost 15 pounds in the past month. He reported that he had passed gas and moved his bowels recently. He stated that for breakfast he had had a bite of toast and some milk but became full quickly. He drank a few sips of Ensure for lunch, with the

same experience. He stated this had been typical for him over the past 2 weeks but had been getting worse recently. He denied pain, reported occasional nausea with vomiting, and denied shortness of breath, coughing, anxiety, and depression.

MM's psychosocial history revealed that he was single with an adult daughter. He did not keep in contact with his daughter's mother and did not have any significant or close relationships. He had been estranged from his daughter most of his daughter's life, but he had been in contact with his daughter in recent years. He stated he lived in a studio apartment in an elevator building. He reported being raised Protestant but did not belong to a church community. Religion or spiritual beliefs and practices did not play a role in his life or his coping with his illness.

The palliative APRN held a goals of care conversation with the patient that revealed that eating was important to him. It was in fact one of his favorite things to do. He wanted to focus on doing what would allow him to eat better. He also stated that he would like to pursue disease-directed therapies, including chemotherapy. He wanted to be resuscitated with a trial of intubation. He appointed his daughter as his healthcare power of attorney. The palliative APRN prescribed metoclopramide 10 mg before meals for nausea and dexamethasone 4 mg three times a day. The APRN ordered physical activity for MM, and the nursing staff was directed to ensure he moved out of bed and ambulated in the hall at least three times a day.

His symptoms improved and he was discharged on this regimen, with a steroid taper after 1 week and follow-up in the palliative care clinic. He gained 2 pounds and reported eating 50% of the meals he received from the local senior meal delivery service.

Conclusion

CAS comprises a complex set of symptoms that are difficult to manage. The cause can be related to treatment, but as the end-of-life nears, it is almost always a manifestation of the progression of disease. Since reversal of this progression is often not possible, alleviating or slowing CAS is difficult, if not impossible. Identifying goals of care for nutrition and weight loss is important. Educating family members and primary care providers about CAS as part of the natural progression of disease is necessary. The palliative APRN can help the patient and family identify a regimen that will maximize the patient's comfort. Though a palliative care focus cannot eliminate CAS, the palliative APRN can help improve some of the symptoms some of the time and can align care with the patient's goals and optimize quality of life.

References

1. Fearon K, Strasser F, Anker SD, et al. Definition and classification of cancer cachexia: an international consensus. *Lancet Oncology.* 2011; 12(5): 489–95.
2. Teunissen SCCM, Wesker W, Kruitwagen C, de Haes HCJM, Voest EE, de Graeff A. Symptom prevalence in patients with incurable cancer: a systematic review. *J Pain Symptom Management.* 2007; 34(1): 94–104.
3. Christensen HM, Kistorp C, Schou M, et al. Prevalence of cachexia in chronic heart failure and characteristics of body composition and metabolic status. *Endocrine.* 2013; 43(3): 626–34.

4. Malafarina V, Uriz-Otano F, Gil-Guerrero L, Iniesta R. The anorexia of ageing: physiopathology, prevalence, associated comorbidity and mortality. A systematic review. *Maturitas.* 2013; 74(4): 293–302.

5. Finley JP. Management of cancer cachexia. *AACN Clinical Issues.* 2000; 11(4): 590–603.

6. Argiles JM, Lopez-Soriano FJ, Busquets S. Mechanisms and treatment of cancer cachexia. *Nutrition, Metabolism, and Cardiovascular Diseases: NMCD.* 2013; 23(Suppl 1): S19–24.

7. Tisdale MJ. Molecular pathways leading to cancer cachexia. *Physiology.* 2005; 20(5): 340–8.

8. Patra SK, Arora S. Integrative role of neuropeptides and cytokines in cancer anorexia–cachexia syndrome. *Clinica Chimica Acta.* 2012; 413(13–14): 1025–34.

9. Clarkston WK, Pantano MM, Morley JE, Horowitz M, Littlefield JM, Burton FR. Evidence for the anorexia of aging: gastrointestinal transit and hunger in healthy elderly vs. young adults. *Am J Physiol.* 1997; 272(1 Pt 2): R243–8.

10. Freeman LM. The pathophysiology of cardiac cachexia. *Curr Opin Support Palliat Care.* 2009; 3(4): 276–81.

11. Blouin G, Fowler BC, Dahlin C. The national agenda for quality palliative care: promoting the National Consensus Project's domain of physical care and the National Quality Forum's preferred practices for physical aspects of care. *J Pain Palliat Care Pharmacother.* 2008; 22(3): 206–12.

12. von Haehling S, Lainscak M, Springer J, Anker SD. Cardiac cachexia: A systematic overview. *Pharmacol Therapeutics.* 2009; 121(3): 227–52.

13. Collins PF, Stratton RJ, Elia M. Nutritional support in chronic obstructive pulmonary disease: a systematic review and meta-analysis. *Am J Clin Nutr.* 2012; 95(6): 1385–95.

14. Remels AH, Gosker HR, Langen RC, Schols AM. The mechanisms of cachexia underlying muscle dysfunction in COPD. *J Appl Physiol.* 2013; 114(9): 1253–62.

15. Watanabe SM, Nekolaichuk C, Johnson L, Myers J, Strasser F. A multi-centre comparison of two numerical versions of the Edmonton Symptom Assessment System in palliative care patients. *J Pain Symptom Management.* 2011; 41: 456–68.

16. Rolland Y, Perrin A, Gardette V, Filhol N, Vellas B. Screening older people at risk of malnutrition or malnourished using the Simplified Nutritional Appetite Questionnaire (SNAQ): a comparison with the Mini-Nutritional Assessment (MNA) tool. *J Am Med Dir Assoc.* 2012; 13(1): 31–4.

17. Dodson S, Baracos VE, Jatoi A, et al. Muscle wasting in cancer cachexia: clinical implications, diagnosis, and emerging treatment strategies. *Annu Rev Med.* 2011; 62: 265–79.

18. Megace. In: McEvoy GK, ed. *AHFS Drug Information®.* 56th ed. Bethesda, MD: American Society of Health-System Pharmacists, Inc.; 2014.

19. Ruiz Garcia V, Lopez-Briz E, Carbonell Sanchis R, Gonzalvez Perales JL, Bort-Marti S. Megestrol acetate for treatment of anorexia-cachexia syndrome. *Cochrane Database of Systematic Reviews.* 2013; 3:CD004310.

20. American Geriatrics Society updated Beers criteria for potentially inappropriate medication use in older adults. *J Am Geriatrics Soc.* 2012; 60(4): 616–31.

21. Yeh SS, Lovitt S, Schuster MW. Usage of megestrol acetate in the treatment of anorexia-cachexia syndrome in the elderly. *J Nutrition Health Aging.* 2009; 13(5): 448–54.

22. Beal JE, Olson R, Laubenstein L, et al. Dronabinol as a treatment for anorexia associated with weight loss in patients with AIDS. *J Pain Symptom Management.* 1995; 10(2): 89–97.

23. Dronabinol. In: McEvoy GK, ed. *AHFS Drug Information®.* 56th ed. Bethesda, MD: American Society of Health-System Pharmacists, Inc.; 2014.

24. Strasser F, Luftner D, et al. Comparison of orally administered cannabis extract and delta-9-tetrahydrocannabinol in treating patients with cancer-related anorexia-cachexia syndrome: a multicenter, phase III, randomized, double-blind, placebo-controlled clinical trial from the Cannabis In Cachexia Study Group. *J Clin Oncol.* 2006; 24(21): 3394–400.

25. Loprinzi CL, Kugler JW, Sloan JA, et al. Randomized comparison of megestrol acetate versus dexamethasone versus fluoxymesterone for the treatment of cancer anorexia/cachexia. *J Clin Oncol.* 1999; 17(10): 3299–306.

26. Moertel CG, Schutt AJ, Reitemeier RJ, Hahn RG. Corticosteroid therapy of preterminal gastrointestinal cancer. *Cancer.* 1974; 33(6): 1607–9.

27. American College of Physicians; Mirtazapine. *ACP Smart Medicine (SM) & AHFS DI® Essentials™.* Philadelphia, PA: American College of Physicians; 2013.

28. Riechelmann RP, Burman D, Tannock IF, Rodin G, Zimmermann C. Phase II trial of mirtazapine for cancer-related cachexia and anorexia. *Am J Hospice Palliat Care.* 2010; 27(2): 106–10.

29. Reid J, Hughes CM, Murray LJ, Parsons C, Cantwell MM. Non-steroidal anti-inflammatory drugs for the treatment of cancer cachexia: a systematic review. *Palliat Med.* 2013; 27(4): 295–303.

30. Reid J, Mills M, Cantwell M, Cardwell CR, Murray LJ, Donnelly M. Thalidomide for managing cancer cachexia. *Cochrane Database of Systematic Reviews.* 2012; 4:CD008664.

31. Dewey A, Baughan C, Dean T, Higgins B, Johnson I. Eicosapentaenoic acid (EPA, an omega-3 fatty acid from fish oils) for the treatment of cancer cachexia. *Cochrane Database of Systematic Reviews.* 2007(1):CD004597.

32. Ashby D, Choi P, Bloom S. Gut hormones and the treatment of disease cachexia. *Proc Nutrition Soc.* 2008; 67(3): 263–9.

33. Miki K, Maekura R, Nagaya N, et al. Ghrelin treatment of cachectic patients with chronic obstructive pulmonary disease: a multicenter, randomized, double-blind, placebo-controlled trial. *PloS One.* 2012; 7(5):e35708.

34. Madeddu C, Dessi M, Panzone F, et al. Randomized phase III clinical trial of a combined treatment with carnitine + celecoxib + megestrol acetate for patients with cancer-related anorexia/cachexia syndrome. *Clinical Nutrition (Edinburgh, Scotland).* 2012; 31(2): 176–82.

35. Mantovani G, Maccio A, Madeddu C, et al. Randomized phase III clinical trial of five different arms of treatment in 332 patients with cancer cachexia. *Oncologist.* 2010; 15(2): 200–11.

36. Ovesen L, Allingstrup L, Hannibal J, Mortensen EL, Hansen OP. Effect of dietary counseling on food intake, body weight, response rate, survival, and quality of life in cancer patients undergoing chemotherapy: a prospective, randomized study. *J Clin Oncol.* 1993; 11(10): 2043–9.

37. Conn VS, Hafdahl AR, Porock DC, McDaniel R, Nielsen PJ. A meta-analysis of exercise interventions among people treated for cancer. *Supportive Care in Cancer.* 2006; 14(7): 699–712.

38. Koretz RL. Should patients with cancer be offered nutritional support: does the benefit outweigh the burden? *Eur J Gastroenterol Hepatol.* 2007; 19(5): 379–82.

39. Meier DE, Ahronheim JC, Morris J, Baskin-Lyons S, Morrison R. High short-term mortality in hospitalized patients with advanced dementia: Lack of benefit of tube feeding. *Arch Intern Med.* 2001; 161(4): 594–9.

40. Solheim TS, Laird BJA. Evidence base for multimodal therapy in cachexia. *Curr Opin Supportive Palliat Care.* 2012; 6(4): 424–31.

41. Reid J, McKenna H, Fitzsimons D, McCance T. Fighting over food: patient and family understanding of cancer cachexia. *Oncol Nurs Forum.* 2009; 36(4):439–45.

42. Porter S, Millar C, Reid J. Cancer cachexia care: the contribution of qualitative research to evidence-based practice. *Cancer Nurs.* 2012; 35(6): E30–8.

43. Reid J, McKenna H, Fitzsimons D, McCance T. The experience of cancer cachexia: A qualitative study of advanced cancer patients and their family members. *Int J Nurs Studies.* 2009; 46(5): 606–16.

44. Millar C, Reid J, Porter S. Healthcare professionals' response to cachexia in advanced cancer: a qualitative study. *Oncol Nurs Forum.* 2013; 40(6): E393–402.

CHAPTER 27

Cough

Justin Engleka

Key Points

- The palliative advanced practice registered nurse (APRN) should treat cough because it is a physically and emotionally draining symptom that can exacerbate other symptoms, such as pain, dyspnea, fatigue, depression, and incontinence.

- There are few high-quality studies addressing interventions for cough in the palliative care population. Therefore, interventions for cough are extrapolated from the research on acute and chronic cough in the general population.

Introduction

Acute and chronic cough can be a debilitating symptom for patients near the end of their lives. Patients can experience the symptom of cough for various reasons. The etiology may come from an advanced disease or terminal process, underlying comorbidities not related to the terminal illness, medications, and therapies that were intended to treat one of the patient's conditions. Although cough is a major symptom in palliative medicine, there are few evidence-based guidelines that focus specifically on the palliative care population. Many of the guidelines are extrapolated from the general research on cough in the general public. The British Thoracic Society,[1] the European Respiratory Society,[2] and the American College of Chest Physicians[3] have produced comprehensive guidelines, but none focuses on cough related to the advanced cancer or nonmalignant life-threatening illnesses that are common to the palliative medicine specialty.[4] Furthermore, few overall quality studies include interventions (pharmacologic and nonpharmacologic) for cough.[5]

Although there is limited research and evidence about cough in patients with life-limiting illnesses, there is a body of research on cough in the general population. Some of this research and evidence can be applied to the palliative care population. In many cases, the cause of chronic cough may be chronic comorbidities that the patient had prior to the diagnosis of a terminal illness. A large majority of chronic cough cases are due to upper airway cough syndrome (UACS). UACS arises from various rhinosinus conditions, asthma, and gastroesophageal reflux disease (GERD).[6] Other common causes of acute and chronic cough in the general population include the common cold/viruses, bronchitis, pneumonia, cough-variant asthma, use of angiotensin-converting enzyme (ACE) inhibitors, smoking, exacerbations of chronic obstructive pulmonary disease (COPD), and chemical or environmental irritants.[7] Overall, cough is one of the leading causes for visits to a healthcare provider and is one of the most common complaints in primary care, accounting for 30 million visits to healthcare providers annually[8] and billions of dollars in evaluation and treatment.[9] The prevalence of chronic cough in the United States among nonsmoking adults is reported to range from 14% to 23%.[8] Similar to other common symptoms in palliative care, the risk/benefit ratio needs to be considered during the course of illness. In many instances, the financial, practical, and emotional implications can be significant.

Aside from conditions that cause cough in the general public, there are several common categories of disease that cause cough in palliative care patients. Lung cancer, primary lung disease, COPD, heart failure, neuromuscular diseases, dementia, and diseases that affect the immune system[10] require additional consideration for diagnosis and treatment. Cough has a prevalence of 47% to 86% in lung cancer and 23% to 37% in general cancer patients.[11] It is present in 38% of patients with advanced cancer.[12] COPD, another major contributor to morbidity and mortality, is often seen as a primary or secondary diagnosis at the end-of-life.

Cough as a primary symptom can also create and exacerbate other symptoms related to the underlying illnesses. It is a constant reminder of the disease state and can reflect further decline. The act of coughing can be exhausting and disruptive to daily living. Associated symptoms include breathlessness, chest pain, rib fracture, insomnia, urinary and fecal incontinence, and feelings of depression and isolation.[13] Psychological effects, such as anger, frustration, anxiety, and depression, have been reported in 55% to 83% of the general public in a cough postal questionnaire.[14]

Case Study

John, a 74-year-old male, was readmitted to the acute care hospital with the primary complaints of cough and shortness of breath. Approximately 1 month earlier, he had been diagnosed with adenocarcinoma of the lung. He initially presented with cough, chest congestion, clear sputum production, retrosternal chest pain without radiation, hoarseness, scant hemoptysis, and dyspnea with minimal exertion. He had lost approximately 40 pounds prior to hospitalization. These findings, in addition to his 35-year smoking history, prompted a comprehensive workup for malignancy. Imaging revealed bilateral lung nodules up to 1.6 cm in diameter, mediastinal lymphadenopathy, and a small pericardial effusion.

After the initial diagnosis, John was referred to an oncologist for the consideration of systemic chemotherapy. However, due to intractable respiratory symptoms and pain, he was admitted back to the hospital and could not initiate chemotherapy. His cough and respiratory symptoms were previously unmanaged by ipratropium bromide/albuterol inhalers, benzonatate, dextromethorphan/guaifenesin, nystatin, omeprazole, prednisone, fentanyl patch, and oxycodone. He had a significant social history of smoking starting at age 14, but stopped approximately 15 years ago. He had no known drug allergies. Significant past medical history was notable for recently diagnosed lung cancer, COPD, coronary artery disease, atrial fibrillation, and hypertension.

During this admission, the patient was reassessed for disease progression with the goal of palliating his respiratory symptoms. A palliative care consultation was placed for symptom management and goals of care discussion. The review of systems revealed primary complaints of increasing cough with clear sputum production, non-radiating chest pain that worsened during coughing exacerbations, anxiety, depression, anorexia, shortness of breath with minimal exertion, and intermittent constipation. On physical examination, he appeared as a frail, anxious male with a forward-leaning, slouched posture. His oral cavity had remnants of thrush, but was otherwise pink and very dry. Heart sounds were regularly irregular without murmurs. Lung sounds were diminished with crackles and rhonchi posteriorly, he was receiving oxygen via nasal cannula, and he used pursed-lip breathing. The abdominal exam revealed a distended appearance, with bowel sounds present, and percussion revealing tympany. His mood appeared very flat with poor eye contact, and he was anxious with restless movements. Extremities were without clubbing or cyanosis, but there was trace lower extremity edema. Medications at the initial time of palliative care consultation were aspirin, ipratropium bromide/albuterol nebulizers, alprazolam, enalapril, benzonatate, diltiazem, docusate sodium, fentanyl patch, furosemide, dextromethorphan/guaifenesin, metoprolol, nitroglycerin ointment, clotrimazole troches, omeprazole, oxycodone, prednisone, and zolpidem. The surgery team noted that the echocardiogram results revealed a large pericardial effusion with right ventricular prolapse suggesting tamponade. The patient eventually had a pericardial window procedure later in his hospital stay. The cardiology findings consisted of a stable pleural effusion. The EKG showed atrial fibrillation with rapid ventricular response. The echocardiogram showed an ejection fraction of 55% with 1 to 2+ mitral regurgitation. He was placed on a diltiazem infusion.

The APRN played multiple roles in this patient's care. Although complex, this case presentation is a common scenario for the palliative APRN. The first step for the APRN is to systematically evaluate all of the potential reasons for cough and respiratory symptoms. This patient presented with numerous medical problems, all of which can contribute to cough. His problem list included lung cancer, pleural effusion, pericardial effusion, COPD, thrush, GERD, partial vocal cord paralysis, and general fatigue/cachexia. In planning the management strategy, the APRN should consider treatments or empiric therapies that will focus on all of the various reasons for cough. In John's case, various medications had previously been attempted, so the interventional strategy, such as the pericardial window, was reasonable since all other strategies had failed, even though the patient was very near the end-of-life. The APRN made additional recommendations, such as a speech therapy consultation, rotation of opioid medication

to oral or intravenous morphine, antidepressant medication, a more aggressive bowel regimen, and a longer-acting benzodiazepine. The APRN's first priority was to manage the patient's acute respiratory and pain symptoms. Once those symptoms were adequately managed, a more focused discussion with the patient could take place.

Normal Cough Physiology

Cough is a physiological mechanism that is inherently protective to the human body. Cough helps to protect the airways and lungs by removing mucus and foreign material from the larynx, trachea, and bronchi and is under both voluntary and involuntary control. The cough reflex is mediated by the vagus nerve in the airways and the glossopharyngeal nerve in the pharynx. Excitatory information is sent from the brain stem to spinal motor neurons innervating the respiratory muscles.[10] Cough can be activated by aggravating stimuli anywhere in the area of the vagus nerve (e.g., inhaled foreign body, gastric reflux irritating the esophagus, or impacted ear wax).[15] Bronchial cilia transfer mucus, fluids, and inhaled foreign bodies to the larynx and then into the pharynx, where they are either expectorated or swallowed. The act of coughing starts with an inspiratory gasp, then a closing of the glottis and a Valsalva maneuver, followed by an expiratory blast.[16]

Cough can be classified into three categories: acute, subacute, or chronic. An acute cough usually lasts less than 3 weeks, a subacute cough 3 to 8 weeks, and chronic cough persists beyond 8 weeks.[17]

Common Non-Cancer Pathology of Cough

UACS

UACS is caused by a variety of upper airway respiratory conditions. It is the most common cause of chronic cough in nonsmoking, immunocompetent adults with normal chest radiograph.[18] Also known as postnasal drainage, it is defined as the posterior drainage of secretions from the nose or paranasal sinuses into the pharyngolaryngeal area, presumably caused by rhinosinus disease. Patients will often complain of secretions in the throat.[19]

Asthma Syndrome and COPD

Asthma is characterized by chronic or recurrent respiratory symptoms associated with airway inflammation and variable airflow obstruction. Most patients experience wheeze, dyspnea, and cough. Some patients with asthma who have cough-predominant symptoms can be classified as having cough-variant asthma. These patients are thought to represent a different phenotype from those with classical asthma.[19] A third disorder of the asthma syndrome is non-asthmatic eosinophilic bronchitis. Patients with non-asthmatic eosinophilic bronchitis are nonsmokers with eosinophilic airway inflammation, normal chest radiographic and spirometric results, and no evidence of variable airflow obstruction.[20] Non-asthmatic eosinophilic bronchitis is not well understood, and bronchoconstriction can mechanically stimulate airway afferent nerves to induce cough.[19]

COPD is a disease that is characterized by cough, sputum production, and shortness of breath. The course of COPD is often aggravated by exacerbations or worsening of the symptoms. Most exacerbations are produced by bronchial infections.[21] Excessive airway mucus may provide a mechanical stimulus to coughing, especially in the presence of ciliary dysfunction, airflow obstruction, and airway collapse (caused by destruction of the supporting parenchyma), all of which impair clearance. If bronchial mucus becomes too thick, uncoupling may occur within it so that the inner part, the sol phase, is cleared by ciliary beating, while the outer part, the gel phase to which bacteria adhere, remains stationary. In addition, the inflammation, infection, and, in some, continuing exposure to cigarette smoke provide chemical stimuli capable of provoking coughing in COPD.[22]

GERD

GERD is the third leading cause of cough[23] but is often overlooked in the palliative care population. Lower esophageal sphincter loosening, either physiological or pathological, is a principal factor in reflux.[15] Acid reflux can stimulate the afferent limb of the cough reflex by irritating the upper respiratory tract without aspiration or by irritating the lower respiratory tract through aspiration. GERD can also cause chronic cough by stimulating esophageal-bronchial cough reflex.[24]

ACE Inhibitors

Cough associated with ACE inhibitors was first reported with captopril in 1985.[25] It is a class effect, but the reported incidence may be as high as 16%. It is not dose-related and time to onset varies; it can occur within hours or more than a year after starting treatment.[26] Patients usually present with a history of dry cough while taking ACE inhibitors or after discontinuation.[2]

Active Infections and Postinfectious Cough

Cough can arise from numerous active bacterial or viral infections. In the general population, many patients seek medical attention for cough that they believe to be infectious in nature. Cough that is viral in nature will not respond to antibiotics and will simply run its natural course. Causes of acute cough with a normal chest radiograph include respiratory syncytial virus, rhinovirus, influenza, parainfluenza, adenovirus, respiratory coronavirus, metapneumovirus, and various bacterial infections (acute bronchitis).

Common Cancer Pathology of Cough

Cancer can cause cough directly or indirectly through various mechanisms. Direct causes of cough include direct stimulation of cough receptors by an invasive tumor and compressive lymphadenopathy. Centrally located tumors, bleeding tumors, and pathologies affecting larger airways are likely to stimulate Aδ-fibers leading to cough via vagal afferent nerves.[27] Indirect causes include pulmonary embolism, atelectasis, pleural effusion, pericardial effusion, and infections, such as pneumonia or empyema.[17] Cough is most commonly associated with primary cancers arising from the airways, lungs, pleura, and other mediastinal structures as well as primary tumors metastasizing to the mediastinum. Cough can also be a side effect of cancer treatment itself.[28]

Pleural Effusions

Cough in patients with advanced lung cancer is often caused by a pleural effusion. Up to 50% of patients with metastatic disease are diagnosed with a pleural effusion during the course of their illness.[29] In the vast majority of cases, malignant pleural effusion signifies an incurable disease with high morbidity and mortality.[30] Pleural effusions can be nonmalignant or malignant. Malignant pleural effusions are characterized by malignant cells in the pleural fluid.[30]

Treatment-Related Pneumonitis

Cancer treatments often cause respiratory symptoms like cough. Erlotinib and other targeted agents administered in patients with advanced lung cancer are known to cause pneumonitis.[31] Radiation therapy has also been known to cause fibrosis of the lung, which can cause chronic cough.[15] It is generally believed that most cough following such therapies relates to the development of pneumonitis, although there are few data to support this statement.[27] Several different pathophysiological patterns of pneumonitis have been described in the literature, the most common of which is diffuse alveolar damage.[32]

Tamponade

Lung cancer is the most common tumor to involve the pericardium.[33] Patients with acute tamponade experience respiratory symptoms and chest pain and present with hemodynamic instability.[31]

Pulmonary Embolus

In patients with cancer, specifically lung cancer, venous thromboembolism is an important cause of respiratory symptoms, including cough. The incidence of venous thromboembolism in patients with cancer is up to three times that of the general population, and recurrent venous thromboembolism is more common in patients with cancer.[34]

Assessment

Assessment of cough in the palliative care patient begins with a thorough review of the patient's medical history, review of systems, medications, and environmental/occupational history, and may require other diagnostic imaging and testing. Understanding the underlying comorbid conditions may help the APRN to focus on likely causes of cough. A review of medications will help determine if the patient is taking medications that may cause cough (i.e., ACE inhibitors) and which medications have been ineffective in controlling cough. Patients who are in the late stages of life and are suffering with advanced illness are more likely to have already been diagnosed with an illness that will cause coughing. Some examples include congestive heart failure (CHF), lung cancer, cancers of the head or neck, asthma or COPD, or neurological conditions, such as stroke and dementia, that carry a high risk of aspiration. Therefore, first-line tests intended to initially diagnose these diseases may already have been conducted. As previously discussed, there is the possibility that patients can develop or have exacerbations of diseases causing cough that affect the general public. In those instances, careful consideration is required to determine which diagnostic tests should be pursued. Assessment beyond simple review of systems and physical exam may be necessary to determine exacerbations of disease or to determine new secondary complications that should be investigated and treated.

Subjective Assessment

The APRN should conduct a thorough patient interview to determine the most bothersome symptoms. The APRN should ask about the intensity and quality of the symptom, its temporal onset, frequency, and course, precipitating, aggravating, and alleviating factors, accompanying symptoms, and the resulting emotional stress.[35] Questions that focus on the most likely organ system should be asked first. For example, patients with COPD should be asked about COPD exacerbations. The APRN should inquire about the presence of fever/chills, productive or nonproductive sputum, and increase in shortness of breath. Patients with a history of CHF should be asked about weight gain, orthopnea, activity intolerance, increased use/need for oxygen, and other factors. In terms of cough quality, it is important to make the distinction between a productive, wet cough and a dry cough.[15] Patients with primary lung or heart disease should also be asked about hemoptysis. Specific questions related to the most common causes of cough should be asked, such as GERD, postnasal drip, asthma, and other frequent etiologies. Social history details, such as current and past occupation, and environmental factors, such as household pets, smoking, or exposure to other irritants that cause cough, should be evaluated.

Objective Assessment

Physical examination is the second step of the comprehensive assessment of cough. Primary consideration should be given to several different organ systems in the evaluation of cough. Physical examination should concentrate on the afferent sites of the vagus nerve most commonly associated with the irritation leading to chronic cough.[1] Physical assessment of the ears, nose, throat, lungs, and heart is clinically valuable. The APRN must also consider that the cough could have more than one cause. Chronic cough has two or more causes in 18% to 62% of patients in the general population, and three causes in 42% of patients.[36] Careful examination of the ears, nose, and throat can produce findings suggestive of the common cold, allergies, cerumen impaction, otitis, and postnasal drip. There may be clinical evidence of rhinitis and pharyngitis with inflamed nasal mucosa and posterior pharynx with adherent or draining secretions.[1] The APRN may also assess the patient's swallowing and gag reflex. Abnormal signs of swallowing and gag reflex may help to further evaluate for the presence of aspiration. Examination of the heart should assess for signs of heart failure and other pathology. This includes auscultation of the heart, inspection of the neck for jugular venous distention, and inspection of the lower extremities for edema. The lung examination should include careful inspection, auscultation, and percussion. Abnormal pulmonary findings include crepitus, rhonchi, rales, and wheezes as well as tachypnea and labored breathing. These abnormal findings can help determine possible pathology, such as COPD exacerbations, pneumonia, bronchitis, or pleural effusions.

Imaging and Other Testing

A significant amount of attention has been placed on the diagnosis and management of chronic cough. Among the most common causes in nonsmoking patients, asthma, GERD, and UACS[1,2,23] have received the most attention. However, much of this work has focused on the general population who do not have life-limiting illnesses. Normal chest radiography usually excludes bronchiectasis, persistent pneumonia, sarcoidosis, and tuberculosis.[37] In addition to chest radiography, there are multiple tests that patients may undergo to determine the pathology. This workup includes (1) asthma (spirometry, methacholine challenge [a drug used to induce bronchoconstriction that can be measured by spirometry], and induced sputum); (2) GERD (24-hour ambulatory pH monitoring, and esophageal manometry); and (3) rhinitis or UACS (plain sinus radiography and computed tomography of the sinuses).[2] Interestingly, "rare" causes are much more common among the palliative care population: aspiration, bronchiolitis, chronic interstitial lung disease, persistent pneumonia, sarcoidosis, cancer, and tuberculosis[23] (Box 27.1).

Differential Diagnosis

Determining the etiology of cough in the palliative care patient can be challenging. Given the likelihood of chronic comorbidities, multiple etiologies need to be considered. The first step is to determine several different factors. It is important to differentiate acute versus subacute/chronic cough, infectious versus non-infectious cough, life-threatening versus non-life-threatening causes,[38] and cancerous versus noncancerous/chronic conditions.[10] Common serious conditions that present with an isolated cough include neoplasm, infection, foreign body aspiration, acute allergy-anaphylaxis, and interstitial lung disease.[1] Signs and symptoms of infectious cough include fever or chills, abnormally colored sputum, and radiologic evidence of pulmonary infiltrates or consolidation.[39] Confirming the diagnosis requires the previously discussed methods, such as history, physical examination, and possibly diagnostic imaging (x-ray[7] or other methods) (Box 27.2).

Box 27.1 Diagnostic Testing	
Disease Category	**Test**
Asthma	Spirometry
	Methacholine challenge
	Induced sputum
GERD	24-hour pH testing
	Esophageal manometry
Rhinitis and UACS	Sinus radiography
	Computed tomography of the sinuses
Cardiac/pulmonary diseases	Chest x-ray
	Computed tomography of the chest/neck
	Bronchoscopy
	Echocardiogram
	Video/fluoroscopy
Esophageal diseases	Modified barium swallow
	Endoscopy
Miscellaneous	Cough monitoring devices
Adapted from references 2, 13, 41, 67.	

Box 27.2 Differential Diagnosis of Cough in Palliative Care Patients

Cough Category Differential	
Noncancerous state	Neuromuscular diseases
	◆ Multiple sclerosis
	◆ Amyotrophic lateral sclerosis
	◆ Late-stage dementia
	◆ Cerebrovascular disease
	◆ Immunocompromised host
	◆ Prolonged neutropenia
	◆ Organ transplant recipients
	◆ HIV infection
	◆ End-stage heart failure
	◆ End-stage respiratory failure
	◆ End-stage renal failure
Cancerous state	
◆ Direct cause	Pulmonary parenchymal involvement
	Lymphangitic carcinomatosis
	Intrinsic or extrinsic airway obstruction
	Pleural effusion
	Pleural tumor
	Multiple tumor microemboli
	Pulmonary leukostasis
	Superior vena cava syndrome
◆ Indirect cause	Anorexia–cachexia
	Aspiration
	Pulmonary embolus
	Paraneoplastic syndrome
	Radiation-induced
	Chemotherapy-induced
	Chemotherapy-induced cardiomyopathy
Unrelated to primary disease	UACS, GERD, asthma, chronic bronchitis, ACE inhibitors

Adapted from references 1, 2, 38.

The diagnosis of primary lung cancer or metastatic disease to the lung requires particular attention in regard to cough symptoms. There are various etiologies within and near the lung that can cause cough. Common causes of respiratory symptoms in advanced lung cancer derive from the airway, parenchyma, pleura, vascular system, neuromuscular system, and extrapulmonary sites.[31]

Aspiration requires special attention in the palliative care setting. It is defined as the misdirection of oropharyngeal or gastric contents into the larynx and lower respiratory tract.[40] Patients with advanced dementia, stroke, amyotrophic lateral sclerosis, Parkinson's disease, and general frailty are particularly susceptible to the effects of aspiration and ultimately are at increased risk for cough and impaired swallowing. A clinical assessment evaluates the structure and function of the oral stage of swallowing. It enables the prediction of the impairment of the pharyngeal, laryngeal, and esophageal swallowing physiology.[41] Trained speech language pathologists can help assist the APRN in determining the presence of dysphagia and aspiration through a bedside evaluation or modified barium swallow. Recognizing basic signs of dysphagia can assist in the eventual diagnosis and recommendations.

Management

APRNs play an instrumental role in the care of patients at the end-of-life. Quality-of-life issues and symptom management should always be the focus and overall goal for patients with advanced illnesses. Management of cough in the palliative care patient may vary considerably from that of the general population. Although the diagnostic workup and treatment may follow prescribed algorithms, those same methods may not always be practical or even feasible for patients at the end-of-life. Managing cough is directed at treating reversible causes. Patients with intractable chronic cough that is believed to be neuropathic in origin, those with abnormal throat sensations or tickle (laryngeal paresthesia), those with increased cough sensitivity to known tussigens (hypertussia), and those with cough triggered in response to nontussive stimuli (allotussia)[42] may respond to neuromodulator medications, such as gabapentin.[43] If those same patients also have neuropathic pain, there may be an added benefit. There is also at least one case study that described the use of the benzodiazepine diazepam for refractory chronic cough.[44] It is unclear if the benefit was realized from a simple reduction in anxiety or if the drug had another effect.

Interventional Techniques

There are several diagnoses causing cough that have possible interventional options for palliation. Patients with pleural effusions secondary to CHF or other non-cancer etiologies may require therapeutic thoracentesis. In addition to the possible therapeutic benefits, thoracentesis should be performed to establish a cytological diagnosis. One of the first steps in managing pleural effusions is to determine whether the patient benefits from the removal of fluid. If the patient does not achieve significant improvement of shortness of breath or exercise tolerance, other comorbid conditions should be considered. For patients with limited prognosis, repeated thoracentesis may be an option. This approach is purely palliative and should not be used in patients on a long-term basis. Consideration of the risks is also warranted: infection, bleeding, and pneumothorax.[30] Similarly, patients with cough secondary to excessive ascites may benefit from intermittent paracentesis or pigtail catheters.[45]

If foreign body aspiration is suspected, bronchoscopy may be undertaken.[1] Although bronchoscopy is typically diagnostic, obvious foreign bodies can be removed. APRNs should consider this intervention in patients with illnesses that have a high rate of aspiration, such as stroke, dementia, Parkinson's disease, amyotrophic lateral sclerosis, cancers of the head and neck, and general frailty, and those with a history of previous aspiration. A retrospective study of 15,420 patients undergoing bronchoscopy without a history of inhaled foreign body, 91% of whom had a persistent cough and 63% of whom had a normal chest radiograph, found that a foreign body was identified in only 0.3%.[46] Therefore, clinical judgment should be used when deciding whether to recommend bronchoscopy.

Review of the literature reveals that there are various interventional techniques for cough in patients with cancer.[10,28,30,31] The majority of the literature details interventions for patients with lung cancer. Surgical intervention may be an early intervention for the treatment of lung cancer and typically occurs initially after diagnosis. When non-small-cell lung cancer can be surgically removed, cough typically resolves postoperatively.[47] Radiation therapy is also a main treatment option for patients with lung cancer. In those with stage III or IV non-small-cell lung cancer, although external beam radiation is more effective for palliating chest pain and hemoptysis than cough, it may be helpful.[13] Studies have reported that up to 82% of people report significant relief of cough, lasting a median of 70 to 78 days, after receiving two fractions of radiotherapy.[48] Brachytherapy may also be used, although the supporting evidence is limited.[28] Nevertheless, these studies suggest that treatment with brachytherapy may be appropriate in selected populations of lung cancer patients. Surgery and radiation therapy may also be considered in treating cancers of the head and neck and the upper airway.

Lung cancer is the most common tumor to involve the pericardium.[33] Patients with tamponade may experience various respiratory symptoms. A single pericardiocentesis is associated with recurrence of the effusion in up to 60% of cases; thus, prolonged catheter drainage is often required. Although the trigger for a surgical approach, such as a pericardial window or pericardiotomy, is not clear, it is generally well tolerated and associated with a very low rate of fluid reaccumulation.[49]

In patients with endobronchial or esophageal tumors, cough can also be a complicating symptom of the underlying disease. Hemoptysis may also be present in patients with lung cancer. At presentation, up to 20% of patients report mild hemoptysis and a much smaller percentage experience severe hemoptysis.[47] Hemoptysis is most notably caused by airway tumors and pulmonary embolus. Bronchial arteries are responsible for the most threatening hemoptysis since these vessels supply the airways and are under higher pressure than pulmonary arteries.

Most interventions target bronchial vessels with either an endobronchial or an endovascular approach. Bronchial artery embolization is commonly used to treat massive hemoptysis, but few studies have included patients with cancer.[31] In a retrospective review of 30 patients with lung cancer who underwent bronchial artery embolization to treat hemoptysis of variable severity, it was effective in 86% of cases.[50] Endobronchial techniques include laser resection and electrocautery; they are most commonly employed to treat obstructive endobronchial lesions but are also indicated for hemoptysis.[51] Stenting of esophagotracheal fistulas (esophageal, tracheal, or double stenting) may offer symptom relief and better quality of life.[52]

Pleural effusions are a common and devastating complication of advanced malignancies.[30] In addition to the myriad of respiratory symptoms caused by pleural effusions, cough can be a common presentation. Palliation should be the primary goal when treating patients with advanced and terminal disease. Long hospital stays and immobility imposed by chest tube insertion, as well as the pain and suffering associated with talc slurry, doxycycline, or similar agents, may not be the most compassionate way of treating this terminal complication. New modalities like pleuroscopy and long-term indwelling pleural catheters are cost-effective,[53] can be done on an outpatient basis,[54] require a minimal hospital stay, produce less discomfort, and give the patient a chance to spend quality time out of the hospital.[30]

The first step in the management of malignant pleural effusion (MPE) is to determine the symptomatic benefit from removal of the pleural fluid. In patients who have not received symptomatic benefit from an initial thoracentesis, the utility of removing pleural fluid is limited. The volume of pleural fluid that can be safely removed during thoracentesis is unknown, but removal of only 1.0 to 1.5 liters of fluid per thoracentesis is recommended.[55] A significant number of patients with MPE (up to 50%) may not have improvement in respiratory symptoms, so they may be attributed to other causes.[30]

In addition to thoracentesis, chest tube thoracostomy and chemical pleurodesis with talc are the most commonly used modalities for managing MPE. However, there is significant discomfort and inconvenience associated with this procedure. It is an inpatient procedure that typically requires a hospital stay of 5 to 7 days, and pain and fever often occur following the instillation of talc. Pleurodesis is attempted only after complete lung reexpansion post pleural fluid evacuation with no evidence of trapped lung.[30]

Medical thoracoscopy, also known as pleuroscopy, is another intervention used for the rapid diagnosis and treatment of pleural effusions. It is a single-puncture technique in which some pleural fluid is suctioned out, followed by the introduction of a pleuroscope to inspect the pleural cavity and the lung, diaphragm, and pleural surfaces. Talc poudrage performed during pleuroscopy has a mean pleurodesis success rate of greater than 90%.[56] Video-assisted thoracic surgery is yet another surgical option, but it requires general anesthesia and single-lung ventilation. It is contraindicated for patients with prior contralateral pneumonectomy, airway abnormalities that preclude placement of a double-lumen endotracheal tube, and complex pleural adhesions.[30] For these reasons, the video-assisted thoracic surgery procedure is more invasive and may carry a higher risk than other procedures. Patients at the end-of-life need to consider the risks and benefits and may consider other, less invasive or empiric therapies. Finally, pleuroperitoneal shunts and indwelling, tunneled pleural catheters may be used in patients with MPE. Indwelling pleural catheters and medical thoracoscopy are cost-effective and minimally invasive options that should be considered in the algorithm.[57]

Complex Medication Use

Given the numerous etiologies causing cough, there are also multiple drug classes used to treat this symptom. Targeted therapy should be considered in patients with cough related to conditions that affect the general population, such as GERD, UACS, and asthma. However, in palliative care patients, there is a lower threshold for empirical treatment with stronger opioids and other medications. The simple fact that patients at or near the end-of-life have aggressive disease progression warrants stronger interventions to alleviate suffering. The treatment pyramid for the management of cough in patients with lung cancer[11] provides a systematic approach. The algorithm suggests the following treatment pathway: (1) cancer-specific treatments concurrently with treating comorbidities; (2) simple linctus/glycerol; (3) a trial of oral steroids; (4) opioids; (5) peripherally acting antitussives; (6) local anesthetics; and (7) experimental drugs.

Although there is not much evidence to support pharmacologic treatment of cough, some clinically effective treatments do exist.

There are essentially two ways of treating chronic cough—by treating the underlying cause or by suppressing or alleviating the symptoms.[15] Expectorants and antitussives are two of the major drug classes used to treat cough both in the general population and in palliative care patients. Anticholinergic drugs have also been indicated for the late-stage condition of "death rattle."[58]

Expectorant Medications

In patients with large amounts of mucus, expectorants can help by making the mucus less viscous, liquefying it, and promoting its expulsion. The goal of expectorants is to create a consistency that the patient can more easily cough up. Simple nebulized saline solution and substances that lessen irritation, such as thyme cough syrup, can be effective. Other available drugs are acetylcysteine and ambroxol hydrochloride. Additional fluid intake may be necessary to improve the efficacy of expectorants, especially if the patient is dehydrated. The APRN should use caution when prescribing expectorants in patients with neuromuscular diseases, such as amyotrophic lateral sclerosis.[35] Due to their decreased ability to produce an effective cough, these patients may have trouble coughing up the liquefied mucus. Inhaled ipratropium bromide remains the current recommendation for cough due to chronic bronchitis.[59] Nebulized saline is recommended in palliative care, the other options being guaifenesin or carbocysteine, which reduces the viscosity of secretions.[60]

Antitussive Medications

When the cough's etiology has been determined and effectively treated, antitussives may be used with the goal of suppressing the cough. Cough suppressants are classified as central and peripheral antitussive drugs. The main difference between the two is the ability to cross the blood–brain barrier and penetrate the nervous system. Therefore, centrally acting drugs may produce side effects like sedation.[15] Among the centrally acting drugs, opioids, such as codeine and morphine, bind to the μ receptor and suppress the cough center in the brain stem.[35] Codeine's reputation as the best antitussive was recently brought into question[61] after two randomized trials failed to demonstrate any advantage of codeine over placebo.[62,63] However, morphine did reveal benefit compared to placebo.[64] Among central agents in palliative care, morphine is now the agent of first choice. A randomized, double-blind, placebo-controlled trial showed a rapid and highly significant reduction by 40% in the daily cough score with 10 mg of daily morphine sulfate. Response to the treatment was rapid and maximum benefit was achieved by day 5 in those who responded.[64]

In recent years, there has been increased interest in the use of inhaled morphine for the treatment of cough.[65] However, there are no studies supporting its use over that of low-dose oral morphine. However, nebulized morphine can be a potent cause of mast cell degranulation, the resultant histamine release precipitating bronchoconstriction.[15] Dextromethorphan is an opioid derivative with good antitussive efficacy and low toxicity that should be considered for cough suppression. Due to its additional effect at the *N*-methyl-D-aspartate (NMDA) receptor, dextromethorphan is also used to treat pain.[4] Hydrocodone is another commonly prescribed drug for cough. Hydrocodone is the main ingredient in many cough preparations and is quite popular in the United States. There are 96 antitussive and analgesic preparations containing hydrocodone in United States. Some contain homatropine (1.5 mg/5 mL hydrocodone) in addition to hydrocodone.[66] Homatropine is an anticholinergic included to reduce the abuse potential of hydrocodone by causing undesirable side effects, such as dry mouth and hallucinations.[67] In a phase 2 study of hydrocodone in advanced cancer, 19 of 20 patients had at least 50% improvement in their cough frequency. The median best response was 70% improvement in the cough frequency (50–90%), and the median hydrocodone dose associated with the best response was 10 mg/day.[67]

The most commonly used peripherally active antitussives are inhaled local anesthetics, such as bupivacaine 0.25% or lidocaine 2%.[35] They have been used to anesthetize nerve endings involved in the cough reflex,[68] but they may increase the risk of aspiration, and the first dose should be given in the hospital.[15] Lidocaine has been shown to be a safe and effective treatment of asthma and cough secondary to COPD.[69] Inhalation of lidocaine has also been reported to improve intractable cough that has lasted up to several weeks in patients with malignancies as well as intractable cough that is severe enough to disrupt activities of daily living.[70] Nebulized lidocaine has sometimes been advocated for the relief of intractable cough by anesthetizing sensory nerve endings in the hypopharynx, larynx, and upper airways that are involved with generating the cough reflex.[71]

Miscellaneous Medications

Several special disease states may require additional or unique medication therapies outside of the previously mentioned options. Treatment of cough in CHF, for example, should include treatment of the underlying heart failure. Signs of copious, frothy pink sputum may be a sign of left ventricular heart failure. Treatment should include the use of diuretics and/or inotropic medications.[72] Patients with the primary diagnosis of cancer, and more specifically lung cancer, may benefit from chemotherapy administration. Gemcitabine chemotherapy led to improvement in cough lasting for 2 to 5 months in 44% of people with non-small-cell lung cancer and in 73% of those with moderate to severe cough.[73] Patients with active infections should be treated with antibiotics[7] (Box 27.3).

Nonpharmacologic Interventions

Several nonpharmacologic interventions have been proposed to help with cough (Box 27.4) and associated symptoms. Complementary or alternative medicine techniques may be useful: acupuncture, menthol, eucalyptus,[5] relaxation techniques, and guided imagery. In general, these therapies may simply relax the patient and reduce the stress and anxiety produced by chronic cough.

The act of coughing may create dry and irritated airways. Patients with chronically irritated airways may find relief from saline via nebulizer.[10] In patients with copious or difficult-to-expectorate secretions, chest physiotherapy and autogenic drainage may be useful nonpharmacologic interventions. Chest physiotherapy, which involves lightly percussing the patient's chest and back, helps the patient expectorate mucus.[10] Careful technique must be used in frail, elderly, and cachexic patients. Forced expiratory technique, another method to help clear secretions,[74] involves huffing several times, and then inhaling deeply and holding the breath for a few seconds before exhaling forcefully with a strong cough. The use of cool humidified air may also comfort patients

Box 27.3 Pharmacologic Treatment of Cough in Palliative Care Patients

Drug	Starting Dosage
Opioids	
Morphine	5 mg PO/SL q2–4h PRN
Hydrocodone	5 mg PO q4h PRN
Codeine	15–30 mg PO q4h PRN
Oxycodone	5 mg PO q4h PRN
Corticosteroids	
Dexamethasone	4–8 mg PO qd
Prednisone	20–40 mg PO qd
Anesthetics	
Lidocaine	3 mL of nebulized (4%) lidocaine (120 mg) q6h PRN
Anticholinergics	
Scopolamine	0.4–0.6 mg SQ q2–4h PRN or
	0.8–2 mg as a CSI q24h or
	1.5 mg transdermal patch q72h
Hyoscyamine	0.125–0.250 mg SL q2–4h PRN or
	0.25–0.5 mg SQ q2–4h PRN or
	1–2 mg as a CSI q24h
Glycopyrrolate	0.2 mg SL or SQ q2–4h PRN
Atropine	0.4 mg SL or SQ q2–4h PRN or
	2 mg via nebulizer q2–4h PRN
Miscellaneous	
Dextromethorphan	15–30 mg PO q4h PRN

Adapted from references 7, 10, 31.

Box 27.4 Nonpharmacologic Interventions for Cough

Complementary/Alternative Techniques
Acupuncture
Menthol
Eucalyptus
Relaxation/Meditation
Guided imagery

Physical Interventions
Chest physiotherapy
Forced expiratory technique

Devices
Insufflator–exsufflator (cough assist machine—for ineffective cough)

Speech Therapy
Diet modifications
Postural maneuvers
Swallowing exercises

Miscellaneous
Saline nebulizers
Cool humidified air

Adapted from references 10, 41.

while helping to thin secretions.[75] When chest physiotherapy and forced expiratory technique is inadequate, the APRN may consider an insufflator–exsufflator (cough assist machine).

Patients with dysphagia may benefit from evaluation and recommendations from a speech-language pathologist. Patients with dysphagia are at increased risk for aspiration, pneumonia, and cough or ineffective cough. Strategies include modifying food and liquid consistencies, changing volumes, and altering the bolus presentations. Other techniques include compensatory strategies (postural maneuvers) and indirect therapy (exercises to strengthen swallowing muscles). There are also specific strategies for improving airway protection and pharyngeal, laryngeal, and upper esophageal sphincter function[41] (Box 27.4).

Patient and Family Education

Patient and family education is vital when treating palliative care patients for symptoms. The APRN must give adequate education to not only the patient but the caregivers as well. Since patients at the end-of-life are uniquely dependent on their family and caregivers, those caregivers may be making a majority of the care decisions and providing medication administration. Medication education is of paramount importance, particularly about the risks, benefits, side effects, and allergic reactions. The patient or caregiver should be encouraged to contact the provider if any of the serious side effects or allergic reactions are suspected. In the general population, acute cough is a common presentation, along with a request for antibiotics.[76] The APRN should provide education about the appropriate use of antibiotics.

Smoking cessation may be an appropriate part of care for the palliative care patient. The American Cancer Society suggests various methods to help smokers quit,[77] such as support groups, nicotine replacement medications, and cognitive-behavioral strategies.

Conclusion

Cough in the palliative care patient can be an acute or chronic symptom that has a negative impact on the patient's quality of life. Cough in this population has myriad etiologies, and there is little research and literature for the palliative care patient. The majority of research dealing with cough as a symptom has been conducted in the generally healthy outpatient population. GERD, viruses, UACS, and cigarette smoking are among the most common causes. Although patients receiving palliative care may have some of these underlying conditions, they are often faced with other pathological processes that make treating cough even more complex.

One of the main guiding principles in palliative care is to balance the risks and benefits of any diagnostic test. Because many patients receiving palliative care are frail, elderly, immobile, and often homebound, the typical outpatient-based diagnostic tests may be impractical.

The APRN should evaluate and manage cough with the goal of improving the overall quality of life. Treatment consists of pharmacologic, nonpharmacologic, and interventional treatments. Secondary symptoms induced by cough, such as pain, incontinence, depression, anxiety, anorexia, and fatigue, should also be evaluated and managed.

References

1. Morice AH, McGarvey L, Pavord I. Recommendations for the management of cough in adults, on behalf of the British Thoracic Society Cough Guideline. *Thorax.* 2006; 61(Suppl 1): 1–24.
2. Morice AH, Fontana AR, Sovijarvi M, et al. The diagnosis and management of chronic cough. *Eur Resp J.* 2004; 24: 481–92.
3. Irwin RS, Baumann MH, Bolser DC, et al. Diagnosis and management of cough executive summary: ACCP evidence-based clinical practice guidelines. *Chest.* 2006; 129: 1–23.
4. Wee B, Browning J, Adams A, et al. Management of chronic cough in patients receiving palliative care: Review of evidence and recommendations by a task group of the Association for Palliative Medicine of Great Britain and Ireland. *Palliat Med.* 2012; 26(6): 780–7.
5. Molassiotis A, Bailey C, Brunton CA, Smith J. Interventions for cough in cancer (review). *Cochrane Database of Systematic Reviews.* 2010(9): 1–41.
6. Pratter MR. Overview of common causes of chronic cough: American College of Chest Physicians evidence based clinical practice guidelines. *Chest.* 2006; 129 (1Suppl): 59S–62S.
7. Estfan B, LeGrand S. Management of cough in advanced cancer. *J Supportive Oncol.* 2004; 2(6): 523–7.
8. Pratter MR, Bartter T, Akers S, DuBois J. An algorithmic approach to chronic cough. *Ann Intern Med.* 1993; 119(10): 977–83.
9. Morice AH. Epidemiology of cough. *Pulmonary Pharmacol Ther.* 2002; 15: 253–9.
10. Bonneau A. Cough in the palliative care setting. *Canadian Family Physician.* June 2009; 55: 600–2.
11. Hanks GW, Cherny N, Christakis N, Fallon M, Kaasa S, Portenoy R, Eds. *Oxford Textbook of Palliative Medicine.* 4th ed. Oxford: Oxford University Press; 2011.
12. Walsh D, Donnelly S, Rybicki L. The symptoms of advanced cancer: relationship to age, gender, and performance status in 1000 patients. *Supportiv Care Cancer.* 2000; 8: 175–9.
13. Wee B. Chronic cough. *Curr Opin Supportive Palliat Care.* 2008; 2: 105–9.
14. Everett CF, Kastelik JA, Thompson RH, Morice AH. Chronic persistent cough in the community: a questionnaire survey. *Cough.* 2007; 3: 5.
15. Fathi H, Morice A. Cough in palliative care. *Progress Palliat Care.* 2008; 16(1): 31–7.
16. Hagen NA. An approach to cough in cancer patients. *J Pain Symptom Manage.* 1991; 6: 257–62.
17. Truesdale K, Jurdi A. Nebulized lidocaine in the treatment of intractable cough. *Am J Hospice Palliat Med.* 2012; 30(6): 586–9.
18. Pratter MR. Chronic upper airway cough syndrome secondary to rhinosinus diseases (previously referred to as postnasal drip syndrome). *Chest.* 2006; 129 (1suppl): 63S–71S.
19. Goldsobel AB, Kelkar PS. The adult with chronic cough. *J Allergy Clin Immunol.* 2012: 825–825.e6.
20. Gibson PG, Dolovich J, Denberg J, Ramsdale EH, Hargreave FE. Chronic cough: eosinophilic bronchitis without asthma. *Lancet.* 1989; 1: 1346–8.
21. Miravitlles M. Cough and sputum production as risk factors for poor outcomes in patients with COPD. *Resp Med.* 2011; 105: 1118–28.
22. Sumner H, Woodcock A, Kolsum U, et al. Predictors of objective cough frequency in chronic obstructive pulmonary disease. *Am J Respir Crit Care Med.* 2013; 187(9): 943–9.
23. Benich III JJ, Carek J. Evaluation of the patient with chronic cough. *Am Family Physician.* 2011; 84(8): 887–92.
24. Irwin RS. Chronic cough due to gastroesophageal reflux disease: ACCP evidence-based clinical practice guidelines. *Chest.* 2006; 129 (1 suppl): 80S–94S.
25. Sesoko S, Kaneko Y. Cough associated with the use of captopril. *Arch Intern Med.* 1985; 145: 1524.
26. Yeo WW, Foster G, Ramsay LE. Prevalence of persistent cough during long-term enalapril treatment: controlled study versus nifedipine. *Q J Med.* 1991; 80: 763–70.
27. Harle AS, Blackhall FH, Smith JA, Molassiotis A. Understanding cough and its management in lung cancer. *Curr Opin Support Palliat Care.* 2012; 6: 153–62.
28. Molassiotis A, Smith JA, Bennett MI, et al. Clinical expert guidelines for the management of cough in lung cancer: report of a UK task group of cough. *Cough.* 2010; 6(9): 1–8.
29. Sahn SA. Malignancy metastatic to the pleura. *Clin Chest Med.* 1998; 19(3): 351–61.
30. Musani AI. Treatment options for malignant pleural effusion. *Curr Opin Pulm Med.* 2009; 15: 380–7.
31. McCannon J, Temel J. Comprehensive management of respiratory symptoms in patients with advanced lung cancer. *J Supportive Oncol.* 2012; 10(1): 1–9.
32. Camus P, Ebina M. Interstitial lung disease associated with drug therapy. *Br J Cancer.* 2004; 91 (suppl 2)(91): S18–23.
33. Abraham KP, Reddy V, Gattuso P. Neoplasms metastatic to the heart. *Am J Cardiovasc Pathol.* 1990; 3(3): 195–8.
34. Hutten BA, Prins MH, Gent M, Ginsberg J, Tijssen GP, Buller H. Incidence of recurrent thromboembolic and bleeding complications among patients with venous thromboembolism in relation to both malignancy and achieved international normalized ratio: a retrospective analysis. *J Clin Oncol.* 2000; 18(17): 3078–83.
35. Bausewein C, Simon S. Shortness of breath and cough in patients in palliative care. *Deutsches Arzbelatt International.* 2013; 110(33-34): 563–71.
36. Irwin RS, Boulet LP, Cloutier MM, et al. Managing cough as a defense mechanism and as a symptom: a consensus panel report of the American College of Chest Physicians. *Chest.* 1998; 114 (2 suppl managing): 133S–181S.
37. Irwin RS, Madison JM. The diagnosis and treatment of cough. *N Engl J Med.* 2000; 343(23): 1715–21.
38. Pratter MR, Brightling CE, Boulet LP, Irwin RS. An empiric integrative approach to the management of cough. *Chest.* 2006; 129: 228s–231s.
39. Doleh TY, Rehm SJ, Isaacson JH. A 49-year-old woman with a persistent cough. *Cleveland Clin J Med.* 2011; 78(8): 521–8.
40. Marik PE. Aspiration pneumonitis and pneumonia: a clinical review. *N Engl J Med.* 2001; 344: 665–72.
41. Marik PE, Kaplan D. Aspiration pneumonia and dysphagia in the elderly. *Chest.* 2003; 124: 328–36.
42. Vertigan AE, Gibson PG. Chronic refractory cough as a sensory neuropathy: evidence from a reinterpretation of cough triggers. *J Voice.* 2011; 25: 596–601.
43. Ryan NM, Birring SS, Gibson PG. Gabapentin for refractory chronic cough: a randomized, double-blind, placebo-controlled trial. *Lancet.* 2012; 380: 1583–9.
44. Estfan B, Walsh D. The cough from hell: diazepam for intractable cough in a patient with renal cell carcinoma. *J Pain Symptom Management.* 2008; 36(5): 553–8.
45. Economou D. In: Ferrell B, Coyle N, Paice J, eds. *Oxford Textbook of Palliative Nursing.* 4th ed. New York, NY: Oxford University Press; 2015:217–236.

46. Mise K, Sviliicic A, Bradaric A. Foreign bodies in the bronchial system of adults [abstract]. *Eur Respir J Suppl.* 2004; 24: 48S.

47. Kvale PA. Chronic cough due to lung tumors. American College of Chest Physicians evidence-based clinical practice guidelines. *Chest.* 2006; 129 (1Suppl): 147S–153S.

48. Bleehan NM, Girling DJ, Fayers PM, et al. Inoperable nonsmall-cell lung cancer (NSCLC): a Medical Research Council randomised trial of palliative radiotherapy with two fractions or ten fractions. *Br J Cancer.* 1991; 63: 265–70.

49. Cullianane CA, Paz IB, Smith D, et al. Prognostic factors in the surgical management of pericardial effusion in the patient with concurrent malignancy. *Chest.* 2004; 125(4): 1328–34.

50. Wang GR, Ensor JE, Gupta S, et al. Bronchial artery embolization for the management of hemoptysis in oncology patients; utility and prognostic factors. *J Vasc Interv Radiol.* 2009; 20(6): 722–9.

51. Ernst A, Silvestri GA, Johnstone D. Interventional pulmonary procedures: guidelines from the American College of Chest Physicians. *Chest.* 2003; 123(5): 1693–717.

52. Freltag L, Tekolf E, Steveling H, Donovan TJ. Management of malignant esophago-tracheal fistulas with airway stending and double stenting. *Chest.* 1996; 110: 1155–60.

53. Putnam JB, Walsh GL, Swhisher SG, et al. Outpatient management of malignant plerual effusions bya chronic indwelling catheter. *Ann Thorac Surg.* 2000; 69: 369–75.

54. Musani AI, Haas AR, Seijo L, et al. Outpatient management of malignant pleural effusions with a small-bore, tunneled pleural catheters. *Respiration.* 2004; 71: 559–66.

55. Antony VB, Loddenkemper R, Astoul P, et al. Management of malignant plerual effusions. *Am J Respir Crit Care.* 2000; 162: 1987–2001.

56. Menzies R, Charbonneau M. Thoroscopy for the diagnosis of pleural disease. *Ann Intern Med.* 1991; 114: 271–6.

57. Khaleeq G, Musani A. Emerging paradigms in the management of malignant pleural effusions. *Respir Med.* 2008; 102: 939–948.

58. Rousseau P. Nonpain symptom management in the dying patient. *Hospital Physician.* February 2002: 51–56.

59. Bolser DC. Cough suppresant and pharmacologic protussive therapy: American College of Chest Physicians evidence-based clinical practice guidelines. *Chest.* 2008; 129 (1suppl): 238S–249S.

60. McCool FD, Rosen MJ. Nonpharmacologic airway clearance therapies: American College of Chest Physicians evidence-based clinical practice guidelines. *Chest.* 2008; 129 (1Suppl): 250S–259S.

61. Bolser DC, Davenport PW. Codeine and cough: an ineffective gold standard. *Curr Opin Allergy Clin Immunol.* 2007; 7: 32–6.

62. Freestone C, Eccles R. Assessment of the antitussive efficacy of codeine in cough associated with common cold. *J Pharm Pharmacol.* 1997; 49: 1045–9.

63. Smith J, Owen E, Earis J, Woodcock A. Effect of codeine on objective measurement of cough in chronic obstructive pulmonary disease. *J Allerg Clin Immunol.* 2006; 117: 831–5.

64. Morice AH, Menon MS, Mulrennan SA, et al. Opiate therapy in chronic cough. *Am J Respir Crit Care Med.* 2007; 117: 312–5.

65. Ahmedzai S, Davis C. Nebulized drugs in palliative care. *Thorax.* 1997; 552 (suppl 20): S75–S77.

66. Drug Information for the Health Care Professional, 20th ed. Englewood, CO: Micromedex, 2000.

67. Homsi J, Walsh D, Nelson KA, et al. A phase II study of hydrocodone for cough in advanced cancer. *Am J Hospice Palliat Med.* 2002; 19(1): 49–56.

68. Watson MS, Lucas CF, Hoy AM, Black IN. *Oxford Handbook of Palliative Care.* 1st ed. Oxford: Oxford University Press; 2005.

69. Udnzue E. Lidocaine inhalation for cough suppression. *Am J Emerg Med.* 2001; 19(3): 206–7.

70. Stewart CJ, Coady TJ. Suppression of intractable cough. *Br Med J.* 1977; 16077: 1660–1.

71. Lingerfelt BM, Swainey CW, Smith TJ, Coyne PJ. Nebulized lidocaine for intractable cough near the end of life. *J Support Oncol.* 2007; 5(7): 301–2.

72. Zylicz Z, Krajnik M. The use of antitussive drugs in terminally ill patients. *Eur J Palliat Care.* 2004; 11(6): 225.

73. Jassem AR, Krzakowski M, Roszkowski K, et al. A phase II study of gemcitabine plus cisplatin in patients with advanced nonsmall cell lung cancer: clinical outcomes and quality of life. *Lung Cancer.* 2002; 35: 73–9.

74. Janson S, Carrieri-Kohlman V. Respiratory Changes. In: Ropka M, Williams A, eds. *HIV Nursing and Symptom Management.* Sudbury, MA: Jones and Bartlett; 1998.

75. Coyne PJ, Lyne ME, Watson AC. Symptom management in people with AIDS. *Am J Nurs.* 2002; 102(9): 48–57.

76. Ebell MH, Lundgren J, Youngpairoj S. How long does a cough last? Comparing patients' expectations with data from a systematic review of the literature. *Ann Fam Med.* 2013; 11(1): 5–13.

77. Guide to Quitting Smoking. American Cancer Society. 2014. Available at www.Cancer.org. Accessed July 24, 2014.

CHAPTER 28

Challenging Symptoms
Dry Mouth, Hiccups, Fevers, Pruritus, and Sleep Disorders

Barton T. Bobb and Devon Fletcher

Key Points

◆ The advanced practice registered nurse (APRN) must have a working knowledge of the less common symptoms of dry mouth, hiccups, fever, pruritus, and sleep disorders so they can be effectively managed.

◆ Fever may require scheduled antipyretic treatment at end-of-life if it is believed to be distressing.

◆ Dry mouth is a common symptom among palliative care patients, especially cancer patients.

◆ Pruritus can be challenging to treat; determining the cause when possible can help tailor treatment.

Case Study

Mrs. P was a 49-year-old female with advanced pancreatic cancer with associated pain. She had been followed by a palliative APRN in a palliative care clinic. The short-acting opioid that best managed her pain, immediate-release oxycodone, unfortunately caused some pruritus, for which the palliative APRN prescribed hydroxyzine 25 mg PO q6h PRN.

Mrs. P also complained of ongoing dry mouth as well as difficulty sleeping at night. She used sugar-free chewing gum and was prescribed 5 mg pilocarpine PO three times a day to stimulate saliva production. Saliva substitutes were prescribed as well. A variety of sleep hygiene measures were suggested to help her sleep. Temazepam 15 mg PO nightly was prescribed. With sleep medications, pain medications, changes in sleep hygiene, and improved pain control, Mrs. P reported more consecutive hours of uninterrupted sleep.

After several months, Mrs. P's disease progressed and she was actively dying at home with hospice. Because she was running high fevers that appeared to be distressing to her and her family, the attending hospice NP ordered scheduled acetaminophen rectal suppositories q6h. Her oral pain medications were switched to a home patient-controlled analgesia (PCA). The palliative APRN made a home visit to check on her and her family. She appeared to be very comfortable. Her family expressed appreciation for all the care the APRN had provided for her and them over the past several months. Mrs. P died peacefully 3 days later.

Pruritus

The word *pruritus* comes from the Latin *prurire*, meaning "to itch." Pruritus is often associated with pathological or chronic itch causing a desire to scratch. This scratch reflex is meant to be a protective mechanism, but when this sensation becomes chronic, there can be resulting emotional and physical consequences.[1] Pruritus is a frequently underreported symptom.[2] However, the impact on quality of life, sleep, anxiety, and depression can be very distressing, and this symptom must not be overlooked.

The physiology of the itch sensation transmission is not well understood. It was initially thought to be a subset of the pain transmission pathway, but is now believed to be transmitted from the peripheral nervous system by slow, unmyelinated type C nerve fibers to the central nervous system (CNS), distinct from the type C polymodal fibers that carry aching, dull, or burning pain sensations. There are various stimuli and neuropeptide targets associated with itch and its treatment.[1,3–5]

Etiology

Finding the source of the itching can be challenging, but determining the cause may help direct the choice of treatment. The direct cause cannot always be determined, or patients may have overlapping or multiple causes of pruritus.[6,7]

Primary Dermatologic Causes

Pruritus is the most commonly reported symptom in dermatologic disorders as a whole.[2] Often itch-producing stimuli are short-lived or self-limiting and if needed, can be treated effectively by a primary care provider or other first-line providers. Causes of primary dermatologic conditions can range from dry skin and insect bites to dermatologic malignancies. Depending on the severity of the symptoms, the APRN may need to refer the patient to a dermatologist for intervention or consider measures for intractable pruritus.

Systemic Diseases

Pruritus can manifest in many systemic diseases (Table 28.1). Approximately 70% of patients with cholestatic liver disease, from various causes, reported pruritus.[3,8,9] Bilirubin accumulation is thought to be the underlying cause, but how this causes

Table 28.1 Systemic Causes of Pruritus

Biliary and hepatic disease
Chronic renal insufficiency/uremia
Endocrinopathy
Hyper/hypothyroid
Hyperparathyroid
Diabetes mellitus
Carcinoid syndrome
Infectious diseases
AIDS
Infectious hepatitis
Parasitic disease
Prion disease
Hematologic/oncologic
Lymphoma/leukemia
Systemic mastocytosis
Multiple myeloma
Polycythemia vera
Iron deficiency anemia
Autoimmune
Dermatitis herpetiformis
Dermatomyositis
Linear immunoglobulin A
Medications
Opioids
Amphetamines
Cocaine
Niacin
Aspirin

itching is largely unknown.[10–13] Chronic renal insufficiency is another systemic disease with a high symptom burden from pruritus, especially in patients on chronic hemodialysis.[2,14] Metabolic derangements in renal disease such as hypercalcemia, hyperphosphatemia, and hypermagnesemia seem to contribute independently to pruritus as well.[15] Endocrinopathies such as hyperparathyroidism, both hypothyroidism and hyperthyroidism, and diabetes are all associated with itching.[1,2,16,17] Multiple hematopoietic disorders, ranging from more benign iron deficiency anemia to malignancies such as lymphoma and multiple myeloma, can cause itching or chronic pruritus. T-cell lymphomas, in particular Sézary syndrome, are characterized by a high incidence of pruritus and commonly require the assistance of a palliative provider for more advanced interventions.[18,19] Infectious diseases can cause various local and systemic pruritus. There has been an increasing recognition of chronic pruritus seen in HIV-positive patients; it appears to be independent of the incidence of primary dermatologic sources of itch.[20,21]

Medications

Any medication can cause itching from an allergic reaction or sensitivity. Certain medications or illicit drugs commonly known to cause itching include opiates, amphetamines, cocaine, niacin, and aspirin.[1,2]

Neurologic

Patients with stroke or brain tumor (either primary or due to metastatic disease) can have a centrally mediated itch. There are also peripheral neuropathic itch syndromes, such as post-herpetic itch and nostalgia paresthetica.[1,7,22]

Psychiatric

Pruritus is reported to be common in psychiatric conditions, such as psychosis or delirium, but epidemiologic data on the actual prevalence are lacking.[2] In addition to causing pruritus, anxiety and depression are thought to worsen the patient's ability to cope with pruritus of other etiologies.[23] The palliative APRN may need to collaborate with psychiatric colleagues to manage these causes.

Treatment

Treatment of systemic pruritus is often difficult. Particularly frustrating is that the mainstays of treatment for primary dermatologic pruritus are often not helpful for systemic causes. Balancing the side effects against the benefit of a treatment is always at the core of the APRN's decision to administer or prescribe therapeutic agents. If the pruritus is from a disease process or medication that cannot be removed, then treatment modalities range from topical therapies, to systemic medications, or invasive interventions in which the symptom burden should outweigh the risk of the treatment. The APRN should be prepared for a stepwise trial approach to determine what medications are effective at relieving pruritus.

Initial nonpharmacologic interventions include patient and family education on methods to decrease itching, such as wearing light clothing and lowering the room temperature. The APRN should also continue to monitor the patient's skin for excoriation and secondary infections from scratching.[24]

Topical Treatments

Topical ointments and barrier creams are always available and should be used (Box 28.1). However, they are less likely to be helpful when pruritus is due to a systemic cause, the more likely type to be seen within palliative care.[25,26]

Systemic Treatments

Systemic therapies are varied (Table 28.2). When possible, therapy should be directed toward the source of pruritus. Antihistamines are particularly helpful for pruritus that is known to be histamine-mediated. They are generally trialled for all types of pruritus at some point, as they have a relatively benign side-effect profile. Side effects commonly include drowsiness and dry mouth; the former can actually be helpful if the patient is experiencing pruritus at night affecting sleep, but can limit use if causing sedation during the day.[25]

Box 28.1 Topical Treatments of Pruritus

Calamine

Menthol

Oatmeal bath

Antihistamines

Steroids

Capsaicin

Table 28.2 Common Systemic Treatments of Pruritus

Antihistamines
Diphenhydramine (PO, IV)
Doxylamine (PO)
Hydroxyzine (PO, IM)
Rifampicin (PO)
Sequestrants
Cholestyramine (PO)
Colestipol (PO)
Opioid Receptor Antagonists
Naloxone (IV)
Naltrexone (PO, IM)
Neuroleptics
Gabapentin (PO)
Pregabalin (PO)
Antidepressants
SSRIs (PO)
Mirtazapine (PO)
Doxepin (PO)
Antiemetics
Ondansetron (PO, IV)
Aprepitant (PO)

Opiate rotation should be considered for patients experiencing pruritus associated with opiate use. If this is not possible, the use of an opioid receptor antagonist such as naloxone or naltrexone may be helpful. Intravenous naloxone is not a realistic treatment option for outpatient or home management or long-term use. Its half-life is too short, but it can be given by intravenous infusion for acute symptoms.[27,28] Opiate antagonism can produce side effects similar to opiate withdrawal, and patients should be warned of this prior to use.

Sequestrant medications, such as cholestyramine and colestipol, are often used on a first-line basis to control pruritus in cholestatic liver disease.[1,28,29] Compliance difficulties can arise as these medications can be unpleasant to swallow, and there should be a 4-hour interval before taking other oral medications.[28]

Rifampicin has been found to be helpful for pruritus in hepatic cholestasis as a second-line agent. Liver biochemistries should be checked periodically because the antibiotic may cause toxic hepatitis in about 15% of cases, and patients should be counseled about the signs of liver failure.[1,28,29]

Neuroleptics like gabapentin seem to be effective for neurologic causes of itching.[1,28] Both gabapentin and pregabalin are showing promise for the treatment of pruritus associated with uremia.[28,30] Both of these medications can be associated with drowsiness, among other side effects. Serotonin reuptake inhibitors, such as sertraline, paroxetine, and fluvoxamine,[1,7,28] as well as mirtazapine, a tetracyclic antidepressant, and doxepin, a tricyclic antidepressant, have all shown some benefit in pruritus caused by various etiologies.[1,7,25,28]

Antiemetics, such as ondansetron, a type 3 (5-HT3) serotonin receptor antagonist, may relieve some types of pruritus. Further randomized controlled trials suggest antiemetics may not be helpful for pruritus related to hepatic cholestatic disease and chronic renal disease.[1,7,25,31] Aprepitant, a neurokinin receptor-1 (NKR 1) antagonist used as an antiemetic, blocks the binding of substance P and in particular has been helpful in patients with T-cell lymphoma.[7,18,25]

Agents that are less commonly used to treat pruritus include immunosuppressants,[25] tranquilizers, sedatives, and heparin.[28] Topical steroids are frequently used for dermatologic disorders, but oral steroids are thought to help reduce itch only if an inflammatory component is present. Because of the side effects of long-term steroid use, providers should exhaust other treatments before using steroids for systemic pruritus.[25]

Interventional Treatments

Several interventions for pruritus, mostly pruritus caused by liver disease, have been developed for patients with symptoms refractory to less invasive treatments (Box 28.2). Prognosis and ability to withstand these interventions would be dependent on overall clinical status. Patients with primary biliary cirrhosis with cholestatic disease may be liver transplant candidates based on their pruritus symptoms alone.[13] Extracorporeal albumin dialysis[29,32] and biliary drainage have also been shown to relieve intractable pruritus in primary biliary cirrhosis.[27] Additional investigation needs to be performed, but initial observations seem to suggest that phototherapy[1,25,28] and plasmapheresis[25–27] may be beneficial in relieving chronic pruritus as well. Therapies such as acupuncture and transcutaneous nerve stimulation may also be worth exploring.[1]

Hiccups

Most people experience hiccups periodically, but when hiccups are persistent they can become a burdensome symptom, severely affecting quality of life. Persistent hiccup, or *singultus* in medical terms, is derived from the Latin word *singult*, which means "the act of catching one's breath while sobbing."[33] Epidemiologic studies of prevalence are limited, although it is believed that persistent or intractable hiccups are relatively uncommon.[32,34] As a result, minimal research has been done to test the effectiveness of treatments.[34,35]

Hiccups represent an involuntary spasm of the diaphragm and accessory respiratory muscles. The causes of hiccups can be varied, but they generally result from an irritation of the diaphragm directly or of the nervous system controlling this muscle. The

Box 28.2 Interventional Treatments for Pruritus

Acupuncture
Biliary drainage
Hemodialysis
Liver transplantation
Parathyroidectomy
Phototherapy
Plasmapheresis
Transcutaneous nerve stimulation

hiccup reflex involves the afferent vagal, phrenic, and sympathetic nerves, the brain stem, and the efferent phrenic nerve to the diaphragm. Gastric distention and gastroesophageal reflux are among the more common causes of persistent hiccups. Toxicity, such as in infections or uremia, and CNS or direct phrenic nerve irritation are also potential causes of hiccups.[32,33–38] Awareness that medications such as corticosteroids have been linked with hiccups may be beneficial for palliative APRNs working with oncology patients, who are often exposed to corticosteroids for both treatment and symptom management of their cancers.[39,40]

Attempting vagal maneuvers, nasopharyngeal stimulation, and inducing hypercapnia with hyperventilation are among the initial physical interventions that may be successful.[32,40] If symptoms persist or recur at a frequency where the benefit of interventions outweighs the potential side effects, several medications have been tried with some success, although, as mentioned, limited data exist for these treatments.

There are mixed data on medication management. No one medication has been demonstrated to consistently manage hiccups.[34] Thus, the APRN must consider the patient, the current medication profile, and goals of care. Again, management may occur using a process of trial and observation to determine which medication will be effective.

Chlorpromazine, a phenothiazine first-generation antipsychotic, is the only medication approved by the U.S. Food and Drug Administration (FDA) for the treatment of persistent hiccups.[32,38] Doses of oral chlorpromazine for hiccups are typically lower than those for antipsychotic effects. Side effects include dizziness, drowsiness, dystonia, neuroleptic malignant syndrome, and tardive dyskinesia. These side effects can limit the ability to use this medication as a first-line therapy.[38]

Metoclopramide, a prokinetic agent with dopamine receptor antagonist properties, may also be of benefit for hiccups.[41,42] If hiccups are due to gastric distention, this may be a particularly beneficial therapeutic agent to resolve the underlying cause of the hiccups. Side effects include drowsiness, agitation, tardive dyskinesia, dizziness, and confusion, which may limit use. QTc prolongation may occur and monitoring may be indicated, especially if the patient is using other medications that may also prolong QTc and increase the risk of arrhythmias.

Haloperidol, specifically via the intramuscular route, was supported in older literature as a treatment for intractable hiccups based on several case reports,[43] but no new data to confirm this exist, and using the intramuscular route would be discouraged unless intravascular or oral routes were tried and failed. In addition, due to increased risk of tardive dyskinesia, this agent likely should not be used in conjunction with chlorpromazine or metoclopramide.

Baclofen, a GABA analog used as a muscle relaxant, is emerging as a promising treatment for intractable hiccups.[32,44–47] Further evaluation of this treatment in the palliative patient population is needed, however, as most data that exist are specific to neurological conditions. Baclofen's potential side effects include respiratory depression, sedation, and asthenia but are most common in patients with impaired renal function,[46] and overall some data suggest this therapy to have minimal adverse events.[44,47]

Gabapentin has also been identified as a potential low-burden second-line therapy for intractable hiccups, including in advanced cancer patients.[32,38,48,49] Sleepiness is identified as the major potential side effect, but it is otherwise well tolerated.[49]

Antihypertensive medications, such as nifedipine,[50] a calcium channel blocker, and carvedilol,[51] a beta-blocker, have significantly fewer data supporting their use for hiccups. If side effects from more established treatments are limiting use, however, these may be alternative therapies if patients' blood pressures are high enough to tolerate their use.

Various other medications, such as benzodiazepines, methylphenidate, serotonergic agonists,[32,33] olanzapine, valproic acid, cisapride, omeprazole,[45,48] lidocaine,[32,52] amitriptyline, ketamine, and amantadine,[53] all have limited case reports or case series supporting their use.

Therapeutic interventions, such as surgical or radiofrequency nerve ablation,[32,54] diaphragmatic pacing,[32] and alternative therapies such as acupuncture[32,55,56] have shown effectiveness. However, further studies are needed.

Various nonpharmacologic, pharmacologic, and alternative therapies, including invasive interventions, may be beneficial for this relatively rare symptom.[32,34,48,49] No therapies have been extensively studied, and further investigation is needed for definite treatment recommendations.

Dry Mouth

Dry mouth, or xerostomia, is common in cancer patients and patients at the end-of-life.[57-59] The differential diagnosis can be divided into four areas: decreased saliva secretion, dehydration, erosion of the buccal mucosa, and miscellaneous.[58,59]

Saliva secretion is regulated by both sympathetic and parasympathetic processes and involves a number of different pathways, so the pathophysiology of hyposalivation can be traced to several potential causes, including a slight disruption of the muscarinic receptors to outright obliteration of parenchymal tissue.[60] The parotid, submandibular, and sublingual glands work together to produce saliva and maintain proper consistency, so damage to any of them will affect not only the amount but also the viscosity of the saliva.[59]

Decreased saliva secretion can be caused by radiation to the head and neck, chemotherapy, a variety of medications (e.g., anticholinergics, antihistamines, tricyclic antidepressants, opioids, and sedatives), and some medical conditions (e.g., autoimmune disorders, infections, and sarcoidosis).[58,59]

Erosion of the buccal mucosa can also be caused by a variety of medical conditions (e.g., HIV/AIDS, Sjögren syndrome, systemic lupus erythematosus, and diabetes mellitus) plus chemotherapy and radiation, where higher doses and more radiation treatments also directly affect the extent and length of impairment in saliva production.[58,59] Xerostomia from dehydration can occur as a result of vomiting, diarrhea, dysphagia, oxygen use, and fever, while mental health issues, such as depression or anxiety, are potential miscellaneous causes of xerostomia.[59,60]

For the assessment of xerostomia, the APRN can use several precise ways to make the diagnosis, such as measuring salivary flow or salivary gland scintigraphy, but these are usually not appropriate to the palliative care population.[57] A basic clinical history and focused exam should be sufficient to make the diagnosis and determine the likely etiology.[57] The inside of the mouth can be examined for signs of xerostomia, such as dry mucosa and tongue, and ulceration. Two simple bedside tests to evaluate for xerostomia are the cracker biscuit test, where the patient is diagnosed to have xerostomia if unable to eat a cracker or biscuit without drinking something, and the tongue depressor test, which diagnoses xerostomia if the tongue depressor sticks to the tongue after placement.[59] There are also certain assessment tools, such as the University of Michigan Xerostomia tool, that allow patients to rate their symptoms.[59]

The management of xerostomia relies on potentially complex medication use as well as nonpharmacologic interventions (Table 28.3, Box 28.3). A general approach to management involves treating any underlying conditions (e.g., candidiasis), reviewing medications and changing those that may be contributing to xerostomia, finding ways to stimulate salivation, using saliva substitutes to replace lost saliva, and managing the xerostomia holistically in general.[59]

Mucin-based saliva substitutes appear to be better tolerated than carboxymethyl-cellulose-based ones, and sprays overall better than gels.[57,59] Contraindications to taking pilocarpine include asthma, bronchitis/chronic obstructive pulmonary disease, glaucoma, and heart, kidney, or liver disease.[57,59] Cevimeline should not be used in patients with acute iritis, uncontrolled asthma, or narrow-angle glaucoma.[57]

Preventative oral care interventions for patients with xerostomia should be encouraged. This includes brushing teeth regularly with fluoridated toothpaste, rinsing with a cup of warm water containing ½ teaspoon baking soda, and using an antimicrobial rinse daily.[60] Potential interventional techniques to treat xerostomia are acupuncture and intraductal gene therapy, which is inserted via the parotid gland, but acupuncture does not have sufficient evidence to recommend it and gene therapy is in its early stages of research.[61]

The APRN should focus patient and family education on good preventive and nonpharmacologic measures. Oral care is especially important throughout the disease course, including at end-of-life for continued comfort.[59] Ensure that the patient and family know how to use any prescription medications or over-the-counter medications. They should also understand any potential side effects, precautions, contraindications, or drug interactions.

Fevers

Fever is generally defined as a rise in oral body temperature above 38°C (100.4°F).[24] The pathophysiology of fever is based on the presence of pyrogens, substances that produce fever, inducing the hypothalamus to reset the body temperature set point.[62] Pathogens release exogenous pyrogens, and the destruction of pathogens causes the body to produce endogenous pyrogens, namely interleukin-1 and -6, interferons, and tumor necrosis factor, but both types of pyrogens can ultimately induce fever.[62]

Clinically, fever often presents in three stages: chill, fever, and flush.[24] During the chill phase, the body is reacting to the body's

Box 28.3 Nonpharmacologic Xerostomia Treatments

Chewing sugar-free gum

Organic acids (ascorbic acid, citric acid, malic acid)

Water/peppermint water

Electrostimulation (embedded in a custom-made mouthguard)

Diet modifications (e.g., soft foods, increased fluid intake with meals, avoiding sugary and spicy foods)

From references 57, 59, 61.

new temperature set point and generates heat through shivering and tries to prevent heat loss through vasoconstriction.[24] During the fever phase, the body raises its temperature to meet the new set point, resulting in a warm feeling, lethargy, and possible dehydration or even seizures. In the flush stage, the body tries to acclimate to the new set point through diaphoresis and vasodilation.[24] Certain populations, such as immunocompromised patients, older adults, newborns, and those taking steroids, may not mount a fever response with an infection.[63]

The assessment of patients with fever usually begins with a detailed history and exam, but the extent of evaluation and further workup may vary greatly depending on the patient's prognosis and established goals.[63] When appropriate, the APRN conducts a thorough examination, looking for signs of infection and possible disease progression in cancer patients, and reviews the patient's medications; this may be followed by laboratory (e.g., blood and urine cultures, complete blood count) and radiographic (e.g., chest x-ray, computed tomography scan) testing.[63]

Some of the most common differential diagnoses of fever in palliative care patients include infection (by far the most common etiology), medications, paraneoplastic-related fevers, neurologic damage, and inflammation.[62] Neutropenic patients are particularly susceptible to infections; some common sources include wounds, the bloodstream and urinary tract, implanted vascular access devices, pneumonia, and the gastrointestinal tract.[62]

The APRN must decide whether to treat the source of the fever in the first place. How much workup to pursue will depend on the patient's prognosis, potential burden versus benefit, and overall goals of care. If a workup is pursued and the source of the fever is identified, treatment of the underlying condition may involve both interventional techniques (e.g., drainage of an abscess) and complex medication options (e.g., intravenous antibiotics). In some instances, the APRN could initiate empiric antibiotics without further workup. This may be appropriate when patients have a colonized infection and antibiotics curb the infection just enough to ward off fevers.

However, when patients are actively dying, even empiric antibiotics are usually no longer indicated.[24] In fact, even symptomatic treatment of fever is not always necessary or appropriate. Fevers may not cause discomfort, but breaking the fever, and the likely resulting sweats, could cause discomfort.[62] There is also some indication that low-level fevers can have a protective function. It is ultimately the patient's decision whether the fever is bothering him or her; if the patient can no longer communicate, then the patient's family can help the APRN with decision making.[62]

Table 28.3 Pharmacologic Xerostomia Treatments

Saliva Stimulants	Saliva Substitutes
Pilocarpine 5–10 mg tid (primarily muscarinic agonist)	Mucin-based (e.g., Saliva Orthana)
Cevimeline 15–30 mg tid (muscarinic)	Carboxymethyl-cellulose-based (e.g., BioXtra)

From references 57, 59, 61.

For symptomatic treatment of fever, the major medication options include acetaminophen 325 to 650 mg q4–6h (orally, intravenously, or rectally), nonsteroidal anti-inflammatories (e.g., naproxen 225–500 mg orally q12h, intravenous ketorolac 15–30 mg q6h, ibuprofen 200–400 mg orally q4–6h, or indomethacin 50 mg orally or rectally q8h), or aspirin 325 to 650 mg orally or rectally q6h plus corticosteroids.[62] Generally speaking, antipyretics' action centers on preventing the production of prostaglandin E2.[63] When antipyretics are administered for symptomatic relief, it is best to schedule them around the clock to avoid fluctuations in body temperature, and diaphoresis with fever.[24]

Nonpharmacologic interventions to treat fevers need to be chosen carefully. Many of the treatments historically used to bring down fevers, such as ice packs, cooling blankets, cold sponge baths, or a fan blowing directly on the patient, can cause more discomfort by making the patient too cold and inducing shivering.[24] Instead, some measures that can be safely implemented to help maintain patient comfort include keeping the room temperature at a comfortable level, ensuring that the patient's bed linen and clothing are clean and dry, offering cool liquids to drink for those who can drink, and ensuring that the patient's lips are kept moist.[24,62]

The APRN should be aware of the very severe side effects that can occur with excessive use of acetaminophen (liver failure) or nonsteroidal anti-inflammatories (kidney failure, gastrointestinal bleed—a much higher risk with ketorolac). The patient's prognosis and goals of care could once again affect the risk/benefit ratio of administering either of these medications for symptomatic management of fever. In the actively dying patient who is believed to have discomfort from persistent fevers, the potential benefit of giving either medication on a scheduled basis should outweigh the potential risks. The treatment of any underlying infection with antibiotics may also involve careful evaluation of any potential side effects or drug interactions when prescribing them.

When the APRN is treating a fever in a palliative patient, especially one who is actively dying, careful patient and family education is vital. The APRN must ensure that the approach to treatment is properly established and that the patient does not accidentally receive some of the aforementioned nonpharmacologic interventions that may cause more harm than benefit (e.g., cold packs). Cool, not cold, cloths may help, as well as light bedding. Mouth care should be continued since fever causes dry mouth.[24] Patients and family members may need frequent reinforcement when the decision is made not to treat the underlying cause of a fever or its symptoms if it does not appear to be causing discomfort to the dying patient. However, if family members insist that their loved one receive symptomatic fever treatment, it may be an appropriate and palliative measure to do so.[62] When patients require symptomatic treatment for fevers earlier in the course of their disease, patients and families may require extensive education and reminders about the potential dangers of excessive nonsteroidal anti-inflammatory or acetaminophen use.

Sleep Disorders

Sleep disorders, and the associated insomnia or lack of quality sleep, are a potentially very disturbing issue for palliative patients and a challenge for the APRNs treating them. Broadly speaking,

the American Academy of Sleep Medicine classifies sleep disorders into four categories: disorders of extreme somnolence, the sleep–wake cycle, difficulty initiating or maintaining sleep, and dysfunction of sleep, sleep stages, or incomplete arousal.[64] More specifically, the differential diagnoses among the major sleep disorders include primary insomnia (e.g., acute, life-long or chronic, psychological, or poor sleep hygiene), sleep apnea, restless leg syndrome, parasomnia, and narcolepsy.[65] A workup to differentiate primary insomnia from another specific sleep disorder may include: the Epworth Sleepiness Scale questionnaire; an overnight polysomnogram, followed by daytime multiple sleep latency testing if evaluating for narcolepsy; use of an actigraph to study sleep–wake patterns; and other miscellaneous tests.[66] A polysomnogram positive for sleep apnea would likely be followed by a trial of continuous positive airway pressure (CPAP), possibly even done halfway through the night of a polysomnogram, if the results are blatantly positive. A survey of 76 palliative care clinic patients indicated that about 40% met criteria for restless leg syndrome that reduced their quality of life negatively[67] (Box 28.4).

The most common sleep disorder is some form of simple/primary insomnia (occurs in 23% to 61% of cancer patients); it will be the focus of the rest of this section.[64] The normal architecture of sleep involves two major phases, rapid and non-rapid eye movement sleep (REM and NREM).[64] During REM sleep, sometimes also called "dream sleep," the brain is very active, while NREM sleep consists of four increasingly deep, quiet, and restorative periods of sleep that together make up one sleep cycle of approximately 90 minutes.[64] The pathophysiology of insomnia is potentially quite complex as it involves an increased level of arousal of the brain, including higher activity during NREM sleep. Genetic factors may predispose individuals to be more sensitive to external factors, such as caffeine or stress, that can subsequently disrupt the sleep–wake cycle.[64] Some other biological differences found in patients with chronic insomnia include higher levels of adrenocorticotropic hormone (ACTH), cortisol, and adrenaline release and increased body temperature compared to patients who sleep normally.[64]

The assessment of insomnia begins by obtaining a thorough sleep history from the patient and any sleeping partner and involves an evaluation of sleep chronology, environment, and hygiene, in addition to any physical symptoms, medical conditions, and spiritual concerns.[65] The sleep assessment questionnaires that have been used most frequently in research include the Epworth Sleepiness Scale, the Insomnia Severity Index, and the Pittsburgh Sleep Quality Index; the Insomnia Severity Index appears to have the most consistency and reliability regarding cancer patients in particular.[68]

The APRN should determine whether the patient follows generally accepted sleep hygiene behaviors: (a) a regular sleep time and wakeup time, (b) using the bed only for sleep and sexual activity, (c) not lying in bed awake for more than about 30 minutes if unable to fall asleep at night, and (d) subsequently not returning to bed again until sleepy. The APRN should ask whether the patient takes naps during the day. Naps should be avoided, except possibly a short one between 2 and 4 p.m. The APRN should assess the patient's caffeine intake in food and beverages, or the use of alcoholic beverages. Finally, the APRN should assess the patient's activity level. Usually, strenuous exercise from late afternoon on should be avoided unless the patient has a very different sleep cycle. The sleep environment, such as the lighting, an unfamiliar bed, and noises, can also affect the patient's ability to sleep in a strange environment (e.g., a hospital, child's/relative's home).[65]

By assessing the sleep chronology, the course of the patient's insomnia can be determined in more detail and the APRN can pinpoint whether the main issue involves sleep onset, maintenance, or both.[65] If the insomnia is an ongoing problem, there is often a medical, psychological, or neurological disorder that is at least partially responsible.[65] Medications may cause frequent awakening throughout the night, and early morning awakening is often related to depression.[65]

Medical conditions can also contribute to insomnia, including worsening of a chronic problem, such as chronic obstructive pulmonary disease or congestive heart failure, a recent or deepening depression that may also be accompanied by anxiety, a variety of medications to treat such conditions (e.g., corticosteroids, stimulants), or previously mentioned sleep disorders like restless leg syndrome.[65] Physical symptoms such as pain, shortness of breath, or cough may interfere with sleep initiation or maintenance. Spiritual distress associated with the fear of dying while asleep, together with other anxiety and fear of uncertainty, may precipitate reluctance to fall asleep and nightmares.[65] The only sleep disorder that routinely uses an interventional technique for management is obstructive sleep apnea, which may be treated with use of a CPAP machine at night, or in some cases can improve with uvulopalatopharyngoplasty surgery.

The management of insomnia generally consists of complex medication management and nonpharmacologic interventions. The major classes of medications approved by the FDA to treat insomnia are benzodiazepines, benzodiazepine receptor agonists, non-benzodiazepine receptor agonists, and melatonin-receptor agonists.[64] Some of the other major classes of drugs frequently used to treat insomnia include antidepressants, atypical antipsychotics, and antihistamines.[69]

Benzodiazepine and non-benzodiazepine agonists both act on the GABA receptor complex. The APRN should use caution if a patient already taking opioids is started on benzodiazepines. For some patients, a synergistic effect may occur and more sedation may ensue. Non-benzodiazepine agonists do not affect the sleep architecture and tend to have fewer side effects, especially longer-lasting ones (e.g., less risk for abuse, dependence, and lingering oversedation).[64] Melatonin-receptor agonists act on MT1 and MT2 receptors, are believed to be involved in normal sleep–wake cycle regulation, and have fewer side effects and no risk for abuse or dependence; only ramelteon has FDA approval.[64] The other classes of drugs are used due to their sedating properties[64,69] (Table 28.4).

Box 28.4 Differential Diagnosis of Major Sleep Disorders

Primary insomnia

Sleep apnea

Restless leg syndrome

Narcolepsy

Parasomnia

From reference 65.

Table 28.4 Pharmacologic Options to Manage Insomnia

Medication and Dosage	Major Side Effects
Benzodiazepine Receptor Agonists	Drowsiness, confusion
Temazepam 7.5–15 mg	Amnesia, drowsiness
Triazolam 0.125 mg	Respiratory depression, sedation
Lorazepam 0.5–4 mg	
Non-benzodiazepine Receptor Agonists	Sedation, dizziness
Zolpidem 5–10 mg (IR), 6.25–12.5 mg (ER)	Headache, drowsiness, dizziness
Eszopiclone 1–3 mg	
Antidepressants	Sedation, confusion, headache
Trazodone 25–100 mg	Constipation, sedation, xerostomia
Mirtazapine 15–30 mg	
Melatonin-Receptor Agonist	CNS depression, headache
Ramelteon 8 mg	
Atypical Antipsychotics	Extrapyramidal side effects, drowsiness
Olanzapine 5–10 mg	
Antihistamines	Dizziness, headache, sedation
Diphenhydramine 25–50 mg	Paradoxical CNS arousal, dizziness, sedation
Doxylamine 25 mg	

From references 64, 66, 69.

Conclusion

The palliative APRN should be familiar with treatments for these less common and often difficult-to-treat symptoms. Continued investigation into the mechanisms of action of these symptoms and evaluation of novel approaches to treatment is needed.

References

1. Pittelkow MR, Loprinzi CL. Pruritus and sweating in palliative medicine. In: Hanks G, Cherny NI, Christakis NA, Fallon M, Kaasa S, Portenoy RK, eds. *Oxford Textbook of Palliative Medicine.* 4th ed. New York, NY: Oxford University Press; 2011:934–51.
2. Weisshaar E, Matterne U. Epidemiology of itch. Chapter 2 in: Carstens E, Akiyama T, eds. *Itch: Mechanisms and Treatment.* Boca Raton, FL: CRC Press; 2014. Available at: http://www-ncbi-nlm-nih-gov.proxy.library.vcu.edu/books/NBK200924/. Accessed October 8, 2014.
3. Han L, Dong X. Itch mechanisms and circuits. *Annu Rev Biophys.* 2014; 43: 331–55.
4. Ringkamp M, Schepers RJ, Shimada SG, et al. A role for nociceptive, myelinated nerve fibers in itch sensation. *J Neurosci.* 2011; 31: 14841–9.
5. Kuraishi Y. Recent advances in the study of itching: potential new therapeutic targets for pathological pruritus. *Biol Pharm Bull.* 2013; 36 (8): 1228–34.
6. Reamy B, Bunt C, Fletcher S, Bergguist E. A diagnostic approach to pruritus. *Am Fam Physician.* 2011; 84(2): 195–202.
7. Kfoury LW, Jurdi MA. Uremic pruritus. *J Nephrol.* 2012; 25: 644–52.
8. Bunchorntavakul C, Reddy KR. Pruritus in chronic cholestatic liver disease. *Clin Liver Dis.* 2012; 16: 331–46.
9. Oude Elferink RP, Kremer AE, Martens JJ, Beuers UH. The molecular mechanism of cholestatic pruritus. *Dig Dis.* 2011; 29(1): 66–71.

10. Alemi F, Kwon E, Poole DP, et al. The TGR5 receptor mediates bile acid–induced itch and analgesia. *J Clin Investig.* 2013; 123: 1513–30.

11. Kremer AE, Martens JJ, Kulik W, et al. Lysophosphatidic acid is a potential mediator of cholestatic pruritus. *Gastroenterology.* 2010; 139: 1008–18.

12. European Association for the Study of the Liver. EASL Clinical Practice Guidelines: Management of cholestatic liver diseases. *J Hepatol.* 2009; 51(2): 237–67.

13. Mettang T. Pruritus in renal disease. Chapter 5 in: Carstens E, Akiyama T, eds. *Itch: Mechanisms and Treatment.* Boca Raton, FL: CRC Press; 2014. Available at http://www.ncbi.nlm.nih.gov/books/NBK200918/. Accessed October 8, 2014.

14. Narita I, Alchi B, Omori K, et al. Etiology and prognostic significance of severe uremic pruritus in chronic hemodialysis patients. *Kidney Int.* 2006; 69(9): 1626–32.

15. Cheng SP, Lee JJ, Liu TP, et al. Parathyroidectomy improves symptomatology and quality of life in patients with secondary hyperparathyroidism. *Surgery.* 2014; 155(2): 320–8.

16. Tăranu T, Toader S, Eşanu I, Toader MP. Pruritus in the elderly: Pathophysiological, clinical, laboratory and therapeutic approach. *Rev Med Chir Soc Med Nat.* 2014; 118(1): 33–8.

17. Sampogna F, Frontani M, Baliva G, et al. Quality of life and psychological distress in patients with cutaneous lymphoma. *Br J Dermatol.* 2009; 160(4): 815–22.

18. Jiménez Gallo D, Albarrán Planelles C, Linares Barrios M, Fernández Anguita MJ, Márquez Enríquez J, Rodríguez Mateos ME. Treatment of pruritus in early-stage hypopigmented mycosis fungoides with aprepitant. *Dermatol Ther.* 2014; 27(3): 178–82.

19. Kaushik S, Cerci FB, Miracle J, et al. Chronic pruritus in HIV-positive patients in the southeastern United States: Its prevalence and effect on quality of life. *J Am Acad Dermatol.* 2014; 70(4): 659–64.

20. Serling SLC, Leslie K, Maurer T. Approach to pruritus in the adult HIV-positive patient. *Semin Cutan Med Surg.* 2011; 30: 101–6.

21. Dhand A, Aminoff MJ. The neurology of itch. *Brain.* 2014; 137(2): 313–22.

22. Tey HL, Wallengren J, Yosipovitch G. Psychosomatic factors in pruritus. *Clin Dermatol.* 2013; 31: 31–40.

23. Patel T, Yosipovitch G. Therapy of pruritus. *Expert Opin Pharmacother.* 2010; 11(10): 1673–82.

24. Larkin P. Pruritus, fever, and sweats. In: Ferrell BR, Coyle N, Paice J, eds. *Oxford Textbook of Palliative Nursing.* 4th ed. Oxford: Oxford University Press; 2015:325–40.

25. Rika S, Takahiro S, Ayumi T, Kazumi S, Hiroo Y. Anti-pruritic effects of topical crotamiton, capsaicin, and a corticosteroid on pruritogen-induced scratching behavior. *Exp Dermatol.* 2012; 21(3): 201–4.

26. Phan NQ, Lotts T, Antal A, Bernhard JD, Ständer S. Systemic kappa opioid receptor agonists in the treatment of chronic pruritus: a literature review. *Acta Derm Venereol,* 2012; 92: 555–60.

26. Feramisco JD, Berger TG, Steinhoff M. Innovative management of pruritus. *Dermatol Clin.* 2010; 28: 467–78.

27. Kremer AE, Bolier R, van Dijk R, Oude Elferink RP, Beuers U. Advances in pathogenesis and management of pruritus in cholestasis. *Dig Dis.* 2014; 32(5): 637–45.

28. Yue J, Jiao S, Xiao Y, Ren W, Zhao T, Meng J. Comparison of pregabalin with ondansetron in treatment of uraemic pruritus in dialysis patients: a prospective, randomized, double-blind study. *Int Urol Nephrol.* Epub 2014 Aug 7. doi 10.1007/s11255-014-0795-x

29. To THM, Clark K, Lam L, Shelby-James T, Currow DC. The role of ondansetron in the management of cholestatic or uremic pruritus: systematic review. *J Pain Symptom Management.* 2012; 44(5): 725–30.

30. Viegas LP, Ferreira MB, Kaplan AP. The maddening itch: an approach to chronic urticaria. *J Investig Allergol Clin Immunol.* 2014; 24(1): 1–5.

31. Parés A, Herrera M, Avilés J, Sanz M, Mas A. Treatment of resistant pruritus from cholestasis with albumin dialysis: combined analysis of patients from three centers. *J Hepatol.* 2010; 53(2): 307–12.

32. Chang FY, Lu CL. Hiccup: mystery, nature and treatment. *J Neurogastroenterol Motil.* 2012; 18(2): 123–30.

33. Regnard C. Dysphagia, dyspepsia, and hiccup. In: Hanks G, Cherny NI, Christakis NA, Fallon M, Kaasa S, Portenoy RK, eds. *Oxford Textbook of Palliative Medicine.* 4th ed. New York, NY: Oxford University Press; 2011:812–32.

34. Moretto EN, Wee B, Wiffen PJ, Murchison AG. Interventions for treating persistent and intractable hiccups in adults. *Cochrane Database Syst Rev.* 2013; 31: 1.

35. Phillips RA. The management of hiccups in terminally ill patients. *Nursing Times.* 2005; 101(31): 32–3.

36. Bredenoord AJ. Management of belching, hiccups, and aerophagia. *Clin Gastroenterol Hepatol.* 2013; 11(1): 6–12.

37. Kang JH, Hui D, Kim MJ, et al. Corticosteroid rotation to alleviate dexamethasone-induced hiccup: a case series at a single institution. *J Pain Symptom Manage.* 2014; 43(3): 625–30.

38. Marinella MA. Diagnosis and management of hiccups in the patient with advanced cancer. *J Support Oncol.* 2009; 7(4): 122.

39. Peacock ME. Transient hiccups associated with oral dexamethasone. *Case Rep Dent.* 2013; 2013: 426178.

40. Petroianu GA. Treatment of hiccup by vagal maneuvers. *J Hist Neurosci.* 2014; 23: 1–14.

41. Uña E, Alonso P. High dose of prokinetics for refractory hiccups after chemotherapy or the return to a simple drug. *BMJ Case Rep.* 2013; pii: bcr2013201028. doi: 10.1136/bcr-2013-201028.

42. Wang T, Wang D. Metoclopramide for patients with intractable hiccups: A multi-center, randomized, controlled pilot study. *Intern Med J.* Epub 2014 Jul 29. doi: 10.1111/imj.12542.

43. Ives TJ, Fleming MF, Weart CW, Bloch D. Treatment of intractable hiccups with intramuscular haloperidol. *Am J Psychiatry.* 1985; 142(11): 1368–9.

44. Zhang C, Zhang R, Zhang S, Xu M, Zhang S. Baclofen for stroke patients with persistent hiccups: a randomized, double-blind, placebo-controlled trial. *Trials.* 2014; 15(1): 295.

45. Thompson AN, Ehret Leal J, Brzezinski WA. Olanzapine and baclofen for the treatment of intractable hiccups. *Pharmacotherapy.* 2014; 34(1): e4–8.

46. Baumann A, Weicker T, Alb I, Audibert G. Baclofen for the treatment of hiccup related to brainstem compression. *Ann Fr Anesth Reanim.* 2014; 33(1): e27–28.

47. Mirijello A, Addolorato G, D'Angelo C, et al. Baclofen in the treatment of persistent hiccup: a case series. *Int J Clin Pract.* 2013; 67(9): 918–21.

48. Thompson DF, Brooks KG. Gabapentin therapy of hiccups. *Ann Pharmacother.* 2013; 47(6): 897–903.

49. Porzio G, Aielli F, Verna L, Aloisi P, Galletti B, Ficorella C. Gabapentin in the treatment of hiccups in patients with advanced cancer: a 5-year experience. *Clin Neuropharmacol.* 2010; 33(4): 179–180.

50. Quigley C. Nifedipine for hiccups. *J Pain Symptom Manage.* 1997; 13(6): 313.

51. Stueber D, Swartz CM. Carvedilol suppresses intractable hiccups. *J Am Board Fam Med.* 2006; 19: 418–21.

52. Kaneishi K, Kawabata M. Continuous subcutaneous infusion of lidocaine for persistent hiccup in advanced cancer. *Palliat Med.* 2013; 27(3): 284–5.

53. Wilcox SK, Garry A, Johnson MJ. Novel use of amantadine: to treat hiccups. *J Pain Symptom Manage.* 2009; 38: 460–5.

54. Kang KN, Park IK, Suh JH, Leem JG, Shin JW. Ultrasound-guided pulsed radiofrequency lesioning of the phrenic nerve in a patient with intractable hiccup. *Korean J Pain.* 2010; 23: 198–201.

55. Lin YC. Acupuncture for persistent hiccups in a heart and lung transplant recipient. *J Heart Lung Transplant.* 2006; 25(1): 126.

56. Ge AX, Ryan ME, Giaccone G, Hughes MS, Pavletic SZ. Acupuncture treatment for persistent hiccups in patients with cancer. *J Altern Complement Med.* 2010; 16(7): 811.

57. Davies A, Hall S. Salivary gland dysfunction (dry mouth) in patients with advanced cancer. *Int J Palliat Nurs.* 2011; 17(10): 477–82.

58. Center to Advance Palliative Care. Xerostomia. Fast Facts. 182. Available at https://www.capc.org/fast-facts/182-xerostomia/. Accessed August 14, 2015.

59. Dahlin CM, Cohen AK. Dysphagia, xerostomia, and hiccups. In: Ferrell BR, Coyle N, Paice J, eds. *Oxford Textbook of Palliative Nursing.* 4th ed. Oxford: Oxford University Press; 2015:191–216.

60. Lalla RV, Peterson DE. Oral symptoms. In: Walsh D, Caraceni AT, Fainsinger R, et al., eds. *Palliative Medicine.* Philadelphia, PA: Saunders Elsevier; 2009:937–46.

61. Wolff A, Fox PD, Porter S, Konttinen Y. Established and novel approaches for the management of hyposalivation and xerostomia. *Curr Pharm Design.* 2012; 18: 5515–21.

62. Bobb B, Lyckholm L, Coyne P. Fever and sweats. In: Walsh D, Caraceni AT, Fainsinger R, et al., eds. *Palliative Medicine.* Philadelphia, PA: Saunders Elsevier; 2009:890–3.

63. Center to Advance Palliative Care. Fever near the end of life. Fast Facts. 256. Available at https://www.capc.org/fast-facts/256-fever-near-end-life/. Accessed August 14, 2015.

64. Bourdeanu L, Hein MJ, Liu E. Insomnia. In: Ferrell BR, Coyle N, Paice J, eds. *Oxford Textbook of Palliative Nursing.* 4th ed. Oxford: Oxford University Press; 2015:404–10.

65. Center to Advance Palliative Care. Insomnia: patient assessment. 2nd ed. Fast Facts. 101. Available at https://www.capc.org/fast-facts/101-insomnia-patient-assessment/. Accessed August 14, 2015.

66. Khoshknabi DS. Sleep problems and nightmares. In: Walsh D, Caraceni AT, Fainsinger R, et al., eds. *Palliative Medicine.* Philadelphia, PA: Saunders Elsevier; 2009:965–72.

67. Walia HK, Shalhoub G, Ramsammy V, Thornton JD, Auckley D. Symptoms of restless leg syndrome in a palliative care population: frequency and impact. *J Palliat Care.* 2013; 29: 201–16.

68. Davis M, Goforth H. Fighting insomnia and battling lethargy: the yin and yang of palliative care. *Curr Oncol Rep.* 2014; 16(4): 377–95.

69. Center to Advance Palliative Care. Insomnia: drug therapies. Fast Facts. 105. Available at https://www.capc.org/fast-facts/105-insomnia-drug-therapies/. Accessed August 14, 2015.

CHAPTER 29

Fatigue

Tami Borneman

Key Points

◆ Prolonged or chronic fatigue affects approximately 5% to 25% of the general population.[1]

◆ Palliative advanced practice registered nurses (APRNs) are trained to synthesize data, so they can provide care that is centered on patients' goals in the areas of health, quality of life, and function.[2]

◆ Palliative APRNs are positioned to integrate palliative care into their work environment, as they collaborate with interdisciplinary colleagues to address the many needs of patients and family members.

Prevalence and Definitions of Fatigue

Fatigue is a common symptom experienced by patients across several diseases. Solano and colleagues[3] conducted a search of textbooks and medical databases from 64 original studies and identified 11 common patient-reported symptoms among those with cancer, heart disease, AIDS, chronic obstructive pulmonary disease (COPD), or renal disease. Across the five diseases, pain, breathlessness, and fatigue were experienced by more than 50% of the patients.[3] Fatigue is one of the most reported and severe symptoms experienced by patients with cancer due to the disease and its treatment.[4–7] For patients with heart failure and cardiovascular disease, shortness of breath and fatigue are the two most commonly reported symptoms, with fatigue as one of the first symptoms of heart failure.[8,9] In 2014, fatigue was reported as one of the most common symptoms for patients with COPD as well as one of the most distressing symptoms that significantly affects quality of life and functional performance.[10,11] Patients with neurological and autoimmune disorders, such as multiple sclerosis, systemic lupus erythematosus, diabetes, and Parkinson's disease, experience fatigue as one of the most prevalent and debilitating symptoms.[12–16] A synthesis of 26 qualitative studies, involving more than 711 patients with end-stage kidney disease and 178 caregivers, revealed fatigue to be an unrelenting symptom to the point that it became an effort to live.[17] Many breast cancer survivors also experience fatigue that may last from months to years.[18] The Milken Institute reports the 2008–2010 economic burdens of chronic diseases to be $1.5 billion, including treatment and indirect impact. Chronic disease is projected to increase by 42% from 162 million in 2003 to 230 million in 2023, costing approximately $4.2 trillion in lost economic productivity and treatment costs.[19]

In 1998, fatigue was defined by the Multiple Sclerosis Council as "a subjective lack of physical and/or mental energy that is perceived by the individual or caregiver to interfere with usual and desired activities."[20] Another definition, offered by DeLuca from his work in neuroscience, is that fatigue "is the reduction in performance with either prolonged or unusual exertion. Thus fatigue can be sensory, motor, cognitive, or subjective."[21(p 320)] The National Comprehensive Cancer Network (NCCN) defines cancer-related fatigue as "a distressing, persistent, subjective sense of physical, emotional, and/or cognitive tiredness or exhaustion related to cancer or cancer treatment that is not proportional to recent activity and interferes with usual functioning."[22] While there is no one agreed-upon definition of fatigue, a common theme is that fatigue affects the patient's physical function, cognition, emotions, and daily activities and is beyond the norm.

Pathophysiology of Fatigue

There are several descriptions in the literature on the pathophysiology of fatigue. Mitchell[23] organized the various models into four themes: energy balance/energy analysis, fatigue as a stress response, neuroendocrine-based regulatory fatigue, and hybrid models. Energy balance/energy analysis proposes an inequity between energy intake, metabolism, and expenditure, resulting in the progression of fatigue. Fatigue as a stress response suggests that there is an adaptation of tiredness, fatigue, and exhaustion along a continuum and that each state can be differentiated by both behavioral and symptomatic characteristics. The neuroendocrine-based regulatory model posits that the multidimensionality of fatigue is a result of functional dysregulation of the neuroimmunoendocrine system that includes the hypothalamic-pituitary-adrenal axis, cytokines, circadian rhythms, and neurotransmitters.[23–25] Hybrid models propose that stressors caused by cancer and its treatments induce a decline in four main systems (cognitive function, muscle endurance, sleep quality, and nutrition), thus impeding the patient's ability to adapt, while others suggest additional variables that induce fatigue, such as biological, psychological, and functional factors.[23]

Fatigue can also be described as peripheral or central.[1,12] Peripheral fatigue refers to muscle fatigability caused by disorders of muscle and the neuromuscular junction, such as myasthenia gravis and McArdle's disease. Peripheral fatigue can be divided into metabolic myopathies and neurological diseases. Symptoms of metabolic myopathies include premature exertional muscle fatigue, exercise-induced cramps, and myalgia. These symptoms are stimulated by exercise but are usually absent at rest. The major cause of metabolic myopathy is a disorder in carbohydrate and lipid metabolism that begins with sporadic muscle weakness. Between the attacks, histological lab values are normal.[12] Symptoms of neurological peripheral fatigue include exertional fatigue, muscle fatigue, and exercise intolerance that may or may not involve muscle weakness. These diseases are a result of mitochondrial DNA mutations and are best diagnosed with a muscle biopsy.[12]

Central fatigue is a result of either failed transmission of motor impulses or an inability to perform voluntary activities.[1] It affects the body physically and cognitively, thus impairing concentration.[12] Patients with central fatigue feel constantly exhausted, and there are numerous neurological disorders linked with this symptom, such as multiple sclerosis, motor neuron disease, migraine, Parkinson's disease, hypothalamic and pituitary diseases, and idiopathic chronic fatigue syndrome.[12] Interestingly, the severity of central fatigue does not always correlate with the severity of the underlying disease. For example, a patient with multiple sclerosis may experience fatigue in one limb caused by a sustained motor task. When exposed to physiological or psychological stimuli, patients with central fatigue may experience deterioration or sporadic vacillation in the severity of their fatigue.[12] Magnetic resonance imaging is the primary procedure used to rule out other factors, along with a neuropsychological assessment if cognitive impairment is suspected.

Impact of Fatigue on Quality of Life

Fatigue affects not only a patient's physical well-being but also his or her psychological, social, and spiritual well-being.[26–31] Studies exploring cancer-related fatigue have shown a decrease in functional status, interference with activities of daily living, and limits on quality of life, especially in the elderly. It also interferes with employment, relationships, and enjoyment of life, contributes to decreased survival, and reduces the patient's will to combat cancer.[32–34] For cancer patients, fatigue is associated with an increase in depression, mood disturbance, and anxiety, as well as affecting family finances.[32] Non-cancer patients state that fatigue is one of the worst symptoms they experience and describe it as a feeling of tiredness, having little energy, and weakness.[33,35,36] Fatigue can also be demoralizing because it robs patients of who they were, leading to grief over loss of roles and responsibilities.[33]

Similarities exist among patients with cancer-related fatigue and non-cancer-related fatigue in the area of spirituality. Benzein and Berg[27] conducted a study with 40 non-cancer patients receiving palliative care and 45 family members to evaluate the relationship among hope, hopelessness, and fatigue. Results indicated that family members experienced less hope than the patients, which made it difficult for patients to cope at the end-of-life. Additional findings revealed that when patients hoped *for* something (e.g., a cure), fatigue became more of an impediment to hope than for those patients who lived *in* hope (reconciliation with life and death) because hopelessness is equated with loss of control and lack of meaning in life.[27,37]

Similarly, Potter[28] interviewed six patients with advanced cancer in a palliative day care unit who, unprompted, had communicated suffering as a result of their fatigue. In this small phenomenological study, discussion focused on fatigue in relation to their cancer and dying. Patients viewed their fatigue as a measurement to determine where they were on the illness trajectory. Constant struggles included the inability to control fatigue and the limitations it imposed on daily life. Cancer patients and non-cancer patients alike experience the profound effects of fatigue.

Assessment of Fatigue

Like pain, fatigue is a subjective experience. As such, it can be measured by a single-item number as suggested by the NCCN[22] using a 0 (no fatigue) to 10 (severe fatigue) scale. Cella and colleagues[38] also endorse the use of a single number for fatigue among both cancer and non-cancer patients.

Effective fatigue management can be hindered due to patient, professional, and system barriers.[22,39–41] Over a decade ago, Stone and colleagues[42] conducted a study with 576 patients who were being seen in the outpatient and chemotherapy clinics at three regional cancer centers in the United Kingdom. Patients completed a 48-item questionnaire describing various aspects of fatigue. Fifty-two percent reported not discussing fatigue with their doctor; the top six reasons, listed in order, were (1) thinking that fatigue was inevitable (43%), (2) did not think fatigue was an important symptom (34%), (3) belief that the doctor thought nothing could be done (26%), (4) hospital doctor never brought it up (23%), (5) patient hardly experienced it (22%), and (6) did not want to bother the hospital doctor (20%). These findings were confirmed in a later study of barriers to pain and fatigue management in oncology.[41,43] The most common professional barriers to fatigue management were lack of assessment, discussion, management, and documentation.[39,41,43,44] System barriers still exist despite repeated recommendations from the NCCN. These barriers include lack of supportive care referrals, lack of healthcare reimbursement that affects the availability of medications and prescription practices, lack of consistent assessment and documentation between clinical settings, and time to obtain a consult order for supportive services.[22,39,41,43,44]

In addition to the patient's self-report of fatigue, it is helpful for the APRN to use a multidimensional approach to obtain more information to better manage this symptom.[31,44] Table 29.1 provides single-item (NCCN Intensity Scale,[22] Fatigue Intensity Scale,[41] Visual Analogue Scale [VAS][45,46]), multiple-item (Brief Fatigue Inventory [BFI],[47] Cancer-Related Fatigue Distress Scale[48–50]), and multidimensional tools (Cancer Fatigue Scale[50,51], Revised Piper Fatigue Scale,[52–54] Fatigue Assessment Questionnaire[50,55]) that have been developed and well-validated. Other tools, such as the Profile of Mood States Fatigue and Vigor subscales,[56] the Edmonton Symptom Assessment System,[33,57] and the Symptom Distress Scale,[47,58] are single- and multiple-item measures with fatigue items embedded in other scales.

Management of Fatigue

The primary goal of managing fatigue is to treat any underlying contributory factors (e.g., pain, anemia, medication side effects, emotional distress) that are reversible with pharmacologic and/or nonpharmacologic interventions. When that is not possible, mitigating the effects of fatigue through palliation to maximize energy levels becomes the goal.

Table 29.1 Sample Fatigue Assessment Tools

Instrument	Reference	Description
Single-Item Tools		
NCCN Intensity Tool	Mock, Atkinson, et al., 2007[89]	◆ Single item ◆ Assesses severity ◆ 0–10 scale (0 = no fatigue, 10 = worst fatigue)
Fatigue Intensity Scale	Borneman et al., 2007[41]	◆ Single item ◆ Assesses intensity ◆ 0–10 (0—no fatigue, 10 = overwhelming fatigue)
VAS for Fatigue	Glaus, 1993[46] Hauser, Walsh, 2008[45]	◆ Single item ◆ Assesses severity ◆ Uses a 10 cm, 0–100 mm horizontal line. ◆ 0 = does not feel tired, 100 = feels totally exhausted
Multi-item Tools		
Brief Fatigue Inventory	Jean-Pierre et al., 2007[47]	◆ 9 items ◆ Measures intensity or severity (present, usual, worst fatigue during past 24 hours) ◆ 0–10 scale (0 = no fatigue, 10 = fatigue as bad as one can imagine) ◆ Average of 9 items provides a global fatigue severity score (1-3 mild, 4-6 moderate, 7-10 severe)
Cancer-Related Fatigue Distress Scale	Holley, 2000[48] Holley, 2000[49] Piper, 2004[50]	◆ 20 items ◆ Measures distress ◆ 0–10 Likert scale ◆ Assesses fatigue over past 7 days
Multidimensional Cancer-Related Fatigue Tools		
Cancer Fatigue Scale	Piper, 2004[50] Okuyama et al., 2000[51]	◆ 15 items ◆ Assesses physical, cognitive, affective dimensions of fatigue ◆ 1–5 scale (1 = not at all, 5 = very much) ◆ Max score is 60 (physical, 1-28; affective, 0-16; cognitive, 0-16)
Fatigue Assessment Questionnaire	Piper, 2004[50] Beutel et al., 2006[55]	◆ 20 items ◆ Assesses physical, affective, cognitive dimensions of fatigue over past week and month ◆ 0–3 scale (0 = not at all, 3 = strongly; +3 indicates addition of VAS to measure fatigue and distress)
Revised Piper Fatigue Scale	Berger et al., 2007[52] De Jong et al., 2006[53] Piper et al., 1998[54]	◆ 22 items + 5 open-ended items not included in the scoring ◆ Assesses behavioral/severity, affective meaning, sensory, and cognitive/mood ◆ 0–10 scale
Single- and Multi-Item Cancer-Related Fatigue Measures Within Other Scales		
Profile of Mood States Fatigue and Vigor subscales	Meek et al., 2000[56]	◆ 5-7 item subscale ◆ 8 item vigor subscale ◆ Both measure intensity ◆ 5-point Likert scale over past week
Symptom Distress Scale	Jean-Pierre et al., 2007[47] Boehmke et al., 2004[58]	◆ Single item ◆ Measures distress ◆ 5-point Likert scale
Edmonton Symptom Assessment System	Bruera et al., 2007[57] Reddy et al., 2007[90]	◆ Single item ◆ Measures intensity ◆ 0–10 scale (0 = no fatigue, 10 = worst fatigue)

Source: Reprinted from *Journal of Hospice & Palliative Nursing*, Vol. 15 No. 2, Borneman, T., Assessment and management of cancer-related fatigue, Pages No. 77–86, Copyright (2013), with permission from Wolters Kluwer Health. Reference 44.

Pharmacologic Management

Psychostimulants have been used to help patients with fatigue. Psychostimulants act to increase cortical function by interacting with neurotransmitters and receptors in the brain. Different types of psychostimulants work differently in the brain to produce short-term increased energy levels and psychomotor activity.[59] Medications like methylphenidate affect the brain in several areas, whereas modafinil, another type of stimulant, specifically affects the excitatory histamine projections to the hypothalamus.[60] The NCCN[22] reports "some evidence" for using medications for fatigue, but randomized controlled trials have also shown a significant placebo effect. In light of these findings, the NCCN recommends the use of psychostimulants for cancer patients undergoing active treatment after other causes of fatigue have been excluded. In 2010, Peuckmann-Post and colleagues[61] performed a review of pharmacologic treatments for nonspecific fatigue in patients with advanced cancer and other advanced chronic diseases receiving palliative care. After screening more than 2,000 publications, data from 11 drugs and 1,632 patients were analyzed. Studies used in the meta-analysis were those that investigated medications (amantadine, pemoline, and modafinil) for patients with multiple sclerosis-related fatigue and for those with advanced cancer and fatigue (methylphenidate). Even though methylphenidate for cancer patients and amantadine for multiple sclerosis patients showed superior effect, the authors concluded that no specific medication could be recommended for treating fatigue in patients receiving palliative care. This was confirmed by a recent study by Escalente and colleagues on the efficacy of methylphenidate versus placebo for cancer-related fatigue reduction.[62] Results showed that low-dose methylphenidate did not improve cancer-related fatigue.

Results of Peuckmann and colleagues'[61] literature search revealed a lack of research studies investigating the use of corticosteroids for fatigue, even though this is a common clinical practice. Yennurajalingam and colleagues[63] compared the effects of dexamethasone and placebo on cancer-related fatigue. Their primary endpoint was to improve fatigue from baseline to day 15 measured by the Functional Assessment of Chronic Illness-Fatigue (FACIT-F). Anorexia, anxiety, depression, and symptom distress were also evaluated as secondary outcomes. Patients ($n = 84$) were randomly assigned to receive 4 mg dexamethasone or placebo twice daily for 14 days. Patients who received dexamethasone ($n = 43$) showed significant improvement in their fatigue by day 15 ($p = .008$). Physical well-being scores also improved at day 8 ($p = .007$) and day 15 ($p = .002$) in this group. There were no significant differences in the emotional scores or overall symptoms in the dexamethasone group compared with the placebo group. The limitation of this study was the short length of time patients were taking dexamethasone. It is well known that longer-term use of this medication is associated with negative side effects, so future studies are warranted, keeping in mind the risk–benefit ratio.

Antidepressants have also been used to mitigate fatigue. Generally, antidepressants affect the serotonin or norepinephrine system or both. Those affecting the serotonin system (SSRIs) include fluoxetine, paroxetine, escitalopram, and sertraline. Agents affecting the norepinephrine system include bupropion and mirtazapine. Agents like venlafaxine and duloxetine affect both systems.[60] Bupropion has been shown to be more effective for patients with chronic fatigue syndrome, but there are mixed reviews as to its efficacy in patients with cancer-related fatigue.[59,64,65] The SSRIs have been shown to improve depression in cancer patients, but studies have failed to reveal improvement in fatigue.[44,65]

Other supplements have been the subject of evaluation for fatigue, with mixed results. Vitamins have not proven to be effective at reducing cancer-related fatigue.[59] L-Carnitine is thought to be helpful in treating cancer-related fatigue due to its ability to decrease pro-inflammatory cytokines. This was confirmed in a double-blind, placebo-controlled trial with 376 patients with advanced cancer and fatigue randomly assigned to receive either 2 g/day of oral L-carnitine or a matching placebo.[66] The primary outcome, improvement in fatigue measured by the BFI, improved in both groups compared to baseline, but there were no statistically significant differences between the two groups. Secondary outcomes that included fatigue, depression, and pain were measured by the FACIT-F and did not show any statistical differences. Researchers conducted a separate analysis of patients who were carnitine-deficient at baseline, and these results as well did not show any statistical improvement in fatigue.

Ginseng has also been evaluated for treating fatigue. In 2010, Barton and colleagues[67] conducted a phase 2 double-blind dose-finding study with 282 adults with cancer. Patients were randomized into three dosage groups (750, 1,000, or 2,000 mg/day) or a placebo group. Each group received twice-daily doses over 8 weeks. The primary endpoint was to determine dose effectiveness in reducing cancer-related fatigue. Outcome measures included the Vitality subscale of the Medical Outcome Scale Short Form-36 (SF-36), the BFI, and the Global Impression of Benefit Scale. These were completed at 4 and 8 weeks. Those taking ginseng were twice as likely to perceive a benefit and were satisfied with treatment versus those receiving a placebo. The acceptable tolerable dose of ginseng was 1,000 to 2,000 mg/day. These results led to a phase 3 study by the same researchers to evaluate the efficacy of American ginseng on cancer-related fatigue.[68] Three hundred sixty-four cancer survivors with fatigue from 40 institutions participated in this double-blind randomized trial. Patients received 2,000 mg/day of ginseng or a placebo for 8 weeks. The primary endpoint was a change in fatigue scores from baseline to 4 and 8 weeks as measured by the Multidimensional Fatigue Symptom Inventory-Short Form (MFSI-SF). Results showed a statistically significant difference at 8 weeks (change from baseline 20 vs. 10.3 in placebo group, $p = .003$). There were no significant differences at 4 weeks. Patients still receiving cancer treatment reported a greater benefit than those who had completed treatment. Researchers reported no discernible toxicities associated with this treatment.

Nonpharmacologic Interventions

All patients should receive general education on treatment-related fatigue due to chemotherapy and radiation therapy (Table 29.2). General strategies include balancing rest and activity, conserving energy, preventing weight loss, optimizing nutrition, and using distraction (e.g., listening to music, taking short naps, reading).[22,23,44,59,69] Teaching patients how to monitor their fatigue by using a diary lets them see when levels vary and allows them to plan their day accordingly.[70] The NCCN guidelines organize nonpharmacologic interventions into three groups: physical activity (e.g., exercise), physically based therapies (e.g., physical therapy), and psychosocial intervention (e.g., cognitive-behavioral therapy [CBT]).[22]

Table 29.2 Nonpharmacologic Interventions

Nonpharmacologic Interventions	Explanation
Patient Education	
◆ Description of fatigue	◆ Fatigue is a sense of feeling tired that impacts one physically, psychologically, cognitively.
	◆ It is different from being tired, which gets better with rest.
◆ Common causes of fatigue	◆ Anemia, uncontrolled symptoms such as pain, lack of appetite, or sleep problems, comorbidities, infection.
◆ Use of the 0-10 to rate fatigue	◆ 1-3 mild, 4-6 moderate, 7-10 severe.
◆ When to call MD	◆ Call if fatigue is getting worse and prevents patient from ADLs.
◆ What to tell the MD	◆ When it started, what makes it better/worse, description of interference with ADLs (due to the subjective nature of fatigue, helps clinician better understand extent of fatigue impact).
Exercise	
◆ Importance of exercising	◆ Heart, lungs, muscles require exercise to stay healthy.
	◆ Exercise should be tailored to the patient's needs, capabilities and disease status.
	◆ Initiated slowly and increased over time.
	◆ Safety should always be assessed prior to initiating exercise.
	◆ Where warranted, refer to physical/occupational therapy.
Energy Conservation	
◆ Energy conservation can help to reduce the burden of fatigue and use energy more effectively.	◆ Prioritize activities.
	◆ Ask for help or delegate tasks.
	◆ Balance rest and activities, performing activities during times of higher energy.
	◆ Adhere to a regular bedtime.
	◆ Sit instead of standing.
Nutrition and Hydration	
◆ Importance of maintaining good nutrition and hydration	◆ Will help increase energy levels.
	◆ Preserves lean body mass.
◆ Monitor weight	◆ Helps to better tolerate treatment.
	◆ Refer to nutritionist when warranted.
Complementary Therapies to Improve Fatigue	
◆ Acupuncture	
◆ Cognitive behavioral therapy	
◆ Hypnosis	
◆ Massage therapy	
◆ Reiki	
◆ Relaxation breathing	

Source: Reprinted from *Journal of Hospice & Palliative Nursing*, Vol. 15 No. 2, Borneman, T., Assessment and management of cancer-related fatigue, Pages No. 77–86, Copyright (2013), with permission from Wolters Kluwer Health. Reference 44.

Physical Activity

Research studies have shown exercise to be the most effective intervention for managing fatigue.[70–73] If the patient's functional status permits, there are several activities, such as walking, biking, aerobics, and swimming, that may prove beneficial. Empirical evidence for exercise guidelines is lacking.[23,69] Puetz and Herring[74] performed a meta-analysis of controlled trials on the effects of exercise in cancer patients during treatment ($n = 43$) and after treatment ($n = 27$). Results showed that exercise significantly reduced cancer-related fatigue by a mean effect change (95% CI) of 0.32 (0.21, 0.43) for patients in active treatment and

0.38 (0.21, 0.54) for patients having completed treatment. Patients with lower baseline scores who consistently exercised experienced greater improvement. Greater improvement was also seen in trials where patients had more time between completing treatment and initiating exercise, those with shorter exercise time, and those using wait-list comparisons. Exercise for post-treatment patients was more restorative, whereas for those in active treatment, it was more palliative.

In their meta-analysis, McMillan and Newhouse[73] examined the effects of exercise intervention strategies on cancer-related fatigue and to clarify possible exercise prescription guidelines. Sixteen studies with 1,426 total participants (759 exercise, 667 control) were analyzed. Results indicated that a small, significant effect size favored the use of exercise for reducing cancer-related fatigue ($p < .001$). Aerobic exercise was associated with a significant reduction in fatigue ($p < .001$). Overall results indicated that patients who exercised had significantly improved aerobic and musculoskeletal condition compared to the control group ($p < .01$).

All programs should be tailored to the patient's needs and adjusted as his or her functional status changes. Caution should be taken with exercise interventions when patients have bone metastases, thrombocytopenia, anemia, fever or active infection, or any limitations secondary to other illnesses.[22] Physical therapy consultations should be made when patients have comorbidities (e.g., heart disease, COPD), recent major surgery, functional or anatomical deficits, or substantial deconditioning.[22]

Occupational therapists (OTs) assess and analyze patients' functional problems. In the case of cancer-related fatigue, OTs can teach patients practical interventions, such as energy conservation and lifestyle management.[75,76] The most common interventions provided by OTs include mobility, self-care skills, upper extremity strength and function, educational needs, home management skills, and need for assistive devices.[75–77] OTs can adapt activities according to the effects of fatigue on patients' functional abilities and ensure that proper equipment is accessible so patients can maintain as much independence as possible. This, in turn, empowers patients to continue making their own healthcare decisions and at the same time preserves their dignity.[75,76]

Physical Therapies

Physical therapies, such as acupuncture and massage therapy, are likely to be effective, according to the NCCN and the Pan-Canadian Practice Guidelines.[22,78] Evidence from randomized controlled trials shows promising results using acupuncture in conjunction with patient education to reduce cancer-related fatigue and improve quality of life.[79,80] In Johnston and colleagues'[79] randomized trial, 13 patients (7 control, 6 treatment) received education to improve self-care through exercise, nutrition, and CBT (four weekly, 50-minute sessions on stress management). The second part of the intervention involved providing patients with eight weekly, 50-minute acupuncture sessions. Results indicated positive, but not statistically significant results, with the treatment group only experiencing a 2.38-point decline (66%) in cancer-related fatigue after 10 weeks compared with the control group. Although the results were not statistically significant in their small sample, the authors believe the results were clinically significant.

Molassiotis and colleagues[80] conducted a randomized controlled trial comparing acupuncture with enhanced usual care in patients with breast cancer. Seventy-five patients were randomly assigned to receive usual care and 227 patients to receive acupuncture plus usual care. Patients received acupuncture once a week for 6 weeks using three pairs of acupoints. The usual care group received a booklet providing information on fatigue and fatigue management. The primary endpoint was general fatigue at 6 weeks, measured with the Multidimensional Fatigue Inventory along with other measures for secondary outcomes. Results showed the trial arm effect to be highly significant ($p < .001$); beneficial effects were also noted on all secondary outcomes.

Similar to acupuncture, massage studies have shown clinical significance in helping with fatigue, but larger-scale trials are needed to substantiate its efficacy.[23,81] Karagozoglu and Kahve[82] conducted a quasi-experimental and cross-sectional study to determine the efficacy of using back massage to relieve chemotherapy-induced fatigue and to reduce anxiety during treatment. Data were collected on 40 patients (20 intervention, 20 control) with solid tumors. Measures used included the BFI, the Personal Information form, and the State Anxiety scale of the Spielberger State-Trait Anxiety Inventory. Results showed a statistically significant decrease in fatigue in the intervention group on post-chemotherapy day 1 ($p = .020$; effect size .84). Mean anxiety scores also decreased in this group on post-chemotherapy day 1 ($p = .109$; effect size .37). Back massage given during chemotherapy significantly reduced acute fatigue and state anxiety.

An earlier randomized controlled trial with 86 breast cancer patients examined the efficacy of massage for reducing symptoms and improving mood.[83] Patients with primary breast cancer randomized to the massage group received biweekly 30-minute classical massages on the back and neck twice a week for 5 weeks. The control group received usual care. Intervention patients completed three sets of questionnaires: at baseline, at the end of the intervention, and at 11 weeks of follow-up. Results showed reduced fatigue at the end of the intervention that was sustained over time. Compared to the control group, results were statistically significant at 11 weeks.

Psychosocial Therapies

Psychosocial therapies are aimed at helping patients cope with their fatigue. These therapies teach patients how their thoughts can influence feelings and behaviors. CBT has been shown to be effective for both non-cancer and cancer patients.[69,84–88] In a randomized controlled trial, Knoop and colleagues[84] studied chronic fatigue in patients with multiple sclerosis to determine whether CBT or relaxation training was more effective in changing cognition and behaviors thought to perpetuate fatigue in multiple sclerosis. Seventy patients (CBT 35, relaxation training 35) participated and completed questionnaires before and after the intervention. The instruments included the Cognitive and Behavioural Responses to Symptoms Questionnaire, the Brief Illness Perception Questionnaire (modified to measure negative representations of fatigue), the Hospital Anxiety and Depression Scale, and the Chalder Fatigue questionnaire. Researchers also used multiple mediation analysis to determine if any variables mediated the change in fatigue. Results indicated that avoidance behavior, focusing on symptoms, believing symptoms indicate damage, and a negative representation of fatigue were significantly improved more in the CBT group versus the relaxation group. When patients were able to view themselves as having more control, fatigue was seen as something that could be understood, was time-limited, and had fewer actual and emotional consequences, which helped reduce its severity. The overall change in the perception of fatigue was more important than changes in behavior (avoidance, sleep problems) in mediating the positive effects of CBT.

Another randomized controlled trial looked at CBT plus hypnosis to relieve fatigue in patients receiving radiotherapy for breast cancer.[85] Two hundred patients were randomly assigned to either the CBT group ($n = 100$) or the control group ($n = 100$). The primary endpoint was a change in fatigue scores from baseline to the end of radiotherapy to 4 weeks and 6 months after radiotherapy, measured by the FACIT-F and Visual Analogue Scores (VAS) scores for fatigue and muscle weakness. Results were positive for the CBT group for significantly lower levels of fatigue (FACIT-F) at the end of radiotherapy ($p < .001$), at 4 weeks ($p < .001$), and at 6 months ($p < .001$). VAS scores were also significantly lower in this group at the end of treatment ($p < .001$) and at 6 months ($p < .001$). Muscle weakness VAS scores followed suit, with significantly lower scores at the end of treatment ($p < .001$) and at 6 months ($p < .02$). Results indicate that CBT as an evidence-based intervention provides extended benefits in helping to control fatigue.

Case Study

Jean was a 75-year-old Caucasian female with newly diagnosed metastatic lung cancer who presented to the cancer center for treatment options. Her past medical history included controlled type II diabetes with nonpainful peripheral neuropathy, a pacemaker for atrial fibrillation, and hypertension. Jean had begun having shortness of breath, especially on exertion, approximately 3 months prior to coming to the cancer center. Prior initial diagnostics included a CT angiogram revealing a right-sided pleural effusion that was drained of 3 liters of fluid. Her shortness of breath improved, but 2 months later it recurred and a CT scan revealed a mass. Biopsy results of the mass were consistent with adenocarcinoma of the lung. MRI/PET/CT revealed widely metastatic disease to the brain, bones, and liver. ECOG performance status was 2. Her medications included antihypertensive and cardiac agents, a diuretic, an anticoagulant, an antidepressant, and several vitamins. She did not have pain, but she rated her fatigue at 10/10. Jean's family history included a paternal grandfather with lung cancer.

Jean had been married to her husband, Matt, for 52 years; he owned a construction company. They had two grown children with whom Jean had very strained relationships, due to marital and financial issues when the children were young. The adult children were much closer to their father, but rarely offered to help their parents in any way. Jean and Matt had many friends who stopped by throughout the week to visit and/or bring a meal. Jean never worked outside the home, except for the two years she ran her own business selling specialty gift cards. She and her husband loved the outdoors, especially being near water and fishing. Matt shared that Jean cried frequently, had little energy to do much of anything around the house or go out with friends, and did not eat as much. In addition, she had become complacent and rather negative. Jean confirmed this and added that she "just couldn't seem to get moving" and she had "never been this tired in my life." She loved spending time with friends but even when they came to her home, she was glad when they left because she could then lie down and take a nap. Jean stated that she had very poor quality of life.

Review of systems was negative except for current increasing shortness of breath and fatigue. Physical exam confirmed decreased breath sounds at the right base with dullness to percussion. The left lung was clear and all else was negative. Several lab values were abnormal, including a hemoglobin of 8.1 g/dL. Jean had received 25 palliative radiation treatments concurrent with carboplatin and Taxol, of which she had completed six treatments. The APRN asked Jean if she wanted to meet with the palliative care team. She explained the purpose of the palliative care

team and said that her medical oncologist also thought she would benefit from this service. The APRN asked Jean and Matt if they wanted to include their adult children when meeting with the palliative care team, but they preferred not to, as both children were very busy with work. A palliative care consult was ordered and the appointment was scheduled for 2 weeks later.

Prior to the meeting, the APRN discussed Jean's case with the palliative care team, answered their questions, and discussed possible goals of care. At the appointment with the palliative care team, the APRN reviewed the purpose of the meeting with Jean and Matt. She asked Jean to share what she understood about her lung cancer, treatments, and side effects, and invited Matt to share his view of what Jean has been going through, as well as how that has affected him. Asking Jean and Matt to share their perspectives provided the team with insight into their understanding of the disease trajectory and their expectations of treatment. The medical oncologist, as well as the APRN, had previously explained to them that Jean's lung cancer could not be cured but that treatment would be focused on stabilizing the cancer and providing an acceptable quality of life, for as long as possible. Jean talked about her experience with her lung cancer, and both she and Matt acknowledged knowing the ultimate outcome of her disease and that treatment would not cure her. She knew she needed to complete an advance directive, but stated, "I can't bring myself to think about it yet." She said, "I'm just so very tired." Matt stated that he was at a loss as to how to help her.

The APRN explained to Jean and Matt that fatigue is a common symptom of both treatment and cancer. It was not an easy symptom to describe to patients so that they can prepare for it, nor is it easy for patients to describe to others just how much it affects their lives. The APRN recommended a consult with pulmonary rehab so that Jean could learn how to maximize her breathing through breathing exercises and techniques. Based on prior discussion with Jean, the APRN confirmed her willingness to meet with a social worker. The social worker confirmed that she would call Jean and set up a time for them to meet and that their meeting would not be limited to a one-time appointment. The social worker asked Jean if she would be willing to just review the advance directive form between that visit and the next appointment. The APRN told Jean that she understood how hard it was for her to do this, but that it was also for Matt. The form would provide him with a legal document stating what she wanted regarding her healthcare, relieving him of undue stress on top of profound grief when that time came. The APRN suggested seeing the nutritionist about her decreased appetite, but Jean declined, stating that she still liked to eat and didn't view nutrition as a problem.

The APRN had previously inquired about Jean's religious/spiritual preferences and learned that Jean and Matt were nonpracticing Protestants. She asked if Jean would be interested in a visit from the chaplain. Jean hesitated but accepted. The chaplain stated that he could either call her at home or visit with her during her next clinic appointment. Jean agreed to see him at her next appointment. Prior to her next appointment, the chaplain called to confirm visiting with her. Jean declined, but mentioned that Matt would enjoy talking with him while she was receiving treatment. Matt and the chaplain met at the following appointment over coffee.

Over the next 4 months, Jean saw some improvement in her fatigue levels. Her energy never returned to baseline, but she was able to carry on with most household activities and she enjoyed visiting with friends. Jean stated that the appointments with pulmonary rehab were very helpful, teaching her strategies to breathe more effectively and to conserve energy. The social worker discussed with her ways to reframe her outlook on life in coping with fatigue, as well as the disease overall. She was also able to teach Matt ways to support Jean both emotionally and around the house, in addition to taking care of himself. Jean and Matt both enjoyed talking with the chaplain. He became a strong source of emotional and, later, spiritual support, especially when Jean's health began to rapidly decline.

When Jean was ready, the APRN set up a home hospice visit. Jean died a peaceful death 3 weeks later on hospice. Matt expressed deep gratitude for all that was done for his wife and him. He was thankful that she did not suffer with pain.

References

1. Jason LA, Evans M, Brown M, Porter N. What is fatigue? Pathological and nonpathological fatigue. *PM R*. 2010; 2(5): 327–31.
2. Hospice and Palliative Nurses. HPNA position statement: value of the advanced practice registered nurse in palliative care. 2010. Available at www.hpna.org/DisplayPage.aspx?Title=Position%20Statements. Accessed July 29, 2014.
3. Solano JP, Gomes B, Higginson IJ. A comparison of symptom prevalence in far advanced cancer, AIDS, heart disease, chronic obstructive pulmonary disease and renal disease. *J Pain Symptom Manage*. 2006; 31(1): 58–69.
4. Minton O, Strasser F, Radbruch L, Stone P. Identification of factors associated with fatigue in advanced cancer: a subset analysis of the European palliative care research collaborative computerized symptom assessment data set. *J Pain Symptom Manage*. 2012; 43(2): 226–35.
5. Wang XS, Cleeland CS, Mendoza TR, et al. Impact of cultural and linguistic factors on symptom reporting by patients with cancer. *J Natl Cancer Inst*. 2010; 102(10): 732–8.
6. Wang XS, Zhao F, Fisch MJ, et al. Prevalence and characteristics of moderate to severe fatigue: a multicenter study in cancer patients and survivors. *Cancer*. 2014;1 20(3): 425–32.
7. Yanez B, Pearman T, Lis CG, Beaumont JL, Cella D. The FACT-G7: a rapid version of the functional assessment of cancer therapy-general (FACT-G) for monitoring symptoms and concerns in oncology practice and research. *Ann Oncol*. 2013; 24(4): 1073–8.
8. Casillas JM, Damak S, Chauvet-Gelinier JC, Deley G, Ornetti P. Fatigue in patients with cardiovascular disease. *Annals Phys Rehab Med*. 2006;49(6):392–402.
9. Evangelista LS, Moser DK, Westlake C, Pike N, Ter-Galstanyan A, Dracup K. Correlates of fatigue in patients with heart failure. *Prog Cardiovasc Nurs*. 2008; 23(1): 12–7.
10. Stridsman C, Lindberg A, Skar L. Fatigue in chronic obstructive pulmonary disease: a qualitative study of people's experiences. *Scand J Caring Sci*. 2014; 28(1): 130–8.
11. Wong C, Goodridge D, Marciniuk D, Rennie D. Fatigue in patients with COPD participating in a pulmonary rehabilitation program. *Int J COPD*. 2010;5:319–26.
12. Chaudhuri A, Behan PO. Fatigue in neurological disorders. *Lancet*. 2004; 363(9413): 978–88.
13. Fonseca R, Bernardes M, Terroso G, de Sousa M, Figueiredo-Braga M. Silent burdens in disease: fatigue and depression in SLE. *Autoimmune Dis*. 2014; 2014: 9.
14. Metta V, Logishetty K, Martinez-Martin P, et al. The possible clinical predictors of fatigue in Parkinson's disease: a study of 135 patients as part of international nonmotor scale validation project. *Hindawi Access to Research*. 2011; 2011: 7. Available at www.hindawi.com/journals/pd/2011/125271. Accessed July 30, 2014.
15. Rubin S. Management of multiple sclerosis: an overview. *Disease-a-Month*. 2013; 59(7): 253–60.
16. Strupp J, Romotzky V, Paed D, Galushko M, Golla H, Voltz R. Palliative care for severely affected patients with multiple sclerosis: when and why? Results of a delphi survey of health care professionals. *J Palliat Med*. 2014; 17(10): 1128–36.
17. Tong A, Cheung KL, Nair SS, Kurella Tamura M, Craig JC, Winkelmayer WC. Thematic synthesis of qualitative studies on patient and caregiver perspectives on end-of-life care in CKD. *Am J Kidney Dis*. 2014; 63(6): 913–27.
18. Schmidt ME, Chang-Claude J, Seibold P, et al. Determinants of long-term fatigue in breast cancer survivors: results of a prospective patient cohort study. *Psychooncology*. 2015; 24(1): 40–6.
19. Chatterjee A, Kubendran S, King J, DeVol R. Checkup time: chronic disease and wellness in America. 2014. Available at http://www.chronicdiseaseimpact.com/. Accessed July 28, 2014.
20. Consortium of Multiple Sclerosis Centers. Fatigue and multiple sclerosis: clinical practice guidelines. 1998. Hackensack, NJ: CMSC Available at http://www.pva.org/site/apps/ka/ec/catalog.asp?c=ajIRK9 NJLcJ2E&b=6423003&en=5nIGILNfE9JGLGPfE6KFJINfH8ILLYPuE cKEIKOoEdLPJ0PEG&CategoryID=322152. Accessed August 11, 2014.
21. DeLuca J. Fatigue: its definition, its study, and its future. In: DeLuca J, ed. *Fatigue as a Window to the Brain*. Cambridge, MA: The MIT Press; 2005:336.
22. National Comprehensive Cancer Network. NCCN guidelines version 1.2014 Cancer-related fatigue. 2014. Available at http://www.nccn.org/professionals/physician_gls/pdf/fatigue.pdf. Accessed August 11, 2014.
23. Mitchell SA. Cancer-related fatigue: state of the science. *PM R*. 2010; 2(5): 364–83.
24. Chesnokova V, Melmed S. Minireview: Neuro-immuno-endocrine modulation of the hypothalamic-pituitary-adrenal (HPA) axis by GP130 signaling molecules. *Endocrinology*. 2002; 143(5): 1571–4.
25. Illi J, Miaskowski C, Cooper B, et al. Association between pro- and anti-inflammatory cytokine genes and a symptom cluster of pain, fatigue, sleep disturbance, and depression. *Cytokine*. 2012; 58(3): 437–47.
26. Baetz M, Bowen R. Chronic pain and fatigue: associations with religion and spirituality. *Pain Res Manage*. 2008; 13(5): 383–8.
27. Benzein EG, Berg AC. The level of and relation between hope, hopelessness and fatigue in patients and family members in palliative care. *Palliat Med*. 2005; 19(3): 234–40.
28. Potter J. Fatigue experience in advanced cancer: a phenomenological approach. *Int J Palliat Nurs*. 2004; 10(1): 15–23.
29. Reif K, de Vries U, Petermann F, Gorres S. A patient education program is effective in reducing cancer-related fatigue: a multi-centre randomised two-group waiting-list controlled intervention trial. *Eur J Oncol Nurs*. 2013; 17(2): 204–13.
30. Wu HS, Davis JE. Definition, prevalence and characteristics of sudden exhaustion: a possible syndrome of fatigue in cancer? *Support Care Cancer*. 2013; 21(2): 609–17.
31. Koornstra RH, Peters M, Donofrio S, van den Borne B, de Jong FA. Management of fatigue in patients with cancer—A practical overview. *Cancer Treat Rev*. 2014; 40(6): 791–9.
32. Hofman M, Ryan J, Figuero a-Moseley C, Jean-Pierre P, Morrow G. Cancer-related fatigue: the scale of the problem. *Oncologist*. 2007; 12(S1): 4–10.
33. Ream E. Fatigue in patients receiving palliative care. *Nursing Standard*. 2007; 21(28): 49–58.
34. Scott JA, Lasch KE, Barsevick AM, Piault-Louis E. Patients' experiences with cancer-related fatigue: a review and synthesis of qualitative research. *Oncol Nurs Forum*. 2011; 38(3): E191–203.
35. Radbruch L, Strasser F, Elsner F, et al. Fatigue in palliative care patients—an EAPC approach. *Palliat Med*. 2008; 22(1): 13–32.
36. Smith OR, van den Broek KC, Renkens M, Denollet J. Comparison of fatigue levels in patients with stroke and patients with end-stage heart failure: application of the Fatigue Assessment Scale. *J Am Geriatr Soc*. 2008; 56(10): 1915–9.

37. Benzein E, Norberg A, Saveman BI. The meaning of the lived experience of hope in patients with cancer in palliative home care. *Palliat Med.* 2001; 15(2): 117–126.

38. Cella D, Lai JS, Stone A. Self-reported fatigue: one dimension or more? Lessons from the Functional Assessment of Chronic Illness Therapy—Fatigue (FACIT-F) questionnaire. *Support Care Cancer.* 2011; 19(9): 1441–50.

39. Piper B, Borneman T, Sun V, et al. Assessment of cancer-related fatigue: role of the oncology nurse in translating NCCN assessment guidelines into practice. *Clin J Oncol Nurs.* 2008; 12(Suppl 5): 37–47.

40. Prue G, Rankin J, Allen J, Gracey J, Cramp F. Cancer-related fatigue: A critical appraisal. *Eur J Cancer.* 2006; 42(7): 846–63.

41. Borneman T, Piper BF, Sun VC, Koczywas M, Uman G, Ferrell B. Implementing the Fatigue Guidelines at one NCCN member institution: process and outcomes. *J Natl Compr Canc Netw.* 2007; 5(10): 1092–101.

42. Stone P, Richardson A, Ream E, Smith AG, Kerr DJ, Kearney N. Cancer-related fatigue: inevitable, unimportant and untreatable? Results of a multi-centre patient survey. Cancer Fatigue Forum. *Ann Oncol.* 2000; 11(8): 971–5.

43. Borneman T, Koczywas M, Sun V, et al. Effectiveness of a clinical intervention to eliminate barriers to pain and fatigue management in oncology. *J Palliat Med.* 2011; 14(2): 197–205.

44. Borneman T. Assessment and management of cancer-related fatigue. *J Hosp Palliat Nurs.* 2013; 15(2): 77–88.

45. Hauser K, Walsh D. Visual analogue scales and assessment of quality of life in cancer. *J Support Care.* 2008; 6(6): 277–82.

46. Glaus A. Assessment of fatigue in cancer and non-cancer patients and in healthy individuals. *Support Care Cancer.* 1993; 1(6): 305–15.

47. Jean-Pierre P, Figueroa-Moseley CD, Kohli S, Fiscella K, Palesh OG, Morrow GR. Assessment of cancer-related fatigue: implications for clinical diagnosis and treatment. *Oncologist.* 2007; 12(Suppl 1): 11–21.

48. Holley S. Cancer-related fatigue. Suffering a different fatigue. *Cancer Pract.* 2000; 8(2): 87–95.

49. Holley SK. Evaluating patient distress from cancer-related fatigue: an instrument development study. *Oncol Nurs Forum.* 2000; 27(9): 1425–31.

50. Piper B. Measuring fatigue. In: Frank-Stromberg M, Olsen SJ, eds. *Instruments for Clinical Healthcare Research.* 3rd ed. Sudbury, MA: Jones and Bartlett; 2004:538–53.

51. Okuyama T, Akechi T, Kugaya A, et al. Development and validation of the Cancer Fatigue Scale: a brief, three-dimensional, self-rating scale for assessment of fatigue in cancer patients. *J Pain Symptom Manage.* 2000; 19(1): 5–14.

52. Berger AM, Farr LA, Kuhn BR, Fischer P, Agrawal S. Values of sleep/wake, activity/rest, circadian rhythms, and fatigue prior to adjuvant breast cancer chemotherapy. *J Pain Symptom Manage.* 2007; 33(4): 398–409.

53. de Jong N, Candel MJ, Schouten HC, Abu-Saad HH, Courtens AM. Course of the fatigue dimensions "activity level" and the interference of fatigue with daily living activities for patients with breast cancer receiving adjuvant chemotherapy. *Cancer Nurs.* 2006; 29(5): E1–E13.

54. Piper BF, Dibble SL, Dodd MJ, Weiss MC, Slaughter RE, Paul SM. The revised Piper Fatigue Scale: psychometric evaluation in women with breast cancer. *Oncol Nurs Forum.* 1998; 25(4): 677–84.

55. Beutel ME, Hinz A, Albani C, Brahler E. Fatigue assessment questionnaire: standardization of a cancer-specific instrument based on the general population. *Oncology.* 2006; 70(5): 351–7.

56. Meek PM, Nail LM, Barsevick A, et al. Psychometric testing of fatigue instruments for use with cancer patients. *Nurs Res.* 2000; 49(4): 181–90.

57. Bruera E, El Osta B, Valero V, et al. Donepezil for cancer fatigue: a double-blind, placebo-controlled trial. *J Clin Oncol.* 2007; 25(23): 3475–81.

58. Boehmke MM. Measurement of symptom distress in women with early-stage breast cancer. *Cancer Nurs.* 2004; 27(2): 144–52.

59. National Cancer Institute: PDQ Fatigue. 2014. Available at http://cancer.gov/cancertopics/pdq/supportivecare/fatigue/HealthProfessional. Accessed August 14, 2014.

60. Braun I, Pirl W. Psychotropic medications in cancer care. In: Holland J, Breitbart W, Jacobsen P, Lederberg M, Loscalzo M, McCorkle R, eds. *Psycho-Oncology.* 2nd ed. New York, NY: Oxford University Press, Inc.; 2010:378–85.

61. Peuckmann V, Elsner F, Krumm N, Trottenberg P, Radbruch L. Pharmacological treatments for fatigue associated with palliative care. *Cochrane Database Syst Rev.* 2010(11): CD006788.

62. Escalante CP, Meyers C, Reuben JM, et al. A randomized, double-blind, 2-period, placebo-controlled crossover trial of a sustained-release methylphenidate in the treatment of fatigue in cancer patients. *Cancer J.*2014; 20(1): 8–14.

63. Yennurajalingam S, Frisbee-Hume S, Palmer JL, et al. Reduction of cancer-related fatigue with dexamethasone: a double-blind, randomized, placebo-controlled trial in patients with advanced cancer. *J Clin Oncol.* 2013; 31(25): 3076–82.

64. Breitbart W, Alici Y. Pharmacologic treatment options for cancer-related fatigue: current state of clinical research. *Clin J Oncol Nurs.* 2008; 12(5 Suppl): 27–36.

65. Escalante C. Cancer-related fatigue: treatment. In: Hesketh P, Savarese D, eds. *UpToDate.* Waltham, MA: UpToDate; 2014.

66. Cruciani RA, Zhang JJ, Manola J, Cella D, Ansari B, Fisch MJ. L-carnitine supplementation for the management of fatigue in patients with cancer: an Eastern Cooperative Oncology Group phase III, randomized, double-blind, placebo-controlled trial. *J Clin Oncol.* 2012; 30(31): 3864–9.

67. Barton DL, Soori GS, Bauer BA, et al. Pilot study of *Panax quinquefolius* (American ginseng) to improve cancer-related fatigue: a randomized, double-blind, dose-finding evaluation: NCCTG trial N03CA. *Support Care Cancer.* 2010; 18(2): 179–87.

68. Barton DL, Liu H, Dakhil SR, et al. Wisconsin Ginseng (*Panax quinquefolius*) to improve cancer-related fatigue: a randomized, double-blind trial, N07C2. *J Natl Cancer Inst.* 2013; 105(16): 1230–8.

69. Bower JE, Bak K, Berger A, et al. Screening, assessment, and management of fatigue in adult survivors of cancer: an American Society of Clinical oncology clinical practice guideline adaptation. *J Clin Oncol.* 2014; 32(17): 1840–50.

70. Berger AM, Abernethy AP, Atkinson A, et al. Cancer-related fatigue. *J Natl Compr Canc Netw.* 2010; 8(8): 904–31.

71. Cramp F, Byron-Daniel J. Exercise for the management of cancer-related fatigue. *Cochrane Database of Systematic Reviews.* 2012(11): CD006145. doi: 10.1002/14651858.CD006145.pub3. Accessed August 12, 2014.

72. Keeney C, Head B. Palliative nursing care of the patient with cancer-related fatigue. *J Hosp Palliat Nurs.* 2011; 13(5): 270–8.

73. McMillan EM, Newhouse IJ. Exercise is an effective treatment modality for reducing cancer-related fatigue and improving physical capacity in cancer patients and survivors: a meta-analysis. *Appl Physiol Nutr Metab.* 2011; 36(6): 892–903.

74. Puetz TW, Herring MP. Differential effects of exercise on cancer-related fatigue during and following treatment: a meta-analysis. *Am J Prev Med.* 2012; 43(2): e1–24.

75. Kealey P, McIntyre I. An evaluation of the domiciliary occupational therapy service in palliative cancer care in a community trust: a patient and carers perspective. *Eur J Cancer Care (Engl).* 2005; 14(3): 232–43.

76. Vockins H. Occupational therapy intervention with patients with breast cancer: a survey. *Eur J Cancer Care (Engl).* 2004; 13(1): 45–52.

77. Wilson D, Michael D. Rehabilitation and palliative care. In: Ferrell B, Coyle N, eds. *Oxford Textbook of Palliative Nursing.* 3rd ed. New York, NY: Oxford University Press, Inc.; 2010:935–48.

78. Howell D, Keller-Olaman S, Oliver T, et al. A pan-Canadian practice guideline: screening, assessment and care of cancer-related fatigue in

adults with cancer. 2011. Available at http://www.capo.ca/Fatigue_
Guideline_FR.pdf. Accessed August 11, 2014.

79. Johnston MF, Hays RD, Subramanian SK, et al. Patient education
integrated with acupuncture for relief of cancer-related fatigue
randomized controlled feasibility study. *BMC Complement Altern
Med.* 2011; 11: 49.

80. Molassiotis A, Bardy J, Finnegan-John J, et al. Acupuncture for
cancer-related fatigue in patients with breast cancer: a pragmatic
randomized controlled trial. *J Clin Oncol.* 2012; 30(36): 4470–6.

81. Fernandez-Lao C, Cantarero-Villanueva I, Diaz-Rodriguez L,
Cuesta-Vargas A, Fernandez-Delas-Penas C, Arroyo-Morales M.
Attitudes towards massage modify effects of manual therapy in
breast cancer survivors: a randomised clinical trial with crossover
design. *Eur J Cancer Care.* 2012; 21(2): 233–41.

82. Karagozoglu S, Kahve E. Effects of back massage on
chemotherapy-related fatigue and anxiety: supportive care
and therapeutic touch in cancer nursing. *Appl Nurs Res.* 2013;
26(4): 210–7.

83. Listing M, Reisshauer A, Krohn M, et al. Massage therapy reduces
physical discomfort and improves mood disturbances in women with
breast cancer. *Psychooncology.* 2009; 18(12): 1290–9.

84. Knoop H, van Kessel K, Moss-Morris R. Which cognitions and
behaviours mediate the positive effect of cognitive behavioural

therapy on fatigue in patients with multiple sclerosis? *Psychol Med.*
2012; 42(1): 205–13.

85. Montgomery GH, David D, Kangas M, et al. Randomized controlled
trial of a cognitive-behavioral therapy plus hypnosis intervention to
control fatigue in patients undergoing radiotherapy for breast cancer.
J Clin Oncol. 2014; 32(6): 557–63.

86. Schnur JB, Montgomery GH. Hypnosis and cognitive-behavioral
therapy during breast cancer radiotherapy: a case report. *Am J Clin
Hypn.* 2008; 50(3): 209–15.

87. Kwekkeboom KL, Cherwin CH, Lee JW, Wanta B. Mind-body
treatments for the pain-fatigue-sleep disturbance symptom cluster in
persons with cancer. *J Pain Symptom Manage.* 2010; 39(1): 126–38.

88. van der Lee ML, Garssen B. Mindfulness-based cognitive
therapy reduces chronic cancer-related fatigue: a treatment study.
Psychooncology. 2012; 21(3): 264–72.

89. Mock V, Atkinson A, Barsevick AM, et al. Cancer-related fatigue.
Clinical practice guidelines in oncology. *J Natl Compr Canc Netw.*
2007; 5(10): 1054–78.

90. Reddy S, Bruera E, Pace E, Zhang K, Reyes-Gibby CC. Clinically
important improvement in the intensity of fatigue in patients with
advanced cancer. *J Palliat Med.* Oct 2007;10(5):1068-1075.

CHAPTER 30

Nausea and Vomiting

Maureen Lynch

Key Points

♦ Nausea and vomiting are different phenomena that require the advanced practice registered nurse (APRN) to perform a comprehensive assessment to determine appropriate interventions for the individual patient.

♦ When antiemetics are used as part of the management plan, the APRN must consider the pharmacologic class of the drug and use only one per class.

♦ The use of nonpharmcologic interventions as appropriate to the patient's condition and convictions are part of the APRN's approach to the management of nausea and vomiting.

Introduction

Nausea and vomiting (N/V) affect all the dimensions of quality of life, particularly if the symptoms are protracted. Dehydration, electrolyte imbalances, malnutrition, aspiration, and esophageal tears are common physical sequelae of N/V. Concerns about eating and declining physical function may lead to feelings of social isolation. The burden of uncontrolled symptoms may lead to feelings of hopelessness and depression. Caregivers may be distressed by their inability to nourish patients. The cost of medications and other direct and indirect care may contribute to distress. If the symptoms are thought to be related to disease-modifying treatments, patients may decide to prematurely stop potentially beneficial therapies. The palliative APRN can have a positive impact on the patient's quality of life and reduce the risk of physical sequelae through a symptom management plan that is based on an understanding of the physiology and pathophysiology of N/V, comprehensive symptom assessment, and formulation of a symptom diagnosis that will direct the rational use of antiemetic therapies.[1–3]

Definitions

Although nausea and vomiting are separate symptoms, they are often viewed as a single entity in practice and in the literature. Either may be experienced acutely, chronically, spontaneously, or in response to specific events, such as eating, activity, or medication use. Nausea is a subjective unpleasant sensation experienced in the back of the throat and epigastrium and is associated with a perceived need to vomit. Patients may describe queasiness or an upset or unsettled stomach or may use other terms. Nausea may be continuous or intermittent and may have a more negative impact on quality of life than vomiting.[1,4–7] Vomiting is the expulsion of gastric contents through the mouth. It may occur as a single episode or be recurrent. Retching or dry heaves refers to spasmodic contractions of abdominal muscles and diaphragm that do not result in vomiting.[1,4,6]

The patterns of chemotherapy-induced N/V describe the temporal occurrence of the symptoms in relation to treatment. These terms may be helpful in describing N/V induced by specific events. Acute nausea occurs within minutes or hours of a specific event, such as chemotherapy. Delayed N/V occur at least 24 hours after the stimulus and lasts for several days. N/V associated with an event may trigger a learned response to similar events in the future, causing anticipatory N/V.[2]

Prevalence and Risk Factors

Much of the research and literature on N/V focuses on the experience and management of these symptoms in oncology practice. Up to 80% of oncology patients undergoing chemotherapy and/or radiation therapy experience N/V.[2] Nausea is more frequently experienced than vomiting. The prevalence rates vary depending on specifics of disease, chemotherapeutic agents used, and anatomic sites of radiation therapy.[2,3] In oncology patients with advanced disease who are no longer receiving active anticancer therapies, the prevalence rate is about 60% for nausea and 30% for vomiting.[2,8]

N/V are also frequently experienced by patients with other life-limiting or life-threatening illnesses and conditions (Table 30.1). N/V may trouble patients with progressive neurological conditions, such as amyotrophic lateral sclerosis and multiple sclerosis.[9] As patients near death, the overall prevalence of N/V is 19%, with a range from 8.4% to 70%.[10] The risk of developing N/V in advanced disease may be higher in patients who are female, who are younger, and who have a history of low alcohol intake.[2] Other risk factors include treatment with chemotherapy, opioids, antibiotics, and digoxin and the presence of hypercalcemia; fluid and electrolyte imbalances; hepatic, renal, gastrointestinal, and central nervous system pathologies; and anxiety.[2]

Physiology

The research surrounding chemotherapy-induced N/V advanced our understanding of the basic physiology of vomiting. Vomiting is a protective reflex designed to rid the body of ingested toxins. It is

Table 30.1 Prevalence of Nausea and Vomiting in Non-Oncology Populations

Disease	Nausea Rate	Vomiting Rate	Nausea and Vomiting Rate
Liver failure	58%		
Heart failure	50%	24%	17–48%
Renal failure			30–43%
HIV			43–49%
COPD	18%	4%	

From references 3, 9.

controlled by the vomiting center or complex located in the medulla oblongata. A number of neurotransmitters and their receptors play an important role in coordination of the reflex. Dopamine/dopamine receptors, serotonin/5-HT-3 receptors, and substance P/neurokinin-1 receptors have the best-described roles.[2–4,9,11] Cannabinoids and their related receptors, present in the central nervous system and the gut, may also play a role, with synergistic effects on dopamine, serotonin, and neurokinin-1 receptors.[12]

The vomiting center responds to input from afferent pathways that include the chemoreceptor trigger zone (CTZ), the vagus nerve, the cerebral cortex, and the vestibular system. The CTZ is a highly vascular area located in the fourth ventricle of the brain. The lack of a blood–brain barrier at the CTZ allows direct exposure to various drugs, toxins, and metabolites circulating in the blood or cerebrospinal fluid. Dopamine, histamine, serotonin, and substance P are the major neurotransmitters in this pathway.[2,4,9,11] Studies suggest that there may be synergistic activity between 5-HT-3 and neurokinin-1 receptors.[13] In addition, the CTZ responds to signaling from the vagal afferents mediated by the release of serotonin from gut enterochromaffin cells in response to injury or inflammation of the gastrointestinal tract, changes in gastrointestinal motility, and the chemistry of the luminal contents. Oropharyngeal irritants signal the CTZ via the pharyngeal branch of the vagus nerve, with histamine and acetylcholine thought to be the major neurotransmitters. The vagal afferents may also directly stimulate the vomiting center.

The cerebral cortex signals the vomiting center via the midbrain. The primary neurotransmitter may be gamma-aminobutyric acid (GABA). Stimuli include anticipation, fear, and memories (e.g., anticipatory vomiting) as well as signals from the senses, such as disturbing sights, smells, or pain. The vomiting center also responds to vestibular input via the inner ear, mediated by histamine and acetylcholine. Motion, certain medications, and changes in intracranial pressure may trigger this pathway. With threshold stimulation of these afferent pathways, the vomiting center triggers the efferent pathways that coordinate the complex sequence of powerful and sustained contractions of the abdominal muscles and diaphragm, and relaxation of pyloric and duodenal sphincters that forces expulsion of gastric contents via the mouth.[2,3,11,12,14,15]

Less is known about the physiological pathways that control nausea. At one time, nausea was thought to be caused by subthreshold stimulation of the vomiting pathways, but more recent research suggests that the physiology of nausea is different.[3,16] While vomiting is a reflex controlled by lower brain structures, nausea seems to require consciousness and cerebral function.[3] Some studies suggest that nausea may result from changes in gastric myoelectrical activity and neuroendocrine responses mediated via the autonomic nervous system and cerebral cortex. The changes in gastric motility are accompanied by a decrease in gastric acid levels and release of cortisol, beta endorphins, epinephrine, and norepinephrine, causing nausea, pallor, cold sweats, tachypnea, tachycardia, and increased salivation.[2,3,14] The CTZ plays a role in the development of nausea through its effect on gastrointestinal motility, taste aversion, and food intake.[2]

These different physiological pathways may explain why N/V do not always respond to the same symptom interventions. An example is the continued higher incidence of post-chemotherapy nausea despite the reduced incidence of chemotherapy-induced vomiting with the use of research-based antiemetic guidelines.[17,18]

Etiology

Nausea, vomiting, and retching are distinct phenomena that may be experienced acutely, chronically, independently, simultaneously, or sequentially. In palliative care, the etiologies of N/V are often multifactorial and may be related to underlying disease and/or comorbidities, treatment effects, or debility.[11] A primary etiology of N/V can be identified in most patients.[11]

N/V are often experienced in relation to other symptoms. Clusters of two or more symptoms that consistently occur concurrently may share a common etiology and be synergistic.[19] Studies of N/V in oncology describe clustering of nausea, vomiting, loss of appetite, taste changes, weight loss, and fatigue.[18,20] While not all concurrent symptoms are clusters, the APRN's attention to other symptoms is part of the comprehensive assessment and may suggest etiologies for N/V.

Gastroparesis, occurring in 34% to 45% of cases, is a common etiology in palliative care that is suggested by intermittent nausea, early satiety, and postprandial bloating relieved by vomiting.[11,21] Bowel obstruction, occurring in 10% to 30% of cases, may be suggested by the presence of N/V, abdominal pain, altered bowel function, and abdominal distention. Pharyngeal stimulation is suggested by vomiting and gagging associated with cough and difficulty clearing secretions.[3,11,14] Persistent nausea unaccompanied by or unrelieved by vomiting may suggest a metabolic and drug-related cause. Opioid use in patients without a previous history of nausea may cause constipation, gastroparesis, and/or stimulation of the CTZ, resulting in a 40% incidence of N/V.[11,22] Early-morning vomiting associated with headache may suggest increased intracranial pressure. Nausea related to movement may suggest a vestibular component.[11]

Other etiologies, both acute and chronic, also need to be considered by the APRN in formulating a differential diagnosis and approach to symptom management. In patients with chronic obstructive pulmonary disease (COPD), N/V may be reactions to antibiotics, theophylline, or steroids, steroid-induced gastrointestinal irritation, gastropathy from circulatory overload, infection, cough and secretions, fatigue, and anxiety. Heart failure may trigger N/V related to cardiac ischemia, digitalis and other medications, congestive gastropathy, impaired renal and/or hepatic function causing hyponatremia, dehydration from diuretics, cough, and anxiety.[3,9,11] Table 30.2 outlines common etiologies of N/V to be considered in formulating a differential diagnosis.

Table 30.2 Common Etiologies of Nausea and Vomiting

Gastrointestinal	Drug-induced
◆ Ascites	◆ Antibiotics
◆ Adhesions	◆ Anticonvulsants
◆ Biliary obstruction	◆ Aspirin and NSAIDs
◆ Cholecystitis	◆ Chemotherapy
◆ Constipation	◆ Digoxin
◆ Gastric irritation/distention	◆ Iron supplements
◆ Gastroparesis	◆ Opioids
◆ Gastric outlet obstruction	◆ Theophylline
◆ Gastric reflux	**Radiation-induced**
◆ Hepatitis	◆ Esophagus
◆ Hepatic capsular distention	◆ Abdominal
◆ Intestinal obstruction	◆ Pelvic
◆ Irritable bowel	◆ Brain
◆ Intra-abdominal cancers: Colon, pancreas, ovarian, gastric, esophageal	
◆ Peritoneal carcinomatosis	
◆ Pancreatitis	
◆ Gastric or duodenal ulcers	

Metabolic	Increased intracranial pressure
◆ Fluid and electrolyte imbalances: Hypercalcemia Hyper/hyponatremia	◆ Cerebral edema
	◆ Intracranial tumor
◆ Dehydration	◆ Intracranial bleeding
◆ Adrenocortical insufficiency	◆ Skull metastases
◆ Liver failure	◆ Carcinomatous meningitis
◆ Renal failure	
◆ Diabetic ketoacidosis	
◆ Pregnancy	

Infections	Psychological
◆ *Candida* esophagitis	◆ Fear
◆ Gastroenteritis	◆ Anxiety
◆ Sepsis	

Vestibular	Pharyngeal
◆ Motion sickness	◆ Chronic cough
◆ Ménière syndrome	◆ Oropharyngeal secretions
◆ Vestibular problems	

Adapted from reference 1. Sources: references 2, 3, 4, 11, 14.

Case Study Part 1

Marion was a 62-year-old woman with metastatic breast cancer involving her liver and bones. Her past medical history included GERD, diverticulitis requiring a surgical intervention 8 months earlier, and intolerance to multiple medications. She reported daily nausea and vomiting over the preceding 3 weeks. The palliative APRN considered whether her symptoms were due to changes in GI function related to tumor growth in, or adjacent to, the GI tract (liver metastasis), GERD, diverticulitis, possible increased intracranial pressure from an undetected CNS tumor, hypercalcemia given the bone involvement, dehydration, reactions to medications, or anxiety.

Assessment

The APRN's comprehensive symptom assessment includes data from multiple sources, including the patient, family, physical examination and clinical observation, the medical record, and diagnostic tests. The assessment data describe the patient, his or her health status, his or her symptom experience, and other patient-specific factors that will affect the symptom management plan. This includes an understanding of the patient's prognosis, overall goals of care, and specific goals for symptom relief.

A synthesis of the patient-specific data and the APRN's knowledge and understanding of the health problems forms the symptom diagnosis. This is a succinct statement of the problem(s) and likely cause(s). In conjunction with patient-specific goals, this guides further diagnostic testing if needed for therapeutic decision making and the selection of therapeutic interventions to eliminate or modify the cause of the symptom, if possible, and to alleviate symptom distress related to N/V.

Identifying the presence of the symptom(s) is the first step in assessment. The subjectivity of nausea makes it harder to identify than vomiting. The patient's report of N/V, either spontaneously or in the clinical interview, is a frequent method of symptom identification. Some patients may be reluctant to report either symptom, in the belief that nothing can be done or that symptom management will detract from disease-directed therapies. Routine screening for common symptoms using symptom inventory tools, such as the Memorial Symptom Assessment Scale or the Edmonton Symptom Assessment System, is another method of symptom identification.[23]

Understanding the patient's experience of N/V begins with the patient's description of the symptom to clarify its nature. The patient's experiential, linguistic, cultural, ethnic, and geographical background may influence the expression and meaning of N/V for the individual. Characteristics of onset, frequency, intensity or severity, and pattern of occurrence; triggering and alleviating factors, such as use of prescription or over-the-counter medications or herbal preparations, activity, and changes in eating and drinking patterns; and associated symptoms help delineate possible etiologies and therapies. The effects of the N/V on function and quality of life are essential parts of the assessment. N/V symptoms often change eating patterns and are accompanied by diminished physical functioning and self-care capacity. In turn, social isolation, uncertainty, and worry about how N/V affect day-to-day life, medical therapies, family caregivers, and survival add to symptom distress.

In addition to the clinician interview and history, patient diaries and journals may aid in understanding the patient's perception of, and response to, N/V. There are also specific assessment tools for evaluating N/V. The Morrow Assessment of Nausea and Vomiting (MANE) and the Rhodes Index of Nausea and Vomiting (INVR) enhance the patient's report of the symptom characteristics. Other tools, such as Functional Living Index-Emesis and Osoba Nausea and Emesis Module, describe the effect of the symptoms on function and well-being[4,6,7,24] (Table 30.3).

Case Study Part 2

Marion described persistent, worsening, continuous, low-level (3 or 4/10) nausea accompanied by vomiting of small amounts of

Table 30.3 Assessment of Nausea and Vomiting

General	*Knowing the Patient*	
	Demographics: age, gender, race, employment, education, place of residence, socioeconomics, health insurance	
	Spiritual: values/beliefs, faith community, practices, rituals, restrictions	
	Psychosocial: marital status, sexual preference, culture, coping, social supports, substance use concerns, past experience with health-related issues	
	Current quality-of-life concerns	
Health status	Current diagnosis, prognosis, disease course and trajectory, including past and current therapies, patient's understanding of disease status, goals of care	
	Past medical history, including history of nausea or vomiting and effective therapies.	

	Nausea	**Vomiting**
Symptom experience	Patient description: nausea, upset stomach, queasiness, sick stomach, other	Description of "throwing up," "upchucking," "barfing"; volume, color, content of emesis
Severity	0 none–10 worst; mild/moderate/severe intensity; episodes per day/week/month; intermittent or constant	Frequency per day/week; intensity of vomiting
Duration and pattern	Onset; pattern and timing of occurrence	
Modulating factors	What makes your nausea or vomiting better or worse (e.g., time of day, medications, eating, activity, bowel function)?	
Distress/Impact	*Meaning of symptom; interference with function and quality of life:*	
	What and how much are you able to eat or drink?	
	What concerns you most about the nausea and/or vomiting?	
	What worries do you have about what is causing it?	
	Do you have an inability to eat or drink?	
	Are you able to eat with family/friends?	
	What effects does it have on energy and activity?	
	Are there family concerns?	
	What have been the effects on treatments?	
	Have you had concerns about your appetite/weight in the past?	
	Overweight?	
	Underweight?	
	History of anorexia/bulimia?	
Associated symptoms	Fever, cough, oropharyngeal secretions, dizziness, headaches, vision changes, anorexia, dysgeusia, dysphagia, abdominal pain, bloating, abdominal distention, heartburn, hiccups, constipation, diarrhea, weight changes	
Physical examination	Temperature	
	Weight: if available, comparison to past weights is helpful	
	Neurological: level of consciousness; cognition, balance, cranial nerve deficits	
	Oropharynx: mucositis, secretions, infection, obstruction	
	Blood pressure and pulse: sitting, lying, standing to assess for postural hypotension from fluid imbalance	
	Abdomen: distention, bowel sounds, tenderness, masses	
	Rectal exam: fecal impaction	
Diagnostic tests as indicated by history and physical findings and patient's health status and goals of care	Laboratory tests for renal and hepatic function, electrolytes, calcium	
	Complete blood count	
	Blood or urine cultures if infection is suspected	
	Therapeutic drug level monitoring, if appropriate (digoxin, theophylline, etc.)	
	Radiological studies	
	Brain scans if CNS pathology suspected	
	Chest x-ray if pneumonia suspected	
	Plain film of abdomen to assess for obstruction or constipation	
	CT scan of abdomen to assess for obstruction, other pathologies	
	Endoscopic evaluation to assess for reflux, esophagitis, obstruction	

From references 1–4, 6.

green to brown liquid once or twice each day over the past 3 weeks. Vomiting temporarily relieved the nausea. She noted the symptoms were worse when she ate, so she restricted her oral intake, resulting in a 4-pound weight loss in the past 3 weeks. Her bowels were "sluggish," with small-volume stools every 2 or 3 days. She noted some abdominal bloating, which she attributed to slow bowel function. She denied abdominal pain. She has continued with her usual activities around the house but has declined social activities because she did not "feel good." She used a fentanyl 25 mcg/hour patch q72h for back pain related to her bone metastasis (changed from long-acting oxycodone after her bowel surgery), senna 2 tablets twice each day, and omeprazole 20 mg daily. In the past, she had rarely used as-needed opioids. However, in the preceding month she took short-acting morphine two or three times per day for back pain, which had increased as she tried to be more active. She wasn't currently receiving anticancer therapies. Her exam noted the weight loss and slight abdominal distention but was otherwise unremarkable. Restaging scans done 4 weeks earlier showed stable liver metastasis. Her laboratory studies were unremarkable. The symptom diagnosis was nausea and vomiting possibly related to increased morphine use and opioid-induced constipation.

Management Strategies

The goal of antiemetic therapy is to modify or alleviate the patient's experience of N/V by reducing the incidence and severity of both, addressing symptom-related distress, and modifying or eliminating the cause if possible. Broad categories of interventions include patient and family education, psychosocial and spiritual support, behavioral and lifestyle changes, medications, invasive procedures, and etiology-directed therapies. The suspected cause of the N/V, the patient's general condition, comorbidities, current medications, prognosis, goals of care, and the patient's preferences and available resources guide selection of interventions. Table 30.4 summarizes management approaches.

Nonpharmacologic Interventions

Pharmacologic management of N/V is often viewed as the mainstay of therapy. However, the APRN's holistic approach encompasses nonpharmacologic interventions suitable for the patient. Patient and family education centers on causes of N/V for the individual, realistic goals for symptom control, and implementation of the symptom management plan. This may include specific instructions regarding how and when to use medications, other therapies, and self-monitoring parameters. Patients and families also need to know how to contact the care team for unexpected or emergent situations.

Psychosocial and spiritual support centers on acknowledging the quality of life and functional concerns, as well as the symptom distress that focuses on the meaning and implications of the symptom for the patient. Nursing's presence and understanding the symptom control plan help to decrease the patient's and family's sense of loss of control and uncertainty. Involving social workers, a chaplain, and/or psychiatric support may also be helpful. This may be particularly helpful if artificial hydration and nutrition and invasive procedures, such as those to bypass obstructions, are being considered.

Lifestyle changes to manage N/V often center on self-care activities dealing with oral intake. Most are based on expert opinion. Oral care; recommendations on the amount, types, and frequency of intake; and maintaining an environment free of emetogenic sights, sounds, and smells are key points.[4,6]

Interest in the use of integrative therapies for management of chemotherapy-induced N/V stimulated research in this area. While few studies have been done in palliative care populations, most of these therapies are relatively nontoxic and can be considered based on cost, availability, the evidence base for managing N/V in other conditions, and patient preference. Behavioral interventions, such as relaxation, progressive muscle relaxation, and guided imagery, reduce the incidence and intensity of anticipatory chemotherapy-related N/V. These techniques can be taught to patients and may increase their sense of control and decrease distress.[2,4,11,25] They may also help with anxiety and stress reduction in general.

Some studies demonstrate that acupuncture reduces the incidence of postoperative and acute chemotherapy-induced N/V.[25,26] Acupressure reduced acute chemotherapy-induced nausea.[27,28] The use of acupressure wristbands produced mixed results.[28]

Interest in the spice ginger as an antiemetic exerting weak inhibition on 5HT3 receptors led to studies and reviews of its use in motion sickness and pregnancy- and chemotherapy-related nausea. Formulations and doses varied, as did reported side effects of heartburn, diarrhea, and bruising. The mixed study results demonstrate no clear evidence of efficacy.[4,29]

If N/V are moderate to severe, recurrent, or prolonged, as with recurrent or persistent gastrointestinal obstructions, the use of intravenous fluids to maintain hydration and electrolyte balance and parenteral nutrition may be considered. For patients in advanced or terminal stages of disease, the use of these therapies beyond the acute phase of management is a highly individual decision based on goals of care, prognosis, and the perceived benefits, burdens, and outcomes of the interventions.[30,31]

Pharmacologic Interventions

There are seven classes of drugs used in antiemetic therapy: dopamine receptor antagonists, including prokinetics and neuroleptics (antipsychotics), serotonin receptor antagonists, antihistamines, anticholinergics, corticosteroids, cannabinoids, and NK1 receptor antagonists (Table 30.5). Drug selection may be guided by a mechanistic/etiological or empiric approach. The mechanistic approach uses an understanding of the neurotransmitters and neuroreceptors involved in the different emetic pathways and the use of drugs to block their activation/effect based on presumed etiology of the symptoms. This is a more evidence-based approach. The empiric approach leaves antiemetic selection to the preference of the clinician. There is no clear evidence that one approach is more effective in palliative care, particularly where the etiology of N/V may be unknown or multifactorial, and limited studies on antiemetic efficacy in this population exist. Understanding the action and side effects of the different antiemetics aids in medication selection.[9,11,32] Regardless of the approach, if initial therapies are unsuccessful, adding or changing to an agent from a different class of antiemetics may be beneficial. The simultaneous use of more than one agent from each class is generally avoided to prevent overlapping side effects/toxicities.[11] The concurrent use of agents from different classes may be beneficial.

Table 30.4 Approaches to Managing Nausea and Vomiting in Palliative Care

Identification and management of etiology and contributing symptoms	
Patient and family education	Likely causes of nausea and vomiting for this patient
	Goals for symptom management
	Directions re: specific interventions and self-monitoring, including emergent situations
	Information about how to contact care team
Psychosocial and spiritual support	Acknowledge the psychological, social, cultural, and religious impact of nausea and vomiting as appropriate for patient and family.
	Refer to social worker, chaplain, or psychiatric support, if needed.
Nutrition counseling	Mouth care*
	Small, frequent meals or snacks*
	Maintain fluid intake but limit fluids with meals.*
	Pleasant eating environment*
	Eat bland, cool temperature foods.*
	Avoid salty, sweet, spicy foods.*
	Use enriched and fortified foods to increased calories and protein.
	Use of commercial oral liquid nutritional supplements
	Consultation with qualified nutritionist
Cognitive-behavioral therapies	Includes relaxation, imagery, distraction, self-hypnosis**
Integrative therapies	Acupuncture**
	Acupressure***
	Ginger***
	Aromatherapy***
Medications	See Table 30.5.
Artificial hydration and nutrition	Generally not tolerated or beneficial in patients who have end-stage disease. Individualized goals of the therapy need to be considered.
	May benefit patients with early-stage disease who have temporary limitations in oral intake or those with GI malfunctions but high performance status
Invasive procedures	For obstructions: surgery, venting gastrostomy tubes, stents

*Expert opinion; **Limited data to support use; ***Mixed or no data to support use.

From references 2–4, 25–31.

Dopamine receptor antagonist (D$_2$) antiemetics are active at the CTZ and in the gut.[33] Commonly used drugs in this class are metoclopramide and neuroleptics, such as prochlorperazine, chlorpromazine, haloperidol, and olanzapine. Except for haloperidol, most drugs in the class also block other receptors in the emetic pathway.[11] These agents may be most useful for N/V related to chemical or metabolic causes. Olanzapine's activity at multiple receptor sites may be useful for nausea of unclear etiology or refractory nausea.[34]

Gastroparesis is a common cause of N/V in palliative care. Thus, the pro-motility effect of metoclopramide on the upper gastrointestinal tract and its activity at the CTZ make it a useful first-line antiemetic.[9,11,32] However, it should be avoided in patients with complete bowel obstruction.[9,11]

Extrapyramidal side effects that range from mild to moderate akathisia (subjective sense of restlessness to motor restlessness), parkinsonian-like changes (masked facies, resting tremor, cogwheel rigidity, shuffling gait, bradykinesia), dystonias (involuntary contraction of major muscles [e.g., torticollis, oculogyric crisis]), and tardive dyskinesia (characterized by lip smacking, rhythmic tongue and/or body movements, grimacing) may be associated with dopamine receptor antagonist use. Management of extrapyramidal symptoms includes discontinuing the drug or reducing the dose. Co-administering a benzodiazepine, a beta-blocker, or an anticholinergic may temporarily reduce akathisia and dystonia.[35]

Selective 5HT$_3$ (serotonin receptor subtype) receptor antagonists (e.g., ondansetron and granisetron) work on receptors in the gut, the CTZ, and the vomiting center. They are primarily used for management of N/V caused by chemotherapy and radiation therapy that affects digestive system organs, and in the postoperative setting. In palliative care, 5HT$_3$ agents are not first-line antiemetics except in managing bowel obstruction, where chemical and mechanical intestinal stimulation causes release of serotonin from enterochromaffin cells. They should also be considered if dopamine antagonist agents are ineffective or not tolerated. Constipation and QT prolongation are potential side effects.[2,11,36] Cost may be a factor in access to these medications.[2]

Antihistamines block H$_1$ receptor activity at the CTZ and the vomiting center. They are primarily used to manage N/V caused

Table 30.5 Commonly Used Antiemetics

Drug	Suggested Doses	Primary Neuroreceptor Affinity	Common Use	Side Effects/Comments
DOPAMINE RECEPTOR ANTAGONISTS				
Prokinetic agent Metoclopramide	Oral, ODT, IV: 10–20 mg, q6–12h	Moderate D_2 (primarily in GI tract) Low $5HT_3$ (only at high doses)	Gastroparesis Ileus in absence of complete obstruction	EPS; esophageal spasm; colic in GI tract obstruction; prolonged half-life in renal failure. QT prolongation Do not use in complete bowel obstruction.
Butyrophenone Haloperidol	Oral: 0.5–5 mg q8–12h IV: 0.5–1 mg q6–8h	High D_2	Chemical and/or metabolic nausea Bowel obstruction	Less sedating than phenothiazines. May cause QT prolongation, EPS, neuroleptic malignant syndrome. Dose reduction may be needed in hepatic insufficiency.
Phenothiazine Prochlorperazine	Oral: 5–10 mg q6–8h PR: 25 mg q12h IV: 10 mg q6h Max dose: 40 mg/24 h	Moderate D_2 Low H_1	Chemical and/or metabolic nausea	EPS, headache, dry mouth, hypotension, drowsiness, QT prolongation
Chlorpromazine	Oral: 10–25 q6h IV: 12.5–25 mg q6–12h	Moderate D_2 Low H_1	Chemical and/or metabolic nausea	More sedating than prochlorperazine EPS, QT prolongation
Atypical Antipsychotic Olanzapine	Oral: 2.5–10 mg q12–24h	D_{1-4}, $5HT_3$, H_1	Refractory nausea/vomiting	Sedation; hyperglycemia; reduced seizure threshold Associated with weight gain and improved appetite Lower risk of EPS QT prolongation
CORTICOSTEROID				
Dexamethasone	Oral: 2–4 mg q6–24h IV: 2–4 mg q6–24h	Possibly reduces release of serotonin or activation of corticosteroid receptors in the CNS	Cerebral edema Intracranial tumors Chemotherapy-induced nausea Bowel obstruction	Insomnia, anxiety, euphoria; perirectal burning with IV administration; GI upset Metabolic effects: glycemic control, infection risk
SEROTONIN ANTAGONISTS				
Ondansetron	Oral/ODT/IV: 4-8 mg q8–12h	High $5HT_3$ Both peripherally and centrally	Chemotherapy-induced nausea Abdominal radiation therapy Postop GI irritants	Constipation Headache Diarrhea Mild sedation QT prolongation
Granisetron	Oral/IV: 1 mg q12h or 2 mg q24h Transdermal patch: 3.1 mg/24 h (lasts 7 days)			
CANNABINOIDS				
Dronabinol	2–10 mg q8–12h Contains sesame oil	CB_1	Second-line antiemetic	Sedation, dizziness, disorientation, concentration difficulties, dysphoria, hypotension, dry mouth, tachycardia
Nabilone	1–2 mg q8–12h (max dose 6 mg/day)	CB_1	Second-line antiemetic	
ANTICHOLINERGICS				
Hyoscyamine	Oral/IV: 0.125–0.25 mg q4h as needed up to 1.5 mg/day	mAChR (in the vomiting center and peripherally)	Intestinal obstruction Peritoneal irritation, Increased intracranial pressure Excess secretions Motion sickness	Dry mouth, ileus, urinary retention, blurred vision, agitation
Scopolamine	Transdermal: 1.5 mg q72h (lasts 72 h)			Onset of effect is up to 24 h.

(continued)

Table 30.5 Continued

ANTIHISTAMNES				
Promethazine	Oral, PR, or IV: 12.5–25 mg q6–8h (max dose 100 mg/day)	High H_1 Low D_2 Low mAChR	Motion sickness Increased intracranial pressure	Sedation Dry mouth Constipation Dizziness Confusion Blurred vision
Cyclizine	Oral: 25–50 mg q6–8h (max dose 200 mg/day)	H_1		
Diphenhydramine	Oral/IV: 12.5–50 mg q6–8h			
BENZODIAZEPINE				
Lorazepam	Oral/IV: 0.5–1 mg q6–24h	GABA	Anxiety Not FDA approved as antiemetic	Sedation, amnesia, delirium, Depression. Reduce dose in renal or hepatic insufficiency.
OTHER				
Octreotide (somatostatin analogue)	SC: 100–150 mg q8h IV continuous infusion: 0.2–0.9 mg/day IM depot: 20–30 mg q3–4 weeks	Somatostatin receptors in brain, pituitary, GI tract	Bowel obstruction. Reduces peristalsis and intestinal secretions	Pain at injection site; worsening GI symptoms. Reduce dose in renal or hepatic insufficiency.
Mirtazapine (antidepressant)	Oral: 7.5–30 mg at bedtime	$5HT_3$, H_1, mAChR	Gastroparesis	Increased appetite; weight gain, somnolence

ODT = oral disintegrating tablet; D_2 = dopamine; H_1 = histamine; $5HT_3$ = serotonin; CB_1 = cannabinoid; mAChR = muscarinic acetylcholine receptors; EPS = extrapyramidal side effects.
Adapted from reference 1. Sources: references 2–4, 9, 11, 32–34, 36, 40–42.

by vestibular stimulation (e.g., motion sickness, raised intracranial pressure). Promethazine, cyclizine, meclizine, and diphenhydramine are commonly used agents. Sedation and anticholinergic side effects may limit use. The elderly and frail may be more prone to delirium as a side effect.[2,11]

Anticholinergic agents are primarily used as antiemetics in combination with other antiemetics for control of N/V associated with dizziness and movement and bowel obstruction.[4,32] They block muscarinic acetylcholine receptors (mAChR) in vestibular nuclei and the autonomic nervous system, resulting in decreased peristaltic tone and movement and reduced intestinal secretions.[4,36] Hyoscyamine and scopolamine are commonly used drugs in this class.

Corticosteroids are often used in antiemetic regimens for chemotherapy-induced N/V, for symptom management in bowel obstruction, and in treatment of raised intracranial pressure. The antiemetic mechanism of these agents is not known. Theorized actions include anti-inflammatory and antisecretory activity and altered permeability of the blood–brain barrier with reduced effect of potential chemical and metabolic stimuli. Concerns about gastric irritation, glycemic control, infection risk, proximal muscle weakness with long-term use, and dysphoria and/or delirium may limit their use.[11,36]

Cannabinoids' activity at the CB_1 receptors in the central and peripheral nervous systems is thought to be the basis of their antiemetic effect. Dronabinol and nabilone are approved by the U.S. Food and Drug Administration (FDA) for use in chemotherapy-induced N/V.[36,37] The effectiveness of other cannabinoid formulations is not yet established. Marijuana remains a schedule 1 substance despite legalization for medical purposes in some states. Reports of cannabinoid hyperemesis syndrome with chronic cannabis use raise the need for further study of this antiemetic class.[38]

Neurokinin-1 receptor antagonists are FDA approved for use in acute chemotherapy-associated N/V and in the postoperative setting. Drugs in this class are aprepitant and fosaprepitant. Use in palliative care has not been studied.[36]

Benzodiazepines act on GABA in the cerebral cortex. They are effective in managing anxiety associated with N/V but do not have antiemetic activity.[11,36] Side effects of sedation and amnesia may limit use.

Mirtazapine, a tetracyclic antidepressant, has activity as a $5HT_3$, H_1, and muscarinic receptor antagonist. Reports of its antiemetic effect in diabetic gastroparesis and idiopathic nausea are indicative of a prokinetic effect that needs further study in the palliative care population.[11,36]

Case Study Part 3

Initial interventions for Marion's presumed opioid-induced nausea and vomiting included adding metoclopramide 10 mg orally twice daily for its pro-motility effect and enhancing her bowel regimen.

Management of Opioid-Induced N/V

Opioid-induced N/V may result from gastroparesis, constipation, CTZ stimulation, and/or vestibular stimulation. Managing associated symptoms, such as constipation, and consideration of changing the opioid or its route of administration when possible are reasonable management strategies. Although there are no specific antiemetic recommendations in the literature, empiric use of antiemetics, especially with initial use of the opioid, also seems reasonable.[24]

Case Study Part 4

After 4 days, Marion had no improvement. At that point, her breakthrough analgesic was changed from morphine to hydromorphone, and metoclopramide was continued. Three days later, her symptoms markedly worsened. She reported the onset of abdominal pain, increased abdominal distention, and more frequent, higher-volume vomiting. Her oral intake was minimal. She was weak and pale and had marked abdominal distention and decreased bowel sounds in the left abdomen. A CT scan of her abdomen showed partial bowel obstruction secondary to peritoneal carcinomatosis.

Management of Bowel Obstructions

Bowel obstruction requires immediate intervention. Decisions about surgical, interventional, and/or medical management are based on the etiology of the obstruction and the patient's condition and goals of care. Symptom management in bowel obstructions focuses on relief of pain, N/V, and abdominal distention. If surgical options are not appropriate, the use of venting gastrostomy tubes or stents may offer symptom relief. If the patient has a high performance status, life expectancy greater than 30 days, and an obstruction at the gastric outlet, proximal small bowel, or colon, then insertion of self-expanding metal stents placed via endoscopy or interventional radiology may be considered. Although often successful in relieving symptoms, stents may cause perforation and bleeding; if the stent migrates, reobstruction may occur.[39] Prolonged nasogastric intubation is possible to relieve distention and vomiting but is limited by discomfort from nasal and pharyngeal irritation and/or infections, difficulty clearing oral secretions, and aspiration pneumonias. An alternative is a venting gastrostomy tube (G-tube) that is placed surgically or percutaneously during an endoscopic procedure to allow drainage of gastric contents. With a venting G-tube in place, limited oral intake may be tolerated, which can be psychosocially satisfying for both the patient and family. Large-volume ascites and tumor infiltration of the stomach may preclude G-tube placement. Complications include pain at the insertion site, leakage of gastric fluid, with resulting skin irritation, and the need for periodic replacement if used in long-term therapy.[39,40]

During the acute phase of managing a bowel obstruction, artificial hydration and nutrition are often given. The parenteral route of medication administration avoids uncertain gastrointestinal absorption. The use of opioids is the mainstay of pain management. Corticosteroids offer analgesic, anti-inflammatory, and antiemetic benefits.

Although haloperidol or serotonin antagonists like ondansetron or granisetron may be of benefit in bowel obstruction management, metoclopramide may be the first-line choice in partial obstructions because of its prokinetic effect. Anticholinergic medications like scopolamine are often used to decrease secretion of gastrointestinal fluids and peristalsis, with a decrease in distention, vomiting, and abdominal cramping. Octreotide, a somatostatin analogue, decreases gastrointestinal secretions and peristalsis by inhibiting the release and action of the gastrointestinal hormones vasopressin and gastrin.[41] It is considered more effective than anticholinergic medications in relieving obstructive symptoms.[40,41] Octreotide has a short half-life, so it requires repeat subcutaneous injection or continuous intravenous dosing. The depot form needs to be repeated monthly to prevent recurrent obstructive symptoms. Initial depot dosing takes about 14 days to establish effectiveness, so short-acting doses should be continued while it takes effect. Although octreotide has an established role in bowel obstruction management, cost may limit its use in some settings.[40,41]

Case Study Part 5

Marion was maintained on intravenous metoclopramide for its prokinetic effect. She was also given octreotide; after initial treatment with subcutaneous injections, she was given a depot form to prevent recurrent obstructive symptoms. Short-acting doses were continued while it took effect. Marion's symptoms improved, and she resumed palliative chemotherapy to treat the cause of the obstruction while continuing on oral metoclopramide and depot octreotide to minimize recurrent symptoms.

Conclusion

N/V are highly distressing symptoms that many palliative care patients experience as a result of disease or therapies, even those that are palliative or symptom-focused. The APRN is positioned to provide expert, compassionate clinical care while contributing to the expanding evidence base for managing these symptoms in palliative care. Successful management of these complex symptoms requires that the APRN conduct an ongoing comprehensive assessment to describe the patient's experience and associated factors, formulate a symptom diagnosis based on an understanding of likely etiologies, and use appropriate nonpharmacologic and pharmacologic management strategies based on best evidence, expert opinion, and patient acceptability.

References

1. Hawkins R, Lynch M. Nausea and vomiting. In: Dahlin CM, Lynch M, eds. *Core Curriculum for the Advanced Practice Hospice and Palliative Registered Nurse*. 2nd ed. Pittsburgh, PA: Hospice and Palliative Nursing Association; 2013.
2. Tipton J. Nausea and vomiting. In: Yarbro CH, Wujcik D, Gobel BH, eds. *Cancer Symptom Management*. Burlington, MA: Jones and Bartlett, Inc.; 2014:213–33.
3. Del Fabbro E. Palliative care: Assessment and management of nausea and vomiting. Up-to-Date®. 2014. Available at http://www.uptodate.com/home Accessed March 26, 2014.
4. Chow K, Cogan, D, Mun S. Nausea and vomiting. In: Ferrell BR, Coyle N, Paice J. *Oxford Textbook of Palliative Nursing*. 4th ed. New York, NY: Oxford University Press Inc., 2015:175–90.
5. Ang SK, Shoemaker LK, Davis MP. Nausea and vomiting in advanced cancer *Am J Hospice Palliat Med*. 2010; 27(3): 219–25.
6. Rhodes VA, McDaniel RW. Nausea, vomiting, retching: complex problems in palliative care. *CA Cancer J Clinicians*. 2001; 51(4): 232–48.
7. Wood JM, Chapman K, Eilers J. Tools for assessing nausea, vomiting, retching. *Cancer Nurs*. 2011; 34(1): E14–E24.

8. Shoemaker LK, Bassam E, Induru R, Walsh TD. Symptom management: an important part of cancer care. *Cleveland Clinic J Med.* 2011; 78(1): 25–34.

9. Benze G, Alt-Epping B, Geyer A, Nauck F. Treatment of nausea and vomiting with prokinetics and neuroleptics in palliative care patients (English version). *Der Schmerz.* 2012; 26: 500–14.

10. Kehl KA, Kowalkowski JA. A systematic review of the prevalence of signs of impending death and symptoms in the last 2 weeks of life. *Am J Hosp Palliat Med.* 2012; 30(6): 601–16.

11. Glare P, Miller J, Nikolova T, Tickoo R. Treating nausea and vomiting in palliative care: A review. *Clin Interventions Aging.* 2011; 6: 243–59.

12. Parker LA, Rock EM, Limebeer CL. Regulation of nausea and vomiting by cannabinoids. *Br J Pharmacol.* 2011; 163: 1411–22.

13. Janelsins MC, Tejani M, Kamen C, et al. Current pharmacotherapy for chemotherapy-induced nausea and vomiting in cancer patients. *Exp Op Pharmacother.* 2013; 14(6): 757–66.

14. Longstreth GF. Approach to adult nausea and vomiting. Up-to-Date®. 2014. Available at http://www.uptodate.com/home. Accessed March 26, 2014.

15. Howard HS, Smith JM, Smith AR. Pathophysiology of nausea/vomiting in palliative medicine. *Ann Palliat Med.* 2012. Accessed July 23, 2014, at http://www.amepc.org/apm/article/view/995/1260.

16. Roscoe JA, Morrow GR, Hickok JT, et al. Biobehavorial factors in chemotherapy induced nausea and vomiting. *J Natl Comp Cancer Netw.* 2004; 2(5): 501–8.

17. National Comprehensive Cancer Network. Antiemesis Guidelines, 2014. Available at http://www.nccn.org/professionals/physician_gls/pdf/antiemesis.pdf Accessed June 1, 2014.

18. Molassiotis A, Farrell C, Bourne K, et al. An exploratory study to clarify the cluster of symptoms predictive of chemotherapy related nausea using random forest remodeling. *J Pain Symptom Manage.* 2012; 44(5): 692–703.

19. Akatas A. Cancer symptom clusters: current concepts and controversies. *Curr Op Support Palliat Care.* 2013; 7(1): 38–44.

20. Cherwin, CH. Gastrointestinal symptom representation in cancer symptoms cluster: a review of the literature. *Oncol Nurs Forum.* 2012; 39(2): 157–65.

21. Bouras EP, Roque V, Aranda-Michel J. Gastroparesis: from concept to management. *Nutr Clin Practice.* 2013; 28(4): 437–47.

22. Laugsand EA, Kaas S, Klepstad. Management of opioid induced nausea and vomiting in cancer patients: systematic review and evidence-based recommendations. *Palliat Med.* 2011; 25(5): 442–53.

23. Bookbinder M, McHugh ME. Symptom management in palliative care and end of life. *Nurs Clin North Am.* 2010; 45(3): 271–327.

24. Saxby C, Acroyd R, Callin S, Mayland C. How should we measure emesis in palliative care? *Palliat Med.* 2007; 21: 369–83.

25. Oncology Nursing Society. Putting Evidence into Practice. Chemotherapy-induced nausea and vomiting. 2011-14. Available at https://www.ons.org/practice-resources/pep/chemotherapy-induced-nausea-and-vomiting. Accessed July 23, 2014.

26. Holmer Patterson P, Wengstrom Y. Acupuncture prior to surgery to minimize postoperative nausea and vomiting: a systematic review. *J Clin Nurs.* 2012; 21(13-14): 1799–805.

27. Lee EJ, Frazier SK. The efficacy of acupressure for symptom management: a systematic review. *J Pain Symptom Manage.* 2011; 42(4): 589–603.

28. Molassiotis A, Russell WH, Breckons M, et al. The effectiveness, and cost effectiveness of acupressure for the control and management of chemotherapy related acute and delayed nausea: Assessment of nausea in chemotherapy research (ANCHoR), a randomized controlled trial. *Health Technology Assessment.* 2013; 17(26): 1–114.

29. Lee J, Oh, H. Ginger as an antiemetic modality for chemotherapy-induced nausea and vomiting: a systematic review and meta-analysis. *Oncol Nurs Forum.* 2013: 40(2): 163–70.

30. Dev R, Dalal S, Bruera E. Is there a role for parenteral nutrition or hydration at end of life? *Curr Op Support Palliat Care.* 2012; 6(3): 365–70.

31. Hospice and Palliative Nursing Association. *HPNA Position Statement: Artificial Hydration and Nutrition in Advanced Illness.* 2011. Available at https://www.hpna.org/DisplayPage.aspx?Title=Position Statements. Accessed July 19, 2014.

32. Davis MP, Hallerberg G. A systematic review of the treatment of nausea and/or vomiting in cancer unrelated to chemotherapy or radiation. *J Pain Symptom Manage.* 2010; 39(4): 756–67.

33. Jordan K, Schmoll HJ, Aapro MS. Comparative activity of antiemetic drugs. *Crit Rev Hematol Oncol.* 2007; 61: 162–75.

34. Pommer E. Olanzapine: Palliative medicine update. *Am J Hospice Palliat Med.* 2012; 30(1): 75–82.

35. Marder S, Stroup TS. Pharmacotherapy for schizophrenia: side effect management. Up-to-Date®. 2013. Available at www.uptodate.com. Accessed July 23, 2014.

36. Benze G, Geyer A, Alt-Epping B, Nauck F. Treatment of nausea and vomiting with 5HT3 receptor antagonists, steroids, antihistamines, anticholinergics, somatostatin analogs, benzodiazepines and cannabinoids in palliative care patients [English version]. *Der Schmerz.* 2012: 26: 481–99.

37. Howard P, Twycross R, Schuster J, et al. Cannabinoids. *J Pain Symptom Manage.* 2013; 46(1): 142–9.

38. Nicholson SE, Denysenko L, Mulcar L, et al. Cannabinoid hyperemesis syndrome: a case series and review of previous reports. *Psychosomatics.* 2012; 53: 212–9.

39. Frago R, Ramirez E, Millan M, Kreisler E, et al. Current management of acute malignant large bowel obstruction: a systematic review. *Am J Surg.* 2014; 207(1): 127–38.

40. Ripamonti C, Mercandante S. Pathophysiology and management of malignant bowel obstructions. In: Hanks G, Cherny NI, Christakis NA, Kassa S, Portemoy R, eds. *Textbook of Palliative Medicine.* 4th ed. New York, NY: Oxford University Press; 2010:850–63.

41. Mercandante S, Porzio G. Octreotide for malignant bowel obstruction: twenty years after. *Crit Rev Oncol Hematol.* 2012; 83(3): 388–92.

42. Pommer E. Role of haloperidol in palliative medicine: an update. *Am J Hospice Palliat Med.* 2012; 29(4): 295–301.

Psychological/ Psychiatric Symptoms

CHAPTER 31

Anxiety

Maria Gatto, Patricia Thomas, and Ann Berger

Key Points

- Anxiety is a universal subjective and objective life experience that crosses all eight palliative care domains of the National Consensus Project (NCP) *Clinical Practice Guidelines*.

- Anxiety and chronic diseases are interchangeable in their causal relationship; chronic diseases can exacerbate symptoms of anxiety, and anxiety disorders can lead to chronic diseases.

- Assessment and treatment of anxiety by the advanced practice registered nurse (APRN) is essential since it affects all four whole-person dimensions of suffering: physical, psychological, social, and spiritual.

Introduction

Anxiety, an aspect of our history that spans the evolutionary process, is inherent in all the domains of the National Consensus Project for Quality Palliative Care's *Clinical Practice Guidelines*. Anxiety is present in the everyday lives of humans, whether patient or clinician. Anxiety is unique and specifically identified within NCP Domain 3 under Psychological and Psychiatric Aspects of Care: "The interdisciplinary team assesses and addresses psychological and psychiatric aspects of care based on the best available evidence to maximize patient and family coping and quality of life".[1] Due to the physical, affective, behavioral, and cognitive responses that anxiety may escalate, it can be clinically implicated in NCP Domain 1, Physical Aspects of Care; NCP Domain 2, Physical Aspects of Care; NCP Domain 4, Social Aspects of Care; and NCP Domain 7, Care of the Patient at the End of Life.

Anxiety is a multidimensional subjective and objective experience with manifestations of physical, affective, behavioral, and cognitive responses.[2] As such, it can be considered both positive and negative. The experience is the physiological reaction that occurs in response to a perceived harmful attack or threat to survival. These include feelings of worry, apprehension, tension, and nervousness that are unpleasant and distressful, but they are a common response for patients and family members when faced with a serious diagnosis.

Anxiety is a natural and expected part of the coping process that helps us adapt to everyday concerns. However, extreme distressful anxiety can impair daily function, causing disability and disruptions in quality of life for patients, family, and caregivers.[3] Specific differentiation between anxiety as a normal response and a specific diagnostic criterion that requires professional intervention and treatment is outlined according to the fifth edition of *The Diagnostic and Statistical Manual of Mental Disorders* (DSM-V-TR).[4] The experience of apparent uncontrollable physical, affective, behavioral, and cognitive symptoms having no specific stimulus warrants consideration of a pathological disorder. Anxiety disorders are categorized according to criteria and range in complexity and severity from panic attacks, acute stress disorder, generalized anxiety disorder, social anxiety disorders, phobias, obsessive–compulsive disorder, post-traumatic stress disorder, anxiety secondary to a medical condition, and substance-induced anxiety disorders.[4]

Common situations, medical conditions, medications, and substances are associated with and can cause nonspecific anxiety symptoms.[5,6] Existential and psychosocial concerns increase anxiety when a person is faced with mortality, long-term or permanent disability, loss of control, family and financial crisis, loss of meaning, hope, and purpose, and religious or spiritual crisis. There is also considerable overlap and confusion among the anxiety, depression, and delirium that commonly arise as part of an illness trajectory and that can either lead, progress to, or continue in a vicious downward cycle when not recognized and treated appropriately (Table 31.1).

Despite the importance of mental health and the increasing prevalence of mental health disorders, U.S. healthcare delivery systems are complex and fragmented, and patients and families are offered little guidance in navigating these systems to manage medical conditions effectively. The result is that anxiety is underestimated, untreated or undertreated, and unrecognized by healthcare professionals. Furthermore, intensified financial stress and social economic burden contribute to anxiety. Given this, anxiety is a contributory factor for caregiver burden, chronic distress, mortality, and comorbidity of the family and caregivers.[7,8] Barriers to appropriate professional intervention are also created by the lack of an integrated palliative care curriculum, inadequate professional resources, personal experiences, limited assessment skills and clinical knowledge, and personal biases associated with the stigma and stereotypes related to diagnosis. This often leads to acceptance of not treating anxiety or its physical, emotional, and psychosocial manifestations.

This chapter presents palliative care from the APRN's perspective, focusing on APRN competencies as an effective team

Table 31.1 Associated Causes and Mimics of Anxiety

Acute emotional disruption	Interpersonal stresses
Anger	Legitimate worries and concerns
Anxiety disorders	Loss of control
Coping style (poor pattern)	Pain
Delirium	Physical symptoms
Fear	Side effects of medications
Financial concerns	Spiritual and existential crisis
Grief and bereavement	Withdrawal states

From references 2, 5, 7.

member or leader for patient-family centered care. Assessment and management of anxiety are based on national quality clinical practice guidelines, evidence-based research, and recommendations by national professional organizations.

Definitions and the Distress Continuum

Any serious illness, such as cancer, is a life-altering experience. In the 1970s, Weissman and Worden identified the first 100 days after the diagnosis of cancer as an "existential plight" in which patients suddenly confront their mortality. This is an extremely fragile period filled with fear and anxiety. Information, communication, and overall psychosocial support are priority needs for the patient's mental well-being.

How anxiety is defined, when an individual is diagnosed with a serious illness, ranges from normal adjustment issues to syndromes that meet the diagnostic criteria for mental disorders. It occurs on a continuum of increasing levels and severity of psychosocial distress, ranging from normal adjustment to adjustment disorders, and subthreshold mental disorders to diagnosable mental disorders (Fig. 31.1).[9,10,11] As healthcare professionals, APRNs must appreciate the variety of related concepts and distinctions of normal adjustment issues from mental disorders along the distress continuum to anticipate potential or actual needs, treatments, and interventions (Table 31.2).

Normal adjustment or psychosocial adaptation is not defined as a single event or in a specific moment in time. Adjustment and adaptation are constant and represent an ongoing process. Coping behaviors are continuous as the individual learns to manage life and relationships that incorporate and integrate a serious illness into daily activities. As personal, professional, and family relationships change, the individual is confronted with solving and

mastering cancer-related emotions, issues, and situations.[12–14] Psychosocial distress has been defined as:

> an unpleasant experience of an emotional, psychological, social, or spiritual nature that interferes with the ability to cope with cancer treatment. It extends along a continuum, from common normal feelings of vulnerability, sadness, and fears, to problems that are disabling, such as depression, anxiety, panic, and feeling isolated or in a spiritual crisis.[9–14]

Adjustment disorders are a diagnostic category in DSM-V-TR. For some, the psychosocial stressors associated with a cancer diagnosis are identifiable with a reactive psychopathology less severe than diagnosable mental disorders that impair social or occupational behavior significantly. The DSM-V-TR anxiety disorders are a group of mental disorders whose common symptoms include excessive, unwarranted, often illogical anxiety, worry, fear, apprehension, and/or dread.[4]

Prevalence and Incidence: Anxiety and Chronic Disease Connection

There is a close relationship between the prevalence of anxiety and the incidence of mental illnesses and chronic diseases. According to the Centers for Disease Control and Prevention (CDC), the National Center for Chronic Disease Prevention and Health Promotion, Division of Population Health, recognized that chronic diseases can exacerbate symptoms of depression, and depressive disorders can lead to chronic diseases.[15] Anxiety, when unrecognized, unassessed, and undertreated, with other comorbid conditions potentiates adjustment disorders. The CDC report *Mental Illness Surveillance Among Adults in the United States*, which supplements the CDC's *Morbidity and Mortality Weekly Report* (MMWR), compiled the first national data to measure the prevalence and effect of anxiety and other mental health conditions for adults in the United States. It underscored the correlation between mental illness and chronic illness.[16] Executive highlights pertaining to chronic disease and anxiety/mental illness are as follows:

◆ 25% of all U.S. adults have a mental illness and nearly 50% of U.S. adults will develop at least one mental illness during their lifetime.

◆ Mental illness is associated with increased occurrence of chronic diseases, such as cardiovascular disease, diabetes, obesity, asthma, epilepsy, and cancer.

◆ Treatment of mental illnesses associated with chronic illness reduces the effects of both and supports better outcomes.

◆ Chronic diseases can coexist in people who have suffered from depression[8] (Table 31.3).

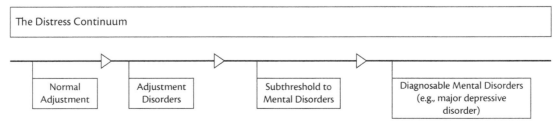

Figure 31.1 The distress continuum

Table 31.2 Summary of Psychosocial Distress Definitions

Normal adjustment	Ongoing life processes and coping responses associated with living with cancer to:
	◆ Manage emotional distress
	◆ Solve specific cancer-related problems
	◆ Gain mastery or control over cancer-related life events
Psychosocial distress	Extends along a continuum ranging from:
	◆ Common normal feelings of vulnerability, sadness, and fears to problems that are disabling (i.e., depression, anxiety, panic)
	◆ Feeling isolated
	◆ Spiritual crisis
	Unpleasant experience of:
	◆ Emotional, psychological, social, or spiritual nature that interferes with the ability to cope with cancer treatment
Adjustment disorders	A diagnostic category of the fifth revised edition of the American Psychiatric Association's *Diagnostic and Statistical Manual of Mental Disorders* (DSM-V-TR):
	◆ Reactions to an identifiable psychosocial stressor with a degree of psychopathology
	◆ Less severe than diagnosable mental disorders yet in excess of what would be expected
	◆ Result in significant impairment in social or occupational functioning (i.e., major depressive disorder, generalized anxiety disorder)
Anxiety disorders	Group of mental disorders whose common symptoms include excessive, unwarranted, often illogical anxiety, worry, fear, apprehension, and/or dread.
	The DSM-V-TR examples include generalized anxiety disorder, panic disorder, agoraphobia, social anxiety disorder, specific phobia, obsessive-compulsive disorder, and post-traumatic stress disorder.

From reference 11.

Anxiety and the Other Side of the Distress Continuum: Adjustment, Integration, and Life Transformation

Anxiety, whether positive or negative, occurs throughout life. It is a continual process with many revolving cycles, not a linear progression. When a patient is diagnosed with a serious illness, anxiety is often identified and separated into categories based on different life experiences. Palliative care practice differs because it embraces and incorporates the integrative nature and multidimensional holistic human needs approach to care, which challenges the assumption that anxiety and disease are separate processes. Anxiety needs to be viewed as a multidimensional experience within an integrated whole.

Cancer and serious illness are experienced within a continuum ranging from positive to negative in terms of adjustment. Positive

adjustment is the patient's psychosocial adaptation process or increased ability to cope. Negative adjustment is the patient's inability to cope or the presence of anxiety and mental disorders that may require professional treatment.[17,18]

Life and serious illness need to be understood as a whole, not as separate entities. The role of the APRN is to understand and address anxiety from an interdisciplinary team perspective and to support adjustment from a medical and holistic perspective.

Integration of Chronic Illness

Palliative care professionals encourage patients and families to focus on living rather than on their illness. The patient's life and illness are not separate but coexist in a way that can be balanced, meaningful, and purposeful, integrating the illness into a whole that also includes the patient's many roles, responsibilities, personal identity, and life experiences.[19] Integration is not just

Table 31.3 Anxiety and Chronic Disease Prevalence

Medical Conditions	Examples
Cardiovascular	Angina, congestive heart failure, hypovolemia, mitral valve prolapse, myocardial infarction, paroxysmal atrial tachycardia
Endocrine	Carcinoid syndrome, Cushing's disease, hyperglycemia, hypoglycemia, hyperthyroidism, hypothyroidism, pheochromocytoma
Immune	AIDS
Metabolic	Anemia, hypercalcemia, hyperkalemia, hypoglycemia, hyponatremia, hyperthermia
Respiratory	Asthma, chronic obstructive pulmonary disease, hypoxia, pneumonia, pulmonary disease, pulmonary edema, pulmonary embolus
Neurological	Akathisia, encephalopathy, brain lesion, seizure disorders, post-concussion syndrome, vertigo, cerebral vascular accident, dementia
Neoplasms	Islet cell adenomas, pheochromocytoma
Cancer	Hormone-producing tumors, pheochromocytoma

From references 2, 5, 7.

Table 31.4 Summary of Adjustment Stages When Diagnosed with Cancer: Pre-Diagnosis and Diagnosis

Pre-Diagnosis	Diagnosis		
Diagnostic process	Phase 1 Initial response	Phase 2 Dysphoria	Phase 3 Adaptation (long term)
1) Anxiety experience: Normal levels of anxiety and concern Crisis: Psychological and existential	1) Anxiety experience: Disbelief Denial Shock High level of distress, emotions Inability to remember, understand	1) Anxiety experience: Distress ranges: Illness-death Depression, anxiety, insomnia, anorexia Poor concentration Inability to function in daily roles Hope: increased with understanding and awareness of treatment	1) Anxiety experience: Coping strategies: Problem-focused Emotion-focused Meaning-focused
2) Normal adjustment & support: Support systems, personal, religious, spiritual	2) Normal adjustment & support: Compassionate communication skills to deliver "bad news,"	2) Normal adjustment & support: Education and information	2) Normal adjustment & support: Personalized coping styles and strategies
3) Adjustment period: 1 week	3) Adjustment period: Variable, 1–2 weeks	3) Adjustment period: Variable, 1–2 weeks	3) Adjustment period: Variable, 1–2 weeks

From reference 21.

a matter of incorporating disease management into one's daily activities but rather integrating the disease experience physically, mentally, emotionally, and spiritually.[18]

The clinical courses of cancer are prediagnosis, diagnosis, treatment, post-treatment, remission, reoccurrence/palliative care, and survivorship.[18] Within each clinical course there is an anxiety experience, normal adjustment and support, and an adjustment period.[20] Anxiety and adjustment are natural parts of the illness experience. The clinical courses should not be considered as separate entities but rather as an ongoing experience of anxiety, challenges, and adjustment (Tables 31.4, 31.5, and 3.16).

Anxiety adjustment goes beyond the natural state of adaptation, coping, and integration. Adjustment outcomes have been identified in different categories, such as healing, psychosocial and spiritual pain in palliative care, posttraumatic growth, stress-related growth, benefit-finding resilience, subjective well-being, and self-actualization.[21, 22,23]

Life-Transforming Change

Life-transforming change can result from the illness experience. Some patients experience a total paradigm shift, where unanticipated discovery of personal abilities and untapped resources helps the patient overcome the challenges of cancer and life challenges outside of cancer. With this shift, the patient's life is taken to a previously unknown level where he or she experiences a more fulfilling, purposeful, and meaningful life, with greater depth psychosocially and spiritually (Fig. 31.2).

Table 31.5 Summary of Adjustment Stages When Diagnosed with Cancer: Treatment, Post-treatment, Remission

Treatment	Post-treatment	Remission
1) Anxiety experience: Treatment fears and focuses: Side effects Disruptions in daily life Effectiveness Survival	1) Anxiety experience: Ranges: positive anticipation, ambivalence, vulnerability Fear: lack of physician and medical care	1) Anxiety experience: Normal anxiety regarding recurrence
2) Normal adjustment & support: Understanding Short-term discomforts outweigh long-term gains	2) Normal adjustment & support: Balance of positive expectations, reality of fears, apprehensions	2) Normal adjustment & support: Coping strategies Expression of emotions (i.e., honesty, nonjudgmental acceptance)
3) Adjustment period: Variable	3) Adjustment period: Variable	3) Adjustment period: Variable

Table 31.6 Summary of Adjustment Stages When Diagnosed with Cancer: Palliative Care & Survivorship

Palliative Care	Survivorship
1) Anxiety experience	1) Anxiety experience
Disbelief, denial, shock, crying, withdrawal, isolation, spiritual/religious anger	Greater appreciation, reprioritizing of life values, strengthening of spiritual or religious beliefs
Shift: palliative curing to healing	
2) Normal adjustment & support:	2) Normal adjustment & support:
Palliative care: hope through what is meaningful	National organizations (i.e., programs, tools, resources)
	Physical, emotional well-being support
3) Adjustment period: Weeks	3) Adjustment period: Gradual over many years

From reference 21.

Some patients describe a reduction in negative experiences; others identify an increase in positive experiences. These changes can occur in the areas of self-care, relationships, spirituality, being true to oneself, personal strength, and priorities or purpose. The "domains" of this change are pre-cancer, cancer, adaptive beliefs and attributes, pragmatic actualization, and transformation. Each domain has its own categories and process themes.[19]

Pre-cancer's category is trauma and healing. The process theme focuses on the pre-cancer state and diagnosis as a challenging event.

The domain of cancer has three subcategories: debilitation, challenges to normal life, and coping. The debilitation subcategory focuses on the process themes of cancer symptoms and treatment side effects. The challenges to normal life subcategory focuses on the process themes of uncertainty, heightened awareness, and loss. The major view expressed by patients in this subcategory is, *it's not just about the cancer.* Support comes in the form of education and lowering distress.

The adaptive beliefs and attributes domain has two subcategories: personal life and hope. Personal life focuses on the process themes of maintaining a personal life, tolerance, and the expectation that life could be improved, mastery of life skills, and improved situational challenges. The hope category's process themes focus on motivation, protection, surrounding oneself with people who provide support, and offer grounding in personal truth and what is found as meaningful.

The domain of pragmatic actualization entails turning hope into reality. It has two subcategories: exploring and resources. Exploring focuses on the process themes of proactive learning,

research, personal decisions and choices, and active experimentation. The resources subcategory focuses on gathering and giving in a wide range of meaningful relationships, unexpected resources, expanded spirituality, and conservation of resources in times of greater need.

The domain of transformation focuses on a recurrent process theme, *it's not just about the cancer,* in terms of applying newly discovered personal resources and heightened skills to non-cancer issues. Applying these new-found personal resources and abilities ultimately leads to a greater sense of gratitude, life appreciation, and empathy and a higher interest in life-fulfilling pursuits.[19]

Screening and Assessment

The sequential screening, evaluation, and referral process is undertaken when anxiety or psychosocial issues arise. A variety of screening tools are available based on the patient's presentation. Screening may include a brief, self-report questionnaire method. The patient's score establishes the level and severity of distress to guide the next steps. If the distress is high, a referral for an in-depth psychosocial assessment by an appropriate mental health professional is made.[24]

Screening and assessment are not just patient-focused but are also family-focused based on the standards of the National Consensus Project for Quality Palliative Care *Clinical Practice Guidelines.*[25] Family members are the most common caregivers and their needs often go unaddressed. Many are easily overwhelmed physically, mentally, socially, and financially. Caregiver stress and burden can lead to increased health risks in terms of

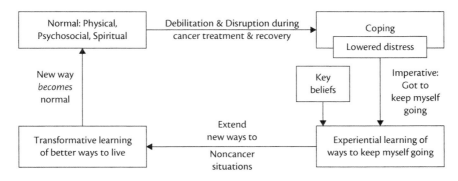

Figure 31.2 Cancer-related life transformation change process

heart disease, hypertension, immune impairment, and cognitive functioning that may meet DSM-V criteria for a psychiatric condition.[26] When assessing caregivers, the APRN should identify the specific problems, needs, strengths, and resources they have for themselves and those that affect the patient's care.[27]

Communication with patients and family members and their participation as partners in care are key. By partnering with them, the APRN can identify their needs and set out the next steps. The patient and family are part of the process, since assessment is a combination of self-report and evaluation by members of the professional team. This approach to assessing caregivers' needs and strengths can improve the overall health and quality of life for both the patient and caregivers.[28] The five major components of the caregiver experience that provide insight into caregiver stress are caregiver context, primary stressors, secondary stressors, resources, and outcomes.[29]

Caregiver context addresses sociodemographic information, history of illness, and caregiving and living arrangements. Primary stressors from the patient experience are symptoms, impairments, activities of daily living, behavioral and cognitive issues, and the caregiver's subjective burden. Secondary stressors are tension and conflicts of employment, relationships, and maintaining roles and responsibility. Resources are social, financial, emotional, and gains from experience. Outcomes are either positive or negative health outcomes related to the caregiver.[8]

The National Caregiver Alliance sponsors the National Center on Caregiving, which provides support and guidance in the development of policy, resources, and programs. It serves as a central source on caregiving and long-term care issues.[30]

The expression of, assessment for, and interventions for anxiety are placed in the cultural and spiritual domains of the National Consensus Project *Clinical Practice Guidelines*. Domain 5 addresses spiritual, religious, and existential aspects of palliative care. Domain 6 addresses cultural aspects of care.[1] Inappropriate or incomplete awareness of cultural, religious, and spiritual beliefs or needs can lead to inappropriate and unacceptable plans of care, resulting in unnecessary and undue anxiety and distress.

To complete the comprehensive anxiety assessment processes and psychosocial spiritual screening and assessments, a physical examination is appropriate; it could reveal anxiety-associated medical conditions, emergent pathophysiology, and medications and substances whose side effects mimic anxiety.

Treatment

The palliative care approach to treatment, occurs across a continuum with many different and simultaneous dependent, independent, and collaborative team approaches and interventions.

Pharmacologic Management

Common medications and substances that can cause nonspecific anxiety symptoms are listed in Table 31.7. Pharmacologic agents used to manage anxiety are listed in Table 31.8.

Most antidepressants are effective for treating anxiety, but full benefit may take several weeks, and lower doses are tolerated best. Many clinicians treating anxiety disorders use selective serotonin reuptake inhibitors (SSRIs) as their first choice due to these agents' reliability and effectiveness for panic, generalized anxiety disorders, post-traumatic stress disorder, and obsessive-compulsive

disorder. Common side effects are managed with low dose titration, and SSRIs have no adjuvant therapeutic effect on pain unlike serotonin-norepinephrine reuptake inhibitors.[5] Tricyclic antidepressants are effective and inexpensive, and serve as an adjuvant for neuropathic pain. Tricyclics can promote sleep and appetite but have a high side-effect burden.

Benzodiazepines are commonly used for the relief of acute anxiety. They have a rapid onset and can reduce nausea, but they are toxic if overdosed, and can suppress respirations, especially in patients with lung disease, and can cause cognitive impairment.[31] There are risks for abuse and addiction with benzodiazepines, but they are effective in the long term. Use of long-acting agents can prevent the loss of efficacy that can occur with shorter-acting agents.

Antipsychotics are reliable, but long-term use can produce the side effect of movement disorders. This risk makes them a second-line treatment. They are valuable when a rapid anxiolytic effect is needed and if patients cannot tolerate benzodiazepines or have respiratory compromise.[32]

The geriatric population has special considerations, and medication adjustments are required. Treatment of anxiety often reflects the balance between goals and the length of time remaining in life. This is especially true in geriatric palliative care evaluation and treatment. For patients with less than a few months to live who are minimally ambulatory, the APRN can prescribe benzodiazepines for rapid relief of symptoms or brief treatment. They are considered a second-line drug based on their longer half-life, which causes adverse drug effects. Benzodiazepines overall have a paradoxical effect that may actually cause more anxiety, especially in the elderly, and are not recommended because they can increase confusion. Typically, tricyclic antidepressants and beta-adrenergic agents are not well tolerated. The most common side effects in the elderly are ataxia, cognitive impairment, and excessive sleepiness. Opioids are indicated for treatment of anxiety secondary to

Table 31.7 Anxiety-Causing Medications and Substances

Alcohol and nicotine withdrawal	Bronchodilators and sympathomimetics
Analgesics	Caffeine (stimulants)
Anticholinergic	Cannabis
Anticonvulsants	Cocaine
Antidepressants	Corticosteroids and anabolic steroids
Antiemetics	Digitalis toxicity
Antihistamines and decongestants	Epinephrine
Antihypertensives	Hallucinogens
Antiparkinsonian drugs	Sedatives (hypnotic withdrawal and paradoxical reaction)
Antipsychotics	
Anesthetics and analgesics	
Benzodiazepines (and their withdrawal)	

From references 2, 5, 7.

Table 31.8 Common Pharmacologic Treatment Options of Anxiety

Generic Name	Approximate daily dose/ranges (mg)	Comment
Benzodiazepines		
Alprazolam	0.25–2 tid–qid	Short-acting
Clonazepam	0.5–2 bid–qid	Long-acting
Diazepam	5–10 bid–qid	Long-acting; rapid onset with single PO dosage
Lorazepam	0.5–2 tid–qid	Short-acting; multiple routes, PO, SL, IV, IM, no metabolites
Azapirones		
Buspirone	5–20 tid	Extended time to peak effect similar to antidepressants
Antidepressants		
Serotonin Reuptake Inhibitors		
Citalopram	20–40 daily	New warning from U.S. Food & Drug Administration about doses above 40 mg
Fluoxetine	10–80 daily	Longest half-life among serotonin reuptake inhibitors
Paroxetine	10–60 daily	
Sertraline	50–200 daily	
Tricyclics		
Desipramine	12.5–150 daily	Least sedating tricyclic antidepressant
Imipramine	12.5–150 daily	
Other Antidepressants		
Duloxetine	40–60 daily	
Venlafaxine	75–375 daily	
Mirtazapine	15–60 daily	Promotes sleep and appetite at low doses; oral disintegrating tablets available
Antipsychotics		
Olanzapine	5–15 daily[a]	Oral disintegrating tablets available
Quetiapine	25–200 daily[a]	Preferred for patients with Parkinson's disease
Risperidone	1–3 daily[a]	
Haloperidol	0.5–5 q2–12h	Inexpensive and multiple routes of administration (IV, PO, and IM)
Antihistamines		
Hydroxyzine	25–50 q4–6h	Risk of anticholinergic side effects and delirium

[a] In divided doses

From reference 5.

dyspnea in terminally ill patients.[33] Antidepressant therapies are often indicated, and cholinesterase inhibitors may be beneficial.

Nonpharmacologic Treatment

Nonpharmacologic therapies used for anxiety are outlined in Table 31.9.

Palliative care includes holistic integrative therapies as well as conventional therapies. Holism and palliative care philosophy are inseparable since they both focus on the total person, with the belief that the mind, body, and spirit are inseparable and interdependent and that health, illness, and dying are manifestations of the life processes of the whole person.[33–38] In both holistic and palliative care, the partnership among the patient, family, and provider generates a sense of empowerment and enables healing (if not necessarily a cure) and transcendence.

There are many integrative holistic therapies that can be used to decrease anxiety. They can improve the overall quality of life for patients and families. Maximum benefits with minimal risk can be achieved when complementary/alternative medicine and therapies are integrated with conventional treatments. This can be accomplished through collaborative interdisciplinary team processes as a component of the overall plan of care (Table 31.10).

Table 31.9 Nonpharmacologic Anxiety Treatment

Mind-Body Therapy	Posture & Mobility	Touch & Body Work Energetic Therapies	Sense Therapy
Biofeedback	Movement therapy	Massage, Reflexology	Aromatherapy
Psychotherapy	Tai Chi	Acupressure, Healing Touch, Reiki, Therapeutic Touch	Music therapy
Guided Imagery	Yoga	Polarity Therapy	Kinesthetics
Hypnosis			
Meditation			
Cognitive Therapy			
Behavioral Therapy			
Reminiscence/Life Review, Centering			
Creating Intention			
Journaling			

From references 34, 35, 36, 37.

Table 31.10 Integrative Holistic Treatment of Anxiety

Nutritional Therapy	Eastern Therapies	Integrative Holistic Providers
Herbology/Herbal Medicine	Traditional Chinese Medicine	Ayurveda Medicine
Nutritional Supplements	Acupuncture	Naturopathic Medicine
	AMMA Therapy	Homeopathic Medicine
	Shiatsu	Integrative Holistic Medicine
	Jin Shin Jyutsu	

From references 34–37.

Conclusion

Palliative care is a comprehensive, evidence-based specialty, provided by a supportive interdisciplinary team, that addresses patient- and family-centered needs. Whether the illness is life-threatening, chronic, progressive, advanced, or terminal, the identification and the management of anxiety are central to effective treatment. Anxiety is a common response in patients and family members and is manifested in various physical, affective, behavioral, and cognitive responses. Palliative care incorporates anxiety in professional practice standards with the goal of anticipating, identifying, assessing, and addressing it via core and interdisciplinary team approaches.

Case Study

Mr. S was a married 61-year-old male Russian immigrant who was self-employed in the construction industry. He had no children and enjoyed traveling with his wife. He was a practicing Catholic but did not have an identified community church. He engaged in mind–body practices and coped with hardship using rituals and clear next steps. The palliative care team followed Mr. S for 2 years from his diagnosis of cancer to his death. At diagnosis, he underwent a thoracotomy, with subsequent pain and anxiety resulting from his new diagnosis of cancer. After the palliative APRN did a thorough palliative care evaluation, his anxiety was initially treated with lorazepam 0.5 mg q6h PRN and acupuncture for pain and anxiety. He also engaged in spiritual ministry.

Several months after diagnosis, Mr. S developed metastatic mesothelioma and was placed on an experimental protocol. His chest pain and dyspnea had increased significantly, and he was extremely anxious when hospitalized for hypercapnic respiratory failure. He was significantly fatigued due to lack of sleep. He was intubated and then sent home on BiPAP, which he remained on for the rest of his life. Duloxetine was started and lorazepam was discontinued by the palliative APRN. Hypnosis was started for the anxiety and acupuncture was continued for pain, anxiety, and fatigue. Several months later, Mr. S discontinued chemotherapy and continued aggressive palliative care.

Two months before his death, Mr. S presented to the ED with severe respiratory distress and was admitted to the ICU with hypercapnia. At this time, the settings on his BiPAP were changed. The palliative APRN visited Mr. S in the ICU to assess how he was doing. He said, "Physically, I am weak because I am dying. But emotionally and spiritually I am great." When the nurse asked what happened, the patient said, "Dying people should not be in an ICU, but I have been transformed." That day he was clearly not anxious and was able to speak to his wife, telling her how much he loved her. He received acupuncture and spiritual ministry. His wife received counseling for her anxiety until his death.

One month before his death, Mr. S was seen in the pain and palliative care outpatient clinic. He was very weak and fatigued and could not sleep. When he stated he was scared to use his BiPAP, the palliative APRN explored this with him. When asked if he was scared he would die at night, he said yes. At this time, the team provided Mr. S with information about the dying process, after which he felt comforted, less frightened, and less anxious. The APRN knew he liked rituals so she framed the conversation about BiPAP as a ritual. Mr. S devised a nightly ritual in which his wife would help him put the machine on his face and then kiss him goodnight.

Mr. S and his wife found this meaningful and the ritual continued until his death. Mr. S died at home with his wife at his side. Mrs. S was followed by the bereavement program.

The case study summarizes the APRN's integrated and collaborative role within the palliative care team. In her roles as clinician and educator, this palliative APRN employed expertise in clinical treatment interventions, communication, listening, and compassion to initiate and maintain a trusting relationship with this patient and family. After conducting a comprehensive assessment, the APRN developed a holistic and purposefully aligned treatment plan. As the patient's and family's needs changed, the treatment plan was adjusted. The continuity of care was coordinated over time in multiple care settings from diagnosis until death. The palliative APRN and her palliative care colleagues were successful in managing the patient's anxiety, pain, and respiratory distress, honoring the wishes of the patient and his wife for information and taking advantage of their past success with rituals. They created an opportunity for transformation at the end-of-life by directing care and treatment toward spiritual healing rather than disease cure. Palliative APRNs, as members of the interdisciplinary team, are prepared to deal with physical, psychological, social, and spiritual suffering using both pharmacologic and complementary approaches to the management of anxiety.

References

1. National Consensus Project. *Clinical Practice Guidelines for Quality Palliative Care*. 3rd ed. Pittsburgh, PA: National Consensus Project for Quality Palliative Care; 2013. Accessed July 20, 2014, from https://www.hpna.org/multimedia/NCP_Clinical_Practice_Guidelines_3rd_Edition.pdf; ISBN 1-934654-35-3.

2. Dahlin CM. Anxiety, depression and delirium. In: Matzo M, Sherman D. *Palliative Care Nursing: Quality Care to the End of Life*. 4th ed. New York, NY: Springer Publishing; 2015:509–39.

3. Thalén-Lindström A, Larsson G, Glimelius B, Johansson B. Anxiety and depression in oncology patients: A longitudinal study of a screening, assessment, and psychosocial support intervention. *Acta Oncol*. 2013; 52(1): 118–27. doi: 10.3109/0284186X.2012.707785.

4. American Psychiatric Association. *Diagnostic and Statistical Manual of Mental Disorders*. 5th ed. Arlington, VA: American Psychiatric Association; 2013. Accessed June 1, 2013, at dsm.psychiatryonline.org.

5. Shuster J. Anxiety. In: Berger A, Shuster J, Von Roenn J. *Palliative Care and Supportive Oncology*. 4th ed. Philadelphia, PA: Lippincott Williams & Wilkins; 2013:552–61.

6. Pasacreta JV, Minarik PA, Nield-Anderson L, Paice J. Anxiety and depression. In: Ferrell B, Coyle N, Paice J, eds. *Oxford Textbook of Palliative Nursing*. 4th ed. New York, NY: Oxford University Press; 2015:366–84.

7. Borneman T, Brown-Saltzman K. Meaning in illness. In: Ferrell B, Coyle N, Paice J, eds. *Oxford Textbook of Palliative Nursing*. 4th ed. New York, NY: Oxford University Press; 2015:554–63.

8. Witt-Sherman D, Cheon J. Family caregivers. In: Matzo M, Sherman D, eds. *Palliative Care Nursing: Quality Care to the End of Life*. 4th ed. New York, NY: Springer Publishing; 2015:147–63.

9. National Comprehensive Cancer Network. NCCN Clinical Practice Guidelines in Oncology (NCCN©). Distress management Ver 3.2015. http://www.nccn.org/professionals/physician_gls/pdf/distress.pdf. Accessed December 10, 2015.

10. Brennan J. Adjustment to cancer: Coping or personal transition? *Psychooncology*. 2001; 10(1): 1–18.

11. Adjustment to Cancer: Anxiety and Distress (PDQ®). Accessed July 16, 2014, at http://www.cancer.gov/cancertopics/pdq/supportivecare/adjustment/HealthProfessional/page2

12. Folkman S, Greer S. Promoting psychological well-being in the face of serious illness: when theory, research and practice inform each other. *Psychooncology*. 2000; 9(1): 11–9.

13. Nicholas DR, Veach TA. The psychosocial assessment of the adult cancer patient. *Prof Psychol*. 2000; 31(2): 206–15.

14. Fashoyin-Aje LA, Martinez KA, Dy SM. New patient-centered care standards from the commission on cancer: Opportunities and challenges. *J Support Oncol*. 2012; 10(3): 107–11.

15. Chapman DP, Perry GS, Strine TW. The vital link between chronic disease and depressive disorders. *Prev Chronic Dis*. 2005; 2(1): A14. Epub December 15, 2004.

16. Centers for Disease Control and Prevention Morbidity and Mortality Weekly Report (MMWR): Mental Illness Surveillance Among Adults in the United States. Available at http://www.cdc.gov/mmwr/preview/mmwrhtml/su6003a1.htm?s_cid=su6003a1.

17. Centers for Disease Control and Prevention. Mental Health and Chronic Disease Expert Workgroup. Accessed July 14, 2014, at http://www.cdc.gov/mentalhealth/about_us/expert-wg.htm.

18. Whittem R, Dixon J. Chronic illness: the process of integration. *J Clin Nurs*. 2008; 17: 177–87. doi: 10.1111/j.1365-2702.2007.0224

19. Skeath P, Norris S, Katheria V, et al. The nature of life-transforming change among cancer survivors. *Qual Health Res*. 2013; 23(9): 1155–67.

20. Holland JC, Gooen-Piels J. Principles of psycho-oncology. In: Holland JC, Frei E, eds. *Cancer Medicine*. 5th ed. Hamilton, Ontario: B.C. Decker Inc.; 2000:943–58.

21. National Cancer Institute: PDQ® Adjustment to Cancer. Bethesda, MD: National Cancer Institute. Available at http://cancer.gov/cancertopics/pdq/supportivecare/adjustment/HealthProfessional/page5. Last modified May 29, 2014. Accessed July 28, 2014.

22. Tartaro J, Roberts J, Nosarti C, et al. Who benefits?: Distress, adjustment and benefit finding among breast cancer survivors. *J Psychosoc Oncol*. 2005; 23(2-3): 45–64.

23. Johnson J. An overview of psychosocial support services: Resources for healing. *Cancer Nurs*. 2000; 23(4): 310–3. doi:10.1097/00002820-200008000-00009

24. Zabora JR. Screening procedures for psychosocial distress. In: Holland JC, Breitbart W, Jacobsen PB, et al., eds. *Psycho-oncology*. New York, NY: Oxford University Press; 2010:653–61.

25. Nicholas DR, Veach TA. The psychosocial assessment of the adult cancer patient. *Prof Psychol*. 2000; 31(2): 206–15.

26. Family Care Giver Alliance. Caregiver assessment: Principles, guidelines, and strategies for change. Report from a national consensus development conference, 2006. Vol 1. San Francisco, CA: Family Caregiver Alliance. Available at http://www.caregiver.org/caregiver/jsp/content/pdfs/v1_consensus.pdf.

27. Vanderwerker LC, Laff RE, Kadan-Lotick NS, McColl S, Prigerson HG. Psychiatric disorders and mental health services use among caregivers of advanced cancer patients. *J Clin Oncol*. 2005; 23(28): 6899–907.

28. Fineberg L, Houser A. Assessing family caregiver needs: Policy and practice considerations. Washington DC: AARP Public Policy Institute. Available at http://www.caregiving.org/wp-content/uploads/2010/11/AARP-caregiver-fact-sheet.pdf.

29. Kutner KS, Kilbourn KM. Bereavement: Addressing challenges faced by advanced cancer patients and their caregivers, and their physicians. *Prim Care*. 2009; 36(4): 825–44.

30. National Alliance for Caregiving. Care for the family: A place to start. Available at http://www.caregiving.org/data/Emblem_CfC10_Final2.pdf.

31. Nutt DJ. Overview of diagnosis and drug treatments of anxiety disorders. *CNS Spectr*. 2005; 10(1): 46–59.

32. Ravindran LN, Stein MB. The pharmacologic treatment of anxiety disorders: A review of progress. *J Clin Psychiatry*. 2010; 71: 839–54.

33. Morrison RS, Meier D. *Geriatric Palliative Care*. New York, NY: Oxford University Press; 2014; 286–298.

34. Freeman L. *Mosby's Complementary and Alternative Medicine: A Research-Based Approach*. 3rd ed. St. Louis, MO: Mosby Elsevier; 2008.

35. Dossey B, Keengan L, eds. *Holistic Nursing, A Handbook for Practice*. 6th ed. Burlington, MA: Jones and Bartlett Learning; 2013.

36. Snyder M, Lunquist R, eds. *Complementary and Alternative Therapies in Nursing*. New York, NY: Springer Publications; 2010.

37. Matzo M, Sherman D. *Palliative Care Nursing: Quality Care to the End of Life*. 4th ed. New York, NY: Springer; 2010.

38. Quinn J. Transpersonal human caring and healing. In: Dossey B, Keengan L, eds. *Holistic Nursing: A Handbook for Practice*. 6th ed. Burlington, MA: Jones & Bartlett, 2013:107–16.

CHAPTER 32

Delirium

Peggy S. Burhenn

Key Points

♦ Delirium is a common, serious medical problem that is underrecognized by healthcare providers. With prevention and comprehensive assessment, the palliative care advanced practice registered nurse (APRN) can promote quality of life.

♦ Evidence suggests that frequent assessment of patients can result in increased recognition of delirium, which will allow for earlier intervention.

♦ Limited data are available on effective interventions for delirium, once it begins; however, proactive prevention strategies have been successful.

Overview

Delirium has been described in the literature since the time of Hippocrates, yet clinicians frequently are unsure how to manage it.[1] Delirium presents in many different ways, and this has led to its misdiagnosis as other mental illnesses, including depression, mania, psychosis, anxiety, dementia, or substance abuse.[2] Delirium is an underrecognized, serious complication suffered by many cancer patients. Patients experiencing delirium have poorer outcomes and may not fully recover after the episode. Delirium typically involves an underlying somatic illness that must be resolved in order to resolve the delirium. Palliative APRNs are frequently unsure how to properly assess for delirium, prevent it, or intervene when delirium occurs. Delirium has been given many names, such as altered mental status, ICU psychosis, toxic metabolic encephalopathy, acute brain failure, and acute confusional state.[3,4] Multiple names and resulting confusion can delay diagnosis and treatment. Therefore, APRNs should use one term consistently to avoid misdiagnosis and delay in treatment and to promote improved outcomes.[2]

Definition

Delirium is defined by the American Psychiatric Association's *Diagnostic and Statistical Manual*, 5th edition (DSM-V), as a disturbance in attention and awareness that develops over a short period of time. It includes an additional cognitive disturbance, and its symptoms are not better explained by another disorder or as a consequence of another medical condition.[5] The hallmarks of delirium are a disturbance in consciousness that has a related change in cognition that occurred over a short period of time (usually hours to days) and is likely caused by a medical condition.[5]

A delirium diagnosis requires the presence of an acute onset or fluctuating course in a change of mental status. Although the APRN should remain vigilant for such changes, usually the family or caregiver reports this information, stating that the change occurred suddenly, and the patient is "not himself." Inattention is the second required feature for a delirium diagnosis. Typically, a patient will be easily distractible and have trouble staying focused on the conversation at hand; this behavior fluctuation may present during the encounter. The patient will also exhibit disorganized thinking or an altered level of consciousness. Disorganized thinking may manifest in the patient's being incoherent and rambling and unable to answer logic questions (e.g., Can a stone float on water?) or follow simple commands. The patient will also exhibit a change in at least one cognitive area, such as memory and learning, disorientation to time or place, alteration in language, or perceptual distortions (hallucinations).[5] Altered level of consciousness is any described level that is not alert. An abnormal level of consciousness may range from being hyperalert or combative, to the opposite end of the spectrum (lethargic or unarousable).[6] Sleep-wake cycle disturbances are common and have been used as a diagnostic criterion; the patient may sleep during the day and become active or agitated at night.

There are three generally recognized subtypes of delirium: hyperactive, hypoactive, and mixed.[5,7]

♦ Hyperactive: characterized by a hyperactive level of psychomotor activity, often combined with mood swings, agitation, refusal to cooperate with medical care, hallucinations, and/or inappropriate behavior.[5,7]

♦ Hypoactive: characterized by a hypoactive level of psychomotor activity that may be accompanied by reduced motor activity, sluggishness, and lethargy that approaches stupor.[5,7]

♦ Mixed: may have a normal level of psychomotor activity, but attention and awareness are disturbed. Also includes individuals whose activity level rapidly fluctuates between hypoactive and hyperactive.[5,7]

Patients may present with hyperactive, hypoactive, or mixed activity states. Hyperactive delirium may seem to be most common, as its symptoms are more noticeable and disruptive. It has also been associated with medications or drug withdrawal.[5] However, the hypoactive state, often associated with fatigue or lethargy symptoms, is actually more frequent than the hyperactive state but is underdiagnosed.[8] Because delirium symptoms tend to fluctuate, an APRN may fail to diagnose delirium if he or she assesses the patient during the patient's lucid periods.

Pathophysiology

The pathophysiology of deliriumis not fully understood. Somatic disturbances, such as infection, toxins, or metabolic processes, interrupt central nervous system areas responsible for arousal, perception, and focus.[4] Reduced acetylcholine signaling and excess dopamine signaling, along with elevated pro-inflammatory cytokines and anti-inflammatory cytokines, are proposed mechanisms for delirium.[4] The physiological basis for delirium has been described as a combination of neurotransmitter imbalance of excess dopamine and reduced cholinergic activity.[2] Reduced acetylcholinergic signals can directly affect cognition, as witnessed in patients who are administered anticholinergic medications (e.g., diphenhydramine, oxybutynin), which can cause confusion.[4] Antidopamine agents given to delirious patients can lessen the symptoms, leading to a theory that excess dopamine plays a role in delirium.[4] Apolipoprotein E epsilon 4 genotype, which is present with an increase in inflammation, was found in a higher percentage of older adults experiencing delirium.[9] Altered melatonin neurotransmission may be a pathway for the development of delirium, as suggested in a study of 67 patients who received nightly ramelteon, a melatonin agonist, for delirium prevention. In this study, ramelteon was associated with a lower risk of delirium when compared to a placebo (32% vs. 3%; p = .003).[10] Delirium is more likely to be caused by a combination of biological mechanisms than a single cause.[11]

Incidence

The prevalence of delirium in the community is low and has been estimated as 1% to 2%, but it can be as high as 14% in individuals over 85 years old.[5] Delirium is present in 10% to 31% of elderly inpatients at admission.[12] In cancer patients admitted to hospice or the hospital, it is noted in 26% to 44% of cases.[13] Palliative care patients with cancer experience delirium at a rate of 47%.[11] In older individuals, the incidence of postoperative delirium ranges from 15% to 53%. The incidence of delirium in ICU patients has been reported to be between 70% and 87%.[5] In a systematic review of delirium prevalence and incidence, the incidence in palliative care patients ranged from 3% to 45%. Prevalence at inpatient admission was 13.3% to 42.3%, compared to 26% to 62% during admission, increasing to 58.8% to 88% in the weeks or hours before death. Hypoactive delirium was the most common subtype, ranging from 68% to 86% in the cases identified.[8]

Assessment Scales

There are multiple scales for delirium assessment. In practice, the APRN should use one tool consistently and regularly, as repeated screening can increase the chance of detection.[8] Daily screening of patients resulted in higher levels of identification of delirium.[8] In a systematic literature search on delirium subtypes, each study used a different method to evaluate delirium, which demonstrates that no consensus exists for classifying subtypes.[14] Nine different instruments were used to classify the cases as hypoactive or somnolent, hyperactive or activated, and mixed.[14] In this review

of primarily older hospitalized patients, rates of delirium ranged from 15% to 44%.[14] The authors hypothesize that different subtypes may have different etiologies and therefore may require different treatment strategies. They found the Memorial Delirium Assessment Scale (MDAS), the Dublin Delirium Assessment Scale (DAS), and the Delirium Rating Scale (DRS-R-98) to be reliable methods of evaluating and classifying delirium symptoms.[14] The following assessment scales are frequently used.

The Confusion Assessment Method (CAM), developed by expert panel consensus in 1990, was constructed to allow non-psychiatric clinicians to assess for delirium quickly (Fig. 32.1). This diagnostic algorithm is based on four of the nine features of delirium originally described in the DSM-III-R: acute onset and fluctuating course, inattention, disorganized thinking, and altered level of consciousness.[6] The presence of the first two features plus one of the second two features would indicate delirium. The CAM assessment, which has been translated into at least 12 languages, showed high sensitivity (94%) and specificity (89%) and is widely used in practice.[11] The English version is available on the Hartford Institute for Geriatric Nursing website or in the original article.[6,15] There is also a smartphone application that contains the CAM: *Confusion: Delirium & Dementia: A Bedside Guide*.[16] For ICU patients, a version of CAM is also available and can be used with patients who cannot speak or with those who are mechanically ventilated.[17] The CAM identifies if delirium is present but does not assess its severity.

The MDAS is a 10-item evaluation to measure delirium severity, with sensitivity and specificity of 87% and 86%, respectively.[18] Each item is scored from 0 to 3, with a maximum of 30 (worst). This scale was used by Marcantonio and colleagues in a 2002 validation study of postsurgical patients. It correlates well with CAM, and nonclinical staff can administer it in 5 minutes.[18] The MDAS measures levels of consciousness/awareness, disorientation, short-term memory, digit span, ability to maintain and shift attention, disorganized thinking, perceptual disturbance, delusion, psychomotor activity, and sleep–wake cycle. See Appendix 1 in the article by Breitbart and colleagues.[19]

The DRS-R-98 is a 16-item scale, containing 13 items focused on severity and 3 items on differential diagnosis, and is useful for longitudinal studies.[20] It is available as Appendix A in the article by Trzepacz and colleagues.[20]

The Delirium Rating Scale (DRS) is a widely used 10-item scale, intended to be completed by a trained psychiatric clinician. It has been translated into seven languages and is used for clinical and research purposes.[21]

The Neelon and Champagne (NEECHAM) Confusion Scale is a scale designed for use by nurses; it takes 10 minutes to complete and can be used while giving routine care.

The Nursing Delirium Screening Scale (NU-DESC) is shorter, takes about 1 minute to complete, and is based on observations made in routine clinical practice.[3]

In a review of published delirium scales, Grover and Kate (2012) considered the CAM to be the most useful scale, based on its accuracy and ability to be done quickly by lay or clinical personnel.[3] The British Geriatrics Society has developed guidelines for delirium prevention and treatment, recommending use of the CAM screening tool on all patients with cognitive impairment or those at high risk, such as those having a severe illness, preexisting dementia, femoral fractures, or vision or hearing impairments.[7]

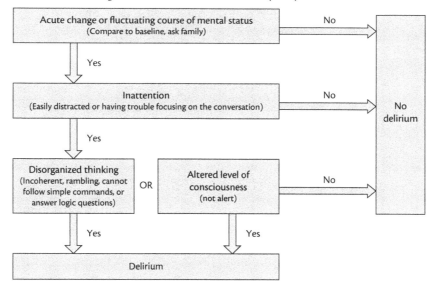

Delirium Diagnostic Criteria
Using the Confusion Assessment Method (CAM)

Figure 32.1 Delirium diagnostic criteria

The National Institute for Health Care and Excellence recommends using a tool based on the DSM, such as the CAM or the CAM-ICU.[22]

Risk Factors

Development of delirium is multifactorial (Table 32.1).[4,11] However, age and preexisting dementia are the strongest risk factors for developing delirium.[12] Delirium is more common in combination with dementia, and dementia is more likely to develop after delirium.[11,23] Age, as an independent factor, may relate to functional age and frailty rather than actual chronological age.

Table 32.1 Factors that Contribute to, or Worsen, Delirium

Predisposing Factors	Precipitating Factors
Older age (≥75)	Polypharmacy, especially anticholinergic or psychoactive medications
Dementia	
Previous delirium	Use of urinary catheters
Immobility	Use of restraints
Dehydration	Hypoxia
Malnutrition	Constipation
Visual impairment	Surgery (especially cardiothoracic and vascular)
Hearing impairment	
Severity of illness	Alcohol excess
Comorbidity	Pain
Depression	Infection
History of transient ischemic attack or stroke	Frequent environmental changes
	Disruption of day/night cycles
Alcohol abuse	Noise and light disturbances

From references 11, 28, 42, 43.

Poor functional status, multiple comorbidities, depression, sensory impairment, fluid and electrolyte imbalances, medications, and alcohol can also be associated with increased delirium.[5,12] In an early predictive model, researchers identified four delirium risk factors: vision impairment, severe illness, preexisting cognitive impairment, and dehydration.[24]

Since the incidence of delirium increases with age and dementia, it is sometimes difficult to distinguish delirium in older adults with known dementia. In these cases, a distinction must be made for the recognition of an acute worsening of a cognitive disturbance. Factors that may contribute to or worsen delirium include immobility, dehydration, anticholinergic or psychoactive medication, use of urinary catheters or restraints, hypoxia, malnutrition, constipation, pain, infection, frequent environmental changes, disruption of day/night cycles, noise, and light disturbances (see Table 32.1).[2,11] Serious medical conditions are frequently associated with the development of delirium. The mnemonic IWATCHDEATH was created to outline those medical conditions: Infections, Withdrawal, Acute metabolic conditions, Trauma, CNS pathology, Hypoxia, Deficiencies, Endocrinopathies, Acute vascular, Toxins or drugs, and Heavy metals (Table 32.2).[2] Using this list as a guide may lead to identifying the cause of the delirium.

Outcomes

Delirium is regarded as a transient condition, but evidence suggests that cognitive and functional impairments can persist.[8] Delirium can last for a week or more, and while most patients will recover, delirium may continue after discharge from the hospital and can lead to stupor, seizures, coma, or death.[5] Poorer outcomes have been associated with delirium, including functional decline, greater morbidity and mortality, increased nursing home placements, longer lengths of stay, and higher healthcare costs.[24,25] A meta-analysis documented the following outcomes of delirium: early risk of death (38% compared to control 27.5%,

Table 32.2 IWATCHDEATH Mnemonic

I	Infections	Upper respiratory or urinary tract infections, meningitis, sepsis, central nervous system (CNS) abscess
W	Withdrawal	Alcohol or sedatives–hypnotics, barbiturates
A	Acute metabolic conditions	Electrolyte imbalances, hepatic/renal failure, acid–base imbalances
T	Trauma	Head trauma, postoperative, heat stroke, burns
C	CNS pathology	Stroke, CNS metastasis, normal-pressure hydrocephalus, hemorrhage, seizures
H	Hypoxia	Pulmonary or cardiac failure, anemia, pulmonary embolus, carbon monoxide poisoning, hypotension
D	Deficiencies	Vitamin B12, niacin, thiamine, hypovitaminosis
E	Endocrine disorders (sometimes listed as Environmental)	Alteration in diabetes, thyroid, parathyroid, or adrenocortical system, hyper/hypothermia
A	Acute vascular	Encephalopathy, shock, hypertensive emergency
T	Toxins or drugs	Medications, industrial poisons, solvents, pesticides, drugs of abuse, cyanide
H	Heavy metals	Lead, mercury, or manganese

From references 2, 27.

$n = 2,957, p < .001$), institutionalization (33.4% vs. 10.7%, $n = 2,579$, $p = < .001$), and development of dementia (62.5% vs. 8.1%, $n = 241$, $p = .009$).[26] The significance of poor long-term outcomes that can occur following delirium suggests that it is important to identify and treat delirium, or ideally to identify at-risk patients and intervene to prevent delirium. Early detection and intervention can shorten the course of delirium, which may lead to improved outcomes. APRNs are in a key position to recognize risk factors and signs of delirium as they assess their patients and can intervene early, which minimizes the occurrence and duration of delirium.[12]

The primary complications that have been associated with delirium are falls, pressure injuries, nosocomial infections, functional decline, incontinence, oversedation, and malnutrition.[7] Measures should be taken to reduce the development of these complications.

Case Study

Mr. C was a 75-year-old widower with metastatic prostate cancer. His daughter lived nearby and checked on him weekly. One evening she noticed that he seemed confused. He seemed to improve the next morning, but when his condition worsened the following evening, his daughter took him to the ED. She stated that he had not been himself. She explained that he had been experiencing memory problems, but since the preceding night, he seemed more confused than usual. He was admitted to the medical oncology unit from the ED. The APRN evaluated Mr. C and found that he had a nagging cough and urinary frequency; he was afebrile, pulse 89, blood pressure 150/90. His once-daily medications included aspirin 81 mg, metoprolol 25 mg, zolpidem 10 mg, omeprazole 40 mg, calcium carbonate 500 mg, and vitamin D3 1,000 IU. He also took oxybutynin 5 mg three times per day, ibuprofen 200 mg as needed for pain, and denosumab 120 mg SC every month. He had been sleeping during the day and was unable to sleep at night unless he took the zolpidem. He was unable to focus on the questions asked of him; instead, he picked at his clothes and mumbled incoherently.

The APRN performed the CAM assessment and determined that Mr. C was experiencing delirium, due to the rapid onset and fluctuating nature of his symptoms, his lack of ability to focus his attention, and his disorganized thinking. The APRN considered the potential etiologies of his delirium.

In considering his medications, he determined that zolpidem was a hypnotic that had been associated with delirium; oxybutynin, an anticholinergic drug, had also been implicated in the development of delirium symptoms. He also considered other risk factors, such as Mr. C's age (delirium occurs in older adults at a higher rate). Mr. C also presented with symptoms of mild dementia, further putting him at risk.

A review of the laboratory results revealed a normal CBC, except a slightly elevated WBC of 10.6 K/μL (normal range 3.6–10.1 K/μL) and a normal comprehensive metabolic panel. A urine culture and chest x-ray were negative.

Once transferred to the medical oncology unit, Mr. C became more paranoid and agitated, lashing out at the nurses and pulling out his intravenous catheter. Later in the same day, he slept soundly and seemed almost lethargic. His cough and urinary frequency may have been signs of a respiratory or urinary tract infection, which had not manifested itself fully.

The zolpidem and oxybutynin were discontinued. Due to Mr. C's continued agitation, the APRN prescribed haloperidol 0.25 mg orally. A repeat CBC the next day revealed a more elevated white count of 13.0 K/μL; subsequently, another chest x-ray and urinalysis were completed. The urinalysis revealed 3+ bacteria, and he was started on intravenous antibiotics.

His daughter stated that he wore glasses and a hearing aid, but in a rush to get him to the ED, she did not bring them. The APRN requested that his daughter bring them, as well as familiar items from home, such as family pictures and favorite items. The APRN told the daughter that he might order an additional staff member for closer monitoring (a continuous observer) if Mr. C became too agitated, as this would provide a safer environment.

A quiet environment was maintained at night and the blinds were kept open during the day. Also, the patient was engaged in activities to prevent daytime sleep, which allowed him to have a more normal sleep–wake cycle.

The APRN promoted nutrition by ordering finger food and high-calorie drinks. The APRN asked the nurses to engage Mr.

C about current events and orientation, using clocks and calendars and comments about his surroundings without disagreeing with him.

As his urinary tract infection resolved and the effect of the discontinued medications, which had anticholinergic and hypnotic effects, subsided, his symptoms improved, while nursing interventions calmed and reassured him. Intravenous fluids were continued to prevent dehydration.

Assessment

The APRN should assess the following:

◆ History: Determine onset, behavior changes such as agitation or withdrawal, presence of inattention, confusion, hallucination, or alteration in sleep–wake cycle.

◆ Initial assessment: Assess mental status and cognitive or perceptual disturbances as compared to baseline, then use the CAM tool (or tool of choice) and continue use of tool each shift for all elderly and at-risk patients (all patients with cognitive impairment or with severe illness, dementia, fracture of the neck of the femur, visual and hearing impairment).[7]

◆ Head-to-toe physical exam: Assess for signs of potential causes of delirium. Key areas include assessment for urinary retention, constipation, or infections in lungs, abdomen, urinary tract, or skin.[27]

◆ Medication review: Anticholinergic drugs have been associated with delirium, but the list of drugs associated with delirium is long, with multiple mechanisms of action, and may include analgesics, benzodiazepines, and hypnotics, among others.[2,27] Consider consultation with pharmacy.

◆ Diagnostic testing: Complete blood count; comprehensive metabolic panel, including urea, electrolytes, glucose, calcium, renal function, and liver function; serum drug levels depending on medications; drug toxicology; C-reactive protein; chest x-ray (review for pneumonia, effusion, and heart abnormalities); blood cultures; pulse oximetry; urinalysis and culture, electrocardiogram.[4,7] Thyroid function and B12 and folate levels may be indicated if the above tests do not reveal a cause.[7] Diagnostic studies may include brain imaging (to evaluate for brain metastases), EEG, or abdominal computed tomography for a patient with severe nausea and vomiting and no bowel movements, to rule out an obstruction.[28] Oxygen saturation levels (hypoxia) or spinal tap can be done if an infectious process is suspected.[27]

Management

The APRN identifies the cause of delirium, if possible, and initiates appropriate therapies:

◆ Manage electrolyte imbalances.

◆ Reduce medications, especially anticholinergics.

◆ Treat infections with antibiotics or antifungals.

◆ Assess for pain and treat it effectively, with scheduled dosing.

◆ Ensure that eyeglasses and/or hearing aids are in place and working (check batteries).

◆ Assess for and treat constipation.

◆ Maintain hydration to prevent dehydration and constipation. Oral route is preferred.

◆ Ensure oxygenation and prescribe oxygen as necessary.

◆ Prescribe appropriate medications. Antipsychotics are the drugs of choice for many clinicians, although there are no approved medications for the treatment of delirium and there is limited evidence to support their use.[2] Titrate starting dose and use lower doses for older adults[7] (Table 32.3).

◆ Institute patient monitoring using a continuous observer or a one-to-one sitter.

◆ Consider consultation with other disciplines, such as a pharmacist (for medication review), geriatrician, neurologist, psychiatrist, or neuropsychologist, who are experienced in cognitive evaluation and treatment.[29] Many patients have underlying dementia, which may need evaluation and treatment by a specialist.

◆ Implement nonpharmacologic measures appropriate for the setting.

◆ Improve orientation to environment and person and ensure continuity of care. Encourage staff to discuss current events and the surroundings. Use clocks and calendars. Discourage aggressive reorientation of patients. Approach patient gently and reduce noises such as pump alarms.

◆ Limit staffing changes to foster familiarity.

◆ Encourage mobility and engagement in social activities. Make referrals to physical therapy, occupational therapy, and/or recreational therapy to evaluate and improve function. Ambulate patients, if possible; at a minimum, have patient sit upright in a chair for all meals.

◆ Promote sleep–wake cycle with appropriate daytime light and sleep hygiene measures. Reduce noise and minimize sleep interruptions by avoiding nighttime nursing or medical interventions.

◆ Involve patient and family in care. Encourage family to visit frequently and bring familiar items from home, including favorite music.

◆ Avoid additional trauma or complications (e.g., eliminate urinary catheters by promoting regular toileting, prevent pressure injury by regularly assessing skin using valid assessment scales, provide adequate nutritional intake by offering nutritional supplements and finger food, limit transfer to other units, avoid restraints).

◆ Provide support and counseling to patients and family after delirium, as there is usually some recollection of events, and it can be very upsetting to patients and families as well.

◆ Delirium is common at the end-of-life and can be prognostic indicator of impending death. Palliative sedation has not been associated with worse survival, and delirium was the most common reason for palliative sedation in a systematic review.[30] This is a controversial subject, as delirium may occur earlier in the disease course, and delirium at end-of-life may not respond to supportive measures.

Prevention

Successful programs for delirium prevention have targeted the reduction of risk factors using multicomponent

Table 32.3 Pharmacologic Management of Delirium

Class	Agent	Dosing	Comments
Typical antipsychotics	Haloperidol	0.5–2 mg may be given PO, SC, IV, IM q2–12h. *In older adults*: 0.25–0.5 mg PO q4h or 1–2 mg IM up to q2h (maximum dose 5 mg/day)	Increased rates of extrapyramidal side effects in higher doses (4.5 mg/day or above). Risk of QT prolongation: monitor ECG at baseline and daily, especially with IV and higher doses. Maintain normal serum potassium and magnesium levels. IM absorption may be poor. IV route not FDA approved. May precipitate with heparin; 2-mL saline flush is recommended prior to IV administration.
	Chlorpromazine	12.5–50 mg q4–6h PO, IV, IM, PR, SC	Higher level of anticholinergic and sedating effects than haloperidol. Monitor in ICU.
Atypical antipsychotics (alternative if intolerant to haloperidol, fewer extrapyramidal side effects)	Olanzapine	2.5–5 mg q12–24h PO, ODT, IM	Poorer response in older adults, those with preexisting dementia, and hypoactive delirium. May cause sedation.
	Risperidone	0.25–1 mg q12–24h PO, ODT	Monitor for orthostatic hypotension and extrapyramidal side effects in higher doses.
	Aripiprazole	5–30 mg q24h PO or IM	May be more effective in hypoactive delirium.
	Quetiapine	12.5–100 mg q12–24h PO	Monitor for orthostatic hypotension. May cause sedation.

No agents are approved by the U.S. Food & Drug Administration (FDA) for use in delirium. Dose recommendations vary by source. Typical and atypical antipsychotics carry an FDA warning of increased mortality in elderly patients with dementia-related psychosis.

ODT = oral disintegrating tablets.

From references 2, 7, 28, 35, 37.

interventions.[31] These interventions can be seen as basic care, but delirium-prevention protocols require consistent implementation to be effective.[31] Patients should be evaluated at admission for risk factors; prevention strategies should be initiated for those at high risk.[7] Inouye described a multi-component delirium-prevention trial that was effective in an inpatient population; the more consistently the protocols were adhered to, the lower the incidence of delirium.[32] This program included protocols for orientation, mobility, sleep, vision and hearing correction, therapeutic activities, and volume replacement strategies.

Marcantonio (2001) conducted a randomized clinical trial for hip surgery patients, with proactive geriatric consultation or usual care. The proactive geriatric care, which involved daily visits and the institution of a structured protocol, reduced delirium incidence by over one-third (32% vs. 50%, $n = 162$, $p = .04$); in severe cases, delirium was reduced by half.[33] The structured geriatrics consultation included assessment and recommendations for oxygen delivery, fluid and electrolyte balance, treatment of pain, eliminating unnecessary medication, regulating bowel and bladder function, nutritional intake, mobilization, postoperative complications, environmental stimuli, and treatment of agitated delirium. They concluded that proactive geriatric consultation may play a role in reducing delirium postoperatively.[33]

Marcantonio and Inouye followed protocols for risk factor reduction and reduced the incidence of delirium. Healthcare professionals can identify high-risk patients and put a prevention plan into place.[7] Inouye and colleagues at the Yale University School of Medicine developed the Hospital Elder Life Program (HELP), designed to prevent delirium in hospitalized, older adults.[34] The HELP materials, including manuals, tools, and resources, are available free of charge to institutions at www.hospitalelderlifeprogram.org.

A multifaceted, interdisciplinary approach to delirium is needed, as the causes can be multiple and diverse, and they are frequently unknown at the time of presentation. Therefore, it is unlikely that a single intervention will resolve the episode.[11] An attempt to determine the cause of delirium and eliminate it (e.g., antibiotics for an infection, fluids for dehydration, eliminating high-risk drugs) is a priority.[2,7] Delirium management is focused on relief of symptoms, simple measures that address risk factors, and a tailored, multidisciplinary approach.[31] Using techniques that reduce risk factors, such as providing a good sensory environment, reorienting patients, managing basic care needs, and eliminating possible causative factors, may help resolve delirious symptoms.[7,31] Many times the cause of the delirium is not identified, and once delirium begins, psychosocial and environmental measures may not be effective.[2] Therefore, drug therapy is typically initiated to when management of severe symptoms is necessary.

Pharmacology

Currently, there are no approved drugs to treat delirium; however, clinicians have widely used sedatives and antipsychotics. In a review of 16 studies evaluating pharmaceuticals for delirium, researchers found no strong evidence recommending any agents.[11] Inouye and colleagues concluded that there is a "preponderance of evidence" against using pharmacologic approaches to prevent or treat delirium in the elderly.[11] If drug therapy is used, the British Geriatric Society guidelines recommend the following:[7]

◆ Keep the use of sedatives to a minimum.

◆ Use one drug at a time. Start at the lowest dose and increase as necessary after 2 hours.

◆ Review all medications at least every 24 hours.

◆ While titrating drugs, provide one-on-one care.

Sedatives may worsen delirium, especially those with anticholinergic effects. The goal of drug treatment is to treat dangerous or distressing behaviors. Drug therapy may also be warranted if patients may harm themselves or others (e.g., highly agitated patients) or if their behavior interferes with essential medical care.[7,11] Sedation should not be used as a form of restraint and should be discontinued as soon as possible.

When drug therapy is required, haloperidol has been the gold standard but may cause extrapyramidal side effects.[35] Injectable haloperidol contains a black box warning for an increased risk of death when used for elderly patients with dementia-related psychoses.[35] A 2007 Cochrane report reviewed the use of antipsychotics in delirium.[36] Studies suggest that atypical antipsychotics, such as risperidone, olanzapine, or quetiapine, can be used to treat delirium. The Cochrane report found no evidence that low-dose haloperidol (<3 mg/day) had any different efficacy than the atypical agents or any greater side effects. However, higher doses of haloperidol (>4.5 mg/day) were associated with more side effects than the atypical antipsychotics. The report noted the small sample size of many studies.

The risks and benefits of drug therapy should be weighed before initiating therapy. The guidelines developed by the British Geriatric Society recommend using haloperidol, if drug therapy is warranted.[7] The National Comprehensive Cancer Network outlines the use of haloperidol and other alternative agents in their palliative care guidelines[37] (see Table 32.3).

Discharge and Follow-Up

The cause of delirium should be investigated and treated prior to discharge; patients should be assessed for functional and cognitive ability as a component of the discharge assessment. The ability to perform activities of daily living can be assessed using the Katz Index of Independence in Activities of Daily Living.[38] Cognition can be assessed using a tool like the Mini-Mental Status Exam (MMSE) or the Mini-Cog.[39] The assessment and a discharge summary can be sent to the geriatrician or primary care provider for continued follow-up. Involvement of the family or caregivers is essential. Practical arrangements are needed to ensure that support for the patient and family is provided in the home setting.

Once discharged, patients need monitoring to ensure that they receive adequate nutrition and hydration. They need to be encouraged to exercise and be active, and to have positive sleep habits and a calm environment. A home health agency can assist with this monitoring, perform a home safety evaluation, and provide home rehabilitation services.

APRN Roles

Staff Education

Interdisciplinary team education and systematic screening for patient impairment, using standardized tools, can improve the detection of delirium.[40] Clinicians should be able to recognize and treat delirium.[7] To determine program effectiveness, regular audits should be performed on patients with delirium to assess the process of care and patient outcomes. Outcomes to measure include length of stay, readmissions, mortality, cognition scores, or patient transfer to long-term facilities.[7] The results of these audits may then provide feedback for future educational programs.[7]

The ability to recognize delirium can be improved by using consistent terminology and by developing training programs that focus on early recognition of cognitive problems.[13] Staff education should include the following:

◆ The term "delirium" is to be used consistently. Staff should understand the definition and criteria for diagnosis.

◆ Preventive measures are reviewed and all high-risk patients targeted.

◆ Staff are able to take a history from the family or caregivers to understand the patient's baseline function and detect any cognitive function changes.

◆ Staff are trained in the use of screening tools (e.g., the CAM tool).

◆ The same delirium screening and assessment tool should be used consistently.

◆ Staff are able to screen for risk factors and precipitating factors of delirium.

◆ Staff are aware of interventions targeted at eliminating potential causes of delirium.

◆ Staff implement measures to reduce delirium symptoms by controlling the environment and orienting the patient to his or her surroundings, person, and time.

Staff education can be provided as a part of a focused orientation program for new hires or as required education at key time points, such as an annual refresher course. An online course can be developed that is tied to a learning management system; course completion can be required as a part of ongoing training. In-service sessions, or short educational programs, can be more effective for busy work areas that have limited time for education breaks. Consideration can be given to developing a delirium care expert nurse who could then serve as a delirium resource nurse, available to assist with more difficult cases. Delirium is considered a geriatric syndrome. Since it has a high incidence in the older population, a nurse with expertise in geriatric syndromes may be a helpful resource.

Consultation

The role of the APRN includes clinical consultation. A clinical nurse specialist, a nurse practitioner, or a nurse educator with special training in the management and prevention of delirium should be available to consult on cases in the inpatient setting. Consultation will focus on assessment, physical examination, differential diagnosis, and coordinating treatment with interdisciplinary measures for the patient. It is recommended that an interdisciplinary team meet daily to discuss a patient with delirium and the treatment interventions that are being implemented. This should be more frequent if the delirium is persistent or worsening. Each team member should share progress made or challenges remaining in the care of the patient. This will allow the team to assess the interventions' impact and to identify if treatment plan changes are warranted.

An APRN is in an ideal position to lead an interdisciplinary work team to create an institutional care plan for delirium. The team would be charged with reviewing the most up-to-date delirium literature as it relates to the patient population being served. Once the literature has been reviewed, recommendations and an institution-specific algorithm or protocol can be developed to prevent, assess for, and treat delirium. Based on this clinical practice guideline, education can be developed, delivered, and evaluated. Audits can monitor the successful implementation of the protocol and its effect on rates of delirium at the institution. The team may consider using materials available from the Hospital Elder Life Program (HELP).[34] Although not all patients who experience delirium are elderly, the program is a comprehensive resource on the management of delirium and can help all patients, regardless of age. Protocols to prevent, recognize, and treat delirium are available. The *Geriatric Nursing Protocol: Delirium: Prevention, Early Recognition, and Treatment*[12] is available on www.ConsultGeriRN.org, a website sponsored by the New York University College of Nursing and the Hartford Institute for Geriatric Nursing. With a goal of reducing delirium in the inpatient older adult population, this protocol provides an overview and background information, as well as specific assessment parameters, nursing care strategies, evaluation with expected outcomes, and recommendations for follow-up monitoring.

Patient and Family Education

Education about delirium is important and should be discussed with those at risk for delirium. Patients and caregivers alike find delirium a distressing experience.[41] Caregivers may question if death is close, or how they will care for the family member in the future. Knowledge of delirium and what to expect may ease caregivers' distress.[41] In the preventive phase, patients and family are advised that delirium is possible; if it occurs, they can be reminded that it is a temporary condition. Family members and friends are generally the first ones to notice subtle changes in a patient's cognition. They should be encouraged to report any changes or fluctuations in behavior to the nursing staff. Caregivers will need emotional support as well; they may feel helpless and will want to know what they can do to participate in the care.[41] An educational program for patients and families may consist of the topics outlined in Table 32.4.

Several online sources contain patient educational materials that can be downloaded. There are many reliable websites with resources on delirium, such as those in Table 32.4. These are reliable sources that provide easy-to-read information that patients and families need to know about delirium. The HELP website contains resources for older adults and caregivers, including links to other educational documents and websites.[34]

Research

Further research is needed to reduce the incidence of delirium and to find ways to reverse it promptly. Data on drug therapy for

Table 32.4 Patient Education Topics to Cover and Online Resources

◆ What is delirium?	◆ Preventive measures that can be taken and how family can help
◆ Who is at risk?	
◆ Potential causes	◆ Complications
◆ Signs and symptoms to watch for and report	◆ Treatments
	◆ Support available

Online resources	Comments	Website
Vanderbilt University	*In the Intensive Care Unit: Delirium—A Guide for Patients and Families:* Focuses on the ICU, where most cases of delirium occur, the information is useful for all patients at risk and their families.	http://www.icudelirium.org/docs/delirium_education_brochure.pdf.
University of Pittsburgh Schools of the Health Sciences	Reviews symptoms, causes, treatments, and how families can help.	http://www.upmc.com/patients-visitors/education/behavioral-health/pages/delirium.aspx
Mayo Clinic	Covers symptoms, causes, complications, tests, treatments, coping, and prevention.	http://www.mayoclinic.org/diseases-conditions/delirium/basics/definition/con-20033982
Memorial Sloan Kettering Cancer Center	Includes symptoms, causes, risk factors, and recovery.	http://www.mskcc.org/cancer-care/patient-education/resources/delirium
HELP website	Includes the article *"10 Tips to Avoid Confusion in the Hospital."*	http://www.hospitalelderlifeprogram.org/public/delirium.php

delirium are limited, and larger, controlled studies to compare agents are needed. Further investigation is indicated to examine delirium's effect on long-term outcomes. Most of the interventions that have been recommended in preventive or treatment protocols are nursing measures, so more studies led by nurse investigators can be done to determine the best use of these interventions and the patient populations in whom they are most effective.

Conclusion

Delirium is a distressing experience for patients, caregivers, and healthcare professionals alike. Although the evidence for effective delirium interventions is limited, systematic assessment and modification of risk factors appear to be an effective approach. APRNs are vital in the identification, assessment, and management of delirium. They may also collaborate with members of an interdisciplinary team. APRNs can bring evidence-based practice to the bedside and lessen the extent and impact of delirium by teaching and serving as consultants.

References

1. Field RR, Wall MH. Delirium: past, present, and future. *Semin Cardiothorac Vasc Anesth*. 2013; 17: 170–9.
2. Caplan JP, Cassem NH, Murray GB, Park JM, Stern TA. Delirious patients. In: Stern TA, Fricchione GL, Cassem NH, Jellinek MS, Rosenbaum JF, eds. *Massachuetts General Hospital Handbook of General Hospital Psychiatry*. 6th ed. Philadelphia, PA: Saunders Elsevier; 2010:93–104.
3. Grover S, Kate N. Assessment scales for delirium: A review. *World J Psychiatry*. 2012; 2: 58–70.
4. Krishnan V, Leung LY, Caplan LR. A neurologist's approach to delirium: diagnosis and management of toxic metabolic encephalopathies. *Eur J Intern Med*. 2014; 25: 112–6.
5. American Psychiatric Association. Delirium. In: *Diagnostic and Statistical Manual of Mental Disorders*. 5th ed. Arlington, VA, American Psychiatric Association; 2013:596–602.
6. Inouye SK, van Dyck CH, Alessi CA, et al. Clarifying confusion: the Confusion Assessment Method. A new method for detection of delirium. *Ann Intern Med*. 1990; 113: 941–8.
7. British Geriatric Society. Guidelines for the prevention, diagnosis and management of delirium in older people in hospital. 2006. Available at http://www.bgs.org.uk/index.php/clinicalguides/170-clinguidedeliriumtreatment. Retrieved July 11, 2014.
8. Hosie A, Davidson PM, Agar M, et al. Delirium prevalence, incidence, and implications for screening in specialist palliative care inpatient settings: a systematic review. *Palliat Med*. 2013; 27: 486–98.
9. van Munster BC, Korevaar JC, Zwinderman AH, et al. The association between delirium and the apolipoprotein E epsilon 4 allele: new study results and a meta-analysis. *Am J Geriatr Psychiatry*. 2009; 17: 856–62.
10. Hatta K, Kishi Y, Wada K, et al. Preventive effects of ramelteon on delirium: a randomized placebo-controlled trial. *JAMA Psychiatry*. 2014; 71: 397–403.
11. Inouye SK, Westendorp RG, Saczynski JS. Delirium in elderly people. *Lancet*. 2014; 383: 911–22.
12. Tullmann D, Fletcher K, Foreman M. Delirium. In: Boltz M, ed. *Evidence-Based Geriatric Nursing Protocols for Best Practice*. 4th ed. New York, NY: Springer Pub. Co.; 2012:186–99.
13. Centeno C, Sanz A, Bruera E. Delirium in advanced cancer patients. *Palliat Med*. 2004; 18: 184–94.
14. de Rooij SE, Schuurmans MJ, van der Mast RC, et al. Clinical subtypes of delirium and their relevance for daily clinical practice: a systematic review. *Int J Geriatr Psychiatry*. 2005; 20: 609–15.
15. Waszynski C. *The Confusion Assessment Method (CAM)*. Hartford Institute for Geriatric Nursing, New York University, College of Nursing; 2012.
16. Proctor Corporation Ltd. *Confusion: Dementia & Delirium: A Bedside Guide*. Ed. 1.2. Proctor Corporation; 2014.
17. Tate J, Happ MB. *The Confusion Assessment Method for the ICU (CAM-ICU)*. The Hartford Institute for Geriatric Nursing New York University, College of Nursing; 2008.
18. Marcantonio E, Ta T, Duthie E, et al. Delirium severity and psychomotor types: their relationship with outcomes after hip fracture repair. *J Am Geriatr Soc*. 2002; 50: 850–7.
19. Breitbart W, Rosenfeld B, Roth A, et al. The Memorial Delirium Assessment Scale. *J Pain Symptom Manage*. 1997; 13: 128–37.
20. Trzepacz PT, Mittal D, Torres R, et al. Validation of the Delirium Rating Scale-revised-98: comparison with the Delirium Rating Scale and the cognitive test for delirium. *J Neuropsychiatry Clin Neurosci*. 2001;13:229–42.
21. Trzepacz PT. The Delirium Rating Scale. Its use in consultation-liaison research. *Psychosomatics*. 1999;40:193–204.
22. National Institute for Health and Care Excellence. Delirium: Diagnosis, prevention and management. 2010. Available at http://www.nice.org.uk/guidance/cg103/resources/guidance-delirium-pdf. Retrieved July 11, 2014.
23. Davis DH, Muniz Terrera G, Keage H, et al. Delirium is a strong risk factor for dementia in the oldest-old: a population-based cohort study. *Brain*. 2012; 135: 2809–16.
24. Inouye SK, Viscoli CM, Horwitz RI, et al. A predictive model for delirium in hospitalized elderly medical patients based on admission characteristics. *Ann Intern Med*. 1993; 119: 474–81.
25. Leslie DL, Inouye SK. The importance of delirium: economic and societal costs. *J Am Geriatr Soc*. 2011; 59(Suppl 2): S241–3.
26. Witlox J, Eurelings LS, de Jonghe JF, et al. Delirium in elderly patients and the risk of postdischarge mortality, institutionalization, and dementia: a meta-analysis. *JAMA*. 2010; 304: 443–51.
27. Gower LE, Gatewood MO, Kang CS. Emergency department management of delirium in the elderly. *West J Emerg Med*. 2012; 13: 194–201.
28. Gershon K. In: Dahlin C, Lynch M, eds. *Core Curriculum for the Advanced Practice Hospice and Palliative Registered Nurse, Delirium*. 2nd ed. Pittsburgh, PA: Hospice and Palliative Nurses Association; 2013.
29. National Comprehensive Cancer Network. Senior Adult Oncology Guideline. 2014. Available at http://www.nccn.org/professionals/physician_gls/pdf/senior.pdf. Retrieved July 16, 2014.
30. Maltoni M, Scarpi E, Rosati M, et al. Palliative sedation in end-of-life care and survival: a systematic review. *J Clin Oncol*. 2012; 30: 1378–83.
31. O'Mahony R, Murthy L, Akunne A, et al. Synopsis of the National Institute for Health and Clinical Excellence guideline for prevention of delirium. *Ann Intern Med*. 2011; 154: 746–51.
32. Inouye SK, Bogardus ST, Jr., Williams CS, et al. The role of adherence on the effectiveness of nonpharmacologic interventions: evidence from the Delirium Prevention Trial. *Arch Intern Med*. 2003; 163: 958–64.
33. Marcantonio ER, Flacker JM, Wright RJ, et al. Reducing delirium after hip fracture: a randomized trial. *J Am Geriatr Soc*. 2001; 49: 516–22.
34. Hospital Elder Life Program (HELP). 2000. Available at http://hospitalelderlifeprogram.org/public/for-clinicians.php?pageid=01.02.00. Retrieved July 20, 2014.
35. Breitbart W, Alici Y. Evidence-based treatment of delirium in patients with cancer. *J Clin Oncol*. 2012; 30: 1206–14.
36. Lonergan E, Britton AM, Luxenberg J, et al. Antipsychotics for delirium. *Cochrane Database Syst Rev*. CD005594, 2007
37. National Comprehensive Cancer Network. Palliative Care. 2014. Available at http://www.nccn.org/professionals/physician_gls/pdf/palliative.pdf. Retrieved September 10, 2014.

38. Wallace M, Shelkey M. Katz Index of Independence in Activities of Daily Living. Try This Series, The Hartford Institute for Geriatric Nursing and the New York University College of Nursing, 2007.

39. McKoy JM, Burhenn PS, Browner IS, et al. Assessing cognitive function and capacity in older adults with cancer. *J Natl Compr Canc Netw.* 2014; 12: 138–44.

40. Yanamadala M, Wieland D, Heflin MT. Educational interventions to improve recognition of delirium: a systematic review. *J Am Geriatr Soc.* 2013; 61: 1983–93.

41. Cohen MZ, Pace EA, Kaur G, et al. Delirium in advanced cancer leading to distress in patients and family caregivers. *J Palliat Care.* 2009; 25: 164–71.

42. Cole MG, Ciampi A, Belzile E, et al. Subsyndromal delirium in older people: a systematic review of frequency, risk factors, course and outcomes. *Int J Geriatr Psychiatry.* 2013; 28: 771–80.

43. Whitlock EL, Torres BA, Lin N, et al. Postoperative delirium in a substudy of cardiothoracic surgical patients in the BAG-RECALL clinical trial. *Anesth Analg.* 2014; 118: 809–17.

CHAPTER 33

Depression and Suicide

John D. Chovan

And, when the moment of our definitive "passage" comes,
grant that we may face it with serenity . . .

—John Paul II[1]

Key Points

- Advanced practice registered nurses (APRNs), as part of the transdisciplinary team, assess patients and families for depressed mood and other depressive symptoms throughout the trajectory of illness to develop a patient-centered plan of care that includes pharmacologic and nonpharmacologic interventions, as well as referrals to psychiatric and mental healthcare providers as needed.

- Although a depressed mood is a natural response of patients and their families to a diagnosis of, being treated for, living with, and dying from, a chronic, life-threatening illness, depression can lead to thoughts and actions of self-harm that can result in death.

- The grief response, before or after the death of a loved one, does not follow a well-defined linear path, but is a journey that is personal to each individual. If not resolved, it can manifest in depressive symptoms.

Case Study

Tom Carson was a 55-year-old Caucasian male who lived with his wife, Cathie, and 20-year-old son, Ben, in their own home in an upper-middle-class neighborhood of a large Midwestern city. Tom was a mechanical engineer for a small jet aircraft design and manufacturing firm. Cathie was a biology teacher who had been teaching from home for the past 10 years at an online high school. The family was very athletic and enjoyed taking long-distance bicycle trips every year. Cathie noticed that Tom was dropping his keys and was tripping over carpets in their home with some frequency. When she brought it to his attention, he reported that he had been noticing it, too, and had been feeling twitching in his hands and feet for several months at least.

After Tom saw his primary care provider—Judy, a family nurse practitioner—and underwent multiple tests, Judy invited a palliative nurse practitioner, Luke, from a local healthcare system, to meet with Tom and Cathie to discuss the findings. Tom and Cathie were very nervous going into the meeting because they had

looked up the symptoms and tests on the Internet, causing them to worry that Tom had a life-threatening illness. Judy asked if they had any questions, which they did not, because they were eager to hear the outcome. She described that the array of findings pointed to a diagnosis of amyotrophic lateral sclerosis (ALS), a progressive disease that would eventually lead to Tom's death.

Introduction

The palliative APRN must understand the psychological aspects that can occur across the spectrum of a diagnosis of a life-limiting illness. The initial response to learning such a diagnosis varies. Disbelief, needing time to let the news sink in, shock, sadness, anger, and denial are all potential psychological responses. This chapter focuses on feelings associated with depression that accompany patients and their family members throughout the trajectory of a chronic, life-threatening illness. Because their needs may change throughout the course of the illness, the framework used to examine the symptoms associated with depression involves the four stages of the illness trajectory: (1) at the time of diagnosis; (2) during treatment—initial treatments and subsequent planned or unplanned treatments; (3) after treatment—when the planned course of treatment is completed or when the goals shift away from treatment; and (4) during active dying.[2]

Definition of Depression

The term *depression* has a technical definition but is often used colloquially in healthcare. When a person says, "I'm depressed," it does not necessarily mean the person has assessed and diagnosed himself or herself according to evidence-based standards. It often means that they are feeling blue, have low spirits, or are unhappy. It may also mean that they are lonely, having physical or psychic pain, or are angry and need to talk. Motivating a person to the point of being able to report "I'm depressed" may be a very complex challenge. For clarity, the terms used in this chapter are:

Mood: The state of one's emotions at a particular point in time[3]

Sadness: The feeling of being in low spirits or being unhappy, also called a depressed mood.[3] The World Health Organization defines depressed mood as "a low mood that may be expressed in a number of ways—sadness, misery, low spirits, inability to enjoy anything, gloom, rejection, feeling blue ... It becomes pathological when it is persistent, pervasive, unresponsive, painful, or out of proportion to the individual's life circumstances."[4(pp 17–18)]

Depressive symptoms: The behavioral indicators associated with a depressed mood. These are described in detail below and include sleep changes, anhedonia, guilt, helplessness, hopelessness, changes in energy level, reduced ability to concentrate, appetite changes, psychomotor slowing, and suicidal ideation or attempts.[3] Depressive symptoms can worsen over time in frequency, severity, duration, and impact on functioning to the point of causing disability, meeting criteria for a depressive disorder.[5]

Depressive episode: A pathological state that meets predefined criteria based on the existence of a depressed mood or anhedonia as well as five of nine particular depressive symptoms, for at least 2 weeks. Most encounters in palliative care and hospice in which the patient says "I'm depressed" will present a constellation of symptoms that very likely do not meet the criteria for a depressive episode.[6]

Depressive disorder: One of the constellation of pathological mood syndromes in which the hallmark feature is severe and persistent depressed mood and associated pathology, limiting one's ability to function in social, occupational, or other important settings. These include major depressive disorder, pervasive depressive disorder, premenstrual dysphoric disorder, substance-induced depression, and depression due to another medical condition. Some palliative care and hospice patients will have a chronic, life-threatening somatic illness in addition to a depressive disorder.[6]

To provide optimal care, the palliative APRN must understand the symptomatology of both somatic and psychiatric illness and the interplay between them.

Depressed Mood and Life-Threatening Illness

Throughout the course of a chronic, life-threatening illness, a patient's response to the illness is often a waxing and waning mood. Patients and their families are often faced with very difficult decisions that can trigger depressive symptoms and thoughts of suicide. As a member of the transdisciplinary team, the APRN assesses for, and plans interventions to alleviate these symptoms.[5–7]

Prior to diagnosis, patients and their families may be anxious but may not show evidence of depressive symptoms. Patients may find that changes they have observed prior to seeking medical attention or the process of going through diagnostic procedures is stressful, triggering depressive symptoms. Persons with preexisting depressive disorder may find that these stressors will make their depression worse or cause a relapse of depression that had been in remission.

At diagnosis, no matter how prepared the person may be, hearing the news for the first time can be a stressor that triggers feelings of sadness, hopelessness, guilt, pain, regret, and helplessness. At any point along the disease trajectory, depressive symptoms can become pathological. Preexisting depression can be made worse.

As treatment begins and continues, difficulties with side effects from the treatments or intermittent and recurring exacerbations can trigger disappointments and depressive symptoms. Feelings of guilt about the impact the diagnosis and treatment have had on the family are related to depressed mood. Discussions about code status, naming a healthcare proxy, and decisions about a living will can cause the patient's or family members' mood to sag. Physical symptoms can trigger depressive symptoms as the patient tries to cope with a new sense of normal, particularly pain. Spiritual angst can also cause depressive symptoms to emerge.

Remissions or return to baseline from exacerbations can offer hope that dangles by a thread. The specter of relapsing or another worse exacerbation is a stressor that can cause depressed mood or make a depressive disorder worse. It can also increase anxiety levels to pathological magnitudes.

During end-stage disease and the dying phase, resolution of depressive symptoms prior to the onset of active dying process is ideal. However, a patient with depressive symptoms may still have trigger stressors, leaving him or her at risk for a difficult death. The focus of the palliative APRN is on comfort, which allows for the mood of the family to concomitantly be managed. For the family (as defined by the patient), the dying process of a loved one can be complex and layered, particularly if there is unfinished business when the patient dies.

At the end-of-life, family members may be asked about the patient's previously expressed wishes. This is a major stressor to those who have not had difficult conversations about the patient's desires, and it can trigger depressive symptomatology and anxiety in the healthcare proxy and family. Grief is a normal response but can become pathological if it persists and has a negative impact on ability to function.[8]

The palliative APRN anticipates these potential responses to a life-limiting illness and living with a life-limiting illness. After comprehensive assessment, the palliative APRN collaborates with the transdisciplinary team to develop a care plan, to marshal community resources, and to organize supportive information in anticipation of patient and family questions and concerns. Although the scope of practice for a palliative APRN clearly includes psychiatric symptom management[9], the extent to which APRNs may manage psychiatric and mental health issues varies according to state laws and institutional policies. Psychiatric and mental health specialist colleagues may be necessary to assist in severe and persistent mental illnesses, such as recurrent, refractory major depressive disorder, schizophrenia, and bipolar disorder. As part of primary care, all APRNs screen for depressive symptoms. Many APRNs can provide therapy and prescribe antidepressants as delineated by scope of practice. As appropriate, referral of a patient or family member to a psychiatric or mental health professional may be necessary. Such transdisciplinary team members include a psychiatric and mental health nurse practitioner or clinical nurse specialist, a social worker, a psychologist, a psychiatrist, an inpatient consultation team, or an outpatient mental healthcare provider.[10]

Epidemiology of Depression in Chronic Illness

Depression is associated with severe, chronic illness.[11] Table 33.1 lists several chronic illnesses and their associated rates of

Table 33.1 Depression in Chronic Illness

Chronic Illness	% Experiencing Depression
Myocardial infarction	40–65%
Parkinson's disease	40%
Multiple sclerosis	40%
Chronic pain syndrome	30–54%
Cancer	25%
Diabetes	25%
Coronary artery disease	18–20%
Stroke	10–27%

Adapted from http://www.webmd.com/

depression. The rate of depression is quite high for cardiac and neurological chronic illnesses and for persons experiencing chronic pain. The palliative APRN should be familiar with this epidemiology to anticipate and monitor for depressive symptoms in persons with these chronic illnesses.

History and Pathology

When a person reports experiencing depressive symptoms, the APRN should consider reversible physical causes of the symptoms (Box 33.1).[3] For example, hypothyroidism causes symptoms that mimic depression and can be corrected medically, often with levothyroxine (Synthroid). It can be detected with a blood test that measures circulating levels of thyroid-stimulating hormone (TSH) and thyroxine (T4). Metastatic disease to the brain can cause mood swings, including depression, as the lesions alter function in mood-related foci of the cerebrum. Normal-pressure hydrocephalus can cause gait and mood changes that mimic depressive symptoms; a consult to neurology or neuropsychiatry would be appropriate. Unmanaged pain is a common cause of stress, and subsequently somatic symptoms and depressive symptoms, yet it is correctible. Pain can include distress from insomnia, anorexia, dysphagia, and existential rumination, which can

---

Box 33.1 Physical Causes of Depression

Brain tumors

Cardiac surgery

Hypothyroidism

Hypoxia

Obstructive sleep apnea

Postpartum

Seizures

Strokes

Traumatic brain injury

From reference 3.

---

lead the patient to ask, "Why me?" Appropriate total pain management can alleviate these stressors and their comorbid depressive symptoms. If potential physiological causes are ruled out, or detected and treated, but the symptoms remain, the APRN can conclude that the symptoms are psychiatric and not due to a correctible physical cause.

Acute stress does not always result in maladaptive responses. The diathesis-stress model of mental illness[3] posits that persons may be genetically predisposed to development of a mental illness. Incipient mental illness is expressed only after stressors trigger the symptoms. Genetic markers have been identified for predisposition to depression and subtypes of depression.[12] The palliative APRN's comprehensive history taking can uncover threads of a genetic predisposition. Evidence of prior depressive symptoms is the best predictor of future depressive symptoms. A family history of depression can also predispose a person to express symptoms of depression when a stressful situation occurs.

The process of taking a history allows the palliative APRN to build rapport with the patient and family when evaluating a new patient for depressive symptoms. Onset, duration, measures that exacerbate it or alleviate it, and amount of debility that the symptoms induce are all features that give insight into how to approach treatment. The therapeutic use of self allows the APRN to defuse any anxiety or reticence about discussing depression, particularly if the distress is in any way related to fear of rejection and the stigma of mental illness.

Understanding of the pathophysiology attributed to depression continues to evolve. For the past 50 years, the monoamine theory of depression has been the paradigm to explain symptoms.[3] The theory states that the lack of monoamine neurotransmitters in sufficient quantities to trigger postsynaptic neurons to fire appropriately in the prefrontal cortex and in the limbic system causes depression. The monoamines, primarily norepinephrine, serotonin, and dopamine, are the major neurotransmitters implicated in this theory. The theory holds up in that monoamine therapy, such as the monoamine oxidase inhibitors (MAOIs; e.g., phenelzine [Nardil]), tricyclic antidepressants (TCAs; e.g., amitriptyline [Elavil]), selective serotonin reuptake inhibitors (SSRIs; e.g., citalopram [Celexa]), and serotonin–norepinephrine reuptake inhibitors (SNRIs; e.g., venlafaxine [Effexor]) do offer symptomatic relief. With these therapies there is often a protracted delay between therapy initiation and onset of symptom relief. Their effect on depressive symptoms is inconsistent. When symptoms are detected before permanent neurological changes take effect, the symptoms can be reversed and treatment eventually can be discontinued. More severe symptoms, however, will require life-long treatment.[13]

The neurotrophic theory of depression complements the monoamine theory. Atrophy and loss of neurons and glia in the structure and function of the cortex, particularly the prefrontal cortex and the limbic system's hippocampal pyramidal neurons, are mechanisms that contribute to depression.[14–17] Stress causes dendrites to retract in these areas and decreases spine density[16] through inflammatory mechanisms, such as pro-inflammatory cytokines, interleukins, tumor necrosis factor, and peripheral growth factors.[16,18,19] Furthermore, the inflammatory response results in an increase of neurotoxic brain amyloid-ß peptides, which causes cell death, particularly in refractory depression.[20] Changes in glutaminergic signaling have been seen in animal models of depression.[21] These findings serve as emerging evidence linking a history of major depressive disorder with Alzheimer's disease.[22]

Assessment

A targeted assessment for depression, performed as part of the complete patient and family assessment, provides evidence on which to plan symptom management. In doing the targeted assessment, the APRN looks for evidence that will support or rule out depression. A focused history and physical examination will determine the need for appropriate diagnostic tests and their interpretation. The palliative APRN should review the patient's history and record for prior history of depression. If the patient has a history of depression, the APRN should find out what treatments were initiated and their effectiveness. The APRN should also inquire about other mental health issues, including bipolar disorder, personality disorders, disorders that emerge in childhood, and schizophrenia. The APRN must be aware of physiological conditions that can contribute to or mimic depression. The family history should examine the patient's and family's history of suicide. Exposure to a suicide or suicide attempt is a major risk factor for suicide. A medication history should help determine

interventions for depression. It should include specific medications that were helpful in the past and those that were not and any allergies to medications or products in pharmaceuticals. The medication review should include all current prescription medication, over-the-counter preparations, supplements, and allergies in order to avoid known sensitivities and to reduce the risk of drug–drug interactions.[2] Finally, there should be discussion about the patient's and the family's knowledge and beliefs about psychiatric illness, pharmacotherapy, and complementary and alternative therapies. The reader is referred to *The Textbook of Palliative Nursing*, Chapter 4, Assessing Patients and Families,[2] for detailed information.

All persons with chronic illness are at risk for depression.[23] Other risk factors for depression are listed in Table 33.2. The physical exam should be focused on mood and psychomotor changes and should include the following:[6]

Depressed mood: A depressed mood is characterized by negative emotions as reported by the patient. Simply asking "How is your mood?" can elicit a response from the patient that indicates an unaltered mood (euthymia) or a mood that is not normal for him or her (dysthymia). "Is this a change from your usual mood?" will help distinguish the patient's current state from his

Table 33.2 Risk Factors for Depression and Suicide in Adults

Domain	Risk Factor	At Risk for Depression	At Risk for Suicide
Mood	Depressed mood	Depression as a child or teen	Feel hopeless, socially isolated, or lonely
Stressors	Stressful life event ◆ Loss ◆ Illness ◆ Military service ◆ Financial/legal problems	Yes	Yes
Substance abuse	Abuse of alcohol, illegal drugs, and/or prescription drugs	Yes	Yes; Can worsen thoughts of suicide and can instill recklessness or impulsivity enough to act on thoughts
Family	Genetic link or environmental exposure to mental illness, substance abuse, or suicide	Blood relatives	Family history; also violence, including physical or sexual abuse
Psychiatric	Any psychiatric disorder but especially anxiety, post-traumatic stress disorder, personality disorders	Yes. Plus: ◆ Borderline personality disorder ◆ Certain personality traits, such as having low self-esteem and being overly dependent, self-critical, or pessimistic	Yes. Plus: ◆ Psychosis ◆ Paranoia
Somatic illness	Chronic or life-threatening illness; pain	Yes	Yes
Medications		Certain medications, such as some high blood pressure medications or sleeping pills	Beginning an antidepressant for symptoms of depression
Development			Identify as bisexual, homosexual, or transgender with an unsupportive family or in a hostile environment. In adolescents and children, being unsure of sexual orientation
Means			Access to firearms
History of suicide			Previous suicide attempt

Adapted from http://psychcentral.com/

or her baseline and will give insight into the duration of a possible depressive episode.

Sleep changes: Decreased need for sleep, early morning wakening, or an increased need for sleep can all indicate depression. Questions can include: "How are you sleeping? Any difficulty falling asleep? Once you fall asleep, do you stay asleep? Once you wake up in the middle of the night, do you have trouble falling asleep? Do you sleep until your planned waking time? Has this changed from your usual sleep schedule?" Changes in sleep patterns are associated with depression, particularly sleep difficulties in the early to the middle part of the sleep cycle.

Lack of interests or anhedonia: The depressed patient may report lack of interest in activities he or she used to enjoy, or a general lack of interest in anything. The APRN might ask, "What sorts of activities are you interested in doing? Has this interest changed recently?"

Beck's Cognitive Triad: Aaron Beck described changes in thinking about the self, the world, and the future as indicators of depression.[24] Excessive guilt and feelings of worthlessness indicate thoughts about the self and can be elicited by asking the patient, "Tell me about your feelings of self-worth. Are there things you feel guilty about?" Thinking about the world is captured by asking the patient to describe how others view him or her from their perspective. "Are you feeling helpless and that others do not want to help you?" And finally, the patient may see the future as dim when depressed and may believe that there is no way out of his or her current situation: "Do you feel hopeless?"

Energy: Changes in level of energy, typically decreases, are associated with depression: "How's your energy level?"

Concentration: Changes in ability to concentrate, typically more difficulty concentrating, are associated with depression: "How is your ability to concentrate?"

Appetite: Changes in appetite, either up or down, and significant weight loss without intentional dieting are features associated with depression. The APRN can ask, "How is your appetite? Is that a change from your usual appetite? Have you lost weight? How much? Over what period of time?"

Psychomotor slowing: Moving more slowly than usual, difficulty initiating activity, such as getting out of bed or off the couch, slower gait, and slower speech are symptoms of depression. Self-report is not as reliable as observation by a friend or family member. The nurse can ask the patient whether the friend or family member has mentioned anything unusual about the patient's ability to move or walk.

Suicidal thoughts or attempts are associated with depression. Risk factors for suicide include exposure to a completed suicide or suicide attempt, thoughts about committing suicide, planning to commit suicide, possessing the means to commit suicide, having access to the means to commit suicide, the potential lethality of the means (e.g., the amount of physical damage that the means could cause), and an unsuccessful attempt at suicide in the past. Other risk factors for suicide are listed in Table 33.2. The APRN screens for suicide by asking these questions:

1. Has anyone close to you attempted or completed suicide?

2. Have you ever tried to hurt yourself?

3. Are you currently thinking about hurting yourself?

4. Do you have a plan?

5. How are you planning on doing it?

6. Do you have means to implement such a plan?

A mnemonic for the features of depression is SIG E CAPS, a play on the prescription to "Take (Sig) energy (E) capsules (Caps)," which stands for **S**leep changes, **I**nterest changes, **G**uilt or hopelessness, **E**nergy decreases, **C**oncentration difficulties, **A**ppetite changes, **P**sychomotor changes, **S**uicidal ideation.

If the patient or family member reports that the patient has thoughts about committing suicide, along with a plan and access to the means, the palliative APRN should make a safety contract with the patient if possible, and then call for help to have the patient taken for more advanced psychiatric help.[3,25,26]

When someone takes his or her own life, the first question typically asked is, "Why?" Even when a suicide note is left behind, questions remain unanswered. Suicide can trigger physical or psychiatric illness in the surviving members of the family and friends. The palliative APRN will be better able to support the survivors if he or she has thought about his or her own beliefs and attitudes about suicide, and how it fits into his or her own philosophy of life. Exploring other people's views, including other members of the transdisciplinary team, is beneficial. It allows the APRN to anticipate his or her own personal reactions and perspectives so he or she can best help members of the patient's family and other team members.

Physician-assisted suicide may be perceived differently. In this case patients legally obtain and use prescription medications to commit suicide. This typically is not done due to depression; rather, they are exercising their own autonomy in determining when and how their life will end. In the states of Washington, Oregon, Vermont, Montana, New Mexico, and California, physician-assisted suicide is legal.[27] The palliative APRN should support persons who request information about assisted suicide according to the laws of the state in which he or she practices.

See Chapter 42, Navigating Ethical Discussions in Palliative Care, and Chapter 51, Palliative Sedation.

Ongoing Assessment

At the initial encounter, the palliative APRN collects baseline data. At subsequent encounters, the APRN assesses the patient and family for any changes from this baseline, using them to measure progress, emerging issues, and the effectiveness of treatments: "Compared to [before or last time] we met, is it the same, better, or worse?"[2] During each encounter, the palliative APRN builds a trusting relationship with the patient and family to facilitate the sharing of information.[3] This is particularly important when discussing mental health issues because of the sensitive nature of mental illness and the stigma associated with it. The palliative APRN continues to build the database from which an appropriate plan of care will be derived, including evidence of risk for and symptoms of depression, as well as related substance abuse and risk for suicide. The acuity of each symptom is also determined[5]: frequency (e.g., nearly every day, most days, 2 or 3 days per week, weekly, once per month or less), duration (e.g., nonstop, months, days, just that day, a few hours), and impact on daily function (e.g., can or cannot work, can or cannot take care of one's own needs, can or cannot cook for oneself, bedbound).

Several standardized tools are available to screen for depression.[28,29] These tools may be categorized by the age of the persons they were designed to measure. For example, the Children's Depression Rating Scale (CDRS) is useful for children under the age of 18. With persons over the age of 14, useful tools include the Beck Depression Inventory (BDI), the Center for Epidemiological Studies Depression Scale (CES-D), the Hamilton Depression Scale (Ham-D), two items on the Palliative Outcomes Scale (POS), the Zung Self-Rating Depression Scale, and the General Well-Being Schedule Depression (GWB-D) Subscale. Elderly patients can be evaluated using the Geriatric Depression Scale (GDS), the Major Depression Inventory (MDI), and the Zung Self-Rating Depression Scale.[28-32]

Newly diagnosed patients without a history of depressive disorder will likely not meet the criteria for a diagnosis of major depressive disorder. They may have fewer symptoms or their symptoms may not have persisted long enough to meet the criteria. In these cases, adjustment disorder with depressed mood may be an appropriate diagnosis. The palliative APRN must remember that depressive symptoms that persist can evolve into a pathologically significant major depressive disorder diagnosis. Although the labels of the diagnoses themselves may not completely inform treatment, the evaluation of the existence of symptoms and their severity, duration, and impact will provide a baseline to direct evaluation of agreed-upon therapeutic interventions.[33] The *Diagnostic and Statistical Manual of Psychiatric Disorders*, fifth edition (DSM-V),[6] lists the specific criteria for these disorders.

Differential Diagnosis

The differential diagnosis for depressive symptoms is shown in Table 33.3.[6] When these symptoms are observed, the palliative APRN collects appropriate data to differentiate sub-pathological conditions, such as normal grief, from higher-acuity conditions based on the constellation of signs and symptoms, their characteristics, and the impact on the individual and family. Only then can appropriate interventions be planned and implemented to address the specific needs of the individual or family.

Management/Interventional Techniques

Evidence-based interventions and approaches for helping patients with depressive symptoms are based on the principles that (a) the patient–clinician relationship is important to the development of a successful plan of care, (b) the patient and the family are at the center of the therapeutic relationship, and (c) an interdisciplinary approach will result in optimal care. Ongoing monitoring of effectiveness is key to managing depression.[3]

Within the context of palliative care, the goal is to maximize quality of life by minimizing symptoms and minimizing the impact of symptoms and therapy on the patient.[34] Techniques for treating depression and depressive symptoms include talk therapy, pharmaceutical interventions, and complementary therapies to achieve this goal. Although the biochemistry of thought and learning is outside the scope of this chapter, the link between the anatomy and physiology of the brain and these processes explains in part the success of various treatment modalities.[34]

Psychotherapy

Current evidence for depression shows that management is best when it includes psychotherapy as well as pharmacologic management. For patients and families with depressive symptoms, processing their feelings aloud can help them find peace, make meaning out of their situation, and develop hope. The challenge for patients with serious illness is finding a supportive and affordable group therapy or therapists at a convenient location. The palliative APRN with training in therapy provides opportunities for the person to process his or her feelings. Otherwise, a referral to a professional trained in brief therapy, cognitive-behavioral therapy, or other therapeutic techniques can be made to manage depressive symptoms in palliative settings.[35,36]

Table 33.3 Differential Diagnosis for Depression

Differential	Description	Comments
Grief	Normal emotional reaction to a loss. Over time, can evolve into a depressive disorder.	The prominent symptom is emptiness, not anhedonia and depressed mood. Self-esteem is preserved, although feelings of sadness come and go. Persons experiencing grief may express a desire to be with the lost loved one, but they do not think of suicide as a way to make the bad feelings go away.[33]
Depressed mood	Sadness or feeling blue	A depressed mood by itself is not a depressive disorder but rather a stand-alone symptom; however, it can be debilitating.
Adjustment disorder	Clinical disorder as defined in DSM-V. Difficulty adapting to a new sense of normal.	The parameters for depressive symptoms (number, severity, duration, and impact) are of a lesser degree and do not meet the criteria for major depressive disorder.
Major depressive disorder	A depressive disorder characterized in DSM-V by multiple symptoms over an extended period of time.	Five or more symptoms (*SIG E CAPS*: *S*leep changes, *I*nterest changes, *G*uilt or hopelessness, *E*nergy decreases, *C*oncentration difficulties, *A*ppetite changes, *P*sychomotor changes, *S*uicidal ideation), including depressed mood, for at least 2 weeks. May be recurrent.
Bipolar disorder	A mood disorder characterized by alternating depression and manic mood states.	Must meet criteria for major depression during depressive episodes and either mania or hypomania as defined in DSM-V (*DIG FAST*: *D*istractibility, *I*rresponsibility, *G*randiosity, *F*light of ideas, *A*ctivity increases, *S*leep is decreased, *T*alkative)

From reference 6.

Table 33.4 Common Pharmacotherapies for Depression

Class	Generic Name	Brand Name
Selective serotonin reuptake inhibitors (SSRIs)	citalopram	Celexa
	escitalopram	Lexapro
	fluoxetine	Prozac
	paroxetine	Paxil
	sertraline	Zoloft
	vilazodone	Viibryd
Serotonin–norepinephrine reuptake inhibitors (SNRIs)	desvenlafaxine	Pristiq
	duloxetine	Cymbalta
	venlafaxine	Effexor
Other Antidepressants		
Serotonin & dopamine reuptake inhibitor	buproprion	Wellbutrin
Serotonin & catecholamine reuptake inhibitor	mirtazapine	Remeron

From reference 13.

Pharmacologic Management

Pharmaceutical therapy is the most common technique used for managing depressive symptoms. This choice, however, may depend on the patient's prognosis. For patients who have a prognosis of longer than 2 to 3 months, there are more options. SSRIs and SNRIs are first-line medications for treating depressive symptoms.[13] Table 33.4 lists the generic and brand names of commonly prescribed antidepressants. Table 33.5 lists the side effects of SSRIs and SNRIs.

A common patient concern is the sexual side effects of the SSRIs, specifically orgasmic delay in men and women and erectile dysfunction in men. These side effects can be treated with psychotherapy or with the addition of buproprion (Wellbutrin).

Table 33.5 Common Side Effects of SSRIs and SNRIs

SSRIs	SNRIs
Agitation	Agitation
Anorexia	Discontinuation syndrome
Anxiety	Headache
Constipation	Hypertension (dose-related)
Diarrhea	Nausea
Discontinuation syndrome	Sleep disturbances
Dizziness	Sweating
Dry mouth	Tremor
Headache	
Insomnia	
Nausea	
Sexual dysfunction	
Somnolence	
Sweating	
Tremor	

From reference 13.

Typically SSRIs and SNRIs are given only after other antidepressants, if any, have been given sufficient time to wash out of the body. Like any other medication in palliative care, the drug is initiated at the lowest therapeutic dose and the dosage is adjusted as needed. Sub-therapeutic effects are often observed in the first few weeks, but full therapeutic effect is achieved in 6 to 8 weeks after pharmacotherapy has started. Citalopram (Celexa) and its levo-isomer escitalopram (Lexapro) have been used to control depressive symptoms while minimizing side effects. Duloxetine (Cymbalta) is used to alleviate depressive symptoms and some somatic symptoms of depression. Mirtazapine (Remeron) has shown to have a more rapid onset than SSRIs when used to treat major depression, but the side-effect profile is often debilitating.[37] Off-label uses of mirtazapine include treating anxiety symptoms, nausea, pruritus, insomnia, and anorexia. When either discontinuing a medication or switching to a new medication, a taper or cross-taper over 2 weeks is required to avoid discontinuation effects.[13]

The rise of the neurotrophic theory of depression creates an opportunity for the emergence of new treatments. Ketamine and scopolamine show a rapid antidepressant action by increasing prefrontal cortex spine synapses.[16] N-Methyl-D-aspartate (NMDA) antagonists increase glutamate transmission and relieve some symptoms of depression.[17] Psychostimulants have shown short-term effectiveness, including rapid onset, in the treatment of depression in palliative patients, but the evidence is limited.[38] Expert consensus states that for patients with prognoses of less than 3 months, methylphenidate 2.5 to 5 mg twice a day may offer some benefit and allow for life closure activities.[36,39]

Current evidence shows that for moderate to severe depression, symptoms are better controlled by a combination of talk therapy and medication than by either modality alone. But mild to moderate depression has been shown to respond equally well to pharmacotherapy or to talk therapy.[35] The European Palliative Care Research Collaborative (EPCRC) derived recommendations for the prevention, detection, and treatment of depression in palliative care patients that include pharmacotherapy and talk therapy. They also recommend open communication, patient involvement in care planning, and regular assessment of symptoms as situations change along the course of illness. For patients with severe depression, the EPCRC recommends a referral to a mental health specialist.[39]

Complex Medication Use

Palliative care patients with longstanding depressive disorders may be taking medications unfamiliar to the palliative APRN. The SSRIs and SNRIs that are used today are third- and fourth-generation medications that manipulate the monoamine neurotransmitters. Earlier medications with similar effects are the MAOIs and the TCAs. If a patient is taking a drug from one of these classes, the palliative APRN needs to be aware of the patient's risk for a life-threatening condition—serotonin syndrome (SS; Box 33.2). Of note, one substance commonly taken by patients is St. John's wort, an over-the-counter herbal medication that is used to augment mood and to treat other ailments by increasing serotonin levels. Although not approved by the U.S. Food and Drug Administration as a pharmaceutical, St. John's wort, in combination with other serotonergic drugs, can cause SS.[40]

Box 33.2 Serotonin Syndrome—A Life-threatening Condition

Sustained levels of serotonin in the synaptic cleft alleviate depressive symptoms. Combinations of medications that increase the level of serotonin in the synaptic cleft, however, can be additive and cause concentrations of serotonin to rise to dangerously high levels. When this happens, evidence of serotonin syndrome (SS) emerges.

SS presents as three or more of the following symptoms: agitation, diarrhea, heavy sweating not due to activity, fever, mental status changes, such as confusion or hypomania, muscle spasms (myoclonus), overactive reflexes (hyperreflexia), shivering, tremor, and uncoordinated movements (ataxia).

This is a crisis situation that is typically treated by stopping the medication and administering benzodiazepines, intravenous fluids, and cyproheptadine, a serotonin antagonist antihistamine.[13]

MAOIs and TCAs must not be taken with SSRIs and SNRIs. If the patient's depressive symptoms become refractory to his or her older medications, then a washout period of 2 weeks is required before starting the more current medications. If the patient is taking an MAOI, diet must be restricted to avoid foods high in tyramine, a precursor to serotonin. These foods include some cheeses; beer; dried meats, such as salami and pepperoni; chicken livers; meat bouillons and gravies; and fermented foods, such as kimchi, sauerkraut, tofu, soy sauce, and fish sauce.[41]

Management of Concomitant Diagnoses

The palliative APRN must note the presence of other mental health diagnoses and the effect of medications on other conditions. Some bipolar disorders are characterized by the existence of a depressed mood and are treated with mood stabilizers. The use of an SSRI or SNRI in a patient with bipolar disorder may trigger a manic episode, a pathological state that may have been revealed in the history. If mania is discovered, SSRI and SNRI antidepressants should be avoided. In these cases, mood elevators (e.g., lithium) are the first-line therapy.[3]

Depression can also be accompanied by psychosis, or not being in touch with reality. If psychotic features are also present, the patient requires antipsychotics in addition to antidepressants. These medications can cause metabolic changes (such as hyperlipidemia, hyperglycemia, and prolonged QTc interval) that can precipitate other comorbid conditions. For example, some antipsychotics cause hyperlipidemia, which can lead to coronary artery disease and distributed atherosclerosis. Hyperglycemia can lead to diabetes mellitus. Cardiac conduction can be affected, such as a prolonged QTc interval, leaving the patient at risk for lethal dysrhythmias. Any side effects should be treated according to evidence-based guidelines. Of note, the palliative APRN should use caution when attempting to manage agitation or delirium in a patient who is already taking antipsychotics as the patient's illness proceeds toward end-of-life. High levels of antipsychotics can lead to neuroleptic malignant syndrome (NMS), a life-threatening emergency characterized by muscle cramps and tremors, fever, symptoms of autonomic nervous system instability like unstable blood pressure, and alterations in mental status (agitation, delirium, or coma). NMS is treated symptomatically, with ice packs for fever, supportive respiratory and circulatory care, and dantrolene for muscle rigidity.[13]

SS and NMS are life-threatening emergencies that must be treated emergently. NMS is distinguished from SS by the presence of bradykinesia, muscle rigidity, elevated white blood cell count and plasma creatine kinase level. Prevention of these conditions should include a referral to a mental health professional for alternative approaches to optimal patient care.[3,13]

Safe Prescribing

Safe prescribing begins with a thorough history that includes diet, allergies, and medications, both historical and current, and herbal supplements. Avoiding concomitant substances (such as St. John's wort) and foods that induce serotonin will decrease the likelihood of SS. Understanding the patient's use of antipsychotics and safe prescribing will help avoid NMS.

Safe prescribing also includes minimizing the availability of lethal doses of any medication that could be used as a means of suicide. For example, consider a patient who has depressive symptoms and is being treated for anxiety with benzodiazepines. The patient has a 30-day supply of lorazepam (Ativan) in 10-mg tablets. In a moment of despair due to new-onset depression, this patient could kill himself by taking all 30 pills at once: the maximum safe dosage of lorazepam in 24 hours is 10 mg.[42] Even acetaminophen in large enough quantities can damage an otherwise healthy liver and cause death.[43] A patient who is planning suicide could hoard pills over time to build a lethal stash. The palliative APRN should consider dosages, amounts, and refills of medication to prevent their lethal use. Interventions and therapy relieve some symptoms, so the patient may be less fatigued and more energetic, while still being at risk for suicide. The palliative APRN must remain vigilant for depression and assess for suicidal ideation, plan, means, and access at every interaction. The challenge is tailoring such practices to promote a supportive encounter that meets the needs of the patient without enabling a dysfunctional response.[3]

Nonpharmacologic Interventions

Depressive symptoms can be co-managed with physical activity, such as walking, swimming, and yoga, and with proper nutrition.[44,45] Talk therapies can assist patients and families to find a new sense of normal and to create meaning in the patient's situation, which can mitigate depressive symptoms.[3] Other modalities, such as meditation, prayer, guided imagery, music therapy, aromatherapy, and acupuncture, have been shown to alleviate depressive symptoms.[46]

Patient and Family Education

Palliative APRNs provide quality care by offering patient and family education that includes information about the following:

1. Stressors trigger depressive symptoms, and reducing exposure to stressors that can be manipulated will reduce the likelihood of the development of longstanding depressive symptoms. Stress management is healthy.

2. Sadness is a normal response to loss. When sadness worsens and impairs functioning over a long period of time, seeking help through individual or group therapy or a healthcare provider can assist patients to cope with the sadness.

3. Depression and depressive symptoms are evidence of psychiatric illness, not lack of moral character, and they can be treated with pharmaceutical and nonpharmaceutical interventions.

4. It is important to take all medications as prescribed. Symptoms take time to go away. The effects of a medication might not be felt for 6 to 8 weeks after initiation.

5. Medications should not be stopped abruptly. Patients and family members should know the signs and symptoms of dangerous conditions like NMS and SS.

6. Patients need to be monitored for thoughts of self-harm or harm to others. This may include identifying a trusted person to report feelings to.

7. The overall strategy for safe treatment is a combination of prescription medications, appropriate diet, and management of alcohol intake to help avoid side effects or dangerous interactions.

Conclusion

Pain and symptom management for persons with chronic, life-threatening illness is profoundly important. It is the most sacred honor to work with patients and families while they are facing enormous physical, emotional, social, and spiritual challenges. Symptoms of depression are very common in patients and their families in these circumstances. The palliative APRN cares for people with symptoms of depression by being fully present, having done his or her own psychic and spiritual work; by understanding what to look for during an assessment; and by offering treatment options based on sound scientific and nursing evidence. Disentangling the causes for the constellation of depression symptoms requires keen insights and a strong base of scientific knowledge. The palliative APRN uses the nursing process to assess patients, diagnose needs, plan interventions, implement care, and evaluate the effectiveness of that care according to professional, legal, and institutional scopes of practice and standards of practice. Helping patients to cope emotionally maximizes their quality of life, the ultimate goal of palliative care. As we improve end-of-life care for people with severe mental illness, we will learn how to provide better care for all.[47(p 734)]

References

1. Wintz J. *A Retreat with Pope John Paul II: Be Not Afraid.* Cincinnati, OH: Franciscan Media (formerly St. Anthony Messenger Press); 2002.

2. Chovan JD, Cluxton D, Rancour P. Assessing patients and families. In: Ferrell B, Coyle N, Paice J, eds. *Textbook of Palliative Nursing.* 4th ed. New York, NY: Oxford University Press; 2015.

3. *Practice Guideline for Treatment of Patients with Major Depressive Disorder.* 3rd ed. Arlington, VA: American Psychiatric Association; 2013.

4. Isaac M, Janca A, Sartorius N, eds. *ICD-10 Symptom Glossary for Mental Disorders.* Geneva, Switzerland: World Health Organization; 1994.

5. Porche K, Reymond L, Callaghan JO, Charles M. Depression in palliative care patients: a survey of assessment and treatment practices of Australian and New Zealand palliative care specialists. *Aust Health Rev.* 2014; 38(1): 44–50.

6. American Psychiatric Association. *Diagnostic and Statistical Manual of Mental Disorders.* 5th ed. Arlington, VA: American Psychiatric Association; 2013.

7. Lloyd-Williams M, Payne S, Reeve J, Dona RK. Thoughts of self-harm and depression as prognostic factors in palliative care patients. *J Affect Disord.* 2014; 166(Sep): 324–9.

8. Lai C, Luciani M, Galli F, et al. Attachment style dimensions can affect prolonged grief risk in caregivers of terminally ill patients with cancer. *Am J Hosp Palliat Care.* 2014. pii: 1049909114547945. [Epub ahead of print]

9. Dahlin CM, Sutermaster DJ. *Palliative Nursing: Scope and Standards of Practice—An Essential Resource for Hospice and Palliative Nurses.* Silver Spring, MD: The American Nurses Association; 2014.

10. Patterson KR, Croom AR, Teverovsky EG, Arnold R. Current state of psychiatric involvement on palliative care consult services: results of a national survey. *J Pain Symptom Manage.* 2014; 47(6): 1019–27.

11. *Depression and Chronic Illness Fact Sheet.* Washington, DC: National Alliance on Mental Illness; 2009.

12. Flint J, Kendler JS. The genetics of major depression. *Neuron.* 2014; 81: 484–583.

13. Stahl SM. *Essential Psychopharmacology: The Prescriber's Guide.* 4th ed. New York, NY: Cambridge University Press; 2013.

14. Duman RS. Pathophysiology of depression and innovative treatments: remodeling glutamatergic synaptic connections. *Dialogues Clin Neurosci.* 2014; 16(1): 11–27.

15. Licznerski P, Duman RS. Remodeling of axo-spinous synapses in the pathophysiology and treatment of depression. *Neuroscience.* 2013; 22(251): 33–50.

16. Ota KT, Duman RS. Environmental and pharmacological modulations of cellular plasticity: role in the pathophysiology and treatment of depression. *Neurobiol Dis.* 2013; 57(Sep): 28–37.

17. Duman RS, Voleti B. Signaling pathways underlying the pathophysiology and treatment of depression: novel mechanisms for rapid-acting agents. *Trends Neurosci.* 2012; 35(1): 47–56.

18. Su JA, Chou SY, Tsai CS, Hung TH. Cytokine changes in the pathophysiology of poststroke depression. *Gen Hosp Psychiatry.* 2012; 34(1): 35–9.

19. Schmidt HD, Shelton RC, Duman RS. Functional biomarkers of depression: diagnosis, treatment, and pathophysiology. *Neuropsychopharmacology.* 2011; 36(12): 2375–94.

20. Pomara N, Sidtis JJ. Brain neurotoxic amyloid-beta peptides: their potential role in the pathophysiology of depression and as molecular therapeutic targets. *Br J Pharmacol.* 2010; 161(4): 768–70.

21. Mitchell ND, Baker GB. An update on the role of glutamate in the pathophysiology of depression. *Acta Psychiatr Scand.* 2010; 122(3): 192–210.

22. Modrego PJ. Depression in Alzheimer's disease: pathophysiology, diagnosis, and treatment. *J Alzheimer Dis.* 2010; 21(4): 1077–87.

23. American Psychological Association. *Coping with a Diagnosis of Chronic Illness.* Psychology Help Center. Available at http://www.apa.org/helpcenter/chronic-illness.aspx. Updated August, 2013. Accessed August 1, 2014.

24. Gotlib IH, Hammen CL, eds. *Handbook of Depression.* 3rd ed. New York, NY: Guildford Press; 2014.

25. Mayo Clinic. *Suicide and Suicidal Thoughts.* Diseases and Conditions. Available at http://www.mayoclinic.org/diseases-conditions/suicide/basics/definition/con-20033954. Published June 9, 2012. Accessed August 1, 2014.

26. Trevino KM, Abbott CH, Fisch MJ, Friedlander RJ, Duberstein PR, Prigerson HG. Patient–oncologist alliance as protection against suicidal ideation in young adults with advanced cancer. *Cancer.* 2014; 120(15): 2272–81.

27. *State by State Guide to Physician Assisted Suicide.* Pro.Con. org. Available at http://euthanasia.procon.org/view.resource.php?resourceID=000132. Updated November 5, 2014. Accessed November 11, 2014.

28. Kelly B, McClement S, Chochinov HM. Measurement of psychological distress in palliative care. *Palliat Med.* 2006; 20: 779–89.

29. Leeds Lloyd-Williams, M, Ward J. Which depression screening tools should be used in palliative care? *Palliat Med.* 2003; 17: 40–3.

30. Krause S, Rydall A, Hales S, Rodin G, Lo C. Initial validation of the death and dying distress scale for the assessment of death anxiety in patients with advanced cancer. *J Pain Symptom Manage.* 2015; 49(1): 126–34. doi: 10.1016/j.jpainsymman.2014.04.012.

31. *Practice Guideline for the Psychiatric Evaluation of Adults.* 2nd ed. Arlington, VA: American Psychiatric Association; 2013.

32. Antunes B, Murtagh F, Bausewein C, Harding R, Higginson IJ. Screening for depression in advanced disease: psychometric properties, sensitivity and specificity of two items of the Palliative Care Outcome Scale (POS). *J Pain Symptom Manage.* 2015; 49(2): 277–88. doi: 10.1016/j.jpainsymman.2014.06.014.

33. Uher R, Payne JL, Pavlova B, Perlis RH. Major depressive disorder in DSM-5: implications for clinical practice and research of changes from depression and anxiety. *Depress Anxiety.* 2014; 31: 459–71.

34. Ferrell B, Coyle N, Paice J, eds. *Textbook of Palliative Nursing.* 4th ed. New York, NY: Oxford University Press; 2015.

35. Okumura Y, Ichikura K. Efficacy and acceptability of group cognitive behavioral therapy for depression: a systematic review and meta-analysis. *J Affect Disord.* 2014; 164(Aug): 155–64.

36. Li M, Fitzgerald P, Rodin G. Evidence-based treatment of depression in patients with cancer. *J Clin Oncol.* 2013; 31(28): 3612.

37. Watanabe N, Omori IM, Nakagawa A, et al. Mirtazapine versus other antidepressive agents for depression. *Cochrane Database of Systematic Reviews.* 2011, Issue 12. Art. No.: CD006528.

38. Candy B, Jones L, Williams R, Tookman A, King M. Psychostimulants for depression. *Cochrane Database of Systematic Reviews.* 2008, Issue 2. Art. No.: CD006722.

39. Rayner L, Price A, Hotopf M, Higginson IJ. The development of evidence-based European guidelines on the management of depression in palliative cancer care. *Eur J Cancer.* 2011; 47(5): 702–12.

40. Davis SA, Feldman SR, Taylor SL. Use of St. John's wort in potentially dangerous combinations. *J Altern Complement Med.* 2014; 20(7): 578–9.

41. Holden KJ. *Meal Ideas and Menus: Avoiding High-Tyramine Foods Made Easy.* North Wales, PA: Teva Neuroscience, Inc; 2006.

42. U.S. Food & Drug Administration. *Ativan (lorazepam) tablets.* FDA Drug Label. Available at http://www.accessdata.fda.gov/drugsatfda_docs/label/2007/017794s034s035lbl.pdf. Accessed August 25, 2014.

43. U.S. Food & Drug Administration. *FDA Drug Safety Communication: Prescription Acetaminophen Products to be Limited to 325 mg Per Dosage Unit; Boxed Warning Will Highlight Potential for Severe Liver Failure.* Drug Safety and Availability. Available at http://www.fda.gov/drugs/drugsafety/ucm239821.htm#aihp. Accessed August 25, 2014.

44. Danielsson L, Papoulias I, Petersson E-L, Carlsson J, Waern M. Exercise or basic body awareness therapy as add-on treatment for major depression: a controlled study. *J Affect Disord.* 2014; 168(Oct): 98–106.

45. O'Neil A, Quirk SE, Housed S, et al. Relationship between diet and mental health in children and adolescents: a systematic review. *Am J Public Health.* 2014; 104(10): e31–42.

46. Purohit MP, Wells RE, Zafonte RD, Davis RB, Phillips RS. Neuropsychiatric symptoms and the use of complementary and alternative medicine. *PM R.* 2013; 5(1): 24–31.

47. Woods A, Willison K, Kington C, Gavin A. Palliative care for people with severe persistent mental illness: a review of the literature. *Can J Psych.* 2008; 53(11): 725–36.

CHAPTER 34

Dual Diagnosis and Post-Traumatic Stress Disorder

Leslie Blatt

Key Points

- The palliative advanced practice registered nurse (APRN) can achieve the most effective treatment and better outcomes for individuals with dual diagnosis by integrating mental health, addiction, and palliative care.

- The palliative APRN should use risk-reduction strategies for the most effective treatment for co-occurring disorders in individuals with a life-threatening illness.

- Research indicates that management of PTSD symptoms is more likely to produce a decrease in substance use than if symptoms were not treated.

Introduction

There are many challenges to treating individuals with mental illness and serious advanced illness. The palliative APRN must understand that each issue brings its own set of challenges; the presence of a dual diagnosis in a patient with serious illness necessitates meticulous assessment, collaboration, and communication. The patient may miss appointments and not adhere to therapeutic regimens, often complicating pain and symptom management.[1] The patient may use substances to avoid difficult feelings. He or she needs assistance in managing his or her behavior, a chance to express his or her feelings through treatment of depression and anxiety, and assistance in discussing existential issues.[1] Alienated family members may try to reconcile with the patient, but this becomes difficult in the face of relapses or manipulative behavior and often leads to caregiver burden and abandonment. Repairing broken relationships, attaining forgiveness of self and others, and reconnecting with a higher power may not be possible if the patient is craving substances.[2]

Both palliative care practitioners and mental health clinicians have a similar philosophy that includes a collaborative framework focused on relieving patients' suffering and improving their quality of life.[3] Patients' wishes are respected whenever possible and pain and other symptoms are relieved. Integrated treatment that addresses physical and mental health and substance use can decrease hospitalization and improve functioning and quality of life.[3]

This chapter reviews the management of patients with dual diagnosis and comorbid psychiatric disorders in the setting of palliative care. It is divided into two parts: the first focuses on co-occurring disorders and serious mental illness and the second on post-traumatic stress disorder (PTSD). The goals are to define dual diagnosis, review assessment and treatment strategies for co-occurring disorders and PTSD, and identify strategies that the palliative APRN can incorporate into practice.

The phrase "substance use disorder," also referred to as chemical dependency or addiction, is used to describe cognitive, behavioral, and physiological symptoms resulting in repeated adverse social consequences, such as missing work, family, or school obligations, interpersonal conflicts, or legal problems.[4] The term "dual diagnosis" is used as a general designation for individuals who have both substance use disorder and a coexisting psychotic, affective, behavioral, or severe personality disorder.[5] "Co-occurring disorders" is sometimes used to replace the term "dual diagnosis," as the latter term also includes other disorders, such as intellectual disability and mental disorders. For the purpose of this chapter, the terms "dual diagnosis" and "co-occurring disorders" are used interchangeably.

Co-occurring Disorders and Serious Mental Illness

Case Study 1

CM was a 50-year-old woman recently diagnosed with Hodgkin's lymphoma. She had a history of untreated chronic paranoid schizophrenia and hepatitis C. She had a history of heroin and cannabis abuse and had been in remission on a methadone maintenance program for 1 year, but she recently relapsed on both substances. CM's recent relapse was due to increased pain, and her symptoms of paranoia worsened. She had a history of suicide attempts, stabbing herself with a knife and a heroin overdose. She smoked one or two packs of cigarettes per day. She lived alone with her five cats, was isolated, and was estranged from her family. She was referred to the palliative care clinic for pain management. The patient was suspicious and distrusting at baseline, but over time a relationship developed. Close collaboration with her methadone maintenance program providers revealed ways to help control her pain and maintain her safety. CM was reassured that she was safe and would not be harmed. The team observed CM for behaviors associated with hallucinations (statement content, scanning, eyes averted, staring, or bolting and running from the room), and the palliative APRN kept in weekly contact with the addictions specialist. Strategies that the palliative APRN employed included brief interactions and clear, concrete statements about pain medication and CM's understanding about her disease and treatment. Active listening and supportive counseling were used, clarifying CM's misconceptions about treatment. Education about substance abuse was given, reinforcing what she had learned from her methadone maintenance clinicians. In addition, the palliative APRN educated the nursing staff on strategies to help manage CM's behavior associated with schizophrenia. CM went through treatment, often missing appointments. It became routine to remind her when her appointments were scheduled and help her make arrangements for transportation. She used morphine in addition to methadone for a brief time, with frequent urine checks, small amounts of medication distributed, and frequent appointments. CM went into remission, remained off morphine, and remained on the methadone maintenance program.

Epidemiology

Based on the National Survey on Drug Use and Health's 2013 estimates, among 9 million adults age 18 or older with serious mental illness, 23.6% (2.1 million) people met criteria for substance use disorder.[6] The Epidemiological Catchment Survey, one of the most comprehensive evaluations of the prevalence of mental illness and addictive disorders, found that 47% of people with schizophrenia and 56% of people with bipolar disorder met criteria for substance use disorder.[7] Over the past 10 years, research has verified that mood and anxiety disorders are associated with risk for substance use. Bipolar disorder had the strongest association with alcohol and drug use. The findings confirmed previous studies.[8] Patients with a diagnosis of panic disorder and social phobia also had a considerable risk for co-occurring disorder.[8] In a study of patients with schizophrenia and bipolar disorder, the majority had experienced at least one traumatic event in their lives, and 43% met criteria for PTSD.[5]

Palliative Assessment of Substance Use Disorder

Early palliative care referrals for people with co-occurring disorders will help establish consistency in relationships during life-threatening illness. Previous substance abuse history should be included as part of the comprehensive assessment. Risk factors for co-occurring disorders, such as schizophrenia, bipolar disorder, and PTSD, should alert the palliative APRN to evaluate the patient for symptoms of substance use. Screening tools can facilitate assessment. Observing behaviors consistent with substance abuse (e.g., frequent missed appointments, poor medication adherence, and financial and legal problems) and obtaining additional information from family members, case managers, and significant others can alert clinicians to potential problems. Mental health and addiction specialists need to be part of the team caring for patients with co-occurring disorders. Using a nonjudgmental approach with the patient will facilitate honest reporting of actual use.

Schizophrenia

The main symptoms of schizophrenia are disorganized speech, impairment in thought process, delusions, and hallucinations. The illness usually begins in late adolescence or early adulthood. The condition is chronic and worsens with stress or substance use. Key treatment issues include antipsychotic medication, compliance, and abstinence from alcohol and drugs.[9] The illicit drugs most frequently used by people with schizophrenia are alcohol, cocaine, and cannabis.[10] Studies have found that co-occurring substance use contributes to poor treatment outcomes, more frequent hospitalizations, medication noncompliance, and increased risk for violence compared to patients with schizophrenia alone.[10] The consequences of comorbid conditions include high rates of treatment noncompliance, relapse, distorted perceptions and cognition, suicidal ideation, homelessness, HIV, hepatitis C, and liver and gastrointestinal disease.[11] Low motivation to reduce substance use is another contributing factor, and this may destabilize the mental illness, undermine treatment adherence, and contribute to psychosocial instability. Family and friends will also experience distress, tension, and conflict within those relationships.[12]

There are four hypotheses as to why substance use rates are so high in patients with schizophrenia: (1) drug abuse can act as an environmental stressor and in vulnerable individuals can precipitate the onset of schizophrenia; (2) substance use offers self-medication for the psychotic symptoms of schizophrenia; (3) patients with schizophrenia have poor cognitive abilities, low social education and vocational functioning, and difficult life circumstances; and (4) people with schizophrenia use substances to counteract the dysfunction of the dopaminergic brain reward circuitry.[10]

Cannabis is the only substance with a demonstrable correlation between use and subsequent development of schizophrenia.[9] Kelly's review of the research revealed an increased risk of psychotic symptoms in individuals using cannabis.[13] When individuals with schizophrenia were asked their reasons for using alcohol and cannabis, answers included to relieve boredom, depression, and anxiety or to relax.[10]

Pharmacologic Treatment for Substance Use Disorder and Schizophrenia

Second-generation antipsychotic agents are more effective for treatment of substance use disorder and schizophrenia. Clozapine appears to be the most effective antipsychotic for reducing alcohol, cocaine, and cannabis use among individuals with schizophrenia.[13] Two studies found that risperidone and olanzapine produced significant reductions in cravings for and use of cocaine, but results of randomized controlled trials have been mixed.[9] The medications that have been approved by the U.S. Food and Drug Administration (FDA) for alcohol treatment—disulfiram, naltrexone, and acamprosate—have also been studied and were shown to be effective in this patient population.[9]

Methadone and buprenorphine are effective in treating opioid addiction in patients with schizophrenia. Close collaboration with methadone maintenance clinics and mental health clinicians is imperative. Treatment of opioid addiction with opioid agonist therapy often puts patients at risk for undertreated pain. Patients will need their baseline opioid requirement met and additional opioid therapy to treat their pain. Doses will need to be higher and more frequent to achieve pain control. Patients will not get pain relief from morphine if their opioid receptors are fully occupied by buprenorphine. Buprenorphine may need to be switched to long-acting morphine or converted to methadone.[14]

Psychotherapy Interventions for Substance Use Disorder and Schizophrenia

Patients with co-occurring disorders require integrated treatment of both their mental illness and substance use. A review of the literature on patients with substance use disorder and schizophrenia revealed that treatment should focus on patient engagement, motivational interviewing, cognitive-behavioral therapy (CBT), and family therapy, along with long-term programs and relapse prevention strategies.[13] Comprehensive services, such as peer support, family education, housing, and vocational rehabilitation, assist with decreasing substance use (Table 34.1).

Palliative APRNs must work collaboratively with their mental health counterparts. Engaging patients in treatment can be difficult, because people with schizophrenia can have an aloof or strange manner. Treatment should focus on routinely asking patients specifically about their use of substances. Often patients with a dual diagnosis deny both of their illnesses, making it difficult for them to comply with treatment or benefit from interventions. Psychotic patients with substance use disorder have impaired short-term thinking. Contacts should be brief to keep social stimulation low. Using a passive, friendly, low-key approach can avoid confrontation, challenge, and criticism. Patients with schizophrenia have trouble learning new information. Educational material needs to be simple and concrete. Repetition is beneficial to help clients understand the connection between substance use and negative consequences. Families benefit from education about both illnesses as well. Involving the family decreases the incidence of relapse and improves outcomes for all illnesses.[5]

Bipolar Disorder

Bipolar disorder is characterized by unpredictable shifts in mood, energy, and activity levels that range from manic to depressive periods that interfere with an individual's ability to function. Mania is characterized by an elevated, expansive, or irritable mood, grandiosity with increased energy, decreased sleep, pressured speech, racing thoughts, impulsivity, distractibility, psychomotor agitation, hallucinations, and delusions.[4]

A review of data of Australians diagnosed with affective or anxiety disorders found that persons with affective disorders had a fivefold increased risk of developing alcohol dependence and people with bipolar disorder had a sevenfold increase.[15] The lifetime prevalence of bipolar disorder and substance use disorder is 60.3%,[16] although the reasons for high rates of substance use in bipolar disorder are not well understood. Similar to schizophrenia, possible explanations include self-medication of mood symptoms, genetic predisposition, substance use leading to bipolar disorder, and overlapping symptoms resulting in mood disorder. The high substance use in this population supports multiple pathways of causality.[16]

Individuals with bipolar disorder and substance use disorder have more frequent hospitalizations, more depressive episodes, and earlier onset of illness. Lack of adherence to treatment in patients with bipolar disorder and substance use disorder has been documented in a number of studies. It leads to delayed symptomatic and functional recovery. Patients with current or past substance use disorder report lower quality of life, have increased aggression and violence, and have a significantly higher lifetime rate of suicide.[16]

Pharmacologic Treatments for Substance Use Disorder and Bipolar Disorder

Pharmacologic treatment of comorbid substance use and bipolar disorder involves mood stabilizers or atypical antipsychotics

Table 34.1 Psychosocial Interventions for Substance Use Disorder and PTSD

Cognitive-behavioral therapy (CBT)	A therapeutic approach that seeks to modify negative, self-defeating thoughts and behaviors. CBT addresses client's cognitive distortions to help promote change. Distortions in thinking are increased with more severe co-occurring disorder. Helps develop coping skills.	Used in substance use disorders and PTSD.
Motivational interviewing	A goal-directed, client-centered counseling method that works on facilitating and engaging in motivation to change behavior. Helps people explore and resolve ambivalence in relation to substance use.	
Seeking Safety	Present-focused therapy to help person attain safety from trauma, PTSD, and substance use. Consists of 25 topics with focus on safety and integrated treatment.	
Exposure therapy	Individuals tell their story, including all sensory and affective responses. The benefits of exposure therapy include exposure to fear over time without any danger, decrease in hyperarousal state, promotion of corrective information into the trauma memory, and help re-establishing the world as a safe place.	Used in PTSD.
Psychoeducation	Education about common symptoms of mental illness and substance use.	Provides information about common symptoms following a traumatic event and helps normalize the response. Education can include information about physiological responses, and psychological responses, such as depression or panic symptoms.

From references 4, 9, 13, 16.

and antidepressants and use of medication like naltrexone for alcohol use disorder.[13] Pettirati and colleagues[16] reviewed the literature for treatment of bipolar disorder and substance use disorder and found a few well-controlled, double-blind studies. Five studies evaluated alcohol and one study evaluated cocaine use. Results of trials revealed no additional benefit from antipsychotic medication in reducing bipolar disorder, with the exception of quetiapine. Medication added to decrease substance use did not reduce substance use in this population.[16] The majority of studies found none of the following medications to be effective: divalproex, bupropion, lamotrigine, gabapentin, and nefazadone.[13]

Psychotherapy Interventions for Substance Use Disorder and Bipolar Disorder

An integrated treatment approach is needed to treat both bipolar disorder and co-occurring substance use disorder. Patients receive comprehensive counseling and treatment of both disorders, which includes case management, vocational rehabilitation, family counseling, housing, and medication. CBT approaches have been used in the treatment of this population. Integrated group therapy is designed for patients with substance use and bipolar disorder. The treatment targets mood and substance use symptoms and has reduced symptoms in outcome measures.[13] Interpersonal Social Rhythm Therapy, developed for bipolar disorder, focuses on helping bipolar patients gain insights between mood and interpersonal events. Structure is an important part of the routine. Outcome studies show that this treatment helps prevent relapse and improve relationships and life satisfaction over medication alone.[13]

PTSD

Case Study 2

MM was a 54-year-old woman who presented with cervical cancer and a history of PTSD resulting from childhood sexual abuse and a sexual assault as a teenager. She had recurrent hospitalizations for increased pain, with positive toxicology screens for cocaine. She lived with her 19-year-old daughter and her boyfriend. MM refused substance abuse treatment and refused to talk to the psychiatrist but was able to engage with the palliative APRN and the social worker. She shared her story of a long history of childhood trauma, abusive relations, and cocaine use. She had tried numerous treatment programs with minimal success; her longest time sober was about 4 years. She relapsed recently due to her cancer diagnosis. MM was vigilant in her home and the hospital, fearful she would be robbed or assaulted. She had difficulty sleeping and had intermittent nightmares; she had trouble recalling the content of her dreams, but they left her feeling anxious and frightened. The nursing staff had difficulty dealing with her behaviors, and education regarding PTSD and substance use disorder was given by the palliative APRN. A comprehensive treatment plan was developed with specific strategies the nurses could use to help with MM's behaviors.

One time when MM came into the clinic for treatment, she was barely responsive; a toxicology screen was positive for cocaine. Prescribing medications for her pain while maintaining her safety became an issue for the providers. Numerous pain regimens were tried, none of which helped her pain: she was sedated, was difficult to arouse, or was in excruciating pain.

The palliative APRN's treatment for MM's substance use disorder and PTSD incorporated risk-reduction strategies. These strategies included a locked box in the home, frequent visits by nurses, and a limited quantity of medication. The palliative APRN continued to treat MM's pain aggressively, as well as her other symptoms of anxiety, depression, and difficulty sleeping. MM was taught and began to incorporate deep breathing and mindfulness techniques. MM's course remained chaotic, with recurrent missed appointments and hospital admissions for increased pain. The palliative APRN closely monitored MM at home through frequent communication with the visiting nurse. When she was found to be using cocaine, she was treated with compassion and understanding. More structure was put into place in the home, with increased visits and closer monitoring to provide as safe an environment as possible. At the end of her life, MM was able to be comfortable and reconciled with one of her estranged daughters. She died peacefully with good pain control.

PTSD differs from other psychiatric disorders in that its cause can be attributed to a life-threatening event, such as a natural disaster, sexual abuse, war, childhood trauma, serious accidents, or life-threatening illness. While it is adaptive to have strong reactions when one's life is threatened, once the threat has subsided, the reactions should resolve. In individuals with PTSD, however, this reaction continues even when the threat has subsided.[17]

The traumatic experiences interfere with processing in the brain, and the dysregulation of neural processing disrupts adaptive processing as mediated by genetics, social supports, developmental period in life, and other factors.[18] PTSD was originally classified as an anxiety disorder, but it is now considered a trauma- and stress-related disorder, with three key elements:

1. Re-experiencing the trauma—intrusive images or thoughts, nightmares, reliving the experience in feelings or actions, and experiencing intense psychological distress when reminded of the trauma through visual, olfactory, auditory, or environmental cues.[4,17,19]

2. Avoidance or numbness response—three or more of the following: avoidance of situations or places that remind the person of the traumatic event, suppressing feelings, not being able to remember the event, decreased participation in outside activities, and feeling detached from others.[4,17,19]

3. Increased arousal—at least two of the following symptoms: difficulty falling or staying asleep, angry outbursts, difficulty concentrating, hypervigilance, and an exaggerated startle response.[4,17,19]

Prevalence of PTSD

Trauma is thought to be the basis for many mental and physical disorders.[5,20] While more than half of people experience a traumatic event, lifetime prevalence rates for PTSD in the United States are approximately 7% for women and 4% for men.[20] Women are twice as likely to develop PTSD than men, but recent military samples found there is less difference in rates of PTSD between men and women.[21] Recent international studies confirm that not everyone exposed to trauma develops PTSD.[20] In one study,

PTSD was associated with other psychiatric disorders, such as major depressive disorder, anxiety disorder, bipolar disorder, and specific phobias.[21] Suicide risk is significant in people with PTSD.[5] Individuals with PTSD and another psychiatric disorder have impaired function and decreased quality of life; the combination can contribute to poor physical health and chronic pain.[5]

Risk Factors for PTSD

The Diagnostic and Statistical Manual of Mental Disorders, 5th edition (DSM-V) has divided risk factors into pretraumatic, peritraumatic, and post-traumatic categories.[4] Variables that have consistently been found to be related to PTSD include female gender, adverse childhood experiences, previous psychiatric problems, lower socioeconomic status, lower education, and minority race. Peritraumatic risk factors include severity of exposure. Post-traumatic risk factors involve social supports and subsequent life stress. Persons in certain occupations are at risk for traumatic reactions and therefore are more vulnerable to PTSD, such as members of the military, law enforcement officers, and mental health professionals.[4] The prevalence of the disorder in the veteran population varies depending on the war.[17]

PTSD and Medical Illness

Typically, people think of PTSD as being related to a traumatic event, such as combat, criminal or sexual assault, natural disaster, or an accident. But the reaction of intense fear, helplessness, or horror and the symptoms of intrusive thoughts, avoidance or numbing, and arousal can also be applied to being diagnosed with a life-threatening illness. In 1994, the American Psychiatric Association added to the criteria for PTSD life-threatening illness (e.g., myocardial infarction, stroke, hemorrhage, heart failure, HIV, and cancer).[22-25] The most abundant data on PTSD in patients with serious illness exist in the diagnosis of cancer, especially breast cancer. A correlation has been shown between chronic pain and PTSD. Table 34.2 discusses PTSD in different populations.

The key point for palliative APRNs is that PTSD can arise in a small percentage of individuals with a wide range of illnesses. Medical trauma can also act as a trigger for people with a predisposition to PTSD. It may take the form of noncompliance with treatment, mood symptoms, or distance from medical providers and family members. It is important to identify patients at risk and help them seek psychiatric treatment.

PTSD and Substance Use Disorder

The relationship between PTSD and substance use disorder has become more evident over the past few decades. Epidemiological studies show high rates of coexisting PTSD and substance use disorder. In people with lifetime PTSD, the lifetime incidence of substance use disorder is estimated to be 21% to 43%, compared to 8% to 25% with substance use disorder alone.[26] Three-quarters of combat veterans with lifetime PTSD also met criteria for alcohol dependence.[26] Patients with PTSD and substance use disorder may use harder drugs, such as amphetamines and opioids.[13] An Australian epidemiological survey found that 24% of individuals with PTSD had amphetamine use disorder and 33% had opioid dependence, compared with 5.4% and 5.2% of individuals with alcohol and cannabis use disorder.[27]

There are several hypotheses about the high correlation between PTSD and substance use disorder. These include the environmental and psychosocial mechanism, the self-medication hypothesis, the susceptibility hypothesis, and the high-risk hypothesis (that childhood trauma increases the risk of PTSD).[26]

PTSD at the End-of-Life

Feldman and Periyakoil have written extensively about PTSD and the end-of-life.[28-30] People with a previous trauma history are at

Table 34.2 PTSD in Different Populations

Condition	Incidence
Cancer	Breast cancer is diagnosis most studied. Prevalence ranges from 0% to 12%.
	Prevalence in cancer patients other than breast cancer ranges from 0% to 22%.
	Stage of disease and type of treatment are not linked to PTSD.
	Risk factors include younger individuals with previous psychiatric diagnosis and women.
	A preexisting coping style of dissociation has been shown to be correlated with PTSD development.
ICU	Prevalence 14–59% (variability in methodology).
	Predictors of PTSD: previous psychiatric illness, greater benzodiazepine administration, and post-ICU memories that remain frightening or psychotic.
Myocardial infarction	Prevalence 0–16%.
	Intrusive thoughts and avoidance are the main symptoms.
Cardiac surgery	10.8–18% intrusive symptoms.
	Predictors of PTSD: previous psychiatric history, female gender, lower social supports, length of ICU stay.
Heart transplant	Patients with PTSD in first year are 13 times more likely to die within 3 years after the transplant.
HIV	Prevalence 30–35%.
	Previous trauma may predispose people to risk-taking behavior.
Chronic pain	Prevalence 15–35%. Pain may serve as a traumatic reminder of the event and make PTSD worse.

From references 22–25, 46.

a higher risk for PTSD in the setting of terminal illness.[28] The feelings of helplessness or horror may be triggers, or the terminal illness itself could trigger symptoms. An avoidant coping style makes communication about prognosis and end-of-life issues difficult. Among men, irritability and anger, along with suspiciousness and disregard of medical advice, may lead to futile treatments. Life review could induce recurrent memories, leading to potential retraumatization.[29,30] Palliative APRNs must be knowledgeable about PTSD symptoms and strategies to deal with the behavior.

Assessment of PTSD

The palliative APRN should assess for PTSD by asking brief, direct questions about trauma exposure and PTSD symptoms as part of a routine assessment. Often insomnia or sleep disturbance is the initial complaint. Asking specific questions about sleep disturbance, including flashbacks, nightmares, or feelings of hyperarousal or agitation, can help identify traumatic events and their impact on quality of life. By detecting PTSD and encouraging the patient to seek treatment, the palliative APRN can develop collaborative relationships with mental health professionals to help care for these complex, challenging patients.

PTSD screening tools assess subjective distress caused by traumatic events (Box 34.1). Primary care physicians and the Department of Veterans Affairs use a four-item screening tool. Respondents are asked to identify a specific stressful life event and indicate how distressed they have been by it in the past week. Items are rated from 0 to 4, with 4 being extreme. The test is positive if the person answers yes to three of the four questions. Individuals screening positive should be fully assessed in a structured clinical interview.[31]

Management of PTSD

Palliative nurses and psychiatrists focus on improving quality of life and relieving suffering. They embrace a respectful, individualized approach to care and work with patients to help cope with stresses in their life.[3] The treatment plan is revised based on changes that have occurred. A comprehensive assessment includes current symptoms, past history, psychiatric and substance use history, responses to medication and prior treatments, social supports, and religious or spiritual affiliations. This is done by the interdisciplinary team.

The palliative APRN must use an interdisciplinary approach in individuals with PTSD and life-threatening illness. These may be challenging patients due to their avoidance behavior and distrust. The palliative APRN may have intense emotional reactions to a patient, especially if the patient is confrontational, suspicious, and nontrusting. It may be hard not to take the patient's behaviors personally. Close collaboration or referral to psychiatry and mental health providers may provide support and assistance to palliative APRNs for issues related to countertransference. Additional education and reassurance will promote comfort in caring for these patients.

There are several strategies to managing this patient population. One strategy is the development of a therapeutic relationship and creation of a safe environment. Feldman[30] in his model suggests that if time is limited, immediate distress should be treated by active listening, providing reassurance, and offering assistance with solving problems. Another strategy is to work with the patient, family, and mental health providers to avoid triggering PTSD symptoms. The palliative APRN can provide and reinforce education about PTSD symptoms and their management.[29] Another strategy is to encourage patients to use coping techniques that they are learning or have learned, such as mindfulness, slow deep breathing, progressive muscle relaxation, meditation, and yoga, to decrease arousal.[29]

Sleep hygiene and regular exercise are important measures in dealing with disrupted sleep, as the patient's condition and energy level permit. Avoidance of nicotine, caffeine, alcohol, and large meals a few hours before bedtime; a quiet, cool environment; and a regular schedule help the patient develop a regular sleep pattern. Medications for insomnia include non-benzodiazepine agents, such as trazodone, antihistamines, zolpidem, zaleplon, and eszopiclone.[32]

Psychotherapy for PTSD

The "gold standard" treatment for PTSD is psychotherapy. Trauma-focused psychotherapies that include directly confronting anxiety triggers, cognitive restructuring techniques, and relaxation techniques are the most effective. Prolonged exposure, cognitive processing therapy, and eye movement desensitization and reprocessing (EMDR) are examples of these therapies.[32] Other therapies include imagery rehearsal, brief psychodynamic therapy, and hypnosis.[32]

Feldman points out that exposure-based CBT and EMDR require time for a session, which hospice and palliative care patients may not be physically able to tolerate given their disease state or other treatments. These therapies often cause the symptoms to worsen before they improve and may contribute to increased suffering at the end-of-life.[29] He suggests a model that relies on cognitive-behavioral techniques to maximize quality of life.[30] Resolving immediate problems, active listening, providing psychoeducation about anxieties and PTSD symptoms, and offering practical assistance with problem solving represent the first step. The second step is to enhance coping skills through education, mindfulness-based acceptance skills, relaxation and breathing exercises, problem-solving interventions, and communication

---

Box 34.1 PTSD Screen

In your life, have you ever had an experience so frightening, horrible, or upsetting that in the past month you:

1. Had nightmares about it or thought about it when you did not want to?

2. Tried hard not to think about it or went out of your way to avoid situations that reminded you of it?

3. Were constantly on guard, watchful, or easily startled?

4. Felt numb or detached from other activities or your surroundings?

The screen is positive if patient answers yes to three of these; this indicates a need for consultation or follow-up.

Prins A, Ouimette P, Kimerling R, et al. The primary care PTSD screen (PC-PTSD): Development and operating characteristics. *Primary Care Psychiatry.* 2003; 9: 9–14.

and social skills training. Family members are also schooled in these techniques. If time permits, the third step is to treat trauma issues through exposure-based or trauma-focused methods, given the patient's prognosis and energy levels.[30]

Researchers are now looking at the concept of resilience and how it can serve as a protective and adaptive mechanism in the face of adversity. Resilience is the ability to overcome or successfully adapt after trauma or severe stress.[33] It is characterized by the ability to "bounce back" from harm, rather than to be immune to harm.[34] Resilience is associated with active coping styles and a positive outlook, exercise, humor, moral courage, social support systems, religion and spirituality, and cognitive flexibility.[35] Cognitive flexibility means finding the silver lining in adverse situations and remaining flexible in one's problem-solving approaches.[35]

Resilience differs from recovery as it often involves a period of dysfunction lasting several months or more, followed by a gradual return to previous functioning.[33] Resilience is best understood as a set of possible trajectories.[33,34] They include relapsing or remitting, in which symptoms display a cyclical course; delayed dysfunction, in which PTSD or other trauma-related disorders develop after a considerable time has passed; and chronic dysfunction.[33]

Palliative APRNs can promote the use of strategies that encourage resilience, including problem solving and managing feelings.[35] Other interventions include physical activity, depending on the patient's stage of illness and energy level; using humor and optimism; and developing nurturing relationships and reconnecting with family and friends even at the end-of-life. Chaplains can be extremely helpful to assist patients and family members find meaning in their life.

Pharmacologic Treatment of PTSD

The palliative APRN should implement concomitant use of medications in conjunction with psychotherapy techniques. The intent of medication therapy is to improve function while addressing comorbidities, such as depression and generalized anxiety disorder, and to decrease symptoms, such as insomnia, nightmares, panic attacks, rage, and paranoia.[36] Selective serotonin reuptake inhibitors (SSRIs) have been found to be the most effective first-line treatment for PTSD.[36] Sertraline and paroxetine are still the only treatments approved by the U.S. Food and Drug Administration and have the most research to support their use. These medications ameliorate the symptoms of re-experiencing, avoidance or numbness, and hyperarousal and can be used to treat other comorbid disorders, such as depression, social phobia, and obsessive–compulsive disorder. There is increasing evidence that other antidepressants, anticonvulsants, and antipsychotic medications may be effective as well.

Because of the significant comorbidity of substance use disorders in patients with PTSD, the use of benzodiazepines is avoided.[36] These medications can contribute to the emotional numbing of PTSD and prevent integration of the traumatic event.[36] Clonazepam has not been demonstrated to benefit those with PTSD. However, if benzodiazepines are necessary, clonazepam is less likely to contribute to dependency than other benzodiazepines because of its long half-life.[37]

Numerous medications have been found to be effective for sleep disruptions in PTSD, including buspirone, gabapentin,

topiramate, imipramine, phenelzine, mirtazapine, prazosin, clonidine, and multiple atypical antipsychotics.[38] In newer research trials, medications like D-cycloserine, a partial agonist at the NMDA glutamate receptor, have been shown to enhance the effectiveness of exposure therapy for both social phobia and acrophobia. While there have not yet been human studies published on D-cycloserine in PTSD, it has shown efficacy in animal models of conditioned fear.[38]

A growing body of literature shows that glutamate plays a major role in mediating the stress response and the formation of traumatic memories and PTSD pathophysiology. Ketamine, an MDS glutamate receptor, has been shown to deliver a rapid antidepressant effect when given intravenously or intranasally in spray form. Researchers found that intravenous ketamine (0.5 mg/kg) was associated with a significant and rapid reduction of PTSD symptom severity when compared to active control.[39]

Other Treatments for PTSD

A systemic review of the literature suggests encouraging results for the use of acupuncture in PTSD patients. However, the ability to make conclusions about the efficacy of acupuncture is hindered due to the limited size of the studies.[40] One study found improvement in PTSD following 12 weeks of biweekly acupuncture sessions, with treatment benefits lasting up to 24 months.

Repetitive transcranial magnetic stimulation is another treatment being researched for PTSD. This is a noninvasive method in which a magnetic coil is held against specific areas of the brain to stimulate underlying neurons. Karsen reviewed primary studies evaluating the effectiveness of this therapy for PTSD. All studies found it to be an effective and well-tolerated treatment that requires additional research.[41]

Treatments for PTSD and Substance Use Disorder

The goal of dual diagnosis treatment is to assist the client in achieving recovery and abstinence. People with serious medical illness may not be able to attend these programs and achieve abstinence. The treatment goal then becomes decreasing use of alcohol or drugs, facilitating compliance with medical treatment, and making sure that pain and other symptoms are treated.[1]

Alleviating suffering is the role of the palliative APRN. Whether suffering is disease-related or within the individual, the focus remains the same: to improve quality of life. Close collaboration with mental health providers is important in helping the patient and his or her family achieve their goals throughout the trajectory of illness. While abstinence is the ideal, this may not be possible. Often the goal is to help provide structure and assistance in managing compliance with both medical and dual diagnosis treatment.

Table 34.1 outlines psychosocial interventions for PTSD and substance use disorder. The literature provides support for improvement in substance use disorder and PTSD symptoms when concurrent treatment is provided. No findings indicated harm to clients when integrated treatment was provided. There is no one specific "gold standard" treatment.[42] Exposure-based therapies and a CBT approach have been studied and found to be beneficial in reducing PTSD symptoms. The CBT approach incorporates psychoeducation, breathing, and exposure therapy. Treatments that use exposure-based therapies have not led to worsened substance use outcomes.[38] Non-exposure-based psychosocial treatment approaches include Seeking Safety, CBT, motivational interviewing, motivational enhancement theory, and 12-step programs.[38]

SSRIs have been helpful for PTSD, but there is little evidence they are effective for treating alcohol dependence.[13] Naltrexone and disulfiram were found to be effective in reducing drinking days per week and increasing nondrinking days compared to the placebo-treated group.[13] Petrakis compared naltrexone and disulfiram in male veterans with alcohol dependence and psychiatric disorders. Patients receiving either disulfiram or no disulfiram were randomized further to naltrexone or placebo. Individuals receiving naltrexone, disulfiram, or both medications had decreased drinking days per week or increased days sober. Patients receiving disulfiram had decreased PTSD symptoms.[43] Trafton found that opiate substitution therapy was equally effective for reducing use of other substances among opioid-dependent patients who had PTSD.[44] There is a strong need for further testing of both psychosocial treatments and medications to treat co-occurring PTSD and substance use disorder.

Mental health clinicians can help manage the comorbidities associated with dual diagnosis, help assess patients' behavior, offer medication and psychotherapy, and help the palliative care team address issues of countertransference. If mental health support is not available, or if patients are reluctant to seek mental health follow-up, the palliative APRN should provide education about PTSD and substance use disorder, schedule regular follow-ups, and monitor symptoms while managing pain. Specifically, the palliative APRN should ask open-ended questions, recognize vague answers, and be gently persistent in obtaining specific information. The palliative APRN can promote a therapeutic relationship, enhance the patient's motivation to stop or decrease substance use, and strengthen the patient's coping skills and social support to help with recovery. The APRN should avoid confrontation and be flexible and understanding if the patient is resistant, expressing empathy through reflective listening. It is important to set realistic goals and establish a commitment to honesty at the beginning of the relationship.

Outside the context of terminal illness, there are high rates of relapse with drug use and addiction. Risk-reduction strategies that decrease adverse consequences associated with ongoing substance use should be employed. These strategies should include weekly sessions to build a therapeutic relationship and assess symptom control and addiction-related concerns. More frequent visits allow for smaller quantities of drugs to be provided, which may decrease the patient's temptation to divert from the plan. It is important to have a written policy about early refills and to explain the policy at the beginning of treatment.[45]

Written agreements are helpful tools in outlining expectations of the patient and the provider, but no research studies show any benefit from this approach.[45] These agreements should clearly state the role of each member of the team and expectations for the patient. Procedures regarding prescription loss and replacement should be outlined in the agreement, with the understanding that to receive medication the patient must be compliant with appointments and any increase in dose requires prior communication with the provider. Periodic urine toxicology screens should be obtained to identify illicit and prescribed drugs and to recognize early drug-related behavior. If a positive drug screen occurs, guidelines for continued treatment should include more frequent visits and smaller quantities of drugs.[1] In the palliative care setting, tolerant policies toward use and relapse should be used to achieve a balance between enabling and rigidity.[1,45] The patient should be encouraged to attend Alcoholics Anonymous or Narcotics Anonymous and other 12-step programs if he or she has the physical capability.

Conclusion

Substance use disorder and PTSD are the most common of all co-occurring disorders. Eighty percent to 90% of patients who seek treatment for substance use have experienced trauma. Women are twice as likely to experience PTSD than men.[4,5] People with PTSD and substance use disorder tend to use and become more dependent on cocaine, cannabis, alcohol, and prescription drugs. People report using medications to help reduce symptoms of depression, anxiety, and hyperarousal.[38] Patients with severe co-occurring disorders and PTSD are susceptible to other mental and medical disorders, relationship problems, housing and employment issues, and social isolation with ineffective coping skills.[5]

The palliative APRN has an essential role in screening for PTSD and substance use disorder when assessing all patients and should be aware of high-risk patient populations. Development of a close collaborative relationship with mental health professionals is important to provide comprehensive care. Some of the strategies used by the palliative APRN include development of a therapeutic relationship, active listening, providing assistance with problem solving, and promoting resilience. Resilience can be strengthened in patients by encouraging exercise appropriate to their level of functioning, incorporating humor and optimism into their coping strategies, fostering nurturing relationships, and encouraging reconnection with family and friends. The use of nonpharmacologic interventions is important. Risk-reduction strategies should be incorporated into the treatment plan through the use of frequent visits, small amounts of medication, and close communication with other providers.

Information regarding the pharmacologic management of patients with a dual diagnosis is essential. The APRN must know the common symptoms and management techniques for depression, anxiety, and sleep disturbance specific to PTSD and substance use disorder. Relaxation techniques can be incorporated into treatment to alleviate symptoms of hyperarousal.

The palliative APRN relieves suffering and promotes healing by treating PTSD and substance use disorder and providing support for the family. Identifying individual strengths, enhancing the patient's motivation to stop or reduce substance use, strengthening coping skills, helping the patient maintain hope, and enhancing social supports can improve the patient's quality of life.

References

1. Rogal L, Starr T, Passik S. Substance abuse and alcohol. In: Holland J, Jacobsen P, Loscalzo M, McCorkle R, eds. *Psycho-oncology*. 2nd ed. New York, NY: Oxford University Press; 2010: 340–7.
2. Gepper C, Volk A. Serious substance use problems and palliative care. In: Cooper D, Cooper J, eds. *Palliative Care within Mental Health*. London: Radcliffe Publishing; 2012:251–64.
3. Foti M. Palliative care for the patients with serious mental illness. In: Chochinov H, Breitbart W, eds. *Handbook of Psychiatry in*

Palliative Medicine. 2nd ed. New York, NY: Oxford University Press; 2012:113–22.

4. American Psychiatric Association. *Diagnostic and Statistical Manual of Mental Disorders.* 5th ed. Arlington, VA: American Medical Association; 2013.

5. Klott J. *Integrated Treatment for Co-Occurring Disorders.* Hoboken, NJ: John Wiley and Sons; 2013.

6. Substance Abuse and Mental Health Services Administration. Revised Estimates of Mental Illness from the National Survey on Drug Use and Health: Mental Health Findings. Retrieved from http://www.samhsa.gov/data//2K13NH/NSDUH148/sr148. Published 2013. Accessed May 8, 2014.

7. Regier DA, Farmer ME, Rae DS, et al. Comorbidity of mental disorders with alcohol and other drug abuse: Results from the Epidemiologic Catchment Area (ECA) Study. *JAMA.* 1990; 264: 2511–8.

8. Swendsen J, Conway K, Degenhardt L, et al. Mental disorders as risk factors for substance use, abuse and dependence: results from the 10-year follow-up of the National Comorbidity Survey. *Addiction.* 2010; 105: 1117–28.

9. Green A. Treatment of schizophrenia and comorbid substance abuse: pharmacological approaches. *J Clin Psychiatry.* 2007; 67(suppl 7): 31–5.

10. Thomas P, Daum I. Comorbid substance use disorder in schizophrenia: A selective overview of neurobiological and cognitive underpinnings. *Psychiatry Clin Neurosci.* 2013; 67: 367–83.

11. Horsfall J, Cleary M, Hunt G, Walter G. Psychosocial treatments for people with co-occurring severe mental illness and substance use disorders (dual diagnosis): a review of empirical evidence. *Harv Rev Psychiatry.* 2009; 17(1): 24–34.

12. Van Nimweegen LJ, de Haan L, van Beveren NJ, van der Heim M, van den Brink W, Linszen D. Effect of olanzapine and risperidone on subjective well-being and craving for cannabis in patients with schizophrenia or related disorders: a double-blind randomized controlled trial. *Can J Psychiatry.* 2008; 53(6): 400–5.

13. Kelly T, Daley D, Douaihy A. Treatment for patients with comorbid psychiatric disorders. *Addictive Behaviors.* 2012; 37: 11–24.

14. Alford D, Comptom P, Samet J. Acute pain management for patients receiving maintenance methadone or buprenorphine therapy. *Ann Intern Med.* 2006; 144(2): 127–34.

15. McEvoy M, Grove R, Slade T. Epidemiology of anxiety disorders in the Australian general population: findings of the 2007 Australian National Survey of Mental Health and Wellbeing. *Australian J Psychiatry.* 2011; 45(11): 957–67.

16. Pettinati H, O'Brien C, Dundon W. Current status of co-occurring mood and substance use disorders: A new therapeutic target. *Am J Psychiatry.* 2013; 170(1): 23–9.

17. PTSD overview. National Center for PTSD. Available at www.PTSD.va.gov. Accessed July 2014.

18. Wheeler K. The neurophysiology of trauma. In: *Psychotherapy for the Advanced Practice Nurse.* 2nd ed. New York, NY: Springer Publishing; 2014: 1706–2937 [Kindle edition].

19. Duckworth K. Post-traumatic stress disorder. National Alliance on Mental Illness. 2013. Available at www.nami.org/factsheets/ptsd_facesheet.pdf. Accessed June 21, 2014.

20. Norris F, Slone L. Epidemiology of trauma and PTSD. In: Friedman M, Keane T, Resick P, eds. *Handbook of PTSD: Science and Practice.* 2nd ed. New York: Guilford Press; 2013: 2960–3548 [Kindle edition].

21. Petrakis I, Rosenheck R, Desai R. Substance use comorbidity among veterans with posttraumatic stress disorder and other psychiatric illness. *Am J Addictions.* 2011; 20: 185–9.

22. Kangas M, Henry J, Bryant R. The course of psychological disorders in the first year after cancer diagnosis. *J Consult Clin Psychol.* 2005; 73(4): 763–8.

23. Kangas M, Milross C., Taylor A, Bryant R. A pilot randomized controlled trial of a brief early intervention for reducing

24. Davydow D, Gifford J, Desai S, Needham D, Bienveno J. PTSD in general ICU survivors: a systematic review. *Gen Hosp Psychiatry.* 2008; 30: 421–34.

25. Tedstone J, Tarrier N. PTSD and medical illness. *Clin Psychol Rev.* 2003; 23: 409–48.

26. Schafer I, Najavitis L. Clinical challenges in the treatment of patients with posttraumatic stress disorder and substance abuse. *Curr Opin Psychiatry.* 2007; 20: 614–8.

27. Liang W, Chikritzhs T. Affective disorders, anxiety disorders and the risk of ETOH dependence and misuse. *Br J Psychiatry.* 2011; 199: 219–24.

28. Feldman D. Periyakoil VJ. Posttraumatic stress disorder at the end of life. *J Pall Med.* 2006; 9: 213–8.

29. Feldman D. Posttraumatic stress disorder at the end of life: Extant research and proposed psychosocial treatment approach. *Pall Support Care.* 2011; 9: 407–18.

30. Feldman D, Sorocco K, Bratkovice K. Treatment of posttraumatic stress disorder at the end of life: Application of the stepwise psychosocial palliative care model. *Pall Support Care.* 2014; 12: 233–43.

31. Prins A, Ouimette P, Kimerling R, et al. The Primary Care PTSD Screen (PC-PTSD): Development and operating characteristics. *Primary Care Psychiatry.* 2003; 9: 9–14.

32. Warner C, Warner C, Appenzeller G, Hoge C. Identifying and managing PTSD. *Am Fam Physician.* 2013; 88(12): 827–34. Erratum in: *Am Fam Physician.* 2014; 89(6): 424.

33. Norris G, Tracy M, Galea S. Looking for resilience: Understanding the longitudinal trajectories of responses to stress. *Soc Sci Med.* 2009; 68: 2190–8.

34. Layne CM, Warren, JS, Watson PJ, Shalev AY. Risk vulnerability resistance and resilience: toward an integrative conceptualization of posttraumatic adaptation. In: Friedman M, Keane T, Resick P, eds. *Handbook of PTSD: Science and Practice.* 2nd ed. New York, NY: Guilford Press; 2014: 497–520 [Kindle edition].

35. Haglund M, Cooper N, Southwick S, Charney D. Six keys to resilience for PTSD and everyday stress. *Curr Psychiatry.* 2007; 6(4): 23–30.

36. Berlin R. Anxiety disorders. *The Carlat Psychiatry Report.* 2011; 9(7): 1–2.

37. Wheeler K. Stabilization for trauma and dissociation. In: *Psychotherapy for the Advanced Practice Nurse.* 2nd ed. New York, NY: Springer Publishing; 2014 [Kindle edition].

38. Cukor J, Olden M, Lee F, Difede J. Evidence-based treatments for PTSD, new directions, and special challenges. *Ann NY Acad Sci.* 2010; 1208: 82–9.

39. Feder A, Parides M, Murrough J, et al. Efficacy of intravenous ketamine for treatment of chronic posttraumatic stress disorder. *JAMA Psychiatry.* 2014; 71(6): 681–8.

40. Kim Y, Heo I, Shin BC, Crawford C, Kang H, Lim J. Acupuncture for posttraumatic stress disorder: A systematic review of randomized controlled trials and prospective clinical trials. *Evidence Based Complementary and Alternative Medicine.* 2013. Article ID 615857. Available at http://dx.doi.org/10.1155.2013/615857.

41. Karsen EF, Watts BV, Holtzheimer PE. Review of the effectiveness of transcranial magnetic stimulation for post-traumatic stress disorder. *Brain Stim.* 2014; 7(2): 151–7.

42. US Department of Veterans Affairs. VA/DoD Clinical Practice Guideline for Management of Post-Traumatic Stress. US Department of Veterans Affairs website. http://www.heathquality.va.gov. Published 2010. Accessed August 8, 2014.

43. Petrakis I, Ralevski E, Nich C, et al. Naltrexone and disulfiram in patients with alcohol dependence and current depression. *J Clin Psychopharmacol.* 2007; 27: 160–5.

44. Trafton JA, Minkel J, Humphrey K. Opioid substitution treatment reduces substance use equivalently in patients with and without posttraumatic stress disorder. *J Studies Alcohol*. 2006; 67: 228–35.

45. Starr T, Rogak L, Casper D, Kirsh K, Passik S. Palliative care for patients with substance abuse and patients with personality disorders. In: Chochinov H, Breitbart W, eds. *Handbook of Psychiatry in Palliative Medicine*. 2nd ed. New York, NY: Oxford University Press; 2012: 122–38.

46. Andrykowski M, Kangas M. PTSD associated with cancer diagnosis and treatment. In: Holland J, Jacobsen P, Loscalzo M, McCorkle R, eds. *Psycho-oncology*. 2nd ed. New York, NY: Oxford University Press; 2010: 348–57.

CHAPTER 35

Grief and Bereavement

Susan Lysaght Hurley and Elizabeth Archer-Nanda

Key Points

◆ Grief theories have evolved to reflect a much more nuanced individual experience, dispelling common myths that there is a specific timeframe for recovery from loss and that failing to confront one's feelings always leads to delayed grief.

◆ Complicated grief is relatively uncommon; but left untreated, it has serious health consequences.

◆ Advanced practice registered nurses (APRNs) should pay attention to self-care around grief and bereavement, particularly while working closely with terminally ill individuals and families.

Case Study: Preparing for Bereavement

Mr. P was a 56-year-old male recently diagnosed with amyotrophic lateral sclerosis (ALS). He lived with his wife and their two children, ages 13 and 17. He struggled with symptoms of weakness for many months before finally receiving the diagnosis in the previous month. His neurologist asked for an outpatient palliative care evaluation for symptom management (weakness, muscle cramping, dyspnea) and to discuss Mr. P's overall goals of care. Following a thorough evaluation of his symptoms, Mr. P expressed great frustration and anger at this diagnosis. He and his wife had just finished marriage counseling and were finally "turning the corner." He felt guilty about the burden that would be placed on her and their children. He had never considered advance care planning and was unsure whether he ever wanted to be on a ventilator for support.

The palliative APRN met with Mr. and Mrs. P for an initial consult. In preparing for the visit, the APRN recalled the many types of loss that Mr. P might be experiencing: physical abilities, loss of his previous role his role as husband and father, and intrapsychic loss of his prior self-image. The APRN probed gently about how the couple were doing with the new diagnosis and encouraged initial conversations about advance directives as a way to help Mr. and Mrs. P plan for the future in a meaningful way. This addressed bereavement by acknowledging loss and helped to prepare for a good quality of death that would meet Mr. P's goals and would also reduce the caregiver burden and risk for complicated bereavement for Mrs. P. The APRN referred this family to a child-life specialist to address loss and bereavement issues with their children.

Case Study: Complicated Grief

Ann's husband Richard had died nearly 18 months earlier during an operation to remove a cancer-related blockage of his colon. While Ann and Richard understood the risks of the surgery, they decided to proceed in the hope that it would improve his quality of life. After his death, Ann withdrew from many of her community activities, including church. She found herself wondering what would have happened had she urged Richard not to have the surgery: could they have made do with his health stressors and reduced quality of life? She reached out to multiple healthcare providers searching for answers and continued to struggle because none could provide her the answer she desired—that she should have prevented Richard from going through with the procedure.

Ann was socially isolated, felt empty, and was struggling to regain a sense of purpose since her husband's death. She said that her children had attempted to reach out, but she didn't think they understood the depth of her pain. She expressed frustration with her situation and wondered if there was anything left worth living for. However, she denied any intent for self-harm, and although she no longer participated in church, she still viewed suicide as against her beliefs.

Ann increasingly found it difficult to keep up with the maintenance of her home and did not want to bother her children for help. She kept repeating that things would be different if only she had talked Richard out of the procedure.

Ann's longing and her guilt related to her husband's death, her preoccupation with the circumstances surrounding the death, and her avoidance of activities were consistent with persistent complex bereavement disorder (PCBD). Given the pervasiveness with which the grief-related experience affected Ann and the length of her suffering, she needed intervention for her complicated persistent bereavement.

The palliative APRN who cared for Richard contacted Ann 6 months after his death. She found Ann severely struggling with her husband's death and helped her find a referral for mental health services. Ann participated in a bereavement support group, received individual psychotherapy, and started taking an antidepressant. Two years after her husband's death, she returned to some of her previous activities and again enjoyed attending social and family gatherings.

The World Health Organization (WHO) reports that 56 million individuals died worldwide in 2012.[1] Each death is believed to directly affect an average of five individuals.[2] Accordingly, an estimated 280 million persons experienced a bereavement in 2012. Although grief-related responses can contribute to painful feelings in the bereaved, fewer than 20% of individuals will develop complicated bereavement requiring intervention for symptoms, with up to 5% of individuals developing PCBD.[3-5] The WHO views bereavement support as an intrinsic aspect of palliative care.[6]

APRNs witness death across the lifespan, and palliative APRNs are uniquely positioned to encounter complications from the impact of death in their daily practice. Located at the front line of the healthcare system, palliative APRNs meet a broad range of health- and illness-related demands, including grief and bereavement assessment. Like any physical symptom in palliative care, grief and bereavement exist on a continuum and may be easy to identify and manage or may become unrelenting, making optimal relief difficult to achieve. Palliative APRNs will encounter a myriad of grief-related experiences: loss of independence and functioning, role strain or changes, disruption in relationships, and the death of an individual. To expertly manage grief and bereavement in palliative care, the APRN should (1) understand common terms, including loss, grief, and bereavement, (2) be able to identify normal grief from complicated bereavement, (3) know when to refer patients for psychiatric services, and (4) employ strategies for self-care.

Common Terms

Common terms for death-related experiences of grief and bereavement are used interchangeably, which may lead to further confusion.[7] **Grief** is defined as an "emotional response to any loss"[8(p 537)] and includes the emotional state and actions of those who experience loss. **Bereavement** is defined as "an event [or] state of being."[8] Special consideration is given to different types of grief, including anticipatory, complicated, and disenfranchised. **Anticipatory grief** refers to the emotions and feelings before an anticipated loss.[8,9] **Complicated grief** "is a chronic, impairing form of grief brought about by interference with the healing process."[7(p 122)] Complicated grief was not officially recognized in the *Diagnostic and Statistical Manual of Mental Disorders*[10] until its most recent edition,[5] when PCBD was recognized as a formal diagnosis. **Disenfranchised grief** is hidden and socially marginalized (e.g., suicide, AIDS).[8]

Loss

Further characterization of loss provides an important framework for understanding the nature of loss and its impact on the palliative care patient. One useful description of six major types of loss is found in the pastoral care literature[11] (Box 35.1).

Patients and families may experience some or all of these types of loss with advanced illness. Acknowledging the possibility of multiple types of loss may help the APRN support a patient and family as they navigate a new diagnosis or worsening prognosis. Additional consideration of categorization of loss is based on the nature of the loss: avoidable and unavoidable loss, temporary and permanent loss, actual and imagined loss, anticipated and unanticipated loss, and leaving versus being left.[11]

Box 35.1 Major Types of Loss

1. **Material loss**: loss of an item or an environment with particular attachment

2. **Relationship loss**: the end of opportunities to engage with others

3. **Intrapsychic loss**: loss of an image of oneself or hopes for the future

4. **Functional loss**: loss of control of bodily function

5. **Role loss**: loss of an individual role in a social group

6. **Systemic loss**: loss experienced by a system (e.g., family or workplace)

Adapted from Mitchell KR, Anderson H. *All Our Losses, All Our Griefs: Resources for Pastoral Care*. Louisville, KY: Westminster John Knox Press; 2010.

Theoretical Models

Theories of grief abound in the literature and have evolved over the past century, with research aimed at confirming or challenging theoretical views.[12] A brief review of some of the key models of grief may assist those working in hospice and palliative care to provide comprehensive bereavement care to their patients.[13] Early psychological models, stage theories, and more current nuanced theoretical models contribute to an overall complex perception of grief.

One of the earliest psychoanalytical theories of grief is found in Freud's writings, where he described grief as profound sadness and something requiring "the work of mourning" to sever ties with a loved one.[14] This work included a process that eventually returns the person to a fully functional, engaged state. Adaptations to loss and coping with grief were first described with a proposed delineation between depression and grief.[15] Attachment theory followed this work. Most notably, Bowlby[16] proposed that children and adults form attachments, and that when one experiences a loss, there is constant tension between that attachment and the knowledge that the person is actually gone. Bowlby also introduced phases of grieving and the concept that early loss influences later loss (e.g., a person experiencing multiple losses in childhood may react more strongly to a loss in adulthood).[12]

The stages of grief were further developed by many theorists, but Elisabeth Kübler-Ross is the best known in both professional and lay literature.[12,15,17] Kübler-Ross hypothesized the stages of grief with the task-oriented goals necessary to achieve relief from mourning.[17] The stages of grief are denial, anger, bargaining, depression, and acceptance. While these stages are somewhat informative about the human experience of grief, not every individual experiences all of these reactions, or in that specific order.[12]

Many of these earlier models stressed breaking off the relationship with the deceased, yet more current research guided theorists to uncover relationships that extend beyond death, just in a different form.[13] Neimeyer's theory of meaning reconstruction[18] stressed the importance of an individual's overall life story and suggested that a loss challenges the overall coherence of that life story. Coping with a loss therefore means uncovering how to keep meaning consistent over time. More recent models include Bonanno's four-component model and the dual-process model outlined by Stroebe and Schut, both of which strive to achieve balance in the aftermath of loss.[19,20] Bonanno[19] emphasized minimizing the negative emotions associated with loss and focusing on positive experiences as a way to cope with loss. Bonanno also devised a framework of four components of grief that influence how an individual responds to loss: the context of the loss, the subjective meaning of the loss, changes in how one maintains a connection with the loved one over time, and the role of coping. Stroebe and Schut[20] describe two processes—loss-oriented and restoration-oriented coping—that individuals use to adapt to loss. Loss-oriented coping involves the memories of the individual and features the loss itself, whereas restoration-oriented coping focuses on present life events.

Numerous other theorists and disciplines have influenced the development of current bereavement research, including neurobiopsychosocial scientists, social constructionists, and cognitive-behavioral clinicians.[8,21] Further research is needed to continue testing these models in a variety of populations and for varying types of loss.

Complicated Grief

Grief is recognized as a normal response that, in most instances, should not be considered pathological.[4] In acute grief, clinicians can anticipate that the intensity of emotional symptoms will dissipate over time, with enhanced integration and a reduction in disturbances to functioning.[4] The person with complicated grief exhibits clinically significant deviations from cultural norms with respect to time and/or the degree to which areas of functioning are affected;[15] a prolonged duration of grief and heightened symptom intensity are characteristics of complicated grief.[4]

Immediately following the death of a loved one, individuals may struggle with ruminative thoughts about the loved one or loss, intense anxiety, or sadness.[8] Grief in the early phase of bereavement is variable and marked by surges of emotions, which can contribute to the clinical difficulty of distinguishing between "normal" and bereavement-related complex disorders. As part of the bereavement process, bereft individuals are faced with the challenge of integrating into the world without the physical presence of the individual who died.[9] Bereaved individuals may experience an intense longing for the deceased, which manifests as emotional pain with a fluctuating preoccupation with the deceased.[5]

Those experiencing loss are at risk for complications resulting from grief. Family caregivers experience burden and are at risk for increased emotional and physical sequelae.[22] Caregivers experiencing loss are at risk for a myriad of negative outcomes, including worsening health, weight loss, and functional impairment.[23] Social and emotional decline is also associated with bereavement, as is loneliness and a reduction in well-being.[23] Although most individuals will naturally start to experience a more integrated grief, allowing them to re-engage in activities, including those bringing pleasure, some will go on to develop PCBD. The prevalence of PCBD is approximately 2.4% to 4.8%.[5]

PCBD criteria include experiencing the death of a loved one, persistent symptoms, difficulties in functioning, or a "bereavement reaction [that] is out of proportion to or inconsistent with

cultural, religious, or age-appropriate norms."[5(p 790)] While symptoms of PCBD can occur as early as the initial months after the death, the onset of full symptoms can appear after several years.[5] The disorder exists across the lifespan; younger children may exhibit symptoms through play or in their behavior.[5] Symptoms must be present for 12 months in adults and 6 months in children to meet criteria for PCBD. Individuals must have a specific number of symptoms; symptoms range from perseverative thoughts of the deceased, rejection of the death, profound avoidance of situations where the loss will be felt, and wishing for death themselves, to an inability to make plans.

Risk factors for the development of PCBD include being female, a history of mood disorders, limited social support, financial distress, positive caregiving experiences, pessimistic tendencies, and the specific conditions of the death (e.g., suicide, dying at a hospital vs. home).[4,5,23,24] Those who do not accept the death initially may be at higher risk.[25] Studies have shown that the risk for complicated grief is higher in individuals who have suffered the loss of a child or life partner. In such cases, the risk for depressive and anxious disorders is present for up to a decade after the death.[7] Individuals with comorbid mood and anxiety disorders are at increased risk to develop PCBD, with associated concern for disability, poor health, and suicidality.[4]

Functional consequences include risks for the development of serious medical illnesses secondary to poor attention to self-care needs, reduced quality of life, and challenges in work and social functioning.[5] APRNs must have a full understanding of the diagnostic criteria for PCBD, so they can differentiate it from other potential diagnoses, including normal grief, depressive disorders, post-traumatic stress disorder (PTSD), and separation anxiety disorder. Shear[7] described a primary difference between acute grief and depression as symptoms occurring *in relation to the deceased*. For example, those with depression may express a general lack of interest in others and activities, but those with acute grief will have those symptoms *because* of the death. The palliative APRN should also understand the risk for comorbid major depressive disorder, PTSD, and substance abuse disorders and should refer individuals, as appropriate, to mental health professionals for ongoing assessment and treatment. Individuals with a history of depression or a vulnerability to depressive disorders may benefit from treatment with an antidepressant.[5]

Assessment

APRNs are intimately involved with individuals approaching end-of-life, as well as their caregivers. In 2002, the national practice standards from the National Organization of Nurse Practitioner Faculties called for the expanded capability for nurses to identify grief responses as a health concern and to address these needs.[26] Individuals in palliative APRN roles are uniquely positioned to assess patients who are experiencing bereavement and to facilitate the grief process through a grief assessment. A full understanding of the development of PCBD provides the foundation for accurate assessment and referral for treatment. Clinicians must balance cultural norms and assess aspects of normal grief while evaluating symptoms common to both depression and bereavement.[27]

Grief ebbs and flows, with periods of intensity remitting with eventual acceptance of the loss and integration. Complicated grief ensues when this integration does not occur. Individuals with complicated grief exhibit impaired healing. Their ability to adapt and accept the loss as final is delayed by prolonged symptoms and increased intensity. Individuals at risk for complicated grief may catastrophize about the future without the loved one or struggle with "what ifs" while describing difficulty with self-blame or a belief that they could have done something different to prevent the death of their loved one.[7,28] They may struggle to identify sources of meaning and purpose in life and may or may not have suicidal thoughts.[7] They often experience intense longing and intrusive rumination related to the circumstances of the loss, struggle to identify sources of meaning, avoid specific activities that the deceased enjoyed, and spend prolonged periods of time going through items reminding them of the deceased.[7,28]

The bereavement experience is complex and often occurs along with other medical illnesses, making it difficult to differentiate the symptoms.[3] Individuals with persistent bereavement are at risk for a number of comorbidities, including cardiovascular disease, cancer, depressive disorders, anxiety disorders, post-traumatic stress, and sleep impairment.[28] Safety assessments should be conducted in individuals with higher levels of bereavement and other risk factors for suicide.

The APRN may use screening instruments to identify individuals who need a higher level of bereavement services or a mental health referral. The most current version of a commonly used tool, the Inventory of Complicated Grief, is referred to now as the PG-13.[29] It measures symptoms along four domains: separation, cognitive/emotional, social impairment, and duration. The PG-13 also has a pre-loss version to use with patients prior to an expected death.[30] The Texas Revised Inventory of Grief is another screening tool commonly used in bereavement research.[31] One study suggests that using a screening tool 6 months following the death of a loved one will predict two-thirds of cases of PCBD at 1 year.[32]

With many individuals at high risk for comorbid medical and mental illnesses, the APRN must become adept at identifying and screening individuals at risk. Forming a network of resources among palliative care, primary care, and mental health providers is increasingly important to meet the complex and changing needs of this population.

Bereavement-related stressors may be comorbid with other psychiatric disorders and can trigger major depression, post-traumatic stress, or substance use disorders.[28] Bereavement with comorbid depressive and anxiety disorders is associated with negative physical and mental health outcomes,[8] making it important to fully explore differential diagnoses. Symptom overlap exists between PCBD and major depression, including feelings of sadness, decreased functional status, and suicide risk.[28]

Strategies for Management

Strategies for management by the palliative APRN include interdisciplinary death preparation, bereavement support, and, when necessary, referral to mental health services. When death is expected, the interdisciplinary team can provide counseling and support to patients and families by establishing a safe plan of care for the impending death, helping caregivers plan for imminent death and ensuring that they have resources to manage the care if at home, and determining risk for complicated grief in advance of the death.[33] Decreasing caregiver stress, use of advance directives,

and focusing on the quality of a loved one's death improve the bereavement outcomes of caregivers.[34] Involvement by hospice may reduce the caregiver's risk for complicated grief, so palliative APRNs should refer patients for hospice services when appropriate.[9,35] Following the death, palliative APRNs can provide additional support by working with an interdisciplinary team to ensure that contact is made with the family to answer any questions and express sympathy for the loss.[9,33] For the team, it may be important to also review the death together to evaluate the quality of death and case management.

For individuals at risk for developing debilitating mental health comorbidities, mental health services may help decrease their maladaptive ways of coping. Many individuals with bereavement-related disorders are never referred to a mental health professional.[8,36] The lack of a bereavement-related disorder in previous versions of the DSM has likely contributed to this gap in care. Now that a bereavement-related disorder is included, there is hope that more individuals will be connected to mental health services aimed at assisting in the grieving process.

Mental health therapies may include bereavement support groups, group therapy, individual psychotherapy, or medication management.[37] Drawing from theoretical models of grief, mental health providers work with individuals to establish necessary tasks for integrating a new sense of meaning and purpose after loss. Mindfulness of individual risk factors and physical and emotional sequelae provides the foundation for achieving optimal recovery; multimodality interventions are often necessary.

Self-Care

An often-forgotten component of grief and bereavement is the care of the palliative practitioner.[38] Increasingly, interdisciplinary colleagues are paying closer attention to the personal demands of palliative care and the effect of witnessing so much loss.[39] Palliative APRNs should pay close attention to personal, situational, and patient factors that may put them at higher risk for feeling as though they have more control over a situation than is possible. Examples of these factors include identification with a patient or family member, a longstanding relationship with a patient, or complicated patient–family dynamics.[39] Four ways to address complicated feelings about the loss of a patient are (1) name the feeling, (2) accept the normalcy of the feeling, (3) reflect on the emotion, and (4) consult a trusted colleague.[39] Using appropriate team support, paying close attention to emotions, particularly in difficult cases, and seeking individual counseling when necessary may help prevent burnout in palliative APRNs.

Conclusion

The field of palliative care and bereavement research continues to grow. A need exists for evidence-based interventions for care of bereaved individuals. Wide-reaching educational efforts should focus on dissemination of best practices in bereavement care for clinicians in primary care, palliative care, psychiatry, and oncology. While the evolution of bereavement research continues along with the creation of evidence-based practice guidelines, APRNs should evaluate the needs of each patient and make referrals to appropriate specialists, including mental health practitioners, to fully support patients struggling with the grieving process.

References

1. World Health Organization. The top 10 causes of death. World Health Organization website. http://www.who.int/mediacentre/factsheets/fs310/en/index2.html. n.d. Accessed September 1, 2014.

2. Zisook S, Pies R, Iglewicz A. Grief, depression, and the DSM-5. *J Psychother Pract*. 2013; 19(5): 386–96. doi: 10.1097/01.pra.0000435037.91049.2f

3. Holland JC, Friedlander MM. Oncology. In: Blumenfeld M, Strain JJ, eds. *Psychosomatic Medicine*. Philadelphia, PA: Lippincott Williams and Wilkins; 2006: 121–44.

4. Shear MK, Simon N, Wall M, et al. Complicated grief and related bereavement issues for DSM-5. *Depress Anxiety*. 2011; 28: 103–17. doi: 10.1002/da.20780.

5. American Psychiatric Association. *Diagnostic and statistical manual of mental disorders*. 5th ed. Washington, DC: American Psychiatric Association; 2013.

6. World Health Organization. Cancer: WHO Definition of Palliative Care. World Health Organization website. http://www.who.int/cancer/palliative/definition/en/. n.d. Accessed September 1, 2014.

7. Shear MK. Grief and mourning gone awry: pathway and course of complicated grief. *Dialogues Clin Neurosci*. 2012; 14(2): 119–28.

8. Lichtenthal WG, Prigerson HG, Kissane DW. Bereavement: a special issue in oncology. In: Holland JC, Breitbart WS, Jacobsen PB, Lederberg MS, Loscalzo MJ, McCorkle R, eds. *Psycho-Oncology*. New York, NY: Oxford University Press; 2010: 537–43. doi: 10.1093/med/9780195367430.001.0001

9. Zisook S, Irwin SA, Shear MK. Understanding and managing bereavement in palliative care. In: Chochinov HM, Breitbart W, eds. *Psychiatry in Palliative Care*. New York, NY: Oxford University Press; 2009: 202–19.

10. American Psychiatric Association. *Diagnostic and Statistical Manual of Mental Disorders*. 4th ed. Washington, DC: American Psychiatric Association; 2000.

11. Mitchell KR, Anderson, H. *All Our Losses, All Our Griefs; Resources for Pastoral Care*. Louisville, KY: Westminster John Knox Press; 2010.

12. Wortman CB, Boerner K. Beyond the myths of coping with loss: prevailing assumptions versus scientific evidence. In: Friedman HS, ed. *The Oxford Handbook of Health Psychology*. New York, NY: Oxford University Press; 2011:438–76. doi: 10.1093/oxfordhb/9780195342819.013.0019

13. Wright PM, Hogan NS. Grief theories and models: applications to hospice nursing practice. *J Hosp Palliat Nurs*. 2008; 10(6): 350–6.

14. Freud S. Mourning and melancholia. In: Strachey J, ed. *The Standard Edition of the Complete Works of Sigmund Freud*. Vol. 14. London: Hogarth Press; 1957:152–70.

15. Guldin MB. Complicated grief: a challenge in bereavement support in palliative care: an update of the field. *Prog Palliat Care*. 2014; 22(3): 136–42. doi: 10.1179/1743291X13Y.0000000078.

16. Bowlby J. Process of mourning. *Int J Psychoanal*. 1961; 42: 317–40.

17. Kübler-Ross E. *On Death and Dying*. New York, NY: Springer; 1969.

18. Neimeyer RA. Narrative strategies in grief therapy. *J Construct Psych*. 1999; 12(1): 65–85.

19. Bonanno GA, Kaltman S. Toward an integrative perspective on bereavement. *Psychol Bulln*. 1999; 125: 760–86.

20. Stroebe M, Schut H. The dual process model of coping with bereavement: rationale and description. *Death Stud*. 1999; 23: 197–224. doi: 10.1080/074811899201046

21. Kacel E, Gao X, Prigerson HG. Understanding bereavement: what every oncology practitioner should know. *J Support Oncol*. 2011; 9(5): 172–80. doi: 10.1016/j.suponc.2011.04.007.

22. Holtslander LF, McMillan SC. Depressive symptoms, grief, and complicated grief among family caregivers of patients with advanced cancer three months into bereavement. *Oncol Nurs Forum*. 2011; 38(1): 60–5. doi: 10.1188/11.ONF.60-65.

23. Shear MKS, Ghesquiere A, Glickman K. Bereavement and complicated grief. *Cur Psych Rep*. 2013; 15(406): 1–7. doi: 10.1007/s11920-013-0406-z.

24. Lobb EA, Kristjanson LJ, Aoun SM, Monterosso L, Halkett GKB, Davies A. Predictors of complicated grief: A systemic review of empirical studies. *Death Stud*. 2010; 34(8): 673–698. doi: 10.1080/07481187.2010.496686

25. Holland JM, Futterman A, Thompson LW, Moran C, Gallagher-Thompson D. Difficulties accepting the loss of a spouse: a precursor for intensified grieving among widowed older adults. *Death Stud*. 2013; 37(2): 126–44. doi: 10.1080/07481187.2011.617489

26. White P, Ferszt G. Exploration of nurse practitioner practice with clients who are grieving. *J Am Acad Nurs Pract*. 2009; 21(4): 231–40. doi: 10.1111/j.1745-7599.2009.00398.x

27. Fox J, Jones KD. DSM-5 and bereavement: the loss of normal grief. *J Counsel Dev*. 2013; 91: 113–9. doi: 10.1002/j.1556-6676.2013.00079.x.

28. Simon NM. Treating complicated grief. *JAMA*. 2013; 310(4): 416–23. doi: 10.1001/jama.2013.8614.

29. Prigerson HG, Horowitz MJ, Jacobs SC, et al. Prolonged grief disorder: psychometric validation of criteria proposed for DSM-V and ICD-11. *PLoS Med*. 2009; 6(8): e1000121. doi:10.1371/journal.pmed.1000121

30. Kiely DK, Prigerson H, Mitchell SL. Health care proxy grief symptoms before the death of nursing home residents with advanced dementia. *Am J Geriatr Psychiatry*. 2008; 16: 664–73. doi: 10.1097JGP.0b013e3181784143.

31. Faschingbauer TR. *Texas Revised Inventory of Grief Manual*. Houston, TX: Honeycomb Publishing; 1981.

32. Thomas K, Hudson P, Trauer T, Remedios C, Clarke D. Risk factors for developing prolonged grief during bereavement in family carers of cancer patients in palliative care: a longitudinal study. *J Pain Symp Manag*. 2014; 47(3): 531–41. doi: 10.1016/j.jpainsymman.2013.05.022.

33. Hudson P, Remedios C, Zordan R. Guidelines for the psychosocial and bereavement support of family caregivers of palliative care patients. *J Palliat Med*. 2011; 15(6): 696–702. doi: 10.1089/jpm.2011.0466.

34. Garrido MM, Prigerson HG. The end-of-life experience: modifiable predictors of caregivers' bereavement adjustment. *Cancer*. 2014; 120: 918–25. doi: 10.1002/cncr.28495.

35. Wright AA, Keating NL, Balboni TA, Matulonis U, Block SD, Prigerson HG. Place of death: Correlations with quality of life of patients with cancer and predictors of bereaved caregivers' mental health. *J Clin Oncol*. 2010; 28: 4457–64. doi: 10.1200/JCO.2009.26.3863.

36. Litchenthal WG, Nilsson M, Kissane DW, et al. Underutilization of mental health services among bereaved caregivers with prolonged grief disorder. *Psych Serv*. 2011; 62(10): 1225–9. doi: 10.1176/appi.ps.62.10.1225.

37. Currier JM, Neimeyer RA, Berman JS. The effectiveness of psychotherapeutic interventions for bereaved persons: a comprehensive quantitative review. *Psychol Bull*. 2008; 134(5): 648–61. doi: 10.1037/0033-2909.134.5.648.

38. Feldstein MA, Gemma PB. Oncology nurses and compounded grief. *Cancer Nurs*. 1995: 18(3): 228–36.

39. Meier DE, Back AL, Morrison RS. The inner life of physicians and care of the seriously ill. *JAMA*. 2001; 286(23): 3007–14. doi:10.1001/jama.286.23.3007.

CHAPTER 36

Symptom Clusters in Various Solid Tumors and Hematologic Malignancies

Tara A. Albrecht

Key Points

- Patients with cancer experience multiple concurrent symptoms that are known to cause a high symptom burden.

- Symptom clusters have deleterious effects on patient health outcomes, including multiple domains of quality of life and ultimately mortality.

- Identification and clinical management of symptom clusters may significantly improve quality of life and health outcomes for patients with cancer.

Introduction

Historically, attention to both symptom research and interventions has focused on single physiological or psychological symptoms experienced by patients with cancer.[1] Yet, it is widely recognized that patients with cancer most often experience multiple concurrent symptoms as a result of their disease and its treatment.[1,2] This pattern suggests that there may be a common mechanism among the symptoms that commonly cluster.[3] The previous use of a single-symptom approach, while important, limits the ability to fully understand and subsequently manage these multiple symptoms in patients with cancer.[1,4,5]

Recognition of this limitation in symptom science has stimulated a shift toward investigating concurrent related symptoms and outcomes for patients with cancer.[1,6] The interest in examining the interaction of multiple symptoms can be traced back to a seminal article written by nurse researchers Dodd, Miaskowski, and Lee in 2001.[1] The following year, the National Institutes of Health held the *State-of-the-Science Conference on Symptom Management in Cancer: Pain, Depression, and Fatigue* that produced recommendations for new directions in research with multiple symptoms.[7] Since that time, there has been a surge in the number of conceptual papers,[8–15] literature reviews,[16–20] and methodological papers,[3,21–23] as well as evolving work on the clinical assessment[24,25] and treatment[26–29] of symptom clusters in patients with cancer. This evolution in symptom research continues to provide the knowledge necessary to fully understand the complex interaction of the multiple symptoms that patients with cancer experience over the entire disease trajectory.[30,31] This is information that is critical to the advanced practice registered nurse (APRN) who must effectively assess and treat the symptom clusters in these patients.

This chapter first reviews the definition of symptom clusters and discusses the current understanding of the symptom cluster etiology. The essential elements of the APRN's clinical assessment of symptom clusters and the challenges related to this assessment are then discussed. Included is a discussion on the deleterious consequences that result when multiple symptoms are not effectively managed in patients with cancer. Symptom clusters in breast cancer and lung cancer as well as hematologic cancers are reviewed. Finally, the current evidence to guide the APRN's management of symptom clusters is addressed.

Case Study

Mrs. Anderson was a 45-year-old woman recently diagnosed with stage II cancer of the right breast. A right mastectomy was performed 2 weeks earlier, with a plan for adjuvant therapy after her incisions healed. During a follow-up clinic visit with Jenny, her APRN, Mrs. Anderson was found to be experiencing severe fatigue (6/10), with accompanying lack of energy (7/10) and pain (5/10), and she reported increased physical weakness. She also reported memory issues and difficulty concentrating while at work. Mrs. Anderson told Jenny that she was feeling really frustrated trying to manage her life, including keeping her house running, getting her children to all the places they needed to be, and coordinating her work responsibilities. Her husband was very supportive, but she was having a hard time imagining how she would be able to do everything once she began her chemotherapy.

Jenny recognized that Mrs. Anderson was experiencing several common symptom clusters that have been identified in women with breast cancer. She also knew that many of these symptoms are very important to monitor as they have long-term implications for quality of life and health outcomes. Jenny was aware that the concurrent use of palliative care during curative treatment in patients with multiple concurrent symptoms has been shown to improve patient outcomes. She explained to Mrs. Anderson that, given the extent of her symptoms and the impact they were having on her life, she believed that Mrs. Anderson would benefit from seeing palliative care specialists, who would work with her through her treatment as her symptoms persisted. Jenny then made a referral for Mrs. Anderson to visit the palliative care clinic at her hospital. She would be seen by a multidisciplinary team comprised of a doctor, a nurse practitioner, a psychologist, and a physical therapist, who would work together to develop a treatment plan for her.

Mrs. Anderson was a little nervous when she arrived at the clinic. She completed the ESAS to rate her current symptoms. She reported her pain as 5/10, tiredness 6/10, nausea 2/10, depression 5/10, anxiety 4/10, drowsiness 5/10, appetite 4/10, well-being 4/10, and shortness of breath 0/10. In the "other" category, she rated her loss of concentration at 6/10.

Anna, the palliative nurse practitioner, recognized that many of these symptoms could be related, so a comprehensive approach was initiated to support Mrs. Anderson through her treatment. Anna reassured Mrs. Anderson that her symptoms could change as she began treatment. Anna taught her about self-care management strategies, physical activity, specialized strengthening exercises, and pharmacologic treatment. She told Mrs. Anderson that she would be followed throughout her treatments and that she should call if she felt worse. Follow-up visits for Mrs. Anderson included repeat administration of the ESAS as well as a detailed assessment of what changes (better and worse) had occurred since her last visit.

Symptom Clusters

A symptom cluster was initially defined as the occurrence of three or more concurrent and related symptoms.[1,6] This definition has evolved to include two or more symptoms that co-occur and are related.[8] While symptom clusters are by definition related, and may share a mechanism or etiology,[4] they do not need to.[1,13] For example, in the common cluster of fatigue, pain, and insomnia, fatigue may be caused by the cancer and treatment, pain by the cancer growth, and insomnia by either the treatment or distress.[1] Regardless, once a symptom cluster is identified, it should occur predictably.[32]

Compared with other specialties in healthcare, such as psychiatry, where historically the identification of symptom clusters has been used to diagnose a disease, the identification of symptom clusters in patients with cancer is often more complicated.[9] This is because symptom clusters in oncology are influenced by a variety of systemic factors, including the disease, treatments, the presence of multiple related and nonrelated symptoms, symptom domains, as well as more arbitrary factors, including the selection of assessment instruments and statistical methods for analysis, all of which may create variations in symptom cluster identification.[13,14,17] Also, individual symptoms can present in multiple symptom clusters.[9,23] As our understanding of symptom clusters continues to evolve, it is important to recognize that symptom clusters are dynamic and for any given cancer may vary over time, just as the prevalence and severity of symptoms may change over time as a result of such transient factors as treatment trajectory and disease state.[13,17]

Mechanisms of Symptom Clusters

Early work in animal models uncovered a biological basis for the presence of what is now commonly referred to as sickness behavior.[33] Sickness behavior is driven by a biobehavioral interaction, mediated by cytokines, hormones, or other immunomediators.[32,34] Common symptom clusters observed in these animal models include fatigue, decreased appetite, sleep disorders, and depression.[14] Building on this theory, Cleeland and colleagues suggested that symptoms experienced by patients with cancer may also share a similar biological mechanism.[35] Subsequently, there has been a growing body of evidence to suggest that some of the most common psychoneurological symptoms, including pain, fatigue, sleep disturbance, depressive symptoms, and cognitive disturbance, likely occur as a result of common neuromolecular pathways. These pathways include dysregulation of the hypothalamic-pituitary-adrenocortical axis, pro-inflammatory cytokines, and serotonin receptors.[15,34,36] While this psychoneurological symptom cluster model likely explains mechanisms responsible for some of the more common symptom clusters that patients with cancer experience, it does not explain the mechanism for all observed symptom clusters.[34] The science of symptom clusters and other biological mechanisms that may be responsible for symptom clusters is still developing. Therefore, while theoretical and supporting biological studies offer convincing evidence that at least some of the common symptom clusters identified in patients with cancer share biological mechanisms, more research is necessary to provide broader and more conclusive evidence that explains whether there are additional shared mechanisms for other prevalent symptom clusters.

Identification of Symptom Clusters

Symptom clusters are identified one of two ways: through either clinical observation or statistical analysis. Given that the entire science of symptom clusters is still developing, the current methods of identification are a work in progress as well. Thus, APRNs, particularly those who work with patients with cancer, must understand the current evidence as well as the current limitations of this evidence.

Clinical Observation

The assessment of symptom clusters in the clinical setting requires empirical identification through observation by the APRN.[3] This method relies upon the APRN's comprehensive understanding of the multidimensional etiologies and relationships of symptoms as well as his or her ability to conduct a thorough clinical assessment. Therefore, the APRN must be familiar with the patient's disease, past and current treatment, psychosocial resources, and comorbid conditions.[25]

There are several different approaches to the assessment of symptoms, including symptom screening, multidimensional assessments, and the use of technology to capture the patient's symptoms.[25,37] Each approach has benefits and limitations. Box 36.1 lists a variety of approaches to the assessment of symptoms and provides details regarding specific features, uses, and limitations.[25]

One challenge to assessing symptom clusters in the clinical setting is the selection of instruments that are not only valid and

Box 36.1 Approaches to Symptom Assessment	
Approach	**Description: Features, Use, and Limitations**
Screening and assessment of intensity	Features: Ask whether patient is experiencing a symptom. Then rate each symptom on scale with 0 = no symptom and 10 = worst possible symptom.
	Use: Screening for multiple symptoms
	Limitations: Does not allow for in-depth assessment of symptoms
Traditional symptom assessment	Features: PQRST Model (provoking factors, quality, region of symptom, severity, timing of onset, peak, and duration for each symptom)
	Use: Gaining deeper perspective on individual symptoms
	Limitations: Focus is on individual symptoms
Multi-symptom assessment tools	Features: This method utilizes a comprehensive, reliable symptom assessment tool to measure symptom presence, intensity, and affect of many diverse symptoms
	Use: These tools are helpful in assessing the overall symptom experience and emerging symptom patterns
	Limitations: These tools are not specific to the assessment of symptom clusters and may be considered as a global symptom measure that requires complex scoring. These tools are suitable to use in symptom research but are generally not practical for frequent clinical use.
Focused assessment of identified clusters	Features: Symptom assessment based upon broad clinical knowledge of disease and treatment
	Use: Tailored assessment to known or expected symptoms
	Limitations: Other symptoms co-occurring with specific symptoms may be missed
Disease- or treatment-specific multi-symptom assessment	Features: Using specific symptom assessment tools based upon assessment of specific expected cancer-related symptoms
	Use: Measurement of known or suspected symptom clusters
	Limitations: Only specific symptoms will be assessed and treated.
Sentinel symptoms	Features: Assessment focuses on the most problematic symptom or a trigger symptom that may lead to development of other related symptoms.
	Use: The presence of sentinel symptoms may lead to specific treatment for a defined symptom cluster or a prioritized approach to assessment.
	Limitations: Patients may not notice specific times when specific symptoms began or are exacerbated; confounding symptoms, such as those characteristic of specific co-morbidities, may make symptoms hard to assess.
Multidisciplinary model	Features: This model includes the collaboration of several disciplines (each contributing their unique perspective) to determine a specific symptom cluster.
	Use: Complex patient populations may require a team approach to determine specific manifestations of cancer and its treatments, co morbidities, and other complex life circumstances.
	Limitations: The team approach to assessment may lead to multiple varying results and opinions on symptom cluster.
Electronic assessment	Features: Individuals log in their assessment into a computer database linked to their medical record, which correlates specific symptoms with each other and the patient's unique history.
	Use: Provides database entry directly into the individual's medical record, which gives clinicians timely information on which to base treatment
	Limitations: Patients may not be comfortable interacting with computers or personal digital assistants (PDAs) and this might prevent accurate, timely assessment of symptom clusters.
Reprinted with permission from reference 25.	

reliable but also clinically useful and feasible. There are approximately 21 instruments to select from that measure at least two symptoms in patients with cancer; of those, 18 instruments assess both physical and psychological symptoms.[38] Table 36.1 reviews descriptions, benefits, and limitations of six instruments that are known to be both clinically useful and feasible in the palliative care setting. The APRN may choose to use one of the more comprehensive symptom instruments,[38] such as either the Memorial Symptom Assessment Scale[39] or the Rotterdam Symptom Checklist,[40] in the initial assessment. Then, once the APRN knows which symptoms are present and bothersome, shorter

instruments, such as the Edmonton Symptom Assessment System,[41] the M.D. Anderson Symptom Inventory,[42] the Symptom Distress Scale,[43] or the Cambridge Palliative Assessment Scale,[44] can be used as appropriate in follow-up assessments[38] (see Box 36.1).

Ultimately, the assessment of symptoms should include collecting information on their presence, frequency, severity, associated distress, and any interference with activities.[24,25] The use of symptom inventories in the clinical setting enables the APRN to identify and prioritize symptoms that require interventions. However, a current limitation to this approach when considering symptom clusters is that it is more akin to general screening for symptoms and

Table 36.1 Symptom Assessment Instruments

Instrument	Description	Benefits	Limitations
ESAS[41]	◆ Assesses 9 items total (physical and psychological) ◆ Provides option for "other" symptoms not included to be scored ◆ Scale: 0–10 numeric rating	◆ Easy to use ◆ Easy to interpret ◆ Provides good validity (accuracy) of what is being assessed	◆ Not as comprehensive as other instruments ◆ Provides moderate reliability (precision) of what is being assessed
MDASI[42]	◆ Assesses 19 items (physical and psychological) ◆ Assesses symptom interference with life ◆ Scale: 0–10 numeric rating	◆ Easy to use ◆ Easy to interpret ◆ Comprehensive in assessment of numerous symptoms ◆ Provides good reliability (precision) and validity (accuracy) of what is being assessed	◆ May be too long for clinic setting ◆ Lacks multidimensional symptom assessment
SDS[43]	◆ Assesses 13 items ◆ Provides symptom distress score ◆ Scale: 1- to 5-point Likert	◆ Easy to use ◆ Easy to interpret ◆ Provides good reliability (precision) of what is being assessed	◆ Not as comprehensive as other instruments ◆ Provides moderate validity (accuracy) of what is being assessed
CAMPAS-R[44]	◆ Assesses 10 items (physical and psychological) ◆ Provides option for "other" symptoms not included to be scored ◆ Provides an option for "not known" ◆ Assesses prevalence and severity ◆ Assesses symptom interference with life ◆ Scale: 0–100 mm Visual Analog	◆ Easy to use ◆ Easy to interpret ◆ Provides good validity (accuracy) of what is being assessed	◆ Not as comprehensive as other instruments ◆ Provides moderate reliability (precision) of what is being assessed
MSAS[39]	◆ Assesses 30 items (physical and psychological) ◆ Provides option for "other" symptom not included to be scored ◆ Assesses frequency, severity, and distress ◆ Scale: 4- and 5-point Likert	◆ Comprehensive in assessment of numerous symptoms and various dimensions of those symptoms ◆ Provides good reliability (precision) and validity (accuracy) of what is being assessed	◆ Can be cumbersome and difficult to complete ◆ Can be difficult to interpret in clinic setting
RSCL[40]	◆ Assesses 30 items (physical and psychological) ◆ Assesses symptom distress ◆ Scale: 4-point Likert	◆ Easy to use ◆ Easy to interpret ◆ Comprehensive in assessment of numerous symptoms and various dimensions of those symptoms ◆ Provides good validity (accuracy) of what is being assessed	◆ Provides moderate reliability (precision) of what is being assessed ◆ May be too long for clinic setting

Abbreviations: ESAS, Edmonton Symptom Assessment System; MDASI, M.D. Anderson Symptom Inventory; SDS, Symptom Distress Scale; CAMPAS-R, Cambridge Palliative Assessment Schedule; MSAS, Memorial Symptom Assessment Scale; RSCL, Rotterdam Symptom Checklist.

From reference 38.

co-occurring symptoms rather than a systematic, scientific-based identification of a symptom cluster.[25]

Cancer patients receiving treatment experience numerous concurrent symptoms.[28] Which symptoms cluster depends on a variety of factors and is still not fully understood. However, current evidence suggests that there is a higher prevalence of pairs of symptoms that cluster rather than multiple symptoms that cluster, which are considered clinically more complex.[28] Patients with higher symptom severity scores may begin to report more symptoms than those with a lower symptom severity. This is clinically very relevant, given that symptom clusters have been linked with poor health outcomes.

Therefore, when caring for patients who are receiving active cancer treatment, the APRN should ask patients about symptoms they are experiencing. Their responses will help the APRN to develop an appropriate treatment plan for the patient. Table 36.2 provides questions that are appropriate to ask patients to elicit the most troubling and perhaps pervasive symptoms.[28] As mentioned earlier, symptom clusters may vary depending on disease types and stages as well as treatment plans. Box 36.2 lists common symptom clusters that have been found to be associated with different treatment modalities.[28] Knowing what symptom clusters are associated with different treatments is useful

Table 36.2 Questions and Clinical Management Considerations when Assessing for the Presence of Symptoms and Symptom Clusters

Symptom Assessment Questions	Clinical Management Considerations
Tell me about your symptom(s). When did the symptom(s) begin?	If symptoms began prior to cancer treatment, suspect a relationship to the disease process.
Did your symptom(s) cluster during one phase of the cancer treatment?	If symptoms worsened during cancer treatment, suspect an etiologic relationship to the cancer treatment, keeping in mind that the symptoms may also be disease-related.
Do you experience fatigue, pain, depression, or sleep disturbance?	If one symptom is present, assess for the presence of other symptoms that are common in the cluster.
What are the most common symptoms you experience with your current treatment?	Diligently assess for the most likely symptoms, keeping in mind the high potential for baseline symptoms of pain, fatigue, depression, and sleep disturbance.
Which symptom is most dominant and distressing to you? Does management of one of your symptoms improve other symptoms?	Consider that management of one symptom, such as pain, may improve fatigue, depression, sleep disturbance, and other related symptoms.

Adapted from reference 28.

Box 36.2 Common Symptom Clusters Caused by Cancer Treatment

Type of Treatment	Subtype	Symptoms
All (baseline symptom cluster)		Fatigue, pain, depression, sleep disturbance
Surgery	Abdominal	Gastrointestinal disturbance
	Brain	Headache, cognitive changes
	Mastectomy	Potential for chronic pain
	Thoracotomy	Potential for dyspnea, chronic pain
	Head/neck	Potential for chronic pain
	Amputation	Potential for chronic pain
Chemotherapy	Alkylating agents	Nausea and vomiting
	Antimetabolites	Diarrhea, mucositis
	Antitumor antibiotics	Mucositis, nausea and vomiting
	Vinca alkaloids	Peripheral neuropathy, constipation
	Taxanes	Peripheral neuropathy, mucositis
Biotherapy and targeted therapies	EGFR antagonists	Rash, itching
	Interferons	Anorexia, fatigue, depression
	Bortezomib	Peripheral neuropathy
	Thalidomide	Drowsiness
Hormonal therapy	SERMS	Hot flashes, pain
	Aromatase inhibitors	Hot flashes, pain
	LHRH agonists	Hot flashes, pain/tumor "flare"
	LHRH antagonists	Hot flashes, pain/tumor "flare"
	Anti-androgens	Nausea, vomiting, diarrhea
	Corticosteroids	Indigestion, nausea, insomnia, restlessness, mood changes, muscle weakness, weight gain, depression, fatigue, headache

Box 36.2 Continued

Type of Treatment	Subtype	Symptoms
Radiation therapy	Brain	Headache, nausea, itching
	Head/neck	Mucositis, dysphagia, dizziness, itching, dry mouth, nausea
	Breast	Skin irritation/itching, pain, lymphedema
	Mantle	Skin irritation/itching, cough
	Lung	Cough, dyspnea, dysphagia, itching
	Upper abdomen	Nausea, vomiting, potential for chronic pain
	Lower abdomen	Diarrhea, potential for chronic pain
	Pelvic	Dysuria, diarrhea, itching, potential for chronic pain
	Radionuclides	Pain flare, fatigue, nausea, vomiting, diarrhea
	Radioimmunotherapy	Fatigue, arthralgias, rash, itching, nausea, vomiting, diarrhea, weakness

Abbreviations: EGFR, epidermal growth factor receptor; SERM, selective estrogen receptor modulators; LHRH, luteinizing hormone-releasing hormone.

Data from references 82 and 83.

Reprinted with permission from reference 28.

Table 36.3 Predictors of Symptom Clusters in Advanced Cancer

Symptom Cluster	Predicting Characteristic
Agitation, confusion, and urinary incontinence	If >70 years of age[84]
Nausea & vomiting	Females[84]
Fatigue, pain, depression	Elevated neuroendocrine levels[85]

From reference 20.

to clinicians as they assess for the presence of symptoms and symptom clusters.

Symptom clusters are also important to assess across treatment plans because the longitudinal pattern of a cluster may provide insights and allow predictions on the patient's response to treatment.[32] For example, it has been suggested that the psychoneuroimmunology symptom cluster of fatigue, insomnia, pain, and depression, when experienced during chemotherapy and radiotherapy, may be an indicator that future treatments will be poorly tolerated.[45] Symptom clusters that do not change during treatment may indicate that the tumor is not responsive to that treatment.[32]

The most current knowledge surrounding symptom clusters in patients with advanced cancer was recently compiled and provides valuable information for clinicians related to the prevalence, predictors, and longitudinal characteristics of symptom clusters.[20] It is helpful for APRNs to identify who might be most at risk for developing a specific cluster of symptoms, including age and gender distributions. Table 36.3 lists several common symptom clusters found in patients with advanced cancer and the patient characteristics associated with each. Table 36.4 lists the most common symptom clusters that have been observed in patients with advanced cancer. Finally, while the overall longitudinal characteristics of symptom clusters in patients with cancer are still being determined,[6] three groups of symptom clusters have been

Table 36.4 Common Symptom Clusters in Advanced Cancer

Symptom Cluster	Prevalence[a]	Independent Cluster[b]	Possible Co-Occurring Symptoms[c]
Anxiety and depression	45%	53%	Sleep disturbance, fatigue, lack of energy, decreased physical strength, loss of concentration
Nausea and vomiting	28%	44%	Dyspnea, abdominal fullness, dizziness, headache, dry mouth, numbness/tingling, diarrhea, sadness, irritable, appetite loss
Nausea and appetite loss	41%	8%	Appetite loss, nausea, dyspnea, diminished well-being, pain, constipation
Fatigue, dyspnea, drowsiness, and pain	45%	7%	Depression, appetite, nausea, diminished well-being, anxiety, loss of concentration, lack of energy, nervous, sleeping difficulty, bloating, worry, weight loss, constipation

[a] In 32 studies included in systematic review.

[b] Cluster existed independently (only these symptoms).

[c] Cluster included additional co-occurring symptoms.

Table 36.5 Longitudinal Symptom Clusters in Advanced Cancer

Symptom Cluster	Time-Frame
Breathlessness, fatigue, and anxiety	Three time points: baseline (1 day prior to palliative radiation), week 3, and week 6[86]
	Four time points: baseline, 1, 2, & 3 months after radiation[87]
Fatigue, pain, nausea, drowsiness, dyspnea, and appetite loss	Three time points: baseline (1 day prior to palliative radiation), week 3, and week 6[86]
	Two time points: baseline and 14-day follow-up[88]
Anxiety and depression	Three time points: baseline (1 day prior to palliative radiation), week 3, and week 6[86]
	Two time points: baseline and 14-day follow-up[88]

From reference 20.

identified that appear to remain stable across multiple studies and time points (Table 36.5).

Barriers to the identification of symptoms and symptom clusters in the clinical setting may be related to the patient, the system, or the provider.[24] First, the subjectivity of the symptom is always a challenge. Two patients may interpret and report their symptoms very differently, which ultimately may alter the APRN's perception of which symptoms commonly occur, and subsequently may affect treatment plans. Patients may also not be forthright in reporting symptoms. They may assume that APRNs are naturally aware of symptoms and thus they do not need to report them.[24] Or they may underreport symptoms, fearing that they will result in treatment changes or will disqualify them from a clinical trial, or just because they do not "want to be a bother" to their provider.[24] Time is another barrier to the assessment of symptoms: it can be time-consuming, and APRNs, who are under pressure to see more patients, have less time per patient visit. Finally, APRNs may assume that patients will voluntarily report the presence of a symptom, and thus bothersome symptoms may go unreported.[24] Ultimately, the best approach an APRN can take is to be vigilant for the presence of symptoms and to promote patient–nurse communication about them during treatment as well as into long-term survivorship.

Statistical Analysis

The second method of symptom cluster identification is through statistical analysis. This method is again not without its challenges. While a variety of statistical methods have been used to identify symptom clusters, there is no one clear gold standard.[3] Ultimately, the aims and conceptual framework of the cluster should guide the analysis.[46]

The identification of symptom clusters can vary, depending on such methodological decisions as the timing of symptom assessment, sample selection, instrument selection, and selection of statistical analysis method.[9] For example, in instrument selection, the assessment of the most common symptoms likely will result in different symptom clusters than when all possible symptoms are assessed.[17] Another consideration is that the selection of different data points across time will likely also introduce variations in the identification of symptom clusters. Therefore, both researchers who develop, and APRNs who read, symptom cluster studies should be aware of these factors as they interpret the findings.

Currently these challenges limit broader understanding of symptom clusters, as there is such variety in the time points used for data collection, the treatments that the study participants received, and their different diseases and stages of disease.[3] Due to these limitations, investigators have started to compare methodological approaches in an attempt to develop recommendations. One of these studies compared the different analysis approaches and reported that using the symptom severity score rather than the prevalence score provided more stable symptom cluster data.[47] APRNs should be aware that the clinical relevance of statistically defined symptom clusters is not well defined at present.[32]

Effect of Symptom Clusters on Patient Outcomes

Clinical APRNs, who care for patients with cancer with frequent concurrent symptoms, must understand the negative effect that these symptom clusters have on health outcomes. For example, symptom clusters have negative effects on multiple domains of quality of life, including physical function, cognitive function, and mood, and ultimately increase patient mortality.[6,8,17,48] Symptoms and symptom clusters that are not effectively managed may delay chemotherapy or radiotherapy treatment[2,35,49] and magnify the patient's distress.[14]

Quality of life and functional status are two measures that are negatively correlated with the severity of symptoms and specific symptom clusters.[50,51] Fatigue, a symptom that is present in the most prevalent symptom clusters, has significant effects on health outcomes for patients with cancer. In general, the cluster of fatigue and depression consistently decreases the quality of life in patients with cancer.[6] The severity of fatigue is influenced by other symptoms, such as pain, dyspnea, insomnia, and nausea, and ultimately it impairs physical functioning.[52] A study by Given and colleagues found that pain, fatigue, and insomnia, when clustered together, impaired physical functioning.[53] Conversely, patients with low pain, sleep disturbance, fatigue, and depression reported the highest functional status.[50,54,55]

Depression is typically examined within a symptom cluster rather than as a consequence of the presence of symptom clusters.[17] However, a few studies have shown that symptom clusters have a negative effect on depressive mood states.[56,57] Specifically, general malaise and nutritional and gastrointestinal symptom clusters independently predicted depression in patients.[57] Given that depression has historically correlated with poorer prognosis, this is a clinically significant finding.

Undoubtedly the most significant consequence for patients who have symptom clusters that are not well controlled is the association with increased mortality. The presence of severe co-occurring symptoms and symptom clusters in patients with lung cancer

Table 36.6 Symptom Clusters Found to Negatively Affect Patient Outcomes

Patient Outcomes Affected	Symptom Cluster	Specific Symptoms in Cluster
Quality of life and functional status	Fatigue and depression	Pain, dyspnea, insomnia, nausea
Depression	Malaise	Feeling unusually tired, feeling weak, with presence of headaches
	Nutritional	Changes to appetite, weight loss/gain
	Gastrointestinal	Vomiting, nausea, pain, constipation
Survival	Fatigue and anorexia-cachexia[59]	Easily fatigued, lack of energy, weakness, dry mouth, anorexia, early satiety, taste change, weight loss
	Aerodigestive[59]	Cough, dyspnea, hoarseness, dysphagia
	Debility[59]	Edema and confusion

6 months after diagnosis has been found to predict mortality.[58] Other studies that compared the influence of symptom clusters in patients in a palliative care program found three different symptom clusters that were significantly associated with poorer survival:[59] fatigue/anorexia-cachexia (easily fatigued, lack of energy, weakness, dry mouth, anorexia, early satiety, taste change, weight loss), aerodigestive (cough, dyspnea, hoarseness, dysphagia), and debility (edema and confusion). Thus, as the science of symptom clusters continues to advance, it may serve as a prognostic tool for survival in the clinical setting. Table 36.6 summarizes these common symptom clusters and the associated patient outcomes.

Symptom Clusters in Solid Tumors

Most patients experience multiple symptoms during their cancer treatment, and the symptoms may last long into survivorship. However, our knowledge regarding symptom clusters during treatment, in specific cancer types and across treatment stages, is limited to date.[28] It is still early in the study of symptom clusters across populations and stages of disease, and in understanding the complex mechanisms that create and influence the presence of symptom clusters.[17,60] The limited research conducted to date has typically focused on specific cancer types in more common solid tumors or in patients with advanced cancer. The following paragraphs discuss the current understanding of symptom clusters in two prevalent solid tumors (breast cancer and lung cancer) and summarize what is known about symptom clusters in hematologic malignancies.

Breast Cancer

Breast cancer is the most common cancer diagnosed in women, and it remains one of the leading causes of death.[61] While a great deal of research has focused on women with breast cancer, there is a limited amount of research on symptom clusters across specific populations, including breast cancer. Fatigue and depression are the most common symptoms that appear to cluster in some form or another across studies and stages of disease and treatment plans in women with breast cancer.[50,62,63] One study comparing symptom clusters across three phases of treatment (women with early-stage breast cancer after surgery but before receiving adjuvant chemotherapy, women with early-stage breast cancer after receiving adjuvant chemotherapy, and women with metastatic breast cancer receiving palliative treatment) found that three

clusters emerged across all stages: fatigue (fatigue, lack of energy, and weakness), perceived cognitive impairment (all three groups reported loss of concentration; women in the two groups with earlier disease reported problems with memory), and mood problems (anxiety, nervousness, depression).[63]

Another study following women through their treatment found that the symptom cluster of fatigue, sleep disturbance, and depression remained constant.[50] Finally, in women who had completed treatment, two symptom clusters appeared consistently: (1) fatigue, sleep disorder, and muscle weakness and (2) fatigue, sleep disturbance, menopausal symptoms, and mood disorders.[64] The amount of research into symptom clusters in women with breast cancer continues to grow, and the available data have clinical applicability for the assessment and management of symptoms throughout treatment.

Lung Cancer

Lung cancer continues to be the leading cause of cancer-related death for both men and women in the United States.[61] The patients typically experience a variety of concurrent symptoms that are very distressing.[64] Findings about the most common symptom clusters in patients with lung cancer have been inconsistent due to a variety of factors discussed earlier in this chapter, such as differing definitions of what constitutes a symptom cluster, the type of assessment instrument administered, the statistical methods used, and population characteristics.[18] One study in patients with lung cancer identified three consistent symptom clusters across various instruments and statistical methods:[18] (1) pain, bowel problems, nausea, appetite loss, and fatigue, (2) mood, outlook, concentration, and insomnia, and (3) dyspnea and cough.[65] Another study found that the cluster of bowel dysfunction, distress with appearance, dyspnea, fatigue, cough, pain, and nausea was associated with poorer performance status in patients with lung cancer.[32] The cluster of anorexia, altered taste, fatigue, nausea, vomiting, weakness, and weight loss was found to be a predictive factor for poor survival in patients with lung cancer.[32] Discrepancies limit the ability to obtain evidence-based clinically relevant information, but as progress continues to be made in the area of symptom clusters and specifically in lung cancer, meaningful information will become available to guide symptom management and predict prognosis, thus opening the door to facilitate transitions in care.[18]

Hematologic Malignancies

Hematologic malignancies are a group of cancers that originate in either the bone marrow or lymphatic tissues. A variety of cancers fall into this classification, including leukemia, lymphoma, myelodysplastic syndrome, and multiple myeloma. Attention to not only symptom clusters but symptoms in general for those with a hematologic malignancy has been limited, especially when compared to the amount of research focusing on such solid tumors as breast and lung cancer.[66-68] However, a few studies have examined symptom clusters in this population. More importantly, researchers are showing a growing interest in symptoms and symptom clusters in patients with hematologic malignancies. One study comparing symptom clusters in solid tumors to those in hematologic malignancies found that the cluster of anxiety, drowsiness, fatigue, and dyspnea occurred only in individuals with a hematologic malignancy.[69] Other symptoms found to be consistent over multiple studies include fatigue, night sweats, and difficulty sleeping.[67] The limitations of these findings include the smaller sample sizes, variations in sample and methodology, and ultimately the limited research that has been conducted to date. Further research is needed to provide evidence to guide best practice.

Management of Symptom Clusters

Current methods for managing symptom clusters often include the use of multiple single agents to treat each symptom. This approach has several consequences: multiple agents may overwhelm the patient and ultimately lead to ineffective management,[52] while also creating the problems of polypharmacy. When multiple medications are prescribed, additional symptoms or comorbidities may result as a consequence of drug side effects or interactions.[32,70] Thus, clinicians should be aware of the potential challenges when prescribing multiple interventions for multiple symptoms.

The clinical management of symptoms and clusters should begin with a comprehensive assessment performed by the APRN to identify priority symptoms. Priority symptoms are ones that have the most detrimental effect on a patient's quality of life at the moment, such as decreasing physical functioning.[52] The APRN should begin symptom control by attempting to alleviate the priority symptom, using current guidelines and recommendations. While management is focused on the priority symptom, other symptoms in the cluster may also improve. This is due to the synergistic relationships that commonly exist between multiple symptoms.[28,52,71,72] For example, a patient with severe pain, fatigue, disrupted sleep, and depression may be helped by decreasing the pain, thereby decreasing fatigue, improving quality of sleep, and lowering depression.[56]

Nonpharmacologic approaches, such as physical activity to manage fatigue, sleep disturbance, anxiety, depression, and pain, have recently received new attention with promising results.[73] Several studies have shown that physical activity reduces the severity of symptom clusters reported in hematologic malignancies[74] and women with breast cancer.[75-77] Other approaches that have been shown to reduce the severity of symptom clusters in patients with cancer include psychoeducational approaches and complementary therapies, such as acupuncture.[29] Table 36.7 lists pharmacologic and nonpharmacologic approaches to the management of symptom clusters in patients with cancer.

Table 36.7 Management of Symptom Clusters

Intervention	Symptom/Symptom Cluster Targeted
Medications	
*Methylphenidate	Depression and fatigue[26,89]
*Analgesic	Pain, sleep disturbance, fatigue[27]
Physical activity	Depression and fatigue;[26] fatigue, anxiety, and depression[27]
Psychoeducational approaches	Nausea and fatigue[27]
Acupuncture	Depression and sleep disturbance;[90] dyspnea, fatigue, depression, anxiety, drowsiness[91]

Given the promising benefits of many nonpharmacologic interventions and the challenges with using multiple pharmacologic agents, the APRN may choose to try a multimodal approach to the management of a symptom cluster. For example, in a patient with the cluster of fatigue, anorexia, and cachexia, the APRN can make a referral to a nutritionist for counseling, encourage the patient to participate in an exercise program, and prescribe an anti-cachexia medication,[78] such as a progestational agent. As our understanding of symptom clusters continues to improve, multimodal and tailored interventions to manage multiple symptoms within a cluster may one day become a part of regular clinical practice.

Conclusion

The science of symptom clusters is evolving. There is a movement to rectify the methodological inconsistencies across studies.[21,67,79] Using common item banks to measure familiar health concepts would allow comparison of findings across multiple settings using a single metric.[80] It is hoped this will lead to broader understanding of the significance that symptom clusters have for patient health outcomes. APRNs play an instrumental role in identifying and managing symptom clusters. With our increasing understanding of symptom clusters, APRNs may be able to offer novel interventions that ameliorate multiple symptoms concurrently.[36,81]

References

1. Dodd MJ, Miaskowski C, Lee K. Occurrence of symptom clusters. *J Natl Cancer Inst Monogr.* 2004; 32: 76–8.
2. Cleeland CS, Reyes-Gibby CC. When is it justified to treat symptoms? Measuring symptom burden. *Oncology.* 2002; 16(9 Suppl 10): 64–70.
3. Aktas A, Walsh D, Hu B. Cancer symptom clusters: An exploratory analysis of eight statistical techniques. *J. Pain Symptom Manage.* 2014; 48(6): 1254–66.
4. Miaskowski C, Dodd M, Lee K. Symptom clusters: The new frontier in symptom management research. *J Natl Cancer Inst Monogr.* 2004; 32: 17–21.
5. Beck S. Symptom clusters: Impediments and suggestions for solutions. *J Natl Cancer Inst Monogr.* 2004; 32: 137–8.
6. Dodd M, Miaskowski C, Paul S. Symptom clusters and their effect on the functional status of patients with cancer. *Oncol Nurs Forum.* 2001; 28(3): 465–70.
7. Patrick D, Ferketich S, Frame P, et al. National Institutes of Health State-of-the-Science Conference Statement: Symptom management

in cancer: Pain, depression, and fatigue, July 15–17, 2002. *J Natl Cancer Inst Monogr.* 2004; 32: 9–16.

8. Kim H-J, McGuire DB, Tulman L, Barsevick AM. Symptom clusters: Concept analysis and clinical implications for cancer nursing. *Cancer Nurs.* 2005; 28(4): 270–82.

9. Barsevick A, Whitmer K, Nail L, Beck S, Dudley W. Symptom cluster research: Conceptual, design, measurement, and analysis issues. *J Pain Symptom Manage.* 2006; 31(1): 85–95.

10. Miaskowski C, Aouizerat BE, Dodd M, Cooper B. Conceptual issues in symptom clusters research and their implications for quality-of-life assessment in patients with cancer. *J Natl Cancer Inst Monogr.* 2007; 2007(37): 39–46.

11. Barsevick AM. The concept of symptom cluster. *Semin Oncol Nurs.* 2007; 23(2): 89–98.

12. Barsevick AM. The elusive concept of the symptom cluster. *Oncol Nurs Forum.* 2007; 34(5): 971–80.

13. Aktas A, Walsh D, Rybicki L. Symptom clusters: Myth or reality? *Palliat Med.* 2010; 24(4): 373–85.

14. Aktas A. Cancer symptom clusters: current concepts and controversies. *Curr Opin Support Palliat Care.* 2013; 7(1): 38–44.

15. Starkweather A, Lyon D, Elswick RK, Montpetit A, Conley Y, McCain N. A conceptual model of psychoneurological symptom cluster variation in women with breast cancer: Bringing nursing research to personalized medicine. *Curr Pharmacogenomics Pers Med.* 2013; 11: 224–30.

16. Fan G, Filipczak L, Chow E. Symptom clusters in cancer patients: A review of the literature. *Curr Oncol.* 2007; 14(5): 173–9.

17. Xiao C. The state of science in the study of cancer symptom clusters. *Eur J Oncol Nurs.* 2010; 14(5): 417–34.

18. Chen E, Nguyen J, Cramarossa G, et al. Symptom clusters in patients with lung cancer: A literature review. *Expert Rev Pharmacoecon Outcomes Res.* 2011; 11(4): 433–9.

19. Thavarajah N, Chen E, Zeng E, et al. Symptom clusters in patients with metastatic cancer: A literature review. *Expert Rev Pharmacoeconomics Outcomes Res.* 2012; 12(5): 597–604.

20. Dong ST, Butow PN, Costa DSJ, Lovell MR, Agar M. Symptom clusters in patients with advanced cancer: A systematic review of observational studies. *J Pain Symptom Manage.* 2014; 48(3): 411–50.

21. Miaskowski C, Meek P. Opportunities and challenges in symptom cluster research. *Commun Nurs Res.* 2009; 41: 29–38.

22. Kim H-J, Abraham I. Statistical approaches to modeling symptom clusters in cancer patients. *Cancer Nurs.* 2008; 31(5): E1–E10.

23. Kirkova J, Aktas A, Walsh D, Davis MP. Cancer symptom clusters: Clinical and research methodology. *J Palliat Med.* 2011; 14(10): 1149–66.

24. Paice J. Assessment of symptom clusters in people with cancer. *J Natl Cancer Inst Monogr.* 2004; 60611(32): 98–102.

25. Lacasse C, Beck SL. Clinical assessment of symptom clusters. *Semin Oncol Nurs.* 2007; 39(2): 106–12.

26. Fleishman SB. Treatment of symptom clusters: Pain, depression, and fatigue. *J Natl Cancer Inst Monogr.* 2004; 10003(32): 119–23.

27. Williams L. Clinical management of symptom clusters. *Semin Oncol Nurs.* 2007; 23(2): 113–20.

28. Honea N, Brant J, Beck SL. Treatment-related symptom clusters. *Semin Oncol Nurs.* 2007; 23(2): 142–51.

29. Berger AM, Yennu S, Million R. Update on interventions focused on symptom clusters: What has been tried and what have we learned? *Curr Opin Support Palliat Care.* 2013; 7(1): 60–6.

30. Temel JS, Greer JA, Muzikansky A, et al. Early palliative care for patients with metastatic non-small-cell lung cancer. *N Engl J Med.* 2010; 363(8): 733–42.

31. Callaway C. Timing is everything: When to consult palliative care. *J Am Acad Nurse Pract.* 2012; 24(11): 633–9.

32. Kirkova J, Walsh D, Aktas A, Davis MP. Cancer symptom clusters: Old concept but new data. *Am J Hosp Palliat Care.* 2010; 27(4): 282–8.

33. Hart B. Biological basis of the behavior of sick animals. *Neurosci Biobehav Rev.* 1988; 12: 123–37.

34. Miaskowski C, Aouizerat BE. Is there a biological basis for the clustering of symptoms? *Semin Oncol Nurs.* 2007; 23(2): 99–105.

35. Cleeland CS, Bennett GJ, Dantzer R, et al. Are the symptoms of cancer and cancer treatment due to a shared biologic mechanism? A cytokine-immunologic model of cancer symptoms. *Cancer.* 2003; 97(11): 2919–25.

36. Kim H-J, Barsevick AM, Fang CY, Miaskowski C. Common biological pathways underlying the psychoneurological symptom cluster in cancer patients. *Cancer Nurs.* 2012; 35(6): E1–E20.

37. Kearney N, McCann L, Norrie J, et al. Evaluation of a mobile phone-based, advanced symptom management system (ASyMS) in the management of chemotherapy-related toxicity. *Support Care Cancer.* 2009; 17(4): 437–44.

38. Kirkova J, Davis MP, Walsh D, et al. Cancer symptom assessment instruments: A systematic review. *J. Clin. Oncol.* 2006; 24(9): 1459–73.

39. Portenoy RK, Thaler HT, Kornblith AB, et al. The Memorial Symptom Assessment Scale: An instrument for the evaluation of symptom prevalence, characteristics and distress. *Eur J Cancer.* 1994; 30A(9): 1326–36.

40. De Haes J, van Knippenberg F, Neigt J. Measuring psychological and physical distress in cancer patients: Structure and application of the Rotterdam Symptom Checklist. *Br J Cancer.* 1990; 62: 1034–8.

41. Chang VT, Hwang SS, Feuerman M. Validation of the Edmonton Symptom Assessment Scale. *Cancer.* 2000; 88(9): 2164–71.

42. Cleeland C, Mendoza T, Wang X, et al. Assessing symptom distress in cancer patients: The M.D. Anderson Symptom Inventory. *Cancer.* 2000; 89: 1634–46.

43. McCorkle R, Young K. Development of a symptom distress scale. *Cancer Nurs.* 1978; 1: 373–8.

44. Ewing G, Todd C, Rogers M, Barclay S, McCabe J, Martin A. Validity of a symptom measure suitable for use among palliative care patients in the community: CAMPAS-R. *J Pain Symptom Manage.* 2004; 27: 287–99.

45. Pasztai L, Mendoza T, Reuben J, et al. Changes in plasma levels of inflammatory cytokines in response to paclitaxel chemotherapy. *Cytokine.* 2004; 7(25): 94–102.

46. Skerman HM, Yates PM, Battistutta D. Multivariate methods to identify cancer-related symptom clusters. *Res Nurs Health.* 2009; 32(3): 345–60.

47. Kim E, Aouizerat BE, Dodd MJ, et al. Differences in symptom clusters identified using occurrence rates versus symptom severity ratings in patients at the end of radiation therapy. *Cancer Nurs.* 2009; 32(6): 429–36.

48. Kim J, Dodd MJ, Aouizerat BE, Jahan T, Miaskowski C. A review of the prevalence and impact of multiple symptoms in oncology patients. *J Pain Symptom Manage.* 2009; 37(4): 715–36.

49. Cleeland CS. Symptom burden: Multiple symptoms and their impact as patient-reported outcomes. *J Natl Cancer Inst Monogr.* 2007; 37: 16–21.

50. Dodd MJ, Cho MH, Cooper B, Miaskowski C. The effect of symptom clusters on functional status and quality of life in women with breast cancer. *Eur J Oncol Nurs.* 2010; 14(2): 101–10.

51. Aktas A, Walsh D, Rybicki L. Symptom clusters and prognosis in advanced cancer. *Support Care Cancer.* 2012; 20(11): 2837–43. doi:10.1007/s00520-012-1408-9.

52. Given B, Given CW, Sikorskii A, Hadar N. Symptom clusters and physical function for patients receiving chemotherapy. *Semin Oncol Nurs.* 2007; 23(2): 121–6.

53. Given B, Given C, Azzous F, Stommel M. Physical functioning of elderly cancer patients prior to diagnosis and following treatment. *Nurs Res.* 2001; 50(4): 222–32.

54. Miaskowski C, Cooper BA, Paul SM, et al. Subgroups of patients with cancer with different symptom experiences and quality-of-life outcomes: A cluster analysis. *Oncol Nurs Forum.* 2006; 33(5): E79–E89.

55. Pud D, Ben Ami S, Cooper B, et al. The symptom experience of oncology outpatients has a different impact on quality-of-life outcomes. *J Pain Symptom Manage.* 2008; 35(2): 162–70.

56. Francoeur R. The relationship of cancer symptom clusters to depressive affect in the initial phase of palliative radiation. *J Pain Symptom Manage.* 2005; 29(2):130–55.

57. Breen S, Baravelli C, Schofield P, Jefford M, Yates P, Aranda S. Is symptom burden a predictor of anxiety and depression in patients with cancer about to commence chemotherapy? *Med J Aust.* 2009; 190(7): S99–104.

58. Gift A, Stommel M, Jablonski A, Given W. A cluster of symptoms over time in patients with lung cancer. *Nurs Res.* 2003; 52(6): 202–12.

59. Aktas A, Rybicki LA, Walsh D. The impact of symptom clusters on survival in patients with advanced cancer. *J Clin Oncol.* 2010; 28(15): 9145.

60. Oh H, Seo Y, Jeong H, Seo W. The identification of multiple symptom clusters and their effects on functional performance in cancer patients. *J Clin Nurs.* 2012; 21(19-20): 2832–42.

61. Howlander N, Noone AM, Krapcho M, et al. SEER Cancer Statistics Review, 1975–2010. National Cancer Institute. Bethesda, MD, 2013, based on November 2012 SEER data submission.

62. Broeckel J, Jacobsen PB, Horton J, Balducci L, Lyman GH. Characteristics and correlates of fatigue after adjuvant chemotherapy for breast cancer. *J Clin Oncol.* 1998; 16(5): 1689–96.

63. Bender CM, Ergÿn FS, Rosenzweig MQ, Cohen SM, Sereika SM. Symptom clusters in breast cancer across 3 phases of the disease. *Cancer Nurs.* 2005; 28(3): 219–25.

64. Fox SW, Lyon DE. Symptom clusters and quality of life in survivors of lung cancer. *Oncol Nurs Forum.* 2006; 33(5): 931–6.

65. Henoch I, Ploner A, Tishelman C. Increasing stringency in symptom cluster research: A methodological exploration of symptom clusters in patients with inoperable lung cancer. *Oncol Nurs Forum.* 2009; 36(6): E282–92.

66. Bevans MF, Mitchell S, Marden S. The symptom experience in the first 100 days following allogeneic hematopoietic stem cell transplantation (HSCT). *Support. Care Cancer.* 2008; 16(11): 1243–54.

67. Johansson E, Wilson B, Brunton L, Tishelman C, Molassiotis A. Symptoms before, during, and 14 months after the beginning of treatment as perceived by patients with lymphoma. *Oncol Nurs Forum.* 2010; 37(2): E105–13.

68. Albrecht T. Physiologic and psychological symptoms experienced by adults with acute leukemia: An integrative literature review. *Oncol Nurs Forum.* 2014; 41(3): 286–95.

69. Cheung WY, Le LW, Zimmermann C. Symptom clusters in patients with advanced cancers. *Support Care Cancer.* 2009; 17(9): 1223–30.

70. Tsai J-S, Wu C-H, Chiu T-Y, Chen C-Y. Significance of symptom clustering in palliative care of advanced cancer patients. *J Pain Symptom Manage.* 2010; 39(4): 655–62.

71. Williams D, Verghese M, Walker LT, Boateng J, Shackelford L, Chawan CB. Flax seed oil and flax seed meal reduce the formation of aberrant crypt foci (ACF) in azoxymethane-induced colon cancer in Fisher 344 male rats. *Food Chem Toxicol.* 2007; 45(1): 153–9.

72. Kwekkeboom K, Wanta B, Bumpus M. Individual difference variables and the effects of progressive muscle relaxation and analgesic imagery interventions on cancer pain. *J Pain Symptom Manage.* 2008; 36(6): 604–15.

73. Albrecht T, Taylor AG. Physical activity in patients with advanced-stage cancer: A systematic review of the literature. *Clin J Oncol Nurs.* 2012; 16(3): 293–300. doi:10.1188/12.CJON.293-300.

74. Jarden M, Nelausen K, Hovgaard D, Boesen E, Adamsen L. The effect of a multimodal intervention on treatment-related

75. symptoms in patients undergoing hematopoietic stem cell transplantation: A randomized controlled trial. *J Pain Symptom Manage.* 2009; 38(2): 174–90.

75. Carson JW, Carson KM, Porter LS, Keefe FJ, Shaw H, Miller JM. Yoga for women with metastatic breast cancer: Results from a pilot study. *J Pain Symptom Manage.* 2007; 33(3): 331–41.

76. Bower JE, Garet D, Sternlieb B, et al. Yoga for persistent fatigue in breast cancer survivors: a randomized controlled trial. *Cancer.* 2012; 118(15): 3766–75.

77. Rogers LQ, Fogleman A, Trammell R, et al. Effects of a physical activity behavior change intervention on inflammation and related health outcomes in breast cancer survivors: Pilot randomized trial. *Integr Cancer Ther.* 2013; 12(4): 323–35.

78. Alesi E, Del Fabbro E. Opportunities for targeting the fatigue-anorexia-cachexia symptom cluster. *Cancer J.* 2014; 20(5): 325–9.

79. Brant JM, Beck S, Miaskowski C. Building dynamic models and theories to advance the science of symptom management research. *J Adv Nurs.* 2010; 66(1): 228–40.

80. Cella D, Yount S, Rothrock N, et al. The Patient-Reported Outcomes Measurement Information System (PROMIS): Progress of an NIH Roadmap Cooperative Group during the first two years. *Med Care.* 2007; 45(5): S3–11.

81. Miaskowski C. Symptom clusters: Establishing the link between clinical practice and symptom management research. *Support Care Cancer.* 2006; 14(8): 792–4.

82. Polovich M, White J, Kelleher L. *Chemotherapy and Biotherapy Guidelines and Recommendations for Practice.* 2nd ed. Pittsburgh, PA: Oncology Nursing Society; 2005.

83. Watkins Bruner D, Haas M, Gosselin-Acomb TK. *Manual for Radiation Oncology Nursing Practice and Education.* 3rd ed. Pittsburgh, PA: Oncology Nursing Society; 2005.

84. Jiménez A, Madero R, Alonso A, et al. Symptom clusters in advanced cancer. *J Pain Symptom Manage.* 2011; 42(1): 24–31.

85. Thornton LM, Andersen BL, Blakely WP. The pain, depression, and fatigue symptom cluster in advanced breast cancer: Covariation with the hypothalamic-pituitary-adrenal axis and the sympathetic nervous system. *Heal Psychol.* 2010; 29(3): 333–7.

86. Chan C, Richardson A, Richardson J. A study to assess the existence of the symptom cluster of breathlessness, fatigue, and anxiety in patients with advanced lung cancer. *Eur J Oncol Nurs.* 2005; 9: 325–33.

87. Chen E, Nguyen J, Khan L, et al. Symptom clusters in patients with advanced cancer: a reanalysis comparing different statistical methods. *J Pain Symptom Manage.* 2012; 44(1): 23–32.

88. Yennurajalingam S, Kwon J, Urbauer D, Hui D, Reyes-Gibby C, Bruera E. Consistency of symptom clusters among advanced cancer patients seen at an outpatient supportive care clinic in a tertiary cancer centre. *Palliat Support Care.* 2013; 11(6): 473–80.

89. Kerr C, Drake J, Milch R, et al. Effects of methylphenidate on fatigue and depression: A randomized, double-blind, placebo-controlled trial. *J Pain Symptom Manage.* 2012; 43(1): 68–77.

90. Feng Y, Wang X, Li S, et al. Clinical research of acupuncture on malignant tumor patients for improving depression and sleep quality. *J Tradit Chinese Med.* 2011; 31(3): 199–202.

91. Lim J, Wong E, Aung S. Is there a role for acupuncture in the symptom management of palliative care for cancer? A pilot study of 20 patients comparing acupuncture with nurse-led supportive care. *Acupunct Med.* 2011; 29: 173–9.

CHAPTER 37

Palliative Emergencies

Marcia J. Buckley and Ann Syrett

Key Points

- Hemorrhage is a frightening experience for both patient and family. The palliative advanced practice registered nurse (APRN) should discuss the potential for hemorrhage with patients at risk for developing a significant bleed and should reassure patients and families that if a significant bleed occurs, a plan of action will be promptly initiated.

- Spinal cord compression is a presenting symptom for 20% of cancer patients. It significantly affects quality of life, so the palliative APRN should maintain vigilance for its onset. With the exception of steroids, the palliative APRN must consider the patient's overall prognosis before initiating therapy.

- Seizures are a medical emergency. Brain metastases are the most common etiology of seizures in palliative care. In a patient experiencing seizures, death can occur from metabolic stress, rhabdomyolysis, lactic acidosis, aspiration pneumonitis, neurogenic pulmonary edema, and respiratory failure. Long-term empiric treatment with antiseizure medications is individualized based on the risk of seizure recurrence, the consequences of seizure recurrence, and potential interactions.

- Superior vena cava syndrome is a true medical emergency if the airway is obstructed. Lung cancer accounts for more than 70% of all cases annually. Early diagnosis and management can lead to a longer time between recurrences.

Introduction

This chapter highlights four emergencies that occur in palliative care: hemorrhage, spinal cord compression, seizures, and superior vena cava syndrome. Palliative APRNs need to understand the etiology, pathophysiology, workup, and management so they can rapidly and expertly respond to these emergencies. Palliative APRNs possess a unique skill set that combines holistic care of patients with the ability to manage acute, often potentially devastating symptoms that often affect patients' goals and wishes. Goals of care can be static, and the disease state needs to be considered when making treatment and management decisions for these palliative emergencies.

Hemorrhage

Bleeding can occur in up to 14% of patients with advanced cancer.[1,2] The thought of an acute hemorrhage is especially frightening for the patient and family. Hemorrhage can occur in patients with advanced cancers of the head, neck, lung, gastrointestinal tract, or genitourinary tract. It can occur as a result of fungating skin lesions, advanced leukemias, or tumors eroding major blood vessels. Medical devices are also a bleeding source (i.e., PICC lines). Small bleeds may be indicative of future trouble. This section focuses on hemorrhage in patients with advanced malignancy. The palliative APRN's understanding of the bleeding risk in cancer patients is key to creating a treatment strategy and determining the prognosis. Preparation of the patient and family for the possibility is emphasized. We discuss treatment of various bleeds and supportive management.

Case Study 1, Part 1

Mr. Edwards was a 64-year-old man who presented to the ED with worsening abdominal pain. Past medical history was significant for cutaneous lymphoma with uveitis and interstitial lung disease. He reported blood "streaking" of his stool that morning. Review of his medications revealed oxycodone, ranitidine, viscous lidocaine mix, lorazepam, and metoprolol. His cytotoxic therapy protocol included prednisone. Physical exam revealed acute right lower quadrant pain on palpation. Relevant laboratory work: Hgb 10.1, WBC 6.5, platelets 514, INR 1.2. His liver function tests were mildly elevated, his pre-albumin was 12. During initial workup, he became increasingly diaphoretic, febrile, and hypotensive. He was given 5 liters of IV fluid; surgery and gastroenterology consults were obtained.

Overview

Although seen in people with advanced-stage diseases, such as liver or lung disease, as well as trauma, catastrophic bleeding is often due to a malignancy. Hemorrhage as a cause of death is relatively rare. Due to the lack of evidence, most management is based on case reports. Bleeding occurs in the form of nosebleeds, hemoptysis, hematemesis, rectal bleeding and melena, vaginal bleeding, direct arterial rupture, and fungating skin lesions/wounds. When bleeding occurs, the psychological effect on the patient, the family, and caregivers can be profound. The palliative APRN must be prepared to manage the event and support the patient, family, and staff.

Incidence

Six percent to 14% of patients with cancer will experience a significant bleed during their cancer course.[1,2] Three percent of patients with lung cancer will have significant hemoptysis.[3] Hemoptysis is a concern in people with lung cancer, particularly those with bronchogenic carcinomas. Patients with head and neck cancer are at risk for uncontrollable bleeding from erosion of their carotid artery, commonly referred to as a carotid artery "blowout." Cancers of the gastrointestinal tract may cause a significant bleed, resulting in hematemesis or melena. A cause of distress for people with genitourinary tumors is clots, which make urination painful if not totally obstructing flow. Disruption in platelet function is concerning for people with advanced hematological malignancies; additional systemic processes would include disseminated intravascular coagulopathy and idiopathic thrombocytopenia.

Other related causes of bleeding in patients with cancer may be chemotherapy, radiation therapy, surgery, anticoagulants, mucosal irritation from nonsteroidal anti-inflammatory drugs (NSAIDS), and steroids. Presentation is often a slow onset with the appearance of petechiae, bruising, and ecchymosis. However, bleeding may present as a "sentinel" or "herald" bleed, thought to be a warning of a more extensive bleed.[2]

Identification of Patients at Risk

The pathophysiology of a bleed is related to the underlying cause or type of cancer a patient has, thereby creating insight into who may be susceptible. In patients with centrally located lung tumors, primarily bronchogenic carcinomas, hemoptysis or massive bleeding results from the creation of multiple collateral vessels, a buildup of vascular pressure, or direct invasion or treatment-related erosion of the bronchotracheal tissue.[1,5,6]

Patients with head and neck cancers are particularly susceptible, although specific statistics are unknown. Fungating tumors may directly invade the arteries in the neck.[7] Direct extension of tumor or damage to the wall of the artery by radiation therapy can weaken the wall, causing collapse. Radiation therapy is the primary cause of bleeding in this subset of cancer patients.[2] Surgery for this type of cancer carries risk as well, particularly in those undergoing radical neck dissection.

Causes of bleeding in patients with genitourinary malignancies are often the result of sloughing of the actual tumor mass, radiation-induced cystitis, and hemorrhagic cystitis from chemotherapy agents like cyclophosphamide.[8] Although it is rare, women with gynecologic cancers can have similar bleeding (bloody vaginal discharge) due to sloughing vaginal tissue or radiation therapy complications.[9] Bleeding from the gastrointestinal system can occur in people with primary cancers of the gastrointestinal system and are often complicated by disease involvement of the liver, which creates coagulopathies. Direct extension, seen in erosion of the wall of the esophagus, stomach, and small and large bowel, is always a possibility.

Treatment will depend on the underlying cause of the bleed, its extent, patient risk factors, and prognosis. Proactive planning about bleeding must occur. The APRN must discuss the possibility of hemorrhage with both patients at risk and their caregivers. McGrath and Leahy[10] delineate the ambivalent feelings nurses and providers have about discussing the possibility of hemorrhage with patients. A qualitative review of interviews with 17 nurses and 15 hematologists revealed significant angst about whether to inform patients and how to do so.[10] Patients and families must understand the potential for hemorrhage and must have realistic information about the chance of survival. A bleeding event is frightening, so both patients and families need reassurance that it *can and will* be managed. This is particularly true if the patient has end-stage disease and desires care at home.[10]

Case Study 1, Part 2

Mr. Edwards had a CT, which revealed (1) prominent mesenteric lymph nodes, (2) pneumoperitoneum with free fluid suggestive of a bowel perforation, (3) small areas of mesenteric hemorrhage, and (4) enlarging lymph nodes. Based upon the CT results and physical findings, the surgical team urged him to consider surgery. He was taken for an emergent exploratory laparotomy and underwent a small bowel resection; there were several segments of bowel perforations on the small bowel and mesenteric border of the distal ileum due to ischemia. Biopsies were taken. Postoperatively, Mr. Edwards was taken to the surgical ICU for management.

Management

The palliative APRN's interventions for bleeding begin with prevention when possible. Factors to be considered include the patient's goals of care, the extent of disease burden, and the ability to control or change the etiology. A thorough review of the patient's medications is essential, identifying medications that may potentiate bleeding (e.g., anti-inflammatory medications, NSAIDs). The benefit/burden ratio of anticoagulants should be discussed. In the context of the patient's goals of care, the aggressiveness of intervention can be determined.

If bleeding occurs via the nose, rectum, or vagina, careful packing of the orifice can help. Hemostatic agents, such as alginates, are used with packing or compression dressings in vaginal packing to slow a bleed.[9] Agents like cocaine can be used with nasal packing.[11] Topical oxymetazoline (Afrin[R]) spray can be an inexpensive and effective method to stop many nosebleeds.[12] Bleeding surface wounds can be treated with hemostatic dressings, such as epinephrine or tranexamic acid syrup. However, limited data support the use of these agents in the control of severe surface wound bleeds.[1] Nonadherent dressings soaked in saline can provide a compression dressing and can, at times, slow or stop even arterial bleeding. A Wound Ostomy Certified Nurse (WOCN) can assist in making financially appropriate product choices since there are numerous supplies, many of them extremely costly.[1,4,13] Cauterizing or vasoconstricting agents are helpful for hemorrhagic cystitis, but these agents are contraindicated if the patient is also experiencing bladder spasm. A review of the literature reveals a lack of randomized clinical trials surrounding the management of hematuria.[8]

For patients with hemoptysis, pulmonary evaluation is imperative. External-beam radiation can control hemoptysis in patients with lung cancer up to 80% of the time, particularly in those with unresectable lung cancer.[2] Often, a patient's performance status and the urgency of therapy may affect the total radiation dosage received and the time course of treatment. One treatment of 10 Gy has demonstrated effectiveness.[4] Endobronchial interventions, such as radiation therapy, can be tried if external-beam treatment is not effective. Endobronchial stenting has also been effective.[4,14]

In addition to these active therapies, opioids control cough to minimize tracheal strain.[1,2] Patients who are bleeding from the skin, rectum, vagina, or bladder can benefit from a radiation oncology consult because external-beam radiation is highly effective at controlling bleeding from these sites.[2,8] For bleeding from the upper gastrointestinal tract, endoscopic interventions can stop or minimize bleeding and are considered to be the treatment of choice.[4,15] Laser coagulation, targeted cauterization of the bleeding lesion or vessels, and the injection of sclerosing agents directly into the site are effective in the management of gastrointestinal bleeds. Cystoscopic cautery is used in bladder cancer, usually after continuous bladder irrigation and lavage have proven ineffective. Bronchoscopy can be used in cases of refractory hemoptysis with topical applications of thrombin or fibrinogen, cold saline lavages, or laser phototherapy.[4]

Case Study 1, Part 3

Mr. Edwards remained in the SICU and was extubated 3 days after his surgery. On day 5, he reported nausea and began to vomit significant amounts of blood. He developed a moderate amount of melena. An NG tube was placed and 800 mL of dark-red blood immediately drained into the wall suction unit. CT of the abdomen revealed a mass lesion in the second and third segments of his duodenum. He required reintubation, and endoscopy revealed fresh blood throughout the duodenum and a large necrotic ulcer in the duodenum. The source of the bleeding was beyond the reach of the endoscope. Mr. Edwards went to interventional radiology, where he underwent coiling of a small branch of his superior mesenteric artery and a prophylactic embolization of the gastroduodenal artery.

Much of the information about the treatment and management of significant bleeds is based on case reports due to the lack of data.[1,2,4,10] Transcutaneous arterial embolization (TAE) is often attempted in a very controlled group of patients. It is frequently employed to control bleeding in patients with metastatic hepatocellular bleeding. The blood vessel supplying the bleeding site is injected with a hemostatic substance after first being located on angiography. Embolization of the bilateral internal iliac arteries using permanent coils can be effective in patients with advanced urological cancer.[4,14]

Surgery is considered to control hemorrhage in patients who have a good functional status. Surgery is usually reserved for patients who have failed to respond to conservative attempts to control their bleeding and can undergo a surgical procedure. The technique involves ligating the artery or resecting the area of the bleed, followed by reconstruction.

Many systemic therapies are available. Phytonadione or vitamin K is important because it aids the liver in producing multiple clotting factors (II, VII, XI, X), if warfarin is found to be a causative therapy in a patient with bleeding or if malignancy has impaired the production of these factors.[4]

Vasopressin slows upper gastrointestinal bleeds as well as those caused by varices. It is a posterior pituitary hormone and is usually given intravenously. Octreotide has been suggested as an effective treatment of upper gastrointestinal bleeding.[4,15] It is given either subcutaneously two or three times daily (not to exceed 600 mcg per day) or via an intravenous continuous infusion at doses no greater than 50 mcg per hour; side effects are minimal. The subcutaneous route or monthly depot administration, although expensive, is not unreasonable for patients desiring to remain at home regardless of their prognosis. Aminocaproic acid, a lysine analog, can be effective as medical management when bleeding occurs due to thrombocytopenias, hematological disorders, solid tumors, hepatic cirrhosis, complications of cardiac surgery, or any situation where fibrinolysis contributes to bleeding. It promotes hemostasis and can be given orally with elixirs or tablets, or intravenously.[16] Despite having medical management available, whenever possible, ligation of bleeding varices remains the most effective treatment.[1,4]

The use of platelet transfusions in a patient with any advanced malignancy depends on many factors, including the patient's prognosis and goals of care and the frequency of transfusions. Pancytopenias are not uncommon in patients who have undergone significant amounts of radiation treatments to their long bones or patients with leukemia, lymphomas, multiple myeloma, and myelodysplastic and myeloproliferative diseases. The half-life of platelets is quite short and, in patients with advanced hematological malignancies, forgoing the administration of platelets can be a pivotal decision. Uncontrollable bleeding becomes most problematic when the platelet count falls below 20,000/mL[3] or, if a patient is afebrile and has no other coagulopathies, below 10,000/mL[3].

In one study, 123 patients developed 232 episodes of significant bleeding, defined as requiring a platelet transfusion. Patients in this study who required platelets also required more red blood cell transfusions. Epistaxis was most common (32%), followed by gingival bleeds (19%), melena (13%), hematuria (11%), rectal bleeding (8%), skin ulcers (5%), cerebral bleeds (4%), hematemesis and hemoptysis (3% each), and conjunctival bleeding and menorrhagia (1% each).[17] Transfusions can have a positive effect on a patient's quality of life, but as the need for infusions increases, frank discussions regarding the patient's goals of care are essential. The cessation of platelet transfusions is a difficult decision because without them, life expectancy is limited.[18,19] See Chapter 42, Navigating Ethical Discussions in Palliative Care.

Case Study 1, Part 4

Unfortunately, Mr. Edwards continued to bleed. His Hgb dropped to 5.8. His surgeon requested a palliative care consultation.

The palliative APRN learned that Mr. Edwards lived his entire life in the same rural town. He taught chemistry and physics at the same high school he had attended. He never cooked, ate two meals per day at the same diner, loved baseball, and was Roman Catholic, attending Mass regularly. The APRN and the surgeon met with Mr. Edwards' brothers and friends. The biopsies taken during surgery revealed recurrent lymphoma. The surgeon explained the interventions that had been done to date and Mr. Edwards' poor prognosis. The palliative APRN reviewed options, acknowledging that Mr. Edwards was dying. He did not appear to be in pain, and midazolam kept him sedated. The APRN encouraged the group to consider Mr. Edwards' preferences for care. His family and friends agreed that he would not want things prolonged. A Do Not Resuscitate and Do Not Escalate Care order was entered into his medical record. A Catholic priest was called.

Mr. Edwards' brothers and friends kept vigil as he was placed on a continuous infusion of midazolam and hydromorphone. The medications were reviewed and only those that provided comfort were maintained. After everyone had had an opportunity to say their goodbyes, he was extubated. He was transferred to the palliative care unit, where he died 4 days later, surrounded by his friends and his brothers.

Anxiolytics, specifically fast-acting medications like midazolam and lorazepam, should be administered if a sudden bleed occurs. Midazolam is the drug of choice over lorazepam or diazepam because of its short half-life. Moreover, it is not always possible to distinguish between a sentinel bleed and a life-ending bleed; many practitioners for that reason favor midazolam.[2] It can be given intravenously or subcutaneously in the acute setting. In the home setting, however, lorazepam may be preferable due to the ease of administration via a butterfly needle device. A standard starting dose would be 2.5 to 5.0 mg every 10 to 15 minutes. Lorazepam can also be administered sublingually but will take longer to take effect. In the out-of-hospital setting, prefilled syringes of midazolam or lorazepam can be used and stored up to 13 days at room temperature. Opioids are suggested as second-line agents unless there is observable pain or increased work of breathing uncontrolled by midazolam.

Proactive Management of Hemorrhage

The possibility of a catastrophic bleed can be unsettling due to the sense of fear and helplessness. Both patients and families need preparation for the possible event and guidance about how management will occur. No matter what the setting, patients and families need assurance that the bleeding will be quickly managed and any distress will be treated. Perhaps the most effective source of comfort providers and families can bring a patient experiencing a terminal hemorrhage is information, guidance, and support. Depending on the site of bleeding, a terminal hemorrhage may cause death within moments and before any sedating medicine has taken effect. The family should be prepared for this potential event. Education should include the use of dark towels and sheets strategically near the patient. Education should include the administration of opioids and anxiolytics if they observe any signs of distress in the patient. In the home setting, hospice services are an invaluable resource.

Summary of Hemorrhage

Early identification of patients at risk for developing a hemorrhage due to malignancy is key to the palliative APRN's development of an individualized comprehensive plan of care. Smaller bleeds should serve as a reminder to prepare for the possibility of a larger one. Ongoing discussions regarding a patient's goals of care, including the use of invasive strategies, need to be part of the nurse's management strategy for these patients. Involving family and friends in the discussion is integral to ensuring that the patient receives the care he or she desires throughout the care continuum.

Spinal Cord Compression

Pathology

Spinal cord compression (SCC) is defined as a compression or invasion of the dural sac and the spinal cord by an extradural tumor mass or hematologically through Batson's venous plexus.[20]

In the literature, it is also known as malignant spinal cord compression. SCC most commonly occurs due to an extradural mass, which may be either osteolytic or osteoblastic. The neurological deficits that occur can be permanent due to direct compression of the cord or cauda equina, interruption of the vascular supply to the cord, or actual fracture of the vertebra. Less common etiologies are direct extension of the tumor through the intervertebral foramina or via leptomeningeal spread (most often seen in melanoma, lymphoma, and lung and breast cancer). The thoracic spine is affected in approximately 60% of all presentations. The lumbar spine accounts for 30% of all cases, followed by 10% in the cervical spine.[5,21] It can occur in non-cancer conditions, such as osteoarthritis, rheumatoid arthritis, infection, any injury to the spine, and abnormal spinal alignment.[22-25] This section focuses on SCC as a palliative care emergency, commonly seen in a malignancy.[20]

Incidence

SCC is a common sequela of malignancy and is considered a medical emergency. Prompt diagnosis can have profound effects on outcomes. Patients who develop an SCC that is not cancer-related (e.g., infections, rheumatoid arthritis, neurological diseases or insults, including primary astrocytomas/ependymomas) often have better outcomes.[5,20-23]

Approximately 20% of all patients diagnosed with a malignancy present with a SCC as their initial symptom.[21] According to a Cochrane review, 40% of all cancer patients develop spinal metastases. Of these, 10% to 20% may have symptoms.[26] Other studies reveal a slightly lower overall cord compression rate of 2.5% to 5%. The cumulative incidence varies by tumor etiology, with cancers of the prostate, lung, and breast accounting for 15% to 25% of all SCCs and renal/kidney, lymphoma, and myeloma accounting for 5% to 10%.[20,21,26,27] Colon cancer, cancer of unknown primary, melanoma, and sarcoma have the lowest incidence, accounting for less than 5% of patients who develop an SCC.[20,23,24,26-29] Loblaw and colleagues reported that 2.5% of patients dying of their cancer had at least one hospital admission for SCC within the last 5 years of their lives. The diagnosis of an SCC is indeed an indication of a poor or worsening prognosis. Median survival following diagnosis of SCC from the Ontario Cancer Registry was 6.7 months for patients with lymphoma, 6.4 months for patients with myeloma, 5 months for breast cancer patients, 4 months for prostate cancer patients, and only 1.5 months in lung cancer patients.[28]

Signs and Symptoms

The palliative APRN must be attentive to the often-subtle signs and symptoms of SCC through a meticulous history and physical exam. Back pain, localized, mechanical, or radicular, is the most common presenting symptom, occurring in 83% to 95% of all cases of SCC and can precede other symptoms by 7 weeks.[21] Differential diagnosis is imperative. If worsening back pain is present with position changes, SCC should be presumed until ruled out. It is especially important to consider SCC as a possibility in patients with thoracic pain. This is because this portion of the spine rarely is affected by pain-producing pathologies like osteoarthritis. Pain that occurs only with movement can be an important indicator of spinal instability, which might need rapid surgical intervention. Nonetheless, weakness with ambulation or the inability to walk combined with increased deep tendon reflexes offers the most significant predictor that the patient may be developing an SCC. In fact, 35% to 75% of all patients will have weakness at the time of diagnosis, and half of them cannot walk.[30] While half of patients experience bladder dysfunction at the time of diagnosis,[21,27,31] this is considered to be a later sign of an SCC, as well as bowel dysfunction.

A thorough physical exam includes gentle spine percussion to elicit pain. This should be done carefully to avoid worsening injury to the cord or causing additional pain, such as a muscle spasm. The palliative APRN should carefully check for changes in sensorium to heat and cold, vibration, light touch, coordination, gait, strength, and reflexes. Sensory testing with neck flexion may reveal Lhermitte's sign (a shock-like sensation) that extends to the back, arm, and legs.[21,31] The phenomenon can also be seen in multiple sclerosis, cervical spondylotic myopathies, neck trauma, and oncologic treatment toxicities due to cisplatin regimens or radiation. A saddle distribution of decreased sensorium below the level of the vertebrae can indicate cauda equina syndrome. This "horse's tail" refers to the lumbar and sacral nerve roots that descend below the distal tip of the vertebral column innervating the lumbosacral areas and is easy to remember. Motor deficits are seen more in thoracic spread, while paresthesias and other sensory changes are seen in lumbar metastasis. Testing reflexes can indicate if nerve root compression could be affecting mobility and other motor movements.[21,26,27,31]

Diagnostics

Magnetic resonance imaging (MRI) of the entire spine is the gold standard of diagnosis. It should be ordered immediately when an SCC is suspected. Patients who have internal hardware may need a CT scan with myelography for optimal spinal imaging. Myelography may also be more tolerable than MRI for a patient whose pain cannot be optimally controlled. Plain spinal radiographs are inappropriate (Fig. 37.1).[28,31] While pain may appear to contraindicate the test, a corticosteroid or opioid bolus may provide relief. Patient and family education about the need for an MRI to determine further treatment is imperative.

Management

The identification of an SCC necessitates urgent treatment to preserve or restore the person's function and quality of life, as well as to control pain. If untreated, SCC carries grave implications in terms of function and quality of life, so treatment is vital. A neurosurgery consult is imperative to determine what treatments are available. Other interventions include glucocorticosteroids, corticosteroids, radiation, and decompressive surgery. Spinal radiosurgery, percutaneous vertebroplasty, and kyphoplasty are common interventions, but thus far these modalities have not been shown to produce better or equal results to corticosteroids, radiation, or decompressive surgery.[20] Though not proven, corticosteroids are frequently initiated if the presumed benefit appears to outweigh the potential for side effects. Gastrointestinal irritation, perforation, and bleeding, as well as mental status changes (particularly in the elderly or those with metastases in the brain), and the presence of, or propensity to, infection all need to be considered.[5,20,25,29] The timing of the steroid should take into account the patient's sleep/wake cycle. Dexamethasone decreases vasogenic edema by

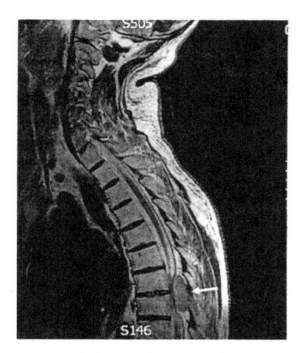

Figure 37.1 Weighted sagittal magnetic resonance imaging

inhibiting prostaglandin E_2 and by inhibiting vascular endothelial growth factor, thereby reducing pain.[30] However, there is not a consensus in the literature about dosing or even efficacy.[20,27]

Radiation therapy, even as a single modality, has been shown to improve the patient's ambulation and neurological status and to decrease or even eliminate pain, thereby improving the patient's quality of life and sometimes lengthening quality survival.[32] Benefits and burdens need to be considered when determining treatment length and expected outcomes. A shorter course of higher fractionated treatment(s) can be given over the course of 1 to 3 days. In this situation, radiation therapy stabilizes the spinal cord and/or provides pain relief. A short course (e.g., 8 Gy for 5 days) can be given in patients with a limited prognosis. Many practitioners administer a single fraction of 8 Gy, depending on the patient's prognosis.[33] For a patient with a longer life expectancy (more than 6 months), a 10-day, 30 Gy (total dose) regimen can be given, or a split course of 5 Gy for 3 days followed by 3 Gy for 5 days.[32,33] Due to the SCC symptom burden, the impact of radiation on their energy, and travel time, many patients will be admitted to the hospital or rehabilitation facility for the duration of treatment. Longer-course therapies are shown to decrease the local recurrence rate and offer better local control overall.[32,34]

Both percutaneous vertebroplasty and spinal radiosurgery have been used in patients with SCC, although neither has been shown to be superior to the aforementioned therapies.[35,36] Box 37.1 summarizes treatment recommendations for patients with an SCC based on overall performance status and prognosis.[20]

Supportive Therapies

There appears to be a role for physical medicine and rehabilitation (PM&R) in select patients with SCC. Research suggests that if a patient's prognosis can support a 2-week PM&R inpatient admission, there are statistically significant improvements in the

---

Box 37.1 Summary Recommendations for Spinal Cord Compression

◆ Malignant spinal cord compression is a serious complication of cancer and should be treated as a medical emergency.

◆ Appropriate treatment depends on the patient's prognosis and the patient's and family's overall goals of care.

  • For patients with a life expectancy of days to a few months or those with complete paraplegia, appropriate treatments include pain management with opioids and consideration of steroids and single-fraction radiation therapy.

  • For patients with a life expectancy of months or longer who have a radiosensitive tumor, management should include immediate treatment with steroids followed by radiation therapy (either a short or longer course depending on the type of cancer).

  • For patients with a life expectancy of months or longer whose cancer is not radiosensitive, management should include immediate treatment with steroids followed by surgery. Radiation and/or chemotherapy may be considered after surgery if appropriate for the type of malignancy.

---

pain score, depression scores, and self-perceived quality-of-life scores.[38-40] Certainly, early entry into a PM&R setting suggests better outcomes.[41] Again, patient selection is key; removing the patient from his or her home for 2 to 4 weeks would have to be justified by measurable outcomes.[37-39] The palliative APRN should consider a physical therapy referral within the home care and hospice setting to optimize function and safety for the patient and caregivers.

Summary

Malignant SCC is a medical emergency requiring rapid identification, location of the compression, timely initiation of appropriate therapies, and a thoughtful, evidence-based approach to treatment and care. Consideration of patients' goals and values, coupled with the providers' ability to offer a realistic prognosis, will enable patients to proceed with appropriate interventions.

Seizures

Epilepsy is a disorder characterized by recurrent unprovoked seizures and categorized by its etiology as genetic, structural/metabolic, or unknown.[42] A seizure is considered a medical emergency. The palliative APRN must have a working knowledge of seizure presentation, predisposing factors, and anticipatory management to relieve symptoms and prevent recurrences. Overall management of seizures is reviewed in this section, with special consideration for those occurring in the palliative or hospice-based setting.

Incidence

Approximately 0.5% of the U.S. population has been affected by epilepsy episodes.[42] Seizure prevalence is highest in those younger than 1 year and older than 65 years. Nearly 50% of seizures occur in persons without a prior history of epilepsy.[43] After two initial unprovoked seizures, approximately 30% to 50% will experience

seizure recurrence and become epileptic.[44] Seizures occurring in the palliative setting account for an estimated 13%; of these, 25% to 50% occur secondary to brain metastases.[45] The actual incidence of seizures in dying patients is unknown. One study focusing on end-of-life symptoms in patients with high-grade glioma reported that an estimated 45% of patients experienced a seizure in their last week of life, even though the majority were taking dexamethasone or an antiseizure medication.[46] The most common cause of seizures in the elderly is stroke; the risk of epilepsy due to seizure is at its highest more than 2 weeks after the initial stroke.[47]

Pathophysiology

Seizures are classified as focal, generalized, or psychogenic. Status epilepticus focal seizures consist of simple partial seizures without loss of consciousness, or complex partial seizures with loss of consciousness. Generalized status epilepticus (tonic-clonic, absence/petit mal, myoclonic) seizures are always associated with loss of consciousness, and these have a greater incidence of associated mortality. Psychogenic status epilepticus is rare and characterized by bilateral rapid jerky motor movements without loss of consciousness. When a seizure involves loss of consciousness, there will be a postictal state that may include somnolence, confusion, and/or headache; it may last several hours.[42]

Clinical Features

Factors influencing the risk of seizure recurrence include a history of long seizure duration and failure to respond to other medications.[49] Table 37.1 outlines predisposing factors for seizures. Mortality from these predisposing factors resulting in acute symptomatic status epilepticus is six times greater compared to chronic epilepsy. Death may occur from metabolic stress related to muscular convulsions, rhabdomyolysis, lactic acidosis, aspiration pneumonitis, neurogenic pulmonary edema, and respiratory failure.[49]

Diagnosis

Status epilepticus of any type is determined by a neurological examination and involves repeated seizures lasting at least

Table 37.1 Predisposing Factors for Seizures

Factor	Examples
Structural	Brain tumor, metastasis, stroke, head trauma, subarachnoid hemorrhage
Degenerative	Cerebral palsy in young patients, Alzheimer's disease in older patients
Systemic	Cerebral anoxia/hypoxia or infections (such as encephalitis, meningitis, abscess), fever, sleep deprivation
Metabolic	Hepatic encephalopathy, uremia, electrolyte abnormalities, such as sodium, calcium, magnesium, phosphorus, or glucose abnormalities
Drug treatments	Use of seizure threshold-lowering drugs, such as antibiotics, antiarrhythmics, psychotropics, chemotherapy
Withdrawal	Rapid withdrawal from alcohol intoxication or antiseizure medications

From references 42, 43, 47, 48.

5 minutes without a recovery period of greater than 30 minutes. Therefore, witnesses' accounts of activity prior to a seizure and description of seizure activity, including any incontinence or loss of consciousness, are crucial in determining the seizure type. Suspect a structural cause if an aura or heightened sensory experience occurs before the seizure. Versive eye movements (deviation to one side) are associated with focal seizures. An electroencephalogram (EEG) is helpful in determining status epilepticus in an unresponsive patient. MRI is the best tool for determining structural lesions that are triggering seizures and is indicated for patients considering palliative radiation.

Management

Primary management when a seizure occurs includes the ABCs: patent airway, effective breathing, and adequate circulation. The workup involves a thorough history from the patient and the witnesses to the seizure, a full neurological exam and individualized neuroimaging, and lab studies as appropriate to the patient's goals of care. Table 37.2 summarizes suggested postseizure laboratory testing and the rationale. The American Academy of Neurology guidelines suggest prudent consideration of testing on an individual basis, as there has not been strong evidence to support or refute the recommendations.[50] When the seizure etiology is unknown, glucose and thiamine should be given together immediately to rule out treatable causes.[43]

Treatment of seizures should be initiated after 5 minutes of sustained seizure activity because they are unlikely to stop spontaneously (Table 37.3). In a hospice situation, 5 minutes can seem like 5 hours to loved ones, and every effort should be made to rapidly treat the seizure, with the goal of comfort. If the patient has an intravenous line, this method would be preferable, although this is not always possible in the palliative/hospice setting. If the patient does not have intravenous access, antiseizure medications may be administered subcutaneously, sublingually, or per rectum.

Table 37.2 Suggested Postseizure Lab Testing

Test	Evaluation
CBC	Leukocytosis, thrombocytopenia, plethora
Blood chemistries	Ammonia, urea, sodium, calcium, magnesium, phosphorus, or glucose abnormalities
TSH	Low TSH indicates hyperthyroidism-associated seizures.
Urinalysis	Increased glucose, infection
C-reactive protein	Inflammatory marker; increased after tonic-clonic seizures
Coagulation studies	Increased risk of intracranial bleeding
Vitamin B_{12}, folate	Vitamin B_{12} deficiency, folate deficiency
Prolactin	Elevated levels seen after seizure
Blood cultures	Infectious cause
Blood gas	Hypoxia and metabolic imbalances
Toxicology	Overdose of tricyclic antidepressants, cocaine
Pregnancy test	Possible eclampsia

From reference 43.

The first-line drug for stopping status epilepticus is either 10 mg midazolam given intramuscularly or, more commonly, a 0.1-mg/kg bolus, usually 4 mg, of intravenous lorazepam.[43,51] Intravenous lorazepam has a rapid onset of 2 to 3 minutes and a long half-life of 4 to 12 hours. Lorazepam is easy to administer and can be given intravenously, subcutaneously, or sublingually in 2-mg doses, repeated every 5 to 10 minutes if the seizure continues. Second-line treatment consists of diazepam 10 mg given intravenously every 5 minutes until effective (maximum dose 40 mg) or a single 30-mg intrarectal gel, or midazolam 5 to 10 mg given intravenously or subcutaneously every 15 minutes up to a total of three doses.[52,53] If in the acute setting the seizure is refractory to these benzodiazepines, consider initiating intravenous phenytoin or valproate.[54] Third-line treatment for status epilepticus includes general anesthesia (phenobarbital or propofol) inducing a chemical coma, with the goal to alleviate suffering while accepting the risk of respiratory failure.[43]

The decision to initiate long-term empiric treatment with antiseizure medication is individualized based on the risk of seizure recurrence, the consequences of seizure recurrence, and potential interactions.[55] After two or more unprovoked seizures on separate days, empiric monotherapy with an antiseizure agent should be initiated to prevent recurrences. In seizures caused by a brain lesion, consider increasing or initiating steroids in addition to starting an anticonvulsant. Patients undergoing cerebral radiation should receive steroids (dexamethasone 4 mg to a maximum of 16 mg daily) to prevent seizures associated with cerebral edema.[45] If the patient is undergoing surgical resection of the brain tumor, then he or she may be weaned off antiseizure medications after surgery. If palliative chemotherapy is an option, preference should be given to antiseizure medications that do not induce cytochrome P450 activity; these include levetiracetam (Keppra), gabapentin (Neurontin), lamotrigine (Lamictal), and pregabalin (Lyrica).[45]

In the hospice setting, it is preferable to avoid enzyme-inducing medications or those that require following blood levels, such as phenytoin, phenobarbital, carbamazepine, oxcarbazepine, and topiramate.[45,55] There are few drug levels routinely monitored by non-neurologists in clinical practice, and blood monitoring may be stopped as the end of life approaches. If the cause of the seizure is reversible, then long-term anticonvulsant treatment is not warranted. Although anticonvulsants are often initiated upon diagnosis of a brain tumor, they have not been shown to prevent seizures in patients with no seizure history.[45] Anticonvulsant prophylaxis does not offer enough benefit in patients with most primary or metastatic brain tumors to justify the potential burdens of using them (e.g., somnolence, drug interactions). In addition, current guidelines do not recommend use of anticonvulsants in stroke patients who have not experienced a seizure.[54,55] Therefore, it is recommended to stop prophylactic dosing of antiseizure medications in patients with no seizure history.[56,57]

Most seizures in the palliative setting can be managed with benzodiazepines. The priority should be to keep the patient as comfortable as possible and to avoid frightening seizure recurrences by instituting maintenance therapy in patients with a history of seizures with no reversible cause identified. Clinical pharmacists may be helpful to evaluate for drug interactions and adverse effects and to simplify medication regimens in order to optimize seizure control.[58]

Table 37.3 Pharmacokinetic Characteristics and Other Administration Considerations of the Major Long-Term Antiseizure Drugs in Adults

Antiepileptic Drug	Usual Dosage (mg/day)	Therapeutic level (mg/L)	Common/Important Side Effects	Main Mechanism of Action	Peak Time (hours)	Half-Life (hours)	Protein Binding (%)	Metabolism and Excretion	Cost of Usual Starting Daily Dose for 1-Month Supply
Carbamazepine	400–2,400	4–12	Dizziness, drowsiness, nausea, leukopenia, aplastic anemia, hepatotoxicity, hyponatremia, Stevens–Johnson syndrome (SJS), toxic epidermal necrolysis (TEN)	Blocks voltage-dependent Na^+ channels	4–8	5–26	75	Hepatic	$$
Clonazepam	0.5–4	0.02–0.08	Sedation, cognitive effects, drowsiness, respiratory depression	GABA receptor agonist	1–4	20–80	86	Hepatic	$
Felbamate	1,200–3,600	30–60	Hepatic failure, SJS, aplastic anemia, insomnia, weight loss, anorexia, nausea, headache	NMDA and Na^+ channel conductance	2–6	13–30	25	Hepatic with renal excretion (40% as unchanged drug)	$$
Gabapentin	900–3,600	2–20	Weight gain, worsening of seizures, dizziness drowsiness, ataxia, peripheral edema	Blocks Ca^+ channels, GABA receptor agonist	2–3	5–7	None	Renal excretion	$$
Lacosamide	200–400	10–20	Dizziness, headache, nausea, diplopia, blurred vision, cognitive dysfunction, skin reactions, ataxia	Slow inactivation of voltage-dependent Na^+ channels	2–4	13	<15	Hepatic with renal excretion (40% as unchanged drug)	$$
Lamotrigine	200–600	1–15	Rash, SJS, TEN, drug reactions with eosinophilia and systemic symptoms (DRESS), headache, blood dyscrasia, ataxia	Blocks voltage-dependent Na^+ channels	1–3	12–60	55	Hepatic with renal excretion (10% unchanged drug)	$$
Levetiracetam	1,000–3,000	3–30	Somnolence, asthenia, irritability, psychosis	Binding to synaptic vesicle protein 2	0.6–1.3	5–11	0 to <10%	Partially hydrolyzed in blood with 60% unchanged drug urinary excretion	$$
Oxcarbazepine	900–2,400	10–35	Somnolence, headache, diplopia, SJS, bone marrow suppression, hyponatremia	Blocks voltage-dependent Na^+ channels	4–6	8–10	38	Hydroxylation, glucuronidation with 95% urinary excretion	$$
Phenobarbital	30–180	15–40	Rash, sedation, dizziness, hepatotoxicity, impaired cognition, ataxia, mood change, SJS/TEN	GABA receptor agonist, glutamate antagonist, blocks voltage-dependent Na^+/Ca^+ channels	1–3	46–136	45–60	Hepatic	$
Phenytoin	150–600	10–20	Sedation, diplopia, hypotension with rapid IV administration, blood dyscrasia, hepatitis, SJS, gum hyperplasia, lupus-like reactions, hirsutism, acne, osteoporosis, cerebellar atrophy, peripheral neuropathy with chronic use	Blocks voltage-dependent Na^+ channels	4–12	24–72	85–95	Hepatic	$

(continued)

Table 37.3 Continued

Antiepileptic Drug	Usual Dosage (mg/day)	Therapeutic level (mg/L)	Common/Important Side Effects	Main Mechanism of Action	Peak Time (hours)	Half-Life (hours)	Protein Binding (%)	Metabolism and Excretion	Cost of Usual Starting Daily Dose for 1-Month Supply
Pregabalin	150–600	2–8	Somnolence, dizziness, ataxia	Binds to Ca+ channels	1.5	6.3	None	Primarily eliminated unchanged in urine	$$
Topiramate	100–600	2–20	Impaired cognition, hepatotoxicity, weight loss, renal calculi, metabolic acidosis, anorexia	Blocks Na+ channels, GABA receptor agonist, blocks NMDA receptors	2–4	19–25	9–17	Minimal metabolism, 70% urinary excretion as unchanged drug	$$$
Valproic acid	500–2,500	50–100	Hepatotoxicity, pancytopenia, tremor, weight gain, hair loss, ovarian cystic syndrome, nausea, vomiting, anorexia	Increases availability of GABA (inhibitory neurotransmitter)	1–10	8–15	85–95	Hepatic	$
Vigabatrin	200–300	0.8–36	Visual field defects (33% permanent), fatigue, drowsiness, weight gain, edema, peripheral neuropathy	GABA transaminase inhibitor	1–2	6–8	None	Trivial metabolism, 80% urinary excretion as unchanged drug	$$$
Zonisamide	200–600	20–30	Somnolence, ataxia, dizziness, renal calculi, anorexia, headache, agitation, behavioral changes, word-finding difficulty	Blocks Na+ and Ca+ channels	2–6	60–70	40–50	Hepatic, 30% urinary excretion as unchanged drug	$$

Key: $ = <$50; $$ = $50–100; $$$ = $100–500.

From references 55, 63, 64.

Experiencing and witnessing a seizure can be terrifying for both patient and family. The palliative APRN should implement measures to avoid recurrence, including assessing for reversible causes and administering anticonvulsants. In the hospice setting, it is reasonable to have available an emergency seizure medication kit for suppression of seizures if they occur. Family education is essential. Instruction should include avoiding putting anything in the mouth and how to protect the seizing person from falls or injury. Patients and families should be reassured through proactive planning that, although status epilepticus may become refractory or terminal, the patient will be cared for and kept as peaceful as possible.

Summary

A seizure is a medical emergency requiring expeditious treatment to stop the seizure and prevent recurrence. The palliative APRN must be knowledgeable about seizure etiology, contributing factors, and treatment. The palliative APRN plays an instrumental role helping to alleviate fears and providing proactive care for seizure patients and their families.

Case Study 2

Mr. Franklin was a 68-year-old man brought to the ED via ambulance after experiencing left visual loss and ataxia immediately before a tonic-clonic seizure at home. This was witnessed by family. Past medical history was significant for diffuse large cell lymphoma diagnosed after he presented with an enlarged cervical lymph node that did not improve with a trial of antibiotics. He achieved primary remission, with a negative PET scan, after four cycles of consolidation chemotherapy and field radiation to his right-sided cerebral mass. He underwent an autologous stem cell transplant 2 months earlier. His current labs and home medications were determined to be unrelated to seizures. A head MRI revealed a new right-sided parieto-occipital lesion concerning for relapsed lymphoma. Mr. Franklin experienced another tonic-clonic seizure in the hospital MRI suite and was given IV lorazepam for seizure cessation. Levetiracetam 750 mg po BID and dexamethasone 6 mg po BID were initiated to decrease cerebral edema and decrease the risk of additional seizure activity. Neuro-oncology and neuro surgery were consulted and advised a lumbar puncture and biopsy of the mass for confirmation of recurrent lymphoma.

After a few days on the antiseizure medication and steroids, Mr. Franklin's visual loss and mental and physical stability improved. An EEG revealed no seizure activity. Mr. Franklin and his family opted to pursue palliative whole-brain radiation and focus on symptom management. He was discharged home and tolerated palliative radiation well. The palliative APRN continued to see him on an outpatient basis and supported him in achieving optimal quality of life as he defined it. The APRN prescribed antiseizure medications in the event of another seizure.

Superior Vena Cave Syndrome

Incidence

Superior vena cava syndrome (SVCS) is a group of symptoms resulting from an obstruction of blood flow from the upper body to the right atrium. It is considered an emergency requiring immediate treatment only when the airway is obstructed or in the setting of cerebral edema not attributed to brain metastases.[59] This relatively rare syndrome was first described in 1757 by Scottish surgeon William Hunter in a patient with syphilis-related aortitis.[59] In most cases, it is caused by a carcinoma of the bronchus or metastases to paratracheal or paracarinal lymph nodes compressing the SVC. The common use of implantable intravenous devices and pacemakers has increased the prevalence of thrombosis-related SVCS. In rare cases, SVCS develops from infections, such as tuberculosis or histoplasmosis, which increase pleural thickening and cause significant systemic-to-pleural venous shunting.[59]

In the United States, approximately 15,000 cases of SVCS occur annually. Lung cancer is responsible for approximately 72% of SVCS cases, with an estimated 50% related to non-small cell lung cancer (NSCLC) and 22% caused by small cell lung cancer (SCLC). Median survival after cancer-related SVCS symptom presentation is about 6 months, although many patients undergoing treatment survive past 2 years. An estimated 35% of SVCS cases are caused by thrombosis or nonmalignant causes.[59]

Pathophysiology

The SVC is a thin-walled blood vessel. The brachiocephalic veins feed into the SVC, which terminates in the right atrium. An extrinsic chest mass generally to the right of midline (i.e., enlarged lymph nodes, lymphoma, thymoma, inflammatory process, or aortic aneurysm) or an internal thrombus compressing the SVC can easily cause obstruction of blood flow because the chest wall and surrounding organs leave little room for compensation. Increased venous pressure caused by the obstruction leads to increased flow through collateral blood vessels.

Clinical Features

SVCS classically presents as progressive swelling of the head and neck. Symptoms associated with increased venous pressure of the upper body usually develop over a period of 2 weeks and include edema of the face, neck, and arms. A blanching rash represents the excess development and dilation of compensatory subcutaneous vessels of the neck and anterior chest. SVCS can also manifest with cerebral edema, causing headaches, dizziness, and syncope, or laryngopharynx-related compression, causing dysphagia, dyspnea, hoarseness, and cough.[60]

Diagnosis

Chest CT imaging with contrast is the most useful study to detect an impeding SVC compression, such as an aortic aneurysm or thrombosis, before symptoms present. MRI can be used when contrast medium is contraindicated. A tissue biopsy is recommended to diagnose malignancy.[59] In approximately 60% of cases, SVCS is the clinical presentation when lung cancer is diagnosed.[61]

Management Strategies

To date there are no evidence-based guidelines for the management of SVCS. The American College of Chest Physicians and the National Comprehensive Cancer Network have made general recommendations supporting radiation and stent placement for symptomatic SVC obstruction due to NSCLC.

If thrombus is related to an indwelling catheter, anticoagulation is the primary treatment. Removal of the catheter and balloon dilation or stenting should be considered if fibrosis remains and is deemed clinically appropriate.[59,61] Management of SVCS related to malignancy is guided by the severity of symptoms and anticipated response to the cancer. In all cases, the goal of treatment should be to alleviate bothersome symptoms of the obstruction.

In cases of SCLC and lymphoma, treatment with radiation or chemotherapy alone has been found to be equally effective in relieving symptoms of SVCS. There was no demonstrated benefit from both chemotherapy and radiation used together.[59] Radiation is best for well-defined tumors that are less chemosensitive, such as NSCLC.[59] SVCS symptoms usually show improvement within 72 hours of radiation and resolve within 1 to 2 weeks from chemotherapy or radiation therapy.[59]

Placement of a stent has low risk and is optimal for symptom management of recurrent SVCS related to malignancy when the goal is to avoid the toxic effects of repeating chemotherapy or radiation.[62] A retrospective study of 149 patients receiving the Wallstent vascular endoprosthesis for treatment of SVCS found that 60% achieved complete resolution of symptoms within 72 hours; symptom-free median survival was 6 months.[62] Once a stent is placed, consideration should be given to anticoagulation and implications for management of SVCS recurrence, which occurs in an estimated 20% to 50% of patients. Researchers have used oral aspirin as antiplatelet preventive maintenance therapy after 3 to 4 days of complete heparinization after stent placement.[62]

Summary

The APRN should be vigilant for SVCS in patients with implanted devices, those with malignant conditions, or those with predisposing risks for cancer (smoking, asbestos). When progressive head and neck swelling occurs, management is focused on determining and treating the root cause of SVCS. Palliative management is focused on addressing symptoms and may include elevating the head, diuretics, steroids, stenting, or surgical removal of the offending mass or intravascular device.

Summary of Palliative Emergencies and the Role of the APRN

Palliative APRNs play a critical and dynamic role in the assessment and treatment of patients with palliative emergencies. An awareness of the current standard of care is critical in helping patients and families make sound management decisions based on outcomes data. Timely recognition, workup, and management of the complication can improve the outcomes.

References

1. Leigh A, Tucker R. What techniques can be used in the hospital or home setting to best manage uncontrollable bleeding. In: Goldstein N, Morrison R, eds. *Evidence-Based Practice of Palliative Medicine.* Philadelphia, PA: Elsevier Saunders; 2013:398–401.
2. Harris D, Noble S. Management of terminal hemorrhage in patients with advanced cancer: a systematic literature review. *J Pain Symptom Manage.* 2009; 38: 913–27.
3. Care management guidelines: Emergencies in Palliative Care. September, 2009 ed. Tasmania: Department of Health and Human Services; 2009:1–12.
4. Pereira J, Phan T. Management of bleeding in patients with advanced cancer. *The Oncologist.* 2004; 9: 561–70.
5. Bobb BT. Urgent syndromes at end of life. In: Ferrell B, Coyle N, Paice J, eds. *Oxford Textbook of Palliative Nursing.* 4th ed. New York, NY: Oxford University Press; 2015:422–39.
6. Corey R, Hla KM. Major and massive hemoptysis: reassessment of conservative management. *Am J Med Sci.* 1987; 294: 301–9.
7. Powitsky R, Vasan N, Krempl G, et al. Carotid blowout in patients with head and neck cancer. *Ann Otol Rhinol Laryngol.* 2010; 119: 476–84.
8. Ghahestani SM, Shakhssalim N. Palliative treatment of intractable hematuria in context of advanced bladder cancer. *Urol J.* 2009; 6: 149–56.
9. Patsner B. Topical acetone for control of life-threatening vaginal hemorrhage from recurrent gynecologic cancer. *Eur J Gynaecol Oncol.* 1993; 14: 33–5.
10. McGrath P, Leahy M. Catastrophic bleeds during end-of-life-care in haematology: controversies from Australian research. *Support Care Cancer.* 2009; 17(5): 527–37.
11. Hulme B, Wilcox S. Guidelines on the management of bleeding for palliative care patients with cancer. 2013; Yorkshire Palliative Medicine Clinical Guidelines Group.
12. Gilman C. Focus on: Treatment of epistaxis. *ACEP News.* 2009. Available at http://www.acep.org/Clinical-Practice-Management/Focus on Epitaxis/. Accessed December 2014.
13. Alexander S. Malignant fungating wounds: managing pain, bleeding and psychological issues. *J Wound Care.* 2009; 18: 418–25.
14. Hague J, Tippett R. Endovascular techniques in palliative care. *Clin Oncol.* 2010; 22: 771–80.
15. D'Amico G, Pietrosi G, Tarantino I. Emergency sclerotherapy versus vasoactive drugs for variceal bleeding in cirrhosis: a Cochrane meta-analysis. *Gastroenterology.* 2003; 124: 1277–91.
16. Roberts SB, Coyne PJ, Thomas,TJ, et al. Palliative use of aminocaproic acid to control upper gastrointestinal bleeding. *J Pain Symptom Manage.* Sept 2010; 40:e1–e3. doi: http://dx.doi.org/10.1016/j.painsymman.20110.06.004
17. Prommer E. Management of bleeding in the terminally ill patient. *Hematology.* 2005;10:167–75.
18. Cartoni C, Delia M, Cupelli L, et al. Hemorrhagic complications in patients with advanced hematological malignancies followed at home: an Italian experience. *Leukemia & Lymphoma.* 2009; 50: 387–91.
19. Salacz ME, Lankiewicz MW, Weissman DE. Management of thrombocytopenia in bone marrow failure. *J Palliat Med.* 2007; 10: 236–244.
20. Nash R. What are the best pharmacological and surgical treatments for patients with spinal cord compression. In: Goldstein NM, ed. *Evidence-Based Practice of Palliative Medicine.* Philadelphia, PA: Elsevier; 2013:394–7.
21. Schiff D. Clinical features and diagnosis of neoplastic epidural spinal cord compression, including cauda equina syndrome. *UpToDate.* 2014; 1–15. Accessed April 2014.
22. Williams K, Lin L, Cuccurullo SJ. Direct extension of a psoas muscle abscess leading to spinal cord compression. *Am J Phys Med Rehabil.* 2013; 92: 370.
23. Stoddard JE, Chiverton N. Thoracic facet joint synovitis causing thoracic spinal cord compression and myelopathy in a patient with rheumatoid arthritis. *Rheumatology.* 2011; 50: 2141–2.
24. Choi SH, Lee SH, Khang SK, Jeon SR. IgG4-related sclerosing pachymeningitis causing spinal cord compression. *Neurology.* 2010; 75: 1388–90.
25. Li MF, Chiu PC, Weng MJ, Lai PH. Atlantoaxial instability and cervical cord compression in Morquio syndrome. *Arch Neurol.* 2010; 67: 1530.
26. George R, Jeba J, Ramkumar G, Chacko AG, Leng M, Tharyan P. Interventions for the treatment of metastatic extradural spinal cord compression in adults. *The Cochrane Database of Systematic Reviews.* 2008(4): Cd006716.
27. Loblaw DA, Perry J, Chambers A, Laperriere NJ. Systematic review of the diagnosis and management of malignant extradural spinal cord compression: the Cancer Care Ontario Practice Guidelines Initiative's Neuro-Oncology Disease Site Group. *J Clin Oncol.* 2005; 23(9): 2028–37.
28. Quraishi NA, Esler C. Metastatic spinal cord compression. *BMJ.* 2011; 342: d2402.
29. Jennelle RL, Vijayakumar V, Vijayakumar S. A systematic and evidence-based approach to the management of vertebral metastasis. *ISRN Surgery.* 2011; 2011: 719715.
30. Abrahm J, Banffy MB, Harris MB. Spinal cord compression in patients with advanced metastatic cancer: "All I care about is walking and living my life." *JAMA.* 2009; 299: 937–46.
31. Nash R. What are the signs and symptoms of spinal cord compression? In: Goldstein NM, ed. *Evidence-Based Practice of Palliative Medicine.* Philadelphia: Elsevier; 2013:390–3.
32. Maranzano E, Bellavita R, Rossi R, et al. Short-course versus split-course radiotherapy in metastatic spinal cord compression: results of a phase III randomized, multicenter trial. *J Clin Oncol.* 2005; 23: 3358–65.
33. Rades D, Dunst J, Schild SE. The first score predicting overall survival in patients with metastatic spinal cord compression. *Cancer.* 2008; 112: 157–61.
34. Rades D, Abrahm JL. The role of radiotherapy for metastatic epidural spinal cord compression. *Nat Rev Clin Oncol.* 2010; 7: 590–8.
35. Patchell RA, Tibbs P, Regine WF, et al. Direct decompressive surgical resection in the treatment of spinal cord compression caused by metastatic cancer: a randomized trial. *Lancet.* 2005; 366: 643–8.
36. Kim JM, Bono CM, Schoenfeld AJ. Clinical outcome of metastatic spinal cord compression treated with surgical excision +/- radiation versus radiation therapy alone: a systematic review of the literature. *Spine.* 2012; 37: 78–84.
37. Sutcliffe P, Connock M, Shyangdan D. A systematic review of evidence on malignant spinal metastases: natural history and technologies for identifying patients at high risk of vertebral fracture and spinal cord compression. *Health Tech Assessment.* 2013; 17: 1–274.
38. Jeba GR, Ramkumar G, Chacko AG. Intervention for the treatment of metastatic extradural spinal cord compression in adults. *Cochrane Database of Systematic Reviews.* 2008;4.doi:10.1002/14651858. CD006716.pub2
39. Ruff RL, Adamson VW, Ruff SS, Wang X. Directed rehabilitation reduces pain and depression while increasing independence and satisfaction with life for patients with paraplegia due to epidural metastatic spinal cord compression. *J Rehabil Res Dev.* 2007; 44: 1–10.
40. Ruff R, Ruff S, Wang X. Persistent benefits of rehabilitation on pain and life quality for nonambulatory patients with spinal epidural metastasis. *J Rehabil Res Dev.* 2007; 44: 271–8.

41. Fattal C, Fabbro M, Gelis A, Bauchet L. Metastatic paraplegia and vital prognosis: perspectives and limitations for rehabilitation care. Part 1. *Arch Phys Med Rehabil*. 2011; 92: 125–33.

42. Aminoff MJ, Kerchner GA. Nervous system disorders. In: McPhee SJ, Papadakis MA, eds. *2012 Current Medical Diagnosis and Treatment*. 51st ed. New York, NY: McGraw-Hill; 2012:942–9.

43. Benedict M, St. Louis EK. Status epilepticus. John Wiley & Sons. http://www.essentialevidenceplus.com/content/eee/459. Accessed June 1, 2014.

44. St. Louis EK, Benedict M. Seizure disorder (adult). John Wiley & Sons. http://www.essentialevidenceplus.com/content/eee/456. Accessed June 1, 2014.

45. Tradounsky G. Seizures in palliative care. *Can Fam Physician*. 2013; 59: 951–5.

46. Sizoo EM, Braam L, Postma TJ et al. Symptoms and problems in the end-of-life phase of high-grade glioma patients. *Neuro Oncol*. 2010; 12(11): 1162–6. doi: 10.1093/neuonc/nop045

47. Creutzfeldt CJ, Holloway RG, Walker M. Symptomatic and palliative care for stroke survivors. *J Gen Intern Med*. 2012; 27: 853–60. doi: 10.1007/s11606-011-1966-4

48. Canoui-Poitrine F, Bastuji-Garin S, Alonso E, et al. Risk and prognostic factors of status epilepticus in elderly: A case-control study. *Epilepsia*. 2011; 52: 1849–56. doi: 10.1111/j.1528-1167.2011.03168.x

49. Alvarez V, Januel JM, Burnand B, Rossetti AO. Role of comorbidities in outcome prediction after status epilepticus. *Epilepsia*. 2012; 53: e89–92. doi: 10.1111/j.1528-1167.2012.03451.x

50. American Association of Neurology. Summary of Evidence-Based Guidelines for Clinicians—Evaluating an Apparent Unprovoked First Seizure in Adults. St. Paul, MN: AAN; 2007. https://www.aan.com/Guidelines/Home/GetGuidelineContent/260. Accessed August 27, 2014.

51. Silbergleit R, Durkalski B, Lowenstein D, et al. Intramuscular versus intravenous therapy for prehospital status epilepticus. *N Engl J Med*. 2012; 366: 591–600.

52. Brophy GM, Bell R, Claassen J, et al. Guidelines for the evaluation and management of status epilepticus. *Neurocrit Care*. Springer Science + Business Media LLC; 2012. doi: 10.1007/s12028-012-9695-2

53. Meirkord H, Boon P, Engelsen B, et al. European Federation of Neurological Societies (EFNS) guideline on the management of status epilepticus in adults. *Eur J Neurol*. 2010; 17: 348–55.

54. American College of Emergency Physicians (ACEP). Clinical policy: critical issues in the evaluation and management of adult patients presenting to the emergency department with seizures. *Ann Emerg Med*. 2014; 63: 437–47.

55. Benit JP, Vecht CJ. Spectrum of side effects of anticonvulsants in patients with brain tumours. *Eur Assoc Neurooncol Mag*. 2012; 2: 15–24.

56. Sykes L, Wood E, Kwan J. Antiepileptic drugs for the primary and secondary prevention of seizures after stroke. *CDSR*. 2014;1. doi: 10.1002/14651858.CD005398.pub3.

57. Ratial BO, Pappmikail L, Costa J, Sampaio C. Anticonvulsants for preventing seizures in patients with chronic subdural haematoma. *CDSR*. 2013;6. doi: 10.1002/14651858.CD004893.pub3.

58. Juba KM, Weiland D. Seizure management in a complex hospice patient. *J Pain Palliat Care Pharmacother*. 2010; 24: 27–32. doi: 10.3109/15360280903583107.

59. McCurdy MT, Shanholtz CB. Oncologic emergencies. *Critical Care Med*. 2012; 40: 2212–22.

60. Ratnarathorn M, Craig E. Cutaneous findings leading to a diagnosis of superior vena cava syndrome: A case report and review of the literature. *Dermatology Online Journal*. 2011; 17: 4.

61. Simoff MJ, Lally B, Slade MG, et al. Symptom management in patients with lung cancer: Diagnosis and management of lung cancer, 3rd ed: American College of Chest Physicians evidence-based clinical practice guidelines. *Chest*. 2013; 143(5 Suppl): e455S–497S.

62. Lanciego C, Pangua C, Chacon JI, et al. Endovascular stenting as the first step in the overall management of malignant superior vena cava syndrome. *AJR Am J Roentgenol*. 2009; 193: 549–58.

63. Lexi-Comp OnlineTM, Lexicomp Drugs Online.™ Hudson, OH: Lexi-Comp, Inc. Accessed May 25, 2014.

64. Rogers SJ, Cavazos JE. Epilepsy. In: DiPiro JT, Talbert RL, Yee GC, Matzke GR, Wells BG, Posey LM, eds. *Pharmacotherapy: A Pathophysiologic Approach*. New York, NY: McGraw-Hill, 2014:855–82.

PART FOUR

COMMUNICATION

CHAPTER 38

Introducing Palliative Care

Marian Grant

Key Points

♦ There is evidence from both the healthcare and the palliative care fields on how best to present palliative care.

♦ The palliative advanced practice registered nurse (APRN) should understand the basic social marketing principles involved in introducing palliative care.

Introduction

This chapter provides evidence and recommendations about how best to introduce palliative care to patients, families, clinicians, and other stakeholders. This is valuable information when seeing patients, meeting with families, persuading colleagues to order palliative care, or working with hospital administrators or other key stakeholders. Many palliative care programs are led by APRNs, so they may be the representatives for that service to the hospital, the clinic, or the community.

Social Marketing and Palliative Care

Social marketing seeks to

> develop and integrate marketing concepts with other approaches to influence behaviors that benefit individuals and communities for the greater social good. Social Marketing practice is guided by ethical principles. It seeks to integrate research, best practice, theory, audience and partnership insight, to inform the delivery of competition sensitive and segmented social change programmes that are effective, efficient, equitable and sustainable.[1]

This is germane to palliative care because the goal is to influence clinicians' and patients' behavior so that palliative care can be provided sooner and to more people with serious illness. Developing social marketing efforts involves a standard process[2] that incorporates the six steps shown in Table 38.1. The first three steps form the framework for this chapter.

Problem Definition: History of Palliative Care

Palliative care evolved out of the hospice movement that began in the 1970s as a way to make death and dying less medical and more personal experience. In 1982, the Medicare Hospice Benefit established funding for hospice services for Medicare patients and their families.[3] Subsequently, private insurance companies also offered hospice benefits, with the result that, by 2012, 1.5 to 1.6 million people received hospice care in the United States.[4]

Even with the growth of home hospice care, most Americans still died in hospitals.[5] This led to the development of hospital-based palliative care programs in the 1980s; there were 600 such programs in 2000 and 1,734 in 2012.[6] Organizations that had previously been hospice-focused, such as the Hospice Nurses Association (established in 1986) or the Academy of Hospice Physicians (established in 1988), expanded to include palliative care and become the Hospice and Palliative Nurses Association in 1998 (HPNA)[7] and the American Academy of Hospice and Palliative Medicine (AAHPM)[8] in 2000. The Center to Advance Palliative Care (CAPC) started as a resource for hospital-based palliative care programs but has broadened its mission to other healthcare settings as well. Today, palliative care is a recognized specialty with certification available for physicians, advanced practice registered nurses, registered nurses, nursing assistants, social workers, chaplains, and administrators.

With the growth in palliative care programs, there has also been an increase in research in the field. A growing evidence base now confirms that palliative care improves the quality of life for those with serious illness and their families without adding to the cost of their care. Recent evidence seems to suggest that implementing palliative care sooner in a serious illness is preferable, as data show that patients who receive earlier care have better outcomes and may even live longer.[9] With healthcare reform, the benefits of palliative care are very timely and the field is seen as a key solution to improving the quality of care for those with serious illness while simultaneously helping to manage costs.[10]

Palliative Care Social Marketing Challenges

While the future of palliative care seems bright, there are barriers preventing it from being more widely available. While some of the barriers are logistical and financial, this chapter focuses on the ones involving knowledge and attitudes about palliative care.

Lack of Awareness

In two national surveys, only 22% to 24% of people were somewhat or very familiar with the term "palliative care."[11,12] This is

Table 38.1 Social Marketing Steps

Step	Activity	Description
1	Problem definition	The issue to be addressed or the outcome sought and its context
2	Market research	Information on either the population or ideal users of a service or program (target audience), their characteristics, beliefs, behaviors, attitudes, needs, etc.
3	Marketing strategy	Plan of action including target audience, the desired behavior change goal, the benefits that will be offered, and the interventions to influence/support the behavior change
4	Interventions	Specific/measurable methods to implement the marketing strategy that will influence, facilitate, or promote desired behavior change
5	Evaluation	Activities to measure outcomes of intervention(s)
6	Implementation	End result of all the previous steps

From reference 2.

a good news/bad news situation. On one hand, having to teach so many people about palliative care is daunting. On the other hand, the public's lack of awareness means there is the opportunity to define palliative care in the most appropriate way.[13]

Confusing Palliative Care with End-of-Life Care

Among those aware of palliative care, some confuse it with end-of-life care or hospice.[9,13] Such confusion is likely justified, since those two concepts/terms are often paired. One example is that the names of the palliative care organizations mentioned earlier in this chapter include hospice: the *Hospice* and Palliative Nurses Association, the National *Hospice* and Palliative Care Organization. The advanced practice registered nurse certification is the Advanced Certified *Hospice* and Palliative Nurse; the medical certification is *Hospice* and Palliative Medicine. This frequent combination of the words "hospice" and "palliative care" may contribute to people's thinking they are one and the same.[13]

In addition, much of the media coverage for palliative care has historically been focused on the end-of-life aspects. These are usually compelling human interest stories but, over time, also contribute to this misunderstanding and make it that much harder to position palliative care as appropriate earlier in an illness.

Many clinicians think palliative care is exclusively for dying patients and therefore avoid considering or involving it until the very end.[9,10] Physicians polled in a national survey described palliative care as "comfort care" for those at the end-of-life.[12] None talked about it being appropriate earlier in a serious illness.[12]

"Death Panel" Fears

Another unfortunate misconception is the public's concern that healthcare reform will involve the government's making care decisions based on cost. This is best reflected in the "death panel" issue

that arose in 2010. This began when a provision in the Affordable Care Act that sought to compensate healthcare providers for having goals-of-care discussions with Medicare patients was singled out and misidentified as a government plan to limit end-of-life care to save money. This provision was termed "death panels" by former Alaska Governor Sarah Palin and other opponents of the legislation.[14] The furor this raised was so strong the provision had to be removed. Four years after passage of the law, 34% of people surveyed still believed there was a "death panel" provision in it,[15] and research done to test the effect of attempts to correct this misinformation found that those who were already supportive of Sarah Palin were even more convinced that death panels existed.[14] Medicare will try, through regulation, to have billing codes that providers can use to be reimbursed for advance care planning. Let's hope the "death panels" are behind us, but, even so, conversations about palliative care should avoid highlighting cost savings as the key benefit, as it only risks raising this previous misconception.

Public Resistance to Thinking About Death

A large body of evidence confirms that people either do not want or are resistant to thinking about and planning for serious illness.[16–20] The low rate of those having advance directives (20% to 30%[20]) is just one confirmation of this. Many people who are in the last stages of illness are either not aware of that fact or do not want to accept it. Efforts to change this situation have largely been unsuccessful. The Robert Wood Johnson Foundation funded a national effort in 1995 to reach over 1,000 consumer and health groups to improve communication and change the culture within healthcare and the American public regarding death and dying. But despite a decade of effort, there was little awareness of this campaign and it had no impact on the public's attitude on these topics.[22] Although almost all those polled in a recent national survey felt that end-of-life and hospice care should be a priority for the country (86% and 91%, respectively), only 50% felt they were themselves somewhat to very prepared for the end-of-life; 49% were somewhat or very unprepared.[11] While people acknowledge the importance of these issues, many have not taken steps to prepare for them personally.

Therefore, from a social marketing standpoint, the problem facing palliative care is that most people are unaware of what palliative care is or think it's synonymous with end-of-life care, which is not appealing. As a result, if it is offered at all, it is offered late in an illness.

There are several different target audiences for palliative care messaging: patients with serious illness and their families, clinicians, administrators, and health policy makers. However, the market research available is primarily for the general public and is summarized below.

The General Public and Palliative Care

There are several different target audiences for palliative care messages, including patients with serious illness and their families, clinicians, administrators, and health policymakers. However, the market research available is primarily for the general public. Two national surveys in 2011 explored attitudes about end-of-life issues and various ways to describe palliative care.[11,12] Their pertinent findings are as follows.

First, palliative care addresses the public's biggest healthcare concerns. Although people surveyed were generally content with the quality of healthcare for serious illness, more than half had concerns about "sharing information between doctor and patient and other doctors, patient control and choice over treatment options, patient understanding about their illness and treatment, and the quality of time doctors spend with patients."[12] This is encouraging, since these are issues that palliative care addresses.

Second, people are interested in palliative care education and coverage. Respondents strongly agreed that education on palliative care should be offered along with curative treatment (78%) and that discussions of palliative care should be fully covered by health insurance (71%) or Medicare (60%).[11] This was tested to explore possible "death panel" concerns. However, when the discussions were presented in a different context, most people felt such discussions were appropriate.

Third, the surveys found that specific words and phrases make a difference. In talking about the kind of conditions palliative care would be most appropriate for, any link to terminal illness was a negative. Instead, people preferred the term "serious illness" because it was less synonymous with terminal illness than "advanced illness"[12] (note that this chapter uses the phrase "serious illness" consistently). In addition, the following phrases about palliative care were found to be very appealing:

◆ It helps provide the best possible quality of life for a patient and family.

◆ It helps patients and families manage the pain, symptoms, and stress of serious illness.

◆ It is a partnership of patient, medical specialists, and family.

◆ It is appropriate at any age and at any stage in a serious illness.[12]

Fourth, palliative care must be differentiated from hospice or end-of-life care. Respondents in one study became confused about the meaning of palliative care when the terms "hospice" or "end-of-life" were included in the definition. The researchers concluded that "it is important to avoid defining palliative care by what it is NOT."[12]

Fifth, different definitions of palliative care result in different levels of interest. There are multiple ways to define palliative care. This is the World Health Organization's definition:

> Palliative care is an approach that improves the quality of life of patients and their families facing the problems associated with life-threatening illness, through the prevention and relief of suffering by means of early identification and impeccable assessment and treatment of pain and other problems, physical, psychosocial and spiritual.[21]

The 2013 National Consensus Project's Clinical Practice Guidelines for Palliative Care uses this definition:

> Palliative care means patient- and family-centered care that optimizes quality of life by anticipating, preventing, and treating suffering. Palliative care throughout the continuum of illness involves addressing physical, intellectual, emotional, social, and spiritual needs and to facilitate patient autonomy, access to information, and choice.[22]

In a national survey done by CAPC, a simple yet more specific definition tested well:

> Palliative care is specialized medical care for people with serious illnesses. This type of care is focused on providing patients with relief from the symptoms, pain, and stress of a serious illness—whatever the diagnosis. The goal is to improve quality of life for both the patient and the family. Palliative care is provided by a team of doctors, nurses, and other specialists who work with a patient's other doctors to provide an extra layer of support. Palliative care is appropriate at any age and at any stage in a serious illness, and can be provided together with curative treatment.[12]

When presented with this definition, 86% of those surveyed said they would be somewhat or very likely to consider palliative care.[12] In addition, 92% felt it would be somewhat or very important for palliative care to be available at all hospitals. That opinion was consistent across Democrats, Republicans, independents, and those who supported the Tea Party, which is helpful when discussing palliative care with policymakers.[12]

While the CAPC definition has been widely disseminated within the palliative care field, there is some evidence that this phrasing might not be appealing to all patient populations. Subsequent research done among those with advanced cancer found there was no difference in terms of understanding or favorable impressions between the CAPC definition and a more traditional one:[13]

> Palliative care (or supportive care) is specialized medical care for patients with life-limiting illness. This type of care is focused on the management of symptoms such as pain, nausea, anxiety, and stress for patients with advanced cancer. The goal is to improve patient's quality of life. Emphasis is placed on communication and coordinated care with the patient's cancer doctors. Palliative care (or supportive care) is appropriate from the time of diagnosis with a life-limiting illness and can be provided together with other cancer treatments such as chemotherapy or radiation.[13]

The researchers felt that the issue was likely more concern about the term "palliative" rather than the specific definition. This concern might be due to cancer patients' possible assumption that this was end-of-life care, as that is typically when "palliative" oncology treatments are offered.[13] The researchers also suggested that patients may have formed a less positive association with "palliative" based on misunderstandings they picked up from their oncologists, who typically equate palliative care with end-of-life care.[13] Since there was little difference between the two definitions in the cancer study and the previous national survey found the CAPC definition very appealing, it is probably appropriate to use the CAPC definition, or key phrases from it, when discussing palliative care.

Table 38.2 gives information on the needs of other potential palliative care stakeholders.

Table 38.2 Palliative Care Target Audiences and Their Needs

Target Audience	Needs
Patients/families	Symptom management, support, education, assistance identifying goals
Clinicians	Education/assistance on symptom management, communication, identifying goals, support
Administrators	Improving quality, satisfaction, controlling costs, staff retention
Policymakers	Information/education on palliative care benefits and fact that public needs/wants this type of care

Marketing Strategy

Given the above market research findings, the next step is to develop a social marketing strategy for palliative care. The key issues to address are what to call it (referred to as branding) and how to position it.

Branding

The "branding" question has probably been around since the beginning of the use of the term "palliative." The Wikipedia page for palliative care begins by saying that palliative care is also called palliative medicine, supportive care, or comfort care and symptom management.[25] This is a problem from a branding standpoint, where consistency is imperative.

Cancer care seems to be the primary place where the issue of palliative-versus-supportive-care branding occurs. Several studies among cancer patients or on behalf of cancer centers have found some benefit to the use of the term "supportive" versus "palliative."[13,26–28] This is likely due to confusion in oncology between the use of the word "palliative" for noncurative treatment and "palliative care," which as a result likely sounds like something for only those with end-stage cancer. Some cancer programs compromise and use both terms (e.g., "palliative and supportive care"). However, "supportive care" comes with its own issues. To some it sounds somewhat "soft" or vague and not necessarily appropriate for a certified specialty that has a growing evidence base. It also has limited use outside of oncology. In the end, it may be appropriate to use "supportive care" with either patients with cancer or their oncologists if that will be more acceptable. Another provocative option would be to rename "palliative" oncology treatments, since they are not typically part of palliative care and often cause worse quality of life.[29]

Some feel the term "palliative" should be abandoned altogether given its potential liabilities. This is ironic when one considers that the very reason the term "palliative" was chosen in 1974 by Dr. Balfour Mount, a surgical oncologist in Montreal, Canada, was to avoid the negative associations with the word "hospice" in French, as the French word meant nursing homes or homes for the poor.[30] Reactions to the term "palliative" will likely change over time as more and more people experience it earlier in an illness, so debating it now is probably unproductive. Therefore, palliative care should be the "brand" used, as, from a social marketing standpoint, it will be difficult to educate the general public, clinicians, and policymakers about this important type of care if the language used to describe it is inconsistent. The most successful brands (e.g., Apple, Nike, Starbucks, and Amazon) are extremely disciplined and consistent in their messaging, and palliative care should follow their example. Also, for 40 years now the field has been called "palliative care," and there will never be enough resources to rebrand it as something else. Therefore, efforts would be better focused on teaching the public and clinicians what palliative care is, since once they have experience with it, it "sells" itself.

Positioning Palliative Care

The next step is to determine how to position palliative care in the most compelling way. The key phrases[12] from the CAPC research are an important start, but there are nuances that go beyond them. To address those nuances, it is helpful to review some principles of persuasive advertising[30] that are relevant to palliative care messaging.

1. Communicate a unique selling proposition (one not claimed by others).[31] This is relevant to palliative care as it is a unique type of care. Few other sets of actions result in improving a patient's and family's quality of life with no additional burden or cost. The position should be that palliative care doesn't cost more, rather than it saves money, since improving quality while reducing cost seems counterintuitive and may frighten those concerned about "death panel" rationing. This is the key message that palliative care leaders have adopted and the one that should be used consistently in messages about the field.

2. Provide news, but only if it's real.[31] Palliative care is a relatively young field that most Americans are unaware of, so its benefits are indeed news to them and, given the growing evidence base, very real. Several studies suggest that palliative care not only improves the quality of life but may also prolong life,[9] which is good news indeed.

3. Use positive statements.[31] This is a critical point. A strong body of advertising evidence and business results show that people are more drawn to positive messages than negative ones and that products or services that provide positive benefits are more persuasive than those that promise to avoid negative ones.[30] As noted earlier in this chapter, many people do not want to think about death and dying, so no amount of "good death" stories are going to change that. This is why palliative care practitioners should avoid talking about horror stories that palliative care can help avoid; instead, they should present inspiring stories enabled by palliative care that people will yearn for. The APRN should focus on what palliative care is and how it can help.

4. Any illustrations should support the basic message.[31] Visuals are very important and should be congruent with the words they accompany.[31] They should show positive, uplifting situations and people enjoying a good quality of life, rather than frail dying patients in sad environments. Such positive visuals are also appropriate since most of the people who could benefit from palliative care are not dying and so are very much alive and want to live their lives to the fullest.

Positioning also refers to how a message is tailored for different target audiences. Table 38.2 is a good reminder of the themes to be reinforced with each target audience to make the message compelling to them.

Pertinent Healthcare Marketing Examples

To bring the above principles to life, it is helpful to note that successful pharmaceutical companies and cancer centers have become masters at marketing, and palliative care could benefit from adopting some of their strategies. The communication challenge these other entities face is the same as for palliative care: how to make treatment for an unpleasant situation appealing. And all offer solutions to people with serious illness. In doing so they also compete, to a certain extent, with palliative care for the attention of those with serious illness. As a result, the communication for palliative care needs to be as compelling and appealing as that of pharmaceuticals and cancer centers to persuade people that it is also worth considering.

Pharmaceutical Advertising

Direct-to-consumer advertising for pharmaceuticals has been around since the early 1980s and is now the predominant health-care communication to the public.[32] Using some of the principles noted above, new medication categories have developed, such as the $9.4 billion antidepressant market in the United States[33] or the $4.3 billion erectile dysfunction category worldwide.[34] And while direct-to-consumer advertising alone is not responsible for the size of these categories, it is a key factor.[35] If we review print advertisements for these categories, we can conclude that: (1) pharmaceutical companies believe consumers are drawn to positive images and experiences; (2) it is possible to talk about unpleasant images in an upbeat, positive way; and (3) businesses that meet people's needs in a positive way will be successful. The ads themselves are very familiar: a confident woman walks on the beach (Zoloft®), and smiling young mothers play with their happy children (Cymbalta®). Missing is the "real" story of depressed, anguished people trapped alone in their rooms. Erectile dysfunction advertising shows happy couples in positive, desirable situations: middle-aged couples dance and laugh together (Viagra®), couples sit in adjoining outdoor bathtubs (Cialis®). These ads do not show the flip side of sad older couples looking dissatisfied in bed. Very little pharmaceutical advertising shows the negatives of the issue they are trying to treat, even though they are required to include side effects and risks in all advertising. Instead, they typically focus on the benefits of their products. And people are drawn to the idea that their lives could be better and happier with these products, which motivates them to want them.

Cancer Center Advertising

Perhaps taking a lesson from the pharmaceutical industry, advertising for cancer centers is also uniformly positive and inspiring. A recent content analysis of such advertising confirmed what most already knew: "clinical advertisements by cancer centers frequently promote cancer therapy with emotional appeals that evoke hope and fear while rarely providing information about risks, benefits, costs, or insurance availability."[36] The current logo for one cancer center has a red line through the word "Cancer." Another's ads feature smiling, healthy-looking people holding up notes addressed to cancer that say things like, "You said I'd never have children. My daughter says you're wrong" or "My hair has grown back. You haven't."

Although many cancer centers also offer palliative care, their advertising doesn't include palliative care messages. Palliative care needs to make its messaging competitive in this context since people are choosing what type of care is right for them in part because of such messaging. For palliative care, this means focusing on success stories, such as people who survived aggressive treatment with the help of palliative care and are now cured or have lived fully and long enough to enjoy important birthdays, graduations, and so forth.

Introducing Hospice and End-of-Life Care

These previous principles are most pertinent to palliative care delivered earlier in a serious illness. The challenge, then, is how to discuss those parts of palliative care that actually do involve death and dying, such as hospice. Awareness of hospice is very high (86%),[11] and most people have a positive opinion about it in the abstract. However, when it comes to actually enrolling, there is resistance as patients and families struggle with what they perceive as a rapid transition from being "sick" to "dying" and that choosing hospice means giving up hope.[37] One way to address this is to introduce the concept of hospice much earlier in a serious illness. Done early, it can be discussed as that form of palliative care for those in the last few months of life, which may eventually be appropriate for that patient. Then, over time, the team can bring hospice up as a way to say that the patient is getting closer to qualifying for hospice. In studies that have tested this approach, patients and families make a smoother and earlier transition to hospice.[38]

There are also examples of successful marketing efforts for hospice. These manage to talk about quality of life versus dying and use visuals that show people enjoying their lives and loved ones. The NHPCO launched a campaign in 2014 called "Moments of Life: Made Possible with Hospice" with a website that shows how "hospice makes more meaningful moments possible" via positive and uplifting visuals and stories.[39] Other hospices have run print ads with positive visuals talking about how a patient is "a person … not an illness," and that hospice is a "choice" that people can make. However, it will always be challenging to discuss this kind of care once people understand that it is linked to death and dying. The hope is that by promoting earlier palliative care for all with serious illness, people will be more emotionally prepared to accept the transition into the final stage and thus more open to services like hospice.

Interventions/Case Study

Based on the principles discussed so far, this section provides examples of how to use them in practice. These examples involve a case study of an APRN named Hannah who is starting a new palliative care service at her community hospital. Hannah has the opportunity to educate people all around her about what palliative care is and to do so in a way that makes it as appealing as possible.

Introducing Palliative Care to Patients and Families

When introducing palliative care to patients and families, it is important to remember the awareness issues covered earlier in this chapter, namely that people may not know what palliative care is or think that it is end-of-life care. What they do have are palliative care needs in terms of symptom management, support, education, and identifying their goals of care and making medical decisions. When discussing how palliative care can help meet these needs, the APRN should remember the key phrases or ideas that are appealing to patients and families:

- "Partners," "team," "support," "extra layer of support"
- "Choice," "independence," "control"
- They can receive palliative care along with curative treatment.
- Palliative care can help them tolerate curative treatment for better outcomes.

Using these phrases and concepts, every APRN should develop a succinct and appealing way to describe what palliative care is when meeting new patients or families. This can be modified for the specific patient or situation but should communicate the same overall message that palliative care is about improving quality of life but not giving up or having to stop other treatment.

Case Study Part 1

After a few weeks of introducing herself to patients or families, Hannah learned that when she describes palliative care by saying it can help keep patients more physically comfortable, that it's a form of support for patients and families, and as a palliative care APRN she can explain medical options and help with decision making, patients or families are usually receptive. She has also found that when she tells patients that their doctor or medical team asked her to come work with them and to see if she could be of help, everyone seems open to her involvement.

When patients or families ask Hannah if palliative care is hospice, she explains that hospice is a form of palliative care but that not all palliative care is hospice. If the patient is appropriate for hospice care, she explores it is an acceptable option for the patient and family members. In either case, she reassures them that palliative care can also be involved. Usually, once she describes how palliative care can be beneficial to patients or families, they become very supportive of this type of care.

Whenever she goes to see a new patient or family, Hannah hands out the brochure her team developed to define palliative care and why it can be helpful. The brochure is available throughout the hospital and uses the key phrases of the CAPC definition, as well as positive images of patients and families. It is printed in a bright, appealing color with a user-friendly design and uses simple, understandable language.

Education

There are various kinds of education that a palliative APRN may be called to do; all of them offer a chance to persuade people of the benefits of palliative care. Persuading while educating should not be too difficult, as much of the education nurses provide has a social marketing aspect. Nurses do not just give patients information. Instead, most try to learn and understand their patients and their needs, and then present health information in such a way as to motivate patients to improve their health. There is usually some attempt at persuasion in the most effective nursing education. So, applying the social marketing principles noted earlier can make education on palliative care more effective.

The palliative APRN may encounter formal clinical education opportunities (e.g., presentations to staff or nursing or medical students, orientations for new hospital employees), and there are also informal day-to-day interaction opportunities with clinicians. In any of those situations, using the CAPC definition or phrases is appropriate. The following phrases and ideas are particularly helpful to clinicians:

- "Partners," "team," "works with the medical team"
- Palliative care can help their patients tolerate curative treatment so they can have better outcomes.
- Palliative care is high-quality care that doesn't increase cost or mortality or reduce longevity.

- Palliative care resources can help with challenging patient/family situations.

The unique needs that clinicians have are education or assistance with symptom management, communication, identifying goals of care, or just support on difficult cases. They also need to feel that they are the ones controlling their patient's care and that while they might appreciate someone working with them as a partner, they are not looking for someone to take over that care.[40]

Case Study Part 2

Hannah studied palliative care consultant etiquette and has found that the nursing staff, house officers, and newer physicians are generally very open to involving palliative care once they see how helpful it is for their patients, the patients' families, and themselves. However, she regularly runs into resistance from some of the older physicians, who feel that ordering palliative care is premature. Although these situations have sometimes been challenging, she has learned to ask the following questions:

- "Would you be surprised if this patient died in the next year?[41,42] If not, then it is not premature to involve palliative care, since it is not just for dying patients."
- "What are your goals for this patient? Palliative care might be able to help you achieve them."
- "Are you thinking that palliative care is end-of-life care? End-of-life care is a form of palliative care for dying patients, but palliative care is appropriate at any time in a serious illness, and the evidence shows that earlier palliative care can improve patient outcomes."

Hannah has developed productive working relationships with most colleagues, but there are some who are still resistant. She has decided not to worry too much about that, but to do the best she can elsewhere in the hope that over time, and with more evidence, they will come around.

Many of these phrases and ideas are also appropriate when introducing palliative care to healthcare administrators, as they may be as unaware of it or as confused as the general public. In addition to understanding what palliative care is and is not, administrators have unique needs, such as improving the quality of care while reducing costs, length of stay, readmission rates, and employee turnover. Evidence shows palliative care can help with all of those things.[9] Talking about cost savings is most appropriate with this target audience. However, it should be presented as a byproduct of the work palliative care does, via identifying goals of care earlier in a hospital stay and helping patients and families choose the right treatment plan for them, rather than an endpoint of its own.

Case Study Part 3

Before her palliative care program was approved, Hannah was part of a team that collaboratively developed the business plan for her hospital. That group used the literature and CAPC information in hospital program development and also included the phrases and ideas about this type of care that have been found to be appealing. They anticipated that administrators might assume that

Table 38.3 Six Social Marketing Steps in Palliative Care

Step	Description	Palliative Care Example(s)
1. Problem definition	The issue to be addressed or the outcome sought and its context	Most people are unaware of what palliative care is or think it's synonymous with end-of-life care. If offered at all, it's offered late in a serious illness.
2. Market research	Information on either the population or ideal users of a service or program (target audience), their characteristics, beliefs, behaviors, attitudes, needs, etc.	◆ Patients with serious illness and their families who need symptom management, support, education, assistance identifying goals ◆ Clinicians who need education/assistance with symptom management, communication, identifying goals, and support ◆ Administrators who need to improve quality and satisfaction, control costs, and retain staff ◆ Policymakers who need information/education about palliative care's benefits and the fact that the public needs/wants this type of care
3. Marketing strategy	Plan of action including target audience, the desired goal of behavior change, the benefits that will be offered, and the interventions to influence/support the behavior change	Messaging to educate and motivate key target audiences to consider/order palliative care earlier in a serious illness
4. Interventions	Specific/measurable methods to implement the marketing strategy that will influence, facilitate, or promote desired behavior change	Educational programs, information sheets, brochures, newsletter articles, community events, presentations to policymakers, and advertisements of programs/services
5. Evaluation	Activities to measure outcomes of interventions	Symptom management scores, patient and family satisfaction scores, hospital length of stay, mortality, cost/hospitalization before and after palliative care intervention, attitude scores of clinicians, and public awareness
6. Implementation	End result of all the previous steps	Combination of those interventions that have been found to be effective

palliative care was just for dying patients only and addressed this in the proposal.

Similar to other target audiences, policymakers and legislators may not know what palliative care is or may confuse it with end-of-life care. Their unique needs are to develop policies that support the health of their constituents while managing or reducing cost, particularly in entitlement programs like Medicare and Medicaid. Therefore they will likely be interested in similar messages as those for healthcare administrators. Depending on their political views, they may need to be reassured that palliative care saves money by allowing people to choose the right care for them, not by persuading them to decline aggressive care.

Palliative APRNs occasionally have the opportunity to talk about palliative care to a more general or public audience. This could be participating in a community health fair or a public education program. Preparing for such educational opportunities is similar to talking about palliative care to patients and families. Using the key phrases, definitions, and examples of how patients and families can benefit is very appropriate.

Case Study Part 4

Hannah was asked to speak at a local church providing education on advance care planning for their congregation. She talked about how palliative care was a resource to help those with serious illness throughout their illness. She explained the difference between palliative care and hospice to make sure those attending understood they were two different but overlapping things. One attendee asked if there was outpatient palliative care, because he knew someone who could benefit from it right away. She responded

that outpatient care was still in development, but was pleased that people could so quickly see the benefits of palliative care and apply them to their personal situations.

Conclusion

There are many opportunities to introduce palliative care to various target audiences. When done properly, most are then interested in this type of care. A summary of the six social marketing steps as applied to palliative care is shown in Table 38.3. Hannah and her team are off to a good start at their hospital and are now trying to recruit another APRN to help with all the demand the service has prompted. She now describes palliative care with great confidence whenever she has that opportunity and is gratified to see how appealing it is when people fully understand it. She looks forward to the day when patients and families will come into the hospital demanding this type of care, and she knows her efforts are contributing to that reality.

References

1. International Social Marketing Association. http://www.i-socialmarketing.org/. Updated 2014. Accessed July 14, 2014.
2. CDCynergy. Gateway to health communication & social marketing practice. http://www.cdc.gov/healthcommunication/cdcynergylite.html. Accessed July 14, 2014.
3. National Hospice and Palliative Care Organization. History of hospice care. http://www.nhpco.org/history-hospice-care. Alexandria, VA. Updated 2014. Accessed July 14, 2014.
4. National Hospice and Palliative Care Organization. NHPCO's facts and figures: Hospice care in America. Alexandria, VA. http://www.nhpco.org/sites/default/files/public/Statistics_Research/2013_Facts_Figures.pdf. Updated 2013. Accessed July 14, 2014.

5. Centers for Disease Control. Health, United States, 2010: With special feature on death and dying. US Department of Health and Human Services, http://www.cdc.gov.proxy-hs.researchport.umd. edu/nchs/data/hus/hus10.pdf. Accessed August 12, 2015.

6. Center to Advance Palliative Care. 2012 national palliative care registry annual survey summary. https://registry.capc.org/cms/ portals/1/Reports/National_Palliative_Care%20Registry_Annual_ Survey_Summary_9.2.2014.pdf. Updated 2014. Accessed October 26, 2014.

7. Hospice and Palliative Nurses Association. History of HPNA. https://hpna.org/DisplayPage.aspx?Title=History%20of%20HPNA. Accessed July 14, 2014.

8. American Academy of Hospice and Palliative Medicine. History of AAHPM. http://aahpm.org/about/history. Updated 2013. Accessed July 14, 2014.

9. Hughes MT, Smith TJ. The growth of palliative care in the united states. *Annu Rev Public Health*. 2014; 35(1): 459–75. http://dx.doi. org/10.1146/annurev-publhealth-032013-182406. doi: 10.1146/ annurev-publhealth-032013-182406.

10. Parikh RB, Kirch RA, Smith TJ, Temel JS. Early specialty palliative care—translating data in oncology into practice. *N Engl J Med*. 2013; 369(24): 2347–51. http://dx.doi.org/10.1056/NEJMsb1305469. doi: 10.1056/NEJMsb1305469.

11. National Journal. Living well at the end of life: A national conversation. http://syndication.nationaljournal.com/events/NJ_ Events_Website/Regence_NationalSurvey_Toplinedata.pdf. Updated 2011. Accessed July 14, 2014.

12. Center to Advance Palliative Care. Public opinion research on palliative care. http://www.capc.org/tools-for-palliative-c are-programs/marketing/public-opinion-research/2 011-public-opinion-research-on-palliative-care.pdf. Updated 2011. Accessed July 14, 2014.

13. Maciasz RM, Arnold RM, Chu E, et al. Does it matter what you call it? A randomized trial of language used to describe palliative care services. *Support Care Cancer*. 2013; 21(12): 3411–9. doi: 10.1007/ s00520-013-1919-z [doi].

14. Nyhan B, Reifler J, Ubel PA. The hazards of correcting myths about health care reform. *Med Care*. 2013; 51(2): 127–32. doi: 10.1097/ MLR.0b013e318279486b.

15. Kaiser Family Foundation. Kaiser health tracking poll: March 2014. http://kaiserfamilyfoundation.files.wordpress.com/2014/03/8565-t2. pdf. Updated 2014. Accessed October 26, 2014.

16. Lake Research Partners. Survey of California voters 40 and older on long-term care. http://healthpolicy.ucla.edu/publications/ Documents/PDF/New%20Poll%20Shows%20California%20 Voters%2040%20and%20Older%20Largely%20Unprepared%20 for%20Costs%20of%20Long-Term%20Care%20Services.pdf. Updated 2010. Accessed July 14, 2014.

17. Kass-Barelmes BL, Hughes R. Advance care planning, preferences for care at the end of life. AHRQ Research in Action, issue 12. http:// www.ahrq.gov/research/findings/factsheets/aging/endliferia/index. html. Updated 2003. Accessed July 14, 2014.

18. Pew Research Social & Demographic Trends. Growing old in America: Expectations vs. reality. http://www.pewsocialtrends. org/2009/06/29/growing-old-in-america-expectations-vs-reality/. Updated 2009. Accessed July 14, 2014.

19. AARP. Planning for long-term care: A survey of midlife and older women. http://assets.aarp.org/rgcenter/general/ltc-planning-women. pdf. Updated 2010. Accessed July 14, 2014.

20. Fried TR, Redding CA, Robbins ML, Paiva A, O'Leary JR, Iannone L. Stages of change for the component behaviors of advance care planning. *J Am Geriatr Soc*. 2010; 58(12): 2329–36. doi: 10.1111/j.1532-5415.2010.03184.x [doi].

21. Rao JK, Anderson LA, Lin FC, Laux JP. Completion of advance directives among U.S. consumers. *Am J Prev Med*. 2014; 46(1): 65–70. doi: 10.1016/j.amepre.2013.09.008.

22. De Milto L. Assessment of last acts program provides recommendations for future direction. Robert Wood Johnson Foundation, October 1, 2002. Available at http://www.rwjf.org/.

23. World Health Organization. WHO definition of palliative care. http://www.who.int/cancer/palliative/definition/en. Updated 2014. Accessed July 28, 2014.

24. National Consensus Project for Quality Palliative Care. C Dahlin, ed. *Clinical Practice Guidelines for Quality Palliative Care*, 3rd ed. 2013. Available at https://www.hpna.org/multimedia/NCP_Clinical_ Practice_Guidelines_3rd_Edition.pdf.

25. Wikipedia. Palliative care. http://en.wikipedia.org/wiki/Palliative_ care. Updated 2013. Accessed July 21, 2014.

26. Morstad Boldt A, Yusuf F, Himelstein BP. Perceptions of the term palliative care. *J Palliat Med*. 2006; 9(5): 1128–36. doi: 10.1089/ jpm.2006.9.1128.

27. Dalal S, Palla S, Hui D, et al. Association between a name change from palliative to supportive care and the timing of patient referrals at a comprehensive cancer center. *Oncologist*. 2011; 16(1): 105–11. doi: 10.1634/theoncologist.2010-0161.

28. Fadul N, Elsayem A, Palmer JL, et al. Supportive versus palliative care: What's in a name? *Cancer*. 2009; 115(9): 2013–21. doi: 10.1002/ cncr.24206.

29. Smith A. "Palliative chemotherapy"—a term that should be laid to rest. Geripal. http://www.geripal.org/2014/05/ palliative-chemotherapy-term-that.html. Updated 2014. Accessed July 14, 2014.

30. Loscalzo MJ. Palliative care: An historical perspective. *ASH Education Program Book*. 2008;2008(1):465–465. doi: 10.1182/ asheducation-2008.1.465.

31. Armstrong JS. Evidence-based advertising: An application to persuasion. *Int J Advertising*. 2011; 30(5): 743.

32. Ventola CL. Direct-to-consumer pharmaceutical advertising: Therapeutic or toxic? *PT*. 2011; 36(10): 669–84.

33. US antidepressant market slides down by 4%: Report. http:// www.biospectrumasia.com/biospectrum/analysis/198165/ us-antidepressant-market-slides-report#.U8bJ71bsr8o;. Updated 2013. Accessed July 28, 2014.

34. Global erectile dysfunction drugs market is expected to reach USD 3.4 billion in 2019: Transparency market research. http://www.prweb. com/releases/2013/11/prweb11294111.htm;. Updated 2014. Accessed July 28, 2014.

35. David G, Markowitz S, Pajerowski W. Side effects of competition. *Harvard Health Policy Review*. 2014; 14(1): 13.

36. Vater LB, Donohue JM, Arnold R, White DB, Chu E, Schenker Y. What are cancer centers advertising to the public? A content analysis. *Ann Intern Med*. 2014; 160(12): 813–20. doi: 10.7326/M14-0500.

37. Ford D, Nietert P, Zapka J, Zoller J, Silvestri G. Barriers to hospice enrollment among lung cancer patients: A survey of family members and physicians. *Palliat Support Care*. 2008; 6(4): 357–62. doi: 10.1017/ S1478951508000564.

38. Dyar S, Lesperance M, Shannon R, Sloan J, Colon-Otero G. A nurse practitioner-directed intervention improves the quality of life of patients with metastatic cancer: Results of a randomized pilot study. *J Palliat Med*. 2012; 15(8): 890–5. doi: 10.1089/jpm.2012.0014.

39. National Hospice and Palliative Care Organization. Moments of life. http://www.momentsoflife.org. Updated 2014. Accessed July 23, 2014.

40. Von Gunten CF, Weissman DE. Fast Facts: Consultation etiquette in palliative care #266. *J Palliat Med*. 2013; 16(5): 578–79. doi: 10.1089/ jpm.2013.9509.

41. Moroni M, Zocchi D, Bolognesi D, et al. The "surprise" question in advanced cancer patients: A prospective study among general practitioners. *Palliat Med*. 2014; 28(7): 959–64. doi: 10.1177/0269216314526273.

42. Pang W, Kwan B, Chow K, Leung C, Li P, Szeto C. Predicting 12-month mortality for peritoneal dialysis patients using the "surprise" question. *Peritoneal Dialysis International*. 2013; 33(1): 60–6. doi: 10.3747/pdi.2011.00204.

CHAPTER 39

Advance Care Planning
Advance Directives, Medical Order Sets, and Surrogate Decision Making

Debra L. Wiegand and Katherine A. Hinderer

Key Points

- Advance care planning is essential to ensure that palliative and end-of-life care is based on patient wishes.

- Toward the end-of-life, patients may lose the ability to participate in decisions, and surrogate decision makers may need to make decisions on their behalf.

- Advanced practice registered nurses (APRNs) need to support patients, surrogates, and family members as they participate in advance care planning and make palliative and end-of-life decisions.

Case Study

Mr. Oates was a 72-year-old widower with advanced heart failure. His palliative APRN was working with the heart failure clinic to help manage his dyspnea. After he was assessed, the APRN discussed goals of care with Mr. Oates and his treatment preferences. When the APRN asked Mr. Oates if he had a living will or a healthcare proxy, he told her he did not and was "really not interested in that kind of stuff." He said his friends had told him that even if you have a living will, no one reads them, so why bother. The palliative APRN spent a few minutes clarifying why advance directives are important and assured Mr. Oates that nurses, physicians, and other members of the healthcare team do read living wills and honor them. He told the APRN that he would think about it. The APRN provided recommendations for ways to minimize and manage his dyspnea. She also asked Mr. Oates to think about advance directives, and Mr. Oates agreed to do so.

At the next visit, Mr. Oates told the APRN that he was interested in identifying someone who could make decisions for him if he was unable to. His sister was the best person, but she had been recently hospitalized and he was not sure what to do.

Advance Care Planning

Advance care planning provides an opportunity for individuals to contemplate what is important to them at the end of life. Advance care planning involves individuals' taking the time to thoughtfully consider their life, their death, and their personal preferences. These preferences are often influenced by personal values, culture, and spiritual beliefs. An important part of advance care planning is documenting personal preferences and talking about preferences with key family members, close friends, and healthcare providers. Advance care planning should include patient and family education, promotion of communication, and helping people to complete advance directives.[1]

Ideally, advance care planning is an ongoing process among patients, families, and healthcare providers that begins while individuals are healthy and able to communicate their wishes.[2,3] Discussions with trusted providers that occur over time as a process are better than one-time discussions. Some patients will choose not to participate in advance care planning, and this decision needs to be respected by the palliative APRN and healthcare team.[4]

Using the transtheoretical model of change as a framework, stages of behavior in advance care planning may include (1) pre-contemplation (the patient has not thought about advance care planning), (2) contemplation (the patient is thinking about advance care planning), (3) preparation (the patient is planning to participate in advance care planning), (4) action (the patient has had discussions and is engaged in advance care planning), and (5) maintenance (the patient has completed documents like a living will or has formally designated a durable power of attorney for healthcare).[5] Palliative APRNs can assess the stage that each person is in and develop a plan to discuss the topic and motivate and help patients as they participate in advance care planning.

Most patients will not initiate advance care planning conversations with the palliative APRN, but if the palliative APRN raises the issue, the patient may welcome the chance to discuss it. Researchers have found that when clinicians initiate advance care planning discussions and are positive about advance care planning, patients are more likely to complete advance directive documents.[6-8]

The palliative APRN should also encourage patients to involve their surrogate decision makers and/or families in the advance care planning process. Family involvement promotes advance care planning engagement and advance directive completion.[8] Involvement may also improve proxy accuracy in decision making.[9]

Healthcare Decision Making

Patients make personal and variable healthcare decisions, decisions that may change over the course of an illness or injury trajectory.[4] Individuals are free to make their own healthcare decisions. These decisions may be simple or quite complex. Autonomous individuals are free to hold certain views, make certain choices, and take certain actions based on personal values and beliefs.[10] Self-determination is based on the principle of autonomy and on respect for the individual.

It is important that the voluntary choice of an informed person with decision-making capacity determines whether any treatment, including life-sustaining therapies, is initiated, continued, or withdrawn.[11] Individuals can make the best decisions when they are informed and if they have the time they need to make decisions.

A person with decision-making capacity makes his or her decisions. This supports free choice of the individual and provides important support of autonomy. These decisions are made based on each person's values, beliefs, and personal preferences. Palliative APRNs assess whether patients have decision-making capacity, provide the information that patients need to make decisions, and determine whether patients understand the information provided.

Often, it is clear if a patient has decision-making capacity, but when it is unclear, the palliative APRN needs to perform an assessment. The APRN may find it helpful to assess decision-making capacity using a set of criteria, such as (1) the patient can make and communicate a decision, (2) the patient is able to articulate an understanding of the medical situation and prognosis, the nature of the recommended care, alternative courses of care, and the risks, benefits, and consequences of each alternative, (3) decisions are consistent with the patient's known values and goals, and (4) the patient uses reasoning to make the choice.[12]

Questions that may be helpful for the palliative APRN to ask while assessing a patient's decision-making capacity include the following:

1. What is your understanding of your health or condition now?

2. What is the therapy/treatment likely to do for you? What are the likely positive and negative outcomes of the therapy/treatment from your perspective?

3. What are you hoping the treatment will do for you?

4. What do you think will happen if you do not have the therapy/treatment?

5. What do you think will happen if you do have the therapy/treatment?

5. How did you decide to accept or refuse the therapy/treatment?

6. What makes the therapy/treatment seem better or worse than the alternatives?[13]

A patient's decision-making capacity can change over even a short period of time based on a variety of issues, including, for example, the time of day (the patient may have clear cognition in the morning after a restful night of sleep) and when certain medications are given (especially medications that impair cognition). Making decisions about care depends on the patient's ability to understand the clinical facts of his or her health status and the consequences of care alternatives.[14] Palliative APRNs must assess each patient's decision-making capacity and have ongoing discussions with patients about their preferences for care, including end-of-life care.

Advance Directives

The Patient Self-Determination Act (PSDA) was passed by the U.S. Congress as an amendment to the Omnibus Budget Reconciliation Act of 1990.[15] The PSDA requires hospitals, nursing homes, home health agencies, hospice providers, and others receiving Medicare or Medicaid reimbursement to ask if adult patients have an advance directive, to inform patients of their rights, and to provide individual and community education about advance directives. Despite legislative efforts and attempts within the healthcare community to promote advance care planning, fewer than 30% of Americans have advance directives.[16] The most common types of advance directives are living wills and durable power of attorney for healthcare documents.

Researchers who conducted the *Study to Understand Prognoses and Preferences for Outcomes and Risks of Treatments* reported shortcomings in the care of seriously ill hospitalized patients, especially in relation to physicians' knowing what treatments patients wanted at the end of life.[17] As a result of this study and other reports, numerous initiatives have been developed in an attempt to promote advance care planning and improve end-of-life care.

In 2008, a grassroots effort started National Healthcare Decisions Day, April 16. The goal is to organize community events to encourage and help individuals to complete advance directives. Table 39.1 lists advance care planning resources.

A living will is a legal document that outlines patient preferences for treatments like cardiopulmonary resuscitation (CPR), artificial nutrition and hydration, life-sustaining treatments, and comfort care. A living will takes effect when a patient can no longer speak on his or her own behalf and when the condition discussed in the advance directive is met. For example, a patient's living will may state, "I do not want life-sustaining treatments if I am in a permanent state of unconsciousness or a persistent vegetative state, or my condition is terminal."

A durable power of attorney for healthcare might also be referred to as a healthcare proxy. In these legal documents, a person designates the person who will make medical decisions on his or her behalf if something happens in the future and the individual no longer has decision-making capacity.

Legal requirements and laws related to advance directives vary from state to state. Palliative APRNs need to know the legal requirements in the state where they practice and whether specific living will and healthcare proxy documents are available in their state. It is also important to know if witnesses are needed and if the documents need to be notarized. Palliative APRNs should know if advance directive documents developed in other states can be honored in the state in which they practice.

It is important for palliative APRNs to ask patients if they have written advance directives. If the patient has a living will

Table 39.1 Advance Care Planning Resources

ACP Decisions

http://www.acpdecisions.org/

Aging With Dignity

Five Wishes

www.agingwithdignity.org

American Bar Association

Consumer's Toolkit for Health Care Advance Planning

http: //www.americanbar.org/groups/law_aging/resources/health_care_
decision_making/consumer_s_toolkit_for_health_care_advance_planning.
html

Compassion and Support at the End of Life

Advance care planning—patients and families

http://www.compassionandsupport.org/index.php/for_patients_families/
advance_care_planning

The Conversation Project

theconversationproject.org

National Cancer Institute

Advance Directives Fact Sheet

http://www.cancer.gov/cancertopics/factsheet/Support/advance-directives

National Hospice and Palliative Care Organization—Caring Connections

Speak4me, It's about how you LIVE, and state-specific documents

http://www.caringinfo.org/i4a/pages/index.cfm?pageid=3285

National Healthcare Decisions Day

www.nhdd.org

National Institute on Aging

http://www.nia.nih.gov/health/publication/advance-care-planning

National POLST Paradigm

Physician Orders for Life-Sustaining Paradigm

www.polst.org

Respecting Choices

Respectingchoices.com

Speak Up

http://www.advancecareplanning.ca/

Take Charge of Your Life

http://www.takechargeofyourlife.org/

and/or a durable power of attorney for healthcare, the palliative APRN should review the document(s) with the patient and ask the patient to confirm that his or her wishes are still the same as what was written in the document(s). If a patient would like to change the documents, the APRN supports the patient in doing so and offers assistance or direction as needed. The palliative APRN should document all advance directive discussions. If patients do not have advance directives, they should be provided with information regarding why they are important, encouraged to develop them, and helped to do so.

Advance directives should be completed early so that there is a clear understanding of what each patient's preferences are for palliative and end-of-life care. The palliative APRN should review each patient's advance directives periodically. Patients should be encouraged to communicate any changes in treatment preferences or in their healthcare proxy with their healthcare providers. Again, all discussions should be documented by the palliative APRN.

Patients should discuss their treatment preferences not only with clinicians but also with their proxy decision maker and close family members and friends. Patients should know that if they would like the palliative APRN's support while discussing or sharing advance directives with family members, the APRN will help them to do this.

The palliative APRN can suggest helpful words to use when asking someone to be a surrogate. Suggestions might include, "If a time should come when I am not able to speak, I would like you to speak for me. You know me well. You know what I value most and you know what I would and would not want at the end of my life. Would you be willing to do this for me?"

If the patient has a living will and/or a durable power of attorney for healthcare, copies of the documents should be distributed to key people. A copy can be given to healthcare providers so the documents can be added to the patient's medical record and placed in an area that can be easily accessed. If an electronic medical record system is used, the advance directive documents can be scanned and included in the electronic record.

Patients should also be advised to keep copies of advance directive documents in several places. One copy may be kept in a personal safe or a safety deposit box. Other copies should be given to the patient's surrogate decision maker. Copies can also be given to other close family members. It is also a good idea to have a card in one's wallet stating that the patient has an advance directive and describing where it is located. People may also keep their advance directive on a flash drive with other personal information that might be kept on a key ring with personal keys.

Online resources are also available to create and store advance directive documents. Most require a fee from the individual or a fee from the healthcare provider or organization. Examples include the National Living Will Registry® and MyDirectives® (mydirectives.com). Another recent technology includes the use of smartphone apps. One example developed by the American Bar Association is My Health Care Wishes (www.MyHealthCareWishes.org). It provides a mechanism for individuals to use mobile technology to create and store advance directive documents and other health-related information. As electronic medical records become the norm, more seamless resources and registries will make access to advance directives easier.[18]

Researchers have identified barriers to, and disparities in, the completion of advance directives. Lack of knowledge about advance directives, not understanding advance directives, and not being asked about advance directives by healthcare providers have been described as barriers to advance directive completion. Rao and colleagues[16] found that individuals who were younger, had lower incomes, and had less education were less likely to complete advance directives. Non-Caucasians are also less likely to complete advance directives.[16,19] Other reasons reported for failure to complete advance directives were (1) healthcare providers did not take the time to discuss advance care planning, (2) individuals wanted to leave it in God's hands, and (3) the belief that family members would know what to do.[19,20]

Medical Order Sets

Out-of-hospital Do Not Resuscitate (DNR) orders were histori-cally developed in an effort to honor individuals' wishes to avoid CPR and to limit aggressive interventions. They were honored by emergency personnel, but they were often not honored if a patient was admitted to an acute care setting.

Many states have now passed legislation regarding medical order sets. There are state variations, but the order sets are commonly referred to as the Medical Orders for Life-Sustaining Treatment (MOLST) or the Physician/Provider Orders for Life-Sustaining Treatment (POLST). The MOLST and POLST documents are portable order sets that were developed for patients with serious health problems. The objective was to respect the patient's wishes regardless of the setting. MOLST and POLST documents are hon-ored in the home, acute care settings, long-term care settings, pal-liative care, and hospice settings. Thus, multiple documents are not needed in different settings; the same document follows the patient as he or she moves from setting to setting.

These medical orders are written to ensure that care is provided according to the patient's wishes. The document includes infor-mation regarding patient preferences for CPR, artificial nutrition and hydration, antibiotic use, other life-sustaining therapies, and comfort care. The documents address the entire spectrum of care, from aggressive treatment to comfort care interventions.

As with other aspects of advance care planning, palliative APRNs need to be aware of state legislation related to these medi-cal order sets. As with living will and durable power of attorney for healthcare documents, it is important that these order sets are completed and reviewed to ensure that care is consistent with the patient's wishes.

A MOLST/POLST differs from an advance directive in that it is a portable medical order. Individuals may have both an advance directive and a MOLST/POLST. The documents should comple-ment each other. Some individuals will have just the MOLST/POLST. MOLST/POLST forms create a legal obligation that medi-cal professionals will honor the patient's end-of-life treatment preferences.

The MOLST and POLST forms are signed by the patient's phy-sician or as allowed in some states, the form can be signed by an APRN or a physician assistant. Depending on the state, the patient and his or her surrogate may sign the document. Orders on the MOLST/POLST form do not expire and can be revised by voiding the form and completing a new one.

Surrogate Decision Making

Another way to ensure that a patient's palliative and end-of-life wishes will be honored is through surrogate decision making. The primary mechanism for facilitating surrogate decision making occurs when a patient designates a durable power of attorney for healthcare or a healthcare proxy. As with other advance care plan-ning documents, the document designating a healthcare proxy should be shared with the patient's healthcare providers. The pal-liative APRN should ask each patient if the person designated as healthcare proxy knows that he or she is aware of this designation. The APRN should also ask the patient if he or she has reviewed the living will and if applicable MOLST/POLST documents with his or her healthcare proxy. Having conversations is an essential part of helping the healthcare proxy to fully understand the patient's wishes.

The healthcare proxy needs to know that he or she will be involved in the decision-making process if the patient no longer has decision-making capacity. The role of the healthcare proxy is to make decisions on the patient's behalf. The healthcare proxy will make decisions based on information that the patient wrote in his or her living will and conversations that the proxy and the patient had about the patient's wishes.

Periodically, when advance directive documents are reviewed, it is important for the palliative APRN to review the health-care proxy document and confirm that the person designated as healthcare proxy has not been changed. If patients want to make changes, they should be encouraged to develop a new document. A healthcare proxy needs to change if the surrogate dies or if the relationship changes between the patient and the surrogate.[21]

If the patient has not designated a healthcare proxy, the pal-liative APRN should discuss this process and provide the patient with information regarding how to do this. Key to successful sur-rogate decision making is selecting the right person. When select-ing a surrogate decision maker, patients should consider someone who can be trusted to make sound decisions, is emotionally stable, who would be comfortable asking healthcare providers questions, and is available.[21]

If the time comes that a patient cannot communicate or no lon-ger has decision-making capacity, then the palliative APRN and other members of the healthcare team will turn to the proxy if important decisions need to be made. The proxy is responsible for making decisions based on what the patient would want done. This supports the patient's previously stated wishes and honors and respects them. If the proxy does not know what the patient would want, then he or she makes decisions based on what he or she thinks would be in the best interest of the patient.

If a patient did not designate a healthcare proxy and cannot communicate his or her wishes, the team turns to the family for advice. Decades ago, the President's Commission for the Study of Ethical Problems in Medicine and Biomedical and Behavioral Research recommended that the family is the patient's best advo-cate if the patient does not have decision-making capacity.[11] The palliative APRN should ask the family if the patient ever stated what he or she would want at the end of life.

Most states have surrogacy laws that specify who can make decisions for a patient. These state laws should be followed when determining which family member has legal authority to make decisions for a patient without decision-making capacity. Legally determined standards are typically set and need to be followed by the palliative APRN. A patient's spouse is typically legally authorized as the primary decision maker. If the patient's spouse has died or the patient is divorced, the next legal decision maker might be the eldest adult child; in other states all adult children need to come together to make a decision. It is important that pal-liative APRNs know and understand surrogacy laws. In cases of conflict, or where no previously designated surrogate is available, it may be necessary to petition a court to appoint a surrogate.[22] The appointed guardian then serves in the role of surrogate.

If the patient does not have decision-making capacity, then the designated healthcare proxy or the family member legally des-ignated to make decisions for the patient does so based on the patient's preferences identified in the living will. If there is no living will, then decisions may be guided by conversations that the surrogate previously had with the patient. If a patient had no living will and did not state what he or she would have wanted at the end-of-life, substituted decisions are made. This is when decisions are made based on what decisions the surrogate decision maker thinks that the patient would make. If the surrogate decision maker has no idea what decision the patient would make, a best interest decision is made. The decision is based on what might be best for an average person.

Although one person is designated as surrogate decision maker, multiple family members are often present and involved when a patient nears death. Even though one decision maker has legal authority for decision making, it is common for the surrogate decision maker to include multiple family members in discussions regarding goals of care, especially in the context of end-of-life care.[13,23] Surrogate decision makers commonly seek advice and help from other family members when making end-of-life decisions.[24] Families have found advance directives helpful when making end-of-life decisions related to life-sustaining therapies.[25-31]

Making end-of-life decisions on behalf of someone else places a tremendous burden on surrogate decision makers.[32,33] Some family members may support and some family members may not support the surrogate decision maker as he or she comes to terms with the decision that needs to be made. It is important for the palliative APRN to help and support the surrogate decision maker and the patient's family through this process. Once decisions are made, the APRN should ensure that the decisions are respected and honored.

Decisions should always be made based on the patient's wishes. Important questions may include, "If your mother could speak with us, what would she want done?" Keeping the conversation focused on patient wishes is important and may prevent conflict and guilt from arising within the family.[13]

Summary and Conclusion

Palliative APRNs must assist and guide patients as they participate in advance care planning. Respect for patient autonomy is essential. Patients need to be supported as they determine their palliative and end-of-life wishes. Palliative APRNs can educate and help patients to develop living wills, designate healthcare proxies, and develop MOLST/POLST documents. Conversations that palliative APRNs have with the patient, surrogate, and family not only help to identify the patient's wishes but also help to ensure that these wishes are honored and respected.

References

1. The National Consensus Project for Quality Palliative Care. C Dahlin, ed. *Clinical Practice Guidelines for Quality Palliative Care.* 3rd ed. Pittsburgh, PA: The National Consensus Project for Quality Palliative Care; 2013.
2. Hickman SE, Hammes BJ, Moss AH, Tolle SW. Hope for the future: Achieving the original intent of advance directives. Improving End of Life Care: Why Has it Been so Difficult? *Hastings Center Special Report.* 2005; 35(6): S26–S30.
3. Tilden VP, Corless I, Dahlin C, Ferrell B, Gibson R, Lentz J. Advance care planning as an urgent public health concern. *Nursing Outlook* 2011; 59(1): 55–6.
4. Hospice and Palliative Nurses Association. *Position Statement: The Nurse's Role in Advance Care Planning.* Pittsburgh, PA: Hospice and Palliative Nurses Association; 2010.
5. Fried TR, Redding CA, Robbins ML, Paiva A, O'Leary JR, Iannone L. Stages of change for the component behaviors of advance care planning. *J Am Geriatrics Soc* 2010; 58: 2329–36.
6. Alano GJ, Pekmezaris R, Tai JY, et al. Factors influencing older adults to complete advance directives. *Palliat Support Care.* 2010; 8(3): 267–75.
7. Detering KM, Hancock AD, Reade MC, Silvester W. The impact of advance care planning on end of lie care in elderly patients: Randomized control trial. *BMJ* 2010; 340: c1345.
8. Levi BH, Dellasega C, Whitehead M, Green MJ. What influences individuals to engage in advance care planning? *Am J Hosp Palliat Care.* 2010; 27(5): 306–12.
9. Barrio-Canteljo IM, Molina-Ruiz A, Simon-Lorda P, et al. Advance directives and proxies' predictions about patient's treatment preferences. *Nursing Ethics* 2009; 16(1): 93–109.
10. Beauchamp TL, Walters L, Kahn JP, Mastroianni AC. *Contemporary Issues in Bioethics.* 8th ed. Belmont, CA: Wadsworth Publishing Co.; 2013.
11. President's Commission for the Study of Ethical Problems in Medicine and Biomedical and Behavioral Research. *Deciding to Forgo Life-Sustaining Treatment: A Report on Ethical, Medical and Legal Issues in Treatment Decisions.* Washington, DC: U.S. Government Printing Office; 1983.
12. Lo B. *Resolving Ethical Dilemmas: A Guide for Clinicians.* 4th ed. Philadelphia, PA: Lippincott Williams & Wilkins; 2009.
13. Wiegand DL, Russo MM. Ethical considerations. In: Dahlin M, Lynch MT, eds. *Core Curriculum for the Advanced Practice Hospice and Palliative Registered Nurse.* 2nd ed. Pittsburgh, PA: Hospice and Palliative Nurses Association, 2013: 39–59.
14. Hamilton JB. The ethics of end-of-life care. In: Poor B, Poierrier GP. *End of Life Nursing Care.* National League for Nursing. Sudbury, MA: Jones and Bartlett; 2001:73–103.
15. Patient Self-Determination Act 4206-4751, Pub L No. 101-508 (1990).
16. Rao JK, Anderson LA, Lin F, Lauz JP. Completion of advance directives among U.S. consumers. *Am J Prev Med.* 2014; 46(1): 65–70.
17. The Support Principal Investigators. A controlled trial to improve care for seriously ill hospitalized patients: The study to understand prognoses and preferences for outcomes and risks of treatments (SUPPORT). *JAMA* 1995; 274(20): 1591–8.
18. Waldrop DP, Meeker MA. Communication and advance care planning in palliative and end-of-life care. *Nurs Outlook.* 2012; 60(6): 365–9.
19. Johnson RW, Zhao Y, Newby LK, Granger CB, Granger BB. Reasons for noncompetion of advance directives in a cardiac intensive care unit. *Am J Crit Care.* 2012; 21(5): 311–20.
20. Schickedanz AD, Schillinger D, Landerfeld CS, Knight SJ, Wialliams BA, Sudore RL. A clinical framework for improving the advance care planning process: Start with patients' self-identified barriers. *J Am Geriatr Soc.* 2009; 57: 31–9.
21. McMahan RD, Knight SJ, Fried TR, Sudore RL. Advance care planning beyond advance directives: Perspectives from patients and surrogates. *J Pain Symptom Manage.* 2013; 46(3): 355–65.
22. Pope TM. Legal fundamentals of surrogate decision making. *Medical Ethics.* 2012; 141(4): 1074–81.
23. Kelly B, Rid A, Wendler D. Systematic review: Individuals' goals for surrogate decision-making. *J Am Geriatr Soc.* 2012; 60: 884–95.
24. Wiegand DL. In their own time: The family experience during the process of withdrawal of life-sustaining therapy. *J Palliat Med.* 2008; 11(8): 1115–21.
25. Hickman RL, Pinto MD. Advance directives lessen the decisional burden of surrogate decision-making for the chronically critically ill. *J Clin Nurs.* 2013; 23(5-6):756–65.
26. Jacob DA. Family members' experiences with decision making for incompetent patients in the ICU: a qualitative study. *Am J Crit Care.* 1998; 7: 30–6.
27. Mayer SA, Kossoff SB. Withdrawal of life support in the neurological intensive care unit. *Neurology.* 1999; 52: 1602–9.

28. O'Callahan JG, Fink C, Pitts LH, Luce JM. Withholding and withdrawing of life support from patients with severe head injury. *Crit Care Med.* 1995; 23(9): 1567–75.

29. Swigart V, Lidz C, Butterworth V, Arnold R. Letting go: family willingness to forgo life support. *Heart Lung* 1996; 25(6): 483–94.

30. Tilden VP, Tolle SW, Nelson CA, Fields J. Family decision-making to withdraw life-sustaining treatments from hospitalized patients. *Nurs Res.* 2001; 50(2): 105–15.

31. Tilden VP, Tolle SW, Nelson CA, Thompson M, Eggman SC. Family decision making in foregoing life-extending treatments. *J Family Nurs.* 1999; 5(4): 426–42.

32. Fritsch J, Petronio S, Helft PR, Torke A. Making decisions for hospitalized older adults: Ethical factors considered by family surrogates. *J Clin Ethics.* 2013; 24(2): 125–34.

33. Wengler D, Rid A. Systematic review: The effect on surrogates of making treatment decisions for others. *Ann Intern Med.* 2011; 154(5): 336–46.

CHAPTER 40

Family Meetings

Jennifer Gentry

Key Points

- Excellent communication is the foundation for effective family meetings.
- The advanced practice registered nurse (APRN) must prepare for a family meeting.
- When there is conflict, the palliative APRN must address the emotion from the patient and/ or the family.

Case Study

Mr. Johnson was a 69-year-old man with end-stage renal disease on hemodialysis. He was admitted to the hospital with sepsis, and during this admission was diagnosed with stage IV lung cancer. Mr. Johnson was nonambulatory and unable to tolerate sitting up in a chair for more than a few minutes. The oncologist was unwilling to discuss chemotherapy unless Mr. Johnson could walk into the office. Mr. Johnson was unable to tolerate ongoing dialysis because of hypotension. The palliative APRN was consulted to discuss goals and next steps in the plan of care with Mr. Johnson and his wife. The APRN reviewed symptoms and assessed the Johnsons' knowledge and perception of the situation during the initial visit:

APRN: "Mr. Johnson, what have you heard so far?"
MR. JOHNSON: "Nothing good . . ." (pause of several seconds)
MRS. JOHNSON: "I know that there is a mass . . . is it cancer?"
APRN: "I have some sad news . . . the biopsy showed that the mass is cancer and the x-rays indicate that the cancer has spread."
Mrs. Johnson begins to cry.
APRN: (extended pause) "I am sensing that this is really sad and difficult for you."
MRS. JOHNSON: (crying more) "I am sad . . . I don't know what to do . . ."

After allowing time for expression of emotion and questions, the APRN recognized that the Johnsons were overwhelmed and made plans to meet again the following day, when their daughter could be present along with the oncologist.

Over subsequent visits and family meetings, the APRN reviewed the medical facts and the prognosis and clarified the goals of care. Ultimately, the Johnsons opted to make the transition to an inpatient hospice setting.

Introduction

Caught in the tangled web of healthcare, patients and families may have limited insight into their situation. Nonexistent or poorly delivered communication during the course of an illness may result in conflict, confusion, frustration, and mistrust. Thoughtful communication and facilitated family meetings can go far to bridge the communication gap. Leading a family meeting is an essential skill for the APRN.[1] By its nature, palliative care is interdisciplinary and collaborative. As leaders on the interdisciplinary team, APRNs frequently lead formal and informal family meetings, discuss prognosis, clarify goals of care, assist with advance care planning, deliver bad news, and provide care when death is imminent.

Communication expertise is a core competency for APRNs and is woven throughout the scope and standards of palliative nursing practice.[1] Principles of good communication include use of open-ended questions, sitting down, maintaining eye contact, being present, listening, and addressing emotion.[2,3] Whether practicing in an inpatient acute care setting, an outpatient clinic, or hospice, APRNs lead and participate in complex communication episodes with patients and families.[1–3]

While no standard definition of a family meeting exists, these meetings may be described as a facilitated, dynamic means of exchanging information about illness, prognosis, and treatment options with the patient, family, and healthcare team. Family meetings provide a vehicle for two-way communication about goals, values, concerns, and decisions needed to formulate a plan of care. Family meetings are sometimes referred to as one of the major "procedures" of palliative care.

For this "procedure" to be effective, the palliative APRN must use excellent communication skills, including active listening and observation.[2,3] To best facilitate these meetings, the APRN must have a basic knowledge of common disease processes and their prognoses, as well as potential technology and treatment options, to guide patients and families in making informed decisions about their healthcare.[1] Basic elements of communication required during a family meeting include listening, information gathering, imparting information, therapeutic presence, and sensitivity.[2,3] Information must be provided in a manner that is educationally, culturally, and developmentally appropriate without overwhelming the recipients' coping styles.[2]

APRNs frequently provide palliative care and associated communication in many different settings. Care provided by APRNs is rated highly in terms of satisfaction and the achievement of comfort.[4,5] In a systematic review of outcomes, care provided by APRNs has been shown to be similar to that provided by physicians.[6] APRNs provide care that is of high quality and highly satisfying to patients.[6] APRNs should be allowed to function fully within the scope of their education and training. It is within the APRN's scope of practice to lead family meetings and to discuss prognosis, disease process, and therapeutic options.[1]

Liu and colleagues examined the palliative care provided by APRNs for dementia patients in a skilled nursing facility.[5] High levels of family satisfaction and excellent symptom management were found and were attributed to the APRNs' emphasis on advance care planning, communication, and comfort.[5] Hudson and colleagues looked at the effectiveness of family meetings using trained nurse facilitators.[7] The nurses in this study reported increased levels of confidence in their ability to lead family meetings based on the training and protocols they received.[7] The family meetings described in this study were noted to be useful in addressing important caregiver needs, such as information, decision making, and expression of emotion.[7]

Despite the importance of communication skills, there has been a lack of emphasis on training in nursing education programs.[8] Palliative care team members without specific counseling backgrounds, such as nurses and physicians, may not have received training in meeting facilitation or conflict resolution.[2,3] Fortunately, like other clinical skills, communication and facilitation skills can be effectively taught using simulated patients and expert observation and feedback.[9]

Regular communication and family meetings have immediate and long-term benefits for patients and families. One of the most common reasons for palliative care consultation is to facilitate communication.[10,11] In one study, over 70% of palliative care consultations were obtained to determine goals of care and to facilitate transitions in care from one setting to another.[11] Most palliative care consultations in this study involved the introduction of palliative care to promote ongoing discussions, symptom management, or a strategic family meeting.[11]

Communication in the context of palliative care consultation has been shown to improve respect for treatment preferences, emotional and spiritual support, and symptom management.[3,12] Without the information that may be gained in a family meeting, clinicians are very poor at predicting patient preferences.[13] The preponderance of the evidence has demonstrated that physicians do not accurately assess a patient's quality of life, functioning, or preferences for cardiopulmonary resuscitation (CPR) even if there is a relationship with the patient over time.[13,14] Palliative care consultation teams have been shown to identify unrecognized problems as well as improve processes of care, such as opioid prescribing and documentation of patient goals.[12] After the death of the patient, family members who participated in a proactive family meeting had a lower incidence of anxiety, depression, and post-traumatic stress disorder.[15]

Poor communication has been identified as the greatest source of anxiety and frustration for family members.[11] Weiner and Roth describe five counterproductive behaviors that clinicians may unintentionally use that may result in conflict and suffering in a family meeting (Table 40.1): (1) forcing the discussion, (2) linking relief of suffering with limited life expectancy, (3) pressuring through repeated attempts to persuade, (4) misdiagnosing denial, and (5) presenting information out of context.[16]

Communication during family meetings can lead to misunderstandings, missed opportunities, and distress for all.[17,18] Medical jargon may not be well understood, and the importance of every

Table 40.1 Common Clinician Errors in Communication

Proceeding without assessing readiness: forcing the goals-of-care discussion when the patient or family is not ready.
Linking relief of suffering with demands to accept limited life expectancy (e.g., "I'm sorry, but there is nothing else we can do for you. Should we just keep you comfortable now?")
Misdiagnosing denial: patients and families may have the initial, "This is not happening" response as part of normal grief, self-protection, and coping
Destructive debates: repeated attempts to convince the patient and family of a certain viewpoint (e.g., repeated attempts to "get the DNR")
Presenting hypothetical decisions in an impersonal manner without a context (e.g., "If your heart and lungs stop, what do you want us to do?")

From reference 16.

single word must be measured. It is not surprising that family members view communication as being more important than a provider's clinical skill.[19]

Although there is extensive literature on the benefits of communication and palliative care consultation, less is known about the specific outcomes and effectiveness of family meetings in palliative care.[7] Family meetings are thought to help meet caregivers' needs in such areas as information, decision making, and expression of emotion. In one study, nurse facilitators reported improved confidence in their ability to lead family meetings after receiving extensive training and protocols.[7] From the nurse facilitator's point of view, the meetings were useful for getting information, clarifying goals of care, and resolving conflicts.[7] Proactive palliative care consultation for patients at a high risk of dying in a medical intensive care unit (ICU) was associated with a significantly shorter ICU stay, care more congruent with patient goals, and accelerated decision making, all attributed to better communication.[20]

If family meetings are beneficial, why do they happen late in the course of illness or not at all?[20,21] Several barriers to timely family meetings have been identified (Table 40.2). Wright and colleagues suggest that conversations about difficult things like poor prognosis and end-of-life are avoided for fear that the patient will "lose hope" or experience distress.[21] Despite the ambivalence that patients and providers may have about difficult discussions, terminally ill cancer patients who participated in these discussions were less likely to receive aggressive ICU care, mechanical ventilation, or attempts at resuscitation and did not experience higher rates of depression.[21] When patients underwent more aggressive medical treatments at the end-of-life, they experienced a lower quality

Table 40.2 Barriers to Family Meetings

Fear of loss of hope/patient distress
Lack of time
Lack of training/low confidence in communication ability
Cultural differences
Logistics (lack of space, multiple providers, scheduling conflicts)
Provider burnout/low priority

From references 21, 22.

Table 40.3 Triggers for Family Meetings

Long length of stay
Significant clinical change
High risk of mortality
Multiple organ system dysfunction for 3 or more days
Global cerebral ischemia after resuscitation
Stage IV malignancy
Age >80 years with two or more comorbidities
Interventions like tracheostomy or percutaneous endoscopic gastrostomy (PEG) tube

From reference 22.

of life before death and the caregivers were at a higher risk for depression.[20] Other potential barriers to family meetings include lack of time, involvement of multiple providers, lack of provider training in communication and facilitation, cultural differences, lack of space, and provider burnout.[21,22]

Ensuring adequate preparation is an essential component for a successful family meeting.[22] Gay and colleagues have suggested addressing potential barriers to family meetings by identifying and setting aside specific times for family meetings, supporting communication skills training for clinicians, and using assistance from members of the interdisciplinary team to help with the logistics of scheduling, coordinating, and finding a location for the meeting.[22] It has been suggested that identifying triggers for family meetings and palliative care consultation may promote palliative care consultation and family meetings (Table 40.3). The need for a family meeting could be triggered by being included in a pre-procedure checklist for interventions like tracheostomy or percutaneous endoscopic gastrostomy (PEG) tube placement.[22]

Setting the Stage for Family Meetings

Several essential components of family meetings have been identified.[15,22–25] Lautrette and colleagues developed a communication strategy and brochure to facilitate proactive family meetings for patients dying in the ICU (Table 40.4).[15] The authors concluded that fewer nonbeneficial interventions were done in those who received a proactive family meeting, and there was a lower incidence of depression, anxiety, and post-traumatic stress disorder among survivors 90 days after their loved one died.[15] In another study, researchers developed a model for family conferences containing four major components: (1) conference organization, including the setting, participants, and structure of the meeting; (2) negotiation

Table 40.4 Steps in Communication Using Menomic **VALUE**

Value and appreciate what family members have to say.
Acknowledge emotion.
Listen to concerns expressed.
Understand/learn about who the patient is through open-ended questions.
Elicit questions from the family.

From reference 15.

or building consensus and reaching decisions; (3) personal stance or the attitude and mode of information delivery; and (4) emotional work or use of empathic responses[25] (Table 40.5).

The Steps of a Family Meeting
Preparation

Identifying the Decision Maker and Who Should Be Present
Patients with capacity have a right to self-determination and should be included in decisions about their medical care, per their preference.[26] But the reality is that many deaths occur in the hospital and ICU, where patients are frequently too ill to participate in decision making.[27–30] Deaths commonly occur after the decision is made in a family meeting to withdraw life-sustaining measures or to limit treatment.[28,29,31]

Family members often serve as surrogate decision makers for incapacitated patients.[28,29,31] The definition of "family" is very individual, and family members may include anyone who is important to the patient, rather than just a legal or biological relative. A surrogate decision maker or next-of-kin status is individually defined by the state via statute or through written advance directives.[30] All 50 states and the District of Columbia have laws that allow for the use of instructional advance directives.[32] The ethical principle of substituted judgment is applied when there is no advance directive and the patient lacks decision-making capacity. APRNs must be knowledgeable about the laws in their practice location so they can determine the appropriate legal decision maker. The APRN must also identify other persons important to the patient who should be included in a family meeting. Although the legal surrogate may be authorized to act on behalf of the patient, there may be others who hold great influence in the decision-making process. They may include relatives, close friends, or spiritual care providers who know the patient's wishes and can contribute to the meeting. Even with a written advance directive, surrogate decision making can be difficult. Surrogate decision makers' ability to predict what the patient would have wanted in a given situation may be inaccurate, and authorizing overtreatment is a common error.[32]

Table 40.5 Essential Elements of a Family Meeting

1. Preparation
◆ Appropriate decision maker
◆ Meeting place
◆ Medical facts
◆ Information needs
◆ Participants
2. Meeting structure
◆ Introductions and ground rules
◆ Elicit understanding and information needs
◆ Provide information (if delivering bad news, consider giving a warning or preparatory statement first)
3. Respond to emotions
4. Develop the plan (summarize, next steps)
5. Documentation

From references 3, 23, 26.

Table 40.6 Sample Questions to Clarify Roles in Decision Making

"How has your family made decisions in the past?"
"Some families make decisions as a group and others appoint a spokesperson. Can you help me understand how your family makes decisions?"
"I can see how difficult that this is for you. Would it help if I make a recommendation?"
"Would it be helpful to include your family in these discussions and decisions?"

From reference 3.

Shared decision making, a dynamic process in which the responsibility is shared by the treating provider and the patient's family, has been endorsed by numerous professional societies.[28] It is best carried out using a stepwise approach.[28] Family members who are involved in decision making frequently report feeling overwhelmed and overburdened by the responsibility (Table 40.6).[33] Exploring the family's preferred role in the decision-making process and the uncertainty about the prognosis is essential and should be reassessed frequently. Some families prefer that the provider make recommendations; others prefer to accept ultimate responsibility for the decisions made.

Meeting Place

Finding an appropriate setting and space for the meeting may seem like a simple task, but healthcare facilities are designed for utility and may not provide the patient- and family-friendly space needed for family meetings.[24] An ideal space would allow for privacy, adequate seating, and use of technology, such as speakerphones and computers.[2,24] While technology can facilitate communication, it may also be a distraction. Clinicians should silence their cellphones and pagers prior to the meeting and may consider asking family members to do the same. Evidence to support the best physical arrangements for family meetings is lacking, but arranging the room/seating to allow good eye contact and observation of participants' nonverbal communication may be helpful.[23] In some cases, a patient with decision-making capacity may be too ill to move to a separate location, requiring the meeting to be held in the patient's room. The space may not accommodate seating for everyone, but at a minimum the person leading the meeting should be seated.

History and Medical Facts

Another element of preparation includes being knowledgeable about the medical facts in the case.[24] Prior to a family meeting, the APRN should review the medical history, consult with members of the team knowledgeable about the patient's situation, and become familiar with the patient's psychosocial, spiritual, and family background. The APRN should identify key stakeholders and subspecialists to be included or consulted prior to the meeting.[27] "Who is the health provider you trust the most (on the medical team)?" can be a helpful question to pose ahead of time to patients and families in an effort to identify important stakeholders. If other team members will be attending the meeting, set aside a few minutes to discuss key facts, such as prognosis, treatment options, and concerns, before the meeting.[28] In the pre-meeting conference, everyone attending should be clear which team member is leading the meeting and what role each team member will play.

Meeting Structure

Introductions

Everyone present in the room should be introduced, and their role and relationship to the patient should be made clear. In large groups, the person leading the meeting or a designee may wish to discreetly jot down this information to refer to later. Consider establishing ground rules if there is a large group or a history of conflict.[34] Ground rules can include clarifying the legal decision maker if the patient lacks decision-making capacity and noting that there will be an opportunity for everyone to ask questions and participate during the meeting.

Elicit Understanding and Information Needs

Beginning the discussion by asking an open-ended question like "What have you heard so far?" or "How do you feel things are going at this point?" provides important information about the patient and family's perception and allows the APRN to use active listening skills.[23,24] Using the phrase "What do you understand?" may get at the information needed but should be used cautiously, as patients and families may perceive this as condescending or may conclude that the clinician views them as uninformed. While many patients and families want as much information as possible, this is not always the case.[23-35] The need for information is very individual and should be determined prior to the meeting.[23,24] The APRN should avoid making assumptions about the type and amount of information that should be disclosed. Culture and developmental level may dictate what and how information is shared, particularly if children are involved in the discussion.[23]

Provide Information

Deliver information using an honest and direct manner while continually assessing the response and nonverbal communication. A good operating rule is to give no more than three pieces of information before pausing and checking in with those present.[23] Checking in about the group's understanding must be done with tact and diplomacy. A question like "Am I making sense to you so far?" or "Sometimes I forget that I use medical jargon. Would you mind sharing what you heard me say, so that I know I am being clear?" puts the responsibility for communication difficulties on the provider and not on the recipient's lack of understanding.

Respond to Emotion

The APRN should pause after information is delivered and allow the group to process it and express emotion. The natural inclination may be to "fill the space" with words, but the APRN must recognize that silence and presence are vital communication tools.[2,3,36,37] Expressions of emotion and distress are common during palliative care consultation.[38] In a study by Alexander and colleagues, 69% of the conversations contained at least one expression of emotional distress.[38] Anxiety and fear were the most frequently encountered emotion, followed by sadness, anger, and frustration.[38] Fortunately, most of these expressions of distress and emotion were handled by clinicians with a compassionate response.[38] Allowing time to speak and express emotion has been correlated with higher levels of satisfaction when patients and families speak more than the clinician.[39,40] Addressing emotions, while intuitive for some, is a skill that can be learned like any other.[41] The **NURSE** mnemonic has been suggested as a way to remember five different skills for handling emotions (Table 40.7).[3,35,42] In some instances, the patient or family members may state how they are feeling and the APRN can reflect this; in other instances it may be helpful for the APRN to name what he or she observes and allow the patient or family to validate or clarify. Although no one can fully appreciate another person's exact situation, the APRN can still convey empathy for what the patient and family are experiencing. Acknowledging and offering respect for the emotions being expressed can go far to build a trusting and supportive therapeutic relationship. Respect and affirmation can be conveyed through the APRN's body language and facial expression as well as with words.

There may be a point in the conversation where the APRN is unsure where things stand based on the clues the person is giving. Using empathic curiosity is a way of exploring using an pen-ended question, such as "Are you able to tell me what you are thinking at this point?" or "We have been discussing some difficult things. How are you doing with this?"[41]

All of the skills to address emotion ultimately offer patients and families support, but none of them specifically addresses the fear of abandonment.[36] In today's healthcare environment, continuity is lacking. Patients and families may fear being abandoned at a time when they need the most support.[43] Assuring patients that they will continue to receive care and support no matter what happens or what decisions they make about their care will go far to allay this fear. Offering false promises of support that is not possible should be avoided, however. Support can be conveyed by making good handoffs and communicating this.

Developing the Plan (Summarize and Strategize)

In some cases, the emotion of the situation is so overwhelming that it may be best to summarize, plan another meeting, and adjourn. In other situations further conversation and goal setting flow naturally from the conversation. Clarifying goals through open-ended questions like "Given what you have heard, what is most important to you now?" and "What things are you hoping for?" can help the APRN make recommendations based on the values and expectations of the patient.[24] Realistically, it may take several communication episodes or meetings to fully develop the plan of care. While a "meeting before the meeting" can be helpful for the team, a postmeeting debriefing can be just as useful. Delivering bad news and attending to emotion can be stressful for healthcare providers who may not have a longstanding relationship with the patient.[22,23] Taking time to talk about what went well and areas that could be improved upon and assessing the patient's and family's response can be therapeutic as well as educational.

Documentation

Documentation of the family meeting is part of the process of communicating with other members of the team and promoting continuity (Table 40.8). Several important pieces of information should be included in the documentation for both communication and billing purposes.[2,20]

Delivering Bad News

In addition to leading family meetings and facilitating communication for patients and families, the APRN may be in the position of delivering bad news, much like in the case study. Back and colleagues define "bad news" as any information that

Table 40.7 Emotion-Handling Skills Using the Mnemonic **NURSE**

Emotion-Handling Skills	Phrases to Use/Questions to Ask
N: Recognizing and **naming** emotion	"I'm hearing that you are really concerned and upset about this situation."
	"I wonder if you are feeling angry about this?"
U: Expressing **understanding** and "normalizing" the emotion	"I can't imagine how difficult that it must be, seeing your loved one go through this."
	"I wouldn't be surprised if you were feeling really sad."
R: Acknowledging and offering **respect**	"I really appreciate your commitment to your loved one and all the time that you have spent at the hospital."
	"I have great respect for the care that you have given your loved one."
S: Offering **support** and demonstrating commitment to the patient and family	"We will continue to adjust your pain medications until you are comfortable."
E: Explore to gain clarity and insight into the story/experience	"Tell me more about …"
	"I heard you say that you felt confused. Can you say more about this?"

From references 3, 36.

Table 40.8 Key Elements of Documentation Following a Family Meeting

Those who attended the meeting from the family and the medical team. If the patient was unable to participate, note the reason (e.g., "the patient lacked decision-making capacity and was unable to participate")
The necessity of the meeting for medical decision making
A brief summary of information discussed, including: ◆ Current state of illness ◆ Prognosis ◆ Treatment plan ◆ Specific discussions of bad news
The patient and family response (e.g., "After the prognosis was discussed, Mrs. Johnson cried and expressed feeling sad and overwhelmed by the information presented.")
Specific treatments discussed or decisions made (e.g., advance care planning, resuscitation status, artificial nutrition and hydration, other life-support measures)
Discharge planning, including skilled nursing facility placement, hospice, financial concerns, caregiving concerns
Concerns, questions, and areas of disagreement or agreement
Plan of care
Plan for follow-up
Time the meeting started and ended

From references 2, 22.

adversely alters one's expectations for the future.[36] When delivering bad news, the APRN must use all of the principles of good communication, including active listening, open-ended questions, and attention to emotion, as previously described. Just as with a family meeting, appropriate preparation is essential, including being well versed in the medical history, arranging the best physical setting possible, and ensuring that the right people are present. Beginning with a question to elicit understanding is the best starting place.[23,24] After hearing from the patient and family, correct misunderstandings or validate accurate information. Communication experts recommend using a warning phrase, commonly referred to as a "warning shot," to allow the patient and family to prepare,[2,23,24,36] something like, "I have some serious news to share with you." After delivering the news, pause and allow the information to be absorbed. Give the patient and family adequate time to express emotions and ask questions. Continuously assess their nonverbal communication and response to the news. Whether the meeting ends after the bad news is delivered or if a detailed plan of care is developed, the APRN should summarize and clarify plans for follow-up with the patient and family before adjourning.

Discussing Prognosis

Discussions of prognosis are common during family meetings and palliative care consultation.[44] Predictions of survival may weigh heavily in decisions to pursue aggressive treatments or to choose a less aggressive plan of care.[23,44] The APRN must be prepared for these discussions and knowledgeable about both prognostic indicators and limitations in the ability to prognosticate. In several studies, surrogate decision makers have indicated that (1) avoiding these discussions is an unacceptable way to maintain hope and (2) they wanted to receive more than only bad news.[45,46] "Hope for the best and prepare for the worst" addresses the challenge of providing an honest prognosis with hope and optimism.

Apatira and colleagues found that the need for surrogate decision makers to maintain hope was sometimes at odds with their need for more information, and some surrogate decision makers only wanted to hear good news.[45] The researchers identified four coping strategies that surrogate decision makers employed to manage the tension between honesty and hope:

1. Focusing on minutia: Small positive changes, such as improvement in urine output or respiratory rate or the patient's level of consciousness, provided both information and hope.[45]

2. Relying on personal knowledge and beliefs about the patient: The decision maker believes he or she can interpret a patient's response that a stranger would not be able to identify. For example, the family may believe a facial expression is special communication meant only for them and not the medical team.[45]

3. Seeking information from sources outside of the medical team: The decision maker may contact friends, family, and others with similar experience or a medical background, as well as online resources. This serves as an alternative way to seek hopeful information when the team caring for the patient gives bad news.[45]

4. Avoidance and disbelief: Some surrogates avoided doctors whom they perceived as pessimistic or they expressed blatant disbelief.[45]

Research has illustrated the limitations of the palliative care clinician's ability to predict life expectancy. Studies have demonstrated that the most common prognostic error among providers, including palliative care clinicians, is overestimating life expectancy.[44,47] Estimates of shorter survival are more likely to be accurate, such as when a patient has hours to days or days to weeks to live.[44,47] Even scoring systems like APACHE (Acute Physiology and Chronic Health Evaluation) have not demonstrated accuracy in predicting life expectancy.[48] Given the challenges of providing precise estimates of life expectancy, a common approach is to provide ranges (e.g., hours to days, days to weeks, weeks to months).

Predictions of survival for patients with specific diagnoses have also been studied. For example, in cancer patients, functional status is the single greatest prognostic factor.[49] The Karnofsky Performance Status score, Palliative Performance Scale score, and ECOG (Eastern Cooperative Oncology Group) score are commonly used to score a patient's performance status.[49,50] For patients with a poor functional status (defined as spending more than 50% of their day in bed or chair), a rough estimate of survival is less than 3 months.[49-51] For patients with end-stage renal disease on maintenance hemodialysis, several variables have been independently associated with mortality, including older age, dementia, peripheral vascular disease, decreased albumin, and a negative answer to the "surprise question" ("Would I be surprised if my patient died within the next 6 months?").[52] Predicting survival in disease states like congestive heart failure remains difficult given the increasing use of advanced therapies, such as transplantation and ventricular assist devices, as well as the risk of sudden death.[53]

Prognosis can include much more than just survival estimates. Medical decisions should not be made in isolation, and discussing the long-term implications may help patients and families make more informed choices. Treatments like feeding tube insertion may lead to other consequences, such as skilled nursing facility placement or use of physical and chemical restraints.[54] In one study, patients who underwent prolonged mechanical ventilation and/or tracheostomy were followed over time. After one year, 65% of the patients who survived the hospital stay were totally dependent for their care or had died.[55]

Discussing Technology and Withholding or Withdrawing Treatments in Family Meetings

Use of aggressive therapies and technology is common in seriously ill patients and those at the end-of-life.[56] APRNs must be knowledgeable about commonly used technologies and how the use of technology fits into the context of the patient's goals of care. In family meetings, use of technology should be closely tied to the patient's values and goals as well as what is feasible and the long-term implications of particular decisions.[56] Although withholding and withdrawing therapies are viewed as ethically equivalent, they may be perceived very differently.[30] Families may feel they are playing a more active role or are the cause of a poor outcome by discontinuing a therapy already in use rather than never initiating it in the first place. Clinicians may also make a moral distinction between withholding and withdrawing and are more comfortable withholding than withdrawing therapies.[30]

The APRN must recognize and support families who are struggling with these painful decisions. Reframing the situation may be helpful. For example, if a decision is made to discontinue ventilator use in a patient with end-stage lung disease, based on knowledge of the patient's wishes, the disease is allowed to follow its natural course and is actually the cause of death, not the removal of the ventilator. Words matter greatly in these discussions. Well-intended clinicians may use phrases like "withdrawing care" when they really mean discontinuing a specific treatment.[30] The APRN must communicate that, although specific treatment is no longer to be used, attention to care and comfort will continue. See Part Six, Withdrawal of Technology, which includes chapters on withdrawal of cardiac, respiratory, and other interventions.

Resuscitation

CPR techniques were developed in the 1960s with the purpose of supporting victims of an out-of-hospital event, such as a heart attack, drowning, or accident; they were not intended to become part of routine treatment at the time of death from a terminal illness.[56] In our current healthcare system, though, use of CPR is an "opt out" request, and the default assumption is that everyone desires CPR.[55] Many patients and families do not understand the low likelihood of survival in a person with advanced disease and may believe that the chances of a good outcome are much higher.[23,24,57] Discussing Do Not Resuscitate status during a family meeting is best done in the context of the overall goals of care. Making recommendations tied to the ability of resuscitation attempts to meet the patient's goals rather than asking a question is often a more effective approach. Phrases like "If your heart and lungs stop, do you want to us to do everything?," "Restarting your heart," and "Putting on a breathing machine" convey a false assurance of success and reversibility.[24] Families may worry that if doing everything possible includes CPR, then the opposite is doing nothing.[24] Patients and families may be under the false assumption that "Do Not Resuscitate" is the same as "Do Not Treat" or being abandoned. The APRN should reassure the patient and family that they will continue to be cared for and that treatments that support their goals will continue.

PATIENT: "I would never want to be kept alive on machines . . ."
APRN: "You have told me that you would prefer your death to be natural and that you want to be at home. I would recommend that we make your wishes clear to the medical team and place a 'Do Not Attempt Resuscitation Order' in your medical record. We will continue to provide all the appropriate treatments to manage your symptoms and support the quality of life that we have discussed."

Implantable Cardiac Devices

Despite the benefits of implantable cardiac devices, such as pacemakers, ventricular assist devices, and defibrillators, in terms of improving and lengthening life, all of the patients who receive them will eventually reach the end of their lives.[58,59] As many as 20% of patients with implantable cardiac defibrillators receive shocks in the last weeks of life, which can lead to significant distress for patients and families alike.[58] Ideally, conversations about deactivation should occur when the devices are implanted and the issue should be readdressed as the underlying heart disease progresses.[58] Decisions about device deactivation should occur in the context of goals of care and resuscitation discussions during a family meeting. The APRN should obtain a history from the patient and family about their past experience with a device (e.g., prior defibrillator activations). Some patients may have little memory; others may describe the episode as being painful

or frightening ("being kicked in the chest" or "an explosion").[59] If a decision is made to deactivate the device, the APRN should prepare those involved for what to expect when the device is deactivated. Patients may incorrectly assume that deactivation is a surgical procedure or that death will occur when the device is turned off. The APRN should assess the patient's and family's understanding and provide appropriate education about the deactivation process and its implications.[60]

Ventricular assist devices (VADs) are surgically implanted pumps to support damaged left, right, or both ventricles. Discussion related to discontinuation of VAD therapy should be in the context of goals in a family meeting when there are complications or the device no longer supports the desired quality of life. The APRN should advise patients and families that after VAD discontinuation, time of survival may range from a few minutes to a few days.[61] See Chapter 48, Withdrawal of Cardiology Technology.

Artificial Nutrition and Hydration

For many patients and families, artificial nutrition and hydration are not medical treatments but symbols of love and care. Any suggestion that these elements be withheld or withdrawn can be perceived as tantamount to neglect. The majority of the feeding tubes inserted in patients with advanced dementia are done during an acute hospital stay without discussions with surrogate decision makers.[62] During a family meeting, it is important for the APRN to help families make the connection between artificial nutrition and hydration as a treatment and how it supports or does not support the goals of care. For example, use of artificial nutrition and hydration in a frail elderly person with advanced dementia will not help the person get stronger, prevent aspiration, reverse the underlying disease, or prolong life.[54,62] Without the clinician's direction, families may continue to harbor erroneous beliefs about the benefits of artificial nutrition and hydration. The astute APRN can show the family how they can demonstrate love and care in other ways, such as inviting family participation in careful hand feeding or providing oral or other physical care.[24] See Chapter 50, Discontinuation of Life-Sustaining Therapies.

Critical Care/Emergency Department Family Meetings

Twenty percent of all deaths in the United States occur in an ICU.[63] Decisions to withhold or withdraw specific ICU treatments are often done in the context of a family meeting. Family meetings in the ICU have been associated with higher levels of satisfaction, and guidelines recommend that family meetings occur within 72 hours of an ICU admission.[29] Family meetings in the ICU have been associated with higher mortality rates, which may reflect an increased attention to communication in end-of-life situations.[29]

The need for family meetings in the emergency department may parallel those in the ICU. Emergency department visits may be precipitated by a health crisis in which discussion of prognosis and treatment is of vital importance.[64]

When a person is ill enough to require ICU care, it may be too late to discuss values and wishes with the patient, and the information must be obtained from surrogates.[29,30,37] The APRN should use open-ended questions, such as "Tell me about your loved one," "What things did he/she enjoy doing?," "What was life like for him/her prior to this illness?" to construct a picture of the patient and what was important to him or her.[3] Discussions should point surrogates toward what the patient would have expressed for himself or herself rather than what the surrogate would want, or what is in the best interest of the patient when his or her wishes are not known.[31]

Of all of the ICU technologies, mechanical ventilation is the most common life-support measure discontinued.[37] Other ICU technologies that may be discussed during family meetings include continuous venovenous hemodialysis (CVVHD), vasopressors, and extracorporeal membrane oxygenation (ECMO). The APRN should have a basic understanding of these therapies and the implications for their use or discontinuation if they are to be addressed during a family meeting. See Chapter 6, Palliative Care in the Emergency Department.

Dealing with Conflict

Conflict in family meetings is to be expected.[65] Conflict may be defined as a disagreement or difference of opinion on the management of a patient involving more than one individual and requiring a decision or action.[65] The conflict may be between family members, within the team, or between the team and the family. Nurses may be the team member most likely to identify conflicts.[65] In one study, the most common area of disagreement between team and family and between family members was decisions to withhold or withdraw life-sustaining therapies.[65] Families in this study desired more aggressive treatment than the team thought appropriate.[65] Other sources of conflict included the surrogate's inability to make a decision or lack of available decision makers.

The burden of decision making is not insignificant for families, who must process complicated information during a time of uncertainty and unprecedented stress. The shift toward autonomy in decision making has, in some cases, allowed the healthcare team to take a passive approach and avoid the obligation to provide recommendations based on their experience and medical knowledge.[66] APRNs should be aware of the risk factors for conflict that have been identified:[65,66]

1. ICU setting where life-sustaining treatment is in use or being considered

2. Unmarried patient

3. Decision maker (patient or family member) who is medically naïve or views the body in more mechanistic terms

4. Decision maker (patient or family member) who has underlying cognitive or mental health concerns

5. Prior history of poor coping skills (in patient or family member)

6. History of substance abuse (in patient or family member)

7. Culture of patient or family member is traditionally mistrustful of the medical establishment

8. Belief system of patient or family member that allows for miracles as the sole option

When there is conflict about the goals of care and the reality of the medical situation, think about emotion. Grief, anger, mistrust, unfinished personal business, and guilt may lie underneath the more visible conflict.[24] Using emotion-handling skills such as "NURSE" (see Table 40.7) or "wish statements" can help diffuse conflict. By saying "I wish there was a more effective treatment for your mother's condition," the APRN is entering into the patient's situation

empathically but at the same time acknowledging that the situation is not reversible.[3,67] Empathic responses, especially when there is conflict, will help to foster trust and build a therapeutic relationship.

Although lack of information may also precipitate conflict, attempts to convince the family of a certain viewpoint may deepen the divide. Seeking understanding and clarity about the family's position is essential:[23] "I heard you mention that you want everything done for your loved one. Please help me understand what 'everything' means to you." Even when there is disagreement, it is important to seek common ground. It may be that the medical team and the family can only agree that they both want what is best for the patient and a time to meet again.

Conclusion

Family meetings are an essential tool in palliative care. By the nature of their education and expertise, palliative APRNs often lead these meetings. APRNs must be skilled in principles of good communication, including attending to emotion and negotiating conflict, to provide effective care through family meetings. The APRN should pay careful attention to advance preparation and take a "time out" to make sure that everyone is ready before continuing. Above all, proceed with sensitivity, employ empathy, and listen before speaking.

References

1. Hospice and Palliative Nurses Association and the American Nurses Association. *Scope and Standards of Practice: Palliative Nursing, an Essential Resource for Hospice and Palliative Nurses.* Silver Spring, MD: ANA; 2014.

2. Dahlin CM, Wittenberg E. Communication in palliative care: an essential competency for nurses. In: Ferrell BR, Coyle N, Paice J, eds. *The Textbook of Palliative Nursing.* 4th ed. Oxford, England: Oxford University Press; 2015:81–112.

3. Peereboom K, Coyle N. Facilitating goals-of-care discussions for patients with life-limiting disease: communication strategies for nurses. *J Hospice Palliat Nurs.* 2012; 14: 251–8.

4. Parker SM, Remington R, Nannini A, Cifuentes M. Patient outcomes and satisfaction with care following palliative care consultation. *J Hospice Palliat Nurs.* 2013; 15: 225–43.

5. Liu LM, Guarino AJ, Lopez RP. Family satisfaction with care provided by nurse practitioners to nursing home residents with dementia at the end of life. *Clin Nurs Res.* 2012; 21: 350–67.

6. Heinle R, McNulty J, Hebert R. Nurse practitioners and the growth of palliative medicine. *Am J Palliat Med.* 2014; 31: 287–91.

7. Hudson P, Thomas T, Quinn K. Family meetings in palliative care: are they effective? *Palliat Med.* 2009; 23: 150–7.

8. Ferrell BR, Virani R, Grant M. Analysis of end-of-life content in nursing textbooks. *Oncol Nurs Forum.* 1999; 26: 869–76.

9. Curtis JR, Back AL, Ford DW, et al. Effect of communication skills training for residents and nurse practitioners on quality of communications with patients with serious illness. *JAMA.* 2013; 310: 2271–81.

10. Smith RC. *Patient-Centered Interviewing: An Evidence-Based Method.* Philadelphia, PA: Lippincott, Williams & Wilkins; 2002.

11. Nelson JE, Angus DC, Weissfeld LA, et al. End-of-life care for the critically ill: a national intensive care unit survey. *Crit Care Med.* 2006; 34: 2547–53.

12. Cassarett D, Pickard A, Bailey FA, et al. Do palliative care consultations improve patient outcomes? *J Am Geriatr Soc.* 2008; 56: 593–9.

13. Wilson IB, Green ML, Goldman L, Tsevat J, Cook EF, Phillips RS. Is experience a good teacher? How interns and attending physicians understand patients' choices for end-of-life care. *Medical Decision Making.* 1997; 17: 217–27.

14. SUPPORT Principal Investigators. A controlled trial to improve care for seriously ill patients - The study to understand prognoses and preferences for outcomes and risks of treatments (SUPPORT). *JAMA*. 1995; 274: 1591–8.

15. Lautrette A, Darmon M, Megarbane B, et al. A communication strategy and brochure for relatives of patients dying the ICU. *N Engl J Med*. 2007; 356: 469–78.

16. Weiner JS, Roth J. Avoiding iatrogenic harm to patient and family while discussing goals of care near the end of life. *J Palliat Med*. 2006; 9: 451–63.

17. Boyd D, Merkh K, Rutledge DN, Randall V. Nurses' perceptions and experiences with end-of-life communication and care. *Oncol Nurs Forum*. 2011; 38: E229–E239.

18. Baer L, Weinstein E. Improving oncology nurses' communication skills for difficult conversations. *Clin J Oncol Nurs*. 2013; 17: E45–E51.

19. Hickey M. What are the needs of families of critically ill patients? A review of the literature since 1976. *Heart Lung*. 1990; 19:401–15.

20. Norton SA, Hogan LA, Holloway RG, Temkin-Greener H, Buckley MJ, Quill TE. Proactive palliative care in the medical intensive care unit: Effects on length of stay for selected high-risk patients. *Crit Care Med*. 2007; 35: 1530–5.

21. Wright AA, Zhang B, Ray A, et al. Associations between end-of-life discussions, patient mental health, medical care near death and caregiver bereavement adjustment. *JAMA*. 2008; 300: 1665–73.

22. Gay EB, Pronovost PJ, Bassett RD, Nelson JE. The intensive care unit family meeting: making it happen. *J Crit Care*. 2009; 24: 1–12.

23. Barclay JS, Blackhall LJ, Tulsky JA. Communication strategies and cultural issues in the delivery of bad news. *J Palliat Med*. 2007; 10: 958–77.

24. Von Gunten CF, Ferris FD, Emanuel LL. Ensuring competency in end-of-life care: communication and relational skills. *JAMA*. 2000; 284: 3051–7.

25. Fineberg IC, Kawashima M, Asch SM. Communication with families facing life-threatening illness: a research-based model for family conferences. *J Palliat Med*. 2010; 14: 421–7.

26. Omnibus Budget Reconciliation Act of 1990. Patient Self-Determination Act. 1990 P.L. 101-508.

27. Delgado EM, Callhan A, Paganelli G, Reville B, Parks SM, Marik PE. Multidisciplinary family meetings in the ICU facilitate end-of-life decision making. *Am J Hosp Palliat Care*. 2009; 26: 295–302.

28. Curtis JR, White DB. Practical guidance for evidence-based family conferences in the ICU. *Chest*. 2008; 134: 835–43.

29. Kodali S, Stametz RA, Bengier AC, Clarke DN, Layon AJ, Darer JD. Family experience with intensive care unit care: association of self-reported family satisfaction. *J Crit Care*. 2014; 29: 641–4.

30. Truog RD, Campbell ML, Curtis JR, et al. Recommendations for end-of-life care in the intensive care unit: A Consensus Statement by the American College of Critical Care Medicine. *Crit Care Med*. 2008; 36: 953–963.

31. Luce JM. End-of-life decision making in the intensive care unit. *Am J Respir Crit Care Med*. 2010; 182: 6–11.

32. Ditto PH, Danks JH, Smucker WD, et al. Advance directives as acts of communication. *Arch Intern Med*. 2011; 161: 421–30.

33. Sullivan DR, Liu X, Corwin DS, et al. Learned helplessness among families and surrogate decision-makers of patients admitted to medical, surgical, and trauma ICUs. *Chest*. 2012; 142: 1440–6.

34. Weisman D. Preparing for the family meeting. Fast Fact #222. Available at https://www.capc.org/fast-facts/222-preparing-family-meeting/. 2009. Accessed July 31, 2015.

35. Back AL, Arnold RM. "Yes it's sad but what should I do? Moving from empathy to action in discussing goals of care. *J Palliat Med*. 2014; 17: 141–4.

36. Back AL, Arnold RM, Baile WF, Tulsky JA. Fyer-Edwards K. Approaching difficult communication tasks in oncology. *Cancer*. 2009; 55: 164–77.

37. Cook D, Rocker G. Dying with dignity in the intensive care unit. *N Engl J Med*. 2014; 370: 2506–14.

38. Alexander S, Ladwig S, Norton S, et al. Emotional distress and compassionate responses in palliative care decision-making consultations. *J Palliat Med*. 2014; 17: 579–84.

39. Fine E, Reid MC, Shengelia R, Adelman RD. Directly observed patient–physician discussions in palliative and end-of-life care: a systematic review of the literature. *J Palliat Med*. 2010; 13: 595–603.

40. McDonagh JR, Elliott TB, Engelberg RA, Treece PD, Shannon SE, Rubenfeld GD. Family satisfaction with family conferences about end-of-life care in the ICU: increased proportion of family speech is associated with increased satisfaction. *Crit Care Med*. 2004; 32: 1484–8.

41. Ambuel B. Responding to emotion. Fast Fact #29. 2nd ed. Available at https://www.capc.org/fast-facts/29-responding-patient-emotion/. 2009. Accessed August 1, 2015.

42. Smith CB, Nelson JE, Berman AR, et al. Lung cancer physician's referral practices for palliative care consultation. *Ann Oncol*. 2012; 23: 382–7.

43. Sharma G, Freeman J, Zhang D, Goodwin JS. Continuity of care and intensive care use at the end of life. *Arch Intern Med*. 2009; 169: 81–6.

44. Fromme EK, Smith MD, Bascom PB, Kenworthy-Heinige T, Lyons KS, Tolle SW. Incorporating routine survival prediction in a U.S. hospital-based palliative care service. *J Palliat Med*. 2010; 13: 1439–44.

45. Apatira L, Boyd EA, Evans LR, et al. Hope, truth and preparing for death: perspectives of surrogate decision makers. *Ann Intern Med*. 2008; 12: 861–68.

46. Schenker Y, White DB, Crowley-Matoka M, Dohan D, Tiver GA, Arnold RM. "It hurts to know . . . and it helps": exploring how surrogates in the ICU cope with prognostic information. *J Palliat Med*. 2013; 16: 243–9.

47. Zibelman M, Xiang Q, Muchka S, Nickeloff S, Marks S. Assessing prognostic documentation and accuracy among palliative care clinicians. *J Palliat Med*. 2014; 17: 521–6.

48. Swetz KM, Burkle CM, MD, Berge KH, Lanier WL. Ten common questions (and their answers) on medical futility. *Mayo Clin Proc*. 2014; 89: 943–59.

49. Weisman D. Determining prognosis in advanced cancer. Fast Fact #13. Available at https://www.capc.org/fast-facts/13-determining-prognosis-advanced-cancer/. 2009. Accessed August 1, 2015.

50. Wilner LS, Arnold R. The Palliative Performance Scale. Fast Fact #125. Available at https://www.capc.org/fast-facts/125-palliative-performance-scale-pps/. 2009. Accessed September 11, 2015.

51. Lamont EB, Christakis NA. Complexities in prognostication in advanced cancer. *JAMA*. 2003; 290: 98–104

52. Cohen LM, Ruthazer R, Moss AH, Germain MJ. Predicting 6-month mortality for patients who are on maintenance hemodialysis. *Clin J Am Soc Nephrol*. 2010; 5: 72–9.

53. Levy WC, Mozaffarian D, Linker DT, et al. The Seattle Heart Failure Model. Prediction of survival in heart failure. *Circulation*. 2006; 113: 1424–33.

54. American Geriatric Society. Position Statement on Feeding Tubes in Advanced Dementia. Available at www.americangeriatrics.org/files/documents/feeding.tubes.advanced.dementia.pdf. Published May 2013. Accessed July 30, 2014.

55. Unroe M, Kahn JM, Carson SS, et al. One-year trajectories of care and resource utilization for recipients of prolonged mechanical ventilation: A cohort study. *Arch Intern Med*. 2010; 153: 167–75.

56. Weil MH, Weil CJ. How to respond to family demands for futile life support and cardiopulmonary resuscitation. *Crit Care Med*. 2000; 28: 3339–40.

57. Centers for Disease Control and Prevention. Morbidity and Mortality Weekly Report. Out-of-Hospital Cardiac Arrest Registry to Enhance Survival (CARES), United States, October 1, 2005–December 31, 2010. Available at www.cdc.gov/mmrw/preview/mmwrrhtml/ss6008al.htm. Published July 29, 2011. Last accessed July 30, 2014.

58. Lampert R, Hayes DL, Annas GJ, et al. HRH Expert Consensus Statement on the management of cardiovascular implantable electronic devices (CIEDs) in patients nearing end of life requesting withdrawal of therapy. *Heart Rhythm.* 2010; 7: 1008–26.

59. Goldstein NE, Lampert R, Bradley E, Lynn J, Krumholz HM. Management of implantable cardioverter defibrillators in end-of-life care. *Ann Intern Med.* 2004; 141: 835–8.

60. Kalowes P. Implanted cardiac devices. In: Nelson P, ed. *Withdrawal of Life-Sustaining Therapies.* Pittsburgh, PA: Hospice and Palliative Nurses Association; 2010:25–33.

61. Brush S, Budge D, Alharethi R, et al. End-of-life decision making and implementation in recipients of a destination left ventricular assist device. *J Heart Lung Transplant.* 2010; 29: 1337–41.

62. Sampson EL, Candy B, Jones L. Enteral tube feeding for older people with advanced dementia. *Cochrane Database of Systematic Reviews,* 2009, Issue 2. Available at www.thecochranelibrary.com. Accessed June 6, 2014.

63. Norton SA, Hogan LA, Holloway RG, et al. Incorporating routine survival prediction in a U.S. hospital-based palliative care service. *J Palliat Med.* 2010; 13: 1439–44.

64. DiMartino LD, Weiner BJ, Mayer DK, Jackson GL, Biddle AK. Do palliative care interventions reduce emergency department visits among patients with cancer at the end of life? A systematic review. *J Palliat Med.* 2014; 17: 1–16.

65. Studdert DM, Mello MM, Burns JP, et al. Conflict in the care of patients with prolonged stay in the ICU: types, sources, and predictors. *Intens Care Med.* 2003; 29: 1489–97.

66. Roeland E, Cain J, Onderdonk C, Kerr K, Mitchell W, Thornberry K. When open-ended questions don't work: the role of palliative paternalism in difficult medical decisions. *J Palliat Med.* 2014; 17: 415–42.

67. Quill TE, Arnold RM, Platt F. "I wish things were different": expressing wishes in response to loss, futility, and unrealistic hopes. *Ann Intern Med.* 2001; 135: 5551–5.

CHAPTER 41

Communication at the Time of Death

Marlene E. McHugh and Penelope R. Buschman

Key Points

♦ Communication at the time of death requires sensitivity and compassion.

♦ The advanced practice registered nurse (APRN) must communicate effectively and compassionately with the patient, family, and healthcare team at end-of-life.

♦ Using a family systems theoretical framework enhances the ability of palliative APRNs to assess and intervene with patients and families at end-of-life.

Introduction

The work of palliative nursing is born of the knowledge of family systems theory, communication skill, and bereavement theories, as well as expert assessment and patient/family teaching. It is also made manifest in a delicate dance of unspoken communication between the nurse and the relationships served: the intuitive knowing of nurses as relationships change dramatically, as death approaches, and ultimately in the basic tenet of palliative nursing that our care is family centered and if done well is relationship centered.[1]

The American Nurses Association requires nurses to provide comfort, and this includes expertise in the relief of suffering, whether physical, emotional, spiritual, or existential. Increasingly, this means the nurse's role includes discussing end-of-life choices before a patient's death is imminent and after a death, when the family is dealing with the loss.[2] The American Association of Colleges of Nursing has recommended competencies and curricular guidelines for nurses so they can provide high-quality care to patients and families at the end-of-life (Boxes 41.1 and 41.2). The ability to communicate effectively and compassionately with the patient, family, and healthcare team is essential. The National Consensus Project for Quality Palliative Care outlines the importance of communication in Domain 1 of the *Clinical Practice Guidelines for Quality Palliative Care*.

Effective communication skills are requisite in palliative care. These include developmentally appropriate and effective sharing of information, active listening, determination of goals and preferences, assistance with medical decision-making, and effective communication with all individuals involved in the care of patients and their families.[3]

Communication is central to nursing care, especially in the setting of a progressive disease ending in the patient's death. The function of communication is to reduce uncertainty and to provide a basis for action. Information conveyed wisely and with sensitivity can improve the patient's and family's ability to act now and in the future and strengthens the patient–nurse relationship. In contrast, clumsy communication can cause harm, "paralyze" action, and destroy the relationship. Nurses who have the skills necessary for these discussions can provide valuable support for patients to achieve their goals at the end-of-life.[4,5]

What Is Communication?

Essential to every aspect of palliative care nursing is communication. It is woven through the fabric of care that begins at the time of diagnosis and continues throughout the life of the patient and beyond for the family. Communication is so much more than what is said in answer to questions about disease, treatment, and prognosis. It is more about establishing a context of trust and truthfulness. Sourkes writes that truth is neither principle nor rule but rather a state in which there can be exchange, active listening, and deep respect.[6] Communication within this state of trust undergirds the partnership among patient, family, and caregiver that is integral to the practice of palliative care.

Peplau's theory of interpersonal relations provides a conceptual framework derived in part from the empirical study of human interactions that is helpful to an understanding of communication. In this seminal work, Peplau describes the nurse–patient relationship as the human connection central in a most fundamental way to the provision of care. Within this relationship, which is largely unscripted, is the potential to connect and overcome separateness. Is this not the essence of communication, especially at the time of death?[7]

Communication, as a broad construct, includes any behavior or action, intentional or not, that influences the attitudes, ideals, or responses of another human being. Communication is transactional and occurs between and among persons. Yet, Levetown notes that too often caregivers place emphasis on conveying just information, with little regard for feelings, relationships, and continuity in care.[8]

One of the most complex and amazing developments of the first 3 years of life is the transformation of newborns who communicate through body language and vocalizations into children

Box 41.1 Clinical Practice Guidelines Domain 7: Care of the Patient at the End of Life

Guideline 7.1 The interdisciplinary team (IDT) identifies, communicates, and manages the signs and symptoms of patients at the end of life to meet the physical, psychosocial, spiritual, social, and cultural needs of patients and families.

Criteria:

♦ Care of the patient at the end of life is time and detail intensive, requiring expert clinical, social, and spiritual attention to the process as it evolves. Care of the patient is divided into three phases; predeath, perideath, and postdeath.

♦ The IDT recognizes the need for high acuity and high intensity care during the dying process.

♦ The IDT routinely elicits and honestly addresses concerns, hopes, fears, and expectations about the dying process in a developmentally appropriate manner, with respect for the social and cultural context of the family (See Domain 6: Cultural Aspects of Care).

♦ In collaboration with the patient and family, the IDT provides care with respect for patient and family values, preferences, beliefs, culture, and religion.

♦ The IDT acknowledges the patient's needs at the end of life and educates the family and other care providers about what to expect in terms of the death. As death approaches, they communicate signs and symptoms of imminent death, in culturally and developmentally appropriate language, with attention to population specific issues and age appropriateness.

Guideline 7.2 The interdisciplinary team assesses and, in collaboration with the patient and family, develops, documents, and implements a care plan to address preventative and immediate treatment of actual or potential symptoms, patient and family preferences for site of care, attendance of family and/or community members at the bedside, and desire for other treatments and procedures.

Criteria:

♦ The IDT assesses the patient for symptoms and proactively prepares family and other caregivers on the recognition and management of potential symptoms and concerns.

♦ With the patient and family, a plan is developed to meet their unique needs during the dying process as well as the needs of family immediately following the patient's death. Reassessment and revision of the plan occurs in a timely basis.

♦ Any inability to honor the patient's and family's expressed wishes for care immediately leading up to and following the patient's death is documented and communicated in the medical record that is accessible to other health care providers.

♦ For patients who have not accessed hospice services, care planning at this stage may include the introduction or reintroduction of a hospice referral, if such an option is congruent with the patient's and family's goals and preferences.

♦ Before the patient's death, sensitive communication occurs, as appropriate, about autopsy, organ and tissue donation, and anatomical gifts, adhering to institutional and regional policies.

Guideline 7.3 Respectful postdeath care is delivered in a respectful manner that honors the patient and family culture and religious practices.

Criteria:

♦ In postdeath, the focus of care includes respectful care of the body and support of the family.

♦ The interdisciplinary team assesses and documents cultural and religious practices particular to the postdeath period, and delivers care honoring those practices, in accordance with both institutional practice, local laws, and state regulations (see Domain 5: Spiritual, Religious, and Existential Aspects of Care and Domain 6: Cultural Aspects of Care).

Guideline 7.4 An immediate bereavement plan is activated postdeath.

Criteria:

♦ As described in Domain 3 Guideline 3.2, the IDT formulates and activates a postdeath bereavement plan based on a social, cultural, and spiritual grief assessment.

♦ A health care team member is assigned to support the family in the postdeath period and assist with religious practices, funeral arrangements, and burial planning.

From reference 3.

Box 41.2 Clinical Practice Guidelines Related to Communication: Domain 5, Spiritual, Religious, and Existential Aspects of Care, and Domain 6, Cultural Aspects of Care

---

Domain 5: Spiritual, Religious, and Existential Aspects of Care

Guideline 5.3 The palliative care service facilitates religious, spiritual, and cultural rituals or practices as desired by patient and family, especially at and after the time of death.

- The palliative care team ensures postdeath follow up after the patient's death (e.g., phone calls, attendance at wake or funeral, or scheduled visit) to offer support, identify any additional needs that require community referral, and help the family during bereavement (see Domain 3: Psychological and Psychiatric Aspects of Care, Guideline 3.2).

Domain 6: Cultural Aspects of Care

Guideline 6.1 The palliative care program serves each patient, family, and community in a culturally and linguistically appropriate manner.

Criteria:

- Culture is multidimensional. "The word 'culture' implies the integrated pattern of human behavior that includes thoughts, communications, actions, customs, beliefs, values, and institutions of a racial, ethnic, religious, or social group."

- Culture is far reaching. "Cultural identification may include, but is not limited to, race, ethnicity, and national origin; migration background, degree of acculturation, and documentation status; socioeconomic class; age; gender, gender identity, and gender expression; sexual orientation; family status; spiritual, religious, and political belief or affiliation; physical, psychiatric, and cognitive ability; and literacy, including health and financial literacy."

- During the assessment process, the IDT elicits and documents the cultural identifications, strengths, concerns, and needs of the patient and family, with recognition that cultural identity and expression vary within families and communities.

- All palliative care staff consistently convey respect for the patient's and family's cultural perceptions, preferences, and practices regarding illness, disability, treatment, help seeking, disclosure, decision making, grief, death, dying, and family composition.

- Palliative care program staff communicate in a language and manner that the patient and family understand.

- Palliative care staff respect and accommodate dietary and ritual practices of patients and their families.

- Palliative care staff members identify community resources that serve various cultural groups and refer patients and families to such services, as appropriate.

From references 1–3.

---

who use multiword utterances to describe their imaginations, emotions, memories, and wishes. While infants can communicate with their caregivers at birth, the reciprocal partnership in which complex symbolic ideas are exchanged, conflicting agendas are negotiated, and feeling states are shared must await a series of developmental advances. These advances depend both on the hardwiring in the child's central nervous system and, over time, the child's experiences within a family. Thus, the factors that support the evolving development of the ability to communicate are found in the family and social environment.[9] Language, one means of communication, is a complex, conventional system of symbols that are combined and used in a rule-governed way. Language is culturally bound and learned initially within the family of origin and later in education systems.[9] Communication occurs in multiple ways and forms, besides the written and spoken word, through the medium of movement, expression, music, art, and, of course, play.

Communication in palliative care and especially at the end-of-life is the focus of this chapter. Understanding communication in its broadest sense, appreciating the significant barriers altering its effectiveness, and developing strategies both personal and in practice ultimately will enhance the work of palliative nursing.

Conscious nonverbal communication is rarely practiced, yet it can be as powerful as verbal communication at the end-of-life.[10]

The Role of the APRN in Communicating at Critical Junctures

Often there is overlap in roles and functions of palliative interdisciplinary team members. This can be a challenge for nurses, given their educational preparation and the longstanding relationships that APRNs may have with patients and families. It is important for the APRN to recognize that a team that functions well can share responsibility for care.

Before the APRN communicates with the patient and family, essential information must be gathered. The APRN must understand the patient's diagnosis, the underlying pathophysiology of the condition and the etiology, the current medical treatment and plan for future treatment, any side effects of treatment, whether a treatment is curative or palliative, and where the patient is being treated. It is also important that the APRN understand prognostic scores like Palliative Prognostic Score, the Karnofsky, and Eastern Cooperative Oncology Group scales, which will help determine whether treatment is an option. The APRN may need to determine the patient's functional status. The APRN will need to assess the patient's and family's communication style, with attention to primary language, culture, and literacy (both in ability to understand language and medical literacy). When English is not the primary language of the patient or family, a translator (not a family member) must be present.

The APRN will need to organize the team to meet as a group prior to meeting with the family. The purpose of the "meeting before the meeting" is to determine what members of the team will provide information to the patient and family. Various team members should be included in this meeting, with the focus being organized delivery of information.

Communication Across the Trajectory of Advancing Illness

As illustrated in Figure 41.1, communication with patient and family changes over the course of advancing illness, building on early assessment, a growing trust, and a deepening connection. The focus shifts from sharing bad news at the time of diagnosis and discussing advance directives and settings for care, to maintaining connection through transitions in illness. Preference for site of death may change based on the patient's wishes, the symptom burden, and the family's resources. Participants in the process are palliative care team members, primary care providers, the ever-changing staff of physicians and nurses on hospital units, as well as home care providers. Flexibility is required as new information and options are offered and changing goals of care are reviewed. Moving across this trajectory provides an opportunity for APRNs to be proactive in anticipating care issues

and integrating them with the patient and family's individual needs. In addition, APRNs provide guidance in the context of a nurtured trust.

For the patient who expresses the desire to die, Van Loon writes that wishes to die expressed close to the end-of-life have many meanings that require exploration.[11] They may, in fact, reflect the person's wish to end a life that has become increasingly unbearable or burdensome. Wishes may be stated, without plans for execution, as a way to convey the extent of a person's suffering. When these wishes are accompanied by deep depression, further assessment and treatment may improve the person's quality of life for whatever time there may be.[12] The wish to die may also represent acceptance of the inevitability of death and the wish to hasten it. A helpful framework to guide assessment of patients is offered by Van Loon in Figure 41.2.[11]

Finally, at the end-of-life, communication with the patient may be in the form of presence, standing with and bearing witness, providing comfort for the family, discussing any wishes for end-of-life rituals and funerals, and making referrals to hospital- and community-based resources. Holmberg describes poignantly communication in action between family caregivers and palliative care nurses at the time of death in the following passage:

> The nurses made the examinations that are legally required to declare death. Then they and the family all gathered in the kitchen. There was a time to tell about the last hours, there were opportunities to weep, to share hugs. The nurses said they would help out dressing my son and arrange for the rest of the family to say goodbye. His wife changed his clothes and ironed his shirts. One of the nurses

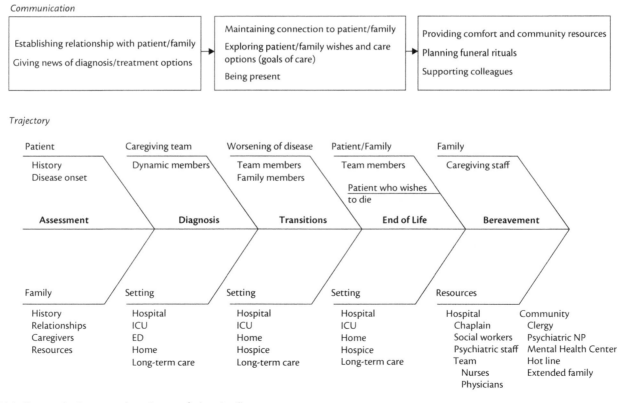

Figure 41.1 Communication across the trajectory of advancing illness

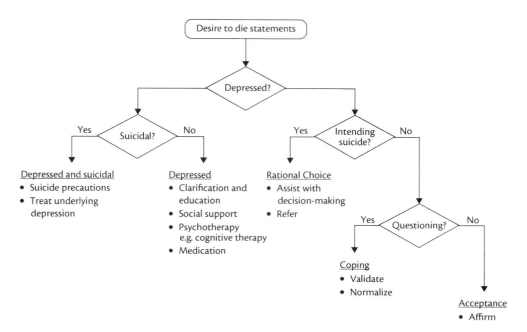

Figure 41.2 Framework for assessment and intervention for those expressing wishes to die
Source: From ref. 11.

and my son's younger brother arranged my son on his bed and lit a candle in the window. The nurses took charge of the practicalities. They arranged for the last transportation. And they stayed as long as the family members wanted them to. There was an atmosphere of respectful silence in the house.[13]

As if knowing that no words could make the loss bearable, the palliative home care nurses simply acted, demonstrating their respectful empathy.

Communication with Families at the Time of Expected Death

Preparing the family for the imminent death of a member and for their bereavement presents challenges to the APRN. In a cooperative study of eight cancer centers, providers reported that they had more difficulty communicating with family members than with patients.[14]

Indeed, family members recall in great detail the sensitivity, or lack of it, shown to them and their dying loved one. Arnold, Gemma, and Cushman studied bereaved parents whose child had died 1 to 62 years prior to the study.[15] Parents recalled in exquisite detail exactly what was said to them by nurses and physicians. In response to an open-ended question, parents reported words used to comfort and small acts of kindness. Communication with families in the form of words, presence, touch, or silence is essential.

Communication with Families About the Stages of Death

The concept of anticipatory guidance is often used by APRNs in clinical practice to prepare a patient and family for a specific developmental milestone or crisis. In working with families whose loved ones are imminently dying, the APRN should expect to discuss the trajectory of death and common concerns they may have and are afraid to ask. Many families will be interested in understanding the process of dying (Box 41.3), and communication may help with their final planning stages as a unit of care. However, some families will choose not to have information shared with them, and this should be respected. Recognition of the trajectory of imminent death is essential for clinicians in order to provide the most appropriate interventions for the patient and family. Some commonly anticipated questions are the following:

◆ How long does my loved one have?

◆ Should I/we stay at the bedside?

◆ Is my loved one in pain/suffering?

◆ What do we do after my loved one has passed away?[16]

Without an invitation, families may be reluctant to initiate discussion, fearful of hastening death by speaking of it. The APRN may use the following questions with patient and family to promote planning for an expected death:

1. Have you thought about what it will be like for your family when your loved one dies?

2. Will it be helpful for you to discuss your thoughts and plans for funeral, memorial service, or some special remembrance for your loved one when he dies? Sometimes families find it helpful to discuss these issues beforehand in a thoughtful manner.

3. Have you considered how you will include family members, particularly young children, in your family ritual of mourning?

Confirmation that Death Has Occurred

The APRN will confirm that death has occurred by assessing that there is no presence of respirations or heartbeat. In some situations,

Box 41.3 Stages of Death		
Early	**Middle**	**Late**
◆ Bedbound ◆ Loss of interest and/or ability to drink/eat ◆ Cognitive changes: increased time spent sleeping and/or delirium	◆ Further decline in mental status to obtundation (slow to arouse with stimulation; only brief periods of wakefulness) ◆ Death rattle—pooled oral sections in the larynx as a result of loss of the swallowing reflex	◆ Coma ◆ Fever ◆ Altered respiratory pattern—periods of apnea, hyperpnea, or irregular breathing ◆ Mottled extremities

From reference 16.

another clinician is required to verify the patient has died. In other settings, an electrocardiogram must be obtained. In many states, a professional nurse may determine and pronounce the death and even sign the death certificate. APRNs should be familiar with their scope of practice regarding death pronouncement and completion of death certificates.

Communication with families at the time of death includes notification that the death has occurred and what to anticipate when the body is viewed immediately after death. Families should be aware that muscles are relaxed after death, resulting in passage of stool and urine, and relaxing of the jaw, causing the mouth to open. Presentation and care of the body after death, including cleaning, is an important nursing intervention.

Sudden, Unexpected Death: Suicide, Homicide, Violence, Accidental Injury, Sudden Onset or Worsening of Disease

The challenges are significant when a person dies unexpectedly and the family does not have an ongoing connection with a caregiver. Much of the initial communication focuses on events surrounding the death as well as on resources in the community for the family (Fig. 41.3). The nurse must remain in the room to answer medical questions and to lend a respectful presence. Because of the unexpected nature of the death and lack of preparation, family members

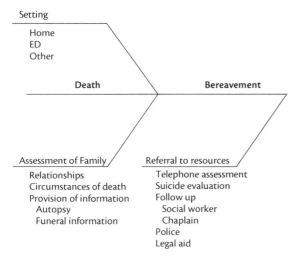

Figure 41.3 Communication at the time of death and beyond with family

may be in shock and require the services of social workers, chaplains, and psychiatric staff. Family members may require assessment for self-harm, harm to others, or damage to the environment.

The APRN meeting the family for the first time will be asked for information and clarification. Accompanying the family to the emergency room or morgue to view the patient's body requires a calm presence and the ability to prepare the family for what they will see, such as changes in skin color or visible injuries. If the family wishes to touch their loved one, they should be prepared for changes in body temperature. Immediately after death, family members may be encouraged to touch the body's core area, rather than the extremities.

In unexpected death, the APRN, in concert with team members, may refer families to community resources for bereavement counseling. Family members who threaten suicide or who may be at risk for suicide may need to be accompanied to a hospital emergency department by family members or by the APRN for a full psychiatric evaluation.

Telephone Management

Communicating with the patient's family by telephone regarding his or her condition, prognosis, and death carries the same responsibilities for the nurse as meeting in person: assessment, listening, and providing concrete medical information (Box 41.4). The one difference in communication over the phone is that the clinician cannot assess the family member's safety using nonverbal clues and unsafe living arrangements. The APRN who believes a family member is at high risk can summon emergency support using 911 and arrange for follow-up by team members.

Barriers to Communication at the End-of-Life

Perhaps the most obvious and far-reaching barrier to the provision of therapeutic communication at the end-of-life lies in our failure to teach and model the process. Levetown notes that far more time is spent focusing on facts and descriptions of procedures than on the process of communication. Moreover, efforts to elevate healthcare communication, empathy, and patient- and family-centered care as competencies within education have thus far failed.[8] Clearly, communication across the trajectory of illness and so importantly at the end-of-life deserves space and time in our curricula and clinical supervision. In specific vulnerable populations of patients, circumstances and conditions impede the communication process and challenge the palliative care nurse to find innovative approaches.

Geriatric Patients with Cognitive and Sensory Deficits

Geriatric patients (those over 65 years of age) lose physiological function and capacity, which serve as more powerful determinants of prognosis than chronological age.[19] Delirium and dementia are the two major cognitive deficits in the elderly population. Both complicate the assessment of pain and symptoms in those with advanced illness and interfere with communication in general. Sutor and colleagues note that when cognition and language are limited, communication becomes behavioral in nature.[20] Contrary to current thinking, behaviors should be seen as forms of communication, rather than as unpredictable or random events with no meaning. To intervene, the palliative APRN must attempt to identify a message in the behavior.

The visual and hearing impairments common in older adults further limit verbal and nonverbal communication.[19] In addition to these deficits, the presence of multiple comorbidities challenges the palliative care nurse's ability to derive goals of care. The APRN should make sure the patient has hearing aids or glasses, if needed, to promote communication.

Patients with Depression, Anxiety, Post-traumatic Stress Disorder, and Serious Persistent Mental Illness

While the recommended therapeutic response to patients with psychological distress at the end-of-life is to listen and provide support, patients with serious persistent mental illness pose significant challenges. Here, too, the APRN observes behaviors and mannerisms as means of communication, respecting the need for space and sometimes the inability to tolerate touch. For many of these patients, their families are disengaged and not involved in care. This population is underserved and truly vulnerable: they may live in jails or shelters or on the streets, unable to access adequate palliative care. Goldenberg, Holland, and Schachter note that palliative patients with serious mental illness have not been studied and the prevalence is unknown.[21] The appalling lack of articulation between the mental health and other healthcare

systems contributes to the lack of palliative and end-of-life care for this population.[22] Baker writes that a combination of factors, including the psychiatric symptoms exhibited by these patients and providers' attitudes and feelings toward the mentally ill, influence planning for end-of-life care.[23] The palliative APRN, in collaboration with a psychiatric nurse practitioner, can provide compassionate end-of-life care, as illustrated in the case study below.

Case Study

Jane was a 36-year-old female who had been diagnosed as an adolescent with major depressive disorder. She contracted HIV as a young adult and was estranged from her family of origin and her only son. She sought services from an agency providing medical and psychiatric services as well as residential care. Jane was enrolled in a methadone maintenance treatment program in her residence. As her HIV/AIDS worsened, Jane was encouraged by staff and her psychiatric nurse practitioner (PMHNP) to agree to inpatient hospitalization, where she would be able to receive palliative care. Jane adamantly refused, stating that she wanted to remain at "home" in the residence, where she was known by staff and other residents. Her PMHNP agreed to coordinate a home hospice program involving a community-based palliative APRN and a trained aide who would provide 24-hour care to address her increasing symptoms. Jane began to experience periods of confusion, delusional thinking, and neuropathic and nociceptive pain in her lower extremities, which was well controlled by methadone 5 mg/mL PO q8h prescribed by the APRN. Jane was at the end-of-life. With the PMHNP, Jane discussed her wish to see her 16-year-old son, who had lived with Jane's sister since birth. Jane was ashamed of her diagnosis and the circumstances of her life, and she firmly believed that her son was better off with her sister. However, as Jane faced the end of her life, her only wish was to see, and perhaps reconcile with, her son. The PMHNP contacted Jane's sister, who agreed to accompany the son to visit Jane and say goodbye. Jane died at "home" in her residence. The palliative APRN met with residents and staff who had known and stood by Jane, providing an opportunity for them to share remembrances of her and to speak of their feelings of loss. The PMHNP agreed to make a follow-up home visit to Jane's sister and son, offering the son an opportunity for bereavement care. In collaboration, the APRN and PMHNP provided pain and symptom management, spiritual and emotional support, and the opportunity for Jane to see and reconcile with her son.

Persons with Developmental Disabilities

When caring for a developmentally delayed patient at the end-of-life, the APRN must engage family members and caregivers in discussion. Goldsmith, Hendrix, and Gentry offer these suggestions to palliative care providers:

- Assist parents and/or caregivers to identify unspoken wishes that may be displayed by their developmentally disabled child/adult, such as repeated self-removal of feeding tubes.

- Invite trusted family friends, physicians, and caregivers to assist parents and/or caregivers with decision making.

- Take time to listen, talk, and develop trust and rapport with the family.

- Introduce the topic of advance directives early. Encourage parents to think about the next potential admission.
- Recognize the differences and similarities between the population of developmentally disabled persons and the general population.[24]

Families and Loss

> Coming to terms with death and loss is the most difficult challenge a family must confront. From a family systems perspective, loss can be viewed as a transactional process involving the dying and deceased with the survivors in a shared life cycle that acknowledges both the finality of death and the continuity of life.[25]

While APRNs view both the patient and family as the focus of care, the major effort at the end-of-life is to prepare the patient and family for death. Bereavement care follows acknowledgment of the loss. Missing is a systematic view of the family and the impact of the loss on the family as an interactional system. This theoretical framework provides caregivers the opportunity to see beyond the number of members and roles in order to view the system as a whole in a particular phase of life-cycle development. Rolland describes three major phases in the unfolding of chronic or advanced illness for the family member: initial crisis, chronic phase, and terminal phase.[26]

In order to respect religious and cultural variations, Rolland recommends helping families during the initial crisis (or time of diagnosis) to establish open and effective disease- and treatment-related communication (Box 41.5). Establishing this pattern early on and knowing the ill person's wishes can benefit both patient and family. With advanced disease, where the timing of loss is ambiguous but the inevitable deterioration is not, family members will grieve at each transition. At key periods, families can be encouraged to shift their roles and responsibilities to other members.

In the crisis phase of illness, families will grieve for the loss of family life prior to the diagnosis. Family members in the chronic phase grieve for the ambiguities they must endure over the long term.[23] As the patient enters the terminal phase, the main question asked is how much time there will be to prepare for death and survivorship. Rolland suggests that family's tasks at this time are as follows:

1. Completing the task of anticipatory grief and unfinished business

2. Supporting the dying member and family survivors to continue their life together for as long as they can

3. Beginning or continuing the family reorganization process[26]

Rolland encourages the palliative care provider to "join with" the family when members are anticipating a final separation. This phase provides an opportunity for some families to experience emotional and relational healing. Relationships in highly dysfunctional families where there is a history of abuse or abandonment may not be mended. Patients who have no families or who are estranged from their families of origin may be content to be surrounded by friends and caregivers.[26] Walsh and McGoldrick describe loss as a powerful nodal event that affects the entire family system and every member.[25] Loss reverberates over time, starting with the threat of death and progressing to the actual approach, the immediate aftermath, and the long-term implications. The authors propose four major tasks that promote immediate and longer-term adaptation for family members and the unit as a whole:

1. Shared acknowledgment of the reality of death

2. Shared experience of loss

3. Reorganization of the family system

4. Reinvestment in other relationships and life pursuits[25]

Self-Care

> The grief that does not speak,
> Whispers the o'er fraught heart and bids it break.
>
> —William Shakespeare, *Macbeth*

As APRNs touch the fringes of family grief and are touched deeply by that grief, they must find ways to share with colleagues and peers so that they can continue to function. Feldstein and Gemma surveyed nurses caring for terminally ill adults. Those who were not able to share their grief with colleagues experienced a chronic, compounded grief that interfered with their personal and professional lives and relationships.[27] Protracted exposure to distressing symptoms and suffering in patients and families at end-of-life generates a high level of stress and dysfunction in APRNs who are not vigilant about caring for themselves.[28] There are many vehicles for nurses to share their grief and find support (Boxes 41.6 and 41.7).

Box 41.5 Samples of Open Questions

- What are your greatest concerns?
- What is your everyday life like right now?
- What do you feel is happening?
- What do you think is happening? What have you heard?
- What really matters for you right now?
- What are your worries?
- What makes you happy in your everyday life?
- What gives you strength every day?
- Who are the people most important to you in life?
- Whom do you rely on for support?
- Are you spiritual?

From reference 16.

Box 41.6 Opportunities for Nurses to Share Grief and Find Support

1. Discussion groups and workshops
2. Support groups
3. Remembrance services
4. Professional meetings/conferences
5. Referral to grief counseling therapists

From reference 29.

Conclusion

Communication at the end-of-life is a complex and therapeutic transactional process between and among human beings. No more so than at the end-of-life does it become the connection, the empathic link between the person whose life is ending and those who will continue to live. Communication occurs through the spoken word, in action, and in silence. For the APRN, communication is an essential tool to be learned, to teach, to model, and to support. Communication as a form of human interaction is not an exact science; it is shaped by the transactional process of the persons who engage in it.

Byock captures the challenge of communication at the end-of-life.[30] Of the fundamental needs of persons as they die, only the need to control physical symptoms is uniquely medical. Their more basic needs are broader than the scope of medicine. They need shelter from the elements, a place to be. They need help with personal hygiene and assistance with elimination. They need nourishment or, as death comes closer, sips of fluid to moisten their mouth and throat. They need companionship, and they need others to recognize their continued existence. In recognizing these needs, we can say to the dying person with our words and, more importantly, with our actions:

> We will keep you warm and we will keep you dry. We will keep you clean. We will help you with elimination, with your bowels and your bladder function. We will always offer you food and fluid. We will be with you. We will bear witness to your pain and your sorrows, your disappointments and your triumphs; we will listen to the stories of your life and will remember the story of your passing.[30]

References

1. Ferrell B. From the Editor. *J Hosp Palliat Nurs.* 2012; 14(1): 1.

2. American Nurses Association (ANA). *Position Statement. Registered Nurses' Roles and Responsibilities in Providing Expert Care and Counseling at the End of Life.* Silver Spring, MD: Author, 2010. Available at http://www.nursingworld.org/MainMenuCategories/EthicsStandards/Ethics-Position-Statements/etpain14426.pdf. Accessed August 1, 2014.

3. National Consensus Project for Quality Palliative Care. *Clinical Practice Guidelines for Quality Palliative Care.* 3rd ed. Pittsburgh, PA: National Consensus Project for Quality Palliative Care; 2013. Available at http://www.nationalconsensusproject.org/NCP_Clinical_Practice_Guidelines_3rd_Edition.pdf. Accessed August 1, 2014.

4. Peereboom K, Coyle N. Facilitating goals-of-care discussions for patients with life-limiting disease—communication strategies for nurses. *J Hosp Palliat Nurs.* 2012; 14: 251–8.

5. White KR, Coyne PJ, White SG. Are hospice and palliative nurses adequately prepared for end-of-life care? *J Hosp Palliat Nurs.* 2012; 14(2): 133–40.

6. Sourkes B. *Armfuls of Time: The Psychological Experience of the Child with a Life-Threatening Illness.* Pittsburgh, PA: University of Pittsburgh Press; 1995.

7. Peplau HE. Peplau's theory of interpersonal relations. *Nurs Sci Q.* 1997; 10: 162–7.

8. Levetown M, American Academy of Pediatrics Committee on Bioethics. Communicating with children and families: from everyday interactions to skill in conveying distressing information. *Pediatrics* 2008; 121(5): e1441–60.

9. Prizant BM, Wetherby AM, Roberts JE. Communication problems. In: Zeanah CH, ed. *Handbook of Infant Mental Health.* 2nd ed. New York, NY: Guilford Press; 2000:282–97.

10. Cook D, Rocker G. Dying with dignity in the intensive care unit. *N Engl J Med,* 2014; 370: 2506–13.

11. Van Loon RA. Desire to die in terminally ill people: a framework for assessment and intervention. *Health & Social Work.* 1999; 24(4): 260–8.

12. Marks S, Rosielle D. Suicide attempts in the terminally ill. *Fast Facts and Concepts.* 2012. Available at https://www.capc.org/fast-facts/210. Accessed September 21, 2015.

13. Holmberg L. Communication in action between family caregivers and a palliative home care team. *J Hosp Palliat Nurs.* 2006; 8: 276–87.

14. Speice J, Harkness J, Laneri H, et al. Involving family members in cancer care: focus group considerations of patients and oncological providers. *Psychooncology.* 2000; 9(2): 101–12.

15. Arnold J, Gemma PB, Cushman LF. Exploring parental grief: combining quantitative and qualitative measures. *Arch Psychiatr Nurs.* 2005; 19(6): 245–55.

16. Weissman DE. Syndrome of imminent death. 2nd ed. *Fast Facts and Concepts.* 2009; 3. Available at https://www.capc.org/fast-facts/3. Accessed September 21, 2015.

17. Brensilver JM, Osias RR, Pomerantz DH. Telephone notification of death—Part I. Fast Facts and Concepts. 2009. Available at https://www.capc.org/fast-facts/76. Accessed September 21, 2015.

18. Brensilver JM, Osias RR, Pomerantz DH. Telephone notification of death—Part II. Fast Facts and Concepts. 2009. Available at https://www.capc.org/fast-facts/77. Accessed September 21, 2015.

19. Delgado-Guay MO, De La Cruz MG, Epner DE. I don't want to burden my family: handling communication challenges in geriatric oncology. *Ann Oncol.* 2013; 24(Suppl 7): vii30–35.

20. Sutor B, Rummans TA, Smith GE. Assessment and management of behavioral disturbances in nursing home patients with dementia. *Mayo Clin Proc.* 2001; 76: 540–50.

21. Goldenberg D, Holland J, Schachter S. Palliative care in the chronically mentally ill. In: Chochinov HM, Breitbart W, eds. *Handbook of Psychiatry in Palliative Medicine.* New York, NY: Oxford University Press; 2000: 91–6.

22. Miller CL, Druss BG, Dombrowski EA, Rosenheck RA. Barriers to primary medical care among patients at a community mental health center. *Psychiatric Services.* 2003; 54(8): 1158–60.

23. Baker, A. Palliative and end-of-life care in the serious and persistently mentally ill population. *J Am Psychiatr Nurses Assoc.* 2005; 11(5): 298–303.

24. Goldsmith B, Hendrix CC, Gentry J. Providing end-of-life palliative care for the developmentally disabled and their families. *J Hosp Palliat Nurs.* 2006; 8: 270–5.

25. Walsh F, McGoldrick M. *Living Beyond Loss: Death in the Family.* 2nd ed. New York: W.W. Norton & Company; 2004:3–14.

26. Rolland JS. Helping families with anticipatory loss and terminal illness. In: Walsh F, McGoldrick M, eds. *Living Beyond Loss: Death in the Family.* New York, NY: Norton; 2004:213–37.

27. Feldstein MA, Gemma PB. Oncology nurses and chronic compounded grief. *Cancer Nurs.* 1995; 18(3): 228–36.

28. Gemma PB, Farley JN, Rushton CH. Chronic and palliative care of pediatric populations. In: Yearwood EL, Pearson GS, Newland JA, eds. *Child and Adolescent Behavioral Health: A Resource for Advanced Practice Psychiatric and Primary Care Practitioners in Nursing*. West Sussex, UK: Wiley-Blackwell; 2012:426–41.

29. Buschman Gemma P, Arnold JH. *Loss and Grieving in Pregnancy and the First Year of Life: A Caring Resource for Nurses*. New York, NY: March of Dimes; 2002.

30. Byock I. *Dying Well: The Prospect for Growth at the End of Life*. East Rutherford, NJ: Putnam-Riverhead; 1997: 247.

CHAPTER 42

Navigating Ethical Discussions in Palliative Care

Nessa Coyle and Timothy W. Kirk

Key Points

◆ The advanced practice registered nurse (APRN) is uniquely trained and situated within palliative care teams to navigate ethical discussions.

◆ Professional codes of ethics, bioethical principles, communication principles, and support of moral agency are the foundation for such discussions.

◆ An ethical framework built on the cornerstone principles of advocacy, clinical sensitivity, truthfulness, and accommodation recommends that *process* rather than *outcome* is the appropriate focus when navigating ethical discussions.

Case Study

Mrs. S was a 65-year-old woman with advanced sarcoma of the left chest wall and an associated fungating chest wall mass. She had been treated with surgery, radiation therapy, and several courses of chemotherapy. No further disease-focused treatment options were available to her, and her care was directed toward symptom management. Mrs. S had completed an advance directive 1 year earlier specifying that, if she were terminally ill and no further treatment options were available to her, she would not want her life to be artificially prolonged with machines or other measures. In the preceding week, Mrs. S was admitted to an inpatient setting for better symptom management. When her code status was addressed upon admission, she said that she wanted "everything done." Concerned that her condition was deteriorating and that her current wishes were diametrically opposed to those expressed in her advance directive, her medical team on the unit invited the palliative APRN to consult on the case.

The APRN met with the patient and her daughter and learned that the daughter's husband had recently died of a brain tumor, and the patient's own husband had been admitted within the last month to a dementia unit. Overwhelmed by these recently changed circumstances, Mrs. S decided that she wanted to live as long as she possibly could—regardless of her medical status—so that she could support her husband through his transition and have more time with her daughter and grandchildren, even if it meant resuscitation and intubation. Mrs. S expressed feeling "hounded" by many different staff members asking her about resuscitation. She felt that she had told the team her wishes, but it was not what they wanted to hear, so they kept asking her again and again. She went on to say, as did her daughter, that if the topic had been addressed in a more compassionate and empathic manner, her decision might have been different.

Introduction

As you read this chapter, we would like you to reflect on ethical discussions you have navigated with patients, families, or staff. What was it about these discussions that left you with a feeling of satisfaction or failure? Was it in the process or was it in the outcome? If in the outcome, how was success or failure measured? This chapter addresses these questions by providing the APRN with a structure and language that complement the classic patient-centered care model of autonomy, beneficence, nonmaleficence, and justice. The chapter builds on the ethical foundation already inherent in the practice of the APRN, emphasizing the importance of presence, listening, and clinical sensitivity. It presents a framework for navigating ethical discussions, using a case study to illustrate ethical principles that are essential to these discussions. The role of the APRN in moral reflection and deliberation—debriefing and supporting staff when their ethical compass has been challenged—is acknowledged. Throughout, the APRN is recognized as being uniquely well trained and situated within palliative care teams to be an advocate to ensure that the values, goals, perspectives, and concerns of patients, families, and fellow clinicians are appropriately heard in patient care conversations.

What is an ethical discussion? When the question "What is the 'right' thing to do in this situation?" is asked, it is an ethical question.[1] When a discussion touches on one or more core values of the participants involved, or the core values of their respective traditions or professions, it is likely ethically significant. The very nature of palliative care, in which patients and their families are faced with many choices and decisions throughout the disease trajectory, but especially during transitions from curative or life-prolonging therapy to end-of-life care, makes such discussions commonplace.[2]

Advances in science and medical technology give healthcare providers the tools to prolong life, but also to prolong the dying process. This double-edged sword has led to challenges for clinicians in palliative care, amplifying the responsibility to provide care that is clinically *and ethically* appropriate. Technological development affects what *can* be done in healthcare but offers no guidance regarding what *ought* to be done. Ethical discussions among patients, loved ones, and clinicians are the processes in which parties work together to decide what should be done. Clinical judgment, sensitivity, and effective communication skills are essential ingredients in such conversations. Progressive illness with a long trajectory provides both the opportunity and the obligation for the APRN to have ongoing conversations with patients and their families about their preferences for present and future healthcare interventions.[3] The importance of having these conversations becomes even more urgent when the patient presents with advanced disease. [4] Notice how the following patient, a 52-year-old woman with refractory breast cancer, communicates the emotional complexity associated with making treatment decisions for herself—acknowledging her autonomy while also implicitly requesting assistance and support.

> I'm near the end psychologically and then I have to make the decision about whether to continue treatment or not. I live each day and try and go along with the most up-to-date medical knowledge that will extend my life. . . . I know my life is foreshortened—I think about death and get frightened. . . . I have a heavy decision whether to have chemo or not. It's my decision because it's my body.

Care decisions are based, among other things, on the quality of information the patient or surrogate has been given about the illness, including the prognosis and the benefits and burdens of the recommended treatment and alternate approaches to care.[5] The Institute of Medicine's 2011 report, *The Future of Nursing: Leading Change, Advancing Health*, states that, although physicians have traditionally been responsible for these difficult end-of-life conversations, with the advancement of nursing practice, nurses are now taking the lead.[6] The Hospice and Palliative Nurses Association emphasizes that, due to their advanced training, visibility, and presence at the bedside, APRNs are ideally placed not only to help staff, patients, and families navigate the difficult decisions to be made, but also to create an ethical environment.[7] The APRN's influence in creating an ethical environment is seen not only in the inpatient setting but also in outpatient clinics, as a clinical palliative care consultant, and in home hospice care. By serving on ethics committees, APRNs can help create ethical environments across their care organizations. An ethical environment is one in which interactions are characterized by trust and respect, where there is encouragement to "speak up" and psychological safety in doing so, and where differences of opinion are welcomed and discussed.[8]

The Foundation of Ethical Discussions

This section briefly reviews four areas: nursing codes of ethics, core principles in clinical healthcare ethics, communication principles, and moral agency. The content of these four areas provides important background knowledge and sets the foundation for the ethical framework explained in the second part of the chapter.

Nursing Codes of Ethics

Nursing codes of ethics articulate defining values that unite individual nurses into a caregiving community with ideals of professional conduct.[4] The International Council of Nurses' (ICN) *Code of Ethics for Nurses* states in its preamble, "Nurses have four fundamental responsibilities: to promote health, to prevent illness, to restore health and to alleviate suffering."[9(p 1)] In addition, the American Nurses Association has a code of ethics with tenets consisting of nine statements that describe the commitment of nurses to patients, duty to self and others, and duties beyond individual patient encounters.[3] These codes are a reminder to nurses of the special responsibilities we have in caring for the sick, and they highlight the responsibility we have to use our knowledge and skills to help individuals and families when they are at their most vulnerable.[4] The APRN has a special responsibility in ensuring that these ideals are actualized at the individual level, the unit level, and the institutional level. At all levels, actualization requires ethical analysis and reasoning specific to the situation at hand.[4] Ethical principles have to be validated by context to be clinically useful.

Ethical Principles

These four ethical principles inform the broad landscape of nursing ethics:[10,11]

1. *Autonomy*: This principle is rooted in the notion of self-governance—the belief that individuals should have the strongest voice in making their own healthcare decisions because such decisions have a significant impact on their lives. Respecting autonomy allows persons with decision-making capacity to make healthcare decisions for themselves by giving them the support and information necessary to integrate their values, beliefs, and preferences into the decision-making process.[12] A patient with capacity may appoint another person to make decisions for him or her, and honoring such decisions when the patient loses capacity becomes one way to respect his or her autonomy.

2. *Beneficence*—This principle asserts that a primary ethical obligation of all clinicians is to do good—to provide care and support that enhances patients' well-being and offers benefit consistent with their goals and values.[13] As such, honoring beneficence requires knowledge about what each patient values in his or her life and discussion with each patient of which treatment options resonate most strongly with those values.

3. *Nonmaleficence*—This principle asserts a duty to avoid harm and reduce the risk of harm.[13] Some treatments may cause a degree of harm, but the benefit to the patient outweighs the harm. For example, palliative sedation will result in a limited ability for a patient to interact with his or her family but will relieve intractable pain or other symptoms. Therefore, nonmaleficence works in concert with beneficence and autonomy, as patient, family, and clinicians need to partner together to discern (a) which values and goals of care are most important and (b) how best to balance likely harms with likely benefits.

4. *Justice*—This principle refers to providing care that is equitable and fair to all and includes the fair distribution of scarce resources. Procedural justice requires that clinicians engage care processes that elicit the goals and preferences of patients and

respect the values and rights of all involved in giving and receiving care. Such processes are considered "fair" when all appropriate voices are heard and considered. Family meetings, for example, benefit from being guided by procedural justice so the patient's and family members' voices are given respect and consideration equal to that given to healthcare providers when decisions about the type and site of care are made. Distributive justice requires that resources be allocated fairly and equitably, using transparent and appropriate criteria. The availability of palliative care is a good example: all patients should have access to palliative care services, interventions, and support, and access to care should be based on transparent, appropriate criteria applied equally to all regardless of socioeconomic state or social status.[10,11,14]

Communication Principles

Principles of communication, discussed in depth in Chapters 39, 40, and 45, provide the foundation for the APRN's approach when navigating ethical discussions. They include (1) making sure that the patient's symptoms are under control and that some privacy has been provided; (2) eliciting, understanding, and validating the patient's perspective of the situation (concerns, feelings, expectations, goals, and values); (3) understanding the patient within his or her own psychological, cultural, social, and spiritual context; (4) reaching a shared understanding of the patient's situation; and (5) supporting the patient or surrogate in the decision made.[15–18] These principles of communication are enhanced by certain APRN behaviors, both nonverbal and verbal. Nonverbal behaviors include maintaining eye contact if culturally appropriate, leaning forward to indicate attentiveness, avoiding interrupting the patient, tolerating silence, and refraining from distracting behavior, such as glancing at a cellphone. Verbal behaviors include soliciting the beliefs, values, and preferences of the patient; exploring the family's social and spiritual context and their explanatory model of health and disease; checking the patient's understanding of what has been said; validating the patient's emotions; and offering reassurance, nonabandonment, and support.[17–19] Understanding the patient's explanatory model of disease—for example, the patient's beliefs about what has caused the illness and, therefore, what kinds of treatments may or may not work—is important as it may shape the patient's response to illness.[20–22] Such an explanatory model may be learned from multiple sources, including culture, mass media, friends, and family.

Moral Agency

Agency is a concept that describes one's ability to develop and exercise a sense of self by engaging with the world in a manner that sets and achieves goals by doing things for oneself. It is linked to concepts like self-efficacy and autonomy and is predictive of improved health outcomes via variables like treatment adherence, self-care, hope, and ability to cope. A person's *moral* agency is the ability to identify and embrace guiding values in life and to execute decisions, participate in actions, and develop character traits that reflect and express those values.[23] Moral agency is the condition on which one can be praised or blamed for actions, held morally responsible for good and bad decisions, and even be considered a good or bad person.

Suffering that arises in the context of life-limiting illness can constitute a threat to the agency of patients and families.[24,25] One

important way that APRNs can address the suffering of their patients, while concurrently honoring the four ethical principles explained above, is to offer support and interventions that restore and engage patients' moral agency. Doing so resonates strongly with the philosophy underpinning palliative care as a model of care.[26,27]

With attention to the basic principles and codes of nursing ethics, evidence-based principles of communication, and moral agency, a foundation has been laid for the integration of ethical communication as a *process* within the larger goals and values of palliative care. The next section offers an ethical framework to guide APRNs through ethical discussions. Other elements essential to navigating any ethical discussion and integral to APRN practice—such as presence, the ability to listen, and a willingness to let go of preconceived judgments—are acknowledged.

An Ethical Framework for Navigating Ethical Discussions

Four principles provide the cornerstones of an ethical framework to guide APRNs in navigating ethical discussions. These principles—advocacy, clinical sensitivity, truthfulness, and accommodation—are all informed by the ultimate goal of palliative care: reducing suffering by supporting and engaging moral agency.[27] The unique balance among these principles will vary in each discussion, paralleling the unique blend of persons, goals, and values involved.

Advocacy

Advocacy is frequently cited as the primary—perhaps even the defining—role of the nurse in the context of healthcare ethics. Two models of advocacy are presented in this section: existential advocacy and advocacy as rights protection.

Existential Advocacy

Gadow's model of "existential advocacy" is an apt model for the APRN and fits well within the framework for this chapter.[28] In it, the nurse as advocate offers care focused on restoring and empowering patients' moral agency. This is done through providing therapeutic presence to create conditions in which patients and families can partner with clinicians to (a) discern the meaning of clinical changes in their condition, (b) explore how such changes interact with their values and goals, and (c) appreciate together which care options might best honor those values and goals.

Explaining the role of existential advocacy in nursing care, Gadow writes:

> The ideal which existential advocacy expresses is this: that individuals be assisted by nursing to authentically exercise their freedom of self-determination. By authentic is meant a way of reaching decisions which are truly one's own decisions that express all that one believes important about oneself and the world, the entire complexity of one's values.
>
> . . .
>
> Individuals can express their wholeness and uniqueness as valuing beings only if their full complexity of values—including contradictions and conflicts—is clearly in mind, having been reexamined and clarified in the new context. Yet, that clarification is the most difficult precisely when it is most needed, when a situation arises which threatens to overturn previously stable values. In such situations, of which health impairment is a paradigm, individuals face

the necessity of either recreating their values or recreating their situation according to their existing hierarchy of values.[28(p 85)]

As Gadow makes clear, the goal in existential advocacy is not for the nurse to put himself or herself in the place of *speaking for* patients. Rather, it is to provide the supportive presence and facilitate the empowering conditions necessary for patients to restore their sense of self by (a) understanding the facts and experiences of their illness, (b) appreciating what they mean in the larger context of their lives, (c) reconnecting to the values that are most important to them and most directly relevant to the situation at hand, and (d) engaging in a decision-making process that integrates such understanding, appreciation, and reconnection. The APRN as a moral advocate directs attention not toward specific decisions or outcomes, but to the ongoing discussion *process* itself that promotes and engages the moral agency of all involved.

Advocacy as Rights Protection

A "rights protection" model of advocacy is a common approach to nursing advocacy in which the nurse represents the wishes of the patient when he or she is in danger of being subsumed to the wishes of someone else—most commonly clinicians or family members.[3] In this model, the nurse functions in the healthcare system in a manner similar to that of a legal advocate in the legal system—protecting the rights of his or her client. This notion of advocacy has two main elements: (a) speaking out for others who cannot speak for themselves and (b) seeking to achieve a particular outcome, presumed to be in the best interest of the party being spoken for.[29] These elements also imply a context in which advocacy occurs: there is some threat in the environment that increases the risk of (a) the voice of the patient or family not being heard on its own and (b) the best outcome for that patient not being prioritized. In other words, the assumed condition in which this model of advocacy is needed is when there is an imbalance of power that creates vulnerability. The role of the nurse advocate is to protect the rights of the vulnerable.

The rights protection model assumes that the patient needs someone else to speak *for* him or her, and that the primary ethical risk in such discussions is that the patient's preferences will be overridden by the preferences of others. Such risks may well be present for certain palliative care patients for whom this model of advocacy is appropriate. An example is when a patient loses decision-making capacity and his or her advance directive is not being honored. Discerning the best way to advocate for patients and families requires clinical sensitivity.

Clinical Sensitivity

> Clinical knowledge rests on the precondition of receptivity and openness to the other . . . When seeing the distress in the face of a person suffering . . . one is exposed to and affected by the person's human condition.[30(p 34)]

Sensitivity in the clinical encounter relies on empathic awareness. The research literature shows that patients who have empathetic nurses are more likely to feel cared for and report that their needs and concerns are being heard. Empathy has three components: affective, cognitive, and behavioral. It has been defined as "a two stage process: (1) the understanding and sensitive appreciation of another person's predicament or feelings and (2) the communication of that understanding back to the patient in a supportive way."[31(p 133)] Clinical sensitivity can be seen as attunement to

the impact of the patient's illness on his or her overall well-being and quality of life.[30] It strives to understand the meaning(s) of the illness experience for each individual patient, as well as his or her vulnerabilities, symptoms, and suffering.[32] The ability to be affected by the suffering of others, to evoke an empathic response, and to relieve their pain are well-established ethical themes in the traditions of nursing and medicine.[30]

Truthfulness

Even in the setting of far-advanced disease, medical technology can make it appear possible to postpone death almost indefinitely—there is always "something else" that can be done. "Something else" may be seen in terms of further invasive interventions that are unlikely to have the outcome desired by the patient or family. Redefining the "something else" within the reality of the patient's clinical situation and helping him or her through that transition requires sensitive communication and truth telling; it is part of the role of the APRN. It is a common, but misinformed, belief among healthcare providers that telling a patient the truth is harmful. In fact, in research primarily done with cancer patients, the opposite has been found to be true.[33,34] Telling the truth fosters trust and demonstrates respect when told in a compassionate and sensitive manner and titrated to the patient's ability to absorb the information.[5] As one patient reflected, "I wonder if my cancer is spreading—I wonder if I am going to get better—I want people to be honest with me but I want them to be hopeful, too."

The purpose of sharing information with patients and families is to enable the kind of understanding, reflection, and deliberation necessary to make informed care decisions that resonate with their goals, values, and beliefs. Navigating between under-disclosure and over-disclosure can be quite challenging for clinicians. In this section we explain the disclosure model of truth telling and supplement that with a concept of truthfulness that captures the shared, relational aspects of how information is given meaning in palliative care.

The dominant model of truth telling in healthcare ethics is the "disclosure" model. The disclosure model begins with the assumption that healthcare providers have access to important information—a diagnosis or prognosis, for example—that patients need to make decisions about their care. Telling the truth, then, focuses on effectively communicating this information to patients so that it can be used in the decision-making process. Hallmarks of truth telling in this model are (a) accuracy (Is what is communicated to the patient consistent with what is known by the provider?); (b) sufficiency (Is the provider telling the patient all of the relevant information?); (c) coherence (Is what is being communicated by the provider integrated with other relevant facts and circumstances such that the patient understands the context of the disclosure?); and (d) timeliness (Is the disclosure shared with the patient at a point in time when it can be effectively integrated into the decision-making process?).

While the spirit of the disclosure model of truth telling is important, we have intentionally opted for the term "truthfulness," as we believe the disclosure model insufficiently captures how truth functions in the giving and receiving of palliative care. As noted earlier, palliative care is family-centered care that seeks to support the moral agency of patients by acknowledging and caring for the web of intimate relationships through which patients already find and create meaning. That relational structure is all the more important in times of distress and serious illness. Patients, loved ones, and clinicians work together in palliative care to interpret the meaning of clinical developments and integrate that meaning into the larger life horizon of the patient. Truth, in other words, is not something possessed by clinicians and disclosed to patients. Rather, the truth of patients' situations is discerned through a shared process of enquiry, discovery, and meaning making.[35-37] Multiple perspectives, histories, spheres of expertise, and value systems combine to develop a plan of care driven by the goal of allowing patients to live their lives authentically as persons, especially during the experience of a serious or final illness.

As an ethical principle, then, "truthfulness" asserts the value of all of these perspectives. This is done by promoting patterns of engagement that create a supportive environment in which all parties can explore, share, and integrate their points of view. The goal is to achieve the fullest understanding of a patient's situation and possibilities. Such integration is likely to require some accommodation—the final principle of the framework—when building and implementing a plan of care.

Accommodation

Originally developed in the context of home care, the principle of accommodation is a very helpful guide in palliative care. Palliative care clinicians are frequently invited into the circle of care for patients whose clinical care is managed by other primary teams. Patients are often in the late stages of progressive illness and may have become dependent on loved ones for rides to appointments, upkeep of their homes, and activities of daily living. As their ability to live independently has slowly eroded, patients have had to accommodate the schedules, preferences, and abilities of others, even when conflicting with their own. Families have had to accommodate in the same way.

> I've accepted it. They clean my bottom for me and they do it with grace and beauty, they don't make me feel like, like some sort of, I don't know—inhuman person. They don't back away from it. Now I have to have them when I use the bedpan 'cause I can't physically—I am paralyzed, I need their strength. They don't turn away from me.

These words from a palliative care patient reflect a tacit level of accommodation on the part of both patient and family. The patient, who in the past had been extremely independent, has accommodated his family by accepting the level of intimate care he needs to remain at home. Family members, in turn, have accommodated their husband and father by adjusting their own needs to provide such care. This is an example of a mutual and reciprocal process that the principle of accommodation acknowledges and promotes.

Sometimes, however, accommodation can be one-sided, or gradually erode into one-sidedness. Collopy and colleagues, in addressing this phenomenon, strive to correct ways in which one-sided accommodation by patients can gradually erode their autonomy:

> In practice, such erosion of autonomy is often incremental. Caregivers intervene when clients function slowly and imperfectly. In the basic, repeated routine of care clients' preferences are not elicited; their efforts to be autonomous are waved aside by paternalistic soothing or efficient impatience on the part of caregivers. The dominant interactive pattern is frequently one in which progressive physical and mental incapacity is expected in clients and is equated with progressive inability to be autonomous.[38(p 8)]

These words may seem harsh and without sensitivity to the needs of family members, discounting the significant accommodations they have had to make in their lives to care for the sick person. Indeed, family members may have many responsibilities to self and others that have been set aside to meet the needs of a seriously ill loved one. It may seem intuitive that healthy family members must do all of the accommodating because they are well. However, this one-sided approach can be destructive for both patients and families. It can be harmful for patients because failing to ask them to accommodate the needs and abilities of loved ones can constitute a significant departure from their usual role as a party in relationships. This can result in a loss of self as a responsible member of a family with the give and take that such a role entails. Similarly, a one-sided model of accommodation can harm family members and their relationships with a sick loved one—they may become resentful and overwhelmed:

> I feel exhausted. Constant demands on me from my boss, husband, and demented half-sister. George expects me to do everything. He doesn't want others to do it. If I go out, he waits for me to come back before catheterizing himself. When I come through the door, he asks for things even though the house is full of people. I'm beginning to resent it. If he loves me, he should think of me.

Accommodation in the palliative care arena is complex. Many different players are involved, including the patient, family members, friends, and members of the healthcare team. Sensitivity and awareness of the ethical issues and complexities implicit in the principle of accommodation will allow the APRN to navigate discussions and make visible the accommodation each person or group is making or being asked to make. This acknowledgment allows people to feel heard and to believe that what they say matters. Because people with advanced disease can be so frail, their voice and agency may be lost inadvertently to the strength of others. It is important that their agency is recognized and re-engaged.

In sum, advocacy, sensitivity, truthfulness, and accommodation constitute the four cornerstones of an ethical framework guiding APRNs in navigating ethical discussions. While there are surely other principles that would be helpful guides, we have chosen these four because they (a) explicitly and effectively support the moral agency of patients, families, and clinicians and (b) are particularly well matched to the training and role of the APRN.

Moral Reflection and Deliberation

In addition to engaging the framework above when navigating ethical discussions with patients and families, teams benefit from ongoing and regularly scheduled opportunities to examine and discuss their own processes. Deliberation and reflection can be an important way for team members to maintain connection with each other, restoring focus on the moral foundation and framework explained above.[8] Moral reflection and deliberation allow for a process in which the APRN can review with the staff the ethical discussions that have taken place—the process involved and the outcomes. Moral reflection and deliberation aim to articulate and explore the various and sometimes conflicting perspectives on the case under consideration. Team members reflect on their ethical questions related to the case at hand. This approach is grounded on the assumption that good care gets defined and redefined in concrete situations wherein a dialogue occurs involving ethical principles, professional standards, constraints, and the unique circumstances of each narrative. Moral reflection and deliberation provide the APRN with a format for educating, debriefing, and supporting the staff following challenging patient interactions or when patients or surrogates have chosen a direction for their care that team members feel is the "wrong choice." Reflection and deliberation allow the APRN to help the staff look at the situation from the viewpoint of the individual, the nurse, and the team, as part of the institution and as part of multiple cultures.[8,39]

Applying Communication and Ethical Principles

The clinical case at the beginning of the chapter illustrates the role of the APRN in navigating ethical discussions. In this case, the patient felt "hounded" by the medical staff to agree to a Do Not Resuscitate (DNR) code status, and staff members felt obligated—individually—to make sure that she understood that attempting cardiopulmonary resuscitation (CPR) would cause harm without benefit. The case raises three questions:

- When should code status be addressed and readdressed with a patient or surrogate?
- Who is the best person to initiate this discussion?
- How can repetitive "confrontations" with the patient or surrogate over code status be prevented?

In this case the APRN was asked by the primary team to help them to communicate more effectively with the patient and family or with other involved services.

Listening to Narratives

In the first step, the APRN attentively listened to separate narratives—that of the primary team and that of the patient and family. It was understood that there might be different narratives among the team members, and, if that were the case, the different narratives would need to be heard. The team's narrative was as follows:

> The patient has far-advanced disease, resuscitation will cause her harm without furthering her stated goals, and we cannot get her to understand this and agree to a DNR status. We are distressed that we will have to run a code for which harm far outweighs any possible benefit, and this violates our core ethical values. Because the patient continues to insist on being resuscitated, we believe she must not fully understand (a) what resuscitation will be like and (b) what the almost certain outcome will be regardless of the attempt of CPR (i.e., death). Her death will be violent rather than peaceful. Indeed, we believe she may have better understood this a year ago when she completed her advance directive, as in that document she clearly stated her preference to *not* be resuscitated in precisely these conditions.

The APRN observed that, perhaps arising out of the team's point of view and associated distress, the manner of their communication with Mrs. S has changed and become focused specifically on the question of code status. This has led them to repeatedly raise the question with her. Because they believe she must not understand the resuscitation process, their discussions with her have become much more (a) insistent and (b) graphic—explaining in harsh detail what will be done if she arrests and emphasizing what a violent process it is. The team's intent arises out of a strong commitment to nonmaleficence: to protect Mrs. S from harm. However, the repeated question about code status has replaced

their usual caring and empathetic interactions. This has caused harm and has interfered with effective patient and clinician communication. The patient's narrative was as follows:

> I was very clear in my initial discussion with the team regarding my code status preference. The team seems unable to hear or understand that preference. My circumstances have changed since I completed my advance directive a year ago. I now want all interventions possible to sustain my life. I want to live as long as possible to be there for my husband, daughter, and grandchildren—even if it means being on a machine. Not only am I not being heard, the team's ongoing hounding of me regarding this status is causing me great distress. I tense up whenever the doctor walks into the room, knowing I have to steel myself to defend my choices. We used to have a great relationship but that has gone.

The APRN observed that now Mrs. S sees the healthcare team as an opposing force and approaches discussions with them from a defensive posture. The current pattern of communication is not effective—on that the team and patient agree. She is grieving for the imminent loss of everything she holds dear: her life, her husband, her daughters, and her grandchildren. Her primary goal now is to be there for them as long as possible. While her views may change, she does not want this question of code status to be raised repeatedly. She wants instead to think and talk about her family and her love for them. Mrs. S has not, however, closed the door to the possibility of reversing her position on resuscitation in the future.

Navigating Ethical Discussion

Eliciting these narratives establishes rapport and opens up space in which the APRN can navigate ethical discussions guided by the principles of sensitivity, truthfulness, accommodation and advocacy:

Sensitivity: The APRN listens to these narratives as they relate to the needs and values of Mrs. S and her care team. In part the team and patient are willing to share their narratives because the APRN is engaging with them in a manner that resonates with the precepts of respect and sensitivity explored earlier.

Truthfulness: All parties appear to have an accurate understanding of Mrs. S's current clinical situation. The patient has acknowledged that she is dying and has explained the reasons for her decision about resuscitation. The team has thoroughly explained the process and likely outcome of resuscitation. As such, truth telling as disclosure has been honored. Where there is a possible disconnect is in the principle of truthfulness as shared meaning informed by multiple perspectives. Resuscitation means something different to Mrs. S than it does to the team, and the parties are struggling to integrate their perspectives to build a shared meaning of (a) what resuscitation is and what it will achieve and (b) if, how, and when to reopen discussion of Mrs. S's resuscitation preferences.

Accommodation: The APRN validates the team's distress and their commitment to nonmaleficence in (a) not wanting to attempt resuscitation in this dying woman and (b) persisting in discussing code status with her to try to get her to change her mind. The APRN also understands that Mrs. S is not willing to discuss the matter further at this time. Revisiting the question of resuscitation has become counterproductive. The APRN helps the team to accommodate and accept Mrs. S's decision to remain a full code. By seeing it as a settled question, the patient's preference shifts from being an ongoing team project—"we need to get her to agree to the DNR"—to being a reality that the team must accept. In accepting this as a reality, the team has had to accommodate her preference despite their best medical judgment. Mrs. S is accommodating insofar as (a) she is willing to talk openly and authentically with the APRN about the reasons for her preference and her experience of repeatedly discussing that preference with the team, (b) she acknowledges and accepts the APRN's explanation of the team's intention behind raising the question, understanding that they do, in fact, care about her as a person and only want what is best for her, and (c) she may reconsider her code status at a future time.

Advocacy: In creating a safe and welcoming environment in which all parties feel supported in reflecting on their values, forming preferences based on those values, and expressing those preferences, the APRN has engaged a process that resonates strongly with the precepts of Gadow's model of existential advocacy. In modeling this pattern of interaction, the APRN has also created a template for a similar pattern of engagement between the team and the patient going forward. Providing a forum in which the team can safely process their feelings as care moves forward is a valuable opportunity for the APRN's advocacy and support to continue.

Further Challenges and Suggestions

The case study has offered an opportunity to consider how APRNs might navigate difficult ethical discussions. Sometimes, however, opportunities for ethical engagement arise not in the form of full discussion but in short—perhaps unforeseen—questions from patients and families. Box 42.1 lists some difficult questions and statements from the patient and/or family that the APRN may be confronted with and on which it can be useful to reflect. Common fears associated with these, and pitfalls to avoid, are also included.

There is an abundance of literature suggesting phrases to use in responding to such questions and statements, and the reader is referred to this literature.[36,37,40–42] Finally, a brief and simple strategy for the APRN to self-monitor and self-reflect on his or her emotional state prior to and following a difficult discussion, and to address it "in the moment," is to take a few seconds to pause, mentally scan one's emotional state using a visual thermometer, and consciously "unhook" from or lower the stress level through focused breathing. Brief, simple stress-reduction exercises can be extremely useful for the APRN.[43,44]

Conclusion

Using the foundation and framework explained above, navigating ethical discussions can be extremely rewarding at the same time as being extremely challenging. These conversations may be fraught with powerful emotions—they are about lives interrupted, a future that has been foreshortened, and the need to face the stark reality of one's mortality. Even the most experienced APRN can worry about saying the "wrong thing" or missing some central aspect of the patient's life story that, if known, contained the key to why particular decisions were being made—decisions that did

---

Box 42.1 Questions to Be Prepared for and Pitfalls to Avoid

Questions/statements that may arise while navigating ethical discussions

1. How long do I have to live?
2. Tell me that everything is going to be alright.
3. Are you saying that I am going to die?
4. Is there no hope for me?
5. Don't tell XX that he is dying.
6. If you don't feed her, she will starve to death.
7. If this were your mother, what would you do?
8. There must be something you can do.
9. She is going to die anyway, so why not give more chemo?
10. Withdrawing the machine is the same as killing her—euthanasia. Call it what it is.
11. Why can't you just dial up the morphine? Why does she have to linger this way? Why does she have to suffer?
12. How can I tell my children that I am dying?
13. How will I die?
14. What is it like to die?
15. I don't like Dr. Q; is he always so rude?

Common fears when navigating ethical discussions

1. Being blamed—"shooting the messenger"
2. Saying the wrong thing
3. Eliciting strong emotional responses
4. Not knowing the answer—not being comfortable saying "I don't know"
5. Expressing one's own emotions (crying)
6. Anxiety about one's own mortality

Pitfalls to avoid

1. Making promises you can't keep
2. Giving information when you don't have the facts
3. Giving premature reassurance

---

not appear to be in the best interest of the patient. Decision making at the end-of-life can be "messy" and conflicted, as reflected in the case study above; that is part of the territory. There may be tensions among ethical principles that are difficult to resolve. There may be tensions between the patient and family, between members of the family, between members of the team, and between the team and the patient or family. The APRN in his or her role as advocate helps by acknowledging these tensions and refocusing discussions on the patient and what is in the best interest of the patient on his or her own terms. Supporting care team members by engaging them in reflection and deliberation creates an opportunity to reexamine the process that unfolded in the interaction. In so doing, clinicians can identify and explore the values and behaviors that shaped the discussion and influenced its outcome.

The focus in this chapter is on the integration of ethical communication as a *process* within the larger goals and values of palliative care. Positive results for the patient from this approach to communication might include feeling understood and supported, actively participating in the discussion, improving his or her understanding of the situation, having a strengthened sense of agency and control, and gaining confidence that the team is there for him or her. The APRN and team, in turn, might feel satisfied with the encounter, have a greater understanding of the patient's perspective (goals, values, concerns, and preferences), feel a rapport with the patient, and feel supported themselves.

References

1. Tarzian AJ, Schwarz JK. Ethical aspects of palliative care. In: Matzo M, Witt Sherman D, eds. *Palliative Care Nursing: Quality Care to the End of Life.* New York, NY: Springer Publishing Company; 2014:33–59.
2. McLennon, SM, Uhrich M, Lasiter S, Chamness BA, Helft PR. Oncology nurses' narratives about ethical dilemmas and prognosis-related communication in advanced cancer patients. *Cancer Nurs.* 2013; 36(2): 114–21.
3. American Nurses Association (ANA). *Code of Ethics for Nurses with Interpretive Statements.* Silver Spring, MD: ANA; 2001. Available at http://www.nursingworld.org/codeofethics. Accessed July 29, 2014.
4. McCabe M, Coyle N. Ethical and legal issues in palliative care. *Semin Oncol Nurs.* 2014; 30(4): 287-95.
5. Siminoff LA. The ethics of communication in cancer and palliative care. In: Kissane DW, Bultz BD, Butow PM, Finlay IG, eds. *Handbook of Communication in Oncology and Palliative Care.* Oxford, England: Oxford University Press; 2010:51–61.
6. Institute of Medicine (IOM). *The Future of Nursing: Leading Change, Advancing Health.* Washington, DC: The National Academies Press; 2011.
7. Wiegand DL, Russo MM. Ethical considerations. In: Dahlin CM, Lynch MT, eds. *Core Curriculum for the Advanced Practice Hospice and Palliative Registered Nurse.* 2nd ed. Pittsburgh, PA: HPNA; 2014:39–59.
8. Altilio T, Coyle N. The interdisciplinary team: Integrating moral reflection and deliberation. In: Kirk TW, Jennings B., eds. *Hospice Ethics: Policy and Practice in Palliative Care.* New York, NY: Oxford University Press; 2014:103–17.
9. International Council of Nurses (ICN). *Code of Ethics for Nurses.* Geneva, Switzerland: ICN; 2012.
10. Beauchamp TL, Childress JF. *Principles of Biomedical Ethics.* 6th ed. New York, NY: Oxford University Press; 2008.
11. Coyle N. Palliative care, hospice care, and bioethics: a natural fit. *J Hosp Palliat Nurs.* 2014; 16(1): 6–14.
12. Moorhouse A, Yeo M, Rodney P. Autonomy. In: Yeo M, Moorhouse A, Khan P, Rodney P, eds. *Concepts and Cases in Nursing Ethics.* 3rd ed. Peterborough, Ontario: Broadview Press; 2010:143–205.
13. Yeo M, Moorhouse A. Beneficence. In: Yeo M, Moorhouse A, Khan P, Rodney P, eds. *Concepts and Cases in Nursing Ethics.* 3rd ed. Peterborough, Ontario: Broadview Press; 2010:103–42.
14. National Health and Medical Research Council. An ethical framework for integrating palliative care principles into the management of advanced chronic or terminal conditions. Canberra, ACT: National Health and Medical Research Council, 2011. Available at https://www.nhmrc.gov.au/guidelines/publications/rec31. Accessed July 20, 2014.
15. Buckman R. Communication in palliative care: A practical guide. In: Doyle D, Hanks G, McDonald N, eds. *Oxford Textbook of Palliative Medicine.* Oxford, England: Oxford University Press; 1998:141–56.
16. Epstein RM, Street RL, Jr. *Patient-Centered Communication in Cancer Care.* Bethesda, MD: National Cancer Institute; 2007.
17. Wittenberg-Lyles E, Goldsmith J, Ferrell B, Ragan SL. *Communication in Palliative Nursing.* Oxford, England: Oxford University Press; 2013.
18. Dahlin CM, Wittenberg E. Communication in palliative care: an essential competency for nurses. In: Ferrell BF, Coyle N, Paice J, eds. *Oxford Textbook of Palliative Nursing.* 4th ed. Oxford, England: Oxford University Press; 2015:81-109.
19. Baile W, Buckman R, Lenzi R, et al. SPIKES: A six-step protocol for delivering bad news: Application to the patient with cancer. *Oncologist.* 2000; 5(4): 302–11.
20. Helman CG. Communication in primary care: The role of patient and practitioner explanatory models. *Soc Sci Med.* 1985; 20(9): 923–31.
21. Kleinman A. *Patients and Healers in the Context of Culture.* Berkeley CA: University of California Press; 1980.
22. Tirodkar MA, Baker DW, Makoul GT, et al. Explanatory models of health and disease among South Asian immigrants in Chicago. *J Immigr Minor Health.* 2011; 13(2): 385–94.
23. Manning RC. Toward a thick theory of moral agency. *Soc Theory Pract.* 1994; 20(2): 203–20.
24. Cassell EJ. *The Nature of Suffering and the Goals of Medicine.* 2nd ed. New York, NY: Oxford University Press; 2004.
25. Ferrell BR, Coyle N. *The Nature of Suffering and the Goals of Nursing.* New York, NY: Oxford University Press; 2008.
26. Dahlin C, ed. *The Clinical Practice Guidelines for Quality Palliative Care.* 3rd ed. Pittsburgh, PA: National Consensus Project for Quality Palliative Care; 2013.
27. Coyle N, Kirk TW, Doolittle M. Communication ethics. In: Wittenberg E, Ferrell B, Goldsmith J, et al., eds. *Textbook of Palliative Care Communication.* New York, NY: Oxford University Press; 2016:27-34.
28. Gadow S. Existential advocacy: philosophical foundation of nursing. In: Gadow S, Spicker SF, eds. *Nursing: Images and ideals.* New York, NY: Springer; 1980:79–101.
29. Kirk TW, Tadel P. Clinical ethics: Supporting and advocating for patient/family choice [webinar]. July 12, 2012. National Hospice and Palliative Care Organization.
30. Nortvedt P. Clinical sensitivity: The inseparability of ethical perceptiveness and clinical knowledge. *Sch Inq Nurs Pract.* 2001; 15(1): 25–43.
31. Silverman J, Kurtz S, Draper D. *Skills for Communicating with Patients.* 3rd ed. London, England: Radcliffe Publishing; 2013.
32. Coyle N. Suffering in the first person: glimpses of suffering through patients' and family narratives. In: Ferrell BF, ed. *Suffering.* Boston, MA: Jones and Bartlett; 1996:29–64.
33. Trice ED, Prigerson HG. Communication in end-stage cancer: Review of the Literature and future research. *J Health Commun.* 2009; 14(1): 95–108.
34. Zhang B, Nilsson ME, Prigerson HG. Factors important to patients' quality of life at end of life. *Arch Intern Med.* 2012; 172(15): 1133–42.
35. Hallenbeck J, Arnold R. A request for nondisclosure: Don't tell mother. *J Clin Oncol.* 2007; 25(31): 5030–4.
36. Lamas D, Rosenbaum L. Freedom from the tyranny of choice: Teaching end-of-life conversation. *N Engl J Med.* 2012; 366(18): 1655–7.
37. Pantilat SZ. Communicating with seriously ill patients: Better words to say. *JAMA.* 2009; 301(12): 1279–81.
38. Collopy B, Dubler N, Zuckerman C. The ethics of home care: autonomy and accommodation. *Hastings Cent Rep.* 1990; 20(2): S1–S16.
39. Abma TA, Molewijk B, Widdershoven GAM. Good care in ongoing dialogue. Improving the quality of care through moral deliberation and responsive evaluation. *Health Care Anal.* 2009; 17(3): 217–35.

40. Back AL, Arnold RM. Dealing with conflict in caring for the seriously ill: "It was just out of the question." *JAMA.* 2005; 293(11): 1374–81.

41. Borowske D. Straddling the fence: ICU nurses advocating for hospice care. *Crit Car Nurs Clin North Am.* 2012; 24(1): 105–16.

42. Quill TE, Arnold R, Back A. Discussing treatment preferences with patients who want "everything." *Ann Intern Med.* 2009; 151(5): 345–9.

43. Schreiner I, Malcolm JP. The benefits of mindfulness meditation: changes in emotional states of depression, anxiety and stress. *Behav Change.* 2008; 25(3): 156–68.

44. Ulrich CM, Taylor C, Soeken K, et al. Everyday ethics: Ethical issues and stress in nursing practice. *J Adv Nurs.* 2010; 66(11): 2510–9.

CHAPTER 43

Culturally Respectful Palliative Care

Polly Mazanec and Joan T. Panke

Key Points

◆ Self-reflection on one's own cultural beliefs, continued life-long learning, and cultural humility are essential to providing culturally sensitive palliative care.

◆ The palliative advanced practice registered nurse (APRN) must assess the patient's and family's cultural values, practices, and beliefs and identify their importance to the patient and family.

◆ Health literacy, health numeracy, and financial literacy are important components of culturally respectful palliative care.

◆ Goals of care must be established in concert with the patient's and family's cultural values, practices, and beliefs.

Introduction

This chapter discusses culturally respectful care and how the APRN can integrate it into clinical practice. Self-reflection about one's own values, practices, and beliefs and their impact on the delivery of culturally sensitive care is emphasized. Communication strategies for assessing the patient's and family's cultural values, practices, and beliefs are presented. Culturally sensitive topics, such as differing languages and health, numeracy, and financial literacy, are addressed, and strategies are offered to deal with these issues. The chapter also includes special considerations in the delivery of culturally respectful palliative care, such as supporting beliefs regarding disclosure of prognosis and medical decision making, recognizing cultural implications of pain and symptom management, integrating cultural rituals and practices into clinical care, and dealing with cultural clashes.

Clinical Practice and Culturally Respectful Palliative Care

Quality palliative care is clearly defined in the third edition of the *Clinical Practice Guidelines for Quality Palliative Care*.[1] Cultural considerations in palliative care are so important that one of the eight domains, Domain 6, is reserved specifically for Cultural Aspects of Care. The clinical implications of this domain emphasize that culture is "a source for resilience for patients and families"[1] and therefore should be incorporated into the delivery of quality palliative care. Criteria that are identified in the guidelines for palliative care practice and that are emphasized in this chapter are summarized in Box 43.1.

The Hospice and Palliative Nurses Association (HPNA) recognizes the importance of cultural competence in its advanced competency statement regarding Cultural and Spiritual Competence. Competency for advanced practice palliative nursing focuses on respecting diversity, in particular ethnicity, culture, spirituality, religion, gender, socioeconomic status, sexual orientation, education level, literacy and location.[2] The second edition of the HPNA *Competencies for the Hospice and Palliative Advanced Practice Nurse* aligns itself with the National Consensus Project (NCP) Guidelines, identifying behaviors that demonstrate competency in cultural aspects of palliative care.

Understanding Culture

The United States is a multicultural society with increasing diversity. Americans have traditionally valued independence and self-reliance and have emphasized the importance of autonomy and each individual's happiness.[3] However, many minority groups in the diverse United States and the non-Western world value collectivism, interdependence, community, and continuity of the generations.[3] Minority groups are expected to make up 57% of the population in the United States by 2060.[4] Because of this increasing diversity, the APRN must understand and respond to a wide variety of customs, norms, beliefs, and languages. Respecting and valuing cultural diversity are keys to delivering culturally sensitive palliative care.

Culture is the "learned, shared and transmitted values, beliefs, norms and life ways of a particular group that guide their thinking, decisions, and actions in patterned ways."[5] Culture is shaped over time, during which the beliefs, values, and lifestyle patterns pass from one generation to another.[5] The biopsychosocial, ecological, organizing system within which a population of people exists is an adaptive, dynamic system, designed to ensure survival and well-being.[3] Culture is the way human beings find meaning and purpose in life and make sense out of life events. In times of crisis, culture can be a source of resilience for the

---

Box 43.1 *Clinical Practice Guidelines for Quality Palliative Care*: Domain 6—Cultural Aspects of Care

Guideline 6.1: The palliative care program serves each patient, family, and community in a culturally and linguistically appropriate manner.

◆ Culture is multidimensional.

◆ Cultural identification of the patient and family is far-reaching.

◆ The palliative care team elicits and documents cultural strengths, concerns, and needs.

◆ The plan of care maximizes the patient's and family's cultural strengths

◆ The palliative care staff consistently conveys respect for the patient's cultural perceptions, preferences, and practices, especially regarding culturally sensitive topics, such as decision making, disclosure, rituals, and bereavement.

◆ The palliative care staff communicates in a language and manner that the patient and family understand and takes into account:

  ◆ Literacy

  ◆ Use of professional interpreter services

  ◆ Written materials that facilitate patient/family understanding

◆ The palliative care staff respects and accommodates dietary and ritual practices of patients and families.

◆ Palliative care staff members identify and refer patients/families to community resources.

Guideline 6.2: The palliative care program strives to enhance its cultural and linguistic competence.

Criteria

◆ Definition of cultural competence

◆ The palliative care program values diversity, demonstrated by creating and sustaining a work environment that affirms multiculturalism.

◆ Palliative care members cultivate cultural self-awareness and recognize how their own cultural values, beliefs, biases, and practices inform their perceptions of patients, families, and colleagues.

◆ The palliative care program provides education to help staff reduce health disparities within and among the communities it serves.

◆ The palliative care program regularly evaluates and, if needed, modifies its services, policies, and procedures to maximize its cultural and linguistic accessibility and responsiveness to a multicultural population.

NCP Guidelines. Abbreviated with permission from references 1 and 14.

---

individual and the family and therefore should be respected by the healthcare team.[3]

A commonly held misconception is that culture is synonymous with race and ethnicity. Race and ethnicity are important components of culture because racial and ethnic disparities exist, in particular in palliative care.[6-8] However, race and ethnicity are merely sociopolitical categories determined by the U. S. Office of Management and Budget.[4] One's culture comprises multiple components, two of which are race and ethnicity. Table 43.1 identifies some components of culture and their implications in the delivery of quality palliative care.

Of course, even though an individual may belong to a cultural group, he or she may or may not adhere to its cultural norms. Members of cultural groups can be very similar or very diverse. Behaviors of individuals within a cultural group can range from totally adherent to group practices, values, and beliefs, to completely nonadherent. Although textbooks and/or respected Internet websites with information on certain cultural groups may be helpful in guiding clinical practice, they may facilitate an understanding of culturally sensitive topics in healthcare and particularly palliative

care. While it is important to seek to understand the practices and values of cultural groups commonly seen in one's clinical setting, the APRN must assess the values, practices, and beliefs of each patient as an individual and determine the importance of these values, practices, and beliefs to the patient and family.

APRNs must be aware of the impact of their own culture on their clinical practice.[7] To provide culturally sensitive care, APRNs must take time to reflect on their individual values, practices, and beliefs. It can be helpful to include this self-reflection in the review of competencies required of all practicing APRNs. A formal self-reflection is recommended annually because one's cultural beliefs are ever-changing, and are heavily influenced by knowledge, experience, and cultural encounters. Box 43.2 contains an example of a self-reflection exercise that can provide great insight into one's own worldview and how it may influence clinical care.[9]

There is a great deal written about cultural competence, cultural sensitivity, and cultural humility, and confusion exists among these terms. The concept of cultural competence inaccurately assumes that competency is an endpoint or something to

Table 43.1 Examples of Components of Culture and Impact on Palliative Care

Component	Palliative Care Considerations
Religion/Spirituality	Identify what gives the patient meaning and purpose to help establish culturally sensitive goals of care.
Race/Ethnicity	Recognize and address the racial and ethnic disparities in hospice and palliative care to improve access and quality care for all.
Age	Advocate for improving pain and symptom management in the very young and the very old.
Gender	Address the disparities in pain and symptom management between men and women.
Sexual orientation	Respect each individual's preferences for sexual orientation and definition of family.
Socioeconomic status	Recognize the challenges to those who struggle with the many burdens of having a life-limiting illness, especially financial burdens, caregiver burdens, and employment issues.
Differing abilities	Respect the right of all persons to be involved in decision making regarding their healthcare, if they so desire, and find appropriate accommodations to ensure their understanding.

be mastered.[10] Cultural humility, a term coined by Trevalon and Murray-Garcia,[11] is a desirable attribute for clinical practice. It is a "process of intercultural exchange, paying attention to clarifying the values and beliefs of provider and of patient and family and incorporating the cultural characteristics of healthcare professionals and individuals into a mutual balanced relationship."[11(p 6)] Cultural humility requires that we enter into each new encounter with an open mind and open heart, recognizing that our individual and professional perspective is but one of many that will be part of the larger context we are encountering. The goal is to create a shared understanding.[10]

In addition to the impact the APRN's individual culture may have on his or her clinical practice, the complex culture of healthcare also contributes to the APRN's clinical practice norms and beliefs. Medical information is often delivered in its own language,

making it impossible for others outside the system to understand.[12] Case Study 1 demonstrates an accidental, miscommunicated message that resulted in needless suffering and distress.

Case Study

Mrs. S was an 84-year-old woman who was recently diagnosed with colon cancer. She had no comorbidities and had never been hospitalized. The resident stopped in to see her one evening several days after she underwent a colon resection and informed her that he would be back in the morning to remove her staples. He left the room before she could ask what he meant. She spent a sleepless night anxious about what they would do to her. Staples? What kind of place was this? Or was it so bad that they had to use staples to hold things together? The APRN on the palliative care team

---

Box 43.2 Cultural Self-Assessment

1. Where were you born? If an immigrant, how long have you lived in this country? How old were you when you came to this country? Where were your grandparents born?

2. What is your ethnic affiliation and how strong is your ethnic identity?

3. Who are your major support people: family members, friends? Do you live in an ethnic community?

4. How does your culture affect decisions regarding your medical treatment? Who makes decisions—you, your family, or a designated family member? What are the gender issues in your culture and in your family structure?

5. What are your primary and secondary languages? What is your speaking and reading ability?

6. How would you characterize your nonverbal communication style?

7. What is your religion? How important is it in your daily life? What are your current religious practices? Is religion an important source of support and comfort?

8. What are your food preferences and prohibitions?

9. What is your economic situation, and is the income adequate to meet your needs?

10. What are your health and illness beliefs and practices?

11. What are your customs and beliefs surrounding birth, illness, and death? What are your experiences with death and bereavement? What are your beliefs about the afterlife and miracles? What are your beliefs about hope?

12. How have the patient and family encounters you have had over the past year influenced your values, practices, and beliefs?

Adapted from reference 8. Reprinted with permission.

came by to meet Mrs. S in the morning and found her confused, agitated, and crying out for help.

Integrating Cultural Assessment into Clinical Practice

Once the APRN recognizes his or her individual cultural values, practices, and beliefs, the next step in developing a culturally respectful palliative care clinical practice is to gain skill in assessing the cultural backgrounds of patients and families. Performing a thorough cultural assessment is essential to understanding the patient's and family's healthcare preferences, especially in the provision of palliative care. Although many cultural assessment tools are available, some are lengthy and require a great deal of time on the part of the clinician and also the patient and family. These tools are actually long checklists, so administration not only may be burdensome but also may hinder the establishment of a trusting clinical relationship, which is the essence of culturally sensitive care.[13]

In the clinical setting, presence, active listening, and strong communication skills are the best tools for assessing cultural considerations in palliative care. Ask the patient and/or the family member to tell you about themselves. Listening intently to their stories is the most effective way to gain an understanding of the patient's and family's cultural norms.[10] Box 43.3 provides an example of open-ended assessment questions that can guide the patient and family in sharing their cultural values, practices, and beliefs.[14]

The Impact of Culture on Communication

Communication is the foundation for all encounters among human beings, and this is especially true in the delivery of palliative care.[15] Communication is an interactive, multidimensional process, often dictated by cultural norms, and provides the mechanism for human interaction and connection.[16] Abiding by general communication principles for quality palliative care in a culturally sensitive manner will ensure the establishment of a trusting relationship between the clinician and the patient and family, regardless of where the interaction takes place (e.g., clinic

---

Box 43.3 Key Cultural Assessment Questions

- We want to make sure we respect how you prefer to be addressed, including how we should act. Is there anything we should avoid? Is it appropriate for you to have male and female healthcare providers?
- Can you tell me a little bit about yourself (e.g., family, mother, father, siblings, etc.)?
- Where were you born and raised? (If an immigrant:) How long have you lived in this country?
- What language would you prefer to speak?
- Is it easier to write things down, or do you have difficulty with reading and writing?
- To whom do you go for support (family, friends, community, or religious or community leaders)?
- Is there anyone we should contact to come be with you?
- I want to be sure I'm giving you all the information you need. What do you want to know about your condition? To whom should I speak about your care?
- Whom do you want to know about your condition?
- How are decisions about healthcare made in your family? Should I speak directly with you, or is there someone else with whom I should be discussing decisions?
- Tell me about your understanding of what has been happening up to this point. What does this illness mean to you?
- We want to work with you to be sure you are getting the best care possible and that we are meeting all your needs. Is there anything we should know about any customs or practices that are important to include in your care?
- Many people have shared that it is very important to include spirituality or religion in their care. Is this something that is important for you? Would you like me to contact our chaplain or another spiritual provider you would like to be involved in your care?
- Are there any foods you would like or that you should avoid?
- Do you have any concerns about how to pay for care, medications, or other services?

Death Rituals and Practices

- What is your belief about what happens after death?
- Is there a way for us to plan for anything you might need during the dying process, at the time of death, or after death?
- Is there anything we should know about care of the body or about rituals, practices, or ceremonies that should be performed during the dying process or at the time of death?

office, hospital room, skilled care facility). Following these principles will help the APRN and the palliative care team understand patient/family norms for communication style and giving and receiving information:

1. Select a setting that is private and as free from interruption as possible.

   - Turn off cellphones and put pagers on vibrate mode.

   - Greet the patient in a respectful, professional manner. Cultural norms related to verbal introduction and nonverbal touch or handshake should be identified early in the initial encounter to avoid making a culturally inappropriate mistake.

   - Determine the dominant language and dialect spoken and the literacy level of both the patient and the family. If there is a language difference between clinician and patient, a professionally trained interpreter of the appropriate gender, if culturally significant, should be contacted prior to proceeding with the visit.

   - Recognize that the professional's message and the understanding of the patient/family can differ, even when they share the same language. When confronted with a life-limiting illness, almost everyone experiences compromise in literacy and difficulties in processing.[10]

2. During the initial interaction, determine how the patient would like to be addressed. Some patients prefer to be called by their last name (e.g., Mr. Jones, Ms. Smith), whereas others may prefer to be called by their first names.

   - Document the patient's preference in the medical record so that all members of the healthcare team can respect this preference.

   - Be cognizant of nonverbal communication that may be culturally insensitive.

   - Ask permission to sit down and maintain a respectful distance that does not invade private space but demonstrates empathy.

   - Introduce yourself to all present at the visit.

3. Once introductions have been made, assess patient and family cultural norms for giving and receiving information and for decision making at the first visit.

   - Share with the patient and family that there will likely be important information about the patient's condition discussed at every visit.

   - Ask the patient with whom he or she would like healthcare information discussed.

   - If there are people important to the patient who cannot be present, such as a long-distance son or daughter, consider ways to use technology to share information with them and to include them in future visits, using telephone or computer conferencing.

4. Find out how much information the patient and family would like to have when decisions need to be made.

   - Normalize the information-gathering process: "Some people like to hear all about the illness, its course and treatments as well as all labs or scan results. Others prefer that we share the information needed to make decisions and limit the detail on the illness, treatment, and testing. How much information would you like us to share with you?"

   - Understand that accepting the family's usual process of decision making will be critical to providing culturally respectful palliative care throughout the patient's disease trajectory.

Disabilities Affecting Communication

Patients and families who are hearing- or sight-impaired face additional challenges when trying to understand communication related to their palliative care needs. One in six individuals experience impaired hearing, with impairment being more common in the geriatric population.[17,18] When caring for a patient who is completely deaf and can use sign language, use a healthcare interpreter fluent in sign language. When caring for a hearing-impaired patient, the APRN can facilitate communication by (1) decreasing background noise and distractions during conversations; (2) encouraging the patient to wear his or her hearing aid during the conversation; (3) ensuring the listener can see the APRN's face; (4) speaking clearly and distinctly, but not shouting; (5) enhancing the discussion with written words and pictures to aid in explanation; and (6) asking the listener to summarize the conversation to ensure understanding.[18] Keep in mind that speech comprehension is more difficult for persons with hearing loss.

Those who have visual impairments are usually very capable of hearing and participating in the verbal part of communication but may be unable to observe nonverbal communication, depending on the severity of the loss of sight. The American Foundation for the Blind[19] offers suggestions to support those with vision impairment. Avoid using nonverbal responses, such as nodding in agreement or shaking your head in disagreement, as the visually impaired person may not see these responses. When entering the room, greet the patient verbally first and then offer a handshake or touch the shoulder, if appropriate. If sight is limited but present, offer written materials in large print. When the visit is over, be certain to inform the patient when you are leaving. Seek additional help from experts like the American Association for the Blind for assistance with Braille materials and other resources.[19]

Preferred Language, Health Literacy, Health Numeracy, and Financial Literacy

The initial communication between the APRN and the patient and family usually goes smoothly when the preferred language of the patient and family is the same as that of the clinician and there are no hearing, visual, or cognitive disabilities. The health literacy, health numeracy, and financial literacy of the patient and family are also important to consider in order for communication to be successful. When there is not a common preferred language between the APRN and the patient, or when the patient and family have low health literacy and numeracy, the APRN must use culturally sensitive strategies to help them navigate the healthcare system.

Preferred Language

A 2010 report by the U.S. Census Bureau revealed that of the 281 million people age 5 and older in the United States in 2007,

20% reported speaking a language other than English at home.[20] Language diversity in the United States is increasing. The 2007 data reflect a 140% increase between the years 1980 and 2007 of those speaking a language other than English at home.[20] In addition to attention to health literacy, financial literacy, and numeracy issues, this population needs to have information and communication available to them in their preferred language, so they can make informed health decisions. The NCP *Clinical Practice Guidelines*[1] Domain 6—Cultural Aspects of Care, defines the current standard in the criteria that outline how palliative care programs should make all reasonable efforts to provide interpreter services and written materials in the preferred language to facilitate patient and family understanding of information.

The APRN should consider the following strategies:

◆ Determine the dominant languages and dialects spoken by individuals in your community.

◆ Consider the literacy level of both the patient and the family.

◆ If the preferred language is not English, a professionally trained interpreter of the appropriate gender should be contacted when verbal communication is required. If no professional interpreter services are available, healthcare providers, preferably trained in palliative care, or those who are willing and able, may serve as interpreters. Keep in mind the nature of the conversation that needs to be interpreted; just because someone knows a language does not mean he or she should act in an interpreter role.

◆ Family members should act as interpreters only in an emergency. Family members are uncomfortable when placed in the interpreter role, especially if sensitive topics are being addressed. In some non-Western cultures, family members have a responsibility to protect the patient from distress or worry, so there is no way to know if the family member is sharing accurate information with the patient; this could lead to major misunderstandings. If a qualified professional interpreter is not available, access a telephone language line to assist in conversations. Examples of language lines that have interpreters for healthcare include Language Line Services[21] and CyraCom[22] International. They offer 24-hour availability, 365 days/year for those with an account. Newer technology services, such as video-remote interpreting (VRI), allow for face-to-face interactions, especially important for those with hearing or speech impairments.[21]

◆ Always remain conscious of your verbal and nonverbal communication when using an interpreter. For example, when speaking, make eye contact with the person you wish information to be directed toward, rather than looking at the interpreter.

◆ Ensure understanding by having the person explain to you or the interpreter what he or she has heard using his or her own words.

Palliative care providers often describe themselves as translators. Training in palliative care requires recognition that patients and families faced with a serious illness may find it difficult at times to take in all the information they have to absorb and understand to make decisions that make sense to them. Add to the mix a complex health system, insurance stipulations, costs of care, and complex testing—not to mention having to learn a new language

with long names of diagnostic tests, medicines, diseases, and even body parts. Cultural humility challenges the nurse to reflect on how the culture and language of the medical world are often foreign to those with little or no knowledge of medical language and culture, regardless of an individual's educational level.[10,12] Literacy and language issues may compound the challenge of understanding the heathcare environment for many.

Individuals facing serious illness must receive information in a format and a language that are easily understood, so they can make informed healthcare decisions.[23] Health literacy, health numeracy, financial literacy, and preferred language affect the person's ability to understand complex medical information and treatment options during serious illness.[24] Even things that seem routine and simple to healthcare providers might be confusing to the public.

Health Literacy

The NCP *Clinical Practice Guidelines*[1] emphasize that palliative care providers should tailor communication to the patient's and family's level of literacy, health literacy, numeracy, and financial literacy. This requires attention to the information that is provided orally and in written formats, and consideration of an individual's or group's language preference. This section focuses on defining terms and offering suggestions about strategies the APRN can use to improve assessment of literacy and language to improve outcomes.

Health literacy is a newly emerging concept, and the scope and definition vary widely. More data are needed, yet new initiatives leading up to and following the passage of the Affordable Care Act in 2010 are focusing on issues related to health literacy. The Institute of Medicine's Committee on Health Literacy defines health literacy as the degree to which individuals can obtain, process, and understand basic health information and services needed to make appropriate health decisions.[25] Only 12% of adults have proficient health literacy, and 14% of adults have below-basic health literacy.[25] Preliminary findings point to a link between lower health literacy and poor health outcomes.[25] Patients with low literacy are less likely to manage chronic conditions effectively and are more likely to be hospitalized, which may lead to poorer health outcomes and higher healthcare costs.

The 2003 National Assessment of Adult Literacy (NAAL) measured the literacy levels of American adults age 16 and older by studying everyday tasks that adults perform and the literacy skills necessary to perform them efficiently.[26] Four levels of literacy were described: below basic (performs no more than the most simple and concrete skills); basic (performs simple, everyday literacy activities); intermediate (performs moderately challenging literacy activities); and proficient (executes complex, challenging literacy activities). Several key findings from NAAL underscore how important it is for the APRN to pay attention to the patient's literacy level (Box 43.4). The APRN can improve how critical information is delivered, received, and understood by asking two important questions:[26]

1. **Is the information appropriate for the individual?**

   ◆ Identify the intended audience and determine whether materials and messages reflect the age, social and cultural background, and language and literacy skills of that audience. Do

---

Box 43.4 Behaviors that May Indicate Literacy Challenges

1. Taking medications incorrectly

2. Offering an excuse when asked to read written materials (e.g., "I forgot my glasses")

3. Identifying medications by shape or color rather than name, or opening medicine bottle rather than reading the label

4. Not looking at written materials or not turning them right side up if handed materials upside down

5. Not being able to fill out simple, age- and language-appropriate forms; providing incorrect information; leaving many items blank

Adapted from reference 27.

Box 43.5 Recommendations for Written Materials for Those with Low Literacy

- Use a 12-point font. Avoid using all capital letters, italics, and fancy fonts.
- Limit line length to between 40 and 50 characters.
- Use headings and bullets, which help to focus attention on key points.
- Leave plenty of white space on the page. Consider using larger margins and increased spacing between sections.

---

the materials account for communication capacities of the individual or group, or are additional strategies necessary to make sure messages are received and understood?

- Evaluate each individual's understanding before, during, and after delivery of information. Consider what information is critical and how it will be used, check for understanding, and consider alternative ways of delivering information as needed, if the information is unclear to the audience.

- Acknowledge and respect cultural variations. Consider components of culture when developing materials or speaking with individuals (see Table 43.1). Acknowledge and respect individual and group preferences and assess for variations within groups.

2. **Is the information easy to use?**

- Limit the number of messages being delivered at any given time. In general, no more than four messages should be conveyed.

- Give specific recommendations and expected actions. Clearly state actions that the person should take based on the information communicated. Focusing on behavior rather than medical principles or concepts may lead to better understanding and outcomes.

- Use plain language that is familiar to the audience. Keep it simple, and avoid long sentences.

- Use pictures when giving instructions. This can help individuals comprehend complicated instructions related to medical conditions, treatments, medications, and abstract concepts they may encounter during the course of an illness. Pictures should reflect the message and should not be merely decorative additions.

Behaviors that may indicate limited health literacy are described in Box 43.4.[27] Resources, instructional materials, and marketing can be made more understandable by following a few simple suggestions from the Department of Health and Human Services[28] (Box 43.5).

Health Numeracy

Case Study 2

Mr. P was a 72-year-old retired economist with congestive heart failure and prostate cancer that had spread to the bone. He was visiting the outpatient palliative care clinic for the first time for his symptoms of dyspnea and pain and was being seen by the clinical nurse specialist. He brought the instructions he received from the hospital, which included two medications prescribed for pain. The instructions read that he was to take oxycodone 5 mg q4h for breakthrough pain or shortness of breath, and to take the extended-release oxycodone q12h for pain. He rated his dyspnea as moderate to severe and his pain as well controlled, yet he was very sleepy. When asked how many of each pill he took, he told the APRN that he took them all so he wouldn't have pain, but he can't remember which one was which since they have the same name. He stated that he was due to start radiation therapy, which he hoped would finally cure his cancer. He had stopped taking his water pill, since it was making him go to the bathroom too much. His main concerns were that his breathing was worse, he was too sleepy from the drugs, and he couldn't walk because his legs were swollen. He reported that he was confused by the instructions for his medications and commented: "What I would really like to know is, who decided to make medical and pharmacy terms so complicated!"

Patients will receive information that involves numbers, and there is a growing recognition that attention to health numeracy is needed to help individuals who cannot fully comprehend or use the information they are given to make informed decisions about their health.[26]

Health numeracy is closely related to health literacy. Health numeracy is the degree to which individuals have the capacity to assess, process, interpret, communicate, and act on numerical, quantitative, graphical, biostatistical, and probabilistic health information to make effective health decisions.[28,29] Four functional categories of health numeracy that individuals should have to navigate today's healthcare system are basic, computational, analytical, and statistical skills.[30] The skills in these categories overlap and are needed throughout the course of a serious illness.

Basic numeracy skills are those required to identify numbers and comprehend data without having to manipulate any figures—for example, the ability to read and understand a prescription label. Computational health numeracy skills include a person's ability to count, quantify, compute, and use simple manipulation of numbers or figures presented in a health context or environment (e.g., lab results). Analytical and statistical numeracy skills are higher-level skills. Analytical skills may include inference, estimation, and proportions. Statistical numeracy proficiencies involve analytical skills as well as the ability to critically analyze information, research findings, complex graphs, and risk/benefit considerations.[30] While more research is needed, studies on numeracy are finding similar results as those on health literacy, in that individuals with lower numeracy skills have poorer health outcomes.[30]

The APRN should be able to assess how numerical information is received and understood by patients and families. If difficulties are uncovered, consider alternative ways of presenting important numerical information. Using pictures and plain language that describe concepts and demonstrate the desired action (e.g., how many morphine pills equal the dose ordered) may improve adherence with medical advice and lead to better outcomes.[30] Pictures can help with the timing of medications. Illustrations of a sunrise may help identify morning medications and a sunset or full moon can signify it is time to take evening medications.

Financial Literacy

The President's Advisory Council on Financial Literacy defines financial literacy as the ability to use knowledge and skills to manage financial resources effectively for a lifetime of financial well-being.[31] Recent healthcare reform goals depend, in part, on the ability of consumers to understand and navigate new rules and options.[30] Individuals who lack experience or proficiency with making decisions about health insurance options and calculating out-of-pocket expenses, copayments, deductibles, and other complex choices, may be confused about what options are best for them, and decision support services are critical to their successful selection of services.[32] The APRN should consider what resources are available to patients and family members who need additional information about financial and insurance options. Collaboration with appropriate team members (e.g., social workers) and other key community and decision support resources can help patients gain access to referral sources.

Culturally Sensitive Palliative Care Topics

Numerous palliative care topics (e.g., disclosure or "truth telling"; medical decision making, including withholding and withdrawing technology; pain and symptom management; and the care of the dying and bereaved) have important cultural implications.

Disclosure of Information and Prognosis

The Patient Self-Determination Act (PSDA) of 1991, grounded in Western cultural values and beliefs, was written to protect individuals' healthcare preferences.[33] Western cultural preferences include the right to be informed of one's diagnosis and prognosis and the risks and benefits of treatment. Autonomy, as the guiding principle, assumes that the individual, rather than the family or other social group, is the appropriate decision maker.[12] This European-American model of patient autonomy has its origin in the present-day U.S. dominant culture, a predominantly white, middle-class perspective that does not consider diverse cultural perspectives.[3]

Some non-Western cultures believe that telling the patient he or she has a terminal illness strips away any and all hope, causes needless suffering, and may actually hasten death.[34,35] If disclosing the patient's diagnosis and/or prognosis violates the patient's and family's cultural norms, or the patient does not wish to receive information, doing so directly violates the patient's right to autonomy. For example, imposing negative information, such as a prognosis of a life-limiting illness, on the person who is ill is a dangerous violation of traditional Navajo values: those who adhere to Navajo traditions believe that talking about death will actually cause death.[36] In families who adhere to Middle Eastern practices, telling the patient, who is perceived by the family as "vulnerable," the diagnosis is considered culturally unacceptable.[37]

Medical Decision Making

The principle of respect for patient autonomy emphasizes the patient's right to participate in decisions about the care he or she receives. The underlying assumption of patient autonomy is that all patients want control over their healthcare decisions, yet this is not always accurate.[34] In some families, patient autonomy may not be viewed as empowering but rather as isolating and burdensome for patients who are too sick to make difficult decisions.[13,34] In fact, depending on patient and family cultural preferences, patient autonomy actually may violate the very principles of dignity and integrity it proposes to uphold.[12,34]

In many non-Western cultures, the concept of interdependence among family and community members is valued more than individual autonomy.[3,34] If the APRN is caring for a patient who adheres to this belief, it is culturally sensitive to include, rather than exclude, the family in decision making. In some religious practices, it is important that the religious leaders also be included in the decision making.[14] Cultural groups that practice family-centered decision making may prefer that the family, or perhaps a particular family member, rather than the patient, receive and process information.

Discontinuation of Life-Prolonging Therapies

Family members may feel that by agreeing to stop potentially life-prolonging therapies, they are, in fact, responsible for the death of their loved one. For families who believe that it is the duty of children to honor, respect, and care for their elders, they may feel obligated to continue futile life-sustaining interventions. Allowing a parent to die may violate the principles of "filial piety" and bring shame and disgrace on the family.[3,38]

Religious beliefs may also play a role in decisions about withholding or withdrawing medical interventions. For example, in the Christian Philippines, removing the ventilator is synonymous with euthanasia.[39] For those practicing Orthodox Judaism, which believes that all life is precious and only God can decide our time to die, agreeing to withdraw life-prolonging therapies may violate their beliefs.[40] In both examples, involving a religious leader from the family's religious community may help the family and the healthcare team integrate religious tenets into the culturally appropriate plan of care.[14]

All healthcare personnel should be acutely aware of the medical jargon and language they use. Many phrases, such as "do not resuscitate" and "withdrawal of life support," have negative connotations. What is standard terminology in healthcare can get lost in translation even if the parties are speaking the same language. "Withdrawal of life support" or "withdrawal of care" may be easily confused with stopping *all* care, which is certainly not the intention.[14,41,42] The family may feel as though the team is giving up on the patient and abandoning him or her, resulting in family suffering, isolation, and distress. Instead, use language that conveys the benefits versus the burdens of all therapies. Focus on what the team will do to care for the patient rather than what burdensome interventions should be stopped.

Pain and Symptom Management

Case Study 3

J.D. was a 24-year-old African-American female admitted to the hospital with a sickle cell pain crisis. J.D. had had multiple admissions in the preceding year for acute chest syndrome, respiratory infections, and painful crises. The admitting nurse called the APRN on the palliative care team to report, "J.D. is back again. Seems like all she wants is to come to the hospital to get narcotics. I'm tired of taking care of her. No matter what I do, she always claims her pain is a 10, even when she's talking on the cellphone or watching television. I need an order for pain medication for her even though she's resting in bed!"

The APRN responded to the nurse in a respectful manner. He heard the nurse's frustration at not being able to control J.D.'s pain and also heard the bias that many healthcare professionals have regarding the self-reporting of pain and the need for opioids to control it. The APRN taught the nurse about the severity of painful crises in sickle cell disease, the principles of chronic pain, and the years of mistrust in the medical system that had influenced J.D.'s self-report of pain. With education and team planning, the APRN was able to work with the patient and the nurse to develop a trusting relationship, skillfully manage this painful crisis with opioids, and deliver care in a culturally respectful manner.

The experience of pain and other symptoms commonly addressed in palliative care (e.g., anorexia, cachexia, nausea and vomiting, fatigue, dyspnea, and depression) can be viewed through a cultural lens. Assessment of both pain and symptoms demands a self-report of the severity and the meaning associated with them. For some, culturally learned responses to pain and symptoms may influence tolerance and behavior. Western culture appears to value individuals who have a high pain threshold; those with a lower threshold may be labeled as "difficult patients." Case Study 3 demonstrates the influence of cultural biases on clinical care.

It is important to remember cultural considerations and health literacy when assessing pain and symptoms. Labels like "pain" or "depression" may be culturally unacceptable for patients to self-report, so asking about a "hurt" or "ache" instead of "pain" and "a tired state" instead of "depression" may elicit a more accurate response from the patient.[43,44]

The meaning of the pain or symptom also influences assessment and treatment. Religious and spiritual practices as well as ethnic values and beliefs may influence a patient's willingness to accept treatment. Enduring pain or severe nausea may be important to a patient who believes that suffering is necessary to achieve a good afterlife.[45] Try to find a common understanding of the suffering experience and the value of pain/symptom management using a team approach, possibly including a religious leader.

Finally, consider that racial, ethnic, age, or gender biases can hinder good pain and symptom management. Pain is often undertreated in minorities.[46] Women, children, and elderly people are also at risk for inaccurate assessment and poor management.[47]

Additional symptoms with cultural implications are anorexia and cachexia. For families who are caring for a loved one who is no longer able to eat or no longer interested in eating, anorexia and cachexia can be a source of distress. Food is seen as essential for life in all cultures.[14,48] It is used in celebrations and rites of passage and as an expression of social relationships and connections with families, friends, and others. The intense meaning attached to food and nutrition can result in cultural and ethical conflicts over providing artificial nutrition and hydration at the end-of-life. The APRN must use listening and presence to understand what feeding the patient means to the family and to help the family develop alternative expressions of comfort and love. If the family's health literacy is low, not feeding the patient may be akin to "starving him to death." The nurse should provide a culturally sensitive explanation of the benefits and burdens associated with feeding.

Death and Bereavement

A conversation about patient and family wishes during the dying process and at the time of death should take place well in advance, provided it is not culturally unacceptable to discuss prior to death.[35] In some cultures, important rituals and customs must take place prior to, or at the time of, death. These need to be identified and integrated into the plan of care. For example, there may be cultural norms regarding which gender or specific family member should be involved in care of the body after death.[49] Beliefs about autopsy or organ donation should be discussed before death. Keep in mind that some cultures and religious communities believe that organ donation and autopsy are disrespectful to the sanctity of the body. The family will hold on to the memory of the patient's final days and death forever, so if cultural practices are not honored, family members may experience complicated grief after the death of their loved one.[49]

The tasks of grief are universal. In all cultures, the process is to accept the reality of the loss, to experience the pain of grief, to begin the adjustment to new social and family roles, and to withdraw emotional energy from the dead individual and turn it over to those who are alive.[50] The experiences of loss, grief, and bereavement are guided by cultural traditions and beliefs, and the expressions of grief can vary significantly among cultures, making it important to assess expressions of grief and individuals' behavior during mourning within a cultural context.[14]

When Cultures Clash

Case Study 4

Mr. T was a 93-year-old Korean-born male. He had lived in the United States since 1950. A grocer all his life, he proudly provided for his wife and three now-grown children. His eldest son told the healthcare team that in his family, he was now the spokesperson for his father's needs and wishes. He asked that the team not share his father's poor prognosis with his dad. He explained it was now his responsibility to care for his father and to protect him from distress and worry.

The new resident on the team, however, believed strongly that Mr. T had a right to know he was dying. The resident was upset with Mr. T's son and told him that, as the resident on his father's team, he had the responsibility to share the prognosis with Mr. T so that Mr. T could "get his affairs in order." The resident also told the son that since Mr. T was cognitively able to make his own treatment decisions, he must know his prognosis so he could decide on what, if any, treatment he might want. The APRN returned to see the family after the team rounds and discovered that Mr. T's son was preparing to sign his father out of the hospital, against medical advice. The APRN respectfully asked the son if he was willing to discuss his decision with the APRN before leaving. The APRN was able to resolve the conflict by promising to honor the son's wishes and by helping the resident to understand the importance of the family's cultural values and the impact of the resident's differing cultural beliefs in this situation. The goal of doing what was best for the patient was actually shared by both parties, and the APRN helped the resident see that the best way to achieve that goal was to honor the patient's and family's values and cultural practices.

The three most common sources of cultural conflict are between the patient and family, among the healthcare team members, and among the healthcare team, patient, and family. In our multicultural society, patients and family members may have different values and beliefs. If one of the parties involved is more assimilated into the Western culture and the other aligns with non-Western values, practices, and beliefs, conflict may occur. Healthcare providers, too, bring the values and beliefs of their own cultures to the clinical setting. The APRN may need to be the advocate for patient and family wishes. An ethics consult and family meeting may help to resolve conflict and reach a shared understanding of the goals of care. Case Study 4 illustrates the distress resulting from a cultural conflict.

Summary

With the increasing cultural diversity in the United States, the APRN must be culturally sensitive to provide quality comprehensive palliative care, as recommended in the NCP guidelines.[1] This requires moving beyond one's own ethnocentric view of the world to appreciate and respect the similarities and differences in each other. There are many situations in which the APRN is challenged to come to appreciate and understand an individual's preferences in care based on cultural values, practices, and beliefs. However, by maintaining a sense of cultural humility, caring for each patient and family member as a unique human being with unique needs, and attending to those needs with dignity and respectfulness, the APRN can provide culturally sensitive care.

References

1. National Consensus Project for Quality Palliative Care. *Clinical Practice Guidelines for Quality Palliative Care.* 3rd ed. Pittsburgh, PA: National Consensus Project for Quality Palliative Care. 2013.
2. Dahlin CM, Lynch MT, eds. *Core Curriculum for the Advanced Practice Hospice and Palliative Registered Nurse.* 2nd ed. Pittsburgh, PA: Hospice and Palliative Nurses Association, 2013.
3. Kagawa-Singer M. Impact of culture on health outcomes. *Pediatr Hematol Oncol.* 2011; 33(suppl 2): S90–S95.
4. U.S. Census Bureau. U.S. Census Bureau Projections show a slower growing, older, more diverse nation a half century from now. December 12, 2012. Available at https://www.census.gov/newsroom/releases/archives/population/cb12-243.html. Accessed July 27, 2014.
5. Leininger M. Quality of life from a transcultural nursing perspective. *Nurs Sci Quart.* 1994; 7: 22–8.
6. Giger JN, Davidhizar RE, Fordham P. Multi-cultural and multi-ethnic considerations and advanced directives: developing cultural competency. *J Cult Divers.* 2006; 13: 3–9.
7. End-of-Life Nursing Education Consortium (ELNEC). Available at http://www.aacn.nche.edu/elnec/. Accessed July 23, 2014.
8. Anderson KC, Green CR, Payne R. Racial and ethnic disparities in pain: causes and consequences of unequal care. *J Pain.* 2009; 10: 1187–204.
9. Zoucha R. The keys to culturally sensitive care. *Am J Nurs.* 2000: 2: 24GG–24II.
10. Wittenberg-Lyles E, Goldsmith J, Ferrell B, Ragan SA. Orientation and opportunity. In: Wittenberg-Lyles E, Goldsmith J, Ferrell B, Ragan SA, eds. *Communication in Palliative Nursing.* New York, NY: Oxford University Press; 2013:59–92.
11. Trevalon M, Murray-Garcia J. Cultural humility versus cultural competence: a critical distinction in defining physician training outcomes in multicultural education. *J Health Care Poor Underserved.* 1998; 9: 117–25.
12. Kagawa-Singer M, Dadia AV, Yu MC, Surbone A. Cancer, culture, and health disparities: time to chart a new course? *CA Cancer J Clin.* 2010; 60: 12–39.
13. Clark D. Cultural considerations in planning palliative and end-of-life care. *J Palliat Med.* 2012; 26: 195–6.
14. Mazanec P, Panke JT. Cultural considerations in palliative care. In: Ferrell BR, Coyle N, Paice J, eds. *Oxford Textbook of Palliative Nursing.* 4th ed. New York, NY: Oxford University Press; 2015: 580–91.
15. Dahlin CM, Wittenberg E. Communication in palliative care: an essential competency for nurses. In: Ferrell BR, Coyle N, Paice J, eds. *Oxford Textbook of Palliative Nursing.* 4th ed. New York, NY: Oxford University Press; 2015: 81–112.
16. Barclay JS, Blackhall LJ, Tulsky JA. Communication strategies and cultural issues in the delivery of bad news. *J Palliat Med.* 2007; 10: 958–77.
17. Bade P. Center to Advance Palliative Care. Fast facts and concepts #241. Improving communication when hearing loss is present. 2010. www.capc.org/fast-facts/241-improving-communication-when-hearing-loss-present/. Accessed July 25, 2015.
18. Hearing Loss Association of America. Available at http://www.hearingloss.org. Accessed July 31, 2014.
19. American Foundation for the Blind. Help for professionals working with the visually impaired. Available at http://www.afb.org/info/programs-and-services/professional-development/12. Accessed July 31, 2014.
20. U.S. Census Bureau. New Census Bureau Report analyzes nation's linguistic diversity: population speaking a language other than English at home increases by 140 percent in past three decades. Available at http://www.census.gov/newsroom/releases/archives/american_community_survey_acs/cb10-cn58.html. Accessed July 12, 2014.
21. Language Line. Available at http://www.languageline.com/solutions/industries/healthcare-interpretation Accessed September 19, 2014.
22. CyraCom International. Available at http://www.cyracom.com/phone-interpretation. Accessed September 19, 2014.
23. Panke JT. Palliative care an hospice care for patients with cancer. In: Camp-Sorrell D, Hawkins R, eds. *In Practice Oncology Nursing.* 2014. Available at www.inpractice.com. Accessed July 19, 2014.
24. Wittenberg-Lyles E, Goldsmith J, Ragan S. The shift to early palliative care: a typology of illness journeys and the role of nursing. *Clin J Oncol Nurs.* 2011; 15(3): 304–10.
25. Institute of Medicine Commission on Health Literacy. Nielsen-Bohlman L, Panzer AM, Kindig DA, eds. Health literacy: a prescription to end confusion. Committee on Health Literacy Board on Neuroscience and Behavioral Health. Washington, DC: The National Academies Press; 2004. Available at http://www.iom.edu/

Reports/2004/health-literacy-a-prescription-to-end-confusion.aspx. Accessed July 13, 2014.

26. National Center for Education Statistics. National Assessment of Adult Literacy (NAAL). Released May 2009. Available at http://nces.ed.gov/NAAL/kf_demographics.asp. Accessed July 19, 2014.

27. Reisfield GM, Wilson GR. Center to Advance Palliative Care. Fast facts and concepts #153: Health literacy in palliative medicine. 2005. www.capc.org/fast-facts/241-improving-communication-when-hearing-loss-present/. Accessed July 19, 2015.

28. U.S. Department of Health and Human Services (DHHS). Office of Disease Prevention and Health Promotion. Quick Guide to Health Literacy. Available at http://www.health.gov/communication/literacy/Default.asp. Accessed July 13, 2014.

29. Ancker JS, Kaufman D. Rethinking health numeracy: a multidisciplinary literature review. *J Am Med Inform Assn*. 2007; 14(6): 713–21.

30. Golbeck AL, Ahlers-Schmidt CR, Paschal AM, Dismuke SE. A definition and operational framework for health numeracy. *Am J Prev Med*. 2005; 29(4): 375–6.

31. President's Advisory Council on Financial Literacy. 2008 Annual Report to the President. Available at http://www.treasury.gov/about/organizational-structure/offices/Domestic-Finance/Documents/exec_sum.pdf. Accessed July 23, 2014.

32. Bauhoff S, Carman KG, Wuppermann A. Financial literacy & consumer choice of health insurance: evidence from low income populations in the U.S. 2013 Working paper from RAND Corporation.

33. Federal Patient Self-Determination Act 19090, 42 U.S.C. 1395 cc(a).

34. Hancock K, Clayton JM, Parker SM, et al. Truth-telling in discussing prognosis in advanced life-limiting illnesses: a systematic review. *Palliat Med*. 2007; 21: 507–17.

35. Johnstone MJ, Kanitsaki O. Ethics and advance care planning in a culturally diverse society. *J Transcult Nurs*. 2009; 20: 405–16. doi:10.1177/104365960934803

36. Carrese JA, Rhodes LA. Western bioethics on the Navajo reservation: benefit or harm? *JAMA*. 1995; 274: 826–9.

37. Abjubran A. Challenges to the disclosure of bad news to cancer patients in the Middle East: Saudi Arabia as an example. In: Surbon A, Zwitter M, Rajer M, et al., eds. *New Challenges in Communication with Cancer Patients*. New York, NY: Springer Science & Business Media, LLC; 2012.

38. Hsiung YY, Ferrans CE. Recognizing Chinese Americans' cultural needs in making end-of-life treatment decisions. *J Hosp Palliat Nurs*. 2007; 9: 132–40.

39. Manalo MF. End-of-life decisions about withholding or withdrawing therapy: medical, ethical, and religio-cultural considerations. *Palliative Care: Research and Treatment*. 2013; 7: 1–5. doi:10.4137/PCRT.S10796

40. Schultz M, Bar-Sela G. Initiating palliative care conversations: lessons from Jewish bioethics. *J Supp Oncol*. Available at http://dx.doi.org/10.1016j.suponc.2012.07.003. Accessed June 20, 2014.

41. Long CO. Ten best practices to enhance culturally competent communication in palliative care. *Pediatr Hematol Oncol*. 2011: 33(suppl 2): S136–9.

42. Curtis JR, Sprung CL, Azolay E. The importance of word choice in the care of critically ill patients and their families. *Intensive Care Med*. 2014; 40: 606–8.

43. Narayan MC. Culture's effects on pain assessment and management. *Am J Nurs*. 2010; 110: 38–48.

44. Pasacreta JV, Minarik PA, Nield-Anderson L, Paice J. Anxiety and depression. In: Ferrell BR, Coyle N, Paice J. eds. *Oxford Textbook of Palliative Nursing*. 4th ed. New York, NY: Oxford University Press; 2015; 366–84.

45. Deal B. Finding meaning in suffering. *Holistic Nursing Practice*. 2011; 25: 205–10.

46. Anderson KC, Green CR, Payne R. Racial and ethnic disparities in pain: causes and consequences of unequal care. *J Pain*. 2009; 10: 1187–204.

47. Wadner LD, Scipio CD, Hirsch AT, Torres CA, Robinson ME. The perception of pain in others: how gender, race and age influence pain expectations. *J Pain*. 2012; 13: 220–7. doi:10.1016/j.pain.2011.10.014

48. HPNA Position Statement on Artificial Nutrition and Hydration in End-of-Life Care. Available at http://www.hpna.org/pdf/Artifical_Nutrition_and_Hydration_PDF.pdfHPNA. Accessed June 24, 2014.

49. Spector R. *Cultural Care: Guides to Heritage Assessment and Health Traditions*. 7th ed. Upper Saddle River, NJ: Pearson Education; 2009.

50. O'Mallon MO. Vulnerable populations: exploring a family perspective of grief. *J Hosp Palliat Nurs*. 2009;11: 91–8.

PART FIVE

SPIRITUAL CARE

CHAPTER 44

The Role of the Advanced Practice Registered Nurse in Spiritual Care

Betty R. Ferrell

Key Points

- Assessment of spiritual needs is a component of comprehensive patient evaluation in palliative care.

- Spirituality encompasses a broad spectrum that includes religion, purpose and meaning, values, beliefs, and hopes.

- Palliative advanced practice registered nurses (APRNs) provide spiritual care through communication, coordination of care, and responding to spiritual distress.

Introduction

Spiritual care becomes especially important as patients face the end-of-life. Spirituality is closely related to culture and encompasses religious beliefs as well as a broad array of dimensions, including meaning, a sense of purpose, hope, and connection.[1-4] Because APRNs provide leadership, serve as mentors, and model expert clinical care, they are very important as agents to ensure quality spiritual care. However, as with other aspects of advanced practice, APRNs need knowledge and skill development to deliver the care patients and families need.

This chapter reviews evidence-based guidelines for delivery of spiritual care, with discussion of both spiritual assessment and interventions. Case examples are provided to illustrate the role of APRNs in spiritual care. The chapter also reviews spiritual assessment tools for application in advanced practice as well as suggested resources for continued learning.

The National Consensus Project (NCP) identifies spiritual, religious, and existential care as one of the eight essential domains of quality care.[2] Spiritual care is often led by the specialist member of the team, the chaplain, but all members of the team must be competent in their roles in assessment and prepared to respond to spiritual needs. As with other aspects of care in serious illness, nursing is the most prevalent discipline across all settings of care, and therefore is centrally involved in provision of spiritual care.

This textbook is devoted to advanced practice, and as is the case with areas like complex pain or symptoms, APRNs need advanced skills in spiritual care. While all nurses in palliative care should

be skilled in basic spiritual assessment and response to spiritual needs,[2-4] APRNs can be a valuable resource for complex spiritual needs. Box 44.1 presents the recommendations for spiritual care from the NCP *Clinical Practice Guidelines for Quality Palliative Care*. Some examples of complex spiritual needs are:

- Conducting a spiritual assessment for patients with less common religious affiliations whose religious beliefs are creating ethical conflicts in care

- Working with the chaplain to reduce spiritual distress in patients who express a sense of abandonment

- Using expert communication skills to support patients as they conduct life reviews, resolve issues of forgiveness, or grasp for miracles, or when conflicting religious beliefs within families create conflicts in care

The role of the APRN is described throughout this text as encompassing many responsibilities, including expert clinician, educator, manager, and researcher. These roles also apply to the domain of spiritual care. The APRN will serve as a clinical exprt in spiritual care, supported by chaplaincy, to model spiritual assessment and care.[5-10] Knowledge and clinical skills are important competencies for staff education provided by the APRN to new graduates or new staff.

APRNs are often involved in developing policies and procedures, documentation, and other structures and processes of care. Spiritual care assessment tools and procedures for documenting spiritual needs and care will need to be selected as palliative care teams are initiated.

As with all other aspects of advanced practice, proficiency in spiritual care requires lifelong learning. This is especially true given the ever-increasing diversity of the population, which includes a vast array of religious traditions and spiritual beliefs that are critical in serious illness.[11-14]

Spiritual Assessment

The importance of spiritual care rests on the foundation of key health-care concepts, such as patient-centered care, respect for the person,

Box 44.1 *National Consensus Project for Quality Palliative Care*, Domain 5—Spiritual, Religious, and Existential Aspects of Care

DOMAIN 5: SPIRITUAL, RELIGIOUS, AND EXISTENTIAL ASPECTS OF CARE

Guideline 5.1. The interdisciplinary team (IDT) assesses and addresses spiritual, religious, and existential dimensions of care.

Criteria

Spirituality is recognized as a fundamental aspect of compassionate patient and family-centered care that honors the dignity of all persons.

♦ Spirituality is defined as, "the aspect of humanity that refers to the way individuals seek and express meaning and purpose and the way they experience their connectedness to the moment, to self, to others, to nature, and/or to the significant or sacred."[1] It is the responsibility of all IDT members to recognize spiritual distress and attend to the patient's and the family's spiritual needs, within their scope of practice.[2]

♦ The interdisciplinary palliative care team, in all settings, includes spiritual care professionals; ideally, a board-certified professional chaplain, with skill and expertise to assess and address spiritual and existential issues frequently confronted by pediatric and adult patients with life-threatening or serious illnesses and their families.

♦ Communication with the patient and family is respectful of their religious and spiritual beliefs, rituals, and practices. Palliative care team members do not impose their individual spiritual, religious, existential beliefs or practices on patients, families, or colleagues.

Guideline 5.2. A spiritual assessment process, including a spiritual screening, history questions, and a full spiritual assessment as indicated, is performed. This assessment identifies religious or spiritual/existential background, preferences, and related beliefs, rituals, and practices of the patient and family, as well as symptoms, such as spiritual distress and/or pain, guilt, resentment, despair, and hopelessness.

Criteria

♦ The IDT regularly explores spiritual and existential concerns and documents these spiritual themes in order to communicate them to the team. This exploration includes, but is not limited to: life review, assessment of hopes, values, and fears, meaning, purpose, beliefs about afterlife, spiritual or religious practices, cultural norms, beliefs that influence understanding of illness, coping, guilt, forgiveness, and life completion tasks. Whenever possible, a standardized instrument is used.

♦ The IDT periodically reevaluates the impact of spiritual/existential interventions and documents patient and family preferences.

♦ The patient's spiritual resources of strength are supported and documented in the patient record.

♦ Spiritual/existential care needs, goals, and concerns identified by patients, family members, the palliative care team, or spiritual care professionals are addressed according to established protocols and documented in the interdisciplinary care plan, and emphasized during transitions of care, and/or in discharge plans. Support is offered for issues of life closure, as well as other spiritual issues, in a manner consistent with the patient's and the family's cultural, spiritual, and religious values.

♦ Referral to an appropriate community-based professional with specialized knowledge or skills in spiritual and existential issues (e.g., to a pastoral counselor or spiritual director) is made when desired by the patient and/or family. Spiritual care professionals are recognized as specialists who provide spiritual counseling.

Guideline 5.3. The palliative care service facilitates religious, spiritual, and cultural rituals or practices as desired by patient and family, especially at and after the time of death.

Criteria

♦ Professional and institutional use of religious/spiritual symbols and language is sensitive to cultural and religious diversity.

♦ The patient and family are supported in their desires to display and use their own religious/spiritual and/or cultural symbols.

♦ Chaplains and other palliative care professionals facilitate contact with spiritual/religious communities, groups or individuals, as desired by the patient and/or family. Palliative care programs create procedures to facilitate patients' access to clergy, religious, spiritual and culturally based leaders, and/or healers in their own religious, spiritual, or cultural traditions.

♦ Palliative professionals acknowledge their own spirituality as part of their professional role. Opportunities are provided to engage staff in self-care and self-reflection of their beliefs and values, as they work with seriously ill and dying patients. Core expectations of the team include respect for spirituality and beliefs of all colleagues and the creation of a healing environment in the workplace.

♦ Non-chaplain palliative care providers obtain training in basic spiritual screening and spiritual care skills.

♦ The palliative care team ensures follow-up after the patient's death (e.g., phone calls, attendance at wake or funeral, or scheduled visit) to offer support, identify any additional needs that require community referral, and help the family during bereavement (see Domain 3: Psychological and Psychiatric Aspects of Care, Guideline 3.2).

and culturally respectful care.[1] Organizations addressing quality in healthcare have recognized the importance of spiritual care even before the development of palliative care. The Joint Commission requires spiritual assessment "to determine the patient's denomination, beliefs and what spiritual practices are important."[5] Spiritual assessment is also closely aligned with the emphasis by many accreditation bodies on culturally competent care, since religious beliefs are very often central to cultural identity.[15–18]

Case Study 1

Joseph was a clinical nurse specialist in a 200-bed Catholic hospital. He had been in a role involving responsibilities in oncology and then devoted half of his time to the developing palliative care service. He was contacted by the ICU to assist in the care of a 70-year-old Iranian man who was visiting his brother in the United States when he had a cerebral aneurysm. The patient was being maintained on a ventilator but death was anticipated soon. The patient's wife was distraught because she was far away from her family and friends and had never been close to the brother they were visiting. She blamed the brother for insisting that her husband come to the United States to work out some family business. The patient and his wife were devout Muslims.

There were two chaplains in the hospital who supported the palliative care service, but their resources were stretched: they provided care in the emergency department, the trauma center, and a large neonatal care unit, as well as conducting daily Mass.

Joseph saw that the ICU nurses were frustrated by the patient situation. They told Joseph the wife was "crazy" and distrustful. She accused the nurses and physicians of trying to kill her husband, and refused to have a visit by the chaplain because he was a Catholic priest. Joseph met with the staff and the neurologist and intensivist physicians and then organized a family meeting. Joseph was familiar with Muslim beliefs and arranged an ICU staff meeting to educate the nurses about the importance of prayer in the Muslim faith, the beliefs prohibiting any discussion of death, the reason why the wife had forbidden completion of an advance directive, and what needs the staff should anticipate as the patient died. The hospital chaplain connected Joseph with an imam (a Muslim spiritual leader) in the community, who arranged a visit. Joseph also worked with the ICU manager to ensure that a male staff member was available to provide postmortem care, since in the Muslim faith only a male is allowed to touch the body after death. Joseph collaborated with the palliative care physician and ICU staff to address the patient's symptoms, including his agitation, fevers, congestion, and pain. Joseph met with the imam when he arrived to explain the patient's condition and plan of care.

Case Study 1 illustrates the APRN's role in spiritual assessment and how that assessment affects care and its outcomes. Through his varied roles as an APRN, Joseph ensured that quality care was provided for the patient and family, provided support for the staff, and avoided further cultural clash, which could have made a difficult situation even worse. When cultural clashes or ethical dilemmas arise in palliative care, it is common for spiritual beliefs to be a key contributing factor. This case study illustrates that the care is contingent on assessment of beliefs, practices, and values of both the patient and family. Thorough spiritual assessment guides palliative care.[19–21]

Spiritual Care

The spiritual care provided to patients and families is as diverse as the cultures represented in our populations. APRNs contribute to palliative teams' attention to spiritual care in many ways. Three case studies illustrate the delivery of spiritual care.

Case Study 2

Madeline was a 62-year-old woman diagnosed with pancreatic cancer. She was referred by her oncologist to the outpatient palliative care clinic for pain, nausea, cachexia, and fatigue. The palliative nurse practitioner, Jane, saw Madeline weekly over the next 3 weeks and was able to provide relief for her symptoms. On follow-up 1 week later, Jane noticed that while Madeline's physical symptoms were well controlled, she seemed very anxious and sad. Jane reviewed the initial assessment completed in the oncology clinic to identify any useful psychosocial information in the medical record. After reviewing with Madeline the plans for ongoing follow-up, she sat next to Madeline and said, "We have spent all our visits focusing on your symptoms, but I would like to hear about how you are doing. How are you managing with all this?"

Madeline began crying intensely, saying repeatedly, "It's so unfair, so unfair." Jane sat quietly and listened as Madeline described how her children had lost their father just a year ago from a heart attack and would soon lose their mother. As Jane listened quietly, Madeline went on to describe the most distressing aspect of her illness, which was that she knew she would die soon, "abandoning" her mother who lived in an Alzheimer's facility. She had promised to always care for her mother, "which we do in my family—Jewish daughters don't abandon their parents."

Case Study 2 illustrates the role of nursing in symptom management and the need for nurses to recognize that it is common for symptom management to move beyond pharmacologic intervention and to address suffering.[6,22–24] In this case, Madeline is not only a patient but also a family caregiver, a role that has important cultural and religious meaning. The case also illustrates the most important skill for APRNs in spiritual care—listening. Presence and listening are essential to understanding and responding to a patient's spiritual needs.

Case Study 3

Mary was an 82-year-old African-American woman living in the South, in a residential care facility. She was experiencing multiple symptoms from her end-stage cardiac disease and was referred to palliative care after three hospital urgent care visits over the preceding 6 weeks due to dyspnea and edema. Mary was preparing for discharge after a hospital admission related to her symptoms. Mary's children lived out of state, and she was described as a lonely woman, fiercely independent, and very stoic.

Mary was seen by a master's-prepared nurse, Jean, who was a case manager in the cardiac care program. Jean did a thorough assessment of Mary, including an assessment of her physical, psychosocial, and spiritual needs. When Jean asked if Mary had a church community that might offer support, Mary angrily stated that she "quit believing in God" as a child after witnessing common hatred and racial discrimination. When asked about her life before retirement, Mary spoke of her career as a high school science teacher, when she was one of the first African-American women to be allowed to teach science in the public school. She said she was proud to have been there at a time "when girls weren't supposed to be smart." She became calm and proud as she told Jean about the many young women she had inspired to get an education.

Jean collaborated with the cardiology service and the palliative care team in arranging for home-based palliative care, as Mary adamantly refused hospice care and insisted on returning home alone. Jean shared with the palliative care service the information she had learned from Mary about her psychosocial and spiritual needs.

Case Study 3 illustrates an instance where the patient's spiritual journey, from early religious affiliation to movement away from religion, was expressed in the final phase of life. Nursing assessment helped move beyond the religious aspect to identify positive aspects of spirituality for this patient through the meaning of her life and her legacy.

Case Study 4

David was a clinical nurse specialist and professional practice leader on a hematology service in an urban academic medical center. One of David's most challenging cases was a 30-year-old Latino patient, Juan, who was admitted 28 days earlier with severe graft-versus-host disease after undergoing a stem cell transplant for leukemia. Juan's large extended family refused to face the seriousness of his illness, despite worsening renal and pulmonary complications. Juan and his family were devout Catholics and believed in miracles.

Over the course of a few days, tensions arose because the family believed the staff had given up on Juan. They became angry when the nurses interrupted their bedside prayer sessions, which they believed were important for God to see they were awaiting a miracle healing. They refused palliative care. The hematology service was becoming frustrated, because they believed Juan's distress and increasing agitation were caused by his family's distress.

The family developed a good relationship with David, who was also a Catholic; they believed that he had not given up on Juan. David arranged a meeting with the family, chaplain, and social worker to gain a better understanding of the family's beliefs and then shared that understanding with the entire team.

Case Study 4 illustrates the challenges that often occur in palliative care related to spirituality. Spiritual beliefs sometimes clash with clinical care goals. The APRN can be the link between the healthcare system and the patient's beliefs, values, and right to dignity.

Spiritual Care in Pediatrics

Nurses in pediatric palliative care can play a significant role in responding to the spiritual needs of children and their families.[26–28] This requires attention to the child's developmental state, how that stage has been affected by the serious illness, and the family's religious or spiritual beliefs.

Spiritual care in pediatrics is an example of the importance of interdisciplinary care, as nurses will need the guidance of chaplaincy to understand the child's and family's religious and spiritual beliefs and practices. Heilferty wrote an excellent paper on spiritual development in dying children, which summarizes needs across developmental stages.[26] Children's understanding of God or a higher power and the meaning of life events is related to their developmental stage, so the APRN's knowledge of childhood development is essential.[25–28] Nurses are also often the primary caregivers as patients, siblings, parents, grandparents, and friends express their emotional responses to spiritual concerns, such as anger toward God, guilt, distress, and blame.[27]

McEvoy provides a model for assessment in pediatrics, the BELIEF mnemonic:

B—Belief system (e.g., participation in religious activities or discussion of an afterlife)

E—Ethics or values

L—Lifestyle (e.g., rituals or practices related to religion)

I—Involvement in a spiritual community

E—Education (religious education in the family)

F—Future events (important rites and the future role of the faith community in the child's care)[28]

Spirituality is also intertwined with culture. The APRN can provide the best care for seriously ill children by doing a cultural assessment, including the cultural meanings of illness, traditions, rituals, and language.

Resources

In addition to the guidelines mentioned earlier, there are many spiritual assessment tools available for clinical use.[29–50] An increasing numbers of textbooks and model projects are advancing the domain of spiritual care.[1,51–53] Boxes 44.2, 44.3, 44.4, and 44.5 and Table 44.1 summarize many of these resources.

Summary

Palliative care is, by definition, based on a foundation of comprehensive care for the whole person. It is incomplete without full attention to the spiritual domain. APRNs contribute to the goal of whole-person care by assessing the spiritual needs of the entire family and applying evidence-based guidelines. Through close collaboration with chaplains and other team members, care can be respectful and inclusive of spiritual needs.

Box 44.2 Items from the *Spiritual Subscale*—the City of Hope Quality of Life Instrument

Spiritual Well-Being

1. How important to you is your participation in **religious activities**, such as praying, going to church?

2. How important to you are other **spiritual activities**, such as meditation?

3. How much has your **spiritual life** changed as a result of the cancer diagnosis?

4. How much **uncertainty** do you feel about your future?

5. To what extent has your illness made **positive changes** in your life?

6. Do you sense a **purpose/mission** for your life or a reason for being alive?

7. How **hopeful** do you feel?

Adapted from the City of Hope Quality of Life Instrument.[54]

Box 44.3 Key Resources for APRNs when Providing Spiritual Care

- George Washington University Institute for Spirituality in Health http://www.GWISH.org

- City of Hope Pain/Palliative Care Resource Center http://prc.coh.org

- Spiritual Parenting http://www.spiritualparenting.com

- Puchalski C, Ferrell B. *Making Health Care Whole*. West Conshohocken, PA: Templeton Press, 2010.

- Cobb M, Puchalski CM, Rumbold B, eds. *Oxford Textbook of Spirituality in Healthcare*. New York, NY: Oxford University Press, 2012.

Box 44.4 Self (or Nurse-Assisted) Spiritual Screening for Palliative Care Patients

Dear _____,

Your palliative care team wants to make sure you receive the physical, emotional, and spiritual care and comfort you need.

Typically, persons receiving palliative care find themselves becoming more aware of their spirituality or religion. Please help us to understand what your spiritual care and comfort needs are.

Directions: Circle the answer that comes closest to describing your experience.

1. How important is spirituality and/or religion to you now?
Not at all important   Very important

Box 44.4 Continued

2. Recently, my spirits have been …
Awful … low … okay … good … great
What can a nurse do to nurture or boost your spirits? (check all that apply)

- pray with me

- allow time and space for my private prayer or meditation

- bring art or music to nurture my spirit

- bring or read inspiring things to me

- listen to my thoughts about certain spiritual matters

- provide assistance so I can record my life story

- just be with me

- help me stay connected to my spiritual community by contacting:
  - my church/temple/mosque/local faith community's name and location _____
  - my clergy or spiritual leader's name (any contact information will be helpful) _____

Is there anything else about your spiritual beliefs or practices that the palliative care team should know? (e.g., diet or lifestyle proscribed by your religion? beliefs guiding your preparation for death?) Please write the information here (or on the back side) or tell your nurse.

From: Johnston-Taylor E. Chapter 32: Spiritual Assessment. In: Ferrell B, Coyle N, Paice J, eds. *Textbook of Palliative Nursing*. 4th ed. New York, NY: Oxford University Press; 2015.

Box 44.5 Chaplaincy Services: Areas of Chaplaincy Assessment

Grief

Concern about death and afterlife

Conflicted or challenged belief systems

Loss of faith

Concern with meaning/purpose of life

Concerns about relationship with deity

Isolation from religious community

Guilt

Hopelessness

Conflict between religious belief and recommended treatments

Ritual needs

Adapted from reference 23.

Table 44.1 Mnemonics to Guide Spiritual Assessment

Author(s)	Components (Mnemonic)	Illustrative Questions
Maugens[48]	◆ S (spiritual belief system)	What is your formal religious affiliation?
	◆ P (personal spirituality)	Describe the beliefs and practices of your religion or spiritual system that you personally accept. What is the importance of your spirituality/religion in daily life?
	◆ I (integration with a spiritual community)	Do you belong to any spiritual or religious group or community? What importance does this group have to you? Does or could this group provide help in dealing with health issues?
	◆ R (ritualized practices and restrictions)	Are there specific elements of medical care that you forbid on religious/spiritual grounds?
	◆ I (implications for medical care)	What aspects of your religion/spirituality would you like me to keep in mind as I care for you? Are there any barriers to our relationship based on religious or spiritual issues?
	◆ T (terminal events planning)	As we plan for your care near the end-of-life, how does your faith impact your decisions?
Anandarajah & Hight[49]	◆ H (sources of hope)	What or who gives you hope?
	◆ O (organized religion)	Are you a part of an organized faith group? What does this group do for you as a person?
	◆ P (personal spirituality or spiritual practices)	What personal spiritual practices, like prayer or meditation, help you?
	◆ E (effects on medical care and/or end-of-life issues)	Do you have any beliefs that may affect how the healthcare team cares for you?
Puchalski & Ferrell[1]	◆ F (faith)	Do you have a faith belief? What is it that gives your life meaning?
	◆ I (import or influence)	What importance does your faith have In your life? How does your faith belief influence your life?
	◆ C (community)	Are you a member of a faith community? How does this support you?
	◆ A (address)	How would you like for me to integrate or address these issues in your care?
LaRocca-Pitts[47]	◆ F (faith)	What spiritual beliefs are important to you now?
	◆ A (availability/accessibility/applicability)	Are you able to find the spiritual nurture that you would like now?
	◆ C (coping/comfort)	How comforting/helpful are your spiritual beliefs at this time?
	◆ T (treatment)	How can I/we provide spiritual support?
Skalla & McCoy[43]	◆ M (moral authority)	Where does your sense of what to do come from? What guides you to decide what is right or wrong for you?
	◆ V (vocational)	What gives your life purpose? What work is important to you? What mission or role do you feel passionate about?
	◆ A (aesthetic)	What brings beauty or pleasure to your life now? How are you able to express your creativity? How do you deal with boredom?
	◆ S (social)	What people or faith community do you sense you belong with most? Do you belong to a community that nourishes you spiritually?
	◆ T (transcendent)	Who or what controls what happens in life? Who/what supports you when you are ill? Is there an Ultimate Other (an entity that is sacred, for example)? If so, how do you relate to it?
McEvoy (pediatric context)[28]	◆ B (belief system)	What religious or spiritual beliefs, if any, do members of your family have?
	◆ E (ethics or values)	What do you value most?
	◆ L (lifestyle)	What standards/values/rules for life does your family think important? What spiritual habits or activities does your family commit to because of spiritual beliefs? (e.g., Any sacred times to observe or diet you keep?)
	◆ I (involvement in spiritual community)	How connected to a faith community are you? Would you like us to help you reconnect with this group now?
	◆ E (education)	Are you receiving any form of religious education? How can we help you keep up with it?
	◆ F (near future events of spiritual significance for which to prepare the child)	Are there any upcoming religious ceremonies that you are getting ready for?

From: Johnston-Taylor E. Chapter 32: Spiritual Assessment. In: Ferrell B, Coyle N, Paice J, eds. *Textbook of Palliative Nursing.* 4th ed. New York, NY: Oxford University Press; 2015.

References

1. Puchalski CM, Ferrell B. *Making Health Care Whole: Integrating Spirituality into Patient Care.* West Conshohocken, PA: Templeton Press; 2010.

2. National Consensus Project for Quality Palliative Care. *Clinical Practice Guidelines for Quality Palliative Care.* 3rd ed. Pittsburgh, PA. 2013. Available at http://www.nationalconsensusproject.org. Accessed July 2, 2013.

3. Taylor EJ. Spiritual responses to cancer. In: Yarbro CH, Wujcik D, Gobel BH, eds. *Cancer Nursing: Principles and Practice.* 7th ed. Sudbury, MA: Jones & Bartlett; 2010.

4. Taylor EJ. *Religion: A Clinical Guide for Nurses.* New York, NY: Springer; 2012.

5. The Joint Commission. Spiritual assessment. 2009. Available at http://www.jointcommission.org/AccreditationPrograms/HomeCare/Standards/09_FAQs/PC/Spiritual_Assessment.htm. Accessed December 31, 2008.

6. Ferrell B, Coyle N. *The Nature of Suffering and the Goals of Nursing.* New York, NY: Oxford University Press, 2008.

7. Ferrell B, Baird P. Deriving meaning and faith in caregiving. *Sem Oncol Nurs.* 2012; 28(4): 256–61.

8. King SD, Fitchett G, Berry DL. Screening for religious/spiritual struggle in blood and marrow transplant patients. *Support Care Cancer.* 2013; 21(4): 993–1001.

9. Taylor EJ. *What Do I Say? Talking with Patients About Spirituality.* Philadelphia, PA: Templeton Press; 2007.

10. Williams AL. Perspectives on spirituality at the end of life: a meta-summary. *Palliat Support Care.* 2006; 4(4): 407–17.

11. Exline JJ, Prince-Paul M, Root BL, Peereboom KS. The spiritual struggle of anger toward God: a study with family members of hospice patients. *J Palliat Med.* 2013; 16(4): 369–75.

12. Newberry AG, Choi CW, Donovan HS, et al. Exploring spirituality in family caregivers of patients with primary malignant brain tumors across the disease trajectory. *Oncol Nurs Forum.* 2013; 40(3): E119–E125.

13. Kalish N. Evidence-based spiritual care: a literature review. *Curr Opin Support Palliat Care.* 2012; 6(2): 242–6.

14. Cobb M, Dowrick C, Lloyd-Williams M. What can we learn about the spiritual needs of palliative care patients from the research literature? *J Pain Symp Manag.* 2012; 43: 1105–19.

15. Chochinov HM, Kristjanson LJ, Breitbart W, et al. Effect of dignity therapy on distress and end-of-life experience in terminally ill patients: a randomised controlled trial. *Lancet Oncol.* 2011; 12(8): 753–62.

16. Delgado-Guay MO, Parsons HA, Hui D, De la Cruz MG, Thorney S, Bruera E. Spirituality, religiosity, and spiritual pain among caregivers of patients with advanced cancer. *Am J Hosp Palliat Care.* 2013; 30(5): 455–61.

17. Skalla KA, McCoy JP. Spiritual assessment of patients with cancer: the moral authority, vocational, aesthetic, social, and transcendent model. *Oncol Nurs Forum.* 2006; 33(4): 745–51.

18. Smith AR, DeSanto-Madeya S, Perez JE, et al. How women with advanced cancer pray: a report from two focus groups. *Oncol Nurs Forum.* 2012; 39(3): E310–6.

19. Vallurupalli M, Lauderdale K, Balboni MJ, et al. The role of spirituality and religious coping in the quality of life of patients with advanced cancer receiving palliative radiation therapy. *J Support Oncol.* 2012; 10: 81–7.

20. Balboni TA, Vanderwerker LC, Block SD, et al. Religiousness and spiritual support among advanced cancer patients and associations with end-of-life treatment preferences and quality of life. *J Clin Oncol.* 2007; 25(5): 555–60.

21. Astrow AB, Wexler A, Texeira K, He MK, Sumasy DP. Is failure to meet spiritual needs associated with cancer patients' perceptions of quality of care and their satisfaction with care? *J Clin Oncol.* 2007; 25(36): 5753–7.

22. Phelps AC, Lauderdale KE, Alcorn S, et al. Addressing spirituality within the care of patients at the end of life: perspectives of patients with advanced cancer, oncologists, and oncology nurses. *J Clin Oncol.* 2012; 30(20): 2538–44.

23. National Comprehensive Cancer Network. Distress Management (Version 2.2013). Available at http://www.nccn.org/professionals/physician_gls/f_guidelines.asp. Accessed May 20, 2014.

24. National Cancer Institute: PDQ® Spirituality in Cancer Care—Patient Version. Bethesda, MD: National Cancer Institute. Available at http://cancer.gov/cancertopics/pdq/supportivecare/spirituality/Patient. Last modified June 15, 2012. Accessed May 27, 2014.

25. National Cancer Institute: PDQ® Spirituality in Cancer Care—Health Professional Version. Bethesda, MD: National Cancer Institute. Available at http://cancer.gov/cancertopics/pdq/supportivecare/spirituality/HealthProfessional. Last modified September 20, 2012. Accessed May 27, 2014.

26. Heilferty CM. Spiritual development and the dying child: the pediatric nurse practitioner's role. *J Pediatr Health Care.* 2004; 18(6): 271–5.

27. Barnes LP, Plotnikoff GA, Fox K, Pendleton S. Spirituality, religion, and pediatrics: intersecting worlds of healing. *Pediatrics.* 2000; 106(4Suppl): 899–908.

28. McEvoy M. An added dimension to the pediatric health maintenance visit: the spiritual history. *J Pediatr Health Care.* 2000; 14(5): 216–20.

29. Taylor EJ, Davenport, F. Spiritual quality of life. In: King CR, Hinds PS, eds. *Quality of Life: From Nursing and Patient Perspectives.* 3rd ed. Sudbury, MA: Jones and Bartlett; 2012.

30. Taylor EJ. New Zealand hospice nurses' self-rated comfort in conducting spiritual assessment. *Inter J Palliat Care Nurs.* 2013; 19(4): 178–85.

31. Hodge DR. Administering a two-stage spiritual assessment in healthcare settings: a necessary component of ethical and effective care. *J Nurs Manag.* 2015; 23(1): 27–38.

32. Steinhauser KE, Voils CI, Clipp EC, Bosworth HB, Christakis NA, Tulsky JA. "Are you at peace?": one item to probe spiritual concerns at the end of life. *Arch Intern Med.* 2006; 166(1): 101–5.

33. Borneman T, Ferrell B, Puchalski CM. Evaluation of the FICA Tool for Spiritual Assessment. *J Pain Symptom Manage.* 2010; 40(2): 163–73.

34. Hodge D. A template for spiritual assessment: a review of the JCAHO requirements and guidelines for implementation. *Social Work.* 2006; 51(4): 317–26.

35. Peterman A, Fitchett, G, Brady MJ, Hernandez L, Cella D. Measuring spiritual well-being in people with cancer: the Functional Assessment of Chronic Illness Therapy-Spiritual Well-Being Scale (FACIT-Sp). *Ann Behav Med.* 2002; 24(1): 49–58.

36. Murphy PE, Canada AL, Fitchett G, et al. An examination of the 3-factor model and structural invariance across racial/ethnic groups for the FACIT-Sp: a report from the American Cancer Society's Study of Cancer Survivors-II (SCS-II). *Psychooncology.* 2010; 19(3): 264–72.

37. King M, Speck P, Thomas A. The royal free interview for spiritual and religious beliefs: development and validation of a self-report version. *Psychol Med.* 2001; 31(6): 1015–23.

38. Pargament K, Feuille M, Burdzy D. Current psychometric status of a short measure of religious coping. 2011; 2(1): 51–76.

39. Sharma RK, Astrow AB, Texeira K, Sulmasy DP. The Spiritual Needs Assessment for Patients (SNAP): development and validation of a comprehensive instrument to assess unmet spiritual needs. *J Pain Symp Manag.* 2012; 44(1): 44–51.

40. Lunder U, Furlan M, Simonic A. Spiritual needs assessments and measurements. *Curr Opin Support Palliat Care.* 2011; 5(3): 273–8.

41. Draper P. An integrative review of spiritual assessment: implications for nursing management. *J Nurs Manag.* 2012; 20(8): 970–80.

42. Monod S, Brennan M, Rochat E, Martin E, Rochat S, Bula CJ. Instruments measuring spirituality in clinical research: a systematic review. *J Gen Intern Med*. 2011; 26(11): 1345–57.

43. Skalla KA, McCoy JP. Spiritual assessment of patients with cancer: the moral authority, vocational, aesthetic, social, and transcendent model. *Oncol Nurs Forum*. 2006; 33(4): 745–51.

44. Byrne M. Spirituality in palliative care: what language do we need? Learning from pastoral care. *Int J Palliat Nurs*. 2007; 13(3): 118–21.

45. Timmins F, Kelly J. Spiritual assessment in intensive and cardiac care nursing. *Nurs Crit Care*. 2008; 13(3): 124–31.

46. Buck HG, McMillan SC. A psychometric analysis of the spiritual needs inventory in informal caregivers of patients with cancer in hospice home care. *Oncol Nurs Forum*. 2012; 39(4): E332–9.

47. LaRocca-Pitts M. A spiritual history tool: FACT. Available at http://www.professionalchaplains.org/uploadedFiles/pdf/FACT%20spiritual%. Accessed December 29, 2008.

48. Maugens TA. The SPIRITual history. *Arch Fam Med*. 1996; 5: 11–6.

49. Anandarajah G, Hight E. Spirituality and medical practice: using the HOPE questions as a practical tool for spiritual assessment. *Am Fam Physician*. 2001; 63(1): 81–9.

50. Vachon ML: Meaning, spirituality, and wellness in cancer survivors. *Semin Oncol Nurs*. 2008; 24(3): 218–25.

51. Otis-Green S, Ferrell B, Borneman T, Puchalski C, Uman G, Garcia A. Integrating spiritual care within palliative care: an overview of nine demonstration projects. *J Palliat Med*. 2012; 15(2): 154–62.

52. Cobb M, Puchalski CM, Rumbold B, eds. *Oxford Textbook of Spirituality in Healthcare*. New York, NY: Oxford University Press; 2012.

53. Puchalski C, Ferrell B, Virani R, et al. Improving the quality of spiritual care as a dimension of palliative care: the report of the consensus conference. *J Palliat Med*. 2009; 12(10): 885–904.

54. City of Hope Pain and Palliative Care Resource Center. COHPPRC Index. http://prc.coh.org. Accessed May 27, 2014.

CHAPTER 45

Communication Principles in Spiritual Care

Joan Carpenter and Patricia Berry

Key Points

◆ Empathetic curiosity is a position or stance the advanced practice registered nurse (APRN) can use that integrates verbal and nonverbal communication techniques to create shared understanding for people with life-limiting illness.

◆ The APRN needs to be aware of personal and professional boundaries, individual culture, and the physical and nonphysical environment when initiating spiritual communication.

◆ Techniques the APRN can use for effective communication include unstructured conversation, open-ended questioning, active listening, recognizing and discussing metaphors, identifying emotions, sharing responsibility for dialogue, and asking curious questions.

Case Study 1

Mr. S was a 70-year-old man with stage IV non-small cell lung cancer, metastatic to the thoracic spine, diagnosed 2 months earlier. He was undergoing chemotherapy and radiation therapy. His pain and symptoms were well managed, but he and his family were struggling with his life being "cut short." He had little social support outside of his family and did not identify with a religious affiliation: "I figure that I am a good person and God sees that … but I don't know why He did this to me." Mr. S had a very successful career in motorcycle sales, owned his dealership, and was financially stable. He had planned on retiring in a few years so he and his wife could travel and spend more time with one another and their grandchildren. Due to his disease, treatment, and resulting fatigue, he turned over his dealership to his two adult children to manage. His wife, 20 years younger than Mr. S, and their sons were not coping well with his illness. His weight loss bothered Mrs. S and she was constantly giving him nutritional supplements he didn't want to take. She tried to cook his favorite food but he was not interested in eating anything. She refused to attend his clinic visits, as she thought the palliative care team had given up on him. Their relationship was tense and getting worse; they barely spoke. Mr. S didn't like the way his sons were running the business he worked so hard to build. He was frustrated with his illness, God,

and his family. The APRN wanted to initiate a conversation about the conflicts he was experiencing and identify ways of coping, as well as provide caring presence and support.

The APRN first asked Mr. S if he had time to talk, confirmed he was comfortable, and found a quiet conference room near the clinic waiting room. The APRN silenced the team cellphone and asked team colleagues to cover the service for the next hour. The APRN pulled the chair out from behind the table and sat at an angle to Mr. S and leaned forward.

APRN: I've been concerned about you, Mr. S. When we first met, I remember you talking about how important your family is to you and how much fun you had when your boys were little. Lately, things don't seem to be going very well. [The APRN sits in silence and maintains eye contact.]

MR. S: [Sighs] It has been so hard. I love my family.

APRN: What are you most fond of about your family?

MR. S: We always had such good times together, even when we had very little money. We lived simply and relied on each other. It seems life was easier when it was simple. Now it's all so complicated. Everything has changed.

APRN: It's so hard when things change.

MR. S: Oh yes, so hard. How can we have fun when I'm going through all of this? I just can't wait until it is all over and I can get back to my life.

APRN: Mm. [APRN reaches out and touches Mr. S on the arm]

MR. S: [Shaking his head] I just don't know how we will continue like this …

APRN: It sounds frustrating.

MR. S: It's as if everyone has left me alone to deal with all of this. I feel abandoned by my wife and children.

After 3 months and two additional clinic visits, Mrs. S and one adult son, Andy, brought Mr. S to the emergency department: even though the dosage of his pain medication had been increased, his pain was worsening. The APRN was called to consult on his pain management and, before seeing him, consulted with the emergency department nurse and physician. They suspected that Mr. S's disease was worsening and was causing the increasing pain. After the APRN greeted them and asked Mr. S if it was okay for his wife and son to remain in the room, the APRN began by addressing Mr. S's pain and other symptoms. The APRN recommended an immediate dose of medication so Mr. S was more comfortable and could participate in the discussion. Suspecting the increased pain might be, in part, due to something more than disease progression, the APRN focused on Mr. S and his family's coping and understanding of his illness. The APRN silenced the pager, closed the door, sat on the stool in the room, and pulled it in to be close to the couple and their son. The APRN offered to get them something to drink and confirmed no one needed a break to use the restroom. The nursing assistant brought in a warm blanket for Mr. S after he stated he was chilly.

APRN: It looks to me like things have changed; what are your thoughts about how things are going?

MRS S: (mouth quivering) It's awful. The cancer isn't shrinking; he is weak and can't do anything anymore. I don't know how to help and feel like I am failing him.

MR. S: (tearfully) No, you're not, and things will get better, just wait.

APRN: This is upsetting to both of you.

MRS S: Yes it is. I don't understand why this is not getting better.

APRN: (leans forward and briefly touches Mrs. S on the sleeve) Mmm.

MRS S: He has had to give up everything. And I have too. We can't travel or do the things we used to enjoy. And our sons have had to completely take over the dealership.

ANDY: Mom, don't worry about that, we've had the best of teachers.

MR. S: Thanks, Andy, I know you and Ben are doing your best, but when it comes to me, I have no hope.

APRN: Hope?

MR. S: For this bad dream to go away.

APRN: How do you mean, "bad dream"?

MR. S: That I am living in this nightmare and suddenly I will wake up and things will be the way they used to be. That I would be strong enough to do the things important to me now.

MRS S: He also had hoped to go and visit his brother again. He and his brother had a silly argument when their father died and haven't spoken since then.

MR. S: I can't get it out of my head. It's all I think about now, isn't that silly?

APRN: Of course not, important things are never silly. (The APRN then sits in silence with the family and bears witness to the tears they share along with the realization that Mr. S's prognosis may be changing.)

The APRN visited the family in their home 2 weeks later. Mr. S was then being cared for by an affiliated hospice, who had requested a visit from the APRN to assess his symptoms. When the APRN arrived at the home, the APRN noticed a crucifix on the wall and a small novena altar with a statue of the Virgin Mary in the living room. The APRN recalled Mr. S describing himself as not religious. The APRN greeted Mr. S, who was in a hospital bed in the living room.

APRN: It is so nice to see you in your home, Mr. S. How have things been going?

MR. S: I feel like I am still living in a nightmare that I can't wake up from.

APRN: Tell me about how this feels like a nightmare. [The APRN leans forward and is quiet, while maintaining eye contact.]

MR. S: [silence and a long pause] This cancer. I'm so tired. I can't even walk up the stairs without being winded. Then, on a day like today I'll sleep all day and not be able to do anything else. But I want to keep on fighting this cancer—it just seems like I should feel better, not worse.[Mrs. S comes in with a bag of groceries and sits down.]

MRS. S: We planned on going on a trip this year—we have had to postpone everything. He doesn't even want to eat anything and we always enjoyed trying new restaurants. It feels like we are

living separate lives in the same house, but he is so sick; I know he can't help it [she begins to cry].

APRN: All of these changes are so hard. [The APRN puts her hand on Mrs. S's arm and leans forward.] What other things do you enjoy doing together?

MRS S: I don't know. Maybe going to the movies?

APRN: What was enjoyable about going to the movies?

MR. S: [smiles] Well, when we were younger we used to make out, do you remember? We used to go out on Friday nights—that was our time together.

MRS. S: [smiles] Oh yes, I remember those days—before children and not a care in the world.

APRN: Have you thought about watching a movie that you both enjoyed together in the past here at home? Maybe the two of you could snuggle together, too.

A month later the hospice nurse notified the APRN that Mr. S's condition had declined and he requested a visit. When the APRN arrived at the home, she was greeted by a tearful Mrs. S and their two sons. Mr. S was bedbound and appeared restless. The APRN knelt by the bed and took Mr. S's hand. He opened his eyes.

MR. S: [with a slight smile] It is so nice to see you. I was hoping you'd come again.

APRN: Your hospice nurse called me and asked me to come and of course, I came. It is nice to see you again, too. [The APRN maintains eye contact during a period of silence.]

MRS S: [to their two sons] Let's go into the other room and let your dad have some time with the nurse.

MR. S: I feel like my time is running out and I have failed everyone.

APRN: [leans forward] Mmm.

MR. S: I am no good to anyone anymore. My brother still won't talk with me and I feel so bad about leaving with this big rift between us. I tried and tried but he is so stubborn.

APRN: That was so important to you.

MR. S: It was [begins to cry] very important to leave here and have everything settled. I'm worried I'll be punished for that.

APRN: Punished?

MR. S: You know, not going to heaven.

APRN: Have you been able to talk to anyone about that, perhaps a trusted friend or a priest?

MR. S: I am not at all religious. My cousin put up that altar a couple of months ago, convinced there would be a miracle. It is nice she cares and all, but it sure didn't work, did it? The priest has come once to visit but we didn't talk about that.

APRN: [after a period of silence] What do *you* think about being punished?

MR. S: I don't believe in a God who punishes, especially when I have tried as hard as I have to get back with my brother. I believe in a God that forgives, too.

APRN: . . . and you have tried so hard to reach out to your brother.

MR. S: I have. Thanks for coming and listening to me. This was important for me.

Introduction

APRNs must be experts in identifying and addressing spiritual suffering, existential distress, and unmet spiritual and supportive care needs. While APRNs work alongside chaplains, social workers, physicians, therapists, and others to provide the best possible interdisciplinary palliative and spiritual care,[1] they must also be ready, within the limits of their preparation, to provide spiritual care directly.

Research demonstrates that patients with terminal illness who receive spiritual support at the end-of-life report improved quality of life.[2] Loss of hope and goal conflicts may lead to more intense symptoms and psychosocial distress for patients and families when making decisions during a serious illness.[3,4] These patients report moving between hope and despair throughout the illness. The APRN is in a position to identify their distress, initiate discussions, and consult the team members for ongoing assistance to reframe hope and develop realistic goals within the context of illness. Therefore, the APRN must promptly identify spiritual needs and initiate appropriate interventions.

Many hospital-based palliative care teams do not have a full-time chaplain on staff. Furthermore, APRNs who practice in nursing homes or assisted living facilities often do not have access to a chaplain on staff.[5] Residents in long-term care who request spiritual support may rely on chaplains from a previous or current religious affiliation. Hospital palliative care team chaplains may have multiple patient care responsibilities with other teams and units. They may be called to the bedside of trauma patients in the emergency department, may be requested at "code blue" resuscitation events, and may be summoned to labor and delivery for critically ill newborn infants and their parents. Therefore, chaplains may not be available for initial and/or ongoing spiritual assessment and management. To ensure that needs related to spirituality, suffering, and hope do not go unmet, APRNs need to be prepared to provide this care.[6]

The APRN serves as an expert clinician, team leader, and educator.[1] This role requires demonstrating effective spiritual communication for patient care, teaching, and serving as a role model for team members and students from all disciplines. The APRN must also coordinate and collaborate with the team chaplain and social worker to best meet patient and family spiritual needs.[4]

During and after assessment, APRNs will use a variety of communication techniques to deliver spiritual, religious, and existential dimensions of care. This chapter presents the principles in which APRNs need to be proficient to effectively provide spiritual interventions to patients with serious illness and their families. The principles are embedded within a framework known as empathetic curiosity.

What Is Empathetic Curiosity?

Empathetic curiosity is a person-centered approach that seeks to equalize the power balance during communication.[7] It integrates verbal and nonverbal communication techniques to create a shared understanding of a situation.[8] An empathetic and curious approach requires that APRNs speak to patients and family members with an openness and willingness to understand their experience of life with serious illness and the consequences (e.g., inconsistent decisions, difficult situations, or goal conflicts). In other words, the APRN creates a large and permissive "space" where patients and families can be who they are and express themselves in a safe, attentive, empathetic, and accepting environment.

The elements of empathetic curiosity are situating self, empathetic listening, allowing for vulnerability, taking a stance of acceptance, and maintaining a curious attitude. The APRN uses many communication techniques with this approach, such as keeping the conversation unstructured; asking short, open-ended questions; active listening; recognizing and discussing metaphors; identifying

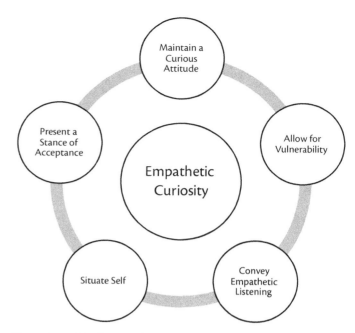

Figure 45.1 Vision for optimal spiritual communication in palliative care.

emotions; allowing shared responsibility for the content of the dialogue; and using curiosity or concern (e.g., conflict, worry, unease) as an impetus to ask questions.[7] Additional skills include employing the therapeutic use of silence and presence, avoiding disruptions, suspending assumptions, approaching the patient as a whole person, gaining permission to discuss confidential information, and displaying mutual understanding and respect[4,9] (Fig. 45.1).

Situating Self

APRNs perform several activities when "situating" themselves before talking with patients dealing with issues related to a life-limiting illness. Situating the self includes the physical setting and nonphysical influences, such as recognizing boundaries and cultural differences. Providing an environment conducive to in-depth personal conversation is essential by avoiding disruptions and being present (both in mind and body) with the patient and family throughout the conversation.[4]

Boundaries

Being aware of our individual beliefs as well as those of others is important. In caring for patients with life-limiting illness and their families, the APRN often enters into an intimate and intense relationship where maintaining a professional relationship can be challenging—but is essential. Boundaries are the guidelines we set in our relationships with other people. Reflecting upon our own experiences, values, faith, and cultural beliefs is the first step to creating these guidelines (Box 45.1). Recognizing when you may be meeting your own needs rather than the patient's or imposing your individual values upon others can be difficult. Checking in with colleagues and mentors on your perception of maintaining boundaries is often helpful.

Maintaining a therapeutic relationship is important in patient and family care and is often a balancing act between over- and

Box 45.1 Questions to Ask Oneself During Communication to Maintain Boundaries

◆ How does this situation make me feel?

◆ Am I separating my beliefs from the patient's/family's beliefs? If so, how?

◆ What am I doing to ensure that my values are not affecting my decisions for this patient/family?

◆ Do I feel comfortable talking with this patient/family?

◆ Am I acting in the best interest of the patient/family? If not, why?

◆ How would my coworkers view this situation?

under-involvement. Signs of over-involvement include revealing an excessive amount of personal information, spending unnecessary time after standard work hours to meet patient needs, and believing that you are the only one on the team who can handle a patient's or family's requests. In Case Study 2, the APRN stepped outside his boundaries and stopped collaborating with his team. Ultimately, it is the patients and families who suffer from this type of behavior.

Case Study 2

John, an APRN, had been working with the palliative care consult team for a little less than a year. The team included John, the full-time APRN, one full-time social worker, a part-time physician, a chaplain, and a clinical pharmacist. John arrived at work at 8 a.m. for the team's morning meeting, but was often rounding on patients well into the evening hours. He had started missing social activities with friends and family, deciding that his work demanded his presence to provide the best care for patients and their families. His work hours had slowly overtaken time he previously set aside for exam preparation for national certification in palliative care, a requirement for his position. He had stopped collaborating with the social worker and chaplain to assist patients with advance directives, "I just do them myself." He became irritated with the other members of the team because he perceived they were not as dedicated as he was to patient care. He was defensive when his supervisor questioned his behavior. He revealed that he felt he was the only one who could meet the patient and family needs. John's supervisor worked with him to limit his work week to 40 hours and to delegate responsibilities to other team members.

Under-involvement also threatens the therapeutic relationship and interrupts successful communication. Behaviors like distancing, lack of concern, or abandonment signal under-involvement.[10]

Culture

We all bring certain beliefs and values to professional relationships. Cultural beliefs help us make sense of the situations we encounter. Our cultural identity can be related to gender, race, ethnicity, religion, nationality, language, or a host of other factors, including socioeconomic class and common interests (e.g.,

political affiliation). Ideally, we are able to maintain our own cultural identity without implying that others must subscribe to our system of behaviors or convictions.[11,12]

The APRN must be sensitive to cultural diversity and recognize how culture affects communication and decision making. This is even more challenging for the APRN during discussions about spiritual issues at the end-of-life as it requires constant awareness of healthcare literacy, use and implications of words and language ("linguistic diversity"),[13(p 1043)] attitudes about curative treatment, and beliefs about dying, while putting one's individual beliefs and faith in the proper place.

The APRN should also consider the patient's and family's cultural background and recognize that in some cultures truth telling and frank or upfront discussions are not preferred for giving information to the patient and family. For example, Zuni Indian elders believe that words can be sealed and you can speak illness into being.[14] Family members who identify with the Asian culture may withhold information from the patient in an effort to help the patient maintain hope.[11] In other situations, low health literacy impedes understanding, and illness comprehension is compromised during periods of great emotional stress.[15] APRNs must never stereotype individuals based on their culture or background. APRNs can best help patients and family members by encouraging them to share their beliefs, perceptions, and understanding about the illness and their preferences for conversation and spiritual support.[16,17]

Language is powerful, and culturally competent APRNs select their words carefully. Being aware of the implications of one's words is key. For example, clinicians may think offering the phrase "There is nothing left to do" will persuade a patient or family to accept impending death. However, in some cultural traditions, words like these may lead to a miscommunication that no one can *help* the patient (e.g., alleviate symptoms, provide support and presence, resolve goal conflicts) before and during imminent death. This may cause the family to lose trust in the palliative care team and APRN.

Physical Presence and Environment

For these serious conversations, space that is private, with minimal opportunities for interruptions, is ideal. Space may be physical (e.g., the capacity of a room) or nonphysical (e.g., feelings or emotions, such as a "safe" space). APRNs should optimize both to provide the most effective environment to communicate and provide presence. The area chosen must be private and comfortable. The room should not be too hot or too cold; simply asking a patient or family member if the temperature is comfortable might be all that is needed.

Maximizing the nonphysical "safe" space includes developing a climate in which patients and family members feel able to express themselves without fearing judgment. Patients must feel free to say anything or ask any question about their illness and receive honest answers. Consider all information as protected health information and keep it confidential unless the patient permits sharing the discussion with family or friends who may be present.

Asking a patient's permission to talk in front of visitors is important. Never assume that, because a person is visiting the patient, it is appropriate to discuss protected and private health information. In addition, ask a patient or family whom they want involved in the discussions. See Chapter 40 on Family Meetings.

Set your phone or pager on vibrate or mute during conversations with patients and families; this demonstrates respect and undivided attention by eliminating distractions. In Case Study 1 at the beginning of the chapter, before beginning to talk with Mr. S, the APRN was proactive and took steps to minimize disruptions. Interruptions hinder good spiritual care.[4]

Spiritual care communication takes time, especially in the beginning, when the APRN is trying to develop a relationship with a patient and family. Setting aside enough time can be difficult, but it is necessary. Both patients and healthcare providers report that inadequate time and "loss of the human touch"[4(p 767)] are barriers to delivering spiritual care. The APRN must be honest about any time constraints and should set up additional meetings as needed to continue the conversation.

Empathetic Listening

The word *empathy* has its origins in the Greek word *pathos*, which translates as *feeling*.[18] To be empathetic means to share in another's emotions or thoughts, as well as his or her feelings. By using empathy, APRNs can display their compassion to a patient and family. In turn, compassion shows concern, sensitivity, and support.

Empathetic listening is best practiced by concentrating on what a speaker is saying and sensing and then matching his or her mood. APRNs demonstrate empathy by using verbal and nonverbal communication strategies.[19] Provide the speaker with your complete and undivided attention. Allow the speaker to finish his or her thoughts without interrupting. Don't hesitate to leave periods of silence. Skills like active and deep listening, compassionate presence, and allowing for shared responsibility in the dialogue help the APRN achieve empathetic listening (Box 45.2).

Active Listening

The use of short phrases like "uh-huh," "mmm-hmm," "okay," along with attentive nonverbal cues, signals to the patient that the APRN is showing interest and trying to understand what is being said.[19] Active listening is a key technique demonstrating empathy.

Often APRNs can paraphrase, rather than parrot or repeat phrases or words to show active listening and to encourage the patient to continue speaking.

Deep listening is another technique closely associated with active listening. It is more closely tied to heightened attention while listening and can lead to an expanded awareness of what is being said. While listening deeply, we can feel another's emotions. Listening deeply requires an APRN to "hold the pain and suffering of another."[9] Deep listening conveys understanding of the real and unspoken meaning of another's expressions (verbal and nonverbal) and does not necessarily require any response on the part of the APRN. The APRN might demonstrate deep listening by practicing self-awareness and self-control. For example, the APRN can minimize his or her own inattention by not planning the next statement, suspending the urge to interrupt the speaker, and setting aside the "agenda" of the meeting. Active and deep listening requires attending to a patient and family beyond just "being there"[20,21] (Box 45.3).

Allow for Shared Responsibility

Throughout the conversations in Case Study 1, the APRN allowed the patient and family to control the pace and content of the exchanges. The APRN took the opportunity to explore Mr. S's "nightmare" comment to learn about the meaning of the illness to the patient and ultimately to identify the source of conflict. The APRN also used invitational silence, creating an environment where Mr. S could take his time to think about his answer.[22] When the APRN visited the family at home, the conversation revealed that Mr. and Mrs. S felt the illness had separated their lives and relationship. They were coping with uncertainty, lacked social support, and were grappling with the meaning of the illness.

Compassionate Presence

Compassionate presence involves offering support and being present in the moment. Deep listening and compassionate presence have been described as spiritual interventions focused on the whole person.[9] Being present in the moment with a patient or

---

Box 45.2 Key Features of Empathetic Listening

- *Body orientation:* Facing toward the patient or family member demonstrates interest in the conversation.
- *Eye contact:* Depending on cultural norms, direct eye contact signals a nonverbal connection between speakers.
- *Head nodding:* Moving the head in an up-and-down motion demonstrates that the spoken words are not just heard, but also understood.
- *Voice tone and rhythm:* Allow the patient or family member to set the speaking style (e.g., serious, humorous, logical, intimate) and attempt to match it.
- *Minimal interruptions:* Permit patients and family members to verbalize their thoughts and emotions.
- *Silence:* Give patients and families the necessary time to absorb, organize, and collect their thoughts.

Box 45.3 Exercise to Practice or Prepare for Deep Listening

- During a conversation with a friend or family member, practice putting aside your beliefs, opinions, and judgment about the topic while the other person is talking.
- Identify a place (office, meeting room) where deep listening is more natural. Spend some time in this space. Imagine staying silent, just sitting and listening while another person is talking.
- Be deliberate in listening. Think about the questions you are asking and whether they seek to improve understanding or intend to judge.
- Prior to a conversation with a patient or family member, take a few minutes alone to mindfully breathe in and out, repeating "breathe in stillness (or silence, calm, quiet, concentration), breathe out distraction (or chaos, confusion, irritation, uncertainty)."

family and really trying to understand and relate to their words, stories, and emotions epitomizes deep and active listening.

When practicing compassionate presence, the APRN also recognizes that it is difficult to "tune out" distractions. It is important to minimize disruptions before starting the conversation and then to actively listen to what is being said and refrain from offering solutions or judgments.[21]

Allowing for Vulnerability

Being vulnerable is an essential element of spiritual care because vulnerability enhances the APRN's ability to demonstrate empathy and can encourage the patient and family to be vulnerable in return.[9,23,24] Identifying emotions and using silence in a therapeutic manner allow for vulnerability. Identifying and supporting the patient and family's emotions and permitting the therapeutic use of silence can be uncomfortable and can make the APRN feel susceptible to the emotions in the room. For example, when a patient or family member is crying, silence and presence are often the only therapeutic intervention necessary.

Deciding when to offer a tissue (which may cause the person to stop crying) is a personal professional practice decision. Some clinicians hesitate to offer tissues when someone is crying so as to not stifle the expression of sadness, grief, or anguish. Crying evokes a powerful personal response, and the APRN may tear up. For some, the only expression of anguish is through crying, and by delaying the expression the APRN may hinder the person's grief and coping. One way to handle this is to have a tissue box in reach of the patient or family members during difficult conversations so they can reach for a tissue if they need one.

The most common negative emotions people with advanced cancer express are anger, sadness, and fear.[25] Other patients describe feeling punished, hopeless, depressed, and frustrated.[4] Recognizing these emotions and taking the opportunity to explore emotions require vulnerability on the part of both the APRN and the patient and family. APRNs will never have all the answers or be able to solve all a patient's problems. This vulnerability, or feeling helpless, is challenging for everyone, including the APRN and the entire interdisciplinary team. Maintaining an openness to being vulnerable, such as feeling helpless and not knowing all the answers, while bearing witness is central to effective communication and professional caregiving.[24]

Identifying Emotions

The APRN needs to be able to identify and differentiate emotions, such as shame, guilt, fear, sadness, or anger. After that, the APRN needs to ask questions about these emotions to prompt further dialogue during discussion about serious illness. This therapeutic communication technique requires the APRN to be open not only to another person's feelings but also to the continued discussion of the emotions. Often this is challenging and difficult for the APRN; researchers have shown that APRNs respond verbally only 30% of the time to emotional concerns during discussions with persons with advanced cancer.[25]

In Case Study 1, notice how the APRN picked up on the emotional cues, in particular "shaking" and "mouth quivering." Paying close attention to nonverbal communication helps the APRN focus on feelings and emotions that the speaker is experiencing. Note there was no parroting, paraphrasing, or summarizing of the spoken

content with this technique. However, the APRN demonstrated an openness and vulnerability by using appropriate touch and silence and by acknowledging emotions and validating feelings.

Therapeutic Silence

Bearing witness and holding silence can also be a healing intervention. Silence does not always need to be broken by the APRN or patient; silence also does not mean people do not want to talk any more. Sometimes there are no words for intense emotions, and the APRN can demonstrate this by remaining silent.

Three types of silence have been described: compassionate, invitational, and awkward.[22] Compassionate silence conveys empathy and the understanding that often there are no words for intense emotions. Invitational silence can be used while exploring metaphors or using open-ended questions (i.e., allowing time to think about an answer, as the APRN did in Case Study 1 when he explored the "bad dream" metaphor). Awkward silence is a forced silence that may seem long and feel unnatural. The danger of awkward silence is the risk that the APRN may appear inattentive or unfocused.

Stance of Acceptance

During communication about spiritual issues, empathetic curiosity requires a stance of acceptance and nonjudgment, which is realized through mutual understanding and respect. Showing respect for another person's worldview by validating his or her thoughts and feelings demonstrates that the APRN accepts the person and what he or she is going through. Recognizing that another person's values are valid and important requires us to suspend assumptions and offer unconditional acceptance.[26] Unconditional acceptance is compassion at work.

Some patients may elect to pursue aggressive treatments that leave them fatigued and too ill to attend an event like a wedding or graduation, even though they identify these events as important to them. APRNs and other team members or family members may feel frustrated knowing that the disease is progressing and the patient's goals for a better quality of life are not aligned with the goals of aggressive treatment. However, maintaining a stance of acceptance during conversations about what appears to be a mismatch between goals and treatment choices upholds acceptance and conveys compassion without judging the patient and his or her decisions. This may open up the space in which the patient feels free to reconsider his or her choices.

Mutual Understanding and Respect

Spirituality and religiosity are different concepts. Spiritual care needs include a great deal more than a connection to religion. Often, to feel well spiritually, patients feel a need to resolve unfinished business, want to continue to control daily and life decisions, or just want to maintain a positive attitude.[4] The APRN demonstrates appreciation for these dimensions of spiritual wellness by encouraging the patient to identify what is most important to him or her and to devise ways to make these things possible.

Having respect for the patient's or family members' hopes and goals for what they want to achieve during the illness is essential. Sharing in the patient's experience builds the relationship.[26] Even though Mr. S could not reconcile with his brother, he was able to start working on forgiveness in order to find peace. The APRN provided respect for his situation and did not attempt to solve the problem or judge Mr. S by telling him he should "not worry about it" or "focus on something else that's more positive." Instead, the APRN continued with active listening and asked curious questions to clarify the meaning of Mr. S's words.

Suspend Assumptions

The phrase *suspend assumptions* means to refrain from making a judgment based on an observation, appearance, or impression. While the APRN recalled Mr. S had no religious connection, the APRN also did not assume that had changed. Instead, in their final visit, the APRN let Mr. S take the conversation where it was meant to go and gently brought up talking with a priest.

Another facet of suspending assumptions is the idea of withholding an opinion. In their final conversation, the APRN did not provide a response like, "God doesn't punish!" or "I also believe in a loving God," nor did the APRN try to resolve the quandary for Mr. S. The APRN asked Mr. S to reflect on his values and beliefs to elucidate meaning from his conflict between feeling punished and forgiven.[27]

Maintaining a Curious Attitude

Maintaining a curious attitude requires the APRN to be "in the moment" with the patient and family and to use unstructured conversation and open-ended questioning. The patient's response to the content of the conversation (e.g., hesitant, eager, with emotion) and his or her willingness to share feelings indicates his or her openness to the topic. Gaining permission to initiate and continue conversations, learning about conflict, and discussing the patient's and family's use of metaphor all help to convey a caring and curious attitude.

Conversation that connects with, and responds to, a patient and family can be described along the continuum of "leading and following."[28] This is a complex process; the APRN lets the patient lead the dialogue and the APRN follows, asking questions that show interest. At other times, the APRN may lead the conversation and encourage the patient to follow by asking curious questions that evoke elaboration on a topic (Case Study 3). During discussions, the APRN must determine or demonstrate readiness to continue talking about difficult topics.

Case Study 3

Susan, an experienced and certifed hospice and palliative APRN, met with a family whose mother was recently diagnosed with dysphagia after a major cerebrovascular infarct. The mother's prognosis was poor and complicated by decisions regarding medically administered nutrition. The family was told that she might live for years with a feeding tube, but her quality of life might never improve over what it was at that time. Without an advance directive, the family members relied on their mother's religious beliefs to make decisions. The APRN led the conversation by asking the daughter, "What decisions did your mother make based on her beliefs and values?" The daughter responded with hesitancy and directed the conversation toward religious teachings. The APRN allowed the daughter to lead the conversation to a Bible verse and asked, "What does that verse mean to you?" and "What did the verse mean to your mother?"

When exploring spiritual issues—how beliefs, rituals, and customs affect decision making and feelings of distress and hope—the nurse must be open to letting the patient and family lead the discussion. This can be challenging for clinicians, who are often seen as the "leader" by patients and peers. Some clinicians find it helpful to put themselves in the position of being the ones who are informed by the patient or family so they can avoid making assumptions and accept the patient and family without judgment.[23,26] Viewing the "patient as teacher" is another way to provide optimal spiritual care.[23(p 1067)]

Clinicians must be mindful of the words that are spoken and the ones left unspoken. Words that are left unsaid can identify areas of distress, avoidance, and an effort to protect oneself. Gaining permission to continue discussing a complex issue is important. If you are unsure if a patient wants to continue a discussion, ask, "Is it okay if we continue talking and I ask a couple of questions to clarify what you said?" (Fig. 45.2).

Unstructured Interview Style

The APRN should adopt an unstructured interview style, as opposed to a structured style (e.g., a set assessment or interview tool). A structured interview shifts the balance of power from the interviewee to the interviewer. In contrast, by trying to equalize their power, the APRN opens a large and permissive space for the patient to talk. Unstructured interviews allow both parties to guide the conversation.[29] Both can raise topics of importance. Unstructured interviews follow the normal course of a conversation.

APRNs might find a structured interview useful during the initial assessment of a patient's spiritual practices, but an ongoing assessment or therapeutic communication should resemble normal conversation. In an attempt to discover important information, an APRN might prepare several questions for the patient and/or family to review or consider ahead of time. This approach allows for flexibility based on the patient's comfort and pace of conversation. In this way, APRNs can build rapport with patients and families.

Open-Ended Questions

Open-ended questions can elicit patient's feelings, perceptions, and understanding about their circumstances.[4] In Case Study 1, a question asked by the APRN elicited fond memories about Mr. S's family. Then Mr. S recalled how things had changed and how he felt abandoned. The contrast of being surrounded by those who care about him yet feeling so alone had created an internal struggle. He felt neglected by those he is closest to and on whom he relied for support.

Open-ended questions or statements can be phrased as follows:

What is this [feeling, symptom] like for you?

Can you tell me about [this experience]?

How does this make you feel?

Tell me about your relationship with your [family or friend].

These statements encourage a meaningful subjective response. Often these questions begin with "why," "what," and "how" phrases. Ask them using a gentle and open cadence and tone.

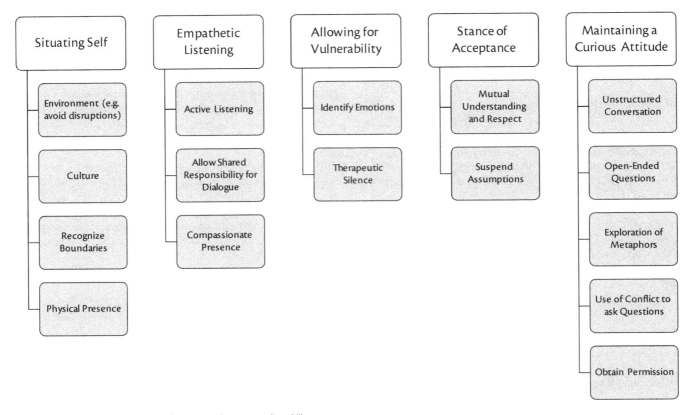

Figure 45.2 Essential communication elements and corresponding skills

Obtain Permission

Communication during family meetings is designed to improve understanding of the illness process and treatments and to clarify the goals of care in the context of the life-limiting illness. The APRN must obtain permission to discuss sensitive aspects of a patient's healthcare and spirituality. Finding out what role the patient wants family members to play and how individual requests for information should be handled demonstrates consideration for the patient's preferences. Building trust in these conversations lays the groundwork for future interactions.[30]

Recall that in Case Study 1, before initiating a conversation with Mr. S, the APRN asked if he wanted his family members to stay in the room, rather than assuming that he would. This demonstrated that the APRN acknowledged who was in control of the situation—the patient, not the APRN.

Recognize and Discuss Metaphor

In Case Study 1, Mr. S used the metaphor "a bad dream" to express how he felt about his illness: he equated it to a nightmare, evoking fear, sadness, and despair. He said he hoped the nightmare would end and suddenly life would be the same way it was before. This was a starting point for the APRN to help reframe Mr. S's hope.

Research demonstrates that higher levels of hope are associated with fewer symptoms, including depression.[3] Hope should focus on meaningful goals that are possible within the patient's goals of care and wishes. Examples include planning leisure activities with friends or family, planning a day or overnight trip, and spending time with loved ones. APRNs can help patients and families to move away from hope for a "miracle" to more realistic short- and long-term activities that exemplify their values and goals within the time remaining. In Case Study 1, Mr. S's desire to reconcile with his brother was unfortunately not an attainable goal.

Using Conflict

In Case Study 1, when the conversation turned toward activities that Mr. and Mrs. S no longer could do together and the phrase "living separate lives" was used, the APRN used this opportunity to ask a question—showing curiosity—about activities the couple enjoyed doing together. This moment provided a time of reflection for them about what kinds of activities brought the couple close and how they might be able to recreate that closeness. This helped the couple plan a way through the illness experience with a short-term, attainable goal.

Summary

The palliative APRN serves as an expert clinician, team leader, and educator. In this role, the APRN must be prepared to collaborate with team members and deliver effective spiritual care. Throughout this chapter, therapeutic communication techniques have been presented in the unique framework called empathetic curiosity. By using this approach to spiritual communication, APRNs can demonstrate all the elements of successful and meaningful communication to deliver the best possible palliative care to patients and their family members with life-limiting illness.

References

1. Hospice and Palliative Nurses Association. *HPNA Position Statement: Value of the Advanced Practice Registered Nurse in Palliative Care*. Pittsburgh, PA: Hospice and Palliative Nurses Association; 2010.

2. Balboni TA, Paulk ME, Balboni MJ, et al. Provision of spiritual care to patients with advanced cancer: associations with medical care and quality of life near death. *J Clin Oncol*. 2010; 28: 445–52.

3. Berendes D, Keefe FJ, Somers TJ, Kothadia SM, Porter LS, Cheavens JS. Hope in the context of lung cancer: relationships of hope to symptoms and psychological distress. *J Pain Symptom Manage*. 2010; 40: 174–82.

4. Edwards A, Pang N, Shiu V, Chan C. Review: The understanding of spirituality and the potential role of spiritual care in end-of-life and palliative care: a meta-study of qualitative research. *Palliat Med*. 2010; 24: 753–70.

5. Nichols SW. Examining the impact of spiritual care in long-term care. *Omega J Death Dying*. 2013; 67: 75–184.

6. Wynne L. Spiritual care at the end of life. *Nursing Standard*. 2013; 28: 41–5.

7. McEvoy P, Plant R. Dementia care: using empathic curiosity to establish the common ground that is necessary for meaningful communication. *J Psychiatric Mental Health Nurs*. 2014; 21: 477–82.

8. McEvoy P, Baker D, Plant R, Hylton K, Mansell W. Empathic curiosity: resolving goal conflicts that generate emotional distress. *J Psychiatric Mental Health Nurs*. 2013; 20: 273–8.

9. Baird P. Spiritual care intervention. In: Ferrell B, Coyle N, Paice J, eds. *Oxford Textbook of Palliative Nursing*. 4th ed. New York, NY: Oxford University Press; 2015; 546–53.

10. National Council of State Boards of Nursing. *A Nurse's Guide to Professional Boundaries*. Chicago, IL: National Council of State Boards of Nursing; 2011.

11. Saccomano SJ, Abbatiello GA. Cultural considerations at the end of life. *Nurse Practitioner*. 2014; 39: 24–32.

12. Amoah CF. The central importance of spirituality in palliative care. *Intl J Palliat Nurs*. 2011; 17: 353–8.

13. Broom A, Good P, Kirby E, Lwin Z. Negotiating palliative care in the context of culturally and linguistically diverse patients. *Intern Med J*. 2013; 43: 1043–9.

14. Moss M. "Thinking inside of the box": Zuni Indian elders' construction of aging. *J Religion Spirituality Aging*. 2008; 19: 37–56.

15. Maciejewski P. Emotional numbness modifies the effect of end-of-life discussions on end-of-life care. *J Pain Symptom Manage*. 2013; 45: 841.

16. Wittenberg-Lyles E, Goldmith J, Ferrell B, Ragan S. Orientation and opportunity. In: *Communication in Palliative Nursing*. New York, NY: Oxford University Press; 2013:59–82.

17. Wiener L, McConnell DG, Latella L, Ludi E. Cultural and religious considerations in pediatric palliative care. *Palliat Support Care*. 2013; 11: 47–67.

18. Agnes M, ed. *Webster's New World Dictionary*. 2nd ed. Boston, MA: Houghton Mifflin Harcourt; 2013.

19. Kelley KJ, Kelley MF. Teaching empathy and other compassion-based communication skills. *J Nurses Prof Dev*. 2013; 29: 321–4.

20. Wright S. The beauty of silence. *Nursing Standard*. 2006; 20: 18–20.

21. Ferrell B. Deriving meaning and faith in caregiving. *Semin Oncol Nurs*. 2012; 28: 256.

22. Back AL, Bauer-Wu SM, Rushton CH, Halifax J. Compassionate silence in the patient—clinician encounter: a contemplative approach. *J Palliat Med*. 2009; 12: 1113–7.

23. Vermandere M, Lepeleire JD, Van Mechelen W, Warmenhoven F, Thoonsen B, Aertgeerts B. Spirituality in palliative home care: a framework for the clinician. *Supportive Care In Cancer*. 2013; 21: 1061–9.

24. Boston P, Towers A, Barnard D. Forum. Embracing vulnerability: risk and empathy in palliative care. *J Palliat Care*. 2001; 17: 248–53.

25. Alexander SC, Pollak KI, Morgan PA, et al. How do non-physician clinicians respond to advanced cancer patients' negative expressions of emotions? *Support Care Cancer*. 2011; 19: 155–9.

26. Ward CC, Reuter T. *Strength-Centered Counseling: Integrating Postomodern Apporaches and Skills with Practice*. Thousand Oaks, CA: Sage Publications, Inc.; 2011.

27. Bruce A, Schreiber R, Petrovskaya O, Boston P. Longing for ground in a ground(less) world: a qualitative inquiry of existential suffering. *BMC Nursing*. 2011; 10: 1–9.

28. Considine J, Miller K. The dialectics of care: communicative choices at the end of life. *Health Communication*. 2010; 25: 165–74.

29. Roulston K. *Reflective Interviewing: A Guide to Theory and Practice*. London: Sage; 2010.

30. Kirk P, Kirk I, Kristjanson LJ. What do patients receiving palliative care for cancer and their families want to be told? A Canadian and Australian qualitative study. *BMJ*. 2004; 328: 1343.

CHAPTER 46

Life Review

Mimi Jenko and James C. Pace

Key Points

- Life review addresses the spiritual components of a person, such as his or her hopes and fears, purpose and meaning, guilt and forgiveness, faith community, inner sources of power, and beliefs about an afterlife.

- Through active listening and a nonjudgmental approach, life review allows the palliative advanced practice registered nurse (APRN) to recast the past in the context of the present.

- Life review can be used to guide goals-of-care conversations, to aid a person in preparing for his or her own death, or to facilitate bereavement interventions with bereaved families.

- The three interconnected components of life review are recontextualizing, forgiving, and living an unclaimed life.

Case Study

A 42-year-old man suffered a massive brain injury in a motorcycle accident. Palliative care was consulted to assist the family members, who had made the agonizing decision to withdraw life support but were sharply divided with regard to organ donation. Their loud, arguing voices had disrupted the trauma intensive care unit, and a stalled treatment plan had prompted a "stat" palliative care consult. To set a less divisive tone, the palliative APRN tried to evoke earlier and happier memories to gain the context of a life lived. Over the next 90 minutes, memories of a "larger-than-life" person arose: romances with multiple women, an infectious laugh, and an adventuresome spirit. The palliative APRN gently guided the conversation to philanthropic themes. Although the patient did not participate in formal nonprofit work, the family recalled that he always contributed to the Girl Scouts during cookie drives, donated to Little League team carwashes, and had a "soft spot" for military veterans. The family realized that their loved one had a charitable, giving spirit toward others, which eventually led to a peaceful family consensus for organ donation.

According to the Hospice and Palliative Nurses Association *Position Statement on Spiritual Care*,[1] human beings are intrinsically spiritual and are in relationship with self, others, nature, and the significant or sacred. Spirituality encompasses universal human needs and includes the belief in the potential of the human spirit. Direct clinical care by the APRN is characterized by the use of a holistic viewpoint that addresses a cohesive and inclusive view of the patient and one's own overall health experience.[2] APRNs embody a holistic perspective that promotes health and wellness, assists with healing, and helps to prevent or alleviate suffering.[2,3]

Holistic nursing embodies the authentic presence of the nurse, which Cumbie[4] views as an essential component of human-to-human interaction. With this viewpoint, human beings are fundamentally good and have an inborn capacity for self-healing.[3] The palliative nurse also recognizes and attends to multiple ways that the environment (to include social, physical, financial, emotional, and spiritual aspects) affects one's health and illness.[2] The palliative nurse strives to assist the patient to find meaning and purpose in his or her life, so that he or she might better find comfort, peace, and harmony.[2,3] The palliative APRN is uniquely educated and prepared to help patients and families find relief, support, and meaning in chronic and potentially life-threatening illness. The palliative APRN understands that a patient's spirituality may be of special concern as health deteriorates. Spiritual care, provided best through an interdisciplinary team approach, entails an assessment and monitoring of the multiple aspects involved with the spiritual dimension of living, to include a life review.[1]

The processes of life review address the spiritual components of a person, such as his or her hopes, fears, purpose and meaning, guilt and forgiveness, faith community, inner sources of power, and beliefs about an afterlife.[1] Empirical patterns of knowing inform the science of nursing practice through scientific data, yet personal patterns of knowing support the nurse–patient relationship through reflections, listening, and centering. This type of knowing is gathered through autobiographical stories.[5] The construct of life review has often been compared and contrasted with several associated constructs, listed in Box 46.1.[6-8] The memory of one's life accomplishments, hopes, and goals has a large role to play in our understanding of emotional health and well-being as well as emotional distress and illness.[7] For some people, life review may be painful and stressful and possibly problematic, indicating the need for further assessment and possible therapy.[7] For others, the process of remembering one's accomplishments, joys, and achievements that define a life well lived sets the stage for a good and peaceful death.[1]

What Is Life Review?

Life review as a formal concept has its roots in lifespan developmental psychology.[12] According to Butler[12] and Erikson,[13] one's development is formed by the myriad events and circumstances

---

Box 46.1 Selected Definitions

Storytelling

According to the National Storytelling Network, storytelling is an ancient art form of human expression that uses words and actions to reveal the content of the story while encouraging the imagination of the listener.[9] Storytelling involves five components: (1) interactive communication between the storyteller and the listener (2) employing the use of words (3) with the use of actions, such as vocalization and physical motions or gestures, (4) that together present a story (narrative) (5) that encourages the imagination of the listener. The completed story "happens" in the mind of the listener, who "co-creates" the story as seen through personal experiences, beliefs, and understandings.[9]

Reminiscence

"Unstructured autobiographical storytelling with the goal of communicating and teaching or informing others, remembering positive past events, and enhancing positive feelings."[8(p 541)] "The process of thinking or telling someone about past experiences that are personally significant ... a therapeutic mode for promoting self-acceptance and psychological health."[8(p 541)]

Remembering/Reminiscence Therapy

A simple form of therapy that "encourages the patient to talk about earlier memories. It's generally offered to people in their later years who have mood or memory problems, or need help dealing with the difficulties that come along with aging ... this treatment has a small but significant effect on mood, self-care, the ability to communicate and well-being."[7(p 1)] In short, it is the use of life histories—written, oral, or both—to improve psychological well-being.[7]

Life Review

The process of life review is much more structured than simple reminiscence. "Usually covers the entire life-span and is most often performed in a one-to-one format. Rather than simply describing past events (as in simple reminiscence), life-review focuses on the (re-)evaluation of life events and on the integration of positive and negative life events in a coherent life story."[8(p 541)] "Life review is the systematic and structured process of recalling past events and memories in an effort to find meaning in and achieve resolution of one's life. Although traditionally used in gerontology, life review is applicable with any person facing the end of life."[10(p 159)]

Life Review Therapy

This type of therapy involves the use of life review with persons with serious mental health issues, such as depression. It is characterized by linking life review to the likely causal factors of the emotional distress. Life-review therapy is focused on diminishing anger, bitterness, and regret while fostering a positive view of one's past. The therapy often explicitly applies therapeutic techniques that have been developed and successfully employed in other therapeutic frameworks, such as cognitive therapy, problem-solving therapy, or narrative therapy. [8]

Dignity Therapy

A brief, individualized psychotherapeutic intervention designed to address psychosocial and existential distress among terminally ill patients. Such distress has often been linked to the notion of suffering and has been described in terms of the challenges that threaten the intactness of a person. The intervention is designed to engender a sense of meaning and purpose, thereby reducing suffering and distress.[11]

---

encountered throughout the entire lifespan. In his seminal article, Butler[12(p 66)] conceptualized life review as:

> a naturally occurring, universal mental process characterized by the progressive return of consciousness of past experiences, and, particularly, the resurgence of unresolved conflicts ... Presumably this process is prompted by the realization of approaching dissolution and death and the inability to maintain one's sense of personal invulnerability.

Life review allows one to recast the past in the context of the present.[14] In so doing, one reviews one's life and is given various opportunities to solve old problems, to make amends, and to restore any lost sense of harmony.[15] Any form of life review involves key questions like "Who am I?" "How did I live my life over time?" and "Did I take every opportunity that I could to live my life well?" For many, there is a distinct difference between periodic episodes of life reminiscence and life review. Life review is not "a random sharing of pleasurable past events, but rather a structured process containing a component of self-evaluation."[16(p 9)] A possible result of such a review is the chance to find new meaning in life, especially when one faces the realities of impending death.[17]

Whether conducted with the patient, the family, or both patient and family together, life review can lead to increased life satisfaction and accomplishment, more peaceful inner feelings, and a renewed state of integrity.[18] Consistent with Erikson's theory of development,[13,19] the final task of ego integrity entails the acceptance of one's life as lived, an awareness of one's place in history, the gradual release of death anxiety, and a greater satisfaction with life overall. Erikson[19] believed that the greater part of adulthood is spent finding creative and meaningful experiences (including one's life work or career) to avoid feeling stagnant; then, during the final stages of living, the person can look back over the years at his or her accomplishments and feel a sense of pride and satisfaction in the summation of the outcomes. The alternative, ego-despair, involves the lack of pride in accomplishment, the absence of hope going forward, and the idea of stagnancy in living.[13] Byock[20] asserts that caring and compassionate healthcare providers are in positions and locations where they can listen and explore patient and family stories during significant moments, and the outcome is a greater sense of meaning and purpose in life. When the APRN actively welcomes and fosters these "critical opportunities" that call for advanced practice responses in terms of interdisciplinary team interventions, the result is a more compassionate healthcare environment that promotes patient awareness, comfort, ease, and satisfaction with life.

Life Review with the Individual Patient

According to Jenko, Gonzalez, and Alley,[10] when a person's goals of care shift definitively from cure to comfort, life review provides an evidence-based approach that brings the members of a family together, alleviates suffering, and focuses specific attention on the patient's holistic care. Storytelling is an ageless form of artful, human communication. It is interactive, uses both verbal and nonverbal forms of expression, and recounts a story that engages the imagination of the listener.[9] Furthermore, in reviewing his or her life story, the storyteller is given the opportunity to find meaning in everyday life problems along with the strengths and the depths of love and devotion that are revealed in his or her story.[21,22] Storytelling is also richly explored in the nursing literature; Smith and Liehr[23] proposed a mid-range nursing theory that uses the story as the central feature. Story theory assists the nurse to determine what "matters most" to a patient by connecting past incidents and future aspirations to the present health challenge. The health challenge is then addressed by the nurse using evidence-based literature and the stories are integrated into the plan of care. The nurse interprets and reinterprets the story, helping the patient to resolve the challenge.[23]

Life Review with the Family

Although the process of life review most often involves exchanges between a patient and the healthcare provider, life review can also involve the family. If the patient is incapacitated, life review is conducted with the family and often involves clarifying goals of care and navigating anticipatory grief.[24] In these instances, an understanding of family systems is vital. Families are seen as an organized whole, comprising both the individuals and the complex relationships between them. When one member of a family experiences a life-limiting situation, the remaining family members struggle between processing rapidly changing contextual realities and maintaining a sense of cohesion and constancy. Families are grappling with impending loss of a loved one as well as the realization of new family patterns and relationships.[25] In addition, at the death of a loved one, the family is in a unique place to talk about the loved one's life and death (as in the case study at the beginning of the chapter). Telling stories allows the family to maintain emotional functioning, retain or regain hope for the future, and find a renewed passion for living.[26]

The therapeutic use of life review provides the palliative APRN with a comprehensive framework for clinical interactions that can provide emotional and spiritual support to dying patients and their families. This approach is consistent with the literature, which supports storytelling as a model for coping with difficult and significant life stressors.[27]

Therapeutic Components of Life Review

The Analysis of a Life Review

A lot of information is shared with the provider during any given session of life review. This can take a significant amount of time if the patient provides detailed accounts and remembrances. As a palliative care intervention, life review is about "having conversations in human-scale time, which means you can't do it in five minutes."[28] When the provider engages in a session of life review, there is an unspoken covenant relationship that takes place between the patient and the healthcare provider. This notion of entering into a covenant relationship presupposes that two people come together; they agree on any promises, stipulations, boundaries, and/or responsibilities that are made.[29,30] The two equal parties are making a bond for therapeutic outcomes. In the case of life review, this covenant relationship incorporates two fundamental nursing assumptions: the promise to listen in a nonjudgmental and therapeutic manner and the unspoken pledge to intervene and address any issues of suffering that may be called forth.

Life review as a spiritual intervention, with its attending covenant relationship, presents unique opportunities to learn about the patient's social, emotional, physical, cultural, religious, and spiritual needs. All life review processes call forth the importance of the nursing process as the guide for providing holistic care to patients and family members. Particularly with end-of-life care, knowledge of the evolving needs of the patient and family better informs all healthcare directives and assists with advance care planning. End-of-life situations can often trigger spiritual and emotional distress, reducing the patient's abilities to cope, communicate, and participate in all care decisions. Knowledge of patient preferences, as they evolve in these areas, can be incorporated into the plan of care and further communicated to staff and the interdisciplinary healthcare team. These nursing actions help to satisfy Joint Commission requirements for advancing effective communication, cultural competence, and patient- and family-centered care.[31]

According to Kaufman,[32] 23 themes commonly evolve from the processes of life review (Box 46.2). With time, the experiences are seen collectively and can be woven into a cohesive whole; when this occurs, the patient's identity is further clarified and meaning making evolves. The person not only comes to conclusions about his or her life but is actively present when communicating that life to others.

In terms of process, the palliative APRN may want to take copious notes while listening or simply take brief notes of key topic areas. The APRN may choose to follow a set format that has worked previously for the gathering of key pieces of data as conversations evolve, or may choose to listen intently to the patient without taking notes and then summarize key points and conversation trends following the session. In any respect, the analysis of the "data" (information gathered) is extremely important in formulating an in-depth understanding of the person, the development of his or

---

Box 46.2 Major Themes that Evolve from Life Reviews

- Affective ties
- Financial status
- Marriage
- Work
- Social status
- Community service
- Self-reliance
- Industry
- Initiative
- Search for spiritual understanding/meaning
- Discipline
- Service
- Acquiescence
- Self-determination
- Financial security
- Religion
- Disengagement
- Family
- Achievement
- Orientation
- Creativity
- Need for relationships
- Selflessness

From reference 32.

---

her personality, the significance of certain key life events, and how aging is playing out in terms of health, disease, distress, integrity, and decline. Data will help to draw out social, psychological, historical, spiritual, and cultural life themes. The life review process has much in common with qualitative research methods in that content analysis of the information gathered is essential. As content themes emerge, the meaning of the information to the patient takes shape. A wide range of experiences are sampled, and those that require further analysis become a part of the ongoing plan of care.

At times during the life review process, the palliative APRN may be tipped off to an episode of a life experience needing further exploration. The patient's face may reveal a brief, fleeting glimpse of a pained affect or there may be words *not* spoken or expressed, the silence indicating a sensitive or controversial key event. This is especially true when an unspoken situation may not be socially acceptable (to the patient) or publicly sanctioned. As an example, while listening to a patient with advanced cancer discuss his family, a palliative APRN noticed a brief shadow cross the patient's face and observed a moment of hesitation in his voice. It was an elusive clue, one that could have been easily dismissed or overlooked, yet there was something that just "was not right." The APRN closed the door to the patient's room and said softly, "I could totally be in left field, but I think there is something you want to tell me—something that causes you great pain in the situation that you were just speaking about." After a long silence, the patient admitted to a son serving a life sentence in a state prison. Their last words, 13 years earlier, were harsh and angry; each blamed the other for the unfortunate situation. With only months

left to live, the patient desired to both offer and receive forgiveness. After two days of work with the staff and chaplain at the prison, a phone call was finally arranged between father and son, and both reported healing after a lengthy conversation.

When facilitating a life review, the provider needs to be prepared to deal with literally anything. In instances of extremely subtle clues of suffering, one might agree with Sir Arthur Conan Doyle, "It has long been an axiom of mine that the little things are infinitely the most important."[33]

Three Key Components in a Life Review

There are at least three interconnected components to life review:[10,34] recontextualizing, forgiving, and reclaiming unlived life.

Recontextualizing

Recontextualizing first takes into account the value and worth of accrued life wisdom. Life experiences, no matter what a person's chronological age, contribute to a "store" of wisdom. Recontextualizing enables the patient to recall and perhaps "reframe" self-defined mistakes and failures. Negative life events and/or situations are reframed in ways that can be positively reconfigured.[10] What is assumed in this process is the willingness of the patient to face the past in a different light, especially when reliving painful or unpleasant memories. Recontextualizing asserts that one is not so much a victim of the past but rather is more in control of life's experiences and can recast one's memories based on perceptions of the past.[12] One can reflect on past experiences and then begin the valued reparation process of those relationships and events formerly perceived as being negative. Changed perceptions can shift a sense of failure to a sense of accomplishment, even success. Recontextualizing asks one to search for the deeper meanings of the often-elusive patterns of life events. Recontextualizing assumes that over time, new-found meanings can heal past scars and wounds. One does not necessarily change the way that one lives, but rather begins to see life through a different filter or lens. Recasting the meanings of past events can give one a new sense of order and can change the way one sees oneself, others, and the world.[12,35]

Regarding the accrual of life wisdom, Baldwin[36] asserts that stories connect one's past, present, and future, allowing one to live in a generational context. Often a life review serves two purposes: it helps to heal the storyteller and also begins the process of healing future generations. For instance, one woman's life review pondered a deathbed conversation with her mother. The mother was trying to reconcile *her* parents' divorce in the 1940s and the challenging economic and painful emotional impact of her father's remarriage. Due to her highly unstable childhood, the mother had based her own marriage and childrearing on traditional values and low-risk choices. The woman was able to "connect the dots" of the generational impact and the limited view of life she unconsciously inherited from her mother. The woman verbalized a desire to change *her* individual view of life; she began a new way of seeing life as abundant and filled with possibility. She vowed to cultivate additional positive, upbeat, and energizing friends to improve the quality of her own life, while significantly affecting the lives of her own children.

Forgiving

In general, forgiveness involves choosing to release retaliation, bitterness, or unfavorable judgments toward a wrongdoer and to attempt to respond with a charitable spirit. Forgiveness is not necessarily predicated on reconciliation, and it does not involve minimizing or forgetting the offense. There are at least two types of forgiveness: offense-specific (which involves a particular action) and a general inclination to forgive others (which is true across settings and is stable over time).[37] The process of forgiveness helps to promote reconciliation between oneself, others, and one's higher power (where applicable).[38] Forgiveness entails the release of anger, resentment, and feelings of being wronged and entails the pardoning, forgiving, and absolving of the other from one's debt, crime, or action.[39]

Forgiveness is a central and potent theme in almost every world religion.[40-42] Peterson[43] categorized world religions into three major groups: the *Abrahamic religions* (Christianity, Judaism, and Islam), the *Indic religions* (Buddhism and Hinduism), and *aboriginal beliefs* (tribal beliefs among indigenous groups). The Abrahamic religions usually frame the relationship between God and human as Forgiver–forgiven and regard forgiveness as a consciously developed pattern of living. Of all the Abrahamic religions, Christianity places the strongest emphasis on an unconditional forgiveness of others. Judaism addresses forgiveness of others, yet the offender has an obligation to make restitution to the offended in order to earn forgiveness. In Islamic thought, absolute forgiveness is commendable but not required.[43] Within the Indic religions, there is an overarching theme of compassion. In Buddhism, there is the nontheistic notion of forgiveness, which is seen as the skillful means of promoting internal harmony, helping to free a person from internal regret and conflict.[40] Both Buddhism and Hinduism believe that personal resentments increase suffering, both to the offender and the offended. Thus, forgiveness is a means to a higher level of mindful living for both parties.[43] Within aboriginal/tribal belief systems, life is seen as holistic, without a distinction between the sacred and the secular. A distinct emphasis is placed on restoration of all parties: victims are mended, transgressors are reinstated, and the community can then return to a healthy equilibrium.[43]

Regardless of one's faith background, obtaining the forgiveness of a higher power is often dependent on or mutually inclusive of the ways that human beings first forgive themselves and others while asking for forgiveness in return. Restoring a sense of personal harmony allows for quietude of the mind, which fosters deeper insights. A careful assessment of the patient's spiritual/religious beliefs and practices better allows the healthcare team to plan for and provide forgiveness-oriented clinical interventions.[38,40]

Several authors[44,45] agree that the final stage of life is a cherished chance to express love and gratitude between oneself, others, and one's higher power. Opportunities to forgive oneself and others yield important results for one at the end-of-life. Jealousies, anger, and negativity can be redirected toward more positive thoughts and attitudes; longstanding resentments and sorrows can be released. Byock[20] cautions that forgiving is not about absolving another's responsibilities; rather, it provides one with a way to reframe what has been fractured, serving as the beginning steps to unfolding healing processes. The repair work that is a part of life review does not discount the pain or the responsibilities of those involved but does give one the tools to begin coming to terms with what was painful or unpleasant.

Reclaiming an Unlived Life

Often, as one reflects on one's life experiences, a multitude of regrets are possible: educational opportunities were ignored, career aspirations and goals went unrealized, healthful living practices were neglected, romances were unfulfilled, relationships were unsuccessful, and personal disappointments seemingly overshadowed any sense of accomplishment in terms of abilities, attitudes, and behaviors. Regrets place sharp boundaries around what should have been limitless possibilities; one's hopes and dreams were gradually shattered ... mere dreams, never fully realized. Using contemplative techniques with the patient, the palliative APRN can take steps to encourage the patient to reframe, repair, or rebuild what was previously perceived as failure and disappointment. Reparation is always possible. Unresolved conflicts can be examined in a new light and through the lens of accumulated life experiences that allow for and bring forward new ways of thinking as well as problem solving. Individual and key events can be placed into the context of one's entire life, and the "value" of the whole can expand one's sense of vision.[10,46]

Initiating Life Review: Further Thoughts and Suggestions

Before any work can begin in regard to life review, the patient must have adequate pain and symptom management and must be comfortable. Once the patient's comfort is reasonably assured, life review activities can begin. The life review process assumes a therapeutic relationship between patient and provider: all of the major therapeutic elements (Box 46.3) are present between the person engaged in review and the healthcare provider who listens, draws forth, extracts, and further develops chains of thought from the patient's unconscious. The provider must be comfortable asking open-ended questions, listening attentively and actively, and being comfortable with periods of silence and reflection. The provider must not interrupt the patient or interpret or attempt to complete the patient's sentences and thoughts.

Life review for the healthcare provider is grounded in cultural competence, often reconceptualized as cultural humility/awareness.[47,48] The provider remains nonjudgmental and is open to all ideas, viewpoints, ways of thinking, conceiving, and ways to integrate life events.

The patient begins with free association, recall, and a personal sense of assessment. Life review has to do with a person's memories and how they are organized and retrieved. The patient's (and often the family's) cultural, emotional, social, and spiritual beliefs and feelings are explored, and respect is shown throughout the entire process.

Typical topics for life review include family and friendships, loves and losses, achievements and disappointments, and adjustments made during the life trajectory. Opening questions to prompt life review can take the form of those found in Box 46.4, balancing both positive and negative aspects of life. If the person has difficulty remembering, various prompts can be used, such as pictures, music, jewelry, tape recordings, letters, or familiar personal items from the past. Prompting may be especially useful

Box 46.3 Elements of a Therapeutic Relationship

◆ Ensuring confidentiality and privacy of shared experiences and collected data
◆ Establishing trust
◆ Providing an open attitude
◆ Possessing a nonjudgmental spirit
◆ Obtaining consent before any life review process begins
◆ Being truthful, transparent, authentic
◆ Maintaining boundaries and having a professional demeanor
◆ Clarifying meaning; restating the patient's thoughts; remembering information shared
◆ Watching for key verbal and nonverbal cues
◆ Using open-ended questions
◆ Being comfortable with periods of silence
◆ Not rushing to complete a session or move to the next topic
◆ Using self-disclosure and self-expression appropriately
◆ Understanding the meaning and potential importance of cultural competence/humility
◆ Knowing about one's own spiritual and religious development/understanding
◆ Having a genuine sense of caring and compassion for the experiences of another

Adapted from references 10 and 14.

when working with the frail elderly who may have mood or memory problems.[7]

There is no single "right" way to initiate a life review. Healthcare providers are adept at finding the perfect teachable, reachable moment in terms of initiating the review process (which may take minutes, hours, weekly sessions, lasting even up to an indefinite end place) and should not press for discussions that are too intimate or sensitive for patients and family members. In every sense of the word, the storyteller is always the "hero" of the story; the provider is a nonjudgmental, open, caring, compassionate, active listener.

Research Implications of Life Review

Robert Butler is perhaps the prime mover in the quest to discover the therapeutic effects of life review, particularly in older people.[14] In evolving reviews of gerontology literature and practice, Butler[14] concluded that life review demonstrated the following positive effects:

Righting old wrongs

Reconciling with old enemies

Coming to a more peaceful acceptance of one's mortality

A sense of serenity

Pride in one's accomplishments

Feeling that one did the best one could in life

Box 46.4 Prompts for Beginning a Life Review

◆ Tell me when and where you were born.
◆ What was life like when you were growing up?
◆ What was school like for you?
◆ If you have siblings, tell me about your brothers and sisters.
◆ Tell me about a particularly enjoyable time or place that you experienced or visited.
◆ Tell me about an event in in your life that you found to be troubling or challenging.
◆ Tell me something that you particularly remember about your childhood.
◆ Talk to me about some of the things you remember as you grew into your teenage years.
◆ Tell me something unique about your family or a close relationship with someone.
◆ Did you ever marry? If so, tell me about how you met, your courtship, and how you proposed/were proposed to.
◆ Tell me something about your friends, particularly your best ones.
◆ Describe an obstacle in your life and tell me how you were able to get through it.
◆ Who are the people who have most influenced your life?
◆ What is that one "most important" event you experienced in your life?
◆ What were the most difficult deaths that you had to deal with in your lifetime?
◆ What do you most enjoy right now?
◆ Do you keep in touch with any of your old friends?
◆ How did you feel (or do you feel) about retirement?
◆ What are your thoughts about death, dying, and the possibility of an afterlife?
◆ Who are the people you most admire in your life?
◆ Describe the way that a person who knows you well would describe you.
◆ What makes you happy now?
◆ Tell me about your work experiences—your career, your business, your vocation.
◆ What do you think you will be remembered for best?
◆ What has been the deepest regret or disappointment in your life as a child, young adult, and middle-aged or older adult?
◆ How do you think you have changed over the course of your life?
◆ What was the hardest thing you had to face as you were growing older?
◆ What is the absolute best thing about being older?
◆ (When appropriate, many find intense satisfaction in discussing significant historical/social events, such as the Great Depression, world wars, political movements, and shared experiences with a community of friends, family, soldiers, or members of a congregation.)

Adapted from references 10 and 14.

More recent research findings indicate that older people who suffered from depression and who participated in life review reported better self-esteem and felt more positive about their life experiences than a similar group who did not participate in life review.[7] The group who participated in life review also had a more favorable view of their past experiences and had greater levels of hope for the future. Caregivers who participated in the sessions gained a deeper knowledge of the patient's experiences, which helped to decrease self-reported stress.[7]

A meta-analysis of 20 studies involving the use of life review as an intervention evaluated its effects in elderly patients with depression and depressive symptomatology.[49] Despite several limitations across studies, there was a statistically significant effect in all studies, indicating that life review is an effective treatment of depressive symptoms in older adults. The effects were comparable to other well-established treatments, including antidepressants and cognitive-behavioral therapy.[49]

Dignity Therapy, a variation of life review, is designed to address psychosocial and existential distress in the terminally ill. Pioneered by Max Chochinov, it involves a brief, individualized psychotherapeutic intervention. There is a considerable amount of evidence for its utility and success in patients who are facing significant end-of-life concerns.[50–52] Each session is designed to engender a sense of meaning and purpose and to reduce the amount of suffering the patient is experiencing. There are seven dignity themes: Generativity, Continuity of Self, Role Preservation, Maintenance of Pride, Hopefulness, Aftermath Concerns, and Care Tenor.[52]

Within a session, which typically lasts 30 to 60 minutes, the patient is asked questions from an interview guide.[53] Sessions are taped and then transcribed; they are edited for clarity, chronology, and possible psychological harm that may be caused to others who may read the content. The edited version ends with an appropriate statement of life closure (a generativity, legacy-making exercise). The final version is given to the patient, who can give it to a loved one. In several studies, patients reported feeling satisfied or highly satisfied with the intervention and believed that it increased their sense of purpose, heightened their sense of meaning, and helped increase their quality of life and feelings of well-being.[50–52]

Possible Risks of Life Review

When one engages in past remembrances, there are risks to the patient and family as well as to the healthcare provider who actively listens and then intervenes to improve the patient's health and well-being. For the patient, the experiences may become an obsession, or anxiety, guilt, or despair may become magnified.[14] Excessive or obsessional rumination on a past event, depression, or panic would lead to increasing rigidity rather than to increased self-awareness and flexibility.[14] A tragic (and fortunately rare) outcome occurs when a patient's increasing (but partial) insight leads to a sense of total squander.[14] In this case, the patient concludes that he or she has never truly lived his or her life as hoped and the patient sees this clearly for the first time as he or she is about to die.[15] A severely depressed patient might contemplate suicide.[14] Another group of individuals at risk are those who believe that forgiveness and redemption are impossible for them.[14] In these situations of spiritual distress, a referral to either a mental health professional or a pastoral care professional (as appropriate) is submitted immediately.

In particularly difficult situations, the palliative APRN may also be subject to the harmful effects of life review. The APRN may feel like he or she "caused" the existential angst and the pain and suffering brought forward. If a patient attempts suicide (successfully or not), the provider may question his or her role in the situation and may bear terrible feelings of guilt. In these situations, the palliative APRN must be aware of the limits of his or her professional capabilities and skills and must be able to refer the patient to others as the need arises. The palliative APRN must also have sufficient self-care habits and emotional/physical support systems to be able to reflect, recharge, reevaluate, renew, and resume.

The inherent nature of palliative care can create a distinct risk to the APRN. In working with the dying, love and compassion are fundamental components.[11] In palliative care, the APRN can develop the ability to "see purely," meaning that one bears witness to the full range of the suffering experienced by the patient while concurrently keeping in mind each person's inherent goodness.[53] One must truly listen to another's story, which gives "our suffering meaning, our dying depth, and our grieving perspective." [54(p 66)] Yet, all of life is interconnected; when patients suffer, practitioners suffer. To be sustainable in the provision of palliative care, personal well-being is not "an optional indulgence but an absolute necessity."[54(p 93)] Palliative APRNs should be mindful of their *literal homes* (an uncluttered physical place that provides refuge) and their *inner homes* (an uncluttered spiritual place that fosters contemplation and reflection).[54]

Viewing one's personal limits as an APRN where compassion is concerned is vital; compassion fatigue and burnout are indeed possible. Neglecting to care for oneself both hurts the self and can lead to harm for others.[54] Several authors[55,56] stress the concept of Sabbath time. This spiritual practice, either for an entire day or for a portion of a day, is when one ceases one's routine, daily activity and consciously takes "time off" to regroup, meditate, and recharge. During Sabbath time, one appreciates the normal rhythms of life—joy and sorrow, death and life, full and empty, acting and waiting. Making time to acknowledge the significant or sacred and to seek personal renewal and reflection is a crucial life lesson for the palliative APRN and one that will promote sustainability for professional growth and ongoing clinical practice.

Entering the Results of a Life Review Session into the Electronic Health Record

Healthcare professionals are entrusted with the most sensitive and private information in regard to their patients and have a strong ethical responsibility to protect their patients from all types of misuse, fraud, and breaches of confidentiality.[10] The information gained from a life review may be highly sensitive health data and may involve information that the patient thought was being shared in confidence with the "listener" only. Make sure that the patient and family members know that any information gained from the life review might be entered into the electronic health record (EHR). The palliative APRN must obtain the patient's consent to have each session become a part of his or her record. Any information shared that may be vital to the patient's care will be handled with the strictest of confidence; however, there can be no assurances that secrets will be kept between patient and provider. The APRN, being respectful of human dignity, should assure the patient and family that minute details (the so-called substance or facts) of the exchanges will be entered sensitively and in "broad strokes." This promotes an up-to-date care plan that continues to direct future interventions, actions, team communications, and ways to secure evidence-based outcomes. Patients and families should be reminded that all data obtained are considered private and confidential and will be honored as such at all times, including all items entered into the EHR.

There are several categories that warrant higher degrees of security when it comes to entering data into the EHR.[57] The law affords special protection to data from patients with mental illness, since they involve the patient's innermost personal communications and information. Patients with HIV/AIDS and sexually transmitted illnesses represent another category with special privacy concerns; sensitive information that may be shared in these areas must be handled cautiously and appropriately. Patients with substance abuse and chemical dependency also require special consideration.[57] Finally, release of these records to any outside source requires patient consent, and recipients must include a written statement prohibiting redisclosure of this information.[57]

Life Review: Religious and Spiritual Implications

Humans are intrinsically spiritual, and spiritual beliefs affect healthcare decisions and outcomes. Spirituality may include specific religious beliefs or may be completely divorced from them, although the relationship between spirituality and religion can change depending on the patient's circumstances. Religion involves specific teachings and customs, a structured approach to life, and a certain moral code as understood in, or structured according to, specific authoritative or holy texts. Religion is most commonly practiced in community with others, whereas spirituality, characterized by meditation and awareness of a universal consciousness, is more of an inner search to find one's individual truth.[58] Spirituality defines those constructs that give a person strength to carry on even in the midst of life's troubles. Spirituality provides comfort, courage, and appreciation. Spirituality encompasses a person's beliefs, values, practices, and rituals and assumes certain spiritual needs: meaning, purpose, life satisfaction, forgiveness, love, and belonging.[1]

It is within the practice of nursing to address the patient's spiritual concerns: one's concept of God or higher power, one's source of hope and strength, the significance of particular rituals or practices, and the correlation between beliefs and health.[59] Appropriate nursing interventions that help to meet the spiritual needs of patients include listening to patient and family concerns, praying with the patient upon request (when the provider feels comfortable doing so), and reading a patient's favorite religious materials.[59] In fact, giving attention to the spiritual dimension of patient care is a Joint Commission requirement, as it contributes to advanced effective communication, cultural competence, and patient- and family-centered care.[31]

In life review, a patient may express themes of spiritual distress: the inability to find meaning in life;[60] an impairment in connectedness, inner peace, and harmony;[61] or an inability to cope with multiple losses and cumulative grief.[62] Spiritual distress can be seen when a person's spiritual beliefs are threatened and through physical and emotional symptoms. Spiritual distress is associated with poorer healthcare outcomes, including emotional despair, depression, mood disorders, anxiety, suicidal thoughts, and substance abuse.[63] To provide spiritual care, the provider must be fully present; identify his or her own boundaries, barriers, and limitations; listen nonjudgmentally; and appreciate his or her own spirituality as a lifelong companion that informs, develops, challenges, and helps with personal growth.

Box 46.5 Recommended Reading

Bowen M. *Family Therapy in Clinical Practice.* Lanham, MD: The Rowman & Littlefield Publishing Group, Inc.; 2004.

Bowen family systems theory is a theory of human behavior that views the family as an emotional unit and uses systems thinking to describe the complex interactions in the unit. It is the nature of a family that its members are intensely connected emotionally. A change in one person's functioning is predictably followed by reciprocal changes in the functioning of others.

Brussat F, Brussat MA. *Spiritual Literacy: Reading the Sacred in Everyday Life.* New York, NY: Touchstone; 1998.

A collection of meaningful examples from contemporary books, movies, and life experiences that promote a new way of looking at and "reading" the world. Helps to answer the age-old question: "How can I live a spiritual life every day?"

Callanan M, Kelley P. *Final Gifts: Understanding the Special Awareness, Needs, and Communications of the Dying.* New York, NY: Bantam Books; 1992.

A classic text that describes a period of time termed "Nearing Death Awareness." During this time, the dying tell stories and attempt communications with friends and family members that are often misunderstood. Learning what to listen for and how to approach various situations allows the reader to respond to the dying in new and authentic ways.

Frankl VF. *Man's Search for Meaning.* New York, NY: Pocket Books; 1997.

This classic book was originally published in 1946 and has been translated into two dozen languages. It recounts psychiatrist Viktor Frankl's experience in Nazi concentration camps and his quest to discover meaning in the midst of horrific and sustained suffering. His subsequent theory, called logotherapy, explores how human beings cope with suffering by creating renewed meaning and purpose for life.

Plante TG, Sherman AC. *Faith and Health: Psychological Perspectives.* New York, NY: The Guilford Press; 2001.

This book focuses on the links between religious faith and health outcomes. A variety of scientific investigators discuss findings from research studies that examine the broader issues involved in the faith–health connection.

Richardson C. *Life Makeovers: 52 Practical and Inspiring Ways to Improve your Life One Week at a Time.* New York, NY: Broadway Books; 2000.

Known for her bestselling books and her series on life makeovers with Oprah Winfrey, Cheryl Richardson speaks about thriving amid the everyday requirements of a fast-paced world. Her simple yet insightful program is filled with thoughtful essays and practical action for sustaining a healthy and joyful life. Her plan is particularly applicable for palliative APRNs, who bear witness to physical and emotional suffering on a daily basis and who work amid the challenges of the modern healthcare system.

During the process of life review, the palliative APRN seeks to recognize and respond to spiritual distress and help the patient to discover deeper meaning in the experience of illness, suffering, grief, and loss.[1] Spiritual distress can be extremely complicated and detrimental to a patient's overall comfort and satisfaction with life. Because the roots of spiritual distress can be extremely complicated, providers should frequently consult with board-certified chaplains, who are trained spiritual care specialists.[1]

Conclusion

Offering life review to a patient is a spiritual intervention that involves active listening; keen and subtle communication skills; attentive behaviors; an open, nonjudgmental, and objective frame of mind; and the luxury of time to allow the patient to develop his or her story. It provides an incredible opportunity for the patient to reflect on life accomplishments, legacies, and achievements. It allows the patient to reframe harsh memories and to celebrate joyous events. Above all, it is an intervention that can promote a peaceful and comfortable death. Box 46.5 lists resources for palliative APRNs interested in learning more about life review.

References

1. Hospice and Palliative Nurses Association (HPNA). *Position Statement on Spiritual Care.* Available at https://www.hpna.org/DisplayPage.aspx?Title1=Position%20Statements. Published 2010. Accessed July 27, 2014.
2. Brown SJ. Direct clinical practice. In: Hamric AB, Spross JA, Hanson CM, eds. *Advanced Practice Nursing: An Integrative Approach.* 3rd ed. St Louis, MO: Elsevier Saunders; 2005:143–86.
3. Mariano C. An overview of holistic nursing. *NSNA Imprint.* February/March 2005:48–51.
4. Cumbie SA. The integration of mind-body-soul and the practice of humanistic nursing. *Holist Nurs Pract.* 2001;15(3): 56–62.
5. Fawcett J, Watson J, Neuman B, Walker PH, Fitzpatrick JJ. On nursing theories and evidence. *J Nurs Scholarship.* 2001; 33(2): 115–9.
6. Chochinov HM. Dignity-conserving care: a new model for palliative care: Helping the patient feel valued. *JAMA.* 2002; 287(17): 2253–60. doi:10.1001/jama.287.17.2253
7. Miller MC. Remembering as a form of therapy. *Harvard Editorial Health Publications.* Available at http://healthyliving.msn.com/health-wellness/remembering-as-a-form-of-therapy. Published 2014. Accessed August 1, 2014.
8. Pinquart M, Forstmeier S. Effects of reminiscence interventions on psychosocial outcomes: A meta-analysis. *Aging and Mental Health.* 2012; 16(5): 541–58. doi: 0.1080/13607863.2011.651434.
9. National Storytelling Network. What is storytelling? Available at http://www.storynet.org/resources/whatisstorytelling.html. Accessed August 10, 2014.
10. Jenko M, Gonzalez L, Alley P. Life review in critical care: Possibilities at end-of-life. *Crit Care Nurse.* 2010; 30(1): 17–28. doi: 10.4037/ccn2010122.
11. Chochinov HM, Hack T, Hassard T, Kristjanson LJ, McClement S, Harlos M. Dignity therapy: A novel psychotherapeutic intervention for patients near the end of life. *J Clin Oncol.* 2014; 23: 5520–5.
12. Butler RN. The life review: An interpretation of reminiscence in the aged. *Psychiatry.* 1963; 26: 65–76.
13. Erikson EH, Erikson JM, Kivnick HQ. *Vital Involvement in Old Age.* New York, NY: WW Norton & Co; 1986.
14. Butler RN. Successful aging and the role of life review. *J Am Geriatr Soc.* 1974; 22(12): 529–35.
15. Lewis MI, Butler RN. Life-review therapy: Putting memories to work in individual and group psychotherapy. *Geriatrics.* 1974; 29(11): 165–73.
16. Black G, Haight BK. Integrality as a holistic framework for the life review process. *Holist Nurs Pract.* 1992; 7(1): 7–15.
17. Wallace JB. Reconsidering the life review: The social construction of talk about the past. *Gerontologist.* 1992; 32(1): 120–5. doi: 10.1093/geront/32.1.120
18. Burnside I, Haight BK. Reminiscence and life review: Analyzing each concept. *J Adv Nurs.* 1992; 17(7): 855–62.
19. Erikson EH. *Life History and the Historical Moment.* New York, NY: Norton; 1975.
20. Byock I. *Dying Well: Peace and Possibilities at the End of Life.* New York, NY: Berkley Publishing Group; 1997.
21. McAdams DP. *The Stories We Live By: Personal Myths and the Making of the Self.* New York, NY: William Morrow; 1993.
22. Bruner J. *Acts of Meaning.* Cambridge, MA: Harvard University Press; 1990.
23. Smith MJ, Liehr P. Story theory to advance nursing practice scholarship. *Holist Nurs Pract.* 2005; 19(6): 272–6.
24. Jenko M. Life review. In: Neimeyer RA, ed. *Techniques of Grief Therapy: Creative Practices for Counseling the Bereaved.* New York, NY: Routledge; 2012:181–3.
25. Shapiro ER. *Grief as Family Process: A Developmental Approach to Clinical Practice.* New York, NY: Guilford Press; 1994.
26. Pennebaker JW. *Opening Up: The Healing Power of Expressing Emotions.* New York, NY: Guilford Press; 1997.
27. Harvey JH, Carlson HR, Huff TM, Green MA. Embracing their memory: the construction of accounts of loss and hope. In: Neimeyer RA, ed. *Meaning Reconstruction and the Experience of Loss.* Washington, DC: American Psychological Association; 2001:231–43.
28. Meier D. Palliative care: the "ah-ha" moment. [YouTube video]. Available at https://www.youtube.com/watch?v=wunepUqZ0DI&list=PL69C2E181A563759A&feature=c4-overview-vl. Published May 29, 2008. Accessed August 13, 2014.
29. D'Aunay D, Rodning CB. Patient–physician interaction: Healing power of a covenant relationship. *Humane Health Care.* 2004: 4(2). Available at http://www.humanehealthcare.com/Article.asp?art_id=222. Accessed August 3, 2014.
30. Rusthoven JJ. Understanding medical relationships through a convenantal ethical perspective. *Perspectives on Science and Christian Faith.* 2010: 62(1): 1–15. Available at http://www.asa3.org/ASA/PSCF/2010/PSCF3-10Rusthoven.pdf. Accessed August 3, 2014.
31. The Joint Commission. *Advancing Effective Communication, Cultural Competence, and Patient and Family Centered Care: A Roadmap for Hospitals.* Oakbrook Terrace, IL: The Joint Commission. Available at http://www.jointcommission.org/assets/1/6/aroadmapforhospitalsfinalversion727.pdf. Published 2010. Accessed August 1, 2014.
32. Kaufman SR. *The Ageless Self: Sources of Meaning in Late Life.* Madison, WI: University of Wisconsin Press; 1986.
33. Goodreads. Quotes of Arthur Conan Doyle. Available at https://www.goodreads.com/author/quotes/2448.Arthur_Conan_Doyle. Published 2014. Accessed August 2, 2014.
34. Schachter-Shalomi Z, Miller RS. *From Age-ing to Sage-ing.* New York, NY: Warner Books; 1995.
35. Garland J, Garland C. *Life Review in Health and Social Care.* Philadelphia, PA: Taylor & Francis, Inc.; 2001.
36. Baldwin C. *Storycatcher: Making Sense of our Lives through the Power and Practice of Story.* Novato, CA: New World Library; 2005.
37. Toussaint LL, Owen AD, Cheadle A. Forgive to live: Forgiveness, health, and longevity. *J Behav Med.* 2012; 35: 375–86. doi 10.1007/s10865-011-9362-4.
38. Baird P. Spiritual care interventions. In: Ferrell B, Coyle N, Paice J, eds. *Textbook of Palliative Care.* 4th ed. New York, NY: Oxford University Press; 2015:546–53.

39. Gehman HS. *The Westminster Dictionary of the Bible*. Philadelphia, PA: The Westminster Press. 1980.

40. Buck G, Lukoff D. Forgiveness: Spiritual perspectives on forgiveness. Spiritual Competency Resource Center. Available at http://www.spiritualcompetency.com/scrcQuiz.aspx?courseID=58. Accessed August 3, 2014.

41. Rye MS, Pargament KI, Ali MA, et al. Religious perspectives on forgiveness. In: McCullough ME, Pargament KI Thoresen CE, eds. *Forgiveness: Theory, Research, and Practice*. New York, NY: The Guilford Press; 2000:17–40.

42. Lutjen LJ, Silton NR, Flannelly KJ. Religion, forgiveness, hostility and health: A structural equation analysis. *J Relig Health*. 2012; 51: 468–78. doi 10.1007/s10943-011-9511-7.

43. Peterson RL. Forgiveness and religion: A schematic approach. *ARA Journal*. 2005–2009; 29–33: 61–4. Retrieved from http://www.bostontheological.org/assets/files/peacebuilding/petersen_religion_forgiveness.pdf.

44. Byock I. *The Four Things That Matter Most: A Book About Living*. New York, NY: Free Press; 2004.

45. Keeley MP, Yingling JM. *Final Conversations: Helping the Living and the Dying Talk to Each Other*. Acton, MA: VanderWyk & Burnham; 2007.

46. Butler RN, Lewis MI. *Aging and Mental Health*. St. Louis, MO: Mosby; 1982.

47. Tervalon M, Murray-Garcia J. Cultural humility versus cultural competence: A critical distinction in defining physician training outcomes in multicultural education. *J Health Care Poor Underserved*. 1998; 9(2):117–25.

48. Austerlic S. Cultural humility and compassionate presence at the end of life. Available at http://www.scu.edu/ethics/practicing/focusareas/medical/culturally-competent-care/chronic-to-critical-austerlic.html. Published February 2009. Accessed August 3, 2014.

49. Bohlmeijer E, Smit F, Cuijpers P. Effects of reminiscence and life review on late-life depression: A meta-analysis. *Int J Geriatr Psychiatry*. 2003; 18(12): 1088–94.

50. Chochinov HM, Hack T, McClement S, et al. Dignity in the terminally ill: An empirical model. *Soc Sci Med*. 2002; 54: 433–43.

51. Chochinov HM, Hack T, Hassard T, et al. Dignity in the terminally ill: A cross-sectional cohort study. *Lancet*. 2002; 360: 2026–30.

52. Chochinov HM. Dying, dignity, and new horizons in palliative end-of-life care. *CA Cancer J Clin*. 2006; 56: 84–103.

53. Halifax J. Compassion and the true meaning of empathy [TED Talk]. Available at https://www.ted.com/talks/joan_halifax#t-13992. Published December 2010. Accessed August 13, 2014.

54. Halifax J. *Being with Dying: Cultivating Compassion and Fearlessness in the Presence of Death*. Boston, MA: Shambhala Publications, Inc.; 2008.

55. Dass R. *Still Here: Embracing Aging, Changing, and Dying*. New York, NY: Riverhead Books; 2000.

56. Muller W. *Sabbath: Finding Rest, Renewal, and Delight in Our Busy Lives*. New York, NY: Bantam Books; 1999.

57. AHIMA e-HIM Work Group on Security of Personal Health Information. Ensuring security of high-risk information in EHRs. American Health Information Management Association (AHIMA). Available at http://library.ahima.org/xpedio/groups/public/documents/ahima/bok1_039956.hcsp?dDocName=bok1_039956. Published September 2008. Accessed July 23, 2014.

58. Shapiro E, Shapiro D. The differences between religion and spirituality. Available at http://www.huffingtonpost.com/ed-and-deb-shapiro/religion-and-spirituality_b_967951.html. Published September 11, 2011. Accessed August 10, 2014.

59. O'Brien ME. *Spirituality in Nursing: Standing on Holy Ground*. 2nd ed. Sudbury, MA: Jones and Bartlett Publishers; 2003.

60. Burnard P. Spiritual distress and the nursing response: theoretical considerations and counseling skills. *J Adv Nurs*. 1987; 12: 377–82.

61. Villagomeza LR. Spiritual distress in advanced cancer patients: toward conceptual clarity. *Holist Nurs Pract*. 2005; 19(6): 285–94.

62. Boston PH, Mount BM. The caregiver's perspective on existential and spiritual distress in palliative care. *J Pain Symptom Manage*. 2006; 32: 13–26.

63. Meraviglia M, Sutter R, Gaskamp CD. Evidence-based guideline: Providing spiritual care to terminally ill older adults. *J Gerontol Nurs*. 2008; 34(7): 8–14.

CHAPTER 47

Interdisciplinary Team Collaboration and the Provision of Spiritual Care

Elaine Wittenberg and Virginia Sun

Key Points

- Quality spiritual care, in the setting of palliative care, should be delivered through interprofessional collaboration.

- The palliative advanced practice registered nurse (APRN) can play a key role in clinical practice, leadership, and research related to interprofessional spiritual care.

- The palliative APRN, as part of an interprofessional team, should have the knowledge and skills to conduct spiritual assessment and manage spiritual distress with respect and trust for all team members.

Spiritual care is delivered through interprofessional collaboration, requiring teamwork and high-quality communication among team members to ensure that interventions are patient-centered.[1] In addition to conducting spiritual assessments and delivering spiritual interventions, APRNs also play a pivotal role in facilitating and leading team collaboration dealing with spiritual care. While previous chapters have reviewed the role of the APRN as a clinical expert in spiritual care, working alongside chaplaincy, we focus here on the APRN's role in teamwork supporting spiritual care. This includes providing team members with an overview of the core elements of spiritual care, determining best practices for documenting spiritual care plans, and assessing spiritual interventions.[2]

Interdisciplinary collaboration and effective teamwork are important factors that contribute to the assessment and delivery of spiritual care and are among the recommended standards for accreditation.[3] The Institute of Medicine defines team-based healthcare as:[4]

> the provision of health services to individuals, families, and/or their communities by at least two health providers who work collaboratively with patients and their caregivers—to the extent preferred by each patient—to accomplish shared goals within and across settings to achieve coordinated, high-quality care.

In 2011, the Interprofessional Education Collaborative (IPEC), comprising representatives from the American Association of Colleges of Nursing, American Association of Colleges of Pharmacy, American Association of Colleges of Osteopathic Medicine, American Association of Medical Colleges, American Dental Education Association, and Association of Schools of Public Health, agreed upon draft interprofessional competencies in four domains: Values/Ethics, Roles and Responsibilities, Interprofessional Communication, and Teamwork.[5]

The IPEC competencies are best illustrated through a model of interdisciplinary collaboration (Fig. 47.1). According to the model, four communication elements characterize interdisciplinary collaboration among team members: (1) team member interdependence and (2) role flexibility, exemplified by new/blended roles and responsibilities for team members; (3) collective ownership of goals; and (4) reflection on team processes.[6] Thus, the team's ability to include spiritual assessment as part of care planning can lead to outcomes that would have otherwise not existed (interdependence and flexibility of team members), and discussion of spiritual concerns and distress can produce different tasks (creating new roles and responsibilities for team members). Team process then includes attention to spiritual distress to produce the team's holistic assessment and plan of care (collective ownership of goals for team members). Finally, team performance is evaluated (team's reflection on development process). This chapter provides an overview of the collaborative process and demonstrates the communication skills palliative APRNs need to meet interprofessional competencies.

Case Study

Daryl was a 72-year-old white male who was diagnosed with lung cancer. The cancer was localized when it was first diagnosed, and he was hopeful that the surgery would result in a "cure." Daryl did well for about 2 years but then experienced a local recurrence of his lung cancer. He underwent several rounds of both radiation and chemotherapy. While the recurrence and treatment-related symptoms were devastating to Daryl and his family, Daryl again was hopeful that the treatments would result in a cure for his cancer. A few months later, a follow-up MRI revealed metastatic disease in the brain. Daryl's medical oncologist suggested a round of palliative radiation to help alleviate symptoms.

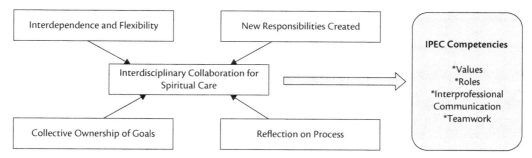

Figure 47.1 Model of interdisciplinary collaboration leading to interprofessional competencies

Daryl came from a large, Italian Catholic family and was the youngest of six siblings. He and his wife, who recently died of pancreatic cancer, had a son and two daughters. Daryl was a practicing and very devout Catholic. He had been a fighter all his life and had strong principles from which he did not often back down. When Daryl's medical oncologist told him that his cancer had spread to the brain, his response was to fight and figure out a way to "beat it." He was determined to live through the next Christmas. Daryl refused a referral to hospice, even though several of his physicians had discussed the option with him. He didn't think he needed hospice and instead wanted to focus on what other treatments he could receive.

Initially, Daryl never talked about dying. He loved talking about his children's and grandchildren's accomplishments. He also kept talking about how he would like to celebrate Christmas. Over the next months, as Daryl gradually declined, he used humor to cope. His faith was tremendously important to him. He prayed regularly, loved to say the rosary, and attended Mass daily as much as he could. His faith was a steady, quiet one. He knew God existed, that his wife was in Heaven, and that he would see her one day. He knew God was good and just and that He would care for his family. Daryl was private and did not talk extensively about God or even his feelings. He just kept stating that he wanted to make it to next Christmas.

Daryl's healthcare team consisted primarily of his medical oncologist and his collaborating APRN. When Daryl was first told about the spread of his lung cancer to the brain, his oncology APRN began to assess his willingness to discuss hospice care. Although this was met with initial resistance ("I don't think I need hospice right now"), the APRN knew that palliative treatments to the brain would be recommended to alleviate symptoms. Knowing how important Daryl's faith had been throughout his cancer experience, the APRN asked if he was willing to speak with a chaplain during his visit for palliative radiation. Daryl accepted the offer, and the oncology APRN informed the chaplain and made a formal referral. The oncology APRN also contacted the medical oncologist regarding her assessment of the importance of involving spiritual counseling for Daryl. Both agreed that they should continue to assess and discuss hospice and palliative care with Daryl.

Daryl started palliative radiation to the brain approximately 1 week after being given the diagnosis of metastatic lung cancer to the brain. The chaplain visited with Daryl each time he came for his treatments and spoke to him on the phone as well. The chaplain also met Daryl's children and was able to assess their needs. The chaplain discussed his assessment of Daryl's and the family's spiritual needs with the APRN. Together, the APRN and the chaplain developed a spiritual care plan for Daryl and his family. It included connecting with Daryl's parish and priest so he could receive the important rituals of his faith (prayers and communion) and could attend Mass as frequently as possible. For Daryl's family, it was important to stay connected and to involve clergy as much as possible. This was particularly important because Daryl's children had already lost their mother to cancer. Both the chaplain and the oncology APRN agreed that discussions on involving palliative and hospice care should be continued.

Three weeks after beginning palliative radiation, Daryl requested a visit with his medical oncologist. The APRN arranged the visit and communicated with the chaplain and medical oncologist about the importance of assessing Daryl's wishes about palliative and hospice care. The team agreed that a family conference was important to assess Daryl's needs and those of his family.

At the family conference, the oncology APRN, chaplain, and medical oncologist used their developed plan and assessed Daryl's needs, the goals of treatment (which were palliative), the needs of his family, and his wishes in relation to palliative and hospice care. At the visit, one of Daryl's daughters was hopeful that he had "outlived" his oncologist's prediction in terms of prognosis, arguing that her father must be getting better. Daryl responded by patting his daughter on the shoulder, saying, "It's not true, but don't burst her bubble. But of course—your Dad is a tough old bird." There was silence, but in that silence everyone knew that a different reality existed. Daryl voiced his wish to enter hospice care, not only for himself but also for his children, so they wouldn't be burdened with the need to care for him at the end-of-life.

One month before Christmas, Daryl was so weak that he could no longer walk without assistance. Home hospice care had been initiated, and Daryl was able to continue to attend Mass or watch it on television. His parish priest and community friends visited regularly to give communion and pray with him. Daryl started to talk more openly about his wishes for his family and would tell people that he was "getting tired." As Daryl fell in and out of consciousness over the days before and after Christmas, his family was at his bedside often.

After Daryl's death, the oncology APRN initiated a meeting with the chaplain and medical oncologist to review the process of caring for Daryl's spiritual needs and to discuss which approaches had worked and what could be improved upon for future cases.

Valuing Interprofessional Collaboration for Spiritual Care

Within the palliative care team, each team member depends on the others to accomplish tasks and goals. Interdependence emerges from formal and informal time spent together, oral and written communication regarding spiritual information, and respecting colleagues' professional input.[6] The values and ethics of the team members' disciplines are different, and each profession socializes individuals differently in regard to their role in spiritual care. Extreme role allegiance, either toward an individual's profession or toward the team, could cause problems among the team. To promote collaboration, reciprocal respect for both the individual's profession and for his or her role as a team member is necessary. Spiritual care requires a team effort, and each team member needs to understand his or her own contribution to the spiritual care plan as well as what other team members can provide.

As a clinical leader, the palliative APRN helps others recognize the value of interdisciplinary collaboration.[7] The APRN role is dependent upon the needs of the team, the patient, and family, and the organization to facilitate the development of spiritual care plans based on an assessment of religious, spiritual, and existential concerns.[6] This requires role flexibility on behalf of the palliative APRN, who sometimes serves as leader, follower, or mediator in the team process. Compromise and adaptability with other team members are ways that the APRN can demonstrate that all team members have valuable information to contribute to care planning. Being flexible with roles and responsibilities in the team environment demonstrates trust and respect for professional colleagues. Palliative APRNs can promote teamwork and a culture of safety by teaching communication skills that aid in solving problems and resolving conflicts.[8]

APRNs can also demonstrate the value and importance of collaboration by mobilizing resources to sustain spiritual care for patients. As a champion for palliative care, the APRN can lobby for the funding of spiritual care positions and can create policy within the organization to incorporate spiritual care in care planning documentation. Fostering a supportive collaborative culture also includes attending to manageable caseloads, securing administrative support, finding time and space conducive to collaboration, and prioritizing professional autonomy.[6] Interdisciplinary collaboration is influenced by the way in which organizations allocate resources and assign work; these choices can either inhibit or advance spiritual care. Team members need to be able to maximize benefits and minimize environmental and agency constraints to positively influence the interdisciplinary team. An unclear mission or one that does not clearly include spiritual care, insufficient time for spiritual care planning discussions, and lack of administrative support can impede collaboration.[6] Teams that have shared leadership and professional diversity can have a positive impact on collaboration.[3]

Team Role in Spiritual Care Planning

Spiritual care plans developed through team collaboration, as described in the case study at the beginning of the chapter, maximize the expertise of all team members.[6] New responsibilities and tasks are created through information shared by team members regarding their clinical interactions and are unique to each patient and family. The overlap between psychological distress and spiritual distress is a good example of how comprehensive care planning can lead to the development of interventions by interdisciplinary team members that address similar symptoms.[9] Given that all palliative care team members interact with the patient, each one captures different information about the patient's care.

Physical, psychological, and social data contribute to existential issues and care-planning decisions. All of these data help the team to understand the patient's existential distress and concerns and inform the subsequent treatment and interventions provided by the palliative care team.

However, professional role conflicts can impede the development of spiritual care plans, which rely on information shared by interdisciplinary team members.[10] For example, a chaplain who experiences conflict as a result of role misunderstandings by other team members may not feel fully valued and integrated into care.[11] Most providers have not received spiritual training as part of their education,[10] so team members often have varying levels of expertise in spiritual care.[12] This can impede the amount of information shared during spiritual care planning discussions or can even result in the absence of spiritual care plan development during team care planning.[13] Moreover, there is confusion over the exact role of nurses in spiritual care, and barriers to providing spiritual care in a hospital include a lack of clear guidelines for the nurse's role.[14]

One of the main responsibilities of the palliative APRN on the team is to ensure that spiritual care is one of the components of the care plan discussion for all patients receiving palliative care. This can be accomplished in one of two ways: (1) based on the clinical relationship with a patient, wherein the nurse and patient have established a therapeutic relationship that facilitates spiritual care, or (2) by ensuring clinical assessment and treatment of spiritual distress through the team model.[9] Working with the team, the APRN should guide the team in developing the components and process of a spiritual assessment.[2] This includes outlining what is done when a patient shares spiritual concerns or shows signs of spiritual distress.[15] All team members should be trained in spiritual assessment, and team care plan discussions should involve contributions from the spiritual care provider on the palliative care team. Spiritual care from a collaborative team also involves supporting the family caregiver, especially following the death of the patient.[16] In the absence of a dedicated spiritual care provider, the team should have a plan in place for sharing this information and obtaining appropriate referrals and support services.

Facilitating Interprofessional Communication for Spiritual Care

Interprofessional communication involves collaborative team discussions and documentation of patient care plans. Team members must be responsible for their part in spiritual assessment and share the collective goal of providing spiritual care as a main component of the care plan. Team members cannot rely on the spiritual care provider or chaplain alone for spiritual care. Teams need clearly defined goals, a shared vision, an agreed-on mission, objectives, and a strategy for making decisions about spiritual care.[6] The team's ability to assess spiritual concerns also influences resource utilization because spiritual interventions can influence decisions by patients and families, especially at the end-of-life.[9]

Importantly, the palliative APRN directs interprofessional communication related to spiritual care by serving as a team leader. This includes advocating for patients and families, serving as a mentor to other team members, focusing on evaluation, organizing educational rounds, and preparing for accreditation.[17] Collaborative skills also include participating in team rounds, working together to develop care plans, participating in strategic meetings, and educating others about the palliative APRN role. Educating other team members about spiritual care is a leadership role to be assumed by the APRN.

Team leadership also includes creating an interdisciplinary collaborative environment that facilitates a safe culture for team members to share.[18] The APRN must help the team overcome the many barriers to interprofessional collaboration, such as the lack of knowledge about team roles, how best to work with other providers outside of the team, understanding the scope of team services, and how to include the patient and family in team care planning.[1] Team processes include communication, collaboration, coordination, conflict resolution, leadership, decision making, and participation.[19] Important communication skills include being able to raise concerns within the team, holding regular debriefings, showing self-control during conflict resolution, and partnering with senior team members, who may be more inclined to answer questions and share during team meetings.[8] Interdisciplinary collaboration skills include approachability, interpersonal skills, listening, and verbal message skills.[20]

Teamwork and the Review of Spiritual Care Plans

Spiritual care plans should be reviewed for their quality and impact on patient care. The team can evaluate itself by thinking back on the process of working together. APRNs need to encourage their teams to think and talk about their work as a team. This should include reflecting on their work together as well as how they work with others (e.g., local clergy, other healthcare providers). First, palliative APRNs should consider how the team uses the chaplain. Extensive spiritual counseling and exploration should come from the team's chaplain or spiritual care provider, either through referral from other interdisciplinary team members or from visits from the chaplain. Evaluation of the effectiveness of spiritual care should be tracked and used to revise processes and develop policy for spiritual care coordination.

Second, an evaluation of teamwork must include attention to collaboration with colleagues.[21] Among the challenges for clinical nurse leaders is the willingness among nurses, support staff, and medical staff to collaborate with them.[18] Palliative APRNs want respect from their peers and honest feedback from their colleagues.[21] The ability to establish teamwork procedures and patterns depends on whether physicians are team leaders or team members.[3] Routine review of the attitudes and perceptions of team members toward collaboration as well as the educational backgrounds and training of team members in existential issues should be considered.[18] To improve teamwork dealing with spiritual care, APRNs should encourage team building and incorporate activities that allow colleagues to share their individual spiritual perspectives and the ways they find meaning and purpose in life.[21]

In addition to evaluating spiritual interventions, the palliative APRN is responsible for drawing the team's attention to the impact of spiritual concerns on other domains of palliative care (e.g., social, cultural, psychological). For example, complementary and alternative medicine may be associated with spirituality in patients.[10] Developing ways to assist with complementary and alternative medicine, if desired, and ensuring that the team knows about the patient's use of these therapies are vital to spiritual care planning.

In reviewing a patient's care plan, APRNs should determine that the patient and family were informed about the availability of spiritual care services and whether spiritual counseling was provided by the team or through local clergy. Recognizing that family members often can provide background information or knowledge of the patient's history that can be important to understanding existential issues in patient care, the APRN should determine how best to include the patient and family in care planning about spiritual distress and concerns.[1] Spiritual distress often creates family discord.[15] The palliative APRN can lead care plan discussions about how team members can mediate family relationships and assist in healing.

Implications for Clinical Practice and Research

The role of APRNs in the delivery of high-quality spiritual care is evident based on professional requirements and recommendations to achieve competence in spiritual care.[22] Team-based spiritual care is essential for the evaluation of effectiveness and quality.[23] Table 47.1 provides an overview of the IPEC core competencies and how they can be applied to interprofessional spiritual care. Based on the core competencies, APRNs should have the following key knowledge and skills to foster and lead team collaborations for spiritual care:[24]

1. Demonstrate professionalism and respect for other disciplines

2. Initiate or lead team spiritual care planning discussions

3. Integrate spirituality assessment principles into clinical practice

4. Serve as team leader for spiritual mentorship

5. Advocate for the provision of spiritual care

6. Serve as liaison between members of the interprofessional team

Table 47.2 presents the Consensus Conference Spiritual Care Guidelines and their application to the APRN's role and responsibilities in providing spiritual care in palliative care settings. First, in their role as leaders and educators, the palliative APRN, with input from spiritual care providers, should have the knowledge and skills to facilitate team training in the integration of evidence-based spiritual assessment in clinical practice.[25] A comprehensive assessment of the patient's and family's spiritual needs and potential distress is the cornerstone of the development of high-quality, interprofessional spiritual care planning. The APRN can play a key role in advocating for the incorporation of assessment into clinical practice.

Second, armed with the knowledge and skills to initiate high-quality communication, the APRN should lead and facilitate spiritual care planning discussions. These discussions, as recommended by the IPEC core competencies, should be conducted with respect and trust for all members of the team, including chaplains and spiritual care providers. There are many strategies to maintain clear communication across team members, such as the clear documentation of spiritual care plans in electronic medical records and debriefing sessions with team members. Regardless of the communication strategy, the palliative APRN should play an integral role in facilitating and sustaining clear communication across team members. Clear communication within the team is critical in providing high-quality spiritual care and ensures that patients and families are provided with consistent information in relation to their spiritual well-being.

Table 47.1 Overview of Interprofessional Core Competencies and Team Collaboration for Spiritual Care

IPEC Core Competency	Team Collaboration for Spiritual Care
Values and Ethics Work with individuals of other professions to maintain a climate of mutual respect and shared values	◆ Show interprofessional professionalism by flexibility in providing spiritual intervention or providing information to team members that aid in spiritual care plan. ◆ Mobilize resources to advocate for a spiritual care provider on the palliative care team. ◆ Demonstrate mutual respect and trust of team members through compromise and by trying to solve team conflicts (i.e., role conflict or ethical dilemmas).
Roles and Responsibilities Use the knowledge of one's own role and those of other professions to appropriately assess and address the healthcare needs of the patients and populations served	◆ Ensure that team care-planning discussions address spiritual care and decide on team roles for spiritual care. ◆ Provide team training on spiritual assessment. ◆ Teach how team roles and responsibilities for spiritual care complement each other. ◆ Communicate your role in spiritual care to other team members. ◆ Understand others' roles in spiritual care. ◆ Establish relationships with others who can aid in spiritual care delivery. ◆ Engage in continued learning about spiritual care.
Interprofessional Communication Communicate with patients, families, communities, and other healthcare professionals in a responsive and responsible manner that supports a team approach	◆ Serve as team leader for spiritual care by mentoring others. ◆ Develop safe team environment for spiritual care planning so that team members are ready to work together, and encourage team members to speak up when they have a concern. ◆ Plan educational rounds to educate others about the APRN role and the importance of spiritual interventions. ◆ Address barriers to interprofessional communication, such as workload assignments, team meetings, hierarchies between professions. ◆ Advocate for patient and family as members of team.
Teamwork Apply relationship-building values and the principles of team dynamics to plan and deliver patient-/population-centered care that is safe, timely, efficient, effective, and equitable	◆ Reflect on team process and how team members work together and with others. ◆ Review how the team uses the chaplain. ◆ Consider interprofessional barriers when working with other healthcare professionals or local clergy. ◆ Assist team members in exploring their own purpose and meaning in life to promote coping. ◆ Organize team-building activities.

Box 47.1 provides a template that palliative APRNs can use to reflect on the effectiveness of team-based approaches in spiritual care in clinical settings. These items can also serve as a tool for discussion and debriefing about the functions within the interprofessional team. APRNs can facilitate reassessment of the spiritual care plan by maintaining knowledge of evidence-based approaches and interventions to treat spiritual distress in palliative care settings. The palliative APRN should be aware of the critical role that physical and psychological suffering plays in spiritual distress, should appropriately promote and advocate for the use of complementary and alternative methods of treating physical and psychological symptoms. Finally, palliative APRNs should be aware of the spiritual care resources available in their own institutions and in the community. APRNs should always advocate for the inclusion of spiritual care providers as integral members of any spiritual care team and should include local

Table 47.2 Consensus Conference on Spiritual Care Guidelines and Implications for the Palliative APRN

Guidelines Regarding Spirituality in Palliative Care	Application to APRN Roles and Responsibilities
All healthcare professionals should be trained to do a spiritual screening or history.	APRN should facilitate team training, and team should agree on what spiritual screening tool to use, with input and guidance from chaplain/spiritual care provider.
Spiritual background/information should be communicated and documented and shared with interprofessional team.	APRN should promote care-planning discussions that address spiritual assessment (by either chaplain/spiritual care provider or another team member) and ensure documentation in electronic medical record.
Follow up on spiritual condition changes as part of routine follow-up.	APRN should incorporate review of spiritual interventions as part of routine care planning.
Address spiritual concerns related to psychological, physical suffering.	APRN should facilitate team meetings that include holistic assessment of pain by including complementary and alternative therapies as part of spiritual interventions.
Spiritual treatment should include referral to trained spiritual care provider.	APRN should advocate for a spiritual care provider on the palliative care team as well as work with local clergy to provide spiritual support.

From reference 9.

Box 47.1 Reflect on Your Team

Practices interdependence and flexibility

Regular sharing of information, tasks, and role responsibilities, with aims to achieve care outcomes through versatility

◆ **Team Process**—What specific responsibilities are designated for each team member for spiritual care? Where are there overlaps in team roles? How do team members complement the spiritual care provider on your team?

Creates new tasks and responsibilities

Members demonstrate interdependence through accessibility, information sharing, and task accomplishment, which maximizes member expertise.

◆ **Team Process**—What information do you share with other team members about your specific discipline? What information do other team members share with you about their discipline?

Collective ownership of goals

Collaboration establishes shared responsibility and a common purpose for this team.

◆ **Team Process**—What is the collaborative team goal for spiritual care planning? Does the team discuss, define, and decide on a goal or is it implicit?

Performs reflection and evaluation

Recognizes shortfalls of team processes, establishes collaborative team goals, and evaluates team communication practices

◆ **Team Process**—What can you do differently as a team to improve spiritual care? What do you think will work well and what currently is not working well?

---

clergy to provide spiritual support for patients and families in the community.

Nursing education programs should also advocate for interprofessional training in palliative care. Although the concept of interprofessional training is evolving, nursing education programs continue to struggle to incorporate interprofessional education into the curriculum.[26] Issues of time and money and the lack of interprofessional curriculum models and outcome measures are slowing down the move toward team-based education.[26] More research is warranted to test the effectiveness of different models of interprofessional education and training in both academic and clinical practice settings. These models will need to be tested for their effectiveness in improving knowledge and communication in team-based approaches of spiritual care. As interdisciplinary team-based care moves forward, future clinical research should focus on ways to identify the impact of interprofessional practice on patient outcomes.[26]

Recent decades have seen an increase in studies focusing on spirituality within the nursing literature.[27,28] While caring for the whole person—including spiritual needs—has always been at the heart of nursing, rigorous research in this area is needed.[29] Researchers should explore the contributions of palliative APRNs and the unique knowledge and skills they contribute to the interdisciplinary team.[30] Future research should include comparing team-based care programs to find similarities and differences, identifying strengths and weaknesses in team design, structure, and processes across care settings. Finally, more research is needed to determine which team practices yield the best outcomes and cost savings for specific patient populations.[4]

Conclusion

This chapter focuses on the ways that palliative APRNs can facilitate teams, mobilize team resources, and facilitate team processes that prioritize spiritual care.[3] Educating the team about existential issues is the first step toward actuating team-based spiritual care planning. As spiritual care planning becomes more defined within palliative care, further research is needed to understand the variables that influence team-based care, such as how to involve patients and families, how best to use technology in healthcare teams, and how to provide appropriate training and assessment.[4]

References

1. McDonald C, McCallin A. Interprofessional collaboration in palliative nursing: what is the patient-family role? *Int J Palliat Nurs.* 2010; 16(6): 286–9.
2. Galchutt P. A palliative care specific spiritual assessment: how this story evolved. *Omega.* 2013; 67(1-2): 79–85.
3. Kilpatrick K, Lavoie-Tremblay M, Ritchie JA, Lamothe L. Advanced practice nursing, health care teams, and perceptions of team effectiveness. *Health Care Manage.* 2011; 30(3): 215–26.
4. Mitchell P, Wynia M, Golden R, et al. *Core Principles & Values of Effective Team-Based Health Care: Discussion Paper.* Washington, DC: Institute of Medicine; 2012. Available at www.iom.edu/tbc.
5. Interprofessional Education Collaborative Expert Panel. *Core Competencies for Interprofessional Collaborative Practice: Report of an Expert Panel.* Washington, DC, 2011.
6. Bronstein LR. A model for interdisciplinary collaboration. *Social Work.* 2003; 48(3): 297–306.
7. Wilson L, Orff S, Gerry T, et al. Evolution of an innovative role: the clinical nurse leader. *J Nurs Manage.* 2013; 21(1): 175–81.
8. Altmiller G. Teaching clinical nurse specialist students to resolve conflict: strategies that promote effective communication and teamwork. *Clin Nurse Spec.* 2011; 25(5): 260–2.
9. Puchalski C, Ferrell B, Otis-Green S, Handzo G. *Overview of Spirituality in Palliative Care.* 2014. Available at www.uptodate.com.
10. Peteet JR, Balboni MJ. Spirituality and religion in oncology. *CA Cancer J Clin.* 2013; 63(4): 280–9.
11. Goldsmith J, Wittenberg-Lyles E, Rodriguez D, Sanchez-Reilly S. Interdisciplinary geriatric and palliative care team narratives: collaboration practices and barriers. *Qual Health Res.* 2010; 20(1): 93–104.
12. Fitchett G, Lyndes KA, Cadge W, et al. The role of professional chaplains on pediatric palliative care teams: perspectives from physicians and chaplains. *J Palliat Med.* 2011; 14(6): 704–7.
13. Oliver DP, Wittenberg-Lyles E, Demiris G, et al. Barriers to pain management: caregiver perceptions and pain talk by hospice interdisciplinary teams. *J Pain Symptom Manage.* 2008; 36(4): 374–82.
14. Rushton L. What are the barriers to spiritual care in a hospital setting? *Br J Nurs.* 2014; 23(7): 370–4.
15. Ellington L, Reblin M, Puchalski C, et al. The religion of "I don't know": naturalistic observations of spiritual conversations occurring during cancer home hospice nurse visits. *Omega.* 2015; 72(1): 3–19.

16. Reblin M, Otis-Green S, Ellington L, Clayton MF. Strategies to support spirituality in health care communication: a home hospice cancer caregiver case study. *J Holist Nurs.* 2014; 32(4): 269–77.

17. Van Soeren M, Hurlock-Chorostecki C, Reeves S. The role of nurse practitioners in hospital settings: implications for interprofessional practice. *J Interprof Care.* 2011; 25(4): 245–51.

18. Bender M, Connelly CD, Brown C. Interdisciplinary collaboration: the role of the clinical nurse leader. *J Nurs Manag.* 2013; 21(1): 165–74.

19. Lemieux-Charles L, McGuire WL. What do we know about health care team effectiveness? A review of the literature. *Med Care Res Rev.* 2006; 63(3): 263–300.

20. O'Brien JL, Martin DR, Heyworth JA, Meyer NR. A phenomenological perspective on advanced practice nurse-physician collaboration within an interdisciplinary healthcare team. *J Am Acad Nurse Pract.* 2009; 21(8): 444–53.

21. Hill KS. Work satisfaction, intent to stay, desires of nurses, and financial knowledge among bedside and advanced practice nurses. *J Nurs Admin.* 2011; 41(5): 211–7.

22. McSherry W, Jamieson S. The qualitative findings from an online survey investigating nurses' perceptions of spirituality and spiritual care. *J Clin Nurs.* 2013; 22(21-22): 3170–82.

23. Matthews SW, Brown MA. APRN expertise: the Collaborative Health Management Model. *Nurse Pract.* 2013; 38(1): 43–8.

24. Balboni MJ, Sullivan A, Amobi A, et al. Why is spiritual care infrequent at the end of life? Spiritual care perceptions among patients, nurses, and physicians and the role of training. *J Clin Oncol.* 2013; 31(4): 461–7.

25. Phelps AC, Lauderdale KE, Alcorn S, et al. Addressing spirituality within the care of patients at the end of life: perspectives of patients with advanced cancer, oncologists, and oncology nurses. *J Clin Oncol.* 2012; 30(20): 2538–44.

26. Jukkala AJ, White ML. The continued need for interprofessional collaboration and research. *Appl Nurs Res.* 2014; 27(2): 95–6.

27. Pesut B, Fowler M, Taylor EJ, et al. Conceptualising spirituality and religion for healthcare. *J Clin Nurs.* 2008; 17(21): 2803–10.

28. Pesut B. Spirituality and spiritual care in nursing fundamentals textbooks. *J Nurs Educ.* 2008; 47(4): 167–73.

29. Reinert KG, Koenig HG. Re-examining definitions of spirituality in nursing research. *J Adv Nurs.* 2013; 69(12): 2622–34.

30. Apold S, Pohl JM. No turning back now. *J Nurse Pract.* 2014; 10(2): 94–9.

PART SIX

Special Situations: Withdrawal of Technology

CHAPTER 48

Withdrawal of Cardiology Technology

Patricia Maani Fogelman and Janine A. Gerringer

Key Points

◆ Heart failure and cardiac advanced practice registered nurses (APRNs) are vital members of the management team for patients with heart failure. APRNs manage a multitude of chronic diseases and follow patients through their often lifelong trajectory of disease management and progression.

◆ The heart failure and/or cardiac APRN is often the primary provider who maintains responsibility for managing the treatment of complex and advancing heart failure.

◆ Ongoing assessment, medication management, symptom management, care planning, goals-of-care discussions, and end-of-life planning are all under the purview of the APRN.

◆ Heart failure, cardiac, and palliative APRNs provide medical care and disease management, education, patient and family counseling, and overall health promotion for patients with advancing and/or terminal heart failure.

Case Study

RR was a 73-year-old male with a past medical history that included coronary artery disease, diabetes, and ischemic cardiomyopathy. He was managed relatively well for about 5 years with routine monitoring by his cardiologist. The patient then went through a 6-month period when he was hospitalized with systolic heart failure three times. An echocardiogram indicated progression of his heart disease to end-stage heart failure. He was deemed ineligible for a heart transplant due to his advanced age and was referred by his cardiologist for destination-therapy LVAD consideration.

The patient and his wife met with the advanced heart failure team, including cardiologists and APRNs, and underwent an extensive preimplantation workup, including meeting with palliative care to ensure that an advance directive was in place and the patient's wishes were expressed and understood. The heart failure and cardiac APRN worked as an integral part of the team, collaborating in the care of the patient, including preoperative testing and extensive education to prepare him and his family for LVAD implantation and life with an LVAD.

The patient underwent an LVAD implant and suffered some immediate complications, including right-sided heart failure. He had a lengthy hospital stay but recovered enough to go to an inpatient rehab facility and then home. The patient enjoyed months of an improved quality of life at home before starting to experience refractory symptoms of heart failure. Throughout this time, the patient was seen regularly by both the cardiologist and heart failure APRN for medication adjustments and continued monitoring of his LVAD.

He then developed worsening right-sided heart failure and a clot within the LVAD pump. Unfortunately, due to his right-sided heart failure and related liver dysfunction, he was not a candidate for an LVAD pump exchange. A family meeting was held with the patient, his wife, members of the LVAD team, including the cardiologist, the heart failure APRN, and nursing staff, and the palliative care team to discuss the patient's wishes at that time. It was decided that he would return home on hospice.

The patient had a preexisting ICD that he did not want deactivated at this time, but he and his wife were open to having a magnet in the home to temporarily deactivate the ICD. The heart failure APRN taught them how to apply the magnet to decrease the risk of excessive defibrillation at the end-of-life. The heart failure APRN also instructed the wife how to turn the LVAD off when the end-of-life occurred. The palliative APRN prescribed morphine and gave instructions on use and administration. The patient returned home with visiting hospice nurse services. Within weeks, he became increasingly unresponsive and the magnet was placed over his chest by the hospice nurse. The LVAD was subsequently deactivated, with the heart failure APRN talking the patient's wife through the process. His wife reported his death as peaceful.

Introduction

APRNs play a key role in caring for cardiac patients. They order and interpret diagnostic data, perform physical examinations, make diagnoses, and formulate treatment plans based on the patient's needs. This includes education about lifestyle modifications that may improve the patient's cardiovascular health, the introduction and titration of cardiac medications, and referral for more advanced cardiac treatments, such as vasoactive or inotropic medications, cardiovascular implantable electronic devices (CIEDs), and ventricular assist devices (VADs). Continual assessment of the patient for symptom management and disease progression and collaboration with other healthcare providers to maximize the quality of care delivered are attributes of the skilled APRN.

Discontinuation of Vasopressors

Vasopressors are medications delivered intravenously to support blood pressure during periods of hemodynamic instability in the acute care setting, most notably in the treatment of shock. Examples of vasopressors are epinephrine, norepinephrine, phenylephrine, and vasopressin (Table 48.1).[1]

The general practice is to stop these medications when their desired effects are no longer elicited. Vasopressors are generally withdrawn when other forms of life support, such as ventilator support or renal dialysis, are withdrawn after the patient's family and medical teams have deemed their use futile. Commonly the medications are withdrawn either at the same time or before or after ventilator support, without the need for medication weaning. The APRN should anticipate the need to provide palliative management of terminal heart failure symptoms (pain, dyspnea, nausea, anxiety). The role of the APRN is to offer treatment to relieve and anticipate distressing symptoms before withdrawing vasopressors and other forms of life support. APRNs should discuss changes patients may move through in the dying process, such as sudden cardiac death, hypotension with loss of perfusion (skin changes, mottling, and cyanosis), sleeping more, disorientation when awake, restlessness, diminished senses and inability to respond to stimulus (although awareness of them remains intact longer), coma, changes in body temperature, respiratory pattern changes, and changes in oral secretions. APRNs should make sure the patient and family members understand these changes and the mutual goal of a peaceful death.

APRNs should always refer to any institutional policies regarding withdrawal of vasopressors. Heart failure APRNs can be critical players in developing these protocols. The palliative care team is especially important in situations where the patient's acute decline was not expected, thereby exacerbating the period of crisis. The heart failure APRN should rapidly assess the patient to ensure that appropriate care is provided. Palliative care consultation will help family members decide what the patient would want under the circumstances and will help the family understand the withdrawal process, including how they can help keep the patient comfortable during the dying process.

Discontinuation of Inotropes

Intravenous inotropic agents are used in acutely ill, hospitalized heart failure patients with a severely reduced ejection fraction. In the acute setting, inotropes are used to establish hemodynamic stability by increasing systemic perfusion and preserving end-organ function. Their use focuses on clinical improvement or as a bridge to a more permanent treatment, such as surgery, cardiac transplant, or left ventricular assist device (LVAD) placement.

In an acute situation, a discussion should be held with the patient and family regarding the limited options available if inotrope therapy is not successful. Treatment goals should be discussed so that appropriate steps can be taken regarding the patient's plan of care.[2] Inotropes may also be used as a long-term palliative treatment in patients whose advanced heart failure is refractory to other guideline-directed oral medications and who are not candidates for a ventricular assist device or a cardiac transplant. The goal of chronic inotrope therapy is symptom relief. Inotrope treatment is initiated based on hemodynamic evidence of clinical benefit and on the patient's wishes. Goals of care and possible end-of-life scenarios should be discussed before starting continuous inotrope therapy.[2]

The most common inotropes used in the home setting are milrinone, dobutamine, and dopamine (Table 48.2). These inotropes can be administered intravenously through a small pump, which allows the patient to remain at home during treatment.[3] Palliative APRNs should monitor patients for the risks of continuous inotropic therapy, such as central line infection, hypotension. and arrhythmias.[4] To minimize the risk of adverse effects such as arrhythmias, the lowest dose needed for symptom relief should be used.[2]

APRNs should monitor the patient for changes in clinical status and goals of care. If the patient is no longer benefiting from inotrope therapy, the palliative APRN should revisit the goals of care. APRNs can manage heart failure patients with the right medications and can perform the tasks associated with withdrawal (if allowed in their practice setting), including writing orders to discontinue medications. Again, the palliative APRN should discuss changes the patient may move through in the dying process and should establish mutual goals with the family regarding a peaceful death for the patient. Many patients express their desire to be at home during the final stages of dying. Taitel and colleagues[5] found that patients who participated in a home inotrope infusion program were more likely to die at home than in the hospital. Patients may be discharged to hospice as well, but this is less common.

Discontinuation of Ventricular Assist Devices

Mechanical circulatory support is becoming a widely accepted treatment for patients with advanced (stage D) heart failure with a reduced ejection fraction refractory to guideline-directed oral medications and cardiac device intervention. VADs are designed

Table 48.1 Vasopressors

Vasopressor Drug	Dose Range
Epinephrine	0.01–0.10 mcg/kg/min
Norepinephrine	0.01–3 mcg/kg/min
Phenylephrine	0.4–9.1 mcg/kg/min
Vasopressin	0.0–0.1 units/min

From reference 1.

Table 48.2 Inotropes

Inotropic Drug	Dose Range
Dobutamine	2.5–20 mcg/kg/min
Dopamine	5–20 mcg/kg/min
Milrinone	0.125–0.75 mcg/kg/min

From reference 2.

to assist the patient's failing native ventricle by improving cardiac output.

VADs can serve patients in both the short term, when patients are acutely decompensated and hemodynamically unstable, and in the long term, when patients have chronic advanced heart failure. VADs can stabilize the patient so decisions can be made regarding the plan of care, such as the need for surgical intervention (e.g., revascularization, correction of valve abnormalities, permanent pump placement, or, when appropriate, pump explant).[2]

Patients who are waiting for a cardiac transplant and need additional support until a donor heart becomes available can receive an LVAD as a bridge to transplant. If the patient's heart failure is severe and irreversible and the patient is not a cardiac transplant candidate, he or she can receive an LVAD as destination therapy. Destination therapy with an LVAD has been proven to prolong survival and improve both quality of life and functional status in select patients with end-stage heart failure.[6]

Long-term LVADs are surgically implanted pumps that connect from the left ventricle to the ascending aorta to assist with systemic circulation. Blood exits the left ventricle through the inflow cannula, enters the pump, and is then directed through an outflow cannula to the aorta. An external driveline and power source are connected to the body to power the pump.[7]

Hospitals that offer LVAD therapy have an interdisciplinary team that participates in the patient's preimplant and long-term care. In October 2014, The Joint Commission mandated that certified destination therapy VAD programs have a palliative care representative who has experience with the VAD population on the institution's interdisciplinary team.[8] Palliative care services should be used from the beginning, while the patient is undergoing evaluation prior to implantation. The palliative care team promotes goals-of-care discussions. Palliative care should be available to support patients who have decided to undergo LVAD implantation, as well as patients who have been deemed ineligible for an LVAD or decline implantation in favor of optimal medical management alone. The APRN provides ongoing assessment of quality of life, goals of care, and health status. Major changes in health status due to device-related complications or other comorbidities not related to the device may lead to revisiting end-of-life discussions. Potential complications that may result in death include stroke, infection, and multiple-organ failure.[7] Again, partnership with the palliative care team is vital in managing patients with an LVAD approaching the end-of-life.[9]

When deactivating an LVAD, many issues need to be considered. Of primary importance is the patient's wishes, expressed either directly or through a living will or designated decision maker. The medical team must agree on the futility of continuing device therapy in a patient with a minimal chance of meaningful recovery. APRNs are integral members of this team, as they develop an intimate relationship with heart failure patients and families due to the chronicity of the disease. Caring for these patients at the end-of-life is just as important as caring for them through their life. If the interdisciplinary medical team cannot reach a consensus regarding device discontinuation, consultation with a hospital ethicist or ethics committee may be necessary.[10]

Swetz and colleagues[11] found that consultation with palliative care before patients received an LVAD for destination therapy was conducive to developing personal preparedness plans, which are expanded advance directives for patients with LVADs. Personal preparedness planning focused on points unique to treatment with an LVAD, including situations where the heart can be supported by the device but other medical conditions or functional limitations may have a significant negative effect on the patient's health status and quality of life. Preparedness planning can be particularly advantageous if a major adverse event or change in quality of life occurs, because palliative care already established a rapport with the patient and family and can focus on the situation at hand.

Petrucci and colleagues[12] devised a 10-point model for addressing ethical concerns in the treatment of VAD patients. It states that advance directives are particularly important in VAD patients because most patients and families are not aware of the issues that may arise while the patient is supported with a VAD. For example, the VAD can continue to mechanically support the blood pressure in an otherwise fatal situation. Discussion should be based on the type of support the VAD will offer, either as destination therapy or a bridge to transplant, keeping in mind that the patient can transition between the two types of support under certain circumstances. The model further states that discussion should occur before an advance directive is formulated regarding complications related to the implant procedure and to VAD therapy, such as bleeding, neurological events, and infection. This is the time when any major conflicts between the patient and designated decision makers should be addressed.

Prior to deactivation of the LVAD, the following points should be discussed with the patient and/or surrogate decision maker: current condition and prognosis, change in benefit of current therapy, how the device will be stopped, how symptoms will be treated, patient and/or surrogate decision maker's readiness to proceed, and the anticipated outcome.[13] Different LVADs have different steps for deactivation. Healthcare professionals should first refer to any institutional protocols regarding VAD deactivation. In the absence of a formal institutional protocol, Gafford and colleagues[14] have outlined key points for LVAD withdrawal, so that the patient can die peacefully:

The APRN should be familiar with the system's alarms and how to turn them off, so as not to cause any additional distress to the patient and the patient's family members.

The APRN should order, and monitor the efficacy of, medications directed toward patient comfort prior to LVAD device deactivation, as the cardiovascular circulation may significantly decrease when the LVAD ceases to function.

Removal of the power sources and the driveline from the controller will cause the LVAD to stop functioning. As with ventilator removal, the APRN should be prepared to act quickly to prevent and treat signs and symptoms of discomfort.

Deactivation can occur in the hospital or at home, depending on the patient's medical condition and wishes and whether the event is acute or chronic. In the hospital, the APRN can oversee the process and be available to support the patient and the staff. This includes writing orders for discontinuation of the device and administering medications for comfort. If deactivation is to occur at home, the APRN may be responsible for teaching the patient's family or hospice staff how to deactivate the device and how to administer medication for the patient's comfort to ensure a peaceful death.

Discontinuation of Pacemakers/Automatic Implantable Cardioverter-Defibrillators

Implantable pacemakers are commonly used to treat patients with symptomatic bradycardia and sinus node dysfunction. Current pacing systems have one or two leads that are positioned in the right atrium and right ventricle with a small computerized pulse generator that is placed under subcutaneous tissue in the shoulder area. The pacemaker can deliver an electrical pulse to the heart, leading to cardiac muscle contraction.[15]

Implantable cardioverter-defibrillators (ICDs) are devices that increase survival by terminating life-threatening arrhythmias. ICDs do not treat heart failure by improving cardiac function or decreasing symptom burden, but they decrease the risk of sudden cardiac death.[16] The 2013 American College of Cardiology Foundation/American Heart Association Guidelines for the Management of Heart Failure address the specific criteria determined through clinical trials, to identify those patients most at risk and make recommendations for the proper use of ICD devices.

Cardiac resynchronization therapy (CRT), on the other hand, synchronizes segmental and global contraction of the left as well as the right ventricle in patients with systolic heart failure who have a left bundle-type wide QRS complex and clinical symptoms of heart failure despite optimal medical therapy.[17] CRT can be combined with a pacemaker or ICD.[18]

CRT and ICD therapy may be available in the same device, but they offer very different options. CRT reduces the altered electrical activation of the left and right ventricles. This sometimes leads to favorable reverse remodeling and decreased severity of mitral regurgitation and left ventricular hypertrophy. CRT has been shown to improve survival and can significantly reduce symptoms and improve quality of life in end-stage heart failure patients. ICDs treat life-threatening tachyarrhythmias but do not improve symptoms. CRT-D (CRT with an ICD) implantation should prompt discussion regarding deactivation of either or both functions.[13]

The patient's goals of care should be assessed prior to implantation of a CIED (cardiovascular implantable electronic device, such as pacemaker or ICD). The healthcare provider is responsible for discussing both the risks and benefits of CIED therapy. The APRN can initiate discussion regarding deactivation and scenarios for the end-of-life prior to CIED implantation. The APRN may recommend that the patient complete an advance directive to outline his or her wishes at the end-of-life and designate a surrogate decision maker. Deactivation should be readdressed should any major changes occur in the patient's health status,[19] such as when prompted for a generator change, notification of device recall, diagnosis of another life-limiting illness, and when a decision is made for hospice care.[20]

Prior to device deactivation, the patient should understand his or her prognosis, any treatment options, and what will happen when the device is withdrawn. For example, the APRN should discuss with the patient how deactivation of an automatic ICD may lead to death if a life-threatening arrhythmia occurs.[11]

Any provider or institution that implants CIEDs should have a protocol in place that clearly outlines the process for deactivating CIEDs when withdrawal of such care is appropriate. Palliative care professionals can facilitate discussions regarding deactivation of CIEDs, including the patient's and family's wishes as well as expected symptom management.[19] The final decision as to whether an ICD is burdensome should be made by the patient or a surrogate decision maker.[21] In a study by Buchhalter and colleagues[22] of patients who underwent cardiac device deactivation, more than half of the requests for device deactivation came from surrogate decision makers.

Whenever possible, deactivation should be performed by healthcare professionals with electrophysiology experience. This may include physicians and device-trained nurses or technologists. In the absence of a device-trained specialist, deactivation can be performed by a healthcare professional such as a physician or a nurse under the guidance of an industry representative.[23] When a patient is at home with hospice or home health, a pacemaker magnet can be used to deactivate an ICD generator if a programmer is unavailable.[14] These general steps can be followed in any setting in which deactivation occurs, including acute care hospitals, patient care facilities, or the patient's home. Pacemakers may be withdrawn by changing the programming mode or the rate may be lowered and the output adjusted so that the device is no longer functional. ICD deactivation can be performed by changing the programming or, for certain pulse generators, constant application of a magnet over the device. Placement of a magnet over a pulse generator of most ICDs will temporarily cease the anti-tachycardia therapies while not affecting the pacemaker function. To spare the patient from multiple painful shocks, a doughnut magnet and instructions for use should be provided to patients with a terminal diagnosis.[19] The patient should be reassured that deactivation of the ICD through reprogramming is not painful.[24] The defibrillator function of an ICD is separate from the pacing function. Pacing does not need to be disabled when the ICD is reprogrammed. Pacing may treat bradyarrhythmias and cardiac resynchronization at the end-of-life for symptomatic relief in patients without causing discomfort.[3]

Palliative Care and the Advanced Heart Failure Patient

Patients with advanced heart failure are living longer and with far more advanced modalities than once thought possible. And while the goal of medical innovation is to prolong or sustain life, the natural endpoint of all life, death, will eventually arrive. APRNs are often the primary providers for these patients over their disease continuum, and it is the time-tested strength of this patient-APRN partnership that builds trust and therapeutic rapport and facilitates discussions about difficult, but necessary, end-of-life topics. The APRN can initiate the discussion about advance illness planning and revisit this discussion during clinic appointments throughout the disease management trajectory.

APRNs can initiate the referral to palliative care for early, upstream involvement to ensure comprehensive, patient-focused care that is not solely "disease-focused" but involves critically assessing the overall needs of the patient, family, and caregivers while allowing for periodic reassessment of needs and preferences. Considerable discussion and attention tends to be given to life-sustaining treatment, while end-of-life issues are often considered the bane of patient-provider dialogue.[25,26] Yet, the literature supports the importance of discussions about the end-of-life, advance illness planning, and goals of care for patients with advanced illness.[27] For patients with advanced heart failure, especially those with assistive devices, early palliative care discussions and interventions are critical.[28]

Thanks to progress in biotechnology, devices can be used as destination therapy, aiming for stable provision of cardiac function; to this end, devices can now be safely and effectively implanted in the human body.[29] With this technology, however, comes the responsibility to ensure that patients are aware of the risks, complications, and adverse outcomes. Medical technology fosters the conviction that one doesn't have to die-yet. This further drives the resistance to discussions about care planning, end-of-life care, and code status. Palliative care provides care across the continuum of illness for patients with advanced medical disease, whether or not therapy is curative in intent. More and more, professional organizations are calling for earlier and more appropriate involvement of palliative care in the care of patients with advanced disease.[30,31] In palliative care, these challenging discussions provide the foundation for optimal care for cardiac failure patients, especially those with implanted devices. Withdrawal of device support is an issue rife with ethical and moral conflict, further emphasizing the need for early involvement of palliative care in partnership with cardiology so that effective, comprehensive care can be delivered to patients with advanced heart failure.[10,11,20,32–35]

There are many challenges to the integration of palliative care in the care of heart failure patients, likely due in part to the difficulty of prognostication in a population with exacerbations and a high risk for sudden death, as well as deficits in provider knowledge.[32] Patients with advanced heart failure have demonstrated preferences to cease therapies or procedures they deem to be ineffective or burdensome and may ask about deactivating devices that had been placed earlier in their disease course, when there was more benefit to be gained. As their disease trajectory evolves, patients demonstrate a desire and willingness to discuss end-of-life planning, to redefine the goals of care, and to establish a plan for pain and symptom management when their disease can no longer be controlled or managed by their present medical regimen.[27,33] Healthcare providers, often perceiving death as a "failure," tend to avoid these discussions.[25,26] The key to breaking down these barriers is continued promotion of palliative care education and awareness.[34,35] APRNs can facilitate the delivery of palliative care to heart failure patients by promoting their educational activities on their units and using resources from the End-of-Life Nursing Education Consortium (ELNEC). This national education initiative strives to enhance the delivery of palliative care by providing education and development tools for nursing staff. The ELNEC project provides APRNs with education in palliative care and advanced disease management and allows these nurse educators to "teach it forward" to their staff, peers, and healthcare colleagues.[36]

Symptom Management

The predominant symptoms of distress for most dying patients, and especially those with cardiopulmonary organ failure, are pain, anxiety, and dyspnea.[30,33,40] The goal of therapy for these symptoms is to ensure relief from suffering while allowing the desired level of interaction for as long as possible. Morphine is the medication most commonly used to relieve pain and dyspnea in heart failure in the non-palliative patient population presenting in florid distress.[37] The intravenous route is fastest for efficacy and relief in the acute inpatient setting, but for syndromes that become more chronic, oral regimens can be developed. Morphine is available in long-acting or short-acting, tablet, liquid, and intravenous

forms. There is no maximum dose of opioids for patients with end-of-life symptoms: patients must receive the dose that controls and relieves their distress and suffering and provides maximal comfort—sometimes in the necessary form of palliative sedation. Stronger medications may be necessary.[37–39] See Chapter 23, Pain, for further information.

The American Pain Society provides excellent guidelines and dosing recommendations for opioid medication management for end-stage or advanced illness.[37] *Principles of Analgesic Use in the Treatment of Acute Pain and Cancer Pain*[37] is a clinical resource that provides well-established guidelines for opioid initiation and management. This publication provides a solid framework and guidance for safe medication administration that can be useful for all practitioners.

The palliative APRN's goals for palliative care of the end-stage heart failure patient are to ensure clear patient and family communication, to provide psychosocial support, and, when indicated, to relieve pain, dyspnea, nausea, and any other distress. The APRN facilitates discussions to determine the goals of care by direct communication with the patient/family, by arranging a family meeting with palliative care and medical teams, or perhaps, if early in the disease trajectory, by simply initiating the referral to palliative care, with a preliminary patient discussion about the importance of planning for advanced illness and the services offered by additional consultants. Common symptoms to anticipate include chest pain, shortness of breath/dyspnea, air hunger, anxiety, nausea, and, later in the process, hallucinations. For patients with an LVAD, one of the most serious risk factors is a traumatic brain bleed, leading to death. For these patients, control of neurotrauma-related symptoms is of utmost importance, as they can often be most distressing to the family. Symptoms can include increased secretions, agitation, and myoclonic or seizure-like activity.

Pain and Dyspnea

Pain and dyspnea are best relieved using a multimodal approach: relief of pain and dyspnea with opioid therapy and additional control of air hunger with supplemental addition of air movement through a ceiling or oscillating fan. Air movement across one's face often reduces the sensation of breathlessness, leading to a decreased sense of air hunger/dyspnea and anxiety. A cooler temperature can also be helpful, as is reducing humidity, because humid air can also lead to feeling short of breath. The room should be comfortable for the patient, and its temperature should not add to his or her distress. For patients who are awake and alert, the use of oral opioids for pain and dyspnea is preferred; for those with refractory or uncontrolled symptoms, escalation to intravenous/continuous therapy is preferred.[30,31,38] See Chapter 23, Pain, for discussion of medications.

End-of-Life Medications Used in Cardiac Patients

Terminal cardiac patients struggle with symptoms that may be physical, psychological, and spiritual. Not all suffering is physical, but the physical symptoms may often cause the most initial distress to the patient and will be what the family members remember after death. In heart failure, the symptom prevalence is as follows: pain (78%), dyspnea (61%), depression (59%), insomnia (45%), anorexia (43%), anxiety (30%), constipation (37%), nausea/vomiting (32%), fatigue, difficulty ambulating, and edema.[40] The APRN should continue to evaluate the patient's comfort and symptom burden and determine when/if additional interventions are warranted.

Lorazepam (Ativan)

Lorazepam is used to treat anxiety due to disease progression, uncontrolled dyspnea, or fear of dying. Cardiac patients become more dyspneic with disease progression, leading to increasing levels of anxiety. They may also have nausea from the effects of hypoperfusion and hypotension, for which lorazepam may also provide relief.[40] It can be given as an elixir, subcutaneously, intravenously, or as a continuous infusion for management of nausea, agitation, anxiety, myoclonus, or seizures.

Dosing varies, based on the patient's history and needs. Begin at 0.5 mg intravenously or orally every 4 hours as needed and rapidly titrate up to an effective dose; doses may be needed every hour for some patients.[37,38]

Furosemide (Lasix)

Heart failure patients at the end-of-life often have fluid overload. Fluid status should be assessed prior to device removal. If fluid overload is noted, additional Lasix can be provided prior to withdrawal. Doses will vary, as heart failure patients through the course of their illness tend to tolerate relatively high doses of diuretics. Therefore, there is no "correct" dose, but instead there is a "right dose for the patient." A urinary catheter should be in place for comfort, as frequent urination could create more distress than relief. To further reduce fluid overload, the APRN should stop therapies that do not provide or contribute to comfort (e.g., intravenous fluids, continuous infusions). Opioids, when given as an infusion, can be concentrated to limit unnecessary fluids: the pharmacy can assist with this higher concentration.

Hyoscyamine (Levsin)

As their level of consciousness decreases, dying patients lose their ability to swallow and clear oral secretions. As air moves over the secretions, which have pooled in the oropharynx and bronchi, the resulting turbulence produces noisy ventilation with each breath, described as "gurgling" or "rattling" noises. While there is no evidence that patients find this "death rattle" disturbing, the noises may be disturbing to family, visitors, or caregivers, who worry the patient is choking to death. The death rattle is a good predictor of approaching death; one study indicated that the median time from onset of the death rattle to death was 16 hours.

Hyoscyamine should be given as an intravenous or subcutaneous injection for the management of oral secretions and is preferred over suctioning, which can cause further damage, swelling, edema, and secretions in the posterior airway and increase patient distress. Dosing generally begins at 0.125 mg given intravenously every 4 hours.[37,38]

Scopolamine (Transderm Scop)

An option for oral secretion management is scopolamine. Scopolamine patches decrease secretions over a longer period of time. While scopolamine should not be used for acute symptoms, it does have the benefit of a steady state of symptom management. The usual dose for scopolamine is a 1.5-mg patch placed on the hairless area of skin just behind one ear. The patch needs to be replaced every 72 hours.[41]

Haloperidol (Haldol)

Haloperidol can be given as a liquid or as a subcutaneous or intravenous injection for management of agitation, restlessness, nausea, or terminal delirium. Terminal delirium is an acute change in the level of arousal; features include an altered sleep/wake cycle, mumbling speech, disturbance of memory and attention, and perceptual disturbances accompanied by delusions and hallucinations. Haloperidol is commonly used for sedation. Haloperidol is administered in a dose-escalation process similar to that used to treat pain: the starting dose is 0.5 to 2 mg given orally or intravenously every hour as needed. [37,38]

Care to Promote Human Dignity

There are many non-pharmacological yet therapeutic options to assist in caring for dying patients that promote human dignity:

- ◆ If patient is feeling warm or uncomfortable: cool mouth swabs, cool compress to forehead

- ◆ For mild dyspnea: oscillating fan, air movement across the face

- ◆ For increased oral secretions (or those not yet controlled by medications like hyoscyamine), position the patient on his or her side or in a semi-prone position to facilitate postural drainage.

- ◆ For mild discomfort: gentle massage, soft music, comforting stimuli (e.g., reading favorite poems or stories, religious music, aromatherapy)

- ◆ Ask the patient and the family members or caregivers, "What helps you relax? What would help you feel more comfortable?" Try to meet their requests whenever possible.[36]

Conclusion

For patients with advanced heart failure, early intervention that represents a collaboration between cardiology and palliative care will optimize patient care and well-being. Truly patient-centered planning entails timely referral to, and partnership with, palliative care so that the plan of care can be customized. Early and ongoing discussions with patients and families are key. The management of heart failure begins with advance care planning. As heart failure worsens, the patient's needs will change, new symptoms will develop (or existing symptoms will intensify), and the goals of care may need to be revised. The heart failure APRN can serve as the advocate for heart failure patients and their families to ensure they receive excellent care throughout the illness and at the end-of-life. Keen assessment skills, partnership with palliative care, and close follow-up will ensure optimal symptom management. Heart failure APRNs manage cardiac medications and partner with palliative care for advanced modalities when the symptom burden intensifies or becomes refractory. APRNs caring for these patients must remember that end-of-life care, like many aspects of medicine, is not a perfect science. There is an art to balancing the needs of the patient and effective symptom management. Assessment and management of symptoms by the APRN can go a long way to facilitate quality of life. As the ancient Swahili proverb says: "When the elephants fight, it is the grass that suffers."[42]

References

1. Havel C, Arrich J, Losert H, Gamper G, Mullner M, Herkner H. Vasopressors for hypotensive shock. *Cochrane Database of Systematic Reviews*. 2011; 5: 1–76.

2. Yancy CW, Jessup M, Bozkut B, et al. 2013 ACCF/AHA Guideline for the Management of Heart Failure: A Report of the American College of Cardiology Foundation/American Heart Association Task Force on Practice Guidelines. *Circulation*. 2013; 1–6.

3. Murthy S, Lipman HI. Management of end-stage heart failure. *Prim Care Clin Office Pract*. 2011; 38: 265–76.

4. Kazory A, Ross EA. Emerging therapies for heart failure: renal mechanisms and effects. *Heart Fail Rev*. 2012; 17: 1–16.

5. Taitel M, Meaux N, Pegus C, Valerian C, Kirkham H. Place of death among patients with terminal heart failure in a continuous inotropic infusion program. *Am J Hosp Palliat Med*. 2012; 29(4): 249–53.

6. Slaughter MS, Rogers JG, Milano CA, et al. Advanced heart failure treated with continuous flow left ventricular assist device. *N Engl J Med*. 2009; 361: 2241–51.

7. Slaughter MS, Pagani FD, Rogers JG, et al. Clinical management of continuous flow left ventricular assist devices in advanced heart failure. *J Heart Lung Transplant*. 2010; 29(1) Supplement: S1–S39.

8. The Joint Commission. Prepublication Requirements. Requirements for Ventricular Assist Device Destination Therapy Advanced Certification. January 2014; 1–21.

9. Goldstein NE, May CW, Meier DE. Comprehensive care for mechanical circulatory support: A new frontier for synergy with palliative medicine. *Circ Heart Fail*. 2011; 4: 519–27.

10. Feldman D, Pamboukian SV, Teuteberg JJ, et al. The 2013 International Society of Heart and Lung Transplantation Guidelines for Mechanical Circulatory Support: Executive Summary. *J Heart Lung Transplant*. 2013; 32(2): 1–26.

11. Swetz KM, Freeman MR, Abou-Ezzeddine OF, et al. Palliative medicine consultation for preparedness planning in patients receiving left ventricular assist devices as destination therapy. *Mayo Clin Proc*. 2011; 86(6): 493–500.

12. Petrucci R, Benish LA, Carrow BL, et al. Ethical considerations for ventricular assist device support: A 10-point model. *ASAIO J*. 2011; 57: 268–73.

13. Allen LA. Stevenson LW, Grady KL, et al. Decision making in advanced heart failure: A scientific statement from the American Heart Association. *Circulation*. 2012; 125: 1928–52.

14. Wiegand DL, Kalowes PG. Withdrawal of cardiac medications and devices. *AACN Adv Crit Care*. 2007; 18(4): 415.

15. Kusumoto FM, Goldschlager N. Device therapy for cardiac arrhythmias. *JAMA*. 2002; 287(14): 1848–52.

16. Bardy GH, Lee KL, Mark DB, Poole JE, Boineau R, Domanski M. Amiodarone or an implantable cardioverter-defibrillator for congestive heart failure. *N Engl J Med*. 2005; 352(3): 225–37.

17. Jarcho JA. Biventricular pacing. *N Engl J Med*. 2006; 355: 288–94.

18. Kramer DB, Reynolds MR, Mitchell SL. Resynchronization: Considering device-based cardiac therapy in older adults. *J Am Geriatr Soc*. 2013; 61: 615–21.

19. Lampert R, Hayes DL, Annas GJ, et al. HRS Expert Consensus Statement on the Management of Cardiovascular Implantable Electronic Devices (CIEDs) in patients nearing end of life or requesting withdrawal of therapy. *Heart Rhythm*. 2010; 7(7): 1008–26.

20. Morganweck CJ. Ethical considerations for discontinuing pacemakers and automatic implantable cardiac defibrillators at end-of-life. *Curr Opin Anesthesiol*. 2013; 26: 171–5.

21. Wiegand DL, Kalowes PG. Withdrawal of cardiac medications and devices. *AACN Adv Crit Care*. 2007; 18(4): 415–25.

22. Buchhalter LC, Ottenberg AL, Webster TL, Swetz KM, Hayes DL, Mueller PS. Features and outcomes of patients who underwent cardiac device deactivation. *JAMA Intern Med*. 2014; 174(1): 80–5.

23. Lindsay BD, Estes MNA 3rd, Maloney JD, Reynolds DW. Heart Rhythm Society Policy Statement Update: Recommendations on the Role of Industry Employed Allied Professionals (IEAPs). *Heart Rhythm*. 2008; 5(11): e8–10.

24. Goldstein N, Carlson M, Livote E, Kutner JS. Brief Communication: Management of implantable cardioverter-defibrillators in hospice: a nationwide survey. *Ann Intern Med*. 2010; 152: 296–9.

25. Hemani S, Letizia MJ. Providing palliative care in end-stage heart failure. *J Hosp Palliat Nurs*. 2008; 10(2): 100–5.

26. O'Neill BJ, Kazer MW. Destination to nowhere: a new look at aggressive treatment for heart failure—a case study. *Crit Care Nurse*. 2014; 34(2): 47–56. doi: 10.4037/ccn2014442.

27. Connors AF Jr, Dawson NV, Desbiens NA, et al. A controlled trial to improve care for seriously ill hospitalized patients: The Study to Understand Prognoses and Preferences for Outcomes and Risks of Treatments (SUPPORT). *JAMA*. 1995; 274(20): 1591–8.

28. Ben Gal T, Jaarsma T. Self-care and communication issues at the end of life of recipients of a left-ventricular assist device as destination therapy. *Curr Opin Support Palliat Care*. 2013; 7(1): 29–35. doi: 10.1097/SPC.0b013e32835d2d50.

29. Rady MY Verheijde JL. End-of-life discontinuation of destination therapy with cardiac and ventilatory support medical devices: physician-assisted death or allowing the patient to die? *BMC Med Ethics*. 2010; 11: 15. doi: 10.1186/1472-6939-11-15

30. Mularski RA, Reinke LF, Carrieri-Kohlman V, et al., on behalf of the ATS Ad Hoc Committee on Palliative Management of Dyspnea Crisis. An Official American Thoracic Society Workshop Report: Assessment and palliative management of dyspnea crisis. *Ann Am Thorac Soc*. 2013; 10(5): S98–S106.

31. Lanken PN, Terry PB, Delisser HM, et al.. An official American Thoracic Society clinical policy statement: Palliative medicine for patients with respiratory diseases and critical illnesses. *Am J Respir Crit Care Med*. 2008; 177(8): 912–27. doi: 10.1164/rccm.200605-587ST

32. McKenna M, Wrightson N, Regnard C, Clark S. Life-sustaining medical devices at the end of life. *BMJ Support Palliat Care*. 2013; 3(1): 5–7. doi: 10.1136/bmjspcare-2012-000364.

33. Whellan DJ, Goodlin SJ, Dickinson MG, et al.; Quality of Care Committee, Heart Failure Society of America. End-of-life care in patients with heart failure. *J Card Fail*. 2014; 20(2): 121–34. doi: 10.1016/j.cardfail.2013.12.003.

34. Kavalieratos DI, Mitchell EM, Carey TS, et al. "Not the 'grim reaper service'": an assessment of provider knowledge, attitudes, and perceptions regarding palliative medicine referral barriers in heart failure. *J Am Heart Assoc*. 2014; 3(1): e000544. doi: 10.1161/JAHA.113.000544.

35. Brush S, Budge D, Alharethi R, et al. End of life decision making and implementation in recipients of a destination left ventricular assist device. *J Heart Lung Transplant*. 2010; 29: 1337–41.

36. American Association of Colleges of Nursing. End-of-Life Nursing Education Consortium (ELNEC). Available at http://www.aacn.nche.edu/elnec. Accessed May 7, 2014.

37. Chou R, Fanciullo GJ, Fine PG, et al; American Pain Society-American Academy of Pain Medicine Opioids Guidelines Panel. Clinical guidelines for the use of chronic opioid therapy in chronic noncancer pain. *J Pain*. 2009; 10(2): 113–30.

38. American Pain Society. 2008. C Miaskowski, M Bair, R Chou, Y D'Arcy, C Hartwick, L Huffman, J Maleki, R Manworren (eds). *Principles of Analgesic Use in the Treatment of Acute Pain and Cancer Pain*. 6th ed. American Pain Society, Chicago, IL.

39. Chou R, Cruciani RA, Fiellin DA, et al. Methadone safety: A clinical practice guideline from the American Pain Society and College on Problems of Drug Dependence, in Collaboration With the Heart Rhythm Society. *J Pain*. 2014; 15(4): 321–37. doi:10.1016/j.jpain.2014.01.494

40. Reisfield GM, Wilson GR. Palliative Care Issues in Heart Failure. Fast Facts and Concepts. October 2005; 144. Available at http://www.eperc.mcw.edu/EPERC/FastFactsIndex/ff_144.htm.

41. Hirsch CA, Marriott JF, Faull CM. Influences on the decision to prescribe or administer anticholinergic drugs to treat death rattle: a focus group study. *Palliat Med*. 2013; 27(8): 732–8. doi: 10.1177/0269216312464407.

42. Healey JG, Sybertz DF. *Towards an African Narrative Theology*. Maryknoll, NY: Orbis Books; 1997.

CHAPTER 49

Withdrawal of Respiratory Technology

Beth Wagner

Key Points

- The palliative advanced practice registered nurse (APRN) must have clinical knowledge of respiratory conditions that warrant respiratory support.

- The palliative APRN must understand the clinical, ethical, and legal aspects of discontinuing respiratory support.

- The palliative APRN should anticipate and proactively manage symptoms associated with discontinuation of respiratory support.

- Standardized protocols for withdrawal of life-sustaining respiratory therapies provide structured guidance, reduce variation in practice, and improve satisfaction of families and healthcare care providers.

Case Study

PC was a 64-year-old male with a history of esophageal cancer. Four years earlier, he underwent surgical resection of the tumor and placement of a tracheostomy and received chemotherapy. Recently, he was admitted to the hospital with esophageal bleeding, weight loss, and shortness of breath. He developed acute shortness of breath that led to respiratory arrest. CPR was administered and PC was transferred to the intensive care unit and was placed on a ventilator. Workup revealed a mass in the mainstem bronchus causing obstruction and pneumonia. A biopsy of the mass was positive for recurrent esophageal cancer. The patient was treated with antibiotics for the pneumonia, and his mental status improved until he was awake and alert. An attempt to place a pulmonary stent to treat the pulmonary obstruction and facilitate weaning from the ventilator was unsuccessful.

The APRN coordinated a family meeting with the patient and his family to address goals of care. After the APRN informed the patient of the inability to wean him from the ventilator and his poor prognosis given his recurrent, metastatic cancer, the patient expressed wishes to remove life support and said he hoped he could be transferred, so he could die at home. He said he wanted to remain as awake and alert as possible so that he could interact with his family, but his priority was relief of his shortness of breath. The APRN ordered a bolus of morphine 10 mg IV followed by the initiation of a morphine infusion at 5 mg/hr. The patient also received lorazepam 1 mg IV.

Once he was comfortable, the ventilator was discontinued. The patient received additional prn boluses of morphine to keep his respiratory rate less than 28 bpm. The morphine infusion was increased to 7.5 mg/hr. After a few hours, the patient had no behavioral indicators of discomfort and had not required any further morphine or lorazepam boluses. The patient was sedated, so an attempt was made to decrease the continuous infusion to allow him to be more alert and interactive, as he requested. However, when the continuous rate was decreased, the patient became restless and his respiratory rate increased to 34 bpm. He was given a PRN morphine bolus and his continuous rate was returned to the previous rate at which he was comfortable. He was transferred to his home with support of hospice care and continued receiving the morphine infusion. He died at home with his family at his bedside 3 days later.

Introduction

Respiratory failure can be fundamentally defined as the inability of the lungs to provide adequate oxygenation or ventilation to sustain life. The symptoms of respiratory failure are distressing for patients and can lead to abrupt clinical deterioration. Respiratory failure accounts for approximately 12% of all hospital costs and 7% of all hospital days. More than 50% of these expenditures involve patients older than 65 years.[1] Advances in technology over the past decade have produced a substantial number of life-sustaining therapies for patients with respiratory failure. Examples of advanced therapies for managing respiratory failure include high-flow oxygen therapy, invasive and noninvasive mechanically-assisted ventilation, prostacyclin therapy, and extracorporeal membrane oxygenation (ECMO). Predicting which patients will benefit from these therapies is often challenging for clinicians.

Guidelines for Withdrawal of Respiratory Support

The transition from curative or restorative therapy to comfort-only care is often difficult for patients, loved ones, and the clinical staff. The majority of deaths in the intensive care unit (ICU) occur after

Table 49.1 Steps for Terminal Weaning from Mechanical Ventilation

- Ensure patient's comfort prior to initiating.

- Reduce FiO₂ to 21% or room air and remove positive end-expiratory pressure (PEEP). Observe for signs of respiratory distress. Adjust opioids and benzodiazepines.

- Reduce IMV rate and/or PS to 4–6 over 5–20 minutes. Observe for signs of respiratory distress. Adjust medication.

- Deflate ETT cuff if present.

- Silence alarm; turn off ventilator.

- Disconnect tubing from the tracheostomy or remove the ETT while covering with a clean towel that will collect the secretions as well as hide the ETT. If not removing the ETT, disconnect connection to ventilator and apply T-piece with humidified air.

- If oropharyngeal secretions are present, suction gently. Avoid deep suction.

- Oxygen is not necessary.

- Move ventilator out of room.

- Encourage family to touch and hold patient. Some may want to lie in bed beside the patient.

From references 3, 15, and 17.

decision to limit or withdraw life-sustaining therapies.[2] Death often occurs rapidly following the removal of respiratory life support, which places a great burden of decision on families and care providers.[3] Removing life-sustaining therapy involves complex decisions filled with a myriad of emotions for all involved. APRNs involved in the withdrawal of respiratory support must understand the ethical principles and legal issues involved and must have top-notch communication skills. See Chapter 42, Navigating Ethical Conversations in Palliative Care.

The palliative APRN guides the process of withdrawing life-sustaining therapies to prevent patient suffering and to diminish family distress. Because of lack of evidence-based protocols, significant variation in practice exists for the withdrawal of respiratory support. Consensus guidelines have emerged to promote quality and improve end-of-life care for critical care patients.[4,5] Table 49.1 lists essential steps to include in clinical pathways, multidisciplinary care plans, or protocols to provide guidance for the care of patients when respiratory life support is withdrawn.

Oxygen

The delivery of supplemental oxygen is an integral medical treatment modality offered across all settings. A wide variety of systems are available to provide oxygen to patients who have dyspnea or cannot maintain adequate oxygenation through spontaneous breathing. The choice of an oxygen delivery system depends on numerous factors, including disease state, clinical status, amount of oxygen required, and patient comfort and acceptance. The goals of oxygen therapy are to attain adequate resting oxygen levels to prevent damage to the tissue from hypoxia, to minimize the risk of oxygen-induced injury, and to provide symptom relief. In general, an oxygen saturation (SpO₂) of more than 90% or a partial pressure of oxygen in arterial blood (PaO₂) of more than 60 mmHg is adequate to meet metabolic demands. Specific goals are individualized for specific disease states or severity of illness,

such as chronic obstructive pulmonary disease (COPD) and acute respiratory distress syndrome (ARDS).

A nasal cannula is the most commonly used method to provide supplemental oxygen in the hospital or ambulatory setting.[6] Both low- and high-flow oxygen rates can be delivered by nasal cannula. The initial nasal cannula design provided only low-flow oxygen, with flow rates up to 6 L/min. In this system, 100% oxygen is directed through a bubbler humidifier at a rate of approximately 1 to 6 L/min. The oxygen mixes with inspired air, resulting in delivery of an oxygen concentration of approximately 25% to 40%, depending on patient's respiratory rate, tidal volume, and use of mouth breathing.[7] Oxygen is used to alleviate dyspnea in people with COPD with severe hypoxia, but there is sparse evidence that oxygen relieves breathlessness in mild hypoxemic or nonhypoxemic conditions.[8]

There is no support for the initiation or continuation of oxygen therapy when the patient is nonhypoxemic or comfortable and near death.[9] A randomized, controlled, double-blind trial comparing oxygen and room air via nasal cannula in outpatients with refractory dyspnea revealed no significant difference in the relief of breathlessness.[10] Although supplemental oxygen is frequently ordered in palliative care, the burdens of uncomfortable masks, interference with communication, and irritation from cold or wet air on the face are likely to mitigate any benefit. The use of a fan directed toward the patient's face or cognitive-behavioral therapy can diminish breathlessness.[8,11]

The high-flow nasal cannula oxygen (HFNCOx) system involves delivery of heated and humidified oxygen via specialized oxygen blenders that are capable of flow rates of 8 L/min in infants and up to 60 L/min in children and adults. In addition, HFNCOx generates a low level of positive airway pressure with greater ease of use and patient comfort compared to therapies with tight face masks, such as bilevel positive airway pressure (BiPAP).[12] HFNCOx maintains an elevated FiO₂ by using high flow rates to increase arterial oxygenation and promote nasopharyngeal washout of entrapped room air, resulting in decreased upper airway resistance and work of breathing.[13] The components of a HFNCOx system include a patient interface, a gas delivery device to control flow and FiO₂, and a humidifier. Unlike non-rebreather systems, high-flow oxygen therapy systems use a nasal cannula, allowing patients to talk and eat while receiving high-flow oxygen; this contributes to the improved tolerability and acceptance.

Patients report improved comfort and greater tolerance with HFNCOx compared to face mask oxygen devices.[6,14] The use of HFNCOx is on the rise in large part because of emerging evidence demonstrating improved tolerability, ease of application, and a potential role in preventing unnecessary ICU admissions in palliative care patients when compared to face masks or noninvasive ventilation therapies.[14] There is a trend toward using HFNCOx as an alternative to noninvasive positive-pressure ventilation for patients with a Do Not Intubate status who are receiving comfort-only care.[12] The clinical indications or guidelines for use, however, are not yet clearly established.[13]

Because oxygen levels naturally will decrease in all imminently dying patients, oxygen provides little to no palliative benefit. Removal of the oxygen may provide further comfort by not prolonging the dying process, and by removing the discomfort caused by the oxygen, such as the feeling of claustrophobia from the equipment or drying and irritation of the nasal mucosa.

The removal of the oxygen may promote interaction between the patient and loved ones, because the patient's face is no longer encumbered by tubes or masks. If patients are awake, they may be able to express their preference for removal of the oxygen. That discussion should include assurance to the patient and family that the symptom of breathlessness will be controlled in either approach. Dyspnea at the end-of-life can be controlled by pharmacologic and nonpharmacologic interventions (detailed later in the chapter). Low-flow oxygen can be provided in any setting, including the home and nursing facilities, so continuation of the oxygen does not affect the transition out of the hospital setting. HFNCOx requires specialized air compression systems to generate the high flow rates, and these are primarily available only in acute care settings and generally not in the home or hospice.

A major challenge arises for patients in the acute care setting who are receiving HFNCOx and who are stable but cannot progress with weaning. With increasing reports of positive outcomes with the use of HFNCOx, more patients are placed on HFNCOx but then do not improve. Because of its limited availability outside the acute care setting, these patients are often faced with the decision to discontinue HFNCOx therapy. Therefore, when contemplating the application of HFNCOx, it should be considered to be like any other form of life support, and a discussion of the goals of care and benefit versus burden should precede its use. New technology is emerging for the administration of HFNCOx in the home or hospice. However, due to the very specialized equipment and high costs, it is unlikely that in the near future it will be routinely available in hospice care. For patients who want to die at home, the benefits and burdens of HFNCOx therapy needs to be addressed.

There are no specific evidence-based guidelines for discontinuation of either high-flow or low-flow oxygen. Patients requiring HFNCOx to maintain adequate oxygenation saturation levels will likely experience dyspnea upon withdrawal. Often, the oxygen is gradually tapered because of theoretical concerns that increased respiratory distress may occur with rapid withdrawal. Proponents of rapid discontinuation argue that gradual tapering will prolong the dying process. Protocols using a gradual taper of HFNCOx often suggest progressive step reductions in flow and FiO_2. One approach for a gradual taper is to reduce FiO_2 levels to less than 40% and then to reduce the flow rate. Throughout the process, the patient is monitored for signs of discomfort or increased work of breathing. Monitoring of the SpO_2 is not necessary. Any symptoms are aggressively treated and controlled as outlined below, before proceeding with the taper. This process is repeated until the patient is comfortable on room air, or death occurs.

Mechanical Ventilation

Mechanical ventilation involves the support of breathing by means of an external machine in patients with respiratory failure. It can be provided either by an invasive technique, such as endotracheal intubation, or a noninvasive technique, such as noninvasive positive-pressure ventilation (NPPV) through a mask applied to the mouth or nose. The indications for mechanical ventilation include the inability to sustain adequate oxygenation, the need for the elimination of carbon dioxide, or maintenance and protection of the airway. Any decision to initiate mechanical ventilation should be preceded by a discussion with the patient and/or family that reviews the goals of care, the benefits and burdens of the intervention, and alternative treatment options.

Invasive Mechanical Ventilation

Invasive mechanical ventilation provides gas exchange in the lungs with an artificial airway that is established via an endotracheal or tracheostomy tube. A large-bore flexible tube is used as the interface between the endotracheal tube (ETT) or the tracheostomy tube and the ventilator. Orotracheal intubation is the most common method of inserting an ETT, but nasotracheal intubation is also possible to maintain the patency of the upper airway. Endotracheal intubation is considered a relatively temporary procedure, because long-term use increases the risk of complications related to cuff pressures or erosion caused by the tube. Guidelines suggest that patients should not be ventilated via an ETT for longer than 3 weeks, with the average time left in place being approximately 2 weeks before converting to the tracheostomy tube. Through an incision into the trachea, a tracheostomy tube is surgically placed to provide long-term airway access.

Detailed planning for withdrawal of invasive mechanical ventilation at the end-of-life ensures the patient's comfort during the process. Many of the recommendations regarding the "how-to's" for withdrawal of the ventilator are based on theoretical considerations and clinical experience, with very little evidence-based research on the specific interventions. The use of protocols, guidelines, standardized order forms, or algorithms that outline steps has been found to be helpful in guiding the process.[15] Dyspnea, respiratory distress, and anxiety should be anticipated with ventilator withdrawal. Opioids and benzodiazepines are the mainstay for the pharmacologic treatment of the dyspnea and anxiety associated with withdrawal of the ventilator. They are discussed later in the chapter. Terminal extubation of alert patients requires some special consideration, as there is the potential risk of suffering longer survival period than expected.[16]

Two methods of ventilator withdrawal have been described. One is a rapid or immediate cessation of mechanical ventilation, sometimes referred to as terminal extubation. The other method is terminal weaning, which is the gradual, stepwise withdrawal of ventilation, with assessment and interventions for discomfort before moving to the next step. Evidence is largely lacking to support one practice over another. Steps for a gradual wean based on principles and recommendations from the literature are outlined in Table 49.1.[3,15,17] There are few data to guide the decision to keep or remove the ETT at the time of extubation. Leaving the tube in place may be a source of discomfort to patients as well as a barrier to interactions or comfort measures by loved ones, such as washing their face with a wet cloth, providing mouth care, and touching or kissing the face. Airway problems can develop after extubation and should be considered when making the decision to keep or remove the ETT. Certain patients are at greater risk for airway compromise if the tube is removed. These include patients experiencing bleeding in the upper respiratory tract, stridor, excessive secretions, and occlusion secondary to external compression by a tumor or a swollen tongue.

NPPV

NPPV refers to assisted ventilation by the application of BiPAP, delivered through an externally placed mask, mouthpiece, or helmet apparatus. The oronasal mask is generally preferred over a nasal mask or nasal prongs during the initiation of NPPV. The full face mask may be an option for patients who experience discomfort, such as excessive device pressure, or fail to achieve adequate improvement in gas exchange. The use of NPPV has gained increasing acceptance as a first-line therapy for patients with acute respiratory failure to temporize pulmonary status while treating the patient to avoid endotracheal intubation. It is less invasive, often requires less sedation, and is associated with lower rates of ventilator-associated pneumonia than endotracheal intubation. The use of NPPV can reduce the rate of endotracheal intubation by providing additional time to assess and correct a reversible process.

Conditions known to respond to NPPV include exacerbations of COPD, respiratory failure in immunocompromised patients and cardiogenic pulmonary edema, and amyotrophic lateral sclerosis (ALS).[18] The escalating use of NPPV as a palliative treatment in patients who have advanced disease or who have decided to forgo life-prolonging therapies has aroused controversy. NPPV may be more effective than oxygen to reduce dyspnea and the amount of administered opioid in some patient populations, but it has significant burdens that lead to poor tolerance and the potential to unnecessarily prolong the dying process. It can be an effective stabilizing measure for a patient who prefers to remain more alert or to delay death until family or loved ones can arrive at the bedside.[19]

Relative contraindications for the use of NPPV include facial trauma or anatomy limiting placement of the mask; inability of the patient to cooperate, protect the airway, or clear secretions; high aspiration risk; severely impaired consciousness; recent esophageal anastomosis; and upper airway obstruction.[20] Factors that may reduce the tolerance or acceptance of therapy include discomfort from a tight-fitting mask or high-pressure air flow, facial skin breakdown, claustrophobia, anxiety, aspiration, dryness of mucous membranes, loud noise of the machine, and interference with communication and family intimacy. Small doses of a benzodiazepine can alleviate anxiety.

To facilitate evaluation of research and decision making in the use of NPPV, a task force of the Society of Critical Care Medicine proposed classifying patients with acute respiratory failure into three categories, with specific recommendations for each:[18]

1. *NPPV as life support in patients who desire full, life-prolonging interventions*: The primary goal is to restore health back to patient's baseline, regardless of the prognosis. Evidence thus far suggests NPPV can offer benefit to patients with COPD exacerbation, hypoxic respiratory failure in the setting of immunocompromise, and congestive heart failure, and possible benefit to patients with neuromuscular diseases like ALS.[17] If the NPPV does not improve respiratory status, intubation and ventilation will be initiated.

2. *NPPV as life support in patients who desire life-prolonging interventions but not use of endotracheal intubation*: The primary goal is to restore health and relieve symptoms without the use of endotracheal intubation. Evidence supporting use of NPPV in patients in this category suggests some benefit in patients with COPD exacerbation, immunocompromise, and congestive heart failure. If the NPPV does not improve respiratory status, or if the dyspnea remains severe, the goal of care will change to comfort-only and the NPPV will be discontinued.

3. *NPPV for palliation of symptoms in patients requesting no endotracheal intubation and comfort measures only*: The primary goal is to maximize comfort by easing dyspnea, reducing the work of breathing, and maintaining alertness. On occasion, the goal may be to prolong life to meet a specific goal, such as allowing time for family or friends to arrive at the bedside. Evidence to support the use of NPPV in patients in this category is lacking. Two randomized feasibility studies suggest that NPPV offers benefit in terms of reducing dyspnea[19,21] and lowering the amount of opioids administered[19] in patients with advanced cancer, but the studies also included patients from category 2 above. There is a need for larger controlled trials to assess NPPV's effectiveness.

Before initiating NPPV, clinicians should engage the patient or family in discussions regarding the goals of care and should outline a plan that defines success or failure, with clear criteria for discontinuation of NPPV. Examples of intended goals may be alleviation of dyspnea within 1 or 2 hours of maximally tolerated settings, acceptable level of alertness and comfort, or delay of death if possible for a limited time.[22] Once it is determined that NPPV is no longer meeting the goals of care, it should be discontinued.

At the time of withdrawal of NPPV, patients can experience significant respiratory distress.[23,24] Removal of NPPV requires many of the same considerations as ETT removal. The APRN must be prepared to intervene for distressing symptoms like dyspnea, increased work of breathing, and anxiety. Prior to weaning NPPV, the initiation of opioids and benzodiazepines may help to ensure patient comfort before proceeding.

There are no evidence-based protocols for weaning NPPV at the end-of-life. Common practice employs incremental reduction of the inspiratory positive airway pressure (iPap) by 2 cm H_2O, in conjunction with gradual reduction in FiO_2. The backup rate setting, which triggers an automatic cycle on some machines if a patient does not spontaneously take a breath, can be turned off in dying patients. Symptoms of respiratory distress are aggressively treated and controlled before proceeding. Once the iPap is approximately 6 cm H_2O or less above expiratory positive pressure and the patient is comfortable, NPPV can be removed. There is no evidence to support automatic placement of nasal cannula oxygen when NPPV is removed in an end-of-life scenario.

Extracorporeal Life Support

Extracorporeal life support (ECLS), also known as ECMO, provides continuous cardiopulmonary support for a temporary period, typically days to weeks, as supportive management of severe respiratory and/or cardiac failure.

This technique uses a modified heart-lung bypass machine that pumps and oxygenates a patient's blood, thus allowing the heart and lungs to rest. The purpose of ECLS is to facilitate recovery of the lungs and heart by minimizing ventilator-induced lung injury, while allowing additional time to diagnose and treat the underlying disease.

ECLS accomplishes bypass of the normal heart-lung circulation through a device (called "the circuit") that transports the blood outside the patient's body through an artificial lung. The artificial lung contains two compartments separated by a gas-permeable membrane, with the blood on one side and the ventilating gas on the other, where carbon dioxide is extracted and the blood is oxygenated. It is then warmed and returned to the heart. Vascular access is usually achieved by cannulation of large vessels in the neck or the groin. The cannula provides the interface between the circuit and the patient and can be placed surgically or percutaneously, depending on the configuration of ECLS used.

The two most common configurations of ECLS are veno-arterial (V-A) and veno-venous (V-V). The V-A configuration provides both cardiac and respiratory support. Blood is withdrawn from venous circulation and returns to arterial circulation through either peripheral or central cannulation. Femoral venous and femoral arterial cannulation are preferred in adult patients.[25] The V-V configuration drains blood from the venous circulation; it is returned to the venous circulation close to the right atrium through peripheral cannulation, typically using the right internal jugular and/or femoral veins in adults. The V-V configuration provides respiratory support only, with no hemodynamic support, and therefore is used when the heart is functioning well and only the lungs require support. If only respiratory support is needed, this method is preferred, because it reduces the risk of complications associated with arterial cannulation, such as limb ischemia and thrombotic or air emboli.

Selecting patients who may benefit from this technology is the key to its success. It was initially used exclusively in newborns but now is increasingly used in adults as a temporary support for patients with respiratory and/or cardiac failure, usually awaiting recovery of organs. Studies are limited and demonstrate a substantial risk of death; however, recent trials showed a reduction in mortality and severe disability in patients with acute respiratory failure receiving ECMO.[25] Potential patients must have severe, but potentially reversible, acute heart or lung failure that is unresponsive to conventional management. Criteria also include patients who have a mortality risk greater than 50% but a treatable underlying disease process with an expectation of the ability to return to a good quality of life.

ECLS has been instituted for cardiac support in patients who cannot be removed from cardiopulmonary bypass following cardiac surgery, post heart transplant with primary graft failure, and severe cardiac failure due to other causes, such as sepsis, decompensated cardiomyopathy, myocarditis, and drug overdose. In addition, ECLS is used to provide support for patients as a bridge to either placement of a ventricular assist device or cardiac transplantation. Common indications for patients requiring pulmonary support include respiratory failure due to pneumonia, ARDS, trauma, or primary graft failure following lung transplant. ECLS for influenza has been performed in neonatal and pediatric populations, with an overall survival rate to discharge of 50%.[25] There is growing interest in the area of influenza for adolescents and adults after a recent report on patients with H1N1-related ARDS demonstrated that referral and transfer to an ECMO center were associated with lower hospital mortality compared with matched patients who did not receive ECMO.[26] As the technology evolves, it is expected that it may increasingly be used as a salvage strategy.

In patients with the V-V configuration, the trial off the system is relatively simple. Once ventilator settings reach levels that can support the patient without ECLS, the sweep gas is stopped and the oxygenator is capped off. If lung function remains acceptable for an hour or more, the patient is ready for decannulation. A trial off the V-A system is more complex, because it requires clamping of the extracorporeal circuit and echocardiography to assess cardiac function. If the trial is successful, the cannulas are heparinized and capped and left in place for 24 hours or more before decannulation.

Venous and arterial cannulas placed by percutaneous access can be removed directly and bleeding controlled by application of direct pressure. Cannulas placed by direct cutdown are removed by direct cutdown, with ligation of the vessel if needed. Femoral artery cannulation by cutdown requires vascular repair at the time of cannula removal.

If the patient does not improve, ECLS should be discontinued as soon as the medical team determines there is no realistic expectation for recovery or organ replacement by a ventricular assist device or transplant. Ideally, the possibility of stopping and the criteria for discontinuing ECLS are discussed with family prior to starting the therapy. This discussion should include an explanation of the therapy, the intended outcome, and a reasonable timeframe for organ recovery or replacement. Guidelines from the Extracorporeal Life Support Organization (ELSO) list criteria (Table 49.2) to consider in the determination of futility and discontinuation of ECLS.[27]

The administration of medications to control end-of-life symptoms in patients supported by ECLS requires knowledge of the unique alterations in pharmacokinetic parameters. Evidence-based studies describing pharmacokinetics during ECMO are sparse but indicate substantial variability and an unpredictable pharmacologic effect. Clinical observations report higher dosing requirements for sedatives and analgesics for patients on ECMO.[28] Studies suggest this is a result of an increased volume of distribution and alteration in renal and hepatic blood flow causing alterations in drug elimination.

In addition, drug sequestration by the ECLS circuit has been observed with several medications, including some commonly used for end-of-life symptom management, such as opioids (morphine, fentanyl), benzodiazepines (midazolam, diazepam, lorazepam), and propofol. It can later result in a prolonged release of the drug from the circuit after the drug is stopped. This presents significant challenges for effective dosing of the analgesics and sedatives necessary to provide comfort in patients undergoing ECLS. A strong correlation exists between the lipophilicity of a drug and the extent of drug absorption.[28,29] Lipophilic drugs, such as fentanyl, and highly protein-bound drugs are significantly sequestered in the circuit, leading to suboptimal drug concentrations in the body.[28] For this reason it appears that morphine, a hydrophilic drug, may be superior to fentanyl in patients on ECLS.[28] Because of numerous variables affecting the sequestration of drugs and rapid advances in the technology, simply increasing the dose administered is not effective and may result in toxic levels. There

Table 49.2 Criteria for Determination of Futility and Discontinuation of ECLS (ELSO Guidelines)

Severe brain damage
No cardiac function after 3 days in a patient who is not a ventricular assist device or transplant candidate
No lung function after 14–50 days in a patient who is not a transplant candidate
Fixed pulmonary hypertension after several weeks
Uncontrolled bleeding
Other irreversible organ failure

Note: The definition of irreversible heart, lung, or brain damage will vary by institution.

are insufficient data, especially in adults, to provide specific recommendations for drug choice and dosing. Until there are further clinical studies to provide dosing guidance and document outcomes in this specific population, drug regimens should be individualized through both clinical and therapeutic drug monitoring whenever possible.

Prostacyclin Therapy

Prostacyclin therapy is commonly used in the treatment of pulmonary arterial hypertension (PAH) as a palliative measure to extend life and control symptoms. PAH is a progressive, terminal illness characterized by dysfunction of the pulmonary arteries. Vasoconstriction and vascular hypertrophy within the pulmonary artery lead to restriction of blood flow, which increases peripheral vascular resistance and eventually right-sided heart failure. Exertional dyspnea with exercise intolerance is the most common and debilitating symptom of PAH. Despite advances in therapies, the prognosis remains poor, with a 15% 1-year mortality rate and 48% 5-year survival. Patients will experience progressive deterioration along with periods of acute decompensation. The goal of therapy for PAH is to slow disease progression and control exertional dyspnea by lowering pulmonary arterial pressure and pulmonary vascular resistance.

Prostacyclin is a naturally occurring prostaglandin that inhibits the aggregation of platelets and is a potent vasodilator used in the treatment of advanced PAH. Currently, three prostacyclin analogues are used in the treatment of PAH: treprostinil (Remodulin), iloprost (Ventavis), and epoprostenol (Flolan, Veletri). Treprostinil is available in intravenous, subcutaneous, or inhaled formulations. Iloprost is administered via inhalation. Epoprostenol has a very short half-life of approximately 6 minutes, so it can be administered only via continuous intravenous infusion. Prostacyclin therapy can be administered in the home, but the complexity of epoprostenol infusion can be arduous for patients and their caregivers.

Prostacyclin therapy presents unique challenges with respect to end-of-life issues. It is a life-sustaining therapy that may be needed for prolonged periods of time. Abrupt withdrawal, large reductions in dosage, or interruptions in drug delivery can lead to sudden rebound pulmonary hypertension and severe respiratory distress. Prostacyclin therapy requires a lifelong commitment, with lifestyle changes, especially with the parenteral infusions, which entail ongoing subcutaneous access or a permanent intravenous catheter and infusion pump, without any break from the therapy. It is difficult to predict when patients will die, because death may come suddenly or slowly.

The high cost of the treatment may be a barrier to enrollment in hospice care. Communication before the initiation of prostacyclin therapy and throughout treatment is vital to ensure a good quality of life for the patient, family, and caregivers. Patients and their caregivers need to understand the practical consequences of the treatment and define their expectations for quality of life. Discussions that address prognosis, goals of care, and preferences regarding cardiopulmonary resuscitation or mechanical ventilation will promote shared decision making. Preparing the patient, family, and caregivers for discontinuation when the therapy is no longer meeting the goals of the patient is important to reduce distress and the possibility of ethical dilemmas.

When the goals of care change to a comfort-only approach, a decision needs to be made regarding discontinuation of the prostacyclin therapy. Most patients with PAH die in the ICU.[30] The high in-hospital mortality rate may be related to numerous factors, including symptom burden, provider experience, moral objection to discontinuation, failure to address goals of care, and barriers to hospice care for patients continuing prostacyclin therapy. There are no published guidelines for managing end-of-life care for patients with PAH. Recommendations come from expert professional opinions and clinical case studies.[31,32] De-escalation of intravenous prostacyclin should occur in a setting with close medical supervision, knowledgeable staff, and sufficient amounts of readily available medications to allow for rapid adjustments and administration to ensure symptom management and comfort.

Recommendations suggest the reduction of the prostacyclin in 10% to 25% increments.[30,33] The medication's half-life affects the rate of taper. Epoprostenol, with a half-life of approximately 6 minutes, can be tapered every 25 to 30 minutes. Treprostinil infusion has a longer half-life of approximately 4 hours, but significant increases in pulmonary pressures were noted within 1 hour of treprostinil discontinuation.[33] A reasonable approach is to reduce the treprostinil infusion every 4 to 6 hours. The patient is closely monitored for symptoms with each dose reduction. Any symptoms are aggressively treated and controlled before proceeding with the taper. The rate of taper can be increased or decreased based on the patient's response. This process is repeated until the infusion is discontinued or death occurs.

Symptom Control During Withdrawal of Respiratory Life-Sustaining Therapies

When the decision has been made to discontinue respiratory support, the initial critical step is to establish the plan for adequate symptom control prior to the extubation. Common symptoms related to withdrawal of respiratory life support include dyspnea, anxiety, accumulation of pulmonary secretions, and dry mouth. Management of symptoms not only is essential for comfort, but also to relieve the family's perceptions and level of distress.[34,35] Controversy exists about the use of proactive medication for symptoms or a reactive approach that treats symptoms as they arise.

Many guidelines suggest prophylactic administration of the medications if the patient is capable of experiencing distress or if distress is likely to occur. Advocates for use of routine premedication with opioids and sedatives argue that it will prevent unnecessary distress and ensure a peaceful death. Other clinicians avoid the use of opioids, citing concerns for hastening the patient's death as reasons for waiting until symptoms appear. The doctrine of double effect gives ethical justification for providing sedatives and opioids at the end-of-life as long as the intention is to relieve suffering and not to hasten death or promote euthanasia. Studies have shown that opioids do not hasten death and in some cases may have slowed the process of dying by reducing the work of breathing.[2,23,36–38]

Difficulties exist in assessing patients receiving life-sustaining therapies because they are rarely able to verbalize distressing symptoms. For patients unable to self-report, the initiation and escalation of sedatives and opioids for control of symptoms should be guided by objective and reliable measurements of distress. Dyspnea is a subjective experience, while respiratory distress is a symptom that can be objectively measured. APRNs must be aware of assessment criteria or instruments that identify the presence of objective indicators of discomfort[39] (Table 49.3). The presence of these behaviors suggests the patient is experiencing discomfort, but it does not identify the source of the distress. The potential causes, such as pain, dyspnea, anxiety, and delirium, must be considered when these behaviors are observed and when decisions are made about interventions. More studies are needed to identify and define behaviors that correlate with respiratory distress.

Standardized assessment tools promote consistency among care providers in the recognition of discomfort. Tools that include nonverbal indicators of discomfort are considered necessary for use in the ICU. The Respiratory Distress Observation Scale (RDOS) is a validated tool to measure and show trends in respiratory distress and response to treatment in adults.[39]

Neuromuscular blocking agents interfere with the ability to assess the patient's comfort because they mask objective signs of discomfort, such as grimacing and tachypnea; therefore, such agents may contribute to patient suffering. These agents should be discontinued prior to life support withdrawal, allowing sufficient time for clearance of the drug, which may be influenced by liver and renal function.

Many APRNs, especially those in the ICU, rely heavily on technology for assessment and monitoring of patients. They often prefer to continue pulse oximetry and cardiac and hemodynamic monitoring even at end-of-life. The objective measurements of discomfort at the end-of-life generally do not require sophisticated technology. The simple use of visual and tactile assessment provides the necessary information to identify the nonverbal indicators of discomfort. In most cases, this allows for the removal of the monitoring devices, which promotes patient comfort and a quieter and more peaceful environment.

Opioids and benzodiazepines are supported by the most evidence as a means to relieve dyspnea at the end-of-life. Given variability in symptom burden, individual responses, and drug tolerance, there is considerable variation in the recommended opioid dose for withdrawal of respiratory life support. Morphine, hydromorphone, and fentanyl are all effective in controlling dyspnea. However, there are specific elements that may influence the selection of one over the other. Factors like whether the patient

is currently on an opioid regimen, allergies, previous side effects, cost, and setting all affect the decision.

Fentanyl is frequently the opioid used in the ICU, so it is often continued in end-of-life care. However, many hospitals do not permit its use outside the ICU. Concerns that fentanyl can increase muscle tone, leading to chest rigidity and thus worsening breathlessness, have been raised, but evidence-based research is lacking.[40] Fentanyl has a shorter duration of action and should be administered as a continuous infusion when managing end-of-life care.[41] Morphine is generally the recommended opioid due to its low cost, efficacy, familiarity to the healthcare team, and potentially beneficial euphoric effects.[41] Morphine is associated with a greater risk of urticaria or pruritus related to histamine release or toxicity manifested as myoclonus, especially in the setting of renal failure. Methadone has an extremely variable half-life, so it would rarely be appropriate in this setting.

There is disagreement on the use of opioids in the severely neurologically impaired patient. It is unclear if the absence of indicators of distress is a result of the patient's inability to perceive discomfort or the inability to manifest the signs. This raises uncertainty for clinicians, resulting in variability in practice. Some suggest that the administration of sedatives and opioids is still guided by the presence of patient behaviors.[42] Others recommend administration of the average doses cited in studies, with adjustments in those doses only if behavioral signs of clinical distress occur during the withdrawal process.

Patients should be made comfortable prior to weaning or removing the respiratory support therapy. In some patients, symptoms can be controlled with intermittent doses of opioid. A continuous opioid infusion should be used for patients who are already experiencing dyspnea, or if it is anticipated that the patient's dyspnea will worsen. For patients who are naïve to opioids, opioid initiation can begin with the recommended bolus doses listed in Table 49.4. In a study to determine opioid doses and the factors influencing their use in adult patients undergoing terminal weaning of mechanical ventilation and extubation, the average dose of morphine during the last hour of mechanical ventilation was 5.3 mg/hr, and the average dose during the last hour before death was 10.6 mg/hr.[2] If initiating an infusion, guidelines generally suggest beginning with a bolus dose and initiating the infusion at a rate 50% to 100% of the bolus dose. For example, if the bolus dose is morphine 10 mg given intravenously, the infusion would begin at 5 mg/hr.

If the patient is already receiving opioids, a bolus of two times the current hourly rate should be administered, and then the continuous infusion rate should be increased by 25%. Increases in doses should be preceded by a bolus so that steady-state levels are achieved rapidly. Increasing the infusion rate alone can

Table 49.3 Objective Correlates of Discomfort

Grimacing
Tachypnea
Tachycardia
Restlessness or agitation
Fearful facial expression
Accessory muscle use (rise and fall of clavicle)
Paradoxical breathing
Nasal flaring
Moaning
Grunting at end-expiration

From reference 39.

Table 49.4 Recommended Initial Parenteral Bolus Dose of Opioid in Opioid-Naïve Patients

Opioid	Initial Bolus Dose
Morphine	2–10 mg
Hydromorphone	0.2–0.6 mg
Fentanyl	50–100 mcg

significantly prolong the time to achieve patient comfort. The common bolus dose of morphine is 5 to 10 mg given intravenously (or another opioid at equianalgesic doses) or 10% of the patient's daily opioid dose every 10 minutes, as needed, to keep the respiratory rate under 28 breaths/minute, with no evidence of other behavioral correlates of distress. The continuous infusion rate should be increased by 25% if the patient requires more than two bolus doses within an hour. Implementation of a standardized order form with guidelines for titration of medications improved caregiver satisfaction and increased the use of narcotics and benzodiazepines without significant decrease in the time from withdrawal of mechanical ventilation to death.[15]

Additional Symptoms

Stridor is a harsh, high-pitched breath sound resulting from a narrowed or obstructed airway that can occur in patients with respiratory failure. The underlying cause can be extrinsic compression by a tumor, edema of the head and neck, or central airway obstruction. Stridor can be disconcerting to the care providers and family, as they may perceive that the patient is choking and suffering. Suggestions for prevention or palliation of stridor include racemic epinephrine or corticosteroids.[43,44] In adults, multiple doses of corticosteroids begun 12 to 24 hours prior to extubation appear beneficial for patients with a high likelihood of postextubation stridor.[45] After a single dose of 100 mg methylprednisolone, 88% of the patients showed no stridor, and 93% showed no stridor after four doses.[44] Other studies report reduced stridor using lower doses of methylprednisolone (40 mg). Use of dexamethasone in doses of 2 to 20 mg given orally, intravenously, or subcutaneously in a daily dose may also be considered to reduce swelling and inflammation. Advantages of dexamethasone over methylprednisolone are the long half-life, which permits once-daily dosing, and fewer mineralocorticoid effects, such as edema. Providing anticipatory guidance to the family members about what to expect may decrease their anxiety should the symptom occur.

Additional symptoms common in end-of-life patients, especially after discontinuation of respiratory life support, include excessive bronchopulmonary secretions, anxiety, and dry mouth. Additional symptom information is provided in other chapters in this text.

Conclusion

The APRN plays a critical role in facilitating communication regarding both the initiation and discontinuation of life-sustaining respiratory therapies. Patients undergoing removal of respiratory life support are prone to distressing symptoms, including dyspnea and anxiety. A primary responsibility of the APRN is to ensure that the patient does not suffer. The APRN must have a plan for the discontinuation of therapy and goals of treatment, should have an extensive understanding of potential symptoms, and need to prepared to intervene immediately when signs of distress occur.

References

1. Cooke CR. Economics of mechanical ventilation and respiratory failure. *Crit Care Clin*. 2012; 28(1): 39–55.
2. Mazer M, Alligood CM, Wu Q. The infusion of opioids during terminal withdrawal of mechanical ventilation in the medical intensive care unit. *J Pain Symptom Manage*. 2011; 42(1): 44–51.
3. Rubenfeld GD, Crawford SW. Principles and practice of withdrawing life-sustaining treatment in the ICU. In: Curtis JR, Rubenfeld GD, eds. *Managing Death in the Intensive Care Unit*. New York, NY: Oxford University Press; 2001:127–47.
4. Hawryluck LA, Harvey WRC, Lemieux-Charles L, Singer PA. Consensus guidelines on analgesia and sedation in dying intensive care unit patients. *BMC Medical Ethics*. 2002; 3:3. doi:10.1186/1472-6939-3-3.
5. Massachusetts General Hospital and Harvard Medical School. Ventilator withdrawal guidelines. American Association of Critical Care Nurses. Available at http://www.aacn.org/WD/Palliative/Content/tools-ventilatorwithdrawalguidelines.content?menu=Practice. Accessed October 1, 2014.
6. Ward J. High-flow oxygen administration by nasal cannula for adult and perinatal patients. *Resp Care*. 2013; 58(1): 98–122.
7. Bazuaye EA, Stone TN, Corris PA, Gibson GJ. Variability of inspired oxygen concentration with nasal cannulas. *Thorax*. 1992; 47: 609.
8. Davidson PM, Johnson M. Update on the role of palliative oxygen. *Curr Opin Support Palliat Care*. 2011; 5: 87–91.
9. Campbell ML, Yarandi H, Dove-Medows E. Oxygen is non-beneficial for most patients who are near death. *J Pain Symptom Manag*. 2013; 45: 517–23.
10. Abernathy AP, McDonald CF, Frith PA, et al. Effect of palliative oxygen versus room air in relief of breathlessness in patients with refractory dyspnoea: A double-blind, randomized controlled trial. *Lancet*. 2010; 376: 784–93.
11. Bausewein C, Booth S, Gysels M, Kuhnbach R, Higginson IJ. Effectiveness of a hand-held fan for breathlessness: a randomized phase II trial. *BMC Palliat Care*. 2010; 9: 22.
12. Peters SG, Holets SR, Gay PC. High-flow nasal cannula therapy in do-not-intubate patients with hypoxemic respiratory distress. *Resp Care*. 2013; 58: 597–600.
13. Lee JH, Rehder KJ, Williford L, Cheifetz IM, Turner DA. Use of high-flow nasal cannula in critically ill infants, children, and adults: a critical review of the literature. *Intens Care Med*. 2013; 39: 247–57.
14. Epstein AS, Hartridge-Lambert SK, Ramaker JS, Voigt LP, Portlock CS. Humidified high-flow nasal oxygen utilization in patients with cancer at Memorial Sloan-Kettering Cancer Center. *J Palliat Med*. 2011; 14(7): 835–9.
15. Treece PD, Engelberg RA, Crowley L, et al. Evaluation of a standardized order form for withdrawal of life support in the intensive care unit. *Crit Care Med*. 2004; 32(7): 1141–8.
16. Billings JA. Terminal extubation of the alert patient. *J Palliat Med*. 2011; 14(7): 800–1.
17. Curtis JR. Interventions to improve care during withdrawal of life-sustaining treatments. *J Palliat Med*. 2005; 8(Supp 1): S116–S131.
18. Curtis JR, Cook DJ, Sinuff T, et al. Noninvasive positive pressure ventilation in critical and palliative care settings: Understanding the goals of therapy. *Crit Care Med* 2007; 35(3): 932–9.
19. Nava S, Ferrer M, Esquinas A, et al. Palliative use of non-invasive ventilation in end-of-life patients with solid tumours: a randomized feasibility trial. *Lancet Oncol*. 2013; 14: 219–27.
20. International Consensus Conferences in Intensive Care Medicine. Noninvasive positive pressure ventilation in acute respiratory failure. *Am J Respir Crit Care Med*. 2001; 163(1): 283.
21. Hui D, Morgado M, Chisholm G, et al. High-flow oxygen and bilevel positive airway pressure for persistent dyspnea in patients with advanced cancer: a phase II randomized trial. *J Pain Symptom Manage*. 2013; 46(4): 463–73.
22. Mehta RS, Szmuilowicz E, White DB, Yeow M. Using noninvasive ventilation at the end-of-life. *Fast Facts and Concepts*. 2010; 230. Available at https://www.capc.org/fast-facts/230-using-non-invasive-ventilation-end-life. Accessed July 15, 2015.
23. Edwards MJ. Opioids and benzodiazepines appear paradoxically to delay inevitable death after ventilator withdrawal. *J Palliat Care*. 2005; 21: 299–302.

24. Rady MY, Verheijde JL. The science and ethics of withdrawing mechanical positive pressure ventilator support in the terminally ill. *J Palliat Med.* 2013; 16(8): 828–30.

25. Park PK, Napolitano LM, Bartlett RH. Extracorporeal membrane oxygenation in adult acute respiratory distress syndrome. *Crit Care Clin.* 2011; 27: 627–46.

26. Noah MA, Peek GJ, Finney SJ, et al. Referral to an extracorporeal membrane oxygenation center and mortality among patients with severe 2009 influenza A (H1N1). *JAMA.* 2011; 306(15): 1659.

27. Extracorporeal Life Support Organization, ELSO Guidelines for Cardiopulmonary Extracorporeal Life Support (www.elsonet. org). November 2013: Version 1.3 Ann Arbor, MI. Accessed Dec. 1, 2014.

28. Shekar K, Fraser JF, Smith MT, Roberts JA. Pharmacokinetic changes in patients receiving extracorporeal membrane oxygenation. *J Crit Care.* 2012; 27: 741.e9–741.e18

29. Wildschut ED, Ahsman MJ, Allegaert K, Mathot R, Tibboel D. Determinants of drug absorption in different ECMO circuits. *Intens Care Med.* 2010; 36: 20109–16.

30. Grinnan DC, Swetz KM, Pinson J, Fairman P, Lyckholm LJ, Smith T. The end-of-life experience for a cohort of patients with pulmonary arterial hypertension. *J Palliat Care.* 2012; 15(10): 10651070.

31. Bartlett C, Landzaat L. Prostacyclin withdrawal in pulmonary hypertension. *Fast Facts and Concepts.* April 2013; 264. Available at http://www.eperc.mcw.edu/EPERC/FastFactsIndex/ff_264.htm

32. Wozencraft CP, Coyne PJ, Grinnan DC, Morel TD, Muzevich KM, Smith TJ. Epoprostenol use for pulmonary arterial hypertension in the palliative care setting. *J Palliat Med.* 2012; 15(5): 619–22.

33. McLaughlin VV, Palevsky HI. Parenteral and inhaled prostanoid therapy in the treatment of pulmonary arterial hypertension. *Clin Chest Med.* 2013; 34: 825–40.

34. Steinhauser KE, Clipp EC, McNeilly M, et al. In search of a good death: observations of patients, families, and providers. *Ann Intern Med.* 2000; 132: 825–32.

35. Steinhauser KE, Christakis NA, Clipp EC, et al. Factors considered important at the end of life by patients, family, physicians, and other care providers. *JAMA.* 2000; 284: 2476–82.

36. Chan JD, Treece PD, Engelberg RA, et al. Narcotic and benzodiazepine use after withdrawal of life support: association with time to death? *Chest.* 2004; 126: 286–93.

37. Bakker J, Jansen TC, Lima A, Kompanje EJ. Why opioids and sedatives may prolong life rather than hasten death after ventilator withdrawal in critically ill patients. *Am J Hosp Palliat Care.* 2008; 25: 152–4.

38. Kompanje EJO, van der Hoven B, Bakker J. Anticipation of distress after discontinuation of mechanical ventilation in the ICU at the end of life. *Intens Care Med* 2008; 24: 1593–9.

39. Campbell ML, Templin T, Walch J. A respiratory distress observation scale for patients unable to self-report dyspnea. *J Palliat Med.* 2010; 13(3): 285–90.

40. Zylicz Z, van Rijn-Van der Plaat LL. Fentanyl may increase breathlessness in a patient with motor neuron disease. *J Pain Symptom Manage.* 2006; 32: 199–200.

41. Truog RD, Campbell ML, Curtis JR, et al. Recommendations for end-of-life care in the intensive care unit: A consensus statement by the American Academy of Critical Care Medicine. *Crit Care Med.* 2008; 36(3): 953–63.

42. Campbell ML. How to withdraw mechanical ventilation: a systematic review of the literature. *AACN Adv Crit Care.* 2007; 18(4): 397–403

43. Campbell ML, Bizek KS, Thill M. Patient responses during rapid terminal weaning from mechanical ventilation: A prospective study. *Crit Care Med.* 1999; 27(1): 73–7.

44. Cheng KC, Hou CC, Huang HC. Intravenous injection of methylprednisolone reduces the incidence of postextubation stridor in intensive care unit patients. *Crit Care Med.* 2006; 34: 1345–50.

45. Khemani RG, Randolph A, Markovitz B. Corticosteroids for the prevention and treatment of post-extubation stridor in neonates, children and adults. *Cochrane Database of Systematic Reviews.* 2009, Issue 3. Art. No.: CD001000. doi: 10.1002/14651858.CD001000.pub3

CHAPTER 50

Discontinuation of Life-Sustaining Therapies

Kathy Plakovic

Key Points

- Withholding and withdrawing antibiotics, blood products, dialysis, and artificial nutrition are important topics that require the palliative advanced practice nurse (APRN) to provide information and participate in shared decision making.

- The APRN should explain the benefits and burdens of treatment versus no treatment to the patient and family, along with the ethical framework that supports them.

- If treatment is withheld or withdrawn, discussions should include the expected course of the dying process.

- Although the phrase "withdrawal of care" is often heard, it is important to distinguish between the withdrawal of life-sustaining interventions and the withdrawal of care. While the former is common, the latter should never occur. Language is important, particularly to patients and their families.[1(p 956)]

Introduction

Technological advances allow healthcare providers to delay the dying process for critically and terminally ill patients. For patients lingering between life and death, decisions frequently need to be made regarding withholding or withdrawing life-sustaining treatments. The ethical principle of autonomy allows patients or their healthcare power of attorney/surrogate decision maker the right to accept or reject any treatment.

Withdrawal of life-sustaining treatment is legally and ethically equivalent to withholding treatment. However, withdrawal feels different not only to families but also to healthcare providers, as it is a more active event that ultimately leads to death. Families often refuse to withdraw life-sustaining treatment because they feel like they are "killing" the patient. Palliative APRNs can help patients and families to understand the dying process by discussing the nature of the underlying illness, including the prognosis. The benefits and burdens of treatments should also be explained so patients and families can make informed decisions about accepting or rejecting treatment.

Palliative APRNs are not ethically obligated to offer a treatment that will not benefit the patient. When there is a conflict between the medical recommendations and the wishes of the patient and family, the ethics committee and legal counsel can be consulted to discuss the options for care and negotiate a mutually acceptable plan of care. There must be respect of the patient's and family's cultural and religious beliefs when discussing end-of-life decisions. Involving the pastoral care department or the patient's spiritual leader can help APRNs to navigate these sensitive topics.

Withdrawing life-sustaining treatment is commonly thought of as disconnecting a ventilator at end-of-life, the proverbial "pulling the plug." However, several other treatments can be withheld or withdrawn in dying patients, including antibiotics, blood products, dialysis, and artificial nutrition. This chapter offers case studies that illustrate several scenarios for withholding or withdrawing life-sustaining treatment at the end-of-life. The burdens and benefits of continuing therapy versus stopping therapy are discussed, and the normal process of dying when these therapies are discontinued is reviewed.

Consensus Regarding Prognosis

Decisions regarding life-sustaining treatment regularly happen in the intensive care unit (ICU). While traditionally patients receive ICU-level care to treat acute, life-threatening illnesses with the goal of returning patients to some measure of health and quality of life, patients with end-stage disease are also transferred to the ICU for treatments that delay the dying process. As deaths often occur in the ICU, palliative APRNs must learn to navigate the end of life in this setting.

It can be challenging for palliative APRNs to initiate discussions with patients and families regarding withdrawal of life-sustaining treatment, especially when there are competing opinions about whether the patient is dying. APRNs must be able to recognize the signs of impending death, so they can have timely discussions with families. The goal of withdrawing treatments is to allow the natural process of death to proceed instead of prolonging the dying process with treatments that may offer little benefit (and potentially high burdens) to the patient.

It is important that there is consensus among healthcare providers regarding the prognosis before discussing it with patients and families. Obtaining consensus can be difficult because physicians are typically overly optimistic in their prognosis.[2] Disagreements can occur between the primary team and consulting specialists.[3] This can present a challenge for the APRN, especially if his or her opinion differs significantly from that of other clinicians. The nurse can explain to other clinicians the basis of the prediction, including evidence-based models and clinical experience, to enhance understanding. Prognostic scoring systems, such as the Palliative Prognostic Score,[4] can assist clinicians in determining a prognosis for patients with diseases like cancer at the end-of-life.

Convening a team meeting prior to holding a family meeting can be beneficial to ensure that all treating clinicians agree how to proceed. The palliative APRN plays a key role in facilitating these meetings, so that all treating clinicians have the opportunity to discuss the patient's overall prognosis. When clinicians' schedules conflict and do not allow for a team meeting, the APRN should reach out to the individual providers to discuss the case prior to meeting with the patient and family.

Once consensus is obtained, honest, frank discussions should take place with patients and families regarding the prognosis with or without continued treatment. Patients with decision-making capacity can elect to forgo or withdraw life-sustaining treatment. For patients who lack capacity, their healthcare power of attorney or legal surrogate decision maker can elect to withhold or stop treatment. These decisions are frequently difficult for families to make because it is uncommon for patients to have discussed their end-of-life wishes, even if they have a designated healthcare power of attorney. Palliative APRNs should present the medical facts and make a recommendation instead of just asking, "What would your loved one want us to do?" When the decision is made to withdraw life-sustaining treatment, the APRN should discuss what to expect as the dying process progresses.

Case Study 1

Mrs. Kapoor was a 48-year-old woman with acute myeloid leukemia. She had received a second stem cell transplant after relapse but failed to engraft. During her hospitalization, she developed mucormycosis requiring surgical removal of half her tongue. Unfortunately, this did not clear the infection, and further resection was needed. Surgery could not be pursued due to ongoing platelet transfusion-dependent thrombocytopenia. Mrs. Kapoor had no further treatment options for her leukemia when it recurred. Her family believed they were getting mixed messages from the various teams involved in her care: some were more optimistic and others were more pessimistic, depending on the specialty represented.

Mrs. Kapoor was in the hospital for almost 2 months before the palliative care team was consulted. The palliative APRN, Mary, arranged a team meeting to discuss the patient's prognosis with all specialty teams: ICU, infectious disease, hematology, and surgery. All agreed it was unlikely Mrs. Kapoor would survive even if full aggressive measures were continued. The teams also agreed that withdrawing life-sustaining treatment, including antibiotics and transfusions, would be recommended to the family.

Mary convened a family meeting with all team members presenting a united voice. Mrs. Kapoor's prognosis was grim even if all treatments were continued, and a recommendation was made to transition to comfort-focused care. It took time for the family to agree to withdraw life-sustaining treatments, but Mrs. Kapoor was eventually sent home with hospice care and died 2 weeks later.

As Case Study 1 illustrates, consulting teams often focus on their specialty and communicate to patients and families the daily progress or regression of that system only. These interactions can give false hope when one specialty's system looks "better" on a given day, but the overall prognosis remains poor. Palliative APRNs can bring together the primary and consulting services to look at the big picture, so that patients and families can receive the information they need to make informed decisions about goals of care.

Antibiotics

Antibiotic use is common and is considered the standard of care for patients with an infection. As patients near the end-of-life, antibiotic use may become a life-sustaining treatment or a death-prolonging treatment. Using antimicrobial medications at the end-of-life is a common practice.[5] Albrecht and colleagues[6] evaluated 3,884 hospice patients and found that 27% received antibiotics in the last week of life, but only 15% of those patients had a documented infectious diagnosis. As with other life-sustaining treatments, the decision to withhold or withdraw antibiotics requires informed decision-making based on the goals of care for the individual patient.

Case Study 2

Mr. McFarlane was a 68-year-old man who had been diagnosed with Alzheimer's disease 10 years earlier. The patient and family had the opportunity early in the disease process to discuss goals of care and to execute an advance directive. Mr. McFarlane agreed not to pursue a feeding tube if he could no longer take oral nutrition. He also decided to forgo antibiotics for infection at the end-of-life and avoid hospitalization if possible.

Mr. McFarlane was admitted to a skilled nursing facility with hospice care when it became too difficult for his spouse to manage his care at home. He was severely, cognitively impaired and frail. Mr. McFarlane had been hand-fed by his spouse for several months and had not had any aspiration events. Even though some level of nutrition had continued, he had hypoalbuminemia and was cachectic.

After admission to the nursing home, Mr. McFarlane aspirated while being fed by staff. He became febrile, and the staff wanted to call 911 to transport the patient to the hospital for intravenous antibiotics. The family referred the staff to the patient's advance directive and called the hospice APRN. The APRN advocated for Mr. McFarlane to stay at the nursing home and provided orders for comfort-focused care. Over the next few hours, he became more lethargic, then comatose. Dyspnea was well controlled with sublingual morphine. Within a few hours, Mr. McFarlane died peacefully with his spouse, sister, and daughter at his bedside.

Case Study 2 presents the decision to withhold antibiotics, which was made early in the disease process after thoughtful conversations among the patient, family, and healthcare providers. Even when all the planning was done in advance and hospice was engaged, other people caring for the patient did not follow the decision and attempted to hospitalize the patient at the end of his life. The hospice APRN played a key role in ensuring that the patient's wishes were followed and allowed him to have a natural death with family present.

Many families and healthcare professionals fail to see dementia as a terminal illness; however, dementia is the sixth leading cause of death in the United States.[7] As dementia progresses, patients lose their ability to swallow food and manage their own secretions, leading to aspiration pneumonia. Several studies have shown pneumonia to be the leading cause of death in patients with dementia.[8] In a study of nursing home patients with severe dementia, the 6-month mortality rate was almost 25%. Those with pneumonia or a febrile episode had adjusted 6-month mortality rates of 46% and 44%, respectively.[9]

In addition, many patients experienced distressing symptoms, including 40% with aspiration. Patients with other disease processes, such as advanced cancer, are at risk for infection due to immune suppression from the disease or neutropenia as a result of cancer treatment. Even when patients are transitioned to comfort-focused care, many patients continue to receive antimicrobial therapy.[10] Patients with hematological malignancies frequently receive antibiotics at the end-of-life; one study showed that almost 90% of dying patients received antimicrobial therapy in the last 7 days of life.[11]

Many healthcare providers believe that because infection is a reversible problem, it should always be treated. Decisions to withdraw antibiotics at the end-of-life can be stressful not only for patients and families but also for clinicians. A common belief is that the treatment of an infection provides comfort by decreasing fever and other distressing symptoms, such as shortness of breath. A study conducted by Givens and colleagues[12] showed that comfort scores for patients receiving antibiotics were worse than those for patients not receiving treatment in pneumonia patients with severe dementia (severe cognitive impairment and a global deterioration score of 7). However, the use of antibiotics did prolong survival up to 9 months. Some clinicians view the use of antibiotics at the end-of-life as a means to palliate the symptoms caused by an infection.

Data from one study showed that antimicrobial use in hospice patients had little effect in relieving symptoms for patients with infections, including bacteremia and pneumonia, although it did decrease symptoms in patients with urinary tract infections.[13] Interestingly, that study also showed no difference in median survival in those patients with an infection versus those without infection: 29.1 and 30.5 days, respectively. Survival was the same for patients treated with antibiotics and those with no antibiotics: 29.3 and 30.7 days.

Despite the frequent use of antibiotics at the end-of-life, many patients with advanced cancer still die of infection. Autopsies of patients with advanced cancer treated with antibiotics in the last 2 weeks of life showed that 75% of them died of pneumonia.[14] The burdens of using antimicrobial therapy include the potential for *Clostridium difficile* infection, side effects or adverse reactions to the medication, and the need for intravenous access, which can be difficult to obtain in patients near the end-of-life. The volume of fluid required to deliver intravenous antibiotics can also place a burden on patients with impaired kidney function or with edema due to hypoalbuminemia.

The healthcare cost, especially for patients on newer antimicrobial medications or those prescribed multiple agents, can place a financial burden on patients, healthcare institutions, and society. Clinicians can explain what to expect if infection is not treated. Symptoms like confusion, dyspnea, fever, and hypotension can occur. Table 50.1 lists likely symptoms or sequelae in various end-of-life situations.[13] Explanations regarding symptoms should also include what can be done to treat the problems.

Palliative APRNs can explain that most symptoms can be successfully managed at the end-of-life. They can also educate families that hypotension in the dying patient is normal and that giving medications like vasopressors or fluid boluses will only prolong the dying process and potentially prolong suffering and is not recommended. The decision to proceed with, withhold, or withdraw treatment should be individualized for each patient based on the goals of care. Determining the goals of care for patients with advanced disease can help guide antibiotic use. If the goal is to prolong life at any cost, then family members may elect to proceed with antimicrobial therapy. However, if comfort is the primary focus, families should be educated on the burdens of antibiotic treatment, including a prolonged dying process and potentially worse symptoms.

Blood Products

Transfusion of blood products, including red blood cells and platelets, is a life-sustaining treatment for patients with anemia and thrombocytopenia due to the disease process or to treatment-related cytopenias. Many patients with advanced disease become transfusion-dependent due to bone marrow infiltration or chronic bleeding from tumor invasion. For these patients, continued transfusions are used not as a bridge to wellness but as a temporary measure.

Many physicians, especially ones with a long-term relationship with a patient, have difficulty discussing goals of care when there are no further treatment options. Aggressive care is frequently continued when patients are actively dying. This can lead to patients and families not having the time to attend to unfinished business prior to death. Patients who are religious use more life-prolonging treatments at the end-of-life.[15] While some patients and families will continue to request ongoing care despite a poor prognosis,[16] they must receive honest, direct information about treatment options, including no treatment, so they can make informed decisions about the goals of care.

Table 50.1 Likely Symptoms or Sequelae at End of Life

Infection Site	Associated Symptoms
Urinary tract	Dysuria, fever, frequency, pain
Respiratory tract	Cough, dyspnea, fever, sputum production
Mouth/pharynx	Fever, mucosal inflammation/pain, odynophagia
Skin/subcutaneous	Fever, pain, skin rash/discoloration
Blood/bacteremia	Fever, disorientation, hypotension
Life-Sustaining Treatment Withdrawn	**Likely Sequelae and/or Symptoms**
Antibiotics	Fever, delirium, cough, dyspnea, hypotension, somnolence
Blood products	Fatigue, weakness, shortness of breath
Dialysis	Pruritus, pain, myoclonus, dyspnea, secretions
Total parenteral nutrition	Hypotension, somnolence

Portions from reference 13. Reprinted with permission from Elsevier.

Advances in medicine have improved survival rates for patients with hematological malignancies, but some patients will succumb to their disease despite aggressive management.[17] Many of these patients are transfusion-dependent due to bone marrow failure or infiltration. These patients often die on the hematology ward or in the ICU.[18] Patients with hematological cancers commonly are not referred to palliative care until they are actively dying, even though treatment of their disease entails a high symptom burden and psychosocial and spiritual distress.[17] Reasons for the late referral to palliative care include the aggressive nature of treatment, including chemotherapy, transfusions, and antibiotics, until the end-of-life. Blood and platelet transfusions become a "normal" part of the patient's life; stopping them is a difficult decision, not only for the patient but also for the hematologist.

Recognizing when patients are near the end-of-life becomes particularly important in this patient population. Kripps and colleagues[19] looked at five factors—low performance status, low platelet count, opioid therapy, high LDH, and low albumin—that would identify patients with a high risk of death (Box 50.1). Patients with four or five risk factors had a median survival of 10 days. Median survival for those with two or three risk factors was 63 days. This information can assist healthcare providers in identifying patients at risk of death, so they can have in-depth discussions with patients and families regarding goals of care.

Continuing transfusions in terminally ill patients can place a tremendous burden on the patient and family and usually requires frequent clinic visits for laboratory tests and transfusions, which can result in unplanned hospitalizations (Case Study 3). Patients requiring frequent transfusions are at risk for fluid overload, transfusion reactions, and alloimmunization, making matched transfusions more difficult. Routine transfusions based on complete blood count results showing anemia or thrombocytopenia should be discouraged. Given the national shortage of blood products, thoughtful consideration should be given before transfusing patients in the terminal phase of their disease.[20] Suggested guidelines for transfusions at the end of life can be found in Box 50.2. Symptomatic treatment for fatigue or active bleeding should guide clinical practice.

Box 50.1 Prognostic Factors in Patients with Hematologic Malignancies

Eastern Cooperative Oncology Group (ECOG) status >2

Platelet count $<90 \times 10^{-9}$/L

LDH >248 U/L

Opioid use World Health Organization (WHO) level 3

Albumin <30 g/L

Median survival with no or one risk factor, 440 days; two or three risk factors, 63 days; four or five risk factors, 10 days.

Adapted from reference 19. Reprinted with permission from Springer.

Box 50.2 Guidelines for Blood Product Use at End-of-Life

1. Exceedingly scarce resources, such as cross-matched and HLA-matched platelets, granulocytes, and rare units of blood should not be used in patients who have transitioned to palliative or comfort care. Routine blood products should be used sparingly, and requests should be reviewed by the transfusion medicine service.

2. Transfusions in medically futile situations should be avoided, if possible, and limited to the minimum number of red blood cell transfusions necessary to ameliorate symptoms of anemia. Platelets should also be limited to the minimum necessary to control bleeding (if it is causing significant patient distress, such as upper airway bleeding). If the frequency of transfusions has an impact on the resources available for other patients (i.e., more than twice a week), the request should be reviewed by the transfusion medicine service.

3. If shortages of blood products arise, attempts should be made to defer transfusion in patients at the end-of-life, so the products can be used for other patients. Unusual requests, such as massive transfusion in a futile situation, should not be filled. If agreement cannot be reached on this, an ethics consult should be requested.

4. Transfusion in stable, terminally ill patients requires a careful analysis of the goals of care. Transfusions should not be discouraged in patients for whom an occasional transfusion is likely to alleviate primary symptoms, such as extreme fatigue. Large numbers of transfusions, however, should be reviewed by the transfusion medicine service.

Adapted from reference 20. Reprinted with permission from Wiley.

Case Study 3

Mrs. Garcia, a 72-year-old female with Waldenström's macroglobulinemia and hemolytic anemia, was admitted from the hematology clinic after being found to have a hemoglobin level of 4.7 g/dL, hypotension, and jaundice. She was dependent on red blood cell and platelet transfusions. Her hospital course was complicated by a fever of unknown origin. Surgical oncology recommended splenectomy for her thrombocytopenia; however, this plan was on hold due to fever. Mrs. Garcia had no further treatment options for her underlying disease according to the hematology service, but the plan was to continue to treat her for infection, although no source had been found after extensive workup. Mrs. Garcia stated that she was tired and just wanted to be at home.

The palliative APRN, Jennifer, discussed options for care with Mrs. Garcia and family, including continued aggressive care or comfort-focused care with home hospice. Jennifer explained to the patient and family the risks and benefits of continued transfusions versus stopping transfusions, and they agreed to forgo further treatment. Mrs. Garcia agreed to home hospice care; however, the primary hematologist insisted on outpatient follow-up in clinic for continued transfusions. Jennifer met with the attending and team to advocate for the patient and discuss the patient's wishes to be home with family. She also explained the hardships Mrs. Garcia and family would endure with regular clinic follow-up. The hematologist agreed to withdraw blood products, and the patient was sent home with hospice care. Over the next 2 weeks, Mrs. Garcia became increasingly fatigued and somnolent. Her family reported she had no pain, and they appreciated her time at home with family before her death.

Dialysis

Dialysis for acute kidney injury (AKI) and end-stage renal disease (ESRD) has saved many lives. Life prolongation is the primary goal of renal replacement therapy (RRT); however, the patient's quality of life must also be taken into consideration. Use of the Renal Physicians Association/American Society of Nephrology *Guidelines for the Initiation and Withdrawal of Dialysis* can help guide discussions with patients and families regarding the appropriate time to start or stop treatment.[21]

Dialysis is a life-prolonging treatment that was initially used as a bridge to either transplant for patients with ESRD or to renal recovery for patients with AKI. Today, it is a destination therapy for many older adults with other chronic diseases. The most rapidly growing group of patients starting dialysis for ESRD is adults older than 65 years, with almost 21% of cases in patients greater than 75 years old.[22] These older adults experience a decrease in functional status after the initiation of dialysis.[23] Mortality of ESRD patients aged 65 and older is two times that of similarly aged patients with cancer, congestive heart failure, diabetes, cerebral vascular accident, or acute myocardial infarction.[22]

Prognosis can be difficult to predict for patients with ESRD once dialysis is initiated. Clearly, there is a survival benefit to initiating treatment versus withholding. However, discussing the short-term prognosis with patients and family members can aid in decision making. A system for predicting 6-month mortality was developed by Couchoud and colleagues[24] to assist with ongoing discussions about the benefits of continued therapy (Box 50.3). Points are assigned based on specific comorbid conditions

and functional status. Patients with a score of 9 or more had a 6-month mortality of 70%. Mortality for those with a score of 0 was 8%. This and similar clinical scores can help palliative APRNs to identify patients at risk of death, so they can assist with ongoing discussion regarding the benefits and burdens of continued treatment.

Withdrawal of RRT also occurs in patients with AKI. Almost 5% of patients in ICUs will require RRT for AKI.[33] Mortality in these patients is high, with more than 50% of patients dying.[25] It is important for patients and families to understand the prognosis with and without dialysis, so they can make informed decisions. Patients with end-stage cancer who are intubated in the ICU for sepsis and then progress to kidney failure will have a dismal prognosis with or without dialysis. Therapy should not be initiated if the underlying disease cannot be treated.

In the ICU, a renal consult is called when it appears the kidneys are failing. Guidelines exist to assist nephrologists with shared decision making regarding the initiation or withdrawal of dialysis.[21] However, Davison and colleagues[26] found that, of nephrologists surveyed, only 21% knew the guidelines existed. In practice, the nephrologist offers dialysis to do the work of the kidneys, but does not always consider other comorbidities or overall prognosis. The question should not be "Do you [or your loved one] want dialysis?" Instead, explaining about the underlying disease, the dying process, and the risks and benefits of the proposed treatment is essential before making a recommendation to withhold or withdraw the treatment. The palliative APRN can explain with words like these: "We are doing everything we can, but your mother is dying and we cannot stop that process. Dialysis will only serve to prolong the dying process. I recommend we allow a natural death without dialysis." Box 50.4 lists other end-of-life situations and suggested messages/wording for APRNs.

Box 50.3 Points Assigned to Each Risk Factor for Mortality in ESRD

Risk Factors	Points
Body mass index (kg/m^2) < 18.5	2
Diabetes	1
Congestive heart failure stage III or IV	2
Peripheral vascular disease stage III or IV	2
Dysrhythmia	1
Active malignancy	1
Severe behavioral disorder	2
Totally dependent for transfers	3
Initial context of dialysis unplanned	2

Adapted from reference 24. Reprinted with permission from Oxford University Press.

Box 50.4 Suggested APRN Communication Regarding Life-Sustaining Therapies at End-of-Life

Patient's Situation	Suggested Wording and/or Messages
Infection in advanced disease	Your father is dying from advanced cancer and has no further treatment options. Antibiotics may prolong the dying process and cause unnecessary suffering. I recommend withholding antibiotic therapy and allowing him to have a natural death.
Blood products in advanced hematological malignancies	Your loved one is anemic because the disease has worsened and is no longer responding to treatment. Transfusions may prolong life for some time but will not help the underlying disease.
Kidney failure in sepsis with underlying terminal illness	Your mother's kidneys are shutting down as a part of the dying process, and dialysis is not medically indicated. As the toxins she normally urinates out build up in her system, she will become more sleepy, then comatose. It is usually a peaceful death.
Total parenteral nutrition (TPN) for malignant gastrointestinal failure	TPN is not likely to prolong life or improve quality of life. Artificial nutrition is not recommended. Most patients with advanced disease do not feel hunger. We can offer pleasure feeds if the patient wants to eat.

One way primary teams can address the situation is not calling a renal consult but placing a palliative care consult instead. The palliative APRN can explain that the kidneys are failing as a normal part of the dying process, which is something that cannot be stopped or changed. Families may still request dialysis; perhaps they know someone who is on dialysis for different medical reasons and assume that their loved one will experience similar medical outcomes (Case Study 4). Although patient and family autonomy should be respected, sound medical decision making should have an equal say. If it is unclear whether dialysis will help, a trial of therapy can be offered for a designated length of time, usually 1 or 2 weeks. If, after the trial, the patient has not shown significant improvement, dialysis is stopped.

The symptom burden in patients receiving RRT is very high and includes pain, pruritus, and fatigue. When the burdens of continued treatment outweigh the benefits, ESRD patients will sometimes elect to discontinue dialysis. In the United States, over 20% of patients withdraw dialysis, with 11% withdrawing within the first 180 days.[22] Withdrawal is the second leading cause of death for dialysis patients.[22]

Patients with ESRD who discontinued chronic dialysis had a mean survival of 7.8 days.[27] Patients with AKI who withdraw from treatment have a much shorter life expectancy.[28] Patients and families can be counseled that death from uremia is usually peaceful because it induces coma. Symptoms like pain, myoclonus, dyspnea, or secretions can occur, and their management should be a priority. Symptom management for patients with end stage renal disease is covered in Chapter 16, The Advanced Practice Registered Nurse Practice in a Specialty Outpatient Setting.

Case Study 4

Mr. Jackson, a 78-year-old male with ESRD who had been on hemodialysis for 12 years, was admitted for lower gastrointestinal bleeding. His history was significant for hypertension, stroke, congestive heart failure, diabetes, multiple line infections, and prostate cancer treated with radiation therapy, which caused radiation proctitis. A colonoscopy revealed ulcerations with fragile mucosa in the rectum. He continued to have ongoing bleeding, and the colorectal surgeon indicated that Mr. Jackson was not a candidate for further surgical intervention due to his poor nutritional and performance status, as well as multiple comorbidities. Throughout his hospitalization, staff members were unable to reach his family.

Mr. Jackson's hospital course was complicated by a non-ST-elevation myocardial infarction requiring a prolonged ICU admission. He expressed his wishes to have a Do Not Resuscitate order placed after this event. Initially, Mr. Jackson wanted to continue dialysis while limiting other life-sustaining treatment. The palliative APRN, Deborah, met with him and discussed that dialysis would likely only prolong the dying process. After the meeting, Mr. Jackson stated he would like to "pull the plug." When asked to clarify, he agreed to discontinue dialysis and pursue inpatient hospice care.

Two days after dialysis was stopped, Mr. Jackson's son arrived at the hospital from out of state. He did not believe his father wanted to stop dialysis and requested it be resumed. Mr. Jackson no longer had decision-making capacity due to worsening uremia. A family meeting was held with the son. The palliative APRN, ethics consultant, gastrointestinal physician, social worker, and chaplaincy were in attendance. The son was notified that Mr. Jackson had completed a Practitioner Orders for Life-Sustaining Treatment (POLST) form and had discussed his wishes to discontinue dialysis on more than one occasion with his healthcare providers. The hospital abided by his wishes and continued to provide comfort-focused care.

The next day, Deborah met with the son at the bedside and stated that the patient's declining blood pressure was an indication he would not live much longer. She encouraged the son to spend time at his father's bedside. The son asked again about resuming dialysis. Deborah reiterated that his father had asked to stop life-sustaining treatment and that the team was obligated to honor his wishes. Mr. Jackson died the following day.

Nutrition

Patients with nonmalignant gastrointestinal failure use TPN as a life-sustaining treatment when adequate nutrition cannot be obtained through the enteral route. The role of TPN in patients with malignant gastrointestinal failure due to bowel obstruction or malnutrition from advanced disease is controversial. Families can have strong feelings about "feeding" patients, and worry that without artificial nutrition the patient will "starve to death."

TPN has a limited role in advanced cancer patients. Bowel obstruction occurs in 25% to 50% of patients with advanced gynecologic cancers.[29] Venting gastrostomy tubes are commonly placed in patients with malignant bowel obstruction for symptomatic relief. There are conflicting data as to whether TPN after gastrostomy tube placement for bowel obstruction provides any survival benefit. One study showed no statistically significant survival benefit for patients started on TPN, with median survival of 6.5 weeks.[30] However, Diver and colleagues[29] found a 5-week survival benefit in patients who received TPN and chemotherapy after gastrostomy tube placement, with median survival of 10.6 weeks in that group versus 5.6 weeks in patients not receiving TPN.

Patients with lower serum albumin levels and older age had decreased overall survival.[29] Patients with prolonged survival times had an increase in complications associated with tube placement, and patients receiving chemotherapy had more unplanned hospitalizations.[29] The authors of these studies questioned whether the small survival benefit was worth the cost and complications associated with more aggressive therapy.

Anorexia is a natural part of the dying process. Patients generally lose their desire to eat as death nears. Often families will request enteral feeding via a nasogastric or percutaneous endoscopic gastrostomy (PEG) tube. The APRN can explain to families that this invasive procedure is not recommended. A recently updated Cochrane review concluded that recommendations regarding artificial nutrition for palliative care patients cannot be made due to lack of good-quality trials.[31] The American Society of Parenteral and Enteral Nutrition (A.S.P.E.N.) guidelines for nutritional support in cancer patients state that "the palliative use of nutrition support therapy in terminally ill cancer patients is rarely indicated."[32] A.S.P.E.N. and Society of Critical Care Medicine recommendations for nutrition at the end-of-life[33] can be found in Table 50.2.

Patients receiving ongoing TPN have reported a decrease in quality of life due to disrupted sleep and limitations on activities, such as travel.[34] The burdens of continuing TPN include ongoing monitoring of laboratory values, electrolyte imbalances, and

Table 50.2 Nutrition Therapy in End-of-Life Situations

Specialized nutrition therapy is not obligatory in cases of futile care or end-of-life situations. The decision to provide nutrition therapy should be based on effective patient/family communication, realistic goals, and respect for patient autonomy.

Rationale. Healthcare providers are not obligated to initiate nutrition support therapy in end-of-life situations. Dehydration and malnutrition are well tolerated and generate little symptomatology in the vast majority of patients. In this unfortunate setting, provision of enteral or parenteral nutrition therapy has not been shown to improve outcome. Nonetheless, cultural, ethnic, religious, or individual patient issues may, in some circumstances, necessitate delivery of nutrition support therapy.

From reference 33. Reprinted with permission from Sage Publishing.

pancreatic and liver dysfunction,[35] as well as edema and worsening respiratory secretions. Patients also incur risks associated with ongoing central venous access, such as line infection leading to sepsis, thrombotic occlusion, and dislocation of the catheter.[36]

Artificial nutrition is often seen by families as the equivalent to eating, and withdrawing it can produce strong emotional responses (Case Study 5). Providing nourishment is a normal part of caregiving, and many people believe artificial nutrition fulfills a basic human need and should never be withheld or withdrawn. Families can be taught that most patients lack an appetite and do not feel hunger at the end-of-life as a natural part of the dying process. Further information about the cultural implications of food and fluids and the meaning of food for families can be found in Chapter 43, Culturally Respectful Palliative Care.

Case Study 5

Dr. Janovich was a 69-year-old retired family medicine physician with stage IV ovarian cancer. She had received multiple chemotherapies and surgeries over the preceding 3 years. She was admitted with nausea, vomiting, and weakness and diagnosed with small bowel obstruction due to disease progression. A PEG tube was inserted for symptom management, and the patient was started on TPN by her oncology team. Her hospital course was complicated by pneumonia and vaginal bleeding due to tumor invasion.

Dr. Janovich understood her life expectancy was limited. She did not want to pursue further chemotherapy and was ready for home hospice care. Over the next 24 hours, Dr. Janovich became increasing more somnolent and unable to make her own healthcare decisions. Her daughter, an internal medicine resident, was very involved in the patient's care. She had strong feelings regarding continuing TPN; she believed it would prolong the patient's life by months. The palliative APRN, Kimberly, met with the daughter to explain the burdens and benefits of continued treatment as well as expectations if TPN were stopped. Kimberly explained her mother likely had days to weeks to live. However, the daughter insisted TPN be continued.

Kimberly spoke with local hospice regarding continued TPN and was told it would not be feasible to continue it due to the cost of the prescription. She reached out to another hospice agency with an open access program that agreed to provide "standard recipe" TPN that does not require ongoing laboratory work. The

daughter agreed to home hospice with a change of TPN prescription. Dr. Janovich died 2 weeks later.

Conclusion

Life-sustaining treatments, such as antibiotics, blood products, dialysis, and artificial nutrition, can prolong the dying process in critically and terminally ill patients. These treatments may provide little benefit, and the burdens of these interventions can increase suffering. Families are often faced with decisions regarding withholding or withdrawing life-sustaining treatment as patients near the end-of-life. Recommendations regarding withholding or withdrawing treatments should be made based on medical knowledge and evidence-based practice.

Palliative APRNs can play a key role in explaining the underlying disease process and prognosis to patients and families. They can educate colleagues about prognostic tools that enable clinicians to identify patients who are nearing the end-of-life. Their role includes facilitating team and family meetings to encourage informed decision making. Palliative APRNs can also educate colleagues, patients, and families regarding what to expect during the normal process of dying when treatments are discontinued. Thus, the palliative APRN has an integral role in promoting evidence-based clinical care for patients at the end-of-life.

References

1. Truog RD, Campbell ML, Curtis JR, et al. Recommendations for end-of-life care in the intensive care unit: a consensus statement by the American College of Critical Care Medicine. *Crit Care Med.* 2008; 36(3): 953–63.
2. Glare P, Sinclair C, Downing M, Stone P, Maltoni M, Vigano A. Predicting survival in patients with advanced disease. *Eur J Cancer.* 2008; 44(8): 1146–56.
3. Barnato AE, Tate JA, Rodriguez KL, Zickmund SL, Arnold RM. Norms of decision making in the ICU: a case study of two academic medical centers at the extremes of end-of-life treatment intensity. *Intens Care Med.* 2012; 38(11): 1886–96.
4. Maltoni M, Scarpi E, Pittureri C, et al. Prospective comparison of prognostic scores in palliative care cancer populations. *Oncologist.* 2012; 17(3): 446–54.
5. Chun ED, Rodgers PE, Vitale CA, Collins CD, Malani PN. Antimicrobial use among patients receiving palliative care consultation. *Am J Hosp Palliat Care.* 2010; 27(4): 261–5.
6. Albrecht JS, McGregor JC, Fromme EK, Bearden DT, Furuno JP. A nationwide analysis of antibiotic use in hospice care in the final week of life. *J Pain Symptom Manage.* 2013; 46(4): 483–90.
7. National Center for Health Statistics. Detailed Tables for the National Vital Statistics Report. Deaths: Final Data for 2010. Available at http://www.cdc.gov/nchs/data/nvsr/nvsr61/nvsr61_04.pdf. Accessed May 15, 2014.
8. Brunnstrom HR, Englund EM. Cause of death in patients with dementia disorders. *Eur J Neurol* 2009; 16(4): 488–92.
9. Mitchell, SL, Teno JM, Kiely DK, et al. The clinical course of advanced dementia. *N Engl J Med.* 2009; 361(16): 1529–38.
10. Thompson AJ, Silveria MJ, Vitale CA, Malani, PN. Antimicrobial use at the end of life among hospitalized patients with advanced cancer. *Am J Hospice Palliat Care.* 2012; 29(8): 599–603.
11. Cheng BH, Sham MM, Chan KY, Li CW, Au HY. Intensive palliative care for patients with hematological cancer dying in hospice: analysis of the level of medical care in the final week of life. *Am J Hosp Palliat Care.* Published online November 2013. Available at http://ajh.

sagepub.com.proxy.cc.uic.edu/content/early/2013/11/19/10499091135 12412. Accessed June 5, 2014.

12. Givens JL, Jones RN, Shaffer ML, Kiely DK, Mitchell SL. Survival and comfort after treatment of pneumonia in advanced dementia. *Arch Intern Med.* 2010; 170(13): 1102–7.

13. Reinbolt RE, Shenk AM, White PH, Navari RM. Symptomatic treatment of infections in patients with advanced cancer receiving hospice care. *J Pain Symptom Manage.* 2005; 30(2): 175–82.

14. Pautex S, Vayne-Bossert P, Jamme S, et al. Anatomopathological causes of death in patients with advanced cancer: association with the use of anticoagulation and antibiotics at the end of life. *J Palliat Med.* 2012; 16(6): 669–74.

15. Shinall MC, Ehrenfeld JM, Guillamondegui OD. Religiously affiliated intensive care unit patients receive more aggressive end of life care. *J Surg Res.* 2014; 190(2): 623–7.

16. Mack JW, Weeks JC, Wright AA, Block SD, Prigerson HG. End-of-life discussions, goal attainment, and distress at end of life: predictors and outcomes for receipt of care consistent with preferences. *J Clin Oncol.* 2010; 28(7): 1203–8.

17. Manitta VJ, Philip JA, Cole-Sinclair MF. Palliative care and the hemato-oncological patient: can we live together: a review of the literature. *J Palliat Med.* 2010; 13(8): 1021–5.

18. Hill QA. Intensify, resuscitate or palliate: decision making in the critically ill patient with haematological malignancy. *Blood Rev.* 2010; 24(1): 17–25.

19. Kripp M, Willer A, Schmidt C, et al. Patients with malignant hematological disorders treated on a palliative care unit: prognostic impact of clinical factors. *Ann Hematol.* 2014; 93(2): 317–25.

20. Smith LB, Cooling L, Davenport R. How do I allocate blood products at the end of life? An ethical analysis with suggested guidelines. *Transfusion.* 2013; 53(4): 696–700.

21. Moss AH. Revised dialysis clinical practice guideline promotes more informed decision-making. *Clin J Am Soc Nephrol.* 2010; 5(12): 2380–3.

22. U.S. Renal Data System, USRDS 2013 Annual Data Report: Atlas of chronic kidney disease and end-stage renal disease in the United States, National Institutes of Health, National Institute of Diabetes and Digestive and Kidney Diseases, Bethesda, MD, 2013. Available at http://www.usrds.org/atlas.aspx. Accessed June 8, 2014.

23. Kurella Tamura M, Covinsky KE, Chertow GM, Yaffe K, Landefeld CS, McCulloch CE. Functional status of elderly adults before and after initiation of dialysis. *N Engl J Med.* 2009; 361(16): 1539–47.

24. Couchoud C, Labeeuw M, Moranne O, et al. A clinical score to predict 6-month prognosis in elderly patients starting dialysis for end-stage renal disease. *Nephrol Dial Transplant.* 2009; 24(5): 1553–61.

25. Uchino S, Kellum JA, Bellomo R, et al. Beginning and ending supportive therapy for the kidney (BEST Kidney) investigators: acute renal failure in critically ill patients: a multinational, multicenter study. *JAMA.* 2005; 294(7): 813–9.

26. Davison SN, Jhangri GS, Holley JL, Moss AH. Nephrologists' reported preparedness for end-of-life decision-making. *Clin J Am Soc Nephrol.* 2006; 1(6): 1256–62.

27. O'Connor NR, Dougherty M, Harris PS, Casarett DJ. Survival after dialysis discontinuation and hospice enrollment for ESRD. *Clin J Am Soc Nephrol.* 2013; 8(12): 2117–22.

28. Dash T, Mailloux LU. Withdrawal from and withholding of dialysis. UpToDate, 2014. Available at http://www.uptodate.com/contents/withdrawal-from-and-withholding-of-dialysis?source=search_resu lt&search=withdrawal+from+and+withholding+dialysis& selected Title=1%7E150. Accessed May 20, 2014.

29. Diver E, O'Connor O, Garrett L, et al. Modest benefit of total parenteral nutrition and chemotherapy after venting gastrostomy tube placement. *Gynecol Oncol.* 2013; 129(2): 332–5.

30. Rath KS, Loseth D, Muscarell P, et al. Outcomes following percutaneous upper gastrointestinal decompressive tube placement for malignant bowel obstruction in ovarian cancer. *Gynecol Oncol.* 2013; 129(1): 103–6.

31. Good P, Richard R, Syrmis W, Jenkins-Marsh S, Stephens J. Medically assisted nutrition for adult palliative care patients. *Cochrane Database of Systematic Reviews,* 2014. Available at http://onlinelibrary.wiley.com/doi/10.1002/14651858.CD006274.pub3/pdf. Accessed June 17, 2014.

32. August DA, Huhmann MB. American Society of Parenteral and Enteral Nutrition clinical guidelines: nutrition support therapy during adult anticancer treatment and in hematopoietic cell transplantation. *J Parenter Enteral Nutr.* 2009; 33(5): 472–500.

33. McClave SA, Martindale RG, Vanek VW, et al. Guidelines for the provision and assessment of nutrition support therapy in the adult critically ill patient: Society of Critical Care Medicine (SCCM) and American Society for Parenteral and Enteral Nutrition. *J Parenter Enteral Nutr.* 2009; 33(3): 277–316.

34. Winkler MF. Quality of life in adult home parenteral nutrition patients. *J Parenter Enteral Nutr.* 2005; 29(3): 162–70.

35. Mirhosseini M, Fainsinger R. Parenteral nutrition in advanced cancer patients. Fast Facts and Concepts 190. 2009. Available at https://capc.org/fast-facts/190-parental-nutrition-advanced-cancer-patients/. Accessed June 11, 2015.

36. Dy SM. Enteral and parenteral nutrition in terminally ill cancer patients: a review of the literature. *Am J Hosp Palliat Care.* 2006; 23(5): 369–77.

CHAPTER 51

Palliative Sedation

Peg Nelson

Key Points

♦ Palliative sedation is an important therapy of last resort to relieve suffering in patients who have intractable pain and/or other symptoms.

♦ The palliative advanced practice registered nurse (APRN) must understand the ethical framework of palliative sedation.

♦ The palliative APRN should be familiar with the various medications that are used to provide safe and effective sedation.

♦ Palliative sedation necessitates interdisciplinary care of patients and their families.

Case Study

Melanie Eve was 56 years old, twice divorced, and a single parent to five children. She had been employed as a nurse for over 34 years. She was proud of her roles as a mother and a nurse. She presented to her family physician with a 30-pound weight loss over a 4-month period, frequent back pain, and fatigue that interfered with her work and function at home. She was shocked by her diagnosis of stage IV metastatic renal cell carcinoma, which had invaded her spine and bones.

Because of her poor prognosis, Melanie met with the palliative care team, who partnered with the oncology team to help her through her cancer journey. For over 8 months, Melanie did fairly well with chemotherapy and radiation to prolong her life and control symptoms, but over time she began to lose more weight and became weaker. Julianne, her palliative APRN, gently introduced advance care planning and assisted Melanie, during the months of treatment, to complete her advance directives as well as understand the expected outcome of her illness.

Late in the course of her disease, Melanie presented with a stroke that caused left-sided paraplegia and dysphagia, but she retained the ability to communicate and understand. A feeding tube was discussed as a possibility, but after talking with her family and healthcare teams, she decided not to pursue artificial feeding. Melanie also expressed her wish to go home with hospice care. During this time, Melanie voiced distress about her dependence on her fairly young children and feelings of being a burden. She was also devastated that she would not see her children grow and attain their own milestones. Psychosocial support was offered through nursing, social work, and chaplaincy.

Melanie then developed severe back pain, which radiated down her legs and felt like sharp ice picks were stabbing her. She decided against diagnostic testing and focused on pain management. Her pain was difficult to control despite various analgesic trials. Consultation with an interventional pain specialist, the hospital palliative care team, and the hospice team resulted in an unsuccessful trial of an epidural. Melanie found some relief with use of IV fentanyl infusion and IV lorazepam as needed. She was sleepy but able to take comfort in her children's visits, chaplaincy support, and music therapy.

Melanie then sustained a pathological fracture of her femur, with resulting severe intensification of her pain. Additional medications, including ketamine and IV methadone, were unsuccessful in controlling her pain. She also developed pneumonia with cough and felt increasingly short of breath despite aggressive symptom management. Her condition was rapidly deteriorating, with severe discomfort. Melanie told Julianne, "I am so done, I can't take it. Isn't there anything else we can do?" Julianne talked at length with Melanie about her condition and concerns and introduced the concept of palliative sedation.

Melanie met the eligibility criteria for consideration of palliative sedation because her life expectancy was only a matter of days, and her symptoms had become refractory to extensive treatment. Julianne, along with Melanie's oncologist, the palliative care medical director, and the other members of the palliative care team, met with her and explored all aspects of her needs, concerns, hopes, and fears and discussed palliative sedation as an option to relieve the pain and her other distress. Melanie and the team then shared this option with her children and family, who agreed that her suffering warranted sedation. They decided to initiate palliative sedation the next day. The palliative APRN reviewed the procedure with the nursing and hospital unit staff and completed the official consent process.

Melanie spent the night and the early morning with her children, talking about their hopes and dreams for the future and their shared gratitude for their life together. In the morning, Melanie reviewed her decision with the team and agreed to proceed with palliative sedation. A propofol infusion was initiated in addition to her pain medications. For the first time in a long time, she slept peacefully. Her children stayed by her side for 2 more days until she died.

Introduction

Everyone hopes for a peaceful death. Physical comfort can be achieved for many people and the dying experience may become a time for personal growth, reconciliation, strengthening of family relationships, and spiritual enrichment. However, there are rare circumstances when, despite best efforts, distressing symptoms may not be fully managed. This results in not only physical suffering but also psychological and existential suffering that may preclude any hope for a peaceful death. When patients have intractable symptoms, palliative sedation is offered as a treatment of last resort when all other expert palliative care treatments have failed.[1-3] The process of deciding to offer palliative sedation is multifaceted, but its intention, to relieve suffering and not to hasten death, is clear.[4]

Critical and systematic review of the palliative sedation literature reveals differences in the concepts and practice of palliative sedation.[5] The lack of consensus among experts demonstrates that even experienced palliative clinicians may be uncomfortable with palliative sedation. The focus of this chapter is the role of the palliative APRN in palliative sedation, based on expert opinion and evidence-based practice.

Terms and Prevalence of Use

Palliative sedation may also be termed "terminal sedation," "sedation in patients with intractable symptoms," "sedation for intractable distress in the imminently dying," "end-of-life sedation," "total sedation," "controlled sedation," "palliative sedation therapy," and "proportionate sedation."[6] The Hospice and Palliative Nurses Association endorses the term "palliative sedation" in its position statement regarding the practice because "the term palliative sedation more accurately describes the intent and application to palliate the patient's experience of symptoms rather than to cause or hasten the patient's death."[7]

Even though there is no universal definition of palliative sedation, there is agreement that it involves the monitored use of non-opioid medications to induce controlled sedation to the point of unconsciousness in a dying patient, to relieve distress caused by otherwise uncontrolled pain and symptoms. It is typically continued until the patient dies. Palliative sedation is different from procedural or conscious sedation, in which time-limited use of sedation decreases awareness and pain during an anticipated painful procedure in a patient who is going to survive. Respite sedation is a time-limited use of sedative medications in dying patients with the goal of providing reprieve from distress and suffering for a period of time and then returning the patient to consciousness.

Although patients with advanced incurable disease may express a wish for death in the face of suffering,[8,9] palliative sedation is not a veiled type of euthanasia or assisted suicide. Clearly, the intent and practice of palliative sedation are to reduce suffering by inducing an altered consciousness, not by precipitating death. Voluntary active euthanasia is when a physician administers a lethal dose of medication in response to a request from a competent patient for help in ending life.[10] Physician-assisted suicide is when a physician prescribes a lethal dose of medication that is self-administered by a patient who has requested the means to kill himself or herself.[10] Voluntary active euthanasia, physician-assisted suicide, and inappropriate escalation of analgesia with the intention of inducing death are against the Code of Ethics for Nursing as established by the American Nurses Association[11] (Box 51.1).

Box 51.1 Definitions of Types/Uses of Sedation

1. **Palliative sedation**—the controlled induction of sedation to the point of unconsciousness in a dying patient to relieve otherwise uncontrolled suffering; typically continued until the patient dies

2. **Procedural sedation**—the time-limited use of sedation to decrease awareness and pain during a medical procedure in a patient who is going to survive

3. **Respite sedation**—a time-limited use of palliative sedation medications in dying patients with the goal of giving respite from the suffering for a period of time and then returning the patient to consciousness.

4. **Euthanasia**—an act of bringing about the death of a person at his or her request. In euthanasia, someone other than the patient performs an act, such as administering a lethal injection with the intent to end the patient's life. Voluntary active euthanasia is when a physician administers a lethal dose of medication in response to a request for help in ending life by a competent patient.

5. **Assisted suicide**—the means of suicide, such as pills, is made available to a patient, with the knowledge of the patient's intention to kill himself or herself. Physician-assisted suicide is when a physician prescribes a lethal dose of medication that is self-administered by a patient who has requested the means to kill himself or herself.

Adapted from reference 10.

The literature reports extreme variation in the use of palliative sedation, with between 1% and 88% of dying patients receiving palliative sedation.[12-14] The lack of consensus on the definition of palliative sedation and the retrospective nature of palliative sedation studies may contribute to this variation.[5,15,16] Other hypotheses for the wide deviation in its reported use include varied cultural, religious, and ethnic values and beliefs about the ethics and appropriateness of its use.

Legal Justification for the Use of Palliative Sedation

Several important legal cases set the support and precedent for the use of palliative sedation. In the 1997 U.S. Supreme Court decisions in *Vacco v. Quill*[17] and *Washington v. Glucksberg*,[18] Justice O'Connor stated that "a patient who is suffering from a terminal illness and who is experiencing great pain has no legal barriers to obtaining medication, from qualified physicians, to alleviate that suffering, even to the point of causing unconsciousness and hastening death."[19] O'Connor went further to describe the end-of-life: "Death will be different for each of us. For many, the last days will be spent in physical pain and perhaps the despair that accompanies physical deterioration and a loss of control of basic bodily and mental functions. Some will seek medication to alleviate that pain and other symptoms." Justice O'Connor affirmed the distinction between intentionally hastening death and the justifiable use of medication to alleviate suffering, even to point of unconsciousness and hastening death.

Multiple ethical concepts support the use of palliative sedation. Principles of dignity, autonomy, fidelity, beneficence, nonmaleficence and the rule of double effect are often used. A palliative APRN must be familiar with how these concepts relate to decision making about palliative sedation and be able to counsel, educate, and support his or her team. The American Nurses Association's *Code of Ethics for Nurses* states that "A fundamental principle that underlies all nursing practice is the respect for the inherent worth, dignity, and human rights of every individual. Nurses take into account the needs and values of all persons in all professional relationships."[20] Palliative sedation frees a patient from suffering and thereby preserves his or her dignity and self-worth. Furthermore, dignity is the quality or state of being honored or valued. By respecting the values, beliefs, goals, privacy, actions, priorities, and body of an autonomous adult, the APRN respects the dignity of that person.[21]

Autonomy or self-determination is derived from the principle of respect for persons. It is the right of a capable person to decide his or her own course of action based on his or her own personal values and goals of life.[22] This principle is a strongly valued core belief, especially in the United States, and is both a legal right and an ethical concept. Informed consent derives from self-determination. It requires that the patient has the capacity and sufficient information to understand the risks and potential benefits of palliative sedation before it is started. The patient without the capacity to make decisions has the same right to informed consent before treatment, but decisions should be made through a surrogate decision maker who is substituting for the patient.[23]

The principle of fidelity is also an ethical imperative that ensures that healthcare providers keep promises. The commitment to not abandon our patients or their families at the end-of-life, even in the face of great suffering, is often their greatest need, and is based in the ethical principle of fidelity. Beneficence is the ethical duty to act to the benefit or good for the person under our care.[22] Treating physical and psychological distress, creating comfort, and honoring the wishes of our patients are perceived as beneficial. Nonmaleficence is historically linked to the Hippocratic Oath and its stated imperative of doing no harm.[22] This principle is often used as a moral argument against the practice of palliative sedation, as some believe that harm is incurred in the potential for hastening death. The validity of this argument is contradicted by Maltoni and colleagues, who reviewed 30 years of data in patient cohorts matched for prognostic variables. They demonstrated that patients receiving palliative sedation did not die sooner than those not receiving sedation.[24] Moreover, careful use of the therapy in terms of patient selection and impeccable monitoring limit potential harm.

The American Nurses Association's *Code of Ethics for Nurses* states that "the nurse should provide interventions to relieve pain and other symptoms in the dying patient even if those interventions entail the risk of hastening death. However, nurses may not act with the sole intent to end a patient's life even if motivated by compassion, respect for patient autonomy, and quality of life considerations."[20] This reflects the principle of double effect. Billings points out that solely relying on this precept ignores the issue that although the intended effect of palliative sedation is to reduce suffering, it often involves withholding fluids and other life-supporting measures and that death from the underlying disease/condition is actually inevitable.[25,26] Although the Maltoni findings cited above indicated the sedation itself does not hasten death, the rule of double effect can be a helpful construct in the ethics of palliative sedation and has many proponents of its usefulness in supporting palliative sedation[27,28] (Table 51.1).

The Hospice and Palliative Nursing Association, the American Academy of Hospice and Palliative Medicine, the National Hospice and Palliative Care Organization, and other professional organizations endorse palliative sedation for intractable symptoms to relieve suffering.[7,29–32] Despite this general acceptance in the healthcare community for the use of palliative sedation, it is important to understand and acknowledge the concerns of those who do not agree that the practice is morally acceptable. Objections include the fear that the practice is part of a slippery slope that will lead to hastening death or euthanasia, violating the sanctity of life, and the belief that God alone should choose when a patient dies. Also, the withdrawal of life support or withholding of nutrition, although legally permissible and ethically supported in medicine and nursing, is unacceptable in many people's moral framework.[26] Team members, patients, and families may differ in their opinions based on their cultural norms and religious beliefs. The palliative APRN must explore these values while offering nonjudgmental support and negotiating a care plan that is respectful of these other opinions but consistent with the patient's

Table 51.1 Palliative Sedation and Double Effect

Double Effect	Palliative Sedation
The act itself is morally good or indifferent.	Giving medication to relieve suffering is good.
The intent of the act is only to cause a good effect.	The intent is to alleviate suffering and distress from intractable pain and suffering.
A bad effect may be foreseen but is not intended and would have been avoided if a satisfactory alternative method to achieve the good effect could be found.	Death is foreseen but is not intended with palliative sedation.
The desirable effect follows from the intended effect and not from the bad effect (death).	Relief of pain and symptoms and the subsequent suffering is achieved through sedation, not death.
A proportionately grave reason exists for seeking the good effect and thus compensates for risking or permitting the bad effect.	The use of palliative sedation to relieve intolerable suffering from intractable pain and symptoms outweighs the risk of hastening death.

Adapted from reference 26.

wishes and codes of professional conduct. This may result in the APRN's taking the responsibility for care away from others who are uncomfortable with palliative sedation. Such actions include offering to take the lead in care, writing orders, directly initiating the medication administration, and providing ongoing support of the family and staff.

In the final analysis, each clinician must create his or her own personal ethical and moral framework to work with the patient, family, and team to come to a mutually supportive plan that is respectful of each person's values. The use of palliative sedation, although legally supported, will not be morally or ethically permissible to some patients and families and some members of the healthcare team. Thus, the palliative APRN needs to understand the legal and ethical doctrines that support and challenge the use of palliative sedation, while simultaneously initiating and participating in discussions about its use, with sensitivity to the concerns and perspectives of all: patients, families, and members of the healthcare team.

Creating a Model of Care for Palliative Sedation Therapy

To create a model of safe, effective, high-quality care, best practice in all six areas listed in Box 51.2 must be delineated.

Patient Eligibility

For the use of palliative sedation to be considered, the patient must have a terminal condition, with imminent death anticipated, and must be experiencing severe symptoms and suffering, often described as intolerable, intractable, or refractory to aggressive standard palliative interventions. Imminent death is defined as a life expectancy of hours to days based on the person's current condition, the progression of disease, and the symptom constellation.[33]

Cherny and Portenoy define a refractory symptom as having these attributes: (1) aggressive palliative care interventions short of sedation fail to provide relief; (2) additional invasive or noninvasive treatments are unlikely to provide relief; and (3) additional therapies are likely to be associated with excessive or unacceptable morbidity or are unlikely to provide relief within a reasonable timeframe.[34]

The type of refractory patient suffering (physical vs. existential) for which palliative sedation therapy may be considered is another factor. The concepts of existential suffering and spiritual suffering are often interchangeable in the palliative literature.[35] A sense of purpose, freedom, and authenticity in life are fundamental

---

Box 51.2 Fundamental Elements of Patient Care for Palliative Sedation

- Patient eligibility
- Clinician/team member competence, involvement, and care
- Informed consent and decision making (including the use of life support and nutrition and hydration)
- Family involvement and care
- Medications and procedure of palliative sedation

---

existential attributes. The term "existential suffering" relates to the inability to find meaning, purpose, and fulfillment in one's life, a loss of dignity, fear of death, hopelessness, fear of being a burden to others, and loneliness.[36–38] For some patients, such existential distress can be intolerable.

The use of palliative sedation for existential distress is controversial. One argument against its use is the difficulty of defining the intractability of existential distress. While there are objective criteria for quantifying and treating physical distress, evaluating psychological distress is more difficult.[39] Some experts argue that it is not about the cause of the suffering. It is the degree of the distress and the proximity of death that should be considered when determining whether to use palliative sedation. Nonetheless, many clinicians find the idea of sedation for existential suffering to be morally and ethically challenging, as the patient is more frequently awake and interacting with family and the distress appears more subjective.

Refractory psychological distress must be distinguished from other treatable problems, such as depression, anxiety, delirium, other psychiatric illness, and family conflict. The American Medical Association's Opinion 2.201—Sedation to Unconsciousness in End-of-Life Care recommends against the use of palliative sedation for existential distress.[31] The VA Ethics Committee report explores this issue and concludes, "When the patient's suffering is interpersonal, existential, or spiritual, the tasks of the clinician are to remain present, to 'suffer with' the patient in compassion, and to enlist the support of clergy, social workers, family, and friends in healing the aspects of suffering that are beyond the legitimate scope of medical care."[32]

Specific clinical guidelines initially recommended by Rousseau are pertinent and applicable for the use of palliative sedation in the patient with existential suffering include:[15,40]

- All palliative treatments must be exhausted, including treatment for depression, delirium, anxiety, and any other contributing psychiatric illnesses.

- A psychological assessment by a skilled clinician should be completed.

- A spiritual assessment by a skilled clinician or member of the clergy should be done.

- Informed consent should be obtained from the patient or surrogate decision maker.

Consideration should be given to an initial trial of respite sedation, typically 24 to 48 hours. Respite palliative sedation has been found to be helpful for the patient, family, and healthcare team in reevaluating the decision for, and benefit of, palliative sedation. Some patients who were provided with short periods of sedation have been found to be able to break the cycle of anxiety and distress that created the request for palliative sedation in the first place—as a result, further palliative sedation was unnecessary.[41] These criteria seem prudent and appropriate for evaluating the use of palliative sedation not only in patients with existential distress but also in all patients with severe uncontrolled symptoms who are considering palliative sedation.

In practice, some clinicians and protocols limit the use of palliative sedation to only physical distress (or symptoms that are somatic in nature), whereas others include existential and psychological distress, though typically only under special circumstances or for short periods (respite sedation). Although only the patient can determine if a symptom is intolerable, and although the patient has a right to request sedation, the clinician does not have to act to provide sedation. Severe distress in itself should always create urgency for palliative care clinicians to attempt to reduce the suffering. If the treatment of severe symptoms is not successful, the team may consider palliative sedation as an option only if the patient's condition, in terms of both the immediacy of expected death and the intractability of the symptoms and distress, meets established criteria for palliative sedation.

There is general acceptance that when palliative sedation is considered, whether continuously or intermittently, there should be specific policies, procedures, and protocols for its use.[15,40] All treatment and diagnostic options for the previously discussed problems must be addressed adequately before palliative sedation is considered and provided. The decision to begin sedation is often difficult for clinicians, requiring thorough patient assessment and discussions with the patient, family, and other team members.

The literature cites many different reasons palliative sedation has been used. While Muller-Busch, in their analysis of 7 years of data, found anxiety and existential distress (40% anxiety/psychological distress, 35% dyspnea, and 14% delirium/agitation) to be the most commonly cited reason for the use of palliative sedation,[42] a more recent study that looked at 30 years of palliative sedation practice reported delirium as the most common reason for its use (54%), followed by dyspnea (30%), psychological distress (19%), pain (17%), and vomiting (5%). They also reported that some programs never provided palliative sedation for patients with existential psychological distress, while others included it, and it was one of the most often-cited reasons for its use[43] (Box 51.3).

Clinician/Team Member Competence, Involvement, and Care

Interdisciplinary assessment determines the refractory nature of the symptoms. Key roles of the palliative APRN include (1) ensuring that all standard treatments have been aggressively used and (2) determining that the symptom is truly refractory. Involving the social worker and/or the chaplain assists with the assessment and management of the patient's psychological and spiritual distress (which also affects his or her physical distress) and family and patient well-being and coping. The importance of addressing and treating the psychosocial distress that contributes to the patient's total pain expression cannot be overemphasized. A multidimensional approach is important to prevent, detect, and manage risk factors for intractable pain, including psychosocial distress, addictive behavior, and delirium in patients with terminal disease.

Involvement of the palliative care team has been found to successfully treat pain that had been refractory to other symptom management attempts.[44] Even with specialist-level palliative care, cancer pain and other distress can be difficult to treat, especially when it is complicated by profound suffering. Interdisciplinary collaboration among the primary care providers, the palliative clinical experts, and other team members confirms the patient's condition and assists in the essential aspects of the care planning, including assessment (making sure patients meet the conditions of imminently dying, refractory symptoms, assessment of distress), goals-of-care establishment, and care delivery during the sedation period.

Box 51.3 Patient Eligibility for Palliative Sedation

a. Interdisciplinary assessment of the patient includes nursing, medical, social work, chaplaincy providers.

b. The patient must be imminently dying.

  i. Life expectancy is hours to days.

  ii. There is a Do Not Resuscitate order in place.

c. The patient has severe, intolerable pain and/or symptoms refractory to treatment.

  i. Aggressive palliative care management fails to provide relief.

  ii. Additional invasive/noninvasive treatment cannot provide relief.

  iii. Additional therapies are associated with excessive/unacceptable morbidity or are unlikely to provide relief within a reasonable time.

  iv. All palliative treatments must be exhausted, including treatment for depression, delirium, anxiety, and any other contributing psychiatric illnesses.

  v. Expert consultations from other specialties (i.e., psychiatry for delirium, pain service for pain syndromes, pulmonology for respiratory issues) offer no other alternatives.

  vi. Completion of a psychological assessment by a skilled clinician

  vii. Completion of a spiritual assessment by a skilled clinician or member of the clergy

d. Trial of respite sedation may be considered before palliative sedation is provided.

Adapted from references 34 and 40.

The second aspect has to do with competence of the palliative APRN and his or her team in performing the palliative sedation, including their knowledge, critical thinking, and experience. Most protocols require involving the interdisciplinary team in the decision making about palliative sedation. This includes the attending or primary care physician, who consults and/or receives advice from a palliative care clinical expert (typically an experienced palliative physician and/or a palliative APRN), a pain specialist who has interventional expertise, or another expert specialty clinician as appropriate to the symptoms being managed (e.g., pulmonary or cardiology for dyspnea, psychiatry for delirium and to assess for depression and anxiety). The palliative APRN and bedside nurses are critical in the support and coaching of other direct care providers and each other to ensure the patient and family members are given the psychosocial care they need.

Collaboration with the interdisciplinary team not only validates the appropriateness of palliative sedation and facilitates the informed consent process but also reduces the emotional burden for the healthcare providers. Team members have said that one of the worst aspects of their jobs is when they cannot treat a patient's symptoms, especially pain and existential suffering.[45]

These situations often cause increased burden and stress on the care team members.[45] Ongoing care of all members of the team is crucial and should be part of the formal protocols for providing palliative sedation. During the process of palliative sedation, as well as before and after, there should be opportunities for team members to debrief, share concerns, and discuss personal distress.

In addition to ongoing team support, policies must also state how to handle conscientious objection by any member of the team to participating in palliative sedation and give procedures to transfer care to another available team member of equal competence while ensuring ongoing patient care. There should be mechanisms to discuss and resolve conflicts or concerns raised by anyone involved, along with consistent consultation with ethics committees and legal counsel. This promotes open communication within the organization.

Care of patients with life-limiting illness has always been at the core of the practice of professional nursing. Florence Nightingale observed that nursing relieves a patient's suffering from an illness, even when the disease itself cannot be treated, and that suffering includes more than the physical body's response to disease.[46] Ferrell and Coyle further describe a patient's suffering as a personal and multidimensional experience that is expressed in many ways, including grief, loss, pain, discomfort, loss of control or helplessness, hopelessness, inability to cope, loneliness, isolation, and loss of meaning.[47]

Thus, the palliative APRN may first recognize the need to consider palliative sedation in the face of intractable suffering. Collaboration with other practitioners ensures that all reasonable treatment options to manage the distress have been exhausted and that the patient truly is near death. Depending on agency and state regulations, he or she may initiate the sedation, which means that the APRN must have knowledge of the medications commonly used to ensure safe and effective therapy. For safe and consistent practice, the palliative APRN should follow a palliative sedation policy or procedure that he or she developed. He or she must inform and educate colleagues and team members about the process of decision making and implementation of palliative sedation. The palliative APRN must collaborate with the interdisciplinary team to support the patient, family, and other team members. When palliative sedation is part of a treatment plan, the palliative APRN often leads and/or participates in multiple meetings with staff, before, during, and after the procedure to ensure the success of the intervention and to provide ongoing support to team members.

Informed Consent and Decision-Making

Informed consent requires the clinician to provide key information to the patient, so that the patient can weigh the risks and benefits of a procedure or treatment before reaching a voluntary decision about its use in his or her care. The palliative APRN has an essential role in explaining palliative sedation to patients, family, and staff. Some palliative sedation protocols require written consent and some accept verbal consent, but all require that the discussion must occur before palliative sedation starts and must be documented in detail. It is also important to determine the patient's capacity to make informed decisions.

If a patient is deemed to lack decision-making capacity, the surrogate decision maker becomes the voice for the patient. Even if the patient is capable of making a decision, most protocols

mention the importance of family members' being involved with the informed consent discussion along with the patient. Some protocols even require consent from the family.[5] Specific benefits of palliative sedation are relief of suffering and distress and a controlled environment. Burdens include loss of consciousness and awareness and an inability to relate to family and others or engage in personal growth. This has been termed an "existential euthanasia" by some.[48]

Suffering has been described as losing a sense of one's intactness. Physical pain and other unrelieved somatic symptoms, spiritual distress, depression, or the experience of intense loss are sources of suffering.[49-51] When discussing the possibility of using palliative sedation, it is important to consider the patient's sources of suffering and how the loss of perceptual and interactional capacity may affect the benefit/burden balance for him or her. The APRN and team must be sensitive to, and explore, any cultural or religious beliefs of the patient and family.

Complications of the sedation process may include respiratory depression, aspiration, or hemodynamic compromise. One study reported that almost 4% of patients suffered cardiopulmonary arrest or life-threatening aspiration.[52] Although patients who are candidates for palliative sedation are imminently dying and in severe distress, the palliative APRN must discuss death as a potential effect. For clarification, see Chapter 42, Navigating Ethical Discussions in Palliative Care.

Once palliative sedation is initiated, survival can be quite variable but generally is brief. Muller-Busch and colleagues[42] reported survival of 63 to 58 hours after initiation of sedation; Sykes[53] reported that 56% of patients survived less than 48 hours. Before palliative sedation is to be initiated, decisions regarding the use of life support, resuscitation, and artificial nutrition and hydration need to be determined separately from the decision for palliative sedation. Since palliative sedation is only used for the imminently dying, there should be a clear understanding that no attempt at cardiopulmonary resuscitation will occur, and the appropriate order (do not resuscitate [DNR], do not intubate [DNI], do not attempt resuscitation [DNAR]) will be in place before palliative sedation is provided. Other life-prolonging treatments, such as artificial nutrition and hydration, are typically also withdrawn before beginning palliative sedation, except for cases when respite sedation is being considered.

Family Involvement and Care

The palliative APRN should seek to elicit an understanding of the suffering of family members and provide careful, compassionate, and ongoing communication with them. Interdisciplinary care is critical at this time.

When patients are considering or undergoing palliative sedation, family distress may stem from many factors, including inability to interact with patient, anticipatory grief, disagreement or confusion regarding the use of sedation, perceptions that the use of sedation was precipitous or inappropriately delayed, and impressions that sedation hastened or actually caused the death, or that death did not follow sedation as quickly as hoped.[54-56]

Communication and building trust are essential. If a patient or family members do not trust the healthcare team, conflict is likely to result.[57] Experts in palliative nursing stress the importance of deliberate, careful, and compassionate communication. Successful communication involves the principles listed in

Chapter 40, Family Meetings, and Chapter 42, Navigating Ethical Discussions in Palliative Care.

Medications and Procedure of Sedation

The clinical, ethical, and legal decision making for the use of palliative sedation includes determining the best type of sedative to use. In 1958, Dame Cecily Saunders advocated for the use of non-opioid sedative therapy to reduce anxiety and induce a sense of relaxation.[58] She was clear that the use of opioids as analgesia was beneficial but advised against their use to induce drowsiness.[59] Even today, opioids are not recommended as a sedative drug. However, they are used alongside sedatives as part of the management of pain or dyspnea. The most common medications used for palliative sedation are barbiturates, benzodiazepines, and anesthetics. Patient assessment and clinical protocols developed by the interdisciplinary team, including pharmacists, guide drug selection, initial dosing, dose titration, and route of administration.[5]

Drug selection is based on the type of suffering that is present, current medications, response to past medications, the patient's medical problems, and the drug's efficacy, side-effect profile, and potential for success (Box 51.4). Although the intravenous route is preferred because it allows for quick titration and safety, subcutaneous administration is an acceptable alternative for some of the common medications.

Benzodiazepines are commonly used for palliative sedation; midazolam is often chosen due to its rapid onset of action and ease of titration.[60,61] The typical starting dose of midazolam is 2 to 5 mg given via an intravenous bolus (can be given subcutaneously) with a continuous infusion initiated at 1 mg/hour and titrated to achieve the level of sedation needed to provide relief.[62] Dosing may also be based on patient weight, with an initial intravenous bolus of 0.03 to 0.05 mg/kg and a continuous infusion that is initiated at 0.02 to 0.1 mg/kg/hour and titrated to effect.[63] Paradoxical agitation occasionally occurs with benzodiazepine use, especially in elderly patients with reduced liver function.[63] Reports also indicate that benzodiazepines sometimes fail to achieve adequate sedation.[64]

Box 51.4 Decision-Making Considerations for Medication Use

- The intractable pain or symptom being considered for palliative sedation

- History of medications used and their efficacy as well as current medications

- The patient's medical history and comorbid conditions

- Medication selection, including efficacy and rationale for potential for success

- Side-effect profile and potential interactions with current medications

- Best available route to administer medications appropriate to the setting of the patient. In the acute care setting, the intravenous route for palliative sedation is preferred due to the ability for quick titration and safety. However, subcutaneous administration is acceptable as an alternative in the acute care setting or the home.

Barbiturates have been used for many years for palliative sedation.[65,66] Thiopental and pentobarbital have the quickest onsets of action and short durations, so they can be easily titrated. The starting dose for thiopental is an intravenous bolus of 5 to 7 mg/kg/hour and then 20 to 80 mg/hour as a continuous infusion. Pentobarbital is given as an intravenous bolus of 1 to 3 mg/kg, with a continuous infusion usually started at 1 mg/kg/hr.[65,66] Both thiopental and pentobarbital can be titrated to effect. Pentobarbital may offer antiemetic and anticonvulsant effects, making it more advantageous in patients at risk for vomiting and seizures.

Propofol (Diprivan) is considered an excellent agent for palliative sedation.[62] It can be used safely in patients who have renal or liver disease, it has an extremely short onset of action, duration of action, and half-life (shorter than the benzodiazepines and barbiturates), and it is very easy to titrate. It provides anxiolytic, antiemetic, antipruritic, anticonvulsant, antimyoclonic, and muscle relaxant effects.[62] Dosing for propofol is initially based on weight; a continuous infusion of 2.5 to 5 mcg/kg/min can be increased by 2.5 to 5 mcg/kg/min every hour to the desired level of sedation. During the infusion, the palliative APRN may also give bolus doses of propofol (2.5 to 5 mcg/kg) by intravenous push every 10 minutes as needed for rapid control of severe symptoms.[62]

Dexmedetomidine (Precedex) is a newer sedative agent that could be beneficial in palliative sedation, although it has not been studied extensively for this indication. It is an alpha-2 agonist that may induce unconsciousness without causing respiratory depression. The dosing range is typically 0.2 to 0.7 mcg/kg/hour. Loading or intravenous push doses are not needed. Avoiding a loading dose minimizes the risk of developing hypotension or bradycardia. The onset of effect of dexmedetomidine after beginning infusion is 5 to 10 minutes, with action lasting for approximately 60 minutes once the infusion is discontinued.[67,68]

Once the chosen medication is initiated, the level of sedation should be based on the predetermined patient goals and achievement of comfort. Sedation should not be increased unless the patient shows signs of distress, such as restlessness, grimacing, or findings that could reasonably be interpreted as evidence of suffering (including tachypnea and tachycardia). Otherwise, increasing sedation without an overt clinical indication might imply the clinician is intending to hasten death and would ostensibly cross the line between palliative sedation and physician-assisted suicide or euthanasia.[69] Current assessment tools to monitor conscious sedation in hospitals are not appropriate for the dying patient. The level of sedation needed varies with each patient and is based on the achievement of comfort and predetermined goals.

Care of the Dying Patient

As the patient nears death, all members of the team apply their own special skills and abilities to guiding the family and supporting the patient on this final journey. Although basic to nursing care, the care of the imminently dying is a fundamental element of the total care of a patient undergoing palliative sedation. Since most palliative sedation is done in the impersonal, often sterile environs of a facility, the use of favorite music, special clothes, colorful blankets, supportive aromas, and personal mementos in the room can create an environment that supports the patient's comfort, is unique to the individual, and is soothing to the family and patient. See Chapter 35, Grief and Bereavement.

The case study at the beginning of the chapter illustrates the mixed physical and existential components of suffering that patients often experience, and the palliative APRN's role in advocating for the patient while providing physical, psychological, spiritual, and emotional support.

Conclusion

Although palliative sedation is used only when patients experience the most extreme distress, it is a therapy that is a core competency of the palliative APRN. A palliative APRN must be able to demonstrate how he or she uses the fundamental elements of the safe and effective provision of palliative sedation in practice. This begins with a basic competency in understanding the complex issues surrounding palliative sedation decision making. Ideally, palliative sedation is done with the support of a palliative care team and following a policy or protocol. If one does not exist, the palliative APRN must garner support from a team to develop a policy for palliative sedation. The salient points of each step of palliative sedation can be used to develop these protocols and policies, and will assist in the provision of palliative sedation.

In addition, the palliative APRN will need to gain trust from the staff. This often begins with education and requires an individual commitment to be present with nursing and other team members during the often complex process of consideration of the option of palliative sedation, as well as in its delivery. Finally, although palliative care exists to ensure the comfort of patients and their families who are dealing with terminal illness, even an experienced APRN may never be wholly comfortable with palliative sedation. Open dialogue and collaboration with all team members will reduce the emotional burden and create an environment of mutual support and personal growth. Palliative sedation is an option of last resort for patients experiencing the most suffering. It requires the skill and commitment of the palliative APRN.

References

1. Cherny NI, Radbruch L. European Association for Palliative Care (EAPC) recommended framework for the use of sedation in palliative care. *Palliat Med.* 2009; 23: 581–93.
2. McPhee SJ, Winker MA, Rabow MW, Pantilat SZ, Markowitz AJ. *Care at the Close of Life Evidence and Experience.* New York, NY: McGraw Hill Medical; 2011.
3. Onwuteaka-Philipsen BD, Brinkman-Stoppleenburg A, Penning C, DeJong-Krul GJ, Van Delden JM, Vander Heide A. Trends in end-of-life practices before and after the enactment of the euthanasia law in the Netherlands from 1990 to 2010. A repeated cross-sectional survey. *Lancet.* 2012; 380: 908–15.
4. Lo B, Rubenfeld G. Palliative sedation in dying patients. In: McPhee SJ, Winker MA, Rabow MW, Pantilat SZ, Markowitz AJ, eds. *Care at the Close of Life: Evidence and Experience.* New York, NY: McGraw Hill Medical; 2011:403–13.
5. Schildmann MS, Schildmann MA. Palliative sedation therapy: A systemic literature review and critical appraisal of available guidance on indication and decision-making. *J Palliat Med.* 2014; 17(5): 601–11.
6. Sterckx S, Raus K, Mortier F, eds. *Continuous Sedation at End of Life—Ethical, Clinical and Legal Perspectives.* Cambridge, UK: Cambridge University Press; 2013:30.
7. Hospice and Palliative Nurses Association. Position statement: Palliative sedation. HPNA; 2011. Available at www.hpna.org. Accessed June 30, 2014.
8. Rurup ML, Buiting HM, Pasman HR, vander Maas PJ, Onwuteaka-Philipsen BD. The reporting rate of euthanasia and physician-assisted suicide: a study of trends. *Medical Care.* 2008; 46(12): 198–202.
9. Oregon Department of Human Services. Oregon Death with Dignity Act. Available at www.oregon.gov/DHS/ph/pas/index.shtml, Accessed July 27, 2014.
10. Quill TE, Miller FG. Physician-assisted death. In: Quill TE, Miller FG eds. *Palliative Care and Ethics.* New York, NY: Oxford University Press; 2014:247.
11. American Nurses Association. Position statement: Euthanasia, Assisted suicide and Aid in Dying. 2013. Available at http://nursingworld.org/euthanasiaanddying. Accessed September 26, 2014.
12. Claessens P, Menten J. Schotsmans P, Broeckaert B. Palliative sedation: a review of the research literature. *J Pain Symptom Manage.* 2008; 36(3): 310–33.
13. Elsayem A, Curry E, Boohene J, et al. Use of palliative sedation for intractable symptoms in the palliative care unit of a comprehensive cancer center. *Supportive Care in Cancer.* 2009; 17(1): 53–9.
14. Sykes N, Thorns A. The use of opioids and sedatives at end of life. *Lancet Oncol.* 2003; 4: 312–8.
15. Rousseau PC. Palliative sedation: A brief review of ethical validity and clinical experience. *Mayo Clin Proc.* 2000; 75: 1064–9.
16. Fainsinger RL, DeMoissac D, Mancini I, Oneschuk D. Sedation for delirium and other symptoms in terminally ill patients in Edmonton. *J Palliat Care.* 2000; 16: 5–10.
17. *Vacco v. Quill.* 521 U.S. 793 (1997). Available at www.supremecourtus.gov/opinions/boundvolumes/521bv.pdf. 809. Accessed July 5, 2014.
18. *Washington v. Glucksberg,* 521 U.S. 702 (1997), Available at www.supremecourtus.gov/opinions/boundvolumes/521bv.pdf 9737. Accessed July 5, 2014.
19. Burt RQ. The Supreme Court speaks; not assisted suicide but a constitutional right to palliative care. *N Engl J Med.* 1997; 337: 1234–6.
20. American Nurses Association. *Code of Ethics for Nurses with Interpretive Statements.* Washington DC: American Nurses Association; 2001.
21. Dalinis P. Informed consent and decisional capacity. *J Hosp Palliat Nurs.* 2005; 7(1): 52–7.
22. Beauchamp TL, Childress JF. *Principles of Biomedical Ethics.* 7th ed. New York, NY: Oxford University Press; 2012.
23. President's Commission for the Study of Ethical Problems in Medicine and Biomedical and Behavioral Research. *Making Healthcare Decisions: The Ethical and Legal Implications of Informed Consent in the Patient–Practitioner Relationship.* Washington, DC: US Government Printing Office; 1982.
24. Maltoni M, Pittureri C, Scarpi E, et al. Palliative sedation therapy does not hasten death. Results from a prospective multicentre study. *Ann Oncol.* 2009; 20: 1163–9.
25. Billings JA, Churchill LR. Monolithic moral frameworks: how are the ethics of palliative sedation discussed in the clinical literature? *J Palliat Med.* 2012; 15: 709–13.
26. Billings JA. Palliative sedation. In: Quill TE, Miller FG, eds. *Palliative Care and Ethics.* New York, NY: Oxford University Press; 2014: 209–30.
27. Sulmassy DP, Pellegrino ED. The rule of double effect: clearing up the double talk. *Arch Intern Med.* 1999; 159: 545–50.
28. Sulmassy DP, Curlin F, Brungardt GS, Cavanaugh T. Justifying different levels of palliative sedation. *Ann Intern Med.* 2010; 152: 332–3.
29. Kirk T, Mahon M. National Hospice and Palliative Care Organization (NHPCO) Position Statement and Commentary on the Use of Palliative Sedation in Imminently Dying Terminally Ill Patients. *J Pain Symptom Manage.* 2010; 39(5): 914–23.
30. American Medical Association (Council on Ethical and Judicial Affairs). Sedation to unconsciousness end of life care, CEJA Report 5-A-08, American Medical Association; 2008. Available at

www.ama-assn.org/resources/doc/code-medical-ethics/2201a.pdf. Accessed July 5, 2014.

31. American Association of Hospice and Palliative Medicine (Board of Directors). Statement on palliative sedation. September 15, 2006. Available at http://aahpm.org/positions/palliative-sedate. Accessed November 2, 2014.

32. Veterans Health Administration. The ethics of palliative sedation: A report by the national ethics committee of the Veterans Health Administration. March 2006. Available at http://www.ethics. va.gov/docs/reports/NEC_Report_20060301_The_Ethics_Palliative_ Sedation.pdf. Accessed November 2, 2014.

33. Cowan JD, Walsh D. Terminal sedation in palliative medicine—definition and review of the literature. *Supportive Care in Cancer.* 2001; 9: 403–7.

34. Cherny NI, Portenoy RK. Sedation in the management of refractory symptoms: guidelines for evaluation and treatment. *J Palliat Care.* 1994; 10: 31–8.

35. Boston P, Bruce A, Schreiber R. Existential suffering n the palliative care setting; An integrated literature review. *J Pain Symptom Manage.* 2011; 41(3): 604–18.

36. Okon T. Palliative care review: spiritual, religious and existential aspects of palliative care. *J Palliat Med.* 2005; 8: 392–411.

37. Morita T, Tsunoda J, Satoshi I, Chihara S. An exploratory factor analysis of existential suffering in the Japanese terminally ill patients. *Psychooncology.* 2000; 9: 164–8.

38. McSherry W, Cash K. The language of spirituality: an emerging taxonomy. *Intl J Nurs Stud.* 2004; 41: 151–61.

39. Claessens P, Genbregge E, Vannuffelen R, Broeckaert B, Schotsman P, Menten J. Palliative sedation and nursing—the place of palliative sedation with palliative nursing care. *J Hosp Palliat Nurs.* 2007; 9(2): 100–6.

40. Rousseau P. Existential suffering and palliative sedation: a brief commentary with a proposal for clinical guidelines. *Am J Hosp Palliat Care.* 2001; 18(3): 151–3.

41. Cherny NI. Sedation in response to refractory existential distress: Walking the fine line. *J Pain Symptom Manage.* 1998; 16: 406–7.

42. Muller-Busch HC, Andres I, Jehser T. Sedation in palliative care—a critical analysis of 7 years' experience. *BMC Palliat Care.* 2003; 2(1): 2.

43. Maltoni M, Scarpi E. Rosati M, et al. Palliative sedation in end-of-life care: a systematic review. *J Clin Oncol.* 2012; 30(12): 1379–83.

44. Mori M, Elsayem A, Reddy S, Bruera E, Fadul N. Unrelieved pain and suffering in patients with advanced cancer. *Am J Hosp Palliat Care.* 2012; 29(3): 236–40.

45. Luxardo N, Padros CV, Tripodoro V. Palliative care staff perspectives—the challenges of end-of-life care on their professional practices and everyday lives. *J Hosp Palliat Nurs.* 2014; 16(3): 165–72.

46. Nightingale F. *Notes on Nursing: What It Is and What It Is Not.* London, UK: Gerald Duckworth & Co. Ltd, 1970. First published in 1859, Harrison and Sons.

47. Ferrell BR, Coyle N. *The Nature of Suffering and the Goals of Nursing.* New York, NY: Oxford University Press; 2008.

48. Ducharme HM. Total sedation as existential euthanasia. Supplement to *Medical Ethics: Policies, Protocols, Guidelines and Programs.* New York, NY: Aspen Publishers; 2002.

49. Cherny NI, Coyle N, Foley KM. Suffering in the advanced cancer patient: a definition and taxonomy. *J Palliat Care.* 1994; 10: 57–70.

50. Prince-Paul M, Daly BJ. Ethical considerations in palliative care. In: Ferrell BR, Coyle N, Paice J, eds. *Textbook of Palliative Nursing.* 4th ed. New York, NY: Oxford University Press; 2015:987–1000.

51. Cassell EJ. The relationship between pain and suffering. *Adv Pain Res Therapy.* 1989; 11: 63.

52. Morita T, Chinone Y, Ikenaga M, et al. Efficacy and safety of palliative sedation therapy: a multicenter, prospective, observational study conducted on specialized palliative care units in Japan. *J Pain Symptom Manage.* 2005; 30(4): 320–8.

53. Sykes N. Sedative use in the last week of life and the implications for end-of-life decision making. *Arch Intern Med.* 2003; 163: 341–4.

54. Higgins PC, Altillo T. Palliative sedation: an essential place for clinical excellence. *J Social Work End Life Palliat Care.* 2007; 3(4): 3–30.

55. Brajtman S, The impact on the family of terminal restlessness and its management. *Palliat Med.* 2003; 17(5): 454–60.

56. Morita T, Ikenaga M, Adachi I, et al. Concerns of family members of patients receiving palliative sedation therapy. *Support Care Cancer.* 2004; 12 (12): 885–9.

57. Caplan AL. Odds and Ends: Trust and the debate over medical futility. *Ann Intern Med.* 1996; 125: 688–9.

58. Saunders CM. Dying of cancer. *St. Thomas Hospital Gazette* 1958; 56(2): 37–47.

59. Saunders CM. Management of patients in the terminal stage. In: Raven R, ed. *Cancer,* vol. 6: London, UK: Butterworth and Company, 1960:403–17.

60. Levy MH, Cohen SD. Sedation for the relief of refractory symptoms in the imminently dying: a fine intentional line. *Semin Oncol.* 2005; 32: 237–46.

61. Salacz M, Weissman DE. Controlled sedation for refractory suffering—part II. *Fast Facts and Concepts* 2004; 107. Available at www.eperc.mcw.edu. Accessed July 20, 2014.

62. Krakauer EL, Quinn TE. Sedation in palliative medicine. In: Hanks G, Cherny N, Christakis NA, Fallon M, Kaasa S, Portenoy RK, eds. *Oxford Textbook of Palliative Medicine.* 4th ed. New York, NY: Oxford University Press; 2011:1560–7.

63. Shafer A. Complications of sedation with midazolam in the intensive care unit and a comparison with other sedative regimens. *Crit Care Med.* 1998; 26: 947–56.

64. Cheng C, Roemer-Becuwe C, Pereira J. When midazolam fails. *J Pain Symptom Manage.* 2002; 23: 256–65.

65. Truog RD, Berda CB, Mitchell C, Grier HE. Barbiturates in the care of the terminally ill. *N Engl J Med.* 1992; 327: 1678–82.

66. Greene WR, Davis WH. Titrated intravenous barbiturates in the control of symptoms in patients with terminal cancer. *South Med J* 1991; 84: 332–7.

67. Jackson KC, Paul W, Fine PG. Dexmedetomidine: a novel analgesic with palliative medicine potential. *J Pain Palliat Care Pharmacol.* 2006; 20:23–7.

68. Prommer E. Dexmedetomidine: does it have potential in palliative medicine? *J Hosp Palliat Care.* 2011; 28: 276–83.

69. Alpers A, Lo B. The Supreme Court addresses physician-assisted suicide. Can its rulings improve palliative care? *Arch Family Med.* 1999; 8(3): 200–5.

PART SEVEN

SPECIAL POPULATIONS

CHAPTER 52

Recurrent Disease and Long-Term Survivorship

Denice Economou

Key Points

- Cancer survivors experience different trajectories in their cancer experience from diagnosis to the end-of-life.

- Integrating palliative care with survivorship care can provide more effective and efficient management of survivors' needs while conserving costs and sharing resources.

- Palliative Advanced practice registered nurses (APRNs) provide essential care in interdisciplinary teams in palliative care and survivorship care.

Introduction

The goal of survivorship care is to improve the quality of life for patients, their caregivers, and their families from the time their cancer is diagnosed through their lifespan. Integrating palliative care into survivorship care can improve the cancer survivor's quality of life and relieve his or her suffering.[2,3] The overall 5-year survival rate for all cancers is 65%.[4] An estimated half of all cancer survivors in 2014 are 70 years or older; younger survivors under the age of 40 account for only 5%.[4] Although survival rates are growing, cancer remains our country's leading cause of death. Survivor-focused care includes prevention, detection, surveillance, coordination of care, and interventions to relieve symptoms and suffering, with a focus on improving quality of life and health promotion (Table 52.1).

Cancer survivorship occurs over phases from diagnosis to treatment, the immediate post-treatment stage, long-term survivorship for 5 years or greater, to end-of-life care.[4] Cancer survivors may experience multiple symptoms during these phases of survivorship and long-term effects, which begin during the treatment phase and continue into post-treatment and long-term survivorship.[4] These effects include fatigue, chemotherapy-induced peripheral neuropathy (CIPN), sleep dysfunction, and psychosocial problems, such as depression and anxiety.[2,5] Late effects associated with cancer survivorship start after treatment completion and include heart failure related to anthracyclines, osteopenia, hyperlipidemia, sexual dysfunction, infertility, lymphedema, and urinary and bowel dysfunction. These effects vary depending on disease, type of treatments, age, and other comorbidities. Secondary symptoms may accompany primary symptoms, including weight gain, hyperlipidemia, and the development of hypertension.[2] Therefore, it is easy to see how complicated the long-term management of cancer survivors can become.

Relationship Between Survivorship and Palliative Care

The goal of palliative care is to relieve suffering for the patient and family and improve quality of life.[6] Cancer survivorship care is focused not only on treating symptoms associated with late and long-term effects of cancer and its treatment, but also on providing detection, prevention, and surveillance for recurrent or new disease.[1] Communication and education are essential for both cancer survivorship and palliative models of care. Both palliative and survivorship care are focused on relieving suffering and improving quality of life, and the APRN plays a significant role in providing both. Where the APRN roles overlap in these two models of care, there must be integration. Integrating care allows for a shared-care model and the benefit of effective and efficient management of recurrent disease. In the integrated model of care, multidisciplinary experts can help manage the patient's symptoms and plan the patient's goals of care.

Table 52.1 illustrates the overlap of survivorship care and palliative care. In the table, the quality of life model is applied to cancer survivors, while the National Consensus Project for Quality Palliative Care defines the domains of palliative care.[6,7] The overlapping areas of concern are symptom management, psychosocial and supportive care services, education, and coordination of overall care needs for the patient and caregivers. The focus of both models of care is improving quality of life and minimizing or alleviating suffering.

The Roles of the APRN

Nurses are the essential providers in the interdisciplinary models of both palliative and survivorship care. The coordination and handling of patients' needs may vary depending on the different disciplines that make up the palliative care team. Despite this, the responsibilities of the APRN within the multidisciplinary team remain the same: promoting ethical decisions, providing collaboration and consultation, and providing evidence-based interventions for direct patient care.

About one in six cancer survivors will experience recurrence and advanced disease.[8] Table 52.2 describes common late-stage recurrence symptoms. As these patients may experience cycles of

Table 52.1 Overlap of Survivorship Care and Palliative Care

Quality of Life Related to the Cancer Survivor	Clinical Practice Guidelines for Quality Palliative Care
	Domain 1: Structure and Processes of Care overlaps all domains and includes interdisciplinary teams providing assessment of patient and family.
Physical Well-Being Functional Activities Strength/Fatigue Sleep and Rest Overall Physical Health Fertility Pain	*Domain 2: Physical Aspects of Care* Assessment and treatment of physical symptoms, interdisciplinary management of symptoms, including pharmacologic, interventional, behavioral, and complementary interventions
Psychological Well-Being Anxiety, Depression Fear of Recurrence Cognitive/Attention Distress of Diagnosis and Control of Treatment	*Domain 3: Psychological and Psychiatric Aspects* Collaborative assessment of psychological concerns and psychological diagnoses; patient and family communication of assessment, diagnosis, and treatment options for common conditions, including patient and family goals of care. This domain also includes bereavement support.
Social Well-Being Family Distress Roles & Relationships Sexual Function Isolation Finances Work-Related Issues	*Domain 4: Social Aspects of Care* Interdisciplinary evaluation and collaboration with patients and families to identify support and strengths and to facilitate relief of family distress and financial concerns *Domain 8: Ethical and Legal Aspects of Care* Attention to advance care planning, financial issues, ethics, and legal aspects of care
Spiritual Well-Being Meaning of Illness Religiosity Transcendence Hope Uncertainty Inner Strength	*Domain 5: Spiritual, Religious, and Existential Aspects of Care* Stressing assessment, access, and staff collaboration to meet the spiritual concerns of patients throughout their illness trajectory Interdisciplinary team should include an appropriately trained chaplain to help meet the spiritual needs of patient and family. This domain is focused on providing comfort and relief for patients and families based on their individual concerns. *Domain 6: Cultural Aspects of Care* Defines culture and recognizes culture as a "source of resilience and strength" for the patient and family
Peaceful and Respectful Death	*Domain 7: Care of the Patient at the End of Life* Includes the patient, family, and caregivers. Education and support are provided to the family to help them understand what to expect and includes social, spiritual, and cultural aspects of care.

From reference 1, p. 68, and reference 8.

remission, recurrence, and remission again, returning for palliative care support is likely, underscoring the importance of integrating survivorship care with palliative care. Both models of care benefit from the overall guidance of the APRN. Patients whose disease returns in an advanced stage may experience symptoms originally treated by the palliative care team or new symptoms associated with advanced disease. APRNs may have discharged these patients into long-term survivorship care and now will be faced with readmitting them to the palliative care service with new or recurrent symptoms related to advanced disease. It is up to the nurse to perform a comprehensive assessment of the patient's needs and to establish or re-establish a therapeutic relationship with the patient and family. The level of trust and communication that the APRN establishes serves as the foundation for meeting the comprehensive needs of the patient population experiencing

recurrence of disease and approaching the end-of-life.[2,8–10] The APRN provides care that meets the patient's needs, creates a therapeutic relationship, and employs research-based interventions to meet the challenges these complicated patients present.

Palliative Care in Patients with Recurrent Disease

Case Study 1

Mrs. C was a 62-year-old white woman with BRCA 2-positive breast and ovarian cancer who returned for a follow-up exam for possible liver metastases. After her initial breast cancer diagnosis in 2005 with a simultaneous diagnosis of stage III ovarian cancer, she

Table 52.2 Common Late-Stage Recurrence Symptoms

Male		Female	
Cancer	Symptoms Associated with Late Recurrence	Cancer	Symptoms Associated with Late Recurrence
Prostate (43%)	◆ Pain ◆ Osteoporosis/fractures ◆ Urinary and bowel dysfunction ◆ Increased cardiovascular disease risk ◆ Risk of diabetes ◆ Sleep dysfunction	Breast (41%)	◆ Pain ◆ Osteoporosis/fractures ◆ Arthralgias/myalgias ◆ Risk of diabetes ◆ Peripheral neuropathy ◆ Lymphedema ◆ Sleep dysfunction
Colorectal (9%)	◆ Bowel dysfunction (diarrhea, constipation, obstruction) ◆ Peripheral neuropathy	Uterine corpus (8%)	◆ Osteoporosis ◆ Lymphedema lower extremities
Melanoma (8%)	◆ Pain ◆ Depends on where melanoma arises ◆ Cutaneous melanoma or mucosal melanoma: fungating wounds ◆ Brain melanoma: headache, fall risk, weakness, numbness, somnolence, behavioral changes ◆ Lung mets: shortness of breath, cough ◆ Lymphedema ◆ Cord compression: incontinence, paralysis	Colorectal (8%)	◆ Bowel dysfunction (diarrhea, constipation, obstruction) ◆ Peripheral neuropathy
Urinary bladder (7%)	◆ Bladder dysfunction: reduced volume, unable to eliminate; failure of neo-bladder	Melanoma (7%)	◆ Pain ◆ Depends on where melanoma arises ◆ Cutaneous melanoma or mucosal melanoma: fungating wounds ◆ Brain melanoma: headache, fall risk, weakness, numbness, somnolence, behavioral changes ◆ Lung mets: shortness of breath, cough ◆ Lymphedema ◆ Cord compression: incontinence, paralysis
Non-Hodgkin's lymphoma (4%)	◆ Radiation and monoclonal antibody effects ◆ Skin changes ◆ Edema ◆ Stem cell transplant effects	Thyroid (6%)	◆ Thyroglobulin levels changing and difficult to maintain ◆ Potential for distant metastasis ◆ Symptoms depend on location and extent of tumor.

From reference 4.

underwent bilateral mastectomies with bilateral implant reconstruction and debulking of her ovarian cancer. She completed adjuvant chemotherapy with carboplatin and Taxol and was disease-free for 6½ years. She presented with a dry cough and right flank pain, developing over the preceding 2 weeks. She had residual neuropathy in her hands from her chemotherapy and complained of chronic constipation. She and her husband were very saddened about the likelihood of cancer recurrence and new pain sources. Mrs. C stated that she was very spiritual, and she believed that God had watched over her thus far and would continue to do so.

Although survivorship care is defined as care beginning at diagnosis and continuing until death, most survivorship care services focus on the post-treatment care phase. Unless there

are longstanding problems from their cancer treatment, most survivors ultimately return to their primary care physician or oncologist for standard, annual recommended care, depending on their disease or treatment. When these patients have recurrent disease, as in the case study, multiple issues occur at the same time, therefore APRNs will provide important state-of-the-art care.

Assessment

Initially, the APRN evaluates the patient's areas of concern, touching on the four quality-of-life domains. This evaluation can begin a discussion of the patient's goals of care and concerns, as he or she anticipates end-of-life care. By serving as an active listener and taking a whole-person-care approach, the APRN strengthens the relationship with the patient and family. In Case Study 1, Mrs. C and her family were in a period of disbelief and disappointment. The APRN proceeded in a systematic way to complete a comprehensive evaluation of their concerns and to develop a plan of care that reflected her changing health. Standard tools, such as the Edmonton Symptom Assessment System (ESAS) or Patient Health Questionnaire 9 (PHQ-9), may be used to provide a quantitative measure to follow over time and track changes.[11,12] Although Mrs. C reported concerns about pain, constipation, history of neuropathy, and sadness, the APRN must perform a thorough assessment to identify any other issues that may be present.

Long-term cancer survivors experience a variety of symptoms related to their disease type, treatment regimens, age, and comorbidities. The palliative APRN must determine whether the patient is at risk for increased symptoms and, if so, what they might be (see Table 52.1). Mrs. C's genetic findings (she is BRCA2 positive) put her at a very high risk for recurrence. That she lived for such an extended time "disease-free" was remarkable. Long-term cancer survivors are at increased risk for recurrence and long-term complications.[13] A comparative study of women with and without a history of breast cancer found that breast cancer survivors experienced a greater decline in physical function, energy, and social functioning, and increased musculoskeletal pain problems.[14,15]

Physical Well-Being

A primary symptom associated with advanced disease is pain. The palliative APRN has, as his or her goal, relief of the patient's suffering, primarily by focusing on pain sources that are difficult to manage with standard approaches or that require difficult titrations or alternative routes. (See Chapter 23 for pain management strategies for palliative care.) A new pain source may have alerted the patient that something was different and that it was important to explore the pain's implications. In Mrs. C's case, the palliative APRN must establish the patient's pain management history and provide initial, short-acting medications to manage the new flank pain; this is an important first step in improving her quality of life. Studies have shown that 25% to 60% of breast cancer patients may experience chronic pain after treatment.[16] The APRN should also assess Mrs. C's past strategies for managing the late effects of CIPN, along with other potential late effects related to comfort.

Pain with advanced or metastatic disease occurs in 64% of all cancer survivors.[4] Chronic pain syndromes related to surgery, chemotherapy, or radiation therapy may occur. Patients who have received certain chemotherapy drugs may experience peripheral neuropathy, as well as weakness and numbness. Situations where a tumor impinges on bone or nerves or causes a stretching of the viscera surrounding organs can cause the most pain for survivors. Anticipating who is at risk for tumor recurrence in these high-risk areas is a part of the palliative APRN's assessment role.

Fatigue remains a concern in long-term cancer survivors.[17] Fatigue is associated with progressing disease, pro-inflammatory cytokines, and psychosocial issues like anxiety, depression, and unrelieved pain.[15,17,18] Management strategies include understanding fatigue's potential sources, such as stress hormones, anxiety and distress over the new diagnosis, unrelieved pain, possible physical deconditioning, and sleep dysfunction, and attempting to minimize these through support, physical activity, and sleep-promoting interventions.[19]

Psychological Well-Being

Depressive symptoms, anxiety, and distress are all associated with recurrence in long-term cancer survivors.[20] The prevalence in long-term cancer survivors varies widely. Studies do not clarify whether the patient was depressed before the diagnosis.[20] Depression may exist in long-term cancer survivors, but the cause and effect are unclear.

The long-term cancer survivor who is dealing with recurrence may experience post-traumatic stress disorder or may be living with long-term residual cognitive disorders that affect his or her ability to cope with a new and unexpected diagnosis. The rate of post-traumatic stress disorder may be as high as 32% in cancer survivors.[21] Psychological symptoms may fluctuate from diagnosis to long-term survival, and with recurrence, such symptoms may fluctuate again. The burden that the diagnosis and treatment of cancer puts on a patient and family, the resources available to them, and additional indicators, such as culture, educational level, and economic status, all contribute to the psychological effects in a cancer patient throughout the course of disease.[20,22] For breast cancer patients, there may be increased cognitive deficits related to chemotherapy.[17] Assessment and coordination of support to manage these psychological symptoms can help reduce distress and promote quality of life.

Social Well-Being

Social concerns in the cancer survivor include family concerns, work-related issues, and financial debt.[17] The quality-of-life model related to cancer survivors includes affection and sexual function, body image issues, family roles and relationships, social isolation, and ability to find joy.[1,23] This domain of social well-being encompasses many issues that affect quality of life in cancer survivors from diagnosis on. Recurrence brings many of these concerns back to the forefront in cancer survivors' lives.

For a patient like Mrs. C in Case Study 1, the recurrence, after living so many years disease-free, saddened both her and her husband. As a cancer survivor, she probably experienced issues of distress and changes in roles and relationships during her treatment and the post-treatment phases. Late effects like osteopenia can cause bone fractures or changes in ambulation that affect quality of life and contribute to deconditioning with potential inactivity.[2,24] Mrs. C and her family required psychosocial support; this is an area that has been historically undermanaged in cancer survivors.[25] Unmanaged or prolonged stressors increase the risk to patients by reducing their immune system function and raising the potential for fatigue and depressive symptoms. The APRN's role of assessment, with a focus on the patient's social/emotional response to the change in health status, is essential. Reducing distress and helping Mrs. C verbalize her concerns assisted the palliative APRN in coordinating appropriate resources and making them available as part of the interdisciplinary palliative care service.

The risks for other disease types related to cancer recurrence are equally detrimental. Depending on the standard survival associated with certain disease types and the intensity of treatment regimens, patients will experience other social well-being issues. The highest percentage of male survivors have prostate cancer. Prostate cancer, like breast cancer, is sensitive to hormonal influence, which requires surgical removal to protect against recurrence. Treatment may involve only active surveillance for older men or men with less aggressive tumors. Most men, however, are treated with surgery and radiation. For men age 64 or younger, as many as 52% will have a radical prostatectomy, which can contribute to sexual, genitourinary, and colorectal side effects that can severely impair the quality of life in all domains.[4]

Spiritual Well-Being

Spirituality in cancer survivors has been shown to lead to hopefulness and better coping.[2,26] Evans and colleagues[25] evaluated the psychosocial, cultural, and spiritual disparities in end-of-life and palliative care and found barriers to the use of hospice and palliative care services by African-Americans and Hispanic/Latinos. African-Americans as a group have been found to mistrust the healthcare system; they tend to care for ill family members at home and hesitate to complete advance directives. Both of these factors limit their interest in obtaining palliative care. Further, African-Americans as a group are more faith-focused and spiritual than Hispanics or whites and see suffering as part of God's plan.[27,28] Hispanics are also spiritual and follow religious practices to cope with illness rather than seeking hospice or palliative care support.[27] White patients are more likely to complete advance directives and use palliative care services and hospice care.[29]

Terminal illness represents a loss of the future and an opportunity to question the meaning and purpose of life.[30] In Case Study 1, Mrs. C discussed her spiritual beliefs with the palliative APRN. The APRN should have elicited her faith prior to this diagnosis as she began to express her goals of care. Providing spiritual and/or religious support as needed is a key component of good palliative and end-of-life care. There will be moments of reappraisal of beliefs and transcendence or changes in what the patient believes the journey will be like.[30] The APRN's role in providing spiritual care begins with respecting the patient's beliefs and recognizing that the APRN is more of a guide, with the goal of relieving suffering. As patients try to make sense of their recurrent diagnosis and what it means to their future, the APRN's role is to gather appropriate disciplines to assist them through this moment and help them move forward. It is important for the palliative APRN to be present and to listen to the patient. Compassionate listening displays the respect necessary to build the nurse–patient relationship and provide a supportive environment. Prayer, meditation, guided imagery, and breathing techniques may be meaningful interventions for patients.

Palliative Care in Long-Term Survivors

Case Study 2

Mr. B was a 36-year-old male who was diagnosed with stage III Hodgkin's lymphoma 5 years earlier. He was treated with chemotherapy, radiation therapy, and a monoclonal antibody. He was married with a 5-year-old child, who was born just prior to his initial diagnosis. He returned to work full time about 4 years ago. He had extreme fatigue, shortness of breath with exertion, and some residual peripheral neuropathy. He and his wife had intended to have more children but realized this was probably not possible. They were concerned about the risk for recurrence and were saddened about the change in their family plans. Mr. B was frustrated by his symptoms, which he felt impaired his ability to enjoy his life.

Assessment

The palliative APRN's comprehensive training in whole-patient care provides a framework for individualizing patient assessment.

Hodgkin's lymphoma has a 5-year survival of 85%.[4] Standard treatment includes chemotherapy with multiple agents, and 32% of patients also receive radiation therapy. For patients with recurrent disease or disease that does not respond initially to chemotherapy and radiation, a monoclonal antibody is added. If this regimen is not effective, the patient will have the option of undergoing stem cell transplantation. These treatment regimen have multiple side effects.

As illustrated by Case Study 2, surviving cancer does not mean a return to life exactly as it was, but there were palliative care interventions that could improve Mr. B's quality of life. The palliative APRN assessed Mr. B, based on the four quality-of-life domains, and identified such interventions. Mr. B continued to have multiple symptoms associated with his treatment. His disease put him at increased risk for neutropenia, peripheral neuropathy, fatigue, heart and lung damage, and fertility problems.[20]

Physical Well-Being

Mr. B reported peripheral neuropathy associated with his chemotherapy and monoclonal antibody therapy. About 33% of patients who have completed treatment and do not have advanced disease experience pain. Sometimes this pain becomes chronic and needs management, possibly lifelong. Weakness and numbness in the hands and feet are the most common complaints associated with CIPN. Recent guidelines now offer options that may improve this symptom, but treatment continues to reflect a combination of evidence-based recommendations and consensus-based interventions. Pain requires expert management strategies and oversight to change medications and dosages as necessary and is best managed by the palliative care team.

Cardiotoxicity related to chemotherapy and radiation therapy to the chest results in cardiomyopathy, which can lead to heart failure. Depending on the dose of chemotherapy or radiation, the damage can include dysrhythmias, valvular disease, and atherosclerosis or coronary artery disease earlier than expected in a normally aging patient.[31] Monoclonal antibody use also increased Mr. B's already elevated risk of heart failure.[32]

Lung damage was also related to Mr. B's chemotherapy and radiation therapy. Reduced lung function may result in shortness of breath long after treatment is completed.[33] Dyspnea can have a significant impact on quality of life and is related to multiple factors. Increased ventilatory demand is associated with chemotherapy and radiation. This is related to the increased dead space in the lungs, forcing the lungs to work harder to oxygenate blood. Changes in carbon dioxide output and metabolic acidosis result in hypoxemia and dyspnea.[34]

Physical management of Mr. B's symptoms was part of palliative care management. APRNs have a significant part in health promotion by advising patients about smoking cessation techniques, weight control, exercise, and reducing cholesterol levels.[35]

Psychological Well-Being

Mr. B told the palliative APRN he was sad and depressed about his life in general since he completed his cancer treatment. Patients with Hodgkin's lymphoma may experience increased depressive symptoms.[36] The consequences of the disease and the combination of treatments that he received increased his risk for secondary cancers. Mr. B's psychological well-being was impaired by his fatigue, unrelieved pain, and sadness. In addition, if he had not banked his sperm before treatment, he would probably not be able to have more biological children.[37] Providing resources to support both Mr. B and his wife in the areas that are most distressing to them was important to improve his psychological well-being.

Social Well-Being

Palliative care recognizes that the unit of care includes the patient, family, and significant other. Whomever the patient feels most connected to defines "family."[38] Mr. B had multiple social responses related to family distress over fertility issues, as well as concerns about secondary cancer risk. Fear of recurrence can have a negative impact on the patient's quality of life.[39,40] Mr. B's symptoms of shortness of breath, fatigue, and neuropathy interfered with his daily ability to interact with family and maintain the energy needed to work. The APRN's palliative interventions needed to include not only referral for psychosocial support but also referral to fertility experts, who could discuss the options available to Mr. B and his wife. Helping Mr. B redefine his goals in life and find ways to adjust to the limitations his symptoms have imposed played an important part in his long-term care management.[38]

Spiritual Well-Being

Assessing what is important to Mr. B was part of understanding what brings meaning and purpose to his life and where to focus interventions to improve his overall well-being. The spiritual domain for cancer survivors includes understanding what the illness means to the patient. Mr. B had a few years to evaluate the changes that occurred after his cancer treatment. It was important for him to cope with the uncertainty of his illness and to maintain hope for the future. Improving his symptoms and supporting his inner strength made a significant difference in his quality of life.

Conclusion

The role of the palliative APRN includes evaluating the educational needs of patients and families, promoting the palliative model of care, providing evidence-based practice, promoting organizational ethical values, organizing staffing, and providing economic oversight. The APRN's overall advocacy for patients provides leadership to improve the quality of care. The APRN plays a significant role as a clinical consultant to ensure communication among physicians, the palliative care team, support staff, patients, and families.[41] As the ultimate patient advocate and as part of providing whole-person care, the APRN coordinates the care of patients with recurrence of advanced disease and is committed to recognizing and dealing with the health disparities affecting palliative and end-of-life care. Providing care focused on meeting the quality-of-life needs of the cancer survivor with recurrence, integrating the principles of palliative care, and demonstrating expert symptom management, APRNs will provide the comprehensive care necessary to manage this complicated patient population.[9,42]

References

1. Institute of Medicine. *From Cancer Patient to Cancer Survivor: Lost in Transition*. Washington DC: The National Academies Press; 2006. Report No. 0-309-09595-6.

2. Griffith KA, McGuire DB, Russo M. Meeting survivors' unmet needs: an integrated framework for survivor and palliative care. *Semin Oncol Nurs*. 2010; 26: 231–42.

3. Economou D. Palliative care needs of cancer survivors. *Semin Oncol Nurs*. 2014; 30(4): 262–7. doi: 10.1016/j.soncn.2014.08.008.

4. American Cancer Society. Cancer Treatment and Survivorship, Facts & Figures 2014–2015.

5. Deimling GT, Bowman KF, Sterns S, Wagner LJ, Kahana B. Cancer-related health worries and psychological distress among older adult, long-term cancer survivors. *Psychooncology*. 2006; 15: 306–20.

6. National Consensus Project for Quality Palliative Care. *Clinical Practice Guidelines for Quality Palliative Care*. 3rd ed. Pittsburgh, PA; 2013.

7. Ferrell B, Grant M, eds. *Quality of Life Model Applied to Cancer Survivors*. Washington, DC: National Academies Press; 2004.

8. Ng AK, Travis LB. Subsequent malignant neoplasms in cancer survivors. *Cancer J*. 2008; 14: 429–34.

9. Meier DE, Beresford L. Advanced practice nurses in palliative care: a pivotal role and perspective. *J Palliat Med*. 2006; 9: 624–7.

10. Bakitas M, Bishop MF, Caron P, Stephens L. Developing successful models of cancer palliative care services. *Semin Oncol Nurs*. 2010; 26: 266–84.

11. Bruera E, Kuehn N, Miller MJ, Selmser P, Macmillan K. The Edmonton Symptom Assessment System (ESAS): a simple method for the assessment of palliative care patients. *J Palliat Care*. 1991; 7: 6–9.

12. Kroenke K, Spitzer RL, Williams JB. The PHQ-9: validity of a brief depression severity measure. *J Gen Intern Med*. 2001; 16(9): 606–13.

13. Yabroff KR, McNeel TS, Waldron WR, et al. Health limitations and quality of life associated with cancer and other chronic diseases by phase of care. *Medical Care*. 2007; 45: 629–37.

14. Brem S, Kumar N. Management of treatment-related symptoms in patients with breast cancer: current strategies and future directions. *Clin J Oncol Nurs*. 2011; 15: 63–71.

15. Brown LF, Kroenke K. Cancer-related fatigue and its associations with depression and anxiety: a systematic review. *Psychosomatics*. 2009; 50: 440–7.

16. Gartner R, Jensen MB, Nielsen J, Ewertz M, Kroman N, Kehlet H. Prevalence of and factors associated with persistent pain following breast cancer surgery. *JAMA*. 2009; 302: 1985–92.

17. Ness S, Kokal J, Fee-Schroeder K, Novotny P, Satele D, Barton D. Concerns across the survivorship trajectory: results from a survey of cancer survivors. *Oncol Nurs Forum*. 2013; 40: 35–42.

18. O'Neil-Page E, Anderson P, Dean G. Fatigue. In: Ferrell B, Coyle N, Paice J, eds. *Oxford Textbook of Palliative Nursing*. 4th ed. New York, NY: Oxford University Press; 2015:154–166.

19. Stone PC, Minton O. Cancer-related fatigue. *Eur J Cancer*. 2008; 44: 1097–104.

20. Stein KD, Syrjala KL, Andrykowski MA. Physical and psychological long-term and late effects of cancer. *Cancer*. 2008; 112: 2577–92.

21. Kangas M, Henry JL, Bryant RA. Posttraumatic stress disorder following cancer. A conceptual and empirical review. *Clin Psychol Rev*. 2002; 22: 499–524.

22. Giese-Davis J, Collie K, Rancourt KM, Neri E, Kraemer HC, Spiegel D. Decrease in depression symptoms is associated with longer survival in patients with metastatic breast cancer: a secondary analysis. *J Clin Oncol*. 2011; 29: 413–20.

23. Stanton AL. What happens now? Psychosocial care for cancer survivors after medical treatment completion. *J Clin Oncol*. 2012; 30: 1215–20.

24. Vivar CG, Whyte DA, McQueen A. "Again": the impact of recurrence on survivors of cancer and family members. *J Clin Nurs*. 2010; 19: 2048–56.

25. Evans BC, Ume E. Psychosocial, cultural, and spiritual health disparities in end-of-life and palliative care: where we are and where we need to go. *Nurs Outlook*. 2012; 60: 370–5.

26. Clay K, Talley C, Young KB. Exploring spiritual well-being among survivors of colorectal and lung cancer. *J Relig Spiritual Soc Work*. 2010; 29: 14–32.

27. Braun UK, Beyth RJ, Ford ME, McCullough LB. Voices of African American, Caucasian, and Hispanic surrogates on the burdens of end-of-life decision making. *J Gen Intern Med*. 2008; 23: 267–74.

28. Bullock K. The influence of culture on end-of-life decision making. *J Social Work End of Life Pall Care*. 2011; 7: 83–98.

29. Lackan NA, Eschbach K, Stimpson JP, Freeman JL, Goodwin JS. Ethnic differences in in-hospital place of death among older adults in California: effects of individual and contextual characteristics and medical resource supply. *Medical Care*. 2009; 47: 138–45.

30. Borneman T, Brown-Saltzman K. Meaning in illness. In: Ferrell B, Coyle N, Paice J, eds. *Oxford Textbook of Palliative Nursing*. New York, NY: Oxford University Press; 2015:554–565.

31. Groarke JD, Nguyen PL, Nohria A, Ferrari R, Cheng S, Moslehi J. Cardiovascular complications of radiation therapy for thoracic malignancies: the role for non-invasive imaging for detection of cardiovascular disease. *Eur Heart J*. 2014; 35: 612–23.

32. Smith LA, Cornelius VR, Plummer CJ, et al. Cardiotoxicity of anthracycline agents for the treatment of cancer: systematic review and meta-analysis of randomised controlled trials. *BMC Cancer*. 2010; 10: 337.

33. Liles A, Blatt J, Morris D, et al. Monitoring pulmonary complications in long-term childhood cancer survivors: guidelines for the primary care physician. *Cleveland Clin J Med*. 2008; 75: 531–9.

34. Dudgeon D. Dyspnea, death rattle, and cough. In: Ferrell B, Coyle N, Paice J, eds. *Oxford Textbook of Palliative Nursing*. 4th ed. New York, NY: Oxford University Press; 2015:247–261.

35. Hawkins NA, Smith T, Zhao L, Rodriguez J, Berkowitz Z, Stein KD. Health-related behavior change after cancer: results of the American cancer society's studies of cancer survivors (SCS). *J Cancer Surviv*. 2010; 4: 20–32.

36. Winkfield K, Ng A. Hodgkin's disease survivorship. In: *Excellent Care for Cancer Survivors: A Guide to Fully Meet Their Needs in Medical Offices and in the Community*. Santa Barbara, CA: Praeger/ABC-CLIO; US; 2012:297–308.

37. Kort JD, Eisenberg ML, Millheiser LS, Westphal LM. Fertility issues in cancer survivorship. *CA Cancer J Clin*. 2014; 64: 118–34.

38. Steele R, Davies B. Supporting families in palliative care. In: Ferrell B, Coyle N, Paice J, eds. *Oxford Textbook of Palliative Nursing*. 4th ed. New York, NY: Oxford University Press; 2015:500–514.

39. Simard S, Thewes B, Humphris G, et al. Fear of cancer recurrence in adult cancer survivors: a systematic review of quantitative studies. *J Cancer Surviv*. 2013; 7: 300–22.

40. Koch L, Jansen L, Brenner H, Arndt V. Fear of recurrence and disease progression in long-term (>/= 5 years) cancer survivors—a systematic review of quantitative studies. *Psychooncology*. 2013; 22: 1–11.

41. Coyne PJ. The evolution of the advanced practice nurse within palliative care. *J Palliat Med*. 2003; 6: 769–770.

42. Kuebler KK. The palliative care advanced practice nurse. *J Palliat Med*. 2003; 6: 707–14.

CHAPTER 53

Cognitive Impairment

Abraham A. Brody

Key Points

- The palliative advanced practice registered nurse (APRN) must understand the multiple forms of cognitive impairment in order to optimize treatment of each specific form.

- The palliative APRN should use nonpharmacologic interventions as the first line of therapy for treating neuropsychiatric symptoms because pharmacologic interventions have limited efficacy in treating dementia and neuropsychiatric symptoms.

- The APRN's prime focus of treatment should be maintaining physical activity and function.

- Advance care planning should occur early in the disease process, when the patient still has the ability to participate.

Introduction

Cognitive impairment, in its many forms, is a devastating illness that has significant effects on the individual and his or her family and caregivers. The most common form of cognitive impairment is dementia: 5.2 million cases are diagnosed annually in the United States.[1] As the population rises over the next 35 years, this number will increase to 13.8 million cases diagnosed each year. Dementia, however, is a heterogeneous illness; there are over 25 known etiologies, the most common forms being Alzheimer's dementia (approximately 60% of cases), followed by Lewy body dementia, frontotemporal dementia, and vascular dementia. The remaining etiologies combined represent less than 1% of cases of dementia. Palliative APRNs will be caring for many of these patients.[2]

In addition to dementia, there are many other etiologies of cognitive impairment, the most common of which include Down syndrome, delirium, paraneoplastic syndrome, and benign and malignant tumors. While many of the principles laid out here will relate to forms of cognitive impairment other than dementia, particularly advance care planning and goals-of-care conversations, identification and management of symptoms, and caregiving, this chapter primarily frames the discussion in terms of care for persons with dementia (PWD) and Down syndrome.

Clinical Background and Differential Diagnosis of Dementias

PWD are often diagnosed with just "dementia," not a specific form of the disease. However, the different forms of dementia have different presentations, prognoses, disease progressions, and in some cases appropriate therapies. The most common causes of dementia and cognitive impairment to be included in the differential are listed in Box 53.1. While the final diagnosis should be made by a trained geriatrician, neurologist, neuropsychologist, geriatric nurse practitioner, or interprofessional team at an Alzheimer's Disease Center, these resources are not always accessible. Often the primary care provider or inpatient care team may not have arrived at even a preliminary etiology for a dementia. It therefore may become part of the palliative care team members' work, as they care for the patient, to at least develop a working diagnosis of the etiology, and in certain cases even to ensure that a reversible cause of dementia has not been overlooked.

The care process begins by assessing the patient's level of cognitive impairment using an appropriate screening instrument. The most valid, appropriate, and currently available tests are the Montreal Cognitive Assessment (MOCA) and the St. Louis University Mental Status Exam (SLUMS), which are free, have good reliability and validity, are easy and quick to administer, and are not biased toward education and socioeconomic status, as is the more traditionally used Mini Mental Status Exam (MMSE) (Box 53.2). An additional benefit of the MOCA and SLUMS tests are that they are sensitive for mild cognitive impairment.[3,4]

The palliative APRN should obtain a history. If possible, depending on his or her cognitive status, the patient should be allowed to provide a history, including the length and progression of the cognitive impairment as well as the symptoms and their duration and severity. These characteristics will help determine the type of dementia and can also distinguish if the patient has delirium superimposed on dementia. If the patient has sudden onset or clear and sudden worsening of an existing cognitive deficit over a short period, delirium should be strongly considered, as dementia has a slower and more progressive course. One common cause of delirium is medication, so the patient's medication list should be reviewed to rule out the presence of cognition-reducing medications (e.g., anticholinergics, antipsychotics, opioids, antiepileptics, sedatives, anxiolytics). Other common causes of delirium in the seriously ill are infection (urinary tract infection and pneumonia, in particular), recent surgery with or without anesthesia, dehydration, electrolyte imbalances, and encephalopathies caused by renal or hepatic failure or viral infections, such as herpesvirus, which occur particularly in immunocompromised patients.

Box 53.1 Differential Diagnosis of Dementia

Potentially Reversible Causes of Dementia	Common Dementias	Uncommon Dementias
Depression	Alzheimer's disease	Alcoholic dementia
Infection	Vascular dementia	Huntington's disease
Anemia	Mixed dementia	Progressive supranuclear palsy
Hypothyroidism	Dementia with Lewy bodies	Multiple system atrophy
Syphilis	Parkinson's dementia	Corticobasal degeneration
B_{12} deficiency	Frontotemporal dementia	Hydrocephalus
Folate deficiency		AIDS dementia
Drugs (anticholinergic activity)		HSV encephalopathy
Tumors		Traumatic brain injury
Sensory issues (hearing/vision loss)		Prion diseases
Electrolyte disturbances, dehydration		Paraneoplastic syndrome
Increased intracranial pressure		Multiple sclerosis
		Drug-induced
		Progressive multifocal leukoencephalopathy
Other metabolic disorders (hypo/hyperglycemia, storage disorders)		Subacute sclerosing panencephalitis
		Whipple's disease

From reference 2.

Additional screening should include major depression, which is often confused with cognitive impairment and can lead to poor cognitive function. Screening instruments like the Geriatric Depression Scale 15 or PHQ-9 can be used. Those who screen positive should then receive further evaluation for depression. Box 53.3 highlights the chief differences in the presentation of patients with major depression versus dementia.[6] However, depression carries a strong risk for developing Alzheimer's dementia, and up to two out of three older adults with dementia have comorbid depression and dementia, depending on the setting.[5] Thus, the two are not mutually exclusive and often need to be treated simultaneously.

Once a longer-standing cognitive impairment has been established based on the scores from screening instruments and informant and patient interviews, lab tests are performed to rule out potentially reversible causes of dementia (if they have not

already been performed), including B_{12} and folate (deficiency), TSH (hypothyroidism), a complete blood count (severe anemia), and, if the patient has a history of risky sexual behavior, RPR

Box 53.2 Selected Dementia Screening Instrument Cutoff Scores

	SLUMS	MOCA	MMSE
Normal	27–30* 25–30**	27–30	28–30
Mild Cognitive Impairment	21–26* 20–24**	18–26	25–27
Mild Dementia	15–19		19–24
Moderate Dementia	11–14	10–17	10–18
Severe Dementia	>11	<10	>10

* HS education ** Less than HS education
From references 3 and 4.

Box 53.3 Presentation of Depression Versus Dementia

Major Depression	Dementia
Acute	Progressive
Oriented	Impaired orientation
Gives up easily	Tries hard even if incorrect
Fewer symptoms at night	Sundowning
Self-referred	Others refer
Diminished concentration ability	Short-term memory deficit
Normal language	Impaired language capabilities
Draws attention to memory problems	Minimizes memory problems
Severely depressed	Minor or no depression
Blunted or flat affect	Full range of emotions
Apathy or anhedonia over weeks	Apathy or anhedonia gradual over time
Common suicidal thoughts	Rare suicidal thoughts
Guilt is common	Guilt is uncommon
Sudden sleep pattern/ability changes	Gradual sleep disturbance development
Major weight changes	Gradual weight loss over time

From reference 6.

Box 53.4 Presenting Symptoms of Major Types of Dementia

Alzheimer's	Vascular	Mixed	Lewy Body	Frontotemporal
◆ Short-term memory loss	◆ Impaired executive function	◆ Includes symptoms of both Alzheimer's and vascular	◆ Fluctuating cognition	◆ Disinhibition
◆ Forgetfulness	◆ Motor deficits		◆ Recurrent visual hallucinations	◆ Expressive or receptive aphasia
◆ Difficulty learning new tasks	◆ Difficulty retrieving memories		◆ Parkinsonian movement	◆ Emotional distance ◆ Stubbornness
◆ Poor attention	◆ Aphasia		◆ REM sleep disorder	◆ Apathy ◆ Selfishness
◆ Difficulty finding words	◆ Inefficiency of thought		◆ Sensitivity to neuroleptics	◆ Facial recognition difficulty
◆ Difficulty with complex tasks	◆ Poor problem solving		◆ Repeated falls	
◆ Poor recognition			◆ Autonomic dysfunction	
			◆ Systematic delusions	

From reference 7.

(syphilis). Assuming these tests are negative, the next step is to perform a head computed tomography scan without contrast to rule out tumors and hydrocephalus and to examine whether any brain atrophy, white matter changes, or cerebrovascular accidents (CVAs) have occurred.[7]

A specialty positron emission tomography imaging technique using the contrast agent florbetapir F-18 (Amyvid) has been recently approved by the U.S. Food and Drug Administration; it can reveal the presence of amyloid plaques, a major cause of Alzheimer's disease. However, the test is nondefinitive and does not add to certainty in diagnosis in most cases. Therefore, it should be ordered only by a dementia expert in certain highly specific circumstances where there is atypical presentation.[8] There are also now biomarkers of Alzheimer's dementia that can be used for preclinical symptom diagnosis through serum analysis. At this point, the biomarkers, including amyloid-β accumulation levels, should be used only for research purposes, as recognized by an NIH-Alzheimer's Association Expert Panel.[9]

Once test results are available and are combined with the symptomatic presentation, a working diagnosis can be made. Box 53.4 summarizes the presenting symptoms of the five most common forms of dementia. Each is discussed in greater detail below.

Alzheimer's Disease

Alzheimer's disease is characterized by memory loss, beginning with short-term memory loss and progressing to long-term memory loss, including the loss of decades of life memories, loss of ability to perform activities of daily living (ADLs) and instrumental ADLs, and eventually loss of speech and coordinated muscle movements, such as swallowing. The average lifespan following diagnosis is 8 years, and patients usually spend the last 40% of that time in the severe stage.[1] Between 60% and 80% of all dementias diagnosed are of the Alzheimer's type, though up to 40% of patients may have mixed etiology with vascular dementia (see the section on mixed dementia).[10] The disease is caused by a number

of changes in the brain, including formation of amyloid plaques and tau tangles, leading to the damage and destruction of neurons, causing the brain to atrophy. While most individuals diagnosed with Alzheimer's disease are over 65, early-onset Alzheimer's is thought to progress more quickly.[11]

Prior to the onset of Alzheimer's, patients often develop mild cognitive impairment in the form of some memory problems, and perhaps some movement difficulties and changes in smell. Not all patients advance from mild cognitive impairment to Alzheimer's. Mild cognitive impairment is defined as short-term memory deficit and is largely stable over time; it does not affect the patient's functional status.

Alzheimer's disease is generally divided into mild, moderate, and severe categories, and the disease will progress over time. In mild Alzheimer's, patients start to lose short-term memory, which can lead them to become confused in complex situations, such as with driving. They may become lost, have difficulty managing their financial affairs, ask repetitive questions, forget to turn off the stove after starting to cook a meal, and start to show some alteration in personality, particularly due to the frustration of declining memory. Many PWD attempt to hide these deficits, and therefore it is often a family member or friend who will make sure that the deficits are brought to the attention of a medical provider. The mild Alzheimer's stage is where these deficits become clear enough for family to recognize and is therefore where the majority of cases are diagnosed. The median time PWD spend in the mild stage is 4 years.[12]

In moderate Alzheimer's dementia, patients begin losing the ability to learn new tasks or pieces of information, may no longer recognize family and friends, begin to have difficulty performing complex ADLs, such as dressing, and start to have significant impairment in executive function. They start to lose more long-term memory, such as where they went to school, what year they are living in, and the fact that they have grandchildren or their adult children are married. They cannot compare situations and therefore cannot make decisions about most future care (e.g., advance directives). They can no longer live safely and independently in the community and therefore require help with ADLs and instrumental ADLs. Many patients at this stage also start to develop significant neuropsychiatric problems, although they are generally manageable with skilled care. These neuropsychiatric and mood problems include agitation, depression, and aggression. Some individuals may develop delusions or hallucinations, though these are more common in Lewy body dementia. Patients generally remain in the moderate stage of Alzheimer's disease for approximately 1.5 to 2 years.[12]

Severe Alzheimer's disease is characterized by complete loss of ability to communicate needs and by dependence in all ADLs. PWD in this stage may be able to string together a few words, but the words are not generally meaningful, and they will eventually lose speech altogether. Patients at this stage often also develop difficulty with swallowing because they can no longer coordinate movement. Aspiration pneumonias may become frequent and are often a cause of death. Patients generally enter the severe stage 6 years from diagnosis, and the stage generally lasts 1 to 2 years.[12] The median survival time is approximately 8 years from diagnosis, although the older the person is at diagnosis, the shorter the lifespan. Men are also likely to die sooner.

Vascular Dementia

Vascular dementia is caused by ischemic or hemorrhagic damage to the brain, primarily through CVA. It is the second most common form of dementia after Alzheimer's disease, accounting for approximately 10% to 15% of all dementias[13] (excluding mixed dementia). Risk factors for dementia are cerebrovascular in nature (Box 53.5).[14] Unlike in Alzheimer's, progression is variable and highly dependent upon cardiovascular status and risk for future CVAs. Therefore, mortality is also highly variable and difficult to determine, although in general the survival is shorter than in Alzheimer's dementia.[15]

Symptoms of vascular dementia are highly variable and depend on the size and location of the CVA. Early symptoms include impaired executive function, ineffective memory, perseveration, changes in personality, poor verbal fluency, sleep disturbances, and cortical symptoms, such as visual disturbances and difficulty doing mathematical calculations.

Some strokes are major and easily perceived, leading to a clear functional loss. Others may be smaller and occur over time, leading to declines in cognitive capacity. One typical form of small CVA is a lacunar infarct. Multiple, small lacunar infarcts are a common, slow, insidious form of vascular dementia that is often missed until later stages if cognitive screening is not performed frequently; each individual CVA is small and therefore the decline is punctuated over time.

Mixed Dementia

Mixed dementia occurs when the patient develops both Alzheimer's and vascular dementia. Symptoms from both diseases will be present, as discussed earlier. In addition, individuals with mixed dementia experience depressed mood, motor and sensory changes, and gait abnormalities with higher frequency than with either Alzheimer's or vascular dementia separately.[16] While the exact prevalence of mixed dementia is unclear, as studies have varied significantly (0% to 55%),[17] many cases that are diagnosed as Alzheimer's disease

---

Box 53.5 Vascular Dementia Risk Factors

Demographic
- Older age
- Male gender
- Lower education

Atherosclerotic
- Hypertension
- Hyperlipidemia
- Diabetes mellitus
- History of myocardial infarction or cigarette smoking

Genetic
- Familial vascular encephalopathies

Stroke-Related
- Cerebral tissue loss
- Bilateral cerebral infarction
- Strategic infarction
- White matter disease

---

turn out to be mixed dementia, determined at autopsy or through symptomatic and radiographic findings. The median survival time of mixed dementia has been estimated at 5.4 years.[18]

Lewy Body Dementia

Lewy body dementia is an overarching term for two separate diseases, dementia with Lewy bodies and Parkinson's dementia. The primary distinction between the two is whether the cognitive symptoms occur at the same time as movement symptoms (dementia with Lewy bodies) or the movement symptoms are followed at least 2 years later by cognitive symptoms (Parkinson's dementia). Lewy body dementia is caused by the formation in the brain of Lewy bodies, which are abnormal clumps of alpha-synuclein, a protein. It is unclear what causes these bodies to develop, though in most cases it is thought to be genetic–environment interaction. In Parkinson's dementia, Lewy bodies form, but the primary pathophysiology is the degeneration of dopaminergic neurons in the substantia nigra.

The movement disorder features of both include resting tremor, shuffling gait, rigidity, and eventually akinesia, which includes both hypokinesia (decreased frequency or absence of movement) and bradykinesia (slowed movement). Neuropsychiatric symptoms include sleep disturbance, including REM sleep disorder, fluctuation in alertness and attention, recurrent visual hallucinations, visual-spatial problems, and depression. Patients with these diseases have neuroleptic sensitivity, so the correct diagnosis must be made before prescribing a neuroleptic for dementia symptoms. Approximately 4% to 7% of dementia cases are diagnosed as Lewy body dementia,[19] and the average survival time from diagnosis is approximately 4.4 years.[20]

Frontotemporal Dementia

Frontotemporal dementia is a group of dementias caused by progressive neuronal degeneration in the frontal and/or temporal lobes of the brain. It generally occurs in individuals younger than 65 (median in studies is 52 to 60)[21] and is significantly more likely to occur in men than women (14:3).[22] Survival is highly variable and depends on the subtype of disease, ranging from 3 years in motor neuron disease variants to 12 years in semantic dementia and 9 years in neuropsychiatric variant and progressive nonfluent aphasia.[21] Patients with genetic risk factors make up about 30% to 50% of cases, although clinicians do not generally test for these markers, and the remainder of cases occur for unknown reasons, though head trauma and thyroid disease are thought to be potential risk factors.[21] Overall, approximately 12% to 16% of cases of dementia are from frontotemporal dementia.[23]

Neuropsychiatric Variant

The neuropsychiatric variant of frontotemporal dementia, formerly known as Pick's disease, is the most common form. Patients generally present with disinhibition, including inappropriate touching or sexual behavior, impulsiveness, loss of empathy or sympathy, overeating, compulsive behaviors, apathy, and loss of executive function. In the moderate stage, these symptoms will start to worsen, and patients will also begin to have more memory problems and issues with planning and attention. In the severe stage, patients will express severe memory loss and language difficulty, and neuropsychiatric symptoms will continue to decline.

Semantic Dementia

Patients with left-sided semantic dementia commonly present with word-finding difficulties; a "pencil" might be a "writing thing" and an "orange" might be "that fruit." In right-sided semantic dementia, patients tend to present with decreased awareness of other people's emotions. In both cases, memory remains more or less intact. The disease progresses to the moderate phase, generally about 2 to 3 years after diagnosis. At this time, patients with left- and right-sided disease begin to show a more merged symptom presentation, including trouble with comprehending statements and recognizing faces, and some of the neuropsychiatric symptoms common to the behavioral variant. As individuals move into the severe stage of the disease, their neuropsychiatric symptoms worsen and they lose the ability to communicate.

Progressive Nonfluent Aphasia

Unlike those with semantic dementia, patients with progressive nonfluent aphasia retain the ability to understand language and know the words they want to say; the first signs of disease relate to their ability to actually produce the speech they wish. This expressive aphasia will continue to worsen over time, and within 3 to 4 years they will enter the moderate stage, where they will only be able to use short phrases to express their needs. They can still, however, read and write well in most cases, so a dry-erase board or paper and notebook can help with communication in this stage. Approximately 5 to 7 years from diagnosis, patients will become completely unable to speak and will start to develop the neuropsychiatric symptoms common to the behavioral variant of frontotemporal dementia.

Motor Neuron Disease

Motor neuron disease is the most severe form of frontotemporal dementia and causes a precipitous decline. Symptoms are similar to those of the neuropsychiatric variant, but patients also exhibit muscle weakness, stiffness, and atrophy, and loss of coordination and fine motor movement as motor neurons slowly disintegrate, similar to amyotrophic lateral sclerosis. Eventually patients will present with dysphagia and dysarthria and are at high risk for developing aspiration pneumonia.

Down Syndrome

Down syndrome, also known as trisomy 21, is generally diagnosed very early in life or prenatally through chromosomal or blood testing. The disease is caused by the abnormal development of a third full or partial chromosome 21 during early development. Individuals have a distinct facial appearance, which includes some but not always all of the following: upward-slanting eyes, flattened facial features, short hands and fingers, protruding tongue, and short stature. Severity is highly variable: some individuals exhibit mild cognitive deficits and others have severe cognitive difficulty, up to the levels seen in advanced dementias.

Life expectancy in Down syndrome is currently 60 years of age; it has increased dramatically over the past 50 years.[24] While a certain segment of the population will die in childhood, those individuals who live to adulthood generally develop the same health issues as the general public, though in a more rapid fashion. Over 50% may develop Alzheimer's dementia superimposed on Down syndrome if they live past 60.[25] Individuals with Down syndrome generally start to develop functional, cognitive, and health decline around the age of 40. The most prevalent causes of death in this population include congenital heart defect, dementia-related causes (e.g., aspiration pneumonia, falls), and leukemias.[26] Persons with Down syndrome toward the end-of-life often present with similar issues to PWD, specifically issues related to functional decline, such as dysphagia, pressure ulcers, and agitation, particularly around baths and personal care. Persons with Down syndrome are often shuttled between group care homes and nursing homes as they enter the last several years of their lives, and multiple studies have found that the greater the number of transfers, the higher the risk of deterioration; transfers should therefore be limited as much as possible.[27]

Advance Care Planning

Advance care planning in those with cognitive impairment can be a difficult process. Ideally, individuals will have discussed their wishes with their family/proxy before diagnosis, or at least during the early phase of their disease. However, this is often not the case. While studies have shown that those with mild and even early moderate disease may be able to select a healthcare proxy[28] and take part in some noncomplex healthcare decision making,[29] it is not appropriate to give those with even mild cognitive impairment full decision-making capacity for more complex decisions, as they cannot weigh options and conceptualize the long-term risks and benefits of decisions. Therefore, many decisions are discussed with the healthcare proxy. However, to the extent possible, the patient should be consulted in forming a decision.

The most important items to focus on in advance care planning for those with cognitive impairment include the aggressiveness and amount of care versus quality of life (hospitalization, resuscitation status, intubation, antibiotics, feeding tube placement) and the preferred setting of care based on available caregiving and financial status (home, group home, continuing care community, assisted living, nursing home). In states where orders for out-of-hospital life-sustaining treatments (POLST or MOLST) are accepted, these documents should be used to help provide clear, across-setting orders for the patient's wishes. For more information, see Chapter 39, Advance Care Planning.

Management of Symptoms

Cognitive Decline

There are currently no pharmacologic or nonpharmacologic agents to reverse cognitive decline in dementia. Two classes of drugs are approved for slowing the progress of Alzheimer's dementia and Lewy body dementia: acetylcholinesterase inhibitors and NMDA receptor agonists. The former include donepezil (Aricept), galantamine (Razadyne), and rivastigmine (Exelon) and are indicated in mild and moderate dementia. These drugs have been shown to slightly decrease the rate of progression of the disease both cognitively and functionally and are more effective in Lewy body dementia than in Alzheimer's. While these drugs do have some efficacy, they can also have significant side effects that are worse than the slight benefit of the medication. The most prominent side effect is gastrointestinal disturbance and upset, particularly diarrhea; this can lead to reduced oral intake and fluid/electrolyte imbalances. When starting this class of medication, the benefits and risks should be weighed and discussed with the patient and proxy. These drugs are not miracle cures, so it is important to set expectations appropriately. After initiation, if side effects are significant and do not dissipate, then a discussion needs to occur. Once this class of medication is stopped, the patient will lose whatever effect the medication had and will not return to that level if it is restarted.

The second class of drugs, NMDA receptor agonists, consists of only one medication, memantine (Namenda). Memantine is indicated for use in moderate or severe Alzheimer's disease; there is limited evidence for use in other forms of dementia. Studies have shown that combining memantine with an acetylcholinesterase inhibitor when the patient reaches the moderate stage of Alzheimer's disease has a synergistic effect in slowing the disease; however, the effect size is small at best.[30] The drug has limited side effects, so the cost versus small benefit should be discussed and weighed with the patient or family.

There is limited evidence about medication use once a person reaches end-stage dementia (e.g., needs help with all ADLs except walking, limited speech capability). Studies have shown that in severe dementia, there is potentially some improvement in quality of life and reduction in depression symptoms, but these are not at the end stage, and similarly little evidence is available regarding what to do when a PWD has entered hospice care.[30] Therefore, a conversation needs to occur with family about the goals of care and potential pros and cons of continuing the medication.

Functional Decline

As patients decline over the course of disease, more and more issues will arise related to physical function. This decline can lead to aggression and agitation on the part of the PWD and caregiver stress, burden, and burnout, among other issues. The goal is therefore to maintain function or find "workarounds" for function for as long as possible. Generally, even for PWD being followed by palliative care specialists, physical and occupational therapists can be extremely useful. They can suggest home modifications and assistive devices, help train caregivers in how to perform transfers or perform exercises with the patient, or help by providing direct therapy to the patient to assist with function or strength. Especially with the removal of restrictions on physical and occupational therapy services to persons with no potential for improvement, there are greater opportunities to use these skilled rehabilitation therapists in these areas.

Bathing and Personal Care

One of the most difficult areas that PWD and their caregivers struggle with is bathing and personal care. The loss of dignity that occurs when the PWD can no longer care for himself or herself after a long life of independence, coupled with cognitive impairment, often leads to verbal or physical aggression. To prevent or reduce aggression, a highly person-centered approach needs to be taken.[31] Effective, personally tailored interventions may include the following:

Assessing the patient prior to the care for pain and current physical and mental state and altering the routine or stopping the care until these can be better managed

Environmental changes, such as reducing noise, introducing soothing music

Changes to routine, including stopping and interacting with the patient prior to initiating personal care, covering private parts to the extent possible, and ensuring as much privacy as possible

When resistance is encountered, try again a few minutes later (or in the case of a bath, a few hours later), provide reasons for the personal care or bath (e.g., "You've been working hard, wouldn't it feel good to freshen up?"), and/or change the type of bath (e.g., bath, using a shower chair, bed bath with warm wet towels).

Dysphagia

One of the most common problems facing PWD as they reach the severe stage of dementia is dysphagia. This is a normal part of the disease process. PWD often lose their ability to coordinate swallowing movements as well as their ability to feed themselves, leading to a high risk for developing aspiration pneumonias. This often brings up discussions of whether tube feeding would be appropriate. Multiple studies have shown that tube feeding does not prevent aspiration and is no better than spoon feeding, and the potential benefits are far outweighed by the burdens.[32] It is therefore important to educate PWD and family about these benefits and burdens. The earlier in the disease process this can be discussed, the better, allowing time for multiple conversations.

An additional issue that has arisen, particularly recently in hospices, is patients or family members requesting to voluntarily stop eating and drinking or assisting the PWD to eat and drink. Morally, ethically, and legally, if a patient has made a clear statement or advance directive stating he or she would not want to be hand-fed or hydrated, or artificially hydrated, then we must respect these wishes.[33] However, if the patient has not voiced the wishes directly and clearly (and ideally in writing), this is more of a legal, moral, and ethical gray area, and both legal and ethics consults should be called, as laws vary state by state in this regard. Eventually, the patient who stops eating and drinking voluntarily will die (within about 8 to 10 days on average) rather comfortably from dehydration.

Neuropsychiatric Symptoms

PWD may present with a variety of neuropsychiatric symptoms related to the type of dementia they have. There are six primary clusters of symptoms.

Aggression

Physical and verbal aggression is highly prevalent in PWD. The aggression may be caused by any number of problems, so assessment is necessary to treat the baseline problem. The most prevalent causes include bathing and personal care, unidentified or undertreated pain or depression, and a poor relationship between the PWD and the caregiver.[34] Other potential causes include sensory perception issues (hearing, vision), delirium, medication side effects, and environmental factors (noise, temperature). To reduce aggression, the root cause needs to be identified and treated. Pharmacologic measures (e.g., antipsychotics) are not appropriate and do not work for aggressive behaviors; they only sedate the patient. Caregivers need to stay calm, as any show of strong emotion (e.g., yelling, threatening movements) will only make the aggression worse. Redirecting the patient can be a useful method when aggression is not related to an immediately identifiable and treatable cause.

Psychomotor Agitation

Psychomotor agitation includes hyperactive behaviors, such as repetitive actions, pacing, restlessness, and dressing and undressing. This form of agitation is common in Lewy body dementia and can also result from the overuse of antipsychotics. Removing these medications may stop the behaviors. Other options include physical therapy to help patients focus on completing specific tasks rather than aimless hyperactivity. Increasing stimulation and companionship may also help reduce this symptom.

Psychosis

The psychosis cluster includes hallucinations, delusions, and misidentification of people and objects. This is the only time when it may be beneficial to use antipsychotics in PWD. If the hallucination, delusion, or misidentification is not distressing, pharmacologic treatment should not be prescribed, as the risks outweigh any benefits. If, however, the patient is experiencing multiple distressing visual or auditory hallucinations, delusions, or misidentifications, antipsychotic use can be considered. It is important to "start low and go slow." Moreover, different antipsychotics have different properties (e.g., quetiapine is sedating, whereas olanzapine is activating), so the medication must be given at the appropriate time of day, and an activated patient should not be given an activating antipsychotic (or vice versa). Also, for patients with Lewy body dementia or Parkinson's dementia, the only appropriate medications are quetiapine and clozapine, though the latter requires frequent blood testing for agranulocytosis. Finally, whenever considering an antipsychotic, whether typical or atypical, the proxy needs to be informed of the black-box warning and the risks for increased heart attack or stroke and must clearly consent to the medication. Patients are also at a higher risk for falls when taking these medications, and certain medications have other significant side effects. For instance, olanzapine causes disturbances in blood sugar in individuals with diabetes. Therefore, the palliative APRN must be knowledgeable about the specific medication prior to prescribing. The conversation, including all side effects, needs to be documented in the chart.

Apathy

Apathy, including social isolation, withdrawal, and lack of interest, is common in PWD. Nonpharmacologic measures to involve the patient are important: music therapy, multisensory behavioral interventions, physical activity, dancing, singing, and talking have been found to be effective.[35] Pharmacologically, acetylcholinesterase inhibitors have shown to be mildly beneficial, but the side effects likely outweigh the benefits, and other drug classes, such as stimulants and neuroleptics, have not shown any efficacy.[36]

Depression

Depression can be identified using the Geriatric Depression Scale in mild to moderate dementia,[37] and the Cornell Scale for Depression in Dementia,[38] an informant-based interview, can be used for individuals with moderate to severe dementia. Treating depression in PWD can often lead to significant decreases in other neuropsychiatric symptoms, so the patient should be assessed for depression early on. Treatment for depression should include a mixture of pharmacologic treatment (preferably citalopram, sertraline, or escitalopram, which present fewer issues in the geriatric population) and nonpharmacologic measures (e.g., music, reminiscence, and pet therapy).[39]

Sleep Disturbance

Sleep disturbances occur in 40% of PWD[40] and can have significant consequences, including significantly increasing the caregiver's stress.[41] One of the most common disturbances is alteration of the diurnal sleep pattern. Patients are often sleepy and take long naps during the day, becoming restless in the early evening. This early evening agitation is often called sundowning. The most important way to avoid or decrease these sleep-pattern changes is to prevent the patient from taking long naps throughout the day. This requires the patient to be engaged and not socially isolated. The physical environment should be kept bright, if possible with natural light or specialized lights that mimic daylight. Only one nap of no more than an hour should be permitted. Sleep medications in this population can cause significant neuropsychiatric side effects and can lead to falls. Stimulants during the day (pharmacologic or nonpharmacologic, such as caffeine) can cause agitation and should therefore be avoided as much as possible. Melatonin has not been shown to be effective in this population despite common myths that it works. Alcohol should also be avoided. Finally, regular exercise can help to maintain the proper sleep–wake cycle.

A second type of sleep disturbance is REM sleep disorder, which is more prevalent in Lewy body dementia than in other forms. In REM sleep disorder, individuals act out their dreams by walking, talking, screaming, or displaying physical aggression. Clonazepam is the suggested treatment in patients without dementia who have REM sleep disorder, but it is not recommended in PWD due to the risk for rebound agitation. Melatonin has shown some efficacy in treating this disorder, and acetylcholinesterase inhibitors like donepezil have shown some efficacy, though the evidence is limited.[42]

Pain

While pain in and of itself is not associated with dementia, identifying and managing pain in this population can be difficult. PWD still experience pain, though they often cannot communicate that they do. In general, older adults may not identify pain by using the word "pain," instead describing it in terms of soreness, achiness, "the arthritis," or having difficulty with "that" (e.g., using their hands, walking).[43] While rating scales using faces, numbers, or words can all be used in individuals with mild dementia, patients should be assessed at times other than when they are resting, as they may forget that they had pain with movement. The assessment should be done immediately after the patient completes a movement, or even during the movement. The palliative APRN should observe for pain behaviors, such as bracing, verbalizations, and facial expressions indicating pain, and should examine the patient's problem list for potential painful conditions (e.g., osteoarthritis, compression fractures, neuropathies). In individuals with moderate and severe dementia, a pain assessment instrument specifically for use in this population should be used (e.g., the PAINAD) in addition to the patient's subjective report and reporting from the primary caregiver.[44]

Once pain is identified, treatment of pain in this population generally follows the same recommendations as for patients without dementia—with some differences. Mild pain should be treated using nonpharmacologic interventions. Medications should be given on a scheduled basis rather than as needed because the patient may not request, or will forget to request, pain medicine. For mild to moderate pain, acetaminophen is the first-line treatment, not exceeding 3 g/day. If pain is not controlled with acetaminophen, generally a combination opioid/acetaminophen product is the next step.

Spiritual Support

Spiritual support can improve the quality of life for both the patient and caregiver. Higher religiosity has been found to slow cognitive and behavioral decline in dementia.[45] Spiritual support can give meaning to the caregiver's experiences, reducing stress[46] and improving his or her overall mental health.[47] Therefore patients and their caregivers should be encouraged to use spiritual support, whether in the community, an assisted living facility, nursing home, or hospital setting. The palliative APRN should facilitate such services as appropriate and possible.

Working with Caregivers

Caregivers for PWD have a high risk of burden, stress, and burnout. Caregivers, especially spouses, may become ill themselves, even necessitating hospital admission. If the caregiver's needs are not met, the patient is significantly more likely to be placed in a nursing home or other long-term care facility rather than remaining at home. Paid caregivers, if they become burned out, leave, causing further trauma to the patient and family because they have to develop a new therapeutic relationship, which can cause further decline.

Therefore, providing support for the caregiver is just as important as support for the patient. This can take many forms, such as training sessions from the local Alzheimer's Association (applicable regardless of type of dementia), adult day care programs for the patient to give the caregiver some personal time, or respite care in a facility. The most important part of helping the caregiver is to manage neuropsychiatric symptoms as outlined above and to manage the caregiver's expectations.

Caregivers should be monitored for burden, stress, and burnout. The Healthy Aging Brain Care Monitor, available in English and Spanish, measures the caregiver's perception of neuropsychiatric symptoms as well as burden, stress, and burnout.[48] Some additional instruments include the Pines Burnout Inventory[49] and the Zarit Burden Inventory.[50] When the caregiver's stress starts to rise, it is important to identify the source, correct it, and if necessary provide some form of respite.

Hospice Care

While PWD should begin to receive palliative care early in the disease trajectory, they are not eligible for hospice care until they have very severe dementia. Patients must meet the FAST 7C level of debility, which means they cannot speak more than six distinct intelligible words and they have functional dependence with the exception of ambulation, or score at or below a 40 on the Palliative Performance Scale. Patients also must have a secondary condition, which could include a recent history of multiple stage 3 or 4 pressure ulcers, aspiration pneumonia, septicemia, pyelonephritis, recurrent fever, or inability to maintain sufficient intake of food and fluids (as defined by loss of 10% weight in a 6-month period or an albumin level less than 2.5 g/dL). Some hospices have even stricter standards due to increasing pressure from the Office of the Inspector General of the U.S. Government Department of Health and Human Services and the Centers for Medicare and Medicaid Services.

Once a patient is deemed eligible and admitted to hospice, the palliative care team must closely scrutinize standing orders prior to signing the order set. For instance, the emergency kit often provided to patients in homes usually includes lorazepam or another short-acting benzodiazepine. Because benzodiazepines can cause rebound confusion and delirium in older adults, particularly those with cognitive impairment, including this in the kit should be discouraged. Haloperidol, prochlorperazine, and promethazine are often included in these kits; these medications should not be permitted in cases where the patient has Lewy body dementia or Parkinson's dementia because they have dopaminergic blocking activity and may worsen symptoms in these patients.

Once the patient is admitted to hospice, it is important to continue following the patient, as many (though not all) hospice clinicians have limited knowledge of how to care for dementia. They may need help with recognizing and developing a plan of care for treating pain, neuropsychiatric symptoms, or other symptoms. Given that PWD tend to have longer stays in hospice than cancer patients and experience significant functional disability associated with end-stage dementia, special attention needs to be paid to skin integrity. When working with hospice, it is often important to request occupational and physical therapy consultation to help train the caregiver to prevent contractures and prolong function (specifically ambulation) as long as possible, and to evaluate for home safety. Occupational and physical therapists can also train the caregiver in how to perform transfers when the patient cannot ambulate even with assistance, thus preventing caregiver injury. Occupational therapists are experts at providing "workarounds" for functional and cognitive limitations. Physical therapists can be of great help in teaching caregivers about exercises they can use to help the patient maintain strength as long as possible and to prevent contractures once the patient has lost too much strength to bear weight. These services are included within the hospice benefit but are often not provided unless directly requested.

Role of the APRN

The palliative APRN has a wide role in managing the cognitively impaired patient. While a specific diagnosis should probably not be made without consulting a neurologist, geriatrician, Alzheimer's disease center, or geriatric APRN, most treatment falls well within the scope of practice and range of knowledge of the palliative APRN. This includes managing nonpharmacologic and pharmacologic interventions for neuropsychiatric symptoms; advance care planning; referral to physical or occupational therapy for exercise regimens and physical function; assessing and managing caregiver stress, burden, and burnout; and directing care or attending on hospice care.

Case Study

Diane was a 78-year-old Caucasian female admitted to the hospital following left-sided hemiparesis. Her history included hypertension, hyperlipidemia, two past minor CVAs, bilateral knee osteoarthritis, and cognitive impairment, with a MOCA score of 20 1 year earlier. Her medications included clopidogrel, atorvastatin, lisinopril, HCTZ, and amlodipine. According to her daughter, Lisa, her primary caregiver, prior to this most recent CVA, Diane had been experiencing slow, progressive loss of short-term memory and physical function. She also became more socially isolated and spent much of the day inside with the shades drawn, and she had stopped smiling or eating as much. Lisa spent approximately 20 hours per week caring for her mother, who lived in their home. She had two small children and a husband, who was often out of town for work. Regarding care planning, Lisa reported that her mom had previously stated that, when it was her time to go, she didn't want "extra measures," but wanted to be left comfortable. The APRN queried further and found that the patient would not want artificial nutrition or hydration if she wasn't able to eat; however, if she had a simple infection, she would want it treated.

On assessment, the patient was alert and oriented to person and place only, had a new MOCA score of 14, had 2/5 strength of her left leg and arm, and required at maximum 1 person assist to transfer. Diane became physically and verbally aggressive with any attempt to begin physical activity or when passive ROM exercises of the lower extremities were performed. The daughter appeared very stressed and scored a 7/12 on the caregiver burden portion of the HABC-M. A CT scan of Diane's head revealed a new focal hyperattenuation in the primary motor cortex on the right side of the brain (new CVA) and several old deep lesions 10 mm in diameter in the lacunar area of the brain consistent with prior CT (old lacunar infarcts). There was also overall moderate brain atrophy (consistent with Alzheimer's).

Based on this clinical picture, the APRN diagnosed Diane with mixed dementia and depression. After a discussion with the daughter, the APRN began citalopram 5 mg daily PO for 1 week, then increased to 10 mg. The APRN also initiated acetaminophen 1,000 mg three times daily for osteoarthritic knee pain. After the first dose, she reassessed and found the patient was no longer physically or verbally aggressive with ROM exercises or transfer. The APRN ordered PT and OT for post-stroke rehab. The APRN completed a POLST order set for DNAR, limited interventions, no artificial nutrition and hydration, but antibiotics for infection. Diane was discharged home with home PT, OT, safety evaluation, and short-term home health aide services to assist the daughter during the transition period. A follow-up appointment was made for 1 week, at which time there was a discussion of whether to start Diane on an acetylcholinesterase inhibitor and NMDA receptor antagonist (memantine) as well as her long-term plan of care and patient trajectory. While the patient was not eligible for hospice, further palliative follow-up was recommended for symptomatic care. The patient's daughter was also referred to the local Alzheimer's Association chapter for caregiver training.

Conclusion

Most forms of dementia are irreversible and progressive. The most significant problems related to this group of diseases are the presentation and worsening of neuropsychiatric symptoms over time, progressive decline in functional status, and progressive increase in caregiver burden, stress, and burnout, leading to placement in a nursing home. Therefore, the palliative APRN must (1) create a clear plan of care early in the disease, if possible with the patient and proxy present; (2) provide clear expectations to the caregiver about the patient's course; (3) implement nonpharmacologic and pharmacologic interventions to manage functional decline and neuropsychiatric symptoms; and (4) train caregivers to provide appropriate care. These steps can help the patient and caregiver deal with this devastating group of diseases to the greatest extent possible.

References

1. Alzheimer's Association. *Alzheimer's Disease Facts and Figures.* Chicago, IL; 2014.
2. Maalouf M, Ringman JM, Shi J. An update on the diagnosis and management of dementing conditions. *Rev Neurol Dis.* 2011; 8(3-4): e68–87.
3. Cummings-Vaughn LA, Chavakula NN, Malmstrom TK, Tumosa N, Morley JE, Cruz-Oliver DM. Veterans Affairs Saint Louis University Mental Status examination compared with the Montreal Cognitive Assessment and the Short Test of Mental Status. *J Am Geriatr Soc.* 2014; 62(7): 1341–6.
4. Mitchell AJ. A meta-analysis of the accuracy of the Mini-Mental State Examination in the detection of dementia and mild cognitive impairment. *J Psychiatr Res.* 2009; 43(4): 411–31.
5. Rosness TA, Barca ML, Engedal K. Occurrence of depression and its correlates in early onset dementia patients. *Int J Geriatr Psychiatry.* 2010; 25(7): 704–11.
6. Wright SL, Persad C. Distinguishing between depression and dementia in older persons: neuropsychological and neuropathological correlates. *J Geriatr Psychiatry Neurol.* 2007; 20(4): 189–98.

7. Buffington AL, Lipski DM, Westfall E. Dementia: an evidence-based review of common presentations and family-based interventions. *J Am Osteopath Assoc.* 2013; 113(10): 768–75.

8. Johnson KA, Minoshima S, Bohnen NI, et al. Appropriate use criteria for amyloid PET: a report of the Amyloid Imaging Task Force, the Society of Nuclear Medicine and Molecular Imaging, and the Alzheimer's Association. *Alzheimers Dement.* 2013; 9(1): e1–16.

9. Sperling RA, Aisen PS, Beckett LA, et al. Toward defining the preclinical stages of Alzheimer's disease: recommendations from the National Institute on Aging-Alzheimer's Association workgroups on diagnostic guidelines for Alzheimer's disease. *Alzheimers Dement.* 2011; 7(3): 280–92.

10. National Institutes of Health. About Alzheimer's Disease: Other Dementias. 2014. Available at http://www.nia.nih.gov/alzheimers/topics/other-dementias. Accessed September 13, 2014.

11. van der Flier WM, Pijnenburg YA, Fox NC, Scheltens P. Early-onset versus late-onset Alzheimer's disease: the case of the missing APOE varepsilon4 allele. *Lancet Neurol.* 2011; 10(3): 280–8.

12. Brookmeyer R, Johnson E, Ziegler-Graham K, Arrighi HM. Forecasting the global burden of Alzheimer's disease. *Alzheimers Dement.* 2007; 3(3): 186–91.

13. Hebert R, Lindsay J, Verreault R, Rockwood K, Hill G, Dubois MF. Vascular dementia: incidence and risk factors in the Canadian study of health and aging. *Stroke.* 2000; 31(7): 1487–93.

14. Gorelick PB. Risk factors for vascular dementia and Alzheimer disease. *Stroke.* 2004; 35(11 Suppl 1): 2620–2.

15. Rockwood K, Wentzel C, Hachinski V, Hogan DB, MacKnight C, McDowell I. Prevalence and outcomes of vascular cognitive impairment. Vascular Cognitive Impairment Investigators of the Canadian Study of Health and Aging. *Neurology.* 2000; 54(2): 447–51.

16. Corey-Bloom J, Galasko D, Hofstetter CR, Jackson JE, Thal LJ. Clinical features distinguishing large cohorts with possible AD, probable AD, and mixed dementia. *J Am Geriatr Soc.* 1993; 41(1): 31–7.

17. Zekry D, Hauw JJ, Gold G. Mixed dementia: epidemiology, diagnosis, and treatment. *J Am Geriatr Soc.* 2002; 50(8): 1431–8.

18. Fitzpatrick AL, Kuller LH, Lopez OL, Kawas CH, Jagust W. Survival following dementia onset: Alzheimer's disease and vascular dementia. *J Neurol Sci.* 2005; 229–230: 43–9.

19. Vann Jones SA, O'Brien JT. The prevalence and incidence of dementia with Lewy bodies: a systematic review of population and clinical studies. *Psychol Med.* 2014; 44(4): 673–83.

20. Oesterhus R, Soennesyn H, Rongve A, Ballard C, Aarsland D, Vossius C. Long-term mortality in a cohort of home-dwelling elderly with mild Alzheimer's disease and Lewy body dementia. *Dement Geriatr Cogn Disord.* 2014; 38(3-4): 161–9.

21. Onyike CU, Diehl-Schmid J. The epidemiology of frontotemporal dementia. *Intl Rev Psychiatry.* 2013;2 5(2): 130–7.

22. Ratnavalli E, Brayne C, Dawson K, Hodges JR. The prevalence of frontotemporal dementia. *Neurology.* 2002; 58(11): 1615–21.

23. Greicius MD, Geschwind MD, Miller BL. Presenile dementia syndromes: an update on taxonomy and diagnosis. *J Neurol Neurosurg Psychiatry.* 2002; 72(6): 691–700.

24. Bittles AH, Bower C, Hussain R, Glasson EJ. The four ages of Down syndrome. *Eur J Public Health.* 2007; 17(2): 221–5.

25. Tuffrey-Wijne I, Hogg J, Curfs L. End-of-life and palliative care for people with intellectual disabilities who have cancer or other life-limiting illness: a review of the literature and available resources. *J Appl Res Intellect Disabil.* 2007; 20(4): 331–44.

26. Yang Q, Rasmussen SA, Friedman JM. Mortality associated with Down's syndrome in the USA from 1983 to 1997: a population-based study. *Lancet.* 2002; 359(9311): 1019–25.

27. Patti P, Amble K, Flory M. Placement, relocation and end of life issues in aging adults with and without Down's syndrome: a retrospective study. *J Intell Disabil Res.* 2010; 54(6): 538–46.

28. Mezey M, Teresi J, Ramsey G, Mitty E, Bobrowitz T. Decision-making capacity to execute a health care proxy: development and testing of guidelines. *J Am Geriatr Soc.* 2000; 48(2): 179–87.

29. Horton-Deutsch S, Twigg P, Evans R. Health care decision-making of persons with dementia. *Dementia.* 2007; 6(1): 105–20.

30. Smith M, Wells J, Borrie M. Treatment effect size of memantine therapy in Alzheimer disease and vascular dementia. *Alzheimer Dis Assoc Disord.* 2006; 20(3): 133–7.

31. Konno R, Kang HS, Makimoto K. A best-evidence review of intervention studies for minimizing resistance-to-care behaviours for older adults with dementia in nursing homes. *J Adv Nurs.* 2014; 70(10): 2167–80.

32. American Geriatrics Society Ethics Committee. Clinical Practice Models of Care. American Geriatrics Society feeding tubes in advanced dementia position statement. *J Am Geriatr Soc.* 2014; 62(8): 1590–3.

33. Menzel PT, Chandler-Cramer MC. Advance directives, dementia, and withholding food and water by mouth. *Hastings Cent Rep.* 2014; 44(3): 23–37.

34. Kunik ME, Snow AL, Davila JA, et al. Causes of aggressive behavior in patients with dementia. *J Clin Psychiatry.* 2010; 71(9): 1145–52.

35. Ferrero-Arias J, Goni-Imizcoz M, Gonzalez-Bernal J, Lara-Ortega F, da Silva-Gonzalez A, Diez-Lopez M. The efficacy of nonpharmacological treatment for dementia-related apathy. *Alzheimer Dis Assoc Disord.* 2011; 25(3): 213–9.

36. Berman K, Brodaty H, Withall A, Seeher K. Pharmacologic treatment of apathy in dementia. *Am J Geriatr Psychiatry.* 2012; 20(2): 104–22.

37. Lach HW, Chang YP, Edwards D. Can older adults with dementia accurately report depression using brief forms? Reliability and validity of the Geriatric Depression Scale. *J Gerontol Nurs.* 2010; 36(5): 30–7.

38. Alexopoulos GS, Abrams RC, Young RC, Shamoian CA. Cornell scale for depression in dementia. *Biol Psychiatry.* 1988; 23(3): 271–84.

39. Gellis ZD, McClive-Reed KP, Brown E. Treatments for depression in older persons with dementia. *Ann Long Term Care.* 2009; 17(2): 29–36.

40. Savva GM, Zaccai J, Matthews FE, et al. Prevalence, correlates and course of behavioural and psychological symptoms of dementia in the population. *Br J Psychiatry.* 2009; 194(3): 212–9.

41. Beaudreau SA, Spira AP, Gray HL, et al. The relationship between objectively measured sleep disturbance and dementia family caregiver distress and burden. *J Geriatr Psychiatry Neurol.* 2008; 21(3): 159–65.

42. Muntean ML, Sixel-Doring F, Trenkwalder C. REM sleep behavior disorder in Parkinson's disease. *J Neural Transm.* 2014 [Epub before print].

43. Herr KA, Garand L. Assessment and measurement of pain in older adults. *Clin Geriatr Med.* 2001; 17(3): 457–78.

44. Warden V, Hurley AC, Volicer L. Development and psychometric evaluation of the Pain Assessment in Advanced Dementia (PAINAD) scale. *J Am Med Dir Assoc.* 2003; 4(1): 9–15.

45. Coin A, Perissinotto E, Najjar M, et al. Does religiosity protect against cognitive and behavioral decline in Alzheimer's dementia? *Current Alzheimer Res.* 2010; 7(5): 445–52.

46. Marquez-Gonzalez M, Lopez J, Romero-Moreno R, Losada A. Anger, spiritual meaning and support from the religious community in dementia caregiving. *J Religion Health.* 2012; 51(1): 179–86.

47. Hebert RS, Dang Q, Schulz R. Religious beliefs and practices are associated with better mental health in family caregivers of patients with dementia: findings from the REACH study. *Am J Geriatr Psychiatry.* 2007; 15(4): 292–300.

48. Monahan PO, Boustani MA, Alder C, et al. Practical clinical tool to monitor dementia symptoms: the HABC-Monitor. *Clin Interventions Aging.* 2012; 7: 143–57.

49. Malakh-Pines A, Aronson E, Kafry D. *Burnout: From Tedium to Personal Growth.* New York, NY: Free Press; 1981.

50. Bedard M, Molloy DW, Squire L, Dubois S, Lever JA, O'Donnell M. The Zarit Burden Interview: a new short version and screening version. *Gerontologist.* 2001; 41(5): 652–7.

CHAPTER 54

Patients with Substance Use Disorder

Jeannine M. Brant

Key Points

◆ Substance use disorders (SUDs) are a growing concern across the United States and pose significant challenges in assessment and management.

◆ A variety of risk assessment tools exist to help identify and manage patients with SUDs.

◆ DSM criteria are used to diagnose SUDs.

◆ Palliative advanced practice registered nurses (APRNs) who manage patients with SUDS monitor analgesic response, activities of daily living, adverse events, and aberrant behaviors.

Case Study

Allen was a 38-year-old man who had recently completed treatment for head and neck cancer. He had a history of a substance use disorder and prior to his diagnosis he had attended Narcotics Anonymous, a 12-step recovery program. He had undergone a surgical resection followed by combined chemotherapy and radiation therapy. During treatment he suffered severe mucositis and complained of neuropathic pain in the neck and jaw, for which he was prescribed opioids and gabapentin. The palliative APRN saw Allen for his 6-week follow-up appointment. While the oral cavity had improved, Allen continued to complain of neck and jaw pain and requested additional refills of his pain medication. He also reported that the pain had been so severe that he ran out of his prescription early.

The palliative APRN saw Allen following the initial diagnosis and initiated Universal Precautions (see Box 54.1) throughout the treatment trajectory. Allen was initially stratified as high risk and was placed on a substance use agreement. Opioids were prescribed on a weekly basis, and Allen was assessed for the 5 A's (analgesia, adverse events, ADLs, aberrancy, and affect). Random urine drug screens had been positive for opioids but negative for other illicit substances. One early request for a refill occurred during the height of Allen's mucositis.

During this visit, the palliative APRN observed that Allen was also agitated and yawning profusely. The need for a random urine screen was determined by a flip of a coin during the visit, and Allen refused the screen. The APRN reviewed the substance use agreement with him and verbalized concern for his choice. Because Allen continued to refuse the random urine screening, the palliative

APRN informed Allen that she could no longer prescribe opioids for him. She encouraged him to share how he was doing both physically and emotionally. While opioids were not prescribed, Allen was encouraged to return for his 3-month follow-up visit.

Introduction

APRNs are on the frontline of managing symptoms in patients with serious illnesses, and inevitably some of these patients will have a substance use disorder. Managing these patients is challenging for APRNs: prescribing opioids can contribute to the problem, yet underprescribing can lead to suboptimal pain management. Fears about loss of licensure can also surface, reinforcing the need for APRNs to have adequate knowledge about caring for this population.

Substance use disorder is a growing concern in the United States. According to the Substance Abuse and Mental Health Services Administration 2012 survey, 9.2% of the U.S. population had used an illicit drug in the past month, an increase from 8.1% in 2008, and approximately 8.5% of the population was estimated to have a substance use disorder. Of those with a substance use disorder, 13% use alcohol and illicit drugs, 20% use illicit drugs, and 67% are alcohol users. Not just illicit drugs are a concern: 2.6% of the population reportedly used psychotherapeutic prescription drugs nonmedically in the past month.[1] Patients with chronic pain are at a greater risk for substance use disorders: the prevalence of addiction in this population is estimated at 15% to 20%.[2]

The high prevalence of substance abuse in the overall population will be reflected in the palliative care environment, posing significant challenges in terms of managing pain and accompanying symptoms and providing overall care. Palliative APRNs need to understand substance use disorder, how to assess for it, and how to manage pain, according to the risk stratification of the specific patient. A tailored approach to care will ensure the best possible outcomes while minimizing abuse, misuse, and diversion.

Definitions

Many definitions apply to the concepts of addiction and substance abuse. Some definitions, such as tolerance and physical dependence, can be confusing and are often used erroneously when referring to patients with substance use disorder.

Table 54.1 Definition of Terms

Term	Definition
Aberrant behavior	Behaviors to be recognized as indicating prescription opioid abuse
Addiction	A neurobiological disorder with genetic and environmental influences that results in psychological dependence on the use of substances for their psychic effects and is characterized by craving and compulsive use despite harm
Compulsive	An irresistible urge, especially against conscious wishes
Craving	A strong desire to obtain and use a psychoactive substance for its intoxicating effects
Drug misuse	Use of prescription or over-the-counter drugs that does not follow medical indications or prescribed dosing
Drug abuse	Use of a drug for nontherapeutic purposes to obtain psychotropic effects
Diversion	Unlawful channeling of pharmaceuticals from legal sources to the illegal marketplace
Euphoria	A sense of intense happiness and well-being
Illicit drug	A drug that is not legally permitted or authorized
Nonmedical use	Use of a prescription drug without a prescription or in a manner that is not prescribed
Physical dependence	A physiological neuro-adaptation characterized by a withdrawal syndrome if the drug is stopped or decreased abruptly, or if an antagonist is administered
Pseudotolerance	A need to increase dosage that is due not to tolerance but to other factors, such as disease progression, new disease, increased physical activity, lack of compliance, change in medication, drug interaction, addiction, and deviant behavior
Pseudoaddiction	Pattern of drug-seeking behavior in patients with pain who are receiving inadequate pain management; can be mistaken for addiction
Substance abuse	The use of any substance for nontherapeutic purposes to obtain psychotropic effects
Tampering	Manipulating a pharmaceutical to change its drug delivery performance
Tolerance	A physiologic response resulting from the regular use of a drug in which an increased dosage is needed to produce the same effect

Data from references 3, 15, and 41.

For example, addiction involves genetic and biobehavioral influences, while tolerance and physical dependence are strictly physiologic phenomena.[3] Table 54.1 defines terms related to this topic.

Barriers

One of the challenges of working with patients with substance use disorder is the lack of knowledge on the part of healthcare providers. One survey of hospice and palliative care physicians in training revealed that only half stated they had a working knowledge of addiction and only 40% thought their training had prepared them to manage misuse of opioids. While 38% thought they could differentiate between opioid misuse and addiction, 79% were uncomfortable managing symptoms in this population.[4] Often, practitioners feel that opioids should be avoided in patients with substance use disorder; however, current literature suggests that many of these patients can be safely managed using a detailed and vigilant monitoring program.[5–7]

Stigma is another barrier associated with substance use disorder, and it is often rooted in shame and guilt. The more stigmatized patients feel, the less likely they are to disclose a substance use disorder. Using judgment-free language, avoiding terms like *drug-seeking* or *junkie*, and categorizing substance abuse as a disorder can encourage a more open therapeutic relationship.[8]

Using objective measures to assess the risk for substance use can help to eliminate personal biases.[9,10] For example, the palliative APRN may overestimate the risk in an individual who is heavily tattooed and underestimate the risk in a high-profile bank manager. Racial stereotypes can also contribute to inadequate assessment.

One study reported that black patients were more likely to undergo urine drug testing, were required to attend more office visits, and were given more restrictive opioid prescriptions than whites.[9] Patients with poorly managed pain can also exhibit addictive behaviors (i.e., pseudoaddiction). Assessment for substance use disorder risk is further discussed below.

Specific barriers exist for palliative APRNs in managing patients with substance use disorders. State by state variation in APRNs' prescribing privileges for opioids reveals more restriction in medication management. Buprenorphine, in particular, cannot be prescribed by APRNs for addiction.[11]

Pathophysiology

Substance abuse and addiction are complex phenomena that involve an interplay of neurobiological, genetic, and behavioral components. A wide array of neuroadaptive theories apply to the development of, and permanent brain changes that occur with, substance abuse and addiction. Physiologically, neural systems, including dopamine neurons and the mesolimbic system, are sensitized when introduced to a potentially addictive substance.[12,13] Changes in the glutamatergic connections within various parts of the brain (ventral tegmental area, nucleus accumbens, prefrontal cortex, and amygdala) are thought to contribute to this sensitization. Neurocognitive imbalance between the impulsive amygdala, which signals pleasure, and the prefrontal cortex, which signals future decision making, is also thought to occur. These brain changes endure even after the individual stops taking the substance, which explains why relapse rates

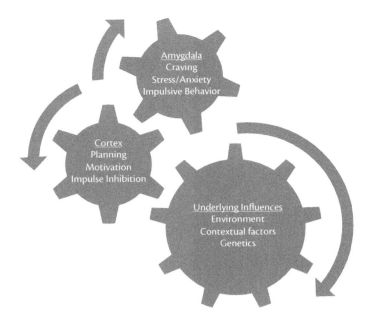

Substance abuse and addiction result from the imbalance between the cortex and the amygdala. Underlying influences can contribute to the phenomena.

Figure 54.1 Pathophysiologic aspects of addiction

for addiction are as high as 80%. Fewer than 50% of addicts remain drug-free following 6 months of abstinence from a substance and fewer than 15% are drug-free at 12 months.[13] Genetic influences are also involved, and over 1,500 human addiction genes have been identified.[14] Further research is needed to determine which genes play the greatest role and to understand the exact influence the genes have on the development of addiction.

Environmental factors, stress, reward-based learning, and conditioning effects also contribute to substance abuse and the development of addiction. Exposure to the drug (e.g., opioid, benzodiazepine, ETOH) can initially create a pleasurable response, thereby reinforcing the desire for the drug when it is not present. Eventually, chronic and excessive levels of the drug correspond with increased salience, producing a greater yearning and physiologic need for the drug.[15] This pattern underlies the stimulus–response habits, aberrant memories, and maladaptive behaviors that characterize addiction (Fig. 54.1).[13] Interestingly, the neurobiological and genetic aspects of substance addiction parallel changes observed in behavioral addictions, such as gambling, Internet/video game use, and shopping.

Assessment for Substance Use Disorder

Routine assessment for substance use disorder is important due to the high prevalence of the problem. A baseline should be obtained, along with subsequent assessments. However, assessment is difficult due to the stigma attached to substance abuse. A perceived lack of trust may lead to nondisclosure of a substance use disorder. The palliative APRN should use interview techniques to promote open dialogue (Box 54.1).

Identifying patients at greatest risk for substance abuse is a key component of the assessment. Sociodemographics, psychological factors, drug-related factors, family history, and genetics have all been linked to addiction risk. The strongest link appears to be the presence of psychosocial, drug-related, and genetic factors

---

Box 54.1 Universal Precautions and Assessment Guide

1. Make a pain diagnosis.

2. Use therapeutic interview skills:
   - Withhold judgment until ample evidence is available.
   - Spend adequate time with the patient to assess verbal and nonverbal behaviors.
   - Focus on the patient, not specifically on the pain or other symptom.
   - Explore patient fears, expectations of treatment, goals.
   - Use reflective listening—reflect back using a slight modification of what the patient said.
     - Clarify understanding.
     - Encourage the patient to keep talking.
     - Communicate a therapeutic alliance.

3. Perform a thorough physical examination, including:
   - Pain and symptom assessment
   - Effect of pain on sleep, mood, function, relationships, sex, recreation
   - Medical history
   - Functional assessment—how the pain and symptoms affect function

4. Conduct a psychosocial history and psychological exam, informing the patient that this is a routine part of the assessment which includes:
   - Adverse childhood events and family upbringing
   - Family and social support
   - History of depression, anxiety, psychiatric disorders
   - Substance use history
   - Screening for addiction risk in all potential candidates for chronic opioid therapy
   - Access the Prescriptive Drug Monitoring Program prior to the visit to determine the patient's use of prior medications, pharmacy use, and and areas of concerns.
   - Urine drug screening at baseline

4. Determine potential treatment options, discuss benefits and burdens of proposed intervention and provide informed consent.

5. Complete a treatment agreement.

6. Conduct an opioid trial or controlled substance.

7. Assess the impact of the opioid intervention on pain and function, with regular assessment of the 5 A's.

8. Periodically review the diagnosis, comorbidities, substance use disorder, and treatment plan.

9 Summarize each visit with the patient, reviewing treatment plan, goals of treatment, and follow-up.

10. Document each visit and ongoing treatment planning.

Data from references 35, 40, and 42.

combined. Therefore, a social history must include a history of drug abuse and a family history of alcoholism.

Mental health screening is especially important in determining risk of addiction, as there is a high prevalence of mood disorders coexisting with both chronic pain and substance use disorder. Patients with a substance use disorder are more likely to have more mental health concerns, use higher doses of opioids, drink more alcohol, smoke more tobacco, use more benzodiazepines, and have a higher rate of depression.[2] Being aware of this cluster can lead to earlier detection of a problem. Once aberrant behaviors are detected, the palliative APRN should discern and carefully interpret the meaning of the behaviors and their influence on the treatment plan. Current guidelines recommend assessment of mood when pain is present.[16] Opioid risk assessment tools, described below, contain items about mood, but further evaluation is warranted. The Beck Depression Inventory and the Profile of Mood States (POMS) are two tools that are routinely used in clinical practice. History of sexual abuse and family history are also included in risk stratification.

Several screening tools exist to identify potential problems (Table 54.2).[17] Some of the more common tools include the CAGE, which is widely used to assess for alcoholism, and the Screener and Opioid Assessment for Patients with Pain-Revised (SOAPP-R)[18,19] and the Opioid Risk Tool (ORT),[20] which screen for opioid abuse. The SOAPP-R has 24 items and takes less than 10 minutes to complete. Items include assessment of psychological responses to situations, pain medication-related perceptions and behaviors, and social and familial influences. The ORT contains five items, including personal and family history of substance use, age, history of sexual abuse, and psychological disease, and takes less than 1 minute to administer and score. While these tools have good internal consistency, they are not "lie detector tests," and the accuracy of the assessment depends on how honestly the individual completes the responses. Aberrant behaviors and risk factors for substance abuse are included in Table 54.3.[21] Risk should be evaluated so that strategies can be employed to regain control over the plan.[22]

The Current Opioid Misuse Measure (COMM), a 17-item measure that takes less than 10 minutes to complete and score, can be used during the monitoring phase.[23] A score of 9 or higher is associated with a higher degree of aberrant behaviors.[24] A systematic review of tools used to monitor ongoing opioid therapy indicated that further testing of these tools is needed, as there is limited evidence to support their ability to detect misuse and substance use disorder in patients taking opioids.[25]

Prescription Drug Monitoring Programs

Prescription Drug Monitoring Program (PDMP) evaluation can be used to evaluate risk but should be used on an ongoing basis to assess for aberrant behaviors. PDMPs are statewide databases

Table 54.2 Substance Use Disorder Risk Screening Tools

Tool	Description	Comments
CAGE (Cut, annoyed, guilty, eye)	4 items	◆ Interview to screen for alcohol use ◆ One positive response warrants caution. ◆ Two affirmative responses are considered a positive result.
CAGE–AID (Adapted to include drugs)	4 items	◆ Interview to screen for drug and alcohol use ◆ Consider modifying yes/no questions to open-ended questions.
COMM (Current Opioid Misuse Measure)	17 items	◆ Self-administered ◆ Use during chronic opioid monitoring. ◆ Score of 9 or higher suggests aberrancy.
DAST (Drug Abuse Screening Test)	20 items	◆ Self-administered ◆ Questions refer to past 12 months.
DSM-V Structured Clinical Interview	Interview	◆ Assessment of the 11 characteristics in the DSM-V criteria ◆ Takes 30–60 minutes to complete
ORT (Opioid Risk Tool)	5 items	◆ Self-administered ◆ For initial visit for pain treatment ◆ Predictive of substance abuse
PDUQ (Prescription Drug Use Questionnaire)	42 items	◆ Interview ◆ Score >15 indicates a substance use disorder. ◆ Predictive of substance abuse
RAFFT (Relax, alone, friends, family, trouble)	5 items	◆ Self-administered ◆ Three affirmative responses are considered a positive result.
SOAPP-R (Screener and Opioid Assessment for Patients with Pain-Revised)	24 items	◆ Self-administered or interview to screen for drug and alcohol use ◆ Intended for patients with chronic pain on long-term opioid therapy ◆ Score of 7 or higher indicates the person is likely to abuse.

Data from references 17 and 35.

Table 54.3 Aberrant Behaviors and Risk Factors for Substance Abuse/Addiction

Behaviors Less Suggestive of Addiction	Behaviors More Suggestive of Addiction	Risk Factors for Addiction
Drug hoarding when symptoms are improved	High opioid dose	Caucasian male
Acquiring drugs from multiple medical sources	Selling prescription drugs	Younger age
Aggressive complaining about the need for a higher dose	Forgery of prescriptions	Higher pain intensity and lower pain tolerance
Unapproved use of a medication to treat a symptom (e.g., use of an opioid to treat anxiety)	Concurrent illicit drug use	More pain complaints
Unsanctioned dose escalation (once or twice)	Multiple prescription/medication losses	More pain-related limitations
Reporting psychic effects	Ongoing unsanctioned dose escalations	Depression and psychotropic medications in younger populations
Requesting specific drugs	Stealing or borrowing drugs	Psychological comorbidity: panic, anxiety, depression, agoraphobia, low self-reported health status
Second opinion for pain requested	Obtaining prescription drugs from nonmedical sources	Substance abuse history
Smoking cigarettes to relieve pain	Repeated resistance to change—inflexibility	Genetic predisposition
Drinking alcohol to relieve pain	Prostitution for drugs or for money to obtain drugs	
Urine toxicology screens positive	Unanticipated positive results in urine toxicology	
Nonadherence to appointments	Frequent pain clinic or emergency department visits	

Data from reference 20, 21, and 42.

containing prescriber- and patient-level data on drugs with high misuse and abuse potential, including opioids and benzodiazepines.[26] The PDMPs are efforts by the states to ensure appropriate prescribing and dispensing of controlled substances in order to prevent misuse, abuse, and diversion. Using their individual Drug Enforcement Agency (DEA) numbers, healthcare providers can register for their state's PDMP and access the databases to examine patterns of prescription drug use in patients. Databases will show if a patient is using multiple prescribers or multiple pharmacies, which both suggest abuse or illegal activities. One study that evaluated the effectiveness of PDMPs found that Poison Center intentional exposures of drugs increased by 1.9% in states without PDMPs and by 0.2% in states with PDMPs. Opioid treatment hospital admissions increased 4.9% per quarter in states without PDMPs versus 2.6% in states with PDMPs.[27] Efforts are underway to link PDMPs between states so that misuse, abuse, or diversion of opioids across state lines can be detected. While not diagnostic, PDMPs are another tool that should be used at baseline and during follow-up to evaluate aberrant behaviors and drug use patterns.[28]

Urine Drug Testing

Urine drug monitoring is another assessment tool available to monitor for controlled substance misuse, abuse, and diversion. Recent recommendations from a panel of experts state that all patients on long-term opioid therapy (more than 3 months) should undergo urine drug monitoring. They further recommended that patients should understand the purpose of monitoring and how the results will be used; this reinforces that testing is not punitive but rather is done to provide consistent monitoring of patients. Guidelines for surveillance are included in Table 54.4. While the American Pain Society and the American Academy of Pain Medicine both

recommend periodic testing in all patients on chronic opioid therapy, it is actually used in only 8% to 30% of them.[29] This may be due to a lack of knowledge about how to interpret the results and how to apply them to practice.[30] Essential information includes which medications are appropriate for urine testing, opioid metabolism that would affect their presence or absence, and other medications that the patient is taking. Being knowledgeable about these factors will enable palliative APRNs to interpret results correctly.[31]

Diagnosis of Substance Use Disorder

The palliative APRN can use the DSM-V criteria to diagnose a substance use disorder.[32] The 11 criteria combine substance abuse and dependence into a single disorder. They include the following:

- Perceptions about use, such as taking more of a substance than intended, desire to cut down or stop using the substance, craving the substance, and being consumed with obtaining the substance

- Functional elements, including inability to manage current roles and responsibilities and forgoing opportunities (e.g., family outings, social relationships)

- Continued use despite harm and endangerment physically, psychologically, and socially

- Development of tolerance and physical withdrawal

Mild substance use disorder requires the presence of two or three symptoms from the list, a moderate substance use disorder includes four or five symptoms, and six or more symptoms indicate severe substance use disorder. A long-standing criticism of the DSM criteria is that patients with cancer often exhibit some of these symptoms and yet they may not have a substance use disorder.

Table 54.4 Urine Drug Testing (UDT) Recommendations

Recommendation Category	Recommendation	Rationale
1. Who to test	◆ Test all patients receiving chronic opioid therapy (>3 months).	Removes APRN subjectivity and makes testing consistent with chronic disease management paradigm
2. How to test	◆ Patients should be clear about UDT purpose.	◆ Removes fear; informs patients that UDT is not punitive but rather part of standard procedures
	◆ UDT parameters can be included in a Controlled Substance Agreement.	◆ Clearly delineates UDT role in therapy
	◆ Comprehensive medication testing should be conducted, which includes illicit drugs, opioids, and other substances, such as benzodiazepines.	◆ Tests for suspected therapeutic metabolites and other substances
	◆ Tests should be performed by a Clinical Laboratory Improvement Amendments (CLIA)-certified laboratory with knowledge about UDT, with results available on same day.	◆ Results can be falsely positive or negative; laboratory proficiency will minimize this variability.
	◆ Point-of-care (POC) testing can be used on the initial visit, but inconsistent results should be verified with UDT.	◆ POC testing is for screening only.
	◆ Test temperature and specific gravity; consider chain of custody (proper administration of the sample to safeguard it from tampering) if concern exists about samples.	◆ Indicates if the sample has been tampered with
3. When to test	◆ Initiate UDT when starting chronic opioid therapy.	◆ Aids in risk stratification
	◆ Test according to risk stratification via SOAPP-R/ORT and other factors.	◆ Allows for more frequent screening for high-risk patients
	◆ Consider developing a procedure to determine frequency of UDT while maintaining minimum requirements (e.g., having patient flip a coin or roll dice at each visit).	◆ Removes burden from staff tracking while providing fairness for random testing
4. How to interpret results	◆ Confirm appropriate interpretation from laboratory that performs testing.	◆ Identifies the type of aberrant behavior present so that behavior can be specifically addressed
	◆ Classify findings as (1) prescribed drug not detected, (2) illicit drug detected, (3) nonprescribed drug of concern detected.	
	◆ Construct a differential diagnosis if (1) drug not detected (e.g., diversion, hoarding, lab error); may need additional testing to determine absence; (2) illicit drug detected (e.g., addiction, seeking additional pain relief, lab error); (3) nonprescribed drug detected (e.g., multiple providers).	◆ Allows the APRN to understand the finding; absence of prescribed drug with presence of illicit drug requires immediate action
5. How to handle test discrepancies	◆ Verify discrepancies with laboratory.	◆ Lab tests should always be verified.
	◆ Schedule an immediate follow-up visit to discuss findings with patient in nonjudgmental manner.	◆ The patient may disclose the reason for the discrepancy; promotes therapeutic communication.
	◆ Develop a plan based on the findings.	◆ The plan will vary and depends on the problem detected.

Data from references 30 and 34.

Pain and Symptom Management

Managing pain and symptoms and providing overall care in patients with substance use disorder can be challenging. Many palliative care patients will require chronic opioid therapy or other treatments, such as benzodiazepines, that may pose risks for those with substance use disorders. Risk of relapse for those in remission is a valid fear, and yet undertreatment of pain and symptoms is also common due to a lack of understanding of appropriate care of these patients.[7] Having a well-defined plan in place that focuses on the goals of care and stratifies patients according to addiction risk allows for individualized pain and symptom care while monitoring patients for aberrant behaviors and signs of addiction. This will provide the best care for the patient while at the same time preventing misuse, abuse, and diversion.[5,6,18]

Goals of Care

Pain and symptom management goals provide a foundation for the plan of care. The 5 A's can be used to measure the success of a management plan: analgesia, activities of daily living, adverse events, aberrant behaviors, and affect[7,33] (Table 54.5). Goals should be clear to the patient when treatment is started. Physiologic and psychosocial functioning should be included in the plan because they reflect an improvement in overall quality of life. Both pain and

Table 54.5 Goals of Pain Management

5 A's	Definition	Assessment
Analgesia	Level of comfort	◆ Decrease in pain intensity ◆ Effectiveness of the intervention on the pain
Activities of Daily Living	Functional status	◆ Increased physical capabilities ◆ Psychologically intact ◆ Family/social relationships intact ◆ Appropriate medication and healthcare utilization
Adverse Events	Side effects related to treatment	◆ Sedation ◆ Euphoria ◆ Other physical and psychological effects
Aberrant Activities	Behaviors that warn of potential substance misuse, abuse, or addiction	◆ Behaviors that suggest concern; see Table 54.3
Affect	Psychological functioning	◆ Improved psychological affect ◆ Ability to cope with illness

Data from references 7 and 21.

substance use disorder lead to dysfunction, so management should lead to optimal functioning. This focus on function allows the palliative APRN to individualize care and prescribing options.[34]

Risk Stratification

A chronic disease management model provides a background for managing patients with substance use disorder, in that

risk assessment, ongoing monitoring, and corrective action as needed can be readily employed.[5] Stratifying patients according to their risk for a substance use disorder is the first step in the management plan. Risk assessment tools can guide stratification, with the understanding that risk may change as the APRN observes the patient's behavior over time (Table 54.6).[18,20]

Substance Use Agreements

Substance use agreements have been shown to improve provider satisfaction, decrease emergency department visits, and improve patient adherence.[34] Substance use agreements should be employed for all patients taking controlled medications or chronic opioid therapy for greater than 3 months, regardless of risk.[5,34] Agreements should spell out the risks and benefits of treatment, provide education about the plan of care, outline the responsibilities of the patient and the palliative APRN, and allow a transparent conversation to occur between the patient and the APRN.[35] Agreements should include the following:

◆ Designated prescriber

◆ Designated pharmacy

◆ Frequency of refills

◆ Times when refills are prohibited (e.g., after hours, weekends)

◆ Dosage changes

◆ Screening and consequences for positive screens (e.g., urine, blood, pill counts)

◆ Need to secure medications and dispose of them safely if needed

◆ Supportive therapy requirements (e.g., psychiatry)

◆ Safe use of medications[35]

Table 54.6 Management According to Risk

Risk Stratification	Risk Assessment Tools	Other Risk Considerations	Management Strategies
Low	SOAPP-R score <10 ORT score <4	◆ No family history ◆ No past/current history of substance use disorder ◆ No psychological comorbidity	◆ Annual adherence monitoring ◆ Review prescription drug monitoring program (PDM) twice per year ◆ Urine drug testing every 1–2 years
Medium	SOAPP-R score 10–21 ORT score 4–7	◆ Family history positive ◆ Treated substance use disorder; can be on pharmacotherapy for addiction ◆ Psychological comorbidity, past or current ◆ <25 years of age	◆ Adherence monitoring every 6 months ◆ Review PDM 3 times per year ◆ Urine drug testing every 6 months to 1 year
High	SOAPP-R score >21 ORT score <7	◆ Current substance use disorder or addiction ◆ Current aberrant behaviors (those more suggestive of addiction) ◆ Major psychiatric disorder that is untreated	◆ Weekly to monthly adherence monitoring ◆ Management by pain and addiction specialists recommended ◆ Review PDM 4 times per year ◆ Urine drug testing every 3–6 months ◆ Prescribe opioids cautiously; chronic opioid therapy may be prohibitive in terms of risk to the patient.

Data from references 7 and 40.

Management of Pain

The pain management plan should be based on a systematic approach that includes the following:

◆ Diagnosis of the problem

◆ Conservative approaches (e.g., physical therapy, non-opioids, co-analgesics) for initial management

◆ Nonpharmacologic modalities

◆ Therapeutic interventions such as anesthetic blocks

◆ Chronic opioid therapy and other controlled co-analgesics (e.g., benzodiazepines) only when conservative approaches are not effective.

See Chapter 23, Pain, for more information.

Risk stratification guides the management plan. The palliative APRN should document the 5 A's at each visit to assess the patient's response to the treatment plan. The higher the risk, the more frequent the monitoring and the more cautious the dosing of opioids should be.

Dosing can be challenging in this population, especially in terms of drug tolerance. Patients with active opioid use will be tolerant of opioids and may require higher doses, but aberrant behaviors may preclude the palliative APRN from prescribing opioids for these patients. Contributing to addiction and diversion can result in loss of licensure, so caution is warranted. The most important component is careful surveillance for all patients: some high-risk patients may show substantially improved function using opioids, while some low-risk patients may experience deterioration in function.

Prescribing medications may be complicated. Palliative APRNs may prescribe certain medications for pain management, but not for substance abuse issues, unless they have completed addiction graduate education or specific coursework. APRNs should refer to their state rules for scope of practice regarding opioid prescribing.

Determining the right opioid can be difficult, as all opioids can be potentially abused. When initiating chronic opioid therapy, long-acting dosing should be optimized while the need for breakthrough doses is minimized. This allows for a therapeutic blood level to control pain while avoiding peaks and troughs and "clock-watching" to take the next dose.[5,35] Abuse-deterrent opioids are another option. These opioids resist manipulation, such as crushing, dissolving, or extracting; any attempts to do so will inactivate the opioid. While this property can be of benefit in high-risk patients, these drug formulations can be expensive, and more evidence is needed to determine their role in managing high-risk patients taking chronic opioid therapy.[36,37]

While methadone cannot be crushed and abused due to its high protein-binding affinity, safety concerns relate to the potential for accumulation, oversedation, and potential death.[38] Palliative APRNs can prescribe methadone for pain, but only licensed methadone maintenance clinics can prescribe it for addiction. Buprenorphine, a partial opioid agonist that is used in opioid addiction, may be useful for pain management. While APRNs can prescribe buprenorphine for pain, restrictions exist on prescribing the agent for addiction. Buprenorphine has a ceiling dose and therefore should be used only in patients with anticipated lower doses of opioids.[39]

Universal Precautions should be used in managing all patients with chronic persistent pain. These precautions allow risk stratification and improved care (see Box 54.1).[40] Misuse, abuse, addiction, and diversion demand immediate action. If misuse or abuse is suspected, counseling may help to change the behavior, or the palliative APRN can decide to discontinue opioids and other controlled substances. The palliative APRN should discuss aberrant behaviors and drug-testing findings with team members. The patient should be given an opportunity to explain the findings, and retesting can be an option if the findings are questioned. When diversion is suspected, the palliative APRNs should follow the 5 S's plan: limiting the opioid supply, selecting a drug with a lower street value, scheduling more frequent visits, scheduling more frequent urine drug testing, and involving a substance abuse specialist. Actual proof of diversion calls for the discontinuation of opioids. APRNs should follow the rules listed in the opioid contract, which may include discharge from the practice, discontinuance of opioids, transition to non-opioids, and the need to include substance abuse providers. All efforts should be made to maintain the patient within the practice, even though opioids may not be continued. When the palliative APRN decides to discontinue opioids, a plan of tapering medications should be initiated.

Conclusion

The palliative APRN should understand the challenges inherent to managing patients with substance use disorder but should still approach patients with compassion and in a nonjudgmental manner. Occasionally, as with Allen in the case study, the palliative APRN may have to cease prescribing opioids for some patients. However, palliative APRNs should understand that by using a systematic approach and a chronic disease model, the majority of patients can be well managed and can achieve both comfort and an improved quality of life.

References

1. Substance Abuse and Mental Health Administration. *Results from the 2012 National Survey on Drug Use and Health: Summary of National Findings.* Research Triangle Park, NC: U.S. Department of Health and Human Services; 2012.
2. Hojsted J, Nielsen PR, Guldstrand SK, Frich L, Sjogren P. Classification and identification of opioid addiction in chronic pain patients. *Eur J Pain.* 2010; 14: 1014–20.
3. Federation of State Medical Boards of the United States. *Model Guidelines for the Use of Controlled Substances for the Treatment of Pain.* Euless, TX: Federation of State Medical Boards; 2013.
4. Childers JW, Arnold RM. "I feel uncomfortable 'calling a patient out'": educational needs of palliative medicine fellows in managing opioid misuse. *J Pain Symptom Manage.* 2012; 43: 253–60.
5. Cheatle MD, Klocek JW, McLellan AT. Managing pain in high-risk patients within a patient-centered medical home. *Transl Behav Med.* 2012; 2: 47–56.
6. Cheatle M, Comer D, Wunsch M, Skoufalos A, Reddy Y. Treating pain in addicted patients: recommendations from an expert panel. *Population Health Manage.* 2014; 17: 79–89.
7. Chang YP, Compton P. Management of chronic pain with chronic opioid therapy in patients with substance use disorders. *Addict Sci Clin Pract.* 2013; 8: 21.
8. Oliver J, Coggins C, Compton P, et al. American Society for Pain Management nursing position statement: pain management in

patients with substance use disorders. *Pain Manag Nurs*. 2012; 13: 169–83.

9. Becker WC, Starrels JL, Heo M, Li X, Weiner MG, Turner BJ. Racial differences in primary care opioid risk reduction strategies. *Ann Fam Med*. 2011; 9: 219–25.

10. Salinas GD, Susalka D, Burton BS, et al. Risk assessment and counseling behaviors of healthcare professionals managing patients with chronic pain: a national multifaceted assessment of physicians, pharmacists, and their patients. *J Opioid Manag*. 2012; 8: 273–84.

11. Substance Abuse and Mental Health Association. Frequently asked questions about buprenorphine 2014. Accessed November 6, 2014, at http://buprenorphine.samhsa.gov/faq.html.

12. Kreek MJ, Levran O, Reed B, Schlussman SD, Zhou Y, Butelman ER. Opiate addiction and cocaine addiction: underlying molecular neurobiology and genetics. *J Clin Invest*. 2012; 122: 3387–93.

13. Le Moal M, Koob GF. Drug addiction: pathways to the disease and pathophysiological perspectives. *Eur Neuropsychopharmacol*. 2007; 17: 377–93.

14. Li CY, Mao X, Wei L. Genes and (common) pathways underlying drug addiction. *PLoS Computational Biol*. 2008; 4: e2.

15. Sinha R. The clinical neurobiology of drug craving. *Curr Opin Neurobiol*. 2013; 23: 649–54.

16. National Comprehensive Cancer Network. *Palliative Care*. Available at www.NCCN.com, 2014. Accessed September 23, 2014.

17. Webster LR, Dove B. *Avoiding Opioid Abuse While Managing Pain*. North Branch, MN: Sunrise River Press; 2007.

18. Koyyalagunta D, Bruera E, Aigner C, Nusrat H, Driver L, Novy D. Risk stratification of opioid misuse among patients with cancer pain using the SOAPP-SF. *Pain Med*. 2013; 14: 667–75.

19. Butler SF, Fernandez K, Benoit C, Budman SH, Jamison RN. Validation of the revised Screener and Opioid Assessment for Patients with Pain (SOAPP-R). *J Pain*. 2008; 9: 360–72.

20. Webster LR, Webster RM. Predicting aberrant behaviors in opioid-treated patients: preliminary validation of the Opioid Risk Tool. *Pain Med*. 2005; 6: 432–42.

21. Passik SD, Kirsh KL, Donaghy KB, Portenoy RK. Pain and aberrant drug-related behaviors in medically ill patients with and without histories of substance abuse. *Clin J Pain*. 2006; 22: 173–81.

22. Bohn TM, Levy LB, Celin S, Starr TD, Passik SD. Screening for abuse risk in pain patients. *Adv Psychosom Med*. 2011; 30: 113–24.

23. Butler SF, Budman SH, Fanciullo GJ, Jamison RN. Cross validation of the current opioid misuse measure to monitor chronic pain patients on opioid therapy. *Clin J Pain*. 2010; 26: 770–6.

24. Chou R, Fanciullo GJ, Fine PG, Miaskowski C, Passik SD, Portenoy RK. Opioids for chronic noncancer pain: prediction and identification of aberrant drug-related behaviors: a review of the evidence for an American Pain Society and American Academy of Pain Medicine clinical practice guideline. *J Pain*. 2009; 10: 131–46.

25. Becker WC, Fraenkel L, Edelman EJ, et al. Instruments to assess patient-reported safety, efficacy, or misuse of current opioid therapy for chronic pain: a systematic review. *Pain*. 2013; 154: 905–16.

26. Alliance of States with Prescription Monitoring Programs. 2014. Accessed July 25, 2014, at http://pmpalliance.org/.

27. Reifler LM, Droz D, Bailey JE, et al. Do prescription monitoring programs impact state trends in opioid abuse/misuse? *Pain Med*. 2012; 13: 434–42.

28. Hildebran C, Cohen DJ, Irvine JM, et al. How clinicians use prescription drug monitoring programs: a qualitative inquiry. *Pain Med*. 2014; 15: 1179–86.

29. Boulanger A, Clark AJ, Squire P, Cui E, Horbay GL. Chronic pain in Canada: have we improved our management of chronic noncancer pain? *Pain Res Manag*. 2007; 12: 39–47.

30. Peppin JF, Passik SD, Couto JE, et al. Recommendations for urine drug monitoring as a component of opioid therapy in the treatment of chronic pain. *Pain Med*. 2012; 13: 886–96.

31. Pesce A, West C, Egan City K, Strickland J. Interpretation of urine drug testing in pain patients. *Pain Med*. 2012; 13: 868–85.

32. American Psychiatric Association. Substance use disorders. In: *Diagnostic and Statistical Manual of Mental Disorders*. Fifth ed. Arlington, VA: American Psychiatric Association; 2013.

33. Nicholson B, Passik SD. Management of chronic noncancer pain in the primary care setting. *South Med J*. 2007; 100: 1028–36.

34. Starrels JL, Becker WC, Alford DP, Kapoor A, Williams AR, Turner BJ. Systematic review: treatment agreements and urine drug testing to reduce opioid misuse in patients with chronic pain. *Ann Intern Med*. 2010; 152: 712–20.

35. Fishman SM. *Responsible Opioid Prescribing: A Physician's Guide*. 2nd ed. Washington, DC: Waterford Life Sciences; 2014.

36. Passik SD. Issues in long-term opioid therapy: unmet needs, risks, and solutions. *Mayo Clin Proc*. 2009; 84: 593–601.

39. Rosenblum A, Cruciani RA, Strain EC, et al. Sublingual buprenorphine/naloxone for chronic pain in at-risk patients: development and pilot test of a clinical protocol. *J Opioid Manage*. 2012; 8: 369–82.

37. Webster L, St Marie B, McCarberg B, Passik SD, Panchal SJ, Voth E. Current status and evolving role of abuse-deterrent opioids in managing patients with chronic pain. *J Opioid Manage*. 2011; 7: 235–45.

38. Chou R, Cruciani RA, Fiellin DA, et al. Methadone safety: a clinical practice guideline from the American Pain Society and College on Problems of Drug Dependence, in collaboration with the Heart Rhythm Society. *J Pain*. 2014; 15: 321–37.

40. Gourlay DL, Heit HA. Universal Precautions revisited: managing the inherited pain patient. *Pain Med*. 2009; 10(Suppl 2): S115–123.

41. Smith SM, Dart RC, Katz NP, et al. Classification and definition of misuse, abuse, and related events in clinical trials: ACTTION systematic review and recommendations. *Pain*. 2013; 154: 2287–96.

42. Sehgal N, Manchikanti L, Smith HS. Prescription opioid abuse in chronic pain: a review of opioid abuse predictors and strategies to curb opioid abuse. *Pain Physician*, 2012; 15(3 Suppl): Es67–92.

CHAPTER 55

Economically Disadvantaged Urban Dwellers

Anne Hughes and Anne Kinderman

Key Points

◆ Economically disadvantaged persons living with serious illness are ethnically, culturally, and linguistically diverse, with differing resources and unique challenges.

◆ By practicing cultural humility, the advanced practice registered nurse (APRN) gains understanding of the impact of serious illness and an appreciation of the particular world of the person who is economically disadvantaged.

◆ Collaboration with community health, social services, housing, substance use treatment services, mental health services, and at times the legal system, may be necessary to meet the palliative care needs of the economically disadvantaged population.

Case Study

Maria was a 58-year-old Central American refugee who fled to the United States almost 40 years earlier while a revolution was occurring in her country. Many family members and friends were killed in the violence, including her husband and baby daughter. She often had nightmares of the violence she witnessed (a symptom of post-traumatic stress disorder). She awakened to vivid flashbacks of the guerrillas and troops fighting in her village and the bloodied, lifeless bodies of her baby and husband. Maria spoke little English. She eventually got a green card (legal immigrant status as a refugee from a war-torn country), but because of language barriers and persistent anxiety regarding her legal immigration status, was forced to work in low-paying jobs with little protection from exploitation. She worked in under-the-table jobs as a dishwasher, a housecleaner, and most recently a nanny/housekeeper to a family with two small children. She received room and board in exchange for her 10-hour-a-day, 6-days-a-week work schedule, plus a small salary. Because Maria could not have guests at her employer's home, and she did not own a car, she took a bus to meet friends across town. Maria had no health insurance or primary care provider and relied on the local safety net system for medical care. After losing weight, finding her work more exhausting than usual, and experiencing rectal bleeding, Maria went to a neighborhood clinic across town that serves a mostly Latino population. The bilingual palliative APRN who evaluated Maria ordered bloodwork and scheduled an urgent colonoscopy, which revealed invasive colon cancer. The staging workup confirmed liver metastasis. Maria was admitted to the city's safety net hospital for surgery and possibly other cancer treatments.

Maria's Evangelical Protestant faith and church community provided spiritual solace and emotional support. Her pastor and congregation members visited her in the hospital and offered prayers for healing and for cure.

When Maria's condition stabilized to the point that acute care was no longer required, she agreed with the recommendation of the palliative care team that she needed additional nursing care and psychosocial support while undergoing outpatient chemotherapy at the cancer center. Maria had refused to allow the palliative care social worker to speak with her employer about modifying her work schedule and allowing Maria to return there while undergoing treatment. When Maria was no longer able to work, she became functionally homeless.

The palliative care team working with Maria identified a skilled nursing facility, also part of the safety net, that had Spanish-speaking staff. This allowed her to receive expert symptom management while receiving outpatient chemotherapy.

Despite this support, over the next few months, Maria developed cytopenias and severe side effects from the FOLFOX chemotherapy regimen. She agreed with the oncologist's recommendation to stop, as the treatment burdens outweighed its benefits. She had not regained her strength and her returning to work was becoming less and less realistic. Nonetheless, Maria continued to hold out the hope that God would save her, while at the same time stating that she would accept whatever God had in store for her.

As Maria's condition progressed, the skilled nursing facility referred Maria to a hospice program. She died in the skilled nursing facility in the presence of hospice volunteers.

Introduction

Of the 46 million Americans living in poverty in 2012, almost 20 million live in cities.[1] Poverty increases illness burden (morbidity) and leads to premature mortality. A recent meta-analysis found lack of education, racial segregation, limited social support, individual-level poverty, and area-level poverty as social factors that contributed to death rates in the United States that were comparable to deaths attributable to pathophysiologic and behavioral causes.[2] Hence, the urban poor are a population at risk for chronic and life-limiting illnesses and therefore a population in need of palliative care. Despite this need, Lewis and colleagues[3] identified a number of barriers to accessing palliative care for those who are economically disadvantaged that resulted in their "dying in the margins" of society.

As a result of these barriers, providing palliative care to the economically disenfranchised requires the palliative APRN to serve in many roles—clinician, advocate, educator, team member/leader, care coordinator, and researcher.[4,5] The goals of this chapter are to identify the needs of the urban poor, to examine services for this population, and to explore aspects of the APRN's role with this vulnerable population.

Poverty profoundly affects rural communities in similar and distinct ways to urban communities (see Chapter 22). Barriers to accessing palliative care services in rural areas may include geographic distance and lack of local services because of minimal population density.

When providers envision the urban poor, often they imagine a mentally ill, substance-using person who is living on the streets or in a single-room-occupancy hotel. However, as the case study shows, not all of the urban poor fit these stereotypes. Some have housing, although not in a place that most of us would call home, and are the "hidden homeless."[6] Some are working poor who are undocumented or otherwise living on the margins of society.[7]

Maria's story introduces us to several issues that are not uncommon in the care of urban poor: the role of essential or safety net hospitals and health systems in care delivery, the skills needed to communicate threatening and emotionally laden information to patients who have limited English proficiency, and the unique knowledge and skills (competencies) required for an APRN working with this population. A growing body of literature identifies the challenges of providing palliative care to the urban poor, such as illness-related issues, resource limitations, healthcare system

Table 55.1 Challenges to Providing Palliative Care to the Economically Disadvantaged

Illness-related	◆ Presentation with advanced disease
	◆ Multiple comorbidities
	◆ End-organ diseases altering pharmacodynamics
	◆ Prevalence of concurrent mental illness and substance abuse
	◆ Decisional incapacity
Resource challenges	◆ Limited English proficiency
	◆ Limited health literacy
	◆ Lack of family or friend caregivers
	◆ Competing role responsibilities
	◆ Functional impairments, geographic distances, and transportation limitations compromise appointment keeping.
	◆ Unstable or marginal housing
	◆ Limited ongoing therapeutic relationships with health or social service providers
	◆ Unable to access healthcare because of lack of insurance, inconvenient service hours, or geographic barriers
	◆ Lack of access to community-based palliative care (either primary or secondary)
	◆ Limited home health or hospice services to remote areas or those with high crime rates
	◆ Limited neighborhood pharmacies to access medications for symptom management
	◆ Need for designated health proxy/agent in the event of decisional incapacity
	◆ Chaotic lives that have little space for day-to-day illness demands
	◆ Survival or addiction may overshadow illness management
	◆ Residential care admission policies that have a low tolerance for drug and alcohol use
	◆ Lack of coordination among providers in community who offer medical and social services to the homeless and otherwise disenfranchised
Relationships with healthcare system or providers	◆ Cultural history of racism, discrimination, or rejection in healthcare system
	◆ Reluctance to be forthcoming about social history because of fear of legal or immigration status consequences
	◆ Healthcare providers often have different cultural and ethnic backgrounds/worldviews
	◆ As a result of disrespectful, rude, or dismissive interactions in past, may present as angry, avoidant, suspicious, or nonadherent with care recommendations
End-of-life preferences	◆ Reluctance to relinquish aggressive medical management
	◆ Different perspectives on optimal end-of-life care, particularly in communities of color
	◆ Lack of advance care planning, as life is experienced moment to moment
	◆ Tendency to equate goals-of-care modification with abandonment or continued poor care
	◆ Spirituality may be a hidden resource for comfort and in guiding decision making

References: Adapted and reprinted with permission from *HPNA Core Curriculum for the Hospice and Palliative Advanced Practice Nurse Curriculum*

interactions, and end-of-life preferences (Table 55.1). These topics will be addressed in this chapter.

Primary Care for the Economically Disadvantaged

Neighborhood health centers play a critical role in providing comprehensive primary healthcare services, chronic illness management, cancer screening, and other healthcare maintenance for underserved and vulnerable populations. These clinics by definition are community-based and patient-directed.[8] But if the location of the clinic is inconvenient and its hours are not conducive to work schedules, the urban poor may have difficulty getting there. Taking time off from work to obtain medical care is a problem for the person who does not have a car, does not have sick leave, is paid on an hourly basis, has more than one job, and does not have coworkers to cover his or her workload. It is especially difficult if the person's income supports many other individuals. Lacking a medical home, many of the urban poor rely on the emergency department with its open-door access to medical care 24 hours a day, 365 days a year.[9,10]

Given these challenges, Maria was never screened for colon cancer, had never received other routine preventive care, and had not participated in an advance care planning conversation with a trusted provider.[11] Given that Maria presented with clinical "red flags" (fatigue, weight loss, and rectal bleeding), the palliative APRN in the neighborhood health center obtained bloodwork and realized that Maria was severely anemic. Her rectal exam was positive for occult fecal blood. With this information, the APRN referred Maria for an urgent colonoscopy to confirm her suspicion: colorectal cancer. Her need for emergent care involved a compressed, high-stakes interaction with the APRN who, until that encounter, was a stranger to Maria. How does an APRN meeting a patient for the first time provide information, support, and anticipatory guidance in this situation, particularly for a patient like Maria who lives on the margins of the dominant society? Very fortunately for Maria, this clinician spoke fluent Spanish and was able to obtain her history, conduct a physical examination, and provide education and support in their one-on-one interaction. The lack of a bilingual clinician would have delayed Maria's treatment further. The palliative APRN must complete a comprehensive social and cultural assessment while simultaneously being truly "present" for patients, listening to their story, attending to their immediate self-identified needs, and creating a therapeutic environment in which they feel safe and cared for as human beings.[5,12,13] The National Consensus Project (NCP) *Clinical Practice Guidelines* outline social and cultural assessment components relevant to the care of patients (Table 55.2).[13]

Role of Safety Net Hospitals/Public Health Care Systems

The term "essential" or "safety net" hospital refers to a loose network of hospitals, clinics/health centers, and local health departments around the country that provide necessary healthcare services for patients and communities who would otherwise "fall through the cracks." Safety net providers serve vulnerable populations at risk for health disparities, such as communities of color, immigrants, and the uninsured or underinsured, and play a critical role as training sites for physician trainees, nursing students, and other allied health professions students. APRNs may be particularly drawn to practice in safety net systems, given their social justice mission of improving the health and well-being of marginalized or underserved communities.[14]

In fiscal year 2013, safety net hospitals reported that almost half of their discharges were from racial/ethnic minorities; more

Table 55.2 National Consensus Project (NCP) Selected Guidelines for Social and Cultural Domains of Palliative Care

Domain 4: Social Aspects of Care;	Criteria:
Guideline 4.2: A comprehensive, person-centered interdisciplinary assessment identifies the social strengths, needs, and goals of each patient and family.	◆ The IDT [interdisciplinary team] assesses and documents the elements of a social assessment, which includes 　◆ Family structure and function: roles, communication and decision making patterns 　◆ Strengths and vulnerabilities: resiliency; social and cultural support networks; effect of illness or injury on intimacy and sexual expression; prior experiences with illness, disability, and loss; risk of abuse, neglect, or exploitation 　◆ Changes in family members' schooling, employment or vocational roles, recreational activities, and economic security 　◆ Geographic location, living arrangements, and perceived suitability of the living environment 　◆ Patient's and family's perceptions about caregiving needs, availability, and capacity 　◆ Needs for adaptive equipment, home modifications, transportation 　◆ Access to medications (prescription and over-the-counter) and nutritional products 　◆ Need for and access to community resources, financial support, and respite
Domain 6: Cultural Aspects of Care;	Criteria [selected]:
Guideline 6.1: The palliative care program serves each patient, family and community in a culturally and linguistically appropriate manner.	◆ During the assessment process, the IDT elicits and documents the cultural identifications, strengths, concerns and needs of the patient and family, with recognition that cultural identity and expression vary within families and communities. ◆ Palliative care program staff communicate in a language and manner that the patient and family understand. ◆ Palliative care staff members identify community resources that serve various cultural groups and refer patients and families to such services, as appropriate.

Reprinted with permission from the National Consensus Project.[13]

than 50% of all inpatient and outpatient visits in these systems were for the uninsured or those who had Medicaid as their insurance payer. Safety net hospitals provided nonemergent outpatient care to 38 million patients and treated more than 7.2 million in emergency departments. Inpatient admissions averaged 23,000 per hospital, nearly three times the inpatient volume of other hospitals.[15] Funding for safety net providers varies by state and by community[16] and will continue to change with the full implementation of the Affordable Care Act (ACA) and the resulting competition for newly qualified persons who may be eligible for Medicaid or other insurance.[17] Nonetheless, persons who are not eligible for coverage under the ACA will likely continue to receive care from safety net hospitals.[18]

While, in general, palliative care services have been integrated more slowly into safety net hospitals,[19] which serve communities with a disproportionate illness burden and limited resources, some recent initiatives offer hope about the positive impact of palliative care services for this population.[20-24] These initiatives included (1) improved family satisfaction following the death of a loved one in an inner-city medical intensive care unit after the introduction of palliative care consultation;[24] (2) increased alignment of end-of-life care wishes as reflected in "Do Not Resuscitate" status among African-Americans cared for in an urban safety net hospital;[22] (3) a statewide initiative that supported the planning, implementation, and expansion of palliative care consultation services in safety net/public health hospitals in California;[21] (4) a 10-year evaluation of palliative care services in a safety net hospital in Texas,[23] which challenged the conventional wisdom that communities of color do not accept hospice care; and (5) a statewide palliative care education and leadership initiative targeting nurses working in safety net hospitals that used the End-of-Life Nursing Consortium program designed for public hospitals (ELNEC-PH); 10,892 nurses were trained.[20]

Overcoming Language Barriers

When patients and healthcare providers cannot communicate in the same language, messages can be misunderstood or lost, resulting in diminished quality of care. Current demographic trends in the United States suggest that healthcare professionals will care for an increasing number of patients with limited English proficiency. The U.S. Census Bureau's American Community Survey of 2011 revealed that most persons living in the United States speak English.[25] However, 21% of those surveyed reported speaking another language at home. Of the more than 60 million who reported speaking another language at home, 42% (over 25 million) reported speaking English less than "very well." Certain states have disproportionately large numbers of persons with limited English proficiency. For example, almost 24% of surveyed Californians reported limited English proficiency in the 2011 American Community Survey.[25] To comply with statutes[26] requiring equal access regardless of race, ethnicity, or national origin, healthcare organizations typically provide some access to professional healthcare interpreters.

Providers can choose from a variety of options when faced with a patient who has limited English proficiency: (1) attempt to "get by" with their limited language skills in the patient's preferred language, (2) use an informal or ad hoc interpreter, or (3) use a professional interpreter. Each of these options has advantages and disadvantages. Although APRNs with limited proficiency in

a second language might attempt to save time by personally conducting important conversations with a patient or family members, the practice of "getting by" with limited second-language skills is inherently problematic.[27]

Given the significance of the subject matter being discussed, as well as the depth of understanding conveyed through word choice and phrasing, communicating through interpreters is recommended.[27,28] In some circumstances, providers will enlist the help of an ad hoc interpreter, an informal, untrained bilingual individual, such as a family member, bystander, or other staff member. Ad hoc interpreters are often used for reasons of convenience or necessity, but several studies suggest that, compared with professional interpreters, ad hoc interpreters make more errors, and these errors are more likely to have clinical significance.[27]

Although professional interpreters are costly and may not be as readily accessible as ad hoc interpreters, they allow family members or other staff to remain in their primary roles, placing the focus on the content of the conversation rather than the additional responsibility of interpretation. Professional interpreters can alert providers to cultural norms, taboos, or traditions that may add important insight into their patients' preferences and values. For all of these reasons, the NCP has supported not only the use of professional interpreters but also the provision of "culturally-sensitive materials in the patient's and family's preferred language."[13]

Given the complexity and emotional weight of the information being communicated in palliative care encounters, even when professional interpreters are used, alterations in meaning can still occur.[28] Surveys of professional interpreters with extensive experience in end-of-life discussions have identified specific techniques to optimize providers' interpreted patient encounters.[29] Guidelines for optimizing communication with healthcare interpreters are summarized in Box 55.1. In addition, Schenker and colleagues reviewed the literature and published recommendations for working with interpreters in palliative care.[27] These best practices emphasize direct communication with the interpreter and outline basic principles of interacting with interpreters, including structural and practical aspects of communication.

Practical Strategies for Communicating Through Professional Interpreters

The palliative APRN should try to meet with the interpreter prior to the patient encounter. Before entering the patient's room or conference room, briefly introduce yourself to the interpreter and inform him or her which patient you will be speaking with. Ask the interpreter whether he or she has worked with or knows this patient, as this may reveal important insights into family dynamics and patient history, or it might uncover confidentiality concerns if the interpreter knows the patient socially. After this brief introduction, discuss your hopes and goals for the encounter, including a brief review of the content you will discuss. Similar to breaking bad news, this serves as a "warning shot" to the interpreter, so that he or she can prepare for the potential emotional weight of the conversation, can ask about necessary vocabulary terms, and can alert you to cultural issues related to the topic you will be addressing. Beyond these practical benefits, meeting with the interpreter ahead of time also communicates mutual respect and value for the interpreter's experience and insight, which may empower the interpreter to offer additional thoughts or hidden information later in the encounter.

Box 55.1 General Guidelines for Working with Healthcare Interpreters

- Ensure that the patient can hear and see the interpreter.

- Introduce the interpreter, and prompt the interpreter to explain his or her role (i.e., patient confidentiality, direct interpretation of everything said).

- Look at and speak directly to the patient, as if he or she spoke English.

- Use short sentences or phrases. Break up lengthy explanations or responses into multiple shorter responses.

- Avoid using euphemisms, proverbs, or cultural references, as they can lead to confusion or may not carry similar meaning when interpreted.

- Check for patient/family understanding frequently, either directly (e.g., teach-back technique) or indirectly (checking with interpreter if he or she perceives that patient is or is not understanding).

- When trying to get the attention of the interpreter, start your comment with "Interpreter" to make it easier for the interpreter to distinguish the person you are addressing.

From references 27 and 53.

In healthcare settings that provide only remote interpreter services (e.g., telephone or video medical interpretation), meeting the interpreter ahead of time is more difficult logistically. The palliative APRN can usually access the remote interpreter before entering the room for the encounter, but if this is impossible, you can simply begin the encounter by performing brief introductions and then telling the patient that you and the interpreter will speak briefly before beginning the visit.

The language barrier creates a gap between the patient and the provider, but sitting down with the patient, looking directly at him or her, and using nonverbal communication can minimize the gap. Palliative care emphasizes using clear language appropriate to the patient's educational level and health literacy and frequently checking for patient understanding. Listen for evidence of miscommunication or misunderstanding. If you ask a question and expect a brief response, but then hear an extended exchange between the interpreter and the patient, this may suggest a misunderstanding. Likewise, pay attention to nonverbal cues like facial expression, which may suggest misunderstanding. If you are concerned that there may be a miscommunication or misunderstanding, directly address the interpreter and relay this concern. To clarify whether a message is for the patient or for the interpreter, begin all statements or questions to the interpreter with the word "interpreter"—for example, "Interpreter, I'm concerned that I may be missing something. Can you please tell me what you and Maria have been talking about? Do you think that she understood the question I was trying to ask?"

After leaving the patient's room or conference room, spend a minute or two debriefing with the interpreter. Ask the interpreter how he or she thought the encounter went, if there were any messages that may have been missed, and if there was any concern about misunderstanding. For example, if there were non-interpreted conversations among others in the room, you might ask if the interpreter was aware of the nature of those conversations. This debriefing session can give you a chance to ask questions about cultural norms or concerns that the interpreter may have noticed. After eliciting feedback from the interpreter, ask the interpreter how he or she is feeling to determine what immediate or long-term support needs, if any, the interpreter might have.

The quality of interpreted sessions in palliative care can also be improved through continuing education and policy. The *Interpreting in Palliative Care* curriculum, created in 2011, is designed to provide professional interpreters with the technical skills, knowledge base, and self-care tools needed to provide high-quality interpretation.[30] Some professional organizations, such as the California Safety Net Institute, have created learning and support communities for healthcare interpreters to provide peer support and disseminate best practices; the link to the curriculum follows (http://learn.hcin.org/). Palliative APRNs who work in settings that employ professional interpreters should consider direct outreach and education in palliative care for their interpreters.

Finally, two qualitative studies using focus groups underscored the challenges of receiving care and providing care when communication barriers exist.[31,32] Non-English-speaking patients in an Australian study said they felt powerless when they could not communicate directly with the professionals caring for them, and acknowledged both the limitations of family members serving as ad hoc interpreters and the importance of professional interpreters in conveying complex medical communication. In a study of British health and social service providers titled "Reduced to Nods and Smiles," the providers expressed concern about their ability to provide high-quality care to cancer patients throughout the illness trajectory when they could not communicate directly with them. Providing information and support was more challenging when they had to work through ad hoc interpreters or when they relied on nonverbal communication. These professionals acknowledged that therapeutic relationships, key to caregiving and care receiving, were compromised due to language and cultural barriers.

Negotiating Hospitalization and Treatment

Given the limited access to, and availability of, outpatient and community-based palliative care for this population,[3] it is most likely that patients will encounter palliative APRNs in the acute care setting. The patient in the case study, Maria, might receive education from an oncology APRN about her cancer diagnosis, treatment side effects, and recovery trajectory; a palliative APRN might assist with symptom management and clarification of goals of care; a wound care APRN might be consulted regarding ostomy teaching or complex surgical wound management; and a psychiatric mental health APRN might assist Maria to identify coping resources for managing her new diagnosis and to acknowledge the impact of past traumas in her life. Regardless of the particular APRN role, an understanding of the hospitalization experience for Maria and others who are economically disadvantaged will be necessary to appreciate their understanding of the illness, its treatment demands, and their future life.

Like many economically disadvantaged persons with serious illness, Maria had a difficult life story.[33–35] She escaped a violent revolution and witnessed the deaths of her husband and infant when she was less than 20 years of age. Many patients with serious illness cared for by safety net systems have been exposed to unimaginable life events prior to the diagnosis of a life-threatening illness, such as child abuse, domestic abuse, homelessness, incarceration, sexual assault, wartime exposure, homicides and suicides of family and friends, and substance abuse. Their lives are trauma-filled.[33,34]

There is a growing awareness of the persistent negative impact of trauma exposure on the mental health and physical well-being of individuals, communities, and healthcare professionals themselves, and along with this awareness is the recognition of the need for services to address the consequences of trauma exposure.[36] Trauma-informed care is an emerging model that will influence program development and is based on the principles of safety, trustworthiness, collaboration, empowerment, and choice.[36] While discussion of trauma-informed care is beyond the scope of this chapter, in the future it undoubtedly will shape palliative care and other services for the economically disadvantaged and other vulnerable populations at high risk for post-traumatic stress disorder, as well as the healthcare and social service professionals working with them.

Perhaps because of their difficult biographies, many persons with limited resources have developed remarkable resiliency.[33,34] Cancer may be viewed as just one more thing in a life of challenges. The palliative APRN can serve a pivotal role in helping to draw on this resiliency to help patients face serious illness and navigate complex healthcare systems.

Beyond linguistic and cultural barriers, the urban poor face many difficulties in the healthcare system, including bureaucratic difficulties accessing care, insensitive or dismissive interactions with healthcare professionals and support staff, and delays in nursing and medical care that result in patients being made to feel less than human.[3,33,34] The following descriptions from participants in a study that explored the meaning of dignity to the urban poor with advanced illness illustrate the difficulty the urban poor may experience receiving person-centered care:[37]

> *Ozzy* (African-American man with metastatic colorectal cancer): "Then . . . when I had . . . diarrhea and everything . . . I always tell her [nurse], I say, 'You know what? I'm shitting on myself.' [She says] 'Oh, I'll be with you in five minutes.' Five minutes go a long way, a long way. Five minutes go by. 30 minutes go by. An hour goes by. I say, 'Nurse, I [messed] in the bed' and [nurse said], 'Oh, well . . . I'll get to you next.' When . . . the nurse tells me that, she's nowhere around. All she's doing is being out in the hallway lollygagging. I told a couple of the man doctors about this here. 'Oh, I will talk to the nurses.' I don't think any of them said anything to them about that, period."[37]
>
> *Eddie* (Caucasian man with metastatic lung cancer): "They [the nurses] just wanted me to stay in bed. They were afraid I was gonna fall . . . they wouldn't even let me even get up to go use the bathroom. I said, 'Well, can't you give me like a walker or something?' And 'uh no' [they said], you know, I kind of got irritable, you might say, because that bathroom was just about as far as this one right here [in his hotel room, approximately 6 feet] . . . Yeah, I could make it over there instead of bringing the nurse. And then she'd be another hour to bring me a bedpan, for crying out loud! You know? Sometimes she'd get back, 'Oh, I forgot all about you.'"
>
> *Interviewer:* "Did that happen very often?"
>
> *Eddie:* "No, not very often. But . . . I guess with the medication and everything . . . I got a little bit of diarrhea, you know. And I messed the bed and it was embarrassing."[37]

If Ozzy and Eddie, both English speakers, had their requests for toileting assistance ignored or, at the very least, delayed without apology or explanation, suffering the embarrassment of incontinence, what might patients who did not speak English experience? They are at a high risk for feeling powerless and not understanding what is happening to and for them.[31]

Being hospitalized and being treated for cancer or any life-threatening illness is scary for most patients. Cancer evokes dread, uncertainty, and death—even in 2014, when many persons with advanced disease are living longer.[38] For many of those who are economically disadvantaged, the diagnosis of a life-threatening illness is one more burden to bear in lives consumed with the struggle to survive every day.[33,39] Struggling or fighting to live is often a way of existence for the urban poor when the basics of life that most of us take for granted—food, housing, transportation, water, electricity, telephone and Internet access, income, healthcare, supportive relationships/community, and safety—are always being renegotiated and prioritized.[9,33,40]

Despite the everyday struggle to survive, many of the urban poor demonstrate remarkable resiliency and courage in the face of adversity. Some of their resilience, in part, may be understood by spiritual and religious beliefs and practices that connect their experiences to something greater than their everyday existence.[41] Similar to findings reported by Moller,[9] some of the urban poor report finding comfort and strength in spiritual beliefs or faith, through a variety of means, including TV evangelists, spending time in nature, organized religious community activities, or meditation. It is important to note the wide spectrum of spirituality, from those who express a spiritual rather than a religious orientation to others who turn over their illness and their fate to God.[42]

APRN Role Competencies Caring for Economically Disadvantaged Persons

For APRNs committed to caring for those who are economically disadvantaged, the knowledge and skills (competencies) are similar to the competencies required when caring for other palliative care populations. The Hospice and Palliative Nurses Association's competencies for the hospice and palliative APRN are listed in Table 55.3, with behaviors of particular relevance to the urban poor noted in Table 55.4.[43] The following discussion examines the implications of some of these competencies and behaviors.

While the HPNA APN communication and cultural competencies and advanced core behaviors do not explicitly include working with non-English-speaking patients, we have included selected NCP guidelines from *Domain 6 – Cultural Aspects of Care* (see Table 55.2) and have already outlined strategies for communicating with non-English-speaking patients/families and working with interpreters (see Box 55.1).

Advocacy and Ethics

All health and social service professionals advocate for patients, families, and communities. However, advocacy and ethics hold particular salience for palliative APRNs working with vulnerable or marginalized populations. McHugh and colleagues contend that nursing's traditions in community health and clinical practice equip nurses to serve as palliative care leaders for at-risk populations

Table 55.3 Skills Necessary for the Care of Economically Disadvantaged Population from the *HPNA Competencies for the Hospice and Palliative Advanced Practice Nurse*

Core Competency	Advanced Competency Statement
Clinical Judgment	Demonstrates advanced clinical judgment and decision making based on expert knowledge and skill in the assessment, physical examination, diagnosis, planning, and management of complex human responses to serious or life-threatening illness.
Advocacy and Ethics	Incorporates ethical principles and advanced practice nursing professional standards in the care of patients and families receiving palliative care, while advocating for patients' and families' rights and access to quality palliative care.
Professionalism	Demonstrates knowledge, skills and behaviors consistent with the *HPNA's Palliative Nursing: Scope and Standards of Practice—An Essential Resource for Hospice and Palliative Nurses*, as well as the HPNA *Code of Ethical Conduct* and the ANA *Code of Ethics for Nurses*.
Collaboration	Promotes an interdisciplinary team approach in the provision of palliative care to the patient and family with serious or life-threatening illness. Promotes palliative care concepts to the public regarding potential or actual physical, psychological, emotional, social and spiritual components of living with a serious or life-threatening illness.
Systems Thinking	Manages and negotiates the health care delivery system to enhance quality of life for patients and families experiencing serious or life-threatening illness and facilitates the provision of comprehensive coordinated care within and across health care settings.
Cultural and Spiritual Competence	Demonstrates and promotes culturally and spiritually competent care by respecting diversity, in regard to ethnicity, culture, spirituality, gender, socioeconomic status, sexual orientation, education level, literacy, and location.
Facilitator of Learning	Demonstrates knowledge, skills, confidence, and the application of adult learning principles inherent to the role of the hospice and palliative advanced practice registered nurse when providing palliative care education to patients/families, healthcare professionals, and the community.
Communication	Communicates effectively with palliative care patients, families, and healthcare professionals by applying knowledge of communication theory and principles.
Evidence-Based Practice and Research	Utilizes research to identify, examine, validate, and evaluate current theories and palliative care practice, with the goal of improved outcomes for palliative care patients, families and the community.

Reprinted with permission from the Hospice and Palliative Nurses Association, 2nd ed.[43]

whether poor, undocumented, homeless, elderly, medically complex, with limited English proficiency, or institutionalized.[44] Others argue that all persons, regardless of sociocultural disadvantages, are vulnerable at the end-of-life, but that the experience of being marginalized, particularly resulting from physical or mental disability, requires inclusive policy changes; such policy changes would welcome the vulnerable into the community and away from its margins.[45] Palliative APRNs must serve on institutional committees and community advisory task forces that promote palliative care for vulnerable and marginalized communities. For example, California APRNs recently served on both a statewide advisory group to explore how Medicaid beneficiaries may gain access to palliative care regardless of setting of care, and a local task force that examined the state of palliative care in their community with the goal of improving access and quality for all. The community palliative care task force's report can be found on the following web site: (https://www.sfdph.org/dph/comupg/knowlcol/palliative/default.asp). Finally, Krakauer argued that palliative care must not and should not be accepted as the alternative for society's failure to address healthcare disparities that result in inadequate prevention efforts and disease-directed therapies[46] in the developing world. To do so, he contends, is unjust and irresponsible and increases the suffering of the poor.[46] We argue the same is true for the developed world: palliative care cannot replace community health and primary care services.

Collaboration and Systems Thinking

While collaboration and systems thinking competencies as described in Tables 55.3 and 55.4 are distinct, we propose that in

caring for the poor, collaboration and systems thinking are inextricably linked. Maria's story underscores the missed opportunities for accessible and quality palliative care[10] that occur when the connections are not made. Persons who have limited English proficiency, are undocumented, or are otherwise disenfranchised often lack a primary care provider or a medical home. They often present in the emergency department with advanced disease that, if diagnosed and treated earlier, may have resulted in a different outcome. Lacking access to primary palliative care compromises the clinical outcomes of those living with serious or life-threatening illness. Working with the urban poor, who have limited resources and options, requires creative, in-the-moment problem solving to honor patients' preferences and goals. To effectively care for vulnerable populations, palliative APRNs must develop collaborative relationships with a wide array of social services and other safety net providers/systems to understand community resources and community providers experienced in caring for the most vulnerable and marginalized. These partnerships provide needed collegial support for the moral distress that may be experienced when caring for the most disenfranchised.

Cultural and Spiritual Competence

Working with persons and communities who are poor, are homeless, have limited English proficiency, or are otherwise isolated and alienated from mainstream society requires attention to the human spirit so that personal and community narratives may be uncovered. These understandings are different from the clinical perspectives we bring to our work.[5] Such work is facilitated by the practice of cultural humility, which is defined as:[4(p 118)]

Table 55.4 Selected Competencies and Advanced Core Behaviors in Caring for the Economically Disadvantaged Population

Competencies	Advanced Core Behaviors
Advocacy and Ethics	◆ Advocates access to quality palliative care for patients and families who meet the definition of the underserved, underresourced, and vulnerable populations ◆ Identifies, acknowledges, and addresses the complex ethical issues arising in the care of people with serious or life-threatening illness ◆ Develops, implements, and evaluates strategies to overcome patient, clinician, and healthcare system obstacles as well as social, legal, or economic barriers to pain and symptom management ◆ Influences professional and health-related outcomes in palliative care in organizational, legislative, and policy settings
Collaboration	◆ Creates a climate of trust, respect, and partnership between patients and families with serious or life-threatening illness and interdisciplinary team members ◆ Collaborates with community agencies to facilitate care in the setting preferred by the patient and family, when feasible, including hospice as provided in a variety of settings, as well as home care or care in a skilled nursing facility ◆ Collaborates with other health professionals to ensure access and fair distribution of healthcare resources across all populations, particularly in vulnerable and underserved populations
Systems Thinking	◆ Analyzes the impact of caring for individuals with serious or life-threatening illness on family, community, and healthcare systems, including identification of available resources and potential barriers across all healthcare settings ◆ Considers access, barriers, cost, efficacy, and quality when making palliative care decisions ◆ Participates in the development of institutional and healthcare systems policies that support quality palliative care ◆ Evaluates implications of contemporary health policy on healthcare providers and patients and families experiencing serious or life-threatening illness
Cultural and Spiritual Competence	◆ Assesses, identifies, and addresses cultural, spiritual, and existential beliefs, behaviors, practices, needs, and concerns of patients and family members according to established protocols and documents in the interdisciplinary care plan ◆ Promotes respect for the patient's and family's cultural perceptions, preferences, and practices regarding illness, disability, treatment, help seeking, disclosure, decision making, grief, death, dying, and family composition ◆ Accesses appropriate cultural as well as spiritual and religious resources to deliver palliative care to patients and families ◆ Addresses conflicts that may arise between patients, families, and healthcare providers resulting from differences in cultural and spiritual perspectives related to palliative care, and plans for effective strategies to allow for and accommodate those differences ◆ Recognizes and educates others about the role of diversity in the application of professional health provider obligations, including information on diagnosis, disclosure, decisional authority, care, and acceptance of decisions to continue, discontinue, or forgo treatments

Reprinted with permission from the Hospice and Palliative Nurses Association, 2nd ed. Ref 43.

a process that requires humility as individuals continually engage in self-reflection and self-critique as lifelong learners and reflective practitioners . . . it requires humility in how [providers] bring into check the power imbalances that exist in the dynamics of [provider]–patient communication by using patient-focused interviewing and care. And it is a process that requires humility to develop and maintain respectful and dynamic partnerships with communities on behalf of individual patients and communities . . .

Garrett and colleagues proposed an inductively derived model of cultural empowerment with patients with limited English proficiency who had been hospitalized in Australia.[31] This model included six competencies: (1) facilitating language, (2) negotiating family involvement, (3) understanding patient beliefs, expectations, experiences, and constructions, (4) being compassionate and respecting patient and human rights, (5) negotiating a care partnership, and (6) providing systems so that services and providers can be competent.[31] Taken together, practicing cultural humility and incorporating actions to promote cultural empowerment honors and respects the lives, and improves the care of, the economically disadvantaged with serious and life-threatening illness.

Conclusion

Caring for persons who are economically disadvantaged and in need of palliative care demands not only expert clinical acumen but also—and equally important—an appreciation of their community and their everyday lives. This chapter examines (1) palliative care across settings; (2) the role of safety net providers; (3) the challenges of communicating serious information indirectly; through an interpreter; and (4) the competencies needed by hospice and palliative APRNs who care for this special population.

References

1. DeNavas-Walt C, Proctor BD, Smith JC. Income, poverty, and health insurance coverage in the United States: 2012. *Current Population Reports*. 2013; 60–245.
2. Galea S, et al. Estimated deaths attributable to social factors in the United States. *Am J Public Health*. 2011; 101(8): 1456–65.
3. Lewis JM, et al. Dying in the margins: understanding palliative care and socioeconomic deprivation in the developed world. *J Pain Symptom Manage*. 2011; 42(1): 105–18.
4. Trevalon M, Murray-Garcia J. Cultural humility versus cultural competence: a critical distinction in defining physician training

outcomes in multicultural education. *J Health Care Poor Underserved.* 1998; 9(2): 117–25.

5. Moller DW. None left behind: urban poverty, social experience, and rethinking palliative care. *J Palliat Med.* 2005; 8: 17–9.

6. Crawley J, et al. Needs of the hidden homeless—no longer hidden: a pilot study. *Public Health.* 2013; 127(3):674–680.

7. Smith AK, Sudore RL, Perez-Stable EJ. Palliative care for Latino patients and their families: whenever we prayed, she wept. *JAMA.* 2009; 301(10): 1047–57.

8. What is a health center? Available from http://bphc.hrsa.gov/about/index.html. Accessed August 18, 2014.

9. Moller DW. *Dancing With Broken Bones: Portraits of Death and Dying Among Inner-City Poor.* New York, NY: Oxford University Press; 2004.

10. Bender M, et al. Missed opportunities in providing palliative care for the urban poor: a case discussion. *J Palliat Med.* 2013; 16(5): 587–90.

11. Ortega AN, et al. Health care access, use of services, and experiences among undocumented Mexicans and other Latinos. *Arch Intern Med.* 2007; 167(21): 2354–20.

12. Hughes A. Meeting the palliative care needs of the underserved. In: Dahlin CM, Lynch MT, eds. *Core Curriculum for the Advanced Practice Hospice and Palliative Care Registered Nurse.* Pittsburgh, PA: Hospice and Palliative Nurses Association; 2013:529–44.

13. National Consensus Project for Quality Palliative Care. *Clinical Practice Guidelines for Quality Palliative Care.* 3rd ed. 2013. Pittsburgh, PA: National Consensus Project. Available at http://www.nationalconsensusproject.org/NCP_Clinical_Practice_Guidelines_3rd_Edition.pdf. Accessed September 21, 2014.

14. Browne AJ, Tarlier DS. Examining the potential of nurse practitioners from a critical social justice perspective. *Nurs Inq.* 2008; 15(2): 83–93.

15. Essential Hospital Institute (Reid KS, Roberson B and Landry C) and America's Essential Hospitals (Linson M, Laycox S) http://essentialhospitals.org/wp-content/uploads/2015/03/Essential-Hospitals-Vital-Data-2015.pdf. Accessed August 23, 2015.

16. Lewin ME, Altman S. *America's Health Care Safety Net: Intact but Endangered.* Washington, DC: The National Academies Press; 2000.

17. Meier DE. Increased access to palliative care and hospice services: opportunities to improve value in health care. *Milbank Q.* 2011; 89(3): 343–80.

18. Coughlin TA, et al. Strategies in 4 Safety-Net Hospitals to Adapt to the ACA. The Kaiser Commission on Medicaid and the Uninsured Issue Brief, 2014: 1–19.

19. Morrison RS, et al. America's care of serious illness: a state-by-state report card on access to palliative care in our nation's hospitals. *J Palliat Med.* 2011; 14(10): 1094–6.

20. Virani R, et al. Creating a fabric for palliative care in safety net hospitals: End-of-Life Nursing Education Consortium for Public Hospitals. *J Hosp Palliat Nurs.* 2014; 16(5): 312–9.

21. Brousseau RT, et al. A multifaceted approach to spreading palliative care consultation services in California public hospital systems. *J Healthcare Qual.* 2012; 34(2): 77–85.

22. Sacco J, Carr DR, Viola D. The effects of the palliative medicine consultation on the DNR status of African Americans in a safety-net hospital. *Am J Hosp Palliat Care.* 2013; 30(4): 363–9.

23. Rhodes RL, et al. An examination of end-of-life care in a safety net hospital system: a decade in review. *J Health Care Poor Underserved.* 2013; 24(4): 1666–75.

24. Kaufer M, et al. Family satisfaction following the death of a loved one in an inner-city MICU. *Am J Hosp Palliat Care.* 2008; 25(4): 318–25.

25. Ryan C. Language use in the United States: 2011 American Community Survey Reports. Available from www.census.gov.

26. U.S. Civil Rights Act in 88-352, U.S. Congress, 1964: Washington, DC, p. 1–29.

27. Schenker Y, et al. "Her husband doesn't speak much English": conducting a family meeting with an interpreter. *J Palliat Med.* 2012; 15(4): 494–8.

28. Pham K, et al. Alterations during medical interpretation of ICU family conferences that interfere with or enhance communication. *Chest.* 2008; 134(1): 109–16.

29. Norris WM, et al. Communication about end-of-life care between language-discordant patients and clinicians: insights from medical interpreters. *J Palliat Med.* 2005; 8(5): 1016–24.

30. Roat C, Kinderman A, Fernandez A. *Interpreting in Palliative Care.* California Health Care Foundation; 2011.

31. Garrett PW, et al. What do non-English-speaking patients value in acute care? Cultural competency from the patient's perspective: a qualitative study. *Ethn Health.* 2008; 13(5): 479–96.

32. Richardson A, Thomas VN, Richardson A. "Reduced to nods and smiles": experiences of professionals caring for people with cancer from black and ethnic minority groups. *Eur J Oncol Nurs.* 2006; 10(2): 93–105.

33. Hughes A, Gundmundsdottir M, Davies B. Everyday struggling to survive: Experiences of the urban poor living with advanced cancer. *Oncol Nurs Forum.* 2007; 34(6): 1113–8.

34. Dzul-Church V, et al. "I'm sitting here by myself . . .": experiences of patients with serious illness at an urban public hospital. *J Palliat Med.* 2010; 13(6): 695–701.

35. Hughes A, Davies B, Gudmundsdottir M. "Can you give me respect?" Experiences of the urban poor on a dedicated AIDS nursing home unit. *J Assoc Nurses AIDS Care.* 2008; 19(5): 342–56.

36. Wolf MR, et al. "We're civil servants": the status of trauma-informed care in the community. *J Social Service Res.* 2014; 40(1): 111–20.

37. Hughes AM. "Can you give me respect?" Experiences of the urban poor with advanced disease. School of Nursing, University of California San Francisco, 2007, p. 202.

38. DeSantis CE, et al. Cancer treatment and survivorship statistics, 2014. *CA Cancer J Clin.* 2014; 64(4): 252–71.

39. Lyckholm LJ, et al. Barriers to effective palliative care for low-income patients in late stages of cancer: report of a study and strategies for defining and conquering the barriers. *Nurs Clin North Am.* 2010; 45(3): 399–409.

40. Williams BR. Dying young, dying poor: a sociological examination of existential suffering among low socio-economic status patients. *J Palliat Med.* 2004; 7(1): 27–37.

41. Sulmasy DP. Spiritual issues in the care of dying patients: ". . . it's okay between me and God." *JAMA.* 2006; 296(11): 1385–92.

42. Hughes A, Gudmundsdottir M, Davies B. Exploring spirituality in the urban poor with advanced cancer. *Oncol Nurs Forum.* 2008; 35: 535.

43. Hospice and Palliative Nurses Association. In: Dahlin C., ed *Competencies for the Hospice and Palliative Advanced Practice Nurse.* Pittsburgh, PA: Hospice and Palliative Nurses Association; 2014:i–26.

44. McHugh ME, Arnold J, Buschman PR. Nurses leading the response to the crisis of palliative care for vulnerable populations. *Nurs Econ.* 2012; 30(3): 140–7.

45. Stienstra D, Chochinov HM. Palliative care for vulnerable populations. *Palliat Support Care.* 2012; 10(1): 37–42.

46. Krakauer EL. Just palliative care: responding responsibly to the suffering of the poor. *J Pain Symptom Manage.* 2008; 36(5): 505–12.

47. Hughes A, Gudmundsdottir M, Davies B. Exploring spirituality in the urban poor with advanced cancer [poster abstract]. *Oncol Nurs Forum.* 2008; 35: 535.

48. Lewis JM, et al. Dying in the margins: understanding palliative care and socioeconomic deprivation in the developed world. *J Pain Symptom Manage.* 2011; 43(2):105–18.

49. Fernandes R, et al. Home-based palliative care services for underserved populations. *J Palliat Med.* 2010; 13(4): 413–9.

50. Dula A, Williams S. When race matters. *Clin Geriatr Med.* 2005; 21(1): 239–253.

51. Hughes A. Poverty and palliative care in the US: Issues facing the urban poor. *Intl J Palliat Nurs.* 2005; 11(1): 6–13.

52. McNeil R, Guirguis-Younger M, Dilley LB. Recommendations for improving the end-of-life care system for homeless populations: a qualitative study of the views of Canadian health and social services professionals. *BMC Palliat Care.* 2012; 11: 14.

53. Association of American Medical Colleges. *AAMC Guidelines for Use of Medical Interpreter Services.* Available at https://www.aamc.org/students/download/70338/data/interpreter-guidelines.pdf Accessed August 23, 2015.

CHAPTER 56

Veterans

Mary E. Davidson

Key Points

◆ The palliative advanced practice registered nurse (APRN) recognizes the unique healthcare needs of veterans across different war and conflict eras.

◆ The palliative APRN incorporates the evaluation of the veteran's military service into palliative care planning.

◆ The palliative APRN recognizes the risks for post-traumatic stress disorder (PTSD) at end-of-life and addresses comfort and support for the veteran and family.

Introduction

A veteran is someone who has served in one, or more, branches of the U.S. military and has now returned to civilian life. There is a great variety in the type of military service that veterans have provided. Eligibility varies for veterans' benefits, such as education, pensions, home loans, and myriad other programs. Eligibility for most VA benefits is based upon discharge from active military service under other than dishonorable conditions. Active service means full-time service, other than active duty for training, as a member of the Army, Navy, Air Force, Marine Corps, Coast Guard, National Guard or Reserve Component, or as a commissioned officer of the Public Health Service, Environmental Science Services Administration, or National Oceanic and Atmospheric Administration.

There are just over 22.5 million living military veterans in the United States, and 17 million of them served in wartime.[1] Forty-four percent of veterans are 65 years of age or older.[2] World War II and Korean War veterans represent the oldest of these military groups.[3] Some healthcare providers are surprised to learn that the majority of veterans die outside of VA facilities: only 4.3% of veterans die in VA facilities.[2(p 49)] Clinically, veterans' needs and preferences at the end-of-life are similar to those of all patients.[4] However, veterans often have "military" wounds that affect their physiologic, social, and spiritual integrity at the end-of-life.[5] The palliative APRN plays an important role in identifying veterans, understanding their unique needs, managing distressing symptoms, and supporting their families. The goal of this chapter is to provide information about the care that is unique to veterans, to review services available to veterans and their loved ones, and to provide basics for navigating the system and accessing these resources.

The care of veterans may occur in VA medical centers, but more frequently it occurs in community settings, including outpatient clinics, home care, and hospice. The unique challenge of providing excellent end-of-life care coordination for veterans often lies in balancing veteran-specific benefits, entitlements, and resources while assessing and responding to the presence of military "wounds," which can worsen as death approaches.

Military culture and a veteran's service experience can have a profound effect on how he or she faces serious illness and death. It is helpful for the palliative APRN to understand military culture, the different military conflicts and wars, and the health challenges that can appear late in life for the veterans of these conflicts. Care of veterans is improved with a basic understanding of the different experiences among veterans of WWII, the Korean War, the Vietnam War, and more recent conflicts in the Persian Gulf, Iraq, and Afghanistan. Psychosocial and spiritual issues, such as post-traumatic stress disorder (PTSD), military sexual trauma, substance abuse, homelessness, and suicide, may cause problems throughout the lives of veterans and may intensify as the end-of-life approaches.

All service members are part of a shared culture that includes a strong sense of respect, honor, and duty. However, each war is different, and it would be a disservice to veterans to think that because they share a common military history, they all culturally integrated that experience similarly. Individual experiences will depend on many factors, such as whether they were drafted or volunteered (either willingly or unwillingly), the military branch, the time and place(s) of service, and military occupation. An excellent reference and review of the different war periods and the effect they have had on veterans can be found at the We Honor Veterans website (www.wehonorveterans.org).

A summary of health concerns applicable to palliative care finds that veterans from WWII and the Korean War may have severe disabling injuries, especially if they were a prisoner of war (POW). Veterans may have problems with cold sensitivity and carcinomas found in areas that were frostbitten.[6] Dangers of radiation exposure from the atomic bombs used during WWII were not fully appreciated, and exposure to active radiation during nuclear cleanup in Japan and during the early years of the Cold War may pose the risk for leukemias and other cancers.

PTSD has been retrospectively recognized after all wars: it was called "soldier's heart" in the Civil War, "shell shock" in World War I, and "combat fatigue" in WWII. The concept of PTSD was not formalized in the diagnostic nomenclature until 1980, after extensive experience in treating Vietnam veterans.[7]

Sixty-three percent of enrolled veterans testing positive for hepatitis C virus are Vietnam-era veterans. Exposure to Agent Orange and other herbicides in Vietnam veterans poses risks for health problems like soft tissue sarcoma, non-Hodgkin's lymphoma, Hodgkin's disease, respiratory cancers, multiple myeloma, prostate cancer, and acute peripheral neuropathy.[8] Environmental exposure to oil-well fire smoke in the Gulf War has exacerbated asthma, and Persian Gulf War veterans are more than twice as likely as other veterans to develop amyotrophic lateral sclerosis.[8]

As part of the VA-wide Office of Public Health and Environmental Hazard, every VA medical facility has a registry physician for Agent Orange, Gulf War, and ionizing radiation.[9] Growing awareness among community health providers about the war-related physical and mental wounds inflicted during military service is a valuable tool when attempting to diagnose confusing and/or complex symptoms presented by veterans.

Veterans represent almost one-quarter of the total homeless population in the United States. There is a Homeless Veteran Program Coordinator at each VA facility; he or she can be an important source of information about the services for homeless veterans provided through the Veterans Health Administration (VHA). Services vary among medical centers and can include outreach, case management, referrals to benefits counselors, linkage to healthcare, and housing assistance.

Many veterans are unaware of the health services available to them as their illnesses progress and they approach the end of their lives. As with their civilian counterparts, critical conversations regarding access to home care, palliative care, hospice care, pain management, and symptom control are sometimes delayed until it is too late to address the needs and wishes of the dying veteran. Healthcare providers are often unaware of the special needs present in the veteran population. The complexity of accessing entitlements and resources through the large infrastructure of the VA can leave professionals frustrated and unsure how to best advocate for the veterans they are serving.

The last journey that an American veteran takes is also the last journey that all humans take. Just as forgiveness is an important task for all who face their death, for those who have war wounds, hospice and palliative care can present a last chance to make peace with wartime memories and guilt.[10]

Understanding Military Cultures

Veteran identity is defined as the self-concept derived from one's military experiences within a social and historical context.[11] This shared experience of serving in the armed forces binds together the people who served. Although the majority of U.S. veterans were not in combat situations, all were prepared for that possibility in their training. Those who fought or who served in the role of chaplain, medic, physician, or nurse are likely to carry some emotional, social, and/or existential suffering as a result of the experience of battle.[12] There is a range of expression of those military experiences, from pride and patriotism to ambiguity to indifference. In some veterans, combat experiences led to profoundly changed and broken lives.

Through a rite of passage that begins with boot camp, men and women from diverse socioeconomic, racial, and ethnic backgrounds assimilate into a distinct group bound to each other with intense camaraderie that is fueled by military purpose and strong survival instinct. The unique values of "duty, honor, valor, courage, loyalty, and commitment to comrades, unit, and nation"[13] that accompany the experience of the military promote a credo of resilience and self-sacrifice. These values are not typically shared values in contemporary U.S. society, and the individual changes that happen in the midst of intense military experiences can leave veterans feeling adrift when they return home.[14] The warrior ethos has become ingrained into their being, along with the beliefs of complete loyalty to team above self, and a constant readiness to complete the mission.[15]

One of the major tenets of military training is stoicism.[16] Stoicism is the automatic suppression of emotions so that hardship, pain, and grief as well as joy and pleasure do not interfere with the all-important military mission. Stoicism is important in military service so that overall strategic goals can be achieved through determined teamwork and adherence to hierarchical authority. This ingrained state of continual readiness and engagement as well as the value of putting the team above the individual can contribute to a deep-seated stoicism. While valuable on the battlefield, stoicism can inflict psychological, emotional, social, and spiritual suffering in civilian life and can be particularly challenging as the end-of-life approaches.

Stoicism typically interferes with symptom management and psychosocial healing. Stoicism can lead to underreporting physical suffering. Pain management for a veteran may require persistent clinical assessment and a fair amount of symptom normalizing to facilitate comfort. Because veterans have often overcome unimaginable hardships in their military experiences, stoicism may also interfere with their ability to reconcile their mortality and make effective planning choices for themselves and their loved ones. Stoicism can rob many veterans of the opportunity for a peaceful death by trapping them in isolation and distancing them from those they love, and it can represent a powerful barrier to knowing and honoring the wholeness of their humanity.

Many of the socioeconomic issues that veterans face can be traced back to issues with adjustment between the military and the civilian world. Veterans may have trouble giving up their warrior identity and reintegrating into the civilian community. Soldiers exposed to combat are more likely than non-combat veterans to be disabled and unemployed in their mid-20s and to remain so throughout their work life.[17] Unemployment and socioeconomic disadvantages in the combat veteran population have a negative impact on health and are often layered atop challenges like addictions, substance abuse, bipolar disorder, and depression.

Discrimination and injustice have occurred in the military. Women, Native Americans, Hispanics, and African-Americans may have experienced various indignities and traumas during their service. These incidents can come back for attention and review at the end-of-life.

Assessment and Initiation of Palliative Care for Veterans

Palliative care has always been patient-centered in its approach to interdisciplinary care. With the majority of veterans dying without support from community healthcare systems, veteran-centered care starts with an understanding and appreciation for the impact that military service has had in the veteran's life. Assessing veteran status and service may provide information about a specific illness, the coping mechanisms that he or she uses, and the VA resources that may be available to meet the unique needs of the veteran and family.

Caring for veterans starts with a basic assessment of the patient's military service history. This provides the foundation for further interdisciplinary collaboration and care coordination across the disease trajectory. One of the basic challenges that arises in caring for veterans is the confusing definition of "veteran." Not everyone who has served in the military considers himself or herself to be a veteran. Some believe that only those who have served during a time of war or conflict, or served outside of the United States, may refer to themselves as veterans.[18] In addition, not all veterans view their time spent in service as a positive one, and they may not value the service they provided. This ambiguity can provoke existential questions. Exploring the value of their service with a simple question about how the veteran perceives his or her time spent in the military may allow the veteran to uncover opportunities for reconciliation through the psychological, spiritual, and emotional work that commonly accompanies dying.

An efficient assessment being used by palliative care providers is the Military History Checklist, which can be found at the We Honor Veterans website.[8] Asking "tell me about your service" and then listening intently is one way to show honor and respect for the veteran's experience. EPEC for Veterans[19] recommends three basic assessment questions:

◆ Where and when did you serve?

◆ What did you do in the service?

◆ Tell me about your time in the service.

Many community hospices and palliative care programs collaborate with VA facilities to organize ceremonies that help make veterans more visible to the larger community. Called a Veteran Pinning Ceremony, this heartfelt recognition ritual typically includes a recitation of gratitude for military service and is often conducted during the veteran's first few days in hospice or palliative care.[8] A pin is then given to or placed on the veteran, often by another veteran volunteer, adding further meaning and value for the veteran and family. The pin can also serve as a reminder to the interdisciplinary team of the special status of the veteran as well as the special care needs he or she may have. More information about pinning ceremonies can be found at the We Honor Veterans website.[8]

Understanding the Department of Veterans Affairs Palliative and Hospice Services

APRNs who work with veterans and their loved ones need to understand the benefits and services offered to veterans. The Department of Veterans Affairs (VA) Services is the governmental agency that distributes entitlements, benefits, and resources. The VA operates the nation's largest integrated healthcare system, with more than 1,400 sites of care, including 151 medical centers, 826 outpatient and community clinics, more than 135 nursing homes (called community living centers), domiciliaries, readjustment counseling centers, and various other facilities.[20] The Veterans Health Administration (VHA) is one of three administrations in the VA—the other two are the Veterans Benefits Administration[21] and the National Cemetery Administration.[22] All three administrations offer veteran benefits and entitlements, which can be helpful at end-of-life. The Veterans Benefits Administration offers a variety of benefits and services to spouses, children, and parents of service members and veterans who are deceased or totally and permanently disabled by a service-connected disability. The National Cemetery Administration offers veterans a variety of burial and memorial benefits that are often a welcome support to surviving families.

The VHA provides healthcare to approximately 6 million veterans annually (approximately 25% of all living veterans).[23] This low rate may be associated with many variables, including difficulty of access, veteran identity, availability of healthcare insurance through private or public sources, confusion about eligibility for services, and perceptions of the VA (including a stigmatization of VA care as "charity" care).

VA healthcare facilities provide a broad spectrum of medical, surgical, rehabilitative, hospice, and palliative care. Individual champions and models of hospice care have been part of the VA since the earliest days of the American hospice movement in the 1970s. Housed under the Geriatrics and Extended Care line in the VA, hospice and palliative care for veterans is a covered service and on equal priority with any other medical care service as authorized in the VA Medical Benefits Package. The Veterans' Health Care Eligibility Reform Act of 1996 (Title 38 Code of Federal Regulations §17.36 and 17.38)[24] mandates that the VHA offer hospice and palliative care services to eligible enrolled veterans who need these services or purchase them from the community. The mission of the VA Hospice and Palliative Care Program is to honor veterans' preferences for care at the end-of-life. The challenge is to work together strategically within the infrastructure of the VA and hospice community to meet the needs of veterans across all settings and levels of care.

For most veterans, entry into the VA healthcare system begins with enrollment application. Veterans can now apply and submit their application for enrollment using VA Form 1010EZ[25] online. In the VA system, enrollment must occur for benefit eligibility to be determined. Enrolled veterans can receive healthcare at VA healthcare facilities anywhere in the country. Eligibility starts with a review of the veteran's eligibility status to determine the veteran's character of discharge from active military service and length of active military service, followed by whether the veteran qualifies for one of the eight enrollment priority groups. Eligibility for hospice in the VA is very similar to the eligibility requirements for the Medicare Hospice Benefit. In addition to the diagnosis of a life-limiting illness and a life expectancy of 6 months or less, veterans must be enrolled in the VA to access hospice in VA medical centers as well as VA-paid hospice services in the community. If the veteran elects Medicare or Medicaid Hospice payment, then VA enrollment may also be helpful to support community care.

Enrolled veterans are also eligible for VA palliative care, which provides symptom control and other supportive therapies without the presence of an imminently terminal condition or time-limited prognosis.[26] A distinct feature of the VA hospice and palliative care program is that, collectively, it represents a continuum of comfort-oriented and supportive services provided in the home, the community, and outpatient or inpatient settings for persons with advanced life-limiting disease. These services include advance care planning, symptom management, inpatient hospice and palliative care services, collaboration with community hospice providers, and access to home hospice care.

To be reimbursed by the VA for hospice care, community hospice providers must confirm a veteran's enrollment status in the VA and secure approval from the veteran's physician prior to starting services. If the veteran is not enrolled in the VA and can no longer remain in the community due to functional decline or symptom progression, community hospice providers can contact the nearest VA facility's palliative care coordinator to explore the possibility of an expedited VA enrollment. Veterans who want to remain in the community with hospice services provided at home are also eligible for expedited enrollment in the VA. The palliative APRN should encourage the veteran to find his or her discharge papers and separation documents, Form DD214, in advance. Veterans who cannot find their DD214 can request the record online (Table 56.1).

Hospice and palliative care services are provided to veterans enrolled in the VA in a variety of settings. In 2008, a National Directive was issued requiring each VA to designate a palliative care consult team consisting of, at a minimum, a physician or advanced practice provider, registered nurse, social worker, chaplain, mental health provider, and administrator[26] (Veterans Health Administration Directive 2008-006). The palliative care teams offer consultation throughout the medical center and assist with planning and guidance on managing pain and other symptoms, especially when they are complex or difficult to control. The palliative care team also recommends policies and procedures to hospital management, assumes a leadership role in promoting quality end-of-life care, facilitates communications with community hospices, and conducts educational programs for the VA and community staff.

The team may provide direct care and consulting services throughout VA hospitals and in outpatient settings, such as a cardiology, oncology, or pain clinic. Outpatient palliative care clinics are often managed by the consult team or in conjunction with one of the other clinics. These clinics help veterans manage their pain and other symptoms and coordinate their care with both inpatient and other outpatient services like home-based primary care. Some VA outpatient palliative care clinics are part of a VA hospital site or located adjacent to it; other outpatient clinics are freestanding and are located many miles from a VA hospital. Remotely located outpatient clinics are always affiliated with a parent VA hospital.

Most hospice and palliative care in VA facilities is provided in an inpatient setting in hospice and palliative care units, which are generally located in long-term care facilities called community living centers. Inpatient care is the preferred option for many

veterans who cannot return to their own homes. Beds are either designated in a particular wing of the community living center or scattered throughout the unit. Not all VA facilities choose to locate their hospice inpatient units in the community living centers, choosing instead to house hospice and/or palliative care patients in designated wings on acute care floors.

Home-based primary care is comprehensive primary care provided by an interdisciplinary team consisting of a physician or advanced practice provider, registered nurse, social worker, rehabilitation therapist, dietitian, and pharmacist that provides home-based care to veterans who are in advanced stages of chronic disabling disease. The interdisciplinary team visits the veteran in his or her home, often assesses for palliative care needs, and when appropriate will refer him or her to a community hospice. Unlike Medicare home-based services, eligibility for home-based primary care does not require the presence of a condition requiring skilled care, nor does it require strict homebound status.

Home-based primary care is generally the preferred way to provide home palliative care services to enrolled veterans. The home-based primary care team can consult palliative care professionals using a variety of technology. One method is e-consults, in which consults are addressed by reviewing the electronic record and/or talking directly with the veteran about symptoms. A second method is clinical video telehealth, in which the veteran is seen remotely at a rural community-based outpatient clinic via video technology). The third method is outpatient consultation, either with the home-based primary care team or at a clinic close to the veteran. If the veteran lives outside of the home-based primary care service area and it is too burdensome to travel to a VA clinic or hospital, the veteran can be referred to a community agency that provides palliative home care, if such an agency exists in that community and the VA hospital offers this option.

VA eligibility for hospice mirrors Medicare Hospice Benefit criteria and includes a diagnosis of a life-limiting illness with a life expectancy of 6 months or less as determined by a VA physician and treatment goals focusing on comfort rather than cure. The payer source can be the VA, Medicare, Medicaid, or another third-party insurer. If eligible for Medicare, the veteran may elect to have hospice services paid for under the Medicare Hospice Benefit, by the VA, or, if applicable, a third-party private insurer. Enrolled veterans who choose Medicare retain their eligibility for VA care and benefits. If the VA pays for hospice care, there should be a written agreement in place that spells out the relationship between the agency and the VA. Veterans should be informed that the VA has no authority to pay for any balances or co-payments that may be due *after* Medicare or any other non-VA source makes payment for hospice care.

The VA does not operate home hospice services or provide duplicative services available through referral or through the purchase of home hospice care from community agencies. The eligible veteran may prefer to receive hospice services in his or her own home or in a community nursing home close to where he or she lives, with costs covered by the insurers listed above. VAs may use community nursing home contracts to purchase inpatient hospice services. Only nursing homes with established hospice agency contracts can be used. The cost of contract nursing home care is covered under the VA hospice benefit (regardless of service-connected status) when an enrolled veteran is placed in the nursing home for purposes of hospice care.

Table 56.1 Sites for Veterans Administration Enrollment Forms

Request military discharge and separation documentation (DD214)[46]	http://www.archives.gov/st-louis/military-personnel/dd-214.html
Dependent or survivor benefits offered through the Veterans Benefits Administration[46]	http://www.va.gov/opa/persona/dependent_survivor.asp
Online benefit enrollment site for veterans, service members or family members[46]	https://www.ebenefits.va.gov/ebenefits-portal/ebenefits.portal

Sometimes an enrolled veteran who is receiving home-based primary care services will become eligible for hospice care and will elect to use his or her Medicare Hospice Benefit. In these cases, the home-based primary care team and the community hospice team will need to work closely together to coordinate and communicate goals and plans of care as well as visit schedules, medications, medical equipment, and the like, to avoid duplication of services. The palliative care coordinator, typically located at a VA medical center, can be very helpful in identifying whom to contact about care planning for veterans receiving community home hospice services.

A separate benefit for veterans who qualify through military retirement or for the spouse/families/survivors of a veteran killed in action is the government healthcare program TRICARE. The TRICARE hospice benefit is very similar to most insurance coverage for hospice care.[27] Veterans eligible for TRICARE can obtain care from military hospitals and clinics. Military hospitals and clinics are not the same as the VA system, nor is TRICARE administered by the VA.

Caring for the Veteran in the Community

Many veterans, as well as community healthcare providers, are unaware that end-of-life care is a VA benefit if they are enrolled in the VA. This is especially important for veterans who do not have third-party insurance or do not qualify for Medicare or Medicaid hospice support. Many factors can contribute to a veteran's awareness of VA benefits, including where he or she lives, his or her type and duration of military service, and whether he or she is enrolled in the VA.

Community partnerships with hospices have been an effective way to reach out to veterans in communities and share information about accessing VA benefits. One well-known collaborative is *We Honor Veterans,* a campaign established in 2010 by the National Hospice and Palliative Care Organization (NHPCO) and the VA's Hospice and Palliative Care program. *We Honor Veterans* seeks to minimize barriers to community veterans receiving hospice care. Its goals are fourfold: to promote "veteran-centric" educational activities, to increase organizational capacity to serve veterans, to support the development of strategic partnerships, and to increase access and improve quality. Hospices, state hospice organizations, community organizations and businesses interested in chronically ill veterans, and VA facilities have been invited to join efforts focused on recognizing the unique needs of America's veterans and their families.

The *We Honor Veterans* website provides many valuable and practical resources and best practices for community hospice professionals to meet the unique needs of dying veterans. The role of the palliative APRN is to coordinate care for the veteran who is enrolled in the VA through the palliative care coordinator at the local VA facility. Statewide or regional coalitions can facilitate ongoing relationships with VA hospitals and remove barriers to securing veteran benefits. Social workers can often be very helpful allies when trying to obtain financial benefits that can assist veterans.

Patients and veterans can search for reviews of community hospices on the *We Honor Veterans* website. To promote life closure and meaning, another community service of particular interest for veterans at the end-of-life is the *Honor Flight* program available throughout much of the United States. This program, which flies veterans to Washington DC to see their war memorials, is funded through generous private donations from pilots and community volunteers through the *Their Last Chance* program. Their Last Chance deals with veterans with terminal illness and helps them with life closure. Priority is given to WWII and Korean War veterans and terminally ill veterans from all wars. Applications can be downloaded from the *Honor Flight* website (honorflight.org).[28]

Addressing Common Veteran Symptoms

Veterans are at risk for emotional distress at the end-of-life, highlighting the possible need for augmented support services, such as palliative and hospice care for veterans and their families.[29] One large study of veterans in VA intensive care units found that 28% of patients have one or more preexisting mental illnesses, including depression (16%), PTSD (7%), anxiety other than PTSD (6%), bipolar disorder (3%), and psychosis (2%).[30]

Specifically, combat exposure can lead to a poorer health-related and psychosocial quality of life in later years. Increasing levels of combat exposure and lower rank have been shown to be associated with a poorer quality of life across all domains.[31] The onset of distressing combat-related memories, agitation, or PTSD-like symptoms in aging combat veterans has gained more recognition. In a study of late-life mortality among 1,448 WWII survivors, the highest hazard rates of mortality were found among military veterans and war survivors who had been seriously wounded. PTSD, suicidal thoughts, and depression were associated with a higher hazard rate.[32] Vietnam veterans have the highest incidence of PTSD.[19]

A study of four groups of WWII and Korean War veterans (those with no trauma, combat trauma only, noncombat trauma only, or both combat and noncombat trauma) revealed changes in general physical health, indexed across multiple organ systems. Men with exposure to both combat and noncombat trauma appeared especially susceptible to health decline, perhaps owing to a postwar "negative adaptive spiral" in which certain traumatized war veterans were vulnerable to additional life stressors. The authors speculated that PTSD could serve a mediating role between trauma and physical health.[33] Another study acknowledged specific late-life physical health outcomes associated with early life trauma and PTSD symptoms, such as the large-scale epidemiological study of cardiovascular diseases in WWII ex-POWs.[34]

Variables like age, greater combat exposure, and premilitary and postmilitary traumas are associated with increased PTSD symptomatology. The likelihood of developing PTSD depends on many factors, including the following:[35]

◆ How intense the trauma was and how long it lasted

◆ If someone close was lost or hurt

◆ Proximity to the event

◆ Strength of the reaction to the event

◆ How much the veteran felt in control of the event

◆ How much help and support the veteran received after the event

◆ History of previous trauma

PTSD symptoms are listed in Box 56.1. Consequences of PTSD can include depression, suicide, anxiety, addiction, relationship problems, employment issues, and existential suffering (guilt

---

Box 56.1 Common Symptoms of PTSD in Veterans

- Difficulty sleeping
- Irritability or outbursts of anger or other negative thoughts and changes in mood
- Intrusive reminders of the trauma
- Difficulty concentrating
- Hypervigilance (on constant "red alert")
- Feeling on edge, jumpy, and easily startled
- Recurring dreams and nightmares

From reference 44.

---

and regret). Several brief screening tools for PTSD have been developed, and Box 56.2 shows the Primary Care PTSD Screen (PC-PTSD) that is used by the VA.[36] Any veteran with a positive screen should be referred to a mental health provider.

Patients at the end of their lives who experience PTSD may also suffer more emotional distress, a lower quality of life, and a poorer medical prognosis than those without PTSD. Research indicates that prior trauma history predicts PTSD in serious medical illness.[37,38] One study of 524 veterans being cared for in VA facilities at the end-of-life found that 17% of the patients reported PTSD-related symptoms.[39]

Key symptom clusters for the APRN to be mindful of at end-of-life include:[19]

1. Reliving the event: Flashbacks or recurring dreams and nightmares about the trauma can be stirred up by common everyday triggers. For example, seeing a news report of sexual trauma can bring back memories of military sexual assault for a woman who was raped, or weather conditions like heavy rainfall may bring back memories of monsoons in Vietnam.

2. Numbing and avoiding the situation that reminded the veteran of the traumatic event: This may involve losing interest in, and

---

Box 56.2 VA PC-PTSD Screening Tool

In your life, have you ever had any experience that was so frightening, horrible, or upsetting that in the past month you

1. have had nightmares about it or thought about it when you did not want to?

2. tried hard not to think about it or went out of your way to avoid situations that reminded you of it?

3. were constantly on guard, watchful, or easily startled?

4. felt numb or detached from others, activities, or your surroundings?

Current research suggests that the results of the PC-PTSD should be considered "positive" if a patient answers "yes" to any three items.

From reference 36.

---

refusing to participate in, activities that were previously enjoyable. If this symptom has been present throughout the post-military life of the veteran, he or she is likely to have strained relationships with family and friends, resulting in limited social support. The veteran typically avoids situations and discussions that remind him or her of the traumatic event, or he or she may not be able to recall the event at all—making clinical assessment difficult.

3. Hyperarousal: This persistent state of increased awareness can result in feelings described as being "keyed up," "jittery," or "on edge." Hyperarousal may be exhibited in behaviors like sudden irritability or anger, difficulty sleeping or concentrating, fearing for one's safety, and feeling continually on one's guard. An invasive medical procedure, such as placement of a nasogastric tube, could trigger a hyperarousal response.

According to Feldman, the threat to life that coexists with a terminal illness may mimic the original trauma and exacerbate PTSD.[40] When immediate traumatic events trigger PTSD for a veteran, Grassman suggests the palliative APRN create an emotionally safe space, which can include:[19]

- **Be willing to hear their story.** Do the initial work to prepare a compassionate place within yourself by addressing your individual concerns and prejudices before working with veterans. This will help to create a safe and welcoming space to hear the veteran's story. Recognize that you may have some feelings about what you are hearing, and be ready to honor your individual response without interfering with the veteran's story. Be aware that veterans may fire warning shots as a "test" to see if you are able and willing to hear their story without prejudice and judgment.

- **Validate their experience.** Ask the veteran about his or her personal experience—or to tell you more about the situation. Consider using the phrase, "Tell me what it was like." If the veteran opens up, be present. Try not to rush the story. This could be the first time the veteran has been able to express his or her feelings about the experience.

- **Normalize the experience and suffering.** Acknowledge, without judgment, the strong emotions that lie behind the experience. Typically these are expressed as fear, shame, anxiety, anger, sadness, and disappointment. Address the emerging emotions through the lens of acceptance. Believing that trauma is an isolated experience that only he or she experiences accentuates feelings of alienation and loneliness for the veteran. Acknowledge that military PTSD experiences are common among veterans.

- **Resist the urge to confuse stoicism with courage.** Look for opportunities to gently soften prideful ways that reinforce military stoicism in civilian situations. Helpful phrases include, "Anyone can hide behind a stoic wall of silence. It takes courage to reach out and connect with others, or say 'I'm wrong' or 'I'm sorry'."

- **Resist the urge to "fix."** Nurses often try to "fix" problems, and it may be hard to bear witness to panic or brokenness. Remember that the story is being told to you as a life review, not because it needs fixing. Try thinking of it as a larger mystery that holds important information for the veteran. Phrases such as, "you were only obeying orders" or "that happened such a long time ago, surely you are forgiven" minimize the veteran's experience.

◆ **Treat PTSD as a war injury**. PTSD, which is an internal conflict, may be a wound that can't be seen. This invisibility can contribute to the agitation and fear about "letting it out" and can lead to a lifetime of "stuffing" the emotions and experience.

Life-review therapy is a method of reviewing significant life events with a person and proceeds in a semistructured manner. The simplicity of life-review therapy lends itself very well to supportive work with veterans. The therapist or healthcare provider should try to reflect to the patient the new story that is emerging as told by the veteran. This helps the veteran see the process as transformative. Forgiveness is part of the spiritual work at the end-of-life, and using a life-review process as a tool to aid this work can be cathartic and instrumental to achieving peace. Including the family in the process can help them learn more about their loved one and provide new insights into the veteran's life experiences.

Maercker[41] addresses the therapeutic effect of life-review technique for elderly patients with PTSD and quantitatively documents reductions in both intrusion and avoidance symptoms in four case reports. The technique may be a more practical approach than traditional PTSD therapies for helping veterans with limited life expectancies and energy levels.[42]

When veterans exhibit PTSD at the end-of-life, treatment options are determined by the symptoms and the prognosis. Rapid pharmacologic assistance may be indicated when life expectancy is short. In general, it is important to allow the veteran as much control of the development of the care plan as possible.

For patients with at least 1 month of life expectancy, antidepressants can be very effective in managing symptoms. Two major classes of drugs effective in palliating PTSD for terminally ill patients are selective serotonin reuptake inhibitors (SSRI) and tricyclic antidepressants (TCAs). Thought to alleviate the avoidance and numbing symptoms of PTSD, SSRIs are effective in relieving anxiety and panic symptoms, whereas TCAs are thought to alleviate intrusive symptoms as well as anxious and depressed affect. Imipramine and desipramine are the generally preferred TCAs because of their lesser anticholinergic effects.[40(p 215)] Typical dosage ranges for SSRIs in the treatment of PTSD are as follows:[43]

◆ Sertraline (Zoloft) 50 to 200 mg daily

◆ Paroxetine (Paxil) 20 to 60 mg daily

◆ Fluoxetine (Prozac) 20 to 60 mg daily

When the veteran is expected to live only days to weeks, the focus of care should be on rapid alleviation of distress and enhancement of comfort using medications with a rapid onset of action. For relief of PTSD symptoms like agitation, hyperarousal, and hostility, short-acting benzodiazepines or neuroleptics can be used.[40(p 216)]

With regard to medications, each VA has its own pharmacy formulary, but with proper documentation, the pharmacy often can get approval for nonformulary medications. The palliative APRN should work with a particular VA if there are problems related to a covered PTSD episode and medications.

Financial Issues

PTSD and mental health problems are now recognized as a source of disability.[44] Since PTSD, traumatic brain injury, and other conditions may not have been fully characterized or appreciated by either the veteran or healthcare providers, some veterans may be able to apply for reevaluation of their healthcare problems that might be related to their time of service. However, the process of evaluation may take months. Veterans with severe illness and a short life expectancy may not survive long enough to complete the process. Veterans with longer life expectancies who are enrolled in palliative care programs may wish to pursue these claims.

Finally, managing veterans with symptoms at end-of-life must take into consideration the prevalence of substance use disorders in this population.[45,46] Veterans at end-of-life who have a history of substance use disorder should still be given opioids and/or benzodiazepines to address pain and anxiety. Individuals with addiction often have a lower tolerance for physical pain. Veterans should not be denied appropriate pain relief because of a past history of substance abuse. It is, however, important to work closely with the veteran to develop mutually appropriate treatment plans to minimize the risk of abuse and diversion.

Case Study

Mr. Carl Smith was an 86-year-old Korean War veteran. He had been recently discharged from the hospital for an episode of CHF, his second hospital admission in 8 months for CHF management. At a palliative care follow-up outpatient visit with the APRN, his wife expressed concern about his increasing nightmares. She stated that he would become more restless through the night, and two nights earlier, he woke up very agitated, saying "get out of the way" over and over. She conveyed her concern about both his and her safety while he was dreaming in such an excitable state.

The palliative APRN addressed this concern by inviting Mr. Smith to share recollections about his time in the Korean War. He stated he was a combat engineer in the Army and his job was planting land mines. She explained that it is not uncommon for veterans to have war experiences re-emerge as they age and approach the end of their life, and she encouraged him to talk further about his experiences. Mr. Smith pointed to the large scar across his left leg and asked the palliative APRN if she know how he sustained the injury. The APRN recalled that it was from his time in Korea and was related to an explosion. She also recognized the importance of respectful silence as a means of creating safe space.

After several seconds passed, Mr. Smith revealed that the scar was all he got; his buddies lost their lives. He said he found himself thinking about this when he woke up and before he tried to sleep at night. Mr. Smith reported that he found himself remembering a particularly awful day in Korea. He was leading a team through Daegu on the Nakdong River where they were burying land mines. Without warning, one of the mines they were attempting to bury went off, immediately killing two of his buddies and mangling the arm of a third team member. Mr. Smith remembers that his life was spared only because he was about 500 feet away, taking care of additional supplies.

The palliative APRN sat quietly, nodding, and expressed wonder at the story. She thanked Mr. Smith for trusting her with this information. She said that veterans sometimes can find talking with a chaplain very helpful. Mr. and Mrs. Smith agreed to think about it. The palliative APRN knew that the palliative care chaplain also served in the Army, and offered to connect with the local VA, since talking with someone who had served in the military might be more comfortable for Mr. Smith. She reviewed Mr. Smith's medications and considered adding an SSRI, which might address his insomnia, disturbing nightmares, and anxiety. She also documented a plan to talk with the VA about counseling through the Vet Centers to see if there could be some home phone assistance available for both Mr. and Mrs. Smith.

Conclusion

Veterans have many unique needs. The palliative APRN needs to understand the issues surrounding the veteran, the military culture that formed the group he or she served with, and potential health sequelae, such as PTSD. The care process begins by identifying the veteran's history of military service. Then the APRN should ascertain whether the veteran is eligible for, or wants to seek, services from the VA. Sensitivity and responsiveness to the unique experiences of veterans allow palliative APRNs to improve care and reduce suffering. Competent, coordinated, compassionate, and comprehensive care is perhaps the best expression of gratitude that healthcare providers can offer veterans at the end-of-life.

Disclaimer

The views expressed in this chapter do not necessarily express the views of the Department of Veterans Affairs or the United States government.

References

1. U.S. Census Bureau, Statistical Abstract of the United States. Table 521. Veterans living by period of service, age, and sex: 2010. Available at https://www.census.gov/compendia/statab/2012/tables/12s0520.pdf Updated 2012. Accessed July 31, 2014.
2. Hallenbeck J. The military mindset. In: Doka KJ, Tucci AS, eds. *Improving Care for Veterans Facing Illness and Death.* Washington, DC: Hospice Foundation of America; 2013:27.
3. National Center for Veteran Analysis and Statistics. Available at http://www.va.gov/vetdata/veteran_population.asp Accessed July 31, 2014.
4. Steinhauser KE, Christakis NA, Clipp AC, McNeilly M, McIntyre L, Tulsky JA. Factors considered important at the end-of-life by patients, family, physicians, and other care providers. *JAMA.* 2000; 284(19): 2476–82.
5. Grassman DL. Forgiveness: A reckoning process that facilitates peace. In: Doka KJ, Tucci AS, eds. *Improving Care for Veterans Facing Illness and Death.* Washington, DC: Hospice Foundation of America; 2013:55–86.
6. U.S. Department of Veteran Affairs. Available at http://www.publichealth.va.gov/exposures/cold-injuries/index.asp Accessed September 14, 2014.
7. Laramie JA. Post-traumatic stress disorder at the end-of-life. *Home Healthcare Nurse.* 2007; 25(4): 293–8.
8. We Honor Veterans. Vietnam War Health Risks. Available at www.wehonorveterans.org. Accessed October 10, 2014.
9. U.S. Department of Veterans Affairs. Office of Public Health and Environmental Hazards. Available at http://www.publichealth.va.gov/index.asp. Updated July 14, 2014. Accessed July 31, 2014.
10. End-of-Life Nursing Education Consortium (ELNEC)—For Veterans 2012. Module 3 Symptom Management. Published in partnership between the American Association of Colleges of Nursing, Washington, DC and City of Hope, Duarte, CA, p. 33.
11. Harada ND, Damron-Rodriguez J, Villa VM, et al. Veteran identity and race/ethnicity: influences on VA outpatient care utilization. *Med Care.* 2002; 40(1 suppl): I117–I128.
12. Smith RT, True G. Warring identities: identity conflict and the mental distress of American veterans of the wars in Iraq and Afghanistan. *Society and Mental Health.* 2014; 4(2): 147–61.
13. Demers A. When veterans return: the role of community in reintegration. *J Loss Trauma.* 2011; 16(2): 160–79.
14. Johnson BS, Boudiab LD, Freundle M, Anthony M, Gmerek GB, Carter J. Enhancing veteran-centered care: A guide for nurses in non-VA settings. *Am J Nurs.* 2013; 113(7): 24–39.
15. Brown WB, Stanulis R, Theis B, Farnsworth J, Daniels D. The perfect storm: veterans, culture and the criminal justice system. *Justice Policy Journal.* 2013; 10 (2): 1–44. Available at http://www.cjcj.org/uploads/cjcj/documents/brown_et_al_fall_2013.pdf. Accessed October 10, 2014.
16. Grassman DL. *Peace At Last: Stories of Hope and Healing for Veterans and Their Families.* St. Petersburg, FL: Vandamere Press; 2009:32–54.
17. MacLean A. The things they carry: combat, disability and unemployment among US men. *Am Sociol Rev.* 2010; 75(4): 563–85.
18. Jones DH. Caring for seriously ill veterans in the community: communication, collaboration, and coordination. In: Doka KJ, Tucci AS, eds. *Improving Care for Veterans Facing Illness and Death.* Washington, DC: Hospice Foundation of America; 2013:133–54.
19. Emanuel LL, Hauser JM, Bailey FA, Ferris FD, von Gunten CF, Von Roenn J, eds. EPEC for Veterans: education in palliative and end-of-life care for veterans. 2011; 3–4. Available at http://www.wehonorveterans.org/epec-veterans-curriculum. Accessed July 31, 2014.
20. U.S. Department of Veterans Affairs FY 2014-2020 Strategic Plan. Available at http://www.va.gov/op3/docs/StrategicPlanning/VA2014-2020strategicPlan.pdf. Accessed July 31, 2014.
21. U.S. Department of Veterans Affairs. I am a Dependent or Survivor. Available at http://www.va.gov/opa/persona/dependent_survivor.asp Updated March 26, 2014. Accessed November 5, 2014.
22. U.S. Department of Veterans Affairs, National Cemetery Administration. Available at http://www.cem.va.gov/. Updated October 24, 2014, Accessed November 5, 2015.
23. U.S. Department of Veterans Affairs, Veterans Health Administration Office of Policy and Planning as of July 18, 2014. Available at http://www.va.gov/vetdata/expenditures.asp. Accessed July 31, 2014.
24. U.S. Department of Veterans Affairs, VHA Handbook 1601A.03. Available at http://www.va.gov/vhapublications/ViewPublication.asp?pub_ID=2917. Accessed November 5, 2014.
25. Veterans Health Administration, Instructions for Completing Enrollment Application for Health Benefits. Available at http://www.va.gov/vaforms/medical/pdf/vha-1010EZ-fill.pdf. Accessed November 5, 2014.
26. Veterans Health Administration Directive 2008-066. Palliative Care Consult Teams. Available at http://www.va.gov/vhapublications/ViewPublication.asp?pub_ID=1784. Accessed July 31, 2014.
27. Erickson-Hurt C. Care of veterans. In: Dahlin CM, Lynch MT, eds. *Core Curriculum for the Advanced Practice Hospice and Palliative Registered Nurse.* 2nd ed. Pittsburgh, PA: Hospice and Palliative Nurses Association, 2013:545–66.
28. Honor Flight Network. Available at www.honorflight.org. Accessed November 5, 2014.
29. Holland JM, Currier JM, Kirkendall A, Keene JR, Luna N. Sadness, anxiety, and experiences with emotional support among veteran and nonveteran patients and their families at the end of life. *J Palliat Med.* 2014; 17(6): 708–11.
30. Abrams TE, Vaughan-Sarrazin M, Rosenthal GE. Preexisting comorbid psychiatric conditions and mortality in nonsurgical intensive care patients. *Am J Crit Care.* 2010; 19(3): 241–9.
31. Ikin JF, Sim MR, McKenzie DP, et al. Life satisfaction and quality in Korean War veterans five decades after the war. *J Epidemiol Commun H.* 2009; 63(5): 359–65.
32. Bramsen I, Deeg DJH, Van der Ploeg E, Fransman S. Wartime stressors and mental health symptoms as predictors of late-life mortality in World War II survivors. *J Affect Disorders.* 2007; 103(1–3): 121–9.

33. Schnurr PP, Spiro A, Aldwin CM, Stukel TA. Physical symptom trajectories following trauma exposure: longitudinal findings from the Normative Aging Study. *J Nerv Ment Dis.* 1998; 186(9): 522–8.

34. Kang HK, Bullman TA, Taylor JW. Risk of selected cardiovascular diseases and posttraumatic stress disorder among former World War II prisoners of war. *Ann Epidemiol.* 2006; 16(5): 381–6.

35. Clancy CP, Graybeal A, Tompson WP, et al. Lifetime trauma exposure in veterans with military-related posttraumatic stress disorder: association with current symptomatology. *J Clin Psychiatry.* 2006; 67(9): 1346–53.

36. Prins A, Ouimette P, Kimerling R, et al. The primary care PTSD screen (PC-PTSD): Corrigendum. *Primary Care Psychiatry.* 2004; 9: 9–14. Available at http://www.ptsd.va.gov/PTSD/professional/articles/article-pdf/id26676.pdf. Accessed July 31, 2014.

37. Green, BL, Krupnick, JL, Rowland JH, et al. Trauma history as a predictor of psychologic symptoms in women with breast cancer. *J Clin Oncol.* 2000; 18(5): 1084–93.

38. Ruzich MJ, Chee Leong Looi J, Robertson MD. Delayed onset of posttraumatic stress disorder among male combat veterans: a case series. *Am J Geriat Psychiat.* 2005; 13(5): 424–7.

39. Alici Y, Smith D, Lu HL, et al. Families' perceptions of veterans' distress due to post-traumatic stress disorder-related symptoms at the end-of-life. *J Pain Symptom Manage.* 2010; 39(3): 507–14.

40. Feldman DB, Periyakoil VS. Posttraumatic stress disorder at the end-of-life. *J Palliat Med.* 2006; 9(4): 213–8.

41. Maercker A. Life-review technique in the treatment of PTSD in elderly patients: rationale and three single case studies. *J Clin Geropsychology.* 2002; 8(3): 239–49.

42. Weller R. Caring for seriously ill veterans in the community: communication, collaboration, and coordination. In: Doka KJ, Tucci AS, eds. *Improving Care for Veterans Facing Illness and Death.* Washington, DC: Hospice Foundation of America; 2013:71–83.

43. Jeffreys M. Clinician's Guide to Medications for PTSD. PTSD: National Center for PTSD. Available at http://www.ptsd.va.gov/professional/treatment/overview/clinicians-guide-to-medications-for-ptsd.asp. Last updated July 28, 2014. Accessed October 14, 2014.

44. U.S. Department of Veterans Affairs. PTSD: National Centers for PTSD. Available at http://www.ptsd.va.gov/public/get_help_with_va.asp. Updated February 14, 2014. Accessed November 5, 2014.

45. Wagner TH, Harris KM, Federman B, Dai L, Luna Y, Humphreys K. Prevalence of substance use disorders among veterans and comparable nonveterans from the National Survey on Drug Use and Health. *Psychol Services.* 2007; 4(3): 149–57.

46. Tsai J, Kasprow WJ, Rosenheck RA. Alcohol and drug use disorders among homeless veterans: prevalence and association with supported housing outcomes. *Addict Behav.* 2014; 39(2): 455–60.

PART EIGHT

THE PEDIATRIC PALLIATIVE ADVANCED PRACTICE REGISTERED NURSE

CHAPTER 57

The Role of the Pediatric Palliative Advanced Practice Registered Nurse

Cheryl Ann Thaxton and Leiann Neubauer

Key Points

♦ The pediatric palliative advanced practice registered nurse (APRN) incorporates an in-depth knowledge of pharmacologic and nonpharmacologic therapies, communication techniques, familiarity with ethical and cultural issues, and ongoing access to bereavement resources for patients and their family members.

♦ Delivery of patient- and family-centered care involves collaboration across several disciplines; the APRN is often the leader of interdisciplinary communication in pediatric palliative care.

♦ Advocacy for the pediatric palliative care population may require the APRN to take on innovative roles, such as a clinical expert, an educator, an entrepreneur, a marketer, and a transformational leader.

Case Study

James* was diagnosed with a low-grade, "benign" brain tumor when he was 11 months old. At that time, the family was informed by the physicians that this type of brain tumor was "the best kind to have." For the next 10 years, James did not have major health issues. He was eventually treated with a chemotherapy regimen, an experimental treatment for 4 years, and then he underwent a craniotomy that left him temporarily without short-term memory. Through it all, James just kept marching on with a smile like it was nothing, defying all odds (Fig. 57.1). Although as his mother, I knew that James could die from this tumor (because that's what the oncology team had told us), in my heart I didn't believe it.

After the craniotomy, the tumor changed. This benign tumor, which had previously grown so slowly that it took 6 months to show any change, now grew 30% in 4 months. After four consecutive brain surgeries working toward a management plan for hydrocephalus over the course of one summer, James was left in a coma with autonomic storming, which appeared as intermittent periods of posturing, dystonia, hypertension, diaphoresis, hyperthermia, and tachypnea (one of the most excruciating things I have ever seen). Being a very independent person, and having dealt with James' illness for 11 years by the time he reached this point, I was not ready to admit that we needed palliative care or hospice care . . . it didn't matter what it was called, I wasn't ready. Of course, I didn't know anything about this area because I didn't think I'd ever need it.

The palliative nurse practitioner and the palliative care team were consulted by the pediatric intensive care staff. When I was introduced to the palliative nurse practitioner, I recall thinking, "Oh, no, you are not needed!" The palliative nurse practitioner may have known what I was thinking; perhaps the team was used to working with families who weren't ready to face the end of life for their loved one. Nonetheless, this dear nurse practitioner came back every day. The palliative nurse practitioner taught me over the next few weeks what palliative care really meant, discussing the plan for managing my son's pain and distressing symptoms in detail. The nurse practitioner wasn't there to help my son die; instead, it was clear that the palliative nurse practitioner was there to help my son live with the best care and the most dignity possible for the time he had left. I was soon looking forward to visits from the team every day rather than hoping they wouldn't show up. The palliative nurse practitioner worked with us over the next few days and developed a plan to transition James to home hospice, and he died peacefully at home (Fig. 57.2).

Since my son's death, I have become a registered nurse and I have had the opportunity to work with a few families who had loved ones nearing the end of life. My greatest joy now is to pass on what this palliative nurse practitioner taught me, what palliative care really is—to let patients and families know that we aren't there to focus on the impending death, but to focus on the remaining life.

*This case study was written by the patient's mother, Ms. Leiann Neubauer, RN, and used with permission of the family.

Figure 57.1 James Printed with permission of his family.

Introduction

Pediatric palliative care (PPC) is a rapidly growing subspecialty, and many tertiary care centers are developing palliative care programs for infants and children. Major advancements have taken place in the role of the pediatric palliative APRN. More attention is being focused on using PPC measures during the early stages for patients receiving aggressive therapies for illnesses like cancer. Based on a study evaluating providers' experiences with neonatal and pediatric palliative care, participants felt that in the acute care environment it is difficult to know when to make the transition from curative to palliative care.[1] Current trends in transitioning from pediatric to adult chronic illnesses have called for advanced practice nursing skills that reflect the differing needs of pediatric patients. Pediatric trajectories of illness, clinical models of care delivery, funding mechanisms, research paradigms, educational initiatives, communication strategies, ethical concerns, staffing ratios and management, and effective pain/symptom management interventions are all significantly different than those in adult patients.[2]

Care provided to patients by the pediatric palliative APRN often takes place within a hospital or in an outpatient, home, or hospice setting. APRNs can serve as front-line nurses to coordinate care and implement strategies to provide services to patients as well as other nurses.[3] APRNs can assist staff nurses with complex patient care procedures, provide hands-on education at the bedside, and support staff in managing challenging situations.[3,4] The APRN's role in PPC is multifaceted and involves "wearing many hats." The APRN contributes to the dynamic organizational infrastructure of PPC programs.

Figure 57.2 James and family. Each year on the anniversary of James' birthday, the family members donate toys and gifts to a home for abused children in honor of his memory and his strong desire to help others in need. Printed with permission of his family.

This chapter's case study offers the story of a mother whose son received palliative care first within the hospital setting and then in home hospice. She had initial fears about engaging the palliative care team and the palliative APRN in the care of the patient, but she became more knowledgeable about the goals of palliative care as she worked with the APRN.

PPC programs across the United States continue to expand. A survey of 226 hospitals identified by the National Association of Children's Hospitals and Related Institutions reported that, of the 162 hospitals that provided data, 69% reported having a PPC program.[5] The overall growth rate of PPC programs across the United States has led to the recognition of this subspecialty by several national organizations. The American Academy of Pediatrics position statement titled Palliative Care for Children calls for the development of clinical policies and minimum standards that promote the welfare of infants and children living with life-threatening or terminal conditions and their families, with the goal of providing equitable and effective support for curative, life-prolonging, and palliative care.[6,7] In January 2013, the AAP endorsed the National Consensus Project *Clinical Practice Guidelines for Quality Palliative Care*.[8,9] This reinforcement of quality initiatives supports best practices in palliative care and serves as the foundation for promoting evidence-based principles. The pediatric palliative APRN should remain aware of these guidelines and ensure that the team is empowered to implement them throughout the evolution of the program.

Role Description and Qualifications

Pediatric palliative APRNs come from a variety of educational and training backgrounds. APRNs employed as providers in PPC programs may have training as family nurse practitioners, family or pediatric clinical nurse specialists, neonatal nurse practitioners, or pediatric nurse practitioners. Programs across the United States offer palliative care nursing fellowships; many of these offer adult palliative care clinical rotations and may not have extensive access to pediatric palliative care patients. Fellowship training can provide exposure to several aspects of palliative care, as well as simulated case reviews.[10]

Pediatric oncology RNs and APRNs often work with children facing chronic and life-threatening illnesses; many of these nurses pursue additional advanced palliative care training. APRNs with clinical backgrounds in oncology, cardiology, pulmonology, neurology, genetics, neonatology, and neuromuscular disorders may encounter patients in need of pain and distressing symptom management. In addition, opportunities exist for APRNs to serve as pioneers for the development of PPC programs within institutions that do not have formal PPC teams or sufficient team support. Funding for PPC programs has been an ongoing issue throughout the healthcare transformation. Many PPC programs rely on hospital funding.[5] In addition, the philanthropic support of PPC initiatives has led to the growth and expansion of programs. Lack of training in PPC has been a barrier to the development of formal programs in some institutions[1]; however, many graduate nurse programs have incorporated principles of palliative care into their curriculum (Fig. 57.3).

Clinical Expert

In collaboration with the PPC attending physicians, fellows, and/or residents, the pediatric palliative APRN should regularly round on patients to assess, diagnose, plan treatment, set priorities and

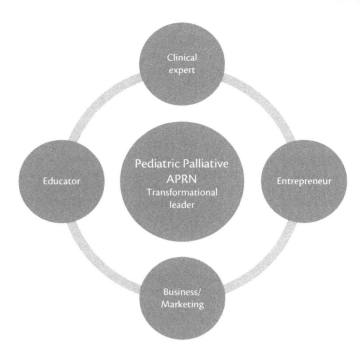

Figure 57.3 Roles of the pediatric palliative APRN in Pediatric palliative care

realistic outcomes, and evaluate the effectiveness and cost efficiency of patient care. The APRN works collaboratively to assess patients and identify quality-of-life issues that may hinder the clinical progression toward a meaningful recovery for pediatric patients, with a consistent focus on addressing the patient's symptom burden.

While serving as a liaison for the patient, family, and staff, the pediatric palliative APRN provides and coordinates clinical care for PPC patients through established protocols. For example, protocols that pertain to the safe use of patient-controlled analgesia can be developed and implemented by the APRN.[11] General pain management policies that are not specific to pediatrics can be reviewed by the pediatric palliative APRN and further developed to support the unique needs of children receiving end-of-life care. As a clinical expert in chronic pain, the pediatric palliative APRN works collaboratively to develop plans that promote pain relief for children with illnesses like juvenile rheumatoid arthritis, sickle cell disease, Crohn's disease, and many other chronic debilitating infirmities. Children with chronic pain are best cared for with interdisciplinary assessment and management, which require a combination of medicine, psychology, and rehabilitation services for all pediatric patients referred for assessment and management of chronic pain.[12,13]

The pediatric palliative APRN should collaborate with APRN colleagues, nurses, case managers, chaplains, child life specialists, clinical social workers, and other healthcare providers to formulate treatment plans and monitor patient progress. Additional plans for improving and promoting the quality-of-life goals for pediatric patients may involve organizing interdisciplinary team meetings that include respiratory therapists, physical and occupational therapists, pharmacists, nutritionists, home health providers, and hospice teams. These team meetings help to outline clear pathways to formulate plans that are based on the patient's and family's preferences. These gatherings can also help to decrease the chance of implementing treatments that are not aligned with these goals and preferences. The APRN is often the lead facilitator of interdisciplinary communication. Care coordination by the APRN involves the ability to implement palliative care procedures specific to the work environment (e.g., conduct family care conference, manage pain and distressing symptoms, provide guidance with advance care planning) while demonstrating competency within the scope of practice and credentialing protocols.

The pediatric palliative APRN should have a clear job description. Regular performance reviews for the APRN can help to evaluate clinical practice patterns, so as to provide the best medical care and to increase effectiveness and efficiency. When using prescriptive privileges for the identified patient population, the APRN must serve as a role model of competence. Pediatric palliative APRN documentation in the medical record should incorporate all relevant data, such as the results of diagnostic tests, laboratory results, the patient's condition and response to therapies and interventions, and any necessary communications with the supervising physician. The documentation should include recommendations for a specific palliative care plan to alleviate suffering and promote the physical, emotional, psychological, and spiritual comfort of the patient and family.

Perhaps the greatest work that the pediatric palliative APRN will encounter is when alleviating suffering in children with pain at the end-of-life; this requires a thorough investigation and intensive exploration of measures used in the past to manage the patient's pain. A retrospective cross-sectional survey conducted at two tertiary care U.S. pediatric institutions revealed that unrelieved pain was associated with parents' past considerations of hastening death in children with cancer.[14] This study surveyed a total of 141 parents of children who died of cancer (response rate 64%). Of the 141 parents, 19 reported that they would have considered hastening their child's death had the child been in uncontrollable pain.

This research supports the significance of the pediatric palliative APRN's role as a clinical expert in managing pediatric pain. The APRN partners with other members of the team to address the pain plan, making referrals when necessary. Thorough knowledge of both pharmacologic and nonpharmacologic measures specific to the pediatric patient population allows the APRN to provide guidance that helps with transition models for patients with chronic illness. For example, the pediatric palliative APRN works with the child life specialist to facilitate methods like pet therapy or other services available within the institution. PPC programs should include music therapy, although recruiting licensed music therapists may be challenging.[15] Finally, the pediatric palliative APRN promotes continuity by providing daily "handoff" of patient care to appropriate physicians, APRNs, residents, and/or interns at the end of the shift while ensuring that proper introductions to the patient and family have taken place before departing.

Educator

The pediatric palliative APRN can assess the educational needs of the patient-care staff and provides one-on-one as well as formal education as needed. Teaching involves serving as a role model of professionalism, while maintaining proper boundaries, and remaining mindful of reactions to challenging clinical situations. Pediatric palliative APRNs work to assess the educational needs of patients and families as well, providing culturally sensitive educational interventions as indicated. It is important to use nontechnical language when educating patients and families. All education must be documented in the patient's medical record. Although

there has been continued growth of PPC programs, there is still limited access to preceptors in the clinical setting; thus, being a resource for new pediatric palliative APRNs is vital.

For APRNs seeking to expand their knowledge base in PPC, there are several evidence-based curriculums for understanding the needs of palliative care patients. An End-of-Life Nursing Education Consortium (ELNEC) curriculum was developed to address the unique needs of APRNs who are starting a palliative care program, leading a hospice/palliative care team, joining and/or participating in a hospice/palliative care team, or incorporating palliative care in their role as an APRN. Participants receive advanced education in pain and symptom assessment/management and communication. Additional training in palliative care-related finances, budgets, quality improvement, education, and leadership is also provided. Participants can choose one of two tracks—adult- or pediatric-focused care.

Another curriculum, Education in Palliative and End of Life Care (EPEC) Pediatrics is a comprehensive adaptation of the EPEC curriculum designed to address the needs of children, their families, and pediatric oncology providers and other pediatric clinicians. It was developed by, and continues to receive input from, experts representing several pediatric disciplines as well as parent advocate advisors. It consists of 23 core and two elective topics in pain and symptom management in palliative care. These topics are taught as a combination of 20 distance-learning modules and six in-person conference sessions. This in-person conference is offered annually.[16] Keeping up with current research in clinical practice can help the pediatric palliative APRN with developing and implementing standards of care. Taking part in a journal club offers the APRN the chance to review literature that reflects developments in PPC.

Analysis of patient care through ongoing case reviews with the interdisciplinary team helps the pediatric palliative APRN to participate in measuring and documenting outcomes. This includes participation in interdisciplinary quality improvement activities, such as chart reviews. Tracking operational data about patients seen by the consultation service (e.g., diagnosis, referring service, disposition) is necessary to assess the effectiveness of program outreach, marketing and education efforts in reaching patients in need, and planning for program staffing to accommodate growth in demand for services. Both program directors and hospital administrators can use these data to gauge the program's impact on the quality of care provided and the use of healthcare services.[17]

As an educator, the pediatric palliative APRN serves as an expert and provides information to other healthcare providers, patients and families, and the community at large on palliative care measures and end-of-life care. This effort should include developing, implementing, and evaluating standards of care for pain and symptom management along with practice guidelines, policies, and procedures within this area of specialization. If there are no clear guidelines for managing distressing symptoms, such as dyspnea, insomnia, nausea, or pruritus, at the end of life for pediatric patients receiving care within the hospital or home hospice setting, the pediatric palliative APRN works to create specific care maps or algorithms that guide the bedside nurse in effective ways.

Entrepreneur

As an entrepreneur, the pediatric palliative APRN serves as a role model of professionalism through his or her conduct, communication, dress, leadership, ethical decision making, critical thinking, compassion, and problem-solving skills. The pediatric palliative APRN is an advocate for PPC on the inpatient and outpatient hospital services and ensures that the availability of PPC as an option for the patient is discussed with clarity. Advocacy may involve speaking at conferences or participating in hospital grand rounds. It can involve participating in small group lunches and learning sessions on the pediatric ward or in hospital orientation sessions to educate new staff about the services provided by PPC teams.

The pediatric palliative APRN can demonstrate responsibility for professional practice by actively participating in professional organizations. The Hospice and Palliative Credentialing Center (HPCC), formerly known as the National Board for Certification of Hospice and Palliative Nurses, is the only nursing specialty organization to offer certification to all members of the nursing team (APRN, RN, pediatric RN, LP/VN, NA) as well as hospice and palliative care program administrators and perinatal loss care professionals.[18]

The pediatric palliative APRN maintains all professional requirements for licensure and certification. Participating in forums to discuss the legislative progress and policies surrounding pediatric healthcare initiatives enables the APRN to talk with colleagues who share similar interests and empowers the APRN to take action in support of best practices. In October 2014, three national nursing organizations joined forces to transform the care and culture of serious illness. Together, the Hospice and Palliative Nurses Association, the Hospice and Palliative Nurses Foundation, and the HPCC launched a campaign aimed at (1) increasing the number of certified hospice and palliative nurses; (2) advancing research into best practices of hospice and palliative care; (3) elevating palliative nursing leadership at the local and national levels; and (4) enhancing nursing competence through certification. Other groups with palliative care initiatives include the Association of Pediatric Hematology/Oncology Nurses, National Hospice and Palliative Care Organization, National Association of Pediatric Nurse Practitioners, American Association of Colleges of Nursing, American Nurses Association, and National Association of Neonatal Nurses.

Building a PPC program requires qualities like self-motivation, creativity, resourcefulness, assertiveness, and perspicacity. Negotiation skills and flexibility help with navigating challenging cases and assist in mediating conflict among staff during ethical quandaries. Pediatric palliative APRNs who are serving in a newly developed PPC team may find it helpful to visit a nearby adult palliative care APRN or neighboring program. Although many aspects of care differ for pediatric patients, the experience of rotating with an already established team can provide valuable insights for the APRN as the program moves forward.

Business/Marketing

As PPC teams become more common, models of excellence and the effectiveness of pediatric palliative APRNs should be documented and shared.[19] With the limited resources available in some institutions, APRNs may have to become creative when marketing the benefits of PPC in an effort to spread awareness. The APRN will find it useful to have a business plan in terms of expansion of service and integration of PPC principles within an environment. This means that the APRN should learn to negotiate with diplomacy and humility. Some providers believe that PPC should only be offered at the end-of-life and the pediatric palliative APRN will spend considerable time dispelling myths about PPC. Working to receive referrals early in the disease course will enable

the pediatric palliative APRN to meet the patient and family at a crucial point in the trajectory. APRNs must remain aware that the relationship between the primary team and the patient/family is at the forefront of the connection and must not be disregarded.

Spreading the word via team brochures, newsletters, or flyers can help to educate the staff about the "who and what" of the PPC service. With marketing savvy, the pediatric palliative APRN can develop a useful way of displaying such literature. Often parents of chronically ill patients meet several different teams, so offering a foldable brochure with the details of the services provided by the PPC team can be helpful. The APRN works with the clinical social work team to provide advance care planning services and ensures that bereavement resources and literature are accessible for the family. The APRN also partners with the chaplaincy team to support the spiritual needs of the patient and family. All members of the team are vital, so the pediatric palliative APRN makes sure that the patient and family understand the various roles of those involved in providing care, remaining available to answer questions when necessary.

Individual care teams may have questions about the types of services provided by PPC teams, and this provides the APRN with the opportunity to develop professional relationships. When trying to increase exposure to PPC services, the pediatric palliative APRN can educate teams about PPC by offering to meet with them. Establishing a relationship with the APRN of the referring team can promote partnerships and helps to maintain the relationship through honest feedback from another APRN. The APRN should solicit feedback and follow-up to review areas that could have been improved during the PPC consultation. Developing consistent goals for follow-up can be vital to the growth of the program. For example, contacting the hospice agency of the patient to discuss transition of care to hospice before and after the death of the patient is important for the growth of the PPC service and more importantly can elicit feedback to review family satisfaction and patient outcomes.

Transformational Leadership

The pediatric palliative APRN seeks to grow as a transformational nurse leader in the midst of an ever-changing healthcare environment in which resources may be limited. The APRN seeks to develop partnerships that lead to improved access to services for patients. Knowledgeable, strong, risk-taking nurse leaders follow a well-articulated, strategic, and visionary philosophy in the day-to-day operations of nursing services.[20] For example, developing partnerships within community settings may include contacting the local home hospice agency to help educate the nursing staff about managing dyspnea in infants. Within an institutional setting, the pediatric palliative APRN may work toward creating a pain management task force in the pediatric intensive care unit to identify patients at risk for having inadequately treated pain. And the APRN would welcome participation on the task force from experts in pharmacology and seeks to build bridges, with the goal of transforming the healthcare environment into a place where all members of the institution are accountable for taking part in the care of the pediatric patient. If there are questions about evidence-based guidelines during the implementation of compassionate extubation, the pediatric palliative APRN may start a journal club and invite others who are interested in establishing protocols to help to model best practices. The APRN is not limited by lack of resources but instead continues with an open mind to promote growth and expansion of the PPC initiatives. Finally, the role as a transformational leader in PPC

Table 57.1 Roles of the Pediatric Palliative APRN

Role	Proposed Actions
Clinical expert	◆ Maintain advanced clinical skills in pain and symptom management
	◆ Acquire knowledge of pharmacologic and nonpharmacologic therapies
	◆ Develop protocols and procedures
	◆ Plan interdisciplinary team meetings
	◆ Facilitate communication
	◆ Provide compassionate care
	◆ Document appropriately
	◆ Demonstrate competency
Educator	◆ Provide information to other healthcare providers, patients/families, and the community at large
	◆ Develop care maps and algorithms for managing distressing symptoms
	◆ Serve as a preceptor for new pediatric palliative APRNs
	◆ Track clinical and/or operational metrics
	◆ Participate in quality improvement activities (e.g., chart reviews)
	◆ Take part in a journal club
Entrepreneur	◆ Join a national palliative care organization
	◆ Participate in hospital grand rounds
	◆ Serve as a role model for professionalism through conduct, communication, dress, leadership, ethical decision making, critical thinking and problem-solving skills
	◆ Make a presentation during a lunch-and-learn session
	◆ Serve as a pioneer for a new PPC program
Business/ marketing	◆ Develop a business plan to expand services
	◆ Create a program brochure, newsletter, or flyer to promote awareness
	◆ Follow up regularly with referring teams
	◆ Elicit patient/family satisfaction through surveys
Transformational leader	◆ Contact local home hospice agencies to offer education for the nursing staff
	◆ Create a pain management task force
	◆ Start a PPC journal club
	◆ Promote the use of evidence-based guidelines and protocols for pain and symptom management in PPC
	◆ Develop partnerships within and outside of the institution

calls for the pediatric palliative APRN to engage patients, family, and staff throughout the patient care experience while serving as a clinical expert, functioning as an educator, using entrepreneurship skills, and developing business/marketing skills (Table 57.1).

Conclusion

Challenges will inevitably arise as a PPC program grows, and the pediatric palliative APRN will need a multifaceted skill set to address these issues while bridging gaps along the way. Ongoing self-awareness and self-care are vital for the pediatric palliative APRN. Personal goals for the nurse may include improving his or her organizational and communication skills. Professional goals may include networking within the field of PPC and assuming a national leadership role in PPC. Finding a mentor within the field may also help tremendously. The goal of relieving pain and suffering for pediatric patients should be the guiding light on whatever path the pediatric palliative APRN takes.

References

1. Docherty SL, Miles MS, Brandon D. Searching for "the dying point:" Providers' experiences with palliative in pediatric acute care. *Pediatr Nurs.* 2007; 33(4): 335–41.
2. National Hospice and Palliative Care Organization. NHPCO Facts and Figures: Hospice Care in America, 2014. Available at http://www.nhpco.org/sites/default/files/public/Statistics_Research/2014_Facts_Figures.pdf.
3. Morgan D. Caring for dying children: Assessing the needs of the pediatric palliative care nurse. *Pediatr Nurs.* 2009; 35(2): 86–91.
4. Chang A, Kicis J, Sangha G. Effect of the clinical support nurse role on work-related stress for nurses on an inpatient pediatric oncology unit. *J Pediatr Oncol Nurs.* 2007; 24(6): 340–9.
5. Feudtner C, Womer J, Augustin A, et al. Pediatric palliative care programs in children's hospitals: A cross-sectional national survey. *Pediatrics.* 2013; 132(6): 1–8.
6. Committee on Bioethics and Committee on Hospital Care. American Academy of Pediatrics: Palliative Care for Children. *Pediatrics.* 2000; 106(2): 351–7.
7. Cassel CK, Foley KM. *Principles for Care of Patients at the End of Life: An Emerging Consensus Among the Specialties of Medicine.* New York, NY: Milbank Memorial Fund; 1999.
8. American Academy of Pediatrics. Statement of Endorsement: Clinical Practice Guidelines for Quality Palliative Care. *Pediatrics.* 2014; 133(4): 1117.
9. National Consensus Project for Quality Palliative Care. *Clinical Practice Guidelines for Quality Palliative Care.* 3rd ed. Pittsburgh, PA; National Consensus Project 2013:1–70.
10. Nursing Fellowship Chart. Hospice and Palliative Nurses Association. Available at https://www.hpna.org/ Updated July 13, 2013. Accessed August 10, 2014.
11. City of Hope. End-of-Life Nursing Education Consortium (ELNEC) Advanced Practice Registered Nurse, 2014. Available at http://www.aacn.nche.edu/elnec/elnec-curricula/aprn. Access July 14, 2015.
12. American Pain Society. Assessment and Management of Children with Chronic Pain: A Position Statement from the American Pain Society. Revised and submitted for approval 1/4/12. Available at http://americanpainsociety.org/uploads/get-involved/pediatric-chronic-pain-statement.pdf. Accessed July 14, 2015.
13. Dell'Api M, Rennick JE, Rosmus C. Childhood chronic pain and health care professional interactions: Shaping the chronic pain experiences of children. *J Child Health Care.* 2007; 11(4): 269–86.
14. Dussel V, Joffe S, Hilden JM, Watterson-Schaeffer J, Weeks JC, Wolfe J. Considerations about hastening death among parents of children who die of cancer. *Arch Pediatr Adolesc Med.* 2010; 164(3): 231–7.
15. Knapp C, Madden V, Wang H, Curtis C, Sloyer P, Shenkman E. Music therapy in an integrated pediatric palliative care program. *Am J Hosp Palliat Care.* 2009; 26(6): 449–55.
16. Education in Palliative and End-of-Life Care (EPEC). EPEC-Pediatrics. 2014. Available at http://epec.net/epec_pediatrics.php. Accessed July 15, 2015.
17. Weissman DE, Meier DE, Spragens LH. Center to Advance Palliative Care Palliative Care Consultation Service Metrics: consensus recommendations. *J Palliat Med.* 2008; 11(10): 1294–8.
18. Hospice and Palliative Credentialing Center. Available at www.gohpcc.org. Accessed August 10, 2015.
19. O'Shea E, Kanarek RB. Understanding pediatric palliative care what it is and what it should be. *J Pediatr Oncol Nurs.* 2013; 30(1): 34–44.
20. Luzinski C. Transformational leadership. *J Nurs Admin.* 2011; 41(12): 501–2.

CHAPTER 58

Pediatric Palliative Care Across the Continuum

Vanessa Battista and Gina Santucci

Key Points

- Pediatric palliative care (PPC) is interdisciplinary family-centered care that focuses on a child's and family's quality of life through the prevention and relief of suffering along a physical, psychological, emotional, spiritual, and social continuum. Care is provided on both an inpatient and outpatient basis.

- The role of the pediatric palliative advanced practice registered nurse (APRN) is to improve the care of children with acute and chronic life-threatening illnesses, through both supportive care and effective pain and symptom management, especially as care transitions to palliative and end-of-life care.

- Many misconceptions and barriers still exist regarding PPC, including that it signifies death giving up hope, no further provision of care, and abandonment.

- The number of children living with a variety of life-threatening illnesses is increasing and families frequently are faced with difficult decisions about what interventions to choose. Pediatric palliative APRNs play a key role in guiding conversations about decision making and goals of care.

- Principles for assessing and managing pain in children are unique and must take into account the child's developmental, cognitive, and biological factors.

- Pediatric palliative APRNs should be knowledgeable in symptom management and the use of opioids, patient-controlled analgesia, and palliative sedation to manage pain effectively.

- A growing number of families choose to have their children die at home, necessitating more home-based PPC and hospice services. A variety of factors must be considered when caring for children and families in their home setting.

Introduction

Care for children living with chronic and/or life-threatening conditions historically has focused upon treatment and cure. Yet, even with our best efforts and expanding scope of knowledge, children continue to get sick and die from illness. Pediatric palliative care (PPC) aims to improve the quality of life of children and their families facing life-threatening illnesses, through the prevention and relief of suffering by early identification and treatment of pain and other problems, whether physical, psychological, social, or spiritual, and is meant to be provided in tertiary care facilities, community health centers, and children's homes.[1] The delivery of high-quality PPC was promulgated by the landmark 2002 Institute of Medicine (IOM) report *When Children Die*,[2] which challenged all healthcare providers to address the needs of children with complex chronic and life-threatening conditions and their families. Since that time, the field of PPC has continued to grow and healthcare providers now have an obligation to provide high-quality PPC for children with life-threatening conditions and their families, as evidenced by the most recently published IOM report, *Dying in America: Improving Quality and Honoring Individual Preferences Near the End of Life* (2014).

By definition, PPC is meant to be performed in a variety of settings. Within the hospital setting, which is the focus of this chapter, pediatric palliative APRNs are positioned to improve the care of children with acute and chronic life-threatening illnesses, especially as care transitions to palliative and end-of-life care. Care along the illness trajectory, from the time of diagnosis to end-of-life, can vary greatly in length and is not always clearly delineated as goals shift from care aimed at a cure to care focused on providing quality of life and comfort. The transition from curative to palliative to end-of-life care can be challenging for both providers and families for several reasons. In pediatrics, prognostic uncertainty continues to be a formidable barrier to shifting the focus of care: it can be difficult to predict if and when a child's condition may improve or continue to progress or for how long the child will remain stable. Without prognostic certainty, initiating discussions regarding a shift from curative to palliative care can be stressful and emotionally charged for everyone involved, including children, family members, and healthcare providers,[3] as it is difficult to isolate the "threshold point" at which goals of care may change.[4]

Another barrier to implementing a transition to palliative care involves providers' uncertainty or inability to have these discussions, which can lead to their avoidance.[3] Even in cases where providers were able to identify specific physiologic factors or conditions that signaled an appropriate shift to palliative care, they found that the transition in goals of care was determined mainly by parents. More education is needed about palliative care for providers to partner with families to make this transition smoother.[4] Currently, a great proportion of hospitalized children die in the pediatric intensive care unit (ICU). Moreover, "many children with life-limiting chronic illnesses still die in a hospital after prolonged periods of inpatient admission and mechanical ventilation"[5]; therefore, an increase in providers' abilities to navigate this shift in care is necessary. Research has shown that although providers in the ICU are skilled in providing high-level care, they have little training in providing palliative care. Thus, they often feel unprepared when goals shift from curative to palliative or end-of-life care; however, this transition in the ICU is attainable.[3] Pediatric palliative APRNs are well positioned to identify the particular needs of hospitalized children and families as they shift toward palliative care and to guide and support them, and the rest of the interdisciplinary team, through the transition in care.

Addressing Misconceptions and Barriers

"If people see me talking with you, will they know my child is dying?" is something that a parent once said upon meeting members of the PPC team. Despite the myriad benefits that PPC provides, many misconceptions about it still exist. It often erroneously signifies death, loss of hope, lack of care provision, and abandonment, all misconceptions that serve as barriers to PPC delivery. One study reported that pediatricians' two greatest barriers were "families' reluctance to accept palliative care (95%) and families viewing palliative care as giving up (94%)."[6] Other barriers include healthcare providers' lack of understanding and training in palliative care and feelings of inadequacy in offering PPC to families, as well as not knowing when and if it is the right time to make a referral to the palliative care team. The challenge then becomes not only providing high-quality PPC but also addressing families' and providers' misconceptions about PPC.

One of the most effective methods to address the misconceptions and barriers is through increased PPC education. Providers not specifically trained in PPC question when to involve the PPC team: Is it at the time of diagnosis, or only when there are no further options for treatment? Can every child with a specific diagnosis benefit from PPC services? Will families be afraid if the PPC team is introduced too early, and would it signify giving up? Should there be specific time points in the illness trajectory, or should the presentation of specific symptoms warrant a referral to the PPC team, or should PPC be involved at all?[7] The answers to these questions differ by situation. As PPC matures, it is necessary for a "focus on educating those who care for patients in primary care and the acute care setting about speaking to patients to find out their goals and preferences for treatment and end-of-life care."[7] Currently, patient-centered care in the acute care setting is often perceived as "too little, too late."[7]

Clinicians need preparation earlier in the educational trajectory and must have an opportunity for clinical placement in a palliative care setting to ensure that they become adept at addressing patients' needs and so palliative care becomes the standard of care for every child who can benefit from it.[7] More healthcare providers require knowledge and skills in palliative care to meet the needs of children living with life-threatening diseases and their families.[7]

Who Receives Pediatric Palliative Care?

"Approximately 55,000 children die every year in the United States, with approximately 80% dying in a hospital setting."[8] Some of these childhood deaths are a result of accidents and trauma. However, approximately 15,000 children ages 0 to 24 years will die annually from complex chronic conditions and could benefit from PPC.[8] There is immense need for PPC, sadly, only a mere fraction of children living with life-threatening illness receive it. A study evaluating the characteristics of dying children who received PPC and those who did not revealed that of the 23,342 children who died after 5 or more days in the hospital, 4% had received documented PPC services during their terminal hospitalization. Older children were more likely to receive PPC, and African-American children were significantly less likely to receive PPC than Caucasian or Hispanic children.[8] The dearth in PPC services is due to a low rate of and access to PPC services. In 2012, 226 identified hospitals were surveyed as to whether or not they had a PPC program. Sixty-nine percent of the 162 hospitals that responded (71.7% response rate) reported having a PPC program.[9] Of those hospitals surveyed, 12 had created new programs in 2008 and 10 in 2011, with most of the programs providing inpatient services only,[9] verifying the increasing need for inpatient PPC.

Child- and Family-Centered Care

Family-centered care can be broadly defined as "a partnership approach to health care decision-making between the family and health care provider."[10] It is an older concept in healthcare, but only in recent years has it been widely applied to pediatric healthcare. The specific definition of family-centered care and its exact parameters remain ambiguous. However, consensus has been reached about the principles that it encompasses: (1) information sharing that is "open, objective, and unbiased"; (2) creating relationships with respect for "diversity, culture, linguistic traditions, and care preferences"; (3) decision making that encompasses the "needs, strengths, values, and abilities of all involved" and includes families "at the level they choose"; and (4) direct medical care and decision making that reflects children "within the context of their family, home, school, daily activities, and quality of life within the community."[10] One of the most notable attributes of family-centered care is the concept of partnership and providing care that considers "the needs of all family members, not just the child."[10] In the inpatient pediatric setting, this translates to care that directly involves family members beyond their mere presence; that is, "family members must participate in the discussion and decision-making."[10] Given the communal nature of PPC (that is, care that is "patient-centered and family-engaged" and "respecting and partnering with patients and families"[11]), one could easily describe PPC as care that is family-centered at its core.

Published guidelines and recommendations for PPC state that all large healthcare organizations that serve children with life-threatening conditions should have dedicated interdisciplinary PPC teams and "that PPC be provided as integrated multimodal care and practiced as a cornerstone of patient safety and quality for patients with life-threatening conditions."[11] PPC is interdisciplinary by nature and includes providing psychological, social, spiritual, and emotional support. This may be delivered by several members of the PPC team, including psychologists/psychiatrists, social workers, child life specialists, art therapists, and/or chaplains, in addition to clinicians, such as nurses, APRNs, and physicians. PPC team members work with the child who is ill, along with other members of the family (parents and siblings, specifically). Thus, PPC is by its true nature family-centered care; it involves facilitating "clear, compassionate, and forthright discussions about medical issues and the goals of care" and supporting "families, siblings, and health care staff,"[11(p 966)] as it would be impossible for the life-threatening illness of a child not to affect the child's whole family.

Impact of Life-Threatening Disease

Child–Family Unit

A large component of providing PPC that is family-centered care involves providing emotional support.[12] This is especially important because a child living with a life-threatening illness frequently spends long amounts of time in the hospital, and this affects the entire family unit in various ways. Parents, family members, siblings, and the child all suffer throughout the course of an illness, and although this may manifest differently, each person's suffering somehow affects the others.[12] Schedules and daily family routines are interrupted, and parents may struggle to find enough time and energy to spend with each other and the ill child's siblings, to transport them to their after-school activities, or to attend events at school.

The entire family experiences stress, and research has shown that this is intensified when ill children are hospitalized. "Hospitalization is a traumatic and harrowing experience for children and even more so for those who spend time in the intensive care unit."[12] The family unit is affected by a child's illness and ongoing hospitalizations, and even the threat or fear of a child dying can cause family members to go through a grieving period.[12] "Mothers felt that they were emotionally supported when they received information, were assured about their child's condition, were prepared for what lay ahead for them and their child in the ICU, and when staff showed them emotional concern."[12] The pediatric palliative APRN has a distinct role in supporting families by providing education and anticipatory guidance, as well as emotional support, through a family-centered model of care in the context of PPC.

Siblings

Although there is little published evidence to support this hypothesis, it is well-recognized that siblings experience a significant amount of stress when their brothers or sisters face life-threatening illness. "Siblings' needs and suffering have not yet been studied extensively, but it has been recognized that they need special attention early on in the course of the disease of another child in the family."[13] It can be difficult, however, for parents to provide enough support for both the child who is ill and his or her siblings, and they may unintentionally overlook the needs of their healthy children given that they are overwhelmed by the disease and the needs of the ill child. For this reason, other supports are crucial for siblings, such as school, community, and camp programs, as well as professional counseling and/or support group services that may be available either at the hospital or through an outpatient setting.[13]

Some hospitals offer specific support programs for siblings, such as Sibshops, a program that exists in ten countries and focuses on meeting the needs of siblings of children living with illness through a mix of unique and developmentally and age-appropriate games, discussions, and friendship.[14] PPC programs may also offer home visits specifically for siblings by social workers, child life specialists, and/or art therapists from the team. Designating a "special person," such as a friend or relative who can take responsibility for each sibling specifically, may be helpful so that siblings get extra attention. Parents and caretakers may also find it helpful to dedicate a specific time of day to spend with siblings and to maintain their normal routine as much as possible.[13]

Parents and other caregivers, including healthcare providers, must pay close attention to signs and symptoms of sibling distress. Siblings can have elevated rates of anxiety and depression, symptoms of post-traumatic stress disorder, decreased participation in activities, difficulties in school, lower cognitive development scores, and overall ratings of poor/diminished quality of life.[15] Role reversal or shift may also be witnessed. Siblings may take on different roles in the family while adjusting to their brother's or sister's illness. Older siblings may regress in behavior and younger siblings may become "parentified" and identify with the role of caretaker in the family. Not all sibling reactions are negative, however. Siblings may demonstrate positive coping strategies and show signs of maturity and leadership, as well as empathy.[15] Other activities can also enhance siblings' abilities to cope, such as allowing them to visit, promoting participation in their brother's or sister's care, and acknowledging the huge sacrifices they are making, when age-appropriate.[13]

Extended Family

As discussed above, PPC is built on a philosophy of family-centered care, with the entire family serving as the unit of care. Everyone considered part of a child's family, including grandparents, aunts and uncles, cousins, and friends, can be affected when a child has a life-threatening illness. Whether a child's illness lasts for a short time or extends over many years, the ramifications of life with an ill child can have lasting effects on marriages/partnerships/relationships, cause stress and physical and/or mental health problems, affect finances and/or employment status, create social isolation or disengagement from peer-related activities, and foster a sense of loss, concern for the future, and grief.[16] Specific family members may also have particular needs or concerns that warrant attention.

Grandparents are often very involved in a child's care and may report feeling helpless as they not only are unable to protect their grandchild from illness, but also cannot protect their own child, the parent, from the pain and suffering he or she is experiencing.

Extended family members may wish to be supportive but are unsure what to do. It may feel overwhelming to parents to manage others' well-intentioned concerns, inquiries, and attempts to be helpful. Because many people are affected by the myriad aspects of a child's illness, it is the role of the PPC team to anticipate the struggles that families will experience and to provide them with anticipatory guidance and education. The pediatric palliative APRN can be helpful in explaining things to other family members, a task that may be difficult for the parents or caregivers who are at the bedside regularly. Evidence shows that clinicians' attention to the needs of family members can enhance their resiliency.[16] Overall, families are amazingly resilient, but they may need guidance in figuring out new roles and ways in which they can support each other, since everyone copes in his or her own unique way.

Community and School

Nearly all families belong to at least one type of community, and children are often at the epicenter of community-based activities. Whether it is through their school, place of worship, neighborhood, sports team, or other recreational activity (e.g., Girl Scouts or Boy Scouts), families find a sense of belonging among others in which camaraderie and relationships form. Similar to the effects on extended family, when a child becomes ill, the whole community may also feel the consequences of the illness. Community members may show concern and play a tremendous role in providing support to the child and family. Often when a child is hospitalized, his or her absence is felt. Community members may visit at the hospital and/or provide support to siblings and family members at home. In addition to family members, multiple professionals, both within the hospital and in the community, are involved in a child's care and are committed to maintaining his or her quality of life. In return, people from a child's community wish to be informed about how he or she is doing during times of hospitalization and may provide invaluable insight into a child's plan of care.

Children living with chronic or life-threatening illnesses often receive much of their care during the school day. Physical, emotional, or developmental challenges may necessitate attendance at a specialized school with an individualized education plan and appropriate therapeutic services in place. Children with life-threatening illness often have an interdisciplinary team of caretakers at school, including teachers, healthcare providers, and a range of therapists (e.g., physical, occupational, recreational, music, art), and school personnel are intimately involved in helping them meet various educational, therapeutic, medical, and basic care needs (e.g., feeding, toileting, hygiene). For these reasons, families rely on school personnel for support, guidance, and responsible execution of care plans. In turn, it is essential to keep educational team members informed of any choices that families make, especially if those decisions affect the care provided to the child or family. The school team should be included in decision-making conversations, yet they are often overlooked when such discussions occur. It is important and helpful to include school-based teams in decision making, to keep them informed of decisions that are made, and to have palliative care conversations in schools.[17,18]

Child's View of Illness and Death

Just as every family and community member will react to a child's illness and grieve in a unique way, every child will have his or her personalized integration of his or her illness experience. Garnering a sense from a child about his or her illness interpretation is not always an easy task, however. Children express themselves in different ways; some use words, some draw pictures, some engage in play, some use body language and behavior, and some don't speak at all. In PPC, one relies on the interdisciplinary nature of the team to interpret children's different modes of expression and to help children and families to come, ideally, to some fluid understanding about what their illness means.

Although every child has a unique perspective on his or her illness experience, it is helpful for the pediatric palliative APRN to have a sense of a child's developmental, emotional, and cognitive abilities. In particular, "different developmental tasks influence how children perceive and cope with illness and possible death, and a crucial aspect of PPC is the consideration of the developmental stage of the child."[19] In short, interventions and approaches for helping children cope with their illness should be influenced by both their chronological age and developmental stage (they do not always coincide), and every child "should be considered as a product of chronological age, developmental stage, medical condition, size, handicap, and cognition."[19] It is also important to recognize that "children, whose disease trajectory spans more than one developmental stage, call for constant evaluation and adaptation of the delivery of support and care,"[19] because some children with advanced illness may progress or regress in developmental age.[19] Table 58.1 summarizes children's developmental stages and perceptions of death in each stage.

Goals of Care, Limitations of Care, and Decision Making

Code Status Discussions

Despite advances in medical technology, the number of children living with life-threatening illness is on the rise. Families frequently are faced with difficult decisions about whether to forgo life-sustaining medical treatment and/or to elect Do Not Attempt Resuscitation (DNAR)/Do Not Resuscitate (DNR)/Do Not Intubate (DNI) orders to be placed for their children. The nomenclature around this topic has changed in recent years: the terms Do Not Attempt Resuscitation (DNAR) and Allow Natural Death (AND) are being used increasingly in more organizations instead of DNR. The code status DNAR signifies that not all attempts at resuscitation will be successful. The code status AND is thought to be more acceptable from a family standpoint as the result of natural disease progression.[1]

Regardless of the terminology used, discussions regarding resuscitation status can be anxiety-provoking for both family members and providers. It is common for providers to feel pressure to "get the DNR" and to consult the PPC team to accomplish this. Therefore, it becomes the role of the PPC team not only to have discussions with children and family members regarding goals of care as they relate to resuscitation status, but also to provide education and mentoring for providers in this arena. It is important to remind providers that DNAR orders are signed by parents/guardians, but are rarely decided upon after one conversation. Thus, it would be inappropriate for a PPC team to meet a

Table 58.1 Developmental Stages and Perceptions of Death

Age	Basic Conflict	View of Death	Suggestions
Birth–18 months	Trust vs. mistrust	◆ No sense of finality and is viewed as continuous with life ◆ Reactive to stress	◆ Use simple physical communication and provide comforting and nurturing care.
Early childhood (2–3 years)	Autonomy vs. shame and doubt	◆ Death is seen as reversible and not final ◆ May feel that death is a punishment ◆ May feel responsible for death	◆ Expect regression, clinging, or aggressive behavior. ◆ Encourage expression, as the child may be concerned about family function after he or she dies. ◆ Use honest and clear language to explain death and dying.
Preschool (3–5 years)	Initiative vs. guilt	◆ Death continues to be understood as temporary ◆ May have a literal understanding of death and will respond with curiosity and questioning	◆ Continue to use open communication with clear language. ◆ Encourage questions about death and dying.
School age (6–11 years)	Industry vs. inferiority	◆ Death is understood as permanent and that the body ceases to function, with heart and respirations stopping ◆ May feel responsible and guilty for the illness ◆ May have spiritual ideas about afterlife ◆ May not want to discuss feelings	◆ Reassure the child that death is not his or her fault. ◆ Strive to maintain as normal a structure as possible. ◆ Include the child in afterlife plans (funeral planning, last wishes).
Adolescence (12–18 years)	Identity vs. role confusion	◆ Understands the finality of death and may develop a mature understanding of death ◆ May try to take responsibility for adult concerns within the family (such as finances and caretaking) ◆ Feelings of anger may be present	◆ Allow time for reflection. ◆ Listen to concerns and questions. ◆ Support efforts for autonomy and control.

Adapted from references 56 and 57; printed in reference 19.

family for the sole purpose of "getting the orders signed." Rather, the PPC team's role is to build trusting relationships with families over time and to have ongoing discussions about goals of care that are based on both a humanistic and ethical framework.[20]

Predicting outcomes for children living with life-threatening illness is a complex and often difficult task. Thus, helping children, when chronologically and developmentally appropriate, and their families decide whether to limit interventions is often a multifaceted task. A good approach to deciding about limitations of care may include discussions with families regarding when "cardiopulmonary resuscitation (CPR) or other medical and procedural interventions may seriously impair the quality of life"[20] or when it may interfere with the ability or desire to achieve important life goals.[20] Most important, however, is to recognize that decisions about resuscitation status are usually the result of several discussions between providers and family members about their goals of care for their children and family. The work of the PPC team, or the teams involved in these discussions, then becomes to help families understand what interventions may or may not be beneficial to their children (e.g., chest compressions, intubation) and ways in which they can "secure for the incurable child a death filled with dignity and free from excessive suffering and treatment-related morbidity."[20]

Decision Making and Honoring Wishes

Decisions about what interventions to choose are seldom "black and white." Having tools to guide decision making and conversations about goals of care is extremely helpful. It is also paramount to include children in age- and developmentally appropriate conversations regarding their goals. Some children may explicitly express their wishes regarding their end-of-life and/or resuscitation status; other children may not want to address these topics. In some cases, children may feel more comfortable talking with the PPC team and other healthcare providers than talking with their family. They may fear disappointing their family if they choose not to pursue particular interventions. At other times, children and their parents/guardians may disagree about what the goals of care should be and/or what particular interventions they should choose to receive. Resources are available to help guide the decision-making process and to aid clinicians in navigating conversations with children of all ages and in some instances their designated decision makers, regarding how they want to be treated throughout their illness and at the time of death from a medical, personal, emotional, and spiritual perspective.[21] Helpful documents include *My Wishes* (for young children), *Voicing My Choices* (for adolescents), and *Five Wishes* (for adults), published by Aging with Dignity and available at www.agingwithdignity.org.

Out-of-Hospital Orders for Life-Sustaining Treatment: POLST/MOLST Forms

There are two documents to reflect Out-of-Hospital Orders for Life-Sustaining Treatment. The Physician/Provider Orders for Life-Sustaining Therapies (POLST) program, referred to as Medical Orders for Life-Sustaining Therapies (MOLST) in some states, "creates a coordinated system for eliciting, documenting, and communicating the life-sustaining treatment wishes of seriously ill patients,"[20] regardless of their age. The POLST program originated in Oregon in 1991 and now exists in most states;[22] it is commonly referred to as an "out-of-hospital DNAR." These POLST forms serve as one aspect of out-of-hospital advance care planning.

The POLST form specifically states it is not meant to replace an advance directive but, as medical orders, they serve to support the surrogate decision maker and support an advance directive. It incorporates specific decisions regarding life-sustaining therapies and is printed on an easily recognizable, brightly colored, and durable stock paper.[22] These documents are divided into the following specific sections: resuscitation preference, life-sustaining medical intervention decisions, and healthcare professional signature. States vary in who can sign the form, such as physicians, nurse practitioners, clinical nurse specialists, and physician assistants.[22]

Children and families deserve to have their wishes honored, whether they opt for full resuscitation or elect to forgo life-sustaining treatments. This is especially important with the current shift toward more children living with life-threatening illness and dying at home with DNAR orders in place.[22] "Clear documentation of advance directives and desired resuscitation status has been demonstrated to lead to effective responses to emergency management issues, even if a parent is not present, without performing unwanted CPR."[20] Families are best prepared for emergency situations when discussions about their wishes have occurred well before the time of the emergency, with ample time to establish goals of care at a time when they are not in crisis. Families should also be informed that they may change their minds at any time about decisions they have made previously should a change in their children's health status necessitate a revision of goals of care.

The POLST/MOLST documents are meant as the basis of discussion with a patient or surrogate decision maker, as in cases where children are under the age of 18, and are completed by healthcare professionals. The patient or decision maker must also sign the form (which differs from inpatient documentation of resuscitation status). The POLST form translates the values and health preferences into out-of-hospital orders for life-sustaining therapies and is intended to travel with the child wherever he or she goes, such as school or other activities.[22] There are state-specific and institutional policies that guide the use of these forms in children. It is incumbent upon pediatric palliative APRNs to be familiar with these.

The pediatric palliative APRN has a specific role in educating families that a POLST/MOLST is intended to protect the parents' and/or child's wishes should the parents not be available at the time a life-threatening event occurs. Families should be advised to inform local emergency medical services, caregivers, and school or daycare providers if a POLST/MOLST has been completed and what their wishes for their child would be should an emergency occur in the parent's absence. Parents should be informed that, if they are present, their verbal instructions will always override what is documented in the forms.

The previous sections provide an overview of some of the basic tenets of PPC. The next part of this chapter discusses commonly seen conditions in PPC.

Disease-Specific Categories

Children die from multiple conditions, including congenital syndromes; chromosomal abnormalities; cancer; metabolic conditions; diseases of the cardiac, pulmonary, gastrointestinal, and nervous systems; infections; and trauma.[23] Regardless of the condition, the addition of PPC can help with pain and symptom management and decision-making support from diagnosis to the end-of-life.

Cardiac Disorders

Heart failure in children is usually seen in those diagnosed with either congenital heart defects or cardiomyopathies; a smaller number will have conditions that directly affect the myocardium (Table 58.2). Children who have surgical palliation of their congenital heart disease are also at risk for developing heart failure. The diagnosis of heart failure is based on several clinical factors, including whether the child has an underlying cardiac defect or a weakened heart muscle. Congenital heart disease occurs in 1:100 live births and is the leading cause of birth defect-related deaths. It is also estimated that 1 in every 100,000 children will be diagnosed with cardiomyopathy.[24] Fifteen percent of congenital heart disease diagnoses are associated with genetic conditions and 20% to 30% of affected children will have a developmental or cognitive disorder.[25,26] Many children born with congenital heart disease will require corrective or palliative surgery.[27]

Children with congenital heart disease often live with increased morbidity and may require frequent hospital stays to manage their complex needs. In infants and children who present in heart failure, signs and symptoms can vary by age. Infants often have feeding difficulties, irritability, failure to thrive, cool extremities, mottled skin, prolonged capillary refill, decreased urinary output, weak pulses, edema, and tachycardia.[28] Children with heart failure tire easily, may appear malnourished, and may develop a persistent cough, fainting spells, dyspnea, tachycardia at rest, abdominal pain, nausea, and vomiting. In the later stages, children can develop hepatic and renal failure, malignant arrhythmias, stroke, or multiple-system organ failure.[29] The hallmark of end-stage heart disease is a significant decrease in a child's condition that often manifests as low cardiac output, respiratory distress, cachexia, and/or anorexia.[30]

Regardless of the etiology, children with end-stage heart failure may be cared for in a variety of settings, including at home, in a community-based hospice, or in an inpatient setting, such as the ICU. The location of care depends on the goals of care, the family's ability to provide care at home, available resources, and,

Table 58.2 Congenital Heart Defects

◆ Transposition of great arteries

◆ Tetralogy of Fallot

◆ Tricuspid or pulmonary atresia

◆ Ebstein's anomaly

◆ Hypoplastic left heart syndrome

◆ Truncus arteriosus

◆ Double outlet right ventricle

◆ Heterotaxy

◆ Atrial and ventricular septal defects

◆ Total or partial anomalous pulmonary venous return

From http://www.cdc.gov/ncbddd/heartdefects/specificdefects.html.

ultimately, where the dying child's and family's needs can be met. Though many children born with congenital heart disease do well, some will require multiple surgeries and frequent hospital admissions for ongoing care. Eventually, the involvement of a PPC team can provide support for children, siblings, and parents; assist with symptom management and decision making; and ultimately prepare the family for care at the end-of-life.

Management for heart failure in children depends on the cause and the child's and family's goals of care. Treatment options should decrease bothersome symptoms, improve function when possible, and maximize quality of life. When prescribing medications for children, careful consideration of dosing is necessary due to differences in pharmacokinetics based on the child's age and weight.[30] Ultimately, the course of treatment includes therapies that will improve function and quality of life by reducing preload, enhancing contractility, decreasing afterload, and improving oxygenation. Most medications used to manage heart failure are available either orally or intravenously (Table 58.3) and should be initiated and managed by a provider with an expertise in cardiology.

Technical support, such as extracorporeal membrane oxygenation (ECMO) or a ventricular assist device (VAD), may be an option for some children, depending on the family's goals of care.[31] Some children in heart failure who are waiting for a transplant may require ECMO or a VAD as a bridge to heart transplantation.[32] However, for children who are not candidates for a heart transplant, implantation of a VAD may provide long-term support in certain settings. In PPC, using a VAD as "destination therapy" is becoming an option in certain centers.[33] The decision to use ECMO or a VAD should not be considered in juxtaposition with the goals of palliative care. Healthcare providers need to balance interventions that may offer some benefit with those that clearly do not. Once a family has made the decision to pursue advanced technologies, it becomes the healthcare provider's responsibility to manage pain, support the family, and provide guidance regarding withdrawal of support, when necessary. Advance planning for children with congenital heart disease should include not only discussions about resuscitation and DNAR but also when the use of advanced technologies like ECMO, VAD, and other invasive procedures would be appropriate and when they would not.[34]

Cystic Fibrosis

Cystic fibrosis is an autosomal recessive genetic disorder caused by a mutation of the cystic fibrosis transmembrane conductance regulator (CFTR) gene. It is the second most common childhood genetic disorder, with approximately 30,000 people living with the disease in North America.[35] Cystic fibrosis occurs in 1 in 3,700 live births, and every year approximately 1,000 patients are newly diagnosed.[36] This progressive, life-threatening disease affects multiple organ systems; chronic respiratory infections, inflammation, and pulmonary decline are the primary causes of morbidity and mortality.[37] Other causes of illness and decline are poor growth, malabsorption, pancreatic insufficiency, diabetes mellitus, hemolytic anemia, and hepatic biliary disease.[38] Currently, there is no cure, but with improvements in technology, aggressive medical management, and supportive care, many children are living into early adulthood, albeit with an increase in morbidity. For certain children with advanced disease, lung transplantation may be an option. The post-transplant survival rate is about 80% after 1 year and 50% after 5 years.[39] Even though a lung transplant may be an option, it poses new challenges for children and their families. Although the new lungs do not have the gene that causes cystic fibrosis, the disease is still present in the child's body and the ability to fight infection is complicated by the need for continuous immune suppression.

From the time of diagnosis, children with cystic fibrosis must endure multiple therapies and frequent hospital stays to manage disease exacerbations. The decision of whether to integrate a palliative approach to care can be challenging, given the misconceptions that PPC teams are consulted only when a patient is at the end-of-life. Initial consultation with PPC may be helpful for the purposes of symptom management; eventually, if the child's condition worsens, the team can be introduced as another layer of support to assist the child and family with goals of care. The PPC team may also be helpful during disease exacerbations requiring hospital admission, when lung transplantation becomes an option, or when the need to balance aggressive interventions with quality of life becomes a challenge (Box 58.1).

Managing progressive dyspnea, fatigue, and pain in cystic fibrosis, especially at the end-of-life, can be challenging. Pain and

Table 58.3 Medication Guidelines for Heart Failure

	Options	Notes
Preload reduction	Furosemide (PO, IV)	Loop diuretic. Indomethacin may reduce effects.
	Hydrochlorothiazide (PO)	Thiazide diuretic. Use with caution in renal disease.
	Bumetanide (PO, IV)	Loop diuretic. Contraindicated in anuria or azotemia.
Afterload reduction	Captopril (PO)	Angiotensin-converting enzyme inhibitor (ACEI). Use caution in bilateral renal stenosis, renal impairment.
	Enalapril (PO)	ACE. Use caution in bilateral renal stenosis, renal impairment.
	Alprostadil (IV)	Maintains patency of ductus arteriosus. Important in ductal dependent defects.
Improve contractility	Digoxin (PO/IV)	Slows ventricular rate. Contraindicated in AV block.
	Dopamine (IV)	Correct hypovolemia prior to starting.
	Milrinone (IV)	Fewer cardiovascular side effects than other medications

Data from (1) http://www.heart.org/HEARTORG/Conditions/HeartFailure/PreventionTreatmentofHeartFailure/Heart-Failure-Medications_UCM_306342_Article.jsp; (2) http://circ.ahajournals.org/content/128/16/e240.extract; (3) http://my.americanheart.org/professional/ScienceNews/2013-ACCFAHA-Guideline-for-the-Management-of-Heart-Failure_UCM_452902_Article.jsp

---

Box 58.1 The Collaborative Benefit of Palliative Care Services in Children with Cystic Fibrosis

◆ Prior to diagnosis, help the primary care team create a supportive approach for infants who screen positive for the disease.

◆ Collaborate with the team to develop strategies to reduce parental grief when given the news their child has a life-threatening disease.

◆ Support the team during admissions, provide strategies to decrease stress, and offer help with pain and symptom management as needed.

◆ As the disease progresses, collaborate with the team and family on: treating bothersome pain and symptoms, answering difficult questions, addressing the "what ifs" and use of aggressive technologies, developing approaches to facilitate discussions related to transplantation, providing support to siblings, and suggesting care settings, including hospice.

◆ Develop a plan to address support for family and medical providers at the time of death, including community services to provide ongoing bereavement services.

Adapted from reference 58.

---

discomfort are intensified by inflammation of the pleura, cough, rib fractures, and the need for aggressive respiratory treatments. Overwhelmingly, evidence supports the benefits of using small doses of opioids to treat dyspnea and benzodiazepines to treat associated anxiety.[40] Some clinicians and family members may fear that using opioids may shorten the child's life (i.e., hasten death) or that the child will become addicted to them. It is the role of the PPC team to help clinicians and families overcome such fears and misconceptions about opioid use. For children with cystic fibrosis, opioids and nonpharmacologic measures may be the only options to palliate progressive symptoms at the end-of-life. Nonpharmacologic measures, such as noninvasive positive pressure ventilation (NIPPV), supplemental oxygen, and use of a fan, may also provide relief of dyspnea. PPC teams, in collaboration with cystic fibrosis teams, can provide the interdisciplinary support that is needed when caring for children with progressive, chronic, life-threatening conditions.

Neoplasms

The overall 5-year survival rate for children with some forms of cancer is currently 80% to 85%. In acute lymphoblastic leukemia, non-Hodgkin's lymphoma, and Wilms tumor, this number can exceed 90%.[41] Until recently, children diagnosed with brain tumors had survival rates of less than 50%, and although there are still uniformly fatal brain tumors, interventions like surgery, chemotherapy, and radiation have increased survival rates to above 75%.[42]

Brain and spinal tumors account for 20% of all pediatric cancers and are the most common type of solid tumors in children. Treatment usually consists of a combination of surgery, chemotherapy, and radiation. Radiation is usually delayed in children under the age of 5 years to preserve neurocognition in the developing brain. Tumor location, cell biology, and metastases will determine what treatments will be offered. Not all brain tumors are malignant, but even nonmalignant ones can be life-threatening due to their location, their impact on the surrounding tissue, and potential to cause increased intracranial pressure. Clinical symptoms depend on the site of involvement and may include headaches, seizures, loss of vision, hemiparesis, ataxia, nerve palsy, macrocephaly in infants, loss of developmental milestones, and vomiting.[43] Depending on tumor location, endocrine disorders such as diabetes insipidus can occur. Treatments can cause personality changes, memory loss, and hormonal dysfunction.

Children with brain tumors require a multidisciplinary approach, and PPC should be introduced as soon as possible to provide ongoing psychosocial support and pain and symptom management. Medications and treatments to cure or palliate can become a source of additional pain, worsening symptoms, and longer hospital stays. Many children require central lines, ventricular-peritoneal shunts, frequent imaging, high-dose corticosteroids, radiation, and chemotherapy. Acute changes in neurological function may require ICU interventions, such as externalization of shunts, mechanical ventilation, and repeat surgeries. When cure is not possible, treatments become a balance of preserving function, maximizing quality of life, and minimizing deficits. Providers are challenged to "do everything possible" to prolong life—but at what burden? PPC teams can facilitate communication, help with decisions regarding aggressive interventions, acknowledge uncertainty, and offer a space for meaningful conversations regarding prognosis.[44]

Spinal Muscular Atrophy

Spinal muscular atrophy (SMA) is an incurable autosomal recessive disorder that causes generalized weakness and atrophy of the voluntary muscles. It is classified into six clinical types; in this chapter we focus on type 1 (Werdnig-Hoffman disease). SMA type 1 is considered a severe form of the disease and occurs in 4.1 per 100,000 live births.[45] Clinical features are hypotonia, symmetrical weakness, poor head control, weak cry and cough, and absent deep tendon reflexes. Cognition and sensation are not affected. SMA is a progressive disease that eventually affects the diaphragm and all voluntary muscles.[46] Hallmark clinical findings include the inability to clear secretions, hypoventilation during sleep, underdeveloped respiratory muscles, and frequent infections that worsen the child's overall weakness.[46] The risk for aspiration, pneumonia, and rapid respiratory decline is considerable, and often these children will have a natural death before 24 months if mechanical ventilation is not pursued. Given the early disease onset, severity of illness, and potential life-threatening complications, involvement of the PPC team is often recommended at the time of diagnosis.

Eventually, without mechanical respiratory support, SMA type 1 is fatal. The type of support a child may require depends on the degree of weakness and overall goal of the family. Noninvasive mechanical intervention (NIPPV), tracheal intubation, and/or a tracheotomy with continuous mechanical ventilation are options many families are given. Initially a child may not require invasive measures and may require respiratory support for only a portion of the day. As muscles become weaker and infections more frequent, continuous noninvasive ventilation can become a source of distress and discomfort for the child. Eventually the family has to make an agonizing decision: to continue NIPPV, accepting its restrictions and impact on quality of life; to agree to tracheal intubation with the hopes of returning to NIPPV, if possible; to agree to a tracheotomy with continuous mechanical ventilation; or to compassionately extubate the child and allow a natural death, with the goal of maintaining comfort and aggressively treating distress. Some families, understandably, have difficulty deciding which path is best for their child, and they should not be forced to make hasty decisions.

Pain Management Considerations

The same guiding principles used for managing pain in adults can be applied to children, with a few caveats. The child's developmental age, cognitive ability, weight, the impact of pain on the child and family, and the maturity of the patient's renal and hepatic systems all affect pediatric pain assessment, management, and appropriate medication use. PPC teams, in consultation with the primary team caring for the child, should develop plans that partner with children and parents. A good pain management plan includes a thorough assessment using appropriate tools, a clarification of the goals of treatment, a description of expected side effects, a discussion of how increased pain will be addressed, and, the incorporation of nonpharmacologic therapies (e.g., distraction, relaxation techniques, acupuncture, guided imagery, play).[47]

Special attention must be given to nonverbal children and those with cognitive or developmental disabilities. This is a vulnerable group, and their inability to self-report pain can result in erroneous and inappropriate management.[48] Children with advanced disease deserve optimal pain control. For children who are at the end-of-life, managing pain and other bothersome symptoms must be a priority. No one wants to see children suffer needlessly in pain, yet many children with advanced illness do not have adequate pain control[49] (Table 58.4).

The World Health Organization (WHO) and the American Academy of Pediatrics offer clear guidelines on how to initiate and escalate pain management in children. The WHO three-step ladder is a universally accepted approach to pain-management escalation in children with cancer pain and is a good guideline for all pain management. It also includes the following concepts: "by the clock," "by the appropriate route," "by the ladder," "by the child," and "attention to detail." Pain medication should be given via the most effective and least traumatic route, at regularly scheduled intervals, with a plan for breakthrough pain. There is no standard dosing for opioids; rather, "the right dose is the dose that works." For children who have been exposed to opioids in the past, start with the drug and dose that were previously safe and effective. For those who are opioid naive, start with a low dose based upon weight and general health and titrate upward, balancing analgesia and sedation or other adverse effects.

Patient-controlled analgesia (PCA) involves an infusion pump that can be programmed to deliver medications at continuous prescribed doses and can also allow the patient (or parent) to deliver boluses of medication. Children as young as 3 or 4 years can be taught how to "press the button" to deliver pain medications. PCA should be considered when (1) pain is not controlled on increasing doses of oral or transdermal medication; (2) pain is not controlled on adequate doses of around-the-clock intravenous opioids; (3) pain is expected to escalate quickly; (4) routine care causes significant pain and may require additional dosing before activity; and (5) the child wants more control or the provider wants to give the child more control over the pain. The two main disadvantages of PCA are a child's unwillingness to use it and the need for intravenous or subcutaneous access. Morphine and hydromorphone are the common PCA opioids utilized, although circumstances may necessitate the use of fentanyl. Depending on the goals of care and resuscitation status, a bag-valve mask, supplemental oxygen, and continuous pulse oximetry may be needed for the first 24 hours on PCA and with subsequent dose increases.

Post-Acute Care

Considerations for Going Home

An increasing number of families are choosing to keep their children at home for the duration of their disease and ultimately their death. This is a very personal choice for families and is based on a variety of factors, such as available resources and support, who lives at home, and the family's past experiences with death. As with other decisions, families must be assured that there is no "right or wrong" choice about keeping the child in the hospital or at home. As with any comprehensive PPC plan, a home care plan should include careful assessment of the child's physical needs and emotional symptoms and the child's and family's developmental level and ability to complete developmental tasks. Practical factors, such as finances, living situation, social support, and religious or spiritual/existential beliefs and practices, should be considered.[50] The role of the pediatric palliative APRN, along with the other members of the interdisciplinary PPC team, is to ensure that families have their physical, emotional, and social needs met, whether they choose to remain in the hospital or transition to home.

Hospice Care

One of the most beneficial resources for the home care of a child is the use of hospice services. The terms "palliative" and "hospice care" are often used interchangeably due to their similar philosophical approaches to care. However, palliative care can be provided at any time during the disease, whereas hospice care focuses

Table 58.4 Pain Behaviors in Children

Infancy (1–12 months)	Inconsolability
	Feeding/sleeping difficulty
	Grimacing
	Change in activity level
	High-pitched cry
	Frequent yawning
	Tachycardia/tachypnea
Toddler (1–4 years)	Lost interest in play
	Moaning
	Irritability
	Loss of appetite
	Difficulty sleeping or excessive sleeping
	Overly clingy
	Guarding
School-age and adolescent (5–17 years)	Change in activity level
	Overly quiet or subdued
	Irritable or angry
	Mismatched cues
	Difficulty sleeping

Adapted from reference 49.

on true end-of-life care.[51] The pediatric palliative APRN should be familiar with the distinct ways in which pediatric hospice care differs from adult hospice. Namely, children go through developmental stages while having more complex, life-long chronic conditions, which may complicate the identification of treatment plans, trajectories, and ethical issues involving legal decision making, all the while having larger community involvement and more complicated grief.[52] Many hospices have nurses and other team members, such as social workers and chaplains, who are dedicated to providing high-quality hospice care for children and their families. It is helpful to identify dedicated pediatric hospice partners in the community. The pediatric palliative APRN is well suited to serve as the direct liaison with hospices nurses. In many instances, the inpatient PPC team will direct the care for children at home with hospice, working directly with hospice providers to adjust medications and care plans to maintain children's comfort and support families while at home. Some hospices have inpatient units where children can go, and it is helpful to identify what resources are available for families in different geographic areas served by the PPC team.

Concurrent Care

Given the wide variability that exists for pediatric prognoses, determining eligibility for hospice care (i.e., prognosis of 6 months or less) and what treatments might be acceptable or affordable under hospice guidelines is difficult. It can be as difficult as the decision for parents about whether to forgo treatment in order for their child to receive palliative or hospice care. On March 23, 2010, the federal government enacted the "concurrent care for children" provision in Section 2302 of the Patient Protection and Affordable Health Care Act (PPACA).[53] This provision allows children with state Medicaid or Children's Health Insurance Programs (CHIP) to receive hospice care while still receiving curative treatment (i.e., blood products, antibiotics, infusions, lab tests) and home nursing services. Enactment of this federal law demonstrated that healthcare providers and government officials understood that the needs of children living with life-threatening illness are distinctly different from those of adults. Although greatly beneficial, the implementation of concurrent care is complex and requires ongoing communication and coordination in order to integrate hospice care into the services and providers already in place for children.[54]

Care While at Home

Aside from resources like hospice, there are several practical aspects that should be considered when providing care for a child at home. It is extremely important to consider who will manage pain and other symptoms in the home and to have a plan in place for medication management. Often this will be managed by a hospice and/or home care nurse in the home, but parents may also be involved in dosing and providing medications. It is also important to make sure that medications are kept in a safe place and are locked up, if necessary. It is the role of the pediatric palliative APRN to create a plan for dosing and titrating medications at home and to communicate with the different people (i.e., hospice, home care, and family members) involved in care to ensure that the child is both safe and comfortable. Some PPC teams also have a system in place with the hospices they work with where the PPC team writes the plan of care and manages all of the medical orders for the child while at home. Many teams also do home visits, when possible. Regardless of the setting, a detailed plan must be established and organized so as to avoid errors and to ensure that pain and other symptoms are being well managed.

Support for Siblings and Other Family Members

Caring for the entire family is an essential component of palliative care, and it is especially important when care is being provided at home. The needs of parents, siblings, and other involved family members, such as grandparents, must be considered in the home setting. Family members may have questions about preparation, what changes may occur in the child's physical and mental status, and whom they should call for additional support. Families may also question who should be invited into the home and will have different opinions regarding sibling involvement. It is important to consider siblings' psychological, emotional, and social needs and to provide age- and developmentally appropriate explanations, as well as opportunities to be included in aspects of the illness experience, although siblings' individual needs will vary, depending on their age and personality, as well as the accepted behavior within a family.[55] Siblings may strive for attention and display a range of emotions and feelings, such as guilt, responsibility, shame, anger, and/or sadness, along with magical thinking (i.e., feeling they caused the illness based on something they once said or did). An important component of PPC is providing resources to support and involve siblings and other family members. Some programs offer specific support for siblings, including home visits with child life specialists and art therapists who are trained to help siblings cope with illness and death.

Care at the Time of Death and Beyond

Many families describe the death of their children at home as a sacred and beautiful event. Therefore, everything possible must be done to allow families this experience and to keep things calm. All necessary medications and other supplies, such as dark towels for potential bleeding, should be in the home in advance. Alternative routes for medication delivery should also be considered. Some families may want private time with their children prior to, surrounding, and following the time of death. Other families may request family members, hospice providers, and even pediatric palliative APRNs to be present. It is helpful to discuss this in advance and to have a plan in place for what will occur at the time surrounding the child's death. Families may have specific cultural and/or spiritual customs and rituals at the time of death, and these practices should be honored and respected. Families may want photos taken of their children and keepsakes created, such as hand molds and prints, and may choose to have siblings and other family members participate in creating these items. Families may participate in the physical care of the child at the time of death, such as bathing and dressing, and this option should be given to families.

The pediatric palliative APRN and other members of the team must recognize that every family copes differently and will have an array of reactions when a child dies. Being flexible and keeping open communication is key, as is providing families with ongoing support following the death. Some PPC teams send cards or make phone calls at regular time intervals and may have bereavement support as part of the team. They also should be familiar with local resources to which they can refer families.

Caring for children and their families at the time of death is important and sacred work, yet it can also be emotionally draining. PPC and hospice providers must be sure to have adequate support to do this very important work, especially when care is provided at home.

Conclusion

PPC is an emerging and multifactorial area of healthcare that is on the rise as more and more attention is being given to children living with life-threatening illnesses and their need for optimal quality of life and pain and symptom management. PPC is family-centered care by nature and focuses on addressing the needs of children living with life-threatening illness as well as the needs of their family and community members. PPC is often initiated as the goals of care shift from a focus on cure to a focus on optimizing quality of life, and a properly trained team of interdisciplinary professionals is necessary to deliver this type of care, both in the hospital and at home. The pediatric palliative APRN plays an important role in providing high-quality PPC by adequately addressing children's and families' needs, collaborating with other providers to provide comprehensive care, and thoroughly assessing and treating pain and other symptoms.

References

1. World Health Organization. Available at www.worldhealthorganization.com and http://www.who.int/cancer/palliative/definition/en/. Accessed October 10, 2014.
2. Field MJ, Behrman RE, eds., for the Institute of Medicine Committee on Palliative and End-of-Life Care for Children and their Families. *When Children Die: Improving Palliative and End-of-Life Care for Children and Their Families.* Washington DC: National Academies Press; 2003.
3. Campbell L. Honouring the wishes of a dying patient: from intensive care to home with palliative care. *Contemp Nurse.* 2013; 45(2): 269–72.
4. Catlin A. Transition from curative efforts to purely palliative care for neonates. *Adv Neonatal Care.* 2011; 11(3): 216–22.
5. Gupta N, Harrop E, Lapwood S, Shefler A, et al. Journey from pediatric intensive care to palliative care. *J Palliat Med.* 2013; 16(4): 397–401.
6. Knapp C, Thompson L. Factors associated with perceived barriers to pediatric palliative care: a survey of pediatricians in Florida and California. *Palliat Med.* 2011; 26(3): 268–74.
7. Maher K, Mitchell G. Panel discussion summary: when is palliative care everyone's business and when are specialists needed? *Int J Palliat Nurs.* 2013; 19(9): 421–2.
8. Keele L, Keenan H, Sheetz J, et al. Differences in characteristics of dying children who receive and do not receive palliative care. *Pediatrics.* 2013; 132(72): 72–8.
9. Feudtner C, Womer J, Augustin R, et al. Pediatric palliative care programs in children's hospitals: a cross-sectional national survey. *Pediatrics.* 2013; 132(6): 1063–70.
10. Kuo D, Houtrow AJ, Arango P, et al. Family-centered care: current applications and future directions in pediatric health care. *Matern Child Health J.* 2012; 16(2): 297–305.
11. American Academy of Pediatrics. Pediatric palliative care and hospice care commitments, guidelines, and recommendations. *Pediatrics.* 2013; 132(5):966–72. http://pediatrics.aappublications.org/content/132/5/966.abstract
12. Roets L, Rowe-Rowe N, Nel R. Family-centered care in the paediatric intensive care unit. *J Nurs Manag.* 2012; 20(5): 624–30.
13. Bergstraesser E. Pediatric palliative care—when quality of life becomes the main focus of treatment. *Eur J Pediatr.* 2013; 172(2): 139–50.
14. Sibshops. Available at http://www.siblingsupport.org/sibshops. Accessed October 7, 2014.
15. Muriel AC, Case C, Sourkes B. Children's voices: the experience of patients and their siblings. In: Hinds PS, Sourkes BM, Wolfe J, eds. *Textbook of Interdisciplinary Pediatric Palliative Care.* Philadelphia, PA: Saunders, 2011:18–29.
16. Jone B, Contro N, Koch KK. The duty of the physician to care for the family in pediatric palliative care: context, communication, and caring. *Pediatrics.* 2014; 133(S1): S8–15.
17. Levetown M. Communicating with children and families: from everyday interactions to skill in conveying distressing information. *Pediatrics.* 2008; 121(5): e1441–60.
18. Ross ME, Hicks J, Furman WL. Preschool as palliative care. *J Clin Oncol.* 2008; 26(22): 3797–9.
19. Mandac C, Battista V. Contributions of palliative care to pediatric patient care. *Semin Oncol Nurs.* 2014; 30(4): 1–15.
20. Baker JN. Resuscitation. In: Hinds PS, Sourkes BM, Wolfe J, eds. *Textbook of Interdisciplinary Pediatric Palliative Care.* Philadelphia, PA: Saunders; 2011:199–203.
21. Aging With Dignity. Available at http://www.agingwithdignity.org/index.php. Accessed October 8, 2014.
22. Citko J, Moss AH, Carley M, et al. The national POLST paradigm initiative. *J Palliat Med.* 2011; 14(2): 241–2.
23. Feudtner C, Hays RM, Haynes G, et al. Deaths attributed to pediatric complex chronic conditions: national trends and implications for supportive care services. *Pediatrics.* 2001; 107(6): E99.
24. American Heart Association. Pediatric cardiomyopathies. Available at http://www.heart.org/HEARTORG/Conditions/More/CardiovascularConditionsofChildhood/Pediatric-Cardiomyopathies_UCM_312219_Article.jsp. Accessed October 6, 2014.
25. Oyen N, Poulsen G, Boyd HA, et al. Recurrence of congenital heart defects in families. *Circulation.* 2009; 120(4): 295–301.
26. Limperopoulou C, Majnemer A, Shevell MI, et al. Neurodevelopment status of newborns and infants with congenital heart defects before and after open heart surgery. *J Pediatr.* 2000; 137(5): 638–45.
27. Children's Heart Foundation. Fact Sheets: Incidence, Morbidity and Mortality. Available at http://childrensheartfoundation.org/about-chf/fact-sheets. Accessed October 6, 2014.
28. McConnell ME, Elixon EM. The neonate with suspected congenital heart disease. *Crit Care Nurs Q.* 2002; 25(3): 17–25.
29. Hsu DT, Pearson GD. Advances in heart failure. Heart failure in children part II: diagnosis, treatment and future directions. *Circ Heart Fail.* 2009; 2(5): 490–8.
30. Satou G, Berger S. Pediatric congestive heart failure treatment and management. Available at http://emedicine.medscape.com/article/2069746-treatment. Prepared February 11, 2013. Accessed October 6, 2014.
31. Fynn-Thompson F, Almond C. Pediatric assisted ventricular devices. *Pediatr Cardiol.* 2007; 28(2): 149–55.
32. De Rita F, Hasan A, Haynes S, et al. Mechanical cardiac support in children with congenital heart disease with intention to bridge to heart transplantation. *Eur J Cardiothorac Surg.* 2014; 46(4): 656–62.
33. Drakos SG, Charitos EI, Nanas SN, et al. Ventricular assist device for treatment of chronic heart failure. *Expert Rev Cardiovasc Ther.* 2007; 5(3): 571–84.
34. Blume E, Green A. Advanced heart disease. In: Hinds PS, Sourkes BM, Wolfe J, eds. *Textbook of Interdisciplinary Pediatric Palliative Care.* Philadelphia, PA: Saunders; 2011:428–37.
35. O'Sullivan BP, Freedman SD. Cystic fibrosis. *Lancet.* 2009; 373(9678): 1891–904.
36. American Lung Association. State of Lung Disease in Diverse Communities. Available at http://www.lung.org/assets/documents/publications/solddc-chapters/cf.pdf. Accessed October 6, 2014.
37. Bonfield TL, Panuska JR, Konstan MW, et al. Inflammatory cytokines in cystic fibrosis lungs. *Am J Respir Crit Care Med.* 1995; 152(6): 2111–8.

38. Genetic Home Reference. Cystic fibrosis. Available at http://ghr.nlm.nih.gov/condition/cystic-fibrosis. Prepared September 2014. Accessed October 6, 2014.

39. Cystic Fibrosis Foundation. Lung transplant. Available at http://www.cff.org/treatments/lungtransplantation/. Prepared May 2, 2012. Accessed October 6, 2014.

40. Bourke SJ, Doe SJ, Gascoigne AD, et al. An integrated model of provision of palliative care to patients with cystic fibrosis. *Palliat Med.* 2009; 23(6): 512–7.

41. LaFond D, Rood B, Jacobs S, et al. Integration of therapeutic and palliative care in pediatric oncology. In: Hinds PS, Sourkes BM, Wolfe J, eds. *Textbook of Interdisciplinary Pediatric Palliative Care.* Philadelphia, PA: Saunders; 2011:460–9.

42. Childhood Cancer: SEER Cancer Statistics Review. Available at http://SEER.cancer.gov. Accessed October 6, 2014.

43. Arland LC, Hendricks-Ferguson VL, Pearson J, et al. Development of an in-home standardized end-of-life treatment program for pediatric patients dying of brain tumors. *J Spec Pediatr Nurs.* 2013; 18(2): 144–57.

44. American Academy of Pediatrics, Committee on Bioethics and Committee on Hospital Care. Palliative care for children. *Pediatrics.* 2000; 106(2): 351–7.

45. Pearn J. Incidence, prevalence and gene frequency studies of chronic childhood spinal muscular atrophy. *J Med Genet.* 1978; 15(6): 409–13.

46. Battista V, Mosher P. Spinal muscular atrophy. In: Ferguson-Hendricks V. *Palliative Care for Pediatric Life-Limiting Conditions.* Pittsburgh, PA: Hospice and Palliative Nurses Association; 2014:165–86.

47. Santucci G. Pain management for children with life-limiting conditions and at the end of life. In: Santucci G, ed. *Core Curriculum for the Pediatric Hospice and Palliative Nurse.* Pittsburgh, PA: Hospice and Palliative Nurses Association; 2011:43–66.

48. Crosta QR, Ward TM, Walker AJ, et al. A review of pain measures for hospitalized children with cognitive impairment. *J Spec Pediatr Nurs.* 2014; 19(2): 109–18.

49. Friedrichsdorf SJ, Kang TI. The management of pain in children with life-limiting illnesses. *Pediatr Clin North Am.* 2007; 54(5): 645–72.

50. McSherry M, Kehoe K, Carroll JM, et al. Psychosocial and spiritual needs of children living with a life-limiting illness. *Pediatr Clin North Am.* 2007; 54(5): 609–29.

51. Crozier F, Hancock LE. Pediatric palliative care beyond the end of life. *Pediatr Nurs.* 2012; 38(4): 198–203, 227; quiz 204.

52. National Hospice and Palliative Care Organization. Standards of Practice for Hospice Programs. Retrieved July 28, 2013, from http://www.nhpco.org/sites/default/files/public/quality/Standards/APXIV.pdf.

53. Office of the Legislative Counsel, U.S. House of Representatives. Compilation of Patient Protection and Affordable Care Act, As Amended Through May 1, 2010, Including Patient Protection and Affordable Care Act Health-Related Portions of the Health Care and Education Reconciliation Act of 2010, Legislative Counsel, 111th Congress 2d Session, Print 111-1, 202–203.

54. Miller EG, LaRagione G, Kang TI, Feudtner C. Concurrent care for the medically complex child: lessons of implementation. *J Palliat Med.* 2012; 15(11): 1281–3.

55. Orloff SF, Jones B, Ford K. Psychosocial needs of the child and family. In: Carter BS, Levetown M, Friebert SE, eds. *Palliative Care for Infants, Children, and Adolescents: A Practical Handbook.* Baltimore, MD: The Johns Hopkins University Press; 2011:202–26.

56. Vern-Gross T. Establishing communication within the field of pediatric oncology: a palliative care approach. *Curr Probl Cancer.* 2011; 35(6): 337–50.

57. Foster TL, Bell CJ, Gilmer MJ. Symptom management of spiritual suffering in pediatric palliative care. *J Hosp Palliat Nurs.* 2012; 14(2): 109–15.

58. Pian P, Goggin J. Cystic fibrosis. In: Ferguson-Hendricks V, ed. *Palliative Care for Pediatric Life-Limiting Conditions.* Pittsburgh, PA: Hospice and Palliative Care Association; 2014:83–112.

CHAPTER 59

Preparing for the Unexpected
Perinatal and Neonatal Palliative Care

Marlene Hardy-Gomez

Key Points

♦ The pediatric palliative advanced practice registered nurse (APRN) can be the anchor for the infant and family, a constant support through the infant's unique life journey.

♦ The pediatric palliative APRN renders comprehensive support for pain and symptom management and attends to emotional, psychological, practical, spiritual, educational, and developmental issues that may contribute to suffering or interfere with infant and family healing.

♦ The pediatric palliative APRN collaborates with the care team to ensure that the principles of pediatric palliative care guide the care of the infant and family.

♦ The APRN is in an ideal position to assess the parents' understanding of the diagnosis, prognosis, and treatment options, in agreement with their cultural and spiritual beliefs, and how they define a good quality of life for their infant. The nurse is also in an ideal position to share the parents' understanding and beliefs with the other providers caring for the child and family.

Introduction

The infant mortality rate in the United States is about 6 out of every 1,000 live births each year.[1] In 2006, more than 28,500 infants died before age 1, and 36% died from preterm-birth-related causes. Of the 543,000 infants who are born prematurely each year in the United States, 4 out of every 1,000 have chronic, complex medical issues that can become life-limiting, leading to death in later childhood.[2] Slightly more than half of all pediatric deaths occur in infancy, with congenital malformations and prematurity/low birth weight being the leading causes of infant death. Of those infants with complex congenital causes of death, 32% have cardiovascular anomalies, 26% have congenital genetic abnormalities, 17% have an underlying congenital respiratory issue, and 14% have congenital neuromuscular issues.[3]

Fetal and infant deaths have a great psychological impact on parents and families, as well as on the providers who care for them. Pediatric APRNs are in a unique position not only to improve the care of these most vulnerable infants and families during a stressful and traumatic time, but also to educate and

support other pediatric providers. This may be achieved by applying the core principles of pediatric palliative care: enhancing the infant's and family's quality of life, using a comprehensive team and individualized approach to pain and other symptoms, as well as addressing the patient's and family's emotional, psychological, practical, and spiritual issues that can contribute to suffering or interfere with healing.

The 2003 Institute of Medicine report *When Children Die: Improving Palliative and End-of-Life Care for Children and Their Families* challenged healthcare providers to develop and implement practice guidelines for palliative, end-of-life, and bereavement care for children and their families. Specifically, it emphasized the importance of good coordination and continuity of care among sites (Box 59.1), educational programs for healthcare providers, palliative care services funded through insurance and Medicaid, and research to move the field forward.[4] This chapter presents the unique role that the pediatric palliative APRN can play in perinatal/neonatal palliative care.

Case Study

Susan and Dennis were married and in their mid-thirties, with a 15-month-old son. Susan had one previous miscarriage. Susan was a manager at a local store and Dennis worked for an insurance company. They described themselves as "planners." They had an extended, supportive family. The couple was Catholic and very active in their local parish.

Susan and Dennis were referred to the Fetal Treatment Center from their OB because their unborn daughter, Grace, had been found to have multiple congenital anomalies, including micrognathia, clubbed feet, clenched hands, skeletal issues, and polyhydramnios. She had a normal echocardiogram. While MRI showed probable vertebral segmentation anomaly in the mid-thoracic spine, no neural tube or intracranial abnormalities were noted. The akinesias panel was negative. Along with cardiology and genetics, the Fetal Treatment Center consulted the pediatric palliative care team offering the parents increased support and assistance with the creation of their birth plan.

Susan and Dennis understood that Grace had a poor prognosis. They wanted to discuss how they could try to remain hopeful for a good outcome for Grace, while being prepared for the worst-case

---

Box 59.1 Cultivation of Interteam Collaboration

Topics for discussion between the Pediatric Palliative Care Team and the Fetal Treatment team:

- What things have been challenging to their teams in the past?
- What types of services/supports does the fetal treatment team want for their parents and infants?
- What do we already know about what parents need and want?
- What types of services/supports can the pediatric palliative care team offer these parents and infants?
- What care standards are already in place?
- How can the palliative care team help meet these standards with the fetal treatment team?
- What would a good collaboration between the teams look like?
- What diagnoses would be appropriate for referral?

---

scenario. Most of all, they wanted to ensure that regardless of what happened, Grace did not suffer. Because the extent of Grace's medical conditions was unknown, it was difficult to prepare for her birth and her future. Susan and Dennis were reassured that all of the medical providers would try to be honest in sharing what information they had about Grace's condition, as well as unknown circumstances that would affect her care.

Dennis and Susan wanted to remain hopeful that Grace could live and have a good quality of life. When asked what a good quality of life would or would not look like to them, they shared that it would not be long-term life-sustaining measures, such as staying on a ventilator and other machines to survive. They expressed that if Grace's issues could be resolved with surgery, then they would agree to those surgeries. However, if she would not have great outcomes and would not be able to live life, then they would choose not to put her through various surgeries.

Susan and Dennis were assured that information learned after Grace's birth would be shared with them. Among their many questions was what her end-of-life would look like in the hospital. The team assured them they would assist and guide them in decision making. Susan and Dennis were told that medications would be administered to ensure Grace's comfort so she would not suffer. They were offered memory making and assistance with funeral planning, and the team detailed the ongoing bereavement support that would be available to them. In her birth plan, the couple stated that to better understand the medical issues and make the best decisions for her, they wanted aggressive treatment for Grace at birth.

Grace was born via a spontaneous vaginal delivery at 37 weeks' gestation. This occurred after artificial rupture of membranes with the presence of meconium-stained fluids. Grace's Apgar scores were 2-6 and 7. Grace presented with many severe problems. At birth, she was cyanotic with no respiratory effort, requiring positive-pressure ventilation with up to 100% oxygen, and improving bradycardia. She had the micrognathia seen prenatally along with retrognathia, a cleft palate, and an inability to fully open her mouth, so her airway was difficult to visualize. She was intubated with some difficulty and transported with admission to the NICU. Because of the polyhydramnios during pregnancy and the frequent requirement for oral suctioning, questions were raised about whether she was able to swallow and maintain her airway. She remained intubated on the vent on minimal settings.

Grace was evaluated by many departments; ENT, Plastics, Orthopedics, Genetics, Neurology, and Palliative Care. There was a strong feeling that jaw distraction surgery could possibly prevent the need for a tracheostomy, but would be the first of many corrective surgeries. The specialists agreed that their surgeries would need to wait until Grace was older. Grace would unlikely be able to walk. Neurology informed Susan and Dennis that the EEG findings were very concerning for a poor neurologic outcome for Grace. However, until they could better determine the extent and future of her neurologic status, a plan was to postpone all invasive procedures. The EEG would be repeated in 2 to 3 weeks.

In the meantime, Grace's parents focused on making memories with Grace and remaining hopeful about her future. The pediatric palliative APRN visited regularly, getting to know Grace and her family better and assisting with practical resources. Unfortunately, Grace's repeat EEG was unchanged, meaning her neurologic status was poor and would not improve. Her parents were heartbroken and requested a meeting to talk the next day.

The pediatric palliative care APRN with Susan and Dennis the next day and reassured them that Grace would be kept comfortable. The plan was to remove life-sustaining therapies to allow nature to take its course. Susan and Dennis were informed that Grace's demise could be quick, over hours or over days. They were offered several locations for Grace's final hours, including their home with hospice support along with the palliative care team. Susan and Dennis preferred the hospital, with the stipulation that if Grace lived beyond a day, they would consider bringing her home to die. They were asked who they would like to be present at her end-of-life. They were told that the palliative care team could be flexible and adjust the process according to what felt right.

Susan and Dennis were informed of the physical changes they would likely see as Grace neared her end-of-life. They were reassured that Grace would be kept comfortable throughout. They were offered memory making and assistance. They were educated about the signs of death. Susan and Dennis were assured they could spend as much time with Grace as they wanted. The post-death process was explained.

One afternoon, Grace was extubated, and she remained comfortable in her parent's arms until she died peacefully that evening. Her parents requested a partial autopsy to try to better understand the presence of her congenital anomalies. They were advised that a meeting would be arranged to discuss the findings and that the palliative care team would be available to them 24/7 to answer any questions or concerns they had. A bereavement folder and resources were given to them, along with the promise of a follow-up call the next day.

One of the most important things that healthcare providers can do for parents is to ensure that they are well informed about their infant's condition and treatment options, so that they can make good decisions for the care of their baby. They need to be able to make difficult decisions and to feel confident they made the best decision, because they will live with their decisions for the rest of their lives. In the case study, Susan and Dennis needed to feel that they had given their daughter every chance to have a good quality of life. When it became clear that it was not going to be the life they had hoped for her, they needed assurance that their wishes for their daughter would continue to be honored, allowing her a natural death, free of pain and suffering, while honoring her life and creating memories. The pediatric palliative APRN has the privilege of being the consistent person who can make sure that the family develops goals of care for their child (adjusted when necessary) and that the whole team caring for them supports and understands those goals and provides good palliative care, regardless of the location.

Perinatal Palliative Care

While there are no evidence-based empirical studies to establish the best standard model of palliative care for the perinatal setting, most experts agree that it must be comprehensive. Therefore, it must address physical, psychological, spiritual, and social concerns, including bereavement issues, and it must be integrated and introduced early (preferably before the baby is born).[5] Carter and Caitlin were instrumental in the development and application of pediatric palliative care in the neonatal intensive care unit (NICU) setting by establishing the neonatal end-of-life care protocol and providing palliative care for newborns.[6] These same principles can be applied to perinatal palliative care. The National Association of Neonatal Nurses' position statement regarding palliative care for newborns and infants states that palliative care is appropriate for neonates with severe prematurity and all of its potential complications, as well as neonates with complex congenital anomalies that may limit their lives, whether prenatally, at birth, during a NICU stay, or at home after discharge. They recommend appropriate support staff at the time of diagnosis, as well as partnering with pediatric palliative care and hospice services to ensure continuity of care.[7]

Dean and McDonald define perinatal palliative care as care that provides comfort and support to patients and their families during the prenatal, intrapartum, and postpartum periods when the pregnancy is not viable, or the infant is born with a life-limiting or life-threatening condition[7] (Box 59.2). They describe a team approach incorporating the core principles of palliative care, with holistic supportive care for the infant and family by creating a birth plan and guiding parents as they explore their options and wishes for their baby. Parents are shown how to create and collect memories throughout the pregnancy and the life of the child.[8]

Creating a Birth Plan

When creating a birth plan, parents must fully understand what each item/decision entails (Box 59.3). Parents need to understand that if they would like the baby to remain with them at all times, they need to have that specified as part of the plan. Specifically, they would need to either eliminate or delay interventions that would be done away from them. Pediatric palliative APRNs must describe what typical interventions can be performed right at the bedside and what can be done later, if the baby survives and stabilizes. Parents should understand that staff can be flexible about when and how they measure and weigh the baby, take footprints, apply the eye ointment, and give vitamin K and hepatitis shots.

Creating a birth plan is a process that may take several meetings. Initially, parents may not understand the realities of specific interventions that they may request for their infant or that would happen routinely unless they specify it in their care plan. Despite saying that they do not want to prolong suffering for their

---

Box 59.2 Appropriate Diagnoses for Neonatal Palliative Care

Extreme prematurity and its complications, which include:

Genetic problems

Trisomy 13, 15, or 18

Triploidy

Thanatophoric dwarfism

Lethal inborn errors of metabolism

Renal problems

Oligo/anhydramnios with pulmonary hypoplasia

Potter syndrome

Renal agenesis

Multicystic/dysplastic kidneys

CNS abnormalities

Anencephaly/acrania

Holoprosencephaly

Congenital severe hydrocephalus with absent or minimal brain growth

Neurodegenerative diseases (spinal muscular atrophy)

Heart problems

Acardia

Complex congenital heart defects like hypoplastic left heart syndrome, Ebstein's anomaly

Pentalogy of Cantrell

Other structural anomalies

Congenital diaphragmatic hernia with hypoplastic lungs

---

baby who has a known lethal diagnosis, parents can sometimes request interventions that do not align with their goals of care. For instance, including cardiopulmonary resuscitation as part of the plan will not give them more time with their baby; in fact, it will take their baby away while it is being done and may cause suffering by prolonging death or delaying comfort medications. It is vital that parents have these details explained so that their birth plan accurately reflects their goals of care for their infant (Box 59.4).

The final birth plan should be one with which the parents are most comfortable and that conveys specific decisions or interventions. The parents should know that the plans are not written in stone and that they can change their minds. Good collaboration and communication are key in the creation of a birth plan. When completed, the birth plan should be shared with everyone involved. The result is appropriate and realistic expectations for the birth for the parents and all the providers involved.

Parents should be encouraged to perform normal activities of infant care: bathing, dressing, and changing the baby's diaper.

Box 59.3 Creating a Birth Plan for Infants with Life-Limiting Conditions

1. Explain the routine interventions that are done with a well-baby birth (suctioning, cleaning, measuring, footprints).

2. Explain how the baby may present at birth given his or her diagnoses. Describe what an aggressive plan of care would look like in the case of respiratory distress/bradycardia/full arrest. Discuss the benefits and burdens of typical emergency interventions. Clarify what would be in alignment with their goals of care for their baby.

3. Discuss what interventions would be done to support their goals of care for their baby and to maximize the time they have with their baby when end-of-life is expected at, or soon after, birth.

4. Understand that it may take more than one conversation to complete the birth plan, and plan accordingly.

5. Share the completed birth plan with all providers involved, including the obstetrics team, the fetal treatment center staff, the palliative care team, and the delivering hospital staff. Extra copies should be given to parents to bring with them.

Taking pictures and videos for memory making should be supported. Spiritual care and rituals should be encouraged.

The very central issue of feeding should be discussed. Since feeding is an essential aspect of a baby's life, there are benefits and burdens for infants with many congenital problems. Depending on the diagnosis, a baby may or may not be able or want to feed. If a parent wants to attempt feeding, encourage him or her to offer a bottle or breast and see what happens, sharing with them that the baby will take what he or she wants; forcing the baby to do more can cause distress. The parents should be informed that feeding can cause discomfort. Parents should be encouraged to perform frequent mouth care and offer a pacifier for comfort. Other siblings should be included; they should be specifically brought in and introduced to the baby.

Adequate preparation for parents and providers for all possible outcomes ensures a smooth transition if a baby with a complex life-limiting diagnosis survives the birth. There should be reassurance that comfort medications are available to continue to keep the baby comfortable. If the baby survives, he or she will stay with the mother during the postpartum hospital stay. When it is time for the mother's discharge, plans will be made for the baby to be discharged home with hospice.

Parents of a child with severe problems may be completely unprepared and overwhelmed at the thought of bringing home a new baby. This is often because they have been so focused on the death

---

Box 59.4 Sample Birth Plan

Mother's name:

Date of birth:

Obstetrician:

Due date:

Planning for _____(Vaginal or C/S)

Birth Plan for: _____

Our baby, _____, has been diagnosed with _____.

Your kindness, compassion and understanding during our labor and delivery experience are greatly appreciated.

We understand that every birthing experience is unique and offer this birth plan only as a guideline and not a script for our birth experience. We also understand that decisions may need to be made after the birth, which we have not anticipated. Our goal is on enhancing _____'s quality of life without causing undue suffering. We ask only that you keep us informed so we can make decisions together for what is best for _____.

1. Our (son or daughter's) name is _____.

2. We would (want or not want)_____intermittent external fetal monitoring. We may ask you to discontinue this as labor progresses.

3. If there is a sudden loss of heartbeat prior to delivery, we (wish or do not wish) _____to be informed.

4. (Mother's name) _____ (would or would not)_____ like an epidural and minimal other pain management. It is important that sedation is avoided for (mother's name)_____so that she can be as alert as possible after delivery.

5. We ask that _____be able to cut the umbilical cord.

6. We (do or do not)_____ want chest compressions or routine emergency medications (epi, atropine, lidocaine) to be initiated under any circumstances for _____.

7. We permit the following to be done to stabilize (his or her) airway/breathing: ____Drying and stimulation, _____suctioning, _____ blow-by oxygen, _____positive pressure ventilation, _____chest compressions.

8. Intubation/mechanical ventilation (will or will not)_____ be considered.

9. After _____is born, we ask that (he or she) quickly be wiped, wrapped in a blanket and handed to _____.

(continued)

Box 59.4 Continued

10. Please delay all routine procedures (weight, measure, footprints, eye ointment, vitamin K, hepatitis shot, etc.) until both parents have held _____. If any of these procedures must be done, please do them only while the parents are holding (him/her).

11. We understand that _____ may be born with more or fewer problems than anticipated. If this is the case, we ask that our options are discussed with us first, and if necessary, further diagnostic testing may be permitted.

12. We would like to have some private time with _____ after delivery. We do not wish to impede staff responsibilities, only to maximize our time together with our (son or daughter).

13. We request that a nurse periodically give updates to the waiting family.

14. We plan for _____ to be (breastfed or bottle fed)_____. If she/he is not able to suck/swallow, a NG tube (may or may not)_____ be placed if possible.

15. We request that a ceremony be performed in accordance with our religious beliefs by _____(baptism, blessing or dedication).

16. Please discuss any medications given to _____ to relieve pain and suffering with us prior to administering.

17. We wish to hold _____ if she/he is dying or has died.

18. We would like to keep the following items as keepsakes: lock of hair, ID band, crib card, hat/blanket/clothes, footprints/handprints, photos, etc.

19. It is important to us that nobody enters the room without knowing our situation. In addition, we would like a room somewhat secluded from other delivering/new parents, if possible.

20. Autopsy (is or is not)_____ being considered.

21. Funeral arrangements are being made with _____in____ phone #_____

22. We would like the Palliative Care Team to be notified when we come into the hospital for delivery. They have been involved with our birth plan and will be available for support. Their phone # is_____

    We appreciate your help in making this event as memorable and special for us as possible. _____

_____

Signature of Parent(s)

---

of their baby that they have not prepared for normal care. They have not allowed themselves to do the enjoyable things to prepare for a new baby, like preparing a baby room, buying clothes, and preparing a crib. Often extended family members are happy to get the essentials for the baby, so that the parents can just stay with the baby prior to their discharge home. The pediatric palliative APRN should ensure that the parents have the essential things needed for their baby prior to discharge and connect them with resources if needed.

The palliative care team should give parents the opportunity to meet with hospice prior to discharge, on the day of discharge, or once they are home. They need to be assured that palliative care will still be involved. The partnership with hospice allows parents to have support close to home, when they need it.

Conflicts over the Birth Plan

Often when the diagnoses are not well known or absolute, there can be conflict between providers or even between parents and providers. Sometimes, providers are uncomfortable with the decisions made by the parents because this would not be their personal choice in a similar situation. They may feel that the interventions are too aggressive or not aggressive enough, based on their own personal values, religious beliefs, or cultural values. When disagreement occurs, these thoughts and feelings need to be discussed and explored. Providers need to be aware of how their personal values and opinions can influence how they are providing care for others. Open communication is essential. Provider reflection is important in a supportive environment that acknowledges individual opinions.

It is important for the pediatric palliative APRN to assess the level of comfort of the providers involved and to explore areas of discomfort or challenges. There may be a need for ethics consultation, legal counsel, or spiritual support for resolution of the issues, or there may be a need for further palliative care education.

A Baby with an Aggressive Plan of Care

Often when a baby is born with a potential life-limiting diagnosis, the parents may desire an aggressive plan of care. In these situations, the parents need to be reminded of realistic expectations regarding the care for their baby, and the likely birth process. Babies who need aggressive therapies usually cannot be initially held by their parents. They are often whisked away to another area where the appropriate supplies/supports are available for those interventions. Once the essential things are done, the healthcare providers should allow a few moments for the mother and father to hold the baby and have a few pictures taken, if possible. The baby may need to be transferred to another facility. In this situation, contact information and directions on where the baby is being transferred should be given, with reassurances of updates to parents.

Admission to the NICU

More research exists about palliative care in the neonatal intensive care unit (NICU) than in the perinatal setting. Carter and Caitlin established a model for palliative care in the NICU to provide consistent clinical guidelines for staff that facilitated family-centered care for the most fragile infants. These guidelines serve as a reference for all healthcare providers to educate others, including families and students.[9]

When a baby with a potential life-limiting condition arrives in the NICU, there is an initial settling-in period. During this time, there is assessment and evaluation to better understand the infant's medical issues and how best to support him or her. Even when an infant has had prenatal evaluation, the actual situation remains unknown until the baby is born. This time is anxiety-provoking for parents because they may not have access to the baby. Mothers may need to recover from a cesarean section or traumatic birthing process.

When a baby is admitted to a critical care unit, it is a time of high stress for parents.[10] Consistent communication when a baby is in the NICU is imperative. Weekly team meetings can strengthen the relationship between the NICU and the palliative care team. Parents find comfort in having compassionate, honest, and cohesive communication about their baby. It also establishes the necessary trust with parents. With the transition from obstetrics to the neonatal team and rotating staff in the NICU, the pediatric palliative APRN provides much-needed continuity through systematic monitoring of the baby and the family. Through this approach, the APRN can put supports in place that represent the core of neonatal palliative care.[11] This offers ongoing updates and ensures that parents understand the baby's needs. The integration of available supports in the NICU, along with appropriate community resources, cultivates and strengthens the relationship of trust between the family and the team members.

End-of-Life in the NICU

The death of an infant with conditions incompatible with life necessitates planning. The pediatric palliative APRN and the healthcare team must prepare families on what to expect at birth, during the dying process, and during the grief and bereavement period. No matter what the circumstances are at the end-of-life, whether expected and planned for or unexpected and sudden, parents and staff must be as prepared as possible. An infant may live with a poor prognosis for several days. Parents may choose to stop interventions that they feel are causing their baby to suffer or they may decide to withdraw interventions when there is no hope of cure or quality of life. The parents should be supported in planning a peaceful death according to their values, preferences, and beliefs. Parents need to understand that this is not "killing" their baby but rather allowing nature to take its course. Parents need reassurance that providers will inform them as they see signs that the baby is close to the end-of-life although prognostication is difficult. The parents should know that death could occur over minutes, hours, or even days.

The role of each person on the NICU team should be clarified to ensure a seamless process. A plan should be in place to manage symptoms when technology is withdrawn, such as respiratory or cardiac support. It is essential to educate the parents about the comfort medications to be used, how and why they will be used, signs and symptoms of pain and discomfort, and physical signs of dying. Opioids and benzodiazepines can offer pain and symptom relief and secretions can be managed (Box 59.5).

It is important to reinforce that each baby and family is unique and that "what is right at the end-of-life" is what feels right to them.

Box 59.5 End-of-Life Medications

Morphine: 0.05–0.1 mg/kg IV prn or 0.2–0.5 mg/kg PO/NG for pain; titrate for comfort

Lorazepam: 0.05 mg/kg IV or PO/NG for dyspnea and agitation (also has antiepileptic properties); titrate for comfort

Midazolam: 0.15 mg/kg IV or if already receiving, adjustment of that dose and/or drip if infusing for agitation; titrate for comfort

Glycopyrrolate: 4–10 mcg/kg IV or 40–100 mcg/kg PO for increased secretions q3–4h

Continue any antiepileptic medications if already ordered to prevent seizures.

From reference 12.

In a situation that is overwhelmingly sad, parents need to be offered control. The pediatric palliative APRN can offer choices, such as when life-sustaining measures will be discontinued, the site of the infant's death (room at the hospital, home, or another specially designated area), who will be present in the room with them, how long they hold the infant after death, and whether they want to participate in a post-death bath or memory making. Parents should know that planning is a fluid process and adjustments can be made during the process, but most important is the reassurance they will not do this alone.

To offer the most control, parents need to be informed of realistic timeframes for planning and arranging a respectful death. For example, if they choose to take their baby home, it may take more time to arrange transport and hospice. Again, parents need to be assured there is no "right way" and that they may change the plan of who is with them and participation in post-death rituals.

The death plan is communicated by the pediatric palliative APRN to the care providers who will be involved in the infant's death. A team meeting should be held to review the plan and to ensure that the correct orders are in place, such as Do Not Resuscitate or Allow Natural Death, as well as the appropriate medications. The discontinuation of life-sustaining measures is ordered as appropriate, such as vasoactive drips, miscellaneous medications, or feeds. The family should be informed about the process of removing life-sustaining measures and the dying process and should be reassured that the infant will be kept comfortable.

The process of allowing an infant's death can begin when the parents and any people they want are in attendance. Although they have received education, parents may ask, "What happens next?" The pediatric palliative APRN may gently guide them through each step of the process: getting ready for withdrawal, administering medications, removing technology, the dying process, and the post-death period. Parents should not feel rushed and should have a provider to attend them at all times to offer support and information. The team ensures the necessary medications and supplies are at hand. Medications are administered to provide comfort and the life-sustaining therapies are discontinued when the medications have taken effect. Usually an endotracheal tube is removed and the ventilator is turned off. The nasogastric tube can also be removed if there is intravenous access for continued medication administration.

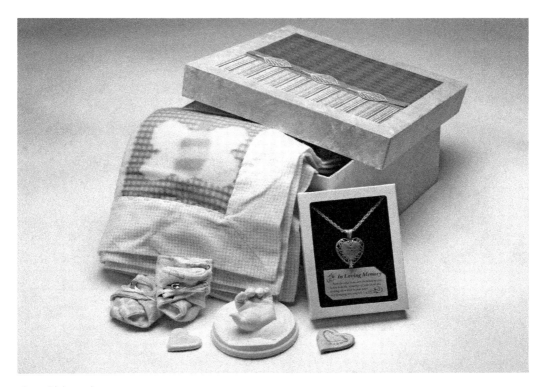

Figure 59.1 Memory box with keepsakes

After an Infant's Death

Once the baby has died and the time of death has been noted, parents should be told that they can take as much time as they need. The period after a death is a sacred time. The parents should be allowed privacy, whether by themselves with the baby or with family members if they wish. They may want to participate in bathing the baby or memory making (Figs. 59.1).

The pediatric palliative APRN can educate the parents about postmortem details, including the role of the medical examiner and the option of autopsy and/or organ donation. An autopsy can often be helpful to better understand what happened to cause the

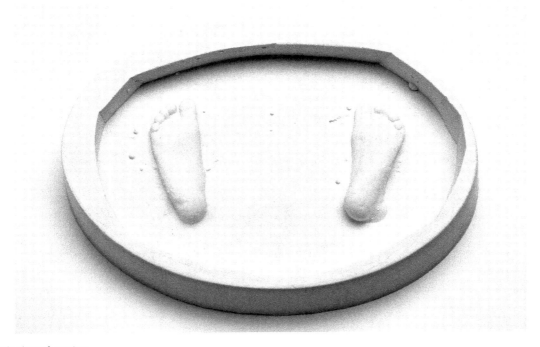

Figure 59.2 Sample plaster footprints

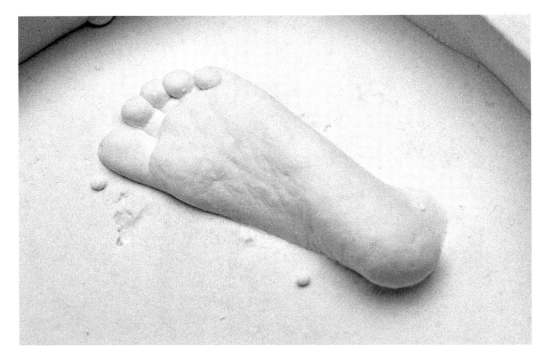

Figure 59.3 Sample plaster footprint (close-up)

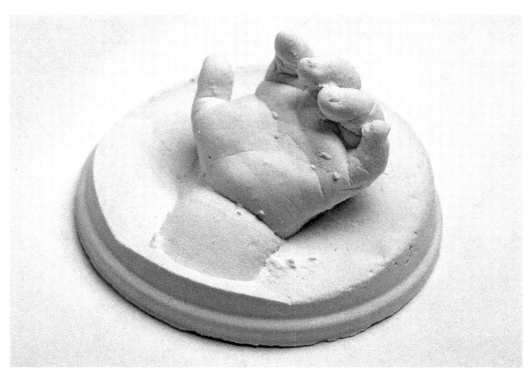

Figure 59.4 Sample plaster handprint

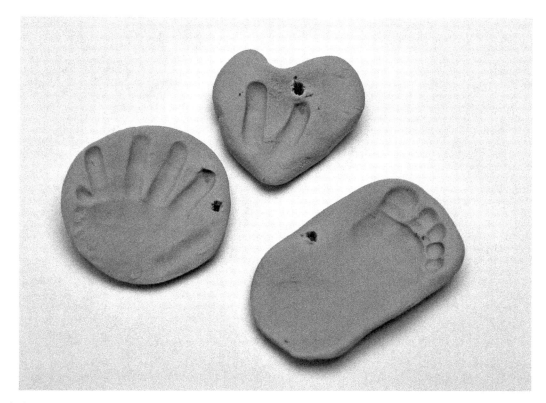

Figure 59.5 Sample clay prints

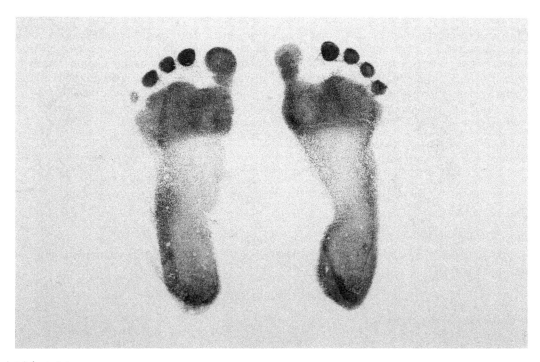

Figure 59.6 Sample ink footprints

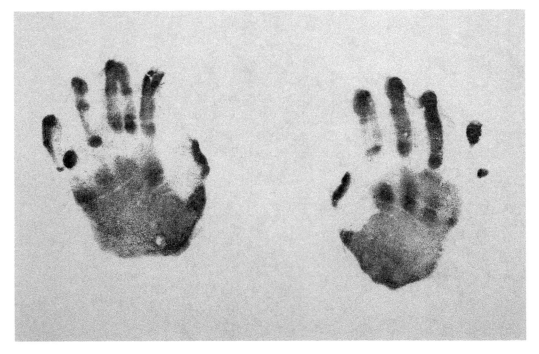

Figure 59.7 Sample ink handprints

baby's medical issues; this can bring them some comfort and can have implications for future pregnancies. The APRN answers any questions and reassures the parents they do not have to make an immediate decision about the autopsy (Box 59.6).

The pediatric palliative APRN is responsible for implementing postmortem care. Constant communication, teaching, and support should occur not only for the parents and family but also for the staff. It is important to include staff members, such as environmental services personnel, cafeteria workers, respiratory therapists, unit secretaries, and others who may be affected by the baby's death, especially if the infant has had a long stay in the NICU. A post-death debriefing allows time for staff bereavement.

It can be comforting for the parents to hear how special their baby was to everyone and how much he or she will be missed.

When the parents are ready to leave, contact information should be confirmed. They should be provided with bereavement resources and a phone number for follow-up with the palliative care team and bereavement specialist. They should also have assistance with collecting their belongings. Safe transportation home should be planned by having another family member or friend drive them home. If they are driving home, they should be accompanied to their vehicle. Reassure them that the palliative care team will continue to follow and support them if they have any questions or concerns (Box 59.7).

Box 59.6 End-of-Life Process

Family Support

Offer privacy

Provide discussion with neonatologist and palliative care

Provide anticipatory guidance regarding what to expect: comfort meds, physical changes, unknown amount of time, support resources available, photos/memory making

Spiritual Needs

Notify chaplain or family clergy/spiritual leader

Perform spiritual rituals

Baby Care

Photograph and/or video record the child and parent holding the child, as requested

Bathe and dress baby in special outfit

(continued)

Box 59.6 Continued

Perform memory-making before or after death (as family prefers)

Make plaster molds of hand and foot, ink hand- and footprints, lock of hair, memory box, bereavement packet with books/resources/support contacts

Remove endotracheal tube and nasogastric tube if present; keep central lines in place

Postmortem

Allow parents/family to have as much time as needed to be with their baby

Provide anticipatory guidance regarding autopsy, organ donation, selection of funeral home, bereavement support resources and coping/grieving process

Prepare body for funeral home or morgue

Place phone calls to organ procurement agency, medical examiner's office, security, hospital operator, nursing supervisor, pathologist (if autopsy), birth hospital (if mother still admitted), Ronald McDonald House (if parents are staying there), funeral home (if chosen)

Complete documentation in electronic health record and information sent to the OB and other consultants involved in care; death certificate information form

---

Box 59.7 Post Mortem Checklist

Name of Child_____   Parent Name_____
Date and Time of Death_____
Funeral Home_____

Notification   Organ Procurement
____Operator   ____yes
____Nursing Supervisor   ____no
____Organ Procurement   Referral # _____
____Security   Organ Procurement Contact Person
____Pathology
                                                                _____

Non-Medical Examiner Case   Medical Examiner Case

____no   ____yes

Autopsy at the request of family   Person contacting Medical Examiner

____yes–permit signed and accompanies body   Name and Empl # _____

____no

____undecided   Disposition of Child's Body

                                                                ____Transported to Morgue

                                                                Released from Floor to Parent

                                                                Name and Empl # _____

                                                                Name _____ Empl # _____

                                                                Release of Body to Funeral Home

                                                                Date _____ Time _____

                                                                Name and Empl # _____

Security   Signature of funeral home staff _____

____Verification of identity of body

Name and Empl # _____

Neonatal Team Support and Education

In addition to supporting the family and infant, pediatric palliative APRNs work closely with their healthcare colleagues as the entire team collaborates about the care for the baby and family. While some curricula have been created for palliative care education, many groups, including the American Academy of Pediatrics, the Institute of Medicine, and the World Health Organization, have recommended increased palliative care-specific training for physicians.[13] Researchers continue to identify the need for education, finding that healthcare providers are inadequately prepared in palliative care and consequently lack confidence in caring for infants and families, causing increased distress.[14,15] Working collaboratively, there can be better assessment of the educational and training needs of nursing and physician colleagues in order to provide opportunities for palliative care education and skills. A positive collaboration and relationship with the NICU team allows team members to be more comfortable sharing their concerns and needs that arise with the challenging and stressful work of caring for palliative care patients and their families.

Conclusion

The pediatric palliative APRN can be the anchor for the infant and family, providing constant support through the infant's unique life journey. The APRN, with the collaboration of the provider team, can ensure that the principles of pediatric palliative care guide the care of the infant and family, rendering comprehensive support for pain and symptom management and assistance with emotional, psychological, practical, spiritual, educational, and developmental issues that may contribute to suffering or interfere with healing. The pediatric palliative APRN is in an ideal position to assess the parents' understanding of the diagnosis, prognosis, and treatment options, in agreement with their cultural and spiritual beliefs, and how they define a good quality of life for their infant. The APRN is also ideally situated to share the parents' understanding and beliefs with the other providers caring for the child and family. While education and training are improving for providers in perinatal/neonatal/pediatric palliative care, the pediatric palliative APRN may educate and support the families and the community.

References

1. Centers for Disease Control and Prevention. National Center for Health Statistics. Deaths: Final Data for 2012. August 31, 2015. NSVR. 2014;63(9):1120. Available at http://www.cdc.gov/nchs/products/nvsr.htm. Accessed September 1, 2015.
2. March of Dimes. Infant Mortality Rates Hit All-Time Low. April 2013. Available at http://www.marchofdimes.org/news/infant-mortality-rates-hit-all-time-low.aspx. Accessed July 15, 2015.
3. Friebert S. *NHPCO Facts and Figures: Pediatric Palliative Care in America*. Alexandria, VA: National Hospice and Palliative Care Organization; April 2009.
4. Field MJ, Behrman RE. Institute of Medicine Committee on Palliative and End-of-Life Care for Children and Their Families. *When Children Die: Improving Palliative and End-of-Life Care for Children and Their Families*. Washington, DC: National Academy Press; 2003.
5. Balaguer A, Martin-Ancel A, Ortigoza-Escobar D, Escribano J, Argemi J. The model of palliative care in the perinatal setting: a review of the literature. *BMC Pediatr.* 2012; 12: 25 http://www.biomedcentral.com/147-2431/12/25.
6. Catlin A, Carter B. Creation of a neonatal end-of-life palliative care protocol. *J Perinatol.* 2002; 22: 184–95. doi:10.1038/sj/jp/7210687
7. National Association of Neonatal Nurses. Palliative Care for Newborn and Infants. Position Statement #3051, 2010. Available at http://www.nann.org/uploads/files/Palliative_Care-final2-in_new_template_01-07-11.pdf. Accessed July 15, 2015.
8. Dean B, McDonald K. Nursing perspectives: building an interprofessional perinatal palliative care team. *NeoReviews.* 2014; 15(10): 422–5. doi: 10.1542/neo.15-10-e422
9. Catlin A, Carter B. Creation of a neonatal end-of-life palliative care protocol. *J Perinatol.* 2002; 22: 184–95. doi:10.1038/sj/jp/7210687
10. Gold KJ. Navigating care after a baby dies: a systematic review of parent experiences with health providers. *J Perinatol.* 2007; 27(4): 230–7.
11. Carter B. Providing palliative care for newborns. *Pediatr Ann.* 2004; 33(11): 770–7. PMID:15559703
12. Lexicomp online. http://www.crlonline.com
13. Petteys A, Goebel J, Wallace J, Singh-Carlson S. Palliative care in neonatal intensive care, effects on parent stress and satisfaction: a feasibility study. *Am J Hosp Palliat Care.* doi:10.1177/1049909114551014
14. Harris L, Placentia F, Arnold J, Minard C, Harris T, Haidet P. A structured end-of-life curriculum for neonatal-perinatal postdoctoral fellows. *Am J Hosp Palliat Care.* doi:10.1177/1049909114523825
15. Wool C. Clinician confidence and comfort in providing perinatal palliative care. *J Obstet Gynecol Neonat Nurs.* 2013; 42: 48–58. doi:10.1111/j.1552-6909.2013.01432.x

CHAPTER 60

Pediatric Oncology

Amy Corey Haskamp and Deborah A. Lafond

Key Points

- Early integration of palliative care may mitigate suffering and fosters improved coping throughout the trajectory of the underlying disease.

- The palliative advanced practice registered nurse (APRN) must appreciate that children with a cancer or blood disease often suffer from a multitude of symptoms, threatening the intactness and quality of life of the child and family.

- The palliative APRN can initiate therapies with curative intent concurrently with those that ease suffering and maximize quality of life.

- While the context of hope may change over time, it is an essential component of the well-being of the patient and family faced with a terminal illness.

Case Study

Eric was a 7-year-old with juvenile xanthogranuloma (JXG), a rare type of non-Langerhans cell histiocytosis leading to accumulation of histiocytes in the skin, adrenal and pituitary glands, central nervous system, bone marrow, and many major organs. Diagnosed at the age of 3 years, he completed chemotherapy treatments. He did well until the age of 5, when he presented with leg pain, refusal to walk at times, and vague abdominal pain. A skeletal survey showed dramatic new and extensive changes in almost every bone. Given these findings, it was decided to proceed with a hematopoietic stem cell transplant (HSCT) with curative intent.

The palliative care team was introduced as a routine service provided for all patients undergoing HSCT to assist with pain and symptom management and to give additional family support. A variety of interventions were provided throughout the trajectory of transplant for symptom management, including a host of integrative therapies, such as acupressure, massage, aromatherapy, music, art, and play therapies. Eric's parents felt well informed by the transplant team about the expected complications. While Eric had multiple admissions after the transplant, they remained optimistic for long-term cure.

Eric did well for 1 year after HSCT, but he subsequently developed increasing symptoms requiring frequent admissions. Many different pharmacologic and nonpharmacologic strategies were implemented without much improvement. Abdominal pain and nausea became very distressing for Eric and his family. The palliative care team continued to follow him during many hospitalizations, and acute symptoms were able to be well managed. Unfortunately, Eric's underlying JXG flared. There were few treatment options for disease recurrence after transplant. Therefore, the family carefully weighed their options to continue aggressive curative-intent therapies with quality of life. The palliative care team worked in collaboration with the primary hematology and transplant teams to help the family explore goals for Eric. Given that Eric had been very vocal and engaged in his treatment for several years, his mother verbalized that she wondered what his wishes were. The palliative care team facilitated a conversation with Eric using the *My Wishes* advance directive document. Using this tool, Eric stated that he did not want to be in the hospital and that he wanted to be home. He realized that treatments were not working and wanted to be home more than he wanted to keep looking for other treatments. Eric conveyed that he wished he was home in his own bed, tucked into his comfy covers. Using this as a guide, his parents made the very loving decision to take him home with home hospice support.

Eric was home for 3 months. Pain was well controlled on a morphine PCA. He was TPN dependent, as he was unable to tolerate enteral feeds. Medications were given primarily via a G-tube. He had outpatient clinic visits twice a week for transfusions. He required one admission after enrolling in hospice. At that time, the pediatric palliative APRN assisted in the development of protocols to manage most symptoms at home to avoid further admissions. Eric was happy and playful and the family was active in making memories at home.

Introduction

The coordination of care between the primary pediatric oncology team and the pediatric palliative APRN is vital for the outcomes of patients and families. Pediatric oncology patients frequently report pain and other physical and psychological symptoms before, during, and after treatment for cancer. The palliative APRN assists with the management of pain and other symptoms and facilitates discussions about goals of care and the end-of-life.

Cancer is much less common in children than in adults. The overall incidence of pediatric cancer is 16.8 cases per 100,000 children[1] in the United States and has increased by an average of 0.6% per year from 1975 to 2010.[2] While the 5-year survival rate for children and young adults 20 years old and younger with cancer improved from 58.8% in 1975 to 84.8% in 2006,[3] pediatric cancers remain the second leading cause of death in children ages 5 to 14 years. In 2010, there were nearly 380,000 survivors of childhood and adolescent cancer living in the United States.[2] In addition to those with a cancer diagnosis, the palliative APRN can provide benefit to children with hematological disorders, such as sickle cell disease, aplastic anemia, or hemophagocytic lymphohistiocytosis.

At diagnosis, patients frequently report cancer-related symptoms caused by the invasion or compression of vital structures of the body. Psychological or social distress may be caused by the uncertainty of the diagnosis, prognosis, or diagnostic testing. During treatment, patients may experience symptoms caused by therapies, such as chemotherapy, radiation therapy, surgery, or hematopoietic stem cell transplant (HSCT); procedures, such as dressing changes, subcutaneous or intramuscular injections, needle sticks, lumbar punctures, bone marrow aspirates, or anxiety related to these treatments and procedures.

While many of the treatments for childhood cancers are administered with a curative intent, more than 15% of children with cancer will die from their illness. Even if long-term survival is achieved, late effects of cancer treatment include neurocognitive impairments, poor motor functioning, and diminished social well-being, all of which may cause significant distress for the child and family.[4] A substantial effort is needed to minimize suffering experienced at the end-of-life. The disease takes an emotional and physical toll on the child's primary caregivers and family members. Distress may be significant whether the child survives or faces the end-of-life. The palliative APRN can help prevent or treat suffering experienced by pediatric oncology patients and families, thereby increasing quality of life throughout the trajectory of the cancer journey.

Early Integration of Palliative Care

Despite the tremendous advances in childhood cancer treatments, children with cancer often experience suffering. Whether suffering is from the side effects of treatment, relapse, imminent death, or perhaps all of these, pediatric palliative APRNs can promote comfort and ease the suffering throughout the trajectory of illness. Even cancer survivors may have a myriad of late effects that affect their quality of life. Thus, early integration of palliative care may mitigate suffering from the time of diagnosis throughout the trajectory of treatment into survivorship, or it may foster a peaceful death. The American Academy of Pediatrics supports the integration of palliative care from the time of diagnosis of a life-limiting illness.[5]

The Case Study illustrates the many advantages of early palliative care involvement with Eric and his family:

- Introduction of palliative care as a normal part of HSCT focused on promoting comfort and quality of life.

- A relationship with Eric and his family developed over time, which allowed better understanding of the family's expectations and wishes when his condition deteriorated.

- The team devoted time and resources that complemented the resources of the transplant team and provided an additional layer of support.

- Trust developed, which allowed the palliative care team to manage home needs in collaboration with hospice and maintain continuity with the primary transplant team.

Introducing Palliative Care into Pediatric Oncology Treatment

The medical team is often the first to recognize that a child is not likely to survive the cancer diagnosis. This may be at the time of diagnosis, where the chance of cure is low, when a cancer is metastatic at the time of diagnosis, or at the time of relapse.[6] Wolfe and colleagues noted that physicians recognize that a child has no realistic chance of cure at a mean of 206 days before the child's death, while parents recognized death as inevitable at 105 days before the child's death.[7] This may lead to missed opportunities for discussion of goals of care with both the child and parents and for legacy making.

There is never a "right time" to talk about death. Healthcare providers are commonly uncomfortable talking with patients and families about this difficult subject. Families never want to have to face the possibility that their child may die. However, asking the question "Would you be surprised if this child died within the next year?" is an accurate prognostic tool.[8] If the answer to this question is "no," then consideration of integrating palliative care is paramount.

Palliative care is more than just end-of-life care. It is about living, whether the outcome is long-term survivorship or death. Prolongation of life is an important goal of pediatric palliative care, but not at the expense of quality of life.[9,10] Introducing palliative care as a means of expert supportive care to promote comfort and quality of life may avoid some of the misperceptions about palliative care (that it is only for dying children).[9] Most families are amenable to focusing on health maintenance and optimizing quality of life.[11] In a recent survey of pediatric oncologists, 90% stated they almost always refer patients to palliative care specialists for significant symptom distress and/or if the child's life expectancy is less than 12 months. However, less than 50% would refer a child with no symptom distress, even if the life expectancy was less than 12 months.[6] This further supports that end-of-life care and planning are only part of palliative care services.

This same survey regarding referral patterns found that 96% of pediatric oncologists identified access to specialized palliative consultation care services and were more likely (73%) to recognize the benefits of early referral at the time of diagnosis of a high-risk cancer than their adult oncology colleagues (43%). Nevertheless, concerns about integration of palliative care included having too many medical teams involved in care (17%), negative reception by parents (60%), terminology attributed to death and dying versus supportive care (58%), and referring only after curative-intent therapies had stopped (13%).[6] Consideration should be given to how palliative care is introduced to families and providers alike.

Parents are usually invested in promoting comfort and quality of life for their child. Providers strive to provide the highest quality of supportive care for their patients and families. While there is no right way to introduce palliative care, it is usually readily accepted if providers explain that it is a way to focus on making every day the best it can be, incorporating strategies for advanced pain and symptom management, optimizing quality of life, and providing additional psychosocial support for the child, as well as the entire family. Exploring what the family understands about palliative care will give opportunities to clarify misconceptions.

As one example, children undergoing HSCT have the potential for intense symptom distress and are more likely to be less prepared for the end-of-life.[12] Parents often do not want to discuss the possibility of death from this and other aggressive anticancer therapies, but these are patients who may die in the ICU, dependent on medical technologies. Early discussion of the benefits of palliative care may provide opportunities to discuss goals and ways to optimize quality of life. In a recent study of early integration of palliative care with curative-intent HSCT, families readily accepted the services (100%), were highly satisfied with integration of palliative care, and often referred other patients and families to the institution because of the availability of palliative care services.[13]

There are many challenges to integrating palliative care into the ongoing care of children with cancer. Normalizing palliative care as part of comprehensive cancer care dispels the fears that it is only introduced when the child is dying and can avoid the common problem of alienating patients, families, and providers.[14]

Some institutions have triggers for integrating palliative care into the ongoing care of pediatric oncology patients. Some proposed automatic triggers include the following:

- Newly diagnosed high-risk cancers, such as diffuse intrinsic pontine gliomas, stage IV neuroblastoma, metastatic solid tumors at diagnosis, or acute myelogenous leukemia
- HSCT
- Progressive, relapsed, and metastatic cancers
- Any patient being enrolled in a phase I clinical trial[15]

Settings for Palliative Care

Palliative care should be provided across the spectrum of care settings: inpatient, outpatient, and in the home.[16] The best setting is the one that the child and family desire, if adequate supports can be put in place. Care should be comprehensive, meeting the patient and family where they are in the journey, and optimizing care from the time of diagnosis. There are many models of pediatric palliative cancer care. The goal for any model is to assess the needs of the child and family and determine the best setting for care.

Symptom Management

Symptom management can be challenging in childhood cancer. A multitude of symptoms have been described in the literature by those undergoing treatment for cancer, childhood cancer survivors, and those at the end-of-life.[17-21] Successful management of symptoms helps to build trust with the child and family[22] and restores quality of life.

Constipation

Acute constipation has been identified in as many as 57% of children in active treatment for cancer.[19] Most common risk factors include inactivity, dehydration, electrolyte imbalance (e.g., hypercalcemia, hypokalemia), bowel compression caused by an abdominal tumor, nerve involvement, and medications (e.g., opioids, neurotoxic chemotherapy agents, such as vincristine). Patients with a preexisting history of constipation are at increased risk for developing constipation during treatment. Receiving vincristine

and/or opioids has been shown to be a significant risk factor due to decreased intestinal motility.[19] Constipation can lead to nausea, vomiting, anorexia, abdominal pain, bloating, and fecal impaction.

Since children and adolescents are often embarrassed when talking about bowel habits, these symptoms may be underreported. Therefore, the pediatric palliative APRN must assess for risk factors critical to constipation. The APRN should speak honestly with the child about the distress caused by constipation and develop a treatment plan. Some adolescents understand the medical management and can be responsible for self-monitoring and treatment without the embarrassment of discussing these issues with their parents. The pediatric palliative APRN should assess the character and frequency of stools; duration of symptoms; presence of blood or intermittent watery diarrhea; presence and character of bowel sounds; presence of abdominal, pelvic, or rectal pain; and presence of abdominal distention and palpable fecal masses.[23] A rectal assessment for hemorrhoids, fissures, tears, or fistulas may be warranted, but a digital exam should be performed only when necessary and with caution. An abdominal x-ray may be warranted to assess the presence of stool in the bowel.

Prevention and prompt treatment are important to constipation management.[23] The pediatric palliative APRN should provide education on prevention, including diet, bathroom measures, and activity. Education to prevent constipation should include the importance of a high-fiber diet, which includes fruits, vegetables, grains, and non-dairy fluids. Ensuring privacy for bowel elimination and encouraging increased mobility are other nonpharmacologic strategies. If the child has difficulty with mobility, it may be important to obtain a bedside commode or bedpan. Passive range-of-motion exercises to aid in gastric motility are important for the inactive child.

Prophylactic medications should be initiated when appropriate, with a goal of one soft stool per day.[24] Initiating senna within 2 days of starting opioids has been identified as an effective prophylactic agent in children with cancer.[25] Stool softeners may be important to aid in intestinal peristalsis and minimize pain during bowel elimination. Softeners are more effective when the child is well hydrated, so increased fluid intake should be encouraged. If softeners and laxatives are ineffective at treating constipation, other agents, such as magnesium citrate, glycerin suppositories, or enemas, may be required (Box 60.1).[26] Consider the risks before using suppositories or enemas in patients with pancytopenia.

Diarrhea

Diarrhea has been reported in approximately 15% of those undergoing cancer treatment.[18] Parents often greatly underestimate the frequency of the child's diarrhea, likely a result of the child's discomfort discussing bowel patterns. Diarrhea may be caused by partial or intermittent bowel obstruction, medications (e.g., antimicrobials and laxatives), malabsorption, infection, and toxicity of cancer treatment (e.g., abdominal and pelvic irradiation and chemotherapy agents like irinotecan, topotecan, combination cisplatin and docetaxel, and 5-fluorouracil). Four types of diarrhea have been identified as the most common during cancer treatment (Box 60.2).[27] Diarrhea can produce fatigue, impaired perirectal skin integrity, dehydration, electrolyte imbalances, abdominal pain and cramping, problems with body image, and, in severe cases, hypovolemic shock.

Box 60.1 Management of Constipation in Pediatrics

Senna

2–6 years: 3.75 mg PO q hs PO BID, maximum 7.5 mg

6–12 years: 8.6 mg PO q hs PO BID, maximum 25 mg

>12 years: 15 mg PO q hs PO BID, maximum 35–50 mg

Docusate sodium

<3 years: 10–40 mg/day PO in 1–4 divided doses

3–6 years: 20–60 mg/day PO in 1–4 divided doses

6–12 years: 40–150 mg/day PO in 1–4 divided doses

>12 years: 50–500 mg/day PO in 1–4 divided doses

Polyethylene glycol

≥6 months: 0.8 mg/kg PO q day, maximum 17 g/day

Milk of magnesia

2–5 years: 400–1,200 mg/day PO once a day or in divided doses

6–11 years: 1,200–2,400 mg/day PO once a day or in divided doses

≥12 years: 2,400–4,800 mg/day PO once a day or in divided doses

Magnesium citrate

2–6 years: 60–90 mL PO once a day or in divided doses

6–12 years: 90–210 mL PO once a day or in divided doses

≥12 years: 195–300 mL PO once a day or in divided doses

From reference 26.

---

constipation is important, as leakage of stool around impacted stool can be mistaken for diarrhea. A stool culture looking for parasites or other infections may be warranted. Obtaining blood for electrolytes, kidney and liver function tests, amylase, and lipase may be appropriate to determine the cause or effects of diarrhea.

Medical management of diarrhea is aimed at resolving the diarrhea and associated symptoms and treating the underlying cause. Oral hydration is preferred. Small, frequent amounts of fluid (e.g., 1–2 tsp for young children or 1–2 ounces for older children every 15 minutes) may be more tolerable to the child. Parents should be instructed to avoid fatty foods, nutritional supplements like Boost™ or Ensure™, and caffeine, which act as stimulants. A bedpan, bedside commode, or even diapers may be helpful to provide easy access for toileting, but preservation of the child's dignity is important. Application of skin barriers to the perirectal area and gentle cleansing after each stool may help avoid or treat skin breakdown.

Medications directed at constipation management should be discontinued, unless treating an impaction. The administration of antidiarrheal agents or other agents, such as somatostatin, may be appropriate (Box 60.3).[26,28] The administration of octreotide acetate has been shown to be effective for the treatment of chemotherapy-induced diarrhea.[29]

Probiotics contain viable microorganisms that are normally present in a healthy gut and that inhibit pathogenic bacterial growth in the intestines. The use of probiotics in immunocompromised patients has not been well studied, and there may be a concern about introducing new bacteria to the gut.[30] Probiotics are generally nonpathogenic and bacteria can cause infection if the patient is immunocompromised, especially if there are breaches in the host's mucosal barrier.[31] Prebiotics are a nondigestible food stimulating the growth of normal flora. Prebiotics can also be safely used to help prevent diarrhea, but they are generally not well understood. Prebiotics are generally recognized as safe, even in immunocompromised patients, as they serve as sustenance for the healthy microflora.[32]

Nausea and Vomiting

Nausea and vomiting are often the most distressing symptoms described by children undergoing cancer therapy.[18] They occur in about half of these patients.[18,33] Nausea has been more commonly reported in those with longer hospital stays[34] and appears to be more prevalent in adolescents than in younger children.

The pediatric palliative APRN should assess the frequency and duration of symptoms, the character of diarrhea (consistency, color, odor, presence of mucus or blood), volume, and bowel sounds. Associated abdominal, pelvic, or rectal pain should also be assessed, as well as the presence of palpable masses or feces, fever or other signs of infection, skin integrity, hydration status, vital signs, weight loss, and potential risk factors. Assessment for

---

Box 60.2 Classification and Causes of Diarrhea in Children with Cancer

Classification	Cause	Examples
Osmotic diarrhea	Entry of large volume of fluid and electrolytes into the intestinal lumen exceeding the absorptive capacity; commonly referred to as dumping syndrome	Enteral feedings that cannot be absorbed by the intestines, intestinal hemorrhage
Secretory diarrhea	Intestinal wall damage	Graft-versus-host disease, bacterial endotoxins, or surgically resected bowel
Hypermotile	Partial bowel obstruction	Fecal impaction, tumor compression, biliary or pancreatic obstruction causing incomplete digestion of fats
Exudative diarrhea	Mucosal inflammation in the intestinal wall	Abdominal or pelvic radiation, *Salmonella*, *Shigella*

From reference 27.

Box 60.3 Management of Diarrhea in Pediatrics

Loperamide (Imodium)

13–20 kg: 1 mg PO TID × 24 hours followed by maintenance dosing

20–30 kg: 2 mg PO BID × 24 hours followed by maintenance dosing

>30 kg: 2 mg PO TID × 24 hours followed by maintenance dosing

Maintenance dosing: 0.1 mg/kg after each loose stool; daily dose should not exceed the recommended dose for the initial 24 hours

Diphenoxylate and atropine (Lomotil)

2–12 years: 0.3–0.4 mg/kg PO QID; maximum 10 mg/day, then reduce dose as needed

≥12 years: 5 mg PO QID, maximum 20 mg/day, then reduce dose as needed

Octreotide (Sandostatin)

1–2 mcg/kg every 12 hours, may titrate by 0.3 mcg/kg/dose at 3-day intervals to 10 mcg/kg/dose

From references 26, 28.

Nausea may occur with or without vomiting, but vomiting typically is associated with nausea. Many factors may contribute to the presence of nausea and vomiting: side effects of medications (e.g., antimicrobials, chemotherapy agents, and opioids), biliary or intestinal obstruction or tumor invasion, central nervous system tumors, decreased gastric motility, constipation, metabolic disturbances (e.g., hypercalcemia, hyponatremia, and adrenocortical insufficiency), primary renal or hepatic failure, abdominal irradiation, and increased intracranial pressure. Prolonged nausea and vomiting may lead to the development of anticipatory nausea. Chemotherapy-induced nausea and vomiting may occur in two phases: the acute phase, which occurs within the first 24 hours after chemotherapy is administered, and the delayed phase, which may linger for up to a week or more after the administration is complete. Nausea and vomiting may result in fatigue, dehydration, electrolyte imbalances, pain, anorexia, and decreased quality of life. Children find it difficult to attend school and perform schoolwork when nauseated.

The pediatric palliative APRN should assess for risk factors, triggers, frequency and duration, character of bowel sounds, palpable masses, hydration status, and associated neurological sequelae (e.g., headache, ataxia, or changes in consciousness). Electrolytes and kidney and liver function should be monitored, and abdominal radiography may be needed.[35] Treatment is aimed at removing triggers, if possible, alleviating symptoms, and relieving the psychological distress caused by nausea and vomiting. Management should include both a nonpharmacologic and a pharmacologic approach. Parents should encourage small, frequent meals selected by the child, avoiding fatty or greasy foods. Oral care after meals and emesis is also recommended. If gastroesophageal reflux disease is suspected, the head of the bed should be elevated 30 degrees. It is important to eliminate foul odors and keep rooms fresh to relieve any environmental triggers. Anxiety can often provoke or potentiate nausea. Relaxation exercises, guided imagery, distraction, and aromatherapy are integrative approaches to reduce nausea and vomiting. Essential oils of ginger, orange, and mint are the most effective aromatherapies for the treatment of nausea.[36] Acupressure or acupuncture has also been shown to be effective for acute chemotherapy-induced nausea and vomiting.[36]

Pharmacologic management involves a fairly extensive list of agents. 5-HT$_3$-receptor antagonists (ondansetron and granisetron) have been shown to be appropriate for the treatment of chemotherapy-induced nausea and vomiting.[28] H$_1$-receptor antagonists (diphenhydramine and promethazine) are effective antiemetics but may be sedating. Scopolamine, an ACh$_m$-receptor antagonist, can be applied as a transdermal patch and is useful when children are too nauseated to take oral medications and obtaining line access is difficult. NK$_1$-receptor antagonists (aprepitant) have been shown to be highly effective in chemotherapy-induced nausea and vomiting when used in combination with dexamethasone and ondansetron; they are superior to dexamethasone and ondansetron alone.[37] Cannabinoids, corticosteroids, and benzodiazepines are other classes of medications used to treat nausea and vomiting. If gastroesophageal reflux is suspected, antireflux medications may be of benefit. Medications to improve gastric emptying or motility, such as metoclopramide or erythromycin, should not be used if obstruction is suspected, but a nasogastric tube can be used to decompress the stomach and provide relief (Box 60.4).[26,28]

Box 60.4 Treatment of Nausea and Vomiting In Pediatrics

Ondansetron (Zofran)

0.15 mg/kg/dose IV or PO q6–8h, maximum 8 mg/dose

Diphenhydramine (Benadryl)

0.5–1 mg/kg/dose PO or IV q6h, maximum 50 mg

Promethazine (Phenergan)

≥2 years: 0.25–0.5 mg/kg PO or IV q6h, maximum 25 mg

Scopolamine (Transderm Scop)

≥10 years: 1.5-mg transdermal patch q72h

Aprepitant (Emend)

≥12 years: 125 mg PO on day 1, followed by 80 mg PO daily on days 2 and 3

Dronabinol (Marinol)

5 mg/m^2 PO q2–4h, maximum 4–6 doses a day

Lorazepam (Ativan)

≥2 years: 0.025–0.05 mg/kg/dose PO or IV q6h, maximum 2 mg

From references 26, 28.

Anorexia/Cachexia

Anorexia is a decreased appetite and decreased consumption of food. Cachexia is the involuntary loss of more than 10% of a patient's weight, or muscle wasting, whereby the body breaks down skeletal and adipose tissue. These conditions generally lead to weakness and fatigue, body image changes in older children and adolescents, and psychological distress for families. Loss of appetite has been shown to occur in up to 50% of patients undergoing cancer treatment[18,38] and in as many as 80% of children dying of cancer.[21]

Physical factors that contribute to anorexia are uncontrolled pain or other symptoms, feeding or swallowing problems like mucositis, nausea and vomiting, constipation, delayed gastric emptying, and changes in taste. Psychological factors include depression and anxiety.[24] Researchers believe that inflammation plays a role in cachexia. Inflammation is a result of the body's immune response to the tumor, resulting in cytokine production. Cytokines can aid in killing tumor cells, but they also increase the body's metabolism, resulting in breakdown of muscle and fat.[39]

The pediatric palliative APRN should assess the pattern and timing of weight loss, daily caloric intake, changes in taste or smell, and presence of dysphagia, mucositis, nausea, constipation, or pain.[40] Laboratory tests to assess for nutritional depletion may prove beneficial. Albumin is most commonly measured due to the low cost and accuracy of the test when the patient does not have liver or kidney disease.[28] Assessing prognosis and goals of care is necessary to develop a care plan.

Treatment should be aimed at reversing contributing factors. Small, frequent meals of high-calorie foods and fluids, with as much choice as possible, should be encouraged to maximize calorie intake and limit the focus on eating. The choice of when and what to eat allows the child some amount of control. Physical exercise may aid in stimulating an appetite and should be encouraged as tolerated. Pharmacologic management should include agents aimed at treating contributing factors, such as pain medications, laxatives, antiemetics, or antidepressants. Research findings on appetite stimulants is varied, showing some improvement in anorexia, but they have typically been shown to result in only minimal weight gain and do not improve muscle mass, the tissue lost in cachexia[33,41] (Box 60.5). Dexamethasone increases appetite but should be used judiciously due to its side effects. If required, enteral nutrition is favored over parenteral nutrition due to the side effects (e.g., infection, thrombosis, and electrolyte abnormalities) of parenteral nutrition, despite the need for placement of a nasogastric or gastrostomy tube. Enteral nutrition allows for continued stimulation of the intestine, making the transition to oral feedings much more tolerable. However, in the case of a bowel obstruction or severe mucositis or vomiting, parenteral nutrition may be the best nutritional support.

In terminal cancer, the metabolic demands of the tumor may exceed any nutritional supplements provided. Studies in adults have shown no improvement in nutritional status, length of survival, or quality of life with nutritional interventions.[33,40] In fact, any intervention may lead to more suffering and decreased quality of life for the child. Electing to forgo nutritional support is a difficult decision for many families because offering food is generally associated with comfort and plays a significant role in a family's culture. Therefore, the choice to withhold nutrition creates many personal and ethical dilemmas for families. In an irreversible and progressive medical condition, it is ethically and legally permissible to withhold artificial nutrition and hydration.[24]

Fatigue

Cancer-related fatigue is a subjective, distressing side effect of cancer or its treatments. The physical, emotional, or cognitive tiredness or exhaustion is not proportional to the patient's activity level and interferes with daily function and quality of life.[42,43] Fatigue is one of the most commonly reported symptoms in children with cancer: it is reported in 50% to 75% of those undergoing cancer treatments and also occurs in childhood cancer survivors.[18,43] Parents reported that fatigue occurred in nearly 100% of their children with cancer at the end-of-life, with 57% of those children suffering from their fatigue and few cases successfully treated.[21]

There are multiple etiologies of cancer-related fatigue. It may be due to the cancer itself, treatments, or emotional factors. Cancer therapies have been identified as the primary cause, but other factors, such as pain, anemia, sleep/wake disturbances, metabolic abnormalities, nutritional deficiencies, emotional distress, reduced activity, and side effects of medications, may contribute. Physical and psychological factors may develop. The child may be too tired to eat, leading to anorexia. For adolescents, fatigue may lead to a lack of desire to attend school or interact socially with their friends, leading to social isolation and depression. Adolescents may also find it difficult to perform age-appropriate tasks due to the fatigue, leading to an increased dependence on others and a lack of self-confidence, further decreasing their quality of life.[18] In addition, anxiety, sadness, and fear at the end-of-life have been associated with fatigue.[17]

Box 60.5 Treatment for Anorexia/Cachexia in Pediatrics

Megestrol acetate

<50 kg: 7.5–10 mg/kg/day PO in 1–4 divided doses/day

≥50 kg: 400–800 mg PO in 1–4 divided doses/day

Cyproheptadine

2–6 years: 2 mg PO q8–12h

7–14 years: 4 mg PO q8–12h

≥15 years: Start at 2 mg PO q6h and increase over 3 weeks up to 8 mg q6h

Dexamethasone

10–20 kg: 2 mg PO q12h

21–40 kg: 4 mg PO q12h

≥41 kg: 8 mg PO q12h

Dronabinol

2.5 mg/kg/dose PO q6–8h

From reference 33.

Fatigue's multifactorial etiology necessitates a multidimensional approach to assessment. The pediatric palliative APRN should ask if the child feels tired or lacks energy. Then the onset, duration, aggravating and alleviating factors, and its effect on the child's ability to go to school, play, or sleep should be assessed. In children older than 12 years, fatigue can be assessed using a simple numeric rating scale, such as a 0-to-10 scale. A 1- to 5-point scale may be more appropriate in those 7 to 12 years old. For younger children, the word "tired" should be substituted for "fatigue."[44] Scales like the Memorial Symptom Assessment Scale (MSAS) and Childhood/Parent/Adolescent Fatigue Scales are available to screen for fatigue. Objective assessment includes evaluating vital signs, muscle strength, the presence of anxiety or depression, and hemoglobin levels to assess for anemia.

An interdisciplinary approach to the management of fatigue is most effective. Medical management may include blood transfusions for the treatment of anemia and/or medications, such as psychostimulants, antidepressants, sleep agents, or other agents, to combat the cause of the fatigue (e.g., nausea and vomiting, poor nutrition). However, little evidence exists for the use of psychostimulants in fatigue management for children. Nursing interventions include minimizing sleep disturbances and developing a schedule and routine for each day. Child life specialists or psychotherapists can teach techniques for stress management, guided imagery, and other skills to promote relaxation or allow the child to discuss feelings associated with fatigue. Nutritionists can teach families proper nutrition to promote energy. Finally, physical and/or occupational therapy can implement a low-intensity exercise program and age-appropriate activities to minimize boredom and social isolation. Exercise has been shown to have a moderate effect on reducing cancer-related fatigue.[45] Parents should be instructed to establish routines and to schedule activities during times of peak energy. Encouraging good sleep hygiene is also important in managing sleep/wake disturbances (Box 60.6).[26,46]

Pain

Pain has been reported in 45% of children hospitalized with cancer and in as many as 80% at the end-of-life.[18,21] Pain has been referred to as the most frightening and anxiety-provoking component of cancer therapy.[18] Procedural pain is the most common source of pain in this population and can lead to anxiety in cancer

survivors. In addition, pain has been reported in as many as 50% of those with sickle cell anemia, with many of these patients reporting pain daily.[47,48]

Common causes of cancer pain include tumor invasion or obstruction, surgical interventions, and side effects of chemotherapy and radiation therapy (e.g., oral mucositis, peripheral neuropathy, skin burns, perirectal breakdown) or treatment procedures (e.g., bone marrow aspiration/biopsy, lumbar punctures, venipuncture, dressing changes, injections). Vaso-occlusive crises are the most common cause of pain in children with sickle cell disease. Previous pain episodes as well as developmental, environmental, cultural, and psychosocial factors affect the pain experience. The child may report nociceptive and/or neuropathic pain and acute and/or chronic pain (Box 60.7).

Untreated pain can lead to a multitude of other complaints, such as depression, anxiety, sleep disturbance, fatigue, loss of appetite, nausea, loss of trust in the healthcare team, and decreased quality of life. Likewise, many of these symptoms can exacerbate pain, and generally all symptoms must be treated to achieve successful management.

To properly assess pain, the pediatric palliative APRN must acknowledge that pain is a subjective experience and the pain experience is unique to each patient. A history of the child's pain is essential, along with its potential causes or sources. Pain may go underreported in children with cancer if they fear it indicates progression or return of the disease. The APRN should learn the language the child uses to report pain. A self-report represents the gold standard, but behavioral observational scales may be required for a nonverbal patient. It is important to use a developmentally appropriate and evidence-based pain assessment tool. Education to parents and children should include how to use the appropriate pain scale

---

Box 60.6 Treatment of Fatigue in Pediatrics

Sleep agents

Zolpidem ≥12 years: 5 mg (females) or 5–10 mg (males) PO q HS, maximum dose 10 mg/day

Melatonin: 2–5 mg PO q HS

Nonpharmacologic Management

Frequent rest, energy conservation

Physical/occupational therapy

Exploring fears/anxiety that may lead to sleep disturbances

Promoting relaxation through guided imagery and cognitive-behavioral training

From references 26, 46.

Box 60.7 Causes and Descriptors of Nociceptive and Neuropathic Pain

Causes	Descriptors
Nociceptive—Somatic Tissues	
Increased pressure, bony tumor invasion, mucositis, skin breakdown, radiation skin burns, vaso-occlusive crisis in sickle cell disease (SCD), avascular necrosis	Dull, aching, penetrating, sharp, stabbing, throbbing, constant but worse with movement, point tenderness common
Nociceptive—Visceral Organs	
Tumor invasion resulting in organ distention, infiltration, necrosis, or obstruction	Deep, aching, dull, sharp, cramping, pressure
Constipation	Poorly localized
Acute chest syndrome/splenic sequestration in sickle cell disease	
Neuropathic	
Tumor infiltration, nerve compression, peripheral neuropathy, phantom limb pain	Tingling, burning, stabbing, shooting, electric/shooting, prickly, throbbing, aching
Sickle cell pain—has not been well studied	
Avascular necrosis	

to ensure consistent measurement of pain. Parents should also be taught to maintain a daily log of the child's pain, what treatment or intervention was provided, and the effects of that intervention.

Assessment of pain includes pain score, location, characteristics, intensity, quality, pattern, alleviating/aggravating factors, and duration. Behavioral indicators of pain should be observed (restlessness or agitation, grimacing, guarding, or moaning). The impact of pain on the child's interest in playing should also be assessed. A child who does not express interest in play activities may be experiencing pain. Vital sign changes are generally not seen in those with chronic pain or children who have learned to cope with pain in other ways.

The primary goal of pain management is to eliminate or reduce pain with the fewest side effects possible in order to restore quality of life. Acute pain should be treated based on the analgesic ladder approach recommended by the World Health Organization (WHO). See Chapter 23, Pain, for more information and Boxes 60.8[49] and 60.9[26,33] for pediatric dosing recommendations. Pediatric dosing of sustained-release medications can be difficult, particularly if the child cannot swallow pills. Available dosage forms of many long-acting opioids may not be appropriate for smaller children. Methadone is available in a liquid form; it can be easily titrated for pediatric dosing and provide long-acting pain relief.

A total approach to pain that uses both pharmacologic and nonpharmacologic methods is required for adequate pain management. Complementary nonpharmacologic methods can augment opioid administration (Box 60.10).[33] Psychotherapists can introduce cognitive-behavioral therapy to teach the child ways to relax and to learn to think about something other than pain. Physical therapy can be helpful to show the patient ways to move that are less painful or even stretching techniques to reduce pain.

Box 60.8 Pain Management: Initial Opioid Dosing in Pediatrics

Oxycodone

<50 kg: 0.1–0.2 mg/kg q4–6h

>50 kg: 5–10 mg q4–6h

Methadone

<50 kg: 0.1 mg/kg IV OR 0.2 mg/kg PO q8–12h

>50 kg: 2.5 mg IV OR 2.5–5 mg PO q8–12h

Morphine

<50 kg: 0.1 mg/kg IV q2–4h OR 0.3 mg/kg PO q3–4h

>50 kg: 2–4 mg IV q2–4h OR 5–10 mg PO q3–4h

Fentanyl

<50 kg: 0.5–1 mcg/kg q1–2h

>50 kg: 25–50 mcg q1–2h

Hydromorphone

<50 kg: 0.02 mg/kg IV q2–4h OR 0.04–0.08 mg/kg PO q3–4h

>50 kg: 0.5–1 mg IV q2–4h OR 2–4 mg q3–4h

From reference 49.

Box 60.9 Adjuvant Medications—Initial Dosing for Pediatrics

Benzodiazepines

Lorazepam

≥2 years: 0.025–0.05 mg/kg/dose PO or IV q6h, maximum 2 mg

Diazepam

<50 kg: 0.04–0.2 mg/kg PO q6–8h OR 0.04–0.2 mg/kg IV q2–4h

>50 kg: 2–10 mg PO q6–8h OR 5–10 mg IV q2–4h

Tricyclic Antidepressants for Neuropathic Pain

Amitriptyline

<50 kg: 0.1 mg/kg PO q HS, titrate to 0.5–2 mg/kg over 2–3 weeks

>50 kg: 25–50 mg PO q HS; maximum 150 mg/day

Anticonvulsants for Neuropathic Pain

Gabapentin

<50 kg: Day 1: 5 mg/kg PO q HS; day 2: 5 mg/kg PO BID; Day 3: 5 mg/kg PO TID; titrate to effect (dose range 8–35 mg/kg/day)

>50 kg: Day 1: 300 mg PO q HS; Day 2: 300 mg PO BID; Day 3: 300 mg PO TID; titrate to effect (dose range 1,800–2,400 mg/kg/day; maximum 3,600 mg/day)

Pregabalin

>50 kg: 50 mg PO TID; maximum 300 mg/day

From references 26 and 33.

Goals of Care and Decision Making

Goals, in the context of medical decision making, are defined as hopes and expectations for the care of the patient. The goals of care should be established at the time of diagnosis, and discussion should continue throughout the continuum of illness.[50] These discussions generally necessitate a series of conversations between the child, family, and healthcare team. They should be seen as a process rather than a one-time conversation. See Chapter 39 Advance Care Planning: Advance **Directives, Medical Order Sets, and Surrogate Decision Making**.

Box 60.10 Complementary Therapies

Swaddling/cuddling	Distraction
Cognitive-behavioral therapy	Art therapy
Hypnosis	Music therapy
Guided imagery	Heating pads
Biofeedback	Cold packs
Counseling	Reiki
Physical therapy	Acupuncture
Massage	Yoga

Most parents of children with chronic illness have no or limited experience with establishing goals of care, including advance directives.[51] They may fear that their child's needs will be perceived differently or that a different level of care will be given if they elect to have palliative care or put their wishes in writing in the form of an advance directive. In one study of pediatric oncology patients and their families, 66.7% to 99.3% of medical interventions continued after the institution of a Do Not Resuscitate order, and chemotherapy continued in 33.3%.[52] Facilitated discussions with families and the child, as age appropriate, can elucidate their goals and wishes so that they can feel assured that the medical teams know and understand their wishes, and can ensure that goals will be realigned to best honor their wishes.

Goals should be explored in the domains of physical health, the setting of care (environment), and psychosocial and spiritual preferences.[11] Often goals are not discussed fully or assumptions are made that may or may not accurately reflect child and family preferences.[50] The *Clinical Practice Guidelines for Quality Palliative Care* encourages such discussions in pediatric care.[53] Children and families need to be asked what their preferences are, and then a discussion of realistic expectations can occur.

Reframing Goals of Care

Goals may change throughout the trajectory of illness.[50] At diagnosis, goals are often more cure-oriented, including the use of aggressive, life-sustaining therapies. At relapse, the focus may change to prolonging life and balancing the benefits of treatment against symptom distress. At the end-of-life, the focus may turn toward quality of life and relief of symptom distress. Goals for survivorship may include optimizing functionality, quality of life, and sense of well-being in all domains.

Occasionally, families and healthcare team members may disagree on the goals of care. Such disagreement may produce misunderstandings and conflicts. The perceptions and expectations of both the family and the medical team need to be explored to identify differences and similarities.[54] The pediatric palliative APRN is uniquely prepared to facilitate these discussions to develop shared expectations and goals.

Reframing of goals may occur repeatedly within the cancer trajectory.[50] Some families may consider only the goal of cure. While this may be an effective coping mechanism for some, the inability to simultaneously consider other goals may be maladaptive. Crises may occur suddenly, preventing the parent from having adequate time to consider reframing of goals. This can result in regret about the continuation of anticancer therapies or other life-sustaining treatments. Well-meaning family members and friends may ask parents not to "give up" or may comment that the child does not want to "give up." In these situations, parents may feel like they have failed their child if they reconsider the goals of care. Another factor affecting the ability to reconsider goals is the parents' well-being and mental health. Parents may be so emotionally and physically exhausted from trying to meet the care needs of their child that they simply cannot make decisions. Indeed, their self-worth is measured by their caretaking role.[50]

Advance Care Planning and Code Status Discussions

In adult medicine, every patient is given the opportunity to complete an advance directive, but this is often overlooked in the pediatric setting. For children under the age of 18 years, routine advance care planning and code status conversations rarely occur until the clinical situation has deteriorated significantly. Recent studies have shown that adolescents with cancer who participated in discussions about advance care planning were willing to talk about their wishes, wanted their families to do what they thought was best at the time, felt better informed about end-of-life decisions, and were more likely to have congruence with their families about end-of-life care than those who were not engaged in advance care planning discussions.[55]

There are several tools available to facilitate advance care planning discussions (Table 60.1).[56–60] In general, these tools address the following issues:

- Whom the patient wants to make healthcare decisions for him or her if he or she is unable to make those decisions (healthcare proxy/surrogate decision maker)

- The types of medical treatments the patient wants or does not want in certain circumstances (life-sustaining treatments)

- How comfortable the patient wants to be (pain and symptom management preferences)

- How the patient wants people to treat him or her (setting for end-of-life, which people are wanted to be present, how he or she wants to be comforted)

- What the patient wants his or her loved ones to know (special requests, including funeral/burial preferences)

Five Wishes is a recognized legal document in most states for adults over the age of 18 years.[56] This is a paper document that is signed and witnessed by at least two adults who have not or will not be involved in any aspect of medical decision making. The *Voicing My Choices* document is a similar tool for adolescents and young adults; it has more age-appropriate language.[57] The *My Wishes* document is a similar tool for young children.[58] Neither *Voicing My Choices* nor *My Wishes* is a legal document, but they are excellent ways to engage children, adolescents, young adults, and their families in discussing these issues. Families are often relieved when a child or adolescent completes the advance care planning tool, as his or her wishes are less nebulous.[51,52,55] Other creative ways of eliciting the child's voice may include *Shop Talk*, a therapeutic game designed to engage children age 7 to 16 years in conversations about a variety of emotional issues.[59] Topics range from fun facts to more difficult topics, such as what it is like to live with cancer or fears about death and dying. *Go Wish* is a card game asking the player to arrange cards based on what is most important, somewhat important, and least important.[60] The game can be played by the child alone and then discussed with the child, or it can be played by two to four players together. Each of these tools can be used to guide difficult conversations.

Creativity is paramount. The pediatric palliative APRN must be skilled at leading these conversations with all ages of children and types of families. He or she may be the ideal person to facilitate these discussions, although it could be any member of the palliative care or medical team. Many families are accustomed to a team approach to discussing the cancer diagnosis and treatment, so having a few key members of the team discuss these difficult choices with the child and family may be the best approach.

Table 60.1 Examples of Tools for Advance Care Planning in Pediatrics

Tool	Description	Ages	Available from
Five Wishes	Legal advance directive in 42 states Available both online and in print Available in 26 languages	18 years and older	www.agingwithdignity.org
Voicing My Choices	An advance care planning guide to help young people living with a serious illness to communicate their preferences to friends, family, and caregivers. It is not a legal document.	Adolescents and young adults; no specific age ranges	www.agingwithdignity.org
My Wishes	A booklet written in everyday language that helps children express how they want to be cared for in case they become seriously ill. Helps begin conversations among children, parents, and caregivers. It is not a legal document.	Younger children; must be able to understand the questions	www.agingwithdignity.org
Shop Talk	A therapeutic game designed for children living with cancer or another serious illness. Created by Drs. Cindy Mamalian (an artist and psychologist) and Lori Wiener to help therapists lead conversations with pediatric patients about difficult emotional issues related to their illness.	7–16 years	National Cancer Institute
Go Wish Game	An easy, even entertaining way to talk about what is most important. The cards help patients to find words to talk about what is important in living a life that may be shortened by serious illness. Playing the game with relatives or friends can help them learn how best to comfort loved ones. Can be played by one, two, or more people. There is an online version as well. Available in English or Spanish.	Ages 7 years and older	www.gowish.org

From references 56–60.

Education in the art of advance care planning is imperative. It is helpful for the pediatric palliative APRN to find a teacher and mentor to learn better skills in such meetings. Appropriate word choice can be extremely helpful.

Essential Role of Hope

Hope is a very common emotion expressed by children and families in pediatric oncology and can be an effective coping mechanism. Families are better able to provide comfort and support for their child and themselves when they use hope as a source of strength.[61,62] It can give the family a reason for placing one foot in front of the other and continuing with daily routines.

Two categories of hope have been identified in parents of children with cancer: future-oriented hope and present-oriented hope.[63] *Future-oriented hope* involves hope for a cure and treatment success, hope for the child's future, hope for a miracle, and hope for more quality time with the child. *Present-oriented hope* involves hope for each day and each moment, hope for no pain and suffering, and hope for no complications. The hope expressed by families typically vacillates over time depending on how the child is tolerating therapy, but the hope for a cure is typically always present.[63–65] The hope for lack of pain and suffering typically increases if the child is not doing well.

Hope may be strongest when the child is responding positively to cancer treatment but is fragile when the child is responding negatively or if excessive fear or uncertainty exists.[65] A decreased quality of life has been found in those with dampened hope.[66] The pediatric palliative APRN can enrich the family's hope by enhancing the child's quality of life by relieving suffering and optimizing function.[18]

In the setting of relapsed or refractory cancer, families may elect to take part in a phase I study, which is designed to test the safety profile of a new agent with little known benefit. While the medical team is aware that the treatment may be of little benefit to the child, the family may elect to focus on the hope that the treatment will cure their child's cancer. Clinicians may inadvertently intensify the family's hopes by overestimating the outcomes of the clinical trial and their own hopes for the child, out of a desire to support the family's hope and concern that disclosing the likely outcome of the trial may cause further distress for the family. Incorporating the option of palliative care prior to the discussion of a phase I study may weaken recommendations by physicians to enroll in clinical trials.[67] However, they should be explored simultaneously and are not mutually exclusive.

Patients and families will struggle if they have no hope or goals to work toward. Developing realistic goals can give a sense of hope for something they can achieve. Even though the goals may not involve a longer life, developing realistic goals produces more positive emotions in those with terminal illness and their families.[68] Families may need guidance with identifying realistic goals to provide for a new sense of hope when faced with a child with terminal cancer.

Conclusion

The diagnosis of cancer in a child is difficult for both families and medical teams. Palliative care may relieve suffering and promote improved coping and a sense of hope for the family and healthcare teams. Assessment and management of symptoms and re-evaluation of goals are paramount throughout the illness trajectory. Early integration of palliative care in this setting can allow relationships and trust to develop over time and can allow an improved understanding of the patient's and family's wishes. The pediatric palliative APRN has an essential role in care of the child with cancer.

References

1. U.S. Department of Health and Human Services. Surveillance, Epidemiology, and End Results (SEER) Program. Age-Adjusted SEER Cancer Incidence and U.S. Death Rates, 2007–2011. Available at www.seer.cancer.gov. Accessed July 16, 2014.
2. Ward E, DeSantis C, Robbins A, et al. Childhood and adolescent cancer statistics. *CA Cancer J Clin*. 2014; 64(2): 83–103.
3. U.S. Department of Health and Human Services. Surveillance, Epidemiology, and End Results (SEER) Program. 5-Year Relative Survival by Year Dx. by Age at Diagnosis/Death All Sites, All Races, Both Sexes 1975–2006. Available at www.seer.cancer.gov. Accessed July 2, 2014.
4. Cullen J. Because statistics don't tell the whole story: A call for comprehensive care for children with cancer. *CA Cancer J Clin*. 2014; 64(2): 79–82.
5. American Academpy of Pediatrics Committee on Bioethics and Committee on Hospital Care. Palliative care for children. *Pediatrics*. 2000; 106(2): 351–7.
6. Wentlandt K, Krzyanowska MK, Swami N, et al. Referral practices of pediatric oncologists to specialized palliative care. *Support Care Cancer*. 2014; 22(9): 2315–22.
7. Wolfe J, Klar N, Grier HE, et al. Understanding of prognosis among parents of children who died with cancer: Impact on treatment goals and integration of palliative care. *JAMA*. 2000; 284(19): 2469–75.
8. Moroni M, Zocchi D, Bolognesi D, et al. The 'surprise' question in advanced cancer patients: A prospective study among general practitioners. *Palliat Med*. 2014; 28(7): 959–64.
9. Bergstrasser E. Pediatric palliative care—When quality of life becomes the main focus of treatment. *Eur J Pediatr*. 2013; 172: 139–50.
10. Kars MC, Grypdonck MH, de Korte-Verhoef MC, et al. Parental experience at end-of-life in children with cancer: "Preservation" and "letting go" in relation to loss. *Support Care Cancer*. 2011; 19(1): 27–35.
11. Tamburro RF, Shaffer ML, Hahnlen NC, et al. Care goals and decisions for children referred to a pediatric palliative care program. *J Palliat Med*. 2011; 14(5): 607–13.
12. Ullrich CK, Dussel V, Hilden JM, et al. End-of-life experience of children undergoing stem cell transplantation for malignancy: Parent and provider perspectives and patterns of care. *Blood*. 2010; 115(9): 3879–85.
13. Lafond DA, Kelly KP, Hinds PS, et al. Establishing Feasibility of Early Palliative Care Consultation in Pediatric Hematopoietic Stem Cell Transplantation. Baltimore, MD: University of Maryland School of Nursing; 2012. Capstone. Project for completion of Master's Program.
14. Levine D, Lam CG, Cunningham MJ, et al. Best practices for pediatric palliative cancer care: A primer for clinical providers. *J Support Oncol*. 2013; 11(3): 114–25.
15. Friebert S, Osenga K. Pediatric palliative care referral criteria. Center to Advance Palliative Care. Available at https://central.capc.org/eco_download.php?id=588. Accessed July 15, 2015.
16. Harrop E, Edwards C. How and when to refer a child for specialized paediatric palliative care. *Arch Dis Childhood Educ Pract*. 2013; 98: 202–8.
17. Foster TL, Bell CJ, McDonald CF, et al. Palliative nursing care for children and adolescents with cancer. *Nurs Res Rev*. 2012; 2: 17–25.
18. Miller E, Jacob E, Hockenberry MJ. Nausea, pain, fatigue, and multiple symptoms in hospitalized children with cancer. *Oncol Nurs Forum*. 2011; 38(5): E382–E393.
19. Pashankar FD, Season JH, McNamara J, Pashankar DS. Acute constipation in children receiving chemotherapy for cancer. *J Pediatr Hematol Oncol*. 2011; 33(7): e300–e303.
20. Stuber ML, Meeske KA, Krull KR, et al. Prevalence and predictors of posttraumatic stress disorder in adult survivors of childhood cancer. *Pediatrics*. 2010; 125(5): 1124–34.
21. Wolfe J, Grier HE, Klar N, et al. Symptoms and suffering at the end of life in children with cancer. *N Engl J Med*. 2000; 342(5): 326–33.
22. Wittenberg-Lyles E, Goldsmith J, Ragan S. The shift to early palliative care: A typology of illness journeys and the role of nursing. *Clin J Oncol Nurs*. 2011; 15(3): 304–10.
23. Watts A. Constipation. In: Ethier AM, Rollins J, Stewart J, eds. *Pediatric Oncology Palliative and End-of-Life Care Resource*. Glenview, IL: CureSearch Children's Oncology Group & Association of Pediatric Hematology-Oncology Nurses; 2010:21.
24. Hellsten MB, Medellin G. Symptom management in pediatric palliative care. In: Ferrell BR, Coyle N, eds. *Oxford Textbook of Palliative Nursing*. 3rd ed. New York, NY: Oxford University Press; 2010:983–96.
25. Feudtner C, Freedman J, Kang T, et al. Comparative effectiveness of senna to prevent problematic constipation in pediatric oncology patients receiving opioids: A multicenter study of clinically detailed administrative data. *J Pain Symptom Manage*. 2014; 48(2): 272–80.
26. Lexicomp (Version 2.3.0) [Mobile application software]. Retrieved from http://online.lexi.com/lco/action/home/switch.
27. Schmidt D, Guarino J. Diarrhea. In: Ethier AM, Rollins J, Stewart J, eds. *Pediatric Oncology Palliative and End-of-Life Care Resource*. Glenview, IL: CureSearch Children's Oncology Group & Association of Pediatric Hematology-Oncology Nurses; 2010:23–4.

28. Friedrichsdorf SJ, Drake R, Webster ML. Gastrointestinal symptoms. In: Wolfe J, Hinds PS, Sourkes BM, eds. *Textbook of Interdisciplinary Pediatric Palliative Care*. Philadelphia, PA: Elsevier Saunders; 2011:311–34.

29. Pal V, Porter K, Ranalli M. Octreotide acetate is efficacious and safe in children for treating diarrhea due to chemotherapy but not acute graft versus host disease. *Pediatr Blood Cancer*. 2010; 56: 45–9.

30. Thomas DW, Greer FR. Probiotics and prebiotics in pediatrics. *Pediatrics* 2010; 126(6): 1217–31.

31. Redman MG, Ward EJ, Phillips RS. The efficacy and safety of probiotics in people with cancer: A systematic review. *Ann Oncol*. 2014; 25: 1919–29.

32. Ulbrich T, Plogsted S, Geraghty ME, et al. Probiotics and prebiotics: Why are they bugging us in the pharmacy? *J Pediatr Pharmacol Ther*. 2009; 14(1): 17–24.

33. Moody K, Siegel L, Scharbach K, et al. Pediatric palliative care. In: Heidelbaugh JJ, ed. *Palliative Care*. Philadelphia, PA: Saunders; 2011:327–61.

34. Baggott CR, Dodd M, Kennedy C, et al. An evaluation of the factors that affect the hospital-related quality of life of children following myelosuppressive chemotherapy. *Support Care Cancer*. 2011; 19: 353–61.

35. Watts A, Guarino J. Nausea and vomiting. In: Ethier AM, Rollins J, Stewart J, eds. *Pediatric Oncology Palliative and End-of-Life Care Resource*. Glenview, IL: CureSearch Children's Oncology Group & Association of Pediatric Hematology-Oncology Nurses; 2010:26–7.

36. Moody K. An Integrative Approach to Pain and Symptom Management in Children with Cancer. [PowerPoint]. Presented at International Association of Pediatric Hematology/Oncology Nurses Meeting, Indianapolis, IN, 2014.

37. Gore L, Chawla S, Petrilli A, et al. Aprepitant in adolescent patients for prevention of chemotherapy-induced nausea and vomiting: A randomized, double-blind, placebo controlled study of efficacy and tolerability. *Pediatr Blood Cancer*. 2009; 52(2): 242–7.

38. Goldman A, Hewitt M, Collins GS, et al. Symptoms in children/young people with progressive malignant disease: United Kingdom Children's Cancer Study Group/Paediatric Oncology Nurses Forum survey. *Pediatrics*. 2006; 117(6): e1179–e1186.

39. National Cancer Institute. Tackling the conundrum of cachexia in cancer. *NCI Cancer Bull*. 2011; 8(21). Available at http://www.cancer.gov/ncicancerbulletin/110111/page5.

40. Schmidt D, Guarino J. Anorexia and cachexia. In: Ethier AM, Rollins J, Stewart J, eds. *Pediatric Oncology Palliative and End-of-Life Care Resource*. Glenview, IL: CureSearch Children's Oncology Group & Association of Pediatric Hematology-Oncology Nurses; 2010:20.

41. Ruiz GV, López-Briz E, Carbonell SR, et al. Megestrol acetate for treatment of anorexia-cachexia syndrome [review]. *Cochrane Database Syst Rev. (3)*, 2013. Available at http://onlinelibrary.wiley.com/doi/10.1002/14651858.CD004310.pub3/pdf/standard.

42. Chang CW, Mu PF, Jou ST, et al. Systematic review and meta-analysis of nonpharmacological interventions for fatigue in children and adolescents with cancer. *Worldviews Evid Based Nurs*. 2013; 10(4): 208–17.

43. Erickson JM, Beck SL, Christian BR, et al. Fatigue, sleep-wake disturbances, and quality of life in adolescents receiving chemotherapy. *J Pediatr Hematol Oncol*. 2011; 33(1): e17–e25.

44. Hesselgrave J, Hockenberry M. Fatigue. In: Wolfe J, Hinds PS, Sourkes BM, eds. *Textbook of Interdisciplinary Pediatric Palliative Care*. Philadelphia, PA: Elsevier Saunders; 2011:266–71.

45. Tomlinson D, Diorio C, Beyene J, Sung L. Effect of exercise on cancer-related fatigue: a meta-analysis. *Am J Phys Med Rehabil*. 2014; 93(8): 675–86.

46. Wilson K. Insomnia and sleep disturbance. In: Ethier AM, Rollins J, Stewart J, eds. *Pediatric Oncology Palliative and End-of-Life Care Resource*. Glenview, IL: CureSearch Children's Oncology Group & Association of Pediatric Hematology-Oncology Nurses; 2010:50.

47. Smith WR, Penberthy LT, Bovbjerg VE, et al. Daily assessment of pain in adults with sickle cell disease. *Ann Intern Med*. 2008; 148(2): 94–101.

48. Smith WR, Scherer M. Sickle-cell pain: advances in epidemiology and etiology. *Blood*. 2010; 2010(1): 409–15.

49. Collins JJ, Berde CB, Frost JA. Pain assessment and management. In: Wolfe J, Hinds PS, Sourkes BM, eds. *Textbook of Interdisciplinary Pediatric Palliative Care*. Philadelphia, PA: Elsevier Saunders; 2011:284–99.

50. Hill DL, Miller V, Walter JK, et al. Regoaling: a conceptual model of how parents of children with serious illness change medical care goals. *BMC Palliat Care*. 2014; 13(9): 1–8.

51. Libermann DB, Pham PK, Nager AL. Pediatric advance directives: Parents' knowledge, experience, and preferences. *Pediatrics*. 2014; 134(2): 1–8.

52. Baker JN, Kane JR, Rai S, et al. Changes in medical care at a pediatric oncology referral center after placement of a do-not-resuscitate order. *J Palliat Med*. 2010; 13(11): 1349–52.

53. National Consensus Project for Quality Palliative Care. *Clinical Practice Guidelines for Palliative Care*. Pittsburgh, PA: National Consensus Project for Quality Palliative Care; 2013.

54. Weitzman CC, Schlegel S, Murphy N, et al. When clinicians and a parent disagree on the extent of medical care. *J Dev Behav Pediatr*. 2009; 30(3): 242–5.

55. Lyon ME, Jacobs S, Briggs L, et al. Family-centered advance care planning for adolescents with cancer. *JAMA*. 2013; 167(5): 460–7.

56. Aging with Dignity. *Five Wishes*. Tallahassee, FL: Aging with Dignity; 2011.

57. Aging with Dignity. *Voicing My Choices: A Planning Guide for Adolescents and Young Adults*. Tallahassee, FL: Aging with Dignity; 2012.

58. Aging with Dignity. *My Wishes*. Tallahassee, FL: Aging with Dignity; 2006.

59. Wiener L, Battles H, Mamalian C, Zadeh S. Shop Talk: a pilot study of the feasibility and utility of a therapeutic board game for youth living with cancer. *Support Care Cancer*. 2011; 19(7): 1049–54.

60. CODA Alliance. Go Wish game. Available at www.gowish.org. Accessed December 12, 2014.

61. Sumner LH. Pediatric hospice and palliative care. In: Ferrell BR, Coyle N, eds. *Oxford Textbook of Palliative Nursing*. 3rd ed. New York, NY: Oxford University Press; 2010:997–1017.

62. O'Shea ER, Kanarek RB. Understanding pediatric palliative care: What it is and what it should be. *J Pediatr Oncol Nurs*. 2013; 30(1): 34–44.

63. Granek L, Barrera M, Shaheed J, et al. Trajectory of parental hope when a child has a difficult-to-treat cancer: A prospective qualitative study. *Psychooncology*. 2013; 22: 2436–44.

64. Mack JW, Wolfe J, Cook EF, et al. Hope and prognostic disclosure. *J Clin Oncol*. 2007; 25(35): 5636–42.

65. Barrera M, Granek G, Shaheed J, et al. The tenacity and tenuousness of hope. *Cancer Nurs*. 2013; 36(5): 408–16.

66. Sullivan MD. Hope and hopelessness at the end of life. *Am J Geriatr Psychiatry*. 2003; 11(4): 393–405.

67. Miller VA, Cousino M, Leek AC, Kodish ED. Hope and persuasion by physicians during informed consent. *J Clin Oncol*. Available at http://jco.ascopubs.org/cgi/doi/10.1200/JCO.2014.55.2588. Accessed on September 21, 2014.

68. Gum A, Snyder CR. Coping with terminal illness: The role of hopeful thinking. *J Palliat Med*. 2002; 5: 883–94.

CHAPTER 61

Pediatric Palliative Care in the Community

Joan "Jody" Chrastek

Key Points

♦ Family is the unit of care. All interventions must be holistic, taking into account the effect on the physical, psychosocial, emotional, and spiritual aspects of the family.

♦ In the role of a "guide," the pediatric palliative advanced practice registered nurse (APRN) must have the flexibility and humility to collaborate with the family and broader team to support a culturally appropriate, practical, and realistic plan of care while still ensuring excellent pain and symptom management and best practice.

♦ No one does this work alone; team support and excellent professional boundaries are a must to provide best care and to protect the child and family and the professionals caring for them.

Case Study

Joselyn was a 12-year-old with myotonic dystrophy. She had a gastrostomy tube and a portacath. She experienced occasional seizures and was ventilator-dependent. She had frequent hospitalizations due to feeding intolerance, abdominal pain, and family fears of dehydration. For many years, she received artificial nutrition and hydration (ANH) via gastrostomy or jejunostomy or intravenously. Joselyn had two brothers, one of whom was autistic. Her father worked the night shift.

There were more than 25 people involved in Joselyn's care, including five different physicians from three different hospitals, county workers, and school outreach personnel.

Box 61.1 lists the extensive personnel who were invested in Joselyn's care. However, despite everyone's best efforts, her care was often fractured and complex due to suboptimal communication and consultation between the team members as she transitioned in and out of the hospital. Each hospital admission was a time of severe stress and disruption for Joselyn and her family. After each admission, the 24-hour team, including the school- and home-based services, had to be reconfigured, resulting in delays in discharge and increased stress on the family.

The community-based pediatric palliative APRN and her teams were asked to get involved after numerous hospitalizations, miscommunications, and complications. The pediatric palliative APRN met with the family and nursing agency while Joselyn was still in the hospital, establishing trust and learning the family's goals and wishes. She explained that palliative care is total active care to ensure expert symptom management, care coordination, and psychosocial support. The family accepted this, stating they really wanted to keep Joselyn at home but still wanted aggressive life-prolonging treatment when possible. The "goals of care" conversations continued formally and informally throughout the time Joselyn received palliative care at home but began to change as she declined. The APRN clarified the plan of care with the medical team and coordinated with all the home-based services, including the nursing agency, social service workers, and teachers and school personnel, to ensure a smooth transition home. A pediatric palliative APRN and the team planned to follow the patient at home to coordinate the complex team (see Fig. 1.1).

Box 61.1 Joselyn's team members

Primary care physician

Neurologist and office care coordinator

Gastroenterologist and office care coordinator

Pulmonologist and office care coordinator

Physical medicine and rehabilitation, hospital-based

Pediatric Palliative Care Team: physician, speech and language pathologist (SLP),

occupational therapist (OP), physical therapist (PT), and registered nurse

Social worker: hospital-based social worker, disability social worker, and county social worker

School home-based services: physiotherapist,

teacher, social worker, and speech and language pathologist

Nursing agency: 15 home health nurses and home health aides

Insurance company personnel

Medical equipment company personnel and pharmacy

Pediatric palliative APRN and team

Extended family

Religious community

Figure 61.1 Care across the continuum: an achievable goal.

The pediatric palliative APRN made intermittent visits to Joselyn's home and provided care coordination. The 24-hour palliative care telephone line and APRN visits allowed the family to access palliative care expertise quickly by telephone, video visit, or in-person visits. The APRN visits provided opportunities for mentorship to the broad home-based team. Joselyn's care plan was flexible and adapted to meet her needs. Often the pediatric palliative care team visited when team members from the school or county were there providing care. They developed deeper relationships and a strong sense of collaboration. Joselyn's physicians were kept informed by phone and video visits. The visual information provided by the video visits gave the physicians a better understanding of the situation and allowed the family to maintain closer connections with the providers in the hospital when the child was at home.

The pediatric palliative APRN was able to provide consultation for symptom management and leadership as to next steps. Joselyn's team at home worked well together, and for a few weeks she remained relatively stable, with only a few nights of total lack of gastric emptying. One night, the home registered nurse called the 24-hour line to say that Joselyn's feeds were not moving through her gastrointestinal tract, even after attempts had been made to improve the situation though medication and adjustments of her enteral feedings over the past few days. She also had a very low urine output and was developing edema in her feet. The family wanted to start an intravenous line, as this had been successful in the past. The palliative care team was concerned because Joselyn was so much weaker and was already retaining fluid. The pediatric palliative APRN led a "goals of care" discussion with the family in the home to find out what they were thinking about the changes and to talk about options going forward. As Joselyn was not able to digest her food, a "feed to comfort" plan of care was suggested. This plan followed the patient's lead, providing ANH only when she displayed signs of hunger. The parents were interested in trying the intravenous fluids one more time. They were aware of possible complications of this, including increased

Figure 61.2 Drawing by Danny Sauer, a 7-year-old palliative care patient.

edema, pain, retching, and third spacing, but felt that if any of those happened, it would be Joselyn's way of telling them she was "done." Her mother said, "We will let her tell us with those signs if she is really too tired to go on; then we will stop the fluids." They felt like that would take the decision out of their hands, so it would be her decision and not theirs.

Intravenous hydration was started, and two days later Joselyn had positional pitting edema and crackles in the lower lobes of both lungs. The parents accepted this as her sign to them that she was too tired to take in any more fluids. They stopped the continuous ANH but continued the ventilator support. They would use intermittent ANH when she seemed hungry. With the parents' permission, the pediatric palliative APRN talked at length with other family members, the extended-hours nurses, and other members of the team about ANH at the end-of-life. She carefully reviewed how Joselyn could no longer tolerate it and it was increasing her suffering. Some family members had concerns and worries about stopping ANH, but providing open opportunities for discussion was helpful and supportive. During these discussions, it was important to supply both scientific evidence, such as research articles, and emotional support to the extended team. The pediatric palliative APRN's ability to provide literature that discussed benefits and burdens of using ANH at the end-of-life brought comfort to those who needed this education. The palliative care team and family pastor were available to address the fears and concerns on a psychosocial spiritual level.

Joselyn lived for 3 weeks after the discontinuation of ANH. She was comfortable, her lungs were clear, and pain was well controlled with sublingual morphine. She did not struggle with excess secretions at the end-of-life as her body gradually shut down. Her parents, siblings, and extended community had time to make more memories with her. She died peacefully at home one afternoon with her mother and father beside her. Her memorial was a celebration of her life, with standing room only in the large church.

Introduction

Provision of pediatric palliative care (PPC) in the community is a complex and multifaceted subject that cannot be addressed in one chapter of a book. However, this chapter provides a brief overview and resources for further information and learning.

For most of us, "home," be it a house, apartment, or wherever we live, is the place we want to be. This is especially true for many people at the end-of-life.[1] At times, it seems the best comfort measure we can provide for children is to help them be at home. Also, some research has shown that home is the preferred place of death for a child with cancer.[2] However, it can be frightening for families to take a medically fragile loved one home.[3] Yet with education, support, and 24-hour availability of professionals, the families soon find that they are the experts on their child. This expertise is the natural role and privilege of a parent or parent surrogate, whatever the health status of the child.

Support from a strong community palliative care team enables children to remain at home.[4] The role of the visiting community pediatric palliative APRN is essential in these teams. The scope of practice for these nurses is broad but can be divided into five major areas of work: clinical practice, provision of consultation services, teaching, leadership, and research.[5] Each of these areas is interwoven in the work of the nurse.

This chapter discusses ways that the multiple roles of the community pediatric palliative APRN, in clinical practice, provision of consultation services, teaching, and leadership are implemented in the community. When healthcare is provided at home and not in the hospital, family and patient beliefs, culture, and societal pressures can deeply affect the plan of care.

Clinical Practice/Judgment

An important role of the pediatric palliative APRN is to support expert provision of care for patients with serious illness wherever they are. In theory, palliative care in the hospital and community are the same; the nurse must be an expert in both the art and science of the field. However, in practice, providing care in a patient's home requires an additional skill set. This may be due to the environment of the home and neighborhood, the education of caregivers, or social, cultural, or religious issues. As the saying goes, a person's house is his castle, "et domus sua cuique est tutissimum refugium" (each man's home is his safest refuge).[6] The APRN is a guest in the patient's "realm" and must always remember this to provide effective care.

When a child or young person is at home, the family is in charge of the care. The pediatric palliative APRN is in their territory. The nurse may provide sound advice and clinical expertise, but ultimately the family will make the decision of how closely to follow the plan of care. They are the ones who are there 24/7, often doing the tasks that are designated nursing functions in the hospital, everything from enemas to flushing a central line. Nurses must provide expert clinical advice, but it must be paired closely with relationship building, cultural awareness, and good observational skills. The pediatric palliative APRN is a guide, a coach, and a resource for the child or young person and the family. There must be an equal partnership with the parents. Ultimately, they are the decision makers, unless the safety of the child is at stake, in which case child protective services must be involved.

The functions of a hospital APRN and a community pediatric palliative APRN are quite different, as seen in these two scenarios.

> Yosef, age 13, was in hospital room 3127; he had metastatic cancer and now had constant pain relieved by morphine, but only used it on an irregular basis. The hospital APRN initiated him on scheduled morphine. She wrote an order, which was entered into the medication record and was sent to the pharmacy, for an adequate supply. The bedside nurse administered the morphine at the scheduled time. The patient received the medication as planned.

However, in the community, the solution to Yosef's persistent pain must be more holistic than simply writing an order. The APRN must take into account the relationship with the family, the availability of the medication, ability of the caregiver, cultural issues, and individual family preferences.

> Yosef lived in a modest house in suburbia with his parents and six siblings. He had a daily personal care attendant from his community who offered his medications when his mother was out.

The community APRN must think of how to ensure a holistic solution, beyond just assessing the need and writing the order to schedule the opioid every 4 hours to relieve the patient's pain. He or she must consider the social, economic, and logistical issues that arise in the community. For example: Do Yosef and the family trust the APRN enough to be forthright with their opinions about giving morphine routinely? Is expressing an opinion to medical personnel culturally appropriate for them as individuals? Or might they politely agree and then follow their own plan? Does the patient have enough medication to take it routinely? Will he run out on the weekend? Is it available at his pharmacy? If so, does the family have a way to pick it up and pay for it? Are there cultural or religious issues that may affect his choices about pain medications? Culturally, is it acceptable for a man to take pain medications? Some people believe pain is "weakness leaving the body" or "a way of purifying the soul for the next life."

Family members or personal care attendants may be the ones administering the medications, so they must be willing to support the plan, if it is to work. These underlying issues and others, seemingly nonmedical, must be taken into account when developing a plan of care in the community.

Therefore, the clinical judgment of the community pediatric palliative APRN must be more encompassing than that of the palliative APRN in the hospital. It must go beyond the physical act of prescribing medication and educating the patient and family. He or she must educate the caregivers, family, and homecare workers; understand potential cultural and spiritual barriers; build relationships; and assess whether the patient and family trust the care team enough to actually follow the suggested plan of care.

Community pediatric palliative APRNs must be conscious and respectful of the multiple environmental influences on the patient and family. These influences are much stronger in the community, where families may rely heavily on extended family members, online support groups, or neighbors to help them make decisions. This means that these influences often have a greater impact on decisions and actions than advice from the medical team. All of these factors must be taken into account when working with a patient and family to implement a plan of care, even one as simple as scheduling a medication.

Care Across the Continuum—An Achievable Goal

Continuity of care or "seamless care" is a common goal in today's healthcare world for providers and patients alike, but, as seen in Joselyn's case, it can be complex.[7] Continuity of care has been defined simply as the continuous relationship between a provider and a patient as well as the coordination and sharing of information between providers.[8,9] In practice, this can be a challenge, especially if providers, such as home-based services, nursing, physiotherapy, academic education and other school-based therapies, outpatient clinics, and hospitals, operate independently of each other. For children, the provider group extends even farther beyond the medical realm to include all aspects of the child's life. With such a large and diverse team, communication often is incomplete, leaving providers and families frustrated and exhausted trying to fit the pieces together.

Often the communication breakdown occurs when a patient transfers from one setting to another. The community pediatric palliative APRN can be instrumental in making transfers occur smoothly; to do so, he or she will need to collaborate with people from diverse settings, such as home, hospitals, clinics, schools, and daycare centers. Each of these settings will contribute a different aspect of the child's or young person's care, and excellent communication among them is essential for best practice. Building collaborative partnerships means pursuing child- and family-centered goals that are dynamic and require the participation and consensus of the involved parties.[10] The community pediatric palliative APRN is instrumental in building these partnerships and helping to meet these goals across the continuum of care.

Not all pediatric palliative care cases are as complex as Joselyn's, but the concept of inclusivity, adaptability, and respect should flow through all care, simple or complex. The complexity of a situation should not prevent a team with limited resources from providing care. In some situations, nurses and teams may feel overwhelmed and under-resourced when faced with caring for children with palliative care needs in the community. At these times it is good to remember the folk tale of "stone soup":

> A villager was starving and had nothing in her home, only a stone at the foot of her dry garden, but she invited the neighbors to come to dinner and asked each to bring what they had. She put the stone in the pot with water, and as the neighbors arrived she added whatever they brought to the pot: three dried carrots, half a turnip, two onions, a few sprouting potatoes, salt, garlic, and a bunch of leeks. When it was ready they were amazed to find that stone soup tasted so good!

So, too, when a team is faced with providing care for difficult and complex cases but has few resources, an active leader can build collaborations and galvanize individuals from all areas of the child's life to work together to provide what is needed—just like the successful stone soup.

The community pediatric palliative APRN is often the key caretaker and leader on behalf of the child. He or she must be excellent at listening, building collaborations, and sharing information. This model has been used in multiple sites and has been found to be effective.[11] As a key team member, the APRN will use all aspects of the role of clinical practice, provision of consultation services, teaching, leadership, and research. The case study at the beginning of the chapter is an example of how that can be done. It shows the importance of taking a step back to get an overview of the whole situation.

Support and Education

In some cases, children at home have extended hours of nursing, up to 24 hours a day. In these cases, some may wonder why there is a need for a pediatric palliative APRN when there are other nurses already there. But the skills in symptom management and communications that a trained palliative care provider brings must never be underestimated.[12] APRNs without palliative training often lack the confidence and knowledge needed to provide the interventions and support that families need.[9]

The specialist pediatric palliative APRN provides support and education for the team as a whole.[13] This education may be provided in a formal educational session or informally in the home. Palliative APRNs must be able to recognize educational needs in team members and then move quickly and appropriately to fill the knowledge gap. It is important to respond quickly but diplomatically to the educational needs of the caregivers. Pediatric palliative care is a particularly sensitive area, where lay people and professionals alike often have the "mother tiger's instinct" for protection by isolation. Others may see a well-meant tactic to share information or knowledge as a criticism of their care and be angered or offended. Therefore, when collaborating on all levels and sharing knowledge or ideas, the pediatric palliative APRN must act with care and humility. He or she must be current on research and evidence-based practice. It is helpful for all team members to realize that palliative care is characterized by continuous learning for the whole team, even the "experts."[9] Ongoing education, both formal and informal, provides a way for the extended team to have a shared understanding of the situation.

The role of the community pediatric palliative APRN as a teacher and mentor cannot be overemphasized. At times the APRN provides formal and structured educational offerings, but much of the time the APRN's role is to teach by example and "just in time" education. This type of education is done at the point of care and is often more effective and lasting than a formal educational intervention. "Just in time" education is a common need for community-based services that have no prior experience in the provision of palliative or hospice care to children. The pediatric palliative APRN may provide clinical instruction, such as flushing a particular line or care of a wound, but also often provides emotional and psychosocial support to help the home care nurse deal with personal fears concerning caring for a dying child or one with a life-limiting condition.

Both types of education may be needed for the family and home-based extended-hours nurses. Many of the nurses may have worked in the home for years and have a longstanding relationship with the child and family. Yet, it is common for nurses or other team members to have very little or no palliative care training or experience, resulting in fears and misunderstandings about palliative care.

Some of the team members may disagree with the treatment decisions that the family and medical team make together, such as a change in focus from aggressive care to quality-of-life and comfort care. These decisions can bring discord to the team, so they must be appropriately addressed to ensure that the plan of care is correctly followed and the family members receive the support they need. Individual team members who do not agree with the family's and team's decisions must be willing to support the plan of care—or remove themselves from the case. It is the family members who will live permanently with the decisions they made with the medical team. The professional caregiver's role is to support the family, not to judge them.

Providing options in a clear and gentle way, giving advice, and supporting families as they make difficult decisions is an important role for the palliative APRN. When working independently yet interdependently with others in the community, the pediatric palliative APRN must have excellent skills and must ensure that he or she is making decisions based on updated information and evidence. His or her clinical abilities and knowledge must be current and accessible if the APRN is to be a role model and mentor for others. Here the importance of both the "art and science" of expert pediatric palliative care nursing is evident. The APRN must be an insightful communicator but also stay current on research and education in the field. An excellent way of doing this is to become part of a professional hospice and palliative care association that offers ongoing educational and networking opportunities. Box 61.2 includes helpful websites for further information and education.

To return to Joselyn's story, the supervisor at the nursing agency reported that the extended hours home-based nurses were expressing concerns about caring for a child in palliative care. The APRN and social worker met with the homecare nurses to talk about the issues, the anticipated changes, and how they could all work together to provide support for Joselyn, the family, and each other. Many of the nurses had worked with the family on a daily basis for years and had developed close relationships with them, so making the transition to a more comfort-focused plan of care was hard.

Box 61.2 Online Resources

Hospice and Palliative Nurses Association—www.HPNA.org: HPNA is a US-based nursing organization with web-based resources for professionals and families.
Together for Short Lives—www.togetherforshortlives.org.uk: Together for Short Lives is a UK-based organization working to improve care and services for children with life-threatening or terminal conditions and their families. They have a list-serve, resources, and a searchable database.
International Children's Palliative Care Network—www.icpcn.org: The International Children's Palliative Care Network is a worldwide network of individuals and agencies working with children and young people with life-limiting conditions.
Children's Project on Palliative/Hospice Services—http://www.nhpco.org/pediatric: The ChiPPS Curriculum is a collaboration between the Children's International Project on Palliative/Hospice Services and the National Hospice and Palliative Care Organization.
The End-of-Life Nursing Education Consortium—www.aacn.nche.edu/elnec: The ELNEC project is a national education initiative to improve palliative care, providing educational seminars.
Palliative Care Fast Facts—www.capc.org/fast-facts: Palliative Care Fast Facts and Concepts are peer-reviewed summaries of more than 300 palliative care-related topics.
Growth House—www.growthhouse.org: This is a palliative care/grief and bereavement clearinghouse with links for health professionals, families, and volunteers.
The Canadian Virtual Hospice—www.virtualhospice.ca: This website provides information for patients of all ages, their families and friends, healthcare professionals, and healthcare volunteers.
Centre for Pediatric Pain Research—www.pediatric-pain.ca: This website's Pediatric-Pain Mailing List is an international internet forum for informal discussion of any topic related to pain in children.
City of Hope's Pain/Palliative Care Resource Center—www.prc.coh.org: This website has a large number of online resources for professionals and practitioners.

The stress of providing care in these situation affects the whole team. Community-based pediatric palliative APRNs and other team members usually work independently, making visits to multiple patients' homes. They may not see other team members for a number of days, and therefore often miss the opportunity for "curbside" support. Consequently, particularly in community pediatric palliative advanced practice nursing, it is important for the APRN to have a specified plan for self-care. Often, this is ignored, to the detriment of not only the individual but also the team and ultimately the child and family. Therefore, it is important for each team member to have an individualized plan and team support integrated into the normal routine.

Box 61.3 is an example of a simple, individualized care plan especially for nurses and staff who provide palliative care to children in the community. Some programs require every team member to complete a personalized plan and to choose one team member (or more) to share it with and be accountable to for following it. Individuals should select activities in each section that best suit his or her lifestyle and personality. The plan serves as a guide for the individual and for the team to remind them of the importance of self-care so they can continue in this work. In Joselyn's case, each nurse was advised to complete a self-care plan and to develop strategies to cope with ongoing or increasing stress.

Another important part of education is helping nurses learn to support family members and colleagues. Caring for children who are dying or have life-limiting conditions can be emotionally taxing for the family, as well as for the staff.[13,14] To be a sustainable pediatric palliative care team, support must be incorporated into regular practice.[15] There are many different ways that palliative care teams can do this; the important thing is that it is done. One very important aspect of support that is often missed is the skill of listening. In the words of Julian of Norwich (1342–1416):[16]

Box 61.3 Example of a Self-Care Plan

My warning signs of burnout are _____

When I see these signs, I will take the following individualized actions to care for myself:

Physical (e.g., hiking, yoga, exercise, sleep, diet)_____
_____

Emotional (e.g., identify a support person, use your team): _____
_____

Psychosocial (e.g., make specific plans to do fun things, movie, friends)_____

Spiritual (e.g., prayer? meditation? a walk in nature? What nourishes you?)_____

The sorrowing, the sick, the unwanted, the lonely, both young and old, rich and poor, all come to my window. No one listens, they tell me, and so I listen and tell them what they have just told me. And, I sit in silence, listening, letting them grieve. "Julian, you are wise," they say, "You have been gifted with understanding." All I did was listen. For I believe full surely that God's spirit is in us all, giving light, wisdom, understanding, speaking words in us when we cannot speak, showing us gently what we would not see; what we are afraid to see; so that we may show pity, mercy, forgiveness.

Listening and caring for each team member is essential and is a shared responsibility between the team members. Support must be provided for both the individual and the team as a whole. This can be done in a variety of ways, depending on the situation and team, but it must be attended to carefully to ensure excellent care for the children and families.

Figure 61.3 Ben Sauer, age 9

Maintaining Boundaries

"I know you are our nurse, but really you are a member of our family!"

Mother of 3-year-old Tommy

One of the common challenges in pediatrics and other home-based services is maintaining professional boundaries. Boundaries are often difficult to maintain because nurses do grow close to children and families, who often say, "You are closer than my family! I see you every day." or "You are the only nurse who really understands us! It is easier if we just call you." But the relationship between the family and the nursing team is a professional one. It is not a friendship where both parties share confidences equally; rather, it is a relationship where one party can share confidences but the other cannot reciprocate in the same way. This can be difficult to maintain, but if it is not, unfortunate consequences often occur, with resulting harm to the patient and family, as in this example.

> Lee was a great hospice NP. She took wonderful care of Neveah. The family trusted her completely and loved her as one of their own. As Neveah was dying, they wanted only Lee to care for her; after all, she knew her the best.
>
> Neveah stabilized and seemed to be doing well. Lee was invited to a wedding that Saturday but told the family she would be available by pager and cell phone.
>
> Unexpectedly, Neveah took a turn for the worse and died in her sleep. The parents immediately called and paged Lee rather than calling the central hospice number. Unfortunately, the wedding reception hall did not get cell phone reception and the pager was drowned out by festive music. The parents finally called the central hospice number and a nurse came out. By doing what she thought was most supportive, Lee ended up causing the parents more stress because they were delayed in getting help.

The pediatric palliative APRN and the team as a whole have a responsibility to each other and to the families to make sure professional boundaries are followed. A team discussion about the specifics of boundaries can be helpful, as there may be a variety of opinions on the issue. Together the team can outline specific guidelines that they can all agree on and hold each other accountable to. The whole palliative care team must recognize the importance of maintaining professional boundaries for the well-being of the patient, family, and staff.

Telling the Truth

"I knew I was dying, but no one would tell me."

10-year-old boy

The question of how much information to share with a seriously ill child frequently comes up in conversations among professionals and families alike. It is common to hear a parent or a nurse say, "He's too young to really know what is going on." But children often understand much more than adults assume they do. Terminally ill children typically know they are dying.[17] Children are often aware of their diagnosis. Giving age-appropriate information allows the child to create a framework on which to add information as it comes along.[18] If this is not done, the child and adult may feel isolated and abandoned and lose some of their close connections. As one father put it: "I didn't want to talk to my daughter about it because it might upset her, and she did not want to talk to me as it might upset me. We were both suffering until finally we were able to share the burden together. It made all the difference!"

Open sharing of age-appropriate information with a dying child has been shown to have benefits to parents even in the bereavement

Figure 61.4 Drawing by Danny Sauer, 7-year-old palliative care patient: "I am not dying I am going to the beach!"

Box 61.4 Helpful Books

There are many books for children, young people, and families on death and bereavement. These are only a few examples that may be helpful. The age ranges are estimates to be used as suggestions only. It is best to provide the family with a list of books so that they can choose the ones best suited for their children, their family beliefs, and their communication style.

Picture Books (Ages 2–5)

I Miss You: A First Look at Death. By Pat Thomas and Leslie Harker. This book offers a good scope of the core issues faced by younger children when someone dies. This book acknowledges the cycle of life: people are born, people die, and death is natural.

When Dinosaurs Die: A Guide to Understanding Death. By Marc Brown and Laurie Krasney Brown. This book does a nice job of representing various cultures and religions and their different way of grieving. It is a great springboard for discussion.

Someone Special Died. By Joan Prestine. A young girl describes the anger and sadness she feels after someone she loved dies and makes a scrapbook to remember the things they did together. An emotion-based book (sad, mad, lonely, happy) that has an accompanying guide about how to share the book with children.

Where's Jess: For Children Who Have a Brother or Sister Die. By Marvin Johnson. A small child's infant sibling dies and he notices she is gone. The parents tell him what death is about and give permission to remember and talk about Jess. This book has simple language and is geared toward a very young child experiencing the death of a sibling.

Ages 6–12

The Empty Place: A Child's Guide Through Grief. By Roberta Temes and Kim Carlisle. A boy describes the feelings of loss, fear, and guilt he and his friend Betsy felt after each experiences the death of a sibling. The book starts with simple grief issues and progresses to more complex ones. Having a fairly broad emotional array makes it accessible to many children and gives them a good idea of the common range of emotions.

Gentle Willow. By Joyce Mills This powerful book deals with the issue of loss and how to get through it and help others. It addresses core issues of self-worth, legacy, and how one is remembered. It also helps to redefine how one can be of use and be helpful to others.

What on Earth Do You Do When Someone Dies? By Trevor Romain. A broad spectrum that briefly covers many topics: Why do people die? Is it okay to cry?

Water Bugs & Dragonflies. By Doris Stickney and Robyn Henderson Nordstrom. The one-way transition of a water bug (those of us living) to a dragonfly (those who have passed on) is tangible to a young reader.

Teens

Help for the Hard Times. By Earl Hipp and L. K. Hanson. This book helps teens understand how they experience grief and loss, how our culture in general doesn't often acknowledge their losses or give them tools to grieve, and how they can keep their loss from overflowing.

I Will Remember You: What to Do When Someone You Love Dies—A Guidebook Through Grief for Teens. By Laura Dower and Elena Lister. Encourages readers to explore the "long, winding tunnel" of the grieving process and to keep going in the face of terrible loss and sadness.

Losing Someone You Love: When a Brother or Sister Dies. By Elizabeth Richter. Sixteen people ranging in age from 10 to 24 describe the fears, sorrow, and other emotions they experienced when a brother or sister died.

Children of Courage. By Charles Allen. Two children with cystic fibrosis face the certainty of early deaths, while their siblings nurture and watch them and adjust as they bid goodbye to their brother and sister.

Adults

After the Death of a Child. By Ann K. Finkbeiner. This self-help guide for parents examines the continuing love parents feel for their child, ways to preserve the bond, and strategies for coping with loss.

Helping Children Grieve. By Theresa Huntley. This book will help parents listen to their children, answer their questions, and guide them in their passage through grief.

A Child Dies: A Portrait of Family Grief. By Joan Hagan Arnold and Penelope Buschman Gemma. Written by two nurses, this book aims to help parents and health professionals understand the grieving process that follows the death of a child. It describes typical grief symptoms, such as profound emptiness, guilt, and anger; discusses family methods of coping after a loss; and explores possible therapeutic interventions by caregivers.

The Insider's Guide to Grief. By Stacy Remke. The long road of grief can often feel lonely, sometimes even hopeless, but it is a journey that many have traveled before. This book contains warm and sage advice, personal stories, as well as practical suggestions for keeping it together and surviving when faced with the most universal human experience: loss.

CHAPTER 61 PEDIATRIC PALLIATIVE CARE IN THE COMMUNITY 595

period. A study of bereaved parents in Sweden found that none of the parents who spoke openly with their dying child had regrets about their choice. However, for those who had not discussed dying with their child, many regretted their decision and had an increased incidence of depression and anxiety in the bereavement period.[19] However, in some cultures this type of communication is not appropriate, so ultimately the team must respect the parents' wishes. If asked not to tell the child that he or she is dying, the pediatric palliative APRN should agree to not bring it up, but must let the parents know that he or she cannot lie. The parent and APRN should discuss what the child should be told if he or she asks. This opens up an opportunity to ask the parents what they think the child knows and what changes the child may already be aware of. Changes in regularly scheduled chemotherapy appointments or doctor visits often are enough for children to pick up on the change in focus. They may also be aware of how different their body feels. Social workers, child life workers, and spiritual care providers can often be of assistance to the family members as they think about how best to handle this issue.

Children's books can help open the door to difficult conversations. Sometimes an indirect conversation about what is happening in a book can lead to a more natural conversation about what is happening at home. This is true for the ill child and for siblings. A list of some helpful books is included in Box 61.4.

Supporting Siblings

"Sometimes I feel like no one cares about ME, like they don't have any other kids!"

15-year-old sibling of a dying child

The fact that pediatric palliative care is inherently family-centered is an accepted fact. Yet, at times some of the family members are left out, most commonly the siblings. The needs of the healthy siblings are often overshadowed by the concerns and worries for the ill child,[3] yet their needs, which may be less obvious, are urgent and must be a priority. The team must be aware of their needs and must support the parents or family caregivers to do the same.

The role of the siblings is often unclear when there is a seriously-ill child. In some cases, they may take on additional responsibilities and experience a loss in quality of life and attention in the family. In research done with siblings of dying children, they said it was helpful to be given as much information as they wanted, to be allowed to be part of the care, and to be shown care from the medical team.[20] As with care for the ill child, the first step in addressing the need is always a discussion with the decision maker for the child and the siblings (usually a parent). In this discussion, it is important to listen to the parent's understanding of the situation. It is often helpful to help him or her understand how other parents have managed difficult conversations; and how good communication can ease the isolation and suffering of the family as a whole. Good communication is said to involve compassion, clinical accuracy, honesty, and availability.[18] The same holds true when communicating with siblings, making sure it is done with the child's developmental age in mind. Integrating siblings into this process is an essential part of helping families cope with the heavy emotional burdens of grief.[21] An important aspect of the pediatric palliative APRN's role in the community is to reach out and offer support to the siblings. It is also important for the APRN to coordinate with the extended team to ensure the siblings' needs are being met.

Finances

Although it is hard to talk about the financial cost of caring for seriously ill and dying children, programs that provide pediatric

Figure 61.5 Siblings camping, by Noah Sauer, age 12.

palliative care must be fiscally responsible. The complexity of the healthcare reimbursement system in the United States has made this extremely difficult, and regulations can vary from state to state. The pediatric palliative APRN must find out what the insurance benefits will cover and what the care will cost. The Affordable Care Act of 2010 provided an opportunity for concurrent care for children.[22] This means that programs for children funded jointly by the federal and state government must allow terminally ill children to receive hospice care while still pursuing aggressive curative and life-prolonging therapies. As programs learn to use this benefit, some issues are still not clear. Therefore, programs that are not familiar with concurrent care or financing PPC in the community should consult with other agencies that are more familiar with this in practice.

The community pediatric palliative APRN is in a privileged position of being a guide, clinician, and support person for children with life-limiting conditions and their families. He or she can lead the team in providing culturally sensitive and evidence-based care. It is an honor to be a part of a community team that provides holistic care in a family home where the caregivers themselves are empowered to be the expert for their child. The trust, connection, and relationship between the family and nurse is unique because the family members have allowed the APRN into their home, a place of comfort and safety. It is a complex matrix but in every step of the way the focus is on helping the child live fully!

References

1. Higginson I, Sarmento V, Calanzani N, Benalia H, Gomes B. Dying at home—is it better: a narrative appraisal of the state of the science. *Palliat Med.* 2013; 27(10): 918–24.
2. Kassam A, Skiadaresis J, Alexander S, Wolfe J. Parent and clinician preferences of location of end of life care: home hospital or freestanding hospice. *Pediatr Blood Cancer.* 2014; 61(5): 859–64. doi: 10.1002/pbc.24872
3. Goldman A, Hain R, Liben S, eds. *Oxford Textbook of Palliative Care for Children.* New York, NY: Oxford University Press; 2012.
4. Carter B, Levetown M, Friebert S. *Palliative Care for Infants, Children and Adolescents.* Baltimore, MD: The Johns Hopkins University Press; 2011.
5. Skilbeck J, Seymour J. Meeting the complex needs: an analysis of Macmillan nurses' work with patients. *Int J Palliat Nurs.* 2002; 8(12): 574–82.
6. Wikipedia. Castle document http://en.wikipedia.org/wiki/Castle_doctrine. Published December 2013. Accessed June 20, 2014.
7. Steinhorn D, Goldstein R, Orloff S. Relationships with the community: palliative care and beyond. In: Wolfe J, Hinds P, Sourkes B, eds. *Textbook of Interdisciplinary Pediatric Palliative Care.* Philadelphia, PA: Elsevier Saunders; 2011:159–67.
8. Gil J, Mainour A, Nsereko OM. The effect of continuity of care on emergency dept utilization. *Arch Fam Med.* 2000; 9: 333–8.
9. Ionescu-Ittue R, McCusker J, Ciampi A, et al. Continuity of primary care and emergency department utilization among elderly people. *Can Med Assoc J.* 2007; 177(11): 1362–80.
10. Arnaert A, Wainwright M. Providing care and sharing expertise: reflections of a nurse-specialist in palliative home care. *Palliat Supportive Care,* 2009; 7: 357–64.
11. Postier A, Chrastek J, Nugent S, Osenga K, Friedrichsdorf S. Exposure to home-based palliative and hospice care and its impact on hospital and emergency care charges at a single institution. *J Palliat Med.* 2013; 17(2): 183–8. doi: 10.1089/jpm
12. Hospice and Palliative Care Nurses Association. *Value of a Professional Nurse in Palliative Care.* Position Statement. 2011 Available at www.gohpna.org. Accessed July 1, 2014.
13. Aitken A. *Community Palliative Care: The Role of the Clinical Nurse Specialist.* Chichester, UK: John Wiley & Sons Publications; 2009.
14. Gupta V, Woodman C. Managing stress in a palliative care team. *Paediatr Nurs.* 2010; 22(10): 15–21.
15. Morgan D. Caring for dying children: assessing the needs of the pediatric palliative care nurse. *Pediatr Nurs.* 2009; 35(2): 86–9.
16. Julian of Norwich. http://www.julianofnorwich.com/2005. Accessed August 2014.
17. Wolfe J, Hinds P, Sourkes B, eds. *Textbook of Interdisciplinary Pediatric Palliative Care.* Philadelphia, PA: Elsevier Saunders; 2011:128.
18. Levetown M. Communicating with children and families: from everyday interactions to skill in conveying distressing information. *Pediatrics.* 2008; 121(5): 1441–6.
19. Kriecbergs U, Vladimar U, Onelove E, Henter J, Steirneck G. Talking about death with children who have severe malignant disease. *N Engl J Med.* 2004; 351(12): 1175–86.
20. Gaab E, Owens G, MacLeod R. Sibling care for and about pediatric palliative care patients. *J Palliat Med.* 2014; 17(1): 62–7.
21. Kuttner L. Talking with families when their children are dying. *Medical Principles and Practice.* 2007; 1: 16–20. doi: 10.1159/000104542
22. Lindey L. Health care reform and concurrent curative care for terminally ill children: a policy analysis. *J Hosp Palliat Nurs.* 2011; 13(2): 81–8.

CHAPTER 62

Communication in Pediatrics

Janet Duncan and Kathie Kobler

The single biggest problem with communication is the illusion that it has taken place.

—*George Bernard Shaw*

Key Points

◆ Expert communication skills are essential for the pediatric palliative advanced practice registered nurse (APRN) to navigate the myriad of pediatric experiences.

◆ The pediatric palliative APRN is often the pediatric palliative care team's anchor, interacting with family and providers across settings.

◆ The pediatric palliative APRN is in an ideal position to bridge the medical and psychosocial aspects of pediatric care.

Introduction

"Mom, if I die, do you think God would let me see myself as a teenager?"

How do we help families prepare for this kind of question? Nine-year-old Lydia was ready for this kind of honest communication. Whether speaking with the child or with the family members, the APRN must be ready to listen and to respond with compassion, knowledge, and sensitivity to each human being.

Communication is *the* essential component to providing quality pediatric palliative care (PPC) in the inpatient, clinic, and community settings. Standards and guidelines set forth by the National Consensus Project, the American Academy of Pediatrics, and the National Hospice and Palliative Care Organization emphasize the importance of expert, effective, and developmentally appropriate communication among the palliative care team, the child and family.[1-3] The PPC team often meets a child in the moments of critical need or during a significant change in the child's condition. The team works collaboratively, drawing out each member's strengths and expertise to establish a relationship and foster trust with the child and parents. The PPC team strives to understand the child's and parents' perceptions about the serious illness and issues at hand, balancing the family's preferences for care with the team's collective expertise to create together an individualized plan of care.

As vital members of the PPC team, pediatric palliative APRNs are poised to foster effective communication throughout a family's experience with serious or life-limiting illness.[4] Pediatric palliative APRNs serve as key leaders and communication liaisons in a variety of situations, including the following:

Assessing the family's understanding of the child's condition and educating parents (and the child, if parents agree) on issues having an impact on the child's physical, emotional, psychosocial, and spiritual well-being

Honoring the family's cultural and spiritual preferences for receiving and sharing information

Ensuring opportunities for collaborative communication between the family and team to create together a feasible plan of care that honors the family's preferences and optimizes the child's quality of life

Advocating for the family's voice throughout the child's trajectory of care

Encouraging effective communication among all team members, including leading family care conferences or participating in the team discussion before meeting with the family

Modeling effective communication strategies on a daily basis, including mentoring of the child's bedside nurses and all other care team members

Facilitating communication among family members (e.g., parent and child, parent and sibling) while helping parents determine strategies for regulating information with extended family, friends, and the child's community

Acting as a broker, creating a bridge across care settings between the family and the team members: the primary care provider, pediatric subspecialists, psychosocial clinicians, community palliative providers, therapists, and school professionals

Buffering interactions/communication when the child's caregivers become focused on planning end-of-life care during a time when the parents understand death is approaching but also wish to focus on living in the present moment

Communicating changes in prognosis, especially as the transition to end-of-life unfolds

Facilitating care to ensure dignity and to honor relationships during a child's life and death

APRNs need expert communication skills to navigate the myriad of PPC experiences while also striving for integrity in their relationships with children, families, and team members. Parents report that they value genuine, caring relationships with their child's medical team.[5] Entering into such relationships requires knowing one's own expectations, intentions, and motivations while also attempting to understand the other person's perception of the shared experience. Staying connected with oneself and with others is integral to initiating, maintaining, and transitioning relationships.[6] Parents appreciate when PPC team members work to establish relationships with each member of their family, understanding who they are as individuals separate from the child's medical condition.[5,7] This chapter explores the pediatric palliative APRN's role in providing high-quality PPC, focusing on strategies to develop effective communication and honor relationships throughout the child's life and death and the family's bereavement.

Initiating the Relationship

Before meeting with a new child and family, the pediatric palliative APRN must be mindful of his or her own communication preferences and strengths. Limbo and Kobler offer a four-step process for self-awareness and preparation: **P**ause, **R**ecognize, **A**cknowledge, and be **M**indful (PRAM).[8] Pausing to reflect on "What values or feelings do I bring to this encounter?" and "What intentions or expectations do I have for this child?" can be helpful. Such a reflective process also allows the APRN to anticipate personal concerns or limitations that may arise due to the child's specific needs or circumstances. Through mindful self-awareness, pediatric palliative APRNs ground themselves while entering into the tender place of establishing a meaningful relationship with the child and family.

The pediatric palliative APRN usually begins a relationship with the child and family as a member of the PPC team. After the initial consult, the APRN's first task is to identify the best way of connecting with the family. Often the child or parent will lead the initial conversation. The pediatric palliative APRN should be open to exploring creative ways of connecting with children and parents, perhaps through the child's favorite TV shows, books, or hobbies. For one little boy who refused to look any caregiver in the eye, the pediatric palliative APRN's recognition of the Lego figures in his hand elicited a flicker of eye contact and a small nod, thus beginning their eventual caring relationship. Conversation with parents may be initiated over an early morning cup of coffee or while strolling through the hospital garden. The APRN may reach out by texting a teen, e-mailing a parent, or being the team member who consistently meets the family before or after a clinic appointment. Parents report valuing team members who convey an unhurried and available presence.[9] Identifying meaningful ways to establish this initial connection opens the door to deeper communication with the child and family.

Depending on the child's needs, the pediatric palliative APRN may or may not be the palliative team member to make the initial contact with the family. The APRN may not take the leadership role, but instead facilitate the communication with the primary team or home care team members, or with the nurses at the bedside. By working with the interprofessional team, the process of building a relationship with the family can be shared by team members[10] and therefore is not dependent on one clinician when striving to provide 24/7 wraparound care.

To learn each family member's communication preferences, the APRN can simply say, "Help us know how you prefer to receive and process information about your child." When one father shared his intense fear of talking with large numbers of clinicians at the same time, the APRN was able to modify the full team medical rounds and family care conferences to ease the father's anxiety, ultimately enhancing his ability to engage in critical decision making about his baby's care.

In meeting families' communication needs, we must attend to their individualized preferences, using common courtesies that convey respect. Ways to do this include the following:

◆ In the hospital, knock on the door, ask permission to enter, and introduce yourself each time, as families meet a multitude of providers.

◆ Always acknowledge the child by name, regardless of his or her ability to respond.

◆ If there is any question of needing translation services, have an interpreter present.

◆ Ask about, and honor, the family's communication style.

◆ Always ask the child and parents how they prefer to be addressed.

◆ Find out how to pronounce and spell the names of family members you meet.

◆ In the consult note, include names of important family members, pets, and special objects.

One mother shared with the palliative care team that if a caregiver entered the room and did not acknowledge her son immediately, "They're out of here!" This emphasizes the importance of making the first connection in order to be invited back. Through these beginning interactions, the team can start to lay the groundwork for meaningful and helpful strategies to provide symptom management, advance care planning, or memory making.

Maintaining the Relationship

Following the initial encounters, the APRN works as part of the PPC team to establish trust with the child and family. Fostering secure attachments is an essential component to maintaining a relationship with the family receiving pediatric palliative care.[11] Parents perceive the continuity of the relationship with trusted team members and the coordinated provision of information as key elements in the quality of care and caring.[6,12,13] As one mother told the APRN after several months, "I didn't want to have to meet you, and it is only now that I see how much we needed you and your team." Feudtner[14] describes the principle of collaborative communication as a relationship-focused effort by participants to establish common goals, convey mutual respect, understand the other's differing perspectives, verbalize thoughts clearly and correctly, and manage all aspects of personality that may affect the communication process. Pediatric palliative APRNs, along with the entire team, strive to maintain such collaborative communication as the child's trajectory of care unfolds, with the hope that families will embrace this relationship-centered approach.

Fostering continued communication begins with the pediatric palliative APRN and palliative team's assessment of the child's current status and the family's experience of the child's daily needs. It may be a simple intervention, but whether this assessment is led by the palliative APRN or another trusted team member, asking these "5 questions"[15] can help achieve a clear snapshot of the child's needs and the issues at hand:

◆ Who is your child as a person?

◆ What is your understanding of your child's illness?

◆ What are your hopes?

◆ What are your worries?

◆ What sustains you or gives you strength?

In addition to the questions noted above, the APRN and palliative team may find themselves using various phrases to elicit the child's or parents' perception of the issues at hand. Taking the lead from the family, the pediatric palliative APRN may ask the following:

◆ Help me understand what you mean by ...

◆ What are the most important issues for you and your child right now?

◆ I'm confused because I think I heard you say two different things.

◆ It sounds like you feel that you have no control.

◆ What I hear you are saying is ...

◆ Please tell me if I understand you correctly ...

◆ This feels so difficult.

◆ I am so sorry. I don't know what to say.

◆ Some other parents/patients have told me ... it sounds like this is similar for you.

◆ I can't begin to imagine how this feels ...

By addressing the child's or parent's self-identified immediate needs first, the APRN can then discuss the information he or she was planning to share, thus engaging in a collaborative communication experience.

The pediatric palliative APRN and PPC team colleagues should always be mindful of the words they use. Just as a surgeon uses a scalpel, palliative care clinicians use words as their tools.[16] The use of certain words is avoided, such as "narcotic," which has negative connotations, or referring to the parents as "mom and dad" out of respect for them as individuals. Table 62.1 summarizes common themes PPC teams may discuss with families, providing a perspective on the unintended messages we may convey with our words, and offers alternative choices.

In addition to ascertaining a family's perceptions about the child's needs, pediatric palliative APRNs continually assess for distressing symptoms using tools that are developmentally appropriate and that produce consistent, accurate data. While it is always helpful to have the child or teen describe physical symptoms, the PPC team often encounters children who cannot communicate their discomfort in words. For an older, nonverbal child, the Individualized Numeric Rating Scale,[17,18] filled out by the primary caregiver, allows all to recognize and treat pain appropriately. The APRN and PPC team may not have an intervention idea at every visit, but "showing up" demonstrates openness to the evolving course of a child's and family's journey.

It is important for the team to be aware that parents may be holding worries on their mind and heart, yet choose not to communicate them aloud. Parents who receive a prenatal diagnosis of a life-limiting fetal condition describe feeling utterly alone as they struggle with conflicting emotions of grief and hope for their unborn child. They also report that it is difficult to share these feelings with family, friends, and the healthcare team.[19] Other parents of seriously ill children prefer to convey a positive outward expression when inwardly experiencing deep hurt. The result may be emotional miscues and consequent miscommunication with

Table 62.1 Pediatric Palliative Care Discussion Recommendations

Topic	Common Response	Unintended Message	Alternative Wording
Discussion about pain management	"We can best treat your pain by using *narcotics*"	"And you may become a drug addict"	"We can best treat your pain by using opioid or pain medications ... "
Discussion about defining goals of care	"What would you like us to do if ... ?"	Implies that the patient/family can choose from a menu of options	Use open-ended questions to define treatment goals: "What's most important to you/for your child right now?"
Discussion of disease-directed therapy	"We can use this experimental agent or we can *do nothing*"	"If we don't opt for medical management, we are 'giving up.' "	"Whether or not we continue with disease-directed therapy, we will care for you and do our best to manage symptoms and optimize your quality of life."
Discussion about artificial nutrition and hydration	"We could stop the TPN/G-tube feeds."	Discontinuing supplemental nutrition means starving the patient to death.	"Our recommendation is that your child's body is at a point where artificial hydration and nutrition are not going to be of benefit. In fact it may cause harm and/or suffering."
Discussion about resuscitation	"Do you want us to do everything?"	What would a "good parent" do?	"You have made the best decisions possible and done everything to help your child survive. There are no more medical therapies we know of that will change the disease course. Based on our conversations we would recommend limiting attempts at resuscitation."

Adapted from teaching tool by Joanne Wolfe, used with permission.

the healthcare team.[20] The pediatric palliative APRN must mindfully evaluate his or her effectiveness in communicating during each family encounter, assessing and shifting communication strategies as needed. It may take multiple encounters before a parent can verbalize a deep concern. When members of the child's healthcare team comment that "the parents just don't seem to get it," the APRN can clarify that the parents really do "get it," but they just choose carefully when and to whom to acknowledge their understanding, fears, and worries.

Sometimes, when working with seriously ill infants and children, spoken words cannot begin to express the pediatric palliative APRN's thoughts in the midst of witnessing profound suffering or sorrow. During such moments, silence can be used to convey caring while simultaneously honoring the relationship. Compassionate silence stems from reflective practice and involves simply being present to another without expectations for conversation. Instead of attempting to direct the discussion, the caregiver holds silence by focusing on his or her breathing.[21] Compassionate silence allows the child or family members to center on their innermost thoughts or feelings, which in time may find expression in words shared aloud with the caregiver. After periods of silence, it is important to watch for deep sighs, as such expressions often follow reflective thought. Upon hearing a parent's loud sigh, the APRN said, "Help me to know what is on your mind right now." This opened the door for one mother to share a previously unspoken fear: "My first conscious thought each morning is about my son. After that first thought is the same awful question, how do I live through this day knowing that today … today could be the day that he dies?"

During such moments of expressed vulnerability the pediatric palliative APRN may offer words of acknowledgment and affirmation. Validating the strengths of the parents and child is a powerful anchor, as is conveying the belief that family will find its way through the situation at hand. Reminding the parent that he or she is a "good parent"[22] or telling the child that he or she is loved and special is a way to convey caring. Such words, coupled with the pediatric palliative APRN's and PPC team's expressed commitment to "go the distance"[23] with the child and family, foster ongoing trust.

Seeing Through Cultural Lenses

Being grounded in one's own culture provides a sense of security and belonging, offering structure for daily living and influencing how emotions are experienced and communicated. Culture frames our understanding and responses to illness or death.[24] Language and cultural differences may be barriers, restricting the team's ability to discern parents' understanding and emotional responses.[25] Learning about the family's experience of living with the child's life-threatening condition from a cultural perspective can provide profound insight into their values, expectations, and hopes that may guide future care-planning discussions. These questions[24,26] may be helpful in clarifying the family's understanding of the child's condition as influenced by their cultural or spiritual beliefs and values:

- What is happening (has happened) to your child?
- What do you think caused this to happen?
- How have you and your family been affected by what has happened?

- What meaning does this experience have for you and your family?
- Tell me what else I would need to know to understand and help you.

In response to the second question above, one mother confided her belief that her unborn baby's lethal chromosomal disorder was caused by eating too many "hot" foods instead of "cold" foods. She shared her feelings of guilt, which the APRN then acknowledged. The pediatric palliative APRN may also assess for culturally influenced communication cues by watching how family members interact with each other and the medical team, noticing personal space or boundaries, eye contact, or the extent of physical touch. The APRN can then guide the team in regulating their interactions to respect the family's communication preferences.

Watching a parent's body language offers important insights about how best to provide culturally respectful communication. For example, the pediatric palliative APRN observed a father's distraught behavior after participating in his daughter's family-centered PICU rounds. The APRN remarked, "I'm noticing that something is troubling you." To which the father responded in a heightened tone, "All of these medical details are keeping me from my real duty, praying for my daughter's healing. I cannot listen to the details anymore!" The father then shared his beliefs about healing as a practicing Christian Scientist. While the father desired PICU medical interventions for his daughter, something not supported by his church elders, the daily rounding information conflicted with his deeply felt responsibility to pray for healing. The APRN helped the parents and PICU team to determine a rounding compromise, creating a safe environment for the father to remain in uninterrupted prayer.

Medical interpreters should be used whenever English is not the family's primary language. In one study exploring the experiences of Mexican-American and Asian families, parents described more anger, distress, and sadness during their child's illness when interpreters were absent, as trust eroded when parents felt they were provided insufficient information.[25] In preparation, pediatric palliative APRNs should inform the medical interpreter about the nature of the planned discussion and then debrief accordingly, especially if interpretation involves delivering difficult or sad news.

Technology resources, such as Skype or FaceTime, may be helpful communication tools when families wish to incorporate traditions, rituals, or spiritual practices into the child's care. For example, when a baby was nearing the end-of-life, his parents asked for help in facilitating daily afternoon prayers with his grandparents in India. After securing a laptop and Skype connection, the grandparents were able to meet their grandson for the first time. Before he would lead prayers, the grandfather had one request of the pediatric palliative APRN, shared through the medical interpreter: "Show me his feet. I want to see if he has the same big toe as the men in our family!"

In some cultures, the family elder or patriarch is the key decision maker for all important issues pertaining to any member of the family. The pediatric palliative APRN and PPC team must establish a trusting relationship and communicate through this patriarch in order to reach consensus for next steps in a child's care. For other non-Western families, cultural and religious beliefs inform truth telling in decision making. As a result, it is unacceptable or forbidden for a parent to agree to a DNR/DNI order or agree to withdraw mechanical ventilation. There may also be a strong instinct to protect a child from news of a poor prognosis or impending death.[27] With each of these culturally based preferences, the pediatric palliative APRN and PPC team must continue to work creatively to maintain trust and foster communication within the family's parameters to address the child's palliative care needs.

Even though the members of the PPC team do their best to understand a family's cultural lenses, they humbly realize they can never fully understand another's perception. For example, one pediatric palliative APRN entered a baby's room with the goal of learning her family's progress in decision making for a potential surgery. The grandmother was weeping as she rocked her granddaughter. The anguish on her face was evident, prompting the APRN to say, "Your tears reflect much emotion." The grandmother replied, "I weep because I have not received a call today from my family in Syria. They usually call each day, so I can know they are safe from the violence happening in our country. Children are being murdered there by the minute! Here, I safely hold my granddaughter in my arms, knowing your team will do everything to save her life. Yet back home, life is being wasted, thrown away. How … how do I make sense of all of this?" The APRN sat quietly with the grandmother as she rocked and wept, recognizing through this exchange that this family was holding more on their minds than the PPC team could ever comprehend.

Honoring the Child's Voice

Listening carefully to the child's experience of living with serious illness represents the heart of PPC. The child's voice is best heard through the combined skills and expertise of the interprofessional team. A variety of expressive therapies, including art, music, play, pet, and bibliotherapy, can be used to connect with children, helping them to communicate their experiences at their own pace. As play is the language of children, play therapists, child life specialists, or psychologists trust the child's inner direction to lead play and conversation, allowing them to express their fears, hopes, and perceptions of the situation.[28] One psychologist on the oncology unit was known for walking with a stuffed monkey's arms wrapped around her and a PlayMobile® box in one hand filled with figures and objects that children used to "tell their story." Using a creative method of inquiry, Malaysian clinicians invited children to share their experience with serious illness by choosing a miniature model chair and then asking questions such as "What chair would you like to sit in? Would you tell me why you picked this one? Which chair would you like to sit on in the future?"[29] One child chose a two-seat sofa and talked about feeling smothered and needing space. Another child chose a beach chair to sit on in the future, expressing her sadness of never having a family vacation, as she was always sick.

In addition to assessing the child's understanding of his or her illness or prognosis, expressive therapies may be used to determine a child's level of spiritual distress or suffering. Pediatric palliative APRNs may use or suggest a variety of reflective workbooks and books (Box 62.1) to elicit the child's feelings and wishes. Individualized, concrete strategies, such as drawing a picture, using a sand table with figures, making a video, or writing a letter, may help a child or teen address loneliness, express concerns about life after death, explore his or her relationship with God, ask for forgiveness, or find meaning.[30] Lydia was a brave, beautiful 9½-year-old with unrelenting head and neck parameningeal

rhabdomyosarcoma. Lydia drew a picture, which her mother, Paula, titled *Smiling Through Brokenness* (Fig. 62.1). The drawing inspired a large sculpture, which is now a part of the memorial garden created in Lydia's honor at her elementary school (Fig. 62.2).

Listening carefully to children often involves sensing and responding to windows of opportunity for meaningful discussions. Paula shared her experience of hearing Lydia's voice through a story presented at palliative care rounds:

> One evening about 6 months before Lydia's death we were in her bedroom as she was getting ready for bed. "Mom, if I die, do you think God would let me see myself as a teenager?" Lydia asked. "I think so," I said, then seized the opportunity to open this door further and ask the questions I might someday need answers to.

> "So, if you died, what do you think you would want?" I ventured. "Would you want to be buried in Minnesota by Grandma? Would you want to be cremated so I could keep your ashes in an urn in the living room? Or would you want to be buried in the cemetery by your school?" I braced myself for Lydia's response.

> "Oh gross! I would not want you to keep my ashes in the house. You don't want a dead person in your house!" We both laughed as we pictured it. "Minnesota is too far away." Lydia paused, weighing other options, "I like the cemetery by the school."

> And thus our conversations about death began, and continued over the next six months. Once the subject had been broached, honesty and openness replaced fear and anxiety.[31]

Lydia's mother captures well the delicate task of discussing the possibility of dying with one's own child. Pediatric palliative APRNs and PPC team members may find themselves facilitating similar conversations. Understanding the concept of death is a dynamic process that is influenced by the child's cognitive abilities, developmental capacities, life experiences, and ability to communicate his or her feelings and thoughts.[32–34] Hurwitz and Duncan[32] offer a summary of children's specific understandings of death based on developmental stages. Readers are referred to

---

Box 62.1 Suggested Resources to Elicit Conversations with Children About Feelings and Goals

For school-age children

My Wishes (available from www.agingwithdignity.org)

The Invisible String by Patrice Karst

When Someone Has a Very Serious Illness: Children Can Learn to Cope with Loss and Change by Marge Heegaard

When the Wind Stops by Charlotte Zolotow

For teens and young adults

Digging Deep, a Journal for Young People Facing Health Challenges by Rose Offner and Sheri Brisson

Five Wishes (for those over 18 years old; www.agingwithdignity. org)

In My World by Bonnie Byers Crawford and Linda Lazar (available from Centering Corporation)

Voicing My Choices (available from www.agingwithdignity.org)

When You Know You're Dying: 12 Thoughts to Guide You Through the Days Ahead by James E. Miller

Figure 62.1 Lydia's drawing, *Smiling Through Brokenness.*

this reference, as such a detailed discussion is outside the scope of this chapter. As the child progresses in cognitive development, each of these four concepts about death will be understood differently: irreversibility (death cannot be undone); nonfunctionality (death means the body no longer functions); inevitability (death cannot be halted); and universality (death happens to everyone).[35] Comprehension of these concepts about death will be reflected in a child's or teen's consideration of his or her own death, often in ways more eloquent than adults.

Children who live with chronic or life-threatening illnesses, go to camps or regular clinics, or experience extended hospital stays often convey wisdom well beyond their chronological age. Lydia's life experiences with advanced cancer contributed to her mature perspective on the finality of death and her ability to discuss

Figure 62.2 Lydia's school garden.

even her possible gravesite location. Lydia's mother shared this reflection:

> Lydia was able to use her knowledge of impending death to evaluate what she wanted to accomplish with the time she had left. She may have only been nine, but she was a wise soul who reached out to people in her last days. Letting Lydia speak of death, and understand the reality of her situation, allowed her the opportunity to talk with people she cared about as if it were her last chance to do so. In many cases, it *was* her last chance.

> Five days before she died, Lydia said, "I used to judge people by their appearance. If they walked funny or talked funny or looked different. I DON'T DO THAT ANYMORE! After cancer, I know what it is like walking, talking and looking different . . ." This has become Lydia's Legacy quote. It is imprinted on a bench in her memorial garden, in hopes that other children will learn from Lydia's hard-earned wisdom.[31]

However, even though a child may possess a mature understanding of his or her serious illness, he or she may choose to refrain from sharing this knowledge with others. In addition, families may engage in a phenomenon of mutual protection: the child wishes to spare the parents sorrow, and at the same time the parents wish for the child to "keep hope" or "not give up," so honest communication is compromised.[36,37] Just as parents take seriously their role to protect and nurture, children want to please and live up to the expectations of parents, possibly resulting in crucial conversations left unspoken. Other times, parents recognize, understand, and wish to honor their child's cues to not speak of dying out loud, but rather to focus on living.

Myra Bluebond-Langner, an anthropologist whose interviews with terminally ill children provided groundbreaking insights into their experiences, in her book *The Private Worlds of Dying Children*, focuses on determining strategies for child involvement in decision making. She suggests a "shuttle diplomacy" process, whereby the clinician speaks with the parents and then with the child, recognizing that each has a voice that then can be brought to the negotiation or decision, with the goal of reaching a resolution acceptable to all.[36] This strategy is an important reminder for all pediatric palliative APRNs that if the door to discussions with children is not opened, they may be robbed of the opportunity to do what is most important to them, share important words with loved ones, or live out whatever time they have in meaningful ways. Shuttle diplomacy calls for clinicians to be genuine and truthful in all conversations with the child.[36] For instance, if a child asks, "Am I dying?" the pediatric palliative APRN may ask gently, "Are you worried about dying?" or "Help me to know, is that how you feel?" Or the APRN may say, "Right now, we do not believe you are dying. I promise to be honest with you if we think that is happening." These responses convey respect and acknowledgment to the child. Again from Lydia's legacy:

> Several days before Lydia's body gave out completely, she turned to me and said in a matter-of-fact way, "Mom, I'm dying." Our previous conversations had paved the way for her to readily admit this to me.
> "Lydia, if you have to die, you have to die. We have tried everything to keep you alive." I sat facing her in her bed, "If God wants you now, there is nothing else we can do." I grasped her hands in mine and said, "Time will go quickly for you in heaven, and before you know it, I'll be with you." We left nothing unsaid. We apologized for any transgressions and forgave each other. We pledged our undying love, and we comforted each other.[31]

After Lydia's death, her mother drew upon the memory of these poignant conversations, sharing with the pediatric palliative APRN and through her blog (http://plzcontemplate.com/myblog) how the recollection of Lydia's words continues to bring comfort and reassurance. Courageous Parents Network (http://courageousparentsnetwork.org) offers more advice from parents and professionals with videos and a virtual community for families with children facing life-threatening illness.

Discerning Goals of Care

By maintaining a relationship and ongoing communication with the family, the pediatric palliative APRN and the PPC team work to discern goals of care that will optimize the child's quality of life. The team often assumes the role of detective, gathering clues as to a child's or family's preferences and wishes. The APRN may simply ask, "What is most important to you, or for you, in caring for your child right now?" With this approach, the APRN may discern major life goals as well as more subtle and multifaceted goals that can shift and change over time.

Children and teens often possess the wonderful ability to clearly convey their goals and wishes. During a home visit, the pediatric palliative APRN and social work fellow decided to ask a teen with cystic fibrosis to do some homework over the weekend by writing down, without regard to their feasibility, "all the things you wish for or want." On Monday morning, the teen proudly shared the following list, compiled just weeks before her death:[38]

I WISH . . .

. . . to go to heaven.

. . . to swim with the dolphins.

. . . to leave signs for the people I love so they will know I am still with them when I die.

. . . to have a million dollars.

. . . to live in Hawaii or Florida.

. . . to visit the Bahamas.

. . . to ride in a hot air balloon.

. . . to not be so tired.

. . . to have my friends and family at my funeral.

. . . to drive a car and get my license.

. . . to have a water bed.

. . . to have a hot tub.

. . . to have a mansion.

. . . to not have diabetes.

. . . to have people always remember that I am smart, cute, sweet, and loving.

. . . to play horseshoes.

Although not all of the teen's wishes were fulfilled before her death, the exercise of writing out these hopes, along with the discussions that followed as she shared the list with others, proved to be a meaningful experience.

Optimally, the work of discerning care goals or preferences begins at the time of diagnosis, and they are jointly created after a series of relationship-building conversations with the pediatric palliative APRN and PPC team. More commonly, goals of care are determined during times of complex decision making triggered by a significant change or deterioration in the child's condition. Often, these conversations occur in family meetings or care conferences with the entire team, as parents grapple with difficult news and making decisions in their child's best interests.[10,34,39,40] The pediatric palliative APRN plays a crucial role in organizing and facilitating such interprofessional care conferences, including team discussions before the meeting with the family to make sure all perspectives are heard and all possible treatment options are considered.

During the care conference, the pediatric palliative APRN may accept the responsibility of assessing the parents' understanding and reaction to the discussion, calling for a pause in dialogue if the parents appear overwhelmed, and then reframing the issue at hand. Renjilian and colleagues[41] encourage PPC teams to listen for heuristics (verbal shortcuts) that parents of children with life-threatening conditions often use to facilitate understanding of a complex situation or to justify a choice for their child's care—phrases like "everything happens for a reason," "it is best for her," or "I just want her to be comfortable." Upon hearing such expressions, pediatric palliative APRNs can take the lead in discerning the goals, values, or feelings behind the heuristics by statements like, "I noticed you said 'keep fighting.' Can you tell me more?"[41]

It is increasingly common for adult palliative care teams to assist adult patients in creating advance directives, delineating the extent of treatment the adult would prefer if his or her condition declines. Adolescents age 18 years or older are considered to be adults, with decision-making capacity and competency,[42] and thus may use any of the legally recognized advance directive tools to document their care preferences. PPC teams engaged in advance care planning conversations with adolescents and young adults with cancer have found that such discussions foster trust, resilience, and hope, strengthening relationships among participants.[43]

However, there are currently no legal advance directive documents for patients less than 18 years of age. Multiple barriers exist to conducting such conversations in pediatric settings, including limited parental understanding of the child's prognosis, clinicians' concern about destroying a family's hope, and disconnects in clinician–family communication.[44] In addition, parents of children with complex, chronic health conditions may be asked at every emergency department encounter about care preferences, so eventually they decline the invitation to participate in formal advance care planning.[45] As one parent stated, "My child may look different, but I want her treated like any other child here!"

PPC teams who implement advance care planning for children report how these conversations help to relieve anxiety and foster decision making.[46] To facilitate advance planning discussions, the pediatric palliative APRN may wish to access the Decision-Making Tool (DMT) developed by the Pediatric Advance Care Team at Seattle Children's Hospital.[47] The DMT provides a framework to guide conversations regarding a child's treatment options, discharge planning, or future care needs. Or the pediatric palliative APRN may use one of the advance planning tools available from Aging with Dignity.[48] These child-focused tools include *My Wishes* (for younger school-age children to draw or write their responses), *Voicing My Choices* (for teens and young adults), and *Five Wishes* (for those 18 years and older) (see Chapter 60). When completed and signed before witnesses, *Five Wishes* is recognized in many

states as a legal advance directive for persons over the age of 18. These tools offer parents examples of possible language to use in advance planning discussions, while also giving children, teens, and young adults the freedom to express themselves and articulate their wishes in a definitive way. Once the tools are completed by the child and family, the pediatric palliative APRN plays a key role in disseminating the desired plan of care to the entire team.

Maintaining Communication when Expectations Differ

Effective communication takes effort even when all parties have similar perceptions and goals; it is even more intense when expectations differ, often resulting in feelings of frustration that individual concerns are not being heard. Such moments of differing expectations might occur between the parents, between the parents and the child, or between the family and team members.[14] Pediatric palliative APRNs must remember that the family may be experiencing the issue through a filter of intertwining grief and hope.[6] Failure to assess for these deep feelings can lead to differing expectations between the family and the child's healthcare team.

Parents describe their deeply felt responsibility to be bearers of hope, a responsibility taken very seriously throughout the child's care trajectory.[49,50] Parents may also hold tightly to the strong belief that a miraculous healing will occur, often maintaining this belief until the moment of death. The family's focus on a miracle may conflict with the healthcare team's understanding of the child's poor prognosis. The pediatric palliative APRN may take the lead in assessing the parents' hope for a miracle. The APRN may learn more about the family's perception with remarks like, "Help me understand what a miracle would mean to you," followed by, "If that miracle does not come to pass, what else are you hoping for your child?"[51] The family's answers may help the APRN frame a respectful response that acknowledges the family's belief in the miracle, without challenging or offering false hope that it will occur.[49–52]

When conflict arises between parents or with members of the healthcare team, the pediatric palliative APRN can play an instrumental role in discerning the root of the discord. Strong external reactions by parents or team members are often rooted in equally strong internal beliefs of wanting the best for the child. Using phrases like "I am curious" or "help me to understand" and consciously using "and" instead of "but" are useful in drawing out the differing perspectives of the parties.[14]

Conflict may occur when the healthcare team perceives that the child is suffering while parents say, "We want everything done." Often, the hope is that the PPC team will step in and resolve the conflict. Pediatric palliative APRNs play a key role in facilitating conversations about care choices should the child's condition deteriorate significantly. The APRN can help parents consider limitation of treatments or shifting the treatment focus from high-tech, invasive medical interventions to less invasive, yet still intensive, caring measures. Parents' expression of "wanting everything" done for their child is often a reflection of their fear and anticipatory grief. It is this grief that translates into the parents' plea, "care for us, care about us, don't abandon us, we are terrified to think that our child will die."[53] In this situation, the burden of decision making must *not* be placed on the shoulders of families with phrases that reflect an abdication of responsibility, such as, "You (the child/family) need to decide what you want us to do if …"

Rather, the entire team must partner with families, making honest recommendations for next steps in the child's care based on the team's combined medical expertise, while honoring the child's and family's expertise about their values that intertwine with the child's declining physical reality. The pediatric palliative APRN can take the lead in understanding what "doing everything" means to the parents, providing affirmation of both the parents' love for the child and the team's ongoing commitment.[53]

Fostering Seamless Communication

The pediatric palliative APRN is often responsible for reaching out to multiple care providers within the hospital and community when significant events or care decisions arise.[54] By assuming responsibility for ensuring that the child's primary care providers have accurate and thorough discharge summaries, the APRN can help to ease the burden for parents having to communicate such information to multiple providers.[10,54] Without effective communication, it is all too common for the child's community providers (e.g., home care staff, the primary care provider, rehabilitation facility, or other subspecialists involved in the child's care) to feel disconnected during the child's hospitalization. Primary care providers often have longstanding relationships with children and families but may have not previously incorporated palliative care principles. They may need assistance from the pediatric palliative APRN with understanding the concurrent care model of delivering palliative care and disease-directed treatment at the same time, coaching about ways to discuss advance care planning, or locating the appropriate state forms to document treatments to pursue or not pursue (i.e., medical orders for life-sustaining treatments, such as MOLST or POLST). In some states, APRNs may sign these orders with the family. The APRN and PPC team can model communication practices by sharing the initial consult note not only with the family but also with those the family identifies as key players in the child's community, and subsequently reaching out by phone or e-mail to community providers when there are significant changes in the child's care.

When the child's long-term prognosis is unclear, the pediatric palliative APRN can collaborate with the parents to develop an emergency symptom management plan. The APRN outlines pharmacologic and nonpharmacologic interventions that may be used to ameliorate symptoms. Medications are ordered so that they will be available in the home, especially for crises that occur in the middle of the night or on weekends. The APRN sends copies of the plan to the primary care provider, the home PPC, the home hospice team, and other community providers. One family, with the APRN's assistance, took a copy of their emergency plan, along with their daughter on her ventilator, to their neighborhood firehouse to meet those who might be called upon to provide emergent care.

Transitions in the Relationship

Transitions in the relationship occur at different points in time, depending on the progression of the child's condition. Children may receive intensive palliative care measures and then reach a point of relative stability, allowing for a less frequent PPC presence. When this occurs, the pediatric palliative APRN may shift from having daily interactions with the child and family to making periodic checks by calling or sending an e-mail for updates from the family. Maintaining a trusting, consistent relationship allows the APRN and PPC team to reconnect with the family if and when crucial shifts in care occur.

Another significant transition occurs when a teen/young adult with a serious illness starts to receive care from adult providers. The pediatric palliative APRN and PPC team may be in a perfect position to provide ongoing support during this transition, while also finding ways to address the young adult's feelings of reluctance or fear.[55]

Communication as Death Approaches

Early in the disease trajectory and sometimes until the end, parents hold dual goals at the same time: they hope for a miracle or cure, and they hope for comfort and relief of the child's suffering. They share these goals during decision-making meetings or on a daily basis with those who will listen.[36] It is important for the pediatric palliative APRN and PPC team to assess for such dual goals. Parents with higher levels of hopeful thinking are more likely to reset goals of care like cure to that of keeping the child comfortable, and eventually agreeing to limits on emergency treatment efforts.[49,56] One mother poignantly told her APRN, "I will pray for a miracle until her last breath," and the mother's hopes did not preclude important family conversations with the daughter about what songs she wanted sung or readings read at her funeral. Holding hope for cure also did not prohibit the parents from reaching agreement for a DNR/DNI order, so their daughter would be protected from medical interventions that would not change the disease course. Thus, she had a peaceful death surrounded by family and beloved staff on the same hospital unit where she spent many days fighting, laughing, and living over 6 years of treatment.

Likewise, a teen expressed his dual goals by talking about the truck he dreamed of getting once he was well again, even though he could not get out of bed due to pain and metastatic disease. His nurse wondered whether she was being dishonest by entering into this fantasy, but after consulting with the palliative APRN, she learned that this was a healthy way for the teen to cope with his impending death. It reflected his ability to make plans, have a goal, and keep living each day.

A focus on dual hopes and shifting expectations allows the pediatric palliative APRN and PPC team to help parents set new goals for their child, even as death approaches. The APRN may play an integral role, joining the child's care team in providing honest, compassionate communication about the child's prognosis.[57] It is in these moments that the APRN may assist families in creating a plan for what would be most meaningful as the end-of-life nears.[58] Sometimes simple ideas like having a holiday celebration "early" or a sleepover with friends, going outside to feel sunshine and the breeze, or lying cuddled watching a movie in bed together can be determined in advance and then facilitated by the APRN and PPC team.

Unless the patient and family are asked, the APRN and team will not know whether it is helpful for a child or family to talk about end-of-life care. Both health care teams and families may have a great deal of hesitation or fear about discussing death. The PPC team may be told by the child's primary caregivers not to bring up the subject of death to prevent harming the relationship or causing painful emotions.[59] However, parents often readily share, without prompting, that losing their child is their biggest fear. Many who have a child with a chronic, life-threatening illness retell the story of how they were told at the child's birth or shortly thereafter that their child would not survive until the age of 2, then 6 or 10, and now the child is 16 years old. This may lead to disbelief when a crisis is labeled as "due to the worsening of the underlying illness" or when the crisis is seen as part of the unknown individuality of the child and his or her disease course. The children often cannot talk about the end-of-life but may communicate with their eyes or their behaviors.

Other children may be open and able to talk about death if given the opportunity, as Lydia's beautiful story conveys. Teens may be willing to share their fear of not reaching hoped-for goals or their concerns about what will happen to their siblings and parents after their death. One 16-year-old with stable disease, shyly admitted to the palliative APRN that she had already arranged for her best friend to accept her high school diploma if she "didn't make it," and furthermore that she worried about dying every day.

Kreichberg and colleagues learned that no parents in their study regretted speaking to their children about death.[60] A subsequent study found that as the pediatric palliative APRN and PPC team facilitated such discussions, planning about how the child's dying might unfold resulted in more home deaths and fewer hospital admissions.[61] Again, from Lydia's mother's reflections:

> I buried my daughter knowing she would like the casket, the cemetery and the funeral. Lydia had made those decisions. The conversations we had were painful. But **not** having those conversations would have proved more painful. Nothing was left unsaid. In the end, my little girl who could not control what happened to her body in life was given control to make decisions about what happened to her body in death.[31]

It is outside the scope of this chapter to discuss caring for the child and family as the end-of-life approaches. Pediatric palliative APRNs should remember that although they have been present for many patient deaths, this will be the first death for this child, a first experience for this family. The details of those moments will become the parents' permanent memory. Therefore, there is an obligation and privilege to serve families carefully during this time, whether they are in the hospital or at home. Parents report appreciating caregivers who conveyed a caring presence, honored their spiritual needs,[62,63] and offered opportunities for parents to connect in meaningful ways with their child.[64]

Bereavement Support

It is a responsibility of the PPC team to provide bereavement support and help the family access community supports. The pediatric palliative APRN may choose to remain connected to the family after the child's death, transitioning into a new form of relationship. Initially, the APRN, PPC social worker, hospital chaplain, or local spiritual advisor may assist the family with making funeral arrangements, identifying support for siblings, and providing reassurance and validation of feelings and the profound fact that parental grief is unique. Ongoing bereavement contact allows parents to retell their story, while providing support for whatever is most compelling for them. Sending mailings over a year or two is a tangible reminder to parents that they are not forgotten. Parents may have difficulty connecting to other bereaved families and often say they would like to be in a group with parents who have gone through similar losses. Offering a bereavement group for the families of children treated at the same institution, although with a variety of diagnoses, has been successful. Lydia's mother joined the HOPE (Healing Opportunities Parent Exchanges) bereavement support group, driving 1½ hours each way every other week for 7 weeks. The group provided the opportunity for Lydia's mother to share stories of Lydia and to continue her legacy.

After a child's death, the parents may ask the pediatric palliative APRN or social worker to arrange bereavement visits with primary providers so they can reconnect, ask lingering questions, or review autopsy results. Such parent–clinician conferences allow the parents to review events around the child's death, provide feedback to staff on the family's experience, and receive emotional support.[65] The APRN and social worker can also make referrals for individual or family counseling, transitioning the family to community providers who will continue to offer supportive bereavement care.

Reinvesting in Future Relationships

Caring for children with serious illness elicits strong emotions for the entire team as they meet the child's physical, emotional, psychosocial and spiritual needs and support families through difficult transitions. When a child's condition deteriorates or when death approaches, caregivers experience their own grief and heartache. The pediatric palliative APRN and PPC team are often called upon to support staff before and after a child's death, balancing the needs of others while also attending to their own grief.[11] Parents report missing the team after the child's death, and caregivers report difficulty in shifting the relationship and also miss having daily communication with the family.[66] Professional caregivers' grieving is marked by ongoing shifts between experiencing grief by focusing on the loss, and avoiding grief by moving away from the situation.[11] This ongoing fluctuation allows clinicians to adapt to the loss in a healthy manner and to attribute meaning to their experience with the child and family. APRNs need to adopt self-care strategies that foster reflection, healing, and renewal.

Conclusion

Pediatric palliative APRNs are often asked, "How do you do your job? I could never do that. Isn't it so very sad?" The common response is that although this work can be emotion-filled and sometimes overwhelming, primarily it is an immense privilege. Engaging in relationships with children and families experiencing serious illness provides a daily reminder about the importance of living fully each day. Many pediatric palliative APRNs remain humbled and grateful for the opportunity to focus on being present, to offer symptom management to improve a child's day, to engage in honoring relationships, and to delight in small acts of kindness. Pediatric palliative APRNs are aware of how they can make a difference with their words, their touch, their tenacity in showing up, and their ability to be exquisitely present in the moment. We honor these children, their parents, and their extended families throughout the process, and recognize the power of love in birth, life, and death.

References

1. American Academy of Pediatrics Section on Hospice and Palliative Medicine and Committee on Hospital Care. Pediatric palliative care and hospice care commitments, guidelines, and recommendations. *Pediatrics*. 2013; 132(5): 966–72.
2. National Consensus Project for Quality Palliative Care. *Clinical Practice Guidelines for Quality Palliative Care*. 3rd ed. Pittsburgh, PA: National Consensus Project for Quality Palliative Care; 2013.

3. National Hospice and Palliative Care Organization (NHPCO). *Standards for Practice for Pediatric Palliative Care and Hospice.* Alexandria, VA: NHPCO; 2009. Available at www.nhpco.org. Accessed July 15, 2015.

4. Pirie A. Pediatric palliative care communication: Resources for the clinical nurse specialist. *Clin Nurse Spec.* 2012; 26(4): 212–5.

5. Melin-Johansson C, Axelsson I, Grundberg MJ, et al. When a child dies: Parents' experiences of palliative care-an integrative literature review. *J Pediatr Nurs.* 2014; 29(6): 660–9.

6. Kobler K. Honoring relationship in pediatric palliative care. In Cox GR, Stevenson RG, eds. *Final Acts: The End of Life, Hospice and Palliative Care.* Amityville, NY: Baywood Publishing; 2013:45–64.

7. Widger K, Steele R, Oberle K, et al. Exploring the supportive care model as a framework for pediatric palliative care. *J Hospice Palliat Nurs.* 2009; 11(4): 209–16.

8. Limbo R, Kobler K. *Meaningful Moments: Ritual and Reflection When a Child Dies.* La Crosse, WI: Gundersen Medical Foundation; 2013.

9. Kavanaugh, K, Roscigno CI, Swanson, KM, et al. Perinatal palliative care: Parent perceptions of caring in interactions surrounding counseling for risk of delivering an extremely premature infant. *Palliat Support Care.* 2015; 13(2): 145–155.

10. Ogelby M, Goldstein RD. Interdisciplinary care: Using your team. *Pediatr Clin North Am.* 2014; 61(4): 823–34.

11. Papadatou D. *In the Face of Death: Professionals who Care for the Dying and the Bereaved.* New York, NY: Springer; 2009.

12. Contra N, Larson J, Scofield S, et al. Family perspectives on the quality of pediatric palliative care. *Arch Pediatr Adolesc Med.* 2002; 156(1): 14–9.

13. Heller KS, Solomon MZ, for the International Pediatric Palliative Care Investigator Team. Continuity of care and caring: What matters to parents of children with life-threatening conditions. *J Pediatr Nurs.* 2005; 20(5): 335.

14. Feudtner C. Collaborative communication in pediatric palliative care: A foundation for problem-solving and decision-making. *Pediatr Clin North Am.* 2007; 54(5): 583–607.

15. Waldman E, Wolfe J. Palliative care for children with cancer. *Nat Rev Clin Oncol.* 2013; 10: 100–7.

16. Cassel EJ. *Talking with Patients: Volume 2, Clinical Technique.* Boston, MA: MIT Press; 1985:4.

17. Solodiuk J, Curley MA. Pain assessment in nonverbal children with severe cognitive impairments: The Individualized Numeric Rating Scale (INRS). *J Pediatr Nurse.* 2003; 18(4): 295–9.

18. Solodiuk JC, Scott-Sutherland J, Meyers M, et al. Validation of the Individualized Numeric Rating Scale (INRS): A pain assessment tool for nonverbal children with intellectual disability. *Pain.* 2010; 150: 231–6.

19. Côté-Arsenault D, Denney-Koelsch E. "My baby is a person": Parents' experiences with life-threatening fetal diagnosis. *J Palliat Med.* 2011; 14(12): 1302–8.

20. Hexem KR, Miller VA, Carroll KW, et al. Putting on a happy face: Emotional expression in parents of children with serious illness. *J Pain Symptom Manage.* 2012; 45(3): 542–51.

21. Back AL, Bauer-Wu SM, Rushton CH, et al. Compassionate silence in the patient-clinician encounter: A contemplative approach. *J Palliat Med.* 2009; 12(12): 1113–7.

22. Hinds PS, Oakes LL, Hicks J, et al. "Trying to be a good parent." As defined by interviews with parents who made Phase 1, terminal care, and resuscitation decisions for their children. *J Clin Oncol.* 2009; 27(35): 5979–85.

23. Swanson K. Empirical development of a middle range theory of caring. *Nurs Res.* 1991; 40(3): 161–6.

24. Rosenblatt PC. The culturally competent practitioner. In Doka KJ, Tucci AS, eds. *Diversity and End-of-Life Care.* Washington, DC: Hospice Foundation of America; 2009:21–32.

25. Davies B, Contro N, Larson J, et al. Culturally-sensitive information sharing in pediatric palliative care. *Pediatrics.* 2010; 125(4): e859–865.

26. Mazanec P, Panke JT. Cultural considerations in end-of-life care. *Am J Nurs.* 2006; 103(3): 50–8.

27. Hatano Y, Yamada M, Fukui K. Shades of truth: cultural and psychological factors affecting communication in pediatric palliative care. *J Pain Symptom Manage.* 2011; 41(2): 491–5.

28. Van Breemen, C. Using play therapy in paediatric palliative care: Listening to the story and caring for the body. *Internat J Palliat Nurs.* 2009; 15(10): 510–4.

29. Chin LE, Loong LC, Ngen CC, et al. Pediatric palliative care: Using miniature chairs to facilitate communication. *Am J Hosp Palliat Care.* 2013; Oct 21: 1–3.

30. Foster TL, Bell CJ, Gilmer MJ. Symptom management of spiritual suffering in pediatric palliative care. *J Hosp Palliat Nurs.* 2012; 14(2): 109–15.

31. Skelley P. *Caring for a Child with Cancer: A Parent's Reflections on Lessons Learned.* July 10, 2014. Boston Children's Hospital, Palliative Care Rounds offered through the Harvard Medical School Center for Palliative Care and Dana-Farber Cancer Institute's Department of Oncology and Palliative Care. Used with permission.

32. Hurwitz CA, Duncan J, Wolfe, J. Caring for the child with cancer at the close of life: "There are people who make it, and I'm hoping I'm one of them." *JAMA.* 2004; 292(17): 2141–9.

33. Limbo R, Kobler K. "Will our baby be alive again?" Supporting parents of young children when a baby dies. *Nurs Womens Health.* 2009; 13(4): 302–11.

34. Vern-Gross T. Establishing communication within the field of pediatric oncology: A palliative care approach. *Curr Probl Cancer.* 2011; 35(6): 337–50.

35. Hunter SB, Smith DE. Predictors of children's understanding of death: Age, cognitive ability, death experience and maternal communicative competence. *Omega.* 2008; 57(2): 143–62.

36. Bluebond-Langner M, Belasco JB, Wander MD. "I want to live, until I don't want to live anymore": Involving children with life-threatening and life-shortening illnesses in decision making about care and treatment. *Nurs Clin North Am.* 2010; 45(3): 329–43.

37. Liben S, Papadatou D, Wolfe J. Paediatric palliative care: challenges and emerging ideas. *Lancet.* 2008; 371: 852–64.

38. Duncan, J. Personal communication with teen. 2009.

39. Michelson, KN, Pater R, Haber-Barker, et al. End-of-life care decisions in the PICU: Roles professionals play. *Pediatr Crit Care Med.* 2013; 14(1): e34–e44.

40. October TW, Fisher KR, Feudtner C, Hinds PS. The parent perspective: "being a good parent" when making critical decisions in the PICU. *Pediatr Crit Care Med.* 2014; 1594: 291–8.

41. Renjilian CB, Womer JW, Carroll KW, et al. Parental explicit heuristics in decision-making for children with life-threatening illnesses. *Pediatrics.* 2013; 131(2): e566–e572.

42. Linebarger JS, Ajayi TA, Jones BL. Adolescents and young adults with life-threatening illness: Special considerations, transitions in care, and the role of pediatric palliative care. *Pediatr Clin North Am.* 2014; 61: 785–96.

43. Walter JK, Rosenberg AR, Feudtner C. Tackling taboo topics: How to have effective advanced care planning discussions with adolescents and young adults with cancer. *JAMA Pediatr.* 2013; 167(5): 489–90.

44. Durall A, Zurakowski D, Wolfe J. Barriers to conducting advance care discussions for children with life-threatening conditions. *Pediatrics.* 2012; 129(4): e975–982.

45. Liberman DB, Pham PK, Nager AL. Pediatric advance directives: Parents' knowledge, experience and preferences. *Pediatrics.* 2014; 134: e436–e443.

46. Lotz JD., Jox RJ, Borasio GD, et al. Pediatric advance care planning: A systematic review. *Pediatrics.* 2013; 131(3): e873–e880.

47. Seattle Children's Hospital Pediatric Advance Care Team. The Decision-Making Tool. Available at http://www.seattlechildrens. org/clinics-programs/palliative-care-consultation/. Published 1995. Updated 2014. Accessed August 18, 2014.

48. Aging with Dignity. Five Wishes Resources. Available at http://www. agingwithdignity.org/catalog/. Published and updated 2014. Accessed August 18, 2014.

49. Feudtner C, Carroll KW, Hexem KR, et al. Parental hopeful patterns of thinking, emotions, and pediatric palliative care decision making. *Arch Pediatr Adolesc Med*. 2010; 164(9): 831–9.

50. Reder EA, Serwint JR. Until the last breath: Exploring the concept of hope for parents and health care professionals during a child's serious illness. *Arch Pediatr Adolesc Med*. 209; 163(7): 653–7.

51. DeLisser HM. A practical approach to the family that expects a miracle. *Chest*. 2009; 135(6): 1643–7.

52. Hill DL, Miller VA, Hexem KR, et al. Problems and hopes perceived by mothers, fathers and physicians of children receiving palliative care. *Health Expect*. 2013; May 20:1–14.

53. Gillis J. "We want everything done." *Arch Dis Child*. 2008; 93(3): 192–3.

54. Nageswaran S, Radulovic A. Transitions to and from the acute inpatient care setting for children with life-threatening illness. *Pediatr Clin North Am*. 2014; 61: 761–83.

55. Linebarger JS, Toluwalase AA, Jones BL. Adolescents and young adults with life-threatening illness: Special considerations, transitions in care, and the role of pediatric palliative care. *Pediatr Clin North Am*. 2014; 61: 785–96.

56. Hill DL, Miller V, Walter JK, et al. Regoaling: A conceptual model of how parents of children with serious illness change medical care goals. *BMC Palliative Care*. 2014; 13(1): 1–8.

57. Mack JM, Joffe S. Communicating about prognosis: Ethical responsibilities of pediatricians and parents. *Pediatrics*. 2014; 133(Suppl1): S24–S30.

58. Carter BS, Brown JB, Brown S, Meyer EC. Four wishes for Aubrey. *J Perinatol*. 2012; 32(1): 10–4.

59. Gaab EM, Owens RG, MacLeod RD. Primary caregivers' decisions around communicating about death with children involved in pediatric palliative care. *J Hospice Palliat Nurs*. 2013; 15(6): 322–9.

60. Kreicbergs U, Validmarsdóttir U, Onelöve E, et al. Talking about death with children who have severe malignant disease. *N Engl J Med*. 2004; 351(12): 1176–86.

61. Dussel V, Kreicbergs U, Hilden JM, et al. Looking beyond where children die: Determinants and effects of planning a child's location of death. *J Pain Symptom Manage*. 2009; 37(1): 33–43.

62. Meert K, Briller, SH, Schim SM, et al. Examining the needs of bereaved parents in the pediatric intensive care unit: A qualitative study. *Death Stud*. 2009; 33(8): 712–40.

63. Meert KL, Thurston CS, Briller SH. The spiritual needs of parents at the time of their child's death in the pediatric intensive care unit and during bereavement: A qualitative study. *Pediatr Crit Care Med*. 2005; 6(4): 420–7.

64. McGraw SA, Truog RD, Solomon MZ, et al. "I was able to still be her mom"—Parenting at end of life in the pediatric intensive care unit. *Pediatr Crit Care Med*. 2012; 13(6): e350–e356.

65. Meert K, Eggly S, Pollack M, et al. Parents' perspectives regarding a physician-parent conference after their child's death in the pediatric intensive care unit. *J Pediatr*. 2007; 151(1): 50–5.

66. Jankowski JB. Professional boundary issues in pediatric palliative care. *Pediatrics*. 2013; 31(2): 161–5.

Index